University Casebook Series

November, 1992

ACCOUNTING AND THE LAW, Fourth Edition (1978), with Problems Pamphlet (Successor to Dohr, Phillips, Thompson & Warren)

George C. Thompson, Professor, Columbia University Graduate School of Business.
Robert Whitman, Professor of Law, University of Connecticut.
Ellis L. Phillips, Jr., Member of the New York Bar.
William C. Warren, Professor of Law Emeritus, Columbia University.

ACCOUNTING FOR LAWYERS, MATERIALS ON (1980)

David R. Herwitz, Professor of Law, Harvard University.

ADMINISTRATIVE LAW, Eighth Edition (1987), with 1993 Case Supplement and 1983 Problems Supplement (Supplement edited in association with Paul R. Verkuil, Dean and Professor of Law, Tulane University)

Walter Gellhorn, University Professor Emeritus, Columbia University.
Clark Byse, Professor of Law, Harvard University.
Peter L. Strauss, Professor of Law, Columbia University.
Todd D. Rakoff, Professor of Law, Harvard University.
Roy A. Schotland, Professor of Law, Georgetown University.

ADMIRALTY, Third Edition (1987), with 1991 Statute and Rule Supplement

Jo Desha Lucas, Professor of Law, University of Chicago.

ADVOCACY, see also Lawyering Process

AGENCY, see also Enterprise Organization

AGENCY—PARTNERSHIPS, Fourth Edition (1987)

Abridgement from Conard, Knauss & Siegel's Enterprise Organization, Fourth Edition.

AGENCY AND PARTNERSHIPS (1987)

Melvin A. Eisenberg, Professor of Law, University of California, Berkeley.

ANTITRUST: FREE ENTERPRISE AND ECONOMIC ORGANIZATION, Sixth Edition (1983), with 1983 Problems in Antitrust Supplement and 1992 Case Supplement

Louis B. Schwartz, Professor of Law, University of Pennsylvania.
John J. Flynn, Professor of Law, University of Utah.
Harry First, Professor of Law, New York University.

BANKRUPTCY, Second Edition (1989), with 1992 Case Supplement

Robert L. Jordan, Professor of Law, University of California, Los Angeles.
William D. Warren, Professor of Law, University of California, Los Angeles.

BANKRUPTCY AND DEBTOR–CREDITOR LAW, Second Edition (1988)

Theodore Eisenberg, Professor of Law, Cornell University.

[i]

BUSINESS ASSOCIATIONS, AGENCY, PARTNERSHIPS, AND CORPORATIONS (1991)

William A. Klein, Professor of Law, University of California, Los Angeles.
Mark Ramseyer, Professor of Law, University of California, Los Angeles.

BUSINESS CRIME (1990), with 1992 Case Supplement

Harry First, Professor of Law, New York University.

BUSINESS ORGANIZATION, see also Enterprise Organization

BUSINESS PLANNING (1991)

Franklin Gevurtz, Professor of Law, McGeorge School of Law.

BUSINESS PLANNING, Temporary Second Edition (1984)

David R. Herwitz, Professor of Law, Harvard University.

BUSINESS TORTS (1972)

Milton Handler, Professor of Law Emeritus, Columbia University.

CHILDREN IN THE LEGAL SYSTEM (1983), with 1990 Supplement (Supplement edited in association with Elizabeth S. Scott, Professor of Law, University of Virginia)

Walter Wadlington, Professor of Law, University of Virginia.
Charles H. Whitebread, Professor of Law, University of Southern California.
Samuel Davis, Professor of Law, University of Georgia.

CIVIL PROCEDURE, see Procedure

CIVIL RIGHTS ACTIONS (1988), with 1992 Supplement

Peter W. Low, Professor of Law, University of Virginia.
John C. Jeffries, Jr., Professor of Law, University of Virginia.

CLINIC, see also Lawyering Process

COMMERCIAL AND DEBTOR–CREDITOR LAW: SELECTED STATUTES, 1992 EDITION

COMMERCIAL LAW, Third Edition (1992)

Robert L. Jordan, Professor of Law, University of California, Los Angeles.
William D. Warren, Professor of Law, University of California, Los Angeles.

COMMERCIAL LAW, Fourth Edition (1985), with 1991 Case Supplement

E. Allan Farnsworth, Professor of Law, Columbia University.
John Honnold, Professor of Law, University of Pennsylvania.

COMMERCIAL PAPER, see also Negotiable Instruments

COMMERCIAL PAPER, Third Edition (1984), with 1991 Case Supplement

E. Allan Farnsworth, Professor of Law, Columbia University.

COMMERCIAL PAPER AND BANK DEPOSITS AND COLLECTIONS (1967), with Statutory Supplement

William D. Hawkland, Professor of Law, University of Illinois.

COMMERCIAL TRANSACTIONS—Principles and Policies, Second Edition (1991)

Alan Schwartz, Professor of Law, Yale University.
Robert E. Scott, Professor of Law, University of Virginia.

UNIVERSITY CASEBOOK SERIES—Continued

CONTRACTS, Second Edition (1978), with Statutory and Administrative Law Supplement (1978)

Ian R. Macneil, Professor of Law, Cornell University.

COPYRIGHT, PATENTS AND TRADEMARKS, see also Competitive Process; see also Selected Statutes and International Agreements

COPYRIGHT, PATENT, TRADEMARK AND RELATED STATE DOCTRINES, Third Edition (1990), with 1991 Selected Statutes Supplement and 1981 Problem Supplement

Paul Goldstein, Professor of Law, Stanford University.

COPYRIGHT, Unfair Competition, and Other Topics Bearing on the Protection of Literary, Musical, and Artistic Works, Fifth Edition (1990), with 1991 Statutory and Case Supplement

Ralph S. Brown, Jr., Professor of Law, Yale University.
Robert C. Denicola, Professor of Law, University of Nebraska.

CORPORATE ACQUISITIONS, The Law and Finance of (1986), with 1992 Supplement

Ronald J. Gilson, Professor of Law, Stanford University.

CORPORATE FINANCE, Third Edition (1987)

Victor Brudney, Professor of Law, Harvard University.
Marvin A. Chirelstein, Professor of Law, Columbia University.

CORPORATION LAW, BASIC, Third Edition (1989), with Documentary Supplement

Detlev F. Vagts, Professor of Law, Harvard University.

CORPORATIONS, see also Enterprise Organization and Business Organization

CORPORATIONS, Sixth Edition—Concise (1988), with 1992 Case Supplement and 1992 Statutory Supplement

William L. Cary, late Professor of Law, Columbia University.
Melvin Aron Eisenberg, Professor of Law, University of California, Berkeley.

CORPORATIONS, Sixth Edition—Unabridged (1988), with 1992 Case Supplement and 1992 Statutory Supplement

William L. Cary, late Professor of Law, Columbia University.
Melvin Aron Eisenberg, Professor of Law, University of California, Berkeley.

CORPORATIONS AND BUSINESS ASSOCIATIONS—STATUTES, RULES, AND FORMS (1992)

CORRECTIONS, SEE SENTENCING

CREDITORS' RIGHTS, see also Debtor-Creditor Law

CRIMINAL JUSTICE ADMINISTRATION, Fourth Edition (1991), with 1992 Supplement

Frank W. Miller, Professor of Law, Washington University.
Robert O. Dawson, Professor of Law, University of Texas.
George E. Dix, Professor of Law, University of Texas.
Raymond I. Parnas, Professor of Law, University of California, Davis.

CRIMINAL LAW, Fifth Edition (1992)

Andre A. Moenssens, Professor of Law, University of Richmond.
Fred E. Inbau, Professor of Law Emeritus, Northwestern University.
Ronald J. Bacigal, Professor of Law, University of Richmond.

CRIMINAL LAW AND APPROACHES TO THE STUDY OF LAW, Second Edition (1991)

John M. Brumbaugh, Professor of Law, University of Maryland.

CRIMINAL LAW, Second Edition (1986)

Peter W. Low, Professor of Law, University of Virginia.
John C. Jeffries, Jr., Professor of Law, University of Virginia.
Richard C. Bonnie, Professor of Law, University of Virginia.

CRIMINAL LAW, Fourth Edition (1986)

Lloyd L. Weinreb, Professor of Law, Harvard University.

CRIMINAL LAW AND PROCEDURE, Seventh Edition (1989)

Ronald N. Boyce, Professor of Law, University of Utah.
Rollin M. Perkins, Professor of Law Emeritus, University of California, Hastings College of the Law.

CRIMINAL PROCEDURE, Fourth Edition (1992), with 1992 Supplement

James B. Haddad, late Professor of Law, Northwestern University.
James B. Zagel, Chief, Criminal Justice Division, Office of Attorney General of Illinois.
Gary L. Starkman, Assistant U. S. Attorney, Northern District of Illinois.
William J. Bauer, Chief Judge of the U.S. Court of Appeals, Seventh Circuit.

CRIMINAL PROCESS, Fourth Edition (1987), with 1992 Supplement

Lloyd L. Weinreb, Professor of Law, Harvard University.

DAMAGES, Second Edition (1952)

Charles T. McCormick, late Professor of Law, University of Texas.
William F. Fritz, late Professor of Law, University of Texas.

DECEDENTS' ESTATES AND TRUSTS, See also Family Property Law

DECEDENTS' ESTATES AND TRUSTS, Seventh Edition (1988)

John Ritchie, late Professor of Law, University of Virginia.
Neill H. Alford, Jr., Professor of Law, University of Virginia.
Richard W. Effland, late Professor of Law, Arizona State University.

DISPUTE RESOLUTION, Processes of (1989)

John S. Murray, President and Executive Director of The Conflict Clinic, Inc., George Mason University.
Alan Scott Rau, Professor of Law, University of Texas.
Edward F. Sherman, Professor of Law, University of Texas.

DOMESTIC RELATIONS, see also Family Law

DOMESTIC RELATIONS, Second Edition (1990), with 1992 Supplement

Walter Wadlington, Professor of Law, University of Virginia.

EMPLOYMENT DISCRIMINATION, Third Edition (1993)

Joel W. Friedman, Professor of Law, Tulane University.
George M. Strickler, Professor of Law, Tulane University.

EMPLOYMENT LAW, Second Edition (1991), with 1992 Statutory Supplement and 1992 Case Supplement

Mark A. Rothstein, Professor of Law, University of Houston.
Andria S. Knapp, Visiting Professor of Law, Golden Gate University.
Lance Liebman, Professor of Law, Harvard University.

UNIVERSITY CASEBOOK SERIES—Continued

ENERGY LAW (1983), with 1991 Case Supplement

Donald N. Zillman, Professor of Law, University of Utah.
Laurence Lattman, Dean of Mines and Engineering, University of Utah.

ENTERPRISE ORGANIZATION, Fourth Edition (1987), with 1987 Corporation and Partnership Statutes, Rules and Forms Supplement

Alfred F. Conard, Professor of Law, University of Michigan.
Robert L. Knauss, Dean of the Law School, University of Houston.
Stanley Siegel, Professor of Law, University of California, Los Angeles.

ENVIRONMENTAL POLICY LAW, Second Edition (1991)

Thomas J. Schoenbaum, Professor of Law, University of Georgia.
Ronald H. Rosenberg, Professor of Law, College of William and Mary.

EQUITY, see also Remedies

EQUITY, RESTITUTION AND DAMAGES, Second Edition (1974)

Robert Childres, late Professor of Law, Northwestern University.
William F. Johnson, Jr., Professor of Law, New York University.

ESTATE PLANNING, Second Edition (1982), with 1985 Case, Text and Documentary Supplement

David Westfall, Professor of Law, Harvard University.

ETHICS, see Legal Ethics, Legal Profession, Professional Responsibility, and Social Responsibilities

ETHICS OF LAWYERING, THE LAW AND (1990)

Geoffrey C. Hazard, Jr., Professor of Law, Yale University.
Susan P. Koniak, Professor of Law, University of Pittsburgh.

ETHICS AND PROFESSIONAL RESPONSIBILITY (1981) (Reprinted from THE LAWYERING PROCESS)

Gary Bellow, Professor of Law, Harvard University.
Bea Moulton, Legal Services Corporation.

EVIDENCE, Seventh Edition (1992)

John Kaplan, Late Professor of Law, Stanford University.
Jon R. Waltz, Professor of Law, Northwestern University.
Roger C. Park, Professor of Law, University of Minnesota.

EVIDENCE, Eighth Edition (1988), with Rules, Statute and Case Supplement (1992)

Jack B. Weinstein, Chief Judge, United States District Court.
John H. Mansfield, Professor of Law, Harvard University.
Norman Abrams, Professor of Law, University of California, Los Angeles.
Margaret Berger, Professor of Law, Brooklyn Law School.

FAMILY LAW, see also Domestic Relations

FAMILY LAW, Third Edition (1992)

Judith C. Areen, Professor of Law, Georgetown University.

FAMILY LAW AND CHILDREN IN THE LEGAL SYSTEM, STATUTORY MATERIALS (1981)

Walter Wadlington, Professor of Law, University of Virginia.

FAMILY PROPERTY LAW, Cases and Materials on Wills, Trusts and Future Interests (1991)

Lawrence W. Waggoner, Professor of Law, University of Michigan.
Richard V. Wellman, Professor of Law, University of Georgia.
Gregory Alexander, Professor of Law, Cornell Law School.
Mary L. Fellows, Professor of Law, University of Minnesota.

FEDERAL COURTS, Ninth Edition (1992)

Charles T. McCormick, late Professor of Law, University of Texas.
James H. Chadbourn, late Professor of Law, Harvard University.
Charles Alan Wright, Professor of Law, University of Texas, Austin.

FEDERAL COURTS AND THE FEDERAL SYSTEM, Hart and Wechsler's Third Edition (1988), with 1992 Case Supplement, and the Judicial Code and Rules of Procedure in the Federal Courts (1991)

Paul M. Bator, Professor of Law, University of Chicago.
Daniel J. Meltzer, Professor of Law, Harvard University.
Paul J. Mishkin, Professor of Law, University of California, Berkeley.
David L. Shapiro, Professor of Law, Harvard University.

FEDERAL COURTS AND THE LAW OF FEDERAL–STATE RELATIONS, Second Edition (1989), with 1992 Supplement

Peter W. Low, Professor of Law, University of Virginia.
John C. Jeffries, Jr., Professor of Law, University of Virginia.

FEDERAL PUBLIC LAND AND RESOURCES LAW, Third Edition (1993), with 1990 Statutory Supplement

George C. Coggins, Professor of Law, University of Kansas.
Charles F. Wilkinson, Professor of Law, University of Oregon.
John D. Leshy, Professor of Law, Arizona State University.

FEDERAL RULES OF CIVIL PROCEDURE and Selected Other Procedural Provisions, 1992 Edition

FEDERAL TAXATION, see Taxation

FIRST AMENDMENT (1991), with 1992 Supplement

William W. Van Alstyne, Professor of Law, Duke University.

FOOD AND DRUG LAW, Second Edition (1991), with Statutory Supplement

Peter Barton Hutt, Esq.
Richard A. Merrill, Professor of Law, University of Virginia.

FUTURE INTERESTS (1970)

Howard R. Williams, Professor of Law, Stanford University.

FUTURE INTERESTS AND ESTATE PLANNING (1961), with 1962 Supplement

W. Barton Leach, late Professor of Law, Harvard University.
James K. Logan, formerly Dean of the Law School, University of Kansas.

GENDER DISCRIMINATION, see Women and the Law

GOVERNMENT CONTRACTS, FEDERAL, Successor Edition (1985), with 1989 Supplement

John W. Whelan, Professor of Law, Hastings College of the Law.

GOVERNMENT REGULATION: FREE ENTERPRISE AND ECONOMIC ORGANIZATION, Sixth Edition (1985)

Louis B. Schwartz, Professor of Law, Hastings College of the Law.
John J. Flynn, Professor of Law, University of Utah.
Harry First, Professor of Law, New York University.

UNIVERSITY CASEBOOK SERIES—Continued

HEALTH CARE LAW AND POLICY (1988), with 1992 Supplement

Clark C. Havighurst, Professor of Law, Duke University.

HINCKLEY, JOHN W., JR., TRIAL OF: A Case Study of the Insanity Defense (1986)

Peter W. Low, Professor of Law, University of Virginia.
John C. Jeffries, Jr., Professor of Law, University of Virginia.
Richard C. Bonnie, Professor of Law, University of Virginia.

IMMIGRATION LAW AND POLICY (1992)

Stephen H. Legomsky, Professor of Law, Washington University.

INJUNCTIONS, Second Edition (1984)

Owen M. Fiss, Professor of Law, Yale University.
Doug Rendleman, Professor of Law, College of William and Mary.

INSTITUTIONAL INVESTORS (1978)

David L. Ratner, Professor of Law, Cornell University.

INSURANCE, Second Edition (1985)

William F. Young, Professor of Law, Columbia University.
Eric M. Holmes, Professor of Law, University of Georgia.

INSURANCE LAW AND REGULATION (1990)

Kenneth S. Abraham, University of Virginia.

INTERNATIONAL LAW, see also Transnational Legal Problems, Transnational Business Problems, and United Nations Law

INTERNATIONAL LAW IN CONTEMPORARY PERSPECTIVE (1981), with Essay Supplement

Myres S. McDougal, Professor of Law, Yale University.
W. Michael Reisman, Professor of Law, Yale University.

INTERNATIONAL LEGAL SYSTEM, Third Edition (1988), with Documentary Supplement

Joseph Modeste Sweeney, Professor of Law, University of California, Hastings.
Covey T. Oliver, Professor of Law, University of Pennsylvania.
Noyes E. Leech, Professor of Law Emeritus, University of Pennsylvania.

INTRODUCTION TO LAW, see also Legal Method, On Law in Courts, and Dynamics of American Law

INTRODUCTION TO THE STUDY OF LAW (1970)

E. Wayne Thode, late Professor of Law, University of Utah.
Leon Lebowitz, Professor of Law, University of Texas.
Lester J. Mazor, Professor of Law, University of Utah.

JUDICIAL CODE and Rules of Procedure in the Federal Courts, Students' Edition, 1991 Revision

Daniel J. Meltzer, Professor of Law, Harvard University.
David L. Shapiro, Professor of Law, Harvard University.

JURISPRUDENCE (Temporary Edition Hardbound) (1949)

Lon L. Fuller, late Professor of Law, Harvard University.

JUVENILE, see also Children

UNIVERSITY CASEBOOK SERIES—Continued

LEGAL PROFESSION, THE, Responsibility and Regulation, Second Edition (1988)

Geoffrey C. Hazard, Jr., Professor of Law, Yale University.
Deborah L. Rhode, Professor of Law, Stanford University.

LEGISLATION, Fourth Edition (1982) (by Fordham)

Horace E. Read, late Vice President, Dalhousie University.
John W. MacDonald, Professor of Law Emeritus, Cornell Law School.
Jefferson B. Fordham, Professor of Law, University of Utah.
William J. Pierce, Professor of Law, University of Michigan.

LEGISLATIVE AND ADMINISTRATIVE PROCESSES, Second Edition (1981)

Hans A. Linde, Judge, Supreme Court of Oregon.
George Bunn, Professor of Law, University of Wisconsin.
Fredericka Paff, Professor of Law, University of Wisconsin.
W. Lawrence Church, Professor of Law, University of Wisconsin.

LOCAL GOVERNMENT LAW, Second Revised Edition (1986)

Jefferson B. Fordham, Professor of Law, University of Utah.

MASS MEDIA LAW, Fourth Edition (1990)

Marc A. Franklin, Professor of Law, Stanford University.
David A. Anderson, Professor of Law, University of Texas.

MUNICIPAL CORPORATIONS, see Local Government Law

NEGOTIABLE INSTRUMENTS, see Commercial Paper

NEGOTIABLE INSTRUMENTS AND LETTERS OF CREDIT (1992) (Reprinted from Commercial Law) Third Edition (1992)

Robert L. Jordan, Professor of Law, University of California, Los Angeles.
William D. Warren, Professor of Law, University of California, Los Angeles.

NEGOTIATION (1981) (Reprinted from THE LAWYERING PROCESS)

Gary Bellow, Professor of Law, Harvard Law School.
Bea Moulton, Legal Services Corporation.

NEW YORK PRACTICE, Fourth Edition (1978)

Herbert Peterfreund, Professor of Law, New York University.
Joseph M. McLaughlin, Dean of the Law School, Fordham University.

OIL AND GAS, Sixth Edition (1992)

Richard C. Maxwell, Professor of Law, Duke University.
Stephen F. Williams, Judge of the United States Court of Appeals.
Patrick Henry Martin, Professor of Law, Louisiana State University.
Bruce M. Kramer, Professor of Law, Texas Tech University.

ON LAW IN COURTS (1965)

Paul J. Mishkin, Professor of Law, University of California, Berkeley.
Clarence Morris, Professor of Law Emeritus, University of Pennsylvania.

PENSION AND EMPLOYEE BENEFIT LAW (1990), with 1992 Supplement

John H. Langbein, Professor of Law, University of Chicago.
Bruce A. Wolk, Professor of Law, University of California, Davis.

PLEADING AND PROCEDURE, see Procedure, Civil

POLICE FUNCTION, Fifth Edition (1991), with 1992 Supplement

Reprint of Chapters 1–10 of Miller, Dawson, Dix and Parnas's CRIMINAL JUSTICE ADMINISTRATION, Fourth Edition.

PREPARING AND PRESENTING THE CASE (1981) (Reprinted from THE LAWYERING PROCESS)

Gary Bellow, Professor of Law, Harvard Law School.
Bea Moulton, Legal Services Corporation.

PROCEDURE (1988), with Procedure Supplement (1991)

Robert M. Cover, late Professor of Law, Yale Law School.
Owen M. Fiss, Professor of Law, Yale Law School.
Judith Resnik, Professor of Law, University of Southern California Law Center.

PROCEDURE—CIVIL PROCEDURE, Sixth Edition (1990), with 1992 Supplement

Richard H. Field, late Professor of Law, Harvard University.
Benjamin Kaplan, Professor of Law Emeritus, Harvard University.
Kevin M. Clermont, Professor of Law, Cornell University.

PROCEDURE—CIVIL PROCEDURE, Successor Edition (1992)

A. Leo Levin, Professor of Law Emeritus, University of Pennsylvania.
Philip Shuchman, Professor of Law, Rutgers University.
Charles M. Yablon, Professor of Law, Yeshiva University.

PROCEDURE—CIVIL PROCEDURE, Fifth Edition (1990), with 1991 Supplement

Maurice Rosenberg, Professor of Law, Columbia University.
Hans Smit, Professor of Law, Columbia University.
Rochelle C. Dreyfuss, Professor of Law, New York University.

PROCEDURE—PLEADING AND PROCEDURE: State and Federal, Sixth Edition (1989), with 1992 Case Supplement

David W. Louisell, late Professor of Law, University of California, Berkeley.
Geoffrey C. Hazard, Jr., Professor of Law, Yale University.
Colin C. Tait, Professor of Law, University of Connecticut.

PROCEDURE—FEDERAL RULES OF CIVIL PROCEDURE, 1992 Edition

PRODUCTS LIABILITY AND SAFETY, Second Edition (1989), with 1989 Statutory Supplement

W. Page Keeton, Professor of Law, University of Texas.
David G. Owen, Professor of Law, University of South Carolina.
John E. Montgomery, Professor of Law, University of South Carolina.
Michael D. Green, Professor of Law, University of Iowa

PROFESSIONAL RESPONSIBILITY, Fifth Edition (1991), with 1992 Selected Standards on Professional Responsibility Supplement

Thomas D. Morgan, Professor of Law, George Washington University.
Ronald D. Rotunda, Professor of Law, University of Illinois.

PROPERTY, Sixth Edition (1990)

John E. Cribbet, Professor of Law, University of Illinois.
Corwin W. Johnson, Professor of Law, University of Texas.
Roger W. Findley, Professor of Law, University of Illinois.
Ernest E. Smith, Professor of Law, University of Texas.

PROPERTY—PERSONAL (1953)

S. Kenneth Skolfield, late Professor of Law Emeritus, Boston University.

PROPERTY—PERSONAL, Third Edition (1954)

Everett Fraser, late Dean of the Law School Emeritus, University of Minnesota.
Third Edition by Charles W. Taintor, late Professor of Law, University of Pittsburgh.

PROPERTY—INTRODUCTION, TO REAL PROPERTY, Third Edition (1954)

Everett Fraser, late Dean of the Law School Emeritus, University of Minnesota.

PROPERTY—FUNDAMENTALS OF MODERN REAL PROPERTY, Third Edition (1992)

Edward H. Rabin, Professor of Law, University of California, Davis.
Roberta Rosenthal Kwall, Professor of Law, DePaul University.

PROPERTY, REAL (1984), with 1988 Supplement

Paul Goldstein, Professor of Law, Stanford University.

PROSECUTION AND ADJUDICATION, Fourth Edition (1991), with 1992 Supplement

Reprint of Chapters 11–26 of Miller, Dawson, Dix and Parnas's CRIMINAL JUSTICE ADMINISTRATION, Fourth Edition.

PSYCHIATRY AND LAW, see Mental Health, see also Hinckley, Trial of

PUBLIC UTILITY LAW, see Free Enterprise, also Regulated Industries

REAL ESTATE PLANNING, Third Edition (1989), with Revised Problem and Statutory Supplement (1991)

Norton L. Steuben, Professor of Law, University of Colorado.

REAL ESTATE TRANSACTIONS, Revised Second Edition (1988), with Statute, Form and Problem Supplement (1988)

Paul Goldstein, Professor of Law, Stanford University.

RECEIVERSHIP AND CORPORATE REORGANIZATION, see Creditors' Rights

REGULATED INDUSTRIES, Second Edition (1976)

William K. Jones, Professor of Law, Columbia University.

REMEDIES, Third Edition (1992)

Edward D. Re, Professor of Law, St. John's University.
Stanton D. Krauss, Professor of Law, University of Bridgeport.

REMEDIES (1989)

Elaine W. Shoben, Professor of Law, University of Illinois.
Wm. Murray Tabb, Professor of Law, Baylor University.

SALES, Third Edition (1992)

Marion W. Benfield, Jr., Professor of Law, Wake Forest University.
William D. Hawkland, Professor of Law, Louisiana State Law Center.

SALES (1992) (Reprinted from Commercial Law) Third Edition (1992)

Robert L. Jordan, Professor of Law, University of California, Los Angeles.
William D. Warren, Professor of Law, University of California, Los Angeles.

SALES AND SALES FINANCING, Fifth Edition (1984)

John Honnold, Professor of Law, University of Pennsylvania.

SALES LAW AND THE CONTRACTING PROCESS, Second Edition (1991) (Reprinted from Commercial Transactions) Second Edition (1991)

Alan Schwartz, Professor of Law, Yale University.
Robert E. Scott, Professor of Law, University of Virginia.

UNIVERSITY CASEBOOK SERIES—Continued

SECURED TRANSACTIONS IN PERSONAL PROPERTY, Third Edition (1992) (Reprinted from COMMERCIAL LAW, Third Edition (1992))

Robert L. Jordan, Professor of Law, University of California, Los Angeles.
William D. Warren, Professor of Law, University of California, Los Angeles.

SECURITIES REGULATION, Seventh Edition (1992), with 1992 Selected Statutes, Rules and Forms Supplement

Richard W. Jennings, Professor of Law, University of California, Berkeley.
Harold Marsh, Jr., Member of California Bar.
John C. Coffee, Jr., Professor of Law, Columbia University.

SECURITIES REGULATION, Second Edition (1988), with Statute, Rule and Form Supplement (1991)

Larry D. Soderquist, Professor of Law, Vanderbilt University.

SECURITY INTERESTS IN PERSONAL PROPERTY, Second Edition (1987)

Douglas G. Baird, Professor of Law, University of Chicago.
Thomas H. Jackson, Dean of the Law School, University of Virginia.

SECURITY INTERESTS IN PERSONAL PROPERTY, Second Edition (1992)

John Honnold, Professor of Law, University of Pennsylvania.
Steven L. Harris, Professor of Law, University of Illinois.
Charles W. Mooney, Jr., Professor of Law, University of Pennsylvania.

SELECTED STANDARDS ON PROFESSIONAL RESPONSIBILITY, 1992 Edition

SELECTED STATUTES AND INTERNATIONAL AGREEMENTS ON UNFAIR COMPETITION, TRADEMARK, COPYRIGHT AND PATENT, 1991 Edition

SELECTED STATUTES ON TRUSTS AND ESTATES, 1992 Edition

SOCIAL RESPONSIBILITIES OF LAWYERS, Case Studies (1988)

Philip B. Heymann, Professor of Law, Harvard University.
Lance Liebman, Professor of Law, Harvard University.

SOCIAL SCIENCE IN LAW, Second Edition (1990)

John Monahan, Professor of Law, University of Virginia.
Laurens Walker, Professor of Law, University of Virginia.

TAXATION, FEDERAL INCOME (1989)

Stephen B. Cohen, Professor of Law, Georgetown University

TAXATION, FEDERAL INCOME, Second Edition (1988), with 1992 Supplement (Supplement edited in association with Deborah H. Schenk, Professor of Law, New York University)

Michael J. Graetz, Professor of Law, Yale University.

TAXATION, FEDERAL INCOME, Seventh Edition (1991)

James J. Freeland, Professor of Law, University of Florida.
Stephen A. Lind, Professor of Law, University of Florida and University of California, Hastings.
Richard B. Stephens, late Professor of Law Emeritus, University of Florida.

TAXATION, FEDERAL INCOME, Successor Edition (1986), with 1991 Legislative Supplement

Stanley S. Surrey, late Professor of Law, Harvard University.
Paul R. McDaniel, Professor of Law, Boston College.
Hugh J. Ault, Professor of Law, Boston College.
Stanley A. Koppelman, Professor of Law, Boston University.

TAXATION, FEDERAL INCOME, OF BUSINESS ORGANIZATIONS (1991), with 1992 Supplement

Paul R. McDaniel, Professor of Law, Boston College.
Hugh J. Ault, Professor of Law, Boston College.
Martin J. McMahon, Jr., Professor of Law, University of Kentucky.
Daniel L. Simmons, Professor of Law, University of California, Davis.

TAXATION, FEDERAL INCOME, OF PARTNERSHIPS AND S CORPORATIONS (1991), with 1992 Supplement

Paul R. McDaniel, Professor of Law, Boston College.
Hugh J. Ault, Professor of Law, Boston College.
Martin J. McMahon, Jr., Professor of Law, University of Kentucky.
Daniel L. Simmons, Professor of Law, University of California, Davis.

TAXATION, FEDERAL INCOME, OIL AND GAS, NATURAL RESOURCES TRANSACTIONS (1990)

Peter C. Maxfield, Professor of Law, University of Wyoming.
James L. Houghton, CPA, Partner, Ernst and Young.
James R. Gaar, CPA, Partner, Ernst and Young.

TAXATION, FEDERAL WEALTH TRANSFER, Successor Edition (1987)

Stanley S. Surrey, late Professor of Law, Harvard University.
Paul R. McDaniel, Professor of Law, Boston College.
Harry L. Gutman, Professor of Law, University of Pennsylvania.

TAXATION, FUNDAMENTALS OF CORPORATE, Third Edition (1991)

Stephen A. Lind, Professor of Law, University of Florida and University of California, Hastings.
Stephen Schwarz, Professor of Law, University of California, Hastings.
Daniel J. Lathrope, Professor of Law, University of California, Hastings.
Joshua Rosenberg, Professor of Law, University of San Francisco.

TAXATION, FUNDAMENTALS OF PARTNERSHIP, Third Edition (1992)

Stephen A. Lind, Professor of Law, University of Florida and University of California, Hastings.
Stephen Schwarz, Professor of Law, University of California, Hastings.
Daniel J. Lathrope, Professor of Law, University of California, Hastings.
Joshua Rosenberg, Professor of Law, University of San Francisco.

TAXATION OF CORPORATIONS AND THEIR SHAREHOLDERS (1991)

David J. Shakow, Professor of Law, University of Pennsylvania.

TAXATION, PROBLEMS IN THE FEDERAL INCOME TAXATION OF PARTNER-SHIPS AND CORPORATIONS, Second Edition (1986)

Norton L. Steuben, Professor of Law, University of Colorado.
William J. Turnier, Professor of Law, University of North Carolina.

TAXATION, PROBLEMS IN THE FUNDAMENTALS OF FEDERAL INCOME, Second Edition (1985)

Norton L. Steuben, Professor of Law, University of Colorado.
William J. Turnier, Professor of Law, University of North Carolina.

TORT LAW AND ALTERNATIVES, Fifth Edition (1992)

Marc A. Franklin, Professor of Law, Stanford University.
Robert L. Rabin, Professor of Law, Stanford University.

TORTS, Eighth Edition (1988)

William L. Prosser, late Professor of Law, University of California, Hastings.
John W. Wade, Professor of Law, Vanderbilt University.
Victor E. Schwartz, Adjunct Professor of Law, Georgetown University.

University Casebook Series

BASIC
CORPORATION LAW

MATERIALS—CASES—TEXT

THIRD EDITION

By

DETLEV F. VAGTS
Professor of Law, Harvard University

Westbury, New York
THE FOUNDATION PRESS, INC.
1989

Library of Congress Cataloging-in-Publication Data

Vagts, Detlev F.
  Basic corporation law.

  (University casebook series)
  Includes index.
  1. Corporation law—United States—Cases. I. Title.
II. Series.
KF1413.V33   1989   346.73'066   88–24662
ISBN 0–88277–679–7   347.30666

Vagts Basic Corp. Law 3rd Ed. UCB
1st Reprint—1992

PREFACE

As one grapples with a third edition of this casebook one realizes how much has changed since the first edition in 1973, to say nothing of changes since its editor started teaching Corporations in 1959. These changes have made the task of teaching Corporations both more interesting and more difficult. At its root the difference arises from the emergence of new organizing ideas about the subject, generated by new thinking in the world of micro-economics, and from the prominence given to corporations by the wave of mergers and acquisitions of the last decade.

Nobody would now write about corporation statutes what Bayless Manning wrote in 1962—that they were "towering skyscrapers of rusted girders, internally welded together and containing nothing but wind."[1] Corporation law has been impressed on the public consciousness by the obvious way in which takeovers transform the fates not just of stockholders but of managers, employees, headquarters cities, plants, etc. The interest is given extra spice by the lucrative and supposedly fascinating careers of those who arrange, manage or ward off such adventures. Congress has followed the media in debating these developments and there is speculation how much the stock market "adjustment" of October 1987 has done to change this market for corporate power.

Two basic conceptions from the world of economics do a great deal to unify the field of corporations law and to raise challenging questions about it. Both derive from work done by economists trying to understand the securities markets and corporate organizational structure. The securities markets, as the most elaborately organized and most expensively equipped and supported exchanges, are easy to study. Thus one finds a large body of analysis based on the data generated by reports of activity on the exchanges. This body, often referred to as efficient market theory, tends to lead one toward the concept that markets generate good judgments and that government interference with their operations should be as little as possible. It tends to shift the thrust of corporations law in the direction of supporting and enforcing decisions made by informed adults in the pursuit of their self-interest. It also leads courts to try to reach conclusions by asking what such actors would agree upon if their attention had been directed to the problem. Various cautions occur to the observer—not all of the markets in the corporate world are as efficient as others, fraud and theft still exist, perpetrated by people who do not intend to linger around for their bad reputation to impact the market for their next round of offerings, and some people are exposed to the effects of the market without having an effective economic vote.

---

1. Manning, The Shareholder's Appraisal Remedy: An Essay for Frank Coker, 72 Yale L.J. 223, 245 n. 37 (1962).

All of these intellectual and real-world developments are demanding of class time and book space. Students without a background in economics, especially of this special subset of economics, find the new theory difficult. The cases about mergers and acquisitions are long and factually complex. Thus I resist the impulse to shift direction drastically. The older materials about the organizational structure of corporate management, together with some basic points about creating and changing its financial structure seem to me still to be antecedent and basic. While students should know something about mergers and acquisitions law because it is part of the economic constitutional law of the United States that law is not apt to be important to their own practice in the vast majority of cases. Therefore this book gives only limited space to that subject. I have felt it important to set forth a brief explanation of efficient market theory when we study rules about securities transfers in Chapter XI and to provide a short synopsis of modern valuation theory (the capital assets pricing model) when issues of value—that deceptive term—first become relevant. But the fine points of such theory seem better left to courses in Corporate Finance or Mergers and Acquisitions. The object of this book is still to provide a *basic* course.

At the end of the course, one should hope to have accomplished several things. First, the student should have learned the fundamental conceptual framework of corporations law. Actually, that framework turns out to be fairly simple and easily apprehended. It is the details of the rules and the complexity of the factual situations in which they become embedded that give the topic its reputation for difficulty. This book is designed to give the nonspecialist lawyers what law they would need to cope with corporations as they come up in their practice. The specialist should be ready to undertake advanced courses in such fields as securities regulation, corporate finance or business planning. There should not be an excessive amount of overlap though some duplication is not only necessary but may even be beneficial. Second, a student should have obtained some grasp of the basic ideas and terminology of business organization and finance; it seems to be reasonable to aim at roughly the equivalent of what might be learned in a more leisurely way in a semester's college course on corporate operations or finance. Third, the student should have some sense of what a corporation lawyer does. In a curriculum traditionally oriented towards appellate advocacy and now infused with clinical work of a trial-oriented tendency, it seems important to give a countervailing thrust to the less familiar and less spectacular portion of lawyers' work that can be summed up as being a solicitor. Thus the student should have some exercise in planning, preventive counselling and other non-litigious activities. By-products of such education may be an increased sense of what the life of a corporation lawyer is like and a better basis for judging whether to enter on such a career. This exposure should include some exposure to the special ethical problems confronting corporate counsel. Finally, the experience ought to enable the student to get a firmer grasp of the corporation in the economy and society, integrating that aspect with his overall views on politics and economics. It is, I believe, deeply important that lawyers be capable of thinking intelligently about the relationship between corporations and the public interest.

Getting from here to there is an ambitious undertaking. It would be simply impossible to achieve those goals within a book of reasonable size, to be covered in some 60 classroom hours, without finding methods less time and space consuming than a traditional casebook affords. To increase efficiency I have tried various devices. Legal doctrine is developed to only some degree through cases. Traditional use of cases tends to be wasteful not only because of the time taken to extract a two-line rule from a ten-page case but because there is only a very tenuous relation between the corporations problems which come into litigation and the problems about which foresighted lawyers in their offices labor to avoid having arise. Still, I have not felt it wise to dispense with cases completely because they do develop doctrine and rules and because it is impossible to appreciate the flavor of the law here without immersing oneself in some of the factual complexities spread out in the cases. Quite a bit of doctrine is stated straightforwardly in text. As befits the nature of the course, much is left to direct reading of statutes, regulations and private documents. No effort is made to line up the state statutes or cases according to their positions on given issues of law; the book proceeds on the basis of example only. Text, both my own and borrowed, is used to present business and financial data as plainly and compactly as possible. The flow of data is not encumbered with research references, those being concentrated in special bibliography sections for those readers who will actually wish to use them. The result is a book which is lean and spare, even in its third edition, rather than detailed and comprehensive; one should not overlook, however, the fact that the Documentary Supplement is an integral part of the book, which adds length and difficulty.

I have furnished both questions and problems for those instructors who care to use them. The questions sometimes do no more than check the students' comprehension of what they have read; from there they go deeper to more basic issues of the meaning of the cases or statutes. The problems are designed to push the reader into more complex and comprehensive patterns of analysis. Most of them try to develop approaches other than "who-should-win-the-case?" For example, one asks the students to design, step by step, a campaign to gain control of a corporation or to weigh alternative approaches to a transaction (learning that devices that seem very distinguishable to lawyers seem equivalent to business people and vice versa). Review problems appear occasionally, to be dealt with when students are retracing the materials and trying to create a synthesis for themselves. Another device used is a glossary of business-law terms to which students can refer without waiting until the word is explained in due course in its most appropriate point in the structure of the whole book. Some comments have been inserted after cases that seek to develop their business context and also to introduce students to some of the livelier characters of the corporate scene, in the hope that personifying some of these transactions will make them more comprehensible.

Teaching Aspects: A teacher's manual will be made available and the instructor is referred thereto for details as to how I think the book, and in particular the problems, might be used. I will, however, make a few general comments here.

As to coverage, I believe that, using a pace somewhat faster than mine, one could complete the book. I have myself never taught all of Chapters XII, XIII or XIV. I prefer to conclude with at least some of Chapter XIII on fundamental changes because I feel that this pulls together a good many strands of development from earlier portions; particularly in the day of the takeover, students would expect an introduction to that topic. Teachers who prefer to deemphasize corporate finance might prefer to skip not only Chapter XII but also Chapter VI, saving only a note introducing the Securities and Exchange Commission. I have included some materials, including some problems, that may be too discouraging to use with students that have had no background in Accounting; these can easily be identified and severed from the progression of the course. If your students have had Partnership, you would presumably skip Chapter II and, if they have had Agency, you will want to skip or brush lightly over various portions.

The book features the Delaware corporation law as one widely used by a majority of the most important corporations, one revised to meet current problems and copiously annotated by cases. One can obtain a copy (unannotated) of the Delaware law at a modest cost. It should be entirely feasible to use the book to deal with some other statute. Largely as an aid to such conversion, I have included a table of references to sections of the Delaware law with cross references to the Revised Model Business Corporation Act. A corresponding table of references could easily be developed as to another state's code. Some of the problems may come out strangely under another system, but that should be an educational experience for all. I would try to help by correspondence any fellow instructor who encountered difficulties on this. The federal law of corporations is, of course, common to all of us.

Editorial Matters: A separate Documentary Supplement has been published by Foundation Press for use in connection with this book. In deciding whether materials would be included in this book or the Supplement, I have followed two general principles. If references appear in several parts of the book to any one document, it appears in the Supplement. Even if a document is relevant to only one section, it has been included in the Supplement if its length was such as to interfere unduly with the development of a topic. I have not given citations in the book to documents appearing in the Supplement.

PREFACE

The second edition was largely completed as of December 31, 1987, and no systematic attempt has been made to bring matters up to date as of a later time.

Cases are often sharply edited, particularly as to their citations. Omissions are indicated by dots or by parenthetical statements. Footnotes are numbered in sequence through each chapter from 1 to 99. Unless otherwise indicated by a note "Ed.—", a footnote occurring within a case or other quoted statement originally belonged with that material. In the interests of brevity I have omitted noting certiorari denied except as to principal cases.

Acknowledgments: Over the years, my knowledge of corporation law and practice benefited much from the example and instruction of my seniors and colleagues at Cahill, Gordon, Zachry & Reindel and successor firms; thereafter my colleagues at this School and elsewhere in the work of law teaching gave me many useful ideas and warnings. Student research assistants made major contributions to each edition as did Geoffrey Cook to this one. Secretarial work was a vital component of each edition, Marilyn Uzuner's to the present one. In addition to the patience required of the spouse of any casebook editor, my wife assisted with the development of diagrams and tables.

Permissions to reprint works not in the public domain are separately acknowledged at the point at which they appear but are also listed here with designation in parentheses of the work involved: The American Bar Association (excerpts from articles in the Business Lawyer by Marsh and Wheat and Blackstone), Callaghan & Co. (excerpts from Prifti, Securities: Public and Private Offerings), the Harvard University Press (excerpts from The Corporation in Modern Society), the Division of Research, Harvard Business School, Boston (excerpts from Williams' Cumulative Voting for Directors), Richard D. Irwin, Inc. (excerpts from Business Policy by Profs. Learned, Christensen, Andrews & Guth), Harper & Row, Publishers (excerpts from J. A. Livingston, The American Scholar), University of Chicago Press (excerpts from Capitalism and Freedom by Milton Friedman), University of Pennsylvania Law Review (excerpts from Berle's Constitutional Limitations on Corporate Activity). Permissions to reprint matter included in the Documentary Supplement are separately acknowledged therein.

DETLEV F. VAGTS

July, 1988

*

SUMMARY OF CONTENTS

*

TABLE OF CONTENTS

TABLE OF CONTENTS

TABLE OF CASES

Principal cases are in italic type. Cases cited or discussed are in roman type. References are to Pages.

xix

*

TABLE OF STATUTES

DELAWARE GENERAL CORPORATION LAW

The following table is designed primarily to enable the reader to identify where in the book a particular section of the Delaware General Corporation Law is discussed. It has a secondary purpose of being helpful to the instructor reader who prefers to use the Model Business Corporation Act (in its 1984 revision). The third column shows the equivalent section of the Model Act and, hence, where it should be dealt with in the book. The equivalences, it should be noted, are at times only very rough and, in fact, occasionally non-existent. Note that it is possible, by using the annotations to the Model Act, to find the appropriate sections of the corporation laws of other jurisdictions.

* See Model Nonprofit Corporation Act.
** See Model Statutory Close Corporation Supplement.

STATE STATUTES

STATE STATUTES—Continued

FEDERAL STATUTES

POPULAR NAME ACTS

POPULAR NAME ACTS—Continued

BASIC
CORPORATION LAW

*

Chapter I

A GENERAL INTRODUCTION TO CORPORATIONS

To deal realistically with the law of corporations the student needs some sense of the shapes and dimensions of those institutions and of the support and control they need to have from the law. It would be impossible to portray the corporation in all of its facets; what is attempted here is to take pictures of the corporation from the angles suggested by various other disciplines in the hope that this will lend some degree of three-dimensionality to our subject. In the course of this description you will, I hope, gather some impression of the importance of the corporation to the economy and social structure of the United States and of the correspondingly important dangers presented by any major malfunctioning of its machinery.

1. An Historical Perspective

One might pursue the origins of the corporation into very early history but if one's interest is in the present-day business corporation there is no point in trying to go back of the merchant guild system of the Middle Ages in England. These guilds were involved in trade and commerce but not in the same sense as the modern corporation—as entities they regulated and supported the activities which their members carried on but each member made his own investment and reaped his own gains and losses. From these guilds evolved, by the sixteenth century, regulated companies that engaged in foreign trade; these procured a monopoly of the particular trade in question for their membership and laid down regulations for its conduct. In time some companies accumulated substantial assets of their own which might be used to erect trading posts or fortifications abroad. By the seventeenth century we find corporations "trading on a joint stock", that is, engaging in business operations on behalf of their members with assets contributed by them and distributing the gains arising from their common endeavors in proportion to the contributions. At first these joint stocks were not permanent, but rather at the end of a voyage or a given period of years the enterprise was wound up and both the capital and the gains thereon were returned to the members. In the case of a company with as heavy a set of responsibilities as the British East India

1

Company the instability arising from such fluctuations proved intolerable. Thus by 1657 the Company was functioning on a "permanent joint stock" basis with dividends being paid from time to time out of profits.

Incorporation was at this time an expensive and time-consuming process for the crown was stringent, and at times avaricious, in these grants. Thus chartered companies tended to be rather major undertakings including, besides foreign trading companies, banks and water companies. As economic activity grew in tempo and magnitude there came to be more and more loose practice verging on actual fraud. In 1720, in the wake of a disastrous market panic, Parliament struck at the excesses of stock market speculation through the Bubble Act—this statute of which the illustrious Maitland said "[a] panic-stricken Parliament issued a law which, even when we now read it, seems to scream at us from the statute book".[1] It made a crime of "acting or presuming to act as a corporate body or bodies" without being incorporated.[2] Neither this Act nor the greater stringency in granting charters that followed could stem the tide of business organization. Careful research in corporate files and those of contemporary counsel has shown that, with skillful adaptations of trust and partnership laws, legal frameworks for large commercial organizations could be constructed and could support an increasing volume of activity.

The Bubble Act was not repealed until 1825, but it is fair to say that it retained very little of its significance by that time. Rarely did the authorities proceed against companies that were trying, contrary to the Act, to look as much as possible like corporations. England had despite the Act a thriving set of self-made companies to serve as a guide for further legislative action. Within the following 40 years England developed modern companies legislation granting limited liability and offering, in its schedules containing "companies clauses" an optional or suggested framework which made it easy for counsel to prepare constitutive documents for their clients.

English corporation rules carried over to a limited degree to the American colonies, which could be regarded as themselves being chartered companies. The Bubble Act was, for example, specifically extended to the colonies in 1741. One of the results was that it was tremendously expensive and difficult to obtain a charter all the way from London, and it was unclear whether any of the authorities on this side of the Atlantic had chartering authority. Thus there was considerable confusion about the legitimacy of Harvard College as a corporate body during much of the 17th century. Regardless of this, several hundred corporations (as well as bodies looking very much like corporations) did exist before the Revolution.

After independence, power to charter corporations clearly resided in the States (whether the federal government had that power was, of

---

1. 3 F. Maitland, Collected Papers 390 (1911).

2. 6 Geo. 1, c. 18, § 18.

course, settled affirmatively by McCulloch v. Maryland [3]) and they proceeded to make use of that power by calling into being numbers of corporations, at first predominantly in the area of what we would now think of as public utilities, i.e., turnpikes, canals, etc. Banks were another significant category. For the most part legislatures acted through individual grants which involved substantial amounts of log-rolling, haggling and occasionally downright corruption. Quite frequently the grant of corporate character was accompanied by other grants, in particular some sort of monopoly privilege (as in the case of the Charles River Bridge company which, unsuccessfully, claimed protection against competing bridges between Boston and Charlestown).[4] Pressures built up against this system: the staggering burden on the legislature of giving real consideration to the increasing number of requests, the jealousy of competitors towards the exclusive aspects of charters, the mounting Jacksonian antagonism toward special privilege. Thus little by little and one by one, states shifted to a policy of incorporation by general enabling act under which entrepreneurs could achieve corporate status simply by meeting standards, generally rather formal, set out in the statute. These factors were particularly strong in the case of manufacturing companies which grew in importance as time went on. For a time corporation laws still sought to set limits on corporations thus created—the corporation's capital could not be more than so many dollars, it could not own more than so many acres of land, etc. In particular the power to trade and invest in the stock of other corporations was generally withheld. The process of replacing special with general incorporation laws was a gradual one—the first general law was passed in New York in 1811 but New Jersey had none until 1875. In some states many special charters were granted long after incorporation under general laws was possible.

In the latter part of the century a set of changes took place in the nature of corporate enterprise. The corporation as the extension of a single entrepreneur's will, a surrogate for his own resources and capacities, began to prove inadequate. First with railroads and then with manufacturing enterprises, it became necessary on the one hand to aggregate the investments of many individuals who could no longer keep an active eye personally on their investment and on the other hand to develop a more complex managerial structure than the entrepreneur cum private secretary model. In particular, the first merger movement late in the century put heavy pressure on such aspects of the traditional system as the prohibition on holding shares of other companies. As the creators of these firms moved out to acquire other companies they ran into both problems and opportunities arising from the fact that their actions crossed state lines. In the period of specific charters the association between corporation and the chartering state had been so close that it was assumed that their activities would be

---

3. 4 Wheat. 316 (U.S.1819).

4. Proprietors of the Charles River Bridge v. Proprietors of the Warren Bridge, 11 Pet. 420 (U.S.1838).

limited to the home state and that any activity outside the state would be permitted only by the "comity" or tolerance of the foreign jurisdiction. Ingenious lawyers gradually solved these problems first by persuading the legislatures of some states (in particular Maine, New Jersey and finally Delaware) to enact corporation statutes giving broad discretion to management and then by persuading other states to tolerate the in-state activities of foreign corporations. In the latter case they received assistance from cases under the interstate commerce and equal protection clauses which narrowed the effective scope of the theoretically continuing power to exclude foreign companies. Thus by 1914 corporate lawyers had succeeded in constructing a legal framework adequate to support the nation-wide activities of very large industrial combinations.

Legal developments in the post–1914 period tended to focus on problems of the market for corporate securities and on related questions of attempting to shift the balance of power back in the favor of the investor. A peak period of activity on this front occurred in the aftermath of the depression when the Securities Act of 1933 and Securities Exchange Act of 1934 nationalized important parts of the law relating to trading in securities, shareholder control over the management, etc. Meanwhile, the state laws of corporations has continued to grow more flexible and permissive so that management could find within them more or less whatever they needed to create the organizational system they thought best. Restrictions on the growth of corporations in size, complexity and breadth of function now have almost entirely vanished from the corporation law scene and are to be found, if at all, in such fields as antitrust law. In the post World War II era one of the major challenges to the corporation law system has been the extension of the interstate corporation system to the international level so as to permit the operation of multi-national enterprises.

Bibliography: For a start on corporation history, see E.M. Dodd & R. Baker, Cases on Business Associations 1–23 (1940). For successive periods of English history: K. Gross, The Guild Merchant (1890); W.R. Scott, The Constitution and Finance of English, Scottish and Irish Joint–Stock Companies to 1720 (1910–12); A. DuBois, The English Business Company after the Bubble Act, 1720–1800 (1938); B.C. Hunt, The Development of the Business Corporation in England, 1800–1867 (1936). For American firms, see J.S. Davis, Essays on the Earlier History of American Corporations (1917); E.M. Dodd, American Business Corporations until 1860 (1954); A. Chandler, Strategy and Structure (1969), The Visible Hand (1977) (business school views); J.W. Hurst, The Legitimacy of the Business Corporation in the Law of the United States, 1780–1970 (1970); Clark, The Four Stages of Capitalism: Reflections on Investment Management Treatises, 94 Harv.L.Rev. 561 (1981).

2. An Economist's Perspective

Taking first a statistical approach to the corporation we find that its importance on the overall economic scene is difficult to exaggerate. There were in 1982, 2.926 million active corporations and over 600,000 new incorporations per year. Corporations make over 99% of total manufacturing sales, though performing only 67% of service operations and 80% of agriculture and forestry. Thus the sum of the activity of corporations in the United States is overwhelming. Looking at those corporations individually, however, we see many differences. Professor Conard divided them according to their assets into about 300 "billionaire," about 100,000 "millionaire" and over 1,000,000 "thousandaire" corporations.[5] These categories stretch from General Motors at one end of the spectrum to the incorporated hot dog stand at the other. Taking GM alone we find that in 1986 its 876,000 employees produced $102 billion of sales yielding a net after-tax income of $2.9 billion, from which its shareholders received $1.6 billion in dividends.

It is not uncommon for analysts to make comparisons between corporations and nations. For example:

> . . . Exxon had greater sales in 1974 than each of the GNPs of Austria, Denmark, and South Africa. General Motors employs more people—734,000—than are employed in [sic] the states of California, New York, Pennsylvania, and Michigan combined.[6]

Other analysts doubt the meaningfulness of such juxtapositions of state and private measurements.

Economists tend, in fact, to use, as the primary measure of corporate power, ratios which display the percentage of a product market which is possessed by a given corporation, or a group of corporations. These concentration ratios are taken as reflecting the monopolistic or oligopolistic power which those firms hold in the relevant market. There are sharp disputes as to whether, and to what extent, concentration as so measured is presently increasing and as to the effect of antimerger enforcement on that process.[7]

While some large corporations stick to a single product, a number of them are highly diversified, manufacturing numerous lines of related products, as GM makes cars, trucks, diesel locomotives, tractors, etc. In the 1970's there was a spectacular development of conglomerate corporations in which the product lines are quite unrelated so that ITT, for example, runs hotels, rents cars, strings telephone lines, etc. Many of these proved not to be efficient and had to be undone.

5. A. Conard, Corporations in Perspective 152–59 (1976).

6. R. Nader, M. Green & J. Seligman, Taming the Giant Corporation 16 (1976).

7. For a review of this subject see H. Goldschmid, H. Mann & J.F. Weston Industrial Concentration: The New Learning (1974).

Each of these major corporations is thus a formidable aggregate of economic power and their successes or failures (at one point the Penn Central was losing more than $1,000,000 per day, in one quarter of 1977 Bethlehem Steel recorded a loss of $477 million and International Harvester one of $299 million in 1982) have a powerful impact on the fortunes of many people.

From the standpoint of economic theory, one sees the corporation standing in the place of the individual entrepreneur on the marketplace. In the classical model the individual or the firm confronts a market in which an indefinite number of other firms are offering an indistinguishable product to a multitude of buyers. Under those circumstances a firm must offer its wares at a price set by the impersonal operations of the market; it will make as much of its product as it can consistently with its cost position. It cannot increase its profits by cutting back production and charging more per unit since others will fill the gap. The presence of competition will guarantee that it will make no "profit" on these operations but only that return on the capital invested which is needed to attract capital into the industry. The life of such a firm is strenuous and precarious. You may have encountered in college not only this primitive outline of the model, a firm under perfect competition, but might even have elaborated on its implications in some detail.

You may also recall having seen it demonstrated that such conditions do not prevail over wide segments of the economy, that often firms confront a fractionated market in which they can sell greater or lesser quantities of their differentiated product, depending on the price which they choose to charge. Operating with such relative independence from the market, they can select the point at which the gap between costs and sales price is greatest, which may involve producing quantities significantly less than those which would be indicated by a perfectly competitive market. By such operations a firm can generate substantial sums of earnings which it may retain for use in the business. This capacity to realize "monopoly profits" may arise by way of sole possession of a technological innovation, whether or not protected by patent rights, or from a monopolistic or oligopolistic position in the particular market which may be due to either illegal activity or to mere good fortune.

One of the markets in which the corporation functions is the market for capital. Indeed, one of the major advantages of the corporation is the ease with which it can draw upon and unite the resources of many individuals who become holders of its shares and other securities. The Germans sometimes speak of the corporation as a "capital pump". Ideally, the capital market should serve as a judge of the performance of firms, deciding whether or not their past achievements and future prospects warrant channeling more resources into a given field. It was, however, accepted wisdom for some decades that with large corporations the size of their retained earnings ("earned surplus") gave them a considerable independence from the capital market and enabled their managements to run things much as they pleased. But in the 1980's the capital markets were seen to be playing a powerful role in influencing the governance of corporations—through the actual and the feared incidence of hostile takeovers. Managements became very conscious of the market's appraisal of their performance as reflected in the price of their corporation's shares. If their performance was perceived as inefficient and stock prices sank, the scene was set for corporate raiders who could acquire the shares at a discount or who could afford to pay a premium above the depressed price because they could sell off or reorganize the target corporation's assets and still make a profit. Thus the pressure on managements to attend to maximizing shareholder wealth is intense; it has the further troubling aspect that shareholders seem to be intent on wealth maximization over a very short period of time. Arguably this sort of pressure is unhealthy as it inhibits managements from devoting resources to such investments as research and development which tend not to repay the outlay until years have passed.

Bibliography: The Corporation in Modern Society (E. Mason ed. 1959); N.S. Buchanan, The Economics of Corporate Enterprise (1940); A. Berle & G. Means, The Modern Corporation and Private Property (1933, rev. ed. 1968); R. Posner, Economic Analysis of Law chs. 14, 15 (3d ed. 1986); R. Posner & K. Scott, Economics of Corporation Law and Securities Regulation (1980); O. Williamson, The Economic Institutions of Capitalism (1986).

---

3. A Managerial—Sociological Viewpoint

The economist in the strict sense sees the firm as a unit acting in the marketplace trading with and competing with other units. He would distinguish between macro-economics or the study of aggregate behavior in markets and micro-economics or the study of the policy of individual firms confronting their markets. There has, however, been increasing awareness that a corporation is not a monolithic entity, not an irreducible atom. It is in fact an organization arranging a small or large group of people into a working pattern. The study of activity, motivation, patterns, etc., within the firm has been approached by several disciplines from different directions. Sociologists regard study of the corporation as a branch related to the study of other organizations—asylums, prisons, government bureaucracies, etc. Professors of business administration and management consultants approach the corporation from a pragmatic, action-oriented point of view. Psychologists have studied the interactions between persons within corporations, and students of decision theory analyze how corporate management chooses between options. From all of this has grown a large body of material, enlightening in some ways and inconclusive in others.

Management studies tend to view the corporation as a mass of individuals coordinated towards a common purpose. There is a hierarchical element to this. Indeed an organizational chart, with lines running down from top managers to individuals at lower levels, in narrower and more particularized jobs, is a feature of much managerial exposition. However, it becomes plain that people simply will not stay in their little boxes and do precisely what they are told to do by the little labels under them. Frequently only subordinates know enough about the details of a proposed decision to evaluate it with any accuracy; the person or persons titularly at the top can only scrutinize the recommendations brought up to them in a superficial way. Large elements of autonomy must be parcelled out to people at various levels of the large corporation's structure. One can in fact view the top level executive as a mediator, trying to work out solutions that satisfactorily provide for the demands of other executives, workers, clerical staff, and the shareholders. Out of these diverse types must be fashioned a coalition capable of grappling with the business of the corporation.

Another question which such analysts seek to answer is: what are in fact the goals of corporate management? This is a treacherous area to explore since what managers say may not really represent what they do and it may be equally hard to trace back motives from the operating results. In the classic perfectly competitive situation, management had little choice: the goal was survival, to be pursued by maximizing profit as much as possible. Managers may not be able to pursue that goal directly and intelligently and may have to resort to rules of thumb calculated to work out as rough profit-maximizing in the long run. Or, it is suggested, they may prefer a plainly different goal such as maximizing sales or assets or share of the market. These targets may in fact provide more satisfactions to the managers, as distinct from the shareholders, than does profit-maximizing. A dramatic increase in profits one year may simply make the shareholders expect more the next; an increase in size or market share may not only gratify the managers' competitive urges but also be a better base for demanding more pay and perquisites. Managers must, even on this theory, avoid losses, which would jeopardize the position of the firm as well as their own. Some of the targets of managers may lie outside the realm of economics, residing in such things as a sense of contribution to the public interest, the approval of the business or general community, aesthetic interests, etc. Whatever the goals of management may in fact be does not, of course, determine what they should be or whether legal rules should be shaped so as to cause management to lean more in one way than another.

All of this has become more complicated in the 1980's as American industrial performance, once perceived as unparalleled in its efficiency, began to be seen as inferior to its German and Japanese counterparts. American industrial output limped, disadvantaged by an industrial plant that was on an average older and less automated than that of its competition. It also suffered from an overvalued dollar that made

American exports exaggeratedly expensive in foreign markets. The response of American managements was to become "lean and mean." Redundant facilities were closed down, numbers of workers, both blue and white collar, were let go and union contracts were renegotiated. Some of these retrenchments were effectuated by corporate raiders after takeover, some were undertaken by incumbent managements in the face of looming takeover threats and some were not connected with takeovers. In any case, their general effect was to undermine the morale of corporate workers and produce new problems for those who had to manage the truncated enterprises that were left.

Bibliography: Important books on management include C. Barnard, The Functions of the Executive (1958); P. Drucker, The Changing World of the Executive (1982); R. Christensen, N. Berg, M. Salter & H. Stevenson, Policy Formulation and Administration (9th ed. 1985). Practical connections between law and management are made in W. Klein & J. Coffee, Business Organization and Finance (3d ed. 1988).

4. An Accountant's Perspective

In many important senses a corporation is an accounting entity. Its managers appraise its performance and attempt to influence its future in terms of costs and earnings measured through an accounting system. The securities markets in turn appraise the performances of firms, and people buy and sell their shares according to the signals they receive through the accounting system. Thus many of the functions performed by economists and statisticians for the economy at large are performed for the individual corporation by accounting. The implications of accounting for corporation law are pervasive. Some legal rules turn directly on accounting concepts: a corporation may be insolvent if its assets do not equal its liabilities; dividends may be declared only if they do not "impair capital"; shares of stock with par value may not be issued unless the consideration received has a value at least equal to that par. Other corporation law rules call for disclosure designed to enable private parties to make intelligent decisions: whether to buy or sell shares, how to vote on a change of management or a merger. How far a particular corporations course needs to explore these factors is a matter for the instructor's judgment. It is hard to avoid them entirely for we find that even legal ideas such as "unfairness" or "fraud" turn out to have an accounting base. "Cost" and "value" are concepts not to be ignored in a corporations course. However, I believe that they can be treated in a fairly simple yet satisfactory way.

As a minimum there are a few things about accountants and the way in which they operate that you ought to understand. A corporation will employ bookkeepers and accountants to provide it with data needed for its own operations. Financial statements designed to be circulated to the public while prepared by the corporation's staff must generally be audited by an independent accountant or firm of accountants. You will observe that such statements as published are accompanied by a declaration (generally called a "report" or an "opinion" but often referred to as a "certificate") which says that the accountants examined the statements in accordance with generally accepted auditing standards including necessary tests of the underlying accounting records; they then give an opinion that the financial statements present fairly the position of the corporation in conformity with generally accepted accounting principles.

The form of the presentations made and the scope of the investigation to back up those summaries are regulated to some degree by law, primarily by the Securities and Exchange Commission, but to a greater degree by the custom of the accounting profession. Lawyers need to remember that accounting is a proud profession with its own institutions, including some firms much larger than any law firm, its own traditions and its own ethical standards. It not infrequently becomes relevant to lawyers to determine what generally accepted accounting principles or auditing standards are. This may involve an inquiry into accounting treatises and periodicals. Special weight, though not a conclusive one, must be given to the pronouncements of the American Institute of Certified Public Accountants, the body which represents the profession's collective voice. Through various boards and committees it has produced Auditing Standards, Accounting Terminology Bulletins, Accounting Research Bulletins, Opinions of the Accounting Principles Board and, most recently, statements of Financial Accounting Standards. From time to time we refer to such materials when they become relevant to corporation law questions.

Bibliography: The literature of accounting is vast. For a starter for lawyers see D. Herwitz, Materials on Accounting for Lawyers (1980); De Capriles, Modern Financial Accounting, 37 N.Y.U.L.Rev. 1001, 38 id. 1 (1962–63) or J. Cox, Financial Information, Accounting and the Law (1980). For a review of legal aspects of accounting see Symposium, Uniformity in Financial Accounting, 30 Law & Contemp.Prob. 621 (1965). The Journal of Accountancy and the Accounting Review are the leading periodicals. To find authority on specific points consult the Commerce Clearing House loose-leaf service, Accounting Articles, or such a treatise as J. Burton, R. Palmer & R. Key, Handbook of Accounting and Auditing (1981, 1988 update).

---

5. The Legal Context of Corporation Law

There is much misunderstanding about the boundaries of the law of corporations. Some of this originates with the term "corporation lawyer". The person who practices "corporate law" frequently turns out to be involved with something outside the scope of this course, perhaps antitrust law or taxation. Corporation law is in essence the structural, one might say constitutional, law of corporations—it prescribes how the shareholders relate to each other and to the directors and other managers. It tells how meetings are to be conducted and power is to be exercised; it regulates financial transactions between buyers and sellers of shares. Since that law governs the structure of authority within the corporation, outsiders who deal with it, who lend it money or sell it property, must be aware of those rules if they are to be sure that they are dealing on a sound legal basis. In general, however, corporation law deals with insiders, defined in a somewhat arbitrary way. Thus, while corporation law governs the relationship of a corporation to its officers and upper management and its shareholders, relationships with its employees are remitted to labor law and relationships with its dealers are left to contract law, tempered by antitrust. This is true even though the latter groups may have a lasting and intimate relationship to the corporation. Thus in a period when many questions are arising about the impact of the corporation on society as a whole the student is apt to feel somewhat frustrated by the growing realization that the law of corporations only deals tangentially (though, its teachers would say, importantly) with them. For example, changes in the conduct of corporations are essential if pollution is to be curbed, but the central impact will come from a special set of rules on environmental law, backed perhaps by administrative law. Knowledge of corporation law will, however, be necessary in order to gauge the effectiveness of regulations or punitive measures or to use such vehicles as shareholders' meetings or proxy contests to bring demands to bear on management. Thus a very respectable case can be made for the relevance, if not more, of corporation law to many of the critical concerns of society today.

It is useful to consider briefly some of the relationships between corporation law and other fields:

(1) *Contracts.* Basically corporations are the creature of contract; conceptually they are thought of as arising from a contract between the state and the corporate stockholders. Thus they enjoy the protection, such as it is, of the contract clause. Some analysts of corporations use the idea of contract as a base for arguing that whatever is accepted by shareholders is to be accepted as fair and final. One should approach these arguments with a skepticism nourished by an awareness that the shareholder contract is a special one in which possibilities of overreaching are rife. A stock certificate is at best a contract of adhesion. Corporations, of course, also make contracts. In order to do so they must act through agents, who must have authorization along lines provided for in corporation or agency law.

(2) *Antitrust.* In its early years corporation law was concerned with the size and scope of economic activity of the corporate creatures it generated. It characteristically limited them either in individual clauses in the charters creating them or in overall limits. That function has now passed to antitrust law, by default one might say.

Antitrust law must, however, take account of internal corporate arrangements as it seeks to prevent collusion between corporations, as by interlocking directors, or to limit the growth of corporations beyond the point of justification by economies of scale and efficiency.

(3) *Taxation.* How corporations behave is obviously much influenced by taxes, specifically the federal income tax. In particular corporate structures are erected with a view to the Internal Revenue Code's basic rule that a corporation forms a taxable entity separate and distinct from its individual shareholders. The Code does not necessarily classify corporations quite the way nontax laws do.[8] Thus related corporations may file consolidated returns as a unit while remaining separate for liability purposes. Subchapters R and S give groups the right to opt to be corporations or partnerships for tax purposes while being, respectively, partnerships or corporations for nontax purposes.

(4) *Regulatory Law.* Many corporations operate in fields where they are subject to more or less intensive regulation by a federal or state agency. At one time such functions were, in a sense, assigned to the chartering process or to the agency that administered them. At times suggestions are made that we return to such a practice. On the whole, however, practical considerations suggest that such an agent as the Secretary of State of New York cannot supervise all corporations in lines of endeavor ranging from insect extermination to the generation of electric power. Agencies controlling specific industries are concerned with many aspects of corporation law such as the relations between affiliated corporations.

Bibliography: The most complete reference book is the multi-volume Fletcher, Cyclopedia of Corporations. There are compact one volume hornbook-type treatises by H. Henn (3d ed. 1983) and N. Lattin (2d ed. 1971). More theoretically oriented is R. Clark, Corporate Law (1986). There are more practically-oriented treatises such as C.L. Israels, Corporate Practice (4th ed. A. Hoffman 1983), and Lawyer's Basic Corporate Practice Manual (3d ed., R. Deer, 1984). There are a number of treatises on the corporation laws of particular states. The utility of these varies; particular value attaches to the work of lawyers who participated in revising the state legislation in question, e.g., that of Ernest Folk on Delaware and Harold Marsh on California. Others are compendious and thorough and replete with practical hints. Yet others are quite obsolete. Both Commerce Clearing House and Prentice Hall maintain corporation law services. There is now also a Journal of Corporation Law. There is a very substantial quantity of continuing legal education material on corporations at both a state and a national level. Specialized works are cited below in the particular places where they become relevant.

---

8. Klein, Income Taxation and Legal Entities, 20 U.C.L.A.L.Rev. 13 (1972).

6. On Being a Corporation Lawyer

It would be natural to suppose that the course in the Law of Corporations should tell the student something about being a corporation lawyer. I have structured this casebook so that it will at least give glimpses of that way of life but it seems appropriate to make a slightly more extended statement about it here. As indicated above, there is some confusion both about what corporation law is and what corporation lawyers do. The term properly applies to those who spend their time dealing with the subject matter of corporation law and the neighboring field of securities regulation. They deal with prospectuses relating to securities issues, contracts for the sale of securities already issued, mortgages securing corporate debt securities, proxies relating to shareholder meetings, etc.

Mention of the term corporation lawyer tends to evoke a picture of a partner or associate in a large firm on Wall, LaSalle or State Street. Each of these firms does maintain a group (sometimes a formally organized department) of attorneys engaged in advising corporations, often the very largest ones, on their managerial and securities problems. Particular notoriety has attached to law firms specializing in takeovers and other enormous—and enormously rewarding—transactions. However, there are many lawyers in small firms, or on their own, who spend all or some of their time dealing with corporations, often those on a smaller and more intimate scale. There is also a large and growing group of lawyers engaged in the same sort of work within the law departments of major corporations—including many persons who hold the title of "Secretary."

It is difficult to make valid generalizations about the professional experiences of such diverse groups. However, a few can be attempted:

(1) Corporation lawyers need to be able to handle large quantities of paper work with speed and accuracy and to dispose of routine matters in such a way that they can spend time on the exceptional and critical points. I do not mean to imply that litigators can be sloppy or that big cases do not involve masses of paperwork but, in gross terms, there is a contrast.

(2) Corporation lawyers are expected to *know* a complex and involved body of laws and regulations or at least know how to find the pertinent provisions very quickly. They are expected to be able to answer simple questions from their "inventory" of knowledge.

(3) Corporation lawyers have a tendency to give "safe-side" advice about the legality of proposed actions and to regard the cropping up of litigation about them as something to be avoided at all costs. This bias is not always appropriate in certain situations where the hoped-for gains outweigh the risks anticipated, even the legal ones.

(4) Corporation lawyers know a good deal about business, in particular about the financing of businesses. They are familiar with corporate structures, with business terminology and business modes of analysis. While a few have had some formal business school training, most have simply picked it up as they went along. There is always some danger that they will absorb business attitudes so thoroughly as to be unable to advise their clients about their actions and the possible governmental and public reactions thereto with the objectivity that should be forthcoming from them.

(5) There is a reasonable amount of flow from law firms and law departments into general managerial positions. This continues even though there is now more specialized business training available which would seem to afford a more directly relevant foundation for the latter type of position.

(6) It is sometimes thought that corporate work is less emotionally demanding and calls for a less aggressive personality than does litigation work. I know lawyers who have done both who would disagree. They would say that the sort of toughness called for in pressing for the optimum "deal" for one's client, in circumstances where there are many pressures to concede points to be "statesmanlike" or a "good sport", etc., is more difficult than the rather formal confrontations of litigators in the courtroom.

(7) There is a question in the minds of some students though less so in the 1970's whether one can be a corporation lawyer at all and still have a conscience or whether one's involvement with the corporate structure inherently involves one in unacceptable complicity.

(8) Corporation lawyers deal with clients who are demanding and critical of their performance. At the rate which they charge clients feel that they have a right to be! Representative business executives told the American Bar Association in 1977 that they found lawyers to be indecisive, excessively devoted to detail, unnecessarily combative and of doubtful loyalty to their clients in the case of clashes with administrative agencies before which they regularly practice. For all of that, business clients are closer to their counsel in outlook, background and education than clients in other types of practice, especially criminal law.

(9) The most satisfying aspect of corporate practice, for many, are those transactions which are not "zero sum games", as litigation necessarily is. To participate in putting together a new project, for example the building of a plant or a utility, and to see widely differing participants pulling in the same direction for a common goal can be an exciting experience.

Practicing corporation law is apt to raise rather special questions of professional responsibility or legal ethics. In particular, one encounters difficult issues arising from the problem of ascertaining who is the client or speaks for the client. Such issues are pointed out from time to time in this volume and the Documentary Supplement contains excerpts from the 1983 Model Rules of Professional Responsibility that is gradually supplanting the Code of Professional Responsibility.

Bibliography: There is not a great deal of literature that is helpful on the role of the corporation lawyer. For a sociologist's view see E. Smigel, The Wall Street Lawyer (1969). There is quite a lot of interesting background in R.T. Swaine, The Cravath Firm and its Predecessors, 1819–1947 (1946–48), but its picture of practice is necessarily rather dated. For a condensed statement of the same author's views, see Impact of Big Business on the Profession: An Answer to the Critics of the Modern Bar, 35 A.B.A.J. 89 (1949). M. Mayer, The Lawyers ch. 9 (1967), presents some good journalism on the topic. See also, B. Levy, Corporation Lawyer: Saint or Sinner? (1961); P. Hoffman, Lions in the Street (1973); J. Stewart, The Partners: Inside America's Most Powerful Law Firms (1983). For current news on corporate lawyers refer to the tabloids—The National Law Journal and The American Lawyer. Gilson, Value Creation by Business Lawyers, 94 Yale L.J. 239 (1984), makes a carefully reasoned case for the social utility of corporation lawyers.

---

7. Corporation Law and Ideology

Students come to the study of corporations with some sort of predisposition about them, some sort of attitude or set of ideas about them. These they will have picked up in college, from their families or during their work experience. These will not be neatly organized conceptual frameworks, usually, nor will they be free of contradictory ideas. When they come from college business or economics courses they will tend to be more coherent and ideological. Their focus is apt to be on corporations at the upper end of the scale in terms of size and power, ignoring the multitude of small incorporated enterprises that also raise legal questions.

Over time these ideologies clearly change, as any veteran teacher recognizes. In the 1950's and early 1960's there was considerable complacency about American industry and its leadership. It was assumed that our management was the best in the world and that it would continue to grind out economic gains if left alone. There was a general assumption that the New Deal legislation of the 1930's had solved the problems of the past and that the process of expansion would go on fairly automatically. There was a rather dramatic turn-around of mood on many campuses during the period 1964–70. A sizable group of students, though never a majority, were vocally and visibly alienated from the institutions of American society and the establishment, including corporations. Corporations were still regarded as large and powerful but now they were blamed for misusing their power and wealth. A wide variety of evils was laid at their door. They were destroying the environment, they were making possible the imperialist war in Viet–Nam, they were exploiting third world peoples and they were suppressing the individualities of their American workers. The spearhead of this movement was Students for a Democratic Society. Its attitude towards corporations is reflected in the following from New Left Notes, (Sept. 9, 1968, p. 8, col. 2) reporting on an internal squabble within the Liberation News Service:

> "Corporate and criminal laws are the kind of b_____ s_____ to be used as cover and pressure on the Man, not as weapons against each other."

Meanwhile, Ralph Nader and his associates developed a more pragmatic and reformist approach to corporations, seeking to bring them under popular control and to find ways of making them more responsible.

By the 1980's this wave had subsided. What was left was Critical Legal Studies, a movement unique to law schools (and not all of them). Not a great deal of its writing was dedicated to corporations as a subject but attitudes towards them were implicit in its approach to general problems. They saw in corporate structures things they loathed— hierarchy, inequality and bureaucratic rigidity. They tended to equate government agencies and corporations in these respects. To the extent that they proferred a program it concentrated on breaking up large organizations, locating power at lower levels of hierarchy and in smaller groups and opening the way for more spontaneous and flexible, hence enjoyable and fulfilling, group activity. At the same time intellectual forces on the "right" sought to shape the way in which people thought about corporations. Law and economics writers and teachers dealt much more intensively than CLS writers with the specifics of corporation law. Overall their message tended to be that whatever problems there were in the field of corporations would be solved by the operations of the various markets if only interfering governments would stand aside and let natural action proceed. More abstractly, libertarian writers argued that all government incursions upon the untouchability of private property were suspect and that most of them were both immoral and counter-productive.

Students process these messages through their own intellectual systems. More than their predecessors they are conscious of the need to achieve financial security (and pay off heavy educational loans). The slipping position of the United States in the worldwide industrial competition of the 1980s makes them aware that it is important to make sure that the pie is as large as it can possibly be before one starts to decide how it should be sliced. The problems of the securities markets, of takeovers, reorganizations and of industrial restructuring in general are seen as intellectual challenges worthy of the best minds. At the same time students are concerned about losing their identities in large organizations (including the large law firms that service even larger corporate enterprises). They are worried about giving as much of their time and their spirit to the demands of industry. And they tend, after reading about insider trading, corrupt foreign payments, shoddy and dangerous products and other scandals, to believe that there is a great deal of cynicism and amorality prevalent in corporate managements. They note that large corporations are becoming increasingly ruthless in displacing persons who no longer fit into their current strategy so that loyalty to the organization is no longer reciprocated. They even wonder whether countries like Japan have discovered new types of organization and management that are superior to ours. In sum one can describe student attitudes towards corporations as being characterized by a realistic and resigned acquiescence in their permanent importance in the landscape.

It is in the face of these attitudes that we commence the study of Corporations.

Bibliography: For critiques of the corporate system one might begin with L. Brandeis, Other People's Money (1914), and T. Veblen, Absentee Ownership (1923). Of the more recent critical materials consider A. Baran & P. Sweezy, Monopoly Capital (1966); M. Mintz & J. Cohen, America, Inc. (1971). Ralph Nader's views are reported in R. Nader, M. Green & J. Seligman, Taming the Giant Corporation (1976). Conservative views on property (without much reference to corporations) are restated in G. Dietze, In Defense of Property (1971). For a conservative perspective on corporate operations see M. Friedman, Capitalism and Freedom (1962). Two critical legal studies articles that have implications for corporations are Unger, The Critical Legal Studies Movement, 96 Harv.L.Rev. 561 (1983): Frug, The Ideology of Bureaucracy in American Law, 97 Harv.L.Rev. 1276 (1984).

Chapter II

PARTNERSHIP

Before starting to discuss the problems of corporation law you should have some background in the law of partnerships. Partnership law is a topic worth studying for its own sake: it has challenging intellectual problems and is still of substantial concern to the practicing lawyer. Additionally, it serves as a useful introduction to corporation law. Partnership law may be considered as a bridge between the law of agency with which it has many connections, and the law of corporations. Like corporation law it deals with the problems that arise when a business enterprise grows too large to be handled by the law governing individuals and for the law governing individuals acting through agents. It is concerned with one type of organization that aggregates the funds and talents of several individuals towards a common economic goal. Thus it is often enlightening to compare the corporate and the partnership solutions to a problem. Indeed, many cases refer to smaller, more personal corporations as "incorporated partnerships." Finally, it is often part of a lawyer's function to advise as to the choice between corporate and partnership organization.

1. An Historical Note

Like accounting, the law of partnerships is primarily an Italian discovery or, more accurately, a *re*discovery since a "societas" much resembling the partnership was known to the Romans. In the later Middle Ages Italian merchants, operating as partners and very frequently as partners in what we would call limited partnership, brought their commercial customs with them throughout Europe:

The system of limited partnerships, which was introduced by statute into this State, and subsequently very generally adopted in many other States of the Union, was borrowed from the French Code. (3 Kent, 36; Code de Commerce, 19, 23, 24.) Under the name of *la Société en commandite*, it has existed in France from the time of the middle ages; mention being made of it in the most ancient commercial records, and in the early mercantile regulations of Marseilles and Montpelier. In the vulgar Latinity of the middle ages it was styled *commenda*, and in Italy *accomenda*. In the statutes of Pisa and Florence, it is

18

recognized so far back as the year 1160; also in the ordinance of Louisle–Hutin, of 1315; the statutes of Marseilles, 1253; of Geneva, of 1588. In the middle ages it was one of the most frequent combinations of trade, and was the basis of the active and widely-extended commerce of the opulent maritime cities of Italy. It contributed largely to the support of the great and prosperous trade carried on along the shores of the Mediterranean, was known in Languedoc, Provence, and Lombardy, entered into most of the industrial occupations and pursuits of the age, and even travelled under the protection of the arms of the Crusaders to the city of Jerusalem. At a period when capital was in the hands of nobles and clergy, who, from pride of caste, or canonical regulations, could not engage directly in trade, it afforded the means of secretly embarking in commercial enterprises, and reaping the profits of such lucrative pursuits, without personal risk; and thus the vast wealth, which otherwise would have lain dormant in the coffers of the rich, became the foundation, by means of this ingenious idea, of that great commerce which made princes of the merchants, elevated the trading classes, and brought the Commons into position as an influential estate in the commonwealth. Independent of the interest naturally attaching to the history of a mercantile contract, of such ancient origin, but so recently introduced where the general partnership, known to the Common Law, has hitherto existed alone, I have been led to refer to the facts just stated, for the purpose of showing that the special partnership is, in fact, no novelty, but an institution of considerable antiquity, well known, understood, and regulated.[1]

In relatively early times the partnership came to England where it was known in medieval times, and was familiar in Elizabethan days.[2] During the period of Raleigh, Drake and the other great explorers and adventurers, the partnership existed alongside the great joint stock companies which—if they were to achieve true "corporateness"—required a charter from the crown. Malynes, Lex Mercatoria 211 (1622), one of the first English textbooks on commercial law, tells us:

"The other association is done by and between Merchants of their owne authoritie, joyning themselves together for to deale and trade either for yeares or voyages; and this is properly called Partnership, where one man doth adventure £ 1000, another £ 500 [etc.] . . . more or lesse, as they agree amongst themselves, to make a stock, every man to have his profit, or to beare losses and adventure according to their several stockes—wherein the conditions be deverse which must

1. Ames v. Downing, 1 Brad. (N.Y.Surr. Ct.) 321, 329 (1850).

2. 1 Select Cases concerning the Law Merchant 59, 77, 105 (C. Gross ed. 1908); 2 Select Cases concerning the Law Merchant, 18–30 (H. Hall ed. 1929).

be observed truly and the accounts accordingly otherwise all will run into a laborinth and confusion."

(Note already the emphasis on care and exactitude in commercial matters!)

Originally, the common law courts seldom exercised jurisdiction over partnerships, and the principles of the law of partnerships, as of commercial law generally, developed in the courts of the merchants themselves. Only later did the common law courts and Chancery start to hear evidence of commercial custom and to assimilate the custom into the common law. Therefore, the first important court cases on partnership do not emerge before the 17th century.[3] The great period of growth of the common law of partnerships begins in the 1700's and continues until the codification of the law in the 20th century in the form of the Uniform Partnership Act of 1914 (U.P.A.) (adopted in 48 states and the District of Columbia) and the Uniform Limited Partnership Act of 1916 (U.L.P.A.) (with a 1976 revision now adopted in 37 states.) Although the greatest commercial enterprises are now almost uniformly corporations the partnership has not wholly lost its significance. As of 1983, the Statistical Abstract of the United States 506 (1987) had the following findings as to the distribution and productivity of partnerships:

	Number (in thousands)	Receipts (in millions)
Total	1,542	$278,347
Services	306	$ 75,069
Manufacture	26	$ 14,179
Wholesale & Retail	194	$ 59,880
Finance, Insurance & Real Estate	730	$ 76,784

Thus, particularly outside of manufacturing, partnerships retain considerable importance both in numbers and in volume of business done, despite the evidence of a continuing shift towards use of the corporation. In some fields the limited partnership saw increasing use because of its adaptability for use as a tax shelter. The limited partners could take tax losses, induced by rapid depreciation of real estate, natural resources or other investments, into their own income tax returns whereas a corporation, as a separate tax entity, would intercept those benefits. These advantages were sharply curtailed by the "passive investment" rules of the 1986 tax reform. There are some areas, banking and insurance for example, where the law often provides that a company must incorporate. Conversely, there were some types of activity which could be conducted by a partnership but not a corporation. The practice of law was one example and that of medicine (in general) another.[4] This type of restriction has been related to state

---

3. See 1 W. Holdsworth, A History of English Law 459, 466 (7th ed. 1956), 5 id. at 144, 297–98 (2d ed. 1937).

4. See Bittker, Professional Service Organizations, 23 Tax L.Rev. 429 (1968);

Paas, Professional Corporations and Attorney–Shareholders: The Decline of Limited Liability, 11 J.Corp.L. 371 (1986).

laws imposing licensing requirements which a corporation cannot meet. Thus one commentator said:

"A corporation being a fictitious character has no mind and cannot think; consequently it cannot meet educational requirements." [5] In recent years, however, state legislation, responding primarily to federal tax problems, has increasingly come to sanction incorporation for doctors, lawyers and other professionals. Those tax advantages have proved ephemeral and the advantage of limited liability elusive.

REVIEW PROBLEMS

(1) Is the above quotation a satisfactory explanation? Is it relevant that some courts have held that a corporation can be convicted of an offense requiring *mens rea*? Are there other reasons inherent in the differences between partnership and corporation for not permitting such professionals to incorporate?

(2) The typical statute on professional corporations provides that it does "not alter any law applicable to the relationship between a person furnishing professional services and a person receiving such services, including liability arising out of such professional services." Suppose that Jones and Smith, P.C. is a professional corporation consisting of two lawyers. One fails, negligently, to file a claim on time. The client sues and finds the P.C. has inadequate funds. Can the client reach both Jones' and Smith's assets?

2. Formation

While the process of incorporating, as we shall see at p. 76 infra, is a matter of some detail and some tedium, the process of becoming a partnership is simple. With few exceptions, no filing or application or any other contact with a government agency is necessary. Indeed, it is possible to become a partnership without even intending or knowing it. One who fulfills the legal definition of a partnership becomes a partner, even if he does not so intend. In fact one can even—as against outsiders—become a partner by estoppel if he remains inactive knowing that another is representing that he is a partner. (U.P.A. § 16).

Consequently, it is not as easy to be certain whether a group is or is not a partnership as it is to tell whether it is or is not a corporation. Indeed, a distinguished judge, later Justice Lurton, stated: "It is not very prudent to define a partnership." [6] Undeterred, the draftsman of the Uniform Act attempted a definition, which you will find in section 6. The following comment by the Commissioners is worth reading in connection with that section:

5. Note, 27 Marquette L.Rev. 135, 139 (1943); Accord: Painless Parker v. Board of Dental Examiners, 216 Cal. 285, 295, 14 P.2d 67, 72 (1932).

6. Fechteler v. Palm Bros. & Co., 133 Fed. 462, 466 (6th Cir.1904).

"The definition asserts that the associates are 'co-owners' of
the business. This distinguishes a partnership from an agency—an association of principal and agent. A business is a
series of acts directed toward an end. Ownership involves the
power of ultimate control. To state that partners are co-
owners of a business is to state that they each have the power
of ultimate control."

Beneath the surface smoothness of the definition lurk some difficult problems of application. These become more apparent as we put
Section 7 alongside Section 6. You will notice that Section 7 speaks in
terms of a *prima facie* case of partnership arising from sharing in the
profits. It then (in section 7(4)) enumerates certain cases in which a
share in the profits does *not* create a partnership. Paragraph (4)(a) in
particular has a considerable history; its origins go back to the leading
case of Cox v. Hickman [7] in which it was held—discarding prior views—
that repayment of a debt out of the debtor's earnings did not constitute
the creditors partners of the debtor. Are the exceptions in Section 7 in
harmony with the basic conceptions of partnership in Section 6? The
semi-hypothetical problems at the end of this section raise some difficult questions about Sections 6 and 7 and about the idea of "co-
ownership." [8]

It should be emphasized that the fact that no express agreement
and no written agreement is required to form a partnership is no
excuse for failure to exercise care in drafting a partnership agreement.
Indeed, it may be a more challenging task than drafting corporate
papers.[9] Corporation laws tend to form a fairly inflexible mold within
which a certificate of incorporation must be formed. The partnership
law—as far as concerns the relationship of the partners with one
another—affords wider freedom. It largely provides (see especially
U.P.A. § 18) for certain principles that apply in the absence of agreement. Some of these may become highly inconvenient in a specific
case.

There is one exception to the general rule that no application to
any state agency is needed in connection with formation of a partnership. If a *limited* partnership is intended the partners must file a
certificate as provided by state law. The certificate will give the names
of the general and limited partners, the amount of capital contributed
by them, and certain other data. U.L.P.A. § 2. Publication is also
frequently required. The certificate must be kept up to date when
changes take place (U.L.P.A. § 24). Strict compliance with these provisions is essential if the purpose of a limited partnership—that of

---

7. 8 H.L.Cas. 268, 11 Eng.Rep. 431
(1860).

8. For a stimulating attempt to rationalize the rules on the existence of a partnership in terms of risk, profit and control
see W.O. Douglas, Vicarious Liability and

the Administration of Risk II, 38 Yale L.J.
720 (1929).

9. See, generally, M. Volz, C. Trower &
D. Reiss, The Drafting of Partnership
Agreements (7th ed. 1986).

insulating the limited partner from unlimited liability—is to be achieved.

Do not forget that the formation of a partnership to do a certain type of business may bring into play certain laws applicable to all types of business organizations whether partnership, sole proprietorship or corporation. These laws fall into two classes. *First,* if a partnership is doing business under an assumed or fictitious name it should file, if applicable state law so requires, a certificate showing who is doing business under the assumed name. Thus Sam Spade and Mike Hammer may do business as a partnership "Spade & Hammer" but must file a certificate if they do business as "L.A. Private Eyes". *Second,* there may be requirements as to entry into a given business. Spade and Hammer will probably have to have a license to enter into the business of being private detectives and another license to carry concealed weapons.

The absence of organizational requirements cuts down the expense of a partnership. Even the filing fee for a limited partnership is in most states only a few dollars.[10] Certain fees, which may be substantial, are required in connection with the filing of a certificate of incorporation. Where only a small enterprise is concerned this saving may sway an otherwise close decision on the form of organization.

Another corollary of the free access to partnership status is the right to move outside of the state of original formation. Being merely an aggregation of individual citizens, a partnership may do business in any other state under constitutional protection [11] while a corporation may have to do certain acts in order to do business in another state and may incur unpleasant consequences if it does not do them. The right of a limited partnership to do business in a state other than one in which its certificate is filed is open to doubt. An experienced practitioner advises that it is discreet to file a certificate in each state where business is done.[12]

The partnership resulting from the relationship of co-owning a business is not, according to the prevailing interpretation of common law and the Uniform Act, an "entity". It is no more than an aggregation of the partners. This was the result of much discussion at the time the Uniform Act was drafted. Dean Ames of Harvard, the first draftsman, was (roughly speaking) "pro-entity" but his successor, Dean Lewis of Pennsylvania, proceeded on an "anti-entity" basis. You will frequently find in the cases statements to the effect that a given result follows from the basic principle that a partnership is not an entity separate from its members. As you examine the operating results worked out by the draftsmen of the Uniform Act and by the courts ask yourself whether it is helpful to start out by reasoning on the following

10. But see Fla.Stat.Ann. § 620.02(1)(b)(2) (1977) ($4 per thousand of capital—$1000 limit).

11. J. Crane & A. Bromberg, Partnership 108–9 (1968).

12. C. Rohrlich, Organizing Corporate and other Business Enterprises § 2.18 (5th ed. 1975). See U.L.P.A. (rev.) §§ 901–908.

lines: "a partnership is not an entity and therefore. . . ." If the results do not seem to follow from this concept consider what the practical and equitable reasons are for departing from this line of reasoning. Is one of them a belief that the expectations of the business community tend to harmonize more with the entity theory?

PROBLEMS

(1) John Phillips came to the United States from Scotland with his three sons and, starting from poverty, built up a prosperous furniture business. The sons each were to receive 15% of the earnings of the business. However, it often became necessary to plough these funds back into the business. As ancestral traditions dictated, they obeyed their father at all times and made no effort to interfere in the way in which John ran the shop. John was once heard to say:

"Na, na! I will ha' no sons for partners as long as I live. Damn them! They would put me out of the door!"

All transactions were carried on in the name of John Phillips; however, when bills were sent to the office in the name of John Phillips & Sons they were paid without comment.

One of the sons (now 45 years old) leaves home and asks for an accounting for his claimed partnership interest. What result? Would the answer as to partnership be the same if the question were a suit by an outsider against one of the sons on a debt of the business? Does it matter whether the creditor suing was one of those who sent a bill in the partnership format?

(2) John Wilson, a retired broker with considerable financial resources who lives in New York, was approached by two young and energetic entrepreneurs with a promising idea for a new proprietary drug. They, being nearly penniless, are willing to give Wilson a one-third share in the profits in return for $50,000 with which to start up operations. Wilson does not want to have anything to do with running the business and does not even want to have his name associated with the enterprise for fear of the reaction of his conservative friends. He regards the entire transaction as a risky plunge which he is willing to undertake because he can psychologically write off the $50,000 if his worst fears are realized and the firm goes under with heavy losses. How close can the parties come to carrying out their wishes? In particular, can the parties avoid filing and publicity for Wilson?

(3) A severe but temporary crisis in the market for foreign securities brought Mr. Knauth, a private banker, to the verge of ruin since he is unable to pay his creditors, C–1 and C–2, the $10,000 he owes each of them upon the date his notes come due. Sharing Knauth's belief that the crisis would soon pass, C–1 and C–2 have agreed in principle to waive strict performance of the terms of the notes and to advance $5000 more in return for 80% of Knauth's net earnings up to the time when principal and interest of all their loans are fully repaid. Having some doubts of Knauth's business judgment, they want to stipulate for the right to examine Knauth's books and reserved a right to veto all major transactions. Can you carry this arrangement into effect without making C–1 and C–2 partners of Mr. Knauth?

(4) Suppose that a woman lawyer sues a partnership alleging that she was unable to become a partner solely because the firm had a practice that barred women from partnership but allowed them to be hired as associates. Does the

practice violate the Civil Rights Act of 1964, 42 U.S.C.A. § 2000e et seq., forbidding discrimination on account of sex in the "terms, conditions or privileges of employment"? Suppose that a man who had been designated as a partner of one of the "big eight" accounting firms sues the firm for having discriminated against him on account of his age, in violation of the Age Discrimination in Employment Act, 29 U.S.C.A. § 621 et seq. He is able to show that there are 1350 partners in the firm overall (128 in his New York office), that they are compensated largely through pre-set salaries and that they are carefully supervised by managing partners. Is that law violated? [13]

---

3. Capitalization

Generally the formation of a partnership is accompanied by the contribution of capital by the partners. However, there is no requirement that the partners contribute adequate capital or even, except for limited partners, any capital at all. Instead of contributing property and money to the partnership the partners may lease or loan their assets and charge rent thereon (no interest is payable on capital contributions, absent agreement, U.P.A. § 18(d)). A common example has been a seat on a stock or produce exchange which often, by exchange rules, had to be held by an individual. He would then contribute the use of his seat, while he remained a partner, to the partnership.

The property that is contributed to the partnership or acquired by it does not in theory become the property of the partnership. It is held by the partners as co-owners in partnership. This is a tenancy which one might expect to resemble the forms of co-ownership (what are they?) you have encountered in first-year Property. However, practical considerations have caused the incidents of ownership in copartnership to be very much curtailed. Thus a partner's conveyance of his or her interest in specific partnership property conveys nothing (U.P.A. § 25(2)), and his or her creditors cannot attach specific items of partnership property (U.P.A. § 25(2)(c)). Nor does a partner's spouse have rights in partnership realty. However, each partner does have the right to use partnership property for partnership purposes only. Partnership property may be held in the partnership name or in that of a partner; if authorized, a partner may convey title by a sole signature. (U.P.A. § 10(1)).

In addition to receiving an interest (of a rather remote type) in the specific items of partnership property a partner also receives an interest in the partnership itself. (U.P.A. § 26). This interest is a share in the excess of the partnership assets over liabilities and is regarded as personal property. It is assignable to a limited extent.

---

13. Hishon v. King & Spalding, 467 U.S. 69, 104 S.Ct. 2229, 81 L.Ed.2d 59 (1984); Caruso v. Peat, Marwick, Mitchell & Co., 664 F.Supp. 144 (S.D.N.Y.1987).

The amount of capital contributed by the partners to the partnership does not necessarily control the shares of the partners in the earnings, in the losses and in the control of the enterprise. Section 18 of the Act sets forth certain presumptions as to these matters. However, the partners can, if they wish, allocate their shares in earnings, losses and control differently.

REVIEW PROBLEMS

(1) Is it possible for the draftsman of corporate papers to allocate shares in earnings, losses and control in proportions different from that in which capital is contributed? If so, by what means?

(2) Can a corporation be formed without any capital whatever, like a partnership? If not, what policy compels this differentiation?

(3) How different in reality is a stockholder's interest in (a) the specific property of the corporation and (b) the capital and surplus of the corporation from the partner's interest in (a) the specific property of the partnership and (b) the net partnership assets as a whole?

---

4. Operation

Characteristic of the operations of a partnership are (a) informality and speed and (b) danger. Each partner has the sweeping and dangerous powers to bind the other partners to contract, tort or breach of trust liability conferred by Sections 9(1), 13 and 14. These powers may create liability even in violation of an express agreement between the partners. Only a few very drastic actions have been excepted by the specific language of Section 9(3) of the Act from the breadth of this agency. Also the courts have restricted the scope of the partnership general agency in certain directions. Thus the execution of a guaranty may be held to be beyond the scope of a partner's general authority.[14]

As to most matters the vote of the majority of the partners controls (U.P.A. § 18(h)). This is often varied to provide for control of a majority *in interest* of earnings or of the capital contribution of the partners. No action contrary to the terms of the partnership agreement may, however, be undertaken unless there is *unanimous* approval (U.P.A. § 18(h)). Remember that such limitations on partnership activity are very apt to be ineffective as against outside parties without notice. Either majority or unanimous action may be taken with complete informality. An exchange of letters or telephone calls will do.

Corresponding to the broad-ranging power of partners to impose liabilities on each other is their duty to act as fiduciaries with regard to each other. Thus they must make full disclosure to their colleagues,

---

14. Jamestown Banking Co. v. Conneaut Lake Dock & Dredge Co., 339 Pa. 26, 14 A.2d 325 (1940).

maintain records, refrain from competing with the partnership and exercise due care in their business operations. The fiduciary conception of partnership is the product of an old caselaw tradition which the statute does little to make more specific.

In a famous case, involving a man who stole a march on his co-venturer and negotiated secretly a new lease on properties that included a hotel they had been operating together—just before the existing lease expired—Judge Cardozo used the following words. You will see them quoted often.

> Joint adventurers, like copartners, owe to one another, while the enterprise continues, the duty of the finest loyalty. Many forms of conduct permissible in a workaday world for those acting at arm's length, are forbidden to those bound by fiduciary ties. A trustee is held to something stricter than the morals of the market place. Not honesty alone, but the punctilio of an honor the most sensitive, is then the standard of behavior. As to this there has developed a tradition that is unbending and inveterate. Uncompromising rigidity has been the attitude of courts of equity when petitioned to undermine the rule of undivided loyalty by the "disintegrating erosion" of particular exceptions. Wendt v. Fischer, 243 N.Y. 439, 444, 154 N.E. 303. Only thus has the level of conduct for fiduciaries been kept at a level higher than that trodden by the crowd. It will not consciously be lowered by any judgment of this court.[15]

A limited partner has surrendered the right to share in the management of the partnership (except to the extent that consent is required for changes in the agreement and that he or she is still owed duties of disclosure by the general partners). A limited partner who nonetheless intervenes in management forfeits limited partnership immunity. Under the 1916 version of the Uniform Limited Partnership Act (§ 7) there was substantial uncertainty as to the line where a limited partner's rights of review, consultation or veto became a forbidden participation in management. For example, it was not clear whether the reservation in the agreement to the limited partners of the right to set the salary of the active partner, or of the right to veto major transactions, such as the sale of corporate property or the issuance of guarantees, would cross the line. It was, furthermore, not clear what the range of consequences of an act found to violate § 7 would be.[16] The 1976 revision spells out in much more detail what power may be reserved to the limited partners without destroying their status.

---

15. Meinhard v. Salmon, 249 N.Y. 458, 463, 164 N.E. 545, 546 (1928).

16. Feld, The "Control" Test for Limited Partnerships, 82 Harv.L.Rev. 1471 (1969).

REVIEW QUESTIONS

(1) Is the corporate rule on the power to guarantee very different from the partnership rule? Why are the courts reluctant to imply powers to guarantee?

(2) By what sort of proceeding should one of the 150 limited partners of a large real estate venture seek redress for what he believes to be a gross breach of trust by the general partner?

---

5. Transferability and Continuity

Both legal theory and business practicalities combine to cause trouble for partnerships in this area. When one partner wishes to transfer his interest to another he encounters several problems:

(1) The right of *delectus personae* occasioned by the intimacy of the partnership relation which requires the consent of all partners to admission of a new member (U.P.A. § 18(g)).

(2) The fact that a transfer without consent creates in the transferee only the very limited rights conferred by U.P.A. § 27.

(3) The fact that the dropping out of one partner and the insertion of a new one dissolve the old partnership and create a new one. This not only creates complex questions of liability of the incoming and outgoing partners to outsiders (see infra section 6), but also questions as to the income tax basis of the property of the partnership and the partners and, in the case of partnerships owning securities, questions of stock and bond transfer tax liability.

(4) The fact that the valuation of a partnership interest is usually a matter of judgment or guesswork and not of mathematics, since it is not quoted on any exchange and is often dependent on the personal powers of the partners to contribute to earnings.

(5) The fact that it is easier mechanically to transfer shares of stock by endorsing them than it is to convey partnership interests, particularly in real property.

The lack of continuity is a recurrent source of difficulty for a partnership. The maintenance of a stable relationship among partners must reckon with several problems:

(1) The rule that any partner can, even in violation of the partnership agreement, quit and dissolve the firm. U.P.A. § 31(2).

(2) The rule that a partnership is automatically dissolved by various events such as the death, bankruptcy and insanity of any partner. U.P.A. §§ 31 and 32.

(3) The rule that dissolution of the partnership may entail also the termination of the active conduct of the enterprise and the liquidation of the partnership assets and liabilities. Note the rather special and

slightly confusing terminology used in partnership law: a partnership is "dissolved" when the active partnership relation comes to an end. It may thereafter be "liquidated" (the succession of metaphors may bother chemists) or "wound up" which implies a disposition of the partnership assets, payment of its debts and termination of its business. On the other hand, the business of the dissolved partnership may be taken up intact by a new partnership and no liquidation need take place. While the partners cannot by agreement prevent the dissolution of the firm they can provide for its continuation without winding up or liquidation.

(4) The special problems arising on the death of a partner. As long ago as 1591 the charter of the Mines Royal set forth as one of the primary motives for its incorporation the purpose:

> "thereby to avoid divers and sundry great inconveniences which by the several deaths of persons abovesaid or their assigns should else from time to time ensue," [17]

On death, the problems inhering in any change of partnership personnel are complicated by the presence of an inheritance tax which calls for cash which may not be readily available to the partnership and by the disappearance of a valued and trusted partner who is now represented by an unexperienced executor, trustee or offspring. Drafters sometimes try to overcome this problem by having the old partners continue the business, paying the representatives of the deceased the value of the deceased's interest in the partnership in a lump sum or in installments, with or without the aid of insurance. Another solution is to have the executor or heir become a member of the firm, perhaps being a limited partner if active intervention is not desired.

PROBLEMS

(1) A brokerage firm is composed of 3 partners with equal shares in the assets. Of these assets $75,000 is in the form of common stock. A state statute provides that a tax of 10¢ per $100 is due on any transfer of stock. One of the three partners retires and that place in the partnership is taken by a new partner. How much, if any, transfer tax is payable on this transaction? [18]

(2) Which of the following problems of continuity in partnerships can be solved by sound drafting:

(a) the fact that it requires the consent of each partner before a new one can be admitted?

(b) the fact that a partnership can be dissolved at any time by any member?

(c) the problems arising from the loss, through death or disability, of skills that are critical to the firm's success?

17. Select Charters of Trading Companies 5 (C. Carr ed. 1913).

18. The federal stock transfer tax was repealed in 1966. The code provisions and the case law had various answers to the above question. See, e.g., Commissioner v. Lehman, 165 F.2d 383, 386 (2d Cir.1948).

REVIEW PROBLEM

Which of the problems 2(a), (b) and (c) above recur in the corporate framework and how are they handled?

———

6. Liabilities

———

It is common knowledge that partnership (except limited partner-ship) implies the unlimited personal liability of each partner. (See U.P.A. § 15). This does not solve all of the problems as to which partner is liable and for how much.

Problems arise from the dropping out of one partner and the addition of another. Consistent adherence to the theory of dissolution would indicate that the new partnership is not liable for the debts of the old, that creditors of the old partnership must pursue the old partners individually. On the principle of marshalling (see below) the creditors of the old partnership would come after creditors of the new partnership as far as reaching partnership assets. In view of the continuing nature of many partnerships as a business matter this discrimination seems unfair. Therefore a somewhat different solution of the competing claims of theory and practicality has been achieved by the Uniform Act (see §§ 17, 41).

Under this rule the incoming partner is responsible for the old firm's debts but only to the extent of the partnership property. The outgoing partner also has problems of liability. As to debts incurred by the old partnership of which he was a member he is still liable except in the special circumstances treated in Section 36.[19] As to debts incurred after the end of the old partnership the outgoing partner is not liable except to the extent outsiders may still rely on his credit, not being on notice of his departure. (U.P.A. § 35). Both the outgoing and the incoming partners may wish to protect themselves from the conse-quences of these rules of the Act and may be able to achieve some measure of protection, by contractual arrangements.

Another group of problems revolves around the possibility that creditors may not be able to reach all of the partners. Since partners' contractual liability is joint, this might suggest that (a) they could not recover a judgment against less than all partners and (b) if they did, that judgment would constitute a merger of the claims against the unsued partners. These results have been modified in many states by statutes outside of the Partnership Act which are classified as "joint

---

19. See White v. Brown, 292 F.2d 725 (D.C.Cir.1961), for a 2–1 decision that a creditor knowing of the indemnity agree-ment and continuing to accept the notes of the remaining partners, released the retir-ing partner.

debtor acts" or "common name statutes".[20] The net effect of these acts is to provide that a judgment based on service on one partner is collectible from (i) the partner so served and (ii) the partnership, but not from the personal estates of the partners not so served. Partnership tort liabilities do not involve these problems since the partners are jointly *and severally* liable. (U.P.A. § 15(a)).

A third group of problems arises from the fact that along with partnership creditors there may be personal creditors of the partners. The equitable principle of marshalling is applicable here—the partnership creditors have first claim on partnership assets and the individual creditors on the individual assets. (U.P.A. § 40(h)). Any surplus in either category may be applied to the other. This allocation principle, known in the trade as the "jingle rule", was mirrored in § 5 of the Bankruptcy Act but in 1978 the new Bankruptcy Code, 11 U.S.C.A. § 723(c), abolished its symmetry by giving the partnership's bankruptcy trustee the same rights as to the estates of each bankrupt partner as any other claim.

When the outside creditors have been paid off there remains a fourth group of problems: distributing the gains or losses among the partners. It is important to bear in mind that this is a separate problem and quite independent of the partners' liability toward outsiders. Unlike the relationship of partners to outsiders, the rules provided by the Act are ones of construction and are not binding where the partners express a contrary intent. The guiding principles of that Act are those of sharing losses according to the shares in the profits (U.P.A. § 18(a)) and of contribution towards making good any deficit (U.P.A. § 40(d)).

In the case of a limited partner his personal assets will not be subject to further liabilities over and above his capital contribution to the firm. His capital contribution and share of profits are to be returned to him before those of the general partners but after the payment of outside creditors. (U.L.P.A. § 23)

PROBLEMS

(1) What are liabilities of the different partners resulting from the following sequence of events:

    A. W Sr., W Jr. and T form a law partnership.

    B. W Sr. dies.

    C. T commits a breach of trust, abstracting $10,000 from a client.

    D. P is admitted to the firm.

20. See J. Crane & A. Bromberg, Partnership 347–51 (1968).

(2) What additional complications arise from the introduction of the following variations:

    A. After P is admitted to the firm W Jr. resigns.

    B. The $10,000 claim arises from a partnership arrangement to buy law books; $2,000 arose before W Sr. died, another $3,000 before P was admitted and the last $5,000 after W Jr. resigned. Does it matter whether the book seller knew of the death of W Sr.? Of the admission of P? Of W Jr.'s resignation?

(3) To what extent could P safeguard himself from pre-existing liabilities as a result of entering the firm? To what extent could W Jr. safeguard himself by arrangements shifting to those remaining in the firm the burden of partnership losses?

(4) The assets of a partnership, A, B & C, liquidate for $250,000; the firm's debts are $290,000. The other facts are:

	Capital Contribution	Proportion of Profits	Personal Assets	Personal Debts
A	$100,000	50%	$50,000	$5,000
B	75,000	30%	5,000	4,000
C	50,000	20%	2,000	3,000

What are (a) the rights of the partnership creditors against (i) the partnership and (ii) A, B, and C?; (b) the rights of the personal creditors of the partners against (i) the partnership (ii) the individual partners? (c) the rights of A, B and C between themselves?

Assume that all of the above facts remain constant, except that the partnership debts turn out to be only $200,000. How does this change the positions of the parties?

Now assume that the partnership has been successful and that its assets were sold for $400,000 and that only $50,000 of debts needed to be paid. How is the profit shared?

(5) Finally, how would these results vary if B had been a limited, rather than a general, partner? Suppose that a party is found to have violated § 7 by interfering in the operations of a limited partnership in July–September 1986. Should this create liability on the part of the limited partner to a creditor who advanced funds in either January or November 1986? What if the creditor had no suspicion at all that the limited partner existed?

---

7. A Note on Miscellaneous Business Organizations

Besides the partnership, limited partnership and corporation there also exist some relatively rare types of business organization. The purpose of this note is merely to enable you to familiarize yourself with these names so that they will not sound entirely strange to you when you encounter them.

Joint Ventures: The joint venture is basically a partnership limited in duration or scope or both. It is difficult to formulate any usable test for distinguishing the two organizations and it is doubtful whether any special consequences should flow from the distinction.[21] Most of the rules of partnership law apply to joint ventures, such as the fiduciary standards owed to fellow venturers. (See the extract from Meinhard v. Salmon, quoted p. 27 supra.) Recently there has been a tendency for corporations to enter into joint ventures with each other; courts have sometimes said that partnerships between corporations are *ultra vires* but joint ventures are not.

Joint Stock Companies: There still exist, sometimes with special statutory authorizations, some joint stock companies. From a legal point of view they are essentially partnerships with many features of the partnership suppressed by agreement between the members. While it has not been possible to give the members immunity from personal partnership liability, something only the legislature can do, it is possible to alter some traditional partnership qualities by making membership freely transferrable with negotiable shares and by taking the power of control away from the membership at large and centralizing it in a representative board.

Business Trusts: Particularly in Massachusetts the business trust has achieved some popularity. This is a hybrid between the ordinary trust and the joint stock company. If property is given to a trustee to manage for certain investors and they retain no control over the trustee during the term of the trust an ordinary trust results. The trustee and the res may be subject to liability but the beneficiaries seem to be immune. If, however, the beneficiaries have the right to amend the trust deed and elect and remove trustees there is a significant danger that they might be held to be partners. The extent to which such a danger may deter use of this type of organization is indicated from the following opinion of counsel in the prospectus of a Massachusetts business trust in the public utility field:

> "The declaration of trust contains a provision designed to eliminate liability of shareholders to the extent permitted by law. It specifies that every person shall look only to the trust estate for payment or damages or otherwise and that all written obligations shall refer to this provision. The declaration of trust further states that the shares shall be full paid and nonassessable except as otherwise specifically provided in the certificates. In spite of these provisions, the shareholders of a voluntary association such as the Company might, with respect to the liabilities of shareholders under Massachusetts law, be treated in legal contemplation as partners and as such under some circumstances might be held personally liable for certain obligations or liabilities of the Company. Counsel for the Company considers the possibility of any such personal

---

21. Most of the literature about joint ventures is either about their antitrust aspects or about their international character. For an exception devoted to basics see Hand, The Joint Venture—What it is and How to Recognize its Features, 52 J. Kansas B. Ass'n 227 (1983).

liability to be remote because in his opinion under the laws of Massachusetts shareholders are protected from personal liability on contract obligations containing the so-called limited liability clause which the Company customarily inserts in all contract obligations including debt securities, because the Company is a holding company so the possibility of substantial liabilities arising from torts or statutory liabilities, or penalties, other than tax liabilities, is not as great as in the case of companies operating physical properties, and because it has been the experience of the Company over the years since its organization that its liability for taxes of all classes has been adequately covered by its income."

Cooperatives. Like other business organizations, cooperatives are formed to provide goods or services but differ in that their members do not seek returns on their investment but rather reductions in the cost to them of those goods or services. Examples include associations of farmers, rural electricity consumers, small independent grocers and apartment dwellers. Normally each member has an equal share in the ownership and control of the cooperative. Members receive refunds usually on the basis of their patronage of the organization.[22]

REVIEW PROBLEM

Mary Snow, an old and valued client of your firm, comes to confer with you in connection with her business affairs which, she feels, need reorganization. She owns and operates an antique store in Boston which has been profitable for all 20 years of its existence. She has about $80,000 tied up in this enterprise, largely in working capital. A few years ago while in Texas she met a man named Glenn McNamara who is known as a very successful, if rather daring, speculator. Against her conservative instincts, she let herself be talked into participating in a wild cat oil drilling venture that turned out quite successfully. A uranium mining participation was less lucrative, but it was followed by a profitable cattle raising plunge. Although troubled by the risks involved, Mrs. Snow keeps ploughing back the net gains from these operations into ideas suggested by Mr. McNamara. At present that basic stake amounts to $125,000. McNamara, who has full control over the timing of these plunges and over their operation while they continue, has a roughly equal share. They have no formal written agreement but communicate quite often by telephone.

Mrs. Snow has two children one of whom is interested only in abstract impressionist painting; the other shows signs of interest in the antique business. Mrs. Snow is a little over 50 years of age and is beginning to think of retiring and would like to start planning ahead towards making equitable provisions for her children. You may ignore tax considerations, which are being fully taken care of by your tax partner, and concentrate on the question of the advisability of using the corporate form for Mrs. Snow's activities.

Bibliography: The leading modern treatise is still J. Crane & A. Bromberg, Partnership (1968). M. Volz, C. Trower & D. Reiss, The Drafting of Partnership Agreements (7th ed. 1986), is a very useful pamphlet.

   22. I. Packel, The Law of Cooperatives (4th ed. 1970).

Chapter III

CORPORATENESS, OR A BRIEF STUDY OF THE CORPORATE PERSONALITY

1. The Corporation as Subject or Object of Legal Rights

As a preliminary matter, we need to gain some basic familiarity with "corporateness" or the intellectual operation of substituting a single legal conceptual entity for the diverse gaggle of individuals who have some sort of interest in it. This is an intellectual operation without which the complex operations of modern industry could scarcely be understood at all. To imagine life without the corporation concept one might try to think of a grade crossing accident involving a Union Pacific train and a General Motors delivery truck. Treated as partnerships according to the rules developed in Chapter II, these two firms would implicate some 2,000,000 "partners" with at least some hundreds changing every day and having to be dropped out or substituted as parties to the resulting litigation. It would take a computer to keep track of the relationships involved. Not surprisingly, one of the first critical effects of incorporation has been to substitute corporations as entities for their shareholders in litigation (you will have noted the tendency towards permitting that substitution as to partnerships). More complex issues arise when we propose to substitute a corporation for an individual or individuals in some other legal rule, a statutory one for example. Mr. Justice Rutledge thus described this process.[1]

> The process of translating group or institutional relations in terms of individual ones, and so keeping them distinct from the nongroup relations of the people whose group rights are thus integrated, is perennial, not only because the law's norm is so much the individual man, but also because the continuing evolution of institutions more and more compels fitting them into individualistically conceived legal patterns. Perhaps in no other field have the vagaries of this process been exemplified more or more often than in the determination of matters of jurisdiction, venue and liability to service of process in our federal system.

1. United States v. Scophony Corp. of America, 333 U.S. 795, 803, 68 S.Ct. 855, 859, 92 L.Ed. 1091 (1948).

At an early stage courts began to make such translations under the rubric of the corporate personality theory. A classic statement of this theory appears in the *Dartmouth College*[2] case:

> A corporation is an artificial being, invisible, intangible, and existing only in contemplation of law. Being the mere creature of law, it possesses only those properties which the charter of its creation confers upon it, either expressly, or as incidental to its very existence. These are such as are supposed best calculated to effect the object for which it was created. Among the most important are immortality, and, if the expression may be allowed, individuality; properties, by which a perpetual succession of many persons are considered as the same, and may act as a single individual. They enable a corporation to manage its own affairs, and to hold property without the perplexing intricacies, the hazardous and endless necessity, of perpetual conveyances for the purpose of transmitting it from hand to hand. It is chiefly for the purpose of clothing bodies of men, in succession, with these qualities and capacities, that corporations were invented, and are in use. By these means, a perpetual succession of individuals are capable of acting for the promotion of the particular object, like one immortal being . . ..

We open with three cases which discuss the role of the corporation as a plaintiff, including the question whether and when it excludes an action by the shareholders who stand behind it. The latter two cases arise from a complex factual situation. Some students are taken aback by this. It is characteristic of cases in this field that they involve rather intricate facts, and one must get used to unravelling them. Diagrams and other visual aids are often helpful; as to the Old Dominion cases, you may wish to sketch a chart showing the transfers of property, money and stock and indicating their sequence.

GREEN v. VICTOR TALKING MACHINE CO.

United States Court of Appeals, Second Circuit, 1928.
24 F.2d 378, certiorari denied 278 U.S. 602, 49 S.Ct. 9 (1928).

[Mrs. Green brought an action based on diversity, alleging that she had acquired all the stock of the Pearsall Company from her deceased husband, that the Company had been in the business of reselling defendant's products and that defendant had entered into a scheme to take over the business and assets of the Company. She charged defendants had attempted to intimidate and defraud her into selling her stock, had ceased to sell to the Company and by luring away the employees and damaging its reputation, ruined its business. The court, in an opinion by JUDGE SWAN rejected the charge of the use of fraud and

2. Dartmouth College v. Woodward, 4 U.S. (Wheat.) 518, 637, 4 L.Ed. 629, 659 (1819).

intimidation upon Mrs. Green because she had not sold her stock. It went on to deal with the claim based on interference with corporate business.]

Considering first the affirmative interference with the corporation's business: The attempt to induce employees to leave the Pearsall Company, not only is nowhere alleged to have been successful, but, if so, would have given rise to a cause of action to the corporation, rather than to its shareholders. . . . The allegations of disclosure of confidential information, damage to credit, and unfair interference with business are mere conclusions of the pleader; but, even if they were treated as adequately pleaded, they would be subject to the same objection that they charge a breach of duty owing to the corporation rather than to its shareholders. The shareholders' rights are derivative, and, except through the corporation, the shareholders have no relation with one who commits a tort against the corporation's rights. . . .

When there are numerous shareholders, it is apparent that each suffers relatively, depending upon the number of shares he owns, the same damage as all the others, and that each will be made whole if the corporation obtains restitution or compensation from the wrongdoer. Obviously it is sound policy to require a single action to be brought by the corporation, rather than to permit separate suits by each shareholder. In logic the result is justified, because the only right of the shareholder which has been infringed is what may be called his derivative or corporate right. Having elected to conduct their business in a corporate form, the men behind the corporation have, in the phrase of Justice Holmes, "interposed a nonconductor" between themselves and those who deal with them in their corporate enterprise. Donnell v. Herring–Hall–Marvin Safe Co., 208 U.S. 267, 273, 28 S.Ct. 288, 52 L.Ed. 481. Even when all the stock is owned by a sole shareholder, there seems no adequate reason to depart from the general rule that the corporation and its shareholders are to be treated as distinct legal persons. Therefore even a sole shareholder has no independent right which is violated by trespass upon or conversion of the corporation's property. Only his "corporate rights" have been invaded, and consequently he cannot sue the tort-feasor in an action at law. . . .

Admitting this to be the general rule the appellant contends that the result is different when a tort-feasor is animated by malice toward a particular shareholder, and that in such circumstances the principle that intentional harm without justification is actionable gives the shareholder a personal right of action, whether he is a sole shareholder or one of many. With this contention we cannot agree. Assuming that the allegations of the complaint are adequate to charge that the defendant's motive in doing the above-mentioned affirmative acts to the injury of the corporation's credit and business was a malicious desire to damage plaintiff as a shareholder, the cause of action is still the corporation's. The intention of the defendant is to invade the "corporate rights" of the shareholders; that is, the corporation's rights, whether this end is desired as a means of satisfying a grudge against some particular shareholder or all of them, or for some other motive. A defendant's motive in interfering with the corporation's business may be material in determining whether his interference is tortious or privileged, as in the case of fair competition; but his motive will not of itself create an independent cause of action in favor of shareholders, because only their derivative or corporate rights have been infringed. The policy of having their remedy lie in a suit by the corporation is not affected by the wrongdoer's malice toward an individual shareholder.

For a shareholder to obtain a personal right of action there must be relations between him and the tort-feasor independent of those which the shareholder derives through his interest in the corporate assets and business. Thus, in Ritchie v. McMullen, 79 F. 522, 533 (C.C.A. 6), where the shareholder had pledged his stock with defendants who were directors of the corporation, it was held that the pledge created a duty in defendants not to use their power as directors for the purpose of impairing the value of the pledgor's stock. Judge Taft, who wrote the opinion, cited in support of the decision Walsham v. Stainton, 1 De Gex, J. & S. 678. There the plaintiff sold her stock to defendants at less than its real value, as a result of a conspiracy by them to use their powers as controlling shareholders and officers of the corporation, so as to deceive plaintiff as to the value of her shares. The suit was to compel them to account for the actual value of the shares, and the court held there was a direct liability to the plaintiff because they thus acquired her shares. If she had not parted with them, we think her remedy for any impairment of their value due to defendants' conduct would have had to be through a suit by the corporation.

In the instant case defendant is charged with having induced plaintiff's testator to purchase one-third of the shares the plaintiff now owns. Did that fact create a duty to plaintiff's testator, to which plaintiff has succeeded, that the defendant should not thereafter commit torts against the corporation which would impair the value of those shares? There is no allegation of any fraud or deception by defendant at the time it induced the purchase. No tort was committed against the testator which has survived to his executrix. Therefore the defendant owed no duty to the plaintiff, any greater than it would owe to any other transferee of Mr. Green's shares. We cannot think that one who in good faith induces another to buy shares in a corporation owes to him and to all successive owners of those shares a duty, independent of that owed to the corporation, not to do a wrong to the corporation which will impair the value of those shares. The damage to them is the same as to all other shares, the rights of the shareholder which have been injured are derivative rights, and the remedy should lie in a suit by the corporation.

.   .   .

Nor does the allegation of a contractual duty to plaintiff's testator aid her. If it be assumed that the allegations of the complaint are sufficient to charge a contractual duty owing by defendant to the Pearsall Company, despite the indefiniteness of the terms of such a contract, and despite the fact that it was made with a shareholder, not with the corporation, nevertheless a breach of that duty would give a right of action to the corporation, not to its shareholders. Nor can it be maintained that one who breaks a contract with a corporation commits a tort upon its shareholders. If it be assumed that the defendant's contract was with plaintiff's testator, a breach by defendant of this contract would not be a tort against plaintiff, individually or as executrix. And the allegation that this defendant's conduct was pursuant to a conspiracy between defendant and its own directors adds nothing. It is but a reiteration in another form of the allegation of nonfeasance by the defendant corporation, which can act only through its officers or agents.   . . .

We are satisfied that the complaint states no cause of action in tort in the plaintiff. The judgment is affirmed.

COMMENT

(1) In considering Green v. Victor Talking Machine consider the following comment by the court in Watson v. Button, 235 F.2d 235 (9th Cir.1956), a case where plaintiff *had* sold his stock to outside parties before discovering that defendant had misappropriated nearly $14,000 of the corporation's funds:

"Appellant argues that the District Court erred in allowing appellee an individual recovery since any cause of action for misappropriation of corporate assets by a director belongs to the corporation and not its shareholders. He cites Smith v. Bramwell, 1934, 146 Or. 611, 31 P.2d 647, 648 where the Supreme Court of Oregon stated:

'It is a well-established general rule that a stockholder of a corporation has no personal right of action against directors or officers who have defrauded or mismanaged it and thus affected the value of his stock. The wrong is against the corporation and the cause of action belongs to it. Any judgment obtained by reason of such wrongs is an asset of the corporation which inures first to the benefit of creditors and secondly to stockholders.'[3]

"Appellee, who cannot bring a derivative action since he is no longer a stockholder, asserts that the District Court properly awarded him a judgment since this case falls within an exception to the general rule stated in Smith v. Bramwell. Courts in other states have held that a former stockholder, who parted with his shares without knowledge of prior wrongful misappropriation of corporate assets by the directors, may recover from the directors the amount by which the misappropriation had reduced the value of his prior shareholdings.[4]

"Appellee asserts that the Supreme Court of Oregon would recognize such an exception to the general rule stated in Smith v. Bramwell at least in the situation presented here where the rights of creditors are not prejudiced and there are no other shareholders involved. He points out that the reasons behind the general rule are as follows: (1) to avoid a multiplicity of suits by each injured shareholder, (2) to protect the corporate creditors, and (3) to protect all the stockholders since a corporate recovery benefits all equally. These reasons are not applicable in this case. Appellant and appellee were the only stockholders at the time of the misappropriation. The corporate creditors are adequately protected since appellant and appellee are jointly responsible for the corporate liabilities. It is doubtful, in any event, whether under Oregon law the creditors could sue appellant for his misappropriation. The only right apparently would be to enforce the corporate cause of action, but that was given up by the present owners of the corporation when they purchased it from appellant and appellee.

3. This is the rule in most states. See cases collected in Sutter v. General Petroleum Corp., 28 Cal.2d 525, 170 P.2d 898, 167 A.L.R. 279 (1947). See also, Hornstein, Legal Controls for Intracorporate Abuse— Present and Future, 41 Col.L.Rev. 405 (1941).

4. See, e.g., Backus v. Kirsch, 1933, 264 Mich. 73, 249 N.W. 469; Hammer v. Werner, 1933, 239 App.Div. 38, 265 N.Y.S. 172. But cf. Green v. Victor Talking Machine Co., 2 Cir., 1928, 24 F.2d 378, 59 A.L.R. 1091.

"The District Court did not err in concluding that the Oregon court would follow those decisions from other states which allow an individual recovery in this situation, at least in a case where the rights of creditors and other shareholders are not prejudiced. Suits against directors for violations of fiduciary duties are equitable in nature. It is unlikely that the Oregon courts would allow a director to misappropriate funds and leave those injured without a remedy."

OLD DOMINION COPPER MINING & SMELTING CO. v. LEWISOHN

Supreme Court of the United States, 1908.
210 U.S. 206, 28 S.Ct. 634, 52 L.Ed. 1025.

MR. JUSTICE HOLMES delivered the opinion of the court:

This is a bill in equity brought by the petitioner to rescind a sale to it of certain mining rights and land by the defendants' testator, or, in the alternative, to recover damages for the sale. The bill was demurred to and the demurrer was sustained. 136 Fed. 915. Then the bill was amended and again demurred to, and again the demurrer was sustained, and the bill was dismissed. This decree was affirmed by the circuit court of appeals. 79 C.C.A. 534, 148 Fed. 1020. The ground of the petitioner's case is that Lewisohn, the deceased, and one Bigelow, as promoters, formed the petitioner that they might sell certain properties to it at a profit; that they made their sale while they owned all the stock issued, but in contemplation of a large further issue to the public without disclosure of their profit, and that such an issue in fact was made. The supreme judicial court of Massachusetts has held the plaintiff entitled to recover from Bigelow upon a substantially similar bill. 188 Mass. 315, 108 Am.St.Rep. 479, 74 N.E. 653.

The facts alleged are as follows: The property embraced in the plan was the mining property of the Old Dominion Copper Company of Baltimore, and also the mining rights and land now in question, the latter being held by one Keyser, for the benefit of himself and of the executors of one Simpson, who, with Keyser, owned the stock of the Baltimore company. Bigelow and Lewisohn, in May and June, 1895, obtained options from Simpson's executors and Keyser for the purchase of the stock and the property now in question. They also formed a syndicate to carry out their plan, with the agreement that the money subscribed by the members should be used for the purchase and the sale to a new corporation, at a large advance, and that the members, in the proportion of their subscriptions, should receive in cash or in stock of the new corporation the profit made by the sale. On May 28, 1895, Bigelow paid Simpson's executors for their stock on behalf of the syndicate, in cash and notes of himself and Lewisohn, and in June Keyser was paid in the same way.

On July 8, 1895, Bigelow and Lewisohn started the plaintiff corporation, the seven members being their nominees and tools. The next day the stock of the company was increased to 150,000 shares of $25 each, officers were elected, and the corporation became duly organized. July 11, pursuant to instructions, some of the officers resigned, and Bigelow and Lewisohn and three other absent members of the syndicate came in. Thereupon an offer was received from the Baltimore company, the stock of which had been bought, as stated, by Bigelow and Lewisohn, to sell substantially all its property for 100,000 shares of the plaintiff company. The offer was accepted, and then Lewisohn offered to sell the real estate now in question, obtained from Keyser, for 30,000 shares, to be issued to Bigelow and himself. This also was accepted and possession of all the mining property was delivered the next day. The sales "were consummated" by delivery of deeds, and afterwards, on July 18, to raise working capital, it was voted to offer the remaining 20,000 shares to the public at par, and they were taken by subscribers who did not know of the profit made by Bigelow and Lewisohn and the syndicate. On September 18 the 100,000 and 30,000 shares were issued, and it was voted to issue the 20,000 when paid for. The bill alleges that the property of the Baltimore company was not worth more than $1,000,000, the sum paid for its stock, and the property here concerned not over $5,000, as Bigelow and Lewisohn knew. The market value of the petitioner's stock was not less than par, so that the price paid was $2,500,000, it is said, for the Baltimore company's property, and $750,000 for that here concerned. Whether this view of the price paid is correct, it is unnecessary to decide.

Of the stock in the petitioner, received by Bigelow and Lewisohn or their Baltimore corporation 40,000 shares went to the syndicate as profit, and the members had their choice of receiving a like additional number of shares or the repayment of their original subscription. As pretty nearly all took the stock, the syndicate received about 80,000 shares. The remaining 20,000 of the stock paid to the Baltimore company, Bigelow and Lewisohn divided, the plaintiff believes, without the knowledge of the syndicate. The 30,000 shares received for the property now in question they also divided. Thus the plans of Bigelow and Lewisohn were carried out.

The argument for the petitioner is that all would admit that the promoters (assuming the English phrase to be well applied) stood in a fiduciary relation to it, if, when the transaction took place, there were members who were not informed of the profits made and who did not acquiesce, and that the same obligation of good faith extends down to the time of the later subscriptions, which it was the promoters' plan to obtain. It is an argument that has commanded the assent of at least one court, and is stated at length in the decision. But the courts do not agree. There is no authority binding upon us and in point. The general observations in Dickerman v. Northern Trust Co., 176 U.S. 181, 44 L.Ed. 423, 20 Sup.Ct.Rep. 311, were *obiter*, and do not dispose of the case. Without spending time upon the many *dicta* that were quoted to us, we shall endeavor to weigh the considerations on one side and the other afresh.

The difficulty that meets the petitioner at the outset is that it has assented to the transaction with the full knowledge of the facts. It is said, to be sure, that on September 18, when the shares were issued to the sellers, there were already subscribers to the 20,000 shares that the public took. But this does not appear from the bill, unless it should be inferred from the ambiguous statement that on that day it was voted to issue those shares "to persons who had subscribed therefor," upon receiving payment, and that the shares "were thereafter duly issued to said persons," etc. The words "had subscribed" may refer to the time of issue and be equivalent to "should have subscribed," or may refer to an already past event. But that hardly matters. The contract had been made and the property delivered on July 11 and 12, when Bigelow, Lewisohn, and some other members of the syndicate held all the outstanding stock, and it is alleged in terms that the sales were consummated before the vote of July 18, to offer stock to the public, had been passed.

At the time of the sale to the plaintiff, then, there was no wrong done to anyone. Bigelow, Lewisohn, and their syndicate were on both sides of the bargain, and they might issue to themselves as much stock in their corporation as they liked in exchange for their conveyance of their land. Salomon v. A. Salomon & Co. [1897] A.C. 22; Blum v. Whitney, 185 N.Y. 232, 77 N.E. 1159; Tompkins v. Sperry, 96 Md. 560, 54 Atl. 254. If there was a wrong, it was when the innocent public subscribed. But what one would expect to find, if a wrong happened then, would not be that the sale became a breach of duty to the corporation *nunc pro tunc,* but that the invitation to the public without disclosure, when acted upon, became a fraud upon the subscribers from an equitable point of view, accompanied by what they might treat as damage. For it is only by virtue of the innocent subscribers' position and the promoter's invitation that the corporation has any pretense for a standing in court. If the promoters, after starting their scheme, had sold their stock before any subscriptions were taken, and then the purchasers of their stock, with notice, had invited the public to come in, and it did, we do not see how the company could maintain this suit. If it could not then, we do not see how it can now.

But it is said that, from a business point of view, the agreement was not made merely to bind the corporation as it then was, with only 40 shares issued, but to bind the corporation when it should have a capital of $3,750,000; and the implication is that practically this was a new and different corporation. Of course, legally speaking, a corporation does not change its identity by adding a cubit to its stature. The nominal capital of the corporation was the same when the contract was made and after the public had subscribed. Therefore, what must be meant is, as we have said, that the corporation got a new right from the fact that new men, who did not know what it had done, had put in their money and had become members. It is assumed in argument that the new members had no ground for a suit in their own names, but it is assumed also that their position changed that of the corporation, and thus that the indirect effect of their acts was greater than the direct; that facts that gave them no claim gave one to the corporation because of them, notwithstanding its assent. We shall not consider whether the new members had a personal claim of any kind, and therefore we deal with the case without prejudice to that question, and without taking advantage of what we understand the petitioner to concede.

But, if we are to leave technical law on one side, and approach the case from what is supposed to be a business point of view, there are new matters to be taken into account. If the corporation recovers, all the stockholders, guilty as well as innocent, get the benefit. It is answered that the corporation is not precluded from recovering for a fraud upon it, because the party committing the fraud is a stockholder. Old Dominion Copper Min. & Smelting Co. v. Bigelow, 188 Mass. 315, 327, 108 Am.St.Rep. 479, 74 N.E. 653. If there had been innocent members at the time of the sale, the fact that there were also guilty ones would not prevent a recovery, and even might not be a sufficient reason for requiring all the guilty members to be joined as defendants in order to avoid a manifest injustice. Stockton v. Anderson, 40 N.J.Eq. 486, 4 Atl. 642. The same principle is thought to apply when innocent members are brought in later under a scheme. But it is obvious that this answer falls back upon the technical diversity between the corporation and its members, which the business point of view is supposed to transcend, as it must, in order to avoid the objection that the corporation has assented to the sale with full notice of the facts. It is mainly on this diversity that the answer to the objection of injustice is based in New Sombrero Phosphate Co. v. Erlanger, L.R. 5 Ch.Div. 73, 114, 122.

Let us look at the business aspect alone. The syndicate was a party to the scheme to make a profit out of the corporation. Whether or not there was a subordinate fraud committed by Bigelow and Lewisohn on the agreement with them, as the petitioner believes, is immaterial to the corporation. The issue of the stock was apparent, we presume, on the books, so that it is difficult to suppose that at least some members of the syndicate, representing an adverse interest, did not know what was done. But all the members were engaged in the plan of buying for less and selling to the corporation for more, and were subject to whatever equity the corporation has against Bigelow and the estate of Lewisohn. There was some argument to the contrary, but this seems to us the fair meaning of the bill. Bigelow and Lewisohn, it is true, divided the stock received for the real estate now in question. But that was a matter between them and the syndicate. The real estate was bought from Keyser by the syndicate, along with his stock in the Baltimore company, and was sold by the syndicate to the petitioner, along with the Baltimore company's property, as part of the scheme. The syndicate was paid for it, whoever received the stock. And this means that $2/15$ of the stock of the corporation, the 20,000 shares sold to the public, are to be allowed to use the name of the corporation to assert rights against Lewisohn's estate that will inure to the benefit of $13/15$ of the stock that are totally without claim. It seems to us that the practical objection is as strong as that arising if we adhere to the law.

Let us take the business point of view for a moment longer. To the lay mind it would make little or no difference whether the 20,000 shares sold to the public were sold on an original subscription to the articles of incorporation or were issued under the scheme to some of the syndicate and sold by them. Yet it is admitted, in accordance with the decisions, that, in the latter case, the innocent purchasers would have no claim against anyone. If we are to seek what is called substantial justice, in disregard of even peremptory rules of law, it would seem desirable to get a rule that would cover both of the almost equally possible cases of what is deemed a wrong. It might be said that if the stock really was taken as a preliminary to selling to the public, the subscribers would show a certain confidence in the enterprise, and give at least that security for good faith. But the syndicate believed in the enterprise, notwithstanding all the profits that they made it pay. They preferred to take stock at par rather than cash. Moreover, it would have been possible to issue the whole stock in payment for the property purchased, with an understanding as to 20,000 shares.

Of course, it is competent for legislators, but not, we think, for judges, except by a quasi legislative declaration, to establish that a corporation shall not be bound by its assent in a transaction of this kind, when the parties contemplate an invitation to the public to come in and join as original subscribers for any portion of the shares. It may be said that the corporation cannot be bound until the contemplated adverse interest is represented, or it may be said that promoters cannot strip themselves of the character of trustees until that moment. But it seems to us a strictly legislative determination. It is difficult, without inventing new and qualifying established doctrines, to go behind the fact that the corporation remains one and the same after once it really exists. When, as here, after it really exists, it consents, we at least shall require stronger equities than are shown by this bill to allow it to renew its claim at a later date because its internal constitution has changed.

To sum up: In our opinion, on the one hand, the plaintiff cannot recover without departing from the fundamental conception embodied in the law that created it,—the conception that a corporation remains unchanged and unaffected in its identity by changes in its members. Donnell v. Herring–Hall–Marvin Safe Co., 208 U.S. 267, 273, ante, 288, 28 Sup.Ct.Rep. 288; Salomon v. A. Salomon & Co. [1897] A.C. 22, 30. On the other hand, if we should undertake to look through fiction to facts, it appears to us that substantial justice would not be accomplished, but rather a great injustice done, if the corporation were allowed to disregard its previous assent in order to charge a single member with the whole results of a transaction to which $^{13}/_{15}$ of its stock were parties, for the benefit of the guilty, if there was guilt in anyone, and the innocent alike. We decide only what is necessary. We express no opinion as to whether the defendant properly is called a promoter, or whether the plaintiff has not been guilty of laches, or whether a remedy can be had for a part of a single transaction in the form in which it is sought, or whether there was any personal claim on the part of the innocent subscribers, or as to any other question than that which we have discussed.

The English case chiefly relied upon, Erlanger v. New Sombrero Phosphate Co. L.R. 3 App.Cas. 1218, Affirming L.R. 5 Ch.Div. 73, seems to us far from establishing a different doctrine for that jurisdiction. There, to be sure, a syndicate had made an agreement to sell, at a profit, to a company to be got up by the sellers. But the company, at the first stage, was made up mainly of outsiders, some of them instruments of the sellers, but innocent instruments, and, according to Lord Cairns, the contract was provisional on the shares being taken and the company formed. (P. 1239.) There never was a moment when the company had assented with knowledge of the facts. The shares, with perhaps one exception, all were taken by subscribers ignorant of the facts (L.R. 5 Ch.Div. 113), and the contract seems to have reached forward to the moment when they subscribed. As it is put in 2 Morawetz, Priv.Corp.2d ed. § 292, there was really no company till the shares were issued. Here, $^{13}/_{15}$ of the stock had been taken by the syndicate, the corporation was in full life, and had assented to the sale with knowledge of the facts before an outsider joined. There, most of the syndicate were strangers to the corporation, yet all were joined as defendants. (P. 1222.) Here, the members of the syndicate, although members of the corporation, are not joined, and it is sought to throw the burden of their act upon a single one. . . .

Decree affirmed.

————

OLD DOMINION COPPER MINING & SMELTING CO. v. BIGELOW

Supreme Judicial Court of Massachusetts, 1909.
203 Mass. 159, 89 N.E. 193, affirmed 225 U.S. 111, 32 S.Ct. 641,
56 L.Ed. 1009 (1912).

[In this case, JUSTICE RUGG took strong and lengthy issue with his former colleague on the Supreme Court and, over a three judge dissent, affirmed a judgment against Bigelow. Various issues besides the merits were discussed, including the question whether the judgment in favor of Lewisohn protected Bigelow. Extracts follow:]

3. The next inquiry is as to the liability of the defendant. The plaintiff seeks to establish this on the ground that the defendant and Lewisohn framed a scheme, which was an entirety and which as a whole comprised the organization and continued management of the plaintiff by themselves, their agents and representatives, until the completion of the project. This scheme was the capitalization of the plaintiff for $3,750,000; the sale to it of their property, costing and intrinsically worth $1,000,000, but having in the market a value not over $2,000,000, for $3,250,000; the sale to the general public at par for cash of the remaining $500,000 of stock; and all this without providing the plaintiff with any independent board of officers or advisors to pass upon the wisdom of the purchase and without disclosing the substance of the transaction and their extraordinary profit to the purchasers of its stock for cash at par. This scheme was an entity, one part of it was just as essential as any other part, and one part was the procurement of $500,000 in cash from the unenlightened public as a working capital for the new company.

It has been decided, apparently by a unanimous court, that such a transaction creates a liability on the part of the defendant to account for his profits to the plaintiff in this proceeding. Hayward v. Leeson, 176 Mass. 310, 57 N.E. 656, 49 L.R.A. 725. The present suits were before the court in 188 Mass. 315, 74 N.E. 653, 108 Am.St.Rep. 479, and after an elaborate review of the authorities and examination of the grounds for judgment it was held that the defendant was liable, notwithstanding the opposing decision on the precise point by the United States Circuit Court in Old Dominion Copper Mining & Smelting Co. v. Lewisohn, 136 Fed. 915. Since the determination of the present cases on demurrer, the above-entitled case against Lewisohn has been considered by the United States Circuit Court of Appeals (148 Fed. 1020, 79 C.C.A. 534) and by the Supreme Court of the United States (210 U.S. 206, 28 Sup.Ct. 634, 52 L.Ed. 1025) and without dissent a conclusion has been reached contrary to that of this court. The deference due to a decision by the highest court in the land and the intrinsic importance of the question at issue requires a reconsideration of our own cases, a re-examination of the authorities and a careful consideration of the principles involved.

The plaintiff seeks to recover a secret profit made by the promoters in the sale of their own property to the corporation, basing its claim on the general and well recognized proposition that a promoter cannot take lawfully a secret profit and will be held to account for it if he does. Fundamentally the action is to recover profits obtained by a breach of trust. There is a distinct finding by the single justice that the defendant and Lewisohn were the promoters of the plaintiff. This finding is amply justified by the evidence. In their brain it was conceived, by their direction the formalities of its incorporation were carried out, their resources provided its mines, their influence and reputation with those desiring to invest in mines procured its working cash capital. The word promoter has no precise and inflexible meaning in this country. . . . In a comprehensive sense promoter includes those who undertake to form a corporation and to procure for it the rights, instrumentalities and capital by which it is to carry out the purposes set forth in its charter, and to establish it as fully able to do its business. Their work may begin long before the organization of the corporation, in seeking the opening for a venture and projecting a plan for its development, and it may continue after the incorporation by attracting the investment of capital in its securities and providing it with the commercial breath of life. It is now established without exception that a promoter stands in a fiduciary relation to the corporation which he is interested in, and that he is charged with all the duties of good faith which attach to other trusts. In this respect he is held to the high standards which bind directors and other persons occupying fiduciary relations.

That the promoter stands in the relation of a fiduciary to the corporation which he creates seems to be conceded in Old Dominion Copper Mining & Smelting Co. v. Lewisohn, 210 U.S. 206, 28 Sup.Ct. 634, 52 L.Ed. 1025. The point to be determined is whether this rule is applicable, and, if it is, whether the plaintiff is in a position to assert its claim.

Notwithstanding this fiduciary relation the promoter may sell property to the company which he is promoting. But in order that the contract may be absolutely binding he must pursue one of four courses: (a) He may provide an independent board of officers in no respect directly or indirectly under his control, and make full disclosure to the corporation through them. (b) He may make a full disclosure of all material facts to each original subscriber of shares in the corporation. (c) He may procure a ratification of the contract after disclosing its circumstances by vote of the stockholders of the completely established corporation. (d) He may be himself the real subscriber of all the shares of the capital stock contemplated as a part of the promotion scheme. The defendant does not claim upon this report that either of the first two courses was followed. He does rest his claim chiefly upon the third and fourth courses. As applied to the facts of this case these two come to the same thing, for the reason that on the findings of the single justice the defendant and his associate were subscribers for only 130,000 shares out of a total 150,000, and in the light most favorable to them they held all the shares which had been issued at the time of the ratification, but not all which it was proposed to issue as a part of the scheme of promotion. The point to be determined, therefore, is whether the promoter is immune from liability if he and his associates are owners of all the issued stock at the time of the act complained of, although intending as a part of their plan the immediate issue of further stock to the public without disclosure, and whether, while a substantial portion of the stock intended to be issued to the public remains unissued, a vote of ratification of the breach of trust will protect him.

A review of the authorities seems to demonstrate that there is a liability of the promoter to the corporation when further original subscribers to capital stock contemplated as an essential part of the scheme of promotion came in after the transaction complained of, even though that transaction is known to all the then stockholders, that is to say, to the promoters and their representatives.   . . .

[JUSTICE RUGG then addresses himself to the treatment of the Erlanger case by JUSTICE HOLMES:]

We cannot accede to this interpretation. The company was fully formed the moment it was registered. The subscription for the shares required as a prerequisite to registration under the English statute established the company as fully as the 40 shares subscribed and the $1,000 for capital stock, paid into the plaintiff's treasury on or before July 11, 1895, established it. It was enabled to make any contract within the scope of its powers.   . . .

The distinction which appears to be established between the Erlanger Case and the present one, by the decision of the United States Supreme Court, 210 U.S. 206, 28 Sup.Ct. 634, 52 L.Ed. 1025, is that if promoters organize a company with a capital of $3,750,000 and sell to it through their dummy directors property brought by them for this purpose, for $3,250,000, in paid-up shares, and then get by public subscription $500,000 for working capital, the transaction is valid. But if promoters having bought property for £ 55,000 organize a company with a capital of £ 130,000, and while they are the only bona fide stockholders by vote of their directors sell to it their property for £ 110,000, to be paid £ 80,000 in cash and £ 30,000 in paid-up shares, £ 100,000 being subscribed in cash by the public, the transaction is void. The only difference between the two cases is that in the Erlanger Case the promoters were paid a part of the purchase price in money, the proceeds of public subscription, and received paid-up shares, which they took in payment of the balance of the purchase price when the stock was issued to subscribers, while in the present case the whole purchase price was paid in stock, which was issued before any stock was issued to the public although after a substantial public subscription. In other words, the order in which the transaction is carried out, and not its substantial nature, makes the difference between liability and immunity of the promoter. It is true that in the Erlanger Case, until after ratification by the company of the contract previously made in its behalf for the purchase of the lease of the island, the mayor of London by acting as a director was liable to take shares of stock and intended to, and did subsequently, take and pay for 50 shares. He and possibly one other (3 A.C. 1228) appear to have been the only persons up to that time connected with the company, who subsequently became stockholders, who were not agents of the promoters. But it is also the fact (as stated by Jessel, M.R., in 5 Ch.Div., at page 112) that "up to this time there was not really a single bona fide shareholder distinct from the promoters," and of course all these assented to the transaction. If this is a vital circumstance, that case is distinguishable in principle from the one at bar and from the case decided by the United States Supreme Court. This appears to us to be a difference upon an immaterial matter. It is of no consequence whether in fact the dummy directors know of the terms of sale and the breach of trust of the promoters. It does not appear in the present case that the nominees of Bigelow and Lewisohn knew any more about the profit the latter were making than did the directors of the New Sombrero Company of the profits of the syndicate. The point is that in both cases the directors were selected with the purpose that they should be the mere instruments of the promoters and they carried out the will of their masters. Under the English statute the instruments of the promoters in the New Sombrero Company, while its directors were as fully clothed with all the powers of the corporation and as much the holders of all its stock, as were the seven directors of the plaintiff holding in all forty shares of the plaintiff at the time the contract of sale in the present case was made. If the assent of all the stockholders is good in the one case, by the same token it should be equally good in the other; and the breach of trust in the one is equally a breach of trust in the other. This case seems to us an authority in favor of the plaintiff. . . .

This review of decisions seems to establish abundantly the proposition that promoters stand in a fiduciary position toward the corporation, as well when as a part of the scheme of promotion uninformed stockholders are expected to come in after the wrong has been perpetrated, as when at that time there are shareholders to whom no disclosure is made. We find no authority opposed except the Lewisohn Cases in the federal courts. 210 U.S. 206, 28 Sup.Ct. 634, 52 L.Ed. 1025.

If the question is examined on principle apart from authority, the same result appears clear. The starting point is that a promoter is a fiduciary to the corporation. To use the words of Lord Cairns in Erlanger v. New Sombrero Phosphate Co., 3 App.Cas. 1218, at page 1236: "Promoters have in their hands the creation and moulding of the company. They have power to define how and when and in what shape and under what supervision it shall start into existence and begin business." The corporation is in the hands of the promoter like clay in the hands of the potter. It is to this person, absolutely helpless and incapable of independent initiative or uncontrolled action, that the promoter stands as trustee. It is not necessary to inquire how far he may be trustee also for shareholders or associates. In the present case the inquiry relates wholly to his obligation to the corporation. The fiduciary relation must in reason continue until the promoter has completely established according to his plan the being which he has undertaken to create. His liability must be commensurate with the scheme of promotion on which he has embarked. If the plan contemplates merely the organization of the corporation his duties may end there. But if the scheme is more ambitious and includes beside the incorporation, not only the conveyance to it of property but the procurement of a working capital in cash from the public, then the obligation of faithfulness stretches to the length of the plan. It would be a vain thing for the law to say that the promoter is a trustee subject to all the stringent liabilities which inhere in that character and at the same time say that, at any period during his trusteeship and long before an essential part of it was executed or his general duty as such ended, he could, by changing for a moment the cloak of the promoter for that of director or stockholder, by his own act alone, absolve himself from all past, present or future liability in his capacity as promoter. The plaintiff was fully organized and authorized to do business on July 8 and 11, 1895, when only $1,000 in capital stock had been paid in. It would be an idle ceremony indeed to establish for promoters the obligations of trustees, and at the same time hold that by their tools and with only $1,000 paid in, and that as a mere form (for it was soon after repaid to one of them) they could vote to themselves a wholly unwarranted profit of $1,250,000, kept secret from other initial share-holders, because at that moment they were the only stockholders. By such a course the law would be holding out apples of Sodom to the wronged corporation. Corporations can be formed through irresponsible agents with ease. If these agents can vote away a substantial part of the capital stock for property of comparatively small value, and still with immunity to themselves and their principals receive from the uninformed public cash subscriptions for the rest of the capital stock, the organization and management of corporations might readily become a "system of frauds." Peabody v. Flint, 6 Allen, 52–55. It is answered that the plaintiff has assented to the transaction with full knowledge of the facts. But it has not assented when it stood where it could act independently. The assent to the wrongful act of the promoters was given at the behest and by vote of the promoters themselves, while still occupying the position of protectors to their own creature, while it was bound hand and foot by them and prevented from taking any action except through them as a step in its further exploitation, and while their trust was uncompleted. The corporation although by law fully organized was still in its swaddling clothes, so far as the plans of the promoters were concerned. The value of their stock taken in return for their mining property was dependent in a substantial degree upon the corporation having $500,000 in cash for a working capital. They could not perfect their plans nor reap their contemplated profit, except by retaining their hold upon the corporation until the public had made this contribution. In one sense it is true that the plaintiff was completely organized on July 11 and on September 20, 1895. It was fully competent to be bound by its contracts and ratification of contracts with those dealing with it at arm's length. But it was not free from its wardship to its promoters, whose scheme from the first looked forward to a corporation with treasury filled by subscriptions from the unenlightened public. The corporation was not dealing with these fiduciaries upon an independent ground. The plaintiff, although a legal corporation from July 8th leaned wholly upon its promoters, because they made it so to lean, until long after the events here in controversy. An assent under those conditions can be of no greater effect than the assent of a minor under guardianship to the breaches of trust of his guardian.

The situation is akin to the conveyance of property by a man solvent but in contemplation of insolvency. Such conveyance is not wrong until the contemplated indebtedness is incurred which makes him an insolvent. Then the executed evil intent stretches back and invalidates the original conveyance. Here the conveyance to the corporation with the secret profit, when there are no uninformed subscribers to stock, if nothing more is ever done, is not an actionable tort. But the vicious intent looks forward to the procurement of money from the ignorant public by means of original subscriptions and the execution of this evil intent extends backward to contaminate the sale and its profit.

Stress has sometimes been laid upon the fact that the promoters were paid a part of their purchase price out of the public subscriptions. But there is no difference in principle between such a case and the present, where a substantial part of the value of the stock taken by the defendant and Lewisohn depended upon the cash subscriptions to be made by the public for the remaining shares not issued to the promoters.

But it is further argued that the entire capital stock outstanding at the time being in the hands of the promoters, the sale of the property to the corporation was merely changing the form of title of the promoters from owners of real estate to that of shares of stock, and that, there being then no other shareholders, no wrong was done. It has been decided that where persons own the entire authorized capital stock of the company and take it in payment for the conveyance of their property at a grossly exaggerated price, nobody can be heard to complain. . . . The distinction is clear between cases of that class and those like the present, where the promoters took for themselves a large number of shares of stock without adequate consideration and without disclosure to the detriment of the corporation and all its future shareholders, at the same time planning that there should be immediate public subscriptions. It is one thing to take all the shares of a corporation in payment for physical property conveyed. It does not much matter to the stockholders in such a case whether the total is 130,000 shares or 150,000 shares. But it is a very different thing to take $^{130000}/_{150000}$ of capital stock of a corporation whose assets consist of the same physical property, and, in addition, $500,000 in money subscribed by others. The latter course affects the other stockholders and the corporation itself, and it gives the promoters something appreciably more valuable than what they contribute. It is true that in Salomon v. Salomon and in some other cases there was a part of the authorized capital stock which was not issued, but it was not proposed to be issued as a part of the scheme of promotion and the original shareholders intended to remain the only shareholders. It was to be issued or not in the remote future, as the exigencies of the corporation in the actual conduct of its business might require, but, in any event, it was not to be issued for the purpose of starting the corporation on its course. This circumstance materially affects the question here to be considered. Most, if not all, corporation laws provide in some form for an increase of capital stock. It is of no consequence upon such a point as this, whether the capital stock originally authorized is large, but not all issued, or whether it is at first small and subsequently an increase is authorized. . . .

The fundamental reasoning upon which these cases can rest is not that no wrong has been committed, but there is no one to enforce the remedy. All courts recognize the soundness of the doctrine that no man can be on both sides of the same bargain with justice to all interests. The principle that one cannot rightfully sell property, belonging to him in his private right, to himself in a trust capacity is universal.

If this aspect alone is looked at and the corporation is regarded as a distinct person, it cannot be said that the corporation is not wronged by such a breach of duty by promoters. It is only when the corporate personality is disregarded and its component elements as stockholders alone are considered that it can be said that no harm is done on the ground (as was said in Salomon v. Salomon, [1897] A.C., at page 57) that "the company is bound in a matter intra vires by the unanimous agreement of its members." But looking through the form of the corporation to the stockholders and treating them as the corporation is an exception to the otherwise firmly established universal rule that the corporation is a separate legal entity for all purposes, even though all its stock be held by a single interest and it be to all practical intents merely the instrument of the stockholder. . . . We perceive no reason for extending this exception in a case like the present.

The real ground of the decisions of which Salomon v. Salomon is a type is that the corporation is estopped by the circumstance that all persons with financial concern in the matter have assented with knowledge, and thus the lips of everybody are sealed. It is not that no wrong has been done, but that whatever wrong has been done has been condoned. The maxim "Volenti non fit injuria" is invoked. This, however, is setting up confession and avoidance and not a bar to the main cause of action.

The theory upon which corporations are founded is that they are entities, distinct and separate from officers and stockholders. Corporate liabilities do not attach to the latter. The wrong which the defendant and his associate did in this case was in selling property worth intrinsically $1,000,000 and in the market at most $2,000,000 for $3,250,000 without revealing that they were making a secret profit. The wrong was done to the corporation. It affected all its shareholders, present and future alike. It is generally admitted that, if there are existing stockholders ignorant of the wrong, redress may be had. But it is had through the corporation or for the benefit of the corporation, and not by the stockholder in his own right. The wrong is not done to the shareholders as individuals, nor to the shareholders collectively. It is done to the corporation as an independent entity, and thus indirectly the rights of those who are or who may become stockholders are affected. In buying the promoters' mine, the directors of the corporation acted for the corporation, as such, without regard to who were the then stockholders, or even if there were no stockholders. Whoever becomes an originally contemplated shareholder coming in afterwards has as much right to say that the rights of the corporation were not protected and to insist that it should assert its remedy for the wrong done it as one in at first but not informed. Subsequent subscriptions to original stock as a part of the scheme of promotion do not change the identity of the corporation, but remove an impediment to the enforcement of a remedy for a wrong previously done the corporation. The wrong is not done when the innocent public subscribes, but when the sale was made to the corporation at a grossly exaggerated price with secret profit. The occasion for complaining of this wrong comes when the promoters issue to the public the balance of the stock in order to provide the money necessary to set the corporation on its feet and to give thereby the contemplated value to the stock taken by themselves in payment for their mines. The exemption of the promoter from liability to the corporation for a sale without disclosure when he takes the entire issue of capital stock is an exception to the general rule imposing upon him the liabilities of a trustee. If this exception is to be extended to a case like the present, it leaves nothing of substantial value in the original rule. It might still reach small and grosser forms of want of fidelity to corporations, but would leave unharmed the vastly greater and more refined variety illustrated by the present case. It would point the way to general immunity for the wary.

It is also urged that the maintenance of this suit works an injustice to the defendant in requiring a repayment to the corporation, which will result in a benefit to the ¹³/₁₅ of the capital stock taken by the defendant and Lewisohn (who condoned the wrong) as well as to the ²/₁₅ subscribed for by the innocent public. The size of the repayment which may be required of the defendant is due to the enormous profit taken at the outset. Apart from the unjust profit taken by the promoters, their interest in the plaintiff was only $^8/_{17}$ or, tested by the cost and intrinsic value of the property conveyed, $^4/_{17}$. The true answer, however, is given by Jessel, M.R., in New Som. P. Co. v. Erlanger, 5 Ch.D., at page 114: "It is said that it is not doing justice and that the suit cannot be maintained in this form, because it will not do justice. But that argument goes too far because it would apply to a case of the grossest fraud in every instance in which one or more of the actual shareholders of a company took part in that fraud. If the argument were once allowed to prevail, it would only be necessary to corrupt one single shareholder in order to prevent a company from ever setting the contract aside. It may be said, you give to the shareholder, who was a party to the fraud, a profit because he will take it in respect of his shares, and since as between co-conspirators there is no contribution, therefore his brother conspirators, who are made liable for the fraud, cannot make him repay his proportion. But the doctrine of this court has never been to hold its hand and avoid doing justice in favor of the innocent, because it cannot apportion the punishment fully amongst the guilty. A dozen parties to a fraud may be defendants and one decree or judgment go against all, and if there is a fraud of such a character that none of them can bring an action for contribution, the plaintiff may, at his will and pleasure, enforce that judgment against any one of them and perhaps pass over the most guilty of them; still there is no remedy as between those who commit the fraud. It is one of the punishments of fraud that there is no such remedy and that a guilty party, though not the most guilty, may suffer the greatest amount of punishment. It is one of the deterrents to men to prevent their committing fraud." . . .

It is said further that the result reached is harsh from the business man's point of view. A discussion of this aspect of the case involves ethical considerations. Courts are constantly dealing with the various relations of the business world. Legal principles are applied to these transactions, but such principles are "almost always the fundamental ethical rules of right and wrong." Robinson v. Mollett, L.R. 7 H.L.C. 802, 817. Upon its distinctly moral side, there is little to the credit of the defendant and his associate. The offering by the defendant as promoter for public subscription for cash at par a substantial part of the capital stock of a corporation, the rest of whose capital stock had been issued for property conveyed to it under a law which permitted such stock to be issued only for the real value of property, was equivalent to a representation that no fictitious value had been placed upon the property so acquired. But the distinct finding of the single justice is that the real value was less than one-third the price for which the defendant and Lewisohn sold it. Nothing can be said in support of a business enterprise carried on by promoters, which involves the purchase by them of mines, costing and intrinsically worth $1,000,000, with money in substantial part solicited from associates on representations that a corporation is to be formed with a capitalization of $2,500,000 of whose stock $2,000,000 is to be issued for conveyance to it by them of the mines and the rest for cash, the actual organization of the corporation under the laws of a state which permitted the issuance of capital stock for property conveyed only to the real value of the property, with a capital stock of $3,750,000, of which $3,250,000 is issued as fully paid for conveyance of the mines, the settlement with a very great majority of the associates on the basis of a sale for $2,000,000 of stock as at first represented, the promoters retaining $1,250,000 shares as a secret profit, intending also to procure from the public subscriptions for $500,000 of stock in cash at par and actually carrying out this purpose, the promoters themselves during all these manipulations having entire control of all executive offices of the corporation. In the absence of compelling authority, we cannot set the seal of judicial approval upon such business policies. See Bigelow v. Old Dominion Copper M. & S. Co. (N.J.Ch.) 71 Atl., at pages 176, 177.

Both on authority outside of our own cases and on principle, it appears to us that the defendant should be held liable. But in this jurisdiction the matter does not stand quite on the basis of an original proposition . . . added to considerations which otherwise exist, the force of the doctrine of stare decisis. One or both of these cases have frequently been cited by courts of other jurisdictions and always with approval until O.D.C.M. & S. Co. v. Lewisohn, 148 Fed. 1020, 79 C.C.A. 534, s. c. 210 U.S. 206, 28 Sup.Ct. 634, 52 L.Ed. 1025. No arguments have been adduced not considered in those cases, and no points now brought forward were not there discussed. While the rule of stare decisis does not prevent the overruling of those cases, they should not be disturbed unless they now appear to be so clearly wrong as to have no sound support. Mabardy v. McHugh, 202 Mass. 148, 88 N.E. 894. It must appear that the law was "misunderstood or misapplied." 1 Kent's Com. 475. There was no misconception of the points involved when these cases were decided, nor any lack of discernment in their application to the affairs of corporations. It does not appear that they have become archaic or inapplicable by reason of business evolution since they were announced. On the contrary, the tendency of custom since the first case was decided has been rather in the direction of more strict accountability of those owing duties to corporations and their stockholders. At all events, we perceive no occasion to relax these principles of accountability for breaches of trust. The mere fact that the Supreme Court of the United States has since decided the question differently is not alone a sufficient consideration for reversing our decisions. It is only when the reasoning of its decision is of convincing power and compels the conclusion that our cases were wrongly decided that it must command our support in other branches of the law than those where it is supreme under the federal Constitution. With great respect to the decision in 210 U.S. 206, 28 Sup.Ct. 634, 52 L.Ed. 1025, we are constrained to adhere to the law as laid down in the earlier cases in this commonwealth.

[Three justices dissented]

COMMENT

(1) The Supreme Court affirmed the Bigelow decision, finding that it did not deny full faith and credit to the Lewisohn judgment.

(2) As background to the Old Dominion cases it is worth noting that the malfeasance was only discovered 7 years after the corporation was organized. There had been substantial turnover in the stock since the original wrongdoing. The new stockholders obtained the services of Louis D. Brandeis, first to unseat the directors and then to conduct the litigation in New York and Massachusetts. He also helped merge Old Dominion into Phelps Dodge. For this he received fees of $200,000 and apparently the enmity of another group of

Bostonians who helped fight his appointment to the Supreme Court a few years later.

The Lewisohn involved in these cases was Leonard who with his brother Adolph was one of the founders of a family distinguished not only as copper mining magnates but also as donors of such items as the Lewisohn stadium, etc.

(3) The stock watering type of fraud was a rather common and regrettable feature of the promotion of new companies during the late nineteenth century period of stock promotions and corporate consolidations that produced such firms as U.S. Steel and Standard Oil. It involves, as you can observe, the transfer to the new corporation of assets for an amount of stock with a par value in excess of the value of those assets. Now that purchasers are less impressed by a large showing of assets on the balance sheet and look more to past earnings and prospects of future earnings, patterns of fraud have shifted. Also, new types of federal and state controls on the issuance of securities, discussed in Chapter VI, have shifted the emphasis away from common law liabilities discussed in the Old Dominion cases, as well as the special liabilities to creditors for watering stock which are discussed at p. 135, infra. Accordingly these cases are presented primarily as a puzzle in how to structure corporate versus individual recovery in cases where a fraud has been committed.[5]

(4) If the Old Dominion board had refused to bring actions against Bigelow and Lewisohn, one or more of the corporation's shareholders might have brought an action, called a "derivative action," in its name and for its benefit. The major characteristics of this type of action will be explored in Chapter X.

QUESTIONS

(1) Why did the plaintiff in Green bring her action in her own name rather than through the corporate medium? What practical adverse consequences, including those mentioned in the extract from Watson v. Button, might have ensued? Whose interests might have been affected?

(2) The Old Dominion cases are the first really complex situation to confront you. It is advisable to make a chart showing the flow of transactions. What were the consequences of the recovery in the Old Dominion cases? Who benefitted and who lost? Do those consequences seem equitable? If not, can you point to the particular rule that gives rise to those consequences? Does the sequence in which the promotional acts took place affect the results of the cases? Should it? What about different sequences? Do you find it repugnant (champertous) that somebody profited by bringing the lawsuit?

(3) Do the two Old Dominion courts seem to regard the issue as basically substantive or procedural? How do they define the wrong for which relief is sought?

(4) What alternative to the type of action brought in the Old Dominion cases should be explored? What procedural obstacles would be in the way of such relief? Would they have been substantially mitigated by such develop-

5. The obsolescence of the Old Dominion cases can, however, be exaggerated. See, e.g., Whaler Motor Inn, Inc. v. Parsons, 372 Mass. 620, 363 N.E.2d 493 (1977); Miller v. San Sebastian Gold Mines, Inc., 540 F.2d 807 (5th Cir.1976) (both reaffirming Massachusetts' view). Cf. Public Investment Ltd. v. Bandeirante Corp., 740 F.2d 1222, 1234 n. 72 (D.C.Cir.1984).

ments as Federal Rule 23? Would such an action in fact have qualified under that Rule?

---

2. Corporate Personality and the Constitution

In this section we examine the problems of fitting a corporation into a legislative document, the United States Constitution. Not only is this an excellent illustration of the problem of doing so, in a document that was not specifically aimed at corporations, but the subject is of intrinsic importance.

A corporation acquires legal personality only by operation of law, that is through state action of a sort. This much is self-evident, even tautologous. More serious questions arise as to whether the fact that a legal step is involved in the creation of a corporate as opposed to a natural person by itself changes the relationship between the state and the "person". This general question breaks down into three subquestions: (1) is a state free arbitrarily to deny or confer the status of corporate personality? (2) is a state freer to deal with corporate persons (once it has created them) than with live ones—indeed are they "persons" at all in a constitutional sense? (3) is the involvement of the state in the creation of corporate personality enough by itself to make actions by the corporation so created "state action" in such a sense as to subject the corporation to those constitutional restraints applying to the government itself?

The Shapiro case that follows responds to the first question. It involves a not-for-profit corporation, which puts it in a somewhat different category from business corporations. It is indeed rather hard to imagine a state arbitrarily refusing to incorporate a business enterprise in a world where certificates of incorporation are as easy to obtain as under the Delaware practice described below.

ASSOCIATION FOR THE PRESERVATION OF FREEDOM OF CHOICE, INC. v. SHAPIRO

Court of Appeals of New York, 1961.
9 N.Y.2d 376, 214 N.Y.S.2d 388, 174 N.E.2d 487.

[A petition was presented to a Justice of the New York Supreme Court asking him to approve a charter as required by section 10 of the Membership Corporations Law. The certificate listed as among its purposes: "to promote . . . the right of the individual to associate with only those persons with whom he desires to associate." Approval was denied by the Supreme Court and this action was affirmed by the Appellate Division. The Court of Appeals reversed in an opinion by FOSTER, J. that construed the requirement of a "lawful purpose" in section 10 as not excluding a purpose to change the law by peaceful means.

The dissenting opinion of BURKE, J. follows:]

I dissent and vote to affirm. The only issue presented is whether the standard applied by Special Term *in this case* satisfies the constitutional requirement of definiteness. We are not now concerned with what criteria may have been relied on in other situations.

That which is sought here is not solely permission to accomplish a simple act of business, to organize for political purposes and exercise freedom of speech, but rather to obtain "the imprimatur of incorporation", bearing the blessing of the Supreme Court, the benediction of the Secretary of State, and the right to affix the characterization "Incorporated under the Laws of the State of New York" to public matter so as to enable the organizers to assure themselves the prestige which accompanies the privilege. . . .

A State should not be forced to lend its prestige to efforts of a group whose objectives are a contradiction of State law. No decision of the United States Supreme Court is so clearly to the contrary that we should subordinate our policy to that of the Federal Government.

The use of the word "lawful", as describing the purposes for which a membership corporation may be formed (Membership Corporations Law, § 10), does not restrict the Justice of the Supreme Court merely to the performance of a ministerial act, but rather requires the exercise of a judicial function. "That is LAWFUL which is in conformity with . . . the principle or spirit of the law, whether moral or juridical; that is LEGAL which is in conformity with the letter or rules of law as it is administered in the courts" (Webster's New International Dictionary [2d ed., Unabridged], p. 1401; Lewis v. Harlem Dental Co., 189 App.Div. 359, 178 N.Y.S. 533). A "lawful purpose" hence must be in conformity not only with the letter but also the spirit of the law. To be "lawful" then, the purposes of a proposed incorporation, although legal, must also be in harmony with an explicitly defined public policy of a State.

The purposes of the applicant are in conflict with a well-known and recognized public policy of the State of New York, which finds expression in numerous statutes. Consequently the denial of this application by the courts below does not rest on an unconstitutionally vague notion of "what is wholesome public policy" or on any other vague personal philosophy, but on a definite standard of conduct mandated by the Legislature in various statutes. (Section 290 of the Executive Law, Consol.Laws, c. 18, states: "[T]he legislature hereby finds and declares that practices of discrimination against any of its inhabitants because of race, creed, color or national origin are a matter of state concern, that such discrimination threatens not only the rights and proper privileges of its inhabitants but menaces the institutions and foundation of a free democratic state.")

Incorporation, moreover, is a privilege which may be withheld (see Mayor, etc., of City of New York v. Twenty–Third St. Ry. Co., 113 N.Y. 311, 317, 21 N.E. 60, 62). It is as much a privilege whether New York individuals or corporate entities of other States seek it (Ashley v. Ryan, 153 U.S. 436, 14 S.Ct. 865, 38 L.Ed. 773).

When such a franchise is sought and where the Appellate Division has unanimously approved an exercise of discretion, we do not interfere if there is any basis in the evidence or the inferences to sustain the action taken below. The record here supports the unanimous conclusion of the Justices of the Supreme Court, which is the agent of the Legislature.

The policies of the petitioners are, beyond argument, in sharp conflict with those of the People of this State, as announced by the Legislature (e.g., N.Y. Const., art. I, § 11; "Equal protection of laws; discrimination in civil rights prohibited"; see, also, specific provisions in Alcoholic Beverage Control Law, Civil Rights Law, Civil Service Law, Education Law, Executive Law, General Business Law, Military Law, Penal Law and Public Housing Law, Consol.Laws, cc. 3–B, 6, 7, 16, 18, 20, 36, 40, 44–A). Therefore, we could not hold that it was as a matter of law an abuse of discretion for the Justice of the Supreme Court to require, as a basic minimum, that the public policy of the granting body not be abridged (see Matter of General Von Steuben Bund, Inc., 159 Misc. 231, 287 N.Y.S. 527). The discretion delegated by the Legislature may not be found to be improperly exercised or in violation of rights guaranteed by the United States Constitution when it is based on an oft-reaffirmed State policy, and is consistent with the rationale of decisions of the United States Supreme Court.

Each of the individual members of this proposed corporation has all of those rights of freedom of speech and association as may be guaranteed by either the State or Federal Constitution. Special Term did not prohibit or limit them in any such protected activity. They may continue, as they have undoubtedly done, to gather together and exercise their rights in all permissible forms. But the "constitutionally protected right of association" is not tantamount to a right of incorporation (compare N.A.A.C.P. v. State of Alabama, 357 U.S. 449, 463, 78 S.Ct. 1163, 1172, 2 L.Ed.2d 1488 with People of State of New York ex rel. Bryant v. Zimmerman, 278 U.S. 63, 49 S.Ct. 61, 73 L.Ed. 184). Petitioner has no absolute prerogative to have a corporation created or to operate one within this State (National Council U.A.M. v. State Council, 204 U.S. 151, 161, 163, 27 S.Ct. 46, 51 L.Ed. 132).

Although we respect the right of petitioners to share a belief that the exercise of freedom of choice is one of the constitutionally protected, inalienable rights referred to in the Declaration of Independence, we may give effect not only to our State public policy but also to the decisions of the United States Supreme Court, all of which are to the contrary.

Accordingly, the orders of the Appellate Division should be affirmed.

COMMENT

Although none of the opinions reached the constitutional issue that Judge Burke addressed in his dissent, that question might have been raised in State ex rel. Grant v. Brown, 39 Ohio St.2d 112, 313 N.E.2d 847 (1974), appeal dismissed 420 U.S. 916, 95 S.Ct. 1110, 43 L.Ed.2d 388 (1975). It upheld, with three judges dissenting, the refusal of the Secretary of State to accept the proposed articles of incorporation for Greater Cincinnati Gay Society, Inc. because "[w]e agree with the Secretary of State that the promotion of homosexuality as a valid life-style is contrary to the public policy of the state."

QUESTIONS

(1) What does the dissent take to be the meaning of the term "lawful" in the statute? Do you agree?

(2) Suppose that the issue of constitutionality had been reached because the statute was interpreted as Burke, J. argued; how would you have voted?

(3) Do you put any weight on Judge Burke's statement that incorporation is "a privilege"? Is it a "benediction", a "blessing" and a lending of "prestige"?

The next case raises an issue that can come up in innumerable contexts—when a given rule refers to a "person" does it include a corporation? The particular context, the XIVth Amendment, has been a critically important one, especially in those years when economic due process and equal protection were lively creatures. Aside from that intrinsic significance it is illustrative of the techniques to be used in construing a statute or regulation that merely refers to "person" or "citizen" or uses some other word that does not make clear the legislature's intention.

WHEELING STEEL CORP. v. GLANDER
Supreme Court of the United States, 1949.
337 U.S. 562, 69 S.Ct. 1291, 93 L.Ed. 1544.

[The State of Ohio levied a tax on certain intangible property owned by foreign corporations. Appellant corporations challenged the tax as violating the Fourteenth Amendment of the federal Constitution. The Court in an opinion by MR. JUSTICE JACKSON held that discriminations in the Ohio system against nonresidents denied them equal protection. MR. JUSTICE DOUGLAS dissented on the basis that a corporation is not a "person" entitled to equal protection. MR. JUSTICE JACKSON wrote a further opinion responding to that point. Excerpts from the further opinion by MR. JUSTICE JACKSON and from the dissent follow:]

By MR. JUSTICE JACKSON. The writer of the Court's opinion deems it necessary to complete the record by pointing out why, in writing by assignment for the Court, he assumed without discussion that the protections of the Fourteenth Amendment are available to a corporation. It was not questioned by the State in this case, nor was it considered by the courts below. It has consistently been held by this Court that the Fourteenth Amendment assures corporations equal protection of the laws, at least since 1886, Santa Clara Co. v. Southern Pacific R. Co., 118 U.S. 394, 396, 6 S.Ct. 1132, 30 L.Ed. 118, and that it entitles them to due process of law, at least since 1889, Minneapolis R. Co. v. Beckwith, 129 U.S. 26, 28, 9 S.Ct. 207, 32 L.Ed. 585.

It is true that this proposition was once challenged by one Justice. Connecticut General Co. v. Johnson, 303 U.S. 77, 83, 58 S.Ct. 436, 439, 82 L.Ed. 673 (dissenting opinion). But the challenge did not commend itself, even to such consistent liberals as Mr. Justice Brandeis and Mr. Justice Stone, and I had supposed it was no longer pressed. See the same Justice's separate opinion in International Shoe Co. v. State of

Washington, 326 U.S. 310, 322, 66 S.Ct. 154, 161, 90 L.Ed. 95, 161 A.L.R. 1057, making no mention of this issue.

Without pretending to a complete analysis, I find that in at least two cases during this current term the same question was appropriate for consideration, as here. In Railway Express v. New York, 336 U.S. 106, 69 S.Ct. 463, a corporation claimed to be deprived of both due process and equal protection of the law, and in Ott v. Mississippi Barge Line, 336 U.S. 169, 69 S.Ct. 432, a corporation claimed to be denied due process of law. At prior terms, in many cases the question was also inherent, for corporations made similar claims under the Fourteenth Amendment. . . . Although the author of the present dissent was the writer of each of the cited Court's opinions, it was not intimated therein that there was even doubt whether the corporations had standing to raise the questions or were entitled to protection of the Amendment. Instead, in each case the author, as I have done in this case, proceeded to discuss and dispose of the corporation's contentions on their merits, a quite improper procedure, I should think, if the corporation had no standing to raise the constitutional questions. Indeed, if the corporation had no such right, it is difficult to see how this Court would have jurisdiction to consider the case at all.

It may be said that in the foregoing cases other grounds might have been found upon which to defeat the corporations' claims, while in the present case apparently there is none.

However, in at least two cases this Court, joined by both Justices now asserting that corporations have no rights under the Fourteenth Amendment, recently has granted relief to corporations by striking down state action as conflicting with corporate rights under that Amendment. In Times–Mirror Co. v. California, companion case to Bridges v. California, 314 U.S. 252, 62 S.Ct. 190, 86 L.Ed. 192, 159 A.L.R. 1346, a newspaper corporation persuaded this Court that a $500 fine assessed against it violated its rights under the Fourteenth Amendment. In Pennekamp v. Florida, 328 U.S. 331, 66 S.Ct. 1029, 90 L.Ed. 1295, a newspaper corporation was convicted along with an individual defendant, and this Court set aside the conviction upon the ground that the Fourteenth Amendment prohibited such state action. In neither of these cases was the corporation's right to raise the issue questioned and the result in each case was irreconcilable with the position now asserted in dissent.

It cannot be suggested that in cases where the author is the mere instrument of the Court he must forego expression of his own convictions. Mr. Justice Cardozo taught us how Justices may write for the Court and still reserve their own positions, though overruled. Helvering v. Davis, 301 U.S. 619, 639, 57 S.Ct. 904, 908, 81 L.Ed. 1307, 109 A.L.R. 1319.

In view of this record I did not, and still do not, consider it necessary for the Court opinion to review the considerations which justify the assumption that these corporations have standing to raise the issues decided.

Mr. Justice Douglas, with whom Mr. Justice Black concurs, dissenting.

It has been implicit in all of our decisions since 1886 that a corporation is a "person" within the meaning of the Equal Protection Clause of the Fourteenth Amendment. Santa Clara Co. v. South.

Pacific R. Co., 118 U.S. 394, 396, 6 S.Ct. 1132, 30 L.Ed. 118, so held. The Court was cryptic in its decision. It was so sure of its ground that it wrote no opinion on the point, Chief Justice Waite announcing from the bench:

> "The court does not wish to hear argument on the question whether the provision in the Fourteenth Amendment to the Constitution, which forbids a State to deny to any person within its jurisdiction the equal protection of the laws, applies to these corporations. We are all of opinion that it does."

There was no history, logic, or reason given to support that view. Nor was the result so obvious that exposition was unnecessary.

The Fourteenth Amendment became a part of the Constitution in 1868. In 1871, a corporation claimed that Louisiana had imposed on it a tax that violated the Equal Protection Clause of the new Amendment. Mr. Justice Woods (then Circuit Judge) held that "person" as there used did not include a corporation and added, "This construction of the section is strengthened by the history of the submission by congress, and the adoption by the states of the 14th amendment so fresh in all minds as to need no rehearsal." Insurance Co. v. New Orleans, Fed. Cas. No. 7,052, 1 Woods 85, 88.

What was obvious to Mr. Justice Woods in 1871 was still plain to the Court in 1873. Mr. Justice Miller in the Slaughter House Cases, 16 Wall. 36, 71, 21 L.Ed. 394, adverted to events "almost too recent to be called history" to show that the purpose of the Amendment was to protect human rights—primarily the rights of a race which had just won its freedom. And as respects the Equal Protection Clause he stated, "The existence of laws in the States where the newly emancipated negroes resided, which discriminated with gross injustice and hardship against them as a class, was the evil to be remedied by this clause, and by it such laws are forbidden." 16 Wall. at page 81, 21 L.Ed. 394.

Moreover what was clear to these earlier judges was apparently plain to the people who voted to make the Fourteenth Amendment a part of our Constitution. For as Mr. Justice Black pointed out in his dissent in Connecticut General Co. v. Johnson, 303 U.S. 77, 87, 58 S.Ct. 436, 441, 82 L.Ed. 873, the submission of the Amendment to the people was on the basis that it protected human beings. There was no suggestion in its submission that it was designed to put negroes and corporations into one class and so dilute the police power of the States over corporate affairs. Arthur Twining Hadley once wrote that "The Fourteenth Amendment was framed to protect the negroes from oppression by the whites, not to protect corporations from oppression by the legislature. It is doubtful whether a single one of the members of Congress who voted for it had any idea that it would touch the question of corporate regulation at all." [6]

Both Mr. Justice Woods in Insurance Co. v. New Orleans, supra, Fed.Cas. No. 7,052, 1 Woods page 88, and Mr. Justice Black in his

---

6. The Constitutional Position of Property in America, 64 Independent 834, 836 (1908). He went on to say that the Dartmouth College case, 4 Wheat. 518, 4 L.Ed. 629, and the construction given the Fourteenth Amendment in the Santa Clara case "have had the effect of placing the modern industrial corporation in an almost impregnable constitutional position." Id., p. 836.

As to whether the framers of the Amendment may have had such an undisclosed purpose see Graham, The "Conspiracy Theory" of the Fourteenth Amendment, 47 Yale L.J. 371.

dissent in Connecticut General Co. v. Johnson, supra, 303 U.S. at pages 88–89, 58 S.Ct. at pages 441–442, 82 L.Ed. 673, have shown how strained a construction it is of the Fourteenth Amendment so to hold. Section 1 of the Amendment provides:

> "All *persons* born or naturalized in the United States, and subject to the jurisdiction thereof, are *citizens* of the United States and of the State wherein they reside. No State shall make or enforce any law which shall abridge the privileges or immunities of *citizens* of the United States; nor shall any State deprive any *person* of life, liberty, or property, without due process of law; nor deny to any *person* within its jurisdiction the equal protection of the laws." (Italics added.)

"Persons" in the first sentence plainly include only human beings, for corporations are not "born or naturalized."

Corporations are not "citizens" within the meaning of the first clause of the second sentence. Western Turf Ass'n v. Greenberg, 204 U.S. 359, 363, 27 S.Ct. 384, 385, 51 L.Ed. 520; Selover, Bates & Co. v. Walsh, 226 U.S. 112, 126, 33 S.Ct. 69, 72, 57 L.Ed. 146.[7]

It has never been held that they are persons whom a State may not deprive of "life" within the meaning of the second clause of the second sentence.

"Liberty" in that clause is "the liberty of natural, not artificial, persons." Western Turf Ass'n v. Greenberg, supra, 204 U.S. at page 363, 27 S.Ct. at page 385, 386, 51 L.Ed. 520.

But "property" as used in that clause has been held to include that of a corporation since 1889 when Minneapolis R. Co. v. Beckwith, 129 U.S. 26, 9 S.Ct. 207, 32 L.Ed. 585, was decided.

It requires distortion to read "person" as meaning one thing, then another within the same clause and from clause to clause. It means, in my opinion, a substantial revision of the Fourteenth Amendment. As to the matter of construction, the sense seems to me to be with Mr. Justice Woods in Insurance Co. v. New Orleans, supra, Fed.Cas. No. 7,052, 1 Woods at page 88, where he said, "The plain and evident meaning of the section is, that the persons to whom the equal protection of the law is secured are persons born or naturalized or endowed with life and liberty, and consequently natural and not artificial persons."

History has gone the other way. Since 1886 the Court has repeatedly struck down state legislation as applied to corporations on the ground that it violated the Equal Protection Clause. Every one of our decisions upholding legislation as applied to corporations over the objection that it violated the Equal Protection Clause has assumed that they are entitled to the constitutional protection. But in those cases it was not necessary to meet the issue since the state law was not found to contain the elements of discrimination which the Equal Protection Clause condemns. But now that the question is squarely presented I can only conclude that the *Santa Clara* case was wrong and should be overruled.

---

7. Cf. McGovney, A Supreme Court Fiction, 56 Harv.L.Rev. 853, 1090, 1225, dealing with corporations in the diverse citizenship jurisdiction of the federal courts.

One hesitates to overrule cases even in the constitutional field that are of an old vintage. But that has never been a deterrent heretofore and should not be now.

We are dealing with a question of vital concern to the people of the nation. It may be most desirable to give corporations this protection from the operation of the legislative process. But that question is not for us. It is for the people. If they want corporations to be treated as humans are treated, if they want to grant corporations this large degree of emancipation from state regulation, they should say so. The Constitution provides a method by which they may do so. We should not do it for them through the guise of interpretation.

FIRST NATIONAL BANK OF BOSTON v. BELLOTTI

Supreme Court of the United States, 1978.
435 U.S. 765, 98 S.Ct. 1407, 55 L.Ed.2d 707.

[Two banks (First National Bank of Boston and New England Merchants National Bank) and three business corporations (Gillette Co., Digital Equipment Corp. and Wyman–Gordon Co.) desired to spend money to publicize their views on a proposed amendment to the Massachusetts constitution that was to be submitted to the voters at a general election on November 2, 1976. The amendment would have allowed a graduated individual income tax in the Commonwealth. They confronted a statute, Mass.Gen.Laws Ann. ch. 55, § 8, that forbade banks and business corporations from making contributions or expenditures "for the purpose of. . . . influencing or affecting the vote on any question submitted to the voters, other than one materially affecting any of the property, business or assets of the corporation." The statute further said that "[n]o question submitted to the voters solely concerning the taxation of the income, property or transactions of individuals shall be deemed materially to affect the property, business or assets of the corporation." Violators of the statute, both corporations and their officers, faced fines and imprisonment. The five firms brought suit against the Massachusetts attorney general to have the statute declared unconstitutional. The Supreme Judicial Court of Massachusetts rejected their claims. The Supreme Court, on appeal, disposed of an argument that the case was moot and proceeded to discuss the merits, in an opinion by JUSTICE POWELL.]

III

The court below framed the principal question in this case as whether and to what extent corporations have First Amendment rights. We believe that the court posed the wrong question. The Constitution often protects interests broader than those of the party seeking their vindication. The First Amendment, in particular, serves significant societal interests. The proper question therefore is not whether corporations "have" First Amendment rights and, if so, whether they are coextensive with those of natural persons. Instead, the question must be whether § 8 abridges expression that the First Amendment was meant to protect. We hold that it does.

A

The speech proposed by appellants is at the heart of the First Amendment's protection.

> "The freedom of speech and of the press guaranteed by the Constitution embraces at the least the liberty to discuss publicly and truthfully all matters of public concern without previous restraint or fear of subsequent punishment. . . . Freedom of discussion, if it would fulfill its historic function in this nation, must embrace all issues about which information is needed or appropriate to enable the members of society to cope with the exigencies of their period." Thornhill v. Alabama, 310 U.S. 88, 101–102, 60 S.Ct. 736, 744, 84 L.Ed. 1093 (1940).

The referendum issue that appellants wish to address falls squarely within this description. In appellants' view, the enactment of a graduated personal income tax, as proposed to be authorized by constitutional amendment, would have a seriously adverse effect on the economy of the State. . . . The importance of the referendum issue to the people and government of Massachusetts is not disputed. Its merits, however, are the subject of sharp disagreement.

As the Court said in Mills v. Alabama, 384 U.S. 214, 218, 86 S.Ct. 1434, 1437, 16 L.Ed.2d 484 (1966), "there is practically universal agreement that a major purpose of [the First] Amendment was to protect the free discussion of governmental affairs." If the speakers here were not corporations, no one would suggest that the State could silence their proposed speech. It is the type of speech indispensable to decisionmaking in a democracy, and this is no less true because the speech comes from a corporation rather than an individual. The inherent worth of the speech in terms of its capacity for informing the public does not depend upon the identity of its source, whether corporation, association, union, or individual.

The court below nevertheless held that corporate speech is protected by the First Amendment only when it pertains directly to the corporation's business interests. In deciding whether this novel and restrictive gloss on the First Amendment comports with the Constitution and the precedents of this Court, we need not survey the outer boundaries of the Amendment's protection of corporate speech, or address the abstract question whether corporations have the full measure of rights that individuals enjoy under the First Amendment. The question in this case, simply put, is whether the corporate identity of the speaker deprives this proposed speech of what otherwise would be its clear entitlement to protection. We turn now to that question.

B

The court below found confirmation of the legislature's definition of the scope of a corporation's First Amendment rights in the language of the Fourteenth Amendment. Noting that the First Amendment is applicable to the States through the Fourteenth, and seizing upon the observation that corporations "cannot claim for themselves the liberty which the Fourteenth Amendment guarantees." Pierce v. Society of Sisters, 268 U.S. 510, 535, 45 S.Ct. 571, 573, 69 L.Ed. 1070 (1925), the court concluded that a corporation's First Amendment rights must derive from its property rights under the Fourteenth.

This is an artificial mode of analysis, untenable under decisions of this Court.

. . .

Freedom of speech and the other freedoms encompassed by the First Amendment always have been viewed as fundamental components of the liberty safeguarded by the Due Process Clause, . . . and the Court has not identified a separate source for the right when it has been asserted by corporations.[6] . . .

Yet appellee suggests that First Amendment rights generally have been afforded only to corporations engaged in the communications business or through which individuals express themselves, and the court below apparently accepted the "materially affecting" theory as the conceptual common denominator between appellee's position and the precedents of this Court. It is true that the "materially affecting" requirement would have been satisfied in the Court's decisions affording protection to the speech of media corporations and corporations otherwise in the business of communication or entertainment, and to the commercial speech of business corporations. . . . None of them mentions, let alone attributes significance to, the fact that the subject of the challenged communication materially affected the corporation's business.

The press cases emphasize the special and constitutionally recognized role of that institution in informing and educating the public, offering criticism, and providing a forum for discussion and debate. Mills v. Alabama, 384 U.S., at 219, 86 S.Ct., at 1437; see Saxbe v. Washington Post Co., 417 U.S. 843, 863–864, 94 S.Ct. 2811, 2821–2822, 41 L.Ed.2d 514 (1974) (Powell, J., dissenting). But the press does not have a monopoly on either the First Amendment or the ability to enlighten. . . . Similarly, the Court's decisions involving corporations in the business of communication or entertainment are based not only on the role of the First Amendment in fostering individual self-expression but also on its role in affording the public access to discussion, debate, and the dissemination of information and ideas. . . . Even decisions seemingly based exclusively on the individual's right to express himself acknowledge that the expression may contribute to society's edification. Winters v. New York, 333 U.S. 507, 510, 68 S.Ct. 665, 667, 92 L.Ed. 840 (1948).

Nor do our recent commercial speech cases lend support to appellee's business interest theory. They illustrate that the First Amendment goes beyond protection of the press and the self-expression of individuals to prohibit government from limiting the stock of information from which members of the public may draw. A commercial advertisement is constitutionally protected not so much because it pertains to the seller's business as because it furthers the societal interest in the "free flow of commercial information." Virginia State Bd. of Pharmacy v. Virginia Citizens Consumer Council, Inc., 425 U.S. 748, 764, 96 S.Ct. 1817, 1827, 48 L.Ed.2d 346 (1976); . . . .

6. It has been settled for almost a century that corporations are persons within the meaning of the Fourteenth Amendment. Santa Clara County v. Southern Pacific R. Co., 118 U.S. 394, 6 S.Ct. 1132, 30 L.Ed. 118 (1886); see Covington & Lexington Turnpike R. Co. v. Sanford, 164 U.S. 578, 17 S.Ct. 198, 41 L.Ed. 560 (1896).

C

We thus find no support in the First or Fourteenth Amendment, or in the decisions of this Court, for the proposition that speech that otherwise would be within the protection of the First Amendment loses that protection simply because its source is a corporation that cannot prove, to the satisfaction of a court, a material effect on its business or property. The "materially affecting" requirement is not an identification of the boundaries of corporate speech etched by the Constitution itself. Rather, it amounts to an impermissible legislative prohibition of speech based on the identity of the interests that spokesmen may represent in public debate over controversial issues and a requirement that the speaker have a sufficiently great interest in the subject to justify communication.

Section 8 permits a corporation to communicate to the public its views on certain referendum subjects—those materially affecting its business—but not others. It also singles out one kind of ballot question—individual taxation—as a subject about which corporations may never make their ideas public. The legislature has drawn the line between permissible and impermissible speech according to whether there is a sufficient nexus, as defined by the legislature, between the issue presented to the voters and the business interests of the speaker.

In the realm of protected speech, the legislature is constitutionally disqualified from dictating the subjects about which persons may speak and the speakers who may address a public issue. Police Dept. of Chicago v. Mosley, 408 U.S. 92, 96, 92 S.Ct. 2286, 2290, 33 L.Ed.2d 212 (1972). If a legislature may direct business corporations to "stick to business," it also may limit other corporations—religious, charitable, or civic—to their respective "business" when addressing the public. Such power in government to channel the expression of views is unacceptable under the First Amendment. Especially where, as here, the legislature's suppression of speech suggests an attempt to give one side of a debatable public question an advantage in expressing its views to the people,[8] the First Amendment is plainly offended. Yet the State contends that its action is necessitated by governmental interests of the highest order. We next consider these asserted interests.

IV

The constitutionality of § 8's prohibition of the "exposition of ideas" by corporations turns on whether it can survive the exacting scrutiny necessitated by a state-imposed restriction of freedom of speech. Especially where, as here, a prohibition is directed at speech itself, and the speech is intimately related to the process of governing,

8. Our observation about the apparent purpose of the Massachusetts Legislature is not an endorsement of the legislature's factual assumptions about the views of corporations. We know of no documentation of the notion that corporations are likely to share a monolithic view on an issue such as the adoption of a graduated personal income tax. Corporations, like individuals or groups, are not homogeneous. They range from great multi-national enter-prises whose stock is publicly held and traded to medium-size public companies and to those that are closely held and controlled by an individual or family. It is arguable that small or medium-size corporations might welcome imposition of a graduated personal income tax that might shift a greater share of the tax burden onto wealthy individuals. See Brief for New England Council as Amicus Curiae 23–24.

"the State may prevail only upon showing a subordinating interest which is compelling," Bates v. City of Little Rock, 361 U.S. 516, 524, 80 S.Ct. 412, 417, 4 L.Ed.2d 480 (1960); . . . "and the burden is on the Government to show the existence of such an interest." Elrod v. Burns, 427 U.S. 347, 362, 96 S.Ct. 2673, 49 L.Ed.2d 547 (1976). Even then, the State must employ means "closely drawn to avoid unnecessary abridgment . . .." Buckley v. Valeo, 424 U.S., at 25, 96 S.Ct., at 638; . . . .

The Supreme Judicial Court did not subject § 8 to "the critical scrutiny demanded under accepted First Amendment and equal protection principles," Buckley, supra, 424 U.S., at 11, 96 S.Ct., at 631, because of its view that the First Amendment does not apply to appellants' proposed speech. For this reason the court did not even discuss the State's interests in considering appellants' First Amendment argument. The court adverted to the conceivable interests served by § 8 only in rejecting appellants' equal protection claim. Appellee nevertheless advances two principal justifications for the prohibition of corporate speech. The first is the State's interest in sustaining the active role of the individual citizen in the electoral process and thereby preventing diminution of the citizen's confidence in government. The second is the interest in protecting the rights of shareholders whose views differ from those expressed by management on behalf of the corporation. However weighty these interests may be in the context of partisan candidate elections,[9] they either are not implicated in this case or are not served at all, or in other than a random manner, by the prohibition in § 8.

A

Preserving the integrity of the electoral process, preventing corruption, and "sustain[ing] the active, alert responsibility of the individual citizen in a democracy for the wise conduct of government" [10] are

9. In addition to prohibiting corporate contributions and expenditures for the purpose of influencing the vote on a ballot question submitted to the voters, § 8 also proscribes corporate contributions or expenditures "for the purpose of aiding, promoting or preventing the nomination or election of any person to public office, or aiding, promoting, or antagonizing the interests of any political party." See n. 2, supra. In this respect, the statute is not unlike many other state and federal laws regulating corporate participation in partisan candidate elections. Appellants do not challenge the constitutionality of laws prohibiting or limiting corporate contributions to political candidates or committees, or other means of influencing candidate elections. . . . About half of these laws, including the federal law, 2 U.S.C. § 441b (1976 ed.) (originally enacted as the Federal Corrupt Practices Act, 34 Stat. 864), by their terms do not apply to referendum votes. Several of the others proscribe or limit spending for "political" purposes, which may or may not cover referenda.

See Schwartz v. Romnes, 495 F.2d 844 (CA2 1974).

The overriding concern behind the enactment of statutes such as the Federal Corrupt Practices Act was the problem of corruption of elected representatives through the creation of political debts. . . . The importance of the governmental interest in preventing this occurrence has never been doubted. The case before us presents no comparable problem, and our consideration of a corporation's right to speak on issues of general public interest implies no comparable right in the quite different context of participation in a political campaign for election to public office. Congress might well be able to demonstrate the existence of a danger of real or apparent corruption in independent expenditures by corporations to influence candidate elections. . . .

10. United States v. United Automobile Workers, supra, 352 U.S., at 575, 77 S.Ct., at 533.

interests of the highest importance. Buckley, supra. . . . Preservation of the individual citizen's confidence in government is equally important. Buckley, supra, 424 U.S., at 27, 96 S.Ct., at 638. . . .

Appellee advances a number of arguments in support of his view that these interests are endangered by corporate participation in discussion of a referendum issue. They hinge upon the assumption that such participation would exert an undue influence on the outcome of a referendum vote, and—in the end—destroy the confidence of the people in the democratic process and the integrity of government. According to appellee, corporations are wealthy and powerful and their views may drown out other points of view. If appellee's arguments were supported by record or legislative findings that corporate advocacy threatened imminently to undermine democratic processes, thereby denigrating rather than serving First Amendment interests, these arguments would merit our consideration. Cf. Red Lion Broadcasting Co. v. FCC, 395 U.S. 367, 89 S.Ct. 1794, 23 L.Ed.2d 371 (1969). But there has been no showing that the relative voice of corporations has been overwhelming or even significant in influencing referenda in Massachusetts, or that there has been any threat to the confidence of the citizenry in government.

Nor are appellee's arguments inherently persuasive or supported by the precedents of this Court. Referenda are held on issues, not candidates for public office. The risk of corruption perceived in cases involving candidate elections, simply is not present in a popular vote on a public issue. To be sure, corporate advertising may influence the outcome of the vote; this would be its purpose. But the fact that advocacy may persuade the electorate is hardly a reason to suppress it: . . . Moreover, the people in our democracy are entrusted with the responsibility for judging and evaluating the relative merits of conflicting arguments. They may consider, in making their judgment, the source and credibility of the advocate. But if there be any danger that the people cannot evaluate the information and arguments advanced by appellants, it is a danger contemplated by the Framers of the First Amendment. . . .

B

Finally, appellee argues that § 8 protects corporate shareholders, an interest that is both legitimate and traditionally within the province of state law. Cort v. Ash, 422 U.S. 66, 82–84, 95 S.Ct. 2080, 2089–2091, 45 L.Ed.2d 26 (1975). The statute is said to serve this interest by preventing the use of corporate resources in furtherance of views with which some shareholders may disagree. This purpose is belied, however, by the provisions of the statute, which are both underinclusive and overinclusive.

The underinclusiveness of the statute is self-evident. Corporate expenditures with respect to a referendum are prohibited, while corporate activity with respect to the passage or defeat of legislation is permitted, even though corporations may engage in lobbying more often than they take positions on ballot questions submitted to the voters. Nor does § 8 prohibit a corporation from expressing its views, by the expenditure of corporate funds, on any public issue until it becomes the subject of a referendum, though the displeasure of disapproving shareholders is unlikely to be any less.

The fact that a particular kind of ballot question has been singled out for special treatment undermines the likelihood of a genuine state interest in protecting shareholders. It suggests instead that the legislature may have been concerned with silencing corporations on a particular subject. Indeed, appellee has conceded that "the legislative and judicial history of the statute indicates . . . that the second crime was 'tailor-made' to prohibit corporate campaign contributions to oppose a graduated income tax amendment." Brief for Appellee 6.

Nor is the fact that § 8 is limited to banks and business corporations without relevance. Excluded from its provisions and criminal sanctions are entities or organized groups in which numbers of persons may hold an interest or membership, and which often have resources comparable to those of large corporations. Minorities in such groups or entities may have interests with respect to institutional speech quite comparable to those of minority shareholders in a corporation. Thus the exclusion of Massachusetts business trusts, real estate investment trusts, labor unions, and other associations undermines the plausibility of the State's purported concern for the persons who happen to be shareholders in the banks and corporations covered by § 8.

The overinclusiveness of the statute is demonstrated by the fact that § 8 would prohibit a corporation from supporting or opposing a referendum proposal even if its shareholders unanimously authorized the contribution or expenditure. Ultimately shareholders may decide, through the procedures of corporate democracy, whether their corporation should engage in debate on public issues.[11] Acting through their

---

11. Appellee does not explain why the dissenting shareholder's wishes are entitled to such greater solicitude in this context than in many others where equally important and controversial corporate decisions are made by management or by a predetermined percentage of the shareholders. Mr. Justice White's repeatedly expressed concern for corporate shareholders who may be "coerced" into supporting "causes with which they disagree" apparently is not shared by appellants' shareholders. Not a single shareholder has joined appellee in defending the Massachusetts statute or, so far as the record shows, has interposed any objection to the right asserted by the corporations to make the proscribed expenditures.

The dissent of Mr. Justice White relies heavily on Abood v. Detroit Board of Education, 431 U.S. 209, 97 S.Ct. 1782, 52 L.Ed. 2d 261 (1977), and International Assn. of Machinists v. Street, 367 U.S. 740, 81 S.Ct. 1784, 6 L.Ed.2d 1141 (1961). These decisions involved the First Amendment rights of employees in closed or agency shops not to be compelled, as a condition of employment, to support with financial contributions the political activities of other union members with which the dissenters disagreed.

Street and Abood are irrelevant to the question presented in this case. In those cases employees were required, either by state law or by agreement between the employer and the union, to pay dues or a "service fee" to the exclusive bargaining representative. To the extent that these funds were used by the union in furtherance of political goals, unrelated to collective bargaining, they were held to be unconstitutional because they compelled the dissenting union member " 'to furnish contributions of money for the propagation of opinions which he disbelieves . . . .' " Abood, supra, 431 U.S., at 235 n. 31, 97 S.Ct., at 1799 (Thomas Jefferson as quoted in I. Brant, James Madison: The Nationalist 354 (1948)).

The critical distinction here is that no shareholder has been "compelled" to contribute anything. Apart from the fact, noted by the dissent, that compulsion by the State is wholly absent, the [shareholder] invests in a corporation of his own volition and is [free to withdraw his investment at any time and for any reason.] A more relevant analogy, therefore, is to the situation where an employee voluntarily joins a union, or an individual voluntarily joins an association, and later finds himself in disagreement with its stance on a political issue. The Street and Abood Courts did not address the question whether, in such a situation, the union or association must refund a portion of the dissenter's dues or,

power to elect the board of directors or to insist upon protective provisions in the corporation's charter, shareholders normally are presumed competent to protect their own interests. In addition to intracorporate remedies, minority shareholders generally have access to the judicial remedy of a derivative suit to challenge corporate disbursements alleged to have been made for improper corporate purposes or merely to further the personal interests of management.

Assuming, *arguendo,* that protection of shareholders is a "compelling" interest under the circumstances of this case, we find "no substantially relevant correlation between the governmental interest asserted and the State's effort" to prohibit appellants from speaking. Shelton v. Tucker, 364 U.S., at 485, 81 S.Ct., at 250.

V

Because that portion of § 8 challenged by appellants prohibits protected speech in a manner unjustified by a compelling state interest, it must be invalidated. The judgment of the Supreme Judicial Court is Reversed.

[CHIEF JUSTICE BURGER concurred in an opinion that focused on the First Amendment rights of "the large media conglomerates." He concluded that his "tentative probings" indicated that there should be no differentiation as to First Amendment rights as between different categories of persons or entities. JUSTICE WHITE wrote a dissent, joined by JUSTICES BRENNAN and MARSHALL. Points made in their dissent included: (1) The outcome of this case threatens the constitutionality of federal and state corrupt practices acts limiting corporate (and labor union) political activities. (2) Corporate communications are not fungible with those of individuals since they are not manifestations of creative individuality. (3) The outcome of this case interferes with state efforts to prevent concentrations of wealth from swaying political outcomes. It was noted that $120,000 contributed by corporations, including the appellants in this case, was spent by opponents of the 1972 graduate personal income tax vote, but that proponents of such a tax got only $7000 to spend. Similar imbalances were reported from California and Montana. (4) There is a danger that investment decisions will be significantly affected by ideological views of corporations:]

While the latter concern may not be of the same constitutional magnitude as the former, it is far from trivial. Corporations, as previously noted, are created by the State as a means of furthering the public welfare. One of their functions is to determine, by their success in obtaining funds, the uses to which society's resources are to be put. A State may legitimately conclude that corporations would not serve as economically efficient vehicles for such decisions if the investment preferences of the public were significantly affected by their ideological or political activities. It has long been recognized that such pursuits are not the proper business of corporations. The common law was generally interpreted as prohibiting corporate political participation. Indeed, the Securities and Exchange Commission's rules permit corporations to refuse to submit for shareholder vote any proposal which concerns a general economic, political, racial, religious, or social cause

more drastically, refrain from expressing
the majority's views. . . .

that is not significantly related to the business of the corporation or is not within its control.[12]

The necessity of prohibiting corporate political expenditures in order to prevent the use of corporate funds for purposes with which shareholders may disagree is not a unique perception of Massachusetts.

[JUSTICE REHNQUIST dissented separately; excerpts from that opinion follow:]

Early in our history, Mr. Chief Justice Marshall described the status of a corporation in the eyes of federal law:

> "A corporation is an artificial being, invisible, intangible, and existing only in contemplation of law. Being the mere creature of law, it possesses only those properties which the charter of creation confers upon it, either expressly, or as incidental to its very existence. These are such as are supposed best calculated to effect the object for which it was created." Dartmouth College v. Woodward, 4 Wheat. 518, 636, 4 L.Ed. 629 (1819).

The appellants herein either were created by the Commonwealth or were admitted into the Commonwealth only for the limited purposes described in their charters and regulated by state law. Since it cannot be disputed that the mere creation of a corporation does not invest it with all the liberties enjoyed by natural persons, United States v. White, 322 U.S. 694, 698–701, 64 S.Ct. 1248, 1251–1252, 88 L.Ed. 1542 (1944) (corporations do not enjoy the privilege against self-incrimination), our inquiry must seek to determine which constitutional protections are "incidental to its very existence." Dartmouth College, supra, 4 Wheat. at 636.

There can be little doubt that when a State creates a corporation with the power to acquire and utilize property, it necessarily and implicitly guarantees that the corporation will not be deprived of that property absent due process of law. Likewise, when a State charters a corporation for the purpose of publishing a newspaper, it necessarily assumes that the corporation is entitled to the liberty of the press essential to the conduct of its business. . . . Until recently, it was not thought that any persons, natural or artificial, had any protected right to engage in commercial speech. See Virginia State Board of Pharmacy v. Virginia Citizens Consumer Council, 425 U.S. 748, 761–770, 96 S.Ct. 1817, 1825–1829, 48 L.Ed.2d 346 (1976). Although the Court has never explicitly recognized a corporation's right of commercial speech, such a right might be considered necessarily incidental to the business of a commercial corporation.

It cannot be so readily concluded that the right of political expression is equally necessary to carry out the functions of a corporation organized for commercial purposes. A State grants to a business corporation the blessings of potentially perpetual life and limited liability to enhance its efficiency as an economic entity. It might reasonably be concluded that those properties, so beneficial in the economic sphere, pose special dangers in the political sphere. Furthermore, it might be argued that liberties of political expression are not at all necessary to effectuate the purposes for which States permit commercial corpora-

12. See Rule 14a–8(c) of the Securities and Exchange Commission, 17 CFR § 240.14a–8(c) (1977); SEC v. Medical Committee for Human Rights, 404 U.S. 403, 92 S.Ct. 577, 30 L.Ed.2d 560 (1972).

tions to exist. So long as the Judicial Branches of the State and Federal Governments remain open to protect the corporation's interest in its property, it has no need, though it may have the desire, to petition the political branches for similar protection. Indeed, the States might reasonably fear that the corporation would use its economic power to obtain further benefits beyond those already bestowed.

NOTE ON RELATIONS BETWEEN CORPORATIONS AND THE CONSTITUTION

As the two preceding cases indicate, it is well established that corporations are persons entitled to the protection of at least the First and Fourteenth Amendments. It is not so clear that they are entitled to all of the protections of all of the Amendments. While it is routinely assumed that they are entitled to jury trials and it has been held that they are protected against unreasonable searches and seizures, more controversy has affected the question of their entitlement to the privilege against self-incrimination. Early cases tended to say that by accepting the privilege of limited liability they had impliedly surrendered the other privilege, that under the Fifth Amendment. Later cases have given different rationales but also denied the corporate privilege. The question tends to come up in complex situations. Even the metaphorically inclined cannot visualize the corporation being put on the stand, placed under oath and cross-examined by the prosecution. What is at stake characteristically is the production of corporate documents. That production—including selection of the documents required by the subpoena and their authentication as genuine and the product of the authors in question. This must be done by live persons, frequently the corporate secretary. The documents may have incriminating potential vis-a-vis that individual as well. There are of course cases about the privilege as applicable to one-shareholder corporations and partnerships.[13]

Having decided that a constitutional right applies need not foreclose the issue whether it applies in precisely the same way to corporations as it does to flesh-and-blood individuals. The court has held, contrary to suggestions in the dissent in Wheeling Steel Corp. v. Glander, p. 58 supra, that equal protection does not require exactly the same treatment of corporations as individuals. A search or seizure that might be unreasonable judged by its impact on a private person's home might be thought reasonable as applied to a corporation's office.[14] Since a corporation cannot be executed or imprisoned it is not clear

---

13. The basic case on corporations and the Fifth Amendment was United States v. White, 322 U.S. 694, 64 S.Ct. 1248, 88 L.Ed. 1542 (1944), saying that nobody could assert individually a group privilege. Bellis v. United States, 417 U.S. 85, 94 S.Ct. 2179, 40 L.Ed.2d 678 (1974), held that papers of a dissolved law partnership were subject to production. United States v. Doe, 465 U.S. 605, 104 S.Ct. 1237, 79 L.Ed.2d 552 (1984), complicated the matter by saying that even an individual's papers were not protected by the Fifth, since they had been voluntarily created, but that an individual could not be compelled to produce them.

14. In re Grand Jury Subpoena: Subpoena Duces Tecum, 829 F.2d 1291 (4th Cir.1987).

what crimes it can be accused of that are "capital, or otherwise infamous" so as to require grand jury indictment.[15] It is possible to criticize the outcome in Bellotti as not giving enough effect to the proposition that corporations do not really have personalities that need expression or to the fact that their aggregation of wealth gives them access to the media that individuals cannot match. Be mindful of the interaction between the outcome to the question—are corporations persons under the First Amendment? And the answer to the question—what sorts of speech on commercial or business matters are protected? So long as there was a rule that commercial speech was not protected the typical business corporation was subject to regulation in most of its statements and proclamations.[16]

One must also deal with another side to the corporation and the constitution question. If the two preceding cases conceive of the corporation as part of the people, to be protected by the constitution from the state, what of conceiving of the corporation as part of the state, from which the people need protection?

Professor A.A. Berle is usually associated with the idea that corporate action is state action by virtue of the fact of incorporation. In fact he says:

Remains the final question: is a corporation, having achieved economic power making discrimination possible, subject to constitutional tests as to its practices and regulations *merely* because it is a corporation? Obviously the act done or practice adopted must really invade personality contrary to some constitutional privilege, else there is no wrong. In the absence of very considerable concentration of economic power in a given area, the problem does not arise. But, if there is power, accompanied by invasion of an individual right guaranteed by the Constitution, then it would seem that the mere enjoyment of a state corporate charter is sufficient justification for invoking operation of the Fourteenth and Fifteenth Amendments. It has steadily been held that

"whether the corporate privilege shall be granted or withheld is always a matter of state policy. If granted, the privilege is conferred in order to achieve an end which the State deems desirable." [17]

Though the statement was made by Mr. Justice Brandeis in the course of a dissenting opinion, this doctrine has never been questioned. It is commonly invoked by state courts, and for that matter by corporations, to justify the right of a legislature

15. United States v. Yellow Freight System, Inc., 637 F.2d 1248 (9th Cir.1980), cert. denied 454 U.S. 815, 102 S.Ct. 91, 70 L.Ed.2d 84 (1981).

16. More recent cases on corporations and freedom of speech include Central Hudson Gas & Elec. Corp. v. Public Service Comm'n of N.Y., 447 U.S. 557, 100 S.Ct. 2343, 65 L.Ed.2d 341 (1980), and Pacific Gas and Elec. Co. v. P.U.C. of Cal., 475 U.S. 1, 106 S.Ct. 903, 89 L.Ed.2d 1 (1986), discussed p. 425 infra.

17. Liggett Co. v. Lee, 288 U.S. 517, 545, 53 S.Ct. 481, 488, 77 L.Ed. 929 (1933).

to change or modify stockholders' rights. Implicitly, it would seem, state action in granting a corporate charter assumes that the corporation will not exercise its power (granted in theory at least to forward a state purpose) in a manner forbidden the state itself.

It is here that the phenomenon of concentration becomes controlling. For concentration accomplishes two results. It sets up the large corporations, members of the concentrate, as economic mechanisms on which the community and the public rely for goods or services. Concentration means either no choice or a very limited choice of suppliers of such goods or services. By reason of such a limited choice, the members of the concentrate acquire power substantially to invade constitutionally-created rights of personality. If there are fifty stores in the vicinity from which an individual can satisfy his needs, discriminatory practice by any one of them has little or no effect on the individual. If there is a single chain of stores, the effect may be to drive him out of the neighborhood. . . . The denial by private employees of complainant's right to deliver pamphlets on the streets of one mill town, dealt with in Marsh v. Alabama, involved a mixture of corporate and "public" power. The court argued that this denial of a constitutional right was carried out by the corporation employee in substantial performance of public functions. But what made them "public" except the fact that the one corporation owned the entire town? The whim of a single houseowner directed towards his tenants' religious practices might be private. The prejudice of the owner of ninety per cent of the available housing would be a public matter. One may reasonably forecast, in the future, direct application of constitutional limitations to the corporation, merely because it holds a state charter and exercises a degree of economic power sufficient to make its practices "public" rules.

The article just quoted [18] relies rather heavily on Marsh v. Alabama, 326 U.S. 501, 66 S.Ct. 276, 90 L.Ed. 265 (1946). Marsh held that first amendment restraints applied in a "company town" so that leafleting could not be prohibited by the company's officers where it could not have been curbed by city officials. The court did not in fact emphasize the fact that the company was chartered by the state; it did stress that it had taken over public service functions normally assumed by the state, such as roads, sewers, policing, etc.

The arguments developed in Berle's article have had little impact on later court decisions, with the possible exception of the concurring opinion by Justice Douglas in Bell v. Maryland, 378 U.S. 226, 84 S.Ct. 1814, 12 L.Ed.2d 822 (1964), in which he seems to argue that trespass

18. Constitutional Limitations on Corporate Activity, 100 U.Pa.L.Rev. 933, 951 (1952). Reprinted by permission of the holder of the copyright, the University of Pennsylvania Law Review.

convictions for sit-ins by black students in corporation-owned lunch-rooms involved state action and thus violated the Fourteenth Amendment. He may however, simply have been responding to an argument that lunchroom owners had a right to select those with whom they would have a "personal" relationship. Perhaps the clearest evidence that the courts have not accepted the position that a charter carries with it the limitations of state action is to be found in Jackson v. Metropolitan Edison Co.,[19] where the entity sought to be held to due process standards not only had a certificate of incorporation but also a certificate of convenience and necessity. Despite that fact and the fact that it was a lawful monopoly and was in a business affected with the public interest, the majority (6–3) held that the fourteenth amendment did not apply to its procedures for terminating electric service. Marsh v. Alabama itself has been followed by a number of cases that deal with the issue whether owners of shopping centers, sometimes extensive enough to resemble small municipalities, can control activities related to freedom of speech on those premises in ways that would be prohibited to a town government.[20]

COMMENT

The dissent in the Wheeling Steel case represents the corporate philosophy of Mr. Justice Douglas, a man with an unusually wide experience in the field. After a year as an associate with Messrs. Cravath, Henderson & DeGersdorff in New York, he became a professor at the Yale Law School. There he taught business associations and wrote, in the then dominant "realist" vein, a number of innovative books and articles. He then went to the staff of the new Securities and Exchange Commission, advancing rapidly to membership in the Commission, to Chairman, and, thence, to the bench. He can fairly be regarded as one of the shapers of the New Deal in corporations law and has continued to be interested in developments.[21]

QUESTIONS

(1) Does the textual argument by the dissent convince you? Or could one make an equally strong linguistic case for the orthodox rule? What about the argument about the origins of the Amendment in the Civil War? What category of possible "persons" besides corporations is read out of "due process" protection by the minority view? Assuming history is important, would you give much weight to data indicating (a) that by 1865 lawyers and courts in construing various state statutes had tended to treat corporations as "persons" (b) that senators on the committee preparing the amendment assumed corporations were persons and that some of them had an intent—not generally

19. 419 U.S. 345, 95 S.Ct. 449, 42 L.Ed. 2d 477 (1974). See also Stearns v. Veterans of Foreign Wars, 394 F.Supp. 138 (D.D.C.1975) (VFW's federal charter not enough to make Fifth Amendment apply).

L.Ed.2d 603 (1968); Hudgens v. NLRB, 424 U.S. 507, 96 S.Ct. 1029, 47 L.Ed.2d 196 (1976); Pruneyard Shopping Center v. Robins, 447 U.S. 74, 100 S.Ct. 2035, 64 L.Ed.2d 741 (1980).

20. Compare Amalgamated Food Employees Union Local 590 v. Logan Valley Plaza, Inc., 391 U.S. 308, 88 S.Ct. 1601, 20

21. See Countryman, Mr. Justice Douglas' Contribution to the Law: Business Regulation, 74 Colum.L.Rev. 366 (1974).

disclosed by them—that the amendment should be used to protect the property rights of corporations?[22]

(2) With respect to the Equal Protection side of the dissent's arguments, do you agree that it follows from the conclusion that corporations are persons that the Amendment "puts negroes and corporations into one class"? Could a state, for example, levy property taxes on corporate and individual real estate at different rates? What characteristics of corporations would be relevant to that decision?

(3) Who in fact gets to exercise the freedom of speech afforded corporations in Bellotti? What could stockholders who disagreed with that speech do about it? Is there a respectable way of distinguishing the corporate expenditures in Bellotti from the grants to political candidates, etc. that have long been forbidden by Corrupt Practices Legislation?

Bibliography: For a discussion of Bellotti see Brudney, Business Corporations and Stockholders' Rights under the First Amendment, 91 Yale L.J. 235 (1981). The historical background on corporations and the constitution is traced in Horwitz, Santa Clara Revisited: The Development of Corporate Theory, 88 W.Va.L.Rev. 173 (1985). O'Kelley, The Constitutional Rights of Corporations Revisited, 67 Geo.L.J. 1347 (1979).

22. Graham, An Innocent Abroad: The Constitutional Corporate Person, 2 U.C. L.A.L.Rev. 155 (1954).

Chapter IV

FORMING THE CORPORATION: ITS
LEGAL STRUCTURE

The over 600,000 corporations formed each year in the United States are created without enormous intellectual effort. The procedure, which varies a bit from state to state, centers around the filing of a document (called charter or articles of incorporation) with an office (usually that of the secretary of state) accompanied by a modest fee. Even these formalities are often entrusted to specialized agencies of which the Corporation Trust Company, Prentice–Hall Corporation, Inc. and U.S. Corporation Company are the best known. Where formerly this process was supervised by the younger associates in a law firm, even that is now handled by paralegals. One wonders whether there has not been a certain loss with respect to the basic training provided by starting with such routines. This was not always so; during the period in which corporations were formed by special statute, incorporation involved shepherding a bill through both houses of a legislature, including committees. It seems that the process was occasionally quite expensive. Incorporation is still sometimes achieved by legislative means; the federal statute creating the Communications Satellite Corporation is a conspicuous example.

This chapter will, briefly, describe to you the process of creating a corporation, as it occurs in Delaware. It then goes on to raise some issues about the direct or indirect consequences of slips in the incorporation process. Finally, it considers some issues that arise when the creators of the corporation are not clumsy but, as the British would say, too clever by half.

1. The Incorporation Process

Examine carefully the pertinent portions of the Delaware law: §§ 101–107. You are very likely to have to go through this process at least once in your professional career.

(1) The preparation of the certificate of incorporation;

(2) Its signature and acknowledgment;

(3) Its filing with the secretary of state along with payment of taxes and fees;

(4) The recording of the duplicate with the County Recorder;

(5) The organization meeting.

You should also examine the model articles of incorporation set forth in the Documentary Supplement. Note that the by-laws, which follow them in the Supplement, are *not* filed with any Delaware office.

The Delaware procedure is reasonably typical of that followed in other states. It is, however, somewhat simpler and more streamlined than some others. For example, since 1967 it has permitted the use of a single incorporator. This practice has gradually spread to other states. This type of convenience is one of the attractions of Delaware to corporations that leave home.

Delaware law is highlighted in this casebook for several reasons. That small state has become the preeminent home away from home of large corporations—[1] and of many smaller ones as well. Its statutes are relatively clear and very up to date. It can also boast a substantial body of interesting case law decided by experienced judges. Its closest competitor is the Model Business Corporation Act which was drafted by a committee of the American Bar Association and was revised in 1984. The Act is reflected in a number of state statutes, to a degree that varies from very nearly literal to selective imitation. That Act can be used in conjunction with this book by consulting the cross reference table to the Model Act. This volume also takes into account a third set of prescriptions—the American Law Institute's Principles of Corporate Governance; Analysis and Recommendations. This work has been fighting its way through the Institute since 1980, generating considerable heat in the process. It does not purport to be a comprehensive model statute; it rather endeavors to state principles for the guidance of legislators, judges and corporate managers.

From the practitioner's point of view, Delaware has many advantages. The law is generally clear. Furthermore, it is usually clear in the right direction, that is, it permits management and management's counsel to build a corporate structure that allows for great flexibility and considerable freedom from unwanted interference by shareholders. It is free of cumbersome formalities and the cost in terms of fees is not onerous. Before jumping to the conclusion that Delaware is the preferable solution for your client's problem you should consider the fact that a Delaware corporation doing business in, say, New York, must file various documents and pay various fees in New York in order to qualify to do business there. Furthermore, New York may make some of its provisions applicable to corporations acting within its borders even if they remain basically Delaware creatures. The cost and nuisance may cancel out the benefits of Delaware incorporation.

1. Even before the 1967 revision and its attractions had an effect, 203 of the 500 corporations on *Fortune's* list of the biggest 500 were incorporated in Delaware and as of 1968 more were signing up. Folk, Some Reflections of a Corporation Law Draftsman, 42 Conn.B.J. 409, 412 (1968).

The widespread use of Delaware law by large corporations has not gone without criticism. Writers accuse Delaware of having deliberately sought and bought the position of chief residence of corporations, a position held in prior periods by Maine and then by New Jersey (before the reforms sponsored by Governor Woodrow Wilson). They point to various conveniences for corporate managements tendered by the Delaware legislature and not found in other state statutes (or introduced only later). We will study a number of these elements later. The critics speak of a "race for the bottom", "law for sale" etc. They have suggested the need for federal intervention to arrest this process of deterioration in corporation law. Delaware lawyers and others have defended the institution. They point to the clarity and up-to-dateness of the statute and to the experience and sophistication of the specialized judges of the Court of Chancery who render speedy and knowledgeable service, assisted by a sophisticated bar. They refer to studies which appear to show that there is no damage to the interests of the shareholders of corporations that abandon other states for Delaware reincorporation; these studies rest on findings that the stock market prices of such corporations' shares do not go down when news of the transfer is made public.[2]

The feasibility of incorporating multi-state enterprises in Delaware—or indeed in any one state—depends upon the acceptance by other states of the conflicts of law rule that the internal affairs of a corporation are governed by the law of the place of incorporation. It would be intolerable if, for example, those who planned a meeting of directors or shareholders had to worry about complying with several sets of laws about who had the right to convene the meeting or to vote at it. Subject presumably to some exception for corporations that have the overwhelming bulk of their activity in some other state—sometimes called pseudo-foreign corporations [3]—this rule is so firmly accepted that it seems at times to have a constitutional basis. One guesses that if there were no such rule the needs of large-scale business would have led to the federalization of corporation law or at least the availability of federal incorporation.

Despite the increased simplicity of modern rules on incorporation mistakes do happen. The Secretary of State of New York advised that 20–25% of the 56,000 certificates filed yearly around 1960 were rejected

2. The article that began the debate on Delaware corporation law was Cary, Federalism and Corporate Law: Reflections upon Delaware, 83 Yale L.J. 663 (1974). Responses include Winter, State Law, Shareholder Protection and the Theory of the Corporation, 6 J. Legal Studies 251 (1977); Romano, The State Competition Debate in Corporate Law, 8 Cardozo L.Rev. 709 (1987). For a study that includes Delaware decisional law, see Weiss & White, Of Econometrics and Indeterminacy: A Study of Investors' Reactions to "Changes" in Corporate Law, 75 Calif.L.Rev. 551 (1987).

3. For the current status of this set of issues see Buxbaum, The Threatened Constitutionalization of the Internal Affairs Doctrine in Corporation Law, 75 Calif.L. Rev. 29 (1987). For an old classic, Latty, Pseudo–Foreign Corporations, 65 Yale L.J. 137 (1955).

for failure to comply with formal requirements.[4]　The question then arises what happens if there is something wrong with what is filed or if nothing at all is filed?　One possibility, that of revoking the charter, is illustrated by the case below.　The other, involving making collateral consequences hinge upon the error, is illustrated by succeeding cases. The cases may leave you with the impression that the courts will overlook much and cure defects by equitable doctrines.　Some courts, however, will agree with Farmer, J., in his dissent in People v. Ford and strict constructionists of that ilk.　And, even if the courts forgive you, the partners of the firm that employs you and its clients will not be cheered by the information that, probably, the *de facto* doctrine will save them from the consequences of your carelessness.　Thus, never let the fact that this is routine work lead you into overlooking any of the steps needed to make the process a valid one.　One further warning: even if a corporation is once validly formed, failure to *maintain* its legal existence by filing the required reports and paying the necessary taxes may lead to consequences much like those associated with initial noncompliance.

PEOPLE v. FORD

Supreme Court of Illinois, 1920.
294 Ill. 319, 128 N.E. 479.

DUNN, J.　The Fifty–First General Assembly passed an act in relation to corporations for pecuniary profit, known as the General Corporation Act, which was approved on June 28, and became effective July 1, 1919.　Laws of 1919, p. 316.　Section 4 provides that—

"Whenever three or more adult persons, citizens of the United States of America, at least one of whom shall be a citizen of this state, shall desire to form a corporation under this act, they shall sign, seal and acknowledge before some officer, competent to take acknowledgment of deeds, a statement of incorporation setting forth the following: [Here follow thirteen paragraphs stating the facts to be contained in the statement.]"

The section closes with the sentence that—

"Such statement shall be filed in duplicate in the office of the secretary of state on forms prescribed and furnished by the secretary of state."

Section 5 provides that—

"Upon the filing of such statement, the secretary of state shall examine the same, and, if it is in conformity with the provisions of this act, he shall indorse thereon the word 'Filed' followed by the month, day and year of such filing.　Upon such filing the corporation shall be deemed fully organized and may proceed to business."

4.　Davis, Some Problems in the Preparation of Certificates of Incorporation, N.Y.S. Bar Ass'n Bull., July 1960, p. 166.

On September 5, 1919, a certificate of incorporation of the Washer Maid Company was filed in duplicate in the office of the secretary of state. The Attorney General afterward, by leave of the court, filed in the circuit court of Cook county an information in the nature of quo warranto against E. E. Ford, A. J. Fisher, and C. R. Gilbert, charging them with having unlawfully usurped, intruded into, held, and executed the office of directors of a pretended corporation known as the Washer Maid Company, under color of a void and illegal certificate of incorporation, and calling upon them to show by what warrant they exercised such privileges.

The respondents filed a plea showing the various steps taken for the organization of the corporation, setting forth in haec verba the statement filed by them, alleging that it was made on forms prescribed and furnished by the secretary of state, which were executed and acknowledged by the respondents, and that the respondents had in all respects complied with the requirements of the General Corporation Act. The Attorney General demurred and for special cause of demurrer showed that the respondents in their statement of incorporation did not sign, seal and acknowledge the same, but, on the contrary, failed to seal the same or to affix their seals to said statement of incorporation, as required by the General Corporation Act. The statement set forth in the plea shows the signatures of the respondents as follows:

> E. E. Ford,　　　⎫
> A. J. Fisher,　　　⎬　　　　　　　　Incorporators.
> Chas. R. Gilbert,　⎭

The word "seal" does not appear, nor are there any letters, scrawl, or marks which might be regarded as a seal, unless it is the bracket which joins the names, and neither the statement itself nor the certificate of acknowledgment contains any reference to a seal. The court overruled the demurrer, and, the Attorney General electing to stand by it, the information was dismissed. An appeal was taken, and at the June term the cause was submitted, with a request by both parties for an early decision because of the public importance of the question involved. It was stated that more than 4,300 corporations had been organized under the new act, that the statement of incorporation in each case was made upon the form prescribed and furnished by the secretary of state and was identical with the form used in this case, and that the incorporation of each of those corporations was subject to the same infirmity as that alleged against the appellees. The fees paid to the secretary of state amounted to more than $600,000 and annual franchise taxes to a large amount were about to fall due on July 1. Recognizing the public inconvenience which would arise from a prolonged uncertainty as to the legality of the organization of these corporations, we announced orally our judgment affirming that of the circuit court, stating that the reasons would be given in an opinion to be filed later.

The question presented was whether the requirement that the incorporators shall seal the statement is mandatory or directory. It was argued on behalf of the people that the requirement of the seal is a condition precedent to the legal existence of a corporation. A somewhat similar question arose early in the history of the state in the case of Cross v. Pinckneyville Mill Co., 17 Ill. 54. The act of 1849, to authorize the formation of corporations for manufacturing, agricultural, mining or mechanical purposes, provided that any three or more persons desiring to form a company for such purpose should make, sign, and acknowledge, and file "in the office of the clerk in the county in which the business of the company should be carried on and a duplicate thereof in the office of the secretary of state, a certificate in writing," in which should be stated the name of the company and other facts mentioned in the statute. It was further provided that when the certificate should have been filed as aforesaid the persons who should have signed and acknowledged, and their successors, should be a body politic and corporate. In the case mentioned the duplicate certificate of organization had not been filed in the office of the secretary of state, but the court held that fact unimportant to defeat the organization or rights growing out of it; that there is a well-settled distinction between mandatory and directory provisions, and that carrying out of the true intention of the Legislature and effectuating the object of the law would not be promoted by strict technical constructions, converting every direction and detail of power into a mandatory prerequisite of corporate existence.

More recently a question arose as to the effect of the failure to mail notices of the meeting of subscribers of the capital stock to elect officers, as required by section 3 of the Corporation Act of 1872 (Laws 1871–72, p. 296). We said:

> "The statute prescribes a certain course to be pursued in organizing a corporation in this state. It does not necessarily follow, however, that any departure from that course will prevent a corporation from becoming one de jure. Whether or not such departure will have that effect depends upon the nature of the provision which is violated. If it is a mandatory provision, a failure to substantially comply with its terms will prevent the corporation from becoming one de jure; but if the provision is merely directory, then a departure therefrom will not have that consequence."

It was held that it was immaterial whether or not notice had been given in the manner directed by the statute; the persons entitled to notice having waived it and actually attended the meeting, so that the purpose of the statute in requiring the notices to be given was accomplished. (Butler Paper Co. v. Cleveland, 220 Ill. 128.) . . . In contrast with this case, an illustration of the distinction between mandatory and directory provisions is furnished by another case in the same court, (Utley v. Union Tool Co., 11 Gray 139) in which the articles of agreement of the incorporators did not fix the amount of the capital stock or set forth distinctly the purpose for and the place in which the corporation was established, the court saying: "There is an obvious reason for making such organization by written articles of agreement a condition precedent to the exercise of corporate rights. It is the basis on which all subsequent proceedings are to rest and is designed to take the place of a charter or act of incorporation, by which corporate rights and privileges are usually granted." . . .

The requirement of a seal in the execution of documents by individuals has become a mere formality. It means nothing. Private seals no longer exist as a means of execution of specialties, for even an individual scrawl is not required. In most deeds the word "seal" is printed on the blank form which is used, and the grantor does not know whether he has used a seal or not. It depends upon whether the word was printed on the paper or not. The solemnity of the sealed instrument is purely Pickwickian and no longer represents an idea. While courts of law in this state cannot disregard the legal quality of the sealed instrument, courts of equity frequently relieve parties from the difficulties arising from the application of the rigid rules of the common law to such instruments.

We may look to the intention of the statute in determining the effect of an omission to add the seal. The purpose is to make a public record of the corporation, the definition of its powers, the amount of its stock, the names of its stockholders, its location, and other facts in connection with it, which are of interest to the public to know, and of the state in its supervision over corporations to be acquainted with. The addition of a seal is of no importance for these purposes. It is not of the essence of the thing to be done, and no prejudice can result from its omission. The essential act of making the statement, though not in the precise manner indicated, accomplishes the substantial purpose of the statute, and that is sufficient. It would not be carrying out the intention of the Legislature to hold that the addition of a scrawl by the signers of the statement is mandatory and its omission invalidates the incorporation.

For these reasons the judgment of the circuit court was affirmed.

Judgment affirmed.

FARMER, J. (dissenting). The Legislature saw fit to require the statement to be under seal. Whether this was an important requirement or not, the Legislature had the power to, and did make it. Courts cannot disregard it, on the ground that it was a useless requirement, or that the Legislature did not mean what it said.

QUESTION

What advantage did the State of Illinois hope to gain by bringing the proceeding in Ford? What would have happened if it had been successful? Do you sympathize at all with Judge Farmer's views as to statutory construction? How would a case come out under the Del. §§ 103, 106 in which a certificate of incorporation had never been acknowledged? If one agrees with the Illinois court but feels that formalities ought to be observed, what can the state do to increase compliance?

---

2. Incorporation and Limited Liability

In a certain type of analysis, the absence of liability on the part of the entrepreneurs and investors of a corporation might be deduced directly from thinking about corporate personality. The tort or contract is the obligation of the corporation, a personality separate from that of those behind it; consequently, it is liable and not they. It does seem that the idea of corporate legal personality does imply that the corporation *is* liable. Probably it also implies that it is primarily liable, i.e. that claimants must proceed against it first. However, it does not necessarily imply that there may not be recourse over against the shareholders. In fact there are many examples of shareholder liability. There was serious question, historically, as to whether the grant of incorporation, without specific reference to the liability issue, implicitly bestowed limited liability. The Delaware statute (§ 101(b)(6)) like many others, still gives an opportunity to elect to have the articles of incorporation reflect some degree of liability on the part of the shareholders. Quite apart from such a voluntary provision, some statutes expressly make shareholders liable for certain types of obligations. The notorious example is New York's law requiring that shareholders pay wage claims (a rule specifically inapplicable to publicly traded enterprises).[5] One reason for that exception is that lawyers could not otherwise give the ritual opinion that shares subject to such a risk were "validly issued, fully paid and non-assessable."

Thus, one must recognize that a policy decision has been made that shareholders should not be liable for the debts of their corporation, except to the extent that they lose whatever they contributed to its capital. This decision had become quite universal by about 1860—including continental European countries. The arguments then made for it tended to focus on the problems of the inactive partner who became liable for overwhelming debts incurred by the managers. An oft-cited case was that of Sir Walter Scott who spent years of novel-writing paying off the debts of a publishing firm with which he had been associated. At that time bankruptcy laws did not generally afford a second line of limitation of liability and the unlucky partner might wind up in debtors' prison. In nearly all countries the benefits of limited liability tended at first to be given only to those who associated in large corporations; only by degrees, and sometimes with additional legislation, was it extended to the closed corporation. In particular some judges had serious problems with one-shareholder corporations: Where, as in Germany or France, a company was called a "Gesellschaft" or "société", these words seemed to point towards a plurality of people. So did the use of the term, "contract of association." On the whole this did not prove terribly bothersome in the United States. However, the one shareholder corporation or the corporation wholly owned by another corporation have been abused in some very tricky schemes, and the courts have tried, not too successfully, to distinguish between cases of use and abuse.

Two cases follow: The first deals with the problems of the clumsy lawyer. The second with somebody (perhaps a lawyer) who was very smart—and who seemed to be getting away with it by not too wide a margin.

----

5. Business Corporation Law § 630.

CRANSON v. INTERNATIONAL BUSINESS MACHINES CORP.

Court of Appeals of Maryland, 1964.
234 Md. 477, 200 A.2d 33.

[This was an action by I.B.M. against Cranson to recover the $4,333.40 balance of the price of 8 typewriters sold to "Real Estate Service Bureau". Cranson was one of a group of people who invested in this enterprise and was advised by their attorney that the corporation had been formed. He received a stock certificate and saw a seal and minute book. The business of the venture was done in corporate form. Cranson was elected president and acted as an officer. Due to the attorney's oversight the certificate, signed and acknowledged before May 1961 was not filed until November 24. Between May 17 and November 8 the I.B.M. purchase was made. The trial court entered judgment for I.B.M., which was reversed in an opinion by HORNEY, J.:]

The fundamental question presented by the appeal is whether an officer of a defectively incorporated association may be subjected to personal liability under the circumstances of this case. We think not.

Traditionally, two doctrines have been used by the courts to clothe an officer of a defectively incorporated association with the corporate attribute of limited liability. The first, often referred to as the doctrine of *de facto* corporations, has been applied in those cases where there are elements showing: (1) the existence of law authorizing incorporation; (2) an effort in good faith to incorporate under the existing law; and (3) actual user or exercise of corporate powers . . . The second, the doctrine of estoppel to deny the corporate existence, is generally employed where the person seeking to hold the officer personally liable has contracted or otherwise dealt with the association in such a manner as to recognize and in effect admit its existence as a corporate body . . .

It is not at all clear what Maryland has done with respect to the two doctrines. There have been no recent cases in this State on the subject and some of the seemingly irreconcilable earlier cases offer little to clarify the problem.

In one line of cases, the Court, in determining the rights and liabilities of a defectively organized corporation, or a member or stockholder thereof, seems to have drawn a distinction between those acts or requirements which are a condition precedent to corporate existence and those acts prescribed by law to be done after incorporation. In so doing, it has been generally held that where there had been a failure to comply with a requirement which the law declared to be a condition precedent to the existence of the corporation, the corporation was not a legal entity and was therefore precluded from suing or being sued as such . . . These cases appear to stand for the proposition that substantial compliance with those formalities of the corporation law, which are made a condition precedent to corporate existence, was not only necessary for the creation of a corporation *de jure*, but was also a prerequisite to the existence of a *de facto* corporation or a corporation by estoppel. . . .

On the other hand, where the corporation has obtained legal existence but has failed to comply with a condition subsequent to corporate existence, this Court has held that such nonperformance afforded the State the right to institute proceedings for the forfeiture of the charter, but that such neglect or omission could never be set up by the corporation itself, or by its members and stockholders, as a defense to an action to enforce their liabilities . . . . It seems clear therefore that when a defect in the incorporation process resulted from a failure to comply with a condition subsequent, the doctrine of estoppel may be applied for the benefit of a creditor to estop the corporation, or the members or stockholders thereof, from denying its corporate existence. See Brune (Herbert M., Jr.), Maryland Corporation Law and Practice (rev. ed.), § 339.

In another line of Maryland cases which determined the rights and liabilities of a defectively organized corporation, or a member or stockholder thereof, the Court, apparently disregarding the distinction made between those requirements which are conditions precedent and those which are conditions subsequent to corporate existence, has generally precluded, on the grounds of estoppel or collateral attack, inquiry into the question of corporate existence . . . From these cases it appears that where the parties have assumed corporate existence and dealt with each other on that basis, the Court will apply the estoppel doctrine on the theory that the parties by recognizing the organization as a corporation were thereafter prevented from raising a question as to its corporate existence.

When summarized, the law in Maryland pertaining to the *de facto* and estoppel doctrines reveals that the cases seem to fall into one or the other of two categories. In one line of cases, the Court, choosing to disregard the nature of the dealings between the parties, refused to recognize both doctrines where there had been a failure to comply with a condition precedent to corporate existence, but, whenever such noncompliance concerned a condition subsequent to incorporation, the Court often applied the estoppel doctrine. In the other line of cases, the Court, choosing to make no distinction between defects which were conditions precedent and those which were conditions subsequent, emphasized the course of conduct between the parties and applied the estoppel doctrine when there had been substantial dealings between them on a corporate basis.

Whether or not the decisions in the Boyce and Maryland Tube cases had the effect of repudiating the *de facto* doctrine in this state, as some of the text writers seem to think, is a question we do not reach in this case and therefore need not consider at this time. On the other hand, since it is clear that the Maryland Tube and National Shutter Bar cases are inconsistent with other Maryland cases insofar as they held . . . that the doctrine of estoppel cannot be invoked unless a corporation has at least a *de facto* existence, both cases—Maryland Tube and National Shutter Bar—should be, and are hereby, overruled to the extent of the inconsistency. There is, as we see it, a wide difference between creating a corporation by means of the *de facto* doctrine and estopping a party, due to his conduct in a particular case, from setting up the claim of no incorporation. Although some cases tend to assimilate the doctrines of incorporation *de facto* and by estoppel, each is a distinct theory and they are not dependent on one another in their application. See 8 Fletcher, op. cit., § 3763; France on Corporations (2nd ed.), § 29; 18 C.J.S. op. cit. § 111h. Where there is a concurrence of the three elements necessary for the application of the *de facto* corporation doctrine, there exists an entity which is a corporation *de jure* against all persons but the state. On the other hand, the estoppel theory is applied only to the facts of each particular case and may be invoked even where there is no corporation *de facto*. Accordingly, even though one or more of the requisites of a *de facto* corporation are absent, we think that this factor does not preclude the application of the estoppel doctrine [6] in a proper case, such as the one at bar.

I.B.M. contends that the failure of the Bureau to file its certificate of incorporation debarred *all* corporate existence. But, in spite of the fact that the omission might have prevented the Bureau from being either a corporation *de jure* or *de facto*,[7] . . ., we think that I.B.M. having dealt with the Bureau as if it were a corporation and relied on its credit rather than that of Cranson, is estopped to assert that the Bureau was not incorporated at the time the typewriters were purchased. . . . In 1 Clark and Marshall, Private Corporations, § 89, it is stated:

> "The doctrine in relation to estoppel is based upon the ground that it would generally be inequitable to permit the corporate existence of an association to be denied by persons who have represented it to be a corporation, or held it out as a corporation, or by any persons who have recognized it as a corporation by dealing with it as such; and by the overwhelming weight of authority, therefore, a person may be estopped to deny the legal incorporation of an association which is not even a corporation *de facto*."

In cases similar to the one at bar, involving a failure to file articles of incorporation, the courts of other jurisdictions have held that where one has recognized the corporate existence of an association, he is estopped to assert the contrary with respect to a claim arising out of such dealings. . . .

Since I.B.M. is estopped to deny the corporate existence of the Bureau, we hold that Cranson was not liable for the balance due on account of the typewriters.

QUESTIONS

(1) Suppose that IBM had sued the Real Estate Service Bureau (still solvent) and been met with a claim that it was not really a corporation. Would

6. A third doctrine, called the modern "enterprise-entity theory," which in many respects is not unlike the estoppel theory applied in Maryland, is described in 1 Oleck, Modern Corporation Law, § 592. For an excellent analysis of the law concerning defective incorporation in general, see Chapter 25 of Vol. 1, §§ 584–595. See also the last sentence in § 591 (p. 839) where the author says that "in time the doctrine of 'de facto' corporation may become merely an historic example of legal conceptualism at its worst."

7. Those states which recognize the *de facto* doctrine are not in accord as to whether a corporation *de facto* may be created in spite of the failure to file the

necessary papers. Some courts, without making clear in every instance whether a *de facto* corporation was meant or not, have stated that failure to file the required papers prevented the organizations from becoming a corporation and have held in effect that the persons acting as a corporation are a mere association or partnership . . . Other courts, without expressly deciding whether a *de facto* corporation was created, hold that the statutes of the state imply corporate existence prior to the filing of articles of incorporation . . . Still other courts hold that a *de facto* existence is not precluded by failure to file the articles of incorporation . . .

you have dismissed the suit? If not, on what ground would you have relied? Is this a true estoppel?

(2) Suppose Real Estate Service Bureau had sued IBM, which had defended on the basis of the plaintiff's lack of corporateness—how would you dispose of the defense?

(3) Do you agree with the reasoning of the court in Cranston? Is this a true estoppel or like enough to one to carry over by analogy? What was the defect involved? Suppose that Real Estate Service Bureau had been a Delaware corporation—would the statute have pointed strongly to a result?

(4) Consider the consequences of a decision that a corporation is *not* validly formed. Are the founders of the enterprise partners within the meaning of § 6 of the Uniform Act? Should one distinguish between "officers" and "directors" of the non-existent "corporation" and its "shareholders"? What about the status of the person who purported to represent the "corporation" in the contract being sued upon? See Restatement, Second, Agency § 329. Compare the consequences of failure to perfect a limited partnership, U.L.P.A. § 11, (§ 304 in the 1976 revision) with those of failing to perfect a corporation.

(5) Is imposition of personal liability on entrepreneurs a useful way of achieving a higher level of compliance with the incorporation requirements? If so, is it fair to classify such liability as a "penalty" within the meaning of a conflicts of law principle that prevents one state from enforcing another's "penal laws"?[8] Or does it have a remedial character, that is, does it compensate an innocent party from loss caused him by failure to file or complete some other formality? How would you compare it with the rule, prevailing in some states, that an out-of-state corporation which has not qualified by registering under the local corporation law provisions on foreign corporations cannot use the local courts to enforce contracts—and that such deficit cannot be cured retroactively by later filing?

WALKOVSZKY v. CARLTON

Court of Appeals of New York, 1966.
18 N.Y.2d 414, 223 N.E.2d 6, 276 N.Y.S.2d 585.

[This was an action against a cab driver, the corporation owning the cab and Carlton who owned the stock of 10 taxi corporations each owning 2 cabs and carrying the minimum insurance. The complaint alleged that the corporations were operated as a single entity and that the structure constituted an attempt to "defraud" members of the public. Carlton moved to dismiss for failure to state a cause of action. The trial court granted the motion, the Appellate Division reversed and Carlton obtained leave of the Appellate Division to appeal that order. The Court of Appeals, in an opinion by FULD, J., in turn reversed the Appellate Division's order].

The law permits the incorporation of a business for the very purpose of enabling its proprietors to escape personal liability (see e.g., Bartle v. Home Owners Co-op., 309 N.Y. 103, 106, 127 N.E.2d 832, 833) but, manifestly, the privilege is not without its limits. Broadly speak-

8. Doggrell v. Great Southern Box Co., 206 F.2d 671 (6th Cir.1953), rehearing granted and case reversed, 208 F.2d 310 (6th Cir.1953), after the state court decision in Paper Products Co. v. Doggrell, 195 Tenn. 581, 261 S.W.2d 127 (1953).

ing, the courts will disregard the corporate form, or, to use accepted terminology, "pierce the corporate veil", whenever necessary "to prevent fraud or to achieve equity". (International Aircraft Trading Co. v. Manufacturers Trust Co., 297 N.Y. 285, 292, 79 N.E.2d 249, 252.) In determining whether liability should be extended to reach assets beyond those belonging to the corporation, we are guided, as Judge Cardozo noted, by "general rules of agency". (Berkey v. Third Ave. Ry. Co., 244 N.Y. 84, 95, 155 N.E. 58, 61, 50 A.L.R. 599.) In other words, whenever anyone uses control of the corporation to further his own rather than the corporation's business, he will be liable for the corporation's acts "upon the principle of *respondeat superior* applicable even where the agent is a natural person". (Rapid Tr. Subway Constr. Co. v. City of New York, 259 N.Y. 472, 488, 182 N.E. 145, 150.) Such liability, moreover, extends not only to the corporation's commercial dealings.
. . .

In the case before us, the plaintiff has explicitly alleged that none of the corporations "had a separate existence of their own" and, as indicated above, all are named as defendants. However, it is one thing to assert that a corporation is a fragment of a larger corporate combine which actually conducts the business. (See Berle, The Theory of Enterprise Entity, 47 Col.L.Rev. 343, 348–350.) It is quite another to claim that the corporation is a "dummy" for its individual stockholders who are in reality carrying on the business in their personal capacities for purely personal rather than corporate ends. (See African Metals Corp. v. Bullowa, 288 N.Y. 78, 85, 41 N.E.2d 466, 469.) Either circumstance would justify treating the corporation as an agent and piercing the corporate veil to reach the principal but a different result would follow in each case. In the first, only a larger *corporate* entity would be held financially responsible. . . . Either the stockholder is conducting the business in his individual capacity or he is not. If he is, he will be liable; if he is not, then, it does not matter—insofar as his personal liability is concerned—that the enterprise is actually being carried on by a larger "enterprise entity". (See Berle, The Theory of Enterprise Entity, 47 Col.L.Rev. 343.)

At this stage in the present litigation, we are concerned only with the pleadings, and, since CPLR 3014 permits causes of action to be stated "alternatively or hypothetically", it is possible for the plaintiff to allege both theories as the basis for his demand for judgment. In ascertaining whether he has done so, we must consider the entire pleading, educing therefrom " 'whatever can be imputed from its statements by fair and reasonable intendment.' " . . . Reading the complaint in this case most favorably and liberally, we do not believe that there can be gathered from its averments the allegations required to spell out a valid cause of action against the defendant Carlton.

The individual defendant is charged with having "organized, managed, dominated and controlled" a fragmented corporate entity but there are no allegations that he was conducting business in his individual capacity. Had the taxicab fleet been owned by a single corporation, it would be readily apparent that the plaintiff would face formidable barriers in attempting to establish personal liability on the part of the corporation's stockholders. The fact that the fleet ownership has been deliberately split up among many corporations does not ease the plaintiff's burden in that respect. The corporate form may not be disregarded merely because the assets of the corporation, together with the mandatory insurance coverage of the vehicle which struck the plaintiff, are insufficient to assure him the recovery sought. If Carlton were to be held individually liable on those facts alone, the decision would apply equally to the thousands of cabs which are owned by their individual drivers who conduct their businesses through corporations organized pursuant to section 401 of the Business Corporation Law, Consol.Laws, c. 4 and carry the minimum insurance required by subdivision 1 (par. [a]) of section 370 of the Vehicle and Traffic Law, Consol. Laws, c. 71. These taxi owner-operators are entitled to form such corporations (cf. Elenkrieg v. Siebrecht, 238 N.Y. 254, 144 N.E. 519, 34 A.L.R. 592), and we agree with the court at Special Term that, if the insurance coverage required by statute "is inadequate for the protection of the public, the remedy lies not with the courts but with the Legislature." It may very well be sound policy to require that certain corporations must take out liability insurance which will afford adequate compensation to their potential tort victims. However, the responsibility for imposing conditions on the privilege of incorporation has been committed by the Constitution to the Legislature (N.Y.Const. art. X, § 1) and it may not be fairly implied, from any statute, that the Legislature intended, without the slightest discussion or debate, to require of taxi corporations that they carry automobile liability insurance over and above that mandated by the Vehicle and Traffic Law.

This is not to say that it is impossible for the plaintiff to state a valid cause of action against the defendant Carlton. However, the simple fact is that the plaintiff has just not done so here. While the complaint alleges that the separate corporations were undercapitalized and their assets have been intermingled, it is barren of any "sufficiently particular[ized] statements" (CPLR 3013; see 3 Weinstein–Korn–Miller, N.Y.Civ.Prac., par. 3013.01 et seq., pp. 30–142 et seq.) that the defendant Carlton and his associates are actually doing business in their individual capacities, shuttling their personal funds in and out of the corporations "without regard to formality and to suit their immediate convenience." (Weisser v. Mursam Shoe Corp., 2 Cir., 127 F.2d 344, 345, 145 A.L.R. 467, supra.) Such a "perversion of the privilege to do business in a corporate form" (Berkey v. Third Ave. Ry. Co., 244 N.Y. 84, 95, 155 N.E. 58, 61, 50 A.L.R. 599, supra) would justify imposing personal liability on the individual stockholders. (See African Metals Corp. v. Bullowa, 288 N.Y. 78, 41 N.E.2d 466, supra.) Nothing of the sort has in fact been charged, and it cannot reasonably or logically be inferred from the happenstance that the business of Seon Cab Corporation may actually be carried on by a larger corporate entity composed of many corporations which, under general principles of agency, would be liable to each other's creditors in contract and in tort.

In point of fact, the principle relied upon in the complaint to sustain the imposition of personal liability is not agency but fraud. Such a cause of action cannot withstand analysis. If it is not fraudulent for the owner-operator of a single cab corporation to take out only the minimum required liability insurance, the enterprise does not become either illicit or fraudulent merely because it consists of many such corporations. The plaintiff's injuries are the same regardless of whether the cab which strikes him is owned by a single corporation or part of a fleet with ownership fragmented among many corporations. Whatever rights he may be able to assert against parties other than the registered owner of the vehicle come into being not because he has been defrauded but because, under the principle of *respondeat superior*, he is entitled to hold the whole enterprise responsible for the acts of its agents.

In sum, then, the complaint falls short of adequately stating a cause of action against the defendant Carlton in his individual capacity.

The order of the Appellate Division should be reversed, with costs in this court and in the Appellate Division, the certified question answered in the negative and the order of the Supreme Court, Richmond County, reinstated, with leave to serve an amended complaint.

KEATING, JUDGE (dissenting) . . .

The issue presented by this action is whether the policy of this State, which affords those desiring to engage in a business enterprise the privilege of limited liability through the use of the corporate device, is so strong that it will permit that privilege to continue no matter how much it is abused, no matter how irresponsibly the corporation is operated, no matter what the cost to the public. I do not believe that it is.

Under the circumstances of this case the shareholders should all be held individually liable to this plaintiff for the injuries he suffered. (See Mull v. Colt Co., D.C., 31 F.R.D. 154, 156; Teller v. Clear Serv. Co., 9 Misc.2d 495, 173 N.Y.S.2d 183.) At least the matter should not be disposed of on the pleadings by a dismissal of the complaint. "If a corporation is organized and carries on business without substantial capital in such a way that the corporation is likely to have no sufficient assets available to meet its debts, it is inequitable that shareholders should set up such a flimsy organization to escape personal liability. The attempt to do corporate business without providing any sufficient basis of financial responsibility to creditors is an abuse of the separate entity and will be ineffectual to exempt the shareholders from corporate debts. It is coming to be recognized as the policy of law that shareholders should in good faith put at the risk of the business unincumbered capital reasonably adequate for its prospective liabilities. If capital is illusory or trifling compared with the business to be done and the risks of loss, this is a ground for denying the separate entity privilege." (Ballantine, Corporations [rev. ed., 1946], § 129, pp. 302–303.)

In Minton v. Cavaney, 56 Cal.2d 576, 15 Cal.Rptr. 641, 364 P.2d 473, the Supreme Court of California had occasion to discuss this problem in a negligence case. The corporation of which the defendant was an organizer, director and officer operated a public swimming pool. One afternoon the plaintiffs' daughter drowned in the pool as a result of the alleged negligence of the corporation.

JUSTICE ROGER TRAYNOR, speaking for the court, outlined the applicable law in this area. "The figurative terminology 'alter ego' and 'disregard of the corporate entity'", he wrote, "is generally used to refer to the various situations that are an abuse of the corporate privilege. . . . The equitable owners of a corporation, for example, are personally liable when they treat the assets of the corporation as their own and add or withdraw capital from the corporation at will . . .; when they hold themselves out as being personally liable for the debts of the corporation . . .; *or when they provide inadequate capitalization and actively participate in the conduct of corporate affairs*". (56 Cal.2d, p. 579, 15 Cal.Rptr., p. 643, 364 P.2d, p. 475; italics supplied.)

Examining the facts of the case in light of the legal principles just enumerated, he found that "[it was] undisputed that there was no attempt to provide adequate capitalization. [The corporation] never had any substantial assets. It leased the pool that it operated, and the lease was forfeited for failure to pay the rent. Its capital was 'trifling compared with the business to be done and the risks of loss' ". (56 Cal. 2d, p. 580, 15 Cal.Rptr., p. 643, 364 P.2d, p. 475.)

It seems obvious that one of "the risks of loss" referred to was the possibility of drownings due to the negligence of the corporation. And the defendant's failure to provide such assets or any fund for recovery resulted in his being held personally liable. . . .

The policy of this State has always been to provide and facilitate recovery for those injured through the negligence of others. The automobile, by its very nature, is capable of causing severe and costly injuries when not operated in a proper manner. The great increase in the number of automobile accidents combined with the frequent financial irresponsibility of the individual driving the car led to the adoption of section 388 of the Vehicle and Traffic Law which had the effect of imposing upon the owner of the vehicle the responsibility for its negligent operation. It is upon this very statute that the cause of action against both the corporation and the individual defendant is predicated.

In addition the Legislature, still concerned with the financial irresponsibility of those who owned and operated motor vehicles, enacted a statute requiring minimum liability coverage for all owners of automobiles. The important public policy represented by both these statutes is outlined in section 310 of the Vehicle and Traffic Law. That section provides that: "The legislature is concerned over the rising toll of motor vehicle accidents and the suffering and loss thereby inflicted. The legislature determines that it is a matter of grave concern that motorists shall be financially able to respond in damages for their negligent acts, so that innocent victims of motor vehicle accidents may be recompensed for the injury and financial loss inflicted upon them."

The defendant Carlton claims that, because the minimum amount of insurance required by the statute was obtained, the corporate veil cannot and should not be pierced despite the fact that the assets of the corporation which owned the cab were "trifling compared with the business to be done and the risks of loss" which were certain to be encountered. I do not agree.

The Legislature in requiring minimum liability insurance of $10,000, no doubt, intended to provide at least some small fund for recovery against those individuals and corporations who just did not have and were not able to raise or accumulate assets sufficient to satisfy the claims of those who were injured as a result of their negligence. It certainly could not have intended to shield those individuals who organized corporations, with the specific intent of avoiding responsibility to the public, where the operation of the corporate enterprise yielded profits sufficient to purchase additional insurance. Moreover, it is reasonable to assume that the Legislature believed that those individuals and corporations having substantial assets would take out insurance far in excess of the minimum in order to protect those assets from depletion. Given the costs of hospital care and treatment and the nature of injuries sustained in auto collisions, it would be unreasonable to assume that the Legislature believed that the minimum provided in the statute would in and of itself be sufficient to recompense "innocent victims of motor vehicle accidents . . . for the injury and financial loss inflicted upon them".

The defendant, however, argues that the failure of the Legislature to increase the minimum insurance requirements indicates legislative acquiescence in this scheme to avoid liability and responsibility to the public. In the absence of a clear legislative statement, approval of a scheme having such serious consequences is not to be so lightly inferred.

The defendant contends that the court will be encroaching upon the legislative domain by ignoring the corporate veil and holding the individual shareholder. This argument was answered by MR. JUSTICE DOUGLAS in Anderson v. Abbott, supra, pp. 366–367, 64 S.Ct. p. 540, where he wrote that: "In the field in which we are presently concerned, judicial power hardly oversteps the bounds when it refuses to lend its aid to a promotional project which would circumvent or undermine a legislative policy. To deny it that function would be to make it impotent in situations where historically it has made some of its most notable contributions. If the judicial power is helpless to protect a legislative program from schemes for easy avoidance, then indeed it has become a handy implement of high finance. *Judicial interference to cripple or defeat a legislative policy is one thing; judicial interference with the plans of those whose corporate or other devices would circumvent that policy is quite another.* Once the purpose or effect of the scheme is clear, once the legislative policy is plain, we would indeed forsake a great tradition to say we were helpless to fashion the instruments for appropriate relief." (Emphasis added.)

The defendant contends that a decision holding him personally liable would discourage people from engaging in corporate enterprise.

What I would merely hold is that a participating shareholder of a corporation vested with a public interest, organized with capital insufficient to meet liabilities which are certain to arise in the ordinary course of the corporation's business, may be held personally responsible for such liabilities. Where corporate income is not sufficient to cover the cost of insurance premiums above the statutory minimum or where initially adequate finances dwindle under the pressure of competition, bad times or extraordinary and unexpected liability, obviously the shareholder will not be held liable (Henn, Corporations, p. 208, n. 7).

The only types of corporate enterprises that will be discouraged as a result of a decision allowing the individual shareholder to be sued will be those such as the one in question, designed solely to abuse the corporate privilege at the expense of the public interest.

For these reasons I would vote to affirm the order of the Appellate Division.

DESMOND, C.J., and VAN VOORHIS, BURKE and SCILEPPI, JJ., concur with FULD, J.

KEATING, J., dissents and votes to affirm in an opinion in which BERGAN, J., concurs.

Order reversed, etc.

COMMENT

(1) Apparently this was a pyrrhic victory, for plaintiff was able to file an amended complaint that satisfied the Court of Appeals by including an allegation that defendant conducted business in his individual capacity. 23 N.Y.2d 714, 296 N.Y.S.2d 363, 244 N.E.2d 55 (1968).

(2) Consider the following additional facts about the New York taxi situation set forth in Teller v. Clear Service Co., 9 Misc.2d 495, 173 N.Y.S.2d 183 (1958):

> [T]he principal stockholders of the defendant corporation are a man named Ackerman and some members of his family; that the Ackermans actually have 300 taxicabs, which have been licensed by the City of New York to operate on the city streets; that they have formed 150 corporations, each of which has record title to two taxicabs; that these 300 taxicabs are housed, maintained, and serviced in garages owned by the Ackermans; that the Ackermans and a man named Rosenblatt (who has 200 cabs registered in the name of 100 corporations) own the Mutual Adjustment Company, a licensed private detective agency. This company employs six men and three girls who devote themselves exclusively to the adjustment of claims against the Ackerman and Rosenblatt cabs. The inference is clear that the same employees are used to adjust claims against all 300 Ackerman cabs and that the same mechanics, maintenance men, dispatchers, gas fillers, and bookkeepers are used for all of the cabs. The officers of the 150 corporations are identical. A Mr. Treves and a Mr. Feder, employed by the Mutual Adjustment Company, explained to me that they could not offer more than $3,500 in this case because the statutory bond filed by defendant corporation is limited to $5,000 for injury to one person and the only assets of the corporation are two taxicabs worth $2,300 each. The Ackermans do not carry any insurance for any of their taxicabs, but in pursuance of a provision of the Vehicle and Traffic Law, they do file a bond for each cab guaranteeing payment of any judgment up to $5,000 for injury to one person and $10,000 for injuries to more than one person. By filing a bond, the Ackermans avoid paying the premium for insurance in the amount which would otherwise be required. Where a bond is filed, the Ackermans must pay for the personal injuries themselves up to the limits of the bond. . . .

The situation presented in the present action is not an isolated one. On the contrary, it is a common one—in fact, the common one. A survey discloses that 11.3% of all the personal injury actions brought in the New York County Supreme Court are against taxicab owners for the negligence of their chauffeurs. The Police Department reports indicate that in 1955 taxicabs were involved in 3,685 accidents concerning personal injuries and 2,821 accidents concerning property damage. In 1956 the figures were 3,235 and 2,441, respectively; in 1957, 3,489 and 2,771. In 1937, 8,424 taxicabs were owned by 380 corporate fleet owners. Today, although the number of fleet-owned taxicabs has been reduced to 6,816, the number of corporations owning this smaller number of taxicabs has been increased from 380 to 2,120. Of these 2,120 corporations, only 332 own three or more taxicabs. Although the increase in the number of corporations and the reduction of the number of taxicabs registered in the name of each may, in some instances, have been partially motivated by the legitimate desire to reduce federal income taxes (the corporate federal income tax provides for a tax of 30% on income up to $25,000 per year, whereas the tax is 52% on income over that amount), it is clear that the predominant motive, generally, has been the desire to avoid recovery of more than nominal or negligible amounts on judgments obtained for negligent operation of the taxicabs.

On March 9, 1937, the legislative body of the City of New York enacted chapter 27–a of the Code of Ordinances of the City of New York, which is now section 436–2.0 of the Administrative Code of the City of New York. In this enactment it was declared and found that the taxicab industry in the City of New York is "vested with a public interest", and "financial irresponsible operation whereby the ownership of taxicabs has been transferred in order to avoid tort obligations" was condemned. The number of licensed taxicabs was frozen to the number then existing, viz.: 13,566, consisting of 5,142 individually owned taxicabs and 8,424 fleet-owned (i.e., owned by the same person or corporation). It was also provided that the ratio of individually owned cabs to fleet-owned cabs was to be maintained. In the event that additional licenses are issued, those available for owners of more than one taxicab are to be allocated (Administrative Code, § 436–2.0, subd. 11(a) to the then existing fleet licensees "in the ratio of the number of licenses held by the licensee, to the total number of licenses which is held by owners of more than one taxicab".

One result of this legislation was to confer a monopoly as to taxicab operation upon the then owners of taxicabs and those who acquire their licenses. In 1952 the city permitted a 25% increase in taxi fares. By freezing the number of taxicab licenses permitted to be issued, and increasing the fares the value of *each* taxicab license (popularly referred to as the "medallion") has today reached the market value of approximately $17,000. Ironically enough, the practice of splitting up the registered ownership of fleet-owned taxicabs into many splinter corporations began, as the court is informed by the Police Department, just about the time that the fares were increased. Some idea of the value of this monopoly and of the extent of the public interest involved may be gained from information revealed by a cursory examination of the records of a reputable owner of a large fleet. Each of its cabs is on the city streets approximately 20 hours per day, seven days per week; it travels approximately 60,000 miles per year and brings in an average of $45 per day, carrying 100 passengers per day. It receives, on the average, one claim per cab per year for personal injuries. When we consider that there are almost 12,000 taxicabs roaming the streets of the city today, simple mathematics will disclose that we are dealing with a major industry and public utility. The gross income from this taxi business is approximately $150,000,000 per year. The number of passengers carried annually is well over 300,000,000. The figure is fairly comparable to the number of passengers carried by the surface transportation furnished by the City of New York (buses) to wit, a little over 400,000,000 per year. Here the City has invested untold millions and assumes complete responsibility for the negligence of its drivers. It is also apparent from these figures that about 12,000 persons in New York City file claims for personal injuries each year. This is over 30 personal injury claims per day.

Notwithstanding the valuable monopoly enjoyed by the taxicab owners, they are required to provide protection for injuries to the public (by bond or insurance) only in the amount of $5,000 for injuries to one person and $10,000 for injuries to two or more persons (Vehicle and Traffic Law, § 17). Although the state legislature, in 1952, increased the amounts required to be carried as to vehicles having a seating capacity of eight or more passengers above the amounts theretofore required, the limits for vehicles seating up to seven passengers (primarily taxicabs) were left at $5,000 and $10,000. This despite the increased cost of living since these limits were fixed in 1932 and the increase in the average verdicts throughout the state. We thus have the anomalous situation where there is no limit to the liability of the city for accidents caused by the negligence of its transportation employees and where the owners of private cars must carry insurance of $10,000 for injury to one person and $20,000 for injuries to two or more persons, while the owners of taxicabs, who are the beneficiaries of the valuable monopoly conferred upon them by the 1937 local statute, and whose taxicabs are responsible for a very large number of injuries to the public, are required to protect the public only to the extent of $5,000 for injury to one person and $10,000 for injuries to two or more persons.

To make matters worse, although taxicab licenses may be transferred by *voluntary* sale or transfer, with the approval of the hack bureau, provided that "the applicant assumes, agrees to pay, and satisfies the commissioner of his ability to discharge, all the outstanding tort liabilities of the vendor, or transferor . . . which is in excess of the amount which is covered by any bond or policy of insurance as required by the vehicle and traffic law of the state of New York" (§ 436–2.0, subd. 7, Administrative Code), there is no provision permitting a person holding a judgment, based on the negligence of a taxicab driver, to reach the valuable license (worth about $17,000) issued for the taxicab involved in the accident. In the case of an *involuntary* transfer of a license, a "temporary, non-transferable license" may be issued "for a period not exceeding one year" and not renewable (Administrative Code, § 436–2.0, supra, subd. 9). Why a person injured by the negligence of a taxicab driver, whose claim has been reduced to judgment, may not have the valuable license sold to a purchaser approved by the authorities under the same conditions as apply when a licensee voluntarily transfers his license is a question difficult to answer.

In the court's opinion, the situation here disclosed imperatively demands the enactment of legislation to remedy it. The local legislature should enact legislation eliminating the existing distinction between voluntary and involuntary transfers of licenses, so that the valuable license may be reached by persons injured through the negligence of the taxicab driver. The amounts of the bond or insurance required by the state legislature should be substantially increased. The Superintendent of Insurance informs me that the premium for taxicab insurance (of $5,000 and $10,000) in the City of New York (except the Borough of Richmond) is $34 per month for an individual owner, $80 per month for an individual owner and another driver, and $110 per month for each fleet-owned taxicab; and that the increased cost of a policy with $10,000 and $20,000 limits would be only 30%, and for a policy with limits of $20,000 and $40,000 only 50% . These are small amounts, indeed, in the light of the valuable monopoly enjoyed and the large revenues obtained. It is interesting to note that the taxi industry carried more passengers in 1956 and 1957 than did the Fifth Avenue Coach Company, yet the Fifth Avenue Coach Company in 1956 paid a franchise tax to the City of $909,499, a State franchise tax of $27,324, a gross earnings tax of $165,729, and a public utilities tax of $303,980. The only fee required for the monopoly of which the taxi owners are the beneficiaries is an annual fee of $60 per year.

Medallions, Taxi Licenses are not reachable by creditors

(3) § 370 of the Vehicle and Traffic Law (§ 17 at the time of the Teller case) was amended as of 1959 to increase the amount of coverage per accident from $10,000 to $20,000 and per victim from $5000 to $10,000; in 1979 the limits were again raised to $100,000 per accident and $50,000 per victim. Note that Teller suggests that the taxi medallions, the value of which in 1988 had risen to something like $100,000, are not reachable by creditors. It is not clear to the editor why the provision of $541 of the federal Bankruptcy Code vesting in the trustee all property which the bankrupt might by any means have conveyed would not apply so as to enable a trustee to take possession of them for the benefit of creditors.

(4) "Piercing the veil" cases also arise in the context of attempts to avoid or evade statutes and in contractual cases. For example, in Berger v. Columbia Broadcasting System, Inc., 453 F.2d 991 (5th Cir.1972), a court found parent CBS, Inc. not liable for its subsidiary's actions. It was charged that after CBS Films, Inc. had contracted with plaintiff for a show called International Fashion Festival, CBS, Inc. had proceeded to make a similar show with somebody else. The District Court awarded $200,000 damages, but the judgment was reversed. The Court of Appeals was not impressed by findings that the directors of Films were all employees of CBS, Inc., that the CBS organization chart included Films, or that Films was referred to as a CBS "division." The Court stated that "Just as siamesing is a biological fact, so must corporate umbilication be anatomically demonstrated under New York law." In the absence of evidence that Films had been dominated as to these particular actions by CBS, Inc., the Court found Films was not an alter ego of CBS.

(5) A dramatic episode raising questions of veil-piercing in a modern, multinational context was the catastrophe at Bhopal.[9] Thousands of inhabitants of the Indian city of Bhopal were killed and many more suffered lasting injuries when a poisonous chemical used in the production of a pesticide escaped from a plant owned by Union Carbide of India, a corporation owned 51% by a major American-based corporation, Union Carbide. The rest of UCI's stock was owned by the Indian government and by a substantial number of individual Indian shareholders. The chemical plant involved had been designed after Union Carbide's home plant in West Virginia but a number of engineering changes had been introduced into the blueprints by an outside engineering firm based in India, some at the insistence of the Indian govern-

---

9. See In re Union Carbide Corp. Gas Plant Disaster at Bhopal, India in Dec. 1984, 809 F.2d 195 (2d Cir.1987) (remanding litigation to Indian courts on forum non conveniens grounds). For background see Symposium, 20 Texas Int' L.J. 267 (1985).

ment that maximum possible use be made of local components to save foreign exchange. An inspection team from the United States had identified shortcomings in the safety procedures and equipment in place at Bhopal. Its report was filed by the Indian firm's management without its having produced significant changes in those matters. Intense legal maneuvering in the United States and in India followed the disaster without a definitive ruling on the question of the parent's liability having emerged.

(6) In considering the liability of corporations for the obligations of other members of the corporate "family," one should be aware that it is customary, often obligatory, for the parent to report its financial results on a consolidated basis, including those of the subsidiaries it controls.[10] In consolidating the financial data of the legally separate corporations, the accountants eliminate transactions and obligations running between members of the family. They add the assets, the liabilities and the earnings and expenses of the members. Where the needs of the situation require more emphasis on the status of particular members of the family, a special report may be made on a "consolidating" basis in which separate columns show the figures for separate firms as well as the totals. Note that consolidated financial statements (and consolidated tax returns) tend to reinforce the tendencies of the investing and business communities to see the corporate family as one—tendencies that may influence the results of cases on liability.

QUESTIONS

(1) Note the reference to Judge Cardozo's view, as stated in the *Berkey* case cited at p. 88 supra, that the liability of a parent corporation could be settled on principles of agency. Isn't a 100% subsidiary or one-person corporation always an agent within the definition of § 1 of the Restatement of Agency? Is it any more or less an "agent" if the formalities of board action and accounting are or are not observed?

(2) Is the result of this case dictated by proper respect for legislative action? How would you compare this with People v. Ford in terms of judicial-legislative relations? Suppose that the corporation statute had contained a requirement that the minimum capital of a corporation be $1000 (as 8 Del.C. § 102a(4) once did). Would this affect matters?

(3) What assets did each of the taxi companies have? Draw up a list insofar as you can infer these. How might the company have further minimized its exposure to tort claimants? Is undercapitalization the problem here—if each company had put $20,000 more into the business what would it have done with it? Would such a requirement have helped?

(4) Should the case turn out any differently if the company were (a) owned by another corporation or (b) owned by 30 or 40 individual investors?

(5) Is it possible to formulate a rule for determining when corporate separateness is to be disregarded that will give clearer guidance than the case law does?

PROBLEMS

(1) You are counsel to a group of entrepreneurs who are planning to buy and rehabilitate rundown apartment buildings in rundown portions of the city

---

10. For a brief explanation of consolidated accounting, see S. Siegel & D. Siegel, Accounting and Financial Disclosure 164–66 (1983).

of Megalopolis. Each will cost $100,000 or $200,000 to buy and a similar sum to rehabilitate. They believe that, with assistance from the state and city and some federal funds, they can make a modest profit while still providing decent housing at rents within reason. However, they recognize that their calculations could be thrown off by bad fortune in a number of respects. Adverse possibilities include an unusually high rate of delinquency in the payment of rents as well as the risk that concealed defects in the structures may either necessitate unexpected repair expenses or result in accident claims which cannot be entirely covered by insurance. The entrepreneurs would like to incorporate each building separately so as to prevent losses from dragging down their entire enterprise. They inquire of you whether they may legally do so and if so on what terms. What capitalization would seem appropriate? What reactions should they expect from the banks which will have to provide much of the funds?

(2) Now place yourself in the position of a bank officer contemplating a loan to a corporation set up by these entrepreneurs to own an apartment building called Eveningside Heights Tower, Inc. First, suppose that the projected purchase price, development costs and rental income vs. operating expenditures just meet the bank's criteria. What safeguards will you ask the bank's lawyers to insert in the loan agreement to protect it against manipulation of Eveningside Heights Tower, Inc.? Second, suppose that the financial situation of Eveningside taken by itself falls just a bit below the criteria set by the bank. However, you discern within the total situation including the entrepreneurs personally and the affiliated corporations (parent, "cousins" and a subsidiary) enough value to support the loan. What contract clauses do you need to make sure that that value will be available?

---

3. Liability for Pre–Incorporation Transactions

It is common for at least some transactions looking towards the creation of an enterprise to be concluded before the creation of the corporation which is to serve as the vehicle for the enterprise. This is less common than it was in those days when obtaining a charter was in itself a cumbersome, time consuming and expensive process. Under those circumstances it made sense to nail down certain vital commitments before one went to the trouble of creating a corporation that might prove useless if the venture failed to materialize. There are fewer of these cases nowadays when serious promoters will organize their corporation early in the day and have contracts made in its name. Still, cases do turn up in the advance sheets, enough so as to warrant this brief brush over the topic, a mere shadow of the elaborate treatment once given it.

The essential conceptual conundrum is that the contract is, in a sense, with a non-existent contractor. This has fascinated some judges who went so far as to analogize it with a man who made a contract for "Dobbin, a horse." Suppose, first, that it is clear that the contract was intended to be that of the corporation. It is, for example, signed in orthodox agency manner:

> "Futurcorp
> By <u>P.R. Moter</u>
> Agent"

At this point, no contract exists because the corporate party does not exist. The other party may have a cause of action against the individual signing for the supposed corporation asserting a breach of an implied warranty on the part of the agency (See Restatement of Agency § 329). If the other party is aware of the non-existence of the corporation, that avenue is out; all that remains is the hope that a court might be persuaded that the real intention was to have the promoter bound until the corporation came into existence—this despite the language of the agreement. If the language is ambiguous—e.g., "D. J. Geary for a bridge company to be organized and incorporated" [11]—there is great likelihood that the promoter will be held liable.

If the corporation is organized as intended the situation changes. The corporation may by express action of its directors adopt the contract. If directors or officers or agents of the corporation become aware of the contracts and accept its benefits, the corporation may be held to have adopted it by implication. Note that the courts use the term "adoption" rather than "ratification" on the ground that ratification would date back to the time of original contracting when no corporation existed; adoption takes effect, at the time of adoption.

Does the corporation action affect the liability of the promoter? This is a question of a novation, to be judged according to standard contract analysis. The existence of the necessary consent of the outside party can be drawn from the original contract or from his subsequent conduct, as in dealing with the corporation and accepting payments from it.

None of these legal complications as to who is legally liable to whom is at all important in comparison with the questions of what substantive responsibility the outsider can look to. There may be several obligations to be tied together. Take Mr. Geary's bridge company, for example. The contractor needs to be assured of payment for his work. The bank that will provide most of the money will need to be assured that the project is feasible and will be accomplished for a specified price and that there is a fair amount of shareholders' money invested as a "cushion" for its risk. There may be government permits that will only be granted if the project seems a reasonable risk. Even investigating feasibility, conducting tentative engineering surveys, etc. may cost thousands. Thus somebody's money must be at risk. The promoters may have to invest a convincing amount in the stock of their

---

11. O'Rorke v. Geary, 207 Pa. 240, 56 A. 541 (1903).

corporation or they may have to guarantee some of the obligations of the corporation even after it starts to exist.

Bibliography: For the mechanics of incorporating you can consult G. Seward, Basic Corporate Practice (2d ed. 1977) or The Lawyer's Basic Corporate Practice Manual (3d ed., R. Deer, 1984) published by the joint Committee on Continuing Professional Education of the A.B.A. and the A.L.I. Practical manuals are available in many states. You can also consult corporation service companies.

As to defective incorporation and its consequences see Frey, Legal Analysis and the "De Facto" Doctrine, 100 U.Pa.L.Rev. 1153 (1952).

For stimulating efforts to rationalize the piercing-the-corporate-veil problem see Douglas & Shanks, Insulation from Liability through Subsidiary Corporations, 39 Yale L.J. 193 (1929); Berle, The Theory of Enterprise Entity, 47 Colum.L.Rev. 343 (1947); Easterbrook & Fischel, Limited Liability and the Corporation, 52 U.Chi.L.Rev. 89 (1985). A multi-volume series on corporate systems is appearing in installments by Prof. Philip Blumberg.

As to pre-incorporation transactions Ehrich & Bunsel, Promoters' Contracts, 38 Yale L.J. 1011 (1929); Kessler, Promoters' Contracts: A Statutory Solution, 15 Rutgers L.Rev. 566 (1961).

Chapter V

FORMING THE CORPORATION: PURPOSES AND POWERS

At the time of founding a corporation some consideration has presumably been given to the purpose of that creation. Both business theory and legal doctrine agree that a corporation must have some purpose or goal. As we shall see, this proposition is apt to be blurred from a legal point of view because the draftsman will prefer to make use of the very wide discretion permitted by modern corporation laws in drafting provisions about purposes and powers. From a business point of view we often find some indefiniteness as to what the founders have in mind. However, business schools insist upon the importance of a *strategy* as an element of a successful business operation.

We will let an important business school text speak for itself about the term:

Learned et al., Business Policy.[1]

Our use of the term corporate strategy comprises more than the usual military connotations of this term. For the military, strategy is most simply the positioning of armed forces on the battlefield to accomplish the defeat of the enemy. Less simply, it is the deployment of resources against an enemy in pursuit of goals prescribed by the leaders of the state. When we pass, as we must, from the military to the political sphere, strategy becomes the application of national resources to the accomplishment of national goals.

Our use of the term strategy extends its meaning still further to encompass the choice of goals, as well as the plans for attaining goals. The economist speaks often of strategy as the allocation of scarce resources; we intend more than the closely related selection of product-market relationships. For us strategy is the pattern of objectives, purposes, or goals and major policies and plans for achieving these goals, stated in such a way as to define what business the company is in or is to be in and the kind of company it is or is to be.

Because we are less concerned with exactness of language than we might be if development of theory were our first objective, we do not argue the question whether the term strategy should include the selection of goals or denote only the development of resources marshaled in pursuit of these goals. It is to us a matter of indifference.

1. E. Learned, C. R. Christensen, K. Andrews & W. Guth, Business Policy 15–18 (rev. ed. 1969). Reprinted by permission of the publisher Richard D. Irwin, Inc. Although there is a newer version of this book, C. Christensen, N. Berg, M. Salter & H. Stevenson, Policy Formulation and Administration (9th ed. 1985), I do not find in it as striking a formulation or one as useful for these purposes as this older one.

Little confusion results so long as we make clear what we are doing. In our experience, simplicity and convenience are served by combining the choice of goals and the formulation of major policy into one activity. The choice of goals and the formulation policy cannot in any case be separate decisions. The Stanford Research Institute takes a different path when it equates strategy with the ways in which the firm, reacting to its environment, deploys its principal resources and marshals its main efforts in pursuit of its purpose. Alfred Chandler, in *Strategy and Structure,* takes the direction we favor when he called strategy, ". . . the determination of the basic long-term goals and objectives of an enterprise, and the adoption of courses of action and the allocation of resources necessary for carrying out these goals." [2]

A more important effort to subdivide the idea of strategy seeks to segregate those aspects that are enduring and unchanging over relatively long periods of time from those that are necessarily more responsive to changes in the marketplace and the pressures of other environmental forces. The strategic decision is concerned with the long-term development of the enterprise. The central character of a business organization and the individuality it has for its members and its various publics may, in the instance of mature and highly developed corporations, be determined with some clarity.

Thus the "personality" of firms like Polaroid, Xerox, Control Data, IBM, and General Motors clearly reflects aspects of company intent that are manifested only partially in such activities as research expenditures, choice of product line, and the recruitment and development of organization members. It would be likely to persist through substantial changes in the allocation of resources and in product policy, in part because the basic determinants of organization character would tend to prevent sharp discontinuity. . . . In this view, the basic character of an enterprise and the core of its special competence would be considered separately from the manifestation of these long-range characteristics in changing product lines, markets, and policies designed to make activities profitable from year to year.

A complete summary statement of strategy will in fact say less about what the word means than it does about the company involved. First, it will define products in terms more functional than literal, saying what they do rather than what they are made of. At the same time, it will designate clearly the markets and market segments for which products are now or will be designed, and the channels through which these markets will be reached. The means by which the operation is to be financed will be specified, as will the emphasis to be placed on safety of capital versus income return. Finally, the size and kind of organization which is to be the medium of achievement will be described. It is, of course, more important that the identification of

2. Alfred D. Chandler, Jr., Strategy and Structure: Chapters in the History of the   Industrial Enterprise (Cambridge, Mass.: The M.I.T. Press 1962), p. 13.

strategy capture the present and projected character of the organization than that it elaborate the categories of purpose just cited.

Thus of Continental Watchmakers Company, a Swiss firm, we could say:

> It is Mr. Keller's present plan to produce watches of the highest quality—in a price range between the hand-made ultra-exclusive level and Omega and Rolex. He aims to distribute his watches to all markets of the free world via exclusive wholesale agents and carefully chosen retailers, who are expected to convince customers of the particular value of the product. His growth of about 10% per year is not geared to demand but is deliberately restricted to the productivity of available skilled labor, and to his recognition of cyclical fluctuations in the industry. He aims to maintain within the rules of the industry a stable organization of highly skilled, fully trained workers and a management organization of some breadth, but he apparently wishes to retain personal direction over marketing and a close familiarity with the whole organization.

Companies seldom formulate and publish as complete a statement as we have just illustrated, usually because conscious planning is not carried far enough to achieve the agreement or clarification which publication presumes. These cases enable the student of Policy to do what the managements of the companies usually have not done. In the absence of explicit statements, the student may deduce from operations what the goals and policies are, on the assumption that all normal human behavior is purposeful. Careful examination of the behavior described in the cases will reveal what the strategy must be. At the same time, it is desirable not to infer a degree of conscious planning which does not in fact exist. The current strategy of a company may almost always be deduced from its behavior, but a strategy for a future of changed circumstance may not always be distinguishable from performance in the present.

Corporate strategy has two equally important aspects, interrelated in life but separated to the extent practicable in our study of the concept. The first of these is formulation; the second is implementation. Deciding what strategy should be is, at least ideally, a rational undertaking. Its principal subactivities include identifying opportunities and threats in the company's environment and attaching some estimate of risk to the discernible alternatives. Before a choice can be made, the company's strengths and weaknesses must be appraised. Its actual or potential capacity to take advantage of perceived market needs or to cope with attendant risks must be estimated as objectively as possible. The strategic alternative which results from a matching of opportunity and corporate capability at an acceptable level of risk is what we may call an *economic strategy*.

The process described thus far assumes that the strategist is analytically objective in estimating the relative capacity of his company and the opportunity he sees or anticipates in developing markets. The extent to which he wishes to undertake low or high risk presumably depends on his profit objective. The higher he sets the latter, the more willing he must be to assume a correspondingly high risk that the market opportunity he sees will not develop or that the corporate competence required to excel competition will not be forthcoming.

So far we have described the intellectual processes of ascertaining what a company *might do* in terms of environmental opportunity, of deciding what it *can do* in terms of ability and power, and of bringing these two considerations together in optimal equilibrium. The determination of strategy also requires consideration of what alternative is preferred by the chief executive and perhaps by his immediate associates as well, quite apart from economic considerations. Personal values, aspirations, and ideals do, and in our judgment quite properly should, influence the final choice of purposes. Thus what the executives of a company *want to do* must be brought into the strategic decision.

Finally, strategic choice has an ethical aspect—a fact much more dramatically illustrated in some industries than in others. Just as alternatives may be ordered in terms of the degree of risk that they entail, so may they be examined against the standards of responsibility that the strategist elects. Some alternatives may seem to the executive considering them more attractive than others when the public good or service to society is considered. What a company *should do* thus appears as a fourth element of the fateful decision we have called strategic.

The ability to identify the four components of strategy—(1) market opportunity, (2) corporate competence and resources, (3) personal values and aspirations, and (4) acknowledged obligations to segments of society other than the stockholders—is nothing compared to the art of reconciling their implications in a final choice of purpose. Taken by itself, each consideration might lead in a different direction.

NOTE ON ULTRA VIRES

Corporation law tries to separate out goals and purposes more clearly from the implementation process. The function of such analysis is to distinguish between those goals or purposes that are within and those that are without the bounds set by the certificate of incorporation. The certificate of incorporation is, in legal analysis, a contract between the state and the incorporator(s). Originally, the determining factor as to what purposes were legitimate was the intention of the state for the state had a more or less deliberate purpose in mind when it chartered a corporation. Thus the English crown willed in 1670 that northern Canada be explored and consequently that was the purpose of the Governor & Co. of Adventurers of England Trading into Hudson's Bay. As the role of the state diminishes, the emphasis comes to be on the purpose of the founders and promoters which may receive state approval but does not represent an actively sought governmental objective. Thus the need for a more or less definite purpose originally came from the government's desire to see that an enterprise it had chartered did not become perverted to other ends, particularly if in addition to the grant of a charter and the accompanying privilege of corporateness—themselves valuable assets—the state had conferred some monopoly or other benefit on the organization. If persons proposing to engage in the banking business bought a charter of the Swordmakers Guild the Crown had some reason to feel it had been cheated and to bring a proceeding to terminate the abuse. When Aaron Burr slid into the powers clauses of the Manhattan Company the right to use in the banking business any "surplus capital" left over from supplying water he was getting for his firm a privilege then quite special, so special that the charter was cherished for a century and a half. It was not uncommon for the state to challenge unauthorized steps—by the same action whereby a wrongful assertion of a public power was tested—by a *quo warranto* proceeding.[3]

Increasingly, however, the center of emphasis came to be on keeping the corporation within bounds set by the purposes of the incorporators. From this perspective a violation of a corporate charter is equivalent to one of a partnership agreement—it involves carrying an enterprise into an area where some of the participants never agreed to go.

Considerable skepticism prevails as to whether investors really want such limitations on the activities of management and such skepticism is natural in an age of protean conglomerate enterprises moving into—and out of—a wide variety of businesses. Still, before one invests in a firm one wants to have some concept of what it does or intends to do. The typical prospectus in trying to sell a security describes the issuer's present business and its overall approach in some detail. The Investment Company Act of 1940, which governs mutual funds, requires that such a company advise prospective investors of its policies as to its investments (concentration on industries, the rate of turnover of securities, etc.) and requires that changes in such policy be approved by a shareholder vote.[4]

Closely intertwined with questions of "purpose" are questions of "powers". The law must decide the extent to which a corporation may perform legal acts and create legal relationships. Obviously these acts should be in aid of a corporate purpose. Thus, if a corporation is authorized by its charter to buy land that should be taken in conjunction with its purpose of manufacturing bricks and not taken as a license to engage in real estate speculation. On the other hand a power may

---

3. People v. Ford, p. 79, supra, is an example of quo warranto.

4. Investment Company Act of 1940, §§ 8, 13, 15 U.S.C.A. §§ 80a–8, 80a–13.

have been withheld entirely so that a guarantee may be invalid even if it is intended to further a corporate purpose. Either of these actions might be held to be beyond the corporation's powers or *ultra vires*.

As incorporation laws became looser and more flexible the significance of *ultra vires* receded. The courts contributed to this by becoming more liberal in implying powers not expressed. The legislatures helped by enacting broader and broader statutory grants (see 8 Del.C. §§ 121–126). Most importantly, corporate counsel labored over the powers clauses in charters, making sure that every possible grant to the corporation had been included. Thus, ultra vires problems have tended to appear in recent years only in a few areas. One of these is the legitimacy of corporations entering into partnerships. Such a relationship was long thought to be incompatible with the statutory command [5] that a corporation's business be managed by the board of directors and, more broadly, to put the corporation's assets at risk beyond the scope of the venture originally contemplated. Judicial decisions have, however, softened the impact of the rule by approving corporate entry into relations designated as "joint ventures" (for a reference to the meaningfulness of this distinction see p. 32 supra). A second area is the corporate guarantee.[6] You will recall that partners are not generally given this power and that the Statute of Frauds surrounds the guarantee with special safeguards. The dangers of improvidently committing a corporation to an open-ended risk of loss are fairly evident. Problems also arise in the case of transactions that are not formally guarantees but achieve similar ends. Consider for example the case where corporation X borrows money from a bank and relends it directly to corporation Y which has a weak credit rating. Or suppose that a bank will not lend money to a company that is starting a plant unless a reliable corporation agrees to purchase its output for five years and indeed agrees to make payments to the manufacturer even if it is not producing the product. Is such a "take or pay" contract a guarantee?

Finally, we have the question of corporate contributions to charity or other actions which are aimed at a public welfare purpose other than producing profits for the shareholders. The issues posed by such actions are discussed in the following cases and the excerpt by Dean Rostow.

It is important to recall that *ultra vires* is different from illegality and that the consequences of violation of positive law, such as political contributions by a corporation in violation of the Federal Election Campaign Act of 1971 or [7] the performance by a bank of brokerage functions in violation of the Federal Reserve Act,[8] are quite different

5. See 8 Del.C. § 141(a) and pp. 198, 287 infra.

6. Ragusin, Brother–Sister Corporate Guaranties: Increased Legal Acknowledgment of Business World Realities, 11 J.Corp.L. 391 (1986). For an illustrative case see New England Merchants Nat.

Bank v. Lost Valley Corp., 119 N.H. 254, 400 A.2d 1178 (1979).

7. See First Nat. Bank v. Bellotti, p. 62 supra.

8. 12 U.S.C.A. §§ 377–378.

from acts beyond the scope of the articles of incorporation. As a rule, if the transaction could not have been cured by an appropriate charter amendment, you will find that the question is not really one of ultra vires.

Finally, questions arise about the consequences of an act determined to be *ultra vires*. Modern statutes such as 8 Del.C. § 124, have tended to cut off the *ultra vires* defense to actions by outsiders, leaving it available only for actions by shareholders and against those responsible for over-extending the corporate power. Where no such statute applies, one must look to common law rules. Two rules have prevailed as to contracts: (1) the "state rule" which was that *ultra vires* could not be pleaded as a defense to an action on a contract fully executed by the other side and (2) the "federal rule" (continued in a few states since Erie) that even in such a case recovery could only be on a quantum meruit basis. There is some confusion in the cases as to whether the corporation must have received a benefit in order to be estopped on the executed contract theory; the distinction is crucial in such cases as corporate guarantees where no specific benefit has flowed to the guaranteeing corporation even though the plaintiff has fully performed by rendering benefits to the third party. Similarly, there is doubt as to the consequences of a contract where there has been a performance of some segment—say 3 months of an 18 month rental—as to the status of the later segments. There are problems, too, about the consequences of *ultra vires* torts (for which the corporation is usually liable) and *ultra vires* transfers of property (which are generally left undisturbed).

It is worth noting, parenthetically, that the above paragraphs are written on the assumption that the corporation in question is organized to make a profit. There are, however, corporations organized for nonprofit purposes, to be distinguished from those that try to make a profit but fail. We refer to these as "non-profit," "charitable" or "membership" corporations. The law as to such organizations has been rather sketchy and incomplete. Provisions as to them are scattered through the Delaware General Corporation Law (e.g., 8 Del.C. §§ 125, 127, 141(j), 215, 242(c)(3), 255, 276). The American Bar Association has sponsored a Model Non-Profit Corporation Act to match its Model Business Corporation Act.

DODGE v. FORD MOTOR CO.

Supreme Court of Michigan, 1919.
204 Mich. 459, 170 N.W. 668.

[This was an action brought by the Dodge brothers as shareholders of Ford Motor Co. to compel the payment of a dividend and other relief. The defendants appealed from a decree for plaintiffs. The Ford Motor Co. was founded in 1903 with a capital stock of $150,000 (1500 shares of $100 par value). Henry Ford took 255 shares, the two plaintiffs and two others 50 shares each and other persons took a few shares. "The business of the company continued to expand" says the court. By 1916 its status was represented by the following balance sheet:

Assets

Working—

Cash on hand and in bank	$ 52,550,771	92
Michigan municipal bonds	1,259,029	01
Accounts receivable...............................	8,292,778	41
Merchandise and supplies..........................	31,895,434	69
Investments—outside..............................	9,200	00
Expense inventories...............................	434,055	19

Plant—

Land...	5,232,156	10
Buildings and fixtures	17,293,293	40
Machinery and power plant.......................	8,896,342	31
Factory equipment...............................	3,868,261	02
Tools..	1,690,688	54
Patterns...	170,619	77
Patents..	64,339	85
Office equipment	431,249	37
Total assets	$132,088,219	58

Liabilities

Working—

Accounts payable	$ 7,680,866	17
Contract deposits	1,519,296	40
Accrued pay rolls................................	847,953	68
Accrued salaries.................................	338,268	86
Accrued expenses................................	1,175,070	72
Contract rebates................................	2,199,988	00
Buyers' P.S. rebate	48,099	00

Reserves—

For fire insurance	57,493	89
For depreciation of plant	4,260,275	33
Total liabilities	$ 18,127,312	05
Surplus	111,960,907	53
Capital stock	2,000,000	00
Total..	$132,088,219	58

Note that the rest of the $2,000,000 capital stock represented contributions by the shareholders in the form of surrendering their claims to dividends. On that capital the company for a while paid a dividend equal to 5% per month. It also paid special dividends amounting to $41,000,000 from 1911 through 1915. The plaintiffs charged that Henry Ford had declared that he would pay no further special dividends. They alleged that he had caused the board to approve a great expansion program (which included buying land for a new plant from Henry Ford at cost plus 6%).

The lower court ordered payment of a $19,000,000 dividend, being 50% of "the accumulated cash surplus" of the Company. It further enjoined the construction of a smelting plant or furnaces at River Rouge and the increase of the "fixed capital assets" of the Company or the holding of liquid assets beyond what would be reasonably required for the business. Defendants appealed.

Certain issues considered in the opinion of Ostrander, J., are omitted. These include a charge that the company violated a Michigan statute limiting corporations to a "capital stock" of $50,000,000. This the court disposed of by pointing out that the legislature did not mean to include undistributed profits as part of capital stock. The court also concluded that expansion into the iron ore smelting business was not *ultra vires.*]

The rule which will govern courts in deciding these questions is not in dispute. It is, of course, differently phrased by judges and by authors, and, as the phrasing in a particular instance may seem to lean for or against the exercise of the right of judicial interference with the actions of corporate directors, the context, or the facts before the court, must be considered. This court, in Hunter v. Roberts, Throp & Co., 83 Mich. 63, 71, 47 N.W. 131, 134, recognized the rule in the following language:

> "It is a well-recognized principle of law that the directors of a corporation, and they alone, have the power to declare a dividend of the earnings of the corporation, and to determine its amount. 5 Amer. & Eng.Enc.Law, 725. Courts of equity will not interfere in the management of the directors unless it is clearly made to appear that they are guilty of fraud or misappropriation of the corporate funds, or refuse to declare a dividend when the corporation has a surplus of net profits which it can, without detriment to its business, divide among its stockholders, and when a refusal to do so would amount to such an abuse of discretion as would constitute a fraud, or breach of that good faith which they are bound to exercise towards the stockholders." . . .

It is not necessary to multiply statements of the rule.

To develop the points now discussed, and to a considerable extent they may be developed together as a single point, it is necessary to refer with some particularity to the facts.

When plaintiffs made their complaint and demand for further dividends, the Ford Motor Company had concluded its most prosperous year of business. The demand for its cars at the price of the preceding year continued. It could make and could market in the year beginning August 1, 1916, more than 500,000 cars. Sales of parts and repairs would necessarily increase. The cost of materials was likely to advance, and perhaps the price of labor; but it reasonably might have expected a profit for the year of upwards of $60,000,000. It had assets of more than $132,000,000, a surplus of almost $112,000,000, and its cash on hand and municipal bonds were nearly $54,000,000. Its total liabilities, including capital stock, was a little over $20,000,000. It had declared no special dividend during the business year except the October, 1915, dividend. It had been the practice, under similar circumstances, to declare larger dividends. Considering only these facts, a refusal to declare and pay further dividends appears to be not an exercise of discretion on the part of the directors, but an arbitrary refusal to do what the circumstances required to be done. These facts and others call upon the directors to justify their action, or failure or refusal to act. In justification, the defendants have offered testimony tending to prove, and which does prove, the following facts: It had been the policy of the corporation for a considerable time to annually reduce the selling price of cars, while keeping up, or improving, their quality.

As early as in June, 1915, a general plan for the expansion of the productive capacity of the concern by a practical duplication of its plant had been talked over by the executive officers and directors and agreed upon; not all of the details having been settled, and no formal action of directors having been taken. The erection of a smelter was considered, and engineering and other data in connection therewith secured. In consequence, it was determined not to reduce the selling price of cars for the year beginning August 1, 1915, but to maintain the price and to accumulate a large surplus to pay for the proposed expansion of plant and equipment, and perhaps to build a plant for smelting ore. It is hoped, by Mr. Ford, that eventually 1,000,000 cars will be annually produced. The contemplated changes will permit the increased output.

The plan, as affecting the profits of the business for the year beginning August 1, 1916, and thereafter, calls for a reduction in the selling price of the cars. It is true that this price might be at any time increased, but the plan called for the reduction in price of $80 a car. The capacity of the plant, without the additions thereto voted to be made (without a part of them at least), would produce more than 600,000 cars annually. This number, and more, could have been sold for $440 instead of $360, a difference in the return for capital, labor, and materials employed of at least $48,000,000. In short, the plan does not call for and is not intended to produce immediately a more profitable business, but a less profitable one; not only less profitable than formerly, but less profitable than it is admitted it might be made. The apparent immediate effect will be to diminish the value of shares and the returns to shareholders.

It is the contention of plaintiffs that the apparent effect of the plan is intended to be the continued and continuing effect of it, and that it is deliberately proposed, not of record and not by official corporate declaration, but nevertheless proposed, to continue the corporation henceforth as a semi-eleemosynary institution and not as a business institution. In support of this contention, they point to the attitude and to the expressions of Mr. Henry Ford.

Mr. Henry Ford is the dominant force in the business of the Ford Motor Company. No plan of operations could be adopted unless he consented, and no board of directors can be elected whom he does not favor. One of the directors of the company has no stock. One share was assigned to him to qualify him for the position, but it is not claimed that he owns it. A business, one of the largest in the world, and one of the most profitable, has been built up. It employs many men, at good pay.

"My ambition," said Mr. Ford, "is to employ still more men, to spread the benefits of this industrial system to the greatest possible number, to help them build up their lives and their homes. To do this we are putting the greatest share of our profits back in the business."

"With regard to dividends, the company paid sixty per cent. on its capitalization of two million dollars, or $1,200,000, leaving $58,000,000 to reinvest for the growth of the company. This is Mr. Ford's policy at present, and it is understood that the other stockholders cheerfully accede to this plan."

He had made up his mind in the summer of 1916 that no dividends other than the regular dividends should be paid, "for the present."

"Q. For how long? Had you fixed in your mind any time in the future, when you were going to pay— A. No.

"Q. That was indefinite in the future? A. That was indefinite; yes sir."

The record, and especially the testimony of Mr. Ford, convinces that he has to some extent the attitude towards shareholders of one who has dispensed and distributed to them large gains and that they should be content to take what he chooses to give. His testimony creates the impression, also, that he thinks the Ford Motor Company has made too much money, has had too large profits, and that, although large profits might be still earned, a sharing of them with the public, by reducing the price of the output of the company, ought to be undertaken. We have no doubt that certain sentiments, philanthropic and altruistic, creditable to Mr. Ford, had large influence in determining the policy to be pursued by the Ford Motor Company—the policy which has been herein referred to.

It is said by his counsel that—

"Although a manufacturing corporation cannot engage in humanitarian works as its principal business, the fact that it is organized for profit does not prevent the existence of implied powers to carry on with humanitarian motives such charitable works as are incidental to the main business of the corporation."

And again:

"As the expenditures complained of are being made in an expansion of the business which the company is organized to carry on, and for purposes within the powers of the corporation as hereinbefore shown, the question is as to whether such expenditures are rendered illegal because influenced to some extent by humanitarian motives and purposes on the part of the members of the board of directors."

In discussing this proposition, counsel have referred to decisions such as Hawes v. Oakland, 104 U.S. 450, 26 L.Ed. 827; Taunton v. Royal Ins. Co., 2 Hem. & Miller, 135; Henderson v. Bank of Australia, L.R. 40 Ch.Div. 170; Steinway v. Steinway & Sons, 17 Misc.Rep. 43, 40 N.Y.Supp. 718; People v. Hotchkiss, 136 App.Div. 150, 120 N.Y.Supp. 649. These cases, after all, like all others in which the subject is treated, turn finally upon the point, the question, whether it appears that the directors were not acting for the best interests of the corporation. We do not draw in question, nor do counsel for the plaintiffs do so, the validity of the general proposition stated by counsel nor the soundness of the opinions delivered in the cases cited. The case presented here is not like any of them. The difference between an incidental humanitarian expenditure of corporate funds for the benefit of the employés, like the building of a hospital for their use and the employment of agencies for the betterment of their condition, and a general purpose and plan to benefit mankind at the expense of others, is obvious. There should be no confusion (of which there is evidence) of the duties which Mr. Ford conceives that he and the stockholders owe to the general public and the duties which in law he and his codirectors owe to protesting, minority stockholders. A business corporation is organized and carried on primarily for the profit of the stockholders. The powers of the directors are to be employed for that end. The discretion of directors is to be exercised in the choice of means to attain that end, and does not extend to a change in the end itself, to the reduction of profits, or to the nondistribution of profits among stockholders in order to devote them to other purposes.

There is committed to the discretion of directors, a discretion to be exercised in good faith, the infinite details of business, including the wages which shall be paid to employés, the number of hours they shall work, the conditions under which labor shall be carried on, and the price for which products shall be offered to the public.

It is said by appellants that the motives of the board members are not material and will not be inquired into by the court so long as their acts are within their lawful powers. As we have pointed out, and the proposition does not require argument to sustain it, it is not within the lawful powers of a board of directors to shape and conduct the affairs of a corporation for the merely incidental benefit of shareholders and for the primary purpose of benefiting others, and no one will contend that, if the avowed purpose of the defendant directors was to sacrifice the interests of shareholders, it would not be the duty of the courts to interfere.

We are not, however, persuaded that we should interfere with the proposed expansion of the business of the Ford Motor Company. In view of the fact that the selling price of products may be increased at any time, the ultimate results of the larger business cannot be certainly estimated. The judges are not business experts. It is recognized that plans must often be made for a long future, for expected competition, for a continuing as well as an immediately profitable venture. The experience of the Ford Motor Company is evidence of capable management of its affairs. It may be noticed, incidentally, that it took from the public the money required for the execution of its plan, and that the very considerable salaries paid to Mr. Ford and to certain executive officers and employés were not diminished. We are not satisfied that the alleged motives of the directors, in so far as they are reflected in the conduct of the business, menace the interests of shareholders. It is enough to say, perhaps, that the court of equity is at all times open to complaining shareholders having a just grievance.

Assuming the general plan and policy of expansion and the details of it to have been sufficiently, formally, approved at the October and November, 1917, meetings of directors, and assuming further that the plan and policy and the details agreed upon were for the best ultimate interest of the company and therefore of its shareholders, what does it amount to in justification of a refusal to declare and pay a special dividend or dividends? The Ford Motor Company was able to estimate with nicety its income and profit. It could sell more cars than it could make. Having ascertained what it would cost to produce a car and to sell it, the profit upon each car depended upon the selling price. That being fixed, the yearly income and profit was determinable, and, within slight variations, was certain.

There was appropriated—voted—for the smelter $11,325,000. As to the remainder voted, there is no available way for determining how much had been paid before the action of directors was taken and how much was paid thereafter; but assuming that the plans required an expenditure sooner or later of $9,895,000 for duplication of the plant, and for land and other expenditures $3,000,000, the total is $24,220,000. The company was continuing business, at a profit—a cash business. If the total cost of proposed expenditures had been immediately with-drawn in cash from the cash surplus (money and bonds) on hand August 1, 1916, there would have remained nearly $30,000,000.

Defendants say, and it is true, that a considerable cash balance must be at all times carried by such a concern. But, as has been stated, there was a large daily, weekly, monthly, receipt of cash. The output was practically continuous and was continuously, and within a few days, turned into cash. Moreover, the contemplated expenditures were not to be immediately made. The large sum appropriated for the smelter plant was payable over a considerable period of time. So that, without going further, it would appear that, accepting and approving the plan of the directors, it was their duty to distribute on or near the 1st of August, 1916, a very large sum of money to stockholders.

In reaching this conclusion, we do not ignore, but recognize, the validity of the proposition that plaintiffs have from the beginning profited by, if they have not lately, officially, participated in, the general policy of expansion pursued by this corporation. We do not lose sight of the fact that it had been, upon an occasion, agreeable to the plaintiffs to increase the capital stock to $100,000,000 by a stock dividend of $98,000,000. These things go only to answer other conten-tions now made by plaintiffs, and do not and cannot operate to estop them to demand proper dividends upon the stock they own. It is obvious that an annual dividend of 60 per cent. upon $2,000,000, or $1,200,000, is the equivalent of a very small dividend upon $100,000,000, or more.

The decree of the court below fixing and determining the specific amount to be distributed to stockholders is affirmed. In other respects, except as to the allowance of costs, the said decree is reversed. Plain-tiffs will recover interest at 5 per cent. per annum upon their propor-tional share of said dividend from the date of the decree of the lower court. Appellants will tax the costs of their appeal, and two-thirds of the amount thereof will be paid by plaintiffs. No other costs are allowed.

STEERE, FELLOWS, STONE, and BROOKE, JJ., concurred with OS-TRANDER, J.

MOORE, J. I agree with what is said by Justice OSTRANDER upon the subject of capitalization. I agree with what he says as to the smelting enterprise on the River Rouge. I do not agree with all that is said by him in his discussion of the question of dividends. I do agree with him in his conclusion that the accumulation of so large a surplus establishes the fact that there has been an arbitrary refusal to distribute funds that ought to have been distributed to the stockholders as dividends. I therefore agree with the conclusion reached by him upon that phase of the case.

BIRD, C.J., and KUHN, J., concurred with MOORE, J.

COMMENT [7]

After this case, Ford acquired the dissenters' stock. The Dodge brothers used these funds in developing the rival firm that bore their name and left substantial sums to their heirs, although the firm later passed under the

7. See the multi-volume biography, Ford, by Allen Nevins (1963) for further detail. A more recent history is R. Lacey, Ford, The Men and the Machine (1986).

control of Walter Chrysler. The Ford Motor Company continued to expand, at River Rouge and elsewhere both within the United States and overseas. It was in fact the largest one-man business organization ever known. However, it began to run into difficulties. The more decentralized, bureaucratized and de-personalized regime at General Motors proved to be more flexible and innova-tive than was Mr. Ford himself in his later years—witness his great reluctance to abandon the "Model T." Ford's relations with his employees moved from the paternal to the bitter. The problem of succession was a difficult one and Edsel Ford never got the position of power to which his merits probably entitled him (to add insult to injury his name is now linked to a disastrous styling experi-ment for which he had no responsibility. Nowadays Ford is for most purposes a public corporation like its two major automotive competitors. Henry Ford II is still on the board of directors but a non-Ford is CEO and seems to have a more stable footing than the McNamaras, Knudsens and Iacoccas who preceded him. There is still, however, a closely held class B stock that gives the inner circle potentially more voting power.

A. P. SMITH MFG. CO. v. BARLOW

Supreme Court of New Jersey, 1953.
13 N.J. 145, 98 A.2d 581, appeal dismissed 346 U.S. 861, 74 S.Ct. 107,
98 L.Ed. 373 (1953).

JACOBS, J. The Chancery Division, in a well-reasoned opinion by Judge Stein, determined that a donation by the plaintiff The A. P. Smith Manufacturing Company to Princeton University was *intra vires*. Because of the public importance of the issues presented, the appeal duly taken to the Appellate Division has been certified directly to this court under Rule 1:5–1(a).

The company was incorporated in 1896 and is engaged in the manufacture and sale of valves, fire hydrants and special equipment, mainly for water and gas industries. Its plant is located in East Orange and Bloomfield and it has approximately 300 employees. Over the years the company has contributed regularly to the local communi-ty chest and on occasions to Upsala College in East Orange and Newark University, now part of Rutgers, the State University. On July 24, 1951 the board of directors adopted a resolution which set forth that it was in the corporation's best interests to join with others in the 1951 Annual Giving to Princeton University, and appropriated the sum of $1,500 to be transferred by the corporation's treasurer to the university as a contribution towards its maintenance. When this action was questioned by stockholders the corporation instituted a declaratory judgment action in the Chancery Division and trial was had in due course.

Mr. Hubert F. O'Brien, the president of the company, testified that he considered the contribution to be a sound investment, that the public expects corporations to aid philanthropic and benevolent institu-tions, that they obtain good will in the community by so doing, and that their charitable donations create favorable environment for their busi-ness operations. In addition, he expressed the thought that in contrib-uting to liberal arts institutions, corporations were furthering their self-interest in assuring the free flow of properly trained personnel for administrative and other corporate employment. Mr. Frank W.

Abrams, chairman of the board of the Standard Oil Company of New Jersey, testified that corporations are expected to acknowledge their public responsibilities in support of the essential elements of our free enterprise system. He indicated that it was not "good business" to disappoint "this reasonable and justified public expectation," nor was it good business for corporations "to take substantial benefits from their membership in the economic community while avoiding the normally accepted obligations of citizenship in the social community." Mr. Irving S. Olds, former chairman of the board of the United States Steel Corporation, pointed out that corporations have a self-interest in the maintenance of liberal education as the bulwark of good government. He stated that "Capitalism and free enterprise owe their survival in no small degree to the existence of our private, independent universities" and that if American business does not aid in their maintenance it is not "properly protecting the long-range interest of its stockholders, its employees and its customers." Similarly, Dr. Harold W. Dodds, President of Princeton University, suggested that if private institutions of higher learning were replaced by governmental institutions our society would be vastly different and private enterprise in other fields would fade out rather promptly. Further on he stated that "democratic society will not long endure if it does not nourish within itself strong centers of non-governmental fountains of knowledge, opinions of all sorts not governmentally or politically originated. If the time comes when all these centers are absorbed into government, then freedom as we know it, I submit, is at an end."

The objecting stockholders have not disputed any of the foregoing testimony nor the showing of great need by Princeton and other private institutions of higher learning and the important public service being rendered by them for democratic government and industry alike. Similarly, they have acknowledged that for over two decades there has been state legislation on our books which expresses a strong public policy in favor of corporate contributions such as that being questioned by them. Nevertheless, they have taken the position that (1) the plaintiff's certificate of incorporation does not expressly authorize the contribution and under common-law principles the company does not possess any implied or incidental power to make it, and (2) the New Jersey statutes which expressly authorize the contribution may not constitutionally be applied to the plaintiff, a corporation created long before their enactment. See R.S. 14:3–13, N.J.S.A.; R.S. 14:3–13.1 et seq., N.J.S.A.

In his discussion of the early history of business corporations Professor Williston refers to a 1702 publication where the author stated flatly that "The general intent and end of all civil incorporations is for better government." And he points out that the early corporate charters, particularly their recitals, furnish additional support for the notion that the corporate object was the public one of managing and ordering the trade as well as the private one of profit for the members. See 3 Select Essays on Anglo–American Legal History 201 (1909); 1 Fletcher, Corporations (rev. ed. 1931), 6. See also Currie's Administrators v. Mutual Assurance Society, 4 Hen. & M. 315, 347 (Va.Sup.Ct.App. 1809), where Judge Roane referred to the English corporate charters and expressed the view that acts of incorporation ought never to be passed "but in consideration of services to be rendered to the public." However, with later economic and social developments and the free availability of the corporate device for all trades, the end of private profit became generally accepted as the controlling one in all businesses other than those classed broadly as public utilities. Cf. Dodd, For Whom Are Corporate Managers Trustees?, 45 Harv.L.Rev. 1145, 1148 (1932). As a concomitant the common-law rule developed that those who managed the corporation could not disburse any corporate funds for philanthropic or other worthy public cause unless the expenditure would benefit the corporation. Hutton v. West Cork Railway Company, 23 Ch.D. 654 (1883); Dodge v. Ford Motor Co., 204 Mich. 459, 170 N.W. 668, 3 A.L.R. 413 (Sup.Ct.1919). Ballantine, Corporations, (rev. ed. 1946), 228; 6A Fletcher, supra, 667. During the 19th Century when corporations were relatively few and small and did not dominate the country's wealth, the common-law rule did not significantly interfere with the public interest. But the 20th Century has presented a different climate. Berle and Means, The Modern Corporation and Private Property (1948). Control of economic wealth has passed largely from individual entrepreneurs to dominating corporations, and calls upon the corporations for reasonable philanthropic donations have come to be made with increased public support. In many instances such contributions have been sustained by the courts within the common-law doctrine upon liberal findings that the donations tended reasonably to promote the corporate objectives. See Cousens, How Far Corporations May Contribute to Charity, 35 Va.L.Rev. 401 (1949). . . .

The foregoing authorities illustrate how courts, while adhering to the terms of the common-law rule, have applied it very broadly to enable worthy corporate donations with indirect benefits to the corporations. In State ex rel. Sorensen v. Chicago B. & Q. R. Co., 112 Neb. 248, 199 N.W. 534, 537 (1924), the Supreme Court of Nebraska, through Justice Letton, went even further and without referring to any limitation based on economic benefits to the corporation said that it saw "no reason why if a railroad company desires to foster, encourage and contribute to a charitable enterprise, or to one designed for the public weal and welfare, it may not do so"; later in its opinion it repeated this view with the expression that it saw "no reason why a railroad corporation may not, to a reasonable extent, donate funds or services to aid in good works." Similarly, the court in Carey v. Corporation Commission of Oklahoma, 168 Okl. 487, 33 P.2d 788, 794 (Sup.Ct.1934), while holding that a public service company was not entitled to an increase in its rates because of its reasonable charitable donations, broadly recognized that corporations, like individuals, have power to make them. Cf. New Jersey Bell Telephone Company v. Department of Public Utilities, 12 N.J. 568, 97 A.2d 602 (1953). In the course of his opinion for the court in the Carey case Justice Bayless said:

> "Next is the question of dues, donations, and philanthropies of the Company. It is a matter for the discretion of corporate management in making donations and paying dues. In that respect a corporation does not occupy a status far different from an individual. An individual determines the propriety of joining organizations, and contributing to their support by paying dues, and all contribution to public charities, etc., according to his means. He does not make such contributions above his means with the hope that his employer will increase his compensation accordingly. A corporation likewise should not do so. Its ultimate purpose, from its own standpoint, is to earn and pay dividends. If, as a matter of judg-

ment, it desires to take part of its earnings, just as would an individual, and contribute them to a worthy public cause, it may do so; but we do not feel that it should be allowed to increase its earnings to take care thereof."

Over 20 years ago Professor Dodd, supra, 45 Harv.L.Rev., at 1159, 1160, cited the views of Justice Letton in State ex rel. Sorensen v. Chicago B. & Q. R. Co., supra, with seeming approval and suggested the doctrine that corporations may properly support charities which are important to the welfare of the communities where they do business as soundly representative of the public attitude and actual corporate practice. Developments since he wrote leave no doubts on this score.

When the wealth of the nation was primarily in the hands of individuals they discharged their responsibilities as citizens by donating freely for charitable purposes. With the transfer of most of the wealth to corporate hands and the imposition of heavy burdens of individual taxation, they have been unable to keep pace with increased philanthropic needs. They have therefore, with justification, turned to corporations to assume the modern obligations of good citizenship in the same manner as humans do. Congress and state legislatures have enacted laws which encourage corporate contributions, and much has recently been written to indicate the crying need and adequate legal basis therefor.

. . .

In actual practice corporate giving has correspondingly increased. Thus, it is estimated that annual corporate contributions throughout the nation aggregate over 300 million dollars, with over 60 million dollars thereof going to universities and other educational institutions. Similarly, it is estimated that local community chests receive well over 40% of their contributions from corporations; these contributions and those made by corporations to the American Red Cross, to Boy Scouts and Girl Scouts, to 4–H Clubs and similar organizations have almost invariably been unquestioned.

During the first world war corporations loaned their personnel and contributed substantial corporate funds in order to insure survival; during the depression of the '30s they made contributions to alleviate the desperate hardships of the millions of unemployed; and during the second world war they again contributed to insure survival. They now recognize that we are faced with other, though nonetheless vicious, threats from abroad which must be withstood without impairing the vigor of our democratic institutions at home and that otherwise victory will be pyrrhic indeed. More and more they have come to recognize that their salvation rests upon sound economic and social environment which in turn rests in no insignificant part upon free and vigorous nongovernmental institutions of learning. It seems to us that just as the conditions prevailing when corporations were originally created required that they serve public as well as private interests, modern conditions require that corporations acknowledge and discharge social as well as private responsibilities as members of the communities within which they operate. Within this broad concept there is no difficulty in sustaining, as incidental to their proper objects and in aid of the public welfare, the power of corporations to contribute corporate funds within reasonable limits in support of academic institutions. But even if we confine ourselves to the terms of the common-law rule in its application to current conditions, such expenditures may likewise readily be justified as being for the benefit of the corporation; indeed, if need be the matter may be viewed strictly in terms of actual survival of the corporation in a free enterprise system. The genius of our common law has been its capacity for growth and its adaptability to the needs of the times. Generally courts have accomplished the desired result indirectly through the molding of old forms. Occasionally they have done it directly through frank rejection of the old and recognition of the new. But whichever path the common law has taken it has not been found wanting as the proper tool for the advancement of the general good. Cf. Holmes, The Common Law, 1, 5 (1951); Cardozo, Paradoxes of Legal Science, Hall, Selected Writings, 253 (1947).

In 1930 a statute was enacted in our State which expressly provided that any corporation could cooperate with other corporations and natural persons in the creation and maintenance of community funds and charitable, philanthropic or benevolent instrumentalities conducive to public welfare, and could for such purposes expend such corporate sums as the directors "deem expedient and as in their judgment will contribute to the protection of the corporate interests." L.1930, c. 105; L.1931, c. 290; R.S. 14:3-13, N.J.S.A. See 53 N.J.L.J. 335 (1930). Under the terms of the statute donations in excess of 1% of the capital stock required 10 days' notice to stockholders and approval at a stockholders' meeting if written objections were made by the holders of more than 25% of the stock; in 1949 the statute was amended to increase the limitation to 1% of capital and surplus. See L.1949, c. 171. In 1950 a more comprehensive statute was enacted. L.1950, c. 220; N.J.S.A. 14:3-13.1 et seq. In this enactment the Legislature declared that it shall be the public policy of our State and in furtherance of the public interest and welfare that encouragement be given to the creation and maintenance of institutions engaged in community fund, hospital, charitable, philanthropic, educational, scientific or benevolent activities or patriotic or civic activities conducive to the betterment of social and economic conditions; and it expressly empowered corporations acting singly or with others to contribute reasonable sums to such institutions, provided, however, that the contribution shall not be permissible if the donee institution owns more than 10% of the voting stock of the donor and provided, further, that the contribution shall not exceed 1% of capital and surplus unless the excess is authorized by the stockholders at a regular or special meeting. To insure that the grant of express power in the 1950 statute would not displace pre-existing power at common law or otherwise, the Legislature provided that the "act shall not be construed as directly or indirectly minimizing or interpreting the rights and powers of corporations, as heretofore existing, with reference to appropriations, expenditures or contributions of the nature above specified." N.J.S.A. 14:3-13.3. It may be noted that statutes relating to charitable contributions by corporations have now been passed in 29 states. See Andrews, supra, 235.

The appellants contend that the foregoing New Jersey statutes may not be applied to corporations created before their passage. Fifty years before the incorporation of The A. P. Smith Manufacturing Company our Legislature provided that every corporate charter thereafter granted "shall be subject to alteration, suspension and repeal, in the discretion of the legislature." L.1846, p. 16; R.S. 14:2-9, N.J.S.A. A similar reserved power was placed into our State Constitution in 1875 (Art. IV, Sec. VII, par. 11), and is found in our present Constitution. Art. IV, Sec. VII, par. 9.

. . .

It seems clear to us that the public policy supporting the statutory enactments under consideration is far greater and the alteration of pre-existing rights of stockholders much lesser than in the cited cases sustaining various exercises of the reserve power. In encouraging and expressly authorizing reasonable charitable contributions by corporations, our State has not only joined with other states in advancing the national interest but has also specially furthered the interests of its own people who must bear the burdens of taxation resulting from increased state and federal aid upon default in voluntary giving. It is significant that in its enactments the State has not in anywise sought to impose any compulsory obligations or alter the corporate objectives. And since in our view the corporate power to make reasonable charitable contributions exists under modern conditions, even apart from express statutory provision, its enactments simply constitute helpful and confirmatory declarations of such power, accompanied by limiting safeguards.

In the light of all of the foregoing we have no hesitancy in sustaining the validity of the donation by the plaintiff. There is no suggestion that it was made indiscriminately or to a pet charity of the corporate directors in furtherance of personal rather than corporate ends. On the contrary, it was made to a preeminent institution of higher learning, was modest in amount and well within the limitations imposed by the statutory enactments, and was voluntarily made in the reasonable belief that it would aid the public welfare and advance the interests of the plaintiff as a private corporation and as part of the community in which it operates. We find that it was a lawful exercise of the corporation's implied and incidental powers under common-law principles and that it came within the express authority of the pertinent state legislation. As has been indicated, there is now widespread belief throughout the nation that free and vigorous non-governmental institutions of learning are vital to our democracy and the system of free enterprise and that withdrawal of corporate authority to make such contributions within reasonable limits would seriously threaten their continuance. Corporations have come to recognize this and with their enlightenment have sought in varying measures, as has the plaintiff by its contribution, to insure and strengthen, the society which gives them existence and the means of aiding themselves and their fellow citizens. Clearly then, the appellants, as individual stockholders whose private interests rest entirely upon the well-being of the plaintiff corporation, ought not be permitted to close their eyes to present-day realities and thwart the long-visioned corporate action in recognizing and voluntarily discharging its high obligations as a constituent of our modern social structure.

The judgment entered in the Chancery Division is in all respects

Affirmed.

For affirmance: CHIEF JUSTICE VANDERBILT and JUSTICES HEHER, OLIPHANT, WACHENFELD, BURLING and JACOBS—6.

For reversal: None.

———

NOTE ON RECENT CASES ON CORPORATE
NON-PROFIT ACTIVITY

The sprinkling of cases since Barlow that involve attacks on boards of directors for carrying out non-profit activities is highly indecisive. It illustrates the difficulty of getting a square resolution of this type of problem in the face of the business judgment rule and other procedural obstacles.

(1) In Kelly v. Bell, 254 A.2d 62 (Del.Ch.1969), affirmed 266 A.2d 878 (1970), United States Steel Corp. and several other corporations made "voluntary" payments to Allegheny County. These payments, about $5,000,000 a year, were in lieu of property taxes based on machinery in the county, which tax was abolished by legislation. The law probably would not have passed without the agreement to make these payments since some counties would have been terribly hurt by loss of that tax revenue. The court held that the business judgment rule protected the directors in pursuing the long range self interest of the corporation (which evidently saved the corporation a net sum of $7,000,000 a year).

(2) Sylvia Martin Foundation v. Swearingen, 260 F.Supp. 231 (S.D. N.Y.1966), involved an attack on the management of Standard Oil Co. of New Jersey for borrowing money in Europe at a higher interest rate than that obtainable in the American financial market. This action complied with the President's program, then "voluntary", to redress the balance of payments. The court found it had no jurisdiction but also indicated that it could find the action not beyond the scope of the directors' business judgment.

(3) Shlensky v. Wrigley, 95 Ill.App.2d 173, 237 N.E.2d 776 (1968), upheld the action of the president—majority shareholder of the Chicago Cubs—in refusing to install lights at Wrigley Field and play night games as did the other clubs. It was claimed that Wrigley felt baseball was a daytime game and that nighttime games would damage the neighborhood. The court felt that long term deterioration of the area might adversely affect attendance and refused to override the judgment of the directors that night games would not increase earnings. In 1988 the first night game was played.

(4) Theodora Holding Corp. v. Henderson, 257 A.2d 398 (Del.Ch. 1969), involved the management of a personal holding company that made gifts to a foundation. The Chancellor found that 8 Del.C. § 122(9) permitted this action, that the federal tax deduction made the cost of the gifts only 15¢ per $1.00, that plaintiff was benefitted by the justification such gifts provided "for large private holdings", and that gifts for youth work were "peculiarly appropriate in an age when a large segment of youth is alienated even from parents who are not entirely satisfied with our present social and economic system."

(5) A number of cases have discussed the question of responsibilities broader than shareholder wealth-maximizing in the context of

management's attempts to fend off a threatened hostile take over.[8] Thus the court in GAF Corp. v. Union Carbide Corp., 624 F.Supp. 1016 (S.D.N.Y.1985), said:

> The exercise of independent, honest business judgment is the traditional and appropriate way to deal fairly and even-handedly with both the protection of investors, on the one hand, and the legitimate concerns and interests of employees and management of a corporation who service the interests of investors, on the other.

State statutes on takeovers passed in 1986 and 1987 have made references to such broader interests than shareholder wealth. Sometimes they seem to apply in cases other than resistance to takeovers. Ohio's § 1701.59, (1986 Suppl.) is positioned in the general section on directors' duties: It reads:

> (E) For purposes of this section, a director, in determining what he reasonably believes to be in the best interests of the corporation, shall consider the interests of the corporation's shareholders and, in his discretion, may consider any of the following:

> (1) The interests of the corporation's employees, suppliers, creditors, and customers;

> (2) The economy of the state and nation;

> (3) Community and societal considerations;

> (4) The long-term as well as short-term interests of the corporation and its shareholders, including the possibility that these interests may be best served by the continued independence of the corporation.

NOTE ON THE THEORY OF CORPORATE RESPONSIBILITY

While the case law, as exposed above, is both sparse and inconclusive, the academic and theoretical literature is dense, but inconclusive. The following paragraphs attempt to condense this material. It seems fairly clear that in the early days a charter was granted on the theory that the corporation in question would contribute to the public interest, as well as making some money for the members. Since a majority of the incorporations in question involved what we would think of as public utilities—turnpikes, canals, etc.—this mixture of public and private welfare came naturally. By the late 19th century, however, the view had come into full sway that a corporation was run for the benefit of its shareholders only. This was classically expressed by Bowen, L.J., in 1883:

---

8. See also Unocal Corp. v. Mesa Petroleum Co., 493 A.2d 946, 955 (Del.1985); Norlin Corp. v. Rooney, Pace, Inc., 744 F.2d 255, 266 (2d Cir.1984); Enterra Corp. v. SGS Assoc., 600 F.Supp. 678, 687 (E.D.Pa. 1985).

"The law does not say that there are to be no cakes and ale,
but there are to be no cakes and ale except such as are
required for the benefit of the company. . . . It is not
charity sitting at the board of directors, because as it seems to
me charity has no business to sit at boards of directors *qua*
charity. There is, however, a kind of charitable dealing which
is for the interest of those who practice it, and to that extent
and in that garb (I admit not a very philanthropic garb) charity
may sit at the board, but for no other purpose." [9]

In the United States, too, when a president in the 1920's could say that
the business of America is business, there was not much doubt as to
what the business of a business corporation should be.

A new striving was represented by the famous Dodd–Berle dialogue. I will let Yale's Dean Rostow summarize this:

A classic debate on the question was conducted by Professor Berle and Professor Dodd almost thirty years ago, and
Professor Berle has now concluded that Professor Dodd was
right in the first place. As is the case in many debates, the
theses of the protagonists turn out on inspection to be quite
compatible. Professor Berle starts with the proposition that
all corporate powers are powers in trust, "necessarily and at
all times exercisable only for the ratable benefit of all the
stockholders as their interest appears." In the light of this
premise, he makes illuminating comments on a number of
controversial issues of corporate law and practice. Professor
Dodd agrees that corporate powers are powers in trust, to be
sure. But the use of private property, he urges, is deeply
affected with a public interest, and the development of public
opinion is more and more acutely conscious of that fact. Recognition of the public interest in the use of corporate property,
Professor Dodd contends, requires that directors be viewed as
trustees for the enterprise as a whole—for the corporation
viewed as an institution—and not merely as "attorneys for the
stockholders." To this Professor Berle replied by agreeing that
the use of private property, notably in the case of large
corporations, was indeed a matter of the highest public importance. But, he said, "I submit that you can not abandon
emphasis on the view that business corporations exist for the
sole purpose of making profits for their stockholders until such
time as you are prepared to offer a clear and reasonably
enforceable scheme of responsibilities to someone else." We
have no such directing rule. In its absence, the consequence of
Professor Dodd's argument would be to remit the control of
corporations, and the orientation of their policies, entirely to
the management. The older rule, Professor Berle contended,

9. Hutton v. West Cork Ry., 23 Ch.Div.
654, 673 (C.A.1883).

offers the only chance of ordering business affairs in ways which would minimize managerial over-reaching and self-seeking. With this position Professor Dodd then agreed, although he felt that the rule had lost all contact with reality, and with public aspiration.[10]

Profit-making for absentee owners must be the legal standard by which we measure their conduct until some other legal standard has been evolved. Granted—with some reservations that this is all that the law can do at present, the question remains as to how effectively it can do that. If trusteeship for absentee investors, in addition to being an ideal having little emotional appeal to managers, is an ideal that is losing ground in the community generally and if the signs are multiplying that our economic order is evolving away from it, the prospect of its effective enforcement as an interim legal rule of conduct is not encouraging. Abandon it as yet, we dare not—enforce it with more than moderate success, it is to be feared we cannot.

In 1954, Professor Berle accepted Professor Dodd's initial position, apparently because he concludes that the directors of endocratic corporations, as keepers of the public conscience, can now be safely trusted to exercise their vast powers in the public interest, without the safeguard of either stockholder control or effective public supervision.

The theme was picked up by a number of managers who, one guesses, found satisfaction in thinking of themselves as having higher functions in life than "merely" making profits. From the many, often self-serving, declarations in this field one, by Frank Abrams, Chairman of the Board of Standard Oil, is particularly often cited. He said that the managers of a company must conduct its affairs "in such a way as to maintain an equitable and working balance among the claims of the various directly interested groups—stockholders, employees, customers, and the public at large." [11]

The impact of Ralph Nader, Campaign GM, etc. has been such as to put yet more momentum behind the public interest theory. The context now is apt to be pollution, foreign investment in Angola or South Africa, automotive safety, etc. Business school courses pass on some concepts of public responsibility to their graduates. There are, however, skeptics. Professor Milton Friedman has consistently assailed all of these theories:

Few trends could so thoroughly undermine the very foundations of our free society as the acceptance by corporate officials of a social responsibility other than to make as much

10. Rostow, To Whom and For What Ends are Corporate Managements Responsible? in The Corporation in Modern Society 46 (E. Mason ed. 1959). Reprinted by permission of the publisher, Harvard University Press.

11. Quoted in Mason, The Apologetics of Managerialism, 31 J. of Bus. 1, 3 (1958). Note also his testimony in A. P. Smith Mfg. Co. v. Barlow, p. 115 supra.

money for their stockholders as possible. This is a fundamentally subversive doctrine. If businessmen do have a social responsibility other than making maximum profits for stockholders, how are they to know what it is? Can self-selected private individuals decide what the social interest is? Can they decide how great a burden they are justified in placing on themselves or their stockholders to serve that social interest? Is it tolerable that these public functions of taxation, expenditure, and control be exercised by the people who happen at the moment to be in charge of particular enterprises, chosen for their posts by strictly private groups? If businessmen are civil servants rather than the employees of their stockholders then in a democracy they could sooner or later, be chosen by the public techniques of election and appointment. . . .

The corporation is an instrument of the stockholders who own it. If the corporation makes a contribution, it prevents the individual stockholder from himself deciding how he should dispose of his funds. With the corporation tax and the deductibility of contributions, stockholders may of course want the corporation to make a gift on their behalf, since this would enable them to make a larger gift. The best solution would be the abolition of the corporate tax. But so long as there is a corporate tax, there is no justification for permitting deductions for contributions to charitable and educational institutions. Such contributions should be made by the individuals who are the ultimate owners of property in our society.

People who urge extension of the deductibility of this kind of corporate contribution in the name of free enterprise are fundamentally working against their own interest. A major complaint made frequently against modern business is that it involves the separation of ownership and control—that the corporation has become a social institution that is a law unto itself, with irresponsible executives who do not serve the interests of their stockholders. This charge is not true. But the direction in which policy is now moving, of permitting corporations to make contributions for charitable purposes and allowing deductions for income tax, is a step in the direction of creating a true divorce between ownership and control and of undermining the basic nature and character of our society. It is a step away from an individualistic society and toward the corporate state.[12]

In reacting to his colleagues' exuberance in the report of the Committee for Economic Development, Philip Sporn, retired utilities executive, had some sharp words:

12. M. Friedman, Capitalism and Freedom 133–36 (1962). Reprinted by permission of the publisher, the University of Chicago Press.

What society wants from business is clearly indicated by examining a few typical cases. In the case of the railroad industry, for example, which is in deep trouble, what society wants and has not received is an imaginative modern system of transportation supplying both passenger and freight service. For many years what the railroad industry has been furnishing has not even approached that standard.

If the New York telephone communication system is in trouble today, it is not due to changing conditions or requirements but primarily because what had been for decades the best telephone service in the world has over a period of recent years deteriorated badly to where it is perhaps no better than third rate.

Once more, if many of the electric utilities of the country are in trouble, it is not because of new requirements but because they have not taken care of their basic responsibility to give an adequate power supply, always reliable and not subject to sudden cataclysmic failures. That they have also been careless of their obligations to do so with minimal adverse effect on the environment has not helped them to get public absolution of their failure to discharge their primary responsibility.

And if our automobile manufacturing industry is in difficulty, it is due to the fact that for too many years the manufacturers and purveyors of automobiles have, for competitive reasons, failed to realize that they could not continue to build the same automobiles, making them larger and more expensive, with more chrome plate and more horsepower under the hood, while at the same time neglecting safety and the Frankenstein of environmental pollution they were raising.[13]

Thus, one can say that the present state of opinion is still quite divided about the question and promises to stay that way. In the 1980's one seems to discern a shift in emphasis. There is, both in the world of theory and the world of practice, great emphasis on the bottom line, on shareholder wealth-maximization. The "numbers game" thrust of law and economics approaches and the need to provide for survival in the race with Japan, the newly industrialized countries and Europe, produce an emphasis on doing what produces the best figures. Coupled with a preference for short-run maximization this tends to squeeze out "soft", non-quantifiable factors. It is strongly argued by some that this short-run preference, which has not been shared by business management in Japan and Europe, poses a threat to the

---

13. Committee for Economic Development, Social Responsibilities of Business Corporations 63 (1971). Corporations gave about $3.8 billion to charity in 1984—out of some $74 billion of total private gifts. N.Y. Times. Oct. 28, 1985. Materials and sources on corporate charity are found in Reporters' Notes to § 2.01, ALI Principles of Corporate Governance (Tent. Draft No. 2, 1984). Compare the treatment of political contributions by corporations in the Bellotti case, p. 62 supra.

competitiveness of the United States ten years from now. This argument forms the basis for what one might term a new managerialism that seeks to ward off the threat of takeovers fueled by promises of short term gains. One sees occasionally some curious alliances of hardline management lawyers and public interest writers of the Nader school.

A few points deserve specific mention since overlooking them tends unnecessarily to blur analysis in an area where it is hard to keep arguments straightforward in any case.

First, note that modern securities analysis uses the concept and term "stockholder-wealth-maximization" rather than the more traditional "profit-maximization." This turn of phrase puts emphasis on the fact that stockholders are not concerned solely with maximizing the year's net profits or the year's dividends but with the size of the total value accruing to their stock in dividends and usefully employed reinvested earnings. Since these factors are impounded in the market price of the stock, wealth-maximization is nearly identical to share price maximization (plus dividends).

Second, note that corporate generosity depends upon the possession of some degree of market power. In a perfectly competitive market each firm—by definition—earns just enough to cover its costs, including a return sufficient to attract the capital it needs. Thus any true gifts would push it over the edge into bankruptcy. In fact, of course most substantial firms do not operate on that close a margin and most charitable donations are made by the relatively small minority of big and prosperous firms whose managements have some discretion. Even a big firm if it falls on evil times—as did General Dynamics, Boeing, Penn Central—will rapidly tighten up on contributions. For a comparison, consider the situation where regulation substitutes for competition. If regulation keeps a firm from earning more than a fixed rate of return, such a firm has only two choices: (1) to obtain from the regulatory commission permission to charge rates that will cover the expenditure—thereby passing the cost on to consumers or (2) to reduce the shareholders' return below that to which they are legally entitled, a return supposedly set at no more than the amount needed to attract further investors.[14]

Third, observe that corporate generosity questions become connected with what some economists would call the "externalities" issue. One aspect of this is the "free ride" problem. If A. P. Smith gives $1500 to Princeton it is highly unlikely that it will get anything back for its investment. If 10,000 firms in New Jersey do the same, some or all will benefit from the $15,000,000—from the availability of Princeton physicists, the greater attractiveness of New Jersey to potential employees, etc. Thus a hard headed profit maximizer would be led to say

---

14. E.g., Pacific Tel. & Tel. Co. v. PUC, 62 Cal.2d 634, 668, 401 P.2d 353, 374 (1965).

"let's get a free ride on the others." The gap between the single firm's contributions and its capacity to recapture some of the benefits can be bridged in two ways: the firms involved may each agree to act in parallel (which may bring them in conflict with the antitrust laws) or else the government may require the activity in question so as to make it a mandatory cost. Thus changing the provision of an anti-pollution facility from a voluntary gesture to a legal requirement makes it a regular internalized cost, along with fuel, wages, etc.

Finally, let me note that, until recently there has only once been an attempt to codify a rule that managers need not aim exclusively for profit maximization. The 1937 German statute for publicly held corporations provided that:

> The managing board is, on its own responsibility, to manage the corporation as the good of the enterprise and its retinue [i.e. employees] and the common weal of folk and realm demand.

There seems to have been little material interpreting this section and it was stricken as unnecessary in the 1965 revision.[15] Compare the formulation in § 2.01 of Principles of Corporate Governance: [16]

> A business corporation should have as its objective the conduct of business activities with a view to enhancing corporate profit and shareholder gain, except that, whether or not corporate profit and shareholder gain are thereby enhanced, the corporation, in the conduct of its business
>
> (a) is obliged, to the same extent as a natural person, to act within the boundaries set by law,
>
> (b) may take into account ethical considerations that are reasonably regarded as appropriate to the responsible conduct of business, and
>
> (c) may devote a reasonable amount of resources to public welfare, humanitarian, educational, and philanthropic purposes.

PROBLEM

In 1988 the managers of the small appliance division of General Technology Corporation (GTC) were working on the assigned task of deciding where to place the firm's proposed new factory to produce hand-held miniaturized vacuum cleaners. GTC is a large publicly-held corporation with a major emphasis on household appliances, both large and small, but also some industrial machinery specialties including production robots. One site suggested for the new plant is in South Gobistan, a country on the so-called Asian crescent that, like other newly-industrializing countries in that area, has achieved a surprising degree of economic success through a combination of a tightly

---

15. See Vagts, Reforming the "Modern" Corporation, 80 Harv.L.Rev. 23, 39–41 (1966). For changes see Gruson & Meilicke, The New Co–Determination Law in Germany, 32 Bus.Law. 571 (1977).

16. American Law Institute, Tentative Draft No. 2 (1984).

disciplined and productive work force and laissez faire governmental policies on regulation, taxation and foreign exchange. Its government, presently headed by the former commander-in-chief of South Gobistan's large and well-equipped army, has a reputation for putting down the opposition with scant regard for the niceties of human rights or civil liberties. From time to time there are massive student demonstrations; viewers of American television news can see the troops dispersing crowds with tear gas, water cannons and clubs. Human rights organizations and emigre groups in the United States at regular intervals call upon the United States government to bring pressure to bear on South Gobistan to reform these practices. The country is substantially dependent upon the United States for diplomatic and military support.

The planners in the small appliance division believe that they have found a suitable site for the plant, located in a part of South Gobistan that is near port facilities as well as rail communications with the rest of the country. Preliminary soundings indicate that the country's government would encourage the project and remove bureaucratic difficulties if such should emerge to get in the way of the project. The alternative site would be very near a presently owned site of GTC's located in the midwestern part of the United States. The planners have developed the following tables showing their estimates of the financial results that would follow from the two alternative investments. The calculations are rough and somewhat preliminary but are thought to be sufficiently "within the ballpark" to serve as a basis for making some decisions that need to be finalized in the near future.

EXHIBIT I

First Year Projected Income Statement of Gobistan Alternative

Sales	$40,000,000
Manufacturing costs;	
Labor	16,000,000
Direct material	12,000,000
Factory Overhead	3,000,000
Depreciation	1,500,000
Gross profit	7,500,000
Selling, general and administrative expenses	4,000,000
Interest	500,000
Net income before taxes	3,000,000
Net income after taxes	2,000,000

EXHIBIT II

Second Year Projected Income Statement of Gobistan Alternative

Sales	$60,000,000
Manufacturing costs;	
Labor	21,000,000
Direct material	17,800,000
Factory Overhead	4,000,000
Depreciation	1,500,000
Other	2,000,000
Gross profit	13,700,000
Selling, general and administrative expenses	4,500,000
Interest	500,000
Net income before taxes	8,700,000
Net income after taxes	5,700,000

EXHIBIT III

First Year Projected Income Statement of U.S.A. Alternative

Sales	$50,000,000
Manufacturing costs;	
Labor	28,000,000
Direct material	14,500,000
Factory Overhead	3,000,000
Depreciation	1,500,000
Gross profit	3,000,000
Selling, general and administrative expenses	4,000,000
Interest	500,000
Net income before taxes	(1,500,000)
Net income after taxes	—

EXHIBIT IV

Second Year Projected Income Statement of U.S.A. Alternative

Sales	$60,000,000
Manufacturing costs;	
Labor	32,000,000
Direct material	16,800,000
Factory Overhead	3,000,000
Depreciation	1,500,000
Gross profit	6,700,000
Selling, general and administrative expenses	4,000,000
Interest	500,000
Net income before taxes	2,200,000
Net income after taxes	1,450,000

Assumptions:

1. The composite wage rate in South Gobistan is $6.50 per hour compared with $10 at GTC's plant in the midwest. This wage rate weights the number of personnel of different levels that would be needed times their different wages.

2. Production and, therefore, sales will be less in the Gobistan option in the first year of operation as compared with the American option since it will take longer to build the plant there, train the work force in unfamiliar operations and get the assembly process into full production.

3. Plant construction costs are assumed to be approximately the same in both options, since lower wage rates for construction labor in Gobistan are balanced by additional costs of shipping machinery there and higher costs for specialists and training personnel who will have to be sent to supervise construction.

4. Selling and general costs include, in the case of Gobistan, the ocean freight to bring the products to the United States ports.

5. Taxes will be the same in both cases since the tax rate on corporations in South Gobistan is below that prevailing in the United States and those income taxes can be credited against (deducted from) the taxes payable to the U.S. Treasury.

Various members of the planning team have voiced objections to the calculations and to the end result towards which they seem to point. They have stressed the "iffy" quality of some of the assumptions. Representatives of the firm's office of public affairs have stressed the widespread public hostility towards South Gobistan and have predicted adverse reactions when (and if) an announcement is made that the plant will be located there. Next week the matter is to be put before the executive committee of the board of directors, a body that includes the active managers of the company. It may ultimately be necessary to take the matter before the whole board of directors if no consensus is reached at lower levels. You are among those who are opposed to the move and are trying to line up the arguments in a comprehensive and logical way. The following seem to demand response as you work through the analysis.

(1) Which is in fact the profit-maximizing alternative in the terms in which the report is laid out? What figure represents the "bottom line" comparison? Is there anything which one needs to add to that comparison to close its logic? What assumptions in the report might be subject to challenge on their own terms—that is as elements of the calculation of the expected earnings?

(2) What arguments against the project, not captured by the bottom line, can be made? If the arguments are accepted can the management lawfully refrain from making the investment according to the profit-maximizing calculus? What should be said in the release that announces a negative decision on South Gobistan? Can special arguments be aimed at a director who was previously a university president?

Bibliography: There is a large body of writing on "corporate responsibility, much of it vague and repetitive. The essays in The Corporation in Modern Society (E. Mason ed. 1959) furnish a good introduction. Developments were reviewed from a legal perspective in P. Blumberg, The Megacorporation in American Society: The Scope of Corporate Power (1975); Hetherington, Fact and Legal Theory: Shareholders, Managers and Corporate Social Responsibility, 21 Stanf.L.Rev. 248 (1969); and Romano, Metapolitics and Corporate Law Reform, 36 Stanf.L.Rev. 923 (1984). Solomon & Collins, Humanistic Economics A New Model for the Social Responsibility Debate, 12 J.Corp.L. 331 (1987) seeks to reconcile law and economics.

For a comparative view see Corporate Governance and Directors' Liabilities: The Legal, Economic and Social Analysis of Corporate Social Responsibility (K. Hopt & G. Teubner eds. 1985).

On the regular law of *ultra vires* and its consequences, consult the thorough treatment in R. Baker & E. Dodd, Business Associations 407–62 (1940).

Some special aspects of the corporate responsibility question are covered in E. Epstein, The Corporation in American Politics (1969); R. Eells, Corporate Giving in a Free Society (1956); T. L. Cross, Black Capitalism; Strategy for Business in the Ghetto (1969); and J. Simon, The Ethical Investor: Universities and Corporate Responsibility (1972).

Issues concerning the measurement and reporting of socially responsible corporate behavior are addressed in R. Bauer & D. Fenn, The Corporate Social Audit (1972); Branson, Progress in the Art of Social Accounting and other Arguments for Disclosure on Corporate Social Responsibility, 29 Vand.L.Rev. 539 (1976).

Chapter VI

FORMING THE CORPORATION: ITS FINANCIAL STRUCTURE

1. Introduction

When the legal organizational structure has been established for a corporation and the positions of shareholders, officers, and directors filled, the job is only half done—if that. It is also necessary to establish the financial framework of the corporation and fill it with the necessary funds. While the table of organization describes the new corporation in one dimension, the balance sheet describes it another equally important way. The two dimensions, of course, interrelate very actively; a business corporation is not too inaccurately defined as a set of relationships between people and money.

Since corporate capital substitutes for the individual liability of entrepreneurs, the law has a significant interest in its establishment and its maintenance. Legal requirements and the custom of the market place have caused financial arrangements to fall into certain rather stylized categories rather than being entirely free form contractual improvisations. Within each of these categories a considerable amount of ingenuity can be exercised in adaptation to individual circumstances. Sometimes the adaptations threaten to blur the lines between categories and litigation develops over classification problems.

The broad term for these arrangements is "securities". As used in the federal Securities Act of 1933 [1] it has a scope that is surprising to the uninitiated. It includes, for example, a contract by which one person purchases a lot in an orange grove and contracts with somebody else to manage it for his profit or an arrangement whereby an investor buys a family of minks and entrusts their raising and sale to a contractor. It includes not only corporate obligations but limited partnership interests. In general, any arrangement whereby A turns over funds or assets to B to manage, receiving either a fixed rate or a portion of the profits, is likely to be held to constitute a security.

One can analyze securities on several different scales:

(1) By the types of rights they convey, i.e., stocks versus notes versus bonds;

1. See the definition in Section 2 of the Act.

131

(2) By the types of legal arrangements that create them;

(3) By the classes of persons and institutions who will take them;

On the first scale we find a basic division between stock (equity) and debt. These differences include:

(1) stock *prima facie* has a vote whereas debt obligations do not;

(2) stock participates, via dividends, in profit, its return, though within the discretion of the directors, being roughly in proportion to the earnings of the corporation, whereas debt receives a stipulated rate of interest;

(3) the sum contributed in return for a debt obligation is to be repaid at a fixed time whereas an equity interest has no such claim and is not subject to such a limit;

(4) upon liquidation of the corporation the holders of debt obligations receive payment up to the amount of their claims whereas equity investors receive the residue, if any;

(5) interest on debt is, for accounting purposes and taxation, regarded as an expense, hence deductible, whereas dividends are not.

The differences thus rather sharply stated can be blurred by the creation of intermediate types of security. First and foremost, one can create *preferred stock*. Reviewing the preceding list from this perspective, we note:

(1) preferred stock typically has a vote only when its dividends have been in arrears for a stated period;

(2) preferred stock receives dividends at the discretion of the directors subject to the constraints that they not be paid except out of surplus and that they not exceed the amount stated in the certificate; in any event preferred dividends must usually be paid before anything can be paid on the common; if the stock is "cumulative" that means that dividends unpaid pile up and no dividends can be paid on the common until those areas are taken care of;

(3) preferred stock does not have a fixed maturity date but usually provides for redemption or "call" by the board of directors;

(4) upon liquidation the preferred shareholders are entitled to payment, after creditors and before common stockholders, usually in an amount equal to the original price they paid but sometimes with an additional premium;

(5) for tax and accounting purposes dividends on preferred stock are treated much like dividends on common.

It is also possible to create an intermediate security by starting from a debt security and adapting towards an equity security. Thus one could make the payment of interest on a security contingent on the corporation's having earned income in that period. One can *subordinate* the debt instrument, that is, make its status as debt subordinate to the other indebtedness of the corporation. Intermixture of the two main modes can also be achieved by making a debt security *convertible* into stock at the option of the holder or by giving the holder the option to buy shares of stock at a stated price, sometimes called a warrant. (Preferred stock may also be made convertible). For further treatment of preferred stock see p. 652, infra.

Different securities are created by different instruments, with which you will become familiar if you practice in this field. Stock is embodied in stock certificates but its rights are spelled out in the certificate of incorporation. Both common and preferred are provided for by the sample in the Documentary Supplement. Indebtedness can be created by a variety of instruments. At one extreme an open book account may be reflected only in journal entries. A loan by a bank will be embodied in a more formal document. If it is fairly simple a promissory note will suffice. If it is to be secured it may be necessary to draft a mortgage in proper form to be filed or recorded with the appropriate public office.

Where many members of the public are to hold the debt instruments the form will have to be different. Since it is difficult for bondholders to act together it is common for the constitutive document to create a trustee to act for them. If the indebtedness is secured a mortgage will be involved of which the trustee will be the mortgagee—an unsecured instrument is generally referred to as an *indenture*. The separate indebtedness are evidenced by certificates issued in classes or series which are held by the separate creditors; if they are secured they are commonly referred to as *bonds,* otherwise they are *debentures* or *notes.* The bonds or debentures are cross-referenced to the underlying mortgage or indenture that defines their rights.

A corporation seeking funds may appeal to quite different sources. One rough categorization would be as follows:

    (1) the personal resources of the entrepreneurs and their families and friends;

    (2) banks, both commercial and savings;

    (3) small business investment companies established with special federal advantages to support small new firms;

    (4) insurance companies;

    (5) pension and similar trust funds together with endowment and other charitable foundations;

    (6) specialized federal and state lending agencies;

    (7) the general investing public, reached through the underwriting process described in section 4 below;

    (8) mutual funds or investment companies.

Of course, the security a corporation offers must match the needs of the investor it approaches. An insurance company may be limited by statutory prescriptions as to the type of security it can accept. A trustee for a family trust will wish to buy securities that will provide a fair and rather steady level of income for the family members with a reasonable amount of security and some protection against inflation. A young professional with some surplus income may wish to take risks with investments and pass up current income for the sake of a possibly great ultimate enhancement of the capital investment. Different tax situations will give different motivations to different groups. A large number of individuals in various types of institutions make a more or less comfortable living as intermediaries between such investors and corporations with needs for their funds. A corporation may create a mixed financial structure, drawing on various sources, each to contribute its own type of support. For further review of financing alternatives see Chapter XII.

NOTE: A BRIEF REFRESHER ON SOME ACCOUNTING ASPECTS OF CORPORATE FINANCIAL STRUCTURE

If you have had any accounting of even the most basic type you will recall first that the double entry system requires that each transaction have two aspects and second, that a basic equation is maintained in which assets equal liabilities plus proprietorship. Therefore, the contribution of $10,000 in cash to a corporation at its inception in return for its notes and a like amount of cash for its common stock will produce the following balance sheet:

cash	$20,000	notes	$10,000
		capital	
	———	stock	10,000
	20,000		20,000

You should observe two points that cause difficulty. In accounting terms "capital" is a name for the source and not for the asset. It is common to refer to a corporation's cash, building and investments as its "capital". Marx refers to *Das Kapital* in that sense. For us, capital is a right hand item. "Capital" normally is established as a result of multiplying the number of shares issued times the par (or stated) value of each share. Capital may be changed by amendment of the certificate of incorporation but otherwise it remains fixed. Assets may come and go, increase and decrease but capital is not affected by such changes. If these transactions result in gains by the corporation, that will be reflected in an account entitled surplus, or preferably earned surplus, or even better retained earnings. Dividends may be paid only if the resulting debit can be to such an earned surplus account. The capital account cannot be used to pay dividends. Capital is designed to protect creditors by affording a "cushion" against losses. If losses result there will be a deficit retained earnings account which will "impair" capital and prevent dividends from being paid.

---

2. Problems of Initial Capital Formation

A. "Stock–Watering"

Usually, the capital account (or accounts) arises from the direct "issue" of stock (usually represented by certificates, often elaborately printed or engraved) to the stockholders in exchange for the cash or other assets contributed by them. Sometimes, though not as frequently as formerly, the future stockholders agree in advance to contribute assets for stock which the corporation agrees to create and issue. These agreements are generally known as subscription agreements. The consideration is generally made payable at a single date determined by the board of directors of the corporation, although it may be payable in installments as the corporation (or if affairs go badly, its receiver or trustee in bankruptcy) issues a "call" or "assessment" for additional payments. The law of pre-incorporation subscriptions is not tidy. The basic problem is that there is nobody with whom the subscriber can contract since the corporation does not yet exist. Courts have analyzed the situation in various ways. Some find a "continuing offer" by the subscriber. This implies that he or she may revoke until some point when the offer is, somehow, "accepted". Others find a contract among the subscribers for the benefit of the corporation, an interpretation which seems fairly natural in cases where the subscribers actually know and rely upon each other. Some legislatures, ruthlessly neglectful of classical contractual niceties, have simply made subscriptions irrevocable for a given period. After incorporation there are no longer the same problems about revocability. There are, however, some problems about distinguishing between subscription agreements and executory contracts to buy and sell stock. A subscriber is regarded as already a shareholder, subject to performance of the obligation to pay, and even a disastrous decline in the corporation's fortunes will not relieve one of this duty (nor may it usually be released by agreement, if creditors will be injured thereby). An executory purchaser of shares, on the other hand, is relieved of this obligation since the bankrupt corporation cannot perform its duty to deliver shares in a going concern. Nowadays it is more common to wait until the corporation has been formed before selling any stock to outsiders and many of the niceties of the law of subscriptions are therefore no longer very topical.

If the rules surrounding the capital account are to serve their purposes effectively they must be safeguarded against abuses. One might logically conceive of corporate limited liability as the concession granted by law to the stockholders in exchange for their contribution of capital equivalent to a reasonable advance estimate of the corporation's needs for the risks it proposes to undertake. Human nature being what it is, entrepreneurs keep trying not to perform their end of the bargain. One method of evasion, as we have seen, is openly to contribute only a minimum amount of capital. A more insidious method is to contribute less capital than one purports to do. When shares are simply given away without consideration they are known as "bonus shares". When the property given is overvalued, this is known as "stock watering", after certain agricultural practices allegedly prevalent in rural nineteenth century America. Most state corporation laws, such as Delaware's, prescribe the types of consideration that are acceptable for stock and, in the cases of par value stock assume that an amount equal to the number of shares times their par value will be paid in. Frequently they do not go further and spell out who should be liable and to whom if that payment is not made. Thus these issues have largely been left to the courts. The attitude of the judges towards such conduct parallels that of Calvin Coolidge's preacher towards sin— they are against it. They are less clear about what should be done about it and on what theory liability should be based. The Hospes case represents one of the two leading approaches to this problem, often known as the "holding out" theory.

HOSPES v. NORTHWESTERN MFG. & CAR CO.

Supreme Court of Minnesota, 1892.
48 Minn. 174, 50 N.W. 1117.

MITCHELL, J. This appeal is from an order overruling a demurrer to the so-called "supplemental complaint" of the Minnesota Thresher Manufacturing Company. The Northwestern Manufacturing & Car Company was a manufacturing corporation organized in May, 1882. Upon the complaint of a judgment creditor, (Hospes & Co.,) after return of execution unsatisfied, judgment was rendered in May, 1884, sequestrating all its property, things in action, and effects, and appointing a receiver of the same. This receivership still continues, the affairs of the corporation being not yet fully administered; but it appears that it is hopelessly insolvent, and that all the assets that have come into the hands of the receiver will not be sufficient to pay any considerable part of the debts. The Minnesota Thresher Manufacturing Company, a corporation organized in November, 1884, as creditor, became a party to the sequestration proceeding, and proved its claims against the insolvent corporation. In October, 1889, in behalf of itself and all other creditors who have exhibited their claims, it filed this complaint against certain stockholders (these appellants) of the car company in pursuance of an order of court allowing it to do so, and requiring those thus impleaded to appear and answer the complaint. The object is to recover from these stockholders the amount of certain stock held by them, but alleged never to have been paid for.

The principal question in the case is whether the complaint states facts showing that the thresher company, as creditor, is entitled to the relief prayed for; or, in other words, states a cause of action. Briefly stated, the allegations of the complaint are that on May 10, 1882, Seymour, Sabin & Co. owned property of the value of several million dollars, and a business then supposed to be profitable. That, in order to continue and enlarge this business, the parties interested in Seymour, Sabin & Co., with others, organized the car company, to which was sold the greater part of the assets of Seymour, Sabin & Co. at a valuation of $2,267,000, in payment of which there were issued to Seymour, Sabin & Co. shares of the preferred stock of the car company of the par value of $2,267,000, it being then and there agreed by both parties that this stock was in full payment of the property thus purchased. It is further alleged that the stockholders of Seymour, Sabin & Co., and the other persons who had agreed to become stockholders in the car company, were then desirous of issuing to themselves, and obtaining for their own benefit, a large amount of common stock of the car company, "without paying therefor, and without incurring any liability thereon or to pay therefor;" and for that purpose, and "in order to evade and set at naught the laws of this state," they caused Seymour, Sabin & Co. to subscribe for and agree to take common stock of the car company of the par value of $1,500,000. That Seymour, Sabin & Co. thereupon subscribed for that amount of the common stock, but never paid therefor any consideration whatever, either in money or property. That thereafter these persons caused this stock to be issued to D. M. Sabin as trustee, to be by him distributed among them. That it was so distributed without receipt by him or the car company from any one of any consideration whatever, but was given by the car company and received by these parties entirely "gratuitously." The car company was, at this time, free from debt, but afterwards became indebted to various persons for about $3,000,000. The thresher company, incorporated after the insolvency and receivership of the car company, for the purpose of securing possession of its assets, property, and business, and therewith engaging in and continuing the same kind of manufacturing, prior to October 27, 1887, purchased and became the owner of unsecured claims against the car company, "*bona fide*, and for a valuable consideration," to the aggregate amount of $1,703,000. As creditor, standing on the purchase of these debts, which were contracted after the issue of this "bonus" stock, the thresher company files this complaint to recover the par value of the stock as never having been paid for. The complaint does not allege what the consideration of these debts was, nor to whom originally owing, nor what the intervener paid for them, nor whether any of the original creditors trusted the car company on the faith of the bonus stock having been paid for. Neither does it allege that either the thresher company or its assignors were ignorant of the bonus issue of stock, nor that they or any of them were deceived or damaged in fact by such issue, nor that the bonus stock was of any value. Neither is there any traversable allegation of any actual fraud or intent to deceive or injure creditors. A desire to get something without paying for it, and actually getting it, is not fraudulent or unlawful if the donor consents, and no one else is injured by it; and the general allegation that it was done "in order to evade and set at naught the laws of the state" of itself amounts to nothing but a mere conclusion of law. As a creditors' bill, in the ordinary sense, the complaint is manifestly insufficient. The thresher company, however, plants itself upon the so-called "trust-fund" doctrine that the capital stock of a corporation is a trust fund for the payment of its debts; its contention being that such a "bonus" issue of stock creates, in case of the subsequent insolvency of the corporation, a liability on part of the stockholder in favor of creditors to pay for it, notwithstanding his contract with the corporation to the contrary.

This "trust-fund" doctrine, commonly called the "American doctrine," has given rise to much confusion of ideas as to its real meaning, and much conflict of decision in its application. To such an extent has this been the case that many have questioned the accuracy of the phrase, as well as doubted the necessity or expediency of inventing any such doctrine. While a convenient phrase to express a certain general idea, it is not sufficiently precise or accurate to constitute a safe foundation upon which to build a system of legal rules. The doctrine was invented by Justice STORY in Wood v. Dummer, 3 Mason, 308, which called for no such invention, the fact in that case being that a bank divided up two-thirds of its capital among its stockholders without providing funds sufficient to pay its outstanding bill-holders. Upon old and familiar principles this was a fraud on creditors. Evidently all that the eminent jurist meant by the doctrine was that corporate property must be first appropriated to the payment of the debts of the company before there can be any distribution of it among stockholders,—a proposition that is sound upon the plainest principles of common honesty. In Fogg v. Blair, 133 U.S. 541, 10 Sup.Ct.Rep. 338, it is said that this is all the doctrine means. The expression used in Wood v. Dummer has, however, been taken up as a new discovery, which furnished a solution of every question on the subject. The phrase that "the capital of a corporation constitutes a trust fund for the benefit of creditors" is misleading. Corporate property is not held in trust, in any proper sense of the term. A trust implies two estates or interests,—one equitable and one legal; one person, as trustee, holding the legal title, while another, as the *cestui que trust,* has the beneficial interest. Absolute control and power of disposition are inconsistent with the idea of a trust. The capital of a corporation is its property. It has the whole beneficial interest in it, as well as the legal title. It may use the income and profits of it, and sell and dispose of it, the same as a natural person. It is a trustee for its creditors in the same sense and to the same extent as a natural person, but no further.

Another proposition which we think must be sound is that creditors cannot recover on the ground of contract when the corporation could not. Their right to recover in such cases must rest on the ground that the acts of the stockholders with reference to the corporate capital constitutes a fraud on their rights. We have here a case where the contract between the corporation and the takers of the shares was specific that the shares should not be paid for. Therefore, unlike many of the cases cited, there is no ground for implying a promise to pay for them. The parties have explicitly agreed that there shall be no such implication by agreeing that the stock shall not be paid for. In such a case the creditors undoubtedly may have rights superior to the corporation, but these rights cannot rest on the implication that the shareholder agreed to do something directly contrary to his real agreement, but must be based on tort or fraud, actual or presumed. In England, since the act of 1867, there is an implied contract created by statute that "every share in any company shall be deemed and be taken to have been issued and to be held subject to the payment of the whole amount thereof in cash." This statutory contract makes every contrary contract void. Such a statute would be entirely just to all, for every one would be advised of its provisions, and could conduct himself accordingly. And in view of the fact that "watered" and "bonus" stock is one of *No such* the greatest abuses connected with the management of modern corpora- *Statute* tions, such a law might, on grounds of public policy, be very desirable. *as in* But this is a matter for the legislature, and not for the courts. We *England* have no such statute; and, even if the law of 1873, under which the car company was organized, impliedly forbids the issue of stock not paid for, the result might be that such issue would be void as *ultra vires,* and might be canceled, but such a prohibition would not of itself be sufficient to create an implied contract, contrary to the actual one, that the holder should pay for his stock.

It is well settled that an equity in favor of a creditor does not arise absolutely and in every case to have the holder of "bonus" stock pay for it contrary to his actual contract with the corporation. Thus no such equity exists in favor of one whose debt was contracted prior to the issue, since he could not have trusted the company upon the faith of such stock. First Nat. Bank v. Gustin M. C. Min. Co., 42 Minn. 327, 44 N.W.Rep. 198; Coit v. Amalgamating Co., 119 U.S. 347, 7 Sup.Ct.Rep. 231; Handley v. Stutz, 139 U.S. 435, 11 Sup.Ct.Rep. 530. It does not exist in favor of a subsequent creditor who has dealt with the corpora- tion with full knowledge of the arrangement by which the "bonus" stock was issued, for a man cannot be defrauded by that which he knows when he acts. First Nat. Bank v. Gustin M. C. Min. Co, supra. It has also been held not to exist where stock has been issued and turned out at its full market value to pay corporate debts. Clark v. Bever, supra. The same has been held to be the case where an active corporation, whose original capital has been impaired, for the purpose of recuperating itself issues new stock, and sells it on the market for the best price obtainable, but for less than par, (Handley v. Stutz, supra;) although it is difficult to perceive, in the absence of a statute authorizing such a thing, (of which every one dealing with the corpora- tions is bound to take notice,) any difference between the original stock of a new corporation and additional stock issued by a "going concern." It is difficult, if not impossible, to explain or reconcile these cases upon the "trust-fund" doctrine, or, in the light of them, to predicate the liability of the stockholder upon that doctrine. But by putting it upon the ground of fraud, and applying the old and familiar rules of law on that subject to the peculiar nature of a corporation and the relation which its stockholders bear to it and to the public, we have at once rational and logical ground on which to stand. The capital of a corporation is the basis of its credit. It is a substitute for the individual liability of those who own its stock. People deal with it and give it credit on the faith of it. They have a right to assume that it has paid in capital to the amount which it represents itself as having; and if they give it credit on the faith of that representation, and if the representation is false, it is a fraud upon them; and, in case the corporation becomes insolvent, the law, upon the plainest principles of common justice, says to the delinquent stockholder, "Make that repre- sentation good by paying for your stock." It certainly cannot require the invention of any new doctrine in order to enforce so familiar a rule of equity. It is the misrepresentation of fact in stating the amount of capital to be greater than it really is that is the true basis of the liability of the stockholder in such cases; and it follows that it is only those creditors who have relied, or who can fairly be presumed to have relied, upon the professed amount of capital, in whose favor the law will recognize and enforce an equity against the holders of "bonus" stock. This furnishes a rational and uniform rule, to which familiar principles are easily applied, and which frees the subject from many of the difficulties and apparent inconsistencies into which the "trust-fund" doctrine has involved it; and we think that, even when the trust-fund doctrine has been invoked, the decision in almost every well-considered case is readily referable to such a rule.

It is urged, however, that, if fraud be the basis of the stockholders' liability in such cases, the creditor should affirmatively allege that he believed that the bonus stock had been paid for, and represented so much actual capital, and that he gave credit to the incorporation on the faith of it; and it is also argued that, while there may be a presumption to that effect in the case of a subsequent creditor, this is a mere presumption of fact, and that in pleadings no presumptions of fact are indulged in. This position is very plausible, and at first sight would seem to have much force; but we think it is unsound. Certainly any such rule of pleading or proof would work very inequitably in practice. Inasmuch as the capital of a corporation is the basis of its credit, its financial standing and reputation in the community has its source in, and is founded upon, the amount of its professed and supposed capital, and every one who deals with it does so upon the faith of that standing and reputation, although, as a matter of fact, he may have no personal knowledge of the amount of its professed capital, and in a majority of cases knows nothing about the shares of stock held by any particular stockholder, or, if so, what was paid for them. Hence, in a suit by such creditor against the holders of "bonus" stock, he could not truthfully allege, and could not affirmatively prove, that he believed that the defendants' stock had been paid for, and that he gave the corporation credit on the faith of it, although, as a matter of fact, he actually gave the credit on the faith of the financial standing of the corporation, which was based upon its apparent and professed amount of capital. The misrepresentation as to the amount of capital would operate as a fraud on such a creditor as fully and effectually as if he had personal knowledge of the existence of the defendants' stock, and believed it to have been paid for when he gave the credit. For this reason, among others, we think that all that it is necessary to allege or prove in that regard is that the plaintiff is a subsequent creditor; and that, if the fact was that he dealt with the corporation with knowledge of the arrangement by which the "bonus" stock was issued, this is a matter of defense. Gogebic Inv. Co. v. Iron Chief Min. Co., 78 Wis. 427, 47 N.W.Rep. 726. Counsel cites Fogg v. Blair, supra, to the proposition that the complaint should have stated that this stock had some value; but that case is not in point, for the plaintiff there was a prior creditor; and, as his debt could not have been contracted on the faith of stock not then issued, he could only maintain his action, if at all, by alleging that the corporation parted with something of value.

In one respect, however, we think the complaint is clearly insufficient. The thresher company is here asking the interposition of the court to aid in enforcing an equity in favor of creditors against the stockholders by declaring them liable to pay for this stock contrary to their actual contract with the corporation. While the proceeding is not, strictly speaking, an equitable action, yet the relief asked is equitable in its nature. Under such circumstances, it was incumbent upon the thresher company to show its own equities, and that it was in a position to demand such relief. It was not the original creditor of the car company, but the assignee of the original creditors. By that purchase it, of course, succeeded to whatever strictly legal rights its assignors had; but it is not rights of that kind which it is here seeking to enforce. Under such circumstances, we think it was incumbent upon it to state what it paid for the claims, or at least to show that it paid a substantial, and not a mere nominal, consideration. The only allegation is that it paid "a valuable consideration." This might have been only one dollar. It appears that it bought the claims after the car company had become insolvent, and its affairs were in the hands of a receiver; also that the indebtedness of that company amounted to about $3,000,000, and that there were not corporate assets enough to pay any considerable part of it. The mere chance of collecting something out of the stockholders does not ordinarily much enhance the selling price of claims against an insolvent corporation. If any person or company had gone to work and bought up for a mere song this large indebtedness of the car company for the purpose of speculating on the liability of the stockholders, no court would grant them the relief here prayed for. It would say to them, "We will not create and enforce an equity for the benefit of any such speculation." Counsel for respondent suggests that the thresher company is but an organization of the original creditors, who formed it, and pooled their claims, so as to save something out of the wreck of the car company; but nothing of the kind is alleged. On this ground the demurrer should have been sustained.

In view of further proceedings it may be proper to say that in our opinion there is nothing in the position that the right of recovery against the stockholders was barred by the statute of limitation. The argument in support of the proposition all rests upon the false premise that the cause of action accrued in May, 1882, when the bonus stock was issued. The corporation never had any cause of action against these defendants. As between them and the company, the agreement for the issue of the stock was valid. The creditors are not here seeking to enforce a right of action acquired through or from the corporation, but one that accrued directly to themselves, or for their benefit, and that did not accrue at least until the corporation became insolvent, in May, 1884. . . .

EXCERPTS FROM CH. XI, MINNESOTA GENERAL LAWS, 1873

SEC. 2. The amount of the capital stock in every such corporation shall be fixed and limited by the stockholders in their articles of association, and shall be divided into shares of fifty dollars each, but every such corporation may increase its capital stock, and the number of shares therein at any meeting of the stockholders specially named for that purpose.

SEC. 9. Before any corporation, formed and established by virtue of the provisions of this act, shall commence business the president and directors thereof shall cause their articles of association to be published at full length in two newspapers published in the county in which such corporation is located, or at the capital of the state; and shall also make a certificate of the purpose for which such corporation is formed, the amount of its capital stock, the amount actually paid in, and the names of its stockholders, and the number of shares by each respectively owned, which certificate shall be signed by the president and a majority of the directors, and deposited with the secretary of this state, and a duplicate thereof with the register of deeds of the county in which said corporation is to transact its business. . . .

SEC. 11.   The directors may call in the subscription to the capital stock of such corporation by installments, in such proportion and at such times and places as they shall think proper, by giving such notice thereof as the by-laws shall prescribe, and in case any stockholders shall neglect or refuse payment of any such installment, for the space of sixty days after the same shall have become due and payable, and after he shall have been notified thereof, said corporation may recover the amount of said installment from such negligent stockholder in any proper action for that purpose, or may sell said stock at public auction. . . .

SEC. 18.   The certificate required by the ninth, twelfth and seventeenth sections of this act, shall be made under oath or affirmation, by the person subscribing the same; and if any person shall knowingly swear or affirm falsely as to any material facts, he shall be deemed guilty of perjury, and be punished accordingly.

SEC. 22.   If the president, directors or secretary of any such corporation shall intentionally neglect or refuse to comply with the provisions of this act and to perform the duties therein required of them respectively, such of them as so neglect or refuse shall be jointly and severally liable in an action founded on this statute, for all debts of such corporation contracted during the period of any such neglect or refusal.

QUESTIONS

(1) Can you deduce from the Hospes case what entries were made to reflect the capital contribution transactions?

(2) Prepare a balance sheet for the Northwestern Mfg. & Car Co., involved in the Hospes case, reflecting the issuance of $2,267,000 in par value of preferred stock and $1,500,000 in par value of common stock, and the receipt of the business from Seymour, Sabin & Co.   Which item on the balance sheet constitutes a misrepresentation—and what does it misrepresent?

(3) Why does Hospes court reject the "contract" and "trust fund" approaches to the liability issue?   Is its handling of the trust fund argument consistent with modern accounting terminology?   Is the result in Hospes compelled by (or at least consistent with) the Minnesota statute set forth above?

(4) The Hospes case has been criticized as being "fictional" in its creation of presumptions about reliance.   Critics have said that it is unrealistic to suppose that creditors rely significantly on representations about capital.   Do you agree?

(5) In what respects does the Hospes case go beyond the classic law of liability for misrepresentation?   Are these differences factually justifiable?   How does the Hospes cause of action relate to that in Old Dominion (p. 41 supra)?

(6) Compare the Delaware statute (8 Del.C. §§ 153, 162) with the Minnesota Law.   Would it cause a court to come to the same conclusions as did Mitchell, J. in Hospes?   In what cases, if any, does it seem to require a different result?   Can such results be defended as more equitable than those following from the Hospes approach?

B. Valuation of Consideration Received for Stock

Except in cases where stock is issued for cash, there arises a problem of valuing the assets contributed. These problems are particularly complex when the consideration for stock takes the form of a going business.

SEE v. HEPPENHEIMER

Court of Chancery of New Jersey, 1905.
69 N.J.Eq. 36, 61 A. 843.

PITNEY, V.C. The questions involved in this cause are important, both on account of their intrinsic character and of the amount (over $200,000) involved. They have been argued on each side by distinguished counsel in the most able, thorough, exhaustive, and lucid manner; so that it is but simple truth to say that if the court, in dealing with the case, shall fall into any error, it will not be due in the least degree to a lack of illuminating instruction from counsel. The suit is brought by the creditors, represented by the receiver in insolvency, of the Columbia Straw Paper Company, a corporation organized in this state in the month of December, 1892, and thrown into insolvency in May, 1895. The object of the suit is to hold responsible certain of the stockholders of the company for the debts of the creditors.

The ground on which the defendants are sought to be held is that the stock held by them was issued without any value paid for it, and hence that they occupy the position of subscribers to the capital stock who have not paid their subscriptions, and therefor are liable to the creditors both at common law and under our statute—(1) at common law, on the familiar ground that unpaid subscriptions to capital stock form a trust fund for the benefit of creditors; (2) and under the fifth section of the act concerning corporations of 1875 (1 Gen.St. p. 910), which declares that, "where the whole capital of the corporation shall not have been paid in, and the capital paid shall be insufficient to satisfy the claims of its creditors, each stockholder shall be bound to pay on each share held by him the sum necessary to complete the amount of such share as fixed by the charter of the company, or such proportion of that sum as shall be required to satisfy the debts of the company." The charge of the complainant is that the stock so issued was not issued for cash, but for property purchased at an overvaluation, which overvaluation was arrived at by including in that valuation matters not in any sense property, and that this was done consciously and fraudulently.

The stress of the case is found in the defense set up by the defendants represented by Messrs. Lindabury and Marshall. Counsel for those defendants, whom I shall hereafter call "the defendants," do not contend that the stock held by their clients was issued for cash paid, . . . but they claim that it was issued for property purchased at the value thereof, . . . For convenience I insert here the language of the two sections covering this subject:

"Sec. 54. That nothing but money shall be considered as payment of any part of the capital stock of any company organized under this act, except as hereinafter provided for the purchase of property; and no loan of money shall be made to a stockholder or officer therein; and if any such loan shall be made to a stockholder or officer of the company, the officers who shall make it, or who shall assent thereto, shall be jointly and severally liable, to the extent of such loan and interest, for all the debts of the company contracted before the repayment of the sum so loaned."

"Sec. 213. That the directors of any company incorporated under this act may purchase mines, manufactories or other property necessary for their business, or the stock of any company or companies owning, mining, manufacturing or producing materials, or other property necessary for their business, and issue stock to the amount of the value thereof in payment therefor, and the stock so issued shall be declared and be taken to be full paid stock and not liable to any further call, neither shall the holder thereof be liable for any further payments under any of the provisions of this act; and said stock shall have legibly stamped upon the face thereof 'issued for property purchased,' and in all statements and reports of the company to be published, this stock shall not be stated or reported as being issued for cash paid into the company, but shall be reported in this respect according to the fact."

These defendants assert that the corporation, after being duly organized, purchased from one Emanuel Stein, of Chicago, 39 different mills or plants for the manufacture of straw paper, located in several of the Western states, at the round sum and price of $5,000,000, for which it issued to Stein $1,000,000 of its bonds, secured by a first mortgage on the properties in question, and $1,000,000 of its preferred stock, and $3,000,000 of its common stock, and that their several holdings of stock are parcels of the stock so issued. To this the creditors reply that there was no such actual purchase and sale from Stein to the corporation; that Stein was a mere figurehead for himself and one Beard and the defendant Samuel Untermeyer, and that Stein held for himself and the two just named options from the owners of the 39 mills to purchase their mills at an aggregate price stated at $2,250,000, but actually footing up at less than $2,200,000; and that the mills were paid for on that basis, the owners receiving therefor in round figures, and with certain variations not now necessary to be given in detail, $750,000 in cash, $750,000 in preferred stock of the company, and $1,500,000 of the common stock at 50 cents on the dollar, which would make $3,000,000. In actually working out the scheme, however, it is asserted and proved that the amount actually paid, counting the common stock at par, was less than $2,800,000, and that the balance of the stock, of over $1,000,000, was divided equally between Stein, Beard, and the defendant Samuel Untermeyer without payment therefor; further, that the cash so paid was raised by selling the mortgage bonds at par, with two shares of preferred stock and four shares of common stock added as a bonus to each $1,000 bond.

The clients of Messrs. Lindabury and Marshall, as I interpret their argument, do not seriously dispute the accuracy of the statement just made, but they contend that the valuation of $5,000,000 was arrived at after a careful calculation of the quantity of the paper, viz., 90,000 tons, which the 39 mills were able to produce per year, and the greatly increased price which would be realized from its sale by the suppression of the competition theretofore practiced between the several mill owners. They say that the cost of producing the paper was less than $20 per ton, and that its selling price had been reduced by competition to a trifle over $20 per ton, but that by a concentration of the ownership of the mills they found and believed that the price could be easily maintained, and the whole product of 90,000 tons a year could be marketed, at about $28 per ton, which would pay interest on the bonded debt, with 1 per cent. per year for a sinking fund, and a dividend at 8 per cent. per year on the preferred stock of $1,000,000, and leave a very large dividend, at least 15 per cent. each year, for the common stock of the amount mentioned, $3,000,000. In short, they estimated the value of the property upon a capitalization of the profits expected to be made out of its use by control of the price of its product. So that, taking the aspect of the case most favorable to the defendants, the question which arises out of its ultimate analysis is whether, under our statute above cited, it is competent and lawful to make up the valuation of the visible property to be purchased for stock issued, by adding to the actual market value, or cost of its reproduction, a sum of money ascertained by the capitalization of the annual profits expected to be realized from a favorable marketing of the product of the company by a suppression of competition; or, as I believe I asked counsel in argument, can prospective profits, however promising, be considered as property, as that word is used in the statute above quoted? I repeat its language: "The directors of any company incorporated under this act may purchase mines, manufactories or other property necessary for their business . . . and issue stock to the amount of the value thereof in payment therefor." There the word "property" must evidently be construed by its context, which refers to something visible and tangible and necessary for the business, and the amount of stock to be issued therefor is limited to the value thereof; that is, to the value of that property. If the question above put be the true one, it seems to me that it answers itself, and adversely to the contention of counsel of defendants.

But the defendants attempt to sustain their valuation in question on two grounds: First, that the valuation was made in perfectly good faith, and without any fraudulent intent, and that fraud is, by the rule to be applied here, a necessary ingredient of overvaluation; and, second, that the increased valuation in this case may be justified by, and attributed to, the item of good will. The reply of counsel for complainant to the point of good faith and absence of fraud is twofold: First, that these elements have no place in a transaction of this kind where the thing valued is not, properly speaking, property; and, second, that the good faith and absence of fraud set up by the defendants will not stand the test of close scrutiny, and, further, that the circumstances of the case, given with great detail in the evidence, show that there was no actual appraisement of the property by a competent board of directors, such as is contemplated by the statute.

With regard to the defense based on the item of good will, advanced by the defendants, complainant replies that it is an entire misapplication of the term, and all the law growing out of it, to use it in that connection, and they point out that the conveyances and the contract preceding them, made by the original owners of the 39 mills, included by express terms the good will of the mills, which was included in the original valuation of the mills at $2,250,000, and, besides, that the original contracts were in each case accompanied by an undertaking on the part of the vendor not to engage in the business for five years, and that the preliminary contract with Stein also included the good will. I shall deal with this element of good will at once. Lord Eldon, in Cruttwell v. Lye (1810) 17 Vesey, 335, at page 346, said: "The good will which has been the subject of sale is nothing more than the probability that the old customers will resort to the old place." This definition, though often criticised, seems to me to contain the germ of all the more modern and complete definitions.

Turning to the present case we find, as before remarked, that the individual good will of the different properties was included in the individual valuations thereof and conveyed for the consideration above mentioned to the corporation. Further, the inference is irresistible that the corporation itself could not possibly, at the time of its organization, have acquired any good will in the proper sense of that word, or, indeed, in any sense of that word. It had made no business friends, nor any business reputation. Moreover, an examination in detail of the plan of business laid out and adopted by the promoters of the enterprise, from which they expected to reap such great profits, contemplated a complete destruction of the old good will of the individual establishments. Mr. Stein had, in fact, no good will to convey with the mills, except what he had acquired from the individual owners; hence the increase in price cannot be justified on that basis. It follows that we are driven back to the question first stated, whether prospective and contingent profits of any business, depending, as they always must and do, upon good management and the general course of business of the country, including always the element of competition, can be treated as property in the sense in which that word is used in the statute above cited.

It seems to me that there can be but one opinion as to the soundness of the notion that profits derived, or to be derived, from the prosecution of any business can be properly taken into account, except to a limited extent, in estimating the value of the mere inanimate instrument which is used in conducting that business. Of course, an instrument which is incapable of producing a product to advantage is of no value. On the other hand, an instrument which produces something of great value at little cost is of itself of value, which, however, is limited by the cost of reproducing the instrument itself. Of course, an inanimate instrument which has an extraordinary capacity for producing an article of value is usually covered by a patent, and to the actual cost of its physical reproduction must be added the patentee's fee or license; but, in the absence of any right arising out of a patent, the actual cost of the physical reproduction is the test. Hence, the gross profits to be derived from the carrying on of any ordinary manufacturing business are to be divided, first, into a fair rental for the factory, based on the cost of its reproduction; second, interest on the working capital; third, cost of operating and of administration. The balance, if any, is net profit. For example, if an ordinary manufacturing business should be unusually successful for a series of years, and earn large dividends on the amount of capital invested, no one would think of increasing the valuation of the mill by reason of these profits beyond the cost of its reproduction. The profits were due, in the main, to good management, aided by the general prosperity of the country. Without proper management there might, and probably would, be no profits, and then, on the basis of measuring the value of the mill by the profits of its operations, the mill would be valueless.

The present case is a painful illustration of the utter impossibility of giving the word "property" the construction claimed for it. The rose-colored future, presently to be stated at length, for this enterprise, created with so much confidence by its promoters, failed entirely in the face of actual experience. In the first place the combination did not include all the mills which it was intended to include. There is some dispute and some indefiniteness in the evidence on this subject. The complainant contends that there were, in fact, 73 mills engaged in the manufacture of straw paper, and that the original plan and appraisement included all of them. The defendants admit 41, 2 of which they were unable to purchase, except at prohibitory prices. The proof is clear that there were several more, but just how many is in doubt. It appears from defendants' printed argument, sustained by the proofs, that the failure of the enterprise was due to four causes: first, the financial depression of 1893; second, the starting up of old mills, and the building of new mills as soon as the corporation put up the price of paper; third, bad management of its affairs; and, fourth, the introduction of wood pulp as the basic material of wrapping paper such as was manufactured out of straw. . . .

It will be observed that the consolidation of the ownership of these 39 mills did not increase in the least degree the producing capacity of each, nor did it increase the range of the farming country in the neighborhood of each from which they were to derive their raw material. They were, on the main, widely separated from each other, so that the case is in marked contrast with those which occur where several properties lying contiguous to each other may be applied to a purpose for which they could not be used, except under a combined ownership. Instances of this readily occur to the mind and are found in the books. Several small city lots, covered, if you will, with moderate dwellings, may be worth a great deal more for the purpose of erecting a large hotel or other building requiring considerable of [sic] ground space than the aggregate of the separate value of each for individual dwelling house purposes. So several contiguous lots of unimproved land, under which a large vein of valuable minerals is known to exist, may be more valuable by reason of combined ownership, which enables the minerals to be sought for and brought to the surface much cheaper and to a better advantage than under separate ownerships. So with regard to veins of ore cropping out to the surface under the peculiar mining laws in force in the Rocky Mountain regions, and so leading to insoluble problems of conflict of title. . . .

But the defendants say: The practice of so valuing property under our statute has been indulged in frequently before, and numerous corporations have been organized and have existed upon such a basis, so that, (they argue) the practice has become well-nigh crystalized and sanctioned by long usage. I am sorry to feel constrained to admit that this practice has been frequently indulged in, and, further, that it has brought obloquy upon our state and its legislation. But I am happy to be able to assert with confidence that such practice is entirely unwarranted by anything either in our statute or in the decisions of our courts, and whenever it has been indulged in it has involved a clear infringement of, if not a fraud upon, the plain letter and spirit of our legislation.

But, say the defendants: "We acted in perfectly good faith. We really believed this property was worth the amount at which it was appraised, and we were guilty of no fraud in that behalf. And to show our good faith we invested therein several hundred thousand dollars ($467,000) in cash, besides $50,000 in services and expenses of the law firm of Guggenheimer & Untermeyer and their correspondents in Chicago, and have lost it all." And a powerful appeal was made to the court not to subject the defendants to further loss by saddling these enormous debts upon them. Let us consider the affair from the standpoint of the defendants, and inquire just how and for what they invested their money. The real estate and good will of the 39 mills footed up in value, for purposes of sale to the corporation, to nearly $2,200,000, and, after allowing for the overvaluation which we all know that the individual owners of these industrial properties about to be united usually manage to maintain for that purpose, and of which there is some proof in this case, we may reasonably suppose to be worth $1,500,000, and thus to furnish reasonably good security for $1,000,000 of bonds. Hence it was reasonably safe to invest at par in the bonds to the extent of $1,000,000, secured by a mortgage upon the property. There was little reason to anticipate the completeness of the final catastrophe. The cause of that completeness I have already stated. Now, that investment at par in 6 per cent. bonds secured by a mortgage on property worth at least $1\frac{1}{2}$ times the amount of the sum secured is all that any of the defendants risked. Not one dollar was invested by any of them beyond the par value of the mortgage bonds of the company. For every $1,000 paid into the company they received a mortgage bond for that amount, and, besides, a bonus of two shares of preferred and four shares of common stock. It is thus made clear that, when the faith of these investors in the value of the property purchased was put to the actual test, it went no further than to invest at par in first mortgage 6 per cent. bonds, secured by property estimated to be worth about twice the amount of the mortgage, to which bonds was added as a bonus 60 per cent. of stock representing the value of the property above the mortgage. This transaction is known in the language employed in these financial transactions as "getting in on the ground floor," and was so understood by each of the investors. Mr. Heppenheimer, in fact, uses this very language in his evidence. In answer to a question put by me as to whether he "did not think Mr. Untermeyer was making you a big present," he replied: "No; he was not making me any present, but letting me in on the ground floor. That is the way all these corporations have been formed in the state of New Jersey." No doubt each of these investors really, and therefore in good faith, hoped and expected that the enterprise would prove what they called a success; that is, that the bonds were entirely safe, and so, probably, was the preferred stock. And in like manner it was hoped and expected that the common stock would receive periodical dividends for a period of time long enough at least to enable some, if not all, of it to be marketed, or, to use the apt phrase which has been applied to such transactions, "to be distributed to," and later to be "digested by the public."

I am unable to find that the defendants' belief and faith went beyond this. But I am unwilling to adopt the notion that this sort of good faith is that which is required in order to legalize transactions like this under consideration. And here we find the real motive and reason which gives rise to these inflated values and "watering" of capital stock. It is the desire and intention to sell shares in a property owned by the corporation, for that is what capital stock represents, for more than they are really worth. And therein lies the intrinsically fraudulent character of these transactions. I feel justified in so characterizing them, since the overvaluation of the property does not at all or in any manner increase its intrinsic or practical value, or in the least degree promote the real prosperity of the enterprise. A single paper mill will turn out just as much product capitalized at $100,000 as $200,000, and its rental value will be practically the same. The earnings and profit due to good management and skillful handling of the product will be the same, and these last do not depend at all upon the producing capacity of the mill. Finally, the division of the profits, if any there be, among the stockholders will be on the same basis, and the amount received by each stockholder will be the same, the only difference being in the percentage of the division, and the market values of the shares will finally settle down to the gauge of the dividends earned and declared. But this straightforward mode of doing business does not satisfy the present-day promoter, whose object in making an over-valuation is twofold: First, to sell shares at more than their real value, and thereby secure a profit immediately in hand ("profit" is the word used by Mr. Samuel Untermeyer in his evidence); second, to obtain mercantile credit based on a large capital. . . .

The intention of the Legislature, expressed in these sections in question, in my judgment manifestly was that the capital stock of all corporations should at the start represent the same value, whether paid for in property or money. That result can only be obtained by suppos-ing that the property is to be appraised at its actual cash value, precisely as if a board of directors, with the whole capital stock actually paid in cash, is dealing at actual arm's length as real purchasers with the owner of property proposed to be purchased as a real vendor, without any interest in the directors to overvalue the property, or other interests inconsistent with the real interest of the stockholders as such. I say "at the start," because we all know that property purchased in good faith for cash is liable afterwards to depreciate in value, owing to circumstances not foreseen at the time of its purchase. After all, it seems to me that the true test, under this statute, as applied to the case here in hand, is this: If the company actually had to its credit in bank the sum of $5,000,000, would it have been willing to have paid that price in cash for the property in question for the uses and purposes to which it proposed to devote it? Would the property be worth that sum in cash to the company? Any less severe test will, it seems to me, fail to satisfy the letter and spirit of the two sections of the act before recited, which seem to me clearly to require that the shares of capital stock of any company organized under the act in force when this company was organized should be of equal value, whether paid for in cash or property purchased. . . .

A strong appeal was made to the court in the argument of defen-dants' counsel based on the fact that these defendants had lost between $300,000 and $400,000 of cash, and that no further loss ought to be thrown upon them. With regard to that plea I have this to say: Men of business, who transact their business under the shield of a corporate existence, have the great and peculiar advantage, over those trading as individuals, of avoiding personal pecuniary liability. If the enterprise is prosperous, they make and enjoy its gain. If, on the other hand, it is not prosperous, they lose only their original investment, which may be a part only of their individual fortunes, and any loss beyond that investment falls on the unfortunate creditors. This involves apparent, if not real, unfairness in trade. Be that as it may, under these conditions surely the investors in the stock of trading corporations ought not to complain, or ask any sympathy, if the courts of the country hold them to a strict compliance with the terms of the law under which they claim immunity from pecuniary responsibility. They ought not to complain if the creditors of the corporation shall demand that the original statement of their capital stock shall be made good by those persons who accept it from the company. . . .

Order reversed.

COMMENT

(1) Vice Chancellor Pitney (who took the seat of the senior John Marshall Harlan on the U.S. Supreme Court in 1912) shows concern about the low level of promoters' behavior in New Jersey. Its 1875 statute was one of the first rather liberal laws providing for general incorporation. Many New York enterprises crossed the Hudson to take advantage of that statute and of the low level of corporate taxation. Under the leadership of Governor Woodrow Wilson, the legislature reformed the statute in 1913. The pennant for incorporation attractiveness then passed to Delaware, which in 1915 enacted legislation closely parallel to New Jersey's.

(2) Two of the lawyers involved in the case achieved fame and fortune independently of this case. I refer to Mr. Lindabury in connection with another case.[2] Mr. Untermyer was at this time a highly successful corporation lawyer who made himself wealthy in connection with promotions, mergers, etc. He, too, was active in the affairs of the great insurance firms then growing to national enterprises. He was a flamboyant litigator, always with an orchid in his lapel. He took his expertise over to the other side, so to speak, and acted as counsel for the Pujo Committee of the House of Representatives which first investigated the "money trust" of Wall Street. He later participated in drafting the Federal Reserve Act and fought to retain the five cent fare on the New York subway system. In the 1930's he advocated federal stock exchange legislation. The law firm he founded was active until very recently.

A NOTE ON VALUATION

(1) Obviously, whenever, as in the Hospes case, par stock is issued in exchange for property or services, the consideration received by the corporation must be valued in order to determine whether it is at least equal to the total par value of the stock issued. And, as we have seen, even when no-par stock is used, the consideration received for it must be valued at least for the purpose of preparing financial statements for the enterprise. Almost every corporation statute has some counterpart of 8 Del.C. § 152 casting the responsibility for such valuation upon the directors, at least in the first instance. There has been less uniformity on the question of how conclusive the determination of the directors is. Some of the earlier authorities adopted the "true value" rule, which required a *de novo* determination of whether the value of the property received actually did equal the total par value of the stock issued for it. Many of the more recent statutes go to the opposite extreme and purport to make the directors' valuation conclusive "in the absence of actual fraud." Literally, such statutes would seem to confine attacks

2. Robotham v. Prudential Ins. Co., p. 229 infra.

upon the directors' valuation to cases of conscious wrongdoing; but the courts have refused to be so restricted, particularly where, as is so often true, the directors are in the position of valuing their own contributions. For one thing, the courts have held that the directors' determination need not be respected unless they in fact made efforts to reach a reasonable judgment as to value. In addition, wherever there has been a gross over-valuation when measured by objective standards, it will be regarded as evidence of conscious over-valuation, and if not satisfactorily explained it will be treated as a "badge of fraud" for which the directors' determination may be upset.[3]

(2) This is the first of several places in the book which the concept of *value* as applied to a corporation or its shares becomes relevant. Lawyers at the start have a tendency to assume that they know what this means and to leave it for somebody else to determine as a rather instinctual matter. Accountants also tend to shrink from valuation, regarding value as a dangerous concept and one beyond their expertise; this causes them to cling tenaciously to the use of historical costs, which are objective recorded facts, even where cost figures are not too helpful in answering the question at hand. All of this means that since values must at times be assigned this job falls to appraisers, investment bankers and, often to the board of directors. It can be a very difficult job, one that demands a considerable amount of judgment and experience.

(3) You should now become acquainted, at least in a simplified and preliminary way, with some of the concepts of valuation.

Book value. It is important to recognize—it is often overlooked— that "book value" is a misleading term. It is not a value but cost, less accumulated depreciation. The older the cost the more meaningless it is apt to be as a guide to what the asset is currently worth. Inflation may have done its work in one direction raising the value in current dollars far above the cost in the dollar of twenty years ago. On the other hand obsolescence may have far outstripped the rational and systematic depreciation of the asset so that it is ready for the scrapheap.

Reproduction cost. This is the cost of presently producing the equivalent of the item in question. It does take into account inflationary and other changes in cost. However, it may be rather unhelpful in that nobody would want to reproduce the equivalent of, say, a somewhat obsolescent 10–year old petrochemical plant.

Replacement cost. This attempts to measure the cost of now creating a productive capacity equivalent to that which now exists, even though the form of the replacement plant might be quite different from the existing one.

---

3. In Lewis v. Scotten Dillon Co., 306 A.2d 755 (Del.Ch.1973), the court indicated that a § 152 defense would not be available where the directors valuing the consideration were affected by a conflict of interest.

Liquidation value. This refers to the amount that might be realized on a forced sale, as by an auction. Typically, this is a very low figure since any values arising from having a well-organized and functioning going concern are normally squeezed out.

Market value. Where truly available, market value is the primary indicator. But there are markets and markets. The organized securities exchanges which we will explore hereafter (p. 536 infra), provide finely-tuned indications of what a number of expensive analysts think about the value of a security that is widely traded. Even here there are cautions and limitations. The market reflects what is now being done with an asset and may not take into account the possibility that under different management it might be treated quite differently. Also, the quoted price refers to sales of relatively small blocks of stock and it is unsafe to extrapolate such quotations to large chunks of the security. In other markets such as the real estate market no two parcels are exactly the same and somebody must bridge that gap from the sale price of parcels X and Y to the price that Z would fetch.

Earnings value. It is now the prevailing practice to set the price of productive assets (and securities) through some method based on its net earnings (or its cash flow). In a sense the market value may be the product of calculations by various buyers and sellers of the earnings value of that security. Earnings valuation is a complex process and one can learn about it at various levels of sophistication and complexity. Here we keep it very general and schematic. First, one estimates the expected earnings of the asset for each of the successive years worth thinking about. One discounts the earnings of future years by an appropriate discount rate in order to get their present value. One then adds the successive discounted returns to calculate the present value. Obviously there are complexities to be added on in the real world. It is likely that instead of there being one expected future earning stream there are several likely alternatives. One can calculate each of the streams and multiply it by its probability and then combine the different alternatives to make one probability. It is not always easy to select the correct discount rate. That rate should reflect the risk that inheres in the investment compared so that it is comparable to the yield on similarly chancy investments.

Bibliography: A useful short introduction to valuation is Gould & Caddington, How Do You Know What Your Business is Worth? (Small Business Administration Management Aid No. 166, 1964), reprinted in D. Herwitz, Business Planning 1–7 (1966). B. Graham, D. Dodd & S. Cottle, Security Analysis, Principles and Technique (4th ed. 1962) is the fundamentalist's bible; a new edition is reportedly on the way. Any financial coursebook will spend time on earnings valuation techniques, e.g., R. Brealey & S. Myers, Principles of Corporate Finance 164–88 (2d ed. 1984). Part I of V. Brudney & M. Chirelstein, Corporate Finance (2d ed. 1979) is devoted to valuation, as is Part I of R. Gilson, The Law and Finance of Corporate Acquisitions (1986). For a short introduction to earnings valuation see R. Clark, Corporate Law App. B (1986).

QUESTIONS

(1) Does the opinion in See v. Heppenheimer forbid valuation on the basis of the application of a standardized ratio to (a) the present or (b) the anticipated future earnings of the business taken over by the corporation? Or does it merely forbid shoddy or reckless approaches to such valuation? If you were asked to give an opinion to a New Jersey corporation today, and found no intervening authority, would you approve a valuation on an earnings basis made by a reputable expert after what seems to you to be a careful analysis?

(2) Suppose that the directors of a corporation offer to testify that they had been ready to pay cash for a business in the sum of $5,000,000 but that the purchaser had desired (for tax reasons, perhaps) $5,000,000 par value of stock. Should that have changed the court's view?

C. Low Par and No Par

The designation of a par value for stock seems to stem from the requirement in the early corporation statutes that the capital of a corporation be specified in a total dollar amount, divided into a speci- fied number of shares. See, e.g., Sec. 2 of ch. XI of Minn.Laws of 1873, at p. 141, supra. At that time it was generally provided or assumed that the corporation would not commence business until the total capital had been subscribed. Later the practice evolved of permitting the corporation simply to specify the number of shares of specified par value which the corporation was authorized to issue, leaving it to the incorporators and subsequently the directors how many of such shares would be issued. Under this approach the capital of the corporation was subject to the ready measure of par times the number of shares issued. However, this framework proved rather rigid, and also some- what delusive in lending an importance to the par value that it did not really have in the world of securities traders. Therefore moves were made in two directions that have tended to de-emphasize par value.

"Low par" is not strictly a legal category. It can best be defined as stock which has a par value initially set at a price substantially below the price at which stock is initially issued. Of course no matter what the original par value was, later issues after the corporation had proved successful would be priced at higher figures in fairness to the initial shareholders who got in "on the ground floor." To illustrate, if a stock is originally issued and sold at its par value of $100 a share and the corporation then succeeds in accumulating retained earnings of $50 per share, it would be clearly unfair to sell more stock to new purchasers for only $100. Such a dilution of the rights of the old stockholders would be a windfall to the newcomers and might be restrained by a court of equity.[4] Thus later issues of par stock by prosperous corpora- tions usually involve a price in excess of par, the difference being credited to some account such as capital surplus. What is different about low par is that the issuers know that even at the start there will be a substantial gap between the par value and the sales price. $1 or

4. See p. 642, infra.

even 10¢ par shares are common. Their popularity with management was not impaired by the fact that stock transfer taxes, until 1959, were measured by the amount of the stock's par value even if the par were set as low as a few pennies. Low par provides corporate financers with a certain degree of flexibility in some of the situations which we shall explore in this section. Among other things, it produces a capital surplus account which is more subject to management's discretion than is the legal capital account.

"No par" on the other hand is a creation of statutes (e.g., 8 Del.C. § 153) and is not permitted in those jurisdictions which have not authorized it. Here a corporation does not fix any specific par value. It issues stock from time to time at such prices as its board sees fit, the varying amounts thus received being credited to stated capital except to the extent that the law (e.g., 8 Del.C. § 154) gives the directors a discretion (and they choose to exercise it) to allocate only a part to stated capital. The lawmakers who introduced no par hoped not only that it would permit added flexibility in corporate financing, but also that it would prevent investors and creditors from being misled by statements as to par values and capital and would compel them to make more independent and more intelligent investigation of a corporation's true position. Not all of the hopes of the originators of no par have been met. And a shift from par to no par can entail state tax burdens. Gulf Oil Corp. v. State Tax Comm'n, 65 A.D.2d 157, 411 N.Y.S.2d 698 (3d Dept.1978).

Let us now examine the operative effects of par, low par and no par in three representative situations.

First, suppose that a corporation issued 1000 shares of $100 par stock at par. Its initial operations have exhausted its cash, but its management is optimistic enough to believe that with $50,000 more it can overcome all remaining obstacles. However, it finds that the best offer it can get involves issuing another 1000 shares for $50,000. It could perhaps offer shares with a $50 par value. This would, however, involve amending its certificate of incorporation to authorize such $50 par value shares. Since nobody seems to be very sure what the effect of a corporation having both $50 and $100 par value common shares would be or whether it is legally possible, it would probably also involve an amendment to cut to $50 the par value of the shares already issued at $100. A few courts have adopted a doctrine which permits a corporation to deal with this situation even though it involves an issue at a price below par. This rule is known, after the leading case, as the doctrine of Handley v. Stutz.[5]

Second, note that many states have a statute prescribing that stock can only be issued for specific types of consideration—defined much more narrowly than the general usage employed in connection with the law of contracts. Delaware's Constitution (art. IX, § 3) and laws

---

5. 139 U.S. 417, 11 S.Ct. 530, 35 L.Ed. 227 (1891).

(§ 152) are examples of such provisions. The theory of such statutes perhaps emerges more clearly from a version formerly prevailing in Michigan:

> "*Provided,* that only such property shall be so taken in payment for capital stock as the purposes of the corporation shall require, and only such property as can be sold and transferred by the corporation, and as shall be subject to levy and sale on execution, or other process issued out of any court having competent jurisdiction, for the satisfaction of any judgment or decree against such corporation." [6]

Note that this requirement as to the "quality" of the consideration creates certain problems in the not uncommon situation where one participant promises to furnish services and another cash to the new organization.

Third, any issue of stock for consideration other than cash involves the problem of valuation. The entrepreneurs must agree upon the relative values assigned to their respective contributions; these values in turn have their impact on the actions of creditors and others who deal with the corporation. As we have seen, some promoters have deliberately inflated values for the purpose of affording a false sense of security to creditors. We have also seen that quite apart from promoters with low standards of morality, valuation is a difficult problem about which reasonable and honest observers can differ. It is possible for courts in contemplating the wreckage of a business enterprise to deal too harshly with the promoters. Particularly where a "true value" rule is in force, the trier of fact is invited to "second guess" the entrepreneurs at a time when their original assumptions, however validly based, have been disproved. The debris of an enterprise that failed often retains no hint of the hopes that inspired its creators. Even where a rule is in force that the directors' valuation is final "in the absence of fraud" the stockholders run some risk of being found liable.

It was thought by proponents of no par stock that this sort of problem would be eliminated by that new device, as the following excerpt from Johnson v. Louisville Trust Co.[7] illustrates:

> ". . . the generally, if not universally, accepted theory of the purpose of such statutes is that they are intended to do away with both the 'trust fund' and 'holding out' doctrines . . . As Mr. Cook says:
>
>> 'The whole theory of stock without par value is "let the buyer beware" and "let the creditor beware." ' "

---

6. 2 Mich.Comp.L.1915, § 9018, as construed in Brown v. Weeks, 195 Mich. 27, 161 N.W. 945 (1917) (the case of the Coronet Corset Company). For a case with modern facts see Prickett v. Allen, 475 S.W.2d 308 (Tex.Civ.App.1971) (computer software package may be "labor done" but probably not "property actually received").

7. 293 Fed. 857 (6th Cir.1923).

Some writers find it not so clear that one can transfer assets to a corporation and be certain that no liability will result if it is later determined that the property was worth less than the promoters believed.[8] To form your own opinion on this, read the following case.

G. LOEWUS & CO. v. HIGHLAND QUEEN PACKING CO.

Court of Chancery of New Jersey, 1939.
125 N.J.Eq. 534, 6 A.2d 545.

BIGELOW, V.C.   The receiver of the defendant, Highland Queen Packing Company, an insolvent New Jersey corporation, prays that its three stockholders be assessed a sum sufficient to pay creditors and administration expenses, on the theory that their stock is not fully paid.

The stock is without par value, issued pursuant to R.S. 14:8–6, N.J. S.A. 14:8–6, "Every corporation organized under this title may issue and may sell its authorized shares without nominal or par value, from time to time, for such consideration as may be prescribed in the certificate of incorporation, or, if so provided in the certificate of incorporation, as from time to time may be fixed by the board of directors. . . .

"Any and all shares without nominal or par value issued as permitted by this article shall be deemed fully paid and nonassessable, and the holder of such shares shall not be liable to the corporation or its creditors in respect thereof."

Defendant's certificate of incorporation, pursuant to the statute, authorizes the board of directors to fix the price of the stock. The directors, at their organization meeting, received and accepted an offer from two of the respondents, Jesse B. Triplett and Boice E. Triplett, to sell to the corporation the business then being conducted by them in consideration of the assumption of debts, and especially a note to the third respondent, Edgar H. Lackey, for $950 and for the further consideration of 300 shares of capital stock to be divided among the three respondents: "It is understood that the said shares of stock shall be issued at the price of $20 per share and representing a total value of $6,000."

The sale was consummated, and the stock issued. As part of the transaction, Lackey paid the company $1,050 which he had promised the Tripletts to put in the business. The corporation books show a debt to Lackey of $2,000, namely, the amount of the promissory note, plus his additional payment, but Lackey denies that the company is so indebted to him. "I was not in charge of the books of the defendant corporation nor did I have an opportunity to examine them before the receiver was appointed in this case. In truth, I gave the said sum of $2,000 in payment for the said stock."

The assets and good will of the business turned over by the Tripletts to the corporation were worth only $1,500, so it is alleged. The receiver takes the position that the consideration for the stock

---

8. Israels, Problems of Par and No–Par
Shares: A Reappraisal, 47 Colum.L.Rev.
1279 (1947).

fixed by the directors was $20 per share, or a total of $6,000, of which only $1,500, or $1,500 plus $1,050, has been paid, and that there is owing by the stockholders the difference or so much thereof as may be necessary to satisfy creditors.

The duty of holders of par value stock—as distinguished from non-par stock—to contribute toward the payment of creditors finds three supports: One is the contract of the subscriber to pay a certain amount for his shares. Milliken v. Caruso, 205 N.Y. 559, 98 N.E. 493. Upon the insolvency of the company and the abandonment of its business, he is relieved of his obligation except so far as may be necessary to satisfy creditors. But his contractual debt to that extent remains enforceable at the suit of creditors or receiver. Second comes the trust fund or fraud theory which rests liability upon the representation or holding out to persons extending credit to the company, that its capital, in a certain sum, has been paid in full. The third basis for liability is statutory. "It depends upon the stockholder's voluntary acceptance, for considerations touching his own interest, of a statutory scheme to which watered stock, under whatever device issued, is absolutely alien, and which requires stock subscriptions to be made good for the benefit of creditors of insolvent companies." Easton National Bank v. American Brick Co., 70 N.J.Eq. 732, 738, 64 A. 917, 920, 8 L.R.A.,N.S., 271, 10 Ann.Cas. 84.

The statutory plan on which stockholders' liability depends is found principally in [a section] which provides that where the capital shall not have been paid in full, and the capital paid shall be insufficient to satisfy debts, each stockholder shall be bound to pay the sum necessary to complete the amount of each share held by him or such proportion thereof as shall be required to satisfy the creditors. . . . In the event less than the full amount of the stock is paid and the company becomes insolvent, the stockholders are liable to pay in the balance regardless of any contract or understanding which they had with the corporation, for any agreement by the company to accept less than par is void as to creditors. Liability does not depend on a "holding out" to creditors.

Par value stock has a definite value, fixed by the certificate of incorporation, stated in terms of dollars, but it may be issued for money or property or services. Stock without par value is issued for a "consideration" prescribed by the certificate of incorporation or by directors or stockholders. The consideration fixed may be money or property, or anything that constitutes a good and valuable consideration. Likewise, in the case of insolvency, pretty much the same principles determine the obligations of subscribers and holders of either class of stock. If the consideration for non-par stock is duly fixed at $20 a share, and only $10 a share is paid in, then R.S. 14:8–13, N.J.S.A. 14:8–13, becomes effective and the stockholders may be assessed. Or if the consideration be certain property and the stock is issued though only a part of the property is transferred to the corporation, the stockholders must answer to the call of creditors.

Counsel for respondents direct attention to the provision in R.S. 14:8–6, N.J.S.A. 14:8–6, that "shares without nominal or par value issued as permitted by this article shall be deemed fully paid and nonassessable, and the holder of such shares shall not be liable to the corporation or its creditors in respect thereof." A similar provision relating to par value stock issued for property is found in R.S. 14:3–9,

N.J.S.A. 14:3–9, and has been part of our statute law many years. "The stock so issued shall be fully paid stock and not liable to any further call." Prior to 1917, the statute also declared, "neither shall the holder thereof be liable for any further payment under any of the provisions of this act." Despite these provisions, a holder, with notice, of par value stock issued for property at an inflated valuation is liable to creditors. So when stock without par value is issued for less than the prescribed consideration, it is outside the plan of the statute, and the holder thereof, with notice, is liable for the balance of the consideration, or so much thereof as may satisfy creditors.

Another clause of R.S. 14:8–6, N.J.S.A. 14:8–6, gives the board of directors, within 30 days after issuance of such stock, power to allocate part of the consideration to surplus. Dividends may be made out of the surplus thus created, but not out of the capital. R.S. 14:8–19, N.J.S.A. 14:8–19. Since the directors of the defendant corporation did not exercise this power, I need not consider the possible effect on creditors' rights, of an assignment to surplus of part of the consideration for which the stock was issued.

The question remains whether there was delivered to the corporation in exchange for the stock the full consideration as fixed by the directors. Careful examination of the minutes satisfies me that the only consideration which the Tripletts offered to give and the directors agreed to accept was the transfer of the business conducted by the Tripletts. The directors, by accepting the offer, fixed the consideration for the stock within the intent of R.S. 14:8–13, N.J.S.A. 14:8–13. The meaning of the statement in the minutes that the stock should be issued at the price of $20 per share, or a total value of $6,000, is not clear. Certainly the parties did not intend that $6,000 should be paid in, additional to the transfer of the business, or even that the difference between $6,000 and the value of the business should be paid in. Probably the sentence has some relation to the deal with Lackey, who was paying $2,000 for a third interest in the enterprise.

The duly fixed consideration for the stock was fully satisfied and the stockholders are not assessable.

The receiver also asks that the Tripletts be ordered to deliver to the receiver certain formulas which, he claims, they sold to the corporation. The proofs disclose, however, that they sold only the right to use the formulas so long as the corporation should exist as a going concern. Order denied.

QUESTIONS

(1) Recall the problem presented of a corporation that, because of initial difficulties, can find buyers for its $100 par value stock at no price above $50. Can the Delaware statute (8 Del.C. §§ 153, 162(a)) be so construed as to allow this? If it were possible how would the corporation reflect it on its books? Could adoption initially of a low par or no par approach forestall this problem?

(2) Suppose that three people wish to combine to form a corporation to run a wine business. A has cash, B has some casks of inventory of disputed value and C will agree to run the store. They agree as between themselves that each contribution is about equal, being worth around $10,000. Can one simply issue shares for those amounts? Does no par or low par present a direct solution? Or can they be used to create a solution somewhat more indirectly?

(3) Is it clear that a transaction such as that in Loewus is immune from attack? Consider the issue under 8 Del.C. §§ 153, 154, 162(a) and recollect the entry that must be made to reflect this transaction. Are there advantages to using a low par solution?

---

3. Balancing Debt and Equity

One of the problems encountered in establishing a corporation is the proper mixture of capital and debt. Some of the considerations are strictly business matters. Sophisticated lenders may not be willing to advance funds unless they are assured that there is a reasonable ratio between the equity and debt components. They would fear that without a reasonable "cushion" losses might rather quickly eat away the corporation's assets to the point where not enough was left to pay their claims. They would wish to have funds derived from equity available to cover payments of their interest during periods of unprofitable operation. If they are willing to lend to a corporation with a rather "thin" equity they may charge a very high rate of interest for doing so. Lenders may be willing to tolerate a higher debt/equity ratio if the corporation has a long history of successful operation or if they are given security in a specific piece of collateral that gives them adequate protection. From the entrepreneurs' point of view, then, there are limits to the proportion of debt their firm should have. On the other hand, there are factors pushing them to get as high a ratio as possible. If the enterprise succeeds the holders of the equity will capture all of the gains in income beyond that needed to make the fixed payments on the debt. This leverage factor appeals to the adventurous (it is accompanied by a corresponding danger that nothing will come to the equity if things take even a mild downturn). In some lines of business, such as banking and securities brokerage, debt/equity ratios are specified by legislative or regulatory provisions.

If the same group of entrepreneurs provide all of the funds they may wish to cast that contribution in the form of a mixture of debt and equity. The resulting ratio may be different from that which would have been arrived at as a result of arm's length bargaining between themselves and a bank. They may wish to preserve for the corporation a large deduction for interest paid and for themselves a chance to compete on equal terms with the creditors. The first problem is properly the subject of the course in taxation and the second is dealt with in the following case.

COSTELLO v. FAZIO

United States Court of Appeals, Ninth Circuit, 1958.
256 F.2d 903.

HAMLEY, CIRCUIT JUDGE. Creditors' claims against the bankrupt estate of Leonard Plumbing and Heating Supply, Inc., were filed by J.A. Fazio and Lawrence C. Ambrose. The trustee in bankruptcy objected to these claims, and moved for an order subordinating them to the claims of general unsecured creditors. The referee in bankruptcy denied the motion, and his action was sustained by the district court. The trustee appeals.

The following facts are not in dispute: A partnership known as "Leonard Plumbing and Heating Supply Co." was organized in October, 1948. The three partners, Fazio, Ambrose, and B.T. Leonard, made initial capital contributions to the business aggregating $44,806.40. The capital contributions of the three partners, as they were recorded on the company books in September 1952, totaled $51,620.78, distributed as follows: Fazio $43,169.61; Ambrose, $6,451.17; and Leonard, $2,000.

In the fall of that year, it was decided to incorporate the business. In contemplation of this step, Fazio and Ambrose, on September 15, 1952, withdrew all but $2,000 apiece of their capital contributions to the business. This was accomplished by the issuance to them, on that date, of partnership promissory notes in the sum of $41,169.61 and $4,451.17, respectively. These were demand notes, no interest being specified. The capital contribution to the partnership business then stood at $6,000–$2,000 for each partner.

The closing balance sheet of the partnership showed current assets to be $160,791.87, and current liabilities at $162,162.22. There were also fixed assets in the sum of $6,482.90, and other assets in the sum of $887.45. The partnership had cash on hand in the sum of $66.66, and an overdraft at the bank in the amount of $3,422.78.

Of the current assets, $41,357.76, representing "Accounts receivable—Trade," was assigned to American Trust Co., to secure $50,000 of its $59,000 in notes payable. Both before and after the incorporation, the business had a $75,000 line of credit with American Trust Co., secured by accounts receivable and the personal guaranty of the three partners and stockholders, and their marital communities.

The net sales of the partnership during its last year of operations were $389,543.72, as compared to net sales of $665,747.55 in the preceding year. A net loss of $22,521.34 was experienced during this last year, as compared to a net profit of $40,935.12 in the year ending September 30, 1951.

Based on the reduced capitalization of the partnership, the corporation was capitalized for six hundred shares of no par value common stock valued at ten dollars per share. Two hundred shares were issued to each of the three partners in consideration of the transfer to the corporation of their interest in the partnership. Fazio became president, and Ambrose, secretary-treasurer of the new corporation. Both were directors. The corporation assumed all liabilities of the partnership, including the notes to Fazio and Ambrose.

In June 1954, after suffering continued losses, the corporation made an assignment to the San Francisco Board of Trade for the benefit of creditors. On October 8, 1954, it filed a voluntary petition in bankruptcy. At this time, the corporation was not indebted to any creditors whose obligations were incurred by the pre-existing partnership, saving the promissory notes issued to Fazio and Ambrose.

Fazio filed a claim against the estate in the sum of $34,147.55, based on the promissory note given to him when the capital of the partnership was reduced. Ambrose filed a similar claim in the sum of $7,871.17. The discrepancy between these amounts and the amounts of the promissory notes is due to certain set-offs and transfers not here in issue.

In asking that these claims be subordinated to the claims of general unsecured creditors, the trustee averred that the amounts in question represent a portion of the capital investment in the partnership. It was alleged that the transfer of this sum from the partnership capital account to an account entitled "Loans from Copartners," effectuated a scheme and plan to place copartners in the same class as unsecured creditors. The trustee further alleged, with respect to each claimant:

> ". . . If said claimant is permitted to share in the assets of said bankrupt now in the hands of the trustee, in the same parity with general unsecured creditors, he will receive a portion of the capital invested which should be used to satisfy the claims of creditors before any capital investment can be returned to the owners and stockholders of said bankrupt."

A hearing was held before the referee in bankruptcy. In addition to eliciting the above recounted facts, three expert witnesses called by the trustee, and one expert witness called by the claimants, expressed opinions on various phases of the transaction.

Clifford V. Heimbucher, a certified public accountant and management consultant, called by the trustee, expressed the view that, at the time of incorporation, capitalization was inadequate. He further stated that, in incorporating a business already in existence, where the approximate amount of permanent capital needed has been established by experience, normal procedure called for continuing such capital in the form of common or preferred stock.

Stating that only additional capital needed temporarily is normally set up as loans, Heimbucher testified that ". . . the amount of capital employed in the business was at all times substantially more than the $6,000 employed in the opening of the corporation." He also expressed the opinion that, at the time of incorporation, there was "very little hope [of financial success] in view of the fact that for the year immediately preceding the opening of the corporation, losses were running a little less than $2,000 a month. . . ."

William B. Logan, a business analyst and consultant called by the trustee, expressed the view that $6,000 was inadequate capitalization for this company.[9] John S. Curran, a business analyst, also called by

---

9. He testified:

"A. . . . In 1952, that same year, of about 124 companies in this particular line, the average ratio of turnover of net worth of capital to sales ranged between three and five times. On this basis here,

on $6,000, with a sales of approximately $400,000, it would have better than 60, 65-time turnover which certainly is quite a contrast from a three to five-time turnover. Q. Is a sixty-times turnover feasible at

the trustee, expressed the view that the corporation needed at least as much capital as the partnership required prior to the reduction of capital.

Robert H. Laborde, Jr., a certified public accountant, had handled the accounting problems of the partnership and corporation. He was called by the trustee as an adverse witness, pursuant to § 21, sub. j of the Bankruptcy Act, 11 U.S.C.A. § 44, sub. j. Laborde readily conceded that the transaction whereby Fazio and Ambrose obtained promissory notes from the partnership was for the purpose of transferring a capital account into a loan or debt account. He stated that this was done in contemplation of the formation of the corporation, and with knowledge that the partnership was losing money.

The prime reason for incorporating the business, according to Laborde, was to protect the personal interest of Fazio, who had made the greatest capital contribution to the business. In this connection, it was pointed out that the "liabilities on the business as a partnership were pretty heavy." There was apparently also a tax angle. Laborde testified that it was contemplated that the notes would be paid out of the profits of the business. He agreed that, if promissory notes had not been issued, the profits would have been distributed only as dividends, and that as such they would have been taxable.

Claimants, in their brief, say that Laborde "testified that in his opinion the bankrupt corporation was adequately capitalized at the inception of its corporate existence for several reasons. . . ." We find no support in the record for this statement, and claimants have cited none.[10]

Laborde did express the opinion that the corporation had adequate working capital at the time of incorporation. This was disputed by Heimbucher and Curran. They called attention to the fact that the corporate books showed that current liabilities exceeded current assets at that time, and that there was thus a minus working capital on the opening day of business of the corporation.[11]

---

all? A. Impossible strictly from the capitalization standpoint. . . ."

10. Laborde was asked to state what "opinion" he gave the incorporators and whether he still entertained it. This question was not specifically referenced to adequacy of capital, and the answer given does not reveal the witness' opinion on that subject. The following question was then asked and answered: "Q. And did you express an opinion as to whether or not the stated capital of $6,000.00, having in mind the execution of corporate notes for the remainder of what had been the capital accounts of the partners, would with the other assets of the business be sufficient in your opinion for the corporation to carry on successfully? A. Yes." The witness was not thereafter asked to state what the opinion was that he had expressed, or what was his present opinion on the subject.

11. Current liabilities then exceeded current assets by $1,370.35. Laborde's opinion that there was adequate working capital was apparently based upon the fact that the corporation had a $75,000 line of credit with American Trust Company. Where repayment of loans made under such a line of credit is to be extended over a long term, the result may be to increase working capital. This is because current assets are then offset, not by current liabilities, but by fixed liabilities. But here the loans made under this line of credit were secured by accounts receivable. Where this is the case, the obligations to repay are uniformly classified as current, rather than fixed, liabilities. They were so classified in this case, and in fact the balance sheet of October 1, 1952, lists no fixed liabilities.

Working capital is the excess of current assets over current liabilities. Since the loans made under this line of credit increased current assets and current liabilities in equal amounts, the net change in working capital was nil. Heimbucher's testimony to this effect is undisputed, and

In any event, when we speak of inadequacy of capital in regard to whether loans to shareholders shall be subordinated to claims of general creditors, we are not referring to working capital. We are referring to the amount of the investment of the shareholders in the corporation. This capital is usually referred to as legal capital, or stated capital in reference to restrictions on the declaration of dividends to stockholders.[12] As before stated, Laborde expressed no opinion as to the adequacy of proprietary capital put at the risk of the business. On the other hand, the corporate accounts and the undisputed testimony of three accounting experts demonstrate that stated capital was wholly inadequate.

On the evidence produced at this hearing, as summarized above, the referee found that the paid-in stated capital of the corporation at the time of its incorporation was adequate for the continued operation of the business. He found that while Fazio and Ambrose controlled and dominated the corporation and its affairs they did not mismanage the business. He further found that claimants did not practice any fraud or deception, and did not act for their own personal or private benefit and to the detriment of the corporation or its stockholders and creditors. The referee also found that the transaction which had been described was not a part of any scheme or plan to place the claimants in the same class as unsecured creditors of the partnership.

On the basis of these findings, the referee concluded that, in procuring the promissory notes, the claimants acted in all respects in good faith and took no unfair advantage of the corporation, or of its stockholders or creditors.

Pursuant to § 39, sub. c of the Bankruptcy Act, 11 U.S.C.A. § 67, sub. c, the trustee filed a petition for review of the referee's order. The district court, after examining the record certified to it by the referee, entered an order affirming the order of the referee.

On this appeal, the trustee advances two grounds for reversal of the district court order. The first of these is that claims of controlling shareholders will be deferred or subordinated to outside creditors where a corporation in bankruptcy has not been adequately or honestly capitalized, or has been managed to the prejudice of creditors, or where to do otherwise would be unfair to creditors.

As a basis for applying this asserted rule in the case before us, the trustee challenges most of the findings of fact noted above.

The district court and this court are required to accept the findings of the referee in bankruptcy, unless such findings are clearly erroneous.

The factual conclusion of the referee, that the paid-in capital of the corporation at the time of its incorporation was adequate for the continued operation of the business, was based upon certain accounting data and the expert testimony of four witnesses. The accounting data, summarized above, is contained in the opening balance sheet and the

is in accord with recognized principles of accounting. See "Accounting and the Law," Dohr–Thompson–Warren, 2d Ed., The Foundation Press, Inc., 1955, pages 25, 259–263.

12. Capital in the sense of legal or stated capital measures the amount of the margin of assets over debts and liabilities

required to be retained as a condition of granting the shareholders of the privilege of trading in a corporate capacity with limited liability. 23 Cal.L.Rev. 229, "Corporate Capital and Restrictions upon Dividends under Modern Corporation Laws," Ballantine and Hills.

comparative profit and loss statements of the corporation, and is not in dispute.

It does not require the confirmatory opinion of experts to determine from this data that the corporation was grossly undercapitalized. In the year immediately preceding incorporation, net sales aggregated $390,000. In order to handle such a turnover, the partners apparently found that capital in excess of $50,000 was necessary. They actually had $51,620.78 in the business at that time. Even then, the business was only "two jumps ahead of the wolf." A net loss of $22,000 was sustained in that year; there was only $66.66 in the bank; and there was an overdraft of $3,422.78.

Yet, despite this precarious financial condition, Fazio and Ambrose withdrew $45,620.78 of the partnership capital—more than eighty-eight per cent of the total capital. The $6,000 capital left in the business was only one-sixty-fifth of the last annual net sales. All this is revealed by the books of the company.

But if there is need to confirm this conclusion that the corporation was gross[ly] undercapitalized, such confirmation is provided by three of the four experts who testified. The fourth expert, called by appellees, did not express an opinion to the contrary.

We therefore hold that the factual conclusion of the referee, that the corporation was adequately capitalized at the time of its organization, is clearly erroneous.

The factual conclusion of the trial court, that the claimants, in withdrawing capital from the partnership in contemplation of incorporation, did not act for their own personal or private benefit and to the detriment of the corporation or of its stockholders and creditors, is based upon the same accounting data and expert testimony.

Laborde, testifying for the claimants, made it perfectly clear that the depletion of the capital account in favor of a debt account was for the purpose of equalizing the capital investments of the partners and to reduce tax liability when there were profits to distribute. It is therefore certain, contrary to the finding just noted, that, in withdrawing this capital, Fazio and Ambrose did act for their own personal and private benefit.

It is equally certain, from the undisputed facts, that in so doing they acted to the detriment of the corporation and its creditors. The best evidence of this is what happened to the business after incorporation, and what will happen to its creditors if the reduction in capital is allowed to stand. The likelihood that business failure would result from such undercapitalization should have been apparent to anyone who knew the company's financial and business history and who had access to its balance sheet and profit and loss statements. Three expert witnesses confirmed this view, and none expressed a contrary opinion.

Accordingly, we hold that the factual conclusion, that the claimants, in withdrawing capital, did not act for their own personal or private benefit and to the detriment of the corporation and creditors, is clearly erroneous.

Recasting the facts in the light of what is said above, the question which appellant presents is this:

Where, in connection with the incorporation of a partnership, and for their own personal and private benefit, two partners who are to become officers, directors, and controlling stockholders of the corporation, convert the bulk of their capital contributions into loans, taking promissory notes, thereby leaving the partnership and succeeding corporation grossly undercapitalized, to the detriment of the corporation and its creditors, should their claims against the estate of the subsequently bankrupted corporation be subordinated to the claims of the general unsecured creditors?

The question almost answers itself.

In allowing and disallowing claims, courts of bankruptcy apply the rules and regulations of equity jurisprudence. Pepper v. Litton, 308 U.S. 295, 304, 60 S.Ct. 238, 84 L.Ed. 281. Where the claim is found to be inequitable, it may be set aside (Pepper v. Litton, supra), or subordinated to the claims of other creditors. As stated in Taylor v. Standard Gas Co., supra, 306 U.S. at page 315, 59 S.Ct. at page 547, the question to be determined when the plan or transaction which gives rise to a claim is challenged as inequitable is "whether, within the bounds of reason and fairness, such a plan can be justified."

Where, as here, the claims are filed by persons standing in a fiduciary relationship to the corporation, another test which equity will apply is "whether or not under all the circumstances the transaction carries the earmarks of an arm's length bargain." Pepper v. Litton, supra, 308 U.S. at page 306, 60 S.Ct. at page 245.[13]

Under either of these tests, the transaction here in question stands condemned.

Appellees argue that more must be shown than mere undercapitalization if the claims are to be subordinated. Much more than mere undercapitalization was shown here. Persons serving in a fiduciary relationship to the corporation actually withdrew capital already committed to the business, in the face of recent adverse financial experience. They stripped the business of eighty-eight per cent of its stated capital at a time when it had a minus working capital and had suffered substantial business losses. This was done for personal gain, under circumstances which charge them with knowledge that the corporation and its creditors would be endangered. Taking advantage of their fiduciary position, they thus sought to gain equality of treatment with general creditors.

In Taylor v. Standard Gas & Electric Co., 306 U.S. 307, 59 S.Ct. 543, 83 L.Ed. 669, and some other cases, there was fraud and mismanagement present in addition to undercapitalization. Appellees argue from this that fraud and mismanagement must always be present if claims are to be subordinated in a situation involving undercapitalization.

This is not the rule. The test to be applied, as announced in the Taylor case and quoted above, is whether the transaction can be justified "within the bounds of reason and fairness." In the more recent Heiser case, supra, 327 U.S. pages 732–733, 66 S.Ct. at page 856,

13. Claims based on transactions involving officers, directors, or controlling stockholders of the bankrupt corporation are always suspect. As the court said in Pepper v. Litton, supra, 308 U.S. at pages 307–308, 60 S.Ct. at page 246: ". . . In the exercise of its equitable jurisdiction the bankruptcy court has the power to sift the circumstances surrounding any claim to see that injustice or unfairness is not done in administration of the bankrupt estate. And its duty so to do is especially clear when the claim seeking allowance accrues to the benefit of an officer, director, or stockholder. . . ."

the Supreme Court made clear, in these words, that fraud is not an essential ingredient:

> ". . . In appropriate cases, acting upon equitable principles, it [bankruptcy court] may also subordinate the claim of one creditor to those of others in order to prevent the consummation of a course of conduct by the claimant, which, as to them, would be fraudulent *or otherwise inequitable.* . . ." (Emphasis supplied.)

The fact that the withdrawal of capital occurred prior to incorporation is immaterial. This transaction occurred in contemplation of incorporation. The participants then occupied a fiduciary relationship to the partnership; and expected to become controlling stockholders, directors, and officers of the corporation. This plan was effectuated, and they were serving in those fiduciary capacities when the corporation assumed the liabilities of the partnership, including the notes here in question.

Nor is the fact that the business, after being stripped of necessary capital, was able to survive long enough to have a turnover of creditors a mitigating circumstance. The inequitable conduct of appellees consisted not in acting to the detriment of creditors then known, but in acting to the detriment of present or future creditors, whoever they may be.

In our opinion, it was error to affirm the order of the referee denying the motion to subordinate the claims in question. We do not reach appellant's other major contention, that the notes are not provable in bankruptcy because they were to be paid only out of profits, and there were no profits.

Reversed and remanded for further proceedings not inconsistent with this opinion.

QUESTIONS

(1) To understand what happened in Costello v. Fazio try to construct, insofar as possible, the balance sheet of the firm before and after these transactions. In what sense did Fazio and Ambrose withdraw the partnership capital? What is the difference between legal capital and working capital? Which is significant for purposes of cases like this? If there had been no withdrawal but only an original contribution, would the case come out differently?

(2) From what source does the court derive its ruling in this case? Would its precedential value be affected by a later contrary ruling of the California Supreme Court? Or by the 1978 revision in the Bankruptcy Code (11 U.S.C.A. § 510(c)?

(3) Suppose that corporation X has $100,000 worth of debts and $10,000 of capital stock. The capital stock is owned entirely by a parent corporation Y which holds $50,000 of the debt as well. Y owes $20,000 to various creditors. Both X and Y become insolvent. X has $30,000 of assets and Y has nothing except its investment in X. How should the $30,000 be divided?

(4) In a projected revision of the Bankruptcy Act it was proposed that *all* debt claims of parent corporations and other stockholders be subordinated. Is such a solution justified? Superior to that in Costello v. Fazio?

(5) What is the relationship between veil-piercing (discussed in Chapter 4) and subordination? Which has the more drastic effect upon the entrepreneur involved?

Bibliography: For further review of capitalization problems, see D. Herwitz, Business Planning Ch. 1 (1966). Israels, Problems of Par and No Par Shares: A Reappraisal, 47 Colum.L.Rev. 1279 (1947), is still a classic. Manne, Accounting for Share Issues Under Modern Corporation Laws, 54 N.W.U.L.Rev. 285 (1959), covers accounting aspects. A comprehensive and straightforward student approach is offered by B. Manning, A Concise Textbook on Legal Capital (2d ed. 1981).

Both veil-piercing and subordination are treated in Clark, The Duties of the Corporate Debtor to its Creditors, 90 Harv.L.Rev. 505 (1977) and in a dialogue between Professors Landers and Posner, 42 U.Chi.L.Rev. 589, 43 id. 499, 43 id. 527 (1975–76).

---

4. Public Distribution of Securities and its Regulatory Framework

A careful consideration of the process of distributing securities to the public and of the complex body of federal and state regulation that has been imposed on it would amount to a course in itself. However, it seems that a basic conception of the field should be part of the equipment of any corporation lawyer.

The treatment in this Section assumes that it has been decided not to resort for financing to a single institution but to seek to lodge the securities with a broader group. This may be accomplished by the issuing corporation itself but ordinarily one needs the help of a professional—an underwriter. Only the underwriter will usually have the broad network of contacts with potential investors and the expertise in timing and pricing the securities one decides to issue. An underwriter is usually a broker/dealer and thus has a list of investors and some knowledge of their needs and preferences. Note that the term "underwriter" is a bit misleading since what an underwriter really does is buy the security and resell it. An underwriter does not normally guarantee the sale of the security except in that sense.

The first step is to decide whether the offering the corporation proposes to make must in fact be registered with the Securities and Exchange Commission (and secondarily what state-level proceedings must be taken care of). It is obviously desirable in terms of speed and economy from the entrepreneur's view to bypass that registration process. A brief description of what has to be done if registration cannot be avoided follows the treatment of exemptions.[14]

---

14. The issuance and distribution of securities to the public involves their introduction into the securities market in which issues are further traded. Thus it may be desirable now to read pp. 536–543 infra, in which those markets are described.

NOTE ON STATE REGULATION OF SECURITIES ISSUES

Before 1933 state law governed alone in this field. To illustrate, consider the following episode. William Z. Ripley, Harvard economics professor and author of a minatory book, Main Street and Wall Street (1927), obtained an interview with President Coolidge. He described to the President "the prestidigitation, double-shuffling, honey-fugling, horn swoggling and skulduggery" of Wall Street. William A. White [15] then recounts:

> "The President again leaned back in his chair, put his feet on the desk, closed and opened his eyes occasionally, clearly absorbing the Ripley story. His face was troubled. Finally he asked sadly: 'Well, Mr. Ripley, is there anything we can do down here?' In 1927, Ripley did not consider the organization of public utilities a federal matter. He answered: 'No, it's a state matter.'

> Trouble rolled away like a cloud, and the sunshine of sweet complacence bathed the Yankee head like a sunset in the Green Mountains. It was the ideal situation, a chance for that masterly inactivity for which he was so splendidly equipped."

With the disastrous crash of October, 1929 and the gradual emergence of revelations about misbehaviour in high places, not least the conviction for embezzlement of Richard Whitney, president of the New York Stock Exchange federal action became inevitable.[16]

The state rules are often referred to as "blue sky" laws, supposedly after an exclamation by a legislator during the passage of one of the early laws that stock salesmen were willing to sell investors anything, even the blue sky itself. These statutes vary a great deal both in their coverage and in their burdensomeness. There has been a tendency to make them relate better to the processes of the Securities and Exchange Commission so as to remove problems of inconsistent requirements. However, state law was not preempted by the 1933 federal rules. A number of state commissions still exercise the authority to disapprove issues of securities on substantive grounds such as a determination that they represent an unfair imposition on the public. California is regarded as particularly active in this respect. Thus it is a demanding job for an expert lawyer to clear through all the state commissions a securities issue for which the underwriters wish nationwide distribution.

---

15. A Puritan in Babylon 338 (1939).   **16.** J. Brooks, Once in Golconda (1969).

NOTE ON THE SECURITIES AND EXCHANGE COMMISSION

At this point it is appropriate to introduce one of the leading actors on the corporate stage today—the SEC. This agency, consisting of 5 commissioners with a moderate sized staff, was created by § 4 of the Securities Exchange Act of 1934. For a brief period, the Federal Trade Commission exercised functions under the Securities Act of 1933. It administers two far-reaching statutes, the Securities Act of 1933 and the 1934 Act. It also has functions under other, narrower, statutes such as the Public Utility Holding Company Act, the Investment Company Act, and the Trust Indenture Act. These Acts were not passed as an integrated whole and you will find their relations confusing at times. A comprehensive Federal Securities Code was drafted by the American Law Institute and published in 1980. Its enactment, which seems unlikely, would solve many of these discrepancies. Meanwhile the SEC is using its own authority to integrate the statutory mandates as far as possible.

The core of SEC's approach, unlike some of the state systems, has been not regulation but disclosure, a philosophy that the market would function best if investors were left to make their own decisions on the basis of full information. In recent years, there has been a tendency to reexamine the idea of disclosure, to ask whether it is in fact possible to convey complex data about corporations to an audience of millions of shareholders and, if so, how that can best be done. Disclosure was restudied in the SEC's Wheat Report [17] of 1969 which was reflected in various changes in the regulations, and then again in 1977 by a committee of outside experts headed by former Commissioner A.A. Sommer. The challenge of the 1980's comes from a somewhat different direction. Proponents of the efficient market theory (see p. 542 infra) assert that regulation is not necessary, that quite aside from regulation, the self-interest of those who seek to sell securities to the public would propel them into providing the information that security analysts would need. There is resistance to that theory and in particular supporters of mandatory requirements respond that there *is* a history of securities fraud and that there are operators who will take the money and run before the mechanisms of the efficient market catch up with them. [18]

The SEC differs in a number of respects from other regulatory commissions, particularly those in the transportation field. Its functions, at least with regard to the two principal statutes, are largely limited to compelling adequate disclosure. It does not approve or disapprove offerings of securities nor does it set rates or prices. The securities industry which it regulates is a relatively small world composed of relatively sophisticated people, including their lawyers. Un-

---

17. Disclosure to Investors—A Reappraisal of Federal Administrative Policies under the '33 and 34 Acts (S.E.C. 1969).

18. Seligman, The Historical Need for a Mandatory Corporate Disclosure System, 9 J.Corp.L. 1 (1983).

like railroad or air travel rates, most of the SEC's operations do not arouse intense public interest or generate widely-based political pressures. For these and other reasons the SEC has managed to keep up with its business with a relatively small staff. In the early, "heroic" days the Commissioners included several of the great names of the New Deal: William O. Douglas, Jerome Frank, Joseph Kennedy, and James M. Landis. More recently, most commissioners have been lawyers with practice in the securities field, persons of respectable standards at the very least. Thus while not immune from difficulties, specifically in the wake of Watergate, the SEC has not been in the center of the storms that have swirled about such regulatory agencies as the Interstate Commerce Commission.

The SEC is empowered to make rules by various portions of the acts it administers. It also has formal adjudicatory powers in several instances. In many cases it resorts to the federal courts to obtain injunctions against violations of law (it turns over some cases to the Department of Justice to be prosecuted criminally). By far the greatest portion of its employees' time is taken up with reviewing materials filed with the SEC—such as proxy materials, prospectuses, etc. In most cases the private parties will accede to the staff's requests or suggestions, giving way to its expertise and to its powerful position, particularly powerful when one considers how the factors of delay and adverse publicity would affect delicate financial operations. Actions by the SEC are made reviewable by §§ 9 and 25 of the Securities Act and the Exchange Act, respectively. Precisely what actions are so reviewable is a matter of some dispute.[19]

NOTE ON EXEMPTIONS

(1) To understand when it is that one can avoid registration you must orient yourself in the Securities Act of 1933 that governs this process; you should first examine Section 5 that sets forth the requirements that a registration statement be filed and a prospectus be furnished to each purchaser. Section 5 on its face casts a very wide net over all sorts of transactions, particularly if one recalls the generous construction given to the term "security". Sections 3 and 4 withdraw a good deal of the apparent scope of Section 5 by their exemptions. The lawyer advising a client involved in a fairly modest offering will normally consider three possibilities: (a) The intrastate exemption (§ 3(a)(11)); (b) the private offering exemption under § 4(2), which needs to be read in connection with the special definition of "underwriter" in § 2(11); and (c) exemptions, whole or partial, for small issues under § 3(b) as related to § 4(6). Each of these exemptions is explained below.

(2) The intrastate exemption has been the subject of SEC Rule 147 which states that it does not raise any presumption that the exemption "is not available for transactions by an issuer which do not satisfy all of the provisions of the rule." Nonetheless, it would take some temerity to

---

19. See, e.g., p. 409 infra.

give an opinion in a case that fell outside the Rule. Rule 147 gives more detail than the Act does about the qualifications of the issuer, which shall be deemed to do business within a state or territory if it derives 80% of gross revenues from business or property in the territory, has 80% of its assets there, intends to use 80% of the proceeds of the issue there and has its principal office there. Residence of offerees and purchasers is defined as the "principal residence" as to individuals and the "principal office" as to corporations. Securities sold under Rule 147 can be resold only to residents of the state for 9 months after the last sale by the issuer and precautions must be taken to nail this down: placing a legend on the certificate, giving instructions to the transfer agent and obtaining a written representation as to residence from each purchaser.

(3) The two cases which follow explore the meaning of the "private offering" exemption, which is plainly the most difficult of all to understand and probably the most difficult to use. In considering that exemption you should be aware of the differing contexts in which it is likely to be claimed. In a private placement blocks of securities, sometimes very large, are placed with insurance companies, banks or other institutions. Another context is the close corporation in which friends and associates of the entrepreneurs are to be invited to participate. Finally, there are transactions that attempt to be, in effect, minature public offerings going to the limit of the exemption. Ralston Purina, despite its relative age, is still *the* authoritative exposition of the exemption, particularly as it relates to the initial offering directly by the issuer. The Gilligan, Will case discusses the problems presented by the fact that purchasers buying directly from the issuer may be underwriters and may be, therefore, a part of the offering process. The SEC has attempted to create greater certainty in the application of the exemption while still protecting persons unable to fend for themselves. The present fruit of that attempt is Regulation D; you should examine the excerpts from that rule set forth in the Documentary Supplement. Regulation D states that failure to comply with its precise conditions shall not raise any presumption that the exemption provided by § 4(2) of the Act is not available. Still, issuer's counsel must necessarily feel somewhat concerned about going outside of the safe harbor provided by the Regulation. Observe that Rules 504, 505 and 506 provide slightly different exemptions. The emphasis on the dollar amounts of the offers shows that Regulation D is tied to § 3(b) of the Act as well as to § 4(2).

Since offerees under Regulation D are going to want to be able to resell their securities eventually one must also take account of Rule 144 on resales.

(4) The SEC has also exercised the exempting authority given it by § 3(b) of the Act through Regulation A. Rule 254 specifies that the offering cannot exceed a total of $1.5 million of all securities of the issuer in a twelve month period. An offering statement must be filed with the Commission 10 days before the first offering and an offering

circular must be used—but these are much simpler than the materials required for a regular registration.

(5) Counsel's opinion is of great importance in connection with exemptions and no sensible issuer would proceed to claim one without such an opinion. An erroneous opinion may provide a defense, in particular as to criminal prosecutions, but only if the reliance on it was reasonable. Giving an erroneous opinion may, on the other hand, create problems for a lawyer who may be faced with disqualification from practice before the SEC, with an injunction and with liability for damages.[20]

SECURITIES AND EXCHANGE COMMISSION v. RALSTON PURINA CO.

Supreme Court of the United States, 1953.
346 U.S. 119, 73 S.Ct. 981, 97 L.Ed. 1494.

MR. JUSTICE CLARK, delivered the opinion of the Court.

Section 4(1) of the Securities Act of 1933 exempts "transactions by an issuer not involving any public offering" from the registration requirements of § 5. We must decide whether Ralston Purina's offerings of treasury stock to its "key employees" are within this exemption. On a complaint brought by the Commission under § 20(b) of the Act seeking to enjoin respondent's unregistered offerings, the District Court held the exemption applicable and dismissed the suit. The Court of Appeals affirmed. The question has arisen many times since the Act was passed; an apparent need to define the scope of the private offering exemption prompted certiorari. 345 U.S. 903, 73 S.Ct. 643.

Ralston Purina manufactures and distributes various feed and cereal products. Its processing and distribution facilities are scattered throughout the United States and Canada, staffed by some 7,000 employees. At least since 1911 the company has had a policy of encouraging stock ownership among its employees; more particularly, since 1942 it has made authorized but unissued common shares available to some of them. Between 1947 and 1951, the period covered by the record in this case, Ralston Purina sold nearly $2,000,000 of stock to employees without registration and in so doing made use of the mails.

In each of these years, a corporate resolution authorized the sale of common stock "to employees . . . who shall, without any solicitation by the Company or its officers or employees, inquire of any of them as to how to purchase common stock of Ralston Purina Company." A memorandum sent to branch and store managers after the resolution was adopted, advised that "The only employees to whom this stock will be available will be those who take the initiative and are interested in buying stock at present market prices." Among those responding to these offers were employees with the duties of artist, bakeshop foreman, chow loading foreman, clerical assistant, copywriter, electrician,

---

20. See United States v. Custer Channel Wing Corp., 376 F.2d 675, 683 (4th Cir. 1967) (more buyers included than counsel advised); Matter of Schwebel, 40 S.E.C. 347 (1960) (lawyer is disqualified from practice before SEC for giving exemption opinions without adequate inquiry). Compare Popham, Haik, Schnobrich, Kaufman & Doty, Ltd. v. Newcomb Securities Co., 751 F.2d 1262 (D.C.Cir.1985).

stock clerk, mill office clerk, order credit trainee, production trainee, stenographer, and veterinarian.   The buyers lived in over fifty widely separated communities scattered from Garland, Texas, to Nashua, New Hampshire and Visalia, California.   The lowest salary bracket of those purchasing was $2,700 in 1949, $2,435 in 1950 and $3,107 in 1951.   The record shows that in 1947, 243 employees bought stock, 20 in 1948, 414 in 1949, 411 in 1950, and the 1951 offer, interrupted by this litigation, produced 165 applications to purchase.   No records were kept of those to whom the offers were made; the estimated number in 1951 was 500.

The company bottoms its exemption claim on the classification of all offerees as "key employees" in its organization.   Its position on trial was that "A key employee . . . is not confined to an organization chart.   It would include an individual who is eligible for promotion, an individual who especially influences others or who advises others, a person whom the employees look to in some special way, an individual, of course, who carries some special responsibility, who is sympathetic to management and who is ambitious and who the management feels is likely to be promoted to a greater responsibility."   That an offering to all of its employees would be public is conceded.

The Securities Act nowhere defines the scope of § 4(1)'s private offering exemption.   Nor is the legislative history of much help in staking out its boundaries.   The problem was first dealt with in § 4(1) of the House Bill, H.R. 5480, 73d Cong., 1st Sess., which exempted "transactions by an issuer not with or through an underwriter; . . .."   The bill, as reported by the House Committee, added "and not involving any public offering."   H.R.Rep. No. 85, 73d Cong., 1st Sess. 1.   This was thought to be one of those transactions "where there is no practical need for . . . [the bill's] application or where the public benefits are too remote."   Id., at 5.[21]   The exemption as thus delimited became law.[22]   It assumed its present shape with the deletion of "not with or through an underwriter" by § 203(a) of the Securities Exchange Act of 1934, 48 Stat. 906, a change regarded as the elimination of superfluous language.   H.R.Rep. No. 1838, 73d Cong., 2d Sess. 41.

Decisions under comparable exemptions in the English Companies Acts and state "blue sky" laws, the statutory antecedents of federal securities legislation have made one thing clear—to be public, an offer need not be open to the whole world.   In Securities and Exchange Comm. v. Sunbeam Gold Mines Co., 9 Cir., 1938, 95 F.2d 699, 701, this point was made in dealing with an offering to the stockholders of two corporations about to be merged.   Judge Denman observed that:

"In its broadest meaning the term 'public' distinguishes the populace at large from groups of individual members of the public segregated because of some common interest or charac-

---

21. ". . . the bill does not affect transactions beyond the need of public protection in order to prevent recurrences of demonstrated abuses."   Id., at 7.   In a somewhat different tenor, the report spoke of this as an exemption of "transactions by an issuer unless made by or through an underwriter so as to permit an issuer to make a specific or an isolated sale of its securities to a particular person, but insisting that if a sale of the issuer's securities should be made generally to the public

that that transaction shall come within the purview of the Act."   Id., at 15, 16.

22. The only subsequent reference was an oblique one in the statement of the House Managers on the Conference Report: "Sales of stock to stockholders become subject to the act unless the stockholders are so small in number that the sale to them does not constitute a public offering."   H.R.Rep. No. 152, 73d Cong., 1st Sess. 25.

teristic. Yet such a distinction is inadequate for practical purposes; manifestly, an offering of securities to all redheaded men, to all residents of Chicago or San Francisco, to all existing stockholders of the General Motors Corporation or the American Telephone & Telegraph Company is no less 'public', in every realistic sense of the word, than an unrestricted offering to the world at large. Such an offering, though not open to everyone who may choose to apply, is none the less 'public' in character, for the means used to select the particular individuals to whom the offering is to be made bear no sensible relation to the purposes for which the selection is made. . . . To determine the distinction between 'public' and 'private' in any particular context, it is essential to examine the circumstances under which the distinction is sought to be established and to consider the purposes sought to be achieved by such distinction."

The courts below purported to apply this test. The District Court held, in the language of the Sunbeam decision, that "The purpose of the selection bears a 'sensible relation' to the class chosen," finding that "The sole purpose of the 'selection' is to keep part stock ownership of the business within the operating personnel of the business and to spread ownership throughout all departments and activities of the business." The Court of Appeals treated the case as involving "an offering, without solicitation, of common stock to a selected group of key employees of the issuer, most of whom are already stockholders when the offering is made, with the sole purpose of enabling them to secure a proprietary interest in the company or to increase the interest already held by them."

Exemption from the registration requirements of the Securities Act is the question. The design of the statute is to protect investors by promoting full disclosure of information thought necessary to informed investment decisions.[23] The natural way to interpret the private offering exemption is in light of the statutory purpose. Since exempt transactions are those as to which "there is no practical need for . . . [the bill's] application," the applicability of § 4(1) should turn on whether the particular class of persons affected need the protection of the Act. An offering to those who are shown to be able to fend for themselves is a transaction "not involving any public offering."

The Commission would have us go one step further and hold that "an offering to a substantial number of the public" is not exempt under § 4(1). We are advised that "whatever the special circumstances, the Commission has consistently interpreted the exemption as being inapplicable when a large number of offerees is involved." But the statute would seem to apply to a "public offering" whether to few or many.[24]

---

23. A.C. Frost & Co. v. Coeur D'Alene Mines Corp., 1941, 312 U.S. 38, 40, 61 S.Ct. 414, 415, 85 L.Ed. 500. The words of the preamble are helpful: "An Act To provide full and fair disclosure of the character of securities sold in interstate and foreign commerce and through the mails, and to prevent frauds in the sale thereof, and for other purposes." 48 Stat. 74.

24. See Viscount Sumner's frequently quoted dictum in Nash v. Lynde, " 'The public' . . . is of course a general word. No particular numbers are prescribed. Anything from two to infinity may serve: perhaps even one, if he is intended to be the first of a series of subscribers, but makes further proceedings needless by himself subscribing the whole." [1929] A.C. 158, 169.

It may well be that offerings to a substantial number of persons would rarely be exempt. Indeed nothing prevents the commission, in enforcing the statute, from using some kind of numerical test in deciding when to investigate particular exemption claims. But there is no warrant for superimposing a quantity limit on private offerings as a matter of statutory interpretation.

The exemption, as we construe it, does not deprive corporate employees, as a class, of the safeguards of the Act. We agree that some employee offerings may come within § 4(1), e.g., one made to executive personnel who because of their position have access to the same kind of information that the act would make available in the form of a registration statement.[25] Absent such a showing of special circumstances, employees are just as much members of the investing "public" as any of their neighbors in the community. Although we do not rely on it, the rejection in 1934 of an amendment which would have specifically exempted employee stock offerings supports this conclusion. The House Managers, commenting on the Conference Report, said that "the participants in employees' stock-investment plans may be in as great need of the protection afforded by availability of information concerning the issuer for which they work as are most other members of the public." H.R.Rep. No. 1838, 73d Cong., 2d Sess. 41.

Keeping in mind the broadly remedial purposes of federal securities legislation, imposition of the burden of proof on an issuer who would plead the exemption seems to us fair and reasonable. Schlemmer v. Buffalo, R. & P. R. Co., 1907, 205 U.S. 1, 10, 27 S.Ct. 407, 408, 51 L.Ed. 681. Agreeing, the court below thought the burden met primarily because of the respondent's purpose in singling out its key employees for stock offerings. But once it is seen that the exemption question turns on the knowledge of the offerees, the issuer's motives, laudable though they may be, fade into irrelevance.

The focus of inquiry should be on the need of the offerees for the protections afforded by registration. The employees here were not shown to have access to the kind of information which registration would disclose. The obvious opportunities for pressure and imposition make it advisable that they be entitled to compliance with § 5.

Reversed.

The CHIEF JUSTICE and MR. JUSTICE BURTON dissent.

MR. JUSTICE JACKSON took no part in the consideration or decision of this case.

---

25. This was one of the factors stressed in an advisory opinion rendered by the Commission's General Counsel in 1935. "I also regard as significant the relationship between the issuer and the offerees. Thus, an offering to the members of a class who should have special knowledge of the issuer is less likely to be a public offering than is an offering to the members of a class of the same size who do not have this advantage. This factor would be particularly important in offerings to employees, where a class of high executive officers would have a special relationship to the issuer which subordinate employees would not enjoy." 11 Fed.Reg. 10952.

GILLIGAN, WILL & CO. v. SECURITIES AND EXCHANGE COMMISSION

United States Court of Appeals, Second Circuit, 1959.
267 F.2d 461, certiorari denied 361 U.S. 896, 80 S.Ct. 200, 4 L.Ed.2d 152 (1959).

[The SEC instituted a proceeding to determine whether Gilligan, Will & Co. and its partners had violated the Securities Act of 1933 by acquiring and distributing unregistered common stock and debentures of Crowell–Collier Publishing Company. The Commission heard argument, after waiver of hearing and stipulation of the facts and ordered a 5 day suspension of the firm from membership in the National Association of Securities Dealers, Inc. and found Gilligan and Will each to be a cause of the order. These parties petitioned for review of the order. They claimed that the SEC had committed various procedural violations, not here discussed, and that there was no substantial evidence to support the SEC's findings.

The Court of Appeals affirmed the Commission's order in an opinion by JUDGE LUMBARD. To understand the opinion you should first read Sections 4 and 5 of the 1933 Act in the Documentary Supplement. The opinion starts with a detailed statement of the facts.]

On July 6, 1955, Elliott & Company agreed with Crowell–Collier to try to sell privately, without registration, $3,000,000 of Crowell–Collier 5% debentures, convertible at any time into common stock at $5 a share, and the Elliott firm received an option on an additional $1,000,000 of debentures. Edward L. Elliott, a partner in Elliott & Company, advised Gilligan, one of the two partners of the registrant, Gilligan, Will & Co., of this agreement. He told Gilligan that Gilligan could purchase, but only for investment, as much of the $3,000,000 as he wished, with the exception of $500,000 which Elliott's wife was taking, and that the debentures not taken by Gilligan would be offered to certain friends of Elliott. Gilligan was told by Elliott that Crowell–Collier had "turned the corner" and was then operating on a profitable basis. Elliott also said that the attorneys for Crowell–Collier and his lawyers had stated that the placement was an exempt transaction. Gilligan agreed to purchase $100,000 of debentures for his own account. It does not appear that Gilligan had any information regarding Crowell–Collier and the debenture issue other than what Elliott told him as summarized above.

On August 10, 1955 the $100,000 debentures were delivered to Gilligan, Will & Co., which sent a letter to Crowell–Collier stating: "that said debentures are being purchased for investment and that the undersigned has no present intention of distributing the same."

Nevertheless, by August 10, 1955, almost half of the $100,000 of debentures had already been resold. Either on July 6, or July 7, 1955, Louis Alter, a member of the American Stock Exchange, agreed to buy $45,000 of the debentures. Gilligan also offered $10,000 to a friend and when this was not accepted he sold $5,000 to Michael D. Mooney, who had previously requested that amount of debentures and had been told that none were available; the remaining $5,000 debentures were placed in the registrant's trading account. In early September, when the securities were distributed, Gilligan, Alter and Mooney each signed a statement reading: "I hereby confirm to you that said debentures are being purchased for investment and that I have no present intention of distributing the same."

In May 1956, after Gilligan noticed that the advertising in Crowell–Collier magazines was not increasing, he decided to convert his debentures into common stock and to sell the stock. He advised Alter of his plans and on May 15, 1956 the registrant, Gilligan and Alter converted their debentures into common stock. Later in May they sold the stock at a profit on the American Stock Exchange. The stock had been listed on that Exchange since October 1955, and Gilligan became the specialist in the stock.

In May 1956 Gilligan, Will & Co. also purchased and participated in the sale of additional debentures by Crowell–Collier. Elliott told Gilligan that he was surrendering to Crowell–Collier his option on the remaining $1,000,000 of debentures, and that these debentures were to be sold at 160% of par, based on the stock's price at that time of $8 per share. The proceeds of the sale, Elliott stated, were to be used by Crowell–Collier in the acquisition of certain television stations which would show a profit of $4,000,000 annually. Elliott also told Gilligan that Crowell–Collier would sell him, Elliott, 100,000 stock purchase warrants at 1¢ each, exercisable at $10 per share for five years. Gilligan agreed to take $150,000 face amount debentures and said he would see whether Alter was interested in taking any. After Alter indicated that he wanted $50,000 face amount, Gilligan advised Elliott that the total subscription would be $200,000. Gilligan did not inform Elliott of his and Alter's sales of stock obtained from the conversion of the debentures purchased in 1955.

On May 29, 1956 the registrant subscribed to $200,000 face amount debentures and issued to Alter a confirmation for $50,000 debentures which stated: "we have this day subscribed for your account and risk; over the counter as agents . . ." Alter immediately converted his debentures into stock. On the same day the registrant similarly confirmed $150,000 face amount debentures to a joint specialist's account maintained by it and one Lloyd E. Howard, which debentures were immediately converted into common stock.

In addition, on May 29, the registrant sent Crowell–Collier a letter signed by Will, confirming that $200,000 of debentures were purchased for investment with no present intention to distribute. Howard and Alter made similar representations on copies of the confirmations issued to them by the registrant.

Late in May 1956, Elliott informed Gilligan that $200,000 of debentures were still unsold, that it was necessary to sell these debentures to one party, and that if Gilligan could find a purchaser, Elliott would sell him 50,000 stock warrants at 1¢ each. Gilligan contacted Harry Harris and told him that he would split his warrants with him if he, Harris, could find a purchaser for the debentures. Harris interested Value Line Special Fund, Inc., and Gilligan told Harris to contact Elliott. On May 29, 1956, the Fund's representatives met with Crowell–Collier's president, Paul Smith, and Harris and Elliott, and the Fund later agreed to purchase $200,000 face amount debentures and 15,000 warrants. To accommodate Elliott, Gilligan, Will & Co. as principal sent a confirmation, signed by Will, covering the sale of the debentures to the Fund.

Gilligan, Will & Co. received 50,000 warrants from Elliott, some of which were sold to the Fund and some of which were given to nominees of Harris and others, the 20,000 warrants given to others being subsequently returned to Elliott at his request.

Gilligan, Will & Co. sent Crowell–Collier two investment intention letters, in the usual form, one covering the Fund's purchase of debentures and the other covering the 50,000 warrants received by registrant. The Fund, at the request of Gilligan, Will & Co. signed letters of investment intent covering the debentures and the warrants.

Petitioners assert that they were not "underwriters" within the meaning of the exemption provided by the first clause of § 4(1). Since § 2(11), 15 U.S.C.A. § 77b(11) defines an "underwriter" as "any person who has purchased from an issuer with a view to . . . the distribution of any security" and since a "distribution" requires a "public offering," see H.R.Rep. No. 1838, 73d Cong., 2d Sess. (1934) at p. 41, the question is whether there was a "public offering." Petitioners, disclaiming any reliance on the exemption of the second clause of § 4(1) for "transactions by an issuer not involving any public offering," assert that whether there was a "distribution" must be judged solely by their own acts and intention, and not by the acts or intention of the issuer or others. In other words they claim that whether the total offering was in fact public, their purchases and resales may be found to be exempt on the ground that they were not underwriters if their own resales did not amount to a public offering.

In the view we take of this case we need not decide whether, if the petitioners had purchased with a view to only such resales as would not amount to a distribution or public offering, their acts would be exempt even though the issue was in fact a public offering. We find that the resales contemplated and executed by petitioners were themselves a distribution or public offering as the latter term has been defined by the Supreme Court, and we therefore find that petitioners were underwriters and that their transactions were not exempt under § 4(1).

In S.E.C. v. Ralston Purina Co., 1953, 346 U.S. 119, 73 S.Ct. 981, 97 L.Ed. 1494, the Supreme Court considered the exemptions provided by § 4(1). Two of its holdings are significant here. First, it held that an issuer who claims the benefit of an exemption from § 5 for the sale of an unregistered security has the burden of proving entitlement to it. The rationale of this result applies as well to a broker-dealer who claims the benefit of a similar exemption. We therefore find that the burden was upon the petitioners to establish that they were not underwriters within the meaning of § 4(1).

The Court also defined the standard to be applied in determining whether an issue is a public offering. It held that the governing fact is whether the persons to whom the offering is made are in such a position with respect to the issuer that they either actually have such information as a registration would have disclosed, or have access to such information. 346 U.S. at pages 125–127, 73 S.Ct. at pages 984–985. The stipulation of facts here expressly states that the purchasers "were not supplied with material information of the scope and character contemplated by the Securities Act nor were the purchasers in such a relation to the issuer as to have access to such information concerning the company and its affairs." Such a stipulation, which from the additional stipulated facts, appears equally applicable to Gilligan, the registrant, Alter, Mooney and Mrs. Elliott, concedes the very proposition of which the petitioners had to establish the negative in order to prevail, and we therefore think it dispositive of the question whether petitioners "purchased . . . with a view to . . . distribution."

Petitioners argue, however, that the definition of the Ralston Purina case is not exclusive, and that there is an exception to the standard there announced for cases in which the number of offerees or purchasers is small. In reliance on such a standard they assert that the stipulation discloses the existence of only four specific purchasers, and that therefore the Commission was bound to determine on this record that the petitioners' transactions were exempt because the issue was not public. We do not agree.

First, we think that the Ralston Purina case clearly rejected a quantity limit on the construction of the statutory term, and adopted instead the test set out above under which this issue was a public offering. It stated that "the statute would seem to apply to a 'public offering' whether to few or many," 346 U.S. at page 125, 73 S.Ct. at page 984, and cited with approval the dictum that "anything from two to infinity may serve: perhaps even one . . ." 346 U.S. 125, 73 S.Ct. 985 and note 11. Second, even were this not the case, and if a numerical exemption existed despite an admitted violation of the Purina standard, the stipulation adequately discloses that Gilligan well knew that the sales to Elliott's wife and to and through the registrant were not the only sales that were contemplated. It is stipulated that "Elliott advised Gilligan that . . . Elliott was . . . going to sell as much as was left to certain of his friends" after Gilligan took what he wanted of the $2,500,000 remaining after Elliott's wife took $500,000.

Thus these petitioners, who now assert an exemption based on the small number of resales that they contemplated and made, were admittedly aware that the actual placement involved many others. At the least, to establish entitlement to any numerical exemption in such circumstances, the petitioners would have to establish a reasonable and bona fide belief that the total number involved in the placement would remain within the exemption. Otherwise although a general public placement could be effected by a series of transfers to small numbers of buyers, each distributor would be entitled to an exemption on the ground that it transferred to only a small number of buyers. The stipulation reveals that without any knowledge of the actual number of sales then consummated or contemplated the petitioners effected what they now claim to be a harmless number of resales. Such a record does not require and would not justify a finding that the petitioners had sustained their burden of proving entitlement to an exemption based on the size of the contemplated distribution.

The petitioners separately attack the finding that the registrant was an underwriter on the ground that the stipulation reveals that Gilligan agreed with Elliott that Gilligan would take the $100,000 for his own account and thus it requires the conclusion that the registrant did not participate. But the stipulation also reveals that Will received the debentures on behalf of the registrant and also on its behalf issued an investment intention letter, and that $5,000 were placed in the firm trading account. On such facts the Commission was justified in concluding that the registrant participated in the acquisition and distribution of the unregistered issue.

The Commission also found that "The sales by Gilligan and registrant of the underlying common stock on the American Stock Exchange in May 1956, clearly constituted a public distribution." Petitioners contest this conclusion on the ground that since the conversion and sales occurred more than ten months after the purchase of the debentures the Commission was bound to find that the debentures so converted had been held for investment, and that the sales were therefore exempt under § 4(1) since made by a person other than an issuer, underwriter or dealer. Petitioners concede that if such sales were intended at the time of purchase, the debentures would not then have been held as investments; but it argues that the stipulation reveals that the sales were undertaken only after a change of the issuer's circumstances as a result of which petitioners, acting as prudent investors, thought it wise to sell. The catalytic circumstances were the failure, noted by Gilligan, of Crowell–Collier to increase its advertising space as he had anticipated that it would. We agree with the Commission that in the circumstances here presented the intention to retain the debentures only if Crowell–Collier continued to operate profitably was equivalent to a "purchased . . . with a view to . . . distribution" within the statutory definition of underwriters in § 2(11). To hold otherwise would be to permit a dealer who speculatively purchases an unregistered security in the hope that the financially weak issuer had, as is stipulated here, "turned the corner," to unload on the unadvised public what he later determines to be an unsound investment without the disclosure sought by the securities laws, although it is in precisely such circumstances that disclosure is most necessary and desirable. The Commission was within its discretion in finding on this stipulation that petitioners bought "with a view to distribution" despite the ten months of holding.

It is unnecessary, in the light of our decision sustaining the findings of the Commission as to violations with regard to the 1955 debentures, separately to consider the violations of § 5 found by the Commission as to the issue in 1956. Finally, on the stipulation there is no doubt either that the Commission was justified in finding that the petitioners' acts were "wilful" within the meaning of § 15(b) of the Securities Exchange Act of 1934, see, e.g., Hughes v. S.E.C., 1949, 85 U.S.App.D.C. 56, 174 F.2d 969, 977, or that the penalty imposed was within the Commission's discretion, see, e.g., American Power & Light Co. v. S.E.C., 1946, 329 U.S. 90, 112, 67 S.Ct. 133, 91 L.Ed. 103. . . .

COMMENT

In the mid 1950's Crowell–Collier was in bad shape with problems rather like those that brought down the Saturday Evening Post and the Curtis Publishing Company. While it had a net profit of $775,000 in 1955 it had losses in the millions in 1953, 1954, and 1956. In 1956–57 it disposed of American Magazine, Colliers, and Women's Home Companion. It started then to branch out into other fields such as television. The firm became Crowell Collier and Macmillan, Inc., and then simply Macmillan, Inc. Its subsidiaries, besides Macmillan, the publishing house, include Katherine Gibbs Schools, and the Berlitz Schools. For a time it also owned Gump's, a luxurious San Francisco specialty store, but in a process of restructuring it eliminated such unrelated businesses.

In a related proceeding [26] the SEC ruled that Crowell–Collier as issuer had violated the 1933 Act because the private exemption was not available to it. It

---

26. Securities Act Release No. 3825 of Aug. 12, 1957, set forth in CCH Fed.Sec.L. Rep. ¶ 76,539 (Transfer Binder 1957–61).

found that, although opinions had been given by counsel and assurances received from the purchasers, warning signals should have been recognized by the issuer. These indicia included the speculative character of the securities, the presence of broker-dealers among the buyers, the insistence that the common stock be listed on the American Exchange, etc. The SEC concluded "Counsel and their issuer and underwriter clients cannot base a claim to exemption . . . upon the mere acceptance at face value of representations by purchasers that they take for investment and disclaim responsibility for investigation and consideration of all relevant facts."

PROBLEM

You are counsel for a group of three promoters who are founding a modest corporation in the state of Connecticut. The corporation will make ski bindings in Waterbury, Conn. and have its headquarters there and a small sales office in New York. They plan to issue about $1,200,000 worth of stock and raise another $600,000 by selling notes. They would like to dispense with the delay and expense of registration insofar as possible. They show you a list of their friends among whom they expect to be able to find takers for their shares. These include three experienced elderly members of their investment club, two salespersons in a brokerage firm, the widower of an old associate of theirs, eleven fellow employees in the office of the manufacturing firm where they used to work, a wealthy student from California at Yale whose father was a classmate of one of the promoters, an accountant and two engineers who are going to work for them, a lawyer who lives in Westport and commutes to work in New York, and five fellow members of the local Rotary Club. The notes will probably be taken by a bank in Hartford, Conn., and one in Boston. You are asked the following questions:

(1) Can we get a total exemption from the registration requirements?

(2) In order to do so should we exclude any of the people on the promoters' list?

(3) Are there any contractual or other arrangements which we ought to make in order to maximize our chances of escaping involvement with the Act?

(4) What data about the firm must we provide the persons to whom we make offers? Bearing in mind the fact that we have no financial history and no independent auditors, is it going to be possible to furnish it? Will getting it together leave us with any significant savings in comparison with going via the registration route?

(5) As to the private offering exemption, do you conclude that there are any advantages to pursuing a course of action not within the SEC's Regulation D but within the case law guidelines as you read them? Is it safe?

---

5. The Registration Process and its Consequences

Sometimes it turns out that none of the exemptions will suffice and that the company must "go public" to achieve its financing goals and that therefore the offering must be registered. There follows a description of the registration process. It is deliberately terse because the process lies squarely within the province of the securities regulation specialist; in fact, I doubt that the process can be understood in more than a superficial sense by those who have not groped their way through it at least once. However some apprehension of the work is needed to give an understanding of why the exemptions are so important and to convey a grasp of some of the central ideas of disclosure that permeate all aspects of the securities regulation field and hence of corporation law. These materials describe a traditional single-episode offering; it is now possible in some circumstances to offer securities on a continuous basis with a single registration, referred to as "shelf registration" and governed by Rule 415.

Disclosure. The heart of the registration process is represented by the registration statement and by the prospectus. The registration statement consists of a copy of the prospectus, which is required to be furnished to each offeree, plus other data and various documents designated as exhibits. The registration statement is to be filed with and reviewed by the SEC. On examining the facing page of the Prospectus included in the Documentary Supplement you will see that it prominently bears the legend that the securities offered have been neither approved nor disapproved by the Commission. This statement is fundamental to the statute's and the Commission's perception of the SEC's role. It is not to decide whether the security deserves to be purchased by the public but rather to ensure that the public has the information it needs to make the individual decisions that add up to the judgment of the marketplace. The SEC in fact scrutinizes each registration statement as it comes through, largely to determine that the disclosure materials include the required data and that various forbidden types of claims are not made. It cannot as a routine matter independently ascertain the truth of the claims being made by the drafters of the registration materials.

There are many problems with the concept of disclosure, of which only a few can be discussed here. One is the fact that disclosure requirements have, for better or worse, regulatory effects. Corporate managements that know they will have to disclose "X" will often refrain from doing "X". Sometimes this is consistent with the will of the creators of the requirement, but sometimes it is a rather illegitimate by-product of legislation that had a narrower intent. The pressure of enormous potential liability under the Securities Act induces a special approach to disclosure, one that is designed more to protect the responsible signatories than to enlighten the public. The general tone of the materials is minatory and pessimistic, calling attention to all sorts of risks and uncertainties. The danger is always present that readers of numerous prospectuses will become calloused to the warnings, saying to themselves that, of course, the draftsmen are only trying to cover themselves and that a respected underwriter would not be offering the security if it did not think it worthwhile. There is the further problem that combining the technical nature of the subject matter with the need for protection, the drafters will produce the unreadable prospectus, one that overwhelms the reader with protracted prose, undigested fact and continuous cautions. The question then arises, for whom is the prospectus written? Is it, can it be, written for the millions of individuals who own or consider acquiring securities? The provisions requiring delivery of the prospectus prior to a final purchase assume that it is the buyer who is to be protected. On the other hand, much of the substance of the registration statement can only be deciphered by a trained investment analyst. In one sense, requiring the inclusion of summaries in the prospectus only drives home the point that there are two classes of readers. One might conclude that the process performed quite adequately the task of protecting the public from fly-by-night fraudulent operators of the old school but did not do more than a passable job of creating an enlightened public market. On the other hand, one could say that the professionals in the market can get the data they need from the reports and that others are constrained to get expert advise about investments just as they are about the decisions they have to make that involve law, medicine or engineering.

Two particular aspects of disclosure have received special attention in recent years. One is the disclosure of "soft" information, by which is meant information that goes beyond historical accounting data into the realm of evaluation and prediction. The SEC has generally been skeptical of such information as being too easily colored by managerial optimism but of late it has considerably relaxed its attitude. The other is data that would not influence the simple profit-oriented investor but would affect the judgment of one who either valued nonfinancial data for their own sake or thought that they revealed significant things about management's attitudes. Questions have been raised in particular, about the disclosure of the environmental impact of the corporation's activities and about illegal or questionable payments to government officials—especially those which are too small in amount to be important in terms of their size in relation to the firm's earnings or assets.

The Process. Essentially there are three parts to the labors involved. First, the basic documents must be drafted and agreed upon among the issuer, the underwriter and their respective counsel. These papers include the prospectus, the registration statement, the underwriting agreement and subsidiary papers. The underwriting agreement is basically an agreement to sell and purchase the securities at a specified date, after certain conditions have been met, for a specified price. Where there are several underwriters they must also agree among themselves about the portions of the offering which each will take. Second, there is the process of verifying what is written. This involves talking to the executives, reading minutes, contracts, permits and other documents. Much of this devolves upon lawyers, although law firms are careful to limit their responsibility for the detection of error. The accountants are, meanwhile, going through their familiar work of checking the management's draft financial statements according to the profession's standard auditing procedures. Finally, the product must be processed through the SEC, its comments must be met and amendments filed. The requirements of the state "blue sky" commissioners of the states within which the securities are to be offered must be met.

The time consumed by all of this is substantial. A sample timetable for a modest public offering follows. (The time-frame is probably unrealistically short for the 1980's): [27]

Date	Matter	Responsibility
Feb. 10	Tentative agreement with underwriters	
Feb. 15	Questionnaires to be sent to officers, directors and 10% stockholders as to stockholdings, remuneration for services and interest in material transactions	Company Secretary and Counsel
Feb. 15 March 1	Company documents to be gathered for review and reproduced as exhibits, where required	Company Secretary and Counsel
Feb. 15 March 1	Interviews with Company officers, preparation of memoranda regarding history of business and its operations	Company Counsel, officers and employees
March 1– March 10	Preparation of prospectus (exclusive of financial statements) and of other portions of registration statement	Company Counsel and Underwriter's Counsel
March 10	Audit as of December 31, 1959, to be completed and financial statements to be furnished to printer	CPA firm
March 10	Registration statement to be sent to printer for proof pages	Company Counsel
March 10– March 15	Registration statement proof pages revised and new proof pages obtained	Company Counsel and Underwriter's Counsel
March 18	Registration statement in final form to be printed and signature pages to be signed	Company Counsel, officers, directors and CPA firm
March 21	Registration statement filed with SEC in Washington, D.C.	Printer and Company Counsel
March 21	Preliminary blue sky survey to be distributed	Underwriter's Counsel

---

27. Wheat & Blackstone, Guideposts for a First Public Offering, 15 Bus.Law. 539 (1960). Reprinted by permission of the Business Lawyer. For a 4½ month schedule, with too much detail to reproduce here, see W. Prifti, Securities: Public and Private Offerings App. DD (rev.ed. 1983).

Date	Matter	Responsibility
April 8	Telegraphic delaying amendment to be filed with SEC pursuant to Rule 473, with confirmation mailed to SEC [28]	Company Counsel
April 15	SEC letter of comments ready for delivery (arrangements should be made to have an agent pick up letter in Washington, D.C. and read it over the telephone to a stenographer, to avoid delay in mailing)	Company Counsel
April 15– April 20	Preparation of first amendment to registration statement	Company Counsel and Underwriter's Counsel
April 18	Due Diligence meeting (to acquaint underwriters and dealers with the company and the offering)	Company officers and Underwriters
April 21	First amendment to registration statement filed with SEC with letter requesting acceleration of effective date to April 25	Company Counsel
April 25	Sign Agreement Among Underwriters	Underwriters
	Sign Underwriting Agreement fixing price	Company and Underwriters
April 25	Price amendment filed	Printer and Company Counsel
April 25	Registration statement declared effective by SEC	
April 25	Final blue sky survey distributed	Underwriter's Counsel
May 2	Closing	All hands

Aside from the time cost there is the direct financial burden. The following table [29] compares the costs of different types of offerings, indicating the burdens born by the registration process. You will observe that they do not all vary directly in proportion to the size of the issue or of the issuer.

---

28. [Ed.] One odd timing wrinkle: the Securities Act provides for a 20–day waiting period after filing the registration statement or any amendment thereto. If nothing were done, the registration statement would become effective on April 8 or the SEC would have to issue a stop order. Hence a delaying amendment is filed on April 8. Then a request for acceleration must be filed on April 21st because normally 20 days would run from the last amendment. The SEC derives enhanced power from its capacity to destroy the underwriting by refusing to permit acceleration.

29. Reprinted with permission from W. Prifti, "Securities: Public and Private Offerings" (pp. 1–23, 1984–1987), published by Callaghan & Co., 155 Pfingsten Road, Deerfield, Ill. 60015.

Item	S–1	Reg. A	Private Offering	Intrastate Offering
SEC Registration Fees	1/50 of 1% *	$100	None	None
Underwriting	7–18%	10–18%	10–30%	10–18%
Printing (depending upon quantity and corrections)	$8,500–$30,000 (5000–10,000 prospectuses & S–1)	$3000–$8,500 (5000 offering circulars)	Variable	$5,000 (5000 offering brochures)
Engraving of Certificates	$1200 **	$1200	$750 (1–100 certificates)	$750 (up)
Legal (variable)	¾–3% *	¾–3%	¾–3%	¾–3%
Accounting (variable, depending upon whether reconstruction of prior year statements are needed, condition of company records and availability of records and company personnel)	$7,000–$50,000	$2,500–$15,000	$2,500–$40,000	$3,500–$20,000
Experts, tax, patent, etc. (variable)	$300–$15,000 **	$300–$5,000 **	$300–$500	$50–$1500 (variable in some states)
Blue Sky Filing Fees	$50–$2,000 per state, depending upon the number of states and dollar amount of the offering.	Same as S–1	Variable from zero to $1,500 depending on state	Same as S–1
NASD Filing Fees (applicable to all public offerings)	$100, plus .01% $5,100.	up to $50,000,000 with a maximum fee of		

* Percentages relate to aggregate proceeds of offering.

** Assumes 5,000 certificates sufficient for at least a 300,000–share offering.

Liabilities. The dangers of liability under the 1933 Act have always weighed heavily on the minds of issuers' management, underwriters, accountants and counsel. This is true even though the actual volume of litigation has been small. Read Section 11 of the Act and compare it with what you can recollect of the rules as to common law liability for misrepresentation taught in Torts. In particular, be sure to understand the differences in coverage and in consequences between subsections (a) and (b).

Substantial controversy surrounds the potential liability for inaccuracies under Section 11 of lawyers.[31] In Escott v. BarChris Construction Co., 283 F.Supp. 643 (S.D.N.Y.1968), various persons who were lawyers were held liable, but each of them occupied some other status. Birnbaum was a young lawyer who, as secretary of BarChris, signed the

31. On lawyers and securities regulation, consult Hawes & Sherrard, Reliance on Advice of Counsel as a Defense in Corporate and Securities Cases, 62 Va.L.Rev. 1 (1976); Shipman, The Need for SEC Rules to Govern the Duties and Civil Liabilities of Attorneys under the Federal Securities Statutes, 34 Ohio St.L.J. 231 (1973); Lowenfels, Expanding Public Responsibilities of Securities Lawyers, 74 Colum.L.Rev. 412 (1974); Report of the Special Committee on Lawyers' Role in Securities Transactions, 32 Record N.Y.C.B. 345 (1977).

registration statement, relying on others for its accuracy. Grant was a director of BarChris and a member of the firm that did BarChris' securities work who signed the registration statement, in fact prepared much of it, without doing the checking as far as the court felt was necessary. The court noted that the fact that lawyers prepared the registration statement did not "expertize" the document. Most clients presumably expect more protection from the participation of expert counsel than that, although the standard opinion by underwriters' counsel is cautious. The version that appears in the opinion, after reciting the lawyer's investigations and conversations, says:

> Although we have not otherwise verified the completeness or accuracy of the information furnished to us . . . we have no reason to believe that the Registration Statement or Prospectus contains any untrue statement of any material fact or omits to state a material fact . . .

The SEC has applied increasing pressure on attorneys to act as enforcers of the securities laws in such transactions as public offerings. It might require them to withhold their aid in closing a transaction if they were aware of material falsehoods in the offering materials, SEC v. National Student Marketing Corp., 457 F.Supp. 682 (D.D.C.1978), or of going to the SEC with knowledge that the law had been violated. But see Model Rule 1.6(b) as to such a breach of client confidentiality.

The following case is probably the most spectacular litigation involving the underwriting process. It arose because of almost the only known episode in which an underwriter backed out of a commitment after signing a contract. However, other underwriters have undoubtedly been sorely tempted. For example, major losses were suffered by underwriters when the October 1987 market break took place just before the British government's sale to the public of its holdings in British Petroleum. As a result of this episode there was extensive litigation involving the issuer, the underwriter and the SEC. This is the most significant of these cases.

KAISER–FRAZER CORP. v. OTIS & CO.
United States Court of Appeals, Second Circuit, 1952.
195 F.2d 838, certiorari denied 344 U.S. 856, 73 S.Ct. 89, 97 L.Ed. 664 (1952).

Augustus N. Hand, Circuit Judge. On February 3, 1948, the plaintiff, Kaiser–Frazer Corporation, an automobile manufacturer, entered into a contract for the sale of 900,000 shares of its unissued common stock at $11.50 per share to Otis & Co., First California Company, and Allen & Co., securities underwriters, who in turn were to offer the stock for sale to the public at $13. per share. The purchasers were to take title to the stock severally, Otis and First California having agreed to purchase 337,500 shares each, and Allen & Co. to purchase the remaining 225,000 shares. The contract made the purchasers' obligation to accept the stock subject to certain conditions which, so far as relevant here, may be summarized as follows: (1) Kaiser–Frazer's counsel was to deliver an opinion satisfactory to the purchasers' counsel that there were no material legal proceedings pending against the issuer; and (2) the registration statement (including the prospectus filed with the Securities & Exchange Commission pursuant to the Securities Act of 1933, 15 U.S.C.A. § 77a et seq.,) was to comply with the Act and the Regulations of the SEC ". . . and neither the Registration Statement nor the prospectus [were to] contain any untrue statement of a material fact nor omit to state any material fact required to be stated therein or necessary in order to make the statements therein not misleading . . ." It is undisputed that the registration statement (including the prospectus) was filed with the SEC and became effective on February 3, 1948, the day the contract was signed. The contract set February 9, 1948 as the closing date, at which time Kaiser–Frazer was to have delivered the stock to the purchasers, and the latter were to have paid the purchase price. On the day of the closing, however, the representatives of Otis and First California refused to accept the proffered stock, assigning as their reason therefor, the rejection of the opinion of Kaiser–Frazer's counsel that no material litigation was then pending which would affect the issue of the stock. Apparently, Otis and First California rejected the opinion of Kaiser–Frazer's counsel because a suit to enjoin the pending stock issue had been instituted in Michigan on the morning of February 9, 1948, by a Kaiser–Frazer stockholder named Masterson.[32] Shortly, thereafter, Kaiser–Frazer initiated the present action against Otis in the District Court for the Southern District of New York. Federal jurisdiction was invoked on the ground of diverse citizenship of the parties.[33] The complaint—which was amended—alleged three claims, the first of which charged that Otis was guilty of a breach of contract for failing to accept and pay for 337,500 shares of stock and asked for damages in the total amount of $17,419,819, composed of $1,856,250 general damages and $15,563,569 special damages arising out of manufacturing profits lost by Kaiser–Frazer on account of Otis' breach. The second claim was stated as an alternative to the first and alleged that Otis had inspired the institution of the stockholders' suit by Masterson and had repudiated the contract without excuse; the damages prayed for were the same as under the first claim. The third claim was that Otis had wrongfully induced First California not to perform the latter's obligation under the contract to purchase 337,500 shares of stock and asked for damages in the amount of $1,856,250.

The defendant's answer to the complaint set forth several affirmative defenses, only two of which are in issue on this appeal: The first, that the purchasers were relieved of any obligation under the contract because of the filing of the suit by Masterson, and the second, that the registration statement contained false and misleading statements. After an extensive trial lasting six weeks, the district judge made findings of fact in favor of the plaintiff on substantially all of the points in issue, and entered judgment for the plaintiff in the amount of $3,120,743.51.

Several errors are assigned by the defendant on this appeal, most of which deal with the findings of fact of the trial judge. However,

---

32. The representative of Allen & Co. at the closing expressed a willingness to perform despite the action of Otis and First California.

33. Kaiser–Frazer is a Nevada corporation and Otis is a Delaware corporation qualified to do business in New York.

because of the view we take of the case, we need discuss only one of the alleged errors; namely, whether the district court was correct in finding that the plaintiff had not misrepresented but had adequately disclosed its profit for the month of December 1947 in the statement of earnings which it set forth in the prospectus; for, if the prospectus *Issue* contained such a misrepresentation, as will appear, neither Otis nor First California was under any obligation on February 9, 1948 to accept the stock and Otis would have a complete defense to all the causes of action stated in the complaint.

The stock issue which was the subject of the contract at bar was to have been the third issue of Kaiser–Frazer stock since its organization in 1945, and its first issue after January 1946. In the early part of 1948, when this issue was contemplated, Kaiser–Frazer was as yet a newcomer to the automobile industry; production of its cars did not get underway until late 1946, and volume production was not achieved until the spring of 1947. While the post-war period in the automobile industry was abnormal in the sense that a strong "sellers' " market prevailed, nevertheless the problems of production and competition confronting one in Kaiser–Frazer's position were of sufficient magnitude to make the venture highly speculative. Under such circumstances it is evident that the prospective purchaser of Kaiser–Frazer stock would rely heavily on the corporation's sales and earnings during the last quarters of 1947 as the best and perhaps the only available indication of its ability to compete with the established automobile manufacturers. Indeed, the defendant contends that without a favorable picture of earnings for that period the proposed stock issue could not have been made. In any event, Kaiser–Frazer elected to set forth in the prospectus a table summarizing its sales and earnings in capsule form and "designed to apprise the investor, in a convenient fashion, of the financial results of the operation of the business . . ." SEC Accounting Series Release No. 62, 3 CCH, Fed.Sec.Law Rep. para. 72,081. It is apparent, then, that the table summarizing earnings was an important factor in the sale of the stock and, that being so, failure to make full disclosure therein of all the facts bearing upon the Corporation's earnings constituted a breach of the contract and violated the Securities Act of 1933 as well. 15 U.S.C.A. § 77*l*.

The following is a quotation of the summary earnings table, with text and footnotes, as it appeared in the prospectus:

"Summary of Consolidated Sales and Earnings

"The following summary reflects consolidated sales and earnings of the Corporation from its inception to December 31, 1947. The information for the period ended December 31, 1945, and the year ended December 31, 1946 as shown in the table, and for the six months ended June 30, 1947 (as explained in note 2) has been prepared from profit and loss statements examined by Touche, Niven, Bailey & Smart and should be read in conjunction with the financial statements for such periods included herein and the accountants' report thereon. The information shown in the table for the eleven months ended November 30, 1947, and the breakdown into the three fiscal quarters and the two months period comprising such eleven months, has been taken from profit and loss statements prepared by the Corporation from its books and accounts, without audit, and should be read in conjunction with the unaudited eleven months financial statements and schedule included herein. The tentative information shown in the table for the quarter and for the year ended December 31, 1947, has been prepared by the Corporation from its books and records, without audit, on the basis of a preliminary 1947 closing made at January 23, 1948.

Period	Sales and Miscellaneous Income	Cost of Sales	Selling and Adminis- trative Expenses	Other Deduc- tions or Credits * —Net	Net Profit or Loss*
From August 9 to December 31, 1945	$ 10,979	$ 224,607	$ 551,988	$ 7,104	$ 772,720*
Year ended December 31, 1946	11,657,972	28,092,530	2,940,877	90,754 *	19,284,681*
Eleven months ended November 30, 1947	227,560,032	204,674,595	6,751,960	637,729	15,495,748
Quarter ended March 31, 1947(2)	27,305,035	29,366,660	1,093,542	81,127	3,236,294*(1)
Quarter ended June 30, 1947(2)	53,142,946	50,255,274	1,640,776	198,641	1,048,255 (1)
Quarter ended September 30, 1947	78,527,735	67,890,777	2,150,261	209,388	8,277,309 (1)
Two months ended November 30, 1947	68,584,316	57,161,884	1,867,381	148,573	9,406,478 (1)
* * *					
Quarter ended December 31, 1947(4)	101,999,563	84,519,665	3,850,916	213,121	13,415,861 (1)
Year ended December 31, 1947(4)	260,975,279	232,032,376	8,735,495	702,277	19,505,131 (1)

"Notes:

"(1) But for the operation of the loss carry-over provisions of the Internal Revenue Code, and the loss for the three months ended March 31, 1947, the profits shown above would have been subject to Federal income taxes in approximately the following amounts:

Quarter ended June 30, 1947	$ 420,000
Quarter ended September 30, 1947	3,310,000
Two months ended November 30, 1947	3,765,000
	$7,495,000

Less reduction in tax due to loss for quarter ended March 31, 1947	1,295,000
Eleven months ended November 30, 1947	$6,200,000

"On a similar basis the Federal income taxes applicable to the quarter and to the year ended December 31, 1947 would have been $5,365,000 and $7,800,000 respectively.

"(2) The aggregate information for the six months ended June 30, 1947, agrees with the profit and loss statement for such period included herein and reported upon by Touche,

Niven, Bailey & Smart. However, the segregation of such aggregate information so as to show the two quarters separately has been prepared by the Corporation, without audit.

"(3) The 'excess of fair value of shares issued to Graham–Paige Motors Corporation over book amount of net tangible assets received therefor' is to be written off by charges to profit and loss over a period of five years beginning January 1, 1948. This will result in a charge of $542,943 annually.

"(4) The tentative information for the quarter and year ended December 31, 1947, reflects various substantial year end adjustments including provision for certain reserves and a material increase in inventories to conform to the results of the complete physical inventory taken by the Corporation as of December 31, 1947. In connection with the loss of the Corporation for the fiscal year ended December 31, 1946, attention is called to the fact that the Corporation made no sales until the fourth quarter of such year. Sales in such quarter amounted to $11,504,443, as compared with sales of $78,466,238 in the third quarter of the fiscal year 1947."

The above table contains no figure purporting to be the December 1947 profit as such; however, by subtracting the profit for the two months ending November 30, 1947 from the quarter ending December 31, 1947 profit, a figure of $4,009,383 is obtained which one would naturally assume to represent the profit of the Corporation for the single month of December 1947. Kaiser–Frazer argues that the average person reading the prospectus would not make this arithmetical calculation and hence his judgment would not be affected by any consideration of what the December profit was represented to be.[34] But, as pointed out earlier, because of the comparatively brief earnings record of the Corporation and the speculative nature of the venture in which it was engaged, we think that the average prospective purchaser of Kaiser–Frazer stock would have made the subtraction and would have concluded that the December earnings totalled nearly four million dollars. It is, however, sufficiently clear from the record that December earnings from the Corporation's operations were nowhere near that amount, but were rather in the neighborhood of $900,000. The difference in amount was due to the fact that a physical inventory was taken in the latter part of December 1947, at which time it was discovered that the Corporation had a much larger inventory than had been anticipated. The net amount of the adjustment that was made to reflect this fact was the sum of $3,371,155, which Kaiser–Frazer simply included under the final quarter's earnings in the summary. Actually, the increase in profit resulting from the larger inventory was allocable not only to the month of December or the last quarter of 1947, but to the entire year's operations and in part to prior years; for in effect the larger inventory meant that Kaiser–Frazer had been charging too much to cost of sales for those periods. Indeed, the Corporation's "Consolidat-

34. We do not see how Kaiser–Frazer can derive any comfort from this argument. Even assuming that there was no representation as to the profit for the month of December 1947, nevertheless it cannot be disputed that the profit for the final quarter was shown in the summary as amounting to $13,415,861. This figure, however, included the inventory write-up which should have been reallocated to prior periods. See infra. Using Kaiser–Frazer's own reallocation of the inventory write-up, the final quarter profit was only $11,170,597. Consequently, at best there was a misrepresentation of the final quarter profit to the extent of $2,245,264.

ed Statement of Income and Expense" for December 1947, prepared for its own use, summarized the month's operation as follows:

"Net Profit or (Loss) for the Month of
  December, 1947 .... $ 638,226.97 [35]
Prior Months' Adjustments (see notes) .... 3,371,155.56"

Moreover, Kaiser–Frazer's own expert accounting witness, Hollis, did not deny that the inventory write-up should have been allocated to prior periods. He did, however, give testimony and presented exhibits to the effect that a complete reallocation of expenses that had been charged to December would yield a profit of about $2,900,000, which in turn would mean that the amount of the overstatement of December earnings was only a little over $1,000,000. But his testimony on this point is unacceptable, for his method of reallocation was entirely opposed to the accounting system that had been utilized by the Corporation and upon which the summary was based. For example, he wrote off steel variances [36] in the amount of $1,066,027 paid in December, whereas the Corporation had in the past always charged such variances as an expense to the month in which the steel was purchased; also, he wrote off all advertising expenses for the month of December although it was not disputed that the Corporation had advertised extensively in that month.[37]

The district court found that the "summary of consolidated sales and earnings for the final quarter of the year 1947, set forth on page 7 of the prospectus, was computed in accordance with accepted accounting procedures," and that it was not misleading. With this conclusion we cannot agree. For, regardless of whether its accounting system was a sound one, Kaiser–Frazer stated its earnings in such a way as to represent that it had made a profit of about $4,000,000 in December 1947. This representation was $3,100,000 short of the truth. Concededly, the profits for the year as a whole were substantially unaffected by the overstatement of December earnings, but the prospective purchaser was entitled to a full disclosure of all the facts that were known to the Corporation at the time the prospectus was issued; and the Corporation knew on February 3, 1948 that its profit for the month of December 1947 was less than $1,000,000. The source of the profit as stated in the prospectus for December could have been readily disclosed by a footnote to the earnings table. The footnote that appeared in the prospectus [38] as issued was entirely insufficient for this purpose. No one reading it would have been put on notice that the actual profit for December was less than a fourth of what was indicated by the table.

Kaiser–Frazer urges that since Otis had full knowledge of all the facts prior to the time it entered into the underwriting agreement, Otis

35. Some of the inventory write-up, approximately $260,000, was allocable to the month of December which accounts for the difference between $638,226.97 shown in this statement as December profit and the $900,000 figure referred to earlier in the text.

36. Steel variance is the excess of the price paid by the Corporation for steel purchased over the price at which the steel was included in inventory.

37. The December advertising expenses, amounting to $758,000, were not included

in the summary shown in the prospectus because the billings for that month had not been cleared through Kaiser–Frazer's accounting office when the books were closed. Consequently, when the accountant Hollis wrote off the November advertising expenses, which had been charged to December, his final profit figure of $2,900,000 did not include any charge at all for advertising expenses.

38. This footnote is footnote (4) in the summary earnings table quoted earlier in the text.

cannot now rely on such facts as constituting a breach of warranty. Factually there is some support for Kaiser–Frazer's contention; the testimony at the trial indicates that representatives of Otis at least were informed of the actual December earnings and apparently took part in the preparation of the registration statement and the prospectus. But whatever the rules of estoppel or waiver may be in the case of an ordinary contract of sale, nevertheless it is clear that a contract which violates the laws of the United States and contravenes the public policy as expressed in those laws is unenforceable.[39] E.E. Taenzer & Co. v. Chicago, R.I. & Pa. Ry., 6 Cir., 191 F. 543, certiorari denied 223 U.S. 746, 32 S.Ct. 533, 56 L.Ed. 640; cf. Sola Electric Co. v. Jefferson, 317 U.S. 173, 63 S.Ct. 172, 87 L.Ed. 165. This is so regardless of the equities as between the parties for ". . . the very meaning of public policy is the interest of others than the parties and that interest is not to be at the mercy of the defendant alone." Beasley v. Texas & Pacific Ry., 191 U.S. 492, 498, 24 S.Ct. 164, 48 L.Ed. 274. Any sale to the public by means of the prospectus involved here would have been a violation of the Securities Act of 1933, 15 U.S.C.A. § 77l(2). While it may be argued that the enforcement of the underwriting contract according to its terms would result only in the sale of the stock to Otis and that such a sale would not violate the Act, see 15 U.S.C.A. § 77d(1), we are satisfied that the contract was so closely related to the performance of acts forbidden by law as to be itself illegal. We cannot blind ourselves to the fact that the sale of this stock by Kaiser–Frazer, though, in so far as the particular contract was concerned, was a sale only to the underwriters, was but the initial step in the public offering of the securities which would necessarily follow. The prospectus, which has been found to have been misleading, formed an integral part of the contract and the public sale of the stock by the underwriter was to be made and could only have been made in reliance on that prospectus. 15 U.S.C.A. § 77e(b)(2). We therefore conclude that the contract was unenforceable and that Kaiser–Frazer was not entitled to recover damages for Otis' breach thereof. See Restatement of Contracts, §§ 580, 598. It also follows from what has been said that there having been no enforceable contract, Otis is not liable in damages for interfering with the performance of the underwriting contract by First California.

The judgment is reversed and the case remanded to the district court with directions to enter judgment for the defendant.

COMMENT

This case pitted against each other two of the most formidable exemplars of *homo economicus* on the scene. Henry J. Kaiser (1882–1967) dropped out of school at 13 to work at $1.50 per week in a Utica, New York store. In 1912 he began in the construction business in the Pacific Northwest. He began his own company that, alone or with joint venturers, built the Cuban road system, and the Hoover, Bonneville and Grand Coulee dams. During World War II he built a ship a day or 1,490 in all. To get the steel for them he built the Fontana steel plant, the Pacific Coast's first, and helped break Alcoa's grip on aluminum

---

39. Further support for our holding may be found in § 14 of the Act of 1933, 15 U.S.C.A. § 77n, which provides as follows:

"Any condition, stipulation, or provision binding any person acquiring any security

to waive compliance with any provision of this subchapter or of the rules and regulations of the Commission shall be void."

production. Perhaps his most innovative step was the creation of the Kaiser Foundation Medical Care prepayment program for group medicine. A 16 hour a day worker, he used to say "there's only one time to do anything and that's today." Cyrus Eaton (1883–1979) came from Canada to work for John D. Rockefeller. He started in the utilities industry and in 1916 joined Otis & Co., a Cleveland investment banking firm. He was the organizer of Republic Steel. In his banking capacity he clashed consistently with the forces of Wall Street. Because of the Kaiser–Frazer affair Otis & Co. became involved in much other litigation. It filed a petition for bankruptcy reorganization after losing in the district court, which was withdrawn after the opinion set forth above. However, it was not thereafter active.[40] The SEC investigated the transaction intensively. This produced an interesting opinion when the SEC, represented by its then Associate General Counsel Louis Loss, attempted to subpoena lawyers for Otis & Co. to see whether it had instigated certain litigation in order to have an "out" under the underwriting agreement. Although there was testimony that Eaton had said that "I am going through the purchase agreement and the registration statement with a fine tooth comb and try and find something to hang my hat on," and that "I would rather have a lawsuit on my hands than be broke," the court found that a prima facie case of fraud had not been made out.[41] Eaton later turned his interests more towards promoting east-west harmony. His Nova Scotia estate, "Pugwash", repeatedly served as a meeting place for Russian and American scientists.

QUESTIONS

(1) What was the misrepresentation upon which defendant relied? Can you locate it in the court's excerpts from the registration statement? How did an error in inventory, an asset account, affect the earnings figures? How should the problem have been treated in the financial statement? Do you agree with the court's view as to the likelihood of the public's being misled by this misstatement?

(2) Do you agree with the court's disposition of the question whether the existence of this misrepresentation warranted relieving the underwriter of its obligation to buy? Would your answer be different if the misrepresentation had related to a matter peculiarly within the knowledge of the underwriter (such as the costs of the distribution, etc.)?

(3) What would have been the potential liability of these parties and perhaps others if the underwriting had gone through as planned and the stock had gone down substantially in price? Look at Section 11 of the Securities Act; what differences do you see between that Section and the rules which otherwise prevail in fraud or negligent misrepresentation action? Would counsel for Kaiser–Frazer have incurred any liability? Suppose that counsel had been told by an accountant of the inaccuracy the night before the closing—what should he have done about it? Should he have refused to give an opinion? Informed the SEC?

(4) How would the existence of Section 11 have altered the situation in the Old Dominion cases?

Bibliography: The literature of Securities Regulation is a large and expanding body of material. The *locus classicus* is L. Loss, Securities Regulation, which is, alas, becoming obsolescent since its 1961 edition and 1969 supplement

---

40. See Matter of Otis & Co., 35 S.E.C. 650 (1954).

41. SEC v. Harrison, 80 F.Supp. 226 (D.D.C.1948).

have not been updated. However, his Fundamentals of Securities Regulation (2d ed. 1988) gives one a good start on this subject. For current data one would consult the Commerce Clearing House services—The Federal Securities Law Reporter and Blue Sky Law Reporter, the Bureau of National Affairs Service—Securities Regulation and Law Report, or the Prentice–Hall Securities Regulation Service. The Review of Securities Regulation gathers the commentaries. There is a steady stream of continuing education literature generated by such organizations as the Practising Law Institute and the cooperative efforts of the American Law Institute and American Bar Association.

A casebook approach to the area is offered by R. Jennings & H. Marsh, Securities Regulation—Cases and Materials (6th ed. 1987). A useful introduction is D. Ratner, Securities Regulation in a Nutshell (2d ed. 1982).

Chapter VII

MANAGING THE CORPORATION—THE ROLE OF THE BOARD

1. General Introduction: What Managing Involves

Two very different ideas are expressed in the business concept of the "general manager" and the legal mandate that the business of a corporation "shall be managed by its board of directors", similar though those words may be. The business person, or more strictly speaking the business management theoretician, thinks of the general manager as the one who stands at the apex of the corporate structure, making the ultimate resolution of the conflicting drives within the organization. Management involves the determination of a firm's strategy and its implementation. The functions of a general manager in implementation might be broken down into the following components.[1] What part of these functions are to be handled by the board and what part is to be delegated is explored below.

LEARNED ET AL., BUSINESS POLICY

1. Once strategy is tentatively or finally set, the key tasks to be performed and kinds of decisions required must be identified.

2. Once the size of operations exceeds the capacity of one man, responsibility for accomplishing key tasks and making decisions must be assigned to individuals or groups. The division of labor must permit efficient performance of subtasks and must be accompanied by some hierarchical allocation of authority to insure achievement.

3. Formal provisions for the coordination of activities thus separated must be made in various ways, e.g., through a hierarchy of supervision, project and committee organizations, task forces, and other *ad hoc* units. The prescribed activities of these formally constituted bodies are not intended to preclude spontaneous voluntary coordination.

4. Information systems adequate for coordinating divided functions (i.e., for letting those performing part of the task know what they must know of the rest, and for letting those in supervisory positions

---

1. E. Learned, C. Christensen, K. Andrews & W. Guth, Business Policy 573–74 (rev. ed. 1969). This excerpt should be considered in conjunction with that about the formulation of strategy at p. 101 supra.

know what is happening so that next steps may be taken) must be designed and installed.

5. The tasks to be performed should be arranged in a time sequence comprising a program of action or a schedule of targets. So that long-range planning may not be neglected, this activity should probably be entrusted to a special staff unit. Its influence may be enhanced by attaching it to the president's office, its usefulness by having it work in close cooperation with the line. While long-range plans may be couched in relatively general terms, shorter-range plans will often take the form of relatively detailed budgets. These can meet the need for the establishment of standards against which future performance can be judged.

6. Actual performance, as quantitatively reported in information systems and qualitatively estimated through observation by supervisors and the judgment of customers, should be compared to budgeted performance and to standards in order to test achievement, budgeting processes, and the adequacy of the standards themselves.

7. Individuals and groups of individuals must be recruited and assigned to essential tasks in accordance with the specialized or supervisory skills which they possess or can develop. At the same time, the assignment of tasks may well be adjusted to the nature of available skills.

8. Individual performance, evaluated both quantitatively and qualitatively, should be subjected to influences (constituting a pattern of incentives) which will help to make it effective in accomplishing organizational goals.

9. Since individual motives are complex and multiple, incentives for achievement should range from those that are universally appealing—such as adequate compensation and an organizational climate favorable to the simultaneous satisfaction of individual and organizational purposes—to specialized forms of recognition, financial or nonfinancial, designed to fit individual needs and unusual accomplishments.

10. In addition to financial and nonfinancial incentives and rewards to motivate individuals to voluntary achievement, a system of constraints, controls, and penalties must be devised to contain nonfunctional activity and to enforce standards. Controls, like incentives, are both formal and informal. Effective control requires both quantitative and nonquantitative information which must always be used together.

11. Provision for the continuing development of requisite technical and managerial skills is a high-priority requirement. The development of individuals must take place chiefly within the milieu of their assigned responsibilities. This on-the-job development should be supplemented by intermittent formal instruction and study.

12. Dynamic personal leadership is necessary for continued growth and improved achievement in any organization. Leadership

may be expressed in many styles, but it must be expressed in some perceptible style. This style must be natural and also consistent with the requirements imposed upon the organization by its strategy and membership.

The general manager is principally concerned with determining and monitoring the adequacy of strategy, with adapting the firm to changes in its environment, and with securing and developing the people needed to carry out the strategy or to help with its constructive revision. The manager must also insure that the processes which encourage and constrain individual performance and personal development are consistent with human and strategic needs. In large part, therefore, his leadership consists of achieving commitment to strategy via clarification and dramatization of its requirements and value.

NOTE ON BOARDS OF DIRECTORS

(1) Functions

Rare would be the company in which the chief executive imagined performing all the functions described above. Especially among smaller companies, these types of functions are carried on more or less unconsciously and almost instinctively. In a small enterprise one person could take on all of these functions. When a firm reaches a certain size some element of division of labor necessarily comes into play. The concept of general management is not meant to describe the functions carried on by persons at lower levels within "management" as the overall structure of the "white collar" staff of a corporation is termed, but only the overall command, exercised by a relatively small inner group.

Turning to the legal side we find an almost universal mandate in state corporation law that the business of the corporation be "managed" by the board of directors. (See 8 Del.C. § 141 for a typical formulation, along with qualifications). It is not entirely clear what "manage" is meant to encompass in this context. On the one side, it is intended to delimit the boundaries within which the board is independent of the shareholders and thus excludes certain major decisions, e.g., the sale of all of the corporation's assets, which require the assent of the shareholders.[2]

On the other side "manage" evidently is meant to distinguish some kind of decision-making and supervision relating to major questions as opposed to involvement in relatively routine, detailed and repetitive activities. These other functions are meant to be carried on by other personnel, generally full-time. The addition to the Delaware statute of the words "or under the direction of" seems to recognize this reality. There is then some relationship between the business concept and the legal view of "managing". On close examination, differences do ap-

---

2. See p. 684 infra.

pear. It is rare that a board in fact can take the initiative in managing in the business sense. A board seldom can design a strategy, set up a structure and find the resources for it. These things are done by individuals and generally by full time employees, usually known as the "officers" of the corporation. To confuse matters the president of a company is often regarded as the "general manager" (or "chief executive") of the firm.[3] In a rough sort of way, one could say that what is expected of the board is more fairly designated by the German term "supervisory council" (Aufsichtsrat). It is assumed that the board will pass on major decisions (including those in which it is required by statute to participate), will designate (and if need be, remove) the top executive officers and will watch out for signs of dishonesty, incompetence and error on the part of the full time management. The duties of the board should, of course, vary according to the size of the corporation and the type of activity it is engaged in.

An authoritative study[4] of boards of directors indicated that the *actual* functions performed by boards are substantially less than the above theory might indicate. The actual performance of boards includes (1) serving as sources of advice and counsel to the president, (2) serving as a discipline in requiring top management to produce reasoned arguments for their actions, (3) decision-making in periods of crisis. They do not as a rule establish strategies and objectives, do not ask probing questions or routinely monitor the executives performance or select or discharge them when unsatisfactory.

(2) Composition and Operations

It is useful here to pull together some of the available data as to the present composition of boards of directors. The boards of major corporations tend to have 12 to 15 members, larger boards correlating with larger assets. A basic division is that between "inside" and "outside" directors, i.e., between those who are and those who are not full time employees of the firm. Increasingly the tide is running toward having at least a strong outsider representation. § 3.03 of the American Law Institute's Principles of Corporate Governance (Tent. Draft No. 1, 1982), recommended that a majority of the directors of publicly held corporations should be free of significant relations with management and its supporting data indicated that this the majority of such corporations already had boards with majorities of "outsiders." Even directors who are outsiders in that sense may, however, be tied to the corporation and, in practice, to its chief executive officer. Many provide legal, investment banking, commercial banking or other services to the corporation and are concerned about maintaining those ties. Thus aggressive independence is not to be expected of the bulk of directors. Their acquiescence in management's judgment in normal circumstances is apt to be heightened by their similarities in back-

---

3. See p. 287 infra.

4. M. Mace, Directors—Myth and Reality (1971). See his brief summary in the Symposium on Officers' and Directors' Responsibilities and Liabilities, 27 Bus.Law. 32 (1972).

ground, education, social and financial circumstances, etc. Only quite gradually are small numbers of women, minority members, educators, students and members of other groups diminishing the homogeneity of board membership.

Boards of directors seldom meet more than twelve times a year or about 36 hours; half of them meet only about half as often. Some outside preparation time is also involved, although the materials sent members in advance are seldom very extensive. Outside directors are, therefore, rarely informed as to the details of what is happening within the corporation they direct.

Finally, one ought to note that directors are not particularly well paid *qua* directors. For a long time a $20 or $50 fee per meeting was regarded as standard; of late public firms have been paying annual retainers on the order of $10,000 to $15,000 and very large ones up to $35,000.[5] On the whole, modest sums have not been adequate to assure corporations of a major portion of the time and energy of their directors. Indeed, when liability problems have seemed acute it has been hard to induce people to accept directorships at all. Quite a few directors, particularly those on the boards of smaller, more local, concerns have a different financial incentive for vigilance—they own significant portions of the shares of the corporation or act as the delegates of individuals or institutions that do. Some state laws have *required* that directors own shares or that they own shares unless relieved of the obligation by the charter or by-law. From time to time shareholder groups have demanded that directors invest in their company's stock. Whether the result of director shareholding is worthwhile is questionable. It is in any case hard to enforce a rule calling for significant shareholding when the firm is one of substantial size.

(3) Committees

Observe that a board of directors can assign a large part of its functions to a committee. Read 8 Del.C. § 141 and observe what it reserves to the full board. A cautious lawyer would probably think it inappropriate to delegate such functions, even in the absence of such limits. Committees in effect have moved in two directions in recent years. On the one hand, executive committees composed largely of directors who are full-time executives have taken over many repetitive functions that call for frequent meetings and prompt decisions. On the other, outside directors assume functions which the insiders would, or should, find embarrassing. They can constitute a committee to find a new chief executive officer, one to fix salaries and other compensation, one to meet with the independent auditors to discuss the deficiencies in reports or financial control which they have found or one to consider litigation or other remedial action on accusations made against the management. The American Law Institute's Principles (§§ 3.05–3.07)

---

5. 1 G.T. Washington & V.H. Rothschild, Compensating the Corporate Executive 255 (3d ed. 1962). For more current data see E. Mruk & J. Giardina, Organization and Compensation of Boards of Directors (1983).

would call for such committees in every large publicly held corporation and it appears that this recommendation reflects majority practice.

(4) Movements Toward Change

In recent years the push for change in corporate boardrooms has grown more intense. As of the early 1970's the topic belonged to a few isolated academics and populists. By 1977, however, the question of reconstituting boards of directors was under consideration by groups that could be regarded as hotbeds of conservatism. The SEC experimented with drastic changes in the boards of directors of companies which have been victimized by violations of the securities laws; in various consent decrees companies have agreed to move to boards of outside directors, or to set up special investigating committees of the boards to look into prior misconduct or fend off future misbehavior. Special corporate counsel have been engaged to take over such functions. The SEC called for reactions, by correspondence or by participation in public hearings, to proposals for changes in corporate governance. Congress had hearings upon proposed legislation that would both federalize and drastically change the way in which corporation law controls directors. The New York Stock Exchange pushed for more outside directors and for audit committees. The American Bar Association's Committee on Corporation and Banking Law sponsored repeated Institutes and other symposia on the topic, so that more and more corporation lawyers were exposed to the idea of change. Much excitement has been generated by the process of formulating the American Law Institute's Principles of Corporate Governance and Structure (1982–19___), even though its recommendations seem not to go far beyond what good practice currently indicates. Thus one can look for change within the next few years, without being sure of its direction or of its efficacy.

The changes proposed may be categorized as follows:

(a) *Changes in the Type of Directors.* Reformers push for further development of the trend towards outside directors—toward the 100% line. Outside directors could include representatives of the firm's employees along lines suggested by the German codetermination law and practice. They might include representatives of consumer or environmental protection groups. It has been proposed that directors be "professional", that is, that they should dedicate all or nearly all of their time to one or more corporate directorships.

(b) *Changes in the Selection of Directors.* Instead of the present process of co-opting directors by the existing membership or, in practice, by the chief executive officer, it is proposed that outsiders have an opportunity to place members on boards. Some would streamline the proxy process, discussed in Chapter IX so as to enable minority shareholder groups to nominate and fight for the election of director candidates. Another route to the board might be appointment by some government agency.

(c) *Changes in the Operation of Boards.* There have been suggestions that boards of directors be equipped with staffs of their own and perhaps with special counsel. Thus they could check on management's decisions in a more professional and intensive manner. Individual directors might be given responsibility for specified public aspects of corporate activity such as equal employment, consumer safety, etc. In particular, directors of such specialized types might be chosen where the company or the industry had demonstrated a proclivity towards a particular type of misbehavior.

Bibliography: For an insider's view of boardrooms see M. Mace, Directors— Myth and Reality (1970). Much data is collected in M. Eisenberg, The Structure of the Corporation: A Legal Analysis Pt. III (1976). Periodic surveys by such firms as Korn/Ferry and Heidrick & Struggles keep data current. The Reporters' Notes to the American Law Institute project provide further sources. C. Stone, Where the Law Ends (1975) presents some striking proposals. On committees see McMullen, Committees of the Board of Directors, 29 Bus.Law. 755 (1974). Two older classics are still worth revisiting—Douglas, Directors Who Do Not Direct, 47 Harv.L.Rev. 1305 (1934); R.A. Gordon, Business Leadership in the Large Corporation (1945).

2.   Formal Aspects of Board Action

No corporate lawyer—or for that matter any lawyer at all involved with organizations—can afford to be ignorant of the forms which action by the board of directors takes. This is one of those types of operations which are so routine and recurrent that the best way to avoid having them ruin your life is to master them so thoroughly that they fade into the background, leaving you free to get on with more interesting things.

The fundamental theorem, from which all the other requirements are derived, is that the board act as a board, as a collegial body, rather than a series of individuals. If it is to act as a body, its members must receive notice of the time and place, and preferably the purpose, of the impending meeting; this notice should be of such character as to make attendance reasonably possible. Examine the notice provisions (Art. III, § 2) of the model by-laws in the Documentary Supplement, which are fairly typical. To prevent furtive and unrepresentative meetings from taking action, there have long been quorum requirements. There is a common law rule as to meetings, of quite general applicability, that a majority of the total number of a panel is necessary to have a valid meeting. It is usually for the by-laws to vary that number. See Art. III, § 3 of the model by-laws. The proof of compliance with these formalities, as well as of the substance of what action took place, is usually by means of the minutes taken by the corporate secretary and kept in minute books. Such books together with stock records, seals, etc. can be purchased as "corporate kits"—there is usually an advertisement in the American Bar Association Journal for one called "The Black Beauty"! For making proof of a particular item for an outside party, it is customary for the secretary to prepare extracts from the minutes which he certifies as being true and correct copies, under the seal of the corporation. Look at the sample extract of minutes in the supplement.

One should not leave unexamined the premise that a board is the most desirable form for a corporation's controlling body; that it is so desirable that it should be mandatory. In fact it is mandatory under every American corporation law that I know of, although provisions for one-man boards such as that which appear in 8 Del.C. § 141 (and in some other state statutes but usually only when the number of shareholders is less than 2), in effect eliminate the collegial element. The case for a collegial body has been made by various authorities. I present for you one from an authority not generally associated with that position.[6]

At the end of 1931, Stalin strongly condemned the making of decisions by one man. "Decisions by individuals are always or almost always one-sided. . . ." In each collegium, he said, there are people with opinions which must be considered. They are capable of correcting one-sided views and suggestions and of bringing their own experience to bear on the question under discussion. Decision making by collegia, said Stalin, makes possible the avoidance of serious mistakes.

Clearly, here was an implied criticism of one-man-authority-and-responsibility. Yet that implied criticism has never been developed into a direct attack upon it. Soviet administrators have followed a practice of using the one-man and collegium systems of decision making as alternatives in different situations.

There have been attempts to use modern psychological findings to assess the utility of decision-making by groups as opposed to individuals, with at least some writers coming to conclusions in favor of collegiality.[7]

If a board is necessary or appropriate it follows that it must act as a board, i.e., in a body at a meeting; action taken otherwise should be of no effect. This is the view taken by the cases but the Delaware statute indicates a trend towards loosening this requirement.

---

6. D. Granick, Management of the Industrial Firm in the U.S.S.R. 29 (1959).

7. Haft, Business Decisions by the New Board: Behavioral Sciences and Corporate Law, 80 Mich.L.Rev. 1 (1981); see also Cox & Munsinger, Bias in the Boardroom: Psychological Foundations and Legal Implications of Corporate Cohesion, 48 L. & Contemp.Prob. 83 (Summer 1985.)

BALDWIN v. CANFIELD

Supreme Court of Minnesota, 1879.
26 Minn. 43, 1 N.W. 261.

[In 1871 the Minneapolis Agricultural and Mechanical Association was incorporated to conduct agricultural and mechanical fairs and exhibits. Its affairs were to be managed by a board of directors. It bought 70 acres of land worth about $70,000. The corporation's formal affairs were erratic—no elections of officers or directors were held after the original selection. In November 1872 William King bought all 800 shares of the corporate stock. He sold the buildings on the land and the corporation ceased business.

As a result of various transactions from November 1872 to July 1873 the State National Bank of Minneapolis held 300 and R.J. Baldwin 500 shares of the Association's stock to secure loans to King. In August 1873 King entered into a contract with Canfield to sell him the fairgrounds for $65,000 worth of Northern Pacific bonds and a personal note. Canfield knew that the Association owned the grounds but not about the pledge of stock; he was told that King would furnish him an association deed. Arrangements were made between King and Baldwin to liquidate the loans by Baldwin and the Bank to King out of the proceeds of the Northern Pacific bonds. The Association's stock was to be released to Canfield.

King caused a deed purporting to be a conveyance by the Association to Canfield to be drawn up and had it signed as follows:

"The Minneapolis Agricultural and
"Mechanical Association. [Seal.]

"By R.J. Mendenhall, Thomas Lowry, W.D. Washburn, C.G. Goodrich, G.F. Stevens, Wm. S. King, Levi Butler, W.W. Eastman, W.P. Westfall, Dorilus Morrison, Geo. A. Brackett, directors of said corporation."

No directors' meeting was ever called but King and his attorney found some directors in Hennepin County and others in New York and obtained their signatures. King delivered to Canfield in New York this deed plus a warranty deed to the same property executed by himself. Canfield gave King the railway bonds and a note in exchange. However, he did not ask for the stock, assuming that the deeds gave him title to the land. King kept the bonds and note for himself and did not repay the loans secured by the pledges of Association stock. The pledgees brought suit against King, Canfield and the Association to cancel the two deeds. The trial court entered judgment for plaintiffs and Canfield appealed. Portions of the opinion, per BERRY, J., follow:]

As conclusions of law, the court below finds as follows:

First.—The purchase of all the stock of the Minneapolis Agricultural and Mechanical Association by King did not work a dissolution of the corporation.

Second.—At the time of the conveyance by him to Canfield, King had not the legal title to the real estate purporting to be conveyed thereby, and he has never acquired the legal title thereto.

Third.—At the time of the execution of the deed purporting to be executed by the association mentioned, the legal title to the real estate attempted to be thereby conveyed was in the Minneapolis Agricultural and Mechanical Association.

Fourth.—Said deed was not the act and deed of said association, and did not convey to Canfield the legal title of the real estate purporting to be conveyed thereby.

Fifth.—The plaintiffs are *bona-fide* holders of said eight hundred shares of the stock of said association, as collateral security for the payment of the notes mentioned, and for the return of the gas stock.

Sixth.—By reason of so holding said stock, plaintiffs have a valuable interest in the real estate mentioned, which interest is prior to any claim of King or Canfield in the same.

Seventh.—Canfield is in equity the owner of said eight hundred shares of stock, subject to the right and interest of the plaintiffs therein as found above.

Eighth.—The deed from King to Canfield, and the deed purporting to be executed to Canfield by the association, are a cloud upon the title of such association to said real estate.

Ninth.—Said two deeds are void and of no effect as against the plaintiffs, who are entitled to judgment against King and Canfield, declaring the same and the record thereof void as against plaintiffs, and directing said judgment to be recorded in the registry of deeds for Hennepin county. . . .

The first, second and third of these conclusions of law are obviously right, and require no comment.

The fourth conclusion is called in question by the counsel for defendant Canfield, but we have no doubt of its correctness. As we have already seen, the court below finds that, by its articles of incorporation, the government of the Minneapolis Agricultural and Mechanical Association, and the management of its affairs, was vested in the board of directors. The legal effect of this was to invest the directors with such government and management *as a board,* and not otherwise. This is in accordance with the general rule that the governing body of a corporation, as such, are agents of the corporation only as a board, and not individually. Hence it follows that they have no authority to act, save when assembled at a board meeting. The separate action, individually, of the persons composing such governing body, is not the action of the constituted body of men clothed with corporate powers. [citations omitted] In Vermont a somewhat different rule is allowed, as in the Bank of Middlebury v. Rutland & Washington R. Co., 30 Vt. 159. In that case, and perhaps others in that state, it is held that directors may bind their corporation by acting separately, if this is their usual practice in transacting the corporate business. But we think that the general rule before mentioned is the more rational one, and it is supported by the great weight of authority. From the application of this rule to the facts of this case, it follows that the fourth conclusion of law, viz., that the deed purporting to be made by the association was not the act and deed of such association, and therefore did not convey the title to the premises in question to Canfield, is correct. The directors took no action as a board with reference to the sale of the premises or the execution of any deed thereof. So far as in any way binding the corporation is concerned, their action in executing the deed was a nullity. They could not bind it by their separate and individual action. Hence it follows that the so-called deed is not only ineffectual as a conveyance of real property, but equally so as a contract to convey.

The correctness of the fifth conclusion of law is denied, upon the ground that there was no proper transfer of the stock to plaintiffs, such as is provided for in Gen.St. c. 34, § 49. This section enacts that the stock of corporations like the association aforesaid, shall be transferable only on the books of such corporation, in such form as the directors prescribe. Provisions of this kind are intended solely for the protection and benefit of the corporation; they do not incapacitate a shareholder from transferring his stock without any entry upon the corporation books. McNeil v. Tenth National Bank, 46 N.Y. 325; Grymes v. Hone, 49 N.Y. 17; Field on Corporations, §§ 110, 111. Except as against the corporation, the owner and holder of shares of stock may, as an incident of his right of property, transfer the same as any other personal property of which he is owner. It appearing in this case that the certificates of stock (the evidence of title to the same) were delivered to the plaintiffs in pledge and as security for the payment of the notes and the return of the gas stock loaned, the court below was right in finding the plaintiffs to be *bona-fide* holders of the shares represented by said certificates, as collateral security.

The sixth conclusion of law is, that "by reason of so holding said stock as collateral security as aforesaid, the plaintiffs have a valuable interest in said real estate, which said interest is prior to any claim to or interest in said real estate of defendants King and Canfield." It will be remembered that the court finds that the said association has never owned any other property except said real estate. The stock represents the corporate property. Its value depends upon the value of the corporate property. The holders of the stock, whether holding as general owners or as pledgees, are therefore interested in the preservation of the corporate property, and in preventing it from passing out of the hands of the corporation. Stockholders do not have an "interest" in the corporate real estate, in the sense in which the word "interest" is commonly used in that connection, for such real estate is the property of the corporation. For this reason we think that the court below has used the word "interest" in this finding inaccurately. But this is not important. Upon the facts found, and the preceding conclusions of law, the plaintiffs, as holders of the stock, are interested in the preservation of the corporate property, and in preventing it from passing out of the hands of the corporation. If this is so, they have a right to take legal means to preserve the property, to prevent it from being lost to the corporation, or its value from being impaired. If such value is practically impaired by a cloud upon the title of the corporation to real property, they have a right to have the cloud removed. Their ownership of the stock, either general or special, gives them a right to defend it, as in case of any other property. This right is paramount to any right upon the part of King as general owner of the stock, or of Canfield as equitable owner of it, for the reason that, by the contract of pledge, King has subordinated his rights to theirs, while Canfield's right to the stock accrued while the stock was in the plaintiffs' hands—while they were holding the certificates which are the evidence of its ownership. The certificates were not delivered to Canfield. This fact bound him to take notice of the rights of the plaintiffs as holders of them in pledge.

With that part of the seventh finding which holds that upon the facts in the case, Canfield is in equity the owner of the stock of the association, no fault is found as far as it goes. The remainder of this finding—that such Canfield's ownership is subject to the rights of the plaintiffs therein and thereto—follows from what we have said above.

The ninth finding—to wit, that the two deeds, one purporting to run from the association to Canfield, the other from King to Canfield, are void and of no effect as against the plaintiffs—calls for no remarks beyond what have been already made.

The eighth finding is that the two deeds mentioned are a cloud upon the title of the Minneapolis Agricultural and Mechanical Association to the real estate aforesaid. As respects the deed purporting to run from the association to Canfield, this finding is correct. That deed purports on the face of it to be the deed of the association, and although, for reasons before assigned, it is not the deed of the association, that fact is not apparent upon its face. On the contrary, the deed is, upon its face, regular and valid, and whether it is so in fact and law depends on the extrinsic consideration whether its execution was authorized by the board of directors. As remarked in Story's Eq.Jur. § 700, as "it is a deed purporting to convey lands, * * its existence in an uncancelled state necessarily has a tendency to throw a cloud over the title." Sherman v. Fitch, 98 Mass. 59; Ryan v. Mackmath, 3 Bro.Ch. Rep. 15, note; Colman v. Sarrell, 1 Ves.Jr. 50, note; Van Doren v. Mayor of New York, 9 Paige, 388. Such a cloud a court of equity will remove, by declaring the deed by which it is created, and the record thereof, void. Authorities supra. With regard to this deed, then, the court below properly adjudged it and its record to be void, as respected the plaintiffs.

With regard to the deed from King to Canfield, we see no ground upon which it can be said to cast a cloud upon the title of the association to the real estate mentioned. The title to the real estate was in the association. King's deed is not the deed of the association, and does not purport to be; it is the deed of a total stranger to the title, and in no way of which we can conceive can it possibly affect or cloud the title of the association. As respected the title of the association to the real estate of the association, the deed was void upon its face. For this reason the court below was wrong in adjudging it to be a cloud upon the title of the association . . ..

[The court rejected other points made by Canfield. It affirmed the judgment as to the purported Association deed but modified it as to the deed signed by King.]

SHERMAN v. FITCH

Supreme Judicial Court of Massachusetts, 1867.
98 Mass. 59.

[This was a bill in equity by the assignees in insolvency of Northampton Street Sugar Refinery seeking to declare a record mortgage of personal property held by respondent to be invalid (1) as not a valid corporate deed and (2) violating the insolvency law, a point not relevant to this excerpt.

Respondent was the sales agent of the corporation which owed him about $18,000. One Sampson, the president, director and manager of the manufacturing department delivered the mortgage to him on January 19, 1865 to secure that debt. There were then 3 other directors—Sampson's son and nephew and one Tappan, then in Europe. The directors were also the principal stockholders. All save Tappan knew of the mortgage though no express vote was taken. Neither the directors nor the corporation ever repudiated the mortgage and on February 13, 1866 the stockholders voted "that all contracts, agreements, and other acts, of the president, and directors of the corporation, be and the same are hereby ratified and confirmed." The mortgage was recorded on June 10, 1865. Insolvency proceedings began on April 10, 1866. The case was reserved for determination by the full court.]

WELLS, J. The question submitted to us is whether the instrument of which a copy is annexed to the plaintiff's bill is a valid mortgage of its property by the "Northampton Street Sugar Refinery." The instrument itself is incapable of any other construction than as the mortgage of the corporation. It names the corporation as the party making it; describes the machinery as upon the premises, and in the use and ownership of the corporation; provides for payment by the corporation, and continued possession of the property until default. It is, upon its face, the contract of the corporation, and cannot be made the contract of Sampson by any form of signature whatever. . . .

The signature "Geo. R. Sampson, President of the Northampton Street Sugar Refinery," is consistent with this construction, and, in form, is a good execution by the corporation of a simple contract. Fay v. Noble, 12 Cush. 1. Sampson's seal affixed does not make the instrument his contract; neither does it make it any the less the contract of the corporation . . . If a seal were essential to the validity of the mortgage, it would fail, for the same reasons. If the construction were doubtful upon the face of the instrument, the doubt might be resolved by ascertaining with whose seal it had been executed. But no such conditions exist here. No seal was necessary. As a sealed instrument it could not be construed as the contract of either Sampson or the corporation. But if the seal be disregarded, as it may be, the contract will operate as it was clearly intended, as the mortgage of the corporation.

The remaining consideration relates to the authority of Sampson to execute the mortgage in behalf of the corporation. It is not necessary that the authority should be given by a formal vote. Such an act by the president and general manager of the business of the corporation, with the knowledge and concurrence of the directors, or with their subsequent and long continued acquiescence, may properly be regarded as the act of the corporation. Authority in the agent of a corporation may be inferred from the conduct of its officers, or from their knowledge and neglect to make objection, as well as in the case of individuals . . . The absence of one of the directors in Europe could not deprive the corporation of the capacity to act and bind itself by the acts of the officers in actual charge of its affairs.

If the validity of the mortgage were to depend entirely upon subsequent ratification, such ratification would be effective notwithstanding the recording of the mortgage. No new record would be necessary. The ratification relates back . . .

QUESTIONS

(1) 8 Del.C. § 141(f) goes quite far in permitting informal director action. It formerly contained the words "prior to such action." Would you as a legislator have supported the deletion of that clause? Why?

(2) Are you in accord with the outcome of Baldwin v. Canfield? Do you think it likely that different action would have come out of a proper directors' meeting? What was really wrong with the transaction, anyhow? In allowing plaintiffs to bring the action did the court bypass any significant formalities?

(3) Ought it to make a difference if all of the shareholders of the company assent to the directors' overlooking the formality of a meeting? Should it make a difference whether that assent takes the form of express agreement ahead of time or tacit assent after the event? What if Canfield had owned the stock, free and clear of liens—should the corporation be allowed to disclaim the deal?

(4) Ought the parties with whom the corporation is dealing be made to be concerned about the punctiliousness with which these formalities are observed? Should they have to demand of the corporate officers that they show proof of appropriate action?

(5) What was it about the form of the signature in Sherman v. Fitch that caused difficulties? What would have been the correct form?

(6) You are secretary of the Rapido Corporation, a Delaware corporation, which has a charter and by-laws like those in the Documentary Supplement. The president advises you that a board meeting should be called to carry out a sale and that he *must* have action within 48 hours. You know that two of the directors are on a business trip in Xanadu, one is in the hospital, and another has just resigned and has not been replaced. What possible ways could you suggest as to how you might satisfy the president's demands? How might the by-laws be modified to solve similar future situations, assuming that this is a corporation with a tendency to sudden crises and a peripatetic group of directors? Would resort to an executive committee under 8 Del.C. § 141(c) help?

Bibliography: On the mechanics of directors' meetings, see Encyclopedia of Corporate Meetings, Minutes and Resolutions, Revised (W. Sardell, revisor, 3d ed. 1986). The A.L.I.–A.B.A. volume, The Lawyer's Basic Corporate Practice Manual (R. Deer, Reporter, (3d ed. 1984) and G. Hills, Managing Corporate Meetings (1977).

---

3. The Directors' Duty of Care

One way of examining the issue of what directors are supposed, legally, to do is to look at the cases involving allegations that they have failed to perform these duties. In the next section we will look at cases where that lapse involves a conflict of interest; here we try to isolate cases where the lapse is due to neglect, oversight or incompetence. There is not very much material to work with for "it is unusual for directors to be liable for negligence in the absence of fraud or personal interest".[8] Still, a few of these cases do tell us something not just about the legal rule involved but also about the way in which directors do their business.

The legal rule seems clear at first glance—directors should direct corporations with due care just as drivers should drive cars with due care. But problems begin to enter as we look at the variety of statutory attempts to formulate the rule. The American Law Institute Principles of Corporate Governance [9] categorizes the statutes into those that use "due care", "care that an ordinarily prudent person would exercise in like position and under similar circumstances," "care that an ordinarily prudent person would exercise under similar circumstances", "care exercised by a prudent person in his own affairs" and those that, like the Model Act, add "in a manner he reasonably believes to be in the best interests of the corporation." It is not clear that any of these formulations captures any significant differences in outcome.

We also have the problem of fitting into this formula the business judgment rule enunciated by the courts. Note the following attempt [10] by a New York judge, Judge Shientag, who handled many such cases:

> The fundamental concept of negligence does not vary, whether it is applied to the case of a simple personal injury action or to liability of directors in the management of the affairs of their corporation. A pedestrian crossing the street is under a duty to use reasonable care. He is required to look before he crosses, but "the law does not say how often he must look or precisely how far, or when or from where. . . . If he has used his eyes, and has miscalculated the danger, he may still be free from fault." Knapp v. Barrett, 216 N.Y. 226, 230, 110 N.E. 428, 429. The law does not hold him guilty of negligence although if he had looked oftener the accident might have been avoided. He discharges his duty when he has acted with reasonable prudence. So it is with directors. The law requires the use of judgment, the judgment of ordinary prudence, but it does not hold directors liable simply because they might have used better judgment.

> The question is frequently asked, how does the operation of the so-called "business judgment rule" tie in with the concept of negligence? There is no conflict between the two. When courts say that they will not interfere in matters of business judgment, it is presupposed that judgment—reasonable diligence—has in fact been exercised. A director cannot

8. Bayer v. Beran, 49 N.Y.S.2d 2, 6 (1944). But see DePinto v. Provident Security Life Ins. Co., 374 F.2d 37 (9th Cir. 1967) (holding a doctor liable for negligence as a director of an insurance company—in the amount of $315,000), and DePinto v. United States, 407 F.Supp. 1 (D.Ariz.1975) (rubbing it in by holding that the liability was not deductible because DePinto became a director without fee to accommodate a friend rather than achieve any business purpose of his own).

9. § 4.01, Reporters' Note 1 (Tent. Draft No. 3, 1984).

10. Casey v. Woodruff, 49 N.Y.S.2d 625, 643 (1944).

close his eyes to what is going on about him in the conduct of the business of the corporation and have it said that he is exercising business judgment. Courts have properly decided to give directors a wide latitude in the management of the affairs of a corporation provided always that judgment, and that means an honest, unbiased judgment, is reasonably exercised by them.

In the 1980's a few cases, principally the case that follows, Smith v. Van Gorkom, brought new attention to the negligence field.[11] Indeed, it may not be too strong to say that there was a panic since it coincided with a new skittishness on the part of insurance companies writing director and officer liability policies (see p. 526 infra). Therefore a number of directors found themselves without insurance against the risk of being held liable for negligence and some of them resigned. The legislature of Delaware, with many imitators elsewhere, sought to allay those fears by enacting § 102(7) which authorizes the inclusion of liability-relieving provisions in the certificate of incorporation—subject to limits with respect to misdeeds more serious than negligence. New York amended the above statute to set the level of duty at "that degree of care which an ordinarily prudent person in a like position would use under similar circumstances" and then added a number of sections describing the sort of reliance on others that would satisfy the duty of care. In the midst of this the American Law Institute was attempting to codify its principles of corporate governance and on its second try came up with this (in 1984, before Van Gorkom):

§ 4.01. Duty of Care of Directors and Officers; the Business Judgment Rule

(a) A director or officer has a duty to his corporation to perform his functions in good faith, in a manner that he reasonably believes to be in the best interests of the corporation and otherwise consistent with the principles of § 2.01, and with the care that an ordinarily prudent person would reasonably be expected to exercise in a like position and under similar circumstances.

(b) The duty of care standard set forth in Subsection (a) includes the obligation of a director or officer to make reasonable inquiry in appropriate circumstances.

(c)(1) In performing his duty and functions, a director or officer is entitled to rely on other directors or officers, employees, experts, other persons, or committees of the board in accordance with §§ 4.02–.03. (2) The board may delegate to directors, officers, employees, experts, other persons, or committees of the board the function of identifying matters requiring the attention of the board, and a director, when acting in

---

11. The other case cited by viewers-with-alarm is Hanson Trust PLC v. ML SCM Acquisition, Inc., 781 F.2d 264 (2d Cir. 1986), which also involved directors' reactions to the threat of takeover.

accordance with the standards set forth in §§ 4.02–.03, is entitled to rely on the decisions, judgments, or performance of such persons or committees.

(d) A director or officer does not violate his duty under this Section with respect to the consequences of a business judgment if he:

> (1) was informed with respect to the subject of the business judgment to the extent he reasonably believed to be appropriate under the circumstances;

> (2) was not interested in the subject of the business judgment and made the judgment in good faith; and

> (3) had a rational basis for believing that the business judgment was in the best interests of the corporation.

(e) A director or officer who is subject to liability because of the breach of a duty under this Section will be held liable for damage suffered by his corporation only if the breach of a duty was the proximate cause of the damage suffered by the corporation.

SMITH v. VAN GORKOM

Supreme Court of Delaware, 1985.
488 A.2d 858.

[Transunion Corporation (Trans Union or the Company) was a Delaware corporation, diversified but engaged principally in the business of leasing railcars. Its stock was traded on the New York Stock Exchange, its range in the year prior to the transaction in question having been from 29½ to 38¼. It had an unusual business problem in that its operations generated investment tax credits and accelerated depreciation deductions that exceeded its taxable income. Van Gorkom, the Chairman and Chief Executive Officer of Trans Union, had since 1980 been looking for a solution, including acquisition programs, stock repurchases, etc. In the summer of 1980 events started to move quickly.

August 27, September 5: Van Gorkom reported to senior management about his efforts; Donald Romans, Chief Financial Officer, reported on his study of a "leveraged buyout", i.e., a purchase of the company's stock by management that who would pay for it with sums earned by the corporation. It was said that if management paid $50 a share it would be easy to pay back the purchase price but that at $60 it would be very difficult. Van Gorkom said that he would take $55 for his shares; he vetoed a leveraged buy out as involving conflicts of interest (Van Gorkom was himself close to retirement after 24 years with the company, 17 of them as CEO).

September 13: Van Gorkom met with Jay Pritzker, a corporate takeover specialist and social acquaintance. Without telling the other company managers, Van Gorkom made a proposal using a $55 per share price. Pritzker gave no definite answer though mentioning $50 as more attractive. He reacted negatively to a proposal that Trans Union be free to accept a better offer—and demanded a right to buy 1,750,000 shares of Trans Union at market.

September 15–19: Pritzker advised Van Gorkom that he was interested in a $55 proposal and private meetings took place. Now Van Gorkom was accompanied by several Trans Union executives. The $55 price was not discussed but the number of shares of Trans Union treasury stock to be sold Pritzker was negotiated down to 1 million, the price was to be $38, 75 cents above the market on September 19. Pritzker told Van Gorkom on the 19th that a decision would have to be made by Sunday the 21st. On the 19th consultations with Trans Union's lead bank indicated that financing would be available. Van Gorkom hired a legal adviser, although he did not consult the present head of the firm's legal staff or a director who was its former head. On the 19th Van Gorkom called a special meeting of his board.

September 20: At 11:00 AM Van Gorkom put his proposal before the senior management. Its reaction was negative. Romans objected that the price was too low, that the tax consequence of a cash deal would be bad for low-basis shareholders and that the agreement to sell Pritzer 1 million shares would inhibit other offers. At 12:00 noon Van Gorkom proceeded to the board meeting. There were five inside and five outside directors, all of whom were present except one insider. Of the outsiders four were CEO's of other firms, one was Dean of the University of Chicago Business School. None were investment bankers or financial analysts. They were all familiar with the Company and its operations and financial condition, receiving regular and detailed reports.

The board meeting lasted 2 hours. Van Gorkom began with a twenty-minute oral presentation, reviewing the firm's tax problems and his negotiations with Pritzker. He outlined the terms of Pritzker's offer. He took the position that the $55 figure would be judged by the market since Trans Union was "up for auction." Attorney Brennan told the board that members might be sued if they failed to accept the offer and that a fairness opinion (by a banker) was not required as a matter of law. Romans told the board that he had only learned of the deal that morning. He said that he had not directly addressed the fairness of the price and that, in his opinion, $55 was in the range of a fair price but "at the beginning of the range." Trans Union's President, Chelberg, supported Van Gorkom as to the necessity to act immediately on the offer. Based solely on these oral statements and without seeing a copy of the documents, the board approved the proposed Merger Agreement. However, the Board later claimed to have attached two conditions—(1) that Trans Union had the right to accept any better offer made during the market test period and (2) Trans Union could share proprietary information with other potential bidders. It clearly did not reserve the right actively to solicit other offers. Van Gorkom executed the agreement that night at a formal social event for the opening of the Chicago Lyric Opera. He had not read it.

September 22: Trans Union issued a press release announcing a "definitive" Merger Agreement with Marmon Group Inc., a Pritzker corporation.

October 8: After widespread dissent and threats of resignation by senior Trans Union executives, Van Gorkom negotiated with Pritzker and got several changes in the Agreement in return for promising to persuade the dissidents to stay at least six months. On the 8th Van Gorkom reconvened the board and got approval of the amendments and authorization to hire Salomon Brothers to solicit other offers. The next day another press release announced that Pritzker had gotten the necessary financing and had acquired 1 million shares of Trans Union and that Trans Union was seeking other offers but that if none were received by February, Trans Union's shareholders would meet to vote on the Pritzker proposal. On the next day the amendments to the agreement were executed.

December 19: Plaintiffs began this litigation.

January 21–February 10: On the 21st proxy statements were sent to Trans Union's shareholders, on the 26th the board met and voted to proceed and then a supplement to the proxy statement was approved for mailing. On February 10, the stockholders of Trans Union approved the Pritzker merger proposal—69.9% of the outstanding shares voted in favor and 7.25% against.

The action proceeded, being in effect converted into a class action when the merger became effective and Trans Union ceased to exist. The Chancellor granted judgment for defendants but the Supreme Court reversed and ordered judgment for plaintiffs for the "fair value of the plaintiffs stockholdings." The opinion of the en banc court was written by JUSTICE HORSEY].

Under Delaware law, the business judgment rule is the offspring of the fundamental principle, codified in 8 Del.C. § 141(a), that the business and affairs of a Delaware corporation are managed by or under its board of directors. Pogostin v. Rice, [p. 344 infra] . . . In carrying out their managerial roles, directors are charged with an unyielding fiduciary duty to the corporation and its shareholders. . . . The business judgment rule exists to protect and promote the full and free exercise of the managerial power granted to Delaware directors. . . . The rule itself "is a presumption that in making a business decision, the directors of a corporation acted on an informed basis, in good faith and in the honest belief that the action taken was in the best interests of the company." . . . Thus, the party attacking a board decision as uninformed must rebut the presumption that its business judgment was an informed one.

The determination of whether a business judgment is an informed one turns on whether the directors have informed themselves "prior to making a business decision, of all material information reasonably available to them."

Under the business judgment rule there is no protection for directors who have made "an unintelligent or unadvised judgment." Mitchell v. Highland–Western Glass, Del.Ch., 167 A. 831, 833 (1933). A director's duty to inform himself in preparation for a decision derives from the fiduciary capacity in which he serves the corporation and its stockholders. . . . Since a director is vested with the responsibility for the management of the affairs of the corporation, he must execute that duty with the recognition that he acts on behalf of others. Such obligation does not tolerate faithlessness or self-dealing. But fulfillment of the fiduciary function requires more than the mere absence of bad faith or fraud. Representation of the financial interests of others imposes on a director an affirmative duty to protect those interests and to proceed with a critical eye in assessing information of the type and under the circumstances present here. . . . Thus, a director's duty to exercise an informed business judgment is in the nature of a duty of care, as distinguished from a duty of loyalty. Here, there were no allegations of fraud, bad faith, or self-dealing, or proof thereof. Hence, it is presumed that the directors reached their business judgment in good faith, Allaun v. Consolidated Oil Co., Del.Ch., 147 A. 257 (1929), and considerations of motive are irrelevant to the issue before us.

The standard of care applicable to a director's duty of care has also been recently restated by this Court. In *Aronson*, supra, we stated:

> While the Delaware cases use a variety of terms to describe the applicable standard of care, our analysis satisfies us that under the business judgment rule director liability is predicated upon concepts of gross negligence. (footnote omitted)

473 A.2d at 812.

We again confirm that view. We think the concept of gross negligence is also the proper standard for determining whether a business judgment reached by a board of directors was an informed one.

In the specific context of a proposed merger of domestic corporations, a director has a duty under 8 Del.C. 251(b), along with his fellow directors, to act in an informed and deliberate manner in determining whether to approve an agreement of merger before submitting the proposal to the stockholders. Certainly in the merger context, a director may not abdicate that duty by leaving to the shareholders alone the decision to approve or disapprove the agreement. See Beard v. Elster, Del.Supr., 160 A.2d 731, 737 (1960). Only an agreement of merger satisfying the requirements of 8 Del.C. § 251(b) may be submitted to the shareholders under § 251(c). . . .

It is against those standards that the conduct of the directors of Trans Union must be tested, as a matter of law and as a matter of fact, regarding their exercise of an informed business judgment in voting to approve the Pritzker merger proposal.

The issue of whether the directors reached an informed decision to "sell" the Company on September 20, 1980 must be determined only upon the basis of the information then reasonably available to the directors and relevant to their decision to accept the Pritzker merger proposal. This is not to say that the directors were precluded from altering their original plan of action, had they done so in an informed manner. What we do say is that the question of whether the directors reached an informed business judgment in agreeing to sell the Company, pursuant to the terms of the September 20 Agreement presents, in reality, two questions: (A) whether the directors reached an informed business judgment on September 20, 1980; and (B) if they did not, whether the directors' actions taken subsequent to September 20 were adequate to cure any infirmity in their action taken on September 20. We first consider the directors' September 20 action in terms of their reaching an informed business judgment.

–A–

On the record before us, we must conclude that the Board of Directors did not reach an informed business judgment on September 20, 1980 in voting to "sell" the Company for $55 per share pursuant to the Pritzker cash-out merger proposal. Our reasons, in summary, are as follows:

The directors (1) did not adequately inform themselves as to Van Gorkom's role in forcing the "sale" of the Company and in establishing the per share purchase price; (2) were uninformed as to the intrinsic value of the Company; and (3) given these circumstances, at a minimum, were grossly negligent in approving the "sale" of the Company upon two hours' consideration, without prior notice, and without the exigency of a crisis or emergency.

Under 8 Del.C. § 141(e), "directors are fully protected in relying in good faith on reports made by officers." [citations omitted] The term "report" has been liberally construed to include reports of informal personal investigations by corporate officers, Cheff v. Mathes, Del.Supr., 199 A.2d 548, 556 (1964). However, there is no evidence that any "report," as defined under § 141(e), concerning the Pritzker proposal, was presented to the Board on September 20.[12] Van Gorkom's oral presentation of his understanding of the terms of the proposed Merger Agreement, which he had not seen, and Romans' brief oral statement of his preliminary study regarding the feasibility of a leveraged buy-out of Trans Union do not qualify as § 141(e) "reports" for these reasons: The former lacked substance because Van Gorkom was basically uninformed as to the essential provisions of the very document about which he was talking. Romans' statement was irrelevant to the issues before the Board since it did not purport to be a valuation study. At a minimum for a report to enjoy the status conferred by § 141(e), it must be pertinent to the subject matter upon which a board is called to act, and otherwise be entitled to good faith, not blind, reliance. Considering all of the surrounding circumstances—hastily calling the meeting without prior notice of its subject matter, the proposed sale of the Company without any prior consideration of the issue or necessity therefor, the urgent time constraints imposed by Pritzker, and the total absence of any documentation whatsoever—the directors were duty bound to make reasonable inquiry of Van Gorkom and Romans, and if they had done so, the inadequacy of that upon which they now claim to have relied would have been apparent.

The defendants rely on the following factors to sustain the Trial Court's finding that the Board's decision was an informed one: (1) the magnitude of the premium or spread between the $55 Pritzker offering price and Trans Union's current market price of $38 per share; (2) the amendment of the Agreement as submitted on September 20 to permit the Board to accept any better offer during the "market test" period; (3) the collective experience and expertise of the Board's "inside" and "outside" directors; and (4) their reliance on Brennan's legal advice that the directors might be sued if they rejected the Pritzker proposal. We discuss each of these grounds *seriatim:*

(1)

A substantial premium may provide one reason to recommend a merger, but in the absence of other sound valuation information, the fact of a premium alone does not provide an adequate basis upon which to assess the fairness of an offering price. Here, the judgment reached

---

12. In support of the defendants' argument that their judgment as to the adequacy of $55 per share was an informed one, the directors rely on the BCG study and the Five Year Forecast. However, no one even referred to either of these studies at the September 20 meeting; and it is conceded that these materials do not represent valuation studies. Hence, these documents do not constitute evidence as to whether the directors reached an informed judgment on September 20 that $55 per share was a fair value for sale of the Company.

as to the adequacy of the premium was based on a comparison between the historically depressed Trans Union market price and the amount of the Pritzker offer. Using market price as a basis for concluding that the premium adequately reflected the true value of the Company was a clearly faulty, indeed fallacious, premise, as the defendant's own evidence demonstrates.

The record is clear that before September 20, Van Gorkom and other members of Trans Union's Board knew that the market had consistently undervalued the worth of Trans Union's stock, despite steady increases in the Company's operating income in the seven years preceding the merger. . . . Yet, on September 20, Trans Union's Board apparently believed that the market stock price accurately reflected the value of the Company for the purpose of determining the adequacy of the premium for its sale.

In the Proxy Statement, however, the directors reversed their position. There, they stated that, although the earnings prospects for Trans Union were "excellent," they found no basis for believing that this would be reflected in future stock prices. With regard to past trading, the Board stated that the prices at which the Company's common stock had traded in recent years did not reflect the "inherent" value of the Company. But having referred to the "inherent" value of Trans Union, the directors ascribed no number to it. Moreover, nowhere did they disclose that they had no basis on which to fix "inherent" worth beyond an impressionistic reaction to the premium over market and an unsubstantiated belief that the value of the assets was "significantly greater" than book value. . . .

The parties do not dispute that a publicly-traded stock price is solely a measure of the value of a minority position and, thus, market price represents only the value of a single share. Nevertheless, on September 20, the Board assessed the adequacy of the premium over market, offered by Pritzker, solely by comparing it with Trans Union's current and historical stock price.

Indeed, as of September 20, the Board had no other information on which to base a determination of the intrinsic value of Trans Union as a going concern. As of September 20, the Board had made no evaluation of the Company designed to value the entire enterprise, nor had the Board ever previously considered selling the Company or consenting to a buy-out merger. Thus, the adequacy of a premium is indeterminate unless it is assessed in terms of other competent and sound valuation information that reflects the value of the particular business.

. . .

We do not imply that an outside valuation study is essential to support an informed business judgment; nor do we state that fairness opinions by independent investment bankers are required as a matter of law. Often insiders familiar with the business of a going concern are in a better position than are outsiders to gather relevant information; and under appropriate circumstances, such directors may be fully protected in relying in good faith upon the valuation reports of their management.

Here, the record establishes that the Board did not request its Chief Financial Officer, Romans, to make any valuation study or review of the proposal to determine the adequacy of $55 per share for sale of the Company.   . . .

Had the Board, or any member, made an inquiry of Romans, he presumably would have responded as he testified: that his calculations were rough and preliminary; and, that the study was not designed to determine the fair value of the Company, but rather to assess the feasibility of a leveraged buy-out financed by the Company's projected cash flow, making certain assumptions as to the purchaser's borrowing needs. Romans would have presumably also informed the Board of his view, and the widespread view of Senior Management, that the timing of the offer was wrong and the offer inadequate.

The record also establishes that the Board accepted without scrutiny Van Gorkom's representation as to the fairness of the $55 price per share for sale of the Company—a subject that the Board had never previously considered. . . .

We do not say that the Board of Directors was not entitled to give some credence to Van Gorkom's representation that $55 was an adequate or fair price. Under § 141(e), the directors were entitled to rely upon their chairman's opinion of value and adequacy, provided that such opinion was reached on a sound basis. Here, the issue is whether the directors informed themselves as to all information that was reasonably available to them. Had they done so, they would have learned of the source and derivation of the $55 price and could not reasonably have relied thereupon in good faith.

None of the directors, Management or outside, were investment bankers or financial analysts. Yet the Board did not consider recessing the meeting until a later hour that day (or requesting an extension of Pritzker's Sunday evening deadline) to give it time to elicit more information as to the sufficiency of the offer, either from inside Management (in particular Romans) or from Trans Union's own investment banker, Salomon Brothers, whose Chicago specialist in merger and acquisitions was known to the Board and familiar with Trans Union's affairs.

Thus, the record compels the conclusion that on September 20 the Board lacked valuation information adequate to reach an informed business judgment as to the fairness of $55 per share for sale of the Company.

. . .

(3)

The directors' unfounded reliance on both the premium and the market test as the basis for accepting the Pritzker proposal undermines the defendants' remaining contention that the Board's collective experience and sophistication was a sufficient basis for finding that it reached its September 20 decision with informed, reasonable deliberation.

. . .

(4)

Part of the defense is based on a claim that the directors relied on legal advice rendered at the September 20 meeting by James Brennan, Esquire, who was present at Van Gorkom's request. Unfortunately, Brennan did not appear and testify at trial even though his firm participated in the defense of this action. There is no contemporaneous evidence of the advice given by Brennan on September 20, only the later deposition and trial testimony of certain directors as to their recollections or understanding of what was said at the meeting. Since counsel did not testify, and the advice attributed to Brennan is hearsay received by the Trial Court over the plaintiffs' objections, we consider it only in the context of the directors' present claims. In fairness to counsel, we make no findings that the advice attributed to him was in fact given. We focus solely on the efficacy of the defendants' claims, made months and years later, in an effort to extricate themselves from liability.

Several defendants testified that Brennan advised them that Delaware law did not require a fairness opinion or an outside valuation of the Company before the Board could act on the Pritzker proposal. If given, the advice was correct. However, that did not end the matter. Unless the directors had before them adequate information regarding the intrinsic value of the Company, upon which a proper exercise of business judgment could be made, mere advice of this type is meaningless; and, given this record of the defendants' failures, it constitutes no defense here.

. . .

We conclude that Trans Union's Board was grossly negligent in that it failed to act with informed reasonable deliberation in agreeing to the Pritzker merger proposal on September 20; and we further conclude that the Trial Court erred as a matter of law in failing to address that question before determining whether the directors' later conduct was sufficient to cure its initial error.

[The court made several additional findings. First, it concluded that the directors' decision on October 8 to approve the amendment of the Pritzker Agreement, and thus to permit Trans Union to conduct a "market test," showed the same deficiencies as did their conduct on September 20. The Board approved the amendments without seeing them and adjourned, giving Van Gorkom authority to execute the papers when he received them. The Board further allowed Pritzker to foreclose Trans Union from negotiating any better agreement with third parties.

Second, the Court determined that only one other party, the investment banking firm of Kohlberg, Kravis, Roberts, had actually proposed an alternative agreement. KKR formally offered to purchase all of Trans Union's assets and to assume all of its liabilities for an aggregate cash consideration equivalent to $60 per share. But Van Gorkom apparently convinced the Chief Officer of Trans Union's rail car leasing operation to withdraw from the KKR purchasing group, and the absence of this manager led KKR to withdraw its offer. The court noted that in the face of the terms and time limitations of Trans Union's Merger Agreement with Pritzker as amended October 10, 1980, Trans Union could not conduct an unfettered or free market test.

Finally, the court rejected the directors' argument that they made an informed decision because whatever information the Board lacked on September 20, or on October 8, was fully divulged to the entire Board on January 26, at which time the Board again voted to approve the Pritzker merger. On January 26, the Board was already committed to the merger and could only withdraw from the Pritzker Agreement without liability by establishing fundamental wrongdoing by Pritzker.]

IV.

Whether the directors of Trans Union should be treated as one or individually in terms of invoking the protection of the business judgment rule and the applicability of 8 Del.C. § 141(c) are questions which were not originally addressed by the parties in their briefing of this case. This resulted in a supplemental briefing and a second rehearing en banc on two basic questions: (a) whether one or more of the directors were deprived of the protection of the business judgment rule by evidence of an absence of good faith; and (b) whether one or more of the outside directors were entitled to invoke the protection of 8 Del.C. § 141(e) by evidence of a reasonable, good faith reliance on "reports," including legal advice, rendered the Board by certain inside directors and the Board's special counsel, Brennan.

The parties' response, including reargument, has led the majority of the Court to conclude: (1) that since all of the defendant directors, outside as well as inside, take a unified position, we are required to treat all of the directors as one as to whether they are entitled to the protection of the business judgment rule; and (2) that considerations of good faith, including the presumption that the directors acted in good faith, are irrelevant in determining the threshold issue of whether the directors as a Board exercised an informed business judgment. For the same reason, we must reject defense counsel's *ad hominem* argument for affirmance: that reversal may result in a multi-million dollar class award against the defendants for having made an allegedly uninformed business judgment in a transaction not involving any personal gain, self-dealing or claim of bad faith.

.   .   .

V.

The defendants ultimately rely on the stockholder vote of February 10 for exoneration. The defendants contend that the stockholders' "overwhelming" vote approving the Pritzker Merger Agreement had the legal effect of curing any failure of the Board to reach an informed business judgment in its approval of the merger.

.   .   .

The burden must fall on defendants who claim ratification based on shareholder vote to establish that the shareholder approval resulted from a fully informed electorate. On the record before us, it is clear that the Board failed to meet that burden.

For the foregoing reasons, we conclude that the director defendants breached their fiduciary duty of candor by their failure to make true and correct disclosures of all information they had, or should have had, material to the transaction submitted for stockholder approval.

VI.

To summarize: we hold that the directors of Trans Union breached their fiduciary duty to their stockholders (1) by their failure to inform themselves of all information reasonably available to them and relevant to their decision to recommend the Pritzker merger; and (2) by their failure to disclose all material information such as a reasonable stockholder would consider important in deciding whether to approve the Pritzker offer.

We hold, therefore, that the Trial Court committed reversible error in applying the business judgment rule in favor of the director defendants in this case.

On remand, the Court of Chancery shall conduct an evidentiary hearing to determine the fair value of the shares represented by the plaintiffs' class, based on the intrinsic value of Trans Union on September 20, 1980. Such valuation shall be made in accordance with Weinberger v. UOP, Inc., supra at 712–715. Thereafter, an award of damages may be entered to the extent that the fair value of Trans Union exceeds $55 per share.

.   .   .

[MCNEILLY, JUSTICE, dissented:]

The majority has spoken and has effectively said that Trans Union's Directors have been the victims of a "fast shuffle" by Van Gorkom and Pritzker. That is the beginning of the majority's comedy of errors. The first and most important error made is the majority's assessment of the directors' knowledge of the affairs of Trans Union and their combined ability to act in this situation under the protection of the business judgment rule.

Trans Union's Board of Directors consisted of ten men, five of whom were "inside" directors and five of whom were "outside" directors. The "inside" directors were Van Gorkom, Chelberg, Bonser, William B. Browder, Senior Vice–President–Law, and Thomas P. O'Boyle, Senior Vice–President–Administration. At the time the merger was proposed the inside five directors had collectively been employed by the Company for 116 years and had 68 years of combined experience as directors. The "outside" directors were A.W. Wallis, William B. Johnson, Joseph B. Lanterman, Graham J. Morgan and Robert W. Reneker. With the exception of Wallis, these were all chief executive officers of Chicago based corporations that were at least as large as Trans Union. The five "outside" directors had 78 years of combined experience as chief executive officers, and 53 years cumulative service as Trans Union directors.

The inside directors wear their badge of expertise in the corporate affairs of Trans Union on their sleeves. But what about the outsiders? Dr. Wallis is or was an economist and math statistician, a professor of economics at Yale University, dean of the graduate school of business at the University of Chicago, and Chancellor of the University of Rochester. Dr. Wallis had been on the Board of Trans Union since 1962. He also was on the Board of Bausch & Lomb, Kodak, Metropolitan Life Insurance Company, Standard Oil and others.

William B. Johnson is a University of Pennsylvania law graduate, President of Railway Express until 1966, Chairman and Chief Executive of I.C. Industries Holding Company, and member of Trans Union's Board since 1968.

Joseph Lanterman, a Certified Public Accountant, is or was President and Chief Executive of American Steel, on the Board of International Harvester, Peoples Energy, Illinois Bell Telephone, Harris Bank and Trust Company, Kemper Insurance Company and a director of Trans Union for four years.

Graham Morgan is a chemist, was Chairman and Chief Executive Officer of U.S. Gypsum, and in the 17 and 18 years prior to the Trans Union transaction had been involved in 31 or 32 corporate takeovers.

Robert Reneker attended University of Chicago and Harvard Business Schools. He was President and Chief Executive of Swift and Company, director of Trans Union since 1971, and member of the Boards of seven other corporations including U.S. Gypsum and the Chicago Tribune.

Directors of this caliber are not ordinarily taken in by a "fast shuffle". I submit they were not taken into this multi-million dollar corporate transaction without being fully informed and aware of the state of the art as it pertained to the entire corporate panorama of Trans Union. True, even directors such as these, with their business acumen, interest and expertise, can go astray. I do not believe that to be the case here. These men knew Trans Union like the back of their hands and were more than well qualified to make on the spot informed business judgments concerning the affairs of Trans Union including a 100% sale of the corporation. Lest we forget, the corporate world of then and now operates on what is so aptly referred to as "the fast track". These men were at the time an integral part of that world, all professional businessmen, not intellectual figureheads.

. . .

I have no quarrel with the majority's analysis of the business judgment rule. It is the application of that rule to these facts which is wrong. An overview of the entire record, rather than the limited view of bits and pieces which the majority has exploded like popcorn, convinces me that the directors made an informed business judgment which was buttressed by their test of the market.

At the time of the September 20 meeting the 10 members of Trans Union's Board of Directors were highly qualified and well informed about the affairs and prospects of Trans Union. These directors were acutely aware of the historical problems facing Trans Union which were caused by the tax laws. They had discussed these problems *ad nauseam*. In fact, within two months of the September 20 meeting the board had reviewed and discussed an outside study of the company done by The Boston Consulting Group and an internal five year forecast prepared by management. At the September 20 meeting Van Gorkom presented the Pritzker offer, and the board then heard from James Brennan, the company's counsel in this matter, who discussed the legal documents. Following this, the Board directed that certain changes be made in the merger documents. These changes made it clear that the Board was free to accept a better offer than Pritzker's if one was made. The above facts reveal that the Board did not act in a grossly negligent manner in informing themselves of the relevant and available facts before passing on the merger. To the contrary, this record reveals that the directors acted with the utmost care in informing themselves of the relevant and available facts before passing on the merger. . . .

[In addition] my review of the record leads me to conclude that the proxy materials adequately complied with Delaware law in informing the shareholders about the proposed transaction and the events surrounding it. . . .

[CHRISTIE, JUSTICE, also dissented.]

I respectfully dissent.

Considering the standard and scope of our review under Levitt v. Bouvier, Del.Supr., 287 A.2d 671, 673 (1972), I believe that the record taken as a whole supports a conclusion that the actions of the defendants are protected by the business judgment rule. . . . .

COMMENT

(1) The Transunion litigation was settled for $23.5 million, of which the liability insurance carrier for the directors and officers contributed $10 million; it is said that nearly all of the balance would be paid by the acquiring group. See Manning, Reflections and Practical Tips on Life in the Boardroom after *Van Gorkom*, 41 Bus.Law. 1 (1985).

(2) Note that various federal standards, most notably § 11 of the Securities Act of 1933, discussed at p. 186 supra, set forth a duty of care in different terms from state law and may be applied in different ways by federal courts.

QUESTIONS

(1) Are you as shocked as some commentators by the decision in Van Gorkom? Should the directors have insisted upon a "fairness" opinion by an investment banking firm? Would that have relieved them of liability?

(2) Would any of the formulations of the standard of care set forth at pp. 210–213 supra have made any difference to the way in which the case would come out? Would a provision exercising the powers permitted in § 102(b)(7) of the Delaware law as amended in 1985 have changed the result? Should shareholders be given that option?

(3) Consider the arguments made by adherents of the law and economics school that the imposition of a duty of care upon the members of the board is expensive and counter-productive. One strand of the argument is that other means such as the securities market are adequate to monitor the behavior of corporate managements. Is that the equivalent of telling shareholders that they should simply sell their stock if they think management is not being careful? Another angle to the argument would have it that shareholders can always diversify their securities portfolio against risks, including that of careless management, but that directors cannot diversify *their* risk. One consequence of really enforcing the duty of care, then, is to make directors risk averse, thus not optimizing the behavior of corporations from the point of view of shareholders. There are, after all, complex interrelations between the idea of care and the idea of prudence. Can one safely be bold, the critic of due care asks?

(4) Should there be differences between the liabilities of different directors depending on their specialized skill or their business acumen as demonstrated by other dealings? What of the director who for good reasons is, like O'Boyle in the principal case, unable to come to the critical meeting?

Bibliography: For extensive references see the Reporters' Notes to § 4.01 of the A.L.I. Principles of Corporate Governance: Analysis and Recommendations (Tent. Draft No. 3, 1984). For a generally positive view of Van Gorkom, see Burgman & Cox, Corporate Directors, Corporate Realities and Deliberative Process, 11 J.Corp.L. 311 (1986). For negative views: Fischel, The Business

Judgment Rule and the *Trans Union* Case, 40 Bus.Law. 1437 (1985); Manning, Reflections and Practical Tips on Life in the Boardroom after Van Gorkom, 41 Bus.Law. 1 (1985). See also for a negative view of negligence, Scott, Corporation Law and the American Law Institute Corporate Governance Project, 35 Stanf.L.Rev. 927 (1983).

4. The Duty of Loyalty

One of the foremost functions of the board is to protect the corporation from abuse by self-interested members of management. It cannot fulfill this function unless the board itself is free of corrupting influences. In this section we analyze rules designed to ensure that boards of directors will be able to apply their undivided attention to the best interests of the corporation. A student's reaction is apt to be that all of this can be disposed of by leaning over backwards, by requiring an absolute standard of Caesar's spouse purity. The problem with this approach is that often the very reason why, directors are elected is that they have some other capacity or relationship thought to be valuable to the corporation. Thus if a corporation invites an officer of the local bank to join its board, does it make sense to prevent the corporation from dealing with that bank using its facilities for borrowing, stock transfer services, etc? When some investment bankers have held numerous directorships in important corporations—members of the well known investment banking firm Lehman Brothers held 100 seats, probably a record—it would be a major inconvenience absolutely to debar a banker and the bank firm from engaging in any financial activities with any of those corporations. It would be still more disconcerting to prevent any of those corporations from dealing with any of the other corporations on the board of which the banker happened to be sitting. On the other hand, it would be equally intolerable for the law to acquiesce in business practices simply because they are common practices, without subjecting them to careful scrutiny and imposing rules on them as stringent as is necessary to protect the interests concerned.

While the interest of the corporation, and through it of its shareholders, is the paramount one calling for protection, there are other interests involved as well. The pressure of interlocking directors may make two corporations less anxious to compete and more prone to collusion in terms of prices, markets, etc. This possibility was recognized by Section 8 of the Clayton Act [13] which bars any person from being a director of two or more corporations with capital, surplus and undivided profits aggregating $1,000,000 or more if those two corporations are competitors so that elimination of competition between them by agreement would be illegal. Enforcement has been sporadic but

13. 15 U.S.C.A. § 19.

from time to time the Federal Trade Commission does begin proceedings which usually end in a consent order terminating the relationship. Beyond that, anyone who is concerned about the existence of a "power elite" or an establishment in the United States would be upset by examining data showing the quantity of overlapping directorships among major corporations, for they would confirm one's belief that we are governed by a small group of (by definition) unrepresentative individuals.

We start our examination of the director problem with a slight detour made necessary by changes in the curriculum which have meant that students generally have not been seriously exposed to the law governing agents, trustees, or government officers by the time they begin Corporations. You should examine the following provisions of the Uniform Trusts Act and of the United States Criminal Code (18 U.S.C.A.) as well as §§ 389–392 of the Restatement, Second, Agency and Rules 1.8 and 1.9 of the Code of Professional Responsibility (old DR 5–101, 5–105). Attention has also been focused at times on the conflicts of interest problems of the federal judiciary.

Trustees

Uniform Trusts Act

§ 5.　No trustee shall directly or indirectly buy or sell any property for the trust from or to itself or an affiliate; or from or to a director, officer, or employee of such trustee or of an affiliate; or from or to a relative, employer, partner or other business associate.

§ 18.　Any beneficiary of a trust affected by this Act may if of full legal capacity and acting upon full information by written instrument delivered to the trustee relieve the trustee as to such beneficiary from any or all of the duties, restrictions, and liabilities which would otherwise be imposed on the trustee by this Act, except as to the duties, restrictions, and liabilities imposed by Sections 3, 4 and 5 of this Act. Any such beneficiary may release the trustee from liability to such beneficiary for past violations of any of the provisions of this Act.

Government Officials

§ 208. Acts affecting a personal financial interest

(a) Except as permitted by subsection (b) hereof, whoever, being an officer or employee of the executive branch of the United States Government, of any independent agency of the United States, or of the District of Columbia, including a special Government employee, participates personally and substantially as a Government officer or employee, through decision, approval, disapproval, recommendation, the rendering of advice, investigation, or otherwise, in a judicial or other proceeding, application, request for a ruling or other determination, contract, claim, controversy, charge, accusation, arrest, or other particular matter in which, to his knowledge, he, his spouse, minor child, partner, organization in which he is serving as officer, director, trustee, partner or employee, or any person or organization with whom he is negotiating or has any arrangement concerning prospective employment, has a financial interest—

Shall be fined not more than $10,000, or imprisoned not more than two years, or both.

(b) Subsection (a) hereof shall not apply (1) if the officer or employee first advises the Government official responsible for appointment to his position of the nature and circumstances of the judicial or other proceeding, application, request for a ruling or other determination, contract, claim, controversy, charge, accusation, arrest, or other particular matter and makes full disclosure of the financial interest and receives in advance a written determination made by such official that the interest is not so substantial as to be deemed likely to affect the integrity of the services which the Government may expect from such officer or employee, or (2) if, by general rule or regulation published in the Federal Register, the financial interest has been exempted from the requirements of clause (1) hereof as being too remote or too inconsequential to affect the integrity of Government officers' or employees' services.

§ 218. Voiding transactions in violation of chapter; recovery by the United States

In addition to any other remedies provided by law the President or, under regulations prescribed by him, the head of any department or agency involved, may declare void and rescind any contract, loan, grant, subsidy, license, right, permit, franchise, use, authority, privilege, benefit, certificate, ruling, decision, opinion, or rate schedule awarded, granted, paid, furnished, or published, or the performance of any service or transfer or delivery of anything to, by or for any agency of the United States or officer or employee of the United States or person acting on behalf thereof, in relation to which there has been a final conviction for any violation of this chapter, and the United States shall be entitled to recover in addition to any penalty prescribed by law or in a contract the amount expended or the thing transferred or delivered on its behalf, or the reasonable value thereof.

Where does the director belong in this gallery of fiduciaries of varying degrees of closeness to their beneficiaries and of temptation to misbehave? [14] When the director cases began to come before the courts judges naturally resorted to analogies with older forms of fiduciaries. As their number mounted they began to follow a quite separate pattern. We break the topic down into two major subdivisions. First, what should the formal rule be: an absolute disqualification of directors or something less than that? Subquestions in the same category include whether there ought to be different rules for direct dealings between directors themselves and their corporations as distinct from contracts between two corporations with one or more directors in common, whether similar rules should apply to interest via family members, etc. The second set of questions revolves around the concept of "fairness". If a rule is to embody some sort of fairness concept it must be settled what that concept means—if indeed it has any measurable meaning at all in this context.

We explore the first subdivision by reviewing the development of the law on self-dealing in one important jurisdiction—New Jersey. We examine three important cases and a sharply critical review by Professor Marsh.

STEWART v. LEHIGH VALLEY R.R. CO.

Court of Errors and Appeals of New Jersey, 1875.
38 N.J.L. 505.

[This was an action to recover certain tolls for the passage of boats owned by defendants who pleaded that they had paid all moneys demanded except those waived by a contract between defendants and The Morris Canal and Banking Company from whom the plaintiff Lehigh Valley had leased the Morris canal. The trial court held for plaintiffs and the Court of Errors and Appeals reversed in an opinion by JUDGE DIXON concurred in by 7 other judges, 2 dissenting. The opinion first upheld the validity of the contract against attack on public policy grounds. The portion dealing with conflict of interests follows:]

The plaintiff raises another and a most important question touching the validity of this contract, by a second replication to the second plea before mentioned, upon which no issue was joined, because of the judgment of the Supreme Court holding that plea bad. The main fact averred in the replication also appeared in evidence at the trial, and testimony as to some of the outlying circumstances was offered by the defendants, excluded and exception taken. On the argument before this court, the counsel for the plaintiff urged this main fact as necessarily invalidating the contract relied on by the defendants. This fact is that at the time of the negotiations for, and the execution of, the

---

14. A memorable warning as to the dangers of equating all types of fiduciaries was written by Justice Frankfurter:

But to say that a man is a fiduciary only begins analysis; it gives direction to further inquiry. To whom is he a fiduciary? What obligations does he owe as a fiduciary? In what respect has he failed to discharge these obligations? And what are the consequences of his deviation from duty?

SEC v. Chenery Corp., 318 U.S. 80, 85, 63 S.Ct. 454, 458, 87 L.Ed. 626, 632 (1943).

For a comparison of different types of fiduciaries see Frankel, Fiduciary Law, 71 Calif.L.Rev. 795 (1983).

contract in question, one of the defendants was a director of The Morris Canal and Banking Company—a trustee for it, to manage its affairs—and it is insisted that his relation to the company was, therefore, such that he was prohibited from entering into this contract with it, and that the contract is, *ipso facto,* void.

The position thus assumed by the plaintiff rests upon the broad principle that it was the duty of the director to so deal with the property and franchises of the corporation—to so manage its affairs as would most conduce to the corporate interest, and that he could not perform that duty while contracting with it in his own behalf, or if by possibility his own interest was consistent with the best interest of the company in so contracting, yet, so insidious are the promptings of selfishness and so great is the danger, that it will over-ride duty when brought into conflict with it, that sound policy requires that such contracts should not be enforced or regarded. After an examination of all the cases cited, and such others as I have found, and a careful consideration of the principle and the results of regarding and of disregarding it, I have come to the conviction that the true legal rule is, that such a contract is not void, but voidable, to be avoided at the option of the *cestui que trust,* exercised within a reasonable time. I can see no further safe modification or relaxation of the principle than this. A director of a corporation may have rights not arising out of express contract—such as the right to pass over its railroad, or transport his goods over its canal, on paying reasonable tolls, or to have money which he has loaned it repaid to him; but where the right is one which must stand, if at all, upon an express contract, and which does not arise by operation or implication of law, then he shall not hold it against the will of his *cestui que trust;* for in the very bargain which gave rise to it, in which he should have kept in view the interest of that *cestui que trust,* there intervened before his eyes the opposing interest of himself. The vice which inheres in the judgment of a judge in his own cause, contaminates the contract; the mind of the director or trustee is the forum in which he and his *cestui que trust* are urging their rival claims, and when his opposing litigant appeals from the judgment there pronounced, that judgment must fall. It matters not that the contract seems a fair one. Fraud is too cunning and evasive for courts to establish a rule that invites its presence. There may be isolated cases in which the trustee is willing to make a contract on more favorable terms for the *cestui que trust* than any one else, but the opportunities for self-advancement, at the expense of those whose concerns he has in charge, and under circumstances where concealment is easy, are so much more numerous than these isolated cases, that in declaring a rule the latter are not worthy of consideration. Nor is it proper for one of a board of directors to support his contract with his company, upon the ground that he abstained from participating as director in the negotiations for and final adoption of the bargains by his co-directors, the very words in which he asserts his right declare his wrong; he ought to have participated, and in the interest of the stockholders, and if he did not, and they have thereby suffered loss, of which they shall be the judges, he must restore the rights he has obtained—he must hold against them no advantage that he has got through neglect of his duty towards them. Many authorities exemplifying the rule may be found. [Citations omitted]

The application of the rule is most frequent in the relations between vendor and purchaser, but its reason and force extend to all agents and trustees, public and private. It has not always presented itself to the minds of judges in its full scope. At times they have been seduced into listening to suggestions that the circumstances of the special case showed the absence of fraud and over-reaching. At other times, they have intimated that the *cestui que trust* must seek his relief in equity, but the strongest intellects have enunciated the rule with its utmost vigor, and in its broadest extent.

The qualification, however, which the rule undoubtedly has, saves the case before us from its operation. The *cestui que trust* of the defendant director was not the plaintiff, but the Morris Canal and Banking Company. The right of avoidance was one which belonged to that company and its stockholders, and not to the plaintiff. The act of 1871, empowering the canal company to lease, only authorized it to lease the canal, with its boats, property, works, appurtenances, and franchises; and under this power, it could scarcely transfer so peculiarly personal a privilege as this option to avoid a contract. Nor would a transfer of the contract, and all of the canal company's rights under it, carry this right of choice; for that does not spring out of the contract, but out of the fiduciary relation existing between the parties at the time the contract was made. And, moreover, the case shows that, after the lease to the plaintiff, and during all the time in which it is claimed the tolls sued for were accruing, the plaintiff dealt with the defendants on the basis of the binding efficacy of the contract.

I conclude, therefore, that there appears before us no reason for refusing to give to this contract that force to which our construction of its terms entitles it, and that, upon the case before us, judgment should be rendered for the defendants below, the plaintiffs in error.

ROBOTHAM v. PRUDENTIAL INS. CO. OF AMERICA

Court of Chancery of New Jersey, 1903.
64 N.J.Eq. 673, 53 A. 842.

[This was an action by shareholders of the Prudential Insurance Company of America to block a proposed plan under which a large number of new shares of Prudential were to be issued and sold to Fidelity Trust Company—enough to give Fidelity control over Prudential. Shareholders of Prudential were given a chance to sell their shares to Fidelity. The upshot was that Fidelity would own in all more than 50% of Prudential's stock. Meanwhile Prudential which had somewhat less than ⅓ of the stock of Fidelity was to acquire a majority thereof. As a result Fidelity (i.e., its directors) would control the election of Prudential's directors and vice versa. The President of Prudential asserted that the purpose was to "put the assets of the company beyond the reach of reckless speculators." VICE CHANCELLOR STEVENSON enjoined the plan. He did so in part on the basis that the stock acquisition was ultra vires. However, he also discussed the question whether the fact that half of the 14 Prudential directors were directors and shareholders of Fidelity invalidated the transaction. Excerpts from that portion of the opinion follow:]

How far self-interest of a director in opposition to the interest of his corporation disqualifies him from acting as a director, or exposes corporate action to injunction at the arbitrary election of a dissenting stockholder, or exposes such action to review by the courts at the instance of such stockholder, are matters about which the authorities are not entirely in accord. . . .[15] On the one hand, it may be urged with great force that a minority stockholder has a right to repose upon impartial, unbiased action on the part of the directors who are his trustees, and that he ought not to be obliged, where directors have been acting on both sides of a transaction, or are proposing so to act, to come into court with proofs of actual injury to himself or to the corporation. On the other hand, theoretical rules have to give way to the practical necessities of business. Business eventually is not extended, and great departments of human activity are not developed, by means which are fraudulent. The use of such means in the end is suicidal. In these days the relations of corporations to each other are exceedingly complex. Common directors abound, and common directors are better than dummies. Whether a transaction between two corporations has been accomplished or remains executory, I incline strongly to believe that the safe rule in most cases, in the end, will be found to be that the presence of a director or directors on both sides of the transaction under investigation does not give the dissenting stockholder an arbitrary right to an injunction, but may give him a most ample right to subject the transaction to the scrutiny of the court, and may cast upon the corporations or directors concerned the burden of disclosing and justifying the transaction. To give the dissenting stockholder the arbitrary right to an injunction in this class of cases often will put a deadly weapon in the hands of the blackmailer and the corporation "striker." Such a rule tends to drive the actual wrongdoers to cover,— to induce them to seek concealment while the corporate action is accomplished through apparently impartial directors, who are in fact only agents or "dummies." In several recent cases before this court where the existence of common directors was relied on for injunctive relief, these common directors while the motion was pending were made to disappear, and apparently impartial directors took their place, who proceeded solemnly to approve of the action of the old boards which the injunction was designed to restrain. The fiction of corporate existence goes down in many cases before a charge of fraud, but I incline to think that this fiction in most cases belonging to the class under consideration should be rigidly maintained to defeat a mere arbitrary demand on the part of a stockholder that a corporate transaction should be enjoined, even though all the impartial directors of the corporation and nine-tenths of the stockholders come into court with a demonstration that the transaction was advantageous in all respects to their corporation, and that an injunction upon it would cause great loss. But whether in this case dissenting stockholders can arbitrarily prevent corporate action on the ground of the presence of directors or a majority of directors having a hostile interest, I do not intend to consider. I propose to apply, not to the details of this scheme but to the scheme as a whole, what certainly is a safe rule, viz., that where all the directors of a corporation have a direct, valuable interest in the action which they propose to take, in which interest their stockholders do not participate, these stockholders may compel them, before they will be allowed to carry out their scheme, to prove before the court that it is advantageous to the corporation.

15. [Ed.] Here the court cited, inter alia, the Stewart case, p. 227 supra.

It seems to me that the disqualification of these 14 directors to adjudicate finally that their scheme for exchange of control is advantageous to the Prudential Company is clear and absolute. That the proposed scheme, if carried into effect, will directly and necessarily benefit these 14 directors, and secure to them great emoluments and great influence and power, seems to be a fact beyond dispute. The salaries and other advantages controlled by the directors of an insurance company holding to-day nearly $60,000,000 of assets, and contemplating in the near future the possession of a hundred or even two hundred million dollars of assets, constitute a personal prize of very great magnitude. It is not an answer to this proposition to say that these directors already hold this prize in their possession. They do not hold it in perpetuity for themselves and those successors whom they will personally select from time to time as death makes vacancies in their board. The effect of the scheme is to prevent them and their chosen successors from losing the prize after they have ceased to own beneficially the majority interest in the stock which now keeps the prize in their possession. These 14 directors have never made an independent and unselfish adjudication that this scheme will be beneficial to the Prudential Company. They do not exclude themselves from the charmed circle which their scheme contemplates. They propose to sit therein to the exclusion of the other stockholders. That this is their plan is evident, and is not denied. The Prudential directors are to "dominate," and, if any change in the membership of the Prudential board were contemplated before the scheme is to go into effect, the defendants ought to have proved, and could easily have proved, such fact. If these directors had merely feared that in the future a combination of a majority of stockholders owning eight or ten million dollars worth of Prudential stock might commit a "depredation" not merely upon the salaries and perquisites of the managers of the company, but upon the assets of the company which belong to its policy holders and stockholders, they could easily have arranged their scheme so that in effecting its adoption they would be free from any disqualification arising from selfish interests. If, for instance, they had planned to select 14 men of high character and standing in the business world, and then to see that each of these men was duly qualified with at least one share of Prudential stock to act as a director, and then to make these 14 independent men the personal syndicate for perpetual control, while they themselves unselfishly retired forever from the scheme of their labors and the possession of their emoluments as managers, they would then have presented a scheme which would not be open to the particular objection now under consideration. They have not done this, nor have they apparently considered such a possible situation,—much less, given it their approval as directors. Applying to the situation the very moderate and safe rule above mentioned, the result is that the favorable judgment of these 14 directors, when challenged by a dissenting stockholder, is to be practically excluded from consideration, and the burden is placed upon these directors of making full disclosure of their scheme to the court, and of presenting clear and satisfactory proof that it will in fact be advantageous to the Prudential Company. In the absence of such proof, the scheme cannot receive the commendation of a court of equity; and, as it has not received the commendation of an impartial board of directors, it must be interdicted.

Could a single equity judge, or even a bench of such judges, unaided by experience in the management of insurance companies, and unaided by the favorable judgment of a board of insurance managers and experts qualified to express an impartial opinion, find in the evidence so far produced in this case safe grounds for the affirmative conclusion that this startling novelty in corporation law and corporation business is a safe and prudent thing for the Prudential Insurance Company to adopt and establish? I think not, and on this ground alone, in my opinion, an injunction should go. . . .

COMMENT

(1) In 1903 the big five insurance companies stood at the peak of their power.[16] Their enormous investments enabled them to hold control over banks (the Fidelity was just one example), to exercise wide political powers (the President of the Prudential was also United States Senator from New Jersey), to enjoy great prestige in an age that respected wealth, and to congratulate themselves on their custodianship of the public interest. Lawyers had done much to consolidate this position although the later President of the Equitable (a professor of law at Columbia) could recall:

> "the extraordinary service which insurance lawyers rendered in years gone by, . . . only to develop a public atmosphere and judicial decisions and legislation which puts the insurer under his contract in a worse position . . . than is any other contracting party. That is overservice by the profession."

Among the lawyers involved were Paul D. Cravath and William Nelson Cromwell, the eponymous founders of two great law firms, Samuel Untermyer, then in his pro-management phase, and Richard Lindabury (also involved in See v. Heppenheimer p. 143 supra) who became head of the Prudential.

(2) This picture changed drastically in 1905 when the New York legislature's Armstrong committee began to probe into the insurance business under the leadership of its suave but implacable counsel, Charles Evans Hughes. The immediate impetus for this investigation seems to have been a $200,000 fancy dress party given at Sherry's in New York by James Hazen Hyde, the profligate son of Equitable's able, energetic and domineering founder. Given the then value of the dollar, this was made by the newspapers to seem rather excessive; Mr. Hyde retired to Europe for a 35 year "rest." The investigation resulted in major changes of personnel (including the Prudential's president) and extensive statutory reform.

(3) The Prudential's maneuvers must be considered in the light of the tensions between the stockholders and the policyholders over the management of the firm and its finances. To some extent the scheme was intended to safeguard the policyholder (as well as the directors) against profit-seeking managers. Eventually the large firms were mutualized, i.e. converted to ownership by their policyholders.

---

16. This comment is derived largely from M. Keller, The Life Insurance Enterprise, 1885–1910 (1963). The quotation is at p. 190.

ABELES v. ADAMS ENGINEERING CO., INC.

Supreme Court of New Jersey, 1961.
35 N.J. 411, 173 A.2d 246.

[This was an action on a contract whereby defendant agreed to pay a 6% commission for obtaining a 15 year loan of $1,600,000. The contract ran between defendant, a Florida corporation, and Atwill & Company, a corporation engaged in investment banking. The latter corporation was wholly owned by William Atwill, Jr. who was a director of defendant corporation. The contract was signed by the President of Adams Engineering who, with his family, owned 90% of its stock. After Atwill & Company had assertedly found a suitable lender, it assigned the contract to the plaintiff who brought suit. The trial judge found for plaintiff but the Appellate Division reversed.

The Supreme Court sustained the trial court's finding that Atwill had in fact found a lender and that defendant had agreed to accept the conditions upon which the lender insisted, although the deal was never closed. The portions of JUSTICE FRANCIS' opinion dealing with the conflict of interest issue follow:]

The Appellate Division reversal was predicated also on the ground that plaintiff had produced no proof to establish that the brokerage agreement (which it found to be) between the defendant corporation and its director Atwill was fair and reasonable. We agree with the view expressed in the opinion that a contract between a corporation and one of its directors, made without approval of the stockholders, is not enforceable by the director unless it is honest, fair and reasonable. The burden of demonstrating those elements by clear and convincing proof is on the director. In this area the law of Florida and New Jersey is the same.[17] [Citations omitted]

Plaintiff contends that the brokerage agreement (appearing verbatim supra) was made with Atwill & Company, Inc., a Florida corporation, and not with Atwill as an individual. Therefore, the argument continues, since the contract was between two corporations having common directors or officers, it has the express sanction of the defendant's charter, and thus the doctrine requiring proof of fairness is not applicable. It is true that defendant's certificate of incorporation provides that no contract between it and another corporation shall be affected or invalidated by the fact that the contracting parties have one or more common directors. Assuming validity of such a provision, inquiry by a court with respect to fairness of the agreement to each corporation is not foreclosed. [Citations omitted]

The soundness of the rule authorizing scrutiny regardless of the charter clause becomes manifest in a case like this one. Atwill is the sole owner and operator of Atwill & Company, Inc., and to permit a corporate facade to stand in the way of a fairness inquiry would be to subvert a doctrine which has its roots deep in common law policy.

We find, however, on a consideration of all the circumstances disclosed by the record, that the brokerage contract is in fact a corporate undertaking of Atwill & Company, Inc. The reasons therefor need not be expounded at length because, regardless of that fact, under the

17. [Ed.] At the end of a comparable paragraph in its opinion the Appellate Division had cited the Stewart case, p. 227 supra. See 64 N.J.Super. 167, 181, 165 A.2d 555, 562.

circumstances present here we agree that plaintiff's burden of proof includes the requirement for demonstrating the fairness of the commission agreement.

On the whole record the only respect in which the proof of fairness of the contract may be said to be deficient is the amount of the commission agreed to be paid, i.e., 6% of the loan procured by the broker. Plaintiff appears to have realized the need for such evidence because he began to question Atwill as follows:

"Q. Are there any special problems in securing financing for Florida business companies?

"Mr. Schulter: I object.

"The Court: What is the relevancy of this?

"Mr. Fox: Withdraw this line of questioning.

"Mr. Schulter: Do you mean there is any dispute as to the 6% being reasonable or not?

"The Court: I do not think there is any question about that.

"Mr. Schulter: There is your Honor. The loan was being worked on.

"The Court: I do not see how this can be relevant in this action.

"Sustain the objection."

At that stage the matter was dropped. The court apparently felt that the express contract for 6% was controlling. And the theory of plaintiff's offer of proof or of defendant's objection was not explained to him beyond the excerpt quoted. We agree under the circumstances that the judgment of the trial court must be reversed for that lack of proof and the matter remanded for a new trial on this phase of the case but limited to the single question of fairness and reasonableness of the stipulated 6% commission. If that rate is found to be unreasonable, in the sense of being excessive, it would follow in the peculiar factual context of the case that the necessary adjustment should be ordered.

According to the testimony, by agreement among themselves Levkoff and Abeles were to receive 4% (2% each) and Atwill 2%. Defendant argues that Levkoff and Abeles did most of the work, and that Atwill did nothing but locate a broker with experience in loan transactions and arrange for his services. That circumstance, it is said, is indicative of the unfairness to the corporate defendant of the 6% arrangement. Atwill did say, among other things, that "introducing a borrower to effective people who can make a loan is adequate reason for [his] compensation." It cannot be gainsaid that such participation by itself in ordinary brokerage transactions is commonly recognized as a compensable factor. But the testimony shows also that he participated in meetings and discussions thereafter during the negotiations. And it does not appear specifically that such participation was considered as an integral part of his duties as director of defendant. . . .

Marsh, Are Directors Trustees?: [18]

There have been several different rules adopted by courts and legislatures to deal with this problem of conflict of interest, which correspond roughly with successive periods in the legal history of this country. Therefore in the discussion immediately following, I propose to consider the principles which have been advanced at one time or another, in more or less chronological order, even though the earlier ones have been largely if not completely abandoned.

I. Types of Legal Regulations.

a. *Prohibition.*

In 1880 it could have been stated with confidence that in the United States the general rule was that any contract between a director and his corporation was voidable at the instance of the corporation or its shareholders, without regard to the fairness or unfairness of the transaction. This rule was stated in powerful terms by a number of highly regarded courts and judges in cases which arose generally out of the railroad frauds of the 1860's and 1870's. . . .

Under this rule it mattered not the slightest that there was a majority of so-called disinterested directors who approved the contract. The courts stated that the corporation was entitled to the unprejudiced judgment and advice of all of its directors and therefore it did no good to say that the interested director did not participate in the making of the contract on behalf of the corporation. ". . . the very words in which he asserts his right, declare his wrong; he ought to have participated . . ." [19]

Perhaps the strongest reason for this inflexibility of the law was given by the Maryland Supreme Court which stated that, when a contract is made with even one of the directors, "the remaining directors are placed in the embarrassing and invidious position of having to pass upon, scrutinize and check the transactions and accounts of one of their own body, with whom they are associated on terms of equality in the general management of all the affairs of the corporation." Or, as Justice Davies of the New York Supreme Court expressed the same thought: "The moment the directors permit one or more of their number to deal with the property of the stockholders, they surrender their own independence and self control."

This rule applied not only to individual contracts with directors, but also to the situation of interlocking directorates where even a minority of the boards were common to the two contracting corporations. Not only that, it was also applied to the situation where one corporation owned a majority of the stock of another and appointed its directors, even though they might not be the same men as sat on the

18. 22 Bus.Law. 35 (1966). Reprinted by permission of the Business Lawyer.

19. Stewart v. Lehigh Valley R.R. Co., 38 N.J.Law 505, at 523 (Ct.Err. & App. 1875).

board of the parent corporation. It is interesting to note that the courts during this era had no difficulty in identifying so-called dummy directors, even though their inability to do so was later given as one of the reasons why this rule of law had to be abandoned.[20]

This principle, absolutely inhibiting contracts between a corporation and its directors or any of them, appeared to be impregnable in 1880. It was stated in ringing terms by virtually every decided case, with arguments which seemed irrefutable, and it was sanctioned by age. . . .

Thirty years later this principle was dead.

b. *Approval by a disinterested majority of the board.*

It could have been stated with reasonable confidence in 1910 that the general rule was that a contract between a director and his corporation was valid if it was approved by a disinterested majority of his fellow directors and was not found to be unfair or fraudulent by the court if challenged; but that a contract in which a majority of the board was interested was voidable at the instance of the corporation or its shareholders without regard to any question of fairness.

One searches in vain in the decided cases for a reasoned defense of this change in legal philosophy, or for the slightest attempt to refute the powerful arguments which had been made in support of the previous rule. Did the courts discover in the last quarter of the Nineteenth Century that greed was no longer a factor in human conduct? If so, they did not share the basis of this discovery with the public; nor did they humbly admit their error when confronted with the next wave of corporate frauds arising out of the era of the formation of the "trusts" during the 1890's and early 1900's.

The only explanation which seems to have been given for this change in position was the technical one that a trustee, while forbidden to deal with himself in connection with the trust property, could deal directly with the cestui que trust if he made full disclosure and took no unfair advantage; and that the case of a director who abstained from representing the corporation but dealt in his personal capacity with a majority of disinterested directors was properly analogized to a trustee dealing with the cestui que trust. . . .

Some courts ostensibly took longer to repudiate the previous strict rule than others. The New Jersey Court of Errors and Appeals, for example, reaffirmed Stewart v. Lehigh Valley Railroad in 1920 and again in 1939,[21] and it was not until 1961 that the New Jersey Supreme Court overruled that case [22] (without citing it or even alluding to the

---

20. Robotham v. Prudential Ins. Co. of America, 64 N.J.Eq. 673, at 709, 53 A. 842, at 856 (Ch.1903): "Common directors abound, and common directors are better than 'dummies'."

21. Busch v. Riddle, 92 N.J.Eq. 265, 114 A. 348 (Ct.Err. & App.1920). Wiencke v. Branch–Bridge Realty Corp., 125 N.J.Eq.

135, 4 A.2d 415 (Ct.Err. & App.1939). Cf. Rothenberg v. Franklin Washington Trust Co., 127 N.J.Eq. 406, 13 A.2d 667 (Ch.1940), modified, 129 N.J.Eq. 361, 19 A.2d 640 (Ct. Err. & App.1941).

22. Abeles v. Adams Engineering Co., Inc., 35 N.J. 411, 173 A.2d 246 (1961).

fact that such a rule had ever existed in New Jersey). Similarly, it was not until 1954 that the New York Court of Appeals, with even less courage than the New Jersey court, overruled Munson v. Syracuse, G. & C.R.R. Co. by a shamefaced *per curiam* affirmance of the Appellate Division.[23]

However, this apparent survival of the older rule was nothing but a meaningless facade. As early as 1903 the New Jersey courts decided that the strict rule did not apply to a case of "interlocking directorates."[24] Since the case of a contract between two corporations with common directors was thought to present an entirely different problem than a contract with a director individually, without any inquiry into the question whether the common director or directors owned more stock in one of the two corporations than the other, all that a director had to do in order to avoid the older rule was to incorporate the business in which he expected to have dealings with the corporation on whose board he sat. Since most such businesses would be incorporated anyway for other reasons, this meant that the older rule was virtually abrogated except with respect to approval of salaries.

Under the rule that a disinterested majority of the directors must approve a transaction with one of their number, the question arose whether this meant a disinterested quorum (i.e., normally a majority of the whole board) or merely a disinterested majority of a quorum, so that the interested director or directors could be counted to make up the quorum. Virtually all of the cases held that the interested director could not be counted for quorum purposes.

c. *Judicial review of the fairness of the transaction.*

By 1960 it could be said with some assurance that the general rule was that no transaction of a corporation with any or all of its directors was automatically voidable at the suit of a shareholder, whether there was a disinterested majority of the board or not; but that the courts would review such a contract and subject it to rigid and careful scrutiny, and would invalidate the contract if it was found to be unfair to the corporation.

It is difficult in most States to determine with exactness the point of time at which the rule changed again, or indeed to prove beyond a reasonable doubt that it has in fact changed in a particular State. There are a large number of cases which deal with situations where a majority of the board were interested and which discuss them solely in terms of a review of the fairness of the transaction, without bothering to cite or discuss any of the previous decisions, perhaps in the same State, enunciating the rule that there must be approval by a disinterested majority of the board. Some of these cases could be distinguished from the previous holdings on the basis that they deal with interlocking directorates rather than contracts with interested directors, if one

---

23. La Vin v. La Vin, 283 App.Div. 809, 128 N.Y.S.2d 518 (1954), aff'd per curiam, 307 N.Y. 790, 121 N.E.2d 620 (1954).

24. Robotham v. Prudential Ins. Co. of America, 64 N.J.Eq. 673, 53 A. 842 (Ch. 1903) . . .

wishes to take any stock in that distinction. There is another large group of cases which deal with situations where it does not appear that a majority of the board were interested in the transaction, but the opinions of the courts deal with the problem solely in terms of fairness, without mentioning any requirement of a disinterested majority. These cases are not necessarily inconsistent with such a requirement, but they in all probability indicate that these courts have gone over to the modern rule. . . .

QUESTIONS

(1) How useful do you find the analogies suggested by the above materials between directors and other types of fiduciaries? What factors would you regard as most important in distinguishing between them?

(2) Do you agree with Professor Marsh that Abeles overruled Stewart? Could you have written the latter opinion so as to accommodate the older case? If you think the cases inconsistent, which do you prefer? Where does Robotham stand in the sequence of New Jersey developments? Do you agree with Professor Marsh that it substantially undercut the effect of the Stewart rule?

(3) Is the rule of the disinterested quorum of directors referred to in the Marsh extract a reasonable half way station between the two extremes? What assumptions about individual psychology or group interaction support (or undermine) such a rule?

(4) Consider 8 Del.C. § 144 (largely borrowed from California and duplicated in New York). Is it possible under that law for a transaction to be validated even though it would not pass muster under the present New Jersey case law? Does Clause Eleventh of the Charter in the Documentary Supplement go beyond the authorization in § 144?

"Fairness"

In making up your mind as to the preferable rule among these three you need to suspend final judgment until you can explore the content of the term "fairness". A rule calling for fairness only will mean one thing if fairness can be made a concrete, objective test and another if it continues to float in the realm of subjectivity. If it turns out to be something difficult to establish, the locus of the burden of proof may turn out to be the critical factor. Be on the alert for ambiguities as between "fairness" in a substantive sense and "fairness" in a procedural sense, e.g., as demanding full disclosure by the interested party.

Our review of the fairness problem again focusses upon the case-law of one state, this time that of New York:

GLOBE WOOLEN CO. v. UTICA GAS & ELEC. CO.

Court of Appeals of New York, 1918.
224 N.Y. 483, 121 N.E. 378.

[Plaintiff corporation owned a woolen and a worsted mill in Utica and defendant generated and sold electricity. Maynard was president, director and chief shareholder of plaintiff. He was a director of defendant but held no stock in it. From 1903 to 1906 studies were made by Greenidge, manager of defendant's electric power department, of the feasibility of substituting electricity for the steam used by plaintiff's plants. In December 1906 and February 1907 agreements were arrived at under which defendant was to supply plaintiff with electricity at $.0104 per kilowatt hour with a guaranty that the saving on heat, light and power over the cost for the corresponding month in the last year prior to the change would amount to $300. The contracts were for 5 years renewable by plaintiff for another 5. The executive committee of the defendant approved the contracts. Mr. Maynard presided at each meeting, put the resolution but did not vote or say anything. It cost plaintiff $21,000 to make the changes; it soon appeared that defendant had made a losing contract. Greenidge has miscalculated the amount of steam needed for heating; changes in the type of dyeing done by plaintiff made the situation worse. In February 1911 defendant gave notice of rescission. It had supplied plaintiff with power worth at least $60,000. However, it had received no payment but rather owed $11,721 on its guaranty. Plaintiff sued for specific performance but the referee annulled the contracts.

The Appellate Division affirmed but required defendant to repay the installation cost. The Court of Appeals, in an opinion by JUDGE CARDOZO, affirmed.]

We think the evidence supports the conclusion that the contracts are voidable at the election of the defendant. The plaintiff does not deny that this would be true if the dual director had voted for their adoption. Munson v. Syracuse, G. & C.R.R. Co., 103 N.Y. 58, 8 N.E. 355. But the argument is that by refusing to vote he shifted the responsibility to his associates, and may reap a profit from their errors. One does not divest oneself so readily of one's duties as trustee. The refusal to vote has, indeed, this importance: It gives to the transaction the form and presumption of propriety, and requires one who would invalidate it to probe beneath the surface. Davids v. Davids, 135 App. Div. 206, 209, 120 N.Y.Supp. 350. But "the great rule of law" (Andrews, J., in Munson v. Syracuse, G. & C.R.R. Co., supra, 103 N.Y. at page 73, 8 N.E. at page 358) which holds a trustee to the duty of constant and unqualified fidelity is not a thing of forms and phrases. A dominating influence may be exerted in other ways than by a vote. Adams v. Burke, 201 Ill. 395, 66 N.E. 235; Davids v. Davids, supra. A beneficiary, about to plunge into a ruinous course of dealing, may be betrayed by silence as well as by the spoken word.

The trustee is free to stand aloof, while others act, if all is equitable and fair. He cannot rid himself of the duty to warn and to denounce, if there is improvidence or oppression, either apparent on the surface, or lurking beneath the surface, but visible to his practiced eye. . . .

There was an influence here, dominating, perhaps, and surely potent and persuasive, which was exerted by Mr. Maynard from the beginning to the end. In all the stages of preliminary treaty he dealt with a subordinate, who looked up to him as to a superior, and was alert to serve his pleasure. There was no clean-cut cleavage in those stages between his conflicting offices and agencies. Hoyle v. Platts-burgh & M.R.R. Co., 54 N.Y. 314, 328, 329, 13 Am.Rep. 595. No label identified the request of Mr. Maynard, the plaintiff's president, as something separate from the advice of Mr. Maynard, the defendant's chairman. Superior and subordinate together framed a contract, and together closed it. It came before the executive committee as an accomplished fact. The letters had been signed and delivered. Work had been begun. All that remained was a ratification, which may have been needless, and which, even if needful, took the aspect of a mere formality. There was some attempt to show that Mr. Lewis, the vice president, had seen the letters before. The testimony of Mr. Greenidge indicates the contrary. In support of the judgment, we accept his testimony as true. That the letters had been seen by others, there is not even a pretense. The members of the committee, hearing the contract for the first time, knew that it had been framed by the chairman of the meeting. They were assured in his presence that it was just and equitable. Faith in his loyalty disarmed suspicion.

There was, then, a relation of trust reposed, of influence exerted, of superior knowledge on the one side and legitimate dependence on the other. At least, a finding that there was this relation has evidence to sustain it. A trustee may not cling to contracts thus won, unless their terms are fair and just. Crocker v. Cumberland Mining & Milling Co., supra, and cases there cited; Dongan v. MacPherson, 1902 A.C. 197, 200; Thompson on Corp. 1228, 1231. His dealings with his beneficiary are "viewed with jealousy by the courts, and may be set aside on slight grounds." Twin Lick Oil Co. v. Marbury, 91 U.S. 587, 588 (23 L.Ed. 328). He takes the risk of an enforced surrender of his bargain if it turns out to be improvident. There must be candor and equity in the transaction, and some reasonable proportion between benefits and burdens.

The contracts before us do not survive these tests. The unfairness is startling, and the consequences have been disastrous. The mischief consists in this: That the guaranty has not been limited by a statement of the conditions under which the mills are to be run. No matter how large the business, no matter how great the increase in the price of labor or of fuel, no matter what the changes in the nature or the proportion of the products, no matter even though there be extensions of the plant, the defendant has pledged its word that for ten years there will be a saving of $600 a month, $300 for each mill, $7,200 a year. As a result of that pledge it has supplied the plaintiff with electric current for nothing, and owes, if the contract stands, about $11,000 for the privilege. These elements of unfairness Mr. Maynard must have known, if indeed his knowledge be material. He may not have known how great the loss would be. He may have trusted to the superior technical skill of Mr. Greenidge to compute with approximate accuracy the comparative cost of steam and electricity. But he cannot have failed to know that he held a one-sided contract which left the defen-dant at his mercy. He was not blind to the likelihood that in a term of ten years there would be changes in the business. The swiftness with which some of the changes followed permits the inference that they were premeditated. There was a prompt increase in the proportion of yarns as compared with slubbing when the guaranty of saving charged the defendant with the greater cost of fuel. But, whether these and other changes were premeditated or not, at least they were recognized as possible. With that recognition, no word of warning was uttered to Greenidge or to any of the defendant's officers. There slumbered within these contracts a potency of profit which the plaintiff neither ignored in their making nor forgot in their enforcement.

It is no answer to say that this potency, if obvious to Maynard, ought also to have been obvious to other members of the committee. They did not know, as he did, the likelihood or the significance of changes in the business. There was need, too, of reflection and analysis before the dangers stood revealed. For the man who framed the contracts, there was opportunity to consider and to judge. His fellow members, hearing them for the first time, and trustful of his loyalty, would have no thought of latent peril. That they had none is sufficiently attested by the fact that the contracts were approved. There was inequality, therefore, both in knowledge and in the opportunity for knowledge. It is not important in such circumstances whether the trustee foresaw the precise evils that developed. The inference that he did might not be unsupported by the evidence. But the indefinite possibilities of hardship, the opportunity in changing circumstances to wrest unlooked-for profits and impose unlooked-for losses, these must have been foreseen. Foreseen or not, they were there, and their presence permeates the contracts with oppression and inequity.

We hold, therefore, that the refusal to vote does not nullify as of course an influence and predominance exerted without a vote. We hold that the constant duty rests on a trustee to seek no harsh advantage to the detriment of his trust, but rather to protest and renounce if through the blindness of those who treat with him he gains what is unfair. And, because there is evidence that in the making of these contracts that duty was ignored, the power of equity was fittingly exercised to bring them to an end.

The judgment should be affirmed, with costs.

EVERETT v. PHILLIPS

Court of Appeals of New York, 1942.
288 N.Y. 227, 43 N.E.2d 18, reargument denied 289 N.Y. 625, 43 N.E.2d 841
(1942) and 289 N.Y. 675, 45 N.E.2d 176 (1942).

LEHMAN, CHIEF JUDGE. The plaintiff is the owner of 100 shares of the "participating stock" of Empire Power Corporation. The issued and outstanding capital stock of the corporation consists of 77,000 shares of six per cent cumulative preferred stock with a stated value of $7,133,000; 400,000 shares of "participating" stock with a stated value of $3,150,000 and 400,000 shares of common stock with a stated value of $1,000,000. The directors of the corporation and members of their families owned all the common stock and large amounts of the preferred stock and the "participating" stock. At the same time they also owned or controlled, directly or indirectly, 1,500,000 shares, constituting a majority of the common stock of Long Island Lighting Company. In 1931 and 1932 the Empire Power Corporation loaned to Long Island

Lighting Company large sums of money.[25] Payment of these loans was from time to time extended and the loans are still unpaid. Claiming that these loans and the extension of time of payment were ultra vires and were "not made to promote any business purpose of Empire Power Corporation, but were made for the sole purpose of promoting the interests of the individual defendants and that of Long Island Lighting Company," the plaintiff has brought an action in behalf of himself and other minority stockholders in which he has asked that directors of Empire Power Corporation named as individual defendants be compelled to demand payment of the indebtedness by Long Island Lighting Company and that "in the event that the said indebtedness cannot be collected from Long Island Lighting Company, then that the individual defendants shall be directed to pay the same." At Special Term an interlocutory judgment was granted awarding substantially the relief which the plaintiff asked. The judgment was unanimously reversed by the Appellate Division on the law and the facts and the complaint was dismissed.

To establish his cause of action the plaintiff must show that the individual defendants in causing the Empire Power Corporation to loan the moneys to the Long Island Lighting Company and in failing to demand payment of such loans as they became due, have acted in disregard of the duties they owe Empire Power Corporation and that Empire Power Corporation has suffered, or at least may suffer, some detriment or loss. In a long line of decisions this court has held directors who control corporate action responsible for dereliction of duty where they have used the property of the corporation or managed its affairs to promote their own interests, disregarding the interests of the corporation. Power of control carries with it a trust or duty to exercise that power faithfully to promote the corporate interests, and the courts of this State will insist upon scrupulous performance of that duty. Yet, however high may be the standard of fidelity to duty which the court may exact, errors of judgment by directors do not alone suffice to demonstrate lack of fidelity. That is true even though the errors may be so gross that they may demonstrate the unfitness of the directors to manage the corporate affairs.

The plaintiff here is asserting a cause of action for wrong done to the corporation of which he is a minority stockholder. In such an action it is immaterial whether the minority stockholder who asserts it has a large or a small interest; but in determining whether those who have power to control the corporation have committed a wrong either to the corporation or to its stockholders, the corporate capital structure, the certificate of incorporation, and the corporate constitution or by-laws may be factors of great weight; for within limits prescribed by law these define to whom the power of control is entrusted, its scope and the manner in which it must be exercised. Directors are elected by the holders of stock which have voting rights. Here the certificate of incorporation of Empire Power Corporation provides that only the holders of common stock shall have voting rights. According to the testimony of the defendant Phillips, who has been president of the corporation from its formation in 1924 and who with George W.

---

25. [Ed.] Students introduced to Everett v. Phillips in classes at the Harvard Business School immediately ask a factual question about the loans under attack which Judge Lehman does not answer. Law students seldom do without prodding. Those facts were reported below. See, 22 N.Y.S.2d 852, 857.

Olmsted, its vice-president until he died in 1940, owned or controlled, either directly or indirectly, all of its common stock, the corporation was "formed for the purpose of financing and taking care of the various companies in which we were then interested and later became interested further." They invited the public to subscribe to the capital of the corporation which would be managed by directors in whose election no other stockholders would have any part, and those who might furnish the capital which these directors would manage were not left under any illusion that the directors when acting for the corporation would be free from other interests which might prevent an unprejudiced exercise of judgment. The certificate of incorporation contained a provision that: "No contract or other transaction between the Corporation and any other corporation shall be affected or invalidated by the fact that any one or more of the directors of this Corporation is or are interested in, or is a director or officer, or are directors or officers of such other corporation, . . . and no contract, act or transaction of this Corporation with any person or persons, firm or corporation, shall be affected or invalidated by the fact that any director or directors of this Corporation is a party, or are parties to or interested in such contract, act or transaction, or in any way connected with such person or persons, firm or association, and each and every person who may become a director of this Corporation is hereby relieved from any liability that might otherwise exist from contracting with the Corporation for the benefit of himself or any firm, association or corporation in which he may be in anywise interested." It is against this background that the court must consider the claim of the appellant that he has established by the overwhelming weight of testimony that the directors were faithless to their trust.

The complaint of the plaintiff concerns, as we have said, loans made to Long Island Lighting Company. The defendants controlled that corporation. Their stock interest in it was large. According to the balance sheets of the corporation introduced in evidence by the plaintiff, the corporation in 1931 and also at the time of the trial had a very large surplus and was earning large profits, but needed money for the development of its business. Corporate balance sheets unfortunately do not always present a correct picture of the corporate finances. The Public Service Commission—on appropriate occasions—can and does make independent examinations of the balance sheets of utility corporations; a court can ordinarily consider only the evidence produced by the parties and no evidence was produced which would challenge the correctness of the balance sheets or which would enable the court to reconstruct them. We may not assume that the financial condition of the lighting company was not favorable, but the evidence establishes that unless it had succeeded in borrowing money it would have been obliged to discontinue payment of dividends, at least temporarily, and, to use all its earnings for needed improvements, and that perhaps the earnings might have provided insufficient moneys for its needs. The evidence establishes too that the defendants expected to derive benefit not only as stockholders but also in other ways from the moneys which, as directors, they caused Long Island Lighting Company to borrow. The question remains whether in seeking benefit for themselves and for the Long Island Lighting Company, which they controlled through stock ownership, they caused Empire Power Corporation, which the defendants also controlled through stock ownership, to make a loan, which might work harm to the Empire Power Corporation.

The Long Island Lighting Company at the end of 1930 owed banks approximately $10,500,000 on short term, unsecured notes. Though, according to the balance sheet of the Long Island Lighting Company, it had assets greatly in excess of its indebtedness, and had a net income of more than $3,000,000 a year, its financial position was not entirely safe or sound. The banks might press for payment of short term obligations at a time when Long Island Lighting Company might find it difficult to borrow elsewhere the money to pay such obligations. Moreover, the needs of the territory served by Long Island Lighting Company required constant extension of its plant. We may assume that prudent and conservative directors would, in such circumstances, have sought to obtain by an issue of bonds the money the corporation might require to refund its short term obligations and for new capital. We need not resort to doubtful inferences to find that the directors in their management of Long Island Lighting Company did not feel themselves restricted to conservative plans and methods. The evidence clearly indicates that.

Stocks, bonds, notes or other evidences of indebtedness "payable at periods of more than twelve months after the date thereof" could not be issued by Long Island Lighting Company without approval of the Public Service Commission obtained in accordance with section 69 of the Public Service Law, Consol.Laws, ch. 48. The Long Island Lighting Company did in 1932 apply to the Public Service Commission for permission to issue approximately $15,000,000 of refunding bonds. The directors of the Long Island Lighting Company preferred, however, to borrow the moneys under a plan which would not be subject to the restrictions which the Public Service Commission might impose as conditions to its approval. An inference that the directors were influenced by that consideration when they sought to borrow the moneys for Long Island Lighting Company upon notes payable within one year from that date might reasonably be drawn from the evidence in this case. The transaction would not be unlawful for that reason. The Legislature has in the public interest provided that bonds or notes evidencing loans for a longer period than one year may be issued only with the approval of the Commission. The Legislature has not decreed that the public interest requires similar safeguards for issues where the loans became due within the year. The Legislature has drawn the line, and "the very meaning of a line in the law is that you intentionally may go as close to it as you can if you do not pass it." Superior Oil Co. v. Mississippi, 280 U.S. 390, 395, 50 S.Ct. 169, 170, 74 L.Ed. 504, opinion by Mr. Justice Holmes. True, the inference might reasonably be drawn that the directors of the Long Island Lighting Company arranged that Empire Power Corporation should loan the money on short term notes with the expectation that Empire Power Corporation under their control would continue to renew the loans as they became due, until the time arrived when it would be convenient for Long Island Lighting Company to repay them. The directors regarded these loans as "investments" rather than temporary loans which would be paid at maturity. Nevertheless, the lender could have insisted upon payment of the loans as they became due, and the defendants can be charged with no wrong to the Empire Power Corporation on account of repeated renewals of the loans nor on account of the way in which they were handled, without proof that in these acts the defendants willfully failed to protect the interests of Empire Power Corporation in order to serve better their personal interests and the interests of the Long Island

Lighting Company. There may be difference of opinion as to whether these defendants as directors of Empire Power Corporation acted wisely in the handling of the loans. There are many matters disclosed by the record which cast doubt upon the prudence, the wisdom, and the concern for the public interest shown by these directors. We are constrained, however, to agree with the Appellate Division that there is little, if any, evidence to sustain a finding that they have violated their trust or have failed to protect the interests of the Empire Power Corporation according to the dictates of their judgment, be that judgment good or bad.

It is argued, however, that the transactions in which the defendants acted as directors both of the Empire Power Corporation and the Long Island Lighting Company should be set aside because the dual position of these directors precluded an unprejudiced exercise of judgment. The dual position of the directors making the unprejudiced exercise of judgment by them more difficult, should lead the courts to scrutinize these transactions with care.

It does not, however, alone suffice to render the transactions void, and the provision of the certificate of incorporation of Empire Power Corporation expressly authorizing the directors to act even in matters where they have dual interest, has the effect of exonerating the directors, at least in part, "from adverse inferences which might otherwise be drawn against them." Spiegel v. Beacon Participations, 297 Mass. 398, 417, 8 N.E.2d 895, 907. We may point out here also that if by reason of these loans Empire Power Corporation should sustain a loss, the loss would fall primarily upon these defendants as owners of the entire capital stock. The proportion of stock of all classes owned by these defendants in Empire Power Corporation whose moneys they are claimed to have diverted wrongfully, is indeed, much greater than the proportion of the stock owned by them in Long Island Lighting Company which received these moneys. The loans were not excessive in relation to the capital assets and the income of the borrower as shown in the borrower's balance sheet. The evidence demonstrates that the defendants acting as the directors of the Long Island Lighting Company borrowed moneys from Empire Power Corporation because in their opinion the loans promoted the interests of the borrower and the stockholders of the borrower; the evidence does not demonstrate that the defendants acting as directors of the Empire Power Corporation in loaning its moneys to Long Island Lighting Company did not decide upon sufficient grounds that the loans would also promote the interests of the lender and its stockholders.

The judgment should be affirmed, without costs.

DESMOND, JUDGE (dissenting).

At all the times of which we write, the individual defendants controlled both Long Island Lighting Company and Empire Power Corporation. In dealings between those corporations these individual defendants sat on both sides of the table. They caused Empire Power Corporation, from November, 1930, to February, 1933, to loan Long Island Lighting Company, $5,330,000 on the latter's unsecured notes. These notes and various renewals thereof were all made for periods of less than a year. See Public Service Law, § 69. Interest has been paid regularly but, up to the beginning of this action, nothing was ever paid on principal. The lighting company needed these moneys—and used them—to pay off, from time to time, notes held by banks which were asking for payment. In 1930, when Empire made its first loan to the lighting company, the latter owed the banks more than $10,000,000 and found it increasingly difficult to persuade the banks to accept renewals of their unsecured notes. The banks had suggested to the individual defendants that the lighting company discontinue paying cash dividends, so that it might accumulate in its treasury funds with which to pay off the bank loans. This the individual defendants, who owned or controlled half of the lighting company's common stock, were unwilling to do. An application to the Public Service Commission for authority to issue mortgage bonds to raise money to pay off the banks was pending but undetermined. There was only one other convenient source of funds. A lender had to be found who would supply, without security and without question, the cash needed from time to time to satisfy the banks. Such a lender was ready at hand in Empire Power Corporation, completely controlled by these individual defendants themselves.

During 1930 and 1932 these defendants arranged loans aggregating $4,500,000 from the power corporation to the lighting company, most, if not all, of the proceeds going to pay off the bank loans. In March, 1932, when the lighting company owed the power Corporation about $4,500,000 and the banks about $8,750,000, an agreement was made between the lighting company and the banks whereby the latter accepted renewals of their notes for six months, and agreed to accept renewals for another six months if necessary, on condition that the lighting company make certain payments which were intended to come from, and did come from, Empire Power Corporation. It was part of this arrangement that the whole of the lighting company's debt to Empire Power Corporation should be postdated to that of the banks, postdated rather than subordinated because it was felt that subordination "would be openly subject to attack on account of the unity of interest between Empire Power and Long Island Lighting."

A little later Empire's directors passed a resolution agreeing on behalf of Empire "to extend and keep extended the time of payment" of the lighting company's notes to Empire Power Corporation until the banks should be paid in full. An agreement to the same effect was made by defendant Phillips on behalf of Empire, in 1933, and approved by Empire's board of directors. Later that same year the Public Service Commission granted permission to the lighting company to sell the issue of bonds above referred to, but sale at the stipulated price was found to be impossible. Again the bank notes had to be renewed, and again Empire Power Corporation was caused to agree to subordinate its claims to those of the bank. Finally, in 1934, the authorized bond issue was sold by the lighting company under a contract which provided that the indebtedness to Empire Power Corporation would not be paid, discharged or secured by the issuance of any bonds of the lighting company secured by a lien prior to or on a parity with the lien of the bond issue. All of the proceeds of this bond issue went to the banks, none to Empire Power Corporation. In 1936 the lighting company paid off all its unsecured indebtedness, except that owing to Empire Power Corporation. Among the creditors so paid off were the common directors of the two corporations and their relatives and corporations controlled by them. Thus Empire Power Corporation, starting out with short term loans to the lighting company, ended up with what amounted to a "permanent investment" of $5,000,000 in the lighting company, in the form of unsecured notes, payment of which, if this suit fails, must await the pleasure of the defendants.

In this suit plaintiffs on behalf of Empire Power Corporation asked the court to compel Long Island Lighting Company to repay the moneys loaned to it by the Empire Corporation, to compel the individual defendants, as directors of Long Island Lighting Company, to pay that indebtedness if the lighting company does not, and to restrain the individual defendants from further extending the time of payment. Special Term found, as stated in its opinion, that the conduct of the individual defendants, in making and renewing these loans, was biased in favor of the lighting company, and ordered judgment for plaintiff. The Appellate Division reversed on the law and the facts and rendered final judgment dismissing the complaint. Contracts between two corporations having common officers are, of course, not void per se . . . but are voidable by either corporation, irrespective of the balance of benefits (Globe Woolen Co. v. Utica Gas & Electric Co., 224 N.Y. 483, 121 N.E. 378; Munson v. Syracuse, G. & C.R. Co., 103 N.Y. 58, 8 N.E. 355), or by a court of equity at the instance of either corporation (or its stockholder), where it appears that such a contract was made in bad faith, fraud, other breach of trust or under circumstances preventing "an unprejudiced exercise of judgment." . . . A court will not attempt to pass upon questions of expediency or to control the corporate managers in the faithful exercise of their discretion. City Bank Farmers' Trust Co. v. Hewitt Realty Co., 257 N.Y. 62, 177 N.E. 309, 76 A.L.R. 881; . . . To make a case for the invalidation of such a contract there must be shown circumstances tending to prove that the contract was made in bad faith, fraud or other breach of trust, including a biased exercise of judgment. Globe Woolen Co. v. Utica Gas & Electric Co., . . . Given such a showing, the burden is then upon those who would maintain the contract to establish its fairness . . ., particularly when they themselves are shown to have exercised the dominating influence in effecting the contract. . . . Whether the particular contract between these two corporations having the same directors was or was not made under circumstances amounting to a breach of the directors' fiduciary duty, is a question of fact.

Here the individual defendants who arranged the loans by Empire Power Corporation to Long Island Lighting Company, were completely aware of the latter's financial difficulties at the times the loans and renewals were made. They and their families owned the majority of the lighting company's stock; they directed its policies and managed its affairs; some of them were unsecured creditors of the lighting company in substantial amounts. It was to their interest individually, that the lighting company's urgent need of funds to pay its unsecured and demanding bank creditors be met. They met it by loaning Empire's money to Long Island on such terms that Empire's capital funds were used to pay off Long Island's bank loans in part, then these loans were made subordinate to the balances owing to the banks and finally remained wholly unpaid when all Long Island's other creditors of the same class were taken care of by the proceeds of a bond issue. The inference is unescapable that in the making of these loans, and renewals, the welfare of Empire Power Corporation was ignored and that the purpose of defendants was to benefit Long Island Lighting Company, and themselves. It is no answer to all this that Empire's financial structure may have resilience enough to absorb the risk or the damage of the loans, or that the individual defendant's stake in Empire is large and the plaintiff's small. Plain disclosure of the inequity of the situation and of the unfairness of the risk to the Empire Corporation, makes a strong appeal to the conscience of the court. It is not answered by defendants' protestations that Empire has a good investment in these loans, that they would surely be paid on a liquidation of the lighting company, that the lighting company's credit is good, etc., or by the provision in Empire Power Corporation's charter concerning contracts between that corporation and other corporations with the same officers or directors.

A court of equity in such a case as this does not stand aside and await the outcome of defendants' conduct. It acts promptly and effectively. It sets the whole transaction aside without waiting, or compelling minority stockholders to wait, to see whether those who unlawfully put a corporation's property at risk, may possibly at some undetermined time, have the skill, or luck, to get it back intact for the corporation.

The judgment of the Appellate Division should be reversed and that of the Special Term reinstated, with costs.

LOUGHRAN, LEWIS, and CONWAY, JJ., concur with LEHMAN, C.J.

DESMOND, J., dissents in opinion in which FINCH and RIPPEY, JJ., concur.

Judgment affirmed.

CHELROB v. BARRETT

Court of Appeals of New York, 1944.
293 N.Y. 422, 57 N.E.2d 825.

LEHMAN, CHIEF JUDGE. The defendant corporations, Long Island Lighting Company, Queens Borough Gas & Electric Company and Nassau & Suffolk Lighting Company, are public utility companies organized under the laws of the State of New York, serving sections of Long Island. Prior to 1927 Long Island Lighting Company (hereinafter referred to as "Long Island") acquired the common or voting stock of Queens Borough Gas & Electric Company (hereinafter referred to as "Queens"). Six per cent cumulative preferred stock of Queens of the par value of $6,686,000 remains in the hands of the public. In 1927, Queens acquired the common or voting stock of Nassau & Suffolk Lighting Company (hereinafter referred to as "Nassau"). Seven per cent cumulative preferred stock of Nassau of the par value of $2,726,200 remains in the hands of the public. In 1928 Queens expanded its production plant and transmission facilities to enable it to sell gas to Nassau. Since that time Nassau has purchased from Queens a substantial part of the gas it furnishes to consumers within the territory it serves and in addition has purchased from Queens gas which it resold to Long Island. The price of the gas sold by Queens to Nassau was fixed by the directors of the two corporations. All of them had been elected by Long Island, which directly or indirectly held the voting stock of both corporations. Dividends on the preferred stock of Queens have been in arrears since 1937 and several holders of preferred stock of Queens, claiming that the price paid to Queens by Nassau was unreasonable and caused a loss to Queens, brought actions against the corporate and individual defendants for an accounting of the resulting profits which the defendants may have obtained and the losses which Queens suffered.

The actions were consolidated and, pursuant to the provisions of section 96–a of the Civil Practice Act, the consolidated action was tried together with an action brought by preferred stockholders of Nassau who claimed that Long Island had compelled Nassau to sell to it for an inadequate and unfair price some of the gas which Nassau had purchased from Queens (Espach v. Nassau & Suffolk Lighting Co., 293 N.Y. 463, 57 N.E.2d 835, decided herewith in separate opinion). Mr. Justice McGarey at Special Term (177 Misc. 521, 31 N.Y.S.2d 259) held that Long Island dominated both Queens and Nassau and that the price fixed by the directors of these companies for gas purchased by Nassau from Queens was inadequate and caused loss to Queens, and granted judgment in favor of Queens against Long Island and Nassau in the sum of $387,020, as an additional price for gas supplied after 1934, with interest at the rate of 2%. Any cause of action for additional compensation for gas furnished prior to that date, he held, was barred by the Statute of Limitations. The judgment directs that "as between Nassau and Suffolk Lighting Company and Long Island Lighting Company, said judgment shall be paid by Nassau and Suffolk Lighting Company". The complaints against the individual defendants were "dismissed upon the merits . . . without costs to any party as against any other party and without prejudice to the bringing of an action against the defendant directors in the event that this judgment is not paid".

All parties appealed to the Appellate Division. The plaintiffs acquiesced in the ruling that the six-year Statute of Limitations applied but claim that the judgment in their favor based on alleged wrongs since 1934 is inadequate. The defendants claim that the directors acted honestly and carefully, seeking in good faith to promote the interests of both corporations, and that the price fixed by them was fair. The Appellate Division unanimously reversed on the law and the facts the judgment in favor of the plaintiffs and directed judgment dismissing the complaint on the merits against all the defendants. It expressly reversed some of the findings of the Justice at Special Term and found many of the findings proposed by the defendants. It did not reverse some significant findings of the trial court.

Long Island acquired all the voting stock of Queens and indirectly of Nassau with the written consent and approval of the Public Service Commission of the State. The defendant Ellis L. Phillips and a small group of associates owned and controlled, directly or indirectly, a substantial majority of the voting stock of Long Island. By voting that stock they elected the directors of Long Island who, in turn, chose the directors of Queens and of Nassau. A majority of the directors of Queens and of Nassau were at all times also directors and, in some cases, were paid officers or employees of Long Island and some of the directors of Nassau were also directors of Queens. The three corporations maintained their separate corporate form and conducted their business as separate corporate entities. So long as preferred stock of Queens and of Nassau was outstanding the corporations could not be merged. Nevertheless the three corporations were operated through their interlocking directorate as parts of a single system. Such operation is not forbidden by law or unjust to any of the corporations in the system if the interests of each corporation are zealously safeguarded by its own board of directors. Indeed, such operation may be more economical and efficient and may benefit the public and all the corporations. We may perhaps assume that otherwise the Public Service

Commission would not have given its consent and approval to the acquisition by Long Island of the voting stock of the other corporations.

Nonetheless, the directors of each corporation—though all elected by Long Island—may authorize corporate action by the corporation which they represent only if in their considered opinion such action will promote the best interests of that corporation and is fair to it. That is a fiduciary obligation to the corporation and indirectly to its stockholders and creditors which its directors have assumed. In the operation of separate utility corporations as a single system, agreement must be reached by the directors of the separate corporations in regard to the share of each corporation in such operation and the compensation to be paid by one to the other. The compensation to be paid for benefits received is ordinarily fixed by negotiation or bargaining, but where in negotiations between two corporations the same men represent both, their determinations are subject to judicial scrutiny. In this case we are confronted with the question of what relief may be afforded when such determinations are predicated upon mistake of fact entering into the fixation of the price to be paid by one corporation to the other. The plaintiffs challenge, on that and other grounds, the agreement reached by the boards of directors of Queens and of Nassau. Under its terms Nassau purchases gas from Queens at a price which it is said causes a loss to Queens. The plaintiffs charge that in making the challenged agreement the interests of Queens were disregarded by its directors acting under the domination of Long Island and for the benefit of Long Island and Nassau, rather than of Queens.

Most of the charges of flagrant wrong contained in the complaint were abandoned by the plaintiffs and the Trial Justice found against the plaintiffs in regard to some other charges. These findings were not reversed by the Appellate Division and are sustained by the evidence. The Trial Justice refused to find that the directors had acted wrongfully but did find in favor of the plaintiffs that the price fixed by these directors was unfair to Queens and caused a loss to it. Upon the basis of that finding he concluded that Queens must now receive the difference between the agreed price for the gas it furnished to Nassau and the price which Nassau should have been required to pay. The Appellate Division has held that the price was determined by the directors of the two corporations acting honestly and carefully and that the court may not set aside a price so fixed even if it be the result of bad judgment or error and that the price fixed in this case was not unfair and caused no loss to Queens.

Before 1927 when Queens acquired the common stock of Nassau, Nassau made, at its own plant, the gas which it supplied to consumers within the territory it served and, in addition, gas which it sold to Long Beach Gas Company and to Public Service Corporation of Long Island, utility corporations operating in contiguous territory and controlled by the same group which at that time owned the common stock of Nassau. When Queens acquired the common stock of Nassau it also acquired the common stock of Long Beach, and Long Island then acquired the common stock of Public Service Corporation. Thus, the three affiliated corporations which had obtained gas from the Nassau plant became parts of the same system or group of utility corporations as Queens, all under the stock control of Long Island. The plant owned by Nassau had no access to water where delivery of materials could be made and it could not be operated economically and efficiently unless extended and improved. It could supply the gas needed by Nassau as well as the two affiliated corporations to which Nassau had supplied gas only if it operated with three shifts a day. Queens, on the other hand, owned a plant which could be operated very efficiently and economically. Materials for making gas were delivered at the plant by water and were handled automatically. It produced gas at a low cost—below the average production cost of Nassau. The plant of Queens had a capacity greater than the needs of Queens and its facilities could be extended sufficiently to supply to Nassau the gas required by it and the gas which Nassau had supplied to affiliated corporations. Under these circumstances, commencing in 1928, Nassau reduced the production of gas at its plant and since then has purchased from Queens a substantial part of the gas required by it for distribution to consumers within the territory it served and for resale to Long Island or to Public Service of Long Island.

Gas mains interconnecting the utility corporations were constructed in order to carry out this arrangement. Expenditures were also made by Queens to increase and improve the production and distributing facilities of its plant. The evidence established and the courts below have found that: "The construction of gas mains and the resulting interconnection of the distribution system of the said utility corporations constituted good sound business policy on the part of the respective companies, and said interconnections insured each company of a supply in the case of any emergency, and thereby benefited the general consumers and each of the respective utilities herein." The gas supplied by Queens to Nassau and in part resold by Nassau to Long Island was produced at the plant which could make it at the smallest cost and any agreement by which Nassau and Long Island could obtain gas from Queens at a price lower than either of them could produce gas or obtain it from others and higher than the average cost to Queens of producing and supplying gas would, it is plain, benefit both. By the findings of fact of the court at Special Term, sustained by the weight of the evidence and approved by the Appellate Division, the controversy between the parties to this litigation is reduced to the question whether the price fixed by the directors of the purchasing and selling corporations was fair to each and benefited each.

In 1928 when the intercompany purchases and sales began, both Queens and Nassau had earnings far in excess of the amount required to pay dividends on their outstanding preferred stock and since Long Island owned all the common stock of Queens and Queens owned all the common stock of Nassau, the balance of the earnings of both companies, after payment of the preferred stock dividends, eventually reached the treasury of Long Island. In these circumstances it made little, if any, practical difference to anybody whether the intercompany price was too high or too low. What was important was that all the companies in the system should be efficiently and honestly operated and the record does not show that any of the directors selected for the companies in the system by Long Island or by the group which had voting control of Long Island were remiss in the performance of their duties in that respect, and the courts below agreed that there was no dereliction on their part.

Since the profits of all the corporations—with the exception of the small amount paid out as dividends on the preferred stock, ultimately came into the treasury of Long Island and Long Island elected all of the directors of these corporations, including some who were paid officers of Long Island—the employment of completely independent engineering and legal staffs might have been wasteful. As might be expected, engineers selected for their ability by Long Island at times give advice and assistance to all the companies in the system and there is only one legal department for all the corporations in the system. Where the interests of companies in the system might conflict, the general legal department advises both by assigning one of the attorneys in the department to each side. The joint use of competent expert advisers and professional staffs is doubtless entirely justifiable. We do not refer to it as an indication that any corporation has suffered a wrong. It is, however, a circumstance which may not be overlooked in considering whether the agreement by Queens to supply gas to Nassau for the stipulated price may be challenged by minority stockholders of Queens.

The evidence shows and the courts below have found that engineers retained by Long Island or by the defendant Ellis L. Phillips, its president, who was a director of Long Island and of both Nassau and Queens, made studies of the comparative cost of producing gas at the plants of Queens and of Nassau, of the possibility of enlarging and improving both plants or either, and of the comparative advantages to each corporation of obtaining gas for its own requirements from its own plant or of utilizing the most efficient plan of any company to supply gas to all companies. We shall hereafter refer to the contents of these reports. At this point it is sufficient to say that the evidence establishes, as both courts below agree, that the experts who made these studies were men of ability and integrity.

Upon that evidence the court at Special Term found, and the Appellate Division approved the finding, that "the price at which said gas was sold as set forth in the said contracts was arrived at by study of the physical and operating situation by competent engineers and those experienced in the operation of gas utilities, and the said prices in said contracts were determined after consideration by the boards of directors of said corporations, and that reports recommending the prices at which gas should be sold, as aforesaid, were prepared by competent engineers and fully discussed and considered, and the provisions of said contracts were thoroughly discussed by the officers and directors of said corporations, and contracts for the sale of gas, as aforesaid, were made after an investigation and discussion of the prices to be charged for gas, as stated in said contracts, and that none of the directors of said corporations was guilty of fraud, bad faith or overreaching in negotiating the said contracts." The defendants had proposed a finding in exactly this language except that the proposed finding stated that the prices were determined after "careful" consideration by the directors and the contracts were made after a "full and complete" investigation and discussion. The Appellate Division in its order of reversal made and allowed the finding as proposed by the defendants, thus restoring the words exercised [sic] by the Justice at Special Term.

In the reports of the engineers which the directors considered and studied in fixing the price which Nassau should pay for gas supplied by Queens, the price which the engineers recommended was determined by them upon a formula whereby the cost of the labor and material used in the production of all the gas made at Queens was allocated pro rata to the gas supplied by Queens to consumers within the territory it served and the gas sold to Nassau, so that Nassau paid to Queens the average "direct" or "commodity production cost" of supplying the gas, but the "indirect" cost of supplying gas, that is, such expenses as taxes, insurance, pumping, as well as interest on investments, was allocated on the "increment cost" method, and Nassau paid to Queens only the additional cost which Queens incurred in producing the additional gas supplied to Nassau. Since Queens owned a plant with capacity beyond the needs of Queens, the average cost of labor and material required for the production of the additional amount of gas was lower than the average cost of producing only the amount required by Queens to supply gas to general consumers and was, of course, lower than the average cost of producing gas at the less efficient plant of Nassau; and since Nassau was required to pay to Queens the "average commodity production cost" of gas and the additional "indirect" expenses incurred by Queens in supplying the additional gas, it is plain that both companies would benefit to some extent by the purchase and sale of gas at a price fixed in accordance with that formula. For that reason the court at Special Term held that the price thus fixed and paid until 1936 was not unfair to Queens and should not be set aside by the court though errors in applying the formula should be corrected by the court.

The plaintiffs do not contend that a price fixed in accordance with that formula would cause loss to Queens or would in all circumstances be unfair to that company. In 1936 the price paid by Nassau was, however, reduced. At that time the defendant Maidment, the holder of a considerable amount of preferred stock of Nassau and a director, member of the price committee, and vice-president of that corporation, insisted that the price paid to Queens for gas supplied by it must be reduced or Nassau would proceed to enlarge its plant and itself produce the gas it needed. Maidment was not a director of Queens. Nassau had not bound itself by contract to continue to purchase gas from Queens for a definite term. Though the expenditures by Queens for the extension and improvement of its plant and transmission system without insisting upon such a contract with Nassau might well have been criticised as ill-advised if Nassau had been an entirely independent corporation dealing with Queens at arm's length and able to procure the gas it needed either from a competitive producer or by manufacturing it in its own plant, yet Maidment as a director of Nassau who had assumed no fiduciary obligation to Queens was justified in demanding that no higher price be exacted from Nassau for gas supplied by Queens than the cost at which Nassau could obtain the gas elsewhere. The directors of Queens could not, however, accept from Nassau a price which would not be fair to it.

In a finding approved by the Appellate Division the trial court has stated the limits of what may constitute a fair price: "64. That a fair price to be charged for the gas sold, as aforesaid, falls within certain limits. To the selling company it is the additional cost to the seller, including additional operating expenses incurred by the seller and fixed charges on additional plants installed for the purpose of making the transfer over and above the cost of the operating expenses and fixed charges on plants which would be incurred by the seller if the sale of gas were not made; and to the buying company the maximum reasonable price would be the competitive additional cost at which the buying company could secure the quantity of gas transferred either by manufacturing it itself in its own facilities, or by purchasing it from some alternative source, and this additional competitive cost of the buying company is the limit beyond which the purchasing company would not be justified in buying the gas and the price beyond which it could not be justified in paying."

The general rule so formulated is not challenged upon this appeal. When objection was made to the price of gas which Nassau was then paying to Queens and to the formula upon which that price had been calculated in reports of engineers submitted to Queens and to Nassau, Mr. Phillips, president of Long Island, directed engineers to make new studies of the price which Nassau should thereafter pay to Queens. In their report, they recommended a price based upon the engineers' estimate of the cost to Nassau of enlarging its facilities and itself producing the gas. The report was submitted to Mr. Phillips and considered and approved by the board of directors of Long Island at a meeting in which many of the directors of Queens and Nassau took part. Then the same directors took part in meetings of the boards of directors of Queens and of Nassau, and the same report was approved at these meetings also and the price fixed accordingly.

The evidence establishes, and the trial court has made a finding not reversed by the Appellate Division, that: "19. During all of the time that Queens Borough Gas & Electric Company has been selling and delivering gas to Nassau & Suffolk Lighting Company, there have been restrictions to the expansion of Nassau & Suffolk Lighting Company's production plant, which limited further expansion." That finding completely destroys the basis of the report of the engineers upon which the directors of Queens and Nassau acted in fixing the price. A fair price which Queens should receive for the gas it sells to Nassau cannot be based upon an estimate of the hypothetical cost of expanding the plant belonging to Nassau and of producing there the gas required by Nassau where further expansion is not feasible. It is true that the Trial Justice also found that Nassau "was in a position, in the opinion of its officers and directors to have enlarged its gas manufacturing plant located at Hempstead–Garden City and to have increased the capacity of that plant to an extent sufficient to supply all of its gas requirements, including gas sold to Long Island Lighting Company." We need not pause to consider whether upon this record the directors of Nassau could have been of the opinion that it was "in a position . . . to have enlarged its plant" if they had made any investigation. We may assume arguendo that the directors in good faith were of that opinion. It does not appear that in fact Nassau could have procured gas from a source other than Queens at or near the price which Nassau had theretofore paid. The defendants maintain, nevertheless, that the price so fixed was a fair price because it was not less than the price which might have been fixed by using what is known as the "increment cost formula". The testimony of the expert witnesses produced by the defendants that the price fixed is not less than the price would have been if calculated by the "increment cost" method is persuasive and was for the most part accepted by both courts below, but there is no credible evidence that a price fixed by that method would be fair to Queens.

Queens could operate its plant to full capacity if Nassau agreed to buy gas produced there in excess of the amount required by Queens to supply consumers within the territory served by Queens. The average cost of gas when the plant is operated to its full capacity is lower than the average cost of gas when the plant produces gas only sufficient to meet the requirements of Queens as an independent utility corporation.

A price for the excess gas fixed in accordance with the "increment cost" formula, even though less than the average cost of producing gas at the Queens plant, would, at least, reimburse Queens for the additional cost of producing such excess gas, and it is said that Queens suffered no loss and, in fact, made a profit by accepting the price so fixed. That is true only if Queens could continue to supply gas to consumers in the territory it served at a price not lower than it could have exacted if the average cost of production of gas at its plant had not been reduced by increased production.

Doubtless, at times, when increased production at a plant reduces the average cost, the producer suffers no loss if he obtains a market for the increased output by selling the increase at a price which though less than the average cost is greater than the additional cost of producing such increase—but the producer must inevitably suffer a loss if he cannot sell the remainder at more than the average cost. The rate at which Queens may sell gas to consumers must be fair and must be approved by the Public Service Commission. The cost of the gas sold is a factor in determining the rate that may be charged. The trial court found that in fixing a fair rate which Queens might charge for gas supplied to consumers in its "franchise territory", "the general consumers should benefit to some extent, at least, from the savings resulting from the additional business", and that accordingly the average "commodity production cost" should be allocated both to the gas supplied by Queens to general consumers and to the gas produced as an additional service to Nassau, but that "the increment cost method should apply to all the other elements applicable to such additional service". The Trial Justice indicated that in his opinion the record establishes that this method of combination of "average commodity production cost and increment cost" was used by Queens and by the Public Service Commission in calculating the rate which Queens might exact from general consumers in its "franchise territory". If that be true then Queens would inevitably suffer a loss by selling part of the gas it produced at a price fixed by the "increment cost" method and the remainder at a price fixed by the "average commodity production cost" method or combination method, but the Appellate Division reversed findings in favor of the plaintiff in that regard and the defendants contend that there is no evidence in the record to support it.

Whether or not there is evidence in the record which would support a finding that the rate charged by Queens to general consumers was calculated by the "average commodity production cost" method, depends largely upon the construction placed upon language, possibly equivocal, used in colloquy at the trial. For the purposes of this appeal we accept the sense in which counsel for the defense understood these words. Even so it is plain that there is nothing in the record which could possibly justify an inference that Queens would be permitted to exact from general consumers a rate based on more than the average production or commodity cost of gas supplied from its plant. Extracts from the opinion of the Public Service Commission in the case of Freeport v. Nassau & Suffolk, P.U.R., 1924, at page 96, read into the record upon the cross-examination of a witness, indicate that it is the rule or practice of the Commission to measure the rate which a public utility may charge to general consumers by the average production cost, and that in a case where the public utility can, at a smaller additional cost, produce additional gas to be supplied in bulk to a single customer, the benefit of the consequent reduction in average cost must be apportioned equitably to the general consumers and the customer purchasing the additional gas. Though that rule or practice is not a formal regulation, adopted and published by the Commission and constituting "a public document or record which this court may consider" (Matter of Ackerman v. Kern, 281 N.Y. 87, 94, 22 N.E.2d 247, 249), yet we may certainly not assume that the Public Service Commission would approve a rate measured by a different rule. One expert witness did, it is true, testify that during the years 1934 to 1940, inclusive, Queens made a profit of $53,000 upon its sales of gas to Nassau over and above an annual return of 6% on an average investment of more than $900,000. That is a conclusion drawn by the expert based upon his opinion as to the proper adjustments and deductions to be made from the gross profits in determining the amount of the net profit. To analyze this testimony and to point out the uncertain nature of some of the factors entering into the calculation would extend this opinion unduly. Even if accepted in its entirety it would still remain true that a profit of $53,000 in six years on so large a volume of business would hardly justify a board of directors in authorizing the capital investment required, with its consequent risk, particularly if Nassau could at any time terminate the contract and obtain its gas from another source.

A finding by a court of equity that a contract of sale authorized by a board of directors of a corporation is ill advised or causes loss to a corporation would not by itself constitute ground for setting aside the contract and compelling the purchaser to pay a price which the court considers fair. We have said that: "As a general rule, courts have nothing to do with the internal management of business corporations. . . . All questions within the scope of the corporate powers which relate to the policy of administration, to the expediency of proposed measures, or to the consideration of contracts, provided it is not so grossly inadequate as to be evidence of fraud, are beyond the province of the courts. The minority directors or stockholders cannot come into court, upon allegations of a want of judgment or lack of efficiency on the part of the majority and change the course of administration." Flynn v. Brooklyn City R. Co., 158 N.Y. 493, 507, 53 N.E. 520, 524. Where directors act with undivided loyalty towards the corporation which they direct, their determination that a corporate course of action will promote the interest of the corporation is ordinarily not subject to review by the court, and "errors of judgment by directors do not alone suffice to demonstrate lack of fidelity. That is true even though the errors may be so gross that they may demonstrate the unfitness of the directors to manage the corporate affairs." Everett v. Phillips, 288 N.Y. 227, 232, 43 N.E.2d 18, 20. The test in each case is, whether corporate action is the result of the exercise by the directors of their unbiased judgment in determining that such action will promote the corporate interests. We apply that test here.

The directors of Queens intended to exercise an unbiased judgment and in good faith believed that the price fixed by them was fair. Their good faith is established by persuasive evidence and by the findings of the trial court approved by the Appellate Division. So, too, is the fact that the price was fixed after the directors had considered and discussed reports, in regard to the price at which gas should be sold, made by competent engineers and operating experts. But in this case the determination of directors is open to limited review in the courts because neither they nor the experts who prepared the reports were in a position where their loyalty to the interests of Queens was undivided.

We repeat that the directors were elected by Long Island, which owned directly or indirectly the common stock of both Queens and Nassau. A majority of the directors of each corporation were directors of Long Island and several were directors of all three corporations. We are told that though Long Island elected the directors of Queens and of Nassau, it did not usurp the functions of the directors and dominate and control their actions; but concededly all the corporations were operated as part of a "system" and corporate actions of the separate corporations dictated by directors elected by Long Island would inevitably be influenced by that fact. The directors acted upon the advice of experts retained by the system and often after the board of directors of Long Island had approved a proposed policy. That Long Island selected for the position of director men of ability and integrity and that no officer of Long Island dictated to them what action they should take as directors, does not destroy the significance of these facts. They require the most careful scrutiny of transactions between the corporations represented by common directors, to the end that in the absence of arm's length bargaining the scales may not, even through mistake or inadvertence, be unfairly tipped to one side or the other. Though Long Island in acquiring such control, and even in its exercise within limits imposed by equitable rules, commits no wrong and incurs no liability to Queens, yet where those limits are transgressed to the detriment of Queens, Long Island becomes liable for the consequent damages to Queens and must account for consequent profits to itself. "Power of control carries with it a trust or duty to exercise that power faithfully to promote the corporate interests, and the courts of this State will insist upon scrupulous performance of that duty." Everett v. Phillips, supra, 288 N.Y. at page 232, 43 N.E.2d at page 19. Liability arises not from the power of control, but from breach of the duty which accompanies it. Blaustein v. Pan American Petroleum & Transport Co., 293 N.Y. 281, 56 N.E.2d 705. Here it must be conceded that Long Island and the directors of Queens and of Nassau elected by Long Island sought no personal benefit from the transaction and did not intend to act unfairly towards Queens, and perhaps Long Island obtained no substantial benefit from the inadequacy of the price fixed for gas sold by Queens to Nassau, but the transaction is subjected to judicial scrutiny because the price was fixed by corporate boards having common directors elected by Long Island and these directors had been placed in a position of divided loyalty.

The rule that must be applied in such a situation has been stated by the Supreme Court of the United States. "The relation of directors to corporations is of such a fiduciary nature that transactions between boards having common members are regarded as jealously by the law as are personal dealings between a director and his corporation, and where the fairness of such transactions is challenged the burden is upon those who would maintain them to show their entire fairness and where a sale is involved the full adequacy of the consideration. Especially is this true where a common director is dominating in influence or in character. This court has been consistently emphatic in the application of this rule, which, it has declared, is founded in soundest morality, and we now add in the soundest business policy." Geddes v. Anaconda Mining Co., 254 U.S. 590, 599, 41 S.Ct. 209, 212, 65 L.Ed. 425. Though the dual position of the directors does not itself render such transactions void, it does make "the unprejudiced exercise of judgment by them more difficult" and "should lead the courts to scrutinize these transactions with care." Everett v. Phillips, supra, 288 N.Y. at page 236, 43 N.E.2d at page 22.

The transaction in this case will not bear that scrutiny. The price was fixed upon the basis of reports made by engineers retained by the "system" and these reports are based upon the assumption—which the courts below have agreed is erroneous—that Nassau could expand its plant and manufacture gas for the price it paid to Queens. This erroneous assumption having been accepted as justification of an inadequate price, we cannot doubt that in equity the fixing of a fair price may be required. The defendants have failed to show that the price fixed would not cause a loss to Queens. At best it would make a profit unreasonably small in relation to the volume of the business, the investment of capital and the attendant risk. The proof is insufficient to show justification for the abandonment of the "average production cost" method in calculating the price of gas sold by Queens to Nassau, and the trial court did not err in setting aside the price fixed in 1936 by the "increment cost" method. The Public Service Law, § 110, subds. 3, 4, Consol.Laws, c. 48, confers upon the Public Service Commission jurisdiction to determine whether such an intercompany contract of sale is "not in the public interest," but it does not divest the courts of jurisdiction to determine that it should be set aside on equitable grounds. Since the directors acted in good faith and upon studies prepared by competent engineers, judgment on the merits dismissing the complaint against them is proper.

The question remains whether the trial court's calculation by the "average production cost" method of the price which Nassau should pay is correct. Both sides claim errors there. The controversy involves in large part matters of fact. The Appellate Division, holding that the trial court was not justified in setting aside the price fixed by the directors, has not reviewed the correctness of the calculation of a different price by the trial court. The case should be remitted to it for that purpose.

The judgment of the Appellate Division dismissing the complaint against the Long Island Lighting Company and Nassau & Suffolk Lighting Company should be reversed, with costs to appellants, and the matter remitted to the Appellate Division. The judgment of the Appellate Division dismissing the complaint against the individual defendants should be affirmed, with costs.

LOUGHRAN, RIPPEY, LEWIS, CONWAY, DESMOND, and THACHER, JJ., concur.

Judgment accordingly.

COMMENT

Repetition of the problems of the Long Island system was prevented by action of the Securities and Exchange Commission in 1949. Acting under Section 11 of the Public Utility Holding Company Act of 1935,[26] it approved a plan consolidating Long Island, Queens, and Nassau into one company, assuming the debts of all three and having only one class of stock—a common stock. Section 11 instructed the SEC to examine every utility holding company system and determine whether it could be simplified, whether "unnecessary complexities" could be eliminated and voting power fairly and equitably distributed.

---

26. 15 U.S.C.A. § 79k.

This task was not itself a simple one, as the SEC's opinion—one of a number of related court and commission rulings—covered 105 pages.[27] Meanwhile, Empire Power was liquidated in 1945.

NOTE ON DELAWARE "FAIRNESS" CASES

It would be more consistent with the overall emphasis of this book to test the "fairness" concept with Delaware cases. However, I do not find Delaware cases that afford as much scope for a real attempt at understanding the arms' length test and its application to specific factual problems as do the somewhat elderly, and somewhat discordant, New York cases. The difficulty with the Delaware cases is the very wooliness of the standards they espouse. One from that jurisdiction is Trans World Airlines, Inc. v. Summa Corp., 374 A.2d 5 (Del.Ch.1977), involving a claim by TWA that the late Howard Hughes and his corporate intermediaries had damaged TWA by interfering with the aircraft acquisition program that would have been the most beneficial for it—but not for Hughes who chose to lease aircraft to TWA instead. The Chancellor stated that he was applying the "intrinsically fair" test, which was the test to be applied except where the terms of the transaction are not imposed by the parent corporation but by a third party such as the government, in which case the "business judgment" rule applies. He found that the burden imposed by the intrinsically fair test had not been met. The reference to solutions imposed by third parties refers particularly to Getty Oil Co. v. Skelly Oil Co., 267 A.2d 883 (Del.1970). That case involved a dispute over the parent's unwillingness to allow the subsidiary a share of an oil import quota which the United States allocated to the parent, but which the parent might have shared with the subsidiary. The court held that the fiduciary standard did not require sacrifice though it called for fairness. It said:

> The concept of fairness needs further analysis. Theoretically, the best definition of "fairness" in parent-subsidiary business dealing would be to require that the transaction between the two be reached as though each had in fact exerted its bargaining power against the other at arm's length. It is, of course, obvious that it is impossible, as between parent and subsidiary, to approximate what would have been agreed upon at arm's length. On the other hand, it is possible to set other limits on what is fair.

The upshot of the Delaware jurisprudence then seems to be that the courts will not endeavour to pursue a finely detailed concept of fairness but look for "gross and palpable overreaching," in cases where the business judgment rule applies because of third party interference, and lay a heavy burden on the defendant to come up with justifications

27. 30 S.E.C. 441 (1949).

where no such excuse prevails.[28]   One notes that the enactment of Del. G.C. § 144 seems not to have contributed to the courts' resolution of these problems.   For example, Fliegler v. Lawrence, 361 A.2d 218 (Del. 1976), said that the section did not provide broad immunity for directors but merely provided against invalidation "solely" because of self-dealing.   Conversely Robert A. Wachsler, Inc. v. Florafax Intern., Inc., 778 F.2d 547 (10th Cir.1985), indicated that § 144 did not rule out other ways of validating a self-dealing transaction, such as common law shareholder ratification.

PROBLEM [29]

Midamerican Mining Co. (Mining) is a New York corporation that has for over 60 years been engaged in mining silver, lead and copper in Latin America. You are its general counsel and have been asked to advise on negotiations with Guatador Railway Co. (Railway), likewise a New York corporation, with respect to renewal of arrangements for the carriage of Mining's ore and other commodities and supplies over Railway's lines.   Mining owns 40% of the shares of Railway which it acquired in 1930.   Three of Railway's seven directors are officers of Mining and the other 4 all received Mining's votes in the last annual election; 2 are Guatadorian political figures, 1 is a New York banker and 1 an officer of a major fabricator of copper.

Railway was originally established by Everett Gould who was also a founder of Mining and was laid out in such a way as to serve the function of transporting ore from the mines to a port on the Gulf of Sulaco.   As Guatador has become more developed it has produced other kinds of traffic and now Mining generates only 55% of the volume of goods carried over Railway's lines. It is still, however, by far the single biggest shipper, and ore is by far the largest commodity.

Ever since its origins the relationship between Railway and Mining has been regulated by negotiated contracts running for ten year periods since Guatador in no way effectively regulates the situation.   The last contract, negotiated on behalf of Railway by a board of directors composed of the same members as the present incumbents with the sole exception that one Mining officer was replaced by an outsider, is due to expire in two months.   The key provision governing rates provides that ore shall be carried from the mines to the sea at $130 per ton.   The comparable rate for commodities of other shippers is $150 per ton.   The fixed costs of Railway have worked out to about $110 per ton.   Variable or out of pocket costs run some $25 per ton.   The out-of-pocket costs of Mining's traffic are somewhat (perhaps $5) less if one attributes no advertising costs, etc., to it.   During the last three years the profitability of Railway has been declining; it has gone from a return of 8% on invested capital to 6% to 5%.   This is appreciably lower than that of Mining.   Dividends have also been less than those paid by Mining, which has caused some complaint from holders of substantial blocks of Railway shares.   Mining's

28. See also Sinclair Oil Corp. v. Levien, 280 A.2d 717 (Del.1971); David J. Greene & Co. v. Dunhill International, Inc., 249 A.2d 427 (Del.Ch. 1968).   The court in Weinberger v. UOP, Inc., p. 739 infra, discusses fairness in the context of a merger.

29. In a very general way, this problem is based upon Ripley v. International Ry. of Central Am., 8 A.D.2d 310, 188 N.Y.S.2d 62 (1959), affirmed 8 N.Y.2d 430, 171 N.E.2d 443 (1960).

management has proposed to continue on the same basis except that it will grant a 10% increase roughly parallel to that shown by the rather rudimentary Guatadorian cost of living index.

Concerned about the possibility of litigation or other adverse reaction, the board of Mining has asked you to examine the situation and make recommendations as to the new arrangements. These should include (a) your ideas about the procedure to be followed, (b) your recommendations, if any, as to the substantive terms of the contract and (c) your suggestions as to what investigations of fact might be useful in fixing rates or in substantiating the rates fixed.

A NOTE ON SHAREHOLDER RATIFICATION

It seems best to postpone extended consideration of the concept of shareholder ratification until you have had an opportunity to consider the mechanisms and potentialities and limitations of shareholder action generally, which we will do in Chapter IX. However, rounding out this section seems to call for at least briefly mentioning that almost all jurisdictions permit a contract otherwise infected by self-dealing to be ratified by a vote of the shareholders. Where the difference emerges is in the possibility that ratification might be obtained by the vote of a majority which included shares owned by the director who was interested or by the corporation on the other side of the contractual relationship in question. There is a question as to whether the requirement of fairness is eliminated by ratification. Note the treatment of ratification in 8 Del.C. § 144. Increasingly the key issue is becoming one of the adequacy, tested by common law rules developed by state courts or by the federal rules developed by the federal courts and the Securities and Exchange Commission, of the disclosure made of the transaction which the management seeks to ratify.

---

5. The Corporate Opportunity Doctrine

Alongside the rules we have just reviewed that limit directors in their dealings with the corporation, we find a cluster of rules designed to prevent directors from taking and conducting for their own account or for others activities which they ought to undertake for the corporation. These cases start with situations in which the director (or officer) used corporate property to develop his own private enterprise. Perhaps that is enough, for example, to explain the classic old case of Guth v. Loft, referred to below. Still, it has been used to justify more sweeping applications, when all that the corporation had was an "expectancy", as the courts have called it. There is fairly plainly an "expectancy" when what is involved is a piece of land which has been leased to the corporation for several years but which the insiders then take over in their own name. The language of Judge Cardozo about the level of fiduciary duty in Meinhard v. Salmon, quoted by many courts and commentators (and at p. 27 supra) involves an attempt to do that to a partnership. Suppose the corporation had merely negotiated for the lease or purchase of some asset or stared wistfully at it (perhaps because it lacked ready cash or feared antitrust consequences or ultra vires difficulties). Perhaps there really should be no "expectancy" requirement at all but the duty not to intercept should be extended to all situations where aggressive and single mindedly loyal management would have acted *for* the corporation. Particularly as a counselor to directors you will wonder about the degree to which uneasy questions can be resolved by disclosure and submission of the proposition to the other members of the board. If two or more corporations related by stockholdings or common personnel are involved, there arise issues over which firm's opportunity is involved. Finally, there is a question whether a corporation has a cause of action when its directors enter into a business operation which hurt it by diverting customers but which is one that the corporation could not possibly have acquired and, indeed, did not wish to acquire; no corporate property, including confidential data, was used.

JOHNSTON v. GREENE

Supreme Court of Delaware, 1956.
35 Del.Ch. 479, 121 A.2d 919.

SOUTHERLAND, CHIEF JUSTICE. The ultimate question in this case is the fairness of a transaction between a corporation and its president and dominating director. The court below held that he had appropriated for himself a corporate opportunity belonging to his corporation.

The pertinent facts, either uncontroverted or found by the Chancellor, are as follows:

Airfleets, Inc., is a Delaware corporation, organized in 1948 as a wholly owned subsidiary of Consolidated Vultee Aircraft Corporation (called "Convair"). Convair sometime thereafter distributed all of the Airfleets stock to its own stockholders. Atlas Corporation, an investment company, became Airfleets' largest single stockholder, owning about 18 per cent of its stock. Upon the organization of Airfleets the defendant Odlum became and has since been its president, without compensation. Odlum is also the president of Atlas, owning or controlling about 11 per cent of its stock. He is a man of varied business interests. At the time here material he also was chairman of the Board of Directors of Convair, a director of United Fruit Company, a director of Wasatch Corporation, and a trustee of several foundations.

Airfleets was organized to finance aircraft that might be sold or leased to the air lines. This purpose was never carried out. Airfleets' first business venture was the sale of certain aircraft manufacturing plants, aircraft, and related assets that it had acquired from Convair. By the fall of 1951 it had nearly completed the sale of these assets, and was in a liquid position, with about $2,000,000 in cash. It also held marketable securities worth about $1,500,000. It was looking for investments "without any predisposition as to the type". For example, it had funds in Spain received from the sale of planes to the Spanish

Government. Its management had considered certain investments in Spain, including hotels, mines, motion pictures, and "rainmaking". At this time, therefore, it was not a corporation with any well-defined object or purpose, other than that of employing its liquid assets for the profit of its stockholders. Certainly it was not then engaged in the business of manufacturing aircraft or aircraft accessories.

In late December of 1951 a business opportunity was brought to the attention of Mr. Odlum in the following circumstances:

Mr. Lester E. Hutson was the owner of all the stock of Nutt–Shel Company, a California corporation operating a plant in or near Los Angeles for the manufacture of self-locking nuts used in aircraft. Hutson also owned certain patents and patent applications covering the device. A license agreement was in effect, granting to Nutt–Shel exclusive rights in respect of the patents.

Hutson's health had not been good. In 1950 he told General Ralph P. Cousins, who was interested in a similar business, that he would be willing to sell the Nutt–Shel enterprise. Cousins attempted to interest a company in Pennsylvania, but nothing came of it. During 1951 Hutson entered into negotiations with two individuals, Dohn and Connors. At first he thought of selling only the patents, but later concluded to sell also at least part of the stock. The parties came to an agreement on the price—$350,000 for the patents and $1,000,000 for the stock—but the negotiations were never completed. Dohn and Connors lacked the funds to make an outright purchase. They wanted to buy only 20 per cent of the stock with an option upon the rest. They were planning to separate the ownership of the patents from the ownership of the stock.

Hutson was reluctant to sell the stock on a time basis. He told Cousins of the status of the proposed sale to Dohn and Connors, and Cousins suggested that he (Cousins) talk to Mr. Odlum about it. Hutson assented. Hutson knew of Odlum by reputation as a well-known financier and president of Atlas Corporation, and as a man engaged in various enterprises. Hutson had never heard of Airfleets. Cousins was a friend of Odlum's, having known Odlum since 1942, and was to spend New Year's weekend with Odlum at the latter's ranch in California. He also knew of Odlum's association with Convair and Atlas, but had never heard of Airfleets.

On the Friday before New Year's Cousins broached the subject and outlined to Odlum the history and nature of the Nutt–Shel business. Odlum was interested, and a few days later Hutson came to the ranch to discuss the matter and furnish Odlum with financial data. The price was the same as that offered to Dohn and Connors. Hutson was willing to sell the patents separately but would not sell the stock separately. He would have preferred to retain a controlling interest in the stock but Odlum said he would have to have the controlling interest. Hutson told Odlum that he had been advised by his attorney, and that "the discussion had come up during the Dohn–Connors negotiations", that it would be advisable to have the patents under separate ownership. The reason for this was the possibility of the disallowance of the royalty expense on renegotiation of government contracts, as payments from a wholly-owned corporation to its sole stockholder. About 75 per cent of Nutt–Shel's business in 1952 was subject to renegotiation.

Hutson returned a few days later with additional data. Mr. Rockefeller, Odlum's executive assistant at Convair and a director of

Airfleets, was present. He sat in on the discussions and took the papers home with him. Odlum had the Nutt–Shel plant inspected by Mr. Ryan, of the Convair organization. Ryan's report was very favorable. Odlum also received a telephone call from Rockefeller, advising him of the result of Rockefeller's study of the papers. Odlum decided to make the purchase. On February 10 he talked to Hutson by telephone, confirmed the price—"$350,000 dollars for the patents, $1,000,000 for the stock"—and told Hutson that he had decided to buy the entire deal. He then arranged, through his New York counsel, for the employment of attorneys in California to handle the closing of the transaction.

Odlum appears to have decided almost at once not to take the deal for himself. Because he was in the highest income tax bracket he was interested in capital gains rather than increased income. He discussed the whole matter with his tax adviser. He considered the tax and invested capital situation of Atlas and concluded that the Nutt–Shel investment would not be suitable for Atlas—again, apparently, for tax reasons. He then called a friend in New York who "ran" a foundation, and suggested that Pathé Industries might be interested in it. His friend later reported that Pathé would be prepared to pay the million dollars that was the cost of the stock, plus a bonus in stock of Pathé, but that Pathé would not be interested in the patents because they should be split into different ownership.

At about this time Odlum was advised by his tax consultant that the acquisition of Nutt–Shel might fit very well into the tax problems of Airfleets. Odlum requested further study of the matter, as a result of which he concluded to submit the proposition to Airfleets' Board of Directors.

Between the 24th and 28th of January Odlum had several conversations about the matter with two of his fellow directors of Airfleets, Rockefeller and Johnston. The latter is a member of the legal firm that represents Atlas, Airfleets and Odlum. Odlum told Johnston that he had been advised by Hutson of the desirability of separating the ownership of the stock from the ownership of the patents, because of the possibility of the disallowance of royalty payments on renegotiation of government contracts. Johnston was uninformed on the matter. He called his office and asked that it be checked. They called back and said that they thought there was a possibility of disallowance, and Johnston so advised Odlum.

The three directors reached the conclusion that the stock would be a desirable investment for Airfleets, but that it would be undesirable to acquire the patents. The reasons were two: first, the undesirability of investing the additional $350,000, or a total investment of about two-thirds of Airfleets' net assets, in one enterprise; and second, the possibility of the disallowance of the royalty payments. Odlum told them that in those circumstances, in order to make it possible for the company to buy the stock, he would undertake to find buyers for the patents, and if necessary would take himself whatever interest was not so disposed of.

A formal meeting of the board was held on January 28th, the three named directors being present. The board (Odlum not voting) voted to acquire the stock but not the patents. The Chancellor found that Odlum dominated the other directors and that the decision not to acquire the patents was his. This finding we accept.

On February 8th formal contracts of sale between Hutson and Airfleets, covering the stock, and between Hutson and Odlum, covering the patents, were signed. The transaction was closed in the latter part of the month.

In the meantime Odlum had arranged for the purchase of the patents for $350,000, in undivided interests, by 37 different persons and corporations, including himself. His own retained interest is about 7½ per cent. Odlum testified that he had expected to sell this interest, but after the propriety of the transaction had been questioned by an Airfleets stockholder, his position became "frozen".

The rejection of the opportunity to buy the patents is attacked as a breach of Odlum's fiduciary duty to Airfleets. The complaint charges (1) that Hutson offered to sell the patents to Airfleets for $350,000; (2) that the patents were useful and necessary to Airfleets in the conduct of the Nutt–Shel business, and the opportunity to purchase them was a valuable asset of Airfleets; (3) that the directors, under the domination of Odlum, who controlled the management of Airfleets, caused Airfleets to reject the offer, in violation of their fiduciary duty; and (4) that Odlum caused the patents to be purchased for himself and certain of his associates subject to his control.

The case made by the complaint is thus one of the unlawful diversion of a corporate opportunity for the benefit of the president and dominating director of a corporation.

The general principles of the law pertaining to corporate opportunity are settled in this state. Guth v. Loft, 23 Del.Ch. 255, 5 A.2d 503, 510. Speaking for the Supreme Court, Chief Justice Layton said:

> "It is true that when a business opportunity comes to a corporate officer or director in his individual capacity rather than in his official capacity, and the opportunity is one which, because of the nature of the enterprise, is not essential to his corporation, and is one in which it has no interest or expectancy, the officer or director is entitled to treat the opportunity as his own, and the corporation has no interest in it, if, of course, the officer or director has not wrongfully embarked the corporation's resources therein. . . .

> "On the other hand, it is equally true that, if there is presented to a corporate officer or director a business opportunity which the corporation is financially able to undertake is, from its nature, in the line of the corporation's business and is of practical advantage to it, is one in which the corporation has an interest or a reasonable expectancy, and, by embracing the opportunity, the self-interest of the officer or director will be brought into conflict with that of his corporation, the law will not permit him to seize the opportunity for himself."

The application of these principles depends on the facts. Whether or not the director has appropriated for himself something that in fairness should belong to his corporation "is a factual question to be decided by reasonable inference from objective facts." Guth v. Loft, supra, 23 Del.Ch. 277, 5 A.2d 513.

The Chancellor found that the purchase of the patents was not essential to Airfleets' business, and assumed that it was not one in which the corporation had an expectancy. But he held that it was one in which Airfleets had an interest in the sense that through Odlum it was actively seeking valuable investments, for which it had available funds, and that it was Odlum's duty to find such opportunities.

He also found that Odlum's decision to reject the opportunity to buy the patents was taken in his own interest because by affording friends, associates, and others the opportunity to buy the patents Odlum was satisfying obligations of his own.

The foundation of the Chancellor's reasoning is his holding that when the opportunity came to Odlum to buy the patents, it belonged to Airfleets because Airfleets was seeking opportunities for investment. If that conclusion is sound, Odlum could not take the patents for himself, nor could he divert them to others. Do the admitted facts justify the finding?

The first important fact that appears is that Hutson's offer, which was to sell the patents and at least part of the stock, came to Odlum, not as a director of Airfleets, but in his individual capacity. The Chancellor so found. The second important fact is that the business of Nutt–Shel—the manufacture of self-locking nuts—had no direct or close relation to any business that Airfleets was engaged in or had ever been engaged in, and hence its acquisition was not essential to the conduct of Airfleets' business. Again, the Chancellor so found. The third fact is that Airfleets had no interest or expectancy in the Nutt–Shel business, in the sense that those words are used in the decisions dealing with the law of corporate opportunity.

> "Whether in any case an officer of a corporation is in duty bound to purchase property for the corporation, or to refrain from purchasing property for himself, depends upon whether the corporation has an interest, *actual or in expectancy*, in the property, or whether the purchase of the property by the officer or director may hinder or defeat the plans and purposes of the corporation in the carrying on or development of the legitimate business for which it was created." Colorado & Utah Coal Co. v. Harris, 97 Colo. 309, 49 P.2d 429; quoted in Fletcher, Cyclopedia Corporations, § 861.1 [Italics supplied.]

For the corporation to have an actual or expectant interest in any specific property, there must be some tie between that property and the nature of the corporate business. Cf. Guth v. Loft, supra, in which the Court said: "The tie was close between the business of Loft and the Pepsi–Cola enterprise". 23 Del.Ch. 279, 5 A.2d 515. No such tie exists here. Airfleets had no interest, actual or in expectancy, in the Nutt–Shel business.

We accordingly find ourselves compelled to disagree with the Chancellor's decision. Recognizing that Airfleets had no expectancy in the Nutt–Shel business and that its acquisition was not essential to Airfleets, he nevertheless held that Airfleets' need for investments constituted an "interest" in the opportunity to acquire that business. Now, this is an application of the rule of corporate opportunity that requires careful examination. It is one thing to say that a corporation with funds to invest has a general interest in investing those funds; it is quite another to say that such a corporation has a specific interest attaching in equity to any and every business opportunity that may come to any of its directors in his individual capacity. This is what the Chancellor appears to have held. Such a sweeping extension of the rule of corporate opportunity finds no support in the decisions and is, we think, unsound.

It is, of course, entirely possible that a corporate opportunity might in some cases arise out of a corporate need to invest funds and the duty of the president or any other director to seek such an opportunity. But whether it does arise, in any particular case, depends on the facts— upon the existence of special circumstances that would make it unfair for him to take the opportunity for himself.

We cannot find any such circumstances in this case. At the time when the Nutt–Shel business was offered to Odlum, his position was this: He was the part-time president of Airfleets. He was also president of Atlas—an investment company. He was a director of other corporations and a trustee of foundations interested in making investments. If it was his fiduciary duty, upon being offered any investment opportunity, to submit it to a corporation of which he was a director, the question arises, Which corporation? Why Airfleets instead of Atlas? Why Airfleets instead of one of the foundations? So far as appears, there was no specific tie between the Nutt–Shel business and any of these corporations or foundations. Odlum testified that many of his companies had money to invest, and this appears entirely reasonable. How, then, can it be said that Odlum was under any obligation to offer the opportunity to one particular corporation? And if he was not under such an obligation, why could he not keep it for himself?

Plaintiff suggests that if Odlum elects to assume fiduciary relationships to competing corporations he must assume the obligations that are entailed by such relationships. So he must, but what are the obligations? The mere fact of having funds to invest does not ordinarily put the corporations "in competition" with each other, as that phrase is used in the law of corporate opportunity. There is nothing inherently wrong in a man of large business and financial interests serving as a director of two or more investment companies, and both Airfleets and Atlas (to mention only two companies) must reasonably have expected that Odlum would be free either to offer to any of his companies any business opportunity that came to him personally, or to retain it for himself—provided always that there was no tie between any of such companies and the new venture or any specific duty resting upon him with respect to it. 3 Fletcher, Cyclopedia Corporations, § 862.

It is clear to us that the reason why the Nutt–Shel business was offered to Airfleets was because Odlum, having determined that he did not want it for himself, chose to place the investment in that one of his companies whose tax situation was best adapted to receive it. He chose to do so, although he could probably have sold the stock to an outside company at a profit to himself. If he had done so, who could have complained? If a stockholder of Airfleets could have done so, why not a stockholder of Atlas as well?

It is unnecessary to labor the point further. We are of opinion that the opportunity to purchase the Nutt–Shel business belonged to Odlum and not to any of his companies.

This conclusion requires the rejection of the plaintiffs' contention, and of the Chancellor's holding, that the opportunity to buy the Nutt–Shel business belonged to Airfleets. But it does not in itself dispose of the case.

The refusal of the directors of Airfleets to buy the patents was, under the Chancellor's finding, a transaction between the dominating director and his corporation. It is therefore subject to strict scrutiny, and the defendants have the burden of showing that it was fair.

The facts surrounding the transaction are not in dispute. Odlum had chosen to put Airfleets in the Nutt–Shel business. The patent rights were therefore essential to Nutt–Shel, and ordinarily it would follow that it would be advantageous to Airfleets to acquire the patents, even though Nutt–Shel had an exclusive license to exploit them.   . . . But there are important factual distinctions between these decisions and the case at bar. In those cases the director had acquired the patents for his own profit, although there was no reason why the corporation should not have acquired them.

In the instant case the rejection of the patents was based upon Odlum's judgment that the acquisition would be undesirable for Airfleets, and he did not seek to profit personally by acquiring them for himself. The transaction must of course be viewed in the light of the situation confronting Odlum at the time they were first offered to Airfleets. At that time he had been told by Hutson that the latter's attorney had advised separation, and that Dohn and Connors had also contemplated separate ownership. He had been told that Pathé would not be interested in buying the patents because they should be held in different ownership. Finally, upon requesting the opinion of his own counsel upon the point, he received advice tending to confirm what he had before been told. He thereupon determined to pay Hutson for the patents and distribute the ownership among third persons.

Now, a fair way to determine the propriety of Odlum's action "is to consider whether the proposition submitted would have commended itself to an independent corporation." International Radio Tel. Co. v. Atlantic Communications Co., 2 Cir., 290 F. 698, 702. It is clear to us that if a wholly independent board of directors had determined, upon the information received by Odlum, that it was undesirable for Airfleets to buy the patents and that they should be transferred to third persons, a reviewing court would not think of disturbing its judgment upon the matter. Moreover, it is a fair conclusion that in the light of this information received from four separate sources the separation of the ownership of the patents would have commended itself to an independent board of directors.

As to this question of the hazard of the possible disallowance of royalties on renegotiations, the Chancellor observed that the directors must have known that for sometime the close ownership of the patents had existed as to Hutson, yet he had not suffered thereby. This is to say that because the government had not yet acted in the matter the hazard of adverse action was negligible. This by no means follows. A business man would hardly be justified in making such an assumption and predicating an important decision upon it. In this case it appears that the renegotiation reports covering the Nutt–Shel operations for the year ending October 31, 1951, were not filed until 1954. In any event, there is nothing to show that Odlum could safely assume that the government would decide in Hutson's favor. A hazard of increased tax or other liability, dependent on the future construction and application of a government regulation, is not a matter lightly to be disregarded.

That Hutson subsequently apparently received a clearance from the regional negotiation board in respect to the allowance of royalties, is, of course, immaterial. The question turns on the situation as it existed when Odlum's decision was made.

There is the further circumstance that Odlum thought that one million dollars was sufficient to put into the venture, constituting in itself nearly half of Airfleets' net assets. We cannot say, of course, that on this matter an independent board would have in all likelihood agreed with Odlum; They might, or they might not. But certainly such a consideration is more than a mere pretext or excuse for rejecting the purchase of the patents. The Chancellor thought it not persuasive because Airfleets' existing investments were of a temporary nature, and could readily have been sold to provide more cash. This hardly seems to touch the point of the proportion of the required investment—$1,350,000—to total net assets; moreover, whether and at what time any investment should be sold is peculiarly a matter of business judgment.

Now, as the Chancellor found, Odlum made these decisions on behalf of Airfleets. If, after making them, he had elected to keep the patents for himself, a serious question would be presented whether he had sustained the burden of establishing fairness. In that event there would have been presented a question of conflict between his self-interest and his duty to make these decisions uncolored by his own interests. In such a case a reviewing court might apply the rule, invoked by plaintiff, "that ascribes to self-interest rather than to a sense of duty the motive power of ensuing action". Loft v. Guth, 23 Del.Ch. 138, 169, 2 A.2d 225, 239.

But Odlum did not seek to profit personally by what he had done. He promptly divested himself, prior to the closing of the transaction, of almost the entire interest in the patents. His explanation of the retention of the seven and one-half per cent interest seems entirely reasonable; and we are told that it is still his intention to sell this retained interest if he is permitted to do so. If this is done, there will remain about a four and three-tenths per cent interest owned by himself and his wife. His personal interest in the income from the patents, in the light of his financial situation, is therefore negligible. His financial interest in Airfleets is much greater.

The Chancellor held that Odlum's sale of the patents was a means whereby he satisfied certain "felt" obligations to friends and associates of his own or of his wife. This finding appears to refer to Odlum's testimony that some of the assignees were people for whom he felt "some sort of moral responsibility to help them with their personal affairs". The large majority of the assignees, however, were not of this class. We do not think that it can be fairly said that Odlum profited personally from the sale. The Chancellor's finding that the sale of the patents was improper was, we think, based on his holding that the Nutt–Shel business, including the patents, was a corporate opportunity belonging to Airfleets. If that were so, then his conclusion would be sound, since, as he said Odlum's motive in allowing friends, associates and others to buy the patents could not justify the diversion from Airfleets of an asset belonging to it. But we are of opinion, as above stated, that this is not a case of corporate opportunity, and is to be judged by the test applicable to a transaction between the dominating director and his corporation—the test of fairness.

Plaintiffs contend that Airfleets' assets were used to enable Odlum to buy the patents. The argument runs as follows:

Hutson was unwilling to sell the patents unless a purchaser could be found for the stock; Odlum's ability to purchase the patents was thus wholly dependent on the use of Airfleets' funds to purchase the stock; and this constituted the use of Airfleets' funds to purchase the patents.

The fallacy of this argument is plain. Its implicit major premise is the assumption that Odlum wanted the patents for himself, and merely used Airfleets as a means whereby he got rid of the stock and kept the patents for himself. This is directly contrary to the testimony. Odlum did not want the patents. Because he was in the highest income bracket he was looking for capital gains. And he did not take the patents for himself. Moreover, there is no suggestion that the purchase of the stock was not a sound investment for Airfleets. The whole basis of this contention is unsound.

Our conclusions upon a careful review of this record are: first, that the opportunity to acquire the Nutt–Shel business did not belong to Airfleets; second, that the transaction between Odlum and Airfleets involving the patents was fair and free of any overreaching or inequitable conduct.

It follows that the judgment of the Court of Chancery must be reversed. The cause is remanded to that court, with directions to vacate the judgment and dismiss the complaint.

LEWIS v. FUQUA

Delaware Chancery Court, 1985.
502 A.2d 962.

[Fuqua Industries, Inc., a Delaware corporation, is a diversified enterprise that has engaged in a course of acquiring control of various businesses—and, not infrequently, disposing of them. It has had stakes in banking, Pier I Imports, film processing, movie theatres, sporting goods, power mowers, etc. In 1982 Fuqua Industries became interested in Triton Group, Limited, a Delaware holding company whose primary assets were a $160 million tax loss plus two real estate projects and some cash. It had two classes of stock, both publicly traded. The Preferred was convertible into common at 1:24.5. Fuqua began discussions with American Financial Corporation (AFC) about acquiring AFC's large interest in Triton. On March 3, 1983 Fuqua bought from AFC 425,365 shares of Triton Preferred at $.45 per share. On February 7, 1983 Mr. J.B. Fuqua bought 2 million shares of Triton Common from AFC and on March 7 fourteen individual defendants, at J.B. Fuqua's solicitation, bought the remaining 1,260,450 shares AFC owned of Triton common. Later Fuqua Industries bought the shares of Triton owned by Anthony Walsh and his allies at a price $.30 more per share than paid to AFC. Walsh and his associates resigned from Triton's board. The Fuqua Industries board never rejected the opportunity to buy the common shares of Triton from AFC.

Harry Lewis, a stockholder of Fuqua Industries, began a derivative suit alleging usurpation of a corporate opportunity by J.D. Fuqua, Chairman and CEO of the corporation, and other individual defendants. The board of Fuqua Industries appointed a Special Litigation Committee of one person, Terry Sanford, to review the claim. Sanford had been Governor of North Carolina and President of Duke University. He and a "distinguished law firm" examined the matter and "not surprisingly" recommended that Fuqua Industries not pursue any legal action in the matter. Accordingly the corporation sought to have the suit dismissed. After discussing various procedural matters, VICE CHANCELLOR HARTNETT discussed the corporate opportunity issues as follows].

VI

The Sanford Committee investigation focused on two possible theories of recovery by plaintiff: a corporate opportunity theory and an interested director theory. As to the corporate opportunity theory, the Committee concluded that, under applicable Delaware law, the opportunity to purchase Triton Common Stock was not a corporate opportunity at all, but instead an opportunity which the individuals were entitled to treat as their own. As will be seen, the conclusion reached by the Committee on this issue is flawed and therefore did not have a reasonable basis.

A.

In determining the possible existence of a corporate opportunity the Sanford Committee recognized three possible tests: (1) the expectancy test, (2) the line of business test, and (3) the fairness test. Claiming that the application of any of these tests by this Court has been varying and imprecise, the Sanford Committee chose to find that the most often used test is the fairness test. In reviewing the fairness test, as it applies to the challenged transaction, the Sanford Committee pinpointed a so-called "Delaware Variation". It found that the initial formulation of the fairness test was announced in Guth v. Loft, Del. Supr., 5 A.2d 503 (1939). The Sanford Committee, however, decided that later Delaware cases have modified the Guth fairness test so that, in its view, it is no longer necessary to consider whether an opportunity came to the attention of a corporate manager or director in his individual or corporate capacity. See, Science Accessories v. Summagraphics, Del.Supr., 425 A.2d 957, 963 (1980). The Sanford Committee therefore decided that four elements now must be considered in determining the existence of a corporate opportunity under the fairness test: (1) the "interest or expectancy" test, also called the "essential" test; (2) the "line of business" test; (3) the "practical advantage" test; and (4) the "use of corporate resources" test. The Sanford Committee concluded that none of the elements necessary as to these four tests were present in the challenged transaction and, therefore, no corporate opportunity existed to have been diverted.

B.

In the application of the first so-called "interest or expectancy" test to determine whether a corporate opportunity existed at all, the Sanford Committee found that the opportunity to purchase Triton Common Stock was not essential to Fuqua Industries, nor did the failure to purchase Triton Common Stock cause any affirmative harm to the Corporation. The Sanford Committee concluded that when the directors decided to purchase the Triton Common Stock for themselves, the corporation had no contractual right to purchase the stock and, therefore, had no present interest in the purchase of the stock. The Sanford Committee also decided that Fuqua Industries ceased to have an expectancy in the purchase of the Triton Common Stock because although the corporation had an apparent expectancy in the purchase of the stock, it had rejected the opportunity—thus negating its expectancy.

The Sanford Committee did concede, however, a necessity for a scrutiny of Fuqua Industries' alleged decision not to purchase the Triton Common Stock because the decision was made by the very people who ultimately bought the stock. The Sanford Committee decided, however, that because the Board of Fuqua Industries had rejected the opportunity to purchase the stock on behalf of the corporation before the directors decided to purchase the stock for themselves, the directors were disinterested when they voted to reject the purchase. The Sanford Committee therefore found that a court would scrutinize the decision not to purchase the stock for the corporation under the business judgment test as opposed to the much more burdensome intrinsic fairness test.

By relying on the business judgment test, the Sanford Committee concluded that the directors had a valid business reason for rejecting the opportunity to purchase the Triton Common Stock: the fear of adverse consequences in the reflection of Triton's losses on Fuqua Industries' financial statement. The Sanford Committee therefore concluded that there was no identifiable corporate opportunity under the first "interest", "expectancy", or "essential" test.

Even assuming, arguendo, that the Sanford Committee was correct and the rule of Guth has been modified, the conclusions of the Committee ignore the fact that no Delaware court has yet gone so far as to extend the protection of the business judgment rule to a transaction in which the directors who are passing on the transaction have a conflict of interest or divided loyalties. Cf. Pogostin v. Rice, Del.Supr., 480 A.2d 619 (1984); Aronson v. Lewis, Del.Supr., 473 A.2d 805 (1984); Weinberger v. UOP, Del.Supr., 457 A.2d 701 (1983). It also ignores the fact that it is undisputed that the Board never formally rejected the opportunity and it is a question of fact as to whether the Board actually so agreed. This conclusion of the Sanford Committee therefore did not have a reasonable basis.

C.

The Sanford Committee's analysis of the other three tests to determine if a corporate opportunity existed, also led the Committee to conclude that there was none. In the application of the second or so-called "line of business" test the Sanford Committee conceded that the opportunity to purchase the Triton Common Stock was in Fuqua Industries' line of business. The Committee, however, interpreted case law as suggesting that if there is evidence of a company policy against acquiring a particular opportunity it will negate a finding that the opportunity was in the corporation's line of business.

The Sanford Committee found that Fuqua Industries would have to put Triton's losses on its financial statement, if it acquired any Triton Common Stock, and that this was inconsistent with Fuqua's then policy of maintaining a high earnings profile. This inconsistent policy, in the view of the Sanford Committee, negated the fact that the opportunity to purchase the Triton Common Stock was in Fuqua Industries' line of business. In all the cases cited by the Committee in support of that proposition, however, the Corporations involved were able to show that they had actually turned down a chance to realize a similar prior opportunity. Here, Fuqua Industries had not only not turned down a similar opportunity; it had actually exploited a similar opportunity in the Pier 1 acquisition. As will be discussed, there is also a factual question as to whether Triton's losses would have to be shown on Fuqua Industries' Financial Statement. The Sanford Committee has therefore not borne its burden of showing that its conclusion on this issue had a reasonable basis.

D.

The Sanford Committee further concluded, in analyzing the third so-called "practical advantage" test to determine if a corporate opportunity existed, that the acquisition of the Triton Common Stock would not have been a practical advantage to Fuqua Industries. In making this determination, the Sanford Committee [adopted] the proposition that one must take a short term view in determining the practical advantage to the Corporation. The Committee decided that the application of this principle to the challenged transaction showed that the placement of Triton's losses on Fuqua Industries' financial statements would have hampered the Company's high earnings profile and would therefore have been a short term disadvantage. There is a factual question, however, as to whether Triton's losses would have had to have been shown on Fuqua Industries financial statements. Plaintiff calls attention to Accounting Principles Board Opinion No. 18 which appears to require a corporation which holds 20% or more of the voting stock of an investee company to place the losses of the investee company on its books only in proportion to its share of the investee company's common stock. Plaintiff argues that if Fuqua Industries had purchased the common stock of Triton which the directors ended up purchasing for themselves, Fuqua Industries would have had over 20% of the voting stock of Triton (Triton Preferred Stock has voting rights), but it would have owned only 1.1% of Triton's common stock. Plaintiff therefore argues that Fuqua Industries would only have had to place 1.1% of Triton's losses on its financial statement. Plaintiff has, therefore, raised a question of fact as to whether the purchase of all the available Triton stock by Fuqua Industries would have had an undesirable effect on Fuqua Industries Financial Statements. The Sanford Committee has, therefore, not borne its burden of showing that its conclusion on this issue had a reasonable basis.

E.

Finally, in addressing the fourth so-called "use of corporate resources" test to determine if a corporate opportunity existed, the Sanford Committee found no showing that defendants used any corporate funds in acquiring the opportunity, or that there was any abusive use of corporate resources. The Committee was undoubtedly correct in its finding that no corporate funds were used by the directors when they purchased the Triton stock for themselves but this is not dispositive as to whether a corporate opportunity existed.

VII

The Sanford Committee next addressed the second possible theory of recovery—the interested director issue. This theory of recovery focuses on the Walsh Block transaction in which Fuqua Industries purchased Triton Common and Preferred Stock at $.30 more per share than paid by the individual defendants. In regard to this interested director issue, the Committee recognized three separate tests of liability: (1) a test based on Section 144 of the Delaware General Corporation Law (8 Del.C. § 144); (2) the business judgment test; and (3) the intrinsic fairness test.

[The Vice–Chancellor concluded that the findings of the Sanford Committee on the interested director issue were not "reasonable." He concluded:]

The gravamen of the claim of the plaintiff in this suit is that the directors of Fuqua Industries diverted an opportunity of the corporation to purchase Triton common stock to themselves for their own personal financial gain. If this is true, it is difficult to imagine a more egregious breach of fiduciary duty. In the present corporate litigation climate, a stockholder's welfare rests almost solely on the judgment and independence of his directors. Any reasonably valid claim that the directors acted because of a conflict of interest involving their own selfish economic interest should bear close scrutiny by an impartial tribunal—not a one-man committee appointed by the alleged wrong doers.

It may be that ultimately the directors will be able to show that they did not divert a corporate opportunity to themselves. Thus far they have not done so. Plaintiff should be given an opportunity to pursue discovery so that the truth of his allegations may be tested.

The motion to dismiss is therefore dismissed.[30]

NOTE ON GUTH v. LOFT

At various points each of the preceding opinions refers to, and quotes from, Guth v. Loft,[31] perhaps the "classic" corporate opportunity case. Guth was president of Loft, a Delaware corporation that manufactured candies, syrups, beverages and food and sold them through 115 stores in the Middle Atlantic area and at wholesale. It had $9,000,000 of assets and adequate working capital. Guth became annoyed at Coca–Cola for refusing to give Loft an adequate discount. He learned about Pepsi–Cola which had a formula and a trademark and some sales in the South. In 1931 National Pepsi–Cola went bankrupt. With a friend, Megargel, Guth formed a new Pepsi–Cola Co. which bought the formula and trademark. From 1931 to 1935 Guth poured Loft's resources into Pepsi, using its plant, its working capital, etc. Loft made the concentrate and sold it to Grace, a Guth-owned firm, at a slight mark up. Grace resold the syrup, with sugar and water, to Pepsi's customers, chiefly Loft, at a profit. Replacing Coca–Cola with Pepsi cost Loft losses of profits estimated at $300,000 plus advertising expenses. Guth owed Loft over $100,000. Finally, Guth was discharged and Loft brought suit against him. The Chancellor found that Guth had wrongfully appropriated the opportunity and ordered Guth to turn over to Loft all the shares of Pepsi stock, all dividends thereon, plus all

30. Fuqua Industries sold its holdings in Triton in 1986 for $34 million in cash. 1 Moody's Industrials 1291 (1987).

31. 23 Del.Ch. 255, 5 A.2d 503 (1939).

salary received from Pepsi, and the Supreme Court affirmed. Some portions of the opinion, in addition to those quoted in Johnston follow:

Corporate officers and directors are not permitted to use their position of trust and confidence to further their private interests. While technically not trustees, they stand in a fiduciary relation to the corporation and its stockholders. A public policy, existing through the years, and derived from a profound knowledge of human characteristics and motives, has established a rule that demands of a corporate officer or director, peremptorily and inexorably, the most scrupulous observance of his duty, not only affirmatively to protect the interests of the corporation committed to his charge, but also to refrain from doing anything that would work injury to the corporation, or to deprive it of profit or advantage which his skill and ability might properly bring to it, or to enable it to make in the reasonable and lawful exercise of its powers. The rule that requires an undivided and unselfish loyalty to the corporation demands that there shall be no conflict between duty and self-interest. The occasions for the determination of honesty, good faith and loyal conduct are many and varied, and no hard and fast rule can be formulated. The standard of loyalty is measured by no fixed scale.

[margin note: No conflict b/tw duty & self interest]

If an officer or director of a corporation, in violation of his duty as such, acquires gain or advantage for himself, the law charges the interest so acquired with a trust for the benefit of the corporation, at its election, while it denies to the betrayer all benefit and profit. The rule, inveterate and uncompromising in its rigidity, does not rest upon the narrow ground of injury or damage to the corporation resulting from a betrayal of confidence, but upon a broader foundation of a wise public policy that, for the purpose of removing all temptation, extinguishes all possibility of profit flowing from a breach of the confidence imposed by the fiduciary relation. Given the relation between the parties, a certain result follows; and a constructive trust is the remedial device through which precedence of self is compelled to give way to the stern demands of loyalty. . . .

The rule, referred to briefly as the rule of corporate opportunity, is merely one of the manifestations of the general rule that demands of an officer or director the utmost good faith in his relation to the corporation which he represents. . . .

PROBLEM

You are still general counsel to Mining as in the problem on p. 260 supra. Your client confronts you with a new problem. Recently its vice president Gould, who is also a director of Railway went to negotiate a new deal with the President of Guatador, Guzman Bento, who had just come to power as the head of a military junta. It related to a new copper deposit found in a rather remote region called Azuera. The two hammered out an arrangement providing for the long term exploitation by Mining of the new deposit, the payment of various taxes and royalties, the periodic renegotiation of various terms, etc. Bento then introduced a new topic; he wanted to have Mining build a railroad from Azuera to the Pacific. This line would not only carry ore but ought to speed development of that entire region, Bento thought. It would also, however, draw to itself some traffic that now goes by way of the existing Railroad line to the Atlantic at the Gulf of Sulaco. It would also be possible to extend the latter line to Azuera; indeed, it would be the more economic alternative from a railroading point of view. Gould accepted this additional change without raising these points. The contract is now before the board of directors of Mining and they ask you for your advice as to the legality of their entering into this arrangement. You note that Mining is the more prosperous of the two firms and the only one with the present capacity to raise the necessary funds. However, Railway could probably finance a major project if it could assure lenders of a steady flow of ore traffic over its line.

Bibliography: Corporate opportunity doctrine is dealt with extensively in the ALI Principles of Corporate Governance §§ 5.05 and 5.12 (Tent Draft. No. 5, 1986) (dealing respectively with managers and controlling shareholders). A major effort at rationalizing the field is Brudney & Clark, A New Look at Corporate Opportunities, 94 Harv.L.Rev. 997 (1981).

6. The Role of the Lawyer in Board Action

NOTE ON LEGAL ADVICE AND BOARD ACTION

The function of the lawyer in corporate matters is *par excellence* an advisory one. To some extent he or she carries out instructions of the board by drafting documents, negotiating with other parties, etc. Occasionally—often reluctantly—the attorney litigates on its behalf. But for the most part the attorney advises. This is a more delicate process than appears at first glance. It is hard for one thing, to maintain a division between legal questions and issues of business or public policy. A lawyer may be tempted to express personal business views and ideas as to public policy, especially where legal lines are blurred. The American self-image of the lawyer as generalist tends to exaggerate this. Some clients will resent and resist this tendency. Others will succumb to it, particularly if they have come to know and trust the lawyer outside of the technical role. Still, it must be remembered that there is a difference between advising and deciding, that it is often comfortable to advise a costly but morally attractive course of action but something else again to bear the responsibility for it before the stockholders or the board of directors.

Since corporations are complex organizations it is not always clear who in human terms is the "client." The attorney may visualize a division head or the CEO as the client because of their long-continued course of dealings. But since the board of directors heads the corporation, at least in legal terms, counsel for the corporation must relate to the boards in the last analysis. The complexities of such relationships are revealed, if not resolved, in Rule 1.13 of the Model Rules of Professional Responsibility (1983) (Documentary Supplement).

The situation can get even more complicated if the lawyer is wearing two hats—acting as director of the corporation to which he or she gives advice. While this duality has elements of conveniences for both sides it can create pressures that make fulfillment of either responsibility difficult. Some distinguished lawyers have expressed a wish that bar associations enact a general self-denying rule under which lawyers could not serve in both capacities. A rule of general applicability would ease the competitive pressures that make lawyers anxious to retain a corporation's legal business willing to accept seats on the board.

One aspect of legal advice is its potentiality as a protector from liability. Directors have some reason to hope that they may be shielded from liability vis-a-vis outsiders or the corporation by having previously obtained an opinion of counsel that the step they were about to undertake was in fact lawful. Whether that defense will be successful depends, *inter alia*, on what the cause of action is, whether it requires that the plaintiff show wilfulness, negligence, etc.[32] Conversely, it is possible that the lawyer who clears an arrangement may, in some way, be responsible for it. One possibility would be a suit for malpractice, i.e., negligence. Another possibility is involvement, as a co-conspirator or otherwise, in a substantive offense. Thus in United States v. Union Camp Corp., 5 CCH Trade Reg.Rep. Case No. 1978 (D.Va., May 6, 1968), the indictment for conspiracy to monopolize and restrain trade included an attorney who had advised the company to use a patent known to be invalid as part of the campaign against competitors. In People v. Marcus, a young lawyer was found guilty of participating with directors and officers in a violation of a law against misappropriating bank funds. His conviction was reversed after an eloquent argument by Harold Medina, then a leading New York trial lawyer and subsequently the federal district judge who tried the Communist and investment banking conspiracy cases. His argument stressed the inexperience of the defendant: "I told the judges you know how those boys in law school are—those law clerks of yours—they think they know everything". This theme was picked up in the following portion of Judge Pound's opinion:

> "[I]t is difficult to believe that he intentionally aided or assisted his father and Marcus in willfully misappropriating the funds of corporations of which they were directors. They did not need his assistance in devising or carrying out the plan,

---

32. Holland v. Presley, 255 App.Div. 667, 8 N.Y.S.2d 804 (1939). Gilbert v. Burnside, 11 N.Y.2d 960, 183 N.E.2d 325 (1962). As to liabilities under the Securities Act see p. 186 supra.

other than such assistance as is rendered by lawyers' clerks in drawing necessary papers. No doubt the young man was quite capable in handling these details and profuse in his advice. We are not unfamiliar with the importance frequently assumed by the young practitioner who is apt to magnify his work and worth. It is inconceivable that Saul Singer, who, in thirty-two years after landing in this country, had passed from the crockery, steam laundry and garment business to the position of one of the leading financiers in New York city, could be influenced or directed by the young son he had brought up in the soft places in life. The drive from the bottom to the top develops courage, resolution and determination little swayed by the neophyte, fresh from his books. There is, therefore, no evidence in this case warranting the conclusion that Herbert, the law clerk, aided and assisted criminally in the misappropriation of the funds of those safe deposit companies. That he aided by his work as a clerk is, of course, conceded; that he aided as a participant in the misapplication as a criminal act is not proven." [33]

Martin Mayer relates that young Singer, despite this inauspicious introduction, did become an important member of the New York bar, who in 1966 headed the committee to endow a Medina chair at Columbia Law School.

Some of the issues of attorney-client relationship are pinpointed by questions of privileged communications such as those raised in the following case. Issues that arise in the corporate context are (1) Who is the client? and (2) When is it legal advice? The "who is the client" question brings us back into the scope of the questions raised by Rule 1.15 but with a different twist. If an attorney is communicating with the board of directors it is plain that "the client" is the party. It has generally been assumed that the CEO and some other top level officials represented the client also. Some of the courts developed a "control group" test which extended the privilege to dealings with officers and agents responsible for directing companies' actions in response to legal advice. The Supreme Court in Upjohn Co. v. United States, 449 U.S. 383, 101 S.Ct. 677, 66 L.Ed.2d 584 (1981), rejected that test. It left unclear what test it substituted but one can at least assume coverage in similar fact situations—Upjohn Company had sent a questionnaire to all foreign general and area managers asking them about allegations as to questionable overseas payments (foreign corrupt practices). The letter asked that responses be sent to the firm's general counsel and was signed by the chairman of the board. On the "when is it legal advice" point a number of cases have had to cope with this in the context of memoranda from house counsel to executives, raising the question whether the advice given or sought was legal. Courts have

33. People v. Marcus, 261 N.Y. 268, 295, 185 N.E. 97, 105 (1933); see also M. Mayer, Emory Buckner 277 (1968).

noted a number of factors, including the membership of the lawyer in the local bar, as bearing on this essentially factual issue. A statement by Judge Wyzanski is often quoted: [34]

> The members of law partnership in each case were acting as attorneys giving legal advice. They were not acting as business advisers or officers of United, even though occasionally their recommendations had in addition to legal points some economic or policy or public relations aspect and hence were not unmixed opinions of law. The modern lawyer almost invariably advises his client upon not only what is permissible but also what is desirable. And it is in the public interest that the lawyer should regard himself as more than predicter of legal consequences. His duty to society as well as to his client involves many relevant social, economic, political and philosophical considerations.

Serious questions arise in considering the right of stockholders and other actual or potential investors to learn about the attorney's communications to the management of "their" corporation. The following case represents one context in which that problem can arise—the derivative suit by dissatisfied shareholders. Another is in connection with the periodic reports which management is required to make by federal law. The financial statements included in those reports must include as contingent liabilities significant threats of loss through litigation. In their search for data to substantiate their statements about such liabilities, the accountants have increasingly sought to induce corporate attorneys to supply information as to pending, threatened and even merely potential lawsuits. Attorneys have seen these efforts as undermining the confidentiality necessary to an effective working relation with management and have tried to restrict the scope of these inquiries.[35]

GARNER v. WOLFINBARGER

United States Court of Appeals, Fifth Circuit, 1970.
430 F.2d 1093, certiorari denied 401 U.S. 974, 91 S.Ct. 1191, 28 L.Ed.2d 323 (1971).

[This was a class action by stockholders of First American Life Insurance Company of Alabama (FAL) in a federal district court. Plaintiffs alleged that they had been defrauded by defendants in the purchase of stock in FAL, in violation of federal statutory law and of common law. They also asserted a derivative claim on behalf of FAL in connection with these transactions. FAL filed a cross claim against the other defendants, asserting in its own behalf the derivative claim.

34. United States v. United Shoe Machinery Corp., 89 F.Supp. 357, 359 (D.Mass. 1950).

Requests for Information, 31 Bus.Law. 1709 (1976).

35. See the ABA Statement of Policy regarding Lawyers' Responses to Auditors'

A deposition was taken of one Schwertzer who had been FAL's attorney in connection with the issuance of the stock involved in the suit. He later became FAL's president. He was asked questions about the advice given by him to the corporation about the issuance of that stock and about related discussions with company officials. Objections were made on the ground of attorney-client privilege.

The district court held the privilege not available. It also ordered the case transferred to another district. We here omit discussion of the transfer question and of the appealability of the ruling as to confidentiality. Portions of JUDGE GODBOLD'S opinion as to the merits of the attorney-client privilege question follow:]

B.   Background and choice of law

Turning to the merits, there is no contention by plaintiffs that FAL is outside the ambit of the attorney-client privilege because a corporation is not a client. Their argument is that the privilege is not available to FAL in the circumstances of this case against the demands of the corporate stockholders for access to the communications. The corporation says that its right to assert the privilege is absolute and of special importance where disclosure is sought in a suit brought by the shareholders against the corporation. The American Bar Association appears as amicus curiae and supports the view of an absolute privilege.

The privilege does not arise from the position of the corporation as a party by its status as a client. However, in this instance plaintiffs deny the availability to the corporation of the otherwise existent privilege because of the role of the corporation as a party defending against claims of its stockholders.

We do not consider the privilege to be so inflexibly absolute as contended by the corporation, nor to be so totally unavailable against the stockholders as thought by the District Court. We conclude that the correct rule is between these two extreme positions.

The availability *vel non* of the privilege involves a complex problem of choice of law. 2B Barron & Holtzoff, Federal Practice & Procedure, § 967 at 241–44 (Wright ed. 1961). The order of the District Court appears to treat Alabama standards as controlling. We conclude that the choice of law cannot be settled by reference to any simple talisman, but can be arrived at only after a consideration of state and federal interests that are inseparable from the factors bearing on the availability of the privilege itself.

[A thorough study by the court of the question of reference to Alabama versus federal standards is omitted.]

Our discussion below points up that many of the factors to be weighed in the consideration of federal and state interests are predicated on values long embodied in policies of the states rather than federal law.[36] And it goes without saying that a federal court must take full account of the reasons for any asserted privilege including any especially strong policies of the state in which the court sits. But it must take account of federal interests as well.

---

36. For example, the responsibility of officers and directors toward the stockholders of a corporation, which is an important factor in our decision.

The competing interests in disclosure on the one hand and confidentiality on the other, neither of which lies exclusively within the state or federal realm, are the subject of the next part of our discussion.

C. The availability of the privilege

The privilege must be placed in perspective. The beginning point is the fundamental principle that the public has the right to every man's evidence, and exemptions from the general duty to give testimony that one is capable of giving are distinctly exceptional. 8 Wigmore, Evidence, § 2192 at 70. An exception is justified if—and only if—policy requires it be recognized when measured against the fundamental responsibility of every person to give testimony. *Id.*, § 2285 at 527. Professor Wigmore describes four conditions, the existence of all of which is prerequisite to the establishment of a privilege of any kind against the disclosure of communications:

> § 2285. *General principle of privileged communications.* Looking back upon the principle of privilege, as an exception to the general liability of every person to give testimony upon all facts inquired of in a court of justice, and keeping in view that preponderance of extrinsic policy which alone can justify the recognition of any such exception (§§ 2192 and 2197 *supra*), four fundamental conditions are recognized as necessary to the establishment of a privilege against the disclosure of communications:
>
> (1) The communications must originate in a *confidence* that they will not be disclosed.
>
> (2) This element of *confidentiality must be essential* to the full and satisfactory maintenance of the relation between the parties.
>
> (3) The *relation* must be one which in the opinion of the community ought to be sedulously *fostered.*
>
> (4) The *injury* that would inure to the relation by the disclosure of the communications must be *greater than the benefit* thereby gained for the correct disposal of litigation.
>
> Only if these four conditions are present should a privilege be recognized.

Id., § 2285 at 527. And he points out that in the case of communications between attorney and client all four conditions are present, with the only condition open to dispute being the fourth. Id., § 2285 at 528.

As to this particular type of privileged communication:

> . . . the privilege remains an exception to the general duty to disclose. Its benefits are all indirect and speculative; its obstruction is plain and concrete. . . . It is worth preserving for the sake of a general policy, but is nonetheless an obstacle to the investigation of the truth. It ought to be strictly confined within the narrowest possible limits, consistent with the logic of its principle.

Id., § 2291 at 554.

The policy of the privilege has been plainly grounded since the latter part of the 1700s on subjective considerations. In order to promote freedom of consultation of legal advisers by clients, the apprehension of compelled disclosure by the legal advisers must be removed; hence the law must prohibit such disclosure except on the client's consent. Such is the modern theory.

Id., § 2291 at 545.

The problem before us concerns Wigmore's fourth condition, a balancing of interests between injury resulting from disclosure and the benefit gained in the correct disposal of litigation. We consider it in a particularized context: where the client asserting the privilege is an entity which in the performance of its functions acts wholly or partly in the interests of others, and those others, or some of them, seek access to the subject matter of the communications.

It is urged that disclosure is injurious to both the corporation and the attorney. Corporate management must manage. It has the duty to do so and requires the tools to do so. Part of the managerial task is to seek legal counsel when desirable, and, obviously, management prefers that it confer with counsel without the risk of having the communications revealed at the instance of one or more dissatisfied stockholders. The managerial preference is a rational one, because it is difficult to envision the management of any sizeable corporation pleasing all of its stockholders all of the time, and management desires protection from those who might second-guess or even harass in matters purely of judgment.

But in assessing management assertions of injury to the corporation it must be borne in mind that management does not manage for itself and that the beneficiaries of its action are the stockholders. Conceptualistic phrases describing the corporation as an entity separate from its stockholders are not useful tools of analysis. They serve only to obscure the fact that management has duties which run to the benefit ultimately of the stockholders. For example, it is difficult to rationally defend the assertion of the privilege if all, or substantially all, stockholders desire to inquire into the attorney's communications with corporate representatives who have only nominal ownership interests, or even none at all.[37] There may be reasonable differences over the manner of characterizing in legal terminology the duties of management, and over the extent to which corporate management is less of a fiduciary than the common law trustee. There may be many situations in which the corporate entity or its management, or both, have interests adverse to those of some or all stockholders. But when all is said and done management is not managing for itself.

The representative and the represented have a mutuality of interest in the representative's freely seeking advice when needed and putting it to use when received. This is not to say that management does not have allowable judgment in putting advice to use. But management judgment must stand on its merits, not behind an ironclad veil of secrecy which under all circumstances preserves it from being questioned by those for whom it is, at least in part, exercised.

---

37. Due regard must be paid to the interests of nonparty stockholders, which may be affected by impinging on the privilege, sometimes injuriously (though not necessarily so—in some situations shareholders who are not plaintiffs may benefit). The corporation is vulnerable to suit by shareholders whose interests or intention may be inconsistent with those of other shareholders, even others constituting a majority.

The District Court relied upon two English cases, Gouraud v. Edison Gower Bell Telephone Co., 57 L.T.Ch. 498, 59 L.T. 813 (1888) and W. Dennis & Sons, Ltd. v. West Norfold Farmers' Manure & Chem. Co., 2 All E.R. 94, 112 L.J.Ch. 239, 169 L.T. 74, 59 TLR 298, 87 Sol.Jo. 211 (1943). Both cases treat the relationship between shareholder and company as analogous to that between beneficiaries and trustees, a basis which the defendants in the present case say has no viability for American corporations. Though not binding precedents, these English cases are persuasive recognition that there are obligations, however characterized, that run from corporation to shareholder and must be given recognition in determining the applicability of the privilege.

Apart from the conceptualism that surrounds the management-stockholder relationship, the ABA alternatively contends, implicitly within the framework of Wigmore's fourth condition, that the benefits of disclosure are outweighed by the harm done to both client and attorney. In support of this policy argument, the ABA relies heavily upon In re Prudence Bonds Corp., 76 F.Supp. 643 (E.D.N.Y.1948), which held that a trustee for bondholders in an action for an accounting brought by the bondholders would not be required to produce opinions of counsel rendered to the trustee over a period of eighteen years. That case in turn distinguished the English cases cited above, speculating that the unavailability of the privilege might ultimately harm both attorneys and bondholders.

The ABA urges that the privilege is most necessary where the corporation has sought advice about a prospective transaction, where counsel in good faith has stated his opinion that it is not lawful, but the corporation has proceeded in total or partial disregard of counsel's advice. The ABA urges that the cause of justice requires that counsel be free to state his opinion as fully and forthrightly as possible without fear of later disclosure to persons who might attack the transaction, and that without the cloak of the privilege counsel may be "required by the threat of future discovery to hedge or soften their opinions."

The ABA brief does not always distinguish clearly between the separate interests of the corporate client and of the attorney in freedom from disclosure, nor is it possible always to do so. The privilege's exemptions from the broad duty to divulge are designed not only to protect the individual client who may assert the privilege but also to promote free and open communication between clients and attorneys in all matters. All these interests should properly be taken into account in any decision on the privilege. However, we reject the idea that the prospective decision of the client on whether to abide by advice or disregard it, or the guarantee of a veil of secrecy, either establishes or narrows the attorney's obligation in the giving of advice. And to grant to corporate management plenary assurance of secrecy for opinions received is to encourage it to disregard with impunity the advice sought.[38]

Two traditional exceptions are also persuasive in negativing any absolute privilege in a corporation in the circumstances of this case. These are the exceptions for communications in contemplation of a crime or fraud, and for communications to a joint attorney.

---

38. We do not consider it determinative whether the attorney consulted is corporated or house counsel, or whether his fees are paid for by the corporation or by management on its own account.

Communications made by a client to his attorney during or before the commission of a crime or fraud for the purpose of being guided or assisted in its commission are not privileged. Union Camp Corp. v. Lewis, 385 F.2d 143 (4th Cir.1967); Pollock v. United States, 202 F.2d 281 (5th Cir.1953); United States v. Bob, 106 F.2d 37 (2d Cir.), cert. denied, 308 U.S. 589, 60 S.Ct. 115, 84 L.Ed. 493 (1939).[39] The stockholders claim to have been the victims of improprieties in the issuance and sale of FAL's stock. The questions, and the documents sought, concerned those alleged improprieties, with particular regard to whether the attorney advised the corporation that proposals it had in mind were not legal and that statements to be put in its prospectus were misleading.

The plaintiffs say that some of the matter claimed to be privileged concerned prospective criminal transactions, including issuance by FAL of a misleading prospectus, the circulation of which it is said was a criminal offense under federal securities law, and the granting of options (allegedly as bribes) for securing state registrations of FAL's stock and of its broker-dealer and salesmen. In considering the interplay of interest of management, of stockholders, and of the lawsuit, it must be recognized that management has an obligation to the corporation, to the stockholders and to the public to do what is lawful. But we do not consider unavailability of the privilege to be confined to the narrow ground of prospective criminal transactions. The differences between prospective crime and prospective action of questionable legality, or prospective fraud, are differences of degree, not of principle.[40]

A second exception is also instructive. In many situations in which the same attorney acts for two or more parties having a common interest, neither party may exercise the privilege in a subsequent controversy with the other. This is true even where the attorney acts jointly for two or more persons having no formalized business arrangement between them. 8 Wigmore, § 2312 at 603; Grand Trunk W.R.R. v. H.W. Nelson Co., 116 F.2d 823, 835 (6th Cir.1941). The exception applies to partners, Billias v. Panageotou, 193 Wash. 523, 76 P.2d 987 (1938); makers of mutual wills, Wilson v. Gordon, 73 S.Ct. 155, 53 S.E. 79 (1905), and joint trustors, Boyle v. Kempkin, 243 Wis. 86, 93, 9 N.W.2d 589 (1943); insured and insurer in an automobile death action, Hoffman v. Labutzke, 233 Wis. 365, 377, 289 N.W. 652, 657 (1940); and many others.

In Pattie Lea, Inc. v. District Court, 161 Colo. 493, 423 P.2d 27 (1967) (en banc), a case strikingly similar to this one, the Supreme Court of Colorado held that the statutory privilege for communications between a certified public accountant and his corporate client did not protect the corporation from being required to disclose to its own

---

39. Dictum in at least one famous case states the exception even more broadly, extending it to communications with a lawyer in furtherance of "the purpose of committing a crime or tort." United States v. United Shoe Machinery Corp., 89 F.Supp. 357, 358 (D.Mass.1950).

40. The crime-fraud exception is particularly instructive because it covers advice concerning prospective action. We recognize the much stronger policy justifications behind the confidentiality of communica-tions with one who is already a wrongdoer and seeks legal advice appropriate to his plight as opposed to one who seeks advice concerning proposed future conduct and, having later acted, seeks to maintain the secrecy. See 8 Wigmore, § 2298 at 573. FAL does not recognize the unavailability of the privilege even as to communications about transactions wholly prospective (except, possibly, where relating to commission of a proposed crime).

stockholders in a good faith derivative suit brought by them against the corporation communications from the corporation to the CPA. The Colorado court relied upon the analogy of the joint attorney exception and pointed out that employment of certified public accountants by the corporation was for the benefit of all the stockholders.

In summary, we say this. The attorney-client privilege still has viability for the corporate client. The corporation is not barred from asserting it merely because those demanding information enjoy the status of stockholders. But where the corporation is in suit against its stockholders on charges of acting inimically to stockholder interests, protection of those interests as well as those of the corporation and of the public require that the availability of the privilege be subject to the right of the stockholders to show cause why it should not be invoked in the particular instance.[41]

D.   Good cause

There are many indicia that may contribute to a decision of presence or absence of good cause, among them the number of shareholders and the percentage of stock they represent; the bona fides of the shareholders; the nature of the shareholders' claim and whether it is obviously colorable; the apparent necessity or desirability of the shareholders having the information and the availability of it from other sources; whether, if the shareholders' claim is of wrongful action by the corporation, it is of action criminal, or illegal but not criminal, or of doubtful legality; whether the communication related to past or to prospective actions; whether the communication is of advice concerning the litigation itself; the extent to which the communication is identified versus the extent to which the shareholders are blindly fishing; the risk of revelation of trade secrets or other information in whose confidentiality the corporation has an interest for independent reasons. The court can freely use *in camera* inspection or oral examination and freely avail itself of protective orders, a familiar device to preserve confidentiality in trade secret and other cases where the impact of revelation may be as great as in revealing a communication with counsel.

The order relating to availability of the attorney-client privilege is Vacated. The cause is Remanded for further proceedings not inconsistent with this opinion.

COMMENT

On remand, the district court granted the motion for discovery. The items requested turned out to relate to public offerings of FAL stock and to various permits obtained from state agencies. The court found no reason to safeguard these matters and even raised the question for whom counsel had been acting when they did the work and gave the opinions involved in these transactions. 56 F.R.D. 499 (S.D.Ala.1972).

---

41. This approach is neither new nor worldshaking. At common law the stockholder has the right to see corporate books and records but it is not unlimited. His demand must be germane to his interest as stockholder, and the interests of the corporation and other shareholders may control to deny inspection.

QUESTIONS

(1) Recall Smith v. Van Gorkom, p. 212 supra and the comments which the court makes as to the the legal advice there given. What would full and accurate advice have been? What effect would it have had on the directors' liabilities?

(2) Assume that you are counsel for an industrial corporation and its directors strongly wish to make a contract for certain services with an engineering firm specializing in antipollution devices. One of the client's directors is a director of and shareholder in the engineering firm. New Jersey corporation law is applicable to this transaction. Draft an opinion for your firm to send to the client in this matter. Will the form of your draft be affected at all by your judgment as to whether the letter may be subject to discovery in a later shareholder action? Or in an action by the other side seeking to raise the interlock as a defense? Suppose that you conclude that you simply cannot give an opinion that is favorable on this question. Should you send anything at all?

(3) Suppose that the opinion referred to in question (2) was required by the underwriters in a public offering of securities subject to the 1933 Act. To what extent does that affect the liabilities of the law firm? The reluctance of the firm to give the opinion? The need to qualify or hedge it?

(4) The board of directors of a corporation has been considering an important acquisition. The financial and engineering staffs have presented to the board their recommendations in the following form: a listing of the alternatives, an estimate (in percentage terms) of the likelihood of success or failure of each, and an estimate of the "payoff" or loss to be expected from success or failure. The board is now obviously awaiting from you, as general counsel, an estimate in similar form, of the probabilities of adverse legal reactions by the Department of Justice, regulatory agencies, aggrieved minority shareholders, etc., followed by an estimate of the costs of each. Is it possible, practical, ethical and appropriate to comply with that expectation?

Bibliography: The literature on attorneys' duties in this area is growing rapidly. In addition to newer sources cited p. 186 supra, see McDaniel, Ethical Problems of Counsel for Big Business: Burden of Resolving Conflicting Interests, 38 A.B.A.J. 205, 256 (1952). Much more generally, lawyers, like other experts, can profit from Bryson, Notes on a Theory of Advice, 66 Pol.Sci.Q. 321 (1951).

Chapter VIII

MANAGING THE CORPORATION—THE ROLE OF THE EXECUTIVE

While the management of the corporation is entrusted by law to the board, even the legal system assumes that the board will delegate various operations to the employees, retaining only a rather general supervisory and controlling power. Fact has tended to outrun legal theory here, with power to initiate, suggest and implement projects drifting out of the hands of the board into those of the professional managers. The term "technostructure," coined by J.K. Galbraith, is meant to suggest a largish body of management personnel in a major corporation who share the information and expertise without which decisions cannot be made. It is this stratum of upper level management often called executives which we examine in this chapter.

Corporation statutes expressly contemplate that there will be a group of "officers" or top-level managers and may define their duties and prerogatives to some degree (see 8 Del.C. § 142). The common law of corporations has a good deal to say about their duties; the rules applicable to directors are, with some modifications, applicable to them as well. There is commonly envisaged a chief executive officer (CEO) who is normally entitled the president, although the designation may be "chairman of the board." Below the officer level there may be tiers of agents of one function or another. The rules that govern their activities are part of the law of agency—down to the blue collar level where labor law takes over.

From the point of view of management, law serves the function of sustaining the authority of each successive level of executive over those below, enabling executives to give orders and provide sanctions for disregarding them—this is true even though the resort to legal remedies may be a rare event. The law of corporations also maintains discipline in the sense of compelling adherence to a set of rules of conduct that not only protect the corporation and its shareholders from the self-interest of managers but also serve generally to maintain public confidence in the integrity of these important institutions. Finally it protects, to a degree, the rights of members of management, their tenure and their remuneration.

Lawyers need to be modest about the role of law in keeping the corporate machinery going. It is only the handmaid and backstop to the managerial drive and talent that do so. Creating a sound organizational structure and insuring its reasonably harmonious operation is an act that calls for trained and seasoned talent and something called leadership. There is a tendency on the part of outsiders to take organizational charts as seriously as do their drafters, if not more so, and to assume a greater flow of directives downward. President Truman knew better when he said of his about-to-become successor, "Poor Ike, he'll come in and say 'do this' and 'do that' and, you know, they won't do this or that." It takes will, energy and skill to convert a business strategy once conceived into a functioning mechanism.

The way in which the management component of a firm functions is only partly the result of the will of the people at the top; it is much more a consequence of the objective needs of the organization and general tendencies in society. An American corporation, especially a multi-product, multi-national concern, cannot be managed in the 1980's by the same highly personal, autocratic and paternalistic methods that characterized Henry Ford in the 1920's and that has persisted longer in more authoritarian societies such as those of Germany and Japan.

A number of surveys have tried to capture the American high level executive and I set forth below a summary of their findings. Two cautions are called for: (1) all of these surveys relate to executives of rather large corporations only, (2) each one defines its sample rather differently, both as to the number of corporations and the number of executives within each corporation.

Increasingly, executives are university educated. In 1900 only 40% had degrees. In 1987 out of the 800 "most powerful" executives, 302 had graduate degrees (137 M.B.A.'s and 57 J.D.'s) and only 76 did not have undergraduate degrees.[1] Concern has been expressed that too many come from the world of finance and not enough from the world of production. Fewer executives have family connections with the world of high-level business management—the proportion of them with wealthy parents or parents who are executives is decreasing. There have been striking examples of family continuity over several generations in very large corporations—Fords, Duponts, Watsons (IBM), Sarnoffs (RCA), etc.—but their numbers are declining rapidly. In fact, quite a few firms have rules that prevent nepotism. Most executives have rather small stakes in the equity securities of their corporations, that is, of those whose stock is widely held; however, their holdings of their corporation's stock may represent a high percentage of their own personal wealth. High level managers tend to stay for long periods with the same corporation; of 800 in the Forbes survey 500 had been with the same firm for at least 20 years and only 125 had been their for less than 10. This figure holds even in a day when discharges of CEO's and lesser figures are more frequently in the headlines than ever before. Finally, one notes that Forbes in 1987 wrote of the 797 most

1. The most current data used in the text comes from Forbes, June 15, 1987, p. 145. Comparative data from earlier times is found in M. Newcomer, The Big Business Executives—The Factors that Made Him—1900—1950 (1955); D. Finn, The Corporate Oligarch (1969); Sturdivant & Adler, Executive Origins, Still A Gray Flannel World, Harv.Bus.Rev., Nov.–Dec. 1976, p. 125; M. Hennig & A. Jardim, The Managerial Woman (1977); R. Kanter, Men and Women of the Corporation (1977).

powerful men and 3 most powerful women. At lower levels of the corporate hierarchy the gender proportions are somewhat more even but progress up the ladder has been slow and discouraging. The same is even more true of members of minorities. The figures are in fact rather worse in both categories than as to partnerships in large law firms.

Executives work hard (a 57–60 hour work week was reported in one sampling). As is happening in professional groups, there are increasing signs of differences in attitudes between junior and senior executives and a higher level of questioning and doubt about the values and purposes of corporations and about the way of life that the corporate system entails. Gradually and painfully, corporations are trying to adapt their ways of operating to this new age, experimenting with more collective decision-making, encounter groups, day care, sabbatical leaves for pro bono work, etc.

---

1. The Duty to Supervise

One part of the directors' duty of due care introduced in Chapter VII above is the duty to supervise, to watch over the performance by the rest of the corporate structure of the duties assigned to them. The content of that duty will vary according to the size and function of the corporation involved. In a small corporation the board and the top managers are very close to the operations of the individuals doing the actual work. Thus in a small bank with three or four tellers and two or three secretaries it is not unreasonable to expect the president—and perhaps the directors as well—to know when one of the tellers is showing signs of affluence incompatible with his or her salary or to observe that operations are being carried on in a sloppy way.[2] That can obviously not be the way in which a giant enterprise is run. Functions will have to be delegated to lower echelons. The board, however, retains as part of its general duty of care a generalized duty of supervision, discussed in the Allis–Chalmers case that follows. Also, there are limits in terms of extent and duration as to the board's capacity to delegate its duties to hired managers or others. Jones v. Williams, p. 318 infra, touches on this.

To illustrate the duty of supervisory care, I have chosen a case involving a very large corporation organized along divisional lines. By way of a brief background let me refer to the classic study of the

---

2. See Bates v. Dresser, 251 U.S. 524, 40 S.Ct. 247, 64 L.Ed. 388 (1920), in which the court, per Justice Holmes, found only the president, not the directors of a small bank, liable for failing to detect a new type of fraud: "Some animals must have given at least one exhibition of dangerous propensities before the owner can be held. This fraud was a novelty in the way of swindling a bank so far as the knowledge of any experience had reached Cambridge in 1910."

development of the divisional form of organization, A. Chandler, Strategy and Structure (1962). Chandler breaks down the development of modern American corporate organization into several stages. In Stage I the corporation was largely identical with the entrepreneur who founded or built it—Rockefeller, Ford, Carnegie, etc. These around the turn of the century brought together the resources and funds that made up the foundations of the great American industrial giants. The highly personalized form of administration soon proved incapable of coping with complex nationwide organization. There developed a form of organization in which responsibilities for different functions were delegated to a staff, still quite closely grouped about the chief executive. Thus production, sales, and research were headed by specialists. One problem that this Stage II organization produced was the tendency to bring to the top executives without broad experience outside their own specialties. Difficulties also arose within firms that were evolving rapidly and branching out into different lines of endeavour. The staff found it hard to stretch their skills in engineering, for example, over very disparate products. DuPont in the 1920's was such a firm and it led the way towards a new, Stage III, structure in which all-round responsibility for a given product was given to the heads of the particular divisions. Then in turn could rely on a staff of experts who could concentrate on their specialty within their product line. This method produced division managers who had gained a rounded experience and were ripe for company-level tasks. General Electric adopted such a system and Allis–Chalmers followed suit.

GRAHAM v. ALLIS–CHALMERS MFG. CO.

Supreme Court of Delaware, 1963.
41 Del.Ch. 78, 188 A.2d 125.

WOLCOTT, JUSTICE. This is a derivative action on behalf of Allis–Chalmers against its directors and four of its non-director employees. The complaint is based upon indictments of Allis–Chalmers and the four non-director employees named as defendants herein who, with the corporation, entered pleas of guilty to the indictments. The indictments, eight in number, charged violations of the Federal anti-trust laws. The suit seeks to recover damages which Allis–Chalmers is claimed to have suffered by reason of these violations.

The directors of Allis–Chalmers appeared in the cause voluntarily. The non-director defendants have neither appeared in the cause nor been served with process. Three of the non-director defendants are still employed by Allis–Chalmers. The fourth is under contract with it as a consultant.

The complaint alleges actual knowledge on the part of the director defendants of the anti-trust conduct upon which the indictments were based or, in the alternative, knowledge of facts which should have put them on notice of such conduct.

However, the hearing and depositions produced no evidence that any director had any actual knowledge of the anti-trust activity, or had actual knowledge of any facts which should have put them on notice that anti-trust activity was being carried on by some of their company's employees. The plaintiffs, appellants here, thereupon shifted the theory of the case to the proposition that the directors are liable as a matter of law by reason of their failure to take action designed to learn of and prevent anti-trust activity on the part of any employees of Allis-Chalmers.

By this appeal the plaintiffs seek to have us reverse the Vice Chancellor's ruling of non-liability of the defendant directors upon this theory, and also seek reversal of certain interlocutory rulings of the Vice Chancellor refusing to compel pre-trial production of documents, and refusing to compel the four non-director defendants to testify on oral depositions. We will in this opinion pass upon all the questions raised, but, as a preliminary, a summarized statement of the facts of the cause is required in order to fully understand the issues.

Allis–Chalmers is a manufacturer of a variety of electrical equipment. It employs in excess of 31,000 people, has a total of 24 plants, 145 sales offices, 5000 dealers and distributors, and its sales volume is in excess of $500,000,000 annually. The operations of the company are conducted by two groups, each of which is under the direction of a senior vice president. One of these groups is the Industries Group under the direction of Singleton, director defendant. This group is divided into five divisions. One of these, the Power Equipment Division, produced the products, the sale of which involved the anti-trust activities referred to in the indictments. The Power Equipment Division, presided over by McMullen, non-director defendant, contains ten departments, each of which is presided over by a manager or general manager.

The operating policy of Allis–Chalmers is to decentralize by the delegation of authority to the lowest possible management level capable of fulfilling the delegated responsibility. Thus, prices of products are ordinarily set by the particular department manager, except that if the product being priced is large and special, the department manager might confer with the general manager of the division. Products of a standard character involving repetitive manufacturing processes are sold out of a price list which is established by a price leader for the electrical equipment industry as a whole.

Annually, the Board of Directors reviews group and departmental profit goal budgets. On occasion, the Board considers general questions concerning price levels, but because of the complexity of the company's operations the Board does not participate in decisions fixing the prices of specific products.

The Board of Directors of fourteen members, four of whom are officers, meets once a month, October excepted, and considers a previously prepared agenda for the meeting. Supplied to the Directors at the meetings are financial and operating data relating to all phases of the company's activities. The Board meetings are customarily of several hours duration in which all the Directors participate actively. Apparently, the Board considers and decides matters concerning the general business policy of the company. By reason of the extent and complexity of the company's operations, it is not practicable for the Board to consider in detail specific problems of the various divisions.

The indictments to which Allis–Chalmers and the four non-director defendants pled guilty charge that the company and individual non-director defendants, commencing in 1956, conspired with other manufacturers and their employees to fix prices and to rig bids to private electric utilities and governmental agencies in violation of the anti-trust laws of the United States. None of the director defendants in this cause were named as defendants in the indictments. Indeed, the Federal Government acknowledged that it had uncovered no probative evidence which could lead to the conviction of the defendant directors.

The first actual knowledge the directors had of anti-trust violations by some of the company's employees was in the summer of 1959 from newspaper stories that TVA proposed an investigation of identical bids. Singleton, in charge of the Industries Group of the company, investigated but unearthed nothing. Thereafter, in November of 1959, some of the company's employees were subpoenaed before the Grand Jury. Further investigation by the company's Legal Division gave reason to suspect the illegal activity and all of the subpoenaed employees were instructed to tell the whole truth.

Thereafter, on February 8, 1960, at the direction of the Board, a policy statement relating to anti-trust problems was issued, and the Legal Division commenced a series of meetings with all employees of the company in possible areas of anti-trust activity. The purpose and effect of these steps was to eliminate any possibility of further and future violations of the anti-trust laws.

As we have pointed out, there is no evidence in the record that the defendant directors had actual knowledge of the illegal anti-trust actions of the company's employees. Plaintiffs, however, point to two FTC decrees of 1937 as warning to the directors that anti-trust activity by the company's employees had taken place in the past. It is argued that they were thus put on notice of their duty to ferret out such activity and to take active steps to insure that it would not be repeated.

The decrees in question were consent decrees entered in 1937 against Allis–Chalmers and nine others enjoining agreements to fix uniform prices on condensors and turbine generators. The decrees recited that they were consented to for the sole purpose of avoiding the trouble and expense of the proceeding.

None of the director defendants were directors or officers of Allis–Chalmers in 1937. The director defendants and now officers of the company either were employed in very subordinate capacities or had no connection with the company in 1937. At the time, copies of the decrees were circulated to the heads of concerned departments and were explained to the Managers Committee.

In 1943, Singleton, officer and director defendant, first learned of the decrees upon becoming Assistant Manager of the Steam Turbine Department, and consulted the company's General Counsel as to them. He investigated his department and learned the decrees were being complied with and, in any event, he concluded that the company had not in the first place been guilty of the practice enjoined.

Stevenson, officer and director defendant, first learned of the decrees in 1951 in a conversation with Singleton about their respective areas of the company's operations. He satisfied himself that the company was not then and in fact had not been guilty of quoting uniform prices and had consented to the decrees in order to avoid the expense and vexation of the proceeding.

Scholl, officer and director defendant, learned of the decrees in 1956 in a discussion with Singleton on matters affecting the Industries Group. He was informed that no similar problem was then in existence in the company.

Plaintiffs argue that because of the 1937 consent decrees, the directors were put on notice that they should take steps to ensure that no employee of Allis–Chalmers would violate the anti-trust laws. The difficulty the argument has is that only three of the present directors knew of the decrees, and all three of them satisfied themselves that Allis–Chalmers had not engaged in the practice enjoined and had consented to the decrees merely to avoid expense and the necessity of defending the company's position. Under the circumstances, we think knowledge by three of the directors that in 1937 the company had consented to the entry of decrees enjoining it from doing something they had satisfied themselves it had never done, did not put the Board on notice of the possibility of future illegal price fixing.

Plaintiffs have wholly failed to establish either actual notice or imputed notice to the Board of Directors of facts which should have put them on guard, and have caused them to take steps to prevent the future possibility of illegal price fixing and bid rigging. Plaintiffs say that as a minimum in this respect the Board should have taken the steps it took in 1960 when knowledge of the facts first actually came to their attention as a result of the Grand Jury investigation. Whatever duty, however, there was upon the Board to take such steps, the fact of the 1937 decrees has no bearing upon the question, for under the circumstances they were notice of nothing.

Plaintiffs are thus forced to rely solely upon the legal proposition advanced by them that directors of a corporation, as a matter of law, are liable for losses suffered by their corporations by reason of their gross inattention to the common law duty of actively supervising and managing the corporate affairs. Plaintiffs rely mainly upon Briggs v. Spaulding, 141 U.S. 132, 11 S.Ct. 924, 35 L.Ed. 662.

From the Briggs case and others . . . . it appears that directors of a corporation in managing the corporate affairs are bound to use that amount of care which ordinarily careful and prudent men would use in similar circumstances. Their duties are those of control, and whether or not by neglect they have made themselves liable for failure to exercise proper control depends on the circumstances and facts of the particular case.

The precise charge made against these director defendants is that, even though they had no knowledge of any suspicion of wrongdoing on the part of the company's employees, they still should have put into effect a system of watchfulness which would have brought such misconduct to their attention in ample time to have brought it to an end. However, the Briggs case expressly rejects such an idea. On the contrary, it appears that directors are entitled to rely on the honesty and integrity of their subordinates until something occurs to put them on suspicion that something is wrong. If such occurs and goes unheeded, then liability of the directors might well follow, but absent cause for suspicion there is no duty upon the directors to install and operate a corporate system of espionage to ferret out wrongdoing which they have no reason to suspect exists.

The duties of the Allis–Chalmers Directors were fixed by the nature of the enterprise which employed in excess of 30,000 persons, and extended over a large geographical area. By force of necessity, the company's Directors could not know personally all the company's employees. The very magnitude of the enterprise required them to confine their control to the broad policy decisions. That they did this is clear from the record. At the meetings of the Board in which all Directors participated, these questions were considered and decided on the basis of summaries, reports and corporate records. These they were entitled to rely on, not only, we think, under general principles of the common law, but by reason of 8 Del.C. § 141(f) as well, which in terms fully protects a director who relies on such in the performance of his duties.

In the last analysis, the question of whether a corporate director has become liable for losses to the corporation through neglect of duty is determined by the circumstances. If he has recklessly reposed confidence in an obviously untrustworthy employee, has refused or neglected cavalierly to perform his duty as a director, or has ignored either willfully or through inattention obvious danger signs of employee wrongdoing, the law will cast the burden of liability upon him. This is not the case at bar, however, for as soon as it became evident that there were grounds for suspicion, the Board acted promptly to end it and prevent its recurrence.

Plaintiffs say these steps should have been taken long before, even in the absence of suspicion, but we think not, for we know of no rule of law which requires a corporate director to assume, with no justification whatsoever, that all corporate employees are incipient law violators who, but for a tight checkrein, will give free vent to their unlawful propensities.

We therefore affirm the Vice Chancellor's ruling that the individual director defendants are not liable as a matter of law merely because, unknown to them, some employees of Allis–Chalmers violated the anti-trust laws thus subjecting the corporation to loss.

Plaintiffs concede that they did not prove affirmatively that the Directors knew of the anti-trust violations of the company's employees, or that there were any facts brought to the Directors' knowledge which should have put them on guard against such activities. They argue, however, that they were prevented from doing so by unreasonable restrictions put upon their pre-trial discovery by the Vice Chancellor. They argue before us that this restriction was an abuse by the Vice Chancellor of judicial discretion and, hence, reversible error.

. . .

The judgment of the court below is affirmed.

COMMENT

(1) This case arose from a widely publicized antitrust conspiracy prosecution which saw several executives at such firms as General Electric and Westinghouse sent to jail.[3] Although there was evidence that there had been extensive efforts to conceal the agreements under cover of a "phases of the moon" code as to which supplier was to tender the low bid for a given assignment, there was widespread skepticism in the courts, in Congress and in the press about the claims of the top level management not to have known

3. For a compact account see J. Brooks, Business Adventures ch. 7 (1969).

about the delinquencies. It was claimed, for example, that at one firm repeated formal readings to subordinates of a rule against discussing prices with competitors was, actually or figuratively, accompanied by winks that destroyed their effect. Some firms discharged employees who had been found guilty; others did not. The criminal case was followed by extensive treble damage litigation, chiefly by public utilities that had been overcharged. Allis–Chalmers later left the generator business, but not before it had passed on to New York's Consolidated Edison the large problem-ridden generator unlovingly known as "Big Allis." For a time in the late 1960's a ⅓ interest in Allis–Chalmers was held by the conglomerate Gulf & Western Industries, Inc. which then sold to White Consolidated, another large diversified system. Antitrust and other litigation accompanied these shifts.[4]

(2) The question of liability of executives to criminal prosecution or for damages against outside parties is separate from that of liability to the corporation. While in an antitrust case, such as that involved in Allis–Chalmers, a director or officer would be found guilty only if found to be a conspirator, Congress has at times, as in the Food and Drug Act, drawn the lines more tightly, coming close to imposing a criminal liability without fault on those responsible for the activity in which the lapse was detected.

In United States v. Park[5] the Supreme Court sustained the conviction under that Act of the President of Acme Markets, Inc., a national food chain with 36,000 employees and 874 retail outlets. The evidence showed that, after receiving a written FDA warning about rodent infestation in one of Acme's warehouses, he conferred with the vice-president for legal affairs who advised him that the local division vice-president was investigating and would take corrective action. Park did nothing further, believing that he had properly delegated this as a normal operations duty. The Court ruled proper an instruction to the jury that Park could be found guilty "even if he did not consciously do wrong" so long as he "had a responsible relationship to the issue."

QUESTIONS

(1) Draw an organizational chart of the Allis–Chalmers hierarchy. Where within the structure were the persons who directly committed the violations of law? How far removed were those whom plaintiff sought to charge in this case?

(2) Do you find it inherently implausible that directors such as those of Allis–Chalmers would not know of the activities of their subordinates? If so, why?

(3) After this scandal what should the board do to prevent repetition of such misconduct? Would such restructuring destroy the values which are supposed to inhere in a decentralized structure? If you conclude that such restructuring is not possible, is there any justification for having a corporation of such a size that it cannot be effectively supervised by top management?

4. See, e.g., Allis–Chalmers Mfg. Co. v. White Consol. Industries, Inc., 414 F.2d 506 (3d Cir.1969).

5. United States v. Park, 421 U.S. 658, 95 S.Ct. 1903, 44 L.Ed.2d 489 (1975). Compare Patterson v. United States, 222 F. 599, 631–633 (6th Cir.1915) (Sherman Act).

(4) What role in the difficulties of Allis–Chalmers was played by the way in which top management evidently measured the performance of the corporation's departments?

(5) What differences between the supervisory roles of the board and of executives emerge from this case?

(6) Does the ruling in Allis–Chalmers significantly undercut the intended effect of the Sherman Act's penalties? What is the theory on which criminal penalties are thought to deter violations by corporations, especially those of a size comparable to Allis–Chalmers?

2.   Executives and Their External Representation of the Corporation

NOTE ON AUTHORITY OF EXECUTIVES TO REPRESENT CORPORATION

While the authority of the board of directors to represent the corporation is plenary, within the bounds set by the doctrine of *ultra vires* and by the rules subjecting certain actions to shareholder consent, the authority of officer and executive must be shown to emanate from the board. This subject properly belongs to the law of Agency but since you may not have been exposed to that topic, it becomes necessary to give you the materials for a nodding acquaintance with it. "Authority" is defined (authoritatively, one might say) in the Restatement, Second, Agency § 7 as: "the power of the agent to affect the legal relations of the principal by acts done in accordance with the principal's manifestations of consent to him." This capacity to affect the legal relations of the corporate principal with others can be classified as follows:

Types of Authority	Citation
Actual { express / implied	(Restatement § 144)
Apparent	(Restatement §§ 27, 159)
Agency Power	(Restatement §§ 8A, 161)
Ratification	(Restatement § 82)

In a corporate context, actual express power can be found in the articles of incorporation, in the by-laws or in resolutions of the board of directors. It is common for by-laws to give the president certain specific powers (see art. IV, § 2 of our model), particularly in connection with the borrowing of money and other transactions where there is a tendency to demand formalities. When an arrangement of considerable importance is contemplated, it is customary for counsel handling the transaction to prepare resolutions for the board to pass; extracts of the minutes are then prepared and certified to satisfy counsel that authority has been proved beyond all shadow of doubt (see the Documentary Supplement for an example).

Implied authority may be pieced out by reading between the lines of express authority. To instruct a corporate officer to build a factory may by fair implication convey authority to hire architects, buy land, enter construction contracts and do the other things that have to be done to achieve the end in view. The implication can also arise from a course of acquiescence; a failure to object to a series of two or three expenditures for advertising would give rise to an understanding that a like expenditure in a third or fourth cycle would also be appropriate.

Apparent—as opposed to actual—authority is created by some action on the part of the corporation which creates the impression in the mind of the third party that the agent has authority when in fact there is none. Thus, if the board gives an officer a letter instructing the officer to purchase some equipment and orally imposes some restrictions, such as an injunction not to spend more than $25,000.00, the supplier of the equipment may be able to hold the corporation liable to the full extent of a $35,000 contract signed by the agent—but of course only if the agent keeps silent about the limit so imposed. Apparent authority may thus have the same consequences as between the principal and the third party as does actual authority; however, the consequences as between principal and agent may be quite different: operations in the range of apparent authority involve, by definition, a violation of instructions and such a violation may give the corporation cause to discharge the agent and a cause of action to recover damages for disobedience.

Finally, an outsider may resort to agency power. This is a concept developed in the Restatement and not extensively recognized by the courts. A case clearly covered by agency power and not by apparent authority is that of the "undisclosed principal." Suppose that Panchrome Inc. appoints Antonia to run a store for Panchrome in her own name, setting certain limits on the size of repair contracts she can make. Antonia, nonetheless, has extensive alterations made. Clearly third parties cannot rely on apparent authority since they thought Antonia was acting on her own account. Still courts have held principals like Panchrome liable and modern commentators would approve. They would say that the loss should be assigned to Panchrome because it was in a position to profit from the transaction if it worked out well and because it could control, supervise and discipline Antonia. There are problems about assigning some borderline cases to apparent authority or agency power. If the agent's own false statements to the third party are the only source of the impression relied upon for apparent authority, can that fairly be termed "apparent authority"? If the action is within the scope of the typical similarly situated agent, the principal is likely to be bound and the precise label used is not of very great importance.

Many corporate arrangements are concluded by ratification. The corporate executive who knows the board of directors and is trusted by them will pounce on an opportunity—like President Jefferson on the Louisiana territory—and count upon ratification for his vindication. The pressures on a board to approve such a *fait accompli* are substantial and ratification is thus a very common device. In addition to formal and explicit ratification, a corporation may also be bound by taking the benefits of the transaction, e.g., accepting the goods ordered by the agent while being aware of the arrangements he had made to procure them.

Most of what has been said in this Note applies without regard to the character of the principal as a corporation or of the agent as a corporate officer. Where this relationship exists, however, it may have a definite impact on the question of authority. Vesting an individual with the title "president" in some states will confer a substantial amount of authority *ex officio;* this is even more likely to be true if the by-laws or some other document designate the president as the chief executive, or general manager (recall that term from Ch. VII, supra). Some states, however,[6] take a rather restricted view of this type of authority. The powers of a vice-president *ex officio* are apt to be even more narrowly circumscribed. The secretary has a narrow but often quite critical authority, particularly the power to certify resolutions and other documents in such a way as to permit outsiders to rely upon them even if they are inaccurate or deliberately false. For banking and other purposes, the treasurer may also have a very significant set of powers to handle corporate funds. A great deal of the work of a major corporation is in fact carried out by agents who are hired (and fired) and given (and deprived of) authority by other agents one, two or more steps below the board of directors. Note that these persons ordinarily create liabilities and rights in the corporation and not in their superiors. They are not "subagents" within the meaning of § 5 of the Restatement.

It is apparent from the pattern of the cases that corporations, especially ones that are prosperous and large, seldom choose to interpose the defense of lack of authority vis-a-vis outsiders because of the commercial and public relations values involved. Cases tend to be raised by small firms—or by trustees in bankruptcy.

Parenthetically, let me remind you that executives can cause their corporations to become civilly liable for torts or guilty of crimes—sometimes even when those actions were not authorized or were expressly forbidden by the board. It is sometimes overlooked that while a contract that binds the corporation will not ordinarily impose any obligation on the agent both corporation *and* agent may be liable for a tort or crime.

---

6. E.g., Lucey v. Hero Int. Corp., 361 Mass. 569, 281 N.E.2d 266 (1972).

Finally, a point of terminology. The terms "agency" and "agency costs" are sometimes used in law and economics theory quite without regard to its technical meaning in Restatement terms.

SCHWARTZ v. UNITED MERCHANTS & MANUFACTURERS, INC.

United States Court of Appeals, Second Circuit, 1934.
72 F.2d 256.

[Defendant, a corporation, owned the majority of the stock of two other corporations, Ashland and United Rayon. Its president Loring and vice-president Jewett negotiated with plaintiff about the latter's becoming exclusive sales agent for the two subsidiaries. The proposed arrangement was to be for two years and was to involve creation of a new corporation by plaintiff and defendant. The new company was to receive a percentage of the two subsidiaries' profits. Defendant repudiated the contract, insisting that none had ever been entered into. It is assumed that plaintiff had signed a written contract and that Loring had signed it but never delivered it to plaintiff. The trial court dismissed at the close of plaintiff's case and the Court of Appeals affirmed in opinion by JUDGE LEARNED HAND.]

There is no evidence of any sort that the directors of the defendant had ever heard of Loring's and Jewett's negotiations with the plaintiff; certainly none that they knew that he meant to close on anything like the written draft upon which the plaintiff relies. Such a contract was by no means matter of course in any business, even assuming that the employment of an exclusive selling agent for a textile mill is a routine affair; itself a hardy assumption, for which there is not the least evidence in the record. Indeed this was not even a contract by a mill to employ its own exclusive selling agent; the defendant, by virtue of its holdings in two subsidiaries proposed to impose a selling agent upon them. It is true that the contract recites that the directors of the Ashland company have already so resolved, and this is an admission against the defendant, if we suppose the contract to have been signed and delivered; but nothing of the sort appears as to the Rayon Mill. The exceptional character of this contract did not however stop there; for the defendant reserved more than half the profits of the agency to itself. Though a majority shareholder in the new company it was to contribute nothing to the services, so far as appears, but a trifling capital and a guarantee of the salary to the real selling agent, the plaintiff. For this it might get more than fifteen per cent. of the earnings of the subsidiaries. We need not hold that this made it inevitably unlawful without the assent of the subsidiaries' minority shareholders; but certainly it was not a customary or usual transaction, even if the employment of an exclusive selling agent is such, or the employment of a selling agent for a subsidiary.

The law as to the prima facie authority of a president or other general officer of a corporation is not very clear. Unquestionably there has been a tendency of late to imply greater authority and to throw upon the corporation the duty of showing that in fact the directors have not authorized the particular powers exercised. The Court of Appeals of New York has indeed twice said without limitation that a president presumptively has any powers which the directors have authority to give him or could ratify, Patterson v. Robinson, 116 N.Y. 193, 200, 22 N.E. 372; Hastings v. Brooklyn Life Ins. Co., 138 N.Y. 473, 479, 34 N.E. 289; though the decisions cited do not support so far reaching a doctrine. In Oakes v. Cattaraugus Water Co., 143 N.Y. 430, 436, 38 N.E. 461, 26 L.R.A. 541, it appeared that the president had full charge of the business and the case really does not stand for the rule. In Watkins Salt Co. v. Mulkey (C.C.A.) 225 F. 739, our decision was to the contrary; but in Hotel Woodward v. Ford Motor Co. (C.C.A.) 258 F. 322, we accepted the presumption without limitation, though it appears from the later report of the same case (C.C.A.) 271 F. 625, that it was unnecessary to the decision. How far it was part of our ruling in Ransome Concrete Machinery Co. v. Moody (C.C.A.) 282 F. 29, is not clear. In the last three cases we were professing to follow New York law, and the Court of Appeals has more recently twice expressly decided that there were limitations on the doctrine. Heaman v. Rowell Co., 261 N.Y. 229, 185 N.E. 83; Powers v. Schlicht H.L. & P. Co., 23 App.Div. 380, 48 N.Y.S. 237, affirmed on opinion below, 165 N.Y. 662, 59 N.E. 1129. How far a similar ruling was involved in Bankers' Trust Co. v. International R. Co., 207 App.Div. 579, 202 N.Y.S. 561; Id., 239 N.Y. 619, 147 N.E. 220, and in Large v. Wire Wheel Corp., 223 App.Div. 134, 227 N.Y.S. 449; Id., 250 N.Y. 531, 166 N.E. 312, it is impossible to say, for the Court of Appeals did not write; but at least the opinions below assumed that not all contracts which the directors may authorize are presumptively within the president's authority. In Hardin v. Morgan Lithograph Co., 247 N.Y. 332, 338, 339, 160 N.E. 388, 390, although Hastings v. B.L. Ins. Co., supra, 138 N.Y. 473, 34 N.E. 289, was quoted, the presumption was limited to "such ordinary contracts as custom and the necessities of business would justify or require." The contract there at bar was not an unusual one; nor was that before the court in Twyeffort v. Unexcelled Mfg. Co., Ltd., 263 N.Y. 6, 188 N.E. 138, where the intimation was not justified that Pound, J., had intended in Hardin v. Morgan Lithograph Co., supra, 247 N.Y. 332, 160 N.E. 388, to adopt the unlimited form. The citation of Peck v. Dexter S.P. & P. Co., 164 N.Y. 127, 58 N.E. 6, in Hardin v. Morgan Lithograph Co., supra, shows that the president's authority does not in this regard differ from that of any other officer.

We conclude therefore that there is no absolute rule in New York that any contract which the president of a company may make, however out of the ordinary, throws upon the company the duty of showing that he was unauthorized. It is true that whatever powers are usual in the business may be assumed to have been granted; but the presumption stops there, as much in the case of a president as of any other officer, though naturally in degree they may greatly differ. If so, it seems to us apparent that if any contract needed the express authority of the directors it was this. Not only did it commit the subsidiaries to an exclusive selling agent of the holding company's choosing for two years, a thing most vital to their welfare; but on its face it was a violation of the defendant's obligation to the minority shareholders of those companies, whose earnings were to be diverted to the defendant upon an insufficient consideration. . . .

Surely it would be a curious doctrine which assumed without evidence that a president might bind his corporation to such a questionable undertaking, which might involve it in litigation, if indeed it was valid at all. No desire to free plaintiffs from being obliged to fish in their enemies' water ought so far to fly in the face of probability; nothing could justify such a procedure except the express shifting of the duty of going forward upon the party holding the negative.

Judgment affirmed.

MANTON, CIRCUIT JUDGE, dissents in separate opinion.

MANTON, CIRCUIT JUDGE (dissenting).

On the statement of facts recited in JUDGE HAND's opinion, a jury question was presented as to whether a contract was made and whether or no there was a breach of such contract. Such a contract, made as stated, presumptively had the authority of its maker, the corporation appellee. . . . The contract warranted that the agreement had been approved by the directors of the Ashland Corporation and that its president was authorized to make such a contract. The contract was beneficial to the appellee corporation and was made by the president within the apparent scope of his authority. . . . If the jury found the contract existed and was breached, there should be a recovery.

I dissent.

LEE v. JENKINS BROTHERS

United States Court of Appeals, Second Circuit, 1959.
268 F.2d 357, certiorari denied 361 U.S. 913, 80 S.Ct. 257, 4 L.Ed.2d 183 (1959).

[Lee worked for Crane Company and managed its Bridgeport plant which in 1919 was sold to Jenkins Brothers, a New Jersey corporation. The take-over in 1920 was being managed by one Yardley, president and chairman of the board, a substantial stockholder and son-in-law of Jenkins himself. He wooed a rather reluctant Lee with some vigor. Lee finally agreed to leave Crane and became Jenkins' vice-president and general manager and a director. In 1945 he was discharged at 55 and received settlement of his pension rights under the Jenkins plan. According to Lee part of the "deal" in 1920 had been a promise by Yardley that he would receive a maximum pension of $1500 when he reached 60, his rights under the Crane plan. In 1950, the payments became due and in 1955 Lee brought suit against Jenkins Brothers and Yardley who was then 87 and blind and died before trial. The trial judge dismissed the complaint on two grounds: (1) that the statute of frauds barred the claim and (2) there was no proof as to authorization by the corporation. The Court of Appeals affirmed because it found there was not enough evidence to go to the jury on the existence of a promise to Lee that he would get rights under the Crane program other than having his years of Crane service receive full credit under the Jenkins plan—which is all the other 350 ex-Crane employees got. The opinion by JUDGE MEDINA rejected the trial court's conclusion as to the statute of frauds. The portion dealing with corporate authorization follows.]

Our question on this phase of the case then boils itself down to the following: can it be said as a matter of law that Yardley as president, chairman of the board, substantial stockholder and trustee and son-in-law of the estate of the major stockholder, had no power in the presence of the company's most interested vice president to secure for a "reasonable" length of time badly needed key personnel by promising an experienced local executive a life pension to commence in 30 years at the age of 60, even if Lee were not then working for the corporation, when the maximum liability to Jenkins under such a pension was $1500 per year.

A survey of the law on the authority of corporate officers does not reveal a completely consistent pattern. For the most part the courts perhaps have taken a rather restrictive view on the extent of powers of corporate officials, but the dissatisfaction with such an approach has been manifested in a variety of exceptions such as ratification, estoppel, and promissory estoppel. See Note, 57 Colum.L.Rev. 868 (1957). For the most part also there has been limited discussion of the problem of apparent authority, perhaps on the assumption that if authority could not be implied from a continuing course of action between the corporation and the officer, it could not have been apparent to third parties either.

Such an assumption is ill-founded. The circumstances and facts known to exist between officer and corporation, from which actual authority may be implied, may be entirely different from those circumstances known to exist as between the third party and the corporation. The two concepts are separate and distinct even though the state of the proofs in a given case may cause considerable overlap. . . .

The rule most widely cited is that the president only has authority to bind his company by acts arising in the usual and regular course of business but not for contracts of an "extraordinary" nature. The substance of such a rule lies in the content of the term "extraordinary" which is subject to a broad range of interpretation.

The growth and development of this rule occurred during the late nineteenth and early twentieth centuries when the potentialities of the corporate form of enterprise were just being realized. As the corporation became a more common vehicle for the conduct of business it became increasingly evident that many corporations, particularly small closely held ones, did not normally function in the formal ritualistic manner hitherto envisaged. While the boards of directors still nominally controlled corporate affairs, in reality officers and managers frequently ran the business with little, if any, board supervision. The natural consequence of such a development was that third parties commonly relied on the authority of such officials in almost all the multifarious transactions in which corporations engaged. The pace of modern business life was too swift to insist on the approval by the board of directors of every transaction that was in any way "unusual."

The judicial recognition given to these developments has varied considerably. Whether termed "apparent authority" or an "estoppel" to deny authority, many courts have noted the injustice caused by the practice of permitting corporations to act commonly through their executives and then allowing them to disclaim an agreement as beyond the authority of the contracting officer, when the contract no longer suited its convenience. Other courts, however, continued to cling to the past with little attempt to discuss the unconscionable results obtained or the doctrine of apparent authority. Such restrictive views have been generally condemned by the commentators.

The summary of holdings pro and con in general on the subject of what are and what are not "extraordinary" agreements is inconclusive at best, as shown by the authorities collected in the footnote.[7] But the pattern becomes more distinct when we turn to the more limited area of employment contracts.

7. We note that the following acts have been held to be within either the implied or apparent authority of a corporate president or manager: borrowing money and executing a corporate note, Petition of Mulco Products, Super.Ct., 1956, 11 Terry 28, 50 Del. 28, 123 A.2d 95, affirmed Mulco Products, Inc. v. Black, 11 Terry 246, 50 Del. 246, 127 A.2d 851; Shircliff v. Dixie Drive–In Theatre, 1955, 7 Ill.App.2d 370, 129 N.E.2d 346; Kraft v. Freeman Printing & Publishing Ass'n, 1881, 87 N.Y. 628; even though the moneys obtained might not be used for the benefit of the corporation, Chestnut St. Trust & Savings Fund Co. v. Record Pub. Co., 1910, 227 Pa. 235, 75 A. 1067; pledging security for a loan, Williams v. Hall, 1926, 30 Ariz. 581, 249 P. 755; guaranteeing the note of another corporation, Allis–Chalmers Mfg. Co. v. Citizens Bank & Trust Co., D.C.D.Idaho, 1924, 3 F.2d 316; purchasing merchandise, Blackstone Theatre Corporation v. Goldwyn Distributing Corp., 1925, 86 Ind.App. 277, 146 N.E. 217; White v. Elgin Creamery Co., 1899, 108 Iowa 522, 79 N.W. 283; authorizing an attorney to sue on a corporate claim, Elblum Holding Corp. v. Mintz, 1938, 120 N.J.L. 604, 1 A.2d 204; compromising a corporate claim, Fair Mercantile Co. v. Union–May–Stern Co., 1949, 359 Mo. 385, 221 S.W.2d 751; making a tax closing agreement, E. Van Noorden & Co. v. United States, D.C.D.Mass.1934, 8 F.Supp. 279; executing a time limitations waiver, Philip Carey Mfg. Co. v. Dean, 6 Cir., 1932, 58 F.2d 737, certiorari denied 287 U.S. 623, 53 S.Ct. 78, 77 L.Ed. 541; St. Clair v. Rutledge, 1902, 115 Wis. 583, 92 N.W. 234; pledging a substantial contribution to a hospital, Memorial Hospital Ass'n of Stanislaus County v. Pacific Grape Products Co., 1955, 45 Cal.2d 634, 290 P.2d 481, 50 A.L.R.2d 442; licensing a factory spur track, Anglim v. Sears–Roebuck Shoe Factories, 1926, 255 Mass. 334, 151 N.E. 313; sale of the corporation's only property, Jeppi v. Brockman Holding Co., 1949, 34 Cal. 2d 11, 206 P.2d 847, 9 A.L.R.2d 1299; of all its merchandise and fixtures, Magowan v. Groneweg, 1902, 16 S.D. 29, 91 N.W. 335; or its real estate, Domestic Bldg. Ass'n v. Guadiano, 1902, 195 Ill. 222, 63 N.E. 98.

Other courts have left the question to the jury when the matter involved was: execution of a corporate note, Citizens' Bank v. Public Drug Co., 1921, 190 Iowa 983, 181 N.W. 274; a promise of additional service, Wichita Falls Electric Co. v. Huey, Tex.Civ.App.1923, 246 S.W. 692; a promise

to pay a stale debt, Renault v. L.N. Renault & Sons, Inc., 3 Cir., 1951, 188 F.2d 317; entering a joint venture, Lane v. National Ins. Agency, 1934, 148 Or. 589, 37 P.2d 365; oral waiver of written contract provisions, Van Dusen Aircraft Supplies v. Terminal Construction Corp., 1949, 3 N.J. 321, 70 A.2d 65, and sale of the corporation's sole asset, C.B. Snyder Realty Co. v. National Newark & Essex Banking Co., 1953, 14 N.J. 146, 101 A.2d 544.

On the other hand authority has been found lacking in the following instances: sale of all the company's assets or its major asset, Winsted Hosiery Co. v. New Britain Knitting Co., 1897, 69 Conn. 565, 38 A. 310; Plant v. White River Lumber Co., 8 Cir., 1935, 76 F.2d 155; Gabriel v. Auf Der-Heide–Aragona, Inc., 1951, 14 N.J.Super. 558, 82 A.2d 644; a brokerage contract to effectuate a merger, Abraham Lincoln Life Ins. Co. v. Hopwood, 6 Cir., 1936, 81 F.2d 284, certiorari denied 298 U.S. 687, 56 S.Ct. 955, 80 L.Ed. 1406; modification of directors' resolutions, McMillan v. Dozier, 1952, 257 Ala. 435, 59 So.2d 563; Miller v. Wick Bldg. Co., 1950, 154 Ohio St. 93, 93 N.E.2d 467; Foley v. Wabasha–Nelson Bridge Co., 1940, 207 Minn. 399, 291 N.W. 903; Sattler v. Howe Rubber Corp., Ct.Err. & App.1923, 98 N.J.L. 460, 121 A. 523; employing an architect in a major construction project, Colish v. Brandywine Raceway Ass'n, Inc., Super.Ct., 1955, 10 Terry 493, 49 Del. 493, 119 A.2d 887; giving away corporate property, Fawcett v. New Haven Organ Co., 1879, 47 Conn. 224; Sayre Land Co. v. Borough of Sayre, 1956, 384 Pa. 534, 121 A.2d 579; postponing a mortgage foreclosure, Myrtle Ave. Corp. v. Mt. Prospect B. & L. Ass'n, Ct.Err. & App., 1934, 112 N.J.L. 60, 169 A. 707; suing the corporation's chief stockholder, Ney v. Eastern Iowa Telephone Co., 1913, 162 Iowa 525, 144 N.W. 383; guaranteeing the debt of another, First National Bank of Mason City v. Cement Products Co., 1929, 209 Iowa 358, 227 N.W. 908; and contracts deemed unconscionable from the corporation's point of view, Bowditch, Furniture Co. v. Jones, 1901, 74 Conn. 149, 50 A. 41; Schwartz v. United Merchants & Manufacturers, 2 Cir., 1934, 72 F.2d 256; Bassick v. Aetna Explosives Co., D.C.S.D.N.Y.1917, 246 F. 974.

[Ed.: These cases were reviewed by Judge Friendly in Scientific Holding Co., Ltd. v. Plessey Inc., 510 F.2d 15 (2d Cir. 1974).]

It is generally settled that the president as part of the regular course of business has authority to hire and discharge employees and fix their compensation. In so doing he may agree to hire them for a specific number of years if the term selected is deemed reasonable. But employment contracts for life or on a "permanent" basis are generally regarded as "extraordinary" and beyond the authority of any corporate executive if the only consideration for the promise is the employee's promise to work for that period. Jenkins would have us analogize the pension agreement involved herein to these generally condemned life-time employment contracts because it extends over a long period of time, is of indefinite duration, and involves an indefinite liability on the part of the corporation.

It is not surprising that lifetime employment contracts have met with substantial hostility in the courts, for these contracts are often oral, uncorroborated, vague in important details and highly improbable. Accordingly, the courts have erected a veritable array of obstacles to their enforcement. They have been construed as terminable at will, too indefinite to enforce, *ultra vires,* lacking in mutuality or consideration, abandoned or breached by subsequent acts, and the supporting evidence deemed insufficient to go to the jury, as well as made without proper authority.

However, at times such contracts have been enforced where the circumstances tended to support the plausibility of plaintiff's testimony. Thus when the plaintiff was injured in the course of employment and he agreed to settle his claim of negligence against the company for a lifetime job, authority has been generally found and the barrage of other objections adequately disposed of. And where additional consideration was given such as quitting other employment, giving up a competing business, or where the services were "peculiarly necessary" to the corporation, the courts have divided on the enforceability of the contract.

What makes the point now under discussion particularly interesting is the failure of the courts denying authority to make lifetime contracts to evolve any guiding principle. More often than not we find a mere statement that the contract is "extraordinary" with a citation of cases which say the same thing, without giving reasons. And even in some of the leading cases the question of apparent authority is not even mentioned. All this is a not uncommon indication that the law in a particular area is in a state of evolution, and there seems every reason to believe that the law affecting numerous features of employer-employee relationship, is far from static.

Where reasons have been given to support the conclusion that lifetime employments are "extraordinary," and hence made without authority, a scrutiny of these reasons may be helpful for their bearing on the analogous field of pension agreements. It is said that: they unduly restrict the power of the shareholders and future boards of directors on questions of managerial policy; they subject the corporation to an inordinately substantial amount of liability; they run for long and indefinite periods of time. Of these reasons the only one applicable to pension agreements is that they run for long and indefinite periods of time. There the likeness stops. Future director or shareholder control is in no way impeded; the amount of liability is not disproportionate; the agreement was not only not unreasonable but beneficial and necessary to the corporation; and pension contracts are commonly used fringe benefits in employment contracts. Moreover, unlike the case with life employment contracts, courts have often gone out of their way to find pension promises binding and definite even when labeled gratuitous by the employer. The consideration given to the employee involved is not at all dependent on profits or sales, nor does it involve some other variable suggesting director discretion.

In this case Lee was hired at a starting salary of $4,000 per year plus a contemplated pension of $1500 per year in thirty years. Had Lee been hired at a starting salary of $10,000 per year the cost to the corporation over the long run would have been substantially greater, yet no one could plausibly contend that such an employment contract was beyond Yardley's authority.

The cases on executive authority to make pension agreements are few. . . .

Apparent authority is essentially a question of fact. It depends not only on the nature of the contract involved, but the officer negotiating it, the corporation's usual manner of conducting business, the size of the corporation and the number of its stockholders, the circumstances that give rise to the contract, the reasonableness of the contract, the amounts involved, and who the contracting third party is, to list a few but not all of the relevant factors. In certain instances a given contract may be so important to the welfare of the corporation that outsiders would naturally suppose that only the board of directors (or even the shareholders) could properly handle it. It is in this light that the "ordinary course of business" rule should be given its content. Beyond such "extraordinary" acts, whether or not apparent authority exists is simply a matter of fact.

Accordingly, we hold that, assuming there was sufficient proof of the making of the pension agreement, Connecticut, in the particular circumstances of this case, would probably take the view that reasonable men could differ on the subject of whether or not Yardley had apparent authority to make the contract, and that the trial court erred in deciding the question as a matter of law. We do not think Connecticut would adopt any hard and fast rule against apparent authority to make pension agreements generally, on the theory that they were in the same category as lifetime employment contracts. . . .

[JUDGE LEARNED HAND dissented. As to the authority issue he said, ". . . I cannot agree that Yardley, as president of the corporation, had authority to make a contract that was to last for the life of the promisee. I have not indeed found any decision in Connecticut that decides that question; but in New York, New Jersey, Maryland, Iowa, Wyoming and West Virginia the law is settled and in Texas the same limitation was even imposed on the president's authority to make a contract for three years . . . since the Connecticut courts have indicated no disposition to the contrary, I assume that they would follow so generally accepted a doctrine. There being no relevant corporate by-law, I would say that the accepted doctrine is the law of Connecticut." He would have dismissed the claim against the corporation but not as to Yardley.]

QUESTIONS

(1) There follow a series of rather easy questions so that you can check your understanding of the above materials. In each case ask yourself what kind of authority, if any, is present.

(a) The board of the corporation hands A a copy of a board resolution authorizing A to go to the First National Bank of Peoria and borrow $50,000 for the corporation. A does so.

(b) The board of directors authorizes A to purchase an adequate supply of soybeans, being aware that there is relatively little cash in the corporate treasury.

(c) After borrowing $50,000 on such authorization for three successive seasons to finance the acquisition of an inventory of soybeans, A proceeds to borrow $50,000 again, this time without waiting for the board to meet.

(d) A is acting for a new soybean processing company with no prior borrowing history and, like the other soybean companies in the area, borrows to cover the cost of buying beans, without raising the matter with the board.

(e) The board gives A an undated letter of authorization to borrow which was meant to cover only 1969 borrowings, but A uses it again in 1970.

(f) After several times borrowing at Peoria banks, without ever getting specific authorization, A proceeds to New York and borrows from a bank there.

(g) In which of the above problems is it relevant that A was the president of the corporation?

(2) How does the concept of prima facie, or presumptive authority developed in Schwartz fit with the classification of types of authority represented by the Restatement. Comparing the transactions involved in Lee and Schwartz, how would you rank the transactions in terms of the likelihood that authority existed? How does Lee deal with Schwartz?

REVIEW PROBLEM

You are counsel for a landowner about to rent a large factory for a long period to a new and unknown tenant. Your client would not enter into this transaction on the strength of the tenant's reliability alone. However, the client is impressed by the guaranty being offered by the Tangiers Special Operations Corporation, which he knows to be a company of considerable financial strength but with a rather ugly reputation for raising technical legal points when a deal turns out badly. Thus the client wants from you an explicit opinion that the guaranty is "valid, binding and enforceable in accordance with its terms."

What documents do you need to examine in order to block out all possible internal weaknesses so that you can freely give that opinion? Be sure not to restrict yourself to issues treated in this Chapter only. If in fact one of those weaknesses is undetected, to what extent will legal doctrines protect your client?

Handbook of the Law of Agency (1964), and R. Steffen, Agency—Partnership in a Nutshell (1977). For application of agency law to corporations see Kempin, Corporate Officers and the Law of Agency, 44 Va.L.Rev. 1273 (1958). For "agency" in the broader sense see Principals and Agents: The Structure of Business (J. Pratt & R. Zeckhauser eds. 1985).

3. Loyalty and Tenure

Executives, being agents, are bound by a duty of loyalty and obedience to the corporation, meaning essentially to the mandates of the board of directors. See Restatement (Second) of Agency § 385. In theory, this renders them liable to the corporation in damages for violating instructions given them by the board or by other superiors. In practice, disobedience is usually handled by the corporation in one of the following ways:

(1) reprimand or other unpleasantness

(2) transfer to a less attractive or prestigious post

(3) a fine or denial of some financial advantage

(4) dismissal.

Note that the rules respecting self-dealing, taking of corporate opportunities and due care apply, with some modifications, to officers as well as directors. As befits full-time employees the limitations are sometimes more intense. Corporate executives are protected neither by tenure, as are academicians, nor by union rules, as are unionized employees. Hence discipline at the upper levels can be entirely without due process, can in fact be harsh and arbitrary. Perhaps the most drastic example is the following story from Nevins' biography of Henry Ford:

> The atmosphere which enveloped workers at the Rouge as Bennett took firmer grip on the reins is well indicated by a story told by W.C. Klann. In the fall of 1928 this able official, with his long record of invaluable service, was discharged, receiving a final check for $10,000. When asked a little later to return, he declined, for (he said) he did not wish to get the treatment given Frank Kulick. What had happened to Kulick? He also had been discharged arbitrarily. He had appealed to Henry Ford, who told him to go and see Sorensen, who would put him back to work. Sorensen thereupon sent Kulick to perform a special task for Bennett in getting a defective car ready for use. Inspecting it, Kulick found that a camshaft had been inaccurately ground. With Klann's assistance he made a perfect cam, and after much trouble, for Bennett's service men interposed all kind of obstacles, he delivered it. Klann continues:

Vagts Basic Corp. Law 3rd Ed. UCB—12

Frank Kulick put the camshaft in the car, and he started the motor. It was very quiet. He called up Harry Bennett and told him about it. Bennett said, "We'll take it for a ride."

Bennett told Frank it was still noisy. He told Frank to lie on the running board and listen through the hood. He drove out of the gate on Miller Road and turned the corner so fast he threw Kulick off the running board. Bennett drove back into the plant through another gate and left Kulick outside. Frank started to go back into the plant, but the service men would not let him in.[8]

A well-run corporation of the modern mood will not wish to have a reign of terror in the upper echelons on the ground that it is counterproductive because it distracts its victims from the work at hand. Some corporations, particularly those run by self-made entrepreneurs who regard the firm as their very own, have been famous for the rapid exodus of managers. Even in the modern firm, however, some event such as the failure of a major new product can lead to the purge of numbers of executives found guilty of non-success. These are generally handled in a more civilized manner nowadays; the use of euphemisms such as "dehiring" and "outplacing" indicates the greater sensitivity with which the matter is approached, often through the medium of a management-consulting firm. The American style is, nonetheless, regarded by foreigners as ruthless in its weeding out of executives judged to be unsuccessful; the counterpart is the tendency of managers to leave when a better opportunity appears rather than adhering to a family-like loyalty.

Legally speaking, the level of an executive's security depends on whether or not there is an employment contract. If there is none, the traditional rule was that it was a contract at will and either party could terminate it at any time. As indicated in the Wagenseller case that directly follows, this rule is being eroded from several different directions and a determined discharged employee has at hand materials for contentious action. More and more executives nowadays do have contracts. Often these will specify what compensation will be paid to a discharged employee. Some of them are quite lavish. The term "golden parachute" has been attached to certain contracts that give managers special benefits if their employment relation is severed as a result of a hostile takeover. These contracts are defended on such grounds as the proposition that they enable an executive to weigh disinterestedly the pros and cons of a proposed takeover. General contract or equity principles have tended to limit specific performance of employment contracts. Restatement, Second, Agency § 118. Jones v. Williams may be seen as an exception to that idea.

8. 2 A. Nevins, Ford 593 (1963).

WAGENSELLER v. SCOTTSDALE MEMORIAL HOSPITAL

Supreme Court of Arizona, 1985.
147 Ariz. 370, 710 P.2d 1025.

[Wagenseller brought an action against the Scottsdale Memorial Hospital, its personnel administrators and her supervisor Kay Smith. The trial court entered summary judgment for defendants but the Court of Appeals affirmed only in part and remanded. Wagenseller appealed to the Supreme Court which affirmed in part and reversed in part in an opinion by FELDMAN, J.:]

FACTUAL BACKGROUND

Catherine Wagenseller began her employment at Scottsdale Memorial Hospital as a staff nurse in March 1975, having been personally recruited by the manager of the emergency department, Kay Smith. Wagenseller was an "at-will" employee—one hired without specific contractual term. Smith was her supervisor. In August 1978, Wagenseller was assigned to the position of ambulance charge nurse, and approximately one year later was promoted to the position of paramedic coordinator, a newly approved management position in the emergency department. Three months later, on November 1, 1979, Wagenseller was terminated.

Most of the events surrounding Wagenseller's work at the Hospital and her subsequent termination are not disputed, although the parties differ in their interpretation of the inferences to be drawn from and the significance of these events. For more than four years, Smith and Wagenseller maintained a friendly, professional, working relationship. In May 1979, they joined a group consisting largely of personnel from other hospitals for an eight-day camping and rafting trip down the Colorado River. According to Wagenseller, "an uncomfortable feeling" developed between her and Smith as the trip progressed—a feeling that Wagenseller ascribed to "the behavior that Kay Smith was displaying." Wagenseller states that this included public urination, defecation and bathing, heavy drinking, and "grouping up" with other rafters. Wagenseller did not participate in any of these activities. She also refused to join in the group's staging of a parody of the song "Moon River," which allegedly concluded with members of the group "mooning" the audience. Smith and others allegedly performed the "Moon River" skit twice at the Hospital following the group's return from the river, but Wagenseller declined to participate there as well.

Wagenseller contends that her refusal to engage in these activities caused her relationship with Smith to deteriorate and was the proximate cause of her termination. She claims that following the river trip Smith began harassing her, using abusive language and embarrassing her in the company of other staff. Other emergency department staff reported a similar marked change in Smith's behavior toward Wagenseller after the trip, although Smith denied it.

Up to the time of the river trip, Wagenseller had received consistently favorable job performance evaluations. Two months before the trip, Smith completed an annual evaluation report in which she rated Wagenseller's performance as "exceed[ing] results expected," the second highest of five possible ratings. In August and October 1979, Wagenseller met first with Smith and then with Smith's successor,

Jeannie Steindorff, to discuss some problems regarding her duties as paramedic coordinator and her attitude toward the job. On November 1, 1979, following an exit interview at which Wagenseller was asked to resign and refused, she was terminated.

She appealed her dismissal in letters to her supervisor and to the Hospital administrative and personnel department, answering the Hospital's stated reasons for her termination, claiming violations of the disciplinary procedure contained in the Hospital's personnel policy manual, and requesting reinstatement and other remedies.

THE EMPLOYMENT–AT–WILL DOCTRINE

History

As early as 1562, the English common law presumed that an employment contract containing an annual salary provision or computation was for a one-year term. Murg & Scharman, Employment at Will: Do the Exceptions Overwhelm the Rule? 23 B.C.L.Rev. 329, 332 (1982). Originally designed for the protection of seasonal farm workers, the English rule expanded over the years to protect factory workers as well. Workers were well protected under this rule, for the one-year presumption was not easy to overcome. Id. English courts held an employer liable for breaching the employment contract if he terminated an employee at any time during the year without "reasonable cause to do so." 1 W. Blackstone, Commentaries *413. To uphold an employer's discharge of an employee without a showing of "good cause," the courts required a clear expression of a contrary intent as evidenced either on the face of the contract or by a clearly defined custom of the industry. Murg & Scharman, supra, at 332.

In the early nineteenth century, American courts borrowed the English rule. The legal rationale embodied in the rule was consistent with the nature of the predominant master-servant employment relationship at the time because it reflected the master's duty to make provision for the general well-being of his servants. Id. at 334 and n. 22. In addition, the master was under a duty to employ the servant for a term, either a specified or implied time of service, and could not terminate him strictly at will. Hermann & Sor, Property Rights in One's Job: The Case for Limiting Employment-at-Will, 24 Ariz.L.Rev. 763, 770 (1982). The late nineteenth century, however, brought the Industrial Revolution; with it came the decline of the master-servant relationship and the rise of the more impersonal employer-employee relationship. In apparent response to the economic changes sweeping the country, American courts abandoned the English rule and adopted the employment-at-will doctrine. Murg & Scharman, supra, at 334. This new doctrine gave the employer freedom to terminate an at-will employee for any reason, good or bad.

The at-will rule has been traced to an 1877 treatise by H.G. Wood, in which he wrote:

> With us the rule is inflexible, that a general or indefinite hiring is prima facie a hiring at will, and if the servant seeks to make it out a yearly hiring, the burden is upon him to establish it by proof. . . . [I]t is an indefinite hiring and is determinable at the will of either party. . . .

H.G. Wood, Law of Master and Servant § 134 at 273 (1877). . . .

However unsound its foundation, Wood's at-will doctrine was adopted by the New York courts in Martin v. New York Life Insurance Co., 148 N.Y. 117, 42 N.E. 416 (1895), and soon became the generally accepted American rule. In 1932, this court first adopted the rule for Arizona: "The general rule in regard to contracts for personal services, . . . where no time limit is provided, is that they are terminable at pleasure by either party, or at most upon reasonable notice." Dover Copper Mining Co. v. Doenges, 40 Ariz. 349, 357, 12 P.2d 288, 291–92 (1932). Thus, an employer was free to fire an employee hired for an indefinite term "for good cause, for no cause, or even for cause morally wrong, without being thereby guilty of legal wrong." Blades, Employment at Will v. Individual Freedom: On Limiting the Abusive Exercise of Employer Power, 67 Colum.L.Rev. 1404, 1405 (1967) (quoting Payne v. Western & Allegheny Railroad Co., 81 Tenn. (13 Lea) 507, 519–20 (1884), overruled on other grounds, Hutton v. Watters, 132 Tenn. 527, 179 S.W. 134 (1915)).

Present–Day Status of the At–Will Rule

In recent years there has been apparent dissatisfaction with the absolutist formulation of the common law at-will rule. The Illinois Supreme Court is representative of courts that have acknowledged a need for a less mechanical application of the rule:

> With the rise of large corporations conducting specialized operations and employing relatively immobile workers who often have no other place to market their skills, recognition that the employer and employee do not stand on equal footing is realistic. In addition, unchecked employer power, like unchecked employee power, has been seen to present a distinct threat to the public policy carefully considered and adopted by society as a whole. As a result, it is now recognized that a proper balance must be maintained among the employer's interest in operating a business efficiently and profitably, the employee's interest in earning a livelihood, and society's interest in seeing its public policies carried out.

Palmateer v. International Harvester Co., 85 Ill.2d 124, 129, 52 Ill.Dec. 13, 15, 421 N.E.2d 876, 878 (1981) (citation omitted). Today, courts in three-fifths of the states have recognized some form of a cause of action for wrongful discharge. Lopatka, The Emerging Law of Wrongful Discharge—A Quadrennial Assessment of the Labor Law Issue of the 80s, 40 Bus.Law. 1 (1984).

The trend has been to modify the at-will rule by creating exceptions to its operation. Three general exceptions have developed. The most widely accepted approach is the "public policy" exception, which permits recovery upon a finding that the employer's conduct undermined some important public policy. The second exception, based on contract, requires proof of an implied-in-fact promise of employment for a specific duration, as found in the circumstances surrounding the employment relationship, including assurances of job security in company personnel manuals or memoranda. Under the third approach, courts have found in the employment contract an implied-in-law covenant of "good faith and fair dealing" and have held employers liable in both contract and tort for breach of that covenant. Wagenseller raises all three doctrines.

THE PUBLIC POLICY EXCEPTION

The public policy exception to the at-will doctrine began with a narrow rule permitting employees to sue their employers when a statute expressly prohibited their discharge. See Kouff v. Bethlehem–Alameda Shipyard, 90 Cal.App.2d 322, 202 P.2d 1059 (1949) (statute prohibiting discharge for serving as an election officer). This formulation was then expanded to include any discharge in violation of a statutory expression of public policy. See Petermann v. Teamsters Local 396, 174 Cal.App.2d 184, 344 P.2d 25 (1959) (discharge for refusal to commit perjury). Courts later allowed a cause of action for violation of public policy, even in the absence of a specific statutory prohibition. See Nees v. Hocks, 272 Or. 210, 536 P.2d 512 (1975) (discharge for being absent from work to serve on jury duty). . . .

Before deciding whether to adopt the public policy exception, we first consider what kind of discharge would violate the rule. The majority of courts require, as a threshold showing, a "clear mandate" of public policy. . . . The leading case recognizing a public policy exception to the at-will doctrine is Palmateer v. International Harvester Co., supra, which holds that an employee stated a cause of action for wrongful discharge when he claimed he was fired for supplying information to police investigating alleged criminal violations by a co-employee. Addressing the issue of what constitutes "clearly mandated public policy," the court stated:

> There is no precise definition of the term. In general, it can be said that public policy concerns what is right and just and what affects the citizens of the State collectively. It is to be found in the State's constitution and statutes and, when they are silent, in its judicial decisions. Although there is no precise line of demarcation dividing matters that are the subject of public policies from matters purely personal, a survey of cases in other States involving retaliatory discharges shows that a matter must strike at the heart of a citizen's social rights, duties, and responsibilities before the tort will be allowed.

85 Ill.2d at 130, 52 Ill.Dec. at 15–16, 421 N.E.2d at 878–79 (citation omitted).

[Cases on refusal by employee to commit perjury to engage in price fixing, to perform unauthorized medical procedure, etc. are omitted.]

Similarly, courts have found terminations improper where to do otherwise would have impinged on the employee's exercise of statutory rights or duties. E.g., Glenn v. Clearman's Golden Cock Inn, 192 Cal. App.2d 793, 13 Cal.Rptr. 769 (1961) (right to join a union); Midgett v. Sackett–Chicago, 105 Ill.2d 143, 85 Ill.Dec. 475, 473 N.E.2d 1280 (1984) (filing of a workers' compensation claim by a union member protected by a collective bargaining agreement); Frampton v. Central Indiana Gas Co., 260 Ind. 249, 297 N.E.2d 425 (1973) (filing of a workers' compensation claim); Nees v. Hocks, supra (requesting not to be excused from jury duty). A division of our court of appeals recently adopted the public policy exception, ruling that the discharge of an at-will employee who refused to conceal a violation of Arizona's theft statute was contrary to public policy. Vermillion v. AAA Pro Moving & Storage, 146 Ariz. 215 at 216, 704 P.2d 1360 at 1361 (App.1985). The court's ruling, it stated, was the "logical conclusion" to draw from previous decisions of the court of appeals.

It is difficult to justify this court's further adherence to a rule which permits an employer to fire someone for "cause morally wrong." So far as we can tell, no court faced with a termination that violated a "clear mandate of public policy" has refused to adopt the public policy exception. Certainly, a court would be hard-pressed to find a rationale to hold that an employer could with impunity fire an employee who refused to commit perjury. Why should the law imply an agreement which would give the employer such power? It may be argued, of course, that our economic system functions best if employers are given wide latitude in dealing with employees. We assume that it is in the public interest that employers continue to have that freedom. We also believe, however, that the interests of the economic system will be fully served if employers may fire for good cause or without cause. The interests of society as a whole will be promoted if employers are forbidden to fire for cause which is "morally wrong."

We therefore adopt the public policy exception to the at-will termination rule. We hold that an employer may fire for good cause or for no cause. He may not fire for bad cause—that which violates public policy. . . .

We turn then to the questions of where "public policy" may be found and how it may be recognized and articulated. As the expressions of our founders and those we have elected to our legislature, our state's constitution and statutes embody the public conscience of the people of this state. It is thus in furtherance of their interests to hold that an employer may not with impunity violate the dictates of public policy found in the provisions of our statutory and constitutional law.

We do not believe, however, that expressions of public policy are contained only in the statutory and constitutional law, nor do we believe that all statements made in either a statute or the constitution are expressions of public policy. . . . Thus, we believe that reliance on prior judicial decisions, as part of the body of applicable common law, is appropriate, although we agree with the Hawaii Supreme Court that "courts should proceed cautiously if called upon to declare public policy absent some prior legislative or judicial expression on the subject." Parnar v. Americana Hotels, 65 Hawaii at 380, 652 P.2d at 631. Thus, we will look to the pronouncements of our founders, our legislature, and our courts to discern the public policy of this state.

All such pronouncements, however, will not provide the basis for a claim of wrongful discharge. Only those which have a singularly public purpose will have such force. Lord Truro set forth the classic formulation of the public policy doctrine nearly 150 years ago:

> Public policy is that principle of the law which holds that no subject can lawfully do that which has a tendency to be injurious to the public, or against the public good, which may be termed, as it sometimes has been, the policy of the law, or public policy in relation to the administration of the law.

Egerton v. Earl Brownlow, 4 H.L.Cas. 1, 196 (1853). Where the interest involved is merely private or proprietary, the exception does not apply. . . .

[S]ome legal principles, whether statutory or decisional, have a discernible, comprehensive public purpose. A state's criminal code provides clear examples of such statutes. Thus, courts in other jurisdictions have consistently recognized a cause of action for a discharge in violation of a criminal statute. In a seminal case involving the public policy exception, Petermann v. International Brotherhood of Teamsters Local 396, 174 Cal.App.2d 184, 344 P.2d 25 (1959), the California Court of Appeals upheld an employee's right to refuse to commit perjury. . . .

Although we do not limit our recognition of the public policy exception to cases involving a violation of a criminal statute, we do believe that our duty will seldom be clearer than when such a violation is involved. . . .

In the case before us, Wagenseller refused to participate in activities which arguably would have violated our indecent exposure statute, A.R.S. § 13–1402. She claims that she was fired because of this refusal. The statute provides:

§ 13–1402. Indecent exposure; classifications

A. A person commits indecent exposure if he or she exposes his or her genitals or anus or she exposes the areola or nipple of her breast or breasts and another person is present, and the defendant is reckless about whether such other person, as a reasonable person, would be offended or alarmed by the act.

B. Indecent exposure is a class 1 misdemeanor. Indecent exposure to a person under the age of fifteen years is a class 6 felony.

While this statute may not embody a policy which "strikes at the heart of a citizen's social right, duties and responsibilities" (*Palmateer, supra*) as clearly and forcefully as a statute prohibiting perjury, we believe that it was enacted to preserve and protect the commonly recognized sense of public privacy and decency. The statute does, therefore, recognize bodily privacy as a "citizen's social right." . . . We thus uphold this state's public policy by holding that termination for refusal to commit an act which might violate A.R.S. § 13–1402 may provide the basis of a claim for wrongful discharge. The relevant inquiry here is not whether the alleged "mooning" incidents were either felonies or misdemeanors or constituted purely technical violations of the statute, but whether they contravened the important public policy interests embodied in the law. . . .

From a theoretical standpoint, we emphasize that the "public policy exception" which we adopt does not require the court to make a new contract for the parties. In an at-will situation, the parties have made no express agreement regarding the duration of employment or the grounds for discharge. The common law has presumed that in so doing the parties have intended to allow termination at any time, with or without good cause. It might be more properly argued that the law has recognized an implied covenant to that effect. Whether it be presumption or implied contractual covenant, we do not disturb it. We simply do not raise a presumption or imply a covenant that would require an employee to do that which public policy forbids or refrain from doing that which it commands.

Thus, in an at-will hiring we continue to recognize the presumption or to imply the covenant of termination at the pleasure of either party, whether with or without cause. Firing for bad cause—one against public policy articulated by constitutional, statutory, or decisional law—is not a right inherent in the at-will contract, or in any other contract, even if expressly provided. . . .

THE "PERSONNEL POLICY MANUAL" EXCEPTION

Although an employment contract for an indefinite term is presumed to be terminable at will, that presumption, like any other presumption, is rebuttable by contrary evidence. See Restatement (Second) of Agency § 442; Leikvold v. Valley View Community Hospital, 141 Ariz. 544, 547, 688 P.2d 170, 173 (1984). Thus, in addition to relying on the public policy analysis to restrict the operation of the terminable-at-will rule, courts have turned to the employment contract itself, finding in it implied terms that limit the employer's right of discharge. Two types of implied contract terms have been recognized by the courts: implied-in-law terms and implied-in-fact terms. An implied-in-law term arises from a duty imposed by law where the contract itself is silent; it is imposed even though the parties may not have intended it, and it binds the parties to a legally enforceable duty, just as if they had so contracted explicitly. 1 A. *Corbin, Contracts* § 17, at 38 (1960). The covenant of good faith and fair dealing, discussed post at 1038–1041, is an implied-in-law contract term that has been recognized by a small number of courts in the employment-at-will context.

An implied-in-fact contract term, on the other hand, is one that is inferred from the statements or conduct of the parties. Id. It is not a promise defined by the law, but one made by the parties, though not expressly. Courts have found such terms in an employer's policy statements regarding such things as job security and employee disciplinary procedures, holding that by the conduct of the parties these statements may become part of the contract, supplementing the verbalized at-will agreement, and thus limiting the employer's absolute right to discharge an at-will employee . . .

We do not believe this document, read in its entirety, has the clarity that the court of appeals attributed to its individual portions. One reading the document might well infer that the Hospital had established a procedure that would generally apply in disciplinary actions taken against employees. Although such a person would also note the long list of exceptions, he might not conclude from reading the list that an exception would apply in every case so as to swallow the general rule completely. We do not believe that the provision for unarticulated exceptions destroys the entire articulated general policy as a matter of law. . . . The right of discharge without cause is an implied contractual term which is said to exist in an at-will relationship when there are no factual indications to the contrary. The intent to create a different relationship, as well as the parameters of that relationship, are to be discerned from the totality of the parties' statements and actions regarding the employment relationship. . . .

The general rule is that the determination whether in a particular case a promise should be implied in fact is a question of fact. Where reasonable minds may draw different conclusions or inferences from undisputed evidentiary facts, a question of fact is presented. We believe that reasonable persons could differ in the inferences and conclusions they would draw from the Hospital's published manual regarding disciplinary policy and procedure. Thus, there are questions of fact as to whether this policy and procedure became a part of

Wagenseller's employment contract. The trial court therefore erred in granting summary judgment on this issue.

.   .   .

THE "GOOD FAITH AND FAIR DEALING" EXCEPTION

We turn next to a consideration of implied-in-law contract terms which may limit an employer's right to discharge an at-will employee. Wagenseller claims that discharge without good cause breaches the implied-in-law covenant of good faith and fair dealing contained in every contract. . . . In the context of this case, she argues that discharge without good cause violates the covenant of good faith and is, therefore, wrongful. The covenant requires that neither party do anything that will injure the right of the other to receive the benefits of their agreement. . . . The duty not to act in bad faith or deal unfairly thus becomes a part of the contract, and, as with any other element of the contract, the remedy for its breach generally is on the contract itself. Zancanaro v. Cross, 85 Ariz. 394, 339 P.2d 746 (1959). In certain circumstances, breach of contract, including breach of the covenant of good faith and fair dealing, may provide the basis for a tort claim. . . .

The question whether a duty to terminate only for good cause should be implied into all employment-at-will contracts has received much attention in the case law and other literature. . . . Courts have generally rejected the invitation to imply such a duty in employment contracts, voicing the concern that to do so would place undue restrictions on management and would infringe the employer's "legitimate exercise of management discretion." . . . We think this concern is appropriate.

California has come closer than any other jurisdiction to implying a good cause duty in all employment-at-will contracts. [citations omitted].

We find neither the logic of the California cases nor their factual circumstances compelling for recognition of so broad a rule in the case before us. Were we to adopt such a rule, we fear that we would tread perilously close to abolishing completely the at-will doctrine and establishing by judicial fiat the benefits which employees can and should get *only* through collective bargaining agreements or tenure provisions. Cf. Fleming v. Pima County, 141 Ariz. 149, 685 P.2d 1301 (1984) (county employee protected by a merit system was permitted to bring a tort action for wrongful discharge). While we do not reject the propriety of such a rule, we are not persuaded that it should be the result of judicial decision.

In reaching this conclusion, however, we do not feel that we should treat employment contracts as a special type of agreement in which the law refuses to imply the covenant of good faith and fair dealing that it implies in all other contracts. As we noted above, the implied-in-law covenant of good faith and fair dealing protects the right of the parties to an agreement to receive the benefits of the agreement that they have entered into. The denial of a party's right to those benefits, whatever they are, will breach the duty of good faith implicit in the contract. Thus, the relevant inquiry always will focus on the contract itself, to determine what the parties did agree to. In the case of an employment-at-will contract, it may be said that the parties have agreed, for example, that the employee will do the work required by the employer and that the employer will provide the necessary working conditions and pay the employee for work done. What cannot be said is that one of the agreed benefits to the at-will employee is a guarantee of continued employment or tenure. The very nature of the at-will agreement precludes any claim for a prospective benefit. Either employer or employee may terminate the contract at any time.

We do, however, recognize an implied covenant of good faith and fair dealing in the employment-at-will contract, although that covenant does not create a duty for the employer to terminate the employee only for good cause. The covenant does not protect the employee from a "no cause" termination because tenure was never a benefit inherent in the at-will agreement. The covenant does protect an employee from a discharge based on an employer's desire to avoid the payment of benefits already earned by the employee, such as the sales commissions in *Fortune,* supra, but not the tenure required to earn the pension and retirement benefits in *Cleary,* supra. Thus, plaintiff here has a right to receive the benefits that were a part of her employment agreement with defendant Hospital. To the extent, however, that the benefits represent a claim for prospective employment, her claim must fail. The terminable-at-will contract between her and the Hospital made no promise of continued employment. To the contrary, it was, by its nature, subject to termination by either party at any time, subject only to the legal prohibition that she could not be fired for reasons which contravene public policy.

Thus, because we are concerned not to place undue restrictions on the employer's discretion in managing his workforce and because tenure is contrary to the bargain in an at-will contract, we reject the argument that a no cause termination breaches the implied covenant of good faith and fair dealing in an employment-at-will relationship.

[Portions of the opinion dealing with the claim against Smith for interfering with her employment relationship with the Hospital are omitted.]

SUMMARY AND CONCLUSIONS

The trial court granted summary judgment against Wagenseller on the count alleging the tort of wrongful discharge in violation of public policy. We adopt the "public policy" exception to the at-will termination rule and hold that the trial court erred in granting judgment against plaintiff on this theory. On remand plaintiff will be entitled to a jury trial if she can make a prima facie showing that her termination was caused by her refusal to perform some act contrary to public policy, or her performance of some act which, as a matter of public policy, she had a right to do. The obverse, however, is that mere dispute over an issue involving a question of public policy is not equivalent to establishing causation as a matter of law and will not automatically entitle plaintiff to judgment. In the face of conflicting evidence or inferences as to the actual reason for termination, the question of causation will be a question of fact.

The trial court granted summary judgment against Wagenseller on the count alleging breach of implied-in-fact provisions of the contract. We hold that this was error. On this record, there is a jury question as to whether the provisions of the employment manual were part of the contract of employment.

We affirm the grant of summary judgment on the count seeking recovery for breach of the implied covenant of good faith and fair dealing. We recognize that covenant as part of this and other contracts, but do not construe it to give either party to the contract rights—such as tenure—different from those for which they contracted.

We reverse the grant of summary judgment against Wagenseller on the count alleging tortious interference with a contractual relationship. On this record, there is a question of fact with respect to whether the discharge was tortious. Summary judgment was inappropriate.

For the foregoing reasons, we affirm in part and reverse in part. The decision of the court of appeals is vacated and the case remanded to the trial court for proceedings not inconsistent with this opinion.

[CHIEF JUSTICE HOLOHAN dissented as to the finding that the personnel manual was part of the employment contract. A supplemental opinion as to attorney's fees is omitted].

JONES v. WILLIAMS

Supreme Court of Missouri, 1897.
139 Mo. 1, 39 S.W. 486.

[Joseph Pulitzer founded a daily newspaper in St. Louis, known as the "Post Dispatch". As the court says, he "was an experienced and successful newspaper man, and under his management the Post Dispatch and its good will had become very valuable property." In 1891 he founded the Pulitzer Publishing Company, a Missouri corporation, to which he transferred the paper. As a result he held nearly 90% of the stock and effectively ran the corporation's affairs. Most of the remainder of the shares was held by close relatives. In February 1895, he entered into an agreement with plaintiff, Charles Jones, a successful newspaper editor in the region. Jones was to be editor and manager of the Post Dispatch and director and president of the Company for 5 years at $10,000 a year. For $80,000 Jones was to buy from Pulitzer 1/6 of the stock. Pulitzer agreed to give him "control and management of the paper" and Jones agreed to give "all the time, ability and energy he possesses" to the paper. Shortly thereafter a stockholders meeting was held at which Jones was named director. Pulitzer published in the paper an announcement that Col. Jones had "responsibility and control over its columns." In August 1895 Jones was told that the paper's policy as to "the Silver question" and the "Stone Democratic faction" should be radically changed. When he ignored this notice a second was sent, telling him that "it would be pleasanter and more agreeable if you pledge prompt and loyal compliance" and warning that if he did not, a board meeting would be called to take action to protect the paper. Jones then brought suit to enjoin interference with his contract, defendants being the corporation and its directors, (but not Pulitzer). He alleged that his ouster would irreparably injure his interests. A temporary injunction was granted and, after hearing, made final. Defendants appealed and the Supreme Court, in an opinion by MACFARLANE, J., sustained the injunction (4–2). Portions of the opinion dealing with Pulitzer's authority to act for the corporation are omitted but extracts from the remainder follow:]

5. Is the contract valid and binding on the corporation? Counsel argue that it is not, because against public policy. We have attempted to show in a previous paragraph that the directors, either by their official action or through the president, had the power to appoint plaintiff editor and manager of the Post Dispatch, and to give him control of the same, and that the contract in that particular is not in contravention of the statute which requires that the property and business of a corporation shall be managed and controlled by directors. The corporation does not, by the contract, divest itself of its organic character, or of the powers and obligations incident to its existence, as claimed. It is left entirely free to exercise all its organic functions, but it is bound, as an individual is bound, to perform its agreements. Power to control its business does not imply the right to repudiate contracts lawfully entered into. But it is said that the contract is against public policy, and void, for the reason that it couples with a sale of stock in the corporation an agreement to give to the purchaser a position for five years, at a large salary, and, in addition, the position of director and president of the corporation. Counsel cite many cases in support of their position. It is undoubtedly true that an agreement by one stockholder for the sale, directly or indirectly, of an office in a corporation, or of a permanent position therein, "would be against public policy, and void," though the contracting stockholder had shares sufficient in amount to give him control in the election of officers. By such agreement he might be required to act contrary to the duty he owed the company and other stockholders. West v. Camden, 135 U.S. 507, 10 Sup.Ct. 838. Each shareholder in the corporation has a right to rely upon the judgment of all the others, in the election of directors and officers, and any agreement which puts it out of his power to exercise such judgment is against public policy. An examination of the cases, however, will show that such contracts have generally been declared void, for the reason that the duty the stockholder owes to the company and his associates would be thereby violated. Cone v. Russell, 48 N.J. Eq. 212, 21 Atl. 847; West v. Camden, supra; Fuller v. Dame, 18 Pick. 472; Guernsey v. Cook, 120 Mass. 501. But a corporation—that is to say, the stockholders and officers—has the right to employ the best expert talent it can secure for the management of its affairs. Success depends upon good management. Personal interest in the manager creates an incentive to succeed. The successful management of a large daily paper in a city requires the highest degree of talent, as well as large experience. One possessing these qualifications is difficult to secure, and commands a large salary. During the year 1894 the Post Dispatch had not been as profitable as in previous years. A change of management was thought desirable, at least by Pulitzer. Plaintiff was possessed of experience, talent, and characteristics which were supposed to specially qualify him for increasing the earning power of the paper. The contract was made with a view of securing his services.

It seems to us that all objections to the contract, so far as it relates to the employment of plaintiff as editor and manager, and gives him editorial control, on the ground that it is against public policy, is [sic] removed if the directors and stockholders gave it their unanimous assent. The stockholders or directors of a corporation have the right, in the first instance, to dispose of its stock to such persons as, in their opinion, will be of advantage to it in a business point of view, or to such as will insure its management according to the views of the promoters. It is perfectly manifest that this company was organized with a view of having it managed by Pulitzer. "Continued ill health and loss of sight," says Mr. Pulitzer in his public announcement, "have rendered it impossible for me to give personal attention to the conduct of the Post Dispatch. I have not been able even to visit the city for many years past. Authority implies duty. I relinquish duties to which I am no longer equal at a distance, and responsibilities which should only accompany the actual supervision of affairs." There is no more reason why the manager selected should not be allowed to purchase an interest in the company at this crisis in its affairs than that Pulitzer was allowed, in the original organization, to subscribe for a majority of the stock, and thereby secure the power of control. It could make no difference whether the stock was purchased from the company or from the stockholders, provided, of course, that no wrong was done to the company or the other stockholders, or that they gave their unanimous approval. As has been seen, the directors and stockholders, on being informed of the contract, made no objection thereto, but, on the contrary, immediately installed plaintiff as editor, and at a meeting of the stockholders held on the 16th day of March, 1895, by unanimous vote, elected him a director in the corporation. But, to emphasize the ratification, the new board of directors, on the same day, elected him president. So, the contract, in all particulars material to this controversy, was approved and ratified by all the stockholders. Defendants allege that they were not fully advised of all the terms of the agreement, but their action as stockholders and directors shows that they were advised that plaintiff had secured from Pulitzer 1,667 shares of stock, that he was made editor and manager, with control of the publication of the paper, and that he was to be made a director and president; or, if they were not advised, they blindly voted as directed by Pulitzer. If the latter was the case, then surely they ought not to complain. The contract then stands as though it had been made by the unanimous vote of all the stockholders. The only issue involved in this suit relates to the right of plaintiff, under his contract, to manage the paper and control its policy. Whether the stockholders or Pulitzer, who still owns two-thirds of the stock, could be required to elect plaintiff a director, is not involved, and the legality of the contract in that respect requires no consideration. It seems that Pulitzer, and with him the other stockholders, soon repented of the contract, and under a resolution voted by them, over the protest of plaintiff, undertook to modify it in respect to the control plaintiff should have over the policy of the paper. This they had no right to do. A corporation has no more right to repudiate its valid contracts than an individual has.

6. But it is insisted that a court of equity will not interfere to prevent a breach of the agreement in question, though it is the contract of the corporation, and one it had the power to make. It is urged, in the first place, that an injunction should not be granted because plaintiff has an adequate remedy at law in an action for damages in case he is denied the right to edit and manage the paper according to his own judgment; second, that there is a want of mutuality of remedy, without which a court of equity will not decree specific performance; and, third, that the contract, in substance and effect, is a mere employment of plaintiff as editor and manager of the paper, and equity will never compel an employer, against his will, to retain an employé in his service. There can be no doubt of the correctness of these general

propositions, but do they apply to this contract? In other words, would an action for damages afford plaintiff an adequate remedy? Is there such a want of mutuality in the contract as would prevent a court of equity enforcing it against the corporation and its directors? Is plaintiff, under the contract, a mere employé of the corporation, whose rights cannot be protected by a court of equity?

(a) Under the contract, plaintiff purchased 1,667 shares of stock in the corporation, for which he paid $80,000; and, in consideration thereof, he was to have the "control and management" of the Post Dispatch for five years, at an annual salary of $10,000. In addition to his salary, he was entitled to receive the dividends on his stock, which were shown to have been large in previous years, though not satisfactory to Pulitzer. The value of the tangible property of a newspaper is insignificant when compared with its business value and earning power. The value of the stock of such a corporation depends very largely upon the ability with which the business is managed. Plaintiff had confidence in his own ability to manage this paper, for he stipulates that his appointment and salary shall cease unless the net profits, under his management, should stand the tests imposed by Pulitzer. Plaintiff also had a reputation to sustain, and an opportunity to enlarge it. The management of a metropolitan newspaper also gives to the manager a power and influence among men which is estimated by some as beyond a money value. In this respect it is pretium affectionis. Our statute provides that the remedy by injunction "shall exist in all cases where irreparable injury to real or personal property is threatened, and to prevent the doing of any legal wrong whatever, whenever in the opinion of the court an adequate remedy cannot be afforded by an action for damages." Section 5510. In giving construction to the section, this court has held that "the action of injunction may be resorted to, notwithstanding there may be an adequate remedy at law for the injury, in all cases where an adequate remedy cannot be afforded by an action for damages as such." Towne v. Bowers, 81 Mo. 496; Bank v. Kercheval, 65 Mo. 688. It is perfectly manifest that the control and management of the paper was the chief inducement that actuated plaintiff in entering into the agreement. With the acceptance of the position of editor and manager he gave up his situation on "The World," and removed from New York to St. Louis. He invested his entire capital in the enterprise. His stock was held by the corporation in such a manner that he could not use it for any purpose. The control of the paper was, moreover, a property right, in the nature of a lease, which he had the right to enjoy for five years. Its value to him depended upon the success with which it was managed. Mr. Pulitzer, who was at the time president of the corporation, and manager of the paper, in a letter to Mr. Williams, who was then the editor, in explaining the situation and the reason for the change in editorial management, says, "I am convinced that your paper needs a stronger hand and permanent head;" and in his announcement of plaintiff's appointment, made in the columns of the Post Dispatch, he says, "With this day, Col. Charles H. Jones, having acquired a proprietary interest in the Post Dispatch, becomes its editor and manager, with responsibility and control over its columns." It appears perfectly manifest that taking from plaintiff the right to manage and control the paper according to his own judgment could not be compensated in damages. Every other right acquired rests upon the right to control. It would be impossible to anticipate the effect a successful management might have upon the pecuniary value of the paper, and of the corporate stock, to say nothing of the prestige it would give the manager. Our conclusion is that the contract and the rights acquired thereunder are such that a breach of it by defendants cannot be compensated by an action at law for damages.

(b) Is there such a want of mutuality of remedy as will prevent a court of equity from granting injunctive relief? . . . Should plaintiff fail to perform his contract according to the tests provided, and should then persist in controlling the paper, in disregard of the provision that the appointment should cease, there can be no doubt that a court of equity would enjoin his interference, just as it can enjoin an interference with his rights if threatened. Keeping in view all the time that the right to manage and control the newspaper is the matter in issue, it is apparent that the remedy is mutual. . . .

(c) The law is well settled that personal contracts for service will not, because they cannot, be enforced by courts of equity. But we do not view the duties to be performed by plaintiff under the contract as mere personal service or simple employment. In his control and management of the paper he knows no master or employer. He is answerable to no one for the manner of performing his duty. He is accountable only for the stipulated results. His position gives him a property right in the possession, control, and management of the paper he agrees to edit and manage. A reading of the contract will show that the central idea of the executory part of it is the control and management of the paper. That means the possession and use of the property, and not mere employment to write editorials. The judgment of the circuit court is affirmed.

COMMENT

(1) Colonel Jones' success in the courts was deflated by the defeat of his hero, William Jennings Bryan, in the election of 1896. In June 1897 he sold his interest in the Post–Dispatch back to Pulitzer for a return of his $80,000 plus ⅙ of the profits during his tenure. The paper continued to prosper; some of its earnings can doubtless be traced into the Pulitzer Prizes.[9]

(2) In Staklinski v. Pyramid Elec. Co., 6 N.Y.2d 159, 160 N.E.2d 78 (1959), the Court of Appeals upheld an order by an arbitrator, acting under an arbitration clause in an eleven-year employment contract with a substantial salary plus share of profits, that an executive be reinstated in his position. The board of directors had decided that he should be retired for "permanent disability", pursuant to a special clause in the contract. In a sharp dissent JUDGE BURKE said:

"An arbitrators' award of specific performance of a contract for personal services directing the issuance of a mandatory injunction against a foreign employer in behalf of a nonresident employee who has been wrongfully discharged is without precedent and violates settled principles of equity. In such a situation, the courts of this State are not bound to uphold an arbitration award that offends established principles of law and public policy.

"While a public corporation may be liable in damages for a breach of a long-term contract of employment . . . we have found no case wherein a court

9. W.A. Swanberg, Pulitzer (1967).

has decreed specific performance of these contracts. The reason is that equity has traditionally declined to afford such relief . . .

"While no statute expressly defines the arbitrators' powers to grant relief, the provisions of section 1448 of the Civil Practice Act, making valid and enforcible arbitration submissions and contracts, suggests the adoption of the common-law concept of remedies. This follows from the fact that an arbitration submission and agreements to arbitrate must be capable of being the subject of an action . . .

"In this case the mandatory injunction exceeded the powers of the arbitrator and the decree enforcing it violates both the statutory policy confiding to directors the management of public corporations and the principles of equity barring injunctive relief of this nature. We do not believe that, under a general grant of equitable powers, arbitrators may disregard equitable principles and issue an award not possible either at law or equity. As Judge Pound said, dissenting in Matter of Buffalo & Erie Ry. Co., 250 N.Y. 275, 280–281, 165 N.E. 291, 293, 'It by no means follows that the findings of the arbitrators may be enforced by the court by the remedy of specific performance. *No man may be compelled to work for another or to continue another in his employment.* I hold merely that industrial disputes as to future, wages may be submitted to arbitration where the parties so agree.' (Emphasis added.)

"Cases involving collective bargaining agreements are inapposite here. The reason for this conclusion was stated by the United States Supreme Court in J.I. Case Co. v. National Labor Relations Board, 321 U.S. 332, 334–335, 64 S.Ct. 576, 579, 88 L.Ed. 762, wherein the court stated that: 'Collective bargaining between employer and representatives of a unit, usually a union, results in an accord as to terms which will govern hiring and work and pay in that unit. The result is not, however, a contract of employment except in rare cases; no one has a job by reason of it and no obligation to any individual ordinarily comes into existence from it alone. The negotiations between union and management result in what often has been called a trade agreement, rather than a contract of employment.'

"Further, it has become clear both under the State and National Labor Relations Acts, Labor Law, Consol.Laws, c. 31, § 700 et seq., 29 U.S.C.A. § 151 et seq. as well as in arbitration, that, specific performance is frequently essential to maintain and further the collective relationships involved. See Goldman v. Cohen, 222 App.Div. 631, 227 N.Y.S. 311.

"However, the reasons compelling the courts and arbitrators to grant both specific performance and injunctive relief in collective bargaining agreements do not apply to contracts such as the one in question. A decree for the reinstatement of a nonresident manager in a public corporation is subject to all the obstacles and objections equity has always recognized, and is not justified by the special considerations that make this type of relief desirable in the collective bargaining area. . . . To hold otherwise is to state in effect that under this agreement the corporation itself could seek specific performance of a recalcitrant employee and that arbitrators could award specific performance compelling the employee to work for the corporation. Such a result would be clearly undesirable.

"On a motion to confirm an award, the court does not sit as an administrative rubber stamp over an arbitrator's determination, but rather as a court of equity applying equitable principles and enjoys a certain latitude of discretion. . . ."

(3) At the time New York had a statute which, in substance, read like the present § 716 of the Business Corporation Law:

> (a) Any officer elected or appointed by the board may be removed by the board with or without cause . . .

> (b) The removal of an officer without cause shall be without prejudice to his contract rights, if any. The election or appointment of an officer shall not of itself create contract rights.

(4) Many cases about firings hinge on whether the contract of employment had ever been entered into or whether the officer who represented the corporation in making the contract in fact had authority to commit the corporation. This was in fact an issue in Jones v. Williams and will be considered below in connection with the authority of officers in general.

(5) The question of an executive's contractual status may arise as a result of the arrangements made when a former owner-entrepreneur sells out to a large enterprise, arranging to be continued in an executive position of similar scope. In Rudman v. Cowles Communications, Inc.[10] this resulted in a falling out since "the entrepreneur Rudman could not be housebroken to conform to the large multi-million dollar corporate bureaucracy." The court concluded that Rudman had been fired for insubordination, in violation of contract rights when he had only insisted—forcefully—upon retaining the role of executive and supervisor rather than merely editing educational text books.

QUESTIONS

(1) What brought the court in Jones to disregard the general principle that agents, including corporate officers, may be dismissed? Did the political character of the controversy affect the case? Did the power structure of the Pulitzer family or of the publishing company?

(2) Should additional security of tenure be afforded to nonunionized corporate personnel? Should this take the form of a requirement of "cause"? If so, who should determine this? Can "cause" be defined in any useful way? Should such a rule apply to all corporations and, if not, to which ones? Should the protection apply to "political" firings, for example, discharge of an employee who informs the public of the corporation's concealed pollution practices? Or only to off-the-job exercises of political and free speech privileges?

(3) Could a corporation guarantee a prospective executive that he or she would have a tenure of 5 years in that post? What, if anything, does 8 Del.C. § 142 say about this? What of Art. IV § 1 of the by-laws?

(4) Should specific enforcement (reinstatement) be generally available to wrongfully discharged executives? To those whose contracts so specify? What are the problems in calculating monetary damages if that is the relief granted?

A corporate employee has obligations as well as rights involved in his departure—indeed some of his duties extend beyond the termination of his employment. See Restatement, Second, Agency §§ 386, 396.

10. 30 N.Y.2d 1, 330 N.Y.S.2d 33, 280 N.E.2d 867 (1972).

Some of these obligations are illustrated in the following goings-on down on Madison Avenue.

DUANE JONES CO. v. BURKE

Court of Appeals of New York, 1954.
306 N.Y. 172, 117 N.E.2d 237.

[In 1942, Duane Jones founded the Duane Jones Company, Inc. as an advertising agency; he owned the majority of its stock and was either president or chairman of the board. By 1951 it had a gross billing of $9,000,000. It referred each of its principal customers—about 25 of them—to one or more account executives. There was no contract commitment on the part of the company or the customer to continue the relation. There were no formal contracts with plaintiff's employees, either. In 1951 things began to slip. Several large accounts left and various executives resigned. Apparently Mr. Jones was "guilty of certain behaviour lapses" which can be conjectured to have involved alcohol. In June 1951 a number of officers, directors and employees met at the Park Lane Hotel. One Scheideler told the group that several customers had expressed interest in seeing the group buy out Jones or form a new agency. One Hayes was chosen to make an offer to Jones to buy his stock. He told him that if he did not agree there would be an en masse resignation in 24 hours and that the customers had been "already presold." Jones recalled the conversation as follows:

"In other words, you are standing there with a colt .45, holding it at my forehead, and there is not much I can do except give up?", to which Hayes replied: "Well, you can call it anything you want, but that is what we are going to do."

Jones told the employees the next day that he was retiring and wished them "fair winds and following seas." However, the deal was never consummated by Jones, possibly because it was not "advantageous to him tax-wise." On August 7, 1951, various directors resigned but remained as employees and drew salaries. On August 17, the board voted to fire, for cause, roughly the same group of individuals. On August 21, Scheideler, Beck and Werner, Inc., was organized and it opened for business on September 10. Within six weeks 71 of the 132 persons formerly employed by Duane Jones Co. worked for this firm and a large number of the accounts shifted, including Manhattan Soap Co., G.F. Heublein, International Salt, Wesson Oil and The Borden Company. On August 24th Scheideler wrote a letter to "Dear Duane" advising him that a new agency had started and that customers were being invited to shift; Jones testified that this was the first he knew of such invitations. Duane Jones Co. brought suit against various former officers and employees and the Manhattan Soap Co. and one of its officers. A jury verdict dismissed Manhattan and one ex officer who had not joined the new firm. It awarded $300,000 to plaintiff as to the others. The appellate division affirmed, but dismissed the officer of Manhattan Co. The Court of Appeals in an opinion by LEWIS, J., affirmed.]

The foregoing evidence has led us to conclude that the conduct of the individual defendants-appellants as officers, directors or employees of the plaintiff corporation ". . . fell below the standard required by the law of one acting as an agent or employee of another." Lamdin v. Broadway Surface Adv. Corp., 272 N.Y. 133, 138, 5 N.E.2d 66, 67. Each of these defendants was ". . . prohibited from acting in any manner inconsistent with his agency or trust and [was] at all times bound to exercise the utmost good faith and loyalty in the performance of his duties." 272 N.Y. at page 138, 5 N.E.2d at page 67. . . .

The inferences reasonably to be drawn from the record justify the conclusion—reached by the jury and by a majority of the Appellate Division—that the individual defendants-appellants, while employees of plaintiff corporation, determined upon a course of conduct which, when subsequently carried out, resulted in benefit to themselves through destruction of plaintiff's business, in violation of the fiduciary duties of good faith and fair dealing imposed on defendants by their close relationship with plaintiff corporation. . . .

Nor is it a defense to say that the defendants-appellants did not avail themselves of the benefit of the customers and personnel diverted from plaintiff until after defendants had received notice of discharge or had informed plaintiff of their intention to leave Duane Jones Company. Upon this record the jury might have found that the conspiracy originated in June or July while a fiduciary duty existed, and that the benefits realized when defendant Scheideler, Beck & Werner, Inc., commenced operation in September were merely the results of a predetermined course of action. In view of that circumstance, the individual defendants would not be relieved of liability for advantages secured by them, after termination of their employment, as a result of opportunities gained by reason of their employment relationship. . . .

Defendants-appellants also urge as a basis for reversal of the judgment rendered against them, that plaintiff failed sufficiently to establish a causal relationship between damages sustained by plaintiff and the alleged wrongful conduct by the defendants. For this argument defendants rely upon (1) the fact that none of the accounts serviced by plaintiff were under contract to plaintiff agency, and (2) the fact that there is evidence of record from which it may be inferred that plaintiff had "resigned" all of its accounts in August, 1951, prior to the solicitation of such accounts by the individual defendants. Plaintiff was not required to show interference by defendants with existing contractual relationships in order to impose liability in the present action. . . . As was said in Keviczky v. Lorber, 290 N.Y. 297, 306, 49 N.E.2d 146, 150, 146 A.L.R. 1410: " 'An injury to a person's business by procuring others not to deal with him or by getting away his customers, if unlawful means are employed, such as fraud or intimidation, or if done without justifiable cause, is an actionable wrong.' 2 Cooley on Torts, § 230." Moreover, there is evidence of record from which the jury might have inferred that the loss of customers suffered by plaintiff in August and September, 1951, was the direct result of defendants-appellants' activities immediately prior thereto. Plaintiff introduced evidence of the customers it had serviced for varying periods of time prior to June 28, 1951, and which it was then servicing; it established activities by defendants as to demands made upon plaintiff to surrender the business to defendants, accompanied by threats of mass resignation pursuant to a scheme reputed to have been "presold" to the customers; it proved solicitation by defendants of plaintiff's accounts and personnel, and, finally, it established a mass exodus to the corporate defendant of plaintiff's customers and a majority of its key personnel. Upon that state of the record, the jury was entitled to find that plaintiff's losses were a proximate result of defendants' conduct. . . .

With regard to proof of plaintiff's resignation of accounts, we agree with the statement by one of the Justices at the Appellate Division that "The renunciation of accounts by Jones is of no conclusive significance, if we credit, as apparently the jury did, that Jones was then in a position in which, as he described it, 'a gun' was being held to his head." 281 App.Div. 629, 121 N.Y.S.2d 115. On the record before us the jury could have found that Jones' action was only an intermediate result of defendants' predetermined conduct which, when carried to completion, resulted in the ultimate acquisition by defendant Scheideler, Beck & Werner, Inc., of the accounts formerly serviced by plaintiff. . . .

COMMENT

(1) While Duane Jones Co. v. Burke [11] involves a conspiracy among several officers and directors, a single corporate executive may be liable if he tries to take with him something to which he is not entitled. A classic instance of this is the "Space Suit case." [12] There an Ohio court enjoined one Wohlgemuth who had been hired away from B.F. Goodrich by International Latex from revealing or using confidential information relating to space suits. He had acquired this data while department head at Goodrich Latex which had just gotten the Project Apollo suit contract. The transfer involved a handsome salary increase. When Goodrich protested to Wohlgemuth in the name of company loyalty and ethics, he replied that "loyalty and ethics had their price; insofar as he was concerned, International Latex was paying the price."

(2) Alongside corporation and agency rules, several other bodies of law become involved in executive departure cases. Frequently the thrust of the complaint is that the departing employees took with them the property of the corporation. It is quite evident that they are not allowed to take the electric typewriters, copying machines, etc. Subtler questions affect the taking of plans, drawings and lists and other "trade secrets." [13] Courts have tended to draw a line between what one can take with one in one's head and what one has to have in writing. While this is only a crude way of dividing knowledge which is special to that business and that which is part of one's general background, it has the advantage of administrative convenience. Finally, it is a widespread practice for corporations to seek to enhance their leverage by spelling out in the employment contract the employee's duties upon departure. The courts have long scrutinized such restrictive covenants with care, understanding that they are restraints on competition even if sometimes desirable. They have permitted them only if reasonable in their coverage of (1) time, (2) area and (3) the type of activity. Indeed it is sometimes not clear whether the court is allowing the employer to impose more stringent conditions by means of

11. Limitations on the scope of Duane Jones are suggested by Town & Country House & Home Services, Inc. v. Newbery, 3 N.Y.2d 554, 170 N.Y.S.2d 328, 147 N.E.2d 724 (1958).

12. B.F. Goodrich Co. v. Wohlgemuth, 117 Ohio App. 493, 192 N.E.2d 99 (1963). There is an entertaining summary of this case in J. Brooks, Business Adventures ch. 11 (1969).

13. There was a time when lawyers feared that the Supreme Court would find that the federal patent power would be held to supersede trade secret law. But see Kewanee Oil Co. v. Bicron Corp., 416 U.S. 470, 94 S.Ct. 1879, 40 L.Ed.2d 315 (1974).

a contract than the court would impose in any case by applying fiduciary principles.[14]

PROBLEM

Apricot Company is a significant new actor in the world of computers, in particular of those involved with graphic displays. Three of its officers consult you about leaving this firm, which surprises you a bit because the company has been regarded by the outside world, including the securities markets, as an extraordinarily successful enterprise and a model for other entrepreneurs over the five years it has been operating. Baker is vice president and general manager of operations at Apricot, Coustance is an inventor who played a substantial role in designing the two computers on which Apricot's prosperity is built and Dartagnan is treasurer of the firm.

They advise you that they would like to start a new company to exploit an idea of Coustance's. They believe that it will be possible to market at a reasonable price a printer that will put on paper the multi-colored graphics that appear on the screen of a variety of computers now on the market. At present printers are exceedingly complex and expensive. The new model could be sold to a wide variety of commercial and artistic users and ought to be a major breakthrough. Coustance has done some preliminary work towards developing this machine but has not spoken about it to any of the other employees of Apricot except for Baker and Dartagnan. They regard the idea as quite separate from the products that Apricot has been making to date and assure you that none of Apricot's patents would be infringed by the new device.

Embarking on this new enterprise would be a costly and complex operation. They would be reluctant to plunge into it and give up their comfortable positions at Apricot unless they could be sure that three conditions were in place: (1) they had financial backing which they propose to assure by getting commitments from a venture capital firm which has been helpful to Apricot in its early stages and with which Dartagnan has good connections; (2) they can take with them a small nucleus of designers who can carry out Coustance's ideas and (3) have some assurance that the product will be bought preferably to the extent of a few firm contracts for the first machines made.

Asking a few preliminary questions, you discover that only Baker has a contractual commitment to Apricot, one which expires in six months. It contains a clause saying that if Baker leaves the firm Baker may not work in the computer industry for five years following departure. They feel quite confident that the firm will prosper despite their leaving but say that Eldrige, the president of Apricot, will not be happy at their leaving and is apt to do everything possible to make life difficult for them.

What advice do you give the trio about the legality of their departure? About the things to avoid as they carry out their plan? What further information do you need from them?

Bibliography: The development of limitations on the employment-at-will doctrine is treated in Glendon & Lev, Changes in the Bonding of the Employment Relationship: An Essay on the New Property, 20 B.C.L.Rev. 457 (1979); Summers, The Contract of Employment and the Rights of Individual Employees, 52 Fordham L.Rev. 1082 (1984); Finkin, The Bureaucratization of Work:

----

14. See, e.g., Reed, Roberts Associates, Inc. v. Strauman, 40 N.Y.2d 303, 386 N.Y.S.2d 677, 353 N.E.2d 590 (1976).

Employee Policies and Contract Law, 1986 Wisc.L.Rev. 732. On covenants not to compete see Harty, Competition between Employer and Employee, Drafting and Enforcing Restrictive Covenants in Employment Agreements, 35 Drake L.Rev. 261 (1985–86).

---

4. Executive Compensation

The compensation of top level management raises important questions of theory and is of considerable practical significance to boards of directors and others. Thus it deserves analysis even though case law involving challenges to compensation on corporate law grounds in large corporations is thin. In fact, corporate compensation has become a specialty of its own, more closely allied to tax law than to corporations.

The theoretical problems of compensation start when the firm rises above the simple arrangement in which each member (partner, as it were) commits equal amounts of time and capital to the enterprise and draws equivalent shares of the firm's overall net. As soon as one partner retires from active work the question of the relative "draw" of capital and services arises. While face-to-face bargainers are ready to grapple with this problem there are special difficulties when the capital side of the corporation is represented by thousands of dispersed shareholders. Can the board of directors effectively bargain on their behalf? This is another place where devotees of the market as a solvent of problems call that institution into play. Is there a market for managers? The answer, I believe, is that there is a market but that it is so peculiar a market that it is unsafe to delegate to it untrammeled responsibility for price setting. Note some of the peculiarities. At this level the "goods" are very different. One might quote new MBA's at a general price "F.O.B. business school" but experienced managers have developed specialized skills and demonstrated their individual capacities to such an extent that they are non-standardized, non-interchangeable commodities. The needs of the corporation are individualized also. Thus news about what X is being paid at A Corporation does not help B Corporation to decide what to pay Y in the way that the stock ticker helps other buyers and sellers of B's stock. Other factors complicate the market. Many posts are filled not by hiring from the outside but by promoting from within, even though there is more mobility than there used to be. It is perceived that employing a marginally better manager might increase the earnings of a division by a very large amount over the results of the next best candidate. Thus a firm might bid very high to get the person it thought was best. Meanwhile the "excess" component of management compensation in a large corporation is apt to turn out to be trivially small as compared with the price of the product. Overpaying a General Motors executive by $1 million would cost less than $1 per car sold, not a significant competitive factor.

The sensitivity of high-level compensation issues is intensified by the very large sums that are involved and that receive a great deal of publicity. Each spring after the revelation of compensation for the highest-paid executives of publicly owned corporations the figures are compiled by Forbes and Business Week. Each year the highest figure is more generous than the year before. For a long time there seemed to be a barrier at $1 million. That barrier was broken in the 1980's as such executives as T. Boone Pickens accepted compensation packages in the $5 million range and in 1987 Iacocca received $16 million from Chrysler. These figures can be slightly misleading in that they may involve pay-offs on long term compensation schemes that represent years of effort. They are not equivalent in after-tax purchasing power to the amounts received in the Rogers v. Hill case below. Still, particularly after the market crash of October 1987, they do arouse comment and envy. In part they cause raised eyebrows because they are so far in excess of the sums paid to public sector executives who manage departments that involve every bit as much responsibility.

The basic corporation law attacks upon the quantum of compensation center around the familiar concepts of (1) self-dealing and (2) "waste". Thus the principles, discussed in Chapter VII above, as to contracts between directors and their corporations apply to the employment contracts of director-officers. Where a "disinterested quorum" rule is in effect, a court may well find that rule not satisfied where the officer-directors *seriatim* act upon one another's salaries, each withdrawing graciously in turn.[15] However, there may be no identity of personnel on the two sides if there is a wholly outside board or if compensation is fixed by a committee consisting entirely of outside board members. In such cases the only issue open is that of "waste", a concept of disproportion somehow more extreme than mere unfairness, suggesting that what has happened has been in the nature of a gift. The orthodox body of corporate compensation law has also given prominence to questions of retroactivity. Clearly a corporation cannot pay a director money at the end of a year solely for past services; that would be a gift since the firm need not pay it in order to get what it already has. The situation is complicated by the fact that the officer may have been performing services with the expectation of receiving some salary of an amount to be determined at the end of the period. Or she may have been expecting something beyond the salary fixed for his position. Courts have tended to assume that, unless there is quite a clear understanding, a director serves without expectation of compensation, perhaps even if she is also serving as an officer or makes special contributions beyond those services to be expected of a director. There is an obsolete quality to all of this learning but it is important that you bear in mind the need to draft compensation agreements to allow for it and tie pay to future services rather than to the past.

15. Stoiber v. Miller Brewing Co., 257 Wis. 13, 42 N.W.2d 144 (1950).

Aside from the possibility of derivative litigation, which has been rare in recent years, with the exception of suits about surprisingly small salaries in smaller corporations, there are several restraints.[16] First of all, the proxy rules require quite full and detailed disclosure of compensation. This, coupled with a lively interest on the part of the more vocal shareholder activists, tends to induce managers to exercise some restraint. Second, there is the possibility that the Internal Revenue Service under § 162(a) might conclude that corporate salaries had exceeded the level of a reasonable and hence the permissible deduction; there are in fact more such cases on the books than there are corporate cases. One of these, Home Interiors, is reproduced below.

After the issue of quantum come the questions of form. To a large extent questions of the form of compensation have been driven by the current state of the federal tax rules. When top brackets were in the 20% range, as at the time of Rogers v. Hill, executives cared little about these matters. During the period when the top bracket was over 90% taxes mattered a great deal. There was pressure to channel compensation into forms that benefited from the deduction granted to capital gains (such as in favored stock option arrangements) or that would postpone receipt and taxability to some later time when the executive would be retired and in a lower bracket (pensions, deferred compensation, etc.) The change in 1970 to a system in which the top bracket on "earned income" was placed at 50% encouraged cash payments. The tax reform of 1986 both eliminated the favored treatment shown to capital gains and, by reducing the top level of tax to only 28%, took the edge off the whole tax-avoidance problem (and in particular made postponement of receipts to a later point not particularly useful). The fact that after 1986 the corporate tax rate was higher than the personal had some impact on the tax planning of smaller corporations where the investor and executive roles were held by the same persons. The corporation for its part has interests in shaping the form of compensation so as to achieve its own strategy. It will seek to assure deductibility of its outlays as they are paid. It will wish to ensure that the terms of any incentive program do in fact achieve what they are supposed to do: provide the recipients with motivation for pursuing the best interests of the stockholders and thus of the corporation rather than personal welfare maximization. It will wish to see that the corporation retains the services of the executives it depends on but leaves some flexibility in ridding itself of those that prove unsuitable.

Executive compensation, particularly as it involves pension plans, has become a highly complex and specialized field, with more ties to the law of federal income taxation than to corporation law. The specialist will have to take into account other fields of law—anti-discrimination provisions, economic stabilization rules (when in force) and others. If you become involved in negotiating such contracts you should also be

---

16. The newspapers have reported an occasional settlement involving a major corporation. See, e.g., N.Y. Times, July 15, 1976, p. 49, col. 2 (reduction of Meshulam Riklis' salary from $375,000 to $350,000).

aware of the lurking dangers of conflict of interest. It is easy as counsel for the corporation to fall into the role of advising an executive, perhaps a person whom you have come to know well in the course of working together on behalf of the corporation. The interests of the executive and of the corporation will seem to be in harmony. However, the executive's interests and those of the corporation can become sharply adverse, as in the case of a discharge or a sudden departure to a competitor. The lawyer for the corporation may, for one thing, be held to have estopped the corporation by erroneous advice given as to the meaning of the contract.[17]

The primary forms of remuneration may be listed as follows:

(1) cash salary at a stated level;

(2) cash bonuses geared to a percentage of corporate earnings (discussed in Rogers v. Hill);

(3) plans calling for the issue of stock to executives either solely in return for their services or for a cash price less than the market;

(4) deferred compensation in which cash payments are to be made after the employee's peak income years, generally with a provision about his then availability for consulting purposes designed to help prevent the sums involved from being taxed currently;

(5) pension plans providing for payments after retirement;

(6) stock option programs under which employees are given the right to purchase the corporation's stock, usually at its current market price, in the contemplation that they will exercise the right when—perhaps through their efforts—it has risen substantially (see Pogostin v. Rice p. 344, infra);

(7) "phantom stock" plans in which the recipients do not have to buy stock but are credited with a given number of units each equivalent to a share of stock and receives cash equivalents to the dividends and increments in market value that those shares would have brought them (see Berkwitz v. Humphrey, infra);

(8) fringe benefits of various kinds, including use of corporate vehicles and aircraft, vacations at company lodges, hospitalization at corporate expense. Both the Treasury and the SEC have indicated an unfriendly interest in these "perks", for example those bestowed upon Hugh Hefner in Playboy Enterprises, CCH Sec.L.Rep. ¶ 82,635 (S.E.C.1980).

---

17. Cf. Gediman v. Anheuser Busch, Inc., 299 F.2d 537 (2d Cir.1962).

ROGERS v. HILL

Supreme Court of the United States, 1933.
289 U.S. 582, 53 S.Ct. 731, 77 L.Ed. 1385, 88 A.L.R. 744.

MR. JUSTICE BUTLER delivered the opinion of the Court.

The American Tobacco Company is a corporation organized under the laws of New Jersey. The petitioner, plaintiff below, acquired in 1916 and has since been the owner of 200 shares of its common stock. He also has 400 shares of common stock B. In accordance with by-law XII,[18] adopted by the stockholders at their annual meeting, March 13, 1912, the company for many years has annually paid its president and vice presidents large amounts in addition to their fixed salaries and other sums allowed them as compensation for services.[19]

Hill	Salary	Cash Credits	By-Law	
1921			$ 89,833.84	
1922			82,902.61	
1923			77,336.54	Vice President
1924			88,894.26	
1925			97,059.38	
1926	$ 75,000		188,643.45	
1927	75,000		268,761.45	
1928	75,000		280,203.68	President
1929	144,500	$136,507.71	447,870.30	
1930	168,000	273,470.76	842,507.72	

18. "Section 1. As soon as practicable after the end of the year 1912 and of each year of the company's operations thereafter, the Treasurer of the Company shall ascertain the net profits, as hereinafter defined, earned by the Company during such year, and, if such net profits exceed the sum of $8,222,245.82, which is the estimated amount of such net profits earned during the year 1910 by the business that now belong to the Company, the Treasurer shall pay an amount equal in the aggregate to 10 per cent. of such excess to the President and five Vice–Presidents of the Company in the following proportions, to wit: One-fourth thereof, or 2½ per cent. of such amount, to the President; one-fifth of the remainder or 1½ per cent. of such amount, to each of the five Vice–Presidents as salary for the year, in addition to the fixed salary of each of said officers. . . .

"Section 3. For the purpose of this By–Law the net profits earned by the Company in any year shall consist of the net earnings made by the Company in its business as a manufacturer and seller of tobacco and its products after deducting all expenses and losses, such provisions as shall

be determined by the Board of Directors of the Company for depreciation and for all outstanding trade obligations, and an additional amount equal to 6 per cent. dividends on $52,459,400 of its 6 per cent. preferred stock, to which profits shall be added, or from which profits shall be deducted, as the case may be, the Company's proportion (based on its stock holdings) of the net profits or losses for the year of its subsidiary companies engaged in the manufacture and sale of smoking tobacco, chewing tobacco, cigarettes, or little cigars, except earnings on preference shares of British–American Tobacco, Limited, and shares of Imperial Tobacco Company (of Great Britain and Ireland), Limited. . . .

"Section 5. This By–Law may be modified or repealed only by the action of the stockholders of the Company and not by the directors."

19. The statement below shows for the years specified the amounts alleged to have been paid by the company to the named defendants as salary, credits, and under by-law XII.

Neily	**Salary**	**Cash Credits**	**By–Law**
1929	$ 33,333.32	$ 44,897.89	$115,141.87
1930	50,000.00	89,945.52	409,495.25

Riggio			
1929	$ 33,333.32	$ 45,351.40	$115,141.87
1930	50,000.00	90,854.06	409,495.25

Plaintiff maintains that the by-law is invalid and that, even if valid, the amounts paid under it are unreasonably large and therefore subject to revision by the courts. In March, 1931, he demanded that the company bring suit against the officers who have received such payments to compel them to account to the company for all or such part thereof as the court may hold illegal. The company, insisting that such a suit would be without basis in law or fact, refused to comply with his demand. He brought suit in the Supreme Court of New York against the president and some of the vice presidents to require them so to account, and joined the company as defendant. The case was removed to the federal court for the Southern District of New York. In May, 1931, plaintiff brought suit in that court against Taylor, a vice president, not a defendant in the earlier suit, to require him to account and made the company defendant. The cases were consolidated, plaintiff filed an amended complaint and defendants answered. The officers of the company now before the court are Hill, the president, Neiley, Riggio, and Taylor, vice presidents. The answer, after admissions, denials, and explanations, asserts several separate defenses.

Plaintiff made a motion on the pleadings for judgment that the separate defenses be stricken, the by-law be adjudged invalid, and defendants Hill, Neiley, and Riggio be required to account for amounts so paid them and that further payments be enjoined; and in the alternative that such payments be restrained pendente lite. After argument upon the motion, the court, without decision upon any other question, granted a temporary injunction. Defendants appealed, the Circuit Court of Appeals reversed the interlocutory order and directed that a mandate issue to the District Court "in accordance with this decree." See 60 F.(2d) 109. The mandate directed further proceedings in accordance with "the decision." On the coming down of the mandate, the District Court vacated the temporary injunction and dismissed the bills of complaint upon the merits. Plaintiff appealed, the Circuit Court of Appeals affirmed [62 F.(2d) 1079], citing its opinion on the former appeal, and this court granted plaintiff's petition for writ of certiorari. . . .

Plaintiff suggests that, because the by-law purports to direct payments out of profits, it violates charter provisions which he construes to require the directors to apply all profits to the acquisition of property and the payment of dividends. We need not examine the charter for the contention rests upon a misapprehension of the meaning of "profits" as used in the by-law. As there defined it includes the sums to be paid to the president and vice presidents. Compensation to an officer for his services constitutes a part of operating expenses deductible from earnings in order to ascertain net profits. It is immaterial whether such compensation is a fixed salary or depends in whole or in part upon earnings. There is no conflict between the charter and the by-law.

Bennett v. Millville Improvement Co., 67 N.J.Law, 320, 323, 51 A. 706; Booth v. Beattie, 95 N.J.Eq. 776, 118 A. 257, 123 A. 925.

It follows from what has been shown that when adopted the by-law was valid. But plaintiff alleges that the measure of compensation fixed by it is not now equitable or fair. And he prays that the court fix and determine the fair and reasonable compensation of the individual defendants, respectively, for each of the years in question. The allegations of the complaint are not sufficient to permit consideration by the court of the validity or reasonableness of any of the payments on account of fixed salaries or of special credits or of the allotments of stock therein mentioned. Indeed, plaintiff alleges that other proceedings have been instituted for the restoration of special credits, and his suits to invalidate the stock allotments were recently considered here. Rogers v. Guaranty Trust Co., 288 U.S. 123, 53 S.Ct. 295, 77 L.Ed. 652. The only payments that plaintiff by this suit seeks to have restored to the company are the payments made to the individual defendants under the by-law.

We come to consider whether these amounts are subject to examination and revision in the District Court. As the amounts payable depend upon the gains of the business, the specified percentages are not per se unreasonable. The by-law was adopted in 1912 by an almost unanimous vote of the shares represented at the annual meeting and presumably the stockholders supporting the measure acted in good faith and according to their best judgment. The tabular statement in the margin shows the payments to individual defendants under the by-law. Plaintiff does not complain of any made prior to 1921. Regard is to be had to the enormous increase of the company's profits in recent years. The 2½ per cent. yielded President Hill $447,870.30 in 1929 and $842,507.72 in 1930. The 1½ per cent. yielded to each of the vice presidents, Neiley and Riggio, $115,141.86 in 1929 and $409,495.25 in 1930 and for these years payments under the by-law were in addition to the cash credits and fixed salaries shown in the statement.

While the amounts produced by the application of the prescribed percentages give rise to no inference of actual or constructive fraud, the payments under the by-law have by reason of increase of profits become so large as to warrant investigation in equity in the interest of the company. Much weight is to be given to the action of the stockholders, and the by-law is supported by the presumption of regularity and continuity. But the rule prescribed by it cannot, against the protest of a shareholder, be used to justify payments of sums as salaries so large as in substance and effect to amount to spoliation or waste of corporate property. The dissenting opinion of Judge Swan indicates the applicable rule: "If a bonus payment has no relation to the value of services for which it is given, it is in reality a gift in part, and the majority stockholders have no power to give away corporate property against the protest of the minority." 60 F.(2d) 109, 113. The facts alleged by plaintiff are sufficient to require that the District Court, upon a consideration of all the relevant facts brought forward by the parties, determine whether and to what extent payments to the individual defendants under the by-laws constitute misuse and waste of the money of the corporation. . . .

The separate defenses set up in the answer to the amended complaint are: Failure of plaintiff to comply with Equity Rule 27 (28 U.S. C.A. § 723), ratification, forum non conveniens, laches, and that the payments were justified. As they were not passed on below, we refrain from expressing opinion concerning them. The decree of the Circuit Court of Appeals is reversed, the decree of the District Court dismissing the bills on the merits is vacated, and the case is remanded to the District Court with directions to reinstate its decree granting injunction pendente lite and for further proceedings in conformity with this opinion.

It is so ordered.

COMMENT

(1) Rogers v. Hill was one of a series of cases involving the rather handsomely rewarded officers of the American Tobacco Company. Of these the most famous was George Washington Hill, an aggressive and innovative figure in the development of modern advertising, along with Albert Lasker whose advertising firm was closely associated with American Tobacco. A companion case Rogers v. Guaranty Trust Co.[20] challenged the company's stock bonus plan. As in the Hill case, the Court of Appeals ruled for the defendants, in that case on the basis that a New York federal court should not have assumed jurisdiction over a case involving the internal affairs of a New Jersey corporation. In the Guaranty Trust case the Supreme Court affirmed. Justice Stone wrote a scathing dissent on the merits. He stated that the stock bonus plan was not really a plan since as submitted to the shareholders it gave no details as to who was to receive what. A statement that director-officers would not be *excluded* from the plan was as close as it came to revealing that they would be the chief beneficiaries.

(2) The Court of Appeals opinion in each of the Rogers cases was written by Judge Martin Manton—for a divided court. It was later discovered that while the cases were docketed in the Court of Appeals, Judge Manton had solicited through defendants' counsel a $250,000 loan for a close business associate of his, which loan was extended via the company's advertising firm and was never repaid. Judge Manton resigned and was convicted on other charges. A partner in an important Wall Street firm was disbarred for having arranged the loan.[21]

(3) Although the settlement of Rogers v. Hill after the Supreme Court's ruling resulted in savings to the company of some $8,500,000, seven other stockholders unsuccessfully challenged the arrangement as unduly favorable, asserting that the $525,000 fee paid Rogers was a bribe. Thereafter, they brought a separate action, Heller v. Boylan,[22] challenging the bonus payments in later years—through 1939. Judge Collins rejected the attack but was obviously uncomfortable with the large compensation figures (Hill's own share went down to $137,000 in 1933 but was back up to $420,000 by 1939). He noted that "the unemployed might regard them as fantastic, if not criminal." Yet, he resignedly stated that the court's business "is not the revamping of the social or economic order" and found that he could not establish a "rational or just gauge" or "blueprint" for pruning these salaries. He did, however, order restoration of $2,000,000 representing various errors in calculating or applying the bonus formula plus $150,000 of attorneys' fees which he found had been

20. 288 U.S. 123, 53 S.Ct. 295, 77 L.Ed. 652 (1933).

21. In re Levy, 30 F.Supp. 317 (S.D.N.Y. 1939).

22. 29 N.Y.S.2d 653 (1941), aff'd without opinion 263 App.Div. 815, 32 N.Y.S.2d 131 (1st Dept. 1941).

paid by the company when they should have been paid by the individual defendants who primarily gained thereby.

(4) The 1920's saw a number of very generous arrangements which may have seemed justifiable to the participants in view of the high level of corporate prosperity in general and of their own firm's earnings in particular. During the rude awakening of the 1930's these arrangements were challenged in a series of bruising lawsuits. One of the most famous was the National City Bank Case [23] in which it turned out that Mr. Mitchell, its president, had been receiving from $1,100,000 to $1,300,000 a year at the peak. His own views were expressed as follows:[24]

"Unless the man of energy and perhaps ability can see within the organization for which he is working a point that he can possibly reach that has great material benefit attached to it, I say unless he can see that, . . . that his work is going to be somewhat dulled . . . . That entire organization was spurred to endeavor by a general knowledge that pervaded the institution that I was receiving a very substantial compensation."

Another famous case involved General Motors which had paid individuals compensation up to $500,000, a figure which the court found not excessive in and of itself.[25]

HOME INTERIORS & GIFTS, INC. v. COMMISSIONER OF INTERNAL REVENUE

United States Tax Court, 1980.
73 T.C. 1142.

[The Commissioner of Internal Revenue determined deficiencies in the income taxes of Home Interiors & Gifts, Inc. (Home Interiors) a Texas corporation, Mr. & Mrs. Crowley and Mr. and Mrs. Carter for years 1971 through 1975. The Commissioner's theory was that sums paid by Home Interiors to Mrs. Crowley, Mr. Carter and another officer, Andrew Horner, were in excess of reasonable compensation for services rendered by them, under then section 162(a)(1) of the Internal Revenue Code. If these sums were not reasonable compensation then Home Interiors was not entitled to deduct them in calculating its net income for the years 1974 and 1975 and the individuals were not entitled to use the 50% ceiling on the tax on earned income (as opposed to dividends, etc.) then in force.

Home Interiors was formed by Mrs. Crowley in 1957 to conduct a business of selling home decorations and accessories through the "hostess plan". Under this system the sales representative or displayer would take the products to the homes of cooperating hostesses who would invite potential customers to their homes. The displayer made money by buying the goods from Home Interiors at wholesale prices and selling at retail. Mrs. Crowley had become familiar with this method through her work at other companies that used it. She left that employment in 1957 and with $41,100 of capital from her own

23. Gallin v. National City Bank, 152 Misc. 679, 273 N.Y.S. 87 (1934).

24. Quoted at 2 G. Washington & H. Rothschild, Compensating the Corporate Executive 890 (3d ed. 1962).

25. Winkelman v. General Motors Corp., 44 F.Supp. 960 (S.D.N.Y.1942).

funds and from family and friends started Home Interiors. Mrs. Crowley worked very hard at making the firm a success. She wrote the sales materials and conducted retreats and seminars for displayers and managers. She did much personal counseling as well as selecting them for promotion. Mr. Carter, Mrs. Crowley's son, started with Home Interiors in 1963 after working for IBM. He was basically responsible for the design and procurement of merchandise and the operation of the distribution process. He was also treasurer and controller.

The figures show that these efforts were highly successful. In 1968 Home Interiors grossed $518,000 and netted $27,531 before taxes. In 1971, the first contested year, it earned $21,000,000 gross and brought $2,370,000 down to net income. By 1975, the end of the contested period, its gross was $97,584,000 and its net $12,740,000. During a period when GNP and retail sales went up 2.4 times and corporate profits 1.8 times Home Interior's sales increased over 79 times and profits more than 600 times. Retained earnings grew to $15,333,000 although there were substantial dividends paid after 1970. During the period of context Mrs. Crowley owned 27% of the company's stock and Mr. Carter 19%. The stock's book value grew from $1.27 per share in 1969 to $26.62 in 1975.

Compensation was set by the board of directors. Mr. and Mrs. Crowley, Mr. Carter, Mr. Horner and five other unrelated persons made up the board. Mrs. Crowley received a salary of $300 a month and Mr. Carter $200 a month. However, they also received commissions—2% of gross sales in her case and a commission of 2%. Both of their commissions were reduced in 1973–75 to 1.1875%. Mrs. Crowley's total compensation for the contested years was as follows:

1971	566,364
1972	935,455
1973	1,082,840
1974	1,556,755
1975	1,137,029

Mr. Carter's compensation totalled slightly less each year. The court made various comparisons with the highest paid executives of U.S. public companies, noting that the five highest paid executives in U.S. corporations received between $580,000 and $87,500 in a given year. It noted that top compensation packages for the biggest U.S. retailers' CEOs' ranged from $254,000 to $550,000, in firms that had revenues of up to $10 billion (e.g., Sears Roebuck).

After an elaborate statement of the facts, the Court in an opinion by JUDGE SIMPSON concluded:]

In deciding reasonable compensation cases, the courts have established the propositions that whether the compensation was reasonable is a question to be resolved on the basis of an examination of all the facts and circumstances of the case.

. . .

The determination of the Commissioner is presumptively correct, and the burden of proving the reasonableness of the compensation is upon the petitioners. Botany Worsted Mills v. United States, 278 U.S. 282 (1929). The factors considered relevant in determining reasonableness of compensation include: "the employee's qualifications; the nature, extent and scope of the employee's work; the size and complexities of the business; a comparison of salaries paid with the gross income and the net income; the prevailing general economic conditions; comparison of salaries with distributions to stockholders; the prevailing rates of compensation for comparable positions in comparable concerns; the salary policy of the taxpayer as to all employees; and in the case of small corporations with a limited number of officers the amount of compensation paid to the particular employee in previous years. * * *" [Mayson Mfg. Co. v. Commissioner, 178 F.2d 115, 119 (6th Cir. 1949), revg. a Memorandum Opinion of this Court.]

. . .

No single factor is decisive; rather, we must consider and weigh the totality of facts and circumstances in arriving at our decision. *Mayson Mfg. Co. v. Commissioner*, supra. Where officers-shareholders, who are in control of a corporation, set their own compensation, careful scrutiny is required to determine whether the alleged compensation is in fact a distribution of profits.

. . .

At trial, the Commissioner and the petitioners presented expert testimony to support their positions. The Commissioner's expert and Hay Associates which employs him are recognized experts in designing plans of executive compensation, and the expert presented a carefully prepared report and testimony on the compensation which he considered reasonable for the officers of Home Interiors. His conclusions were primarily based on . . . the "Hay method." Under such method, the expert first interviewed Mrs. Crowley, Mr. Carter, and Mr. Horner to learn about the operations of Home Interiors and the roles they performed in such operations. Then, with that information, he determined, from a survey of approximately 800 companies, the highest amounts those companies paid to employees in positions requiring similar skill, responsibility, and creativity. To check the results obtained by use of the Hay method, the expert also conducted a "market price analysis" of 6 other direct selling companies and 10 other high growth companies with respect to which information was available. He computed the ratio between the compensation paid to the chief executive officers of such other companies and the sales and profits of such companies, and he applied that ratio to the sales and profits of Home Interiors. As a result, he found that the compensation which would be payable to the officers of Home Interiors under the market price analysis was substantially less than the amounts of compensation which he had found by use of the Hay method. Finally, the Commissioner's expert was of the opinion that the following amounts represented reasonable compensation for the officers of Home Interiors:

Year	Mrs. Crowley	Mr. Carter	Mr. Horner
1971	$198,000	$159,000	$ 88,000
1972	248,000	190,000	96,000
1973	268,000	218,000	108,000
1974	338,000	265,000	143,000
1975	411,000	293,000	173,000

In his brief, the Commissioner modified the position taken by him in the notices of deficiency and conceded that the amounts of compensation which his expert found to be reasonable for Mrs. Crowley, Mr. Carter, and Mr. Horner are reasonable nondeferred compensation within the meaning of section 162(a)(1). He also conceded that profit-sharing contributions of 15 percent of such amounts are reasonable and deductible under section 404(a).

The petitioners' experts adopted a different approach. They did not undertake to determine what specific amounts of compensation were reasonable for the officers of Home Interiors; instead, they examined the financial reports of Home Interiors, and compared the amount of compensation paid to its officers with its sales and profits. They selected 18 other companies which they considered to be comparable because those companies were of medium size and involved managers with unusual skills. When they compared the amount of earnings which Home Interiors allocated to the payment of executive compensation with the similar information of the other companies, they concluded that Home Interiors was not paying excessive executive compensation. In reaching their conclusion, the experts also pointed out that Home Interiors' performance over the years was extraordinary.

We have here a most unusual case: the amounts of compensation paid the officers of Home Interiors were very large, but their efforts produced extraordinary results for Home Interiors and everyone connected with it. However measured, the success of Home Interiors was very impressive. . . . Its gross sales in 1968 were $4,284,456 and in 1975, $97,583,835; thus, during such period, the gross sales increased almost 23 times, or at an average annual rate of 57 percent. The after-tax earnings of Home Interiors in 1968 were $60,094 and in 1975, $6,858,947; thus, during such period, such earnings increased 114 times, or at an average annual rate of 110 percent. When the performance of Home Interiors is compared with the growth in the GNP and with sales of retail establishments generally, the results are equally impressive: in 1971 through 1975, the GNP increased about 43 percent; retail store sales generally, about 44 percent; but Home Interiors' sales, 360 percent. What is more, we are convinced that the extraordinary success of Home Interiors was no accident, nor was it merely due to the generally favorable economic conditions prevailing in the 1960's and 1970's.

Mrs. Crowley spent most of a day on the stand as a witness, and it is clear that she possesses rare talent. . . . The profitability of Home Interiors depended upon its sales, and after hearing her describe her policies and practices in leading Home Interiors, we can understand how she was able to recruit a sales organization of over 17,000 by 1975, why the organization was motivated to produce such exceptional results, and why there was little turnover in personnel. . . . We doubt that she could have been replaced.

Mr. Carter also made immense contributions to the success of Home Interiors. Its greatest increase in sales and profitability occurred from 1968 through 1977, a period beginning shortly after he assumed a significant role in managing the affairs of the company. His responsibilities were many and varied. He assisted significantly in conducting the rallies and other activities designed to inspire the sales organization, and he wisely managed the inventory and arranged for the design of products which would have a wide appeal. . . .

Mr. Horner's responsibilities were more limited, but his compensation was also considerably less. . . .

Though Mrs. Crowley, Mr. Carter, and Mr. Horner received large amounts of compensation, the other key employees of Home Interiors also received munificent compensation during the years in issue. . . . [I]n 1975, one area manager received $295,000 in commissions and . . . the average commissions received by an area manager in that year were $226,000. Similarly, the highest commissions of a branch manager in that year were $271,000, and the average for a branch manager for that year was $141,000. Although the area and branch managers were required to pay most of their business expenses out of their commissions, we have found that those expenses averaged around one-third of such commissions; thus, even when those expenses are subtracted, those managers were left with very handsome compensation. Moreover, the compensation of those managers actually increased at approximately the same rate during the years in issue as did the compensation of Mrs. Crowley, Mr. Carter, and Mr. Horner: the aggregate nondeferred compensation of Mrs. Crowley, Mr. Carter, and Mr. Horner rose from $954,091.74 in 1971 to $2,223,384 in 1975—an increase of approximately 133 percent. Whereas, the average commissions of an area manager increased from $103,000 in 1971 to $226,000 in 1975—an increase of 119 percent; and the average commissions of a branch manager increased from $59,000 in 1971 to $141,000 in 1975— an increase of 140 percent.

In judging the reasonableness of the compensation received by Mrs. Crowley, Mr. Carter, and Mr. Horner, it is also significant that all key employees of Home Interiors were compensated on the basis of commissions and that the use of such method of compensation was a longstanding practice of the company. Section 1.162–7(b)(2), Income Tax Regs., provides in part:

> Generally speaking, if contingent compensation is paid pursuant to a free bargain * * * before the services are rendered, not influenced by any consideration on the part of the employer other than that of securing on fair and advantageous terms the services of the individual, it should be allowed as a deduction even though in the actual working out of the contract it may prove to be greater than the amount which would ordinarily be paid.

When Home Interiors was first organized, it decided to compensate Mrs. Crowley and Mr. Amon, its key officers at that time, primarily on the basis of commissions at 2½ percent of sales. At such time, there was no way of knowing the amount of income that would be produced by such commissions. The company continued to pay Mrs. Crowley commissions at that rate through the years while it was experiencing modest success. The rate of her commissions was never increased; but it was decreased in 1973 and again in 1975 when Home Interiors was experiencing such extraordinary success. The rates of commissions paid to Mr. Carter and Mr. Horner were also established before Home Interiors' great success; those rates too were never increased, but the rate paid to Mr. Carter was also reduced in 1974 and again in 1975.

It is true that each year the board of directors of Home Interiors could have changed the rates of commissions paid to these officers, but in view of the sharply increasing profits of the company and in view of the fact that the other shareholders were receiving increasing benefits, the board of directors had no reason to reduce such commissions. It is also true that Mrs. Crowley and Mr. Carter, together with their families, owned slightly more than 50 percent of the stock of Home Interiors; but there were many unrelated shareholders, and together, they held a substantial block of the stock. Thus, this is not a situation in which Mrs. Crowley and her family were free to do as they wished in running the affairs of the company. . . . The company was achieving earnings which must have been gratifying to all of its owners, and all of them had reason to favor continuing the arrangements which had resulted in such success.

Moreover, although the commissions actually received by Mrs. Crowley, Mr. Carter, and Mr. Horner increased greatly from 1968 through 1975, those commissions represented a sharply declining percentage of the earnings of Home Interiors. See Capitol Market, Ltd. v. United States, 207 F.Supp. at 381. In 1968, Mrs. Crowley's nondeferred compensation represented 97 percent of the pre-tax earnings of the company; Mr. Carter's, 67 percent; and Mr. Horner's, 22 percent. However, by 1975, Mrs. Crowley's compensation was equal to only 8 percent of the company's pre-tax earnings; Mr. Carter's, 8 percent; and Mr. Horner's, 2 percent. Thus, a declining percentage of the company's earnings was allocated to compensation of its executive officers.

Over the years, the shareholders of Home Interiors participated handsomely in its earnings. From 1971 through 1975, the average return on equity was 49 percent. From 1968 through 1975, the dividends distributed to shareholders increased dramatically: in 1968, the aggregate dividends were $17,800; in 1971, $63,549; and in 1975, $544,895. Thus, the dividends in 1975 were approximately 9 times the amount in 1971 and approximately 30 times the amount in 1968. The dividends per share increased in an equally impressive manner: in 1969, the dividends were 10 cents per share; in 1973, $1 per share; and in 1975, $1.80 per share.

We recognize that the percentage of after-tax earnings distributed as dividends declined over the years in issue. However, the decline was not the result of the payment of higher compensation to the executive officers; it resulted from a decision to retain additional earnings in the business. Such retained earnings increased from $864,445 at the close of 1970 to $15,333,203 at the close of 1975, and as a result, the book value of Home Interiors stock rose from $1.27 per share at the end of 1969 to $26.62 at the end of 1975. On this record, it is clear that an investment in the stock of Home Interiors was very attractive and that the shareholders were receiving their fair share of the profits of the business. Under such circumstances, there is no ground for concluding that the compensation paid Mrs. Crowley, Mr. Carter, and Mr. Horner represented an arrangement for them to draw off more than their fair share of the profits of the business.

The testimony of the Commissioner's expert was persuasive. We were impressed by the thoroughness of his study, and we are convinced that his conclusions as to the reasonable compensation for Mrs. Crowley, Mr. Carter, and Mr. Horner represent the norms for their services. Yet, such conclusion is not dispositive of the issue in this case. Section 162(a)(1) was not designed to regulate businesses by denying them a deduction for the payment of compensation in excess of the norm. . . . The payment of abnormally high compensation does warrant a careful scrutiny of the arrangement to be sure that the payments were in fact made for services actually rendered. However, in view of the extraordinary services furnished by Mrs. Crowley, Mr. Carter, and Mr. Horner, we are convinced that they earned large compensation. When their compensation is compared to that received by other employees of the company, it is clear that the compensation of the executive officers was not disproportionate. Also, when the return to shareholders in the form of dividends and appreciation in the value of their stock is examined, it is apparent that the exceptional prosperity of the company was shared with the stockholders.

It is true that the compensation received by Mrs. Crowley and Mr. Carter exceeded the compensation paid to the chief executive officers of many other corporations with much larger sales, more employees, and greater profits; but those other corporations did not experience the superb growth achieved by Home Interiors in sales, in earnings, and in return to shareholders. Moreover, in these times of unparalleled inflation, our concept of reasonable compensation must take into consideration such inflation, and as appears in the Forbes information, some other companies were also paying their chief executive officers extraordinary compensation, which might have been considered excessive in other times. Accordingly, after very careful analysis of all the facts and circumstances and careful weighing of those circumstances, we conclude and hold that the compensation paid Mrs. Crowley, Mr. Carter, and Mr. Horner in the years 1971 through 1975 was reasonable within the meaning of section 162(a)(1).

QUESTIONS

(1) If you were advising the directors of a corporation about a compensation package that was generous enough to suggest that legal challenge was not unlikely what data would you think it helpful to gather in support of the plan? What comparisons with what other corporations' behavior seem the most convincing? Would it be useful to employ outside consultants such as Hay Associates to document the justifications? Should one exclude data about corporations much larger (or smaller) than the client?

(2) As you read the materials about the compensation of high level corporate executives do they evoke any reaction as to the compensation of senior partners of law firms? Do the same factors cause executives hiring law firms to ignore differences in cost as compared to attorneys seen as "second best"? What room is there for competitive bidding in such situations, that is for offering a lower price while acknowledging that one is not as well known a quantity?

(3) Does the Rogers case shed any light on the issue raised in Chapter VII above whether the "fairness" of an arrangement is to be judged on the basis of conditions prevailing at the time of contracting or with the benefit of hindsight? Are executive compensation contracts to be treated differently from other corporate contracts in this connection?

(4) To what degree was the drafting of the contract in the Rogers case faulty? How would you correct such flaws? Consider some of the other problems of working out a percentage bonus. What about an executive who performs well but in a declining industry? What of the compensation calculation in the case of an executive responsible only for a portion of the enterprise—say one of the divisions or groups of Allis–Chalmers? Should bonuses be based on divisional performance? Much controversy has surrounded the treatment of "extraordinary" losses or gains. Suppose that the American Tobacco Company had sold its aluminum foil business at a great profit or lost its Cuban operations by expropriation without compensation. Should that affect the bonus of its president? Does the fact that the corporation on its income statement treats such items as from time to time mandated by the pronouncements of the accounting profession determine the question? In other words, should the fact that the item was "by-passed" under the old accounting format

so as to avoid affecting the figure "net income" but would now be treated as a special item before the net income figure change the result? [26]

POGOSTIN v. RICE

Supreme Court of Delaware, 1984.
480 A.2d 619.

[A derivative suit on behalf of City Investing Company (City) charged that (a) defendant directors had wrongfully rejected a tender offer for City's shares at a price of $32.50 when its stock had been trading in the upper 20's and (b) caused excessive payments to be made under City's pre-existing compensation plan, keyed to the market price, when the tender offer increased that market price. The Chancery Court dismissed for failure to state a complaint that would create a reasonable doubt that City's directors were entitled to the protection of the business judgment rule. The Supreme Court affirmed in an opinion by JUSTICE MOORE. Extracts dealing with the compensation question follow.]

[I]t is alleged that in 1971, nine years prior to the tender offer, City, with stockholder approval, had adopted an arrangement for executive compensation, called the Share Unit Plan (the Plan), under which bonuses were awarded in cash, stock, or a combination thereof, to designated employees. The sum ultimately to be paid is based on a pre-existing timetable relative to the market price of City stock. The theory of the plan is that the stock market will reflect successful managerial performance. Thus, when share units are awarded, their value, and the amount ultimately to be paid, are keyed to the price of City's stock as of a later time. Each unit is equivalent to one share of common stock. One-fifth of the units vest in each of the five years after the grant date, and on the fifth anniversary of the grant date, when all units vest, the grantee has the right to receive a cash payment equalling the increase in the market value of the stock from the grant date, plus the assumed reinvestment of non-common stock dividends declared during that five-year period. This reinvestment figure is the market value of the number of common shares represented by the value of the dividends paid over the market value of a share of common stock.

Plaintiffs contend that after the Tamco offer was received and rejected, bonuses were calculated under the Plan at $26 per share, the average market price from June to September 1980. This resulted in abnormally large payments to the four inside directors, based on artificially inflated stock prices caused by heavy trading during the tender offer.

It is claimed that the large payments made to the four officer-directors were not a reward for successful managerial performance, but solely the result of market fluctuations unrelated to the Plan's purpose.

. . .

---

26. Accounting Principles Board Opinion No. 9, reprinted in J. Accountancy, Feb. 1967, p. 55, stated that "extraordinary" items should be listed, labelled as such, *before* the figure captioned "net income". Before that time such items were customarily shown either as an item *after* "net income" or were fully "by passed". A.P.B. Opinion No. 30 in 1973 further narrowed the use of "extraordinary item" treatment.

III.

In assessing plaintiffs' attack on the payments made under the Plan we begin with an analysis of the applicable statutory framework relative to matters of executive compensation. Section 141(h) of the General Corporation Law of Delaware expressly authorizes directors to fix their remuneration. 8 Del.C. § 141(h). Under Section 122(5) a corporation may compensate its officers and agents, and Section 122(15) provides for stock option, incentive, and other compensation plans for directors, officers, and employees. 8 Del.C. § 122(5), (15). See also Folk, The Delaware General Corporation Law, §§ 122, 141 (1972). In addition, Section 157 confers broad discretion upon directors in the issuance of stock options and rights. Moreover, it makes clear that absent "actual fraud", the judgment of the directors as to the consideration for such options or rights is conclusive. 8 Del.C. § 157. Section 157 was enacted to "protect directors' business judgment in consideration inuring to the corporation in exchange for creating and issuing stock options." Michelson v. Duncan, Del.Supr., 407 A.2d 211, 224 (1979). In Michelson, we held that Section 157 did not bar a claim for waste of corporate assets in the cancellation and reissuance of stock options where the claim was an absolute lack of consideration, rather than inadequate consideration. Id. In so holding, we stated that implicit in Section 157 is a requirement of some consideration extant in a stock option plan, and that the existence of such consideration will not be assumed in passing upon a waste of assets claim. Id.

The consideration typically involved in stock options, i.e., continued and greater efforts by employees, is ephemeral and not susceptible of identification and valuation in dollar terms. Beard v. Elster, Del.Supr., 160 A.2d 731, 736 (1960) (use of term "consideration" to identify benefit corporation receives from stock option plan was "ill-advised" because consideration implies some measurable quid pro quo); Lieberman v. Becker, Del.Supr., 155 A.2d 596, 600 (1959). The consideration, in the sense of a legal validation device, implicit in all stock option plans is "the requirement that [all stock option plans] contain conditions or that surrounding circumstances are such, that the corporation may reasonably expect to receive the contemplated benefit from the grant of options." Beard, 160 A.2d at 737. See Gottlieb v. Heyden Chem. Corp., Del.Supr., 90 A.2d 660, 664–66 (1952); Kerbs v. California Eastern Airways, Del.Supr., 90 A.2d 652, 657–58 (1952). In addition, there must be a reasonable relationship between the value of the benefits passing to the corporation and the value of the options granted. Id.

In this action, the essence of plaintiffs' claim is that the substantial sums which became due under the Plan were materially affected by the unrelated Tamco tender offer, and were not a reward for successful managerial performance. The plaintiffs therefore argue that permitting and accepting the payments were breaches of fiduciary duty. Compare Forman v. Chesler, Del.Supr., 167 A.2d 442, 445–46 (1961) (warrants and options provide no incentive if grantee cannot take advantage of appreciation in market price).[27]

---

27. In this respect, plaintiffs' challenges to the Plan are similar to the numerous federal actions brought under section 36(b) of the Investment Company Act of 1940 (ICA) attacking management fees paid to mutual fund advisors. See, e.g., In re Kauffman Mutual Fund Actions, 479 F.2d 257 (1st Cir.1973). Cf. Saxe v. Brady, Del. Ch., 184 A.2d 602, 610 (1962); Meiselman v. Eberstadt, Del.Ch., 170 A.2d 720, 723

However, it is undisputed that the Plan was adopted by a majority of disinterested directors and later ratified by City shareholders in 1971. There is no charge of inadequate disclosure in the proxy materials. Under the circumstances plaintiffs have the burden of demonstrating by particularized allegations that the Plan itself is so devoid of a legitimate corporate purpose as to be a waste of assets. See Michelson v. Duncan, 407 A.2d at 224–225. They have not done so.

Moreover, the Plan is administered by a committee of four outside directors who are themselves ineligible to participate therein. The Plan, as shown by its terms, represents a legitimate attempt to come within the factual context and legal standards of Beard and Lieberman. See Beard, 160 A.2d at 737–39; Lieberman, 155 A.2d at 597–99. Like Lieberman, the Plan is tied to the vagaries of the market, but Lieberman laid to rest any objection to the link between employee efforts and market price. Lieberman, 155 A.2d at 599. Furthermore, Lieberman established that the benefit received under incentive plans is not susceptible of valuation for purposes of determining the validity of such plans. Id. at 600. Plaintiffs' arguments suggest no helpful standard, claiming only that these payments were patently invalid. Given the additional fact that the market appreciation aspect of the Plan was entirely disclosed to the City shareholders in 1971 when they approved it, we conclude that the plaintiffs have failed to allege facts under the Aronson test which would excuse demand. Aronson, 473 A.2d at 815. See Lieberman, 155 A.2d at 601. If anything the Plan by its terms provided reasonable assurance that City would receive the benefits contemplated by it—the continued services of key employees. The benefit of the services of these employees is illustrated by the growth of City's assets from $340 million in 1968 to almost $7.7 billion in 1980 and by City's stock price, which has reached the low thirties on numerous occasions in the three years since the Tamco offer. We also conclude that plaintiffs have failed to allege facts creating a reasonable doubt regarding the independence and disinterestedness of the City board. See Aronson, 473 A.2d at 814. Only the four officer-directors of the fourteen member City board are beneficiaries of the Plan. Plaintiffs do not allege control by these four insiders, nor do they claim that the remaining ten directors have any financial or other interest whatsoever in the Plan. Given the existing legal principles applicable to matters of executive compensation, and the enumerated voids in the pleadings, we must conclude that demand was not excused.

. . .

NOTE ON STOCK OPTIONS AND OTHER STOCK-RELATED PLANS

Since 1945 fashions have changed repeatedly in the incentive plan field, dictated at times by what is happening in the stock market and at times by what is happening in the Internal Revenue Code. In the first

(1961). In these suits, mutual fund directors were attacked for failing to reduce the percentages used to calculate advisor compensation in light of changing economic conditions. Mutual fund shareholders alleged that the demand under Fed.R.Civ.P. 23.1 was excused because fund directors had approved the advisor fee arrangements. Recently, the United States Supreme Court abrogated the demand requirement for ICA actions. Daily Income Fund, Inc., et al. v. Fox, 464 U.S. 523 at 542–543, 104 S.Ct. 831, at 842, 78 L.Ed.2d 645 (1984).

post-war years tax rates at the margin ran above 90% and there was thus intense pressure to defer income or to achieve capital gains treatment. Before 1950 stock options were not dealt with specifically in the Code and were governed by case law. The experts read the cases as dividing options into "compensatory" and "proprietary". If compensation for services was not the motivation the corporation received no deduction but the employee could escape taxation both at the time of the grant and of its exercise. Conversely in compensatory options the corporation got a deduction to the extent that the market price at the time of exercise exceeded the option price and the employee was taxed on that difference at ordinary income rates. Some of the early Delaware cases cited in the preceding case arose because lawyers drafted options with that tax learning in mind and omitted adding provisions that would have made the option seem compensatory but at time would have made it clear that the corporation was getting consideration from the grantee in terms of a commitment to stay and work.

In 1950 Section 130 introduced the restricted stock option which was succeeded in 1964 by the qualified stock option and then the incentive stock option. The 1986 Tax Reform Act changed the whole context of stock option taxation as it ended the capital gains differential, placed corporate income taxes above the individual tax rate and reduced individual rates. Thus a corporate employer might prefer a plan that generated a deduction for it, passing some of the savings on to the employee. On the other hand, the deferral of taxation until the optioned stock was sold makes the incentive option still attractive to some.

There are other stock programs that are still favored by the tax laws. One of these is the employee stock ownership plan referred to as an ESOP (often with a snide reference to the Greek fable-writer). An ESOP is an arrangement under which a trust borrows funds guaranteed by the employer with which to purchase the employer's stock. The borrowings are repaid out of contributions by the company to the trust—the company receives a tax credit for such payments. The trustee holds the stock for the benefit of the employee, with distribution being made when an employee leaves. ESOPS were justified as a means of producing a variety of democratic capitalism. Therefore the tax advantages given to the corporation are matched by a set of restrictions designed to keep the ESOP from being used to favor a few top executives in a manner that is disproportionate to what is being received by the rank and file. The employee stock purchase plan under Section 423 of the Code is similarly limited, the amount of stock to be bought cannot accumulate more rapidly than $25,000 a year, the amount of stock covered must be in uniform proportion to the employee's compensation and only part-time employees may be excluded from the plan.

Executives receiving stock under any variation of these plans must tread carefully around the provisions of the securities laws if they dispose of the stock thus received. In particular, there are technical problems with the "short swing" trading provisions of the Securities Exchange Act of 1934 that penalize "insiders" who buy and sell (or sell and buy) stock within a six month period.[28] Obviously, the rules about misrepresentation or non-disclosure of inside information apply to both the acquisition and the disposition of the stock.

There are some variations on stock option plans which do not involve the actual delivery of stock itself but use the stock as a measure of cash compensation. One of these is the "phantom" stock option discussed in Berkwitz v. Humphrey, the following case. Another was the SAR (stock appreciation rights) plan litigated in Freedman v. Barrow, 427 F.Supp. 1129 (S.D.N.Y.1976). Under that plan executives could, rather than exercising their options, tender them to the corporation which would pay them the amount of appreciation on the optioned shares either in cash or in shares. Thus an executive who was granted an option on 100 shares at $60 per share could, when the stock had risen to $75, surrender the option for $1500 in cash or 20 shares. By dispensing with the requirement that the employee pay cash, such plans avoid some of the difficulties that have plagued option schemes.

The appropriate disclosure of stock plans presents problems. The SEC sets forth items that should be disclosed in the proxy statement by which shareholder approval is sought.[29] In effect it requires a description, in words with some numbers, of the plan and the rights of the persons receiving its benefits. It is customary for these descriptions to be fairly lengthy and the plan may be included as an annex. In Freedman v. Barrow, 427 F.Supp. 1129 (S.D.N.Y.1976), a shareholder challenged the Exxon proxy statement for failing to disclose how the plan would be treated for accounting purposes. The court rejected this attack on the grounds that the accounting treatment would be unhelpful to stockholders. It would, the court said, overwhelm the uninitiated and call for predictions that would not be consistent with the SEC's negative policy on the inclusion of projections. It found the rules somewhat technical and unrealistic.

The accounting profession's view is that a compensatory stock plan should be recognized as creating an expense to the extent of any difference between the option price and the quoted market price on the measurement date.[30] The measurement date is the time at which both the number of shares the employee is to receive and the option price are fixed. In the standard plan that is the date of the grant. The gap will usually be little or nothing so the expense reported will not be significant. In some plans, however, where the number of shares or the option price is subject to adjustment, the measurement date may be the later one, by which time the gap could be substantial.

28. See Chapter XI infra.

29. See Schedule A to Rule 14a, item 8.

30. The relevant accounting prescription is APB No. 25 reprinted in J. Account-

ancy, Jan. 1973, p. 68. It leaves in effect much of Chapter 13B of ARB No. 43.

One possible way of reporting employee options would be to use the method prescribed by Opinion 15 for disclosing the dilution effect of options, warrants and convertible securities upon the claims of the common stock.[31] Most employee stock plans would not register significantly on such a scale because their size in relation to the number of shares of a major corporation already issued and outstanding is generally miniscule. In the Exxon case it was estimated that the impact on earnings would be about ³/₁₀ths of 1%. The technique called for by Opinion No. 15 involves "dual presentation." Dual presentation means that the income statement shows (a) earnings per common share—assuming no dilution and (b) earnings per common share—assuming full dilution. In other words the earnings are divided, first, by the number of outstanding shares of common stock and, second, by the number of shares that would be outstanding if the holders of options, warrants, etc. all exercised their right to convert those securities into common stock. This, by itself, is not enough since it does not account for the fact that exercise of the option will bring in cash to the corporation which should be used so as to expand its earnings. In most cases, the Opinion recommends the use of the "treasury stock" method; in that approach it is assumed that the corporation will take the money and buy up outstanding shares of its stock. Suppose, for example, that an option to buy 10,000 shares at $54 is outstanding and the market price goes up to $60; the corporation already has issued 500,000 shares and has retained earnings of $2,500,000. If the option were exercised, the corporation would receive $540,000 for issuing 10,000 shares; it is assumed, quite unrealistically, that the corporation would use the $540,000 to buy 9,000 shares at the market of $60 so that there is a net increase of 1000 shares. Thus the earnings per share figure, assuming the option not to have been exercised as yet, would show $2,500,000 divided by 500,000 or $5 (assuming no dilution) and then by 501,000 or $4.99 (assuming dilution).

QUESTIONS

(1) Where did the court in Pogostin v. Rice find the consideration flowing to the corporation? What about the other half of the Delaware test—that of equivalency? Is it possible to weigh the value of the option against the services rendered in any meaningful way? What role does 8 Del.C. § 157 play in the case? Coming after the earlier option cases it was evidently meant to change something—but what?

(2) A basic question in this area concerns the value of the option for this underlies the issue of the fairness of the *quid pro quo*. Why is it not possible to establish the value of corporate stock options from the options, known as "calls", offered by brokerage firms in the market and advertised in the financial press? From the point of view of the shareholders the accounting treatment could be significant. If an officer receives an option to buy 1000 shares of $10 par stock at the then market price of $15 what entry should be made? Suppose he exercises the option when it has risen to $25 per share? Is

31. Reprinted in J. Accountancy, July 1969, p. 53.

the type of disclosure prescribed by APB Opinion No. 15 more helpful? The type of verbal disclosure called for by the SEC's proxy rules?

BERKWITZ v. HUMPHREY

United States District Court, Northern District of Ohio, 1958.
163 F.Supp. 78.

[Pittsburgh Consolidation Coal Company was perhaps the world's largest coal producer. It was formed as a result of a merger in 1940 of two not very prosperous companies. This merger resulted in the Mellon family owning some 12% of the stock. Dividends were paid each year since 1945 and the common stock went up steadily in value. In 1946 the board approved a "Management Unit Plan". Under the plan each employee was assigned a number of units, from 400 to 10,000, each unit being tied to the current market value of a share of the company's common stock. When dividends on the stock were paid each employee received one share's worth for each unit. He could elect by signing one of 3 agreements (1) to get all payments at once in cash, (2) to get ½ in cash and ½ credit to the retirement fund or (3) to get all credited to the retirement fund. In addition, the company agreed to pay the unit holder on retirement at age 65 a sum equal to the increase in market value of the corresponding shares of stock over and above the original $18 valuation up to the date of retirement or such date within 5 years after retirement as the employee might select. The retirement benefits would be paid in 10 annual installments. In most cases, an employee had to work for 5 years to realize benefits from the Plan. There were numerous other provisions.

About 105,000 units were assigned to 34 employees at $18 per share. Two of the 34 were directors. The plan was described in the 1947, 1948, and 1949 proxy statements. In 1951 the agreements were amended, after plaintiff's objections, to provide that to choose a date within 5 years after retirement the employee had to give notice 10 days in advance of the date. The 1951 shareholder meeting ratified a proposal to set aside enough shares of unissued stock that could be issued and sold to meet the requirements of the Plan. There was no specific ratification of the Plan as such. The 5 year period was later cut to 2 years. Over $2,000,000 was set aside as a reserve to meet Plan obligations and 16 employees were receiving payments under the retirement plan. Plaintiff, a shareholder of the company, filed a derivation action alleging the invalidity of the Plan as well as attacking three other transactions. DISTRICT JUDGE McNAMEE sustained the complaint as to the Plan. Relevant portions of his opinion follow:]

The question presented is a pioneer one. Although there are many cases in the books involving the propriety and legality of additional compensation paid pursuant to executive compensation plans, diligent research by counsel and the court has failed to reveal any reported decision that is even remotely analogous on its facts. However, the Court may look for guidance to the well settled principle that the authorized compensation must bear a reasonable relation to the value of the services of the employee. Rogers v. Hill, 289 U.S. 582, 53 S.Ct. 731, 77 L.Ed. 1385; Gallin v. National City Bank, 152 Misc. 679, 273 N.Y.S. 87.

Most incentive plans heretofore in effect have provided for stock options, a stipulated bonus or a percentage of net profits as additional compensation to a corporation's key personnel. The Management Unit Plan is novel and unique. It was the first profit sharing and retirement plan to provide additional annual compensation equal in amount to dividends multiplied by the number of units held by an employee plus deferred compensation upon retirement based upon the rise in market value of the stock during the period of employment. Since this plan became effective other corporations have adopted profit sharing and deferred compensation plans based upon the formula of additional current compensation measured by dividends and deferred compensation based upon the increased market value of the corporation's common stock. However, the plan here in question is the first of such plans to be challenged in litigation. . . .

After 5 years of service under the plan, unit holders enjoy all of the financial benefits of shareholders. However, they acquire no proprietary interest in the corporation. They cannot vote at shareholders' meetings. They have no right to inspect the books of the corporation. They cannot institute suit on its behalf nor can they alienate their units or transfer rights thereunder without the corporation's consent. A unit holder's interest in the profits and increased market value of the stock is contingent upon his employment and arises by virtue of his agreement under the plan. In these and other respects the rights of a unit holder differ from those of a stockholder. The issuance of units, unlike the issuance of shares of stock, does not alter the capital structure of a corporation and those who deal with it are not misled as to its apparent resources, as would be the case if shares of watered stock were issued. Houghten v. Restland Memorial Park, 343 Pa. 625, 23 A.2d 497; Grafton v. Marsteller, 3 Cir., 232 F.2d 773. It must be held therefore that a unit issued under the plan is not the legal equivalent of a share of stock.

Notwithstanding the distinction noted above, the assignment of units is tantamount to the allocation of hypothetical shares of stock that entitle the unit holders to all the financial benefits of stock ownership without any investment of capital.

The important question to be determined therefore is whether the financial benefits of such hypothetical shares of stock bear a reasonable relation to the value of the services of the employees to whom the units are issued. Plaintiff makes no objection to that part of the plan that entitles an employee to receive current compensation in addition to his salary in amounts equal to dividends multiplied by the number of units he holds. As to this provision of the plan, plaintiff concedes there is a reasonable relation between such additional current payments and the value of the services rendered by the employees. Plaintiff contends, however, that there is no reasonable relation between the further additional compensation provided by the plan which is based upon the increased market value of the stock at the time of an employee's retirement. It is plaintiff's position that the terms of the plan that provide an award of additional retirement benefits equal to the increase in the market value of the stock during the period of employment are unreasonable and unfair to the corporation and its shareholders. That the market value of the stock of a corporation is an unreliable index of the value of services rendered by its key employees must be conceded. Indeed such a concession is implicit in the provisions of the plan that grant a retiring employee the right to select a market value date at any time within 2 years after the termination of his employment. If a true relationship existed between the increase in market value and the value of an employee's services there would be no need for such provision.

The market value of stock is governed by many factors unrelated to the services of employees of a corporation. It is common knowledge that the general state of the economy of the country—the confidence or lack of confidence of investors—the cost of money—the supply of stock available in the market—inflationary or deflationary trends—the tendency of the market to discount the future and many other extraneous factors, play an important part in the fluctuations of the market. The earnings of a corporation are an important, if not the most important, element in the long range action of the market. But inasmuch as other unrelated factors are considered by the investing public in its evaluation of shares of stock it cannot be said that market value represents the intrinsic worth of a stock or that an increase in market value fairly reflects the value of services rendered by a corporation's key employees. The Management Unit Plan represents a radical departure from all other executive compensation plans. While it cannot be condemned solely on the ground of its novelty, it must meet the test of reasonableness which governs in all cases where the validity of such plans is challenged. This test requires that the compensation provided bear a reasonable degree of equivalence to the value of the services. The governing principles are succinctly stated in Gallin v. National City Bank, 152 Misc. 679, 273 N.Y.S. 87, 113, as follows:

> "We have long since passed the stage in which stockholders, who merely invest capital and leave it wholly to management to make it fruitful, can make absolutely exclusive claim to all profits against those whose labor, skill, ability, judgment and effort have made profits available. *The reward, however, must have reasonable relation to the value of the services for which it is given* and must not be, in whole or in part, a misuse or waste of corporate funds, or a gift to a favored few, or a scheme to distribute profits under a mere guise of compensation but in fact having no relation to services rendered." Rogers v. Hill, 289 U.S. 582, 53 S.Ct. 731, 77 L.Ed. 1385. (Emphasis supplied.)

The plan here in question bears no evidence of any purpose to equate compensation with the value of services. It fixes no percentage of earnings to which those participating in the plan are entitled as a group or as individuals. Nor does the plan prescribe any other rational method of determining compensation in relation to the value of services. The amount of retirement benefits an employee is entitled to receive is governed by aleatory considerations capable of producing incongruous results that could well be avoided if compensation were related reasonably to the value of services. To illustrate: Under the plan, an employee to whom 5,000 units were assigned might work 30 years before reaching the age of 65 and retire at a time the market value of the stock was no higher than it was at the time his units were assigned. This condition might be caused primarily by a sudden and deep decline in market value following many years of profitable operation of the business during which the employee rendered unusually valuable services yet the employee would not be entitled to receive any retirement benefits. Another employee in a less responsible position holding only 1,000 units might terminate his employment after 5 years and at a time when the market value of the stock was $50 a share higher than when his employment commenced. Such an employee would be entitled to retirement benefits of $50,000 even though his services were of less value and of shorter duration than the employee referred to in the first example cited above. A determination of the amount an employee is entitled to receive must await the termination of his employment and is then computed on the basis of the increase in market value at that time irrespective of the length, quality and value of the services rendered during the period of employment.

Another serious defect in the plan is the absence of any limitation on the amount an employee may receive as retirement benefits. This creates a situation where in times of prosperous business and rising market prices the company may be obligated to pay retirement benefits in amounts grossly disproportionate to the value of services and which in whole or in part constitute waste or a misuse of corporate funds. It is sufficient indication of the potentialities of the plan in this regard to note the tremendous increase in the value of the stock since the original units were assigned. At that time the market value of the stock was $18 per share. At the time of the three for one stock split in February 1956 the market value had risen to about $104 per share. In the early part of 1957 the stock sold as high as 46½ for each new share, or a value of $139.50 for each share of the old stock. At the end of 1957 the market value of the shares declined to about 31¾ for each new share, or approximately $95 per share for the old shares. It puts no strain on the imagination to envision the possibilities of waste and misuse of corporate funds that can result from the operation of the plan in a period of general prosperity.

The plan rests on the postulate that an increase in the market value of the stock is attributable solely to the extraordinary services rendered by unit holders in response to the incentive of additional compensation. Such an assumption is demonstrably false. It takes no account of the services rendered by top executives such as Humphrey and Ireland and other executive officers who have declined participation in the plan but whose valuable services have contributed substantially to increase the earnings and net worth of the corporation. The plan also ignores the influence on the net worth of the corporation of nonrecurring capital gains derived from the sale of capital assets in which transactions only one or a few executives participate but in the fruits of which all of the unit holders share. And, as above indicated, the unit holders also share in the increase in the market value of the stock caused by the favorable operation of extraneous factors not even remotely related to the services rendered. Under the design of the plan the unit holder who remains with the corporation for 5 years enjoys all the financial benefits of stock ownership to the same extent as a stockholder who owns shares equal in number to the units assigned to an employee. A shareholder risks the loss of his capital investment and for that reason is entitled to participate fully in the gains of the corporation from whatever source derived. The unit holder who acquires all of such rights incurs no risk of loss of capital or loss of salary. To say that he risks the loss of his retirement benefits is not an accurate statement. Before retirement the unit holder has no enforcible claim for deferred compensation against the corporation. If at the time of retirement the unit holder is entitled to no retirement benefits he suffers no loss. When a stockholder sells his shares the sale is made without expense to the corporation. A stockholder who sells receives his capital investment and the increased value of his shares from a purchaser in the market. However, a unit holder's gains are paid by the corporation and constitute an addition to the cost of operating the business. There may be rare occasions when fortuitously the amount of the awards bear a relation to the value of the services. But the irrational method of compensation provided by the plan is not designed to produce such results. Rather it is calculated to impose obligations upon the corporation which in reason it ought not be required to assume. By way of justifying the generous awards provided by the plan it is urged that they supply a maximum of incentive to the unit holders. While the incentive was designed to stimulate the efforts of the unit holders it did not and could not confer upon them the right to share in the fruits of the efforts of others. Nor does it endow them with competence to control or regulate those extraneous forces upon whose favorable operation the success of the business and an increase in market value of the shares so largely depend. There can be no valid objection to the view that executive employees merit extra compensation for extraordinary effort or ability resulting in increases in the net worth of the corporation. However, the law requires that the amount of the award be measured by the value of the services rendered. This does not mean that the value of services must be balanced precisely or with mathematical accuracy against the amounts of the awards but it does mean that there must be a reasonable approximation of the true relation between compensation and the value of services. The plan provides for no such relation. It was not designed to do so. As stated in the 1951 Proxy Statement quoted above:

> "The Management Unit Plan was designed to provide a method of compensation for key personnel which would bear a relation to the actual increase in value to the shareholders of their investment return and market value."

The stated purpose was accomplished by awarding units representing hypothetical shares of stock which after 5 years of employment under the plan confer upon the holders thereof all the financial benefits of stock ownership without requiring the investment of a single dollar of capital.

No serious objection could be made to the payment of additional current compensation based upon dividends multiplied by the number of units held by an employee if such payments were the only additional compensation provided by the plan. Standing alone, such payments might well be regarded as representing a distribution of current earnings bearing a reasonable relation to the value of services rendered. But the provision of the plan awarding further compensation equal to the increased value of the common stock at the time employment terminates has no relation to the value of services. As shown above, the amount of such award, if any, that a retiring employee receives is determined solely by the market value of the stock at the time his employment ends irrespective of the value of the services rendered during the period of employment. That the corporation was aware of the absence of a relation between compensation based upon increased market value and the value of services of an employee is evidenced by the terms of the plan that grant an employee retiring at age 65 the absolute right to defer his selection of a market value date for a period of 2 years after his retirement; and by the further provision that permits the board of directors to extend the selection of a value date for a similar period in cases where employment is terminated after 5 years of service. Under the increased market value formula employees are entitled to receive awards which if received by a shareholder would be capital gains. Heretofore it has been considered that only shareholders were entitled to such gains. The provision in question introduces a new concept and places unit holders on a parity with shareholders in respect of capital gains and provides for their payment under the guise of compensation having no relation to services rendered. I am of the opinion, and hold, that the method of compensation thus provided is per se unreasonable and invalid. I am of the opinion also that those provisions of the plan that grant retiring employees the right to defer the selection of a value date are per se unreasonable. Manifestly, any payment of an award resulting from an increase in market value occurring after an employee has ceased working for the corporation would be a gift and a clear misuse of corporate funds.

Defendant argues:

"Even if the Unit Plan had been overly generous or otherwise questionable when it was adopted, it has now been approved by 97½% of the shareholders present at the 1951 Annual Meeting and plaintiff is bound by their vote."

I find no evidence in the record tending to show an effective ratification of the Management Unit Plan. After this action was commenced the board of directors on February 12, 1951 voted to submit the plan to the shareholders at the 1951 Annual Meeting. However, the shareholders were not requested to vote on the plan. Instead there was presented to the shareholders a proposal authorizing the setting aside of 200,000 shares of authorized but unissued common stock for issue and sale from time to time in the discretion of the board of directors to provide funds in connection with the retirement of employees covered by the Management Unit Plan. The Proxy Statement forwarded to the shareholders is set out in full in the Statement of Facts. Reference thereto will disclose that the statement contains a summary of the basic compensation provisions of the plan followed by the statement that

"The foregoing summary is intended to bear upon the reason for the reservation of shares as to which the board is recommending action by the shareholders."

The action the shareholders were asked to take is also clearly outlined in the final paragraph of the Proxy Statement as follows:

"The vote of the holders of a majority of the outstanding shares entitled to vote at the meeting is required for the approval of the proposed reservation of 200,000 shares of common stock."

The above quoted statements, together with the general tenor of the Proxy Statement as a whole, show clearly that the proposal submitted to the shareholders did not contemplate or request an approval of the Management Unit Plan. Shareholder approval was sought on the proposal to implement the plan by the issuance and sale of stock but no approval of the plan itself was sought. However, even if contrary to the fact such proposal be considered as a submission of the plan for approval, it must nevertheless be held that there was no effective ratification. While the Proxy Statement fairly summarized the basic compensation provisions of the plan, it contained no summary of numerous other important terms of the plan which were merely referred to in the statement. The shareholders were not informed that if employment was terminated at any time by reason of illness the company would be required to pay the employee an amount equal to the increased market value of the common stock multiplied by the number of units assigned to the employee. Nor were the shareholders advised that if agreements were terminated by the corporation after 5 years or if an employee was discharged or quit after that time the company would be required to pay benefits in similar amounts to the employees in question. There was no reference in the Proxy Statement relative to the increase in the number of units to which an employee would be entitled in the event of a stock dividend or a split in the shares resulting in an overall increase in the number of shares outstanding. These were important matters upon which the shareholders were entitled to be fully informed. As was said in Lutherland, Inc., v. Dahlen, 357 Pa. 143, 53 A.2d 143, 148:

> "When an officer of a corporation seeks the shareholders' approval of a transaction in which he stands to profit at the expense of the corporation every element and fact involved must be revealed by him if such approval is to have any legal effect."

Of primary importance in determining whether there was a ratification of the plan is the type of notice given to the shareholders. The 1951 Proxy Statement did not put the shareholders on notice that they were expected to vote on the plan itself. The absence of such notice is alone sufficient to defeat the claim of ratification. As the court said in Kerbs v. California Eastern Airlines, Inc., 33 Del.Ch. 69, 90 A.2d 652, 659, 34 A.L.R.2d 839:

> "Necessarily the effectiveness of such ratification depends upon the type of notice sent to the stockholders and on the explanation to them of the plan itself. . . ."

The burden of showing that ratification has been made with full knowledge of the facts is upon the party alleging it. Fletcher Cyc. Corporations, Vol. 2, § 780. Defendants have not sustained this burden. I hold, therefore, that there was no effective ratification of the Management Unit Plan.

Although the determinations hereinabove made are adverse to the defendants there is no evidence of fraud or self-dealing on their part in connection with the adoption or operation of the plan. The plan was patterned after a similar plan of The H.J. Heinz Company which provided for the issuance of units and the payment of compensation based upon dividends multiplied by the number of units assigned to the employees. The Heinz plan, however, differed significantly from the Management Unit Plan in that under the former retirement benefits were computed on the basis of the increased book value of the company's shares rather than upon the increased market value thereof. There are other differences in the respective plans unnecessary to be stated. After examining the Heinz plan the president of defendant corporation sought the opinion of counsel on the legality of adapting the principles of the Heinz plan to a similar plan for this corporation. According to the testimony of the president, the Management Unit Plan was approved by counsel in the form in which it was adopted.

The individual defendants in this case had no personal stake in the adoption of the plan and in approving it they undoubtedly acted in the honest belief that it was fair and would be beneficial to the interests of the corporation. These and other circumstances shown by the evidence negate any suggestion of fraud or self-dealing. By reason of their non-participation in the plan the defendants derived no profits therefrom and are entitled to a judgment on the merits on plaintiff's prayer for recovery of profits. The absence of power to determine whether the corporation has suffered a loss compels the dismissal of that part of the complaint seeking the recovery of damages. Such dismissal will be with prejudice to any further action for damages by plaintiff against the defendants but without prejudice to any such claim as may be asserted by the corporation or any other shareholder acting in its behalf. Because of the invalidity of the plan as determined above, plaintiff is entitled to an order restraining the corporation from entering into any agreements or issuing any units in the future pursuant to the Management Unit Plan.

It is perhaps unnecessary to add that no statement, expression of opinion or finding herein made shall be construed as affecting the rights of interested persons not parties to this action.

A decree may be prepared in accordance with the foregoing. . . .

COMMENT

(1) The phantom stock plan has gained in popularity, for various reasons, including the fact that it avoids the problems of financing purchases under options that have troubled many employees. Such plans differ in detail; some of them provide for the current payment of the dividend counterpart to the employee and others defer all payments.

(2) The Delaware courts had occasion to review the Deferred Compensation Unit Plan of Koppers Company, Inc., a large business engaged in making and selling tar and related products. The plan, though generally similar to the Pittsburgh Consolidation Co. plan, did not provide any election to receive current payments equivalent to dividends. The court upheld the plan in Lieberman v. Becker, 38 Del.Ch. 540, 155 A.2d 596 (1959), saying in part:

> We think that there is no substance to the contention that the plan is invalid because of the existence of the possibility of an unlimited liability against the company. As a matter of fact, however, such a reason would not seem to be sufficient in any event to strike down a plan of compensation at the time of its institution. However, in the event matters got out of hand, the courts undoubtedly could prevent the waste of corporate assets if the actual amounts to be paid under the plan became so large as to be wholly unreasonable. Cf. Rogers v. Hill, 289 U.S. 582, 53 S.Ct. 731, 77 L.Ed. 1385.

> We think, fundamentally, there is no difference between the Deferred Compensation Unit Plan and the ordinary stock option plan. Both types of plans are designed to retain the services of valued employees, and we think the Deferred Unit Plan is designed to accomplish this more effectively than is the ordinary stock option plan. In any event, whether or not a corporation should embark upon such a method of compensating its employees is to be decided by the board of directors by the exercise of their business judgment. When a corporate decision is made in the light of the best business judgment of its

management, absent fraud or bad faith, the courts do not interfere. . . .

Finally, one more observation is required. Plaintiff relies strongly
upon the case of Berkwitz v. Humphrey, D.C., 163 F.Supp. 78, which
held invalid a similar plan. The reasons for the ruling of the court in
the Berkwitz case are set forth in a very lengthy opinion. They are
substantially the same as those urged to us by the plaintiff. We have
rejected these reasons. . . .

QUESTIONS

(1) Is there any relationship between effort and reward in a phantom stock
plan such as might make it a useful tool for incentive purposes? Is the
relationship between effort, achievement and reward more remote than in the
case of stock options? Are there practical advantages to a phantom stock plan
from the company's perspective? The executives?

(2) How successful are plans such as these in making the interests of
management coincide with those of the stockholders for whom they are supposed to be working?

(3) How, if at all, would one reflect a phantom stock plan in the corporation's annual income statements?

NOTE ON PENSIONS

A pension is a significant portion of almost every executive's
compensation package. In an age where it seems difficult for even
highly-paid persons to set aside their own savings for their support
after they cease to work, executives expect pensions to cover them in
their last years and at handsome levels.

The field of pension law as a whole is becoming increasingly
complex and would lead us far afield from our topic of high-level
management compensation. Thus we concentrate here on a few points
that relate specifically to that type of situation. As with other types of
compensation, general corporate law rules apply so that pensions must
be judged on a "fairness" or "waste" standard. There have been
problems about the quid pro quo where a pension is granted to an
executive who does not have very long to serve the corporation and
indeed the problem may be most acute where the pension is given to a
widow or widower of the executive. There has been argument, sometimes successful, that where the grant is part of an overall pension plan
the benefits to the corporation of the plans as a whole are what counts
and not the balance between service and pension as to any particular
individual. The fact that some executive received a sizable pension for
having only one year to go would not then undermine the validity of a
plan covering thousands of individuals.

Disclosure is, of course, an issue under the proxy rules and other
portions of federal securities legislation. The proxy rules call for a
rather detailed description of the pension rights of top executives. The
costs of pension programs should appear in the current financial
statements of the paying corporation. There are substantial questions

about the adequacy of the disclosure now being provided to the investing public. Note that the basic theory is fairly plain: the expense of pensions is part of the labor cost of current operations, just like wages now being paid in cash, and should be accrued into present financial accounts as a cost and a liability. The problem is that the amount of the expense and of the liability is a matter of conjecture in several respects. The actuary notes that there is a need to estimate the number of employees who will persevere to the point where their rights vest, when they will retire—if they have a choice—and how long they will live to draw their benefits. Furthermore, since pensions are often promised in terms of the employee's wages during the last X years of employment it is uncertain what years of inflation and promotion will do to the level of payments which the company will ultimately have to make. The investment adviser adds that since the employer is now contributing funds to back its future obligations one must also guess how much those funds will grow (or possibly shrink) through capital appreciation, interest and dividends before they are drawn on. These accounting/actuarial problems differ significantly as between defined *benefit* plans in which a specific level of pension is promised to the employee, with the corporation running the risk of a shortfall in the funds available, and defined *contribution* plans in which the employer makes promised payments into the fund and the employee gets a share of what the funds produce.

Executives do take part in pension plans made available to employees generally including those that partake of special tax benefits. However, the Internal Revenue Code sets some relevant limits; the plan may not discriminate in favor of employees who are officers, shareholders or highly compensated (§ 401(a)(4)) and in defined benefit plans a limit of $90,000 a year in payments is imposed by § 415(b)(1). Thus some top-level employee pension programs do not reap such tax advantages. Congress enacted in 1974 the Employment Retirement Income Security Act (ERISA) which was designed to assure the security of pension programs generally, including those in which executives take part.

A host of issues about the application and administration of ERISA have arisen and given rise to an important and complex specialty for lawyers with its own literature and approaches. There have, for example, been serious problems with firms that went bankrupt so as to default on their ERISA obligations. But these topics do not relate particularly to the executives' part of this field.

One aspect of pension law relates to the subject of the next chapter—the voting power that inheres in the stock held by those who administer the accumulated funds. There have been speculations that pension funds would assume ultimate control over the corporate system by virtue of this great power; [32] to date that power had been exercised

32. P. Drucker, The Unseen Revolution: How Pension Fund Socialism Came to America (1976); Solomon, Institutional Investors Stock Market Impact and Corporate Control, 42 Geo.Wash.L.Rev. 761

in the most hesitant of ways and no such trend is discernible. What does emerge from time to time is a sharp conflict of interests when a take-over bid is made for Corporation X and the trustees of X's pension plan are asked to support the incumbent management in beating off the attempt, even though it seems to offer the greatest enhancement of the shareholders' wealth. It is obvious that the interests of the employees covered by the plan differ, since those who are still working have an interest in their continued employment which may be threatened by the new management whereas those who are at or very near retirement are positioned basically as stockholders.

PROBLEM

Pulsating Products, Inc. (PPI) is a Delaware corporation the stock of which is traded on the American Stock Exchange. It has four divisions, one that produces phosphates and potash at mines in the western part of the United States and in Canada, one that manufactures fertilizers, one that produces detergents for industrial and consumer use, and one that develops and makes rather sophisticated equipment in connection with solar heating and other energy-saving programs on a rather experimental basis. The vice president in charge of the energy division has recently left PPI after a rather unsatisfactory experience on both sides. After initial sales successes, much of the equipment produced turned out not to meet specifications with the consequence not only of a reduction in sales but also of litigation concerning breach of warranty. As a result the division lost $5,000,000 last year. Because of this difficulty and of the general decline in the market PPI stock has gone from 24 to 9. The departed vice president has been making $85,000; he has an advanced degree in mining engineering and spends much of his time outside the country. His division earned $20,000,000 last year. The man in charge of fertilizer manufacture at $80,000 has a Ph.D. in chemistry and has taught at a distinguished technological institution. His division netted $15,000,000. The woman in charge of consumer products at $70,000 has been recently hired from an advertising firm where she was making $60,000. Her division netted $10,000,000. The president of the firm has been earning $100,000. There is also an executive vice president who makes $70,000 a year. There is presently no stock option or profit sharing plan in effect. A pension plan assuring its members of 25% of their salary for their last three years in service is in effect.

The PPI board has set out in search of a suitable new vice president. They believe they have found what they need in the person of Conrad Cornice, aged 54, presently employed as a plant manager at another firm engaged in the production of energy equipment. He is now making $75,000 a year and gives out signals that he would be interested in a move but only if (a) he can be assured of five years tenure (b) he becomes a member of the board of directors of PPI with tenure secured for the like period, and (c) he starts out at $80,000 a year with a reasonable assurance that if he does well he will be making $100,000 by two or three years from now. The board has been told by a management consulting team that its pay for executives is in general a trifle low by comparison with its competition.

(1974); W. Greenough & F. King, Pension
Plans and Public Policy (1976).

As counsel for PPI consider the advice you would give as to the major terms and conditions of the employment contract which PPI should offer Cornice. Consider along with that what other changes in the firm's compensation pattern ought to be introduced. If you prefer, consider from Cornice's point of view what terms you would be willing to accept and what counteroffers you might make.

Bibliography: For two contrasting attempts to relate learning about the markets with executive compensation, see Fischel, Labor Markets and Labor Law Compared with Capital Markets and Corporate Law, 51 U.Chi.L.Rev. 1061 (1984), with my own Challenges to Executive Compensation: For the Markets or the Courts?, 8 J.Corp.L. 231 (1983). For current, practical advice see Executive Compensation: A 1987 Road Map for the Corporate Advisor, 43 Bus. Law. 185 (1987).

Chapter IX

SHAREHOLDERS AND CORPORATE GOVERNMENT

From the manager's point of view shareholders often seem a remote body of faceless people to be placated with dividends and soothed by glossy annual reports. The teacher of managerial theory is apt to see the shareholders as one of several groups whose interests must be balanced and bargained out by management. The law, on the other hand, regards the shareholders as the beneficiaries of the corporation, almost its owners, the objects of management's fiduciary duties and the ultimate source of corporate power. It gives them two basic weapons with which to enforce that control: the vote and the derivative action which we discuss in the next chapter.

1. The Shareholders' Suffrage

Ultimate legal control of the corporation is placed by corporation law in the hands of the shareholder through those provisions which provide for annual elections of directors and for shareholder votes upon basic changes. The orthodox ideology of corporations also insists upon the idea that the shareholders are owners, though indirectly, of the corporation's property and that the corporation and its management are therefore encompassed by the authority and legitimacy owing to private ownership. Between the theory and the reality falls the shadow of certain awkward facts which indicate that such shareholder control is—at least in many cases—purely fictional. Let us examine, in summary, the facts available about shareholders.[1] Among the some 1,900,000 corporations, we find many that are simply incorporated partnerships involving only a few individuals who are at the same time managers and proprietors. These present no issue about the effectiveness of shareholder control. There are then quite a number of corporations where shareholders cannot exercise continuing operating control but where they can follow the management's handling of affairs and intervene when they are dissatisfied or apprehensive about its progress. With from say 25 to 1,000 shareholders, often concentrated in one locality, these corporations possess an electorate capable of carrying out

1. For reviews of this data see M. Eisenberg, The Structure of the Corporation: A Legal Analysis ch. 5 (1976); E. Herman, Corporate Control, Corporate Power (1981).

those duties designed by the statutory model. They are roughly the equivalent of the New England town meeting where there are few enough persons and each has a big enough stake so that they are interested and active. True, the voters do not run the day by day affairs of the organization but that is not the expectation of the law which, as we have seen, assumes that the directors will "manage the business".

As we go on up the scale we find corporations with as many as 2,782,000 shareholders (AT&T) or 868,000 (GM). These are rare numerically. Only some 7500 of the 1,900,000 corporations have 300 or more shareholders. Generally speaking these corporations are also those with more assets, more sales, etc., but there is not necessarily a direct correlation. With such myriads of shareholders it is highly unlikely that they will fuse into an effective challenge to management. A few corporations among the largest ones have a rather tightly knit family ownership, these are tending more and more to disappear. What is commoner is for there to be one important block in a single hand or in an interrelated family group. If such a group can aggregate 51% of the stock it has the equivalent, functionally, of shareholder control at the small corporation level—with the difference that the 49% are more or less excluded from an important function in the process. It is less obviously, but just as practically, true that a block of 20% or more can, in the face of a widely scattered remainder, generally count on making its wishes prevail. Among the major corporations does one or the other of these patterns of distribution prevail? One analysis indicated that, of the 520 largest industrials, about ⅓ had family or individually owned blocks of 10% or more. One should also take account of the presence of holdings by various intermediary financial institutions—banks, pension funds, mutual funds, etc.—which sometimes are often large and could be decisive. An old tradition (the "Wall Street rule") that such institutions would sell rather than exercise their power seems to be gradually eroding. In particular, some institutions will now cast their votes against "shark repellents" or devices that will make it harder for hostile tender offers to succeed—and provide the institutions with substantial gains. It is also true that there are very different types of institutions out there and that some state pension funds, universities, religious foundations, etc., are more rebellious. However, evidence of institutions' intervention into corporate affairs still appears only sporadically. Observers would differ as to the desirability of intensive control over many corporations being held by investment funds, banks, insurance companies and other agencies. Some would welcome the tightening of surveillance over managements they perceive as lax in pursuing shareholder interests. Others would be concerned at the impetus to centralization in a relatively small number of institutions and at the sharpening of profit-maximizing tendencies. Some might prefer to see the voting rights passed through to those who possess the beneficial interests in the funds managed by the institutions.

Thus some observers concentrate on the top corporations, the Fortune's Five Hundred, etc. because of their importance to the nation's economy. They thus tend to see shareholders as basically powerless and proxy fights as hopeless. Even as to quite sizable corporations proxy fights do break out and occasionally succeed. For example, after two years of wrestling with the incumbents an insurgent group succeeded in wresting control of GAF away from the incumbents although it had only 5.2% of the voting stock.[2] A control battle over Gillette Corporation in 1988 was closely contested and the incumbent management's victory was contested. With respect to somewhat smaller corporations there is a respectable chance of success on the part of the challengers. A study of proxy contests examined a sample of 96 contests for New York and American Stock Exchange firms between 1962 and 1978 and found that in 56 the dissidents won some seats and that in 18 they won a majority.[3] Thus the student should recognize that, particularly in smaller corporations the proxy contest should be taken seriously, most in particular where there has been an acquisition of a nucleus of stock by one or more take-over "raiders." Corporate managers tend not to be last ditch fighters and even the threat of stockholder trouble is apt to cause them to make placating gestures. As you will see in Wolfson v. Avery, infra, the leading early takeover/proxy contest case, even a loss at the polls may lead to replacement of management.

In evaluating the prospects of appeals to the shareholders, particularly in support of "public interest" appeals, it is well to bear in mind that stockholdings are narrowly concentrated in our society—even more than income or overall wealth.[4] Thus the body of shareholders is composed of persons from a prosperous stratum of society. The elderly, including retired persons, are rather heavily represented, which enhances the conservatism of this group.

Various commentators, after examining the status of shareholder power particularly in the corporate giants and declaring that it is very low, ask themselves the normative question—what to do about it? Roughly speaking the answers are either go forward or go backward. One can proceed by trying to perfect shareholder power, polish up the proxy system, etc. That is what the SEC has in fact been trying to do ever since 1934. There are additional proposals that have not been acted upon, such as establishing a standing separate shareholder committee to supervise the active managers. Others would proceed to strip

---

2. GAF Corp. v. Heyman, 724 F.2d 727 (2d Cir.1983) (refusing to upset election because of challenger's nondisclosure of a lawsuit with his sister—particularly because management failed to disclose data bearing on its own integrity). The spring of 1988 saw hotly contested proxy fights at Texaco and Gillette.

3. Dodd & Warner, On Corporate Governance—A Study of Proxy Contests, 11 J.Fin.Econ. 401 (1983).

4. Two-tenths of 1% of U.S. families (140,000) receive 27% of the dividends that go to individuals; 1% receive 47% and 6% receive 66%. McLure & Surrey, Integration of Income Taxes, Harv.Bus.Rev. Sept.–Oct. 1977, pp. 169, 171.

the shareholder of what little authority remains to him. Professor Chayes, for example, said:

> The one explicit legal response in terms of structure to the big corporation has nostalgically striven to reverse this process. It has consisted in efforts, supported by legislation, judicial decision and more than a dash of sloganeering, to restore meaning to the shareholder's vote. Elaborate rules for policing proxy solicitation are administered by the SEC with a view to revitalizing "shareholder democracy." With the parody of the honest vote has come the parody of the election campaign: the proxy contest with its attendant minstrelsy of public-relations counselors, professional solicitors, lawyers, ad-men.
>
> I submit this effort is misconceived. Of course the shareholder—and others interested in corporate doings—should be assured of full information about those doings; and certainly purchasers and holders of corporate securities should have protection against fraud and manipulation by those in control of corporate machinery. It is unreal, however, to rely on the shareholder constituency to keep corporate power responsible by the exercise of franchise.
>
> Quite the reverse. Of all those standing in relation to the large corporation, the shareholder is least subject to its power. Through the mechanism of the security markets, his relation to the corporation is rendered highly abstract and formal, quite limited in scope, and readily reducible to monetary terms. The market affords him a way of breaking this relation that is simple and effective. He can sell his stock, and remove himself, qua shareholder, at least from the power of the corporation.
>
> Shareholder democracy, so-called, is misconceived because the shareholders are not the governed of the corporation whose consent must be sought. If they are, it is only in the most limited sense. Their interests are protected if financial information is made available, fraud and overreaching are prevented, and a market is maintained in which their shares may be sold. A priori, there is no reason for them to have any voice, direct or representational, in the catalogue of corporate decisions with which this paper began, decisions on prices, wages, and investment. They are no more affected than non-shareholding neighbors by these decisions. In fine, they deserve the voiceless position in which the modern development left them.
>
> A concept of the corporation which draws the boundary of "membership" thus narrowly is seriously inadequate. It perpetuates—and presses to a logical extreme—the superficial analogy of the seventeenth century between contributors to a joint stock and members of a guild or citizens of a borough.

The error has more than theoretical importance because the line between those who are "inside" and those who are "outside" the corporation is the line between those whom we recognize as entitled to a regularized share in its processes of decision and those who are not.

A more spacious conception of "membership," and one closer to the facts of corporate life, would include all those having a relation of sufficient intimacy with the corporation or subject to its power in a sufficiently specialized way. Their rightful share in decisions on the exercise of corporate power would be exercised through an institutional arrangement appropriately designed to represent the interests of a constituency of members having a significant common relation to the corporation and its power.

It is not always easy to identify such constituencies nor is it always clear what institutional forms are appropriate for recognizing their interests. The effort to answer those questions is among the most meaningful tasks of the American legal system.[5]

From that standpoint one can go in three different directions: (1) "Managerialism" is a tendency to believe that corporate power is well located right where it is—in the managers. They will tend, if left to their own devices, to balance out the claims of the different interest groups in a just manner—free from the pressures of stockholders hungry for dividends. (2) One can seek to give each category of interest group an institutionalized voice somewhere within the corporate structure, most simply through a representative, parliamentary scheme placing members from each group on the board.[6] (3) More remotely, this type of analysis might lead one to advocate state ownership or socialism as a means of taking account of different interests through a more specifically political system.

For present purposes we assume that the shareholder retains his vote. We ask now some basic questions about this right. First of all, is this a basic right of all shareholders or can it be tampered with by the organizers of corporations? The Illinois constitution said "that in all elections for directors or managers of incorporated companies, every stockholder shall have the right to vote in person or by proxy for the number of shares of stock owned by him . . . ." This was held[7] to bar the issue even of preferred stock without voting rights, it having been

---

5. Chayes, The Modern Corporation and the Rule of Law in The Corporation in Modern Society, 25, 40–41 (E. Mason ed. 1959). Reprinted by permission of the publisher, Harvard University Press.

6. See Vagts, Reforming the "Modern" Corporation, 80 Harv.L.Rev. 23 (1966), reviewing the German experience with governing boards of this type.

7. In People ex rel. Watseka Tel. Co. v. Emmerson, 302 Ill. 300, 134 N.E. 707 (1922), construing former Ill. Const. Art. XI § 3. See p. 383 infra. In Stroh v. Blackhawk Holding Corp., 48 Ill.2d 468, 272 N.E.2d 1 (1971), it was held legal to issue stock with nothing but voting power, i.e. no right to dividends or other participation in distribution of assets.

earlier held that it was unconstitutional to give the right to vote to bondholders:

> It is for the interest of the State and of the public that railroad companies be successfully managed, so that they will well and promptly perform the public duties that devolve upon them, and afford all necessary facilities for the safe transportation of persons and property. The interest of the shareholders depends upon the success of the corporation, and the public is interested in having railroad corporations managed and controlled by those who will profit by keeping up the property and by careful management, rather than by bondholders, whose interest, frequently, with a view to foreclosure and future ownership, lies in a depreciation in the condition and value of the property, and in a shrinkage in the revenues of the company. It would seem that a contract which annuls these statutory provisions is against public policy, and a fraud upon the statute under which the corporation is organized and from which it derives all its powers.[8]

Very few states would now take so rigid a position. Examine for example 8 Del.C. §§ 151(a) and 221. The prejudice against non-voting common stock, however, is quite widespread. The New York Stock Exchange long refused to list any company with such shares, and several federal statutes outlaw them as to specific types of companies.[9] However, at the end of 1987 the question of listing non-voting common stock was under consideration by the SEC under its power to make rules for the exchanges.

There are also questions about the weighting of votes—even if one assumes that every shareholder has a vote are they all equal? Note that the ordinary assumption now is not "one-shareholder one-vote" but "one-share one-vote". This was not always so as this passage from an early New Jersey case indicates:

> "Every corporator, every individual member of a body politic, whether public or private, is *prima facie,* entitled to equal rights. . . . In joint stock companies, the owner of one share or a claim of the capital stock is, in general, a member of the company, a corporator; and as such entitled to, and cannot be denied, the entire rights and privileges of a member . . . Those rights and privileges are definite and certain; they cannot be greater or different in one member, than they are in an other . . . A man with one share is just as much *a member* as a man with fifty; and it is difficult to perceive any substantial difference between a by-law excluding a member with one share from voting at all, and a by-law reducing his

---

8. Durkee v. People, 155 Ill. 354, 369, 40 N.E. 626 (1895).

9. Public Utility Holding Company Act § 7(c), 15 U.S.C.A. § 79g(c). Investment Company Act § 18(j), 15 U.S.C.A. § 80a-18(i). The SEC has powers in connection with each of these clauses. See also New York Stock Exchange Manual A-15.

one vote to a cipher, by giving another member fifty or a hundred votes." [10]

NOTE ON ALLOCATION OF VOTING POWER IN VARIOUS RELATIONS

If we assume a block of 100 shares with 100 votes annexed thereto, we find that there may be more than one set of interests in it, raising questions as to which person has the right to vote it. A few of the more common variants are discussed below:

(1) A shareholder may give a proxy. Proxies and their regulation are extensively discussed in Section 4 below. At this point it is enough to note that a proxy basically constitutes the proxyholder an agent of the shareholder, subject to its instructions, with the arrangements being revocable at will.

(2) Parties may not be willing to enter into an arrangement unless they can be assured of a long term commitment of a type that cannot be provided by a proxy. Lawyers invented for them the voting trust. In some of the earlier cases, the courts sharply repudiated this device, as in Warren v. Pim.[11] Justice Pitney had the following to say about a trust to last 50 years (or 20 years after the death of the last descendant of Queen Victoria):

All the clauses of the Corporation act that touch upon the subject seem to me to show a plain purpose and policy that the management of the corporation is to be controlled by the self-interest of its proprietors, voiced at the annual stockholders' meetings, in the election of directors to manage the business. The whole of the act, and especially the provisions to the effect that any lawful business may be conducted by such a company, that the shares of capital stock shall represent money or money's worth equal to the par value of the shares, that the directors are to be elected by the stockholders and are themselves to be stockholders, that the executive officers are to be chosen either by the directors or stockholders, that the stockholders, shall have one vote for each share of capital stock held by them, & c., are eloquent to the same effect. Without multiplying references, it is plain, from every section and line of the act, that the stockholder's vote has no other reason for existence except that the stockholders, who compose the company, who are in truth the company, whose capital is embarked in its enterprises, who are the proprietors of its assets and entitled to its gains and profits, are entitled at the same time, and for that reason and no other, to manage its concerns and business through the formal expression of their will, each in proportion to his interest, at the annual stockholders' meetings. The judgment of the parties interested, actuated by their

---

10. Taylor v. Griswold, 14 N.J.L. 222, 237–38 (1834).

11. 66 N.J.Eq. 353, 380, 59 A. 773, 783 (1904).

interest and guided by the experience of the company from time to time and from year to year, is to dominate the management of the company; that judgment being ascertained by formal expression, according to the majority in interest for the time being, at yearly elections.

In searching for the reason and spirit of the act in this respect it is hardly necessary to say that where the act mentions "stockholders" as entitled to vote, I take it to mean actual stockholders—real stockholders—and not those who, from the fortuitous circumstance that they hold stock certificates without ownership of or interest in the stock itself, assume to vote in respect thereto.

Proponents of voting trusts have had better luck in their appeals to state legislatures. Consider for example, 8 Del.C. § 218.

Voting trusts are perhaps most frequently used in connection with loans to the corporation where the lending party wants assurances of more control than it can get through specific contractual commitments by the corporation itself.[12] It can get specific covenants by the corporation to pay no dividends except under special circumstances, not to encumber its property with mortgages or other liens, not to acquire new property or change its business, etc. Only through a voting trust can the creditor, however, assure itself that a given management in which it has confidence will remain in office. Such trusts may also be used by groups of shareholders who wish to band themselves together to resist "raids" by outsiders seeking to obtain control over their corporation.

Issues about the interpretation of specific voting trust agreement abound. They include disputes as to whether the voting trustees have been or could be empowered to cast the shareholders' votes for major charter changes, to vote themselves into office as directors, etc.

(3) Shares of stock may be held by a trustee, custodian, guardian or other fiduciary. 8 Del.C. § 217(a) provides for the treatment of these cases. Note the distinction between these cases and those of voting trusts covered in the preceding paragraph (2).

(4) Shares may be held in the name of two or more persons—joint tenants, partners, etc. 8 Del.C. § 217(b) disposes of these problems.

(5) Shares of stock may be pledged to secure a debt. 8 Del.C. § 217(a) provides that the owner (pledgor) retains the right to vote, absent specific arrangement to the contrary.

(6) Shares may have been sold very shortly before the meeting. While the new owner has an obvious claim to the voting right as part of what it has bought, its claim may be cut off by rules designed to enable

---

12. A classic example arose when the banks asked to lend money to TWA insisted on the creation of a voting trust for the holdings of Howard Hughes in the airline; that trusteeship set the stage for marathon litigation involving Hughes and the Hughes Tool Co. See Hughes Tool Co. v. Trans World Airlines, 409 U.S. 363, 93 S.Ct. 647, 34 L.Ed.2d 577 (1973).

the corporation to get the very difficult secretarial tasks of marking notices, keeping track of the shares, etc., in hand. A share of stock is kept track of in two ways. One, a certificate is issued. A fairly typical certificate is reproduced (alas, not in color) in the documentary supplement. You should examine it, noting the elaborate precautions taken against forgery or alteration and, on the reverse, the assignment form. Rights as between buyer and seller are governed by article 8 of the Uniform Commercial Code, covering investment securities, and, when properly endorsed on the reverse side, the certificate is negotiable. Meanwhile the corporation needs to keep track of its shareholders. At its simplest the corporation's records might be much like a large checkbook. As shares are issued, the certificates are torn out and the name and address of the shareholder and the number of shares involved are noted on the stub. When shares are transferred the old certificate is cancelled and attached to the corresponding stub; a new certificate (or more) is then issued (the notation this time including a reference to the number of the certificate it replaces). At its most elaborate a stock record system will be computerized and maintained by a bank as transfer agent (the stock exchange requires an outside transfer agent). This system is undergoing change as the blizzard of paperwork threatens to overwhelm brokers, transfer agents, etc. The Securities Acts Amendments of 1975 called for an automated, nationwide system for the settlement and clearance of securities transactions.[13] It appears that eventually the stock certificate will largely disappear, at least for the great corporations, and be replaced by an electronically maintained, "certificateless", record system.

The tension between the desire of shareholders for an immediate reflection in voting power of their newly purchased shares and the needs of the system for time in which to cope have been balanced in § 213 of the Delaware law. There are critics who believe that this resolution of the matter is obsolete and does not give effect to modernization of the transfer system.[14]

(7) Shares of stock in corporation X may be held by corporation Y, while at the same time corporation X holds a controlling block of Y's shares. Other, and more elaborate setups are conceivable, and have been tried. The advantages of these schemes in terms of perpetuation of management control have been obvious; recall, for example, the operations condemned by the New Jersey court in the Robotham case (p. 229 supra). 8 Del.C. § 160 attempts to deal with such problems, but may be too narrow.[15] Consider, for example, the problems posed by substantial stockholdings of corporation Y held by the Y Pension Trust, of which the trustees are corporate officers or the problems of a bank

---

13. On the development of the electronic stock transfer program, see Symposium, 17 Jurimetrics J. 138 (1976).

14. Maidman, Voting Rights of After–Record–Date Shareholders, 71 Yale L.J. 1205 (1962).

15. Apparently stung by the comments on Delaware's literalness in reading corporation law, the court in Speiser v. Baker, 525 A.2d 1001 (Del.Ch.1987), indicated that relations not quite within the proscription of § 160 might lead to disqualification of votes.

which holds large blocks of its own shares in various fiduciary accounts for its customers.

(8) Large quantities of stock are held by brokers. To the extent that they are holding as agents they are obligated to obtain and follow the instructions of the owners. This may result in a single block of shares registered in the name of a brokerage firm being voted in fractions, some for and some against a proposal, in proportion to the owners favoring each position.

NOTE ON PROCEDURE AT SHAREHOLDER MEETINGS

A vote of shareholders is normally obtained at a meeting. Just as modern statutes have loosened up the requirements for directors' meetings or even made it possible to bypass them, so too with shareholder procedures. See, especially, 8 Del.C. § 228. When, however, a meeting does take place, the rules are fairly definite in calling for specific procedures.

(1) *Call.* The corporation by-laws characteristically call for a regular annual meeting at a specified time (see art. II § 2 of our sample). 8 Del.C. § 211 sets forth procedures for use in case that date is missed. Other meetings are special meetings and must be preceded by a call. 8 Del.C. § 211(d) states who may issue such a call. Most other statutes prescribe that calls shall be issued upon demand by specified percentages of the shareholders (California and the Model Act now both specify 1/10th).[16]

(2) *Notice.* The basic prerequisites of notice to be given to the shareholders are set forth in 8 Del.C. § 222 (see also art. II §§ 3, 4 of the sample by-laws). 8 Del.C. § 229 provides for express and in some cases implied, waivers of notice. Among the matters as to which the notice must be specific are the day and hour of the meeting and its place. There was a time when it was very doubtful whether a corporation could hold its meeting outside the state which had chartered it and gave it birth. Even though this doubt evaporated corporations continued to lean toward having meetings at their statutory offices. This often meant Wilmington, Delaware; it not infrequently meant Flemington, New Jersey, where it was handy to have an office since county taxes were significantly lower there. It usually did not bother corporate managements that these places were inconvenient or expensive to get to from centers of shareholder population—the fewer the merrier. However, some companies, conscious of the public relations advantages that might be gained, have been arranging meetings in suitable convention halls in major cities—sometimes rotating them between east coast, west coast and midwestern cities. Particularly when box lunches are served, such a meeting can become a popular spectacle.

---

16. California Corporations Code § 600; Revised Model Business Corporation Act § 7.02.

Whether a notice need state the matter(s) to be discussed and voted on at the meeting is an unresolved question. Note the disposition in 8 Del.C. § 222(a). Some cases have permitted quite drastic changes in corporate structures to be made at meetings called without notice of those proposals. The British system, it has been noted [17] is considerably more rigorous in providing for detailed agenda to be included in the notice. The significance of this issue is now somewhat limited by the federal rules requiring that the solicitation of proxies be accompanied by an explanation of the issues as to which authority is sought.

(3) *Quorum.* A meeting is ordinarily not valid unless a quorum, a proportion of the number of shares outstanding and eligible to vote, is present. As to the proportion needed to constitute a quorum, see 8 Del. C. § 216 and the sample by-laws, art. II, § 5. A quorum is normally determined by a count at the very start of the meeting, since all action depends on its presence. Unlike legislative bodies, shareholder meetings have not uniformly been required to maintain a quorum throughout the proceedings, in other words shares represented at the time of the count cannot thereafter be withdrawn. A number of cases have dealt with variations: (1) shareholders appearing only to object to the meeting who were ejected by management were held not countable toward a quorum, (2) where one group of votes were present at the opening meeting but absent at an adjourned meeting whereas a second group was present at the second only, the court found no quorum had ever existed.[18]

Slight inroads on the quorum requirement should be noted. The New York courts have held that a majority shareholder in a small, partnership-like corporation could not bring the company's operations to a halt by refusing to attend meetings; the Delaware case law appears to go to the contrary.[19] Finally, 8 Del.C. § 211(c) affords a method of overcoming persistent quorum problems.

(4) *Conduct of the Meeting.* Those charged with organizing the meeting need to draw up an agenda; this may be taken care of in the by-laws (though not in our version). Besides the ascertainment of a quorum and the approval of the minutes of the previous meeting, the list would include the substantive concerns of the occasion such as the election of directors. An important step when any contest is involved is the selection of a chairman—if this has not been disposed of already by the by-laws' designation of the chairman of the board or president—or the replacement of the *ex officio* incumbent. The chairman has considerable authority in the conduct of the meeting, recognizing speakers, ruling on motions, etc. His rulings may be appealed to the meeting

---

17. Gower, Some Contrasts between British and American Corporation Law, 69 Harv.L.Rev. 1369, 1391–93 (1956).

18. See e.g., Textron, Inc. v. American Woolen Co., 122 F.Supp. 305 (D.Mass.1954); Duffy v. Loft Inc., 17 Del.Ch. 376, 152 A. 849 (Sup.Ct.1930); Levisa Oil Corp. v. Quigley, 217 Va. 898, 234 S.E.2d 257 (1977).

19. Gearing v. Kelly, 11 N.Y.2d 201, 182 N.E.2d 391, 227 N.Y.S.2d 897 (1962). Cf. Tomlinson v. Loew's Inc., 36 Del.Ch. 516, 134 A.2d 518 (1957), aff'd per curiam, 37 Del.Ch. 8, 135 A.2d 136 (1957).

and overruled by a majority vote. There is some authority to the effect that votes on such matters may be by head count rather than by a per share vote, at least if the by-laws so indicate. In a general way, shareholders' meetings ought to follow normal parliamentary practice but courts will not upset transactions for minor deviations from Roberts' Rules of Order. Important functions as to the counting of votes may be bestowed on inspectors of election.

(5) *Judicial Review.* At one time review of action taken at shareholder meetings could only be had through traditional remedies. For example, the validity of an election of directors could be tested by bringing a *quo warranto* proceeding to challenge their entitlement to their seats. An injunction might lie in some cases to block a merger, for example, that had been improperly approved. Modern statutes provide a specialized proceeding. 8 Del.C. §§ 225–227 show the flexibility and power which can be given to a court.

QUESTIONS

(1) Why should the New York Stock Exchange or the SEC be concerned if shareholders are willing to buy common stock without voting rights? Isn't that something that adult investors can decide upon without guidance or restrictions? Is it also true that shareholders now owning voting common stock can make up their minds as to whether to accept an exchange offer through which they wind up with non-voting common?

(2) It is generally thought that it would be wrong and corrupting to permit shareholders to sell their right to vote at the next stockholders meeting. That is, they should not sell their vote independently of selling the underlying share of stock. Does this assumption survive analysis? Why would a shareholder be willing to sell that share? What would make a party willing to pay for that vote? [20]

Bibliography: A useful review is M. Eisenberg, The Structure of the Corporation: A Legal Analysis (1976). A. Berle & G. Means, The Modern Corporation and Private Property (1932) is still a classic on shareholders and their control over management. Much of the ground is retraced in E. Herman, Corporate Control, Corporate Power (1981). On mechanics see H. Einhorn & J. Robinson, Shareholder Meetings (Prac.L.Inst.1984); Encyclopedia of Corporate Meetings, Minutes and Resolutions (W. Sardell, revisor 3d ed., 1986); Wetzel, Conduct of a Stockholders' Meeting, 22 Bus.Law. 303 (1967) is compact and useful. On stock transfers, see F. Christy, The Transfer of Stock (6th ed., M. Rhodes, 1985); E. Guttman, Modern Securities Transfers (3d ed. 1987).

---

20. See Clark, Vote Buying and Corporate Law, 29 Case West.Res.L.Rev. 776 (1979); Easterbrook & Fischel, Voting in Corporate Law, 26 J.L. & Econ. 395 (1983). Compare Schreiber v. Carney, 447 A.2d 17 (Del.Ch. 1982).

2. Cumulative Voting

One of the noisier ideological issues in the "corporate democracy" field has been the question of cumulative voting. Supporters of corporate democracy, particularly Lewis Gilbert, believe that the position of dissidents will be materially improved by this device. Its opponents view it as creating the possibility of divisive situations, giving openings to opportunists. As in the case below, the arguments have a tendency to depend on political analogies; you will want to decide whether or not these seem appropriate. It is, in a sense, a precursor of the hostile take-over situations of the 1970's and 1980's.

WOLFSON v. AVERY

Supreme Court of Illinois, 1955.
6 Ill.2d 78, 126 N.E.2d 701.

[Wolfson brought an action against Montgomery Ward & Co. and its directors seeking a declaration that § 35 of the Illinois Business Corporation Act providing for classified boards of directors, and the company's by-laws dividing its nine member board into three classes, violated art. XI § 3 of the Illinois constitution providing for cumulative voting. The texts of these two rules follow:

§ 35

"When the board of directors shall consist of nine or more members, in lieu of electing the whole number of directors annually, the by-laws may provide that the directors be divided into either two or three classes, each class to be as nearly equal in number as possible, the term of office of directors of the first class to expire at the first annual meeting of shareholders, after their election, that of the second class to expire at the second annual meeting after their election, and that of the third class, if any, to expire at the third annual meeting after their election. At each annual meeting after such classification the number of directors equal to the number of the class whose term expires at the time of such meeting shall be elected to hold office until the second succeeding annual meeting, if there be two classes, or until the third succeeding annual meeting, if there be three classes."   . . .

Art. XI § 3

"The general assembly shall provide, by law, that in all elections for directors or managers of incorporated companies, every stockholder shall have the right to vote, in person or by proxy, for the number of shares of stock owned by him, for as many persons as there are directors or managers to be elected, or to cumulate said shares, and give one candidate as many votes as the number of directors multiplied by the number of his shares of stock shall equal, or to distribute them on the same principle among as many candidates as he shall think fit; and such directors or managers shall not be elected in any other manner."

Observe that the revision of the Illinois Constitution in 1971 did not carry forward the requirements contained in these two sections.[21]

The circuit court granted plaintiff's motion for judgment on the pleadings and, on a direct appeal, the Supreme Court affirmed in an opinion by KLINGBIEL, J.]

Under cumulative voting, a method designed to enable minority stockholders to gain representation on the board of directors, each shareholder is entitled to votes equal to the number of his shares multiplied by the number of directors to be elected. He may cast all his votes for a single candidate or distribute them among two or more as he sees fit. It is not disputed that in an election of only three members of a nine-member board, approximately 250 per cent as many votes are required to elect a single director as would be necessary if all nine members were to be elected at the same time. In an election of the full board of nine directors, the owners of 10 per cent of the stock voted, plus one share, could elect one out of the nine directors to be elected. On the other hand, if the board of directors is classified so that only three members are elected each year, it would require 25 per cent of the stock voted, plus one share, to gain a single seat on the board. Where all nine members are elected at once, a minority holding 49 per cent of the stock could elect four; and the majority, holding 51 per cent of the shares, by cumulating their votes in the most advantageous manner possible, could elect no more than five out of the nine directors. If only three members of the board are elected each year, however, the holders of 49 per cent would be able to elect only one director at each election, and could never have more than three directors on the board at one time. Similarly, an owner of 25 per cent of the stock could elect two directors if all nine were chosen at once, whereas under the present bylaw such a shareholder would be unable to elect even one director. It is evident, therefore, that as the number of directors up for election decreases the number of share votes necessary to elect one director increases. . . . Classification of directors in fact impairs even majority representation by requiring the majority to wait for two or three years before it can secure representation proportional to its strength.
. . .

Although this State and many others have long had both mandatory cumulative voting and permissive classification of directors, no reported decision has been found in which the precise question presented here has been considered. . . .

Appellants contend the language of section 3 of article XI does not forbid classification of directors and their election for staggered terms, but plainly contemplates a power in the General Assembly to continue the practice which was well known at the time the constitution of 1870 was adopted. In support of the contention it is argued that since the section gives stockholders the right to vote for as many persons as there are directors "to be elected," it contemplates the possibility that less than the whole number may be elected at any particular annual meeting; and that the construction adopted by the circuit court renders meaningless the words "to be elected". Appellee takes the position that the words in question are neutral, and were used merely to describe the persons involved in future elections, to make it clear, for

---

21. However, cumulative voting could be eliminated from existing charters only by unanimous shareholder vote. See Roanoke Agency, Inc. v. Edgar, 101 Ill.2d 315, 78 Ill.Dec. 258, 461 N.E.2d 1365 (1984).

example, that if a corporate board is increased or decreased in size the new number is to be chosen rather than the original number. We may say at once that the failure of the convention to expressly forbid classification is not determinative. This court has not heretofore taken so literal an approach to the constitutional provision. Neither the filling of vacancies by directors, nor the issuance of nonvoting stock is expressly forbidden, yet statutes authorizing both practices have been held invalid. . . . Nor do we think the words "to be elected" can be given the meaning or significance ascribed to them by appellants. The same phrase appears in sections 7 and 8 of article IV of the constitution, dealing with minority representation in the General Assembly. Thus, after stating that three representatives shall be elected in each senatorial district every two years, these provisions declare that "each qualified voter may cast as many votes for one candidate as there are representatives *to be elected,* or may distribute the same, or equal parts thereof, among the candidates, as he shall see fit". (Emphasis supplied.) Since three representatives must always be elected, the phrase in question was obviously not used in reference to the number of representatives to be elected, and we would not be warranted in attributing a different meaning or intent to the words as used in section 3 of article XI, unless the context so requires. A careful examination of the entire section fails to disclose any indication that the words "to be elected," appearing in the first clause, were intended to imply that less than the entire board could be elected at one time. On the contrary, the second clause of the section, which deals expressly with cumulative voting, indicates rather that all directors must be elected at each regular election. It confers on each stockholder the right "to cumulate said shares, and give one candidate as many votes as the *number of directors* multiplied by the number of his shares of stock shall equal, or to distribute them on the same principle among as many candidates as he shall think fit". (Emphasis supplied.) Appellants argue in effect that the words "candidate" and "candidates" in the second part of the section refer to the office or offices of "directors or managers to be elected," mentioned in the first part of the section, and that the phrase "number of directors" must therefore mean only the number which is to be elected at the particular annual meeting. The argument is not convincing. In our opinion these words should be given their ordinary meaning, namely the whole number of directors of the corporation. In People ex rel. Watseka Telephone Co. v. Emmerson, 302 Ill. 300, 134 N.E. 707, 709, we had occasion to construe the present section of the constitution in deciding whether a corporation could provide for preferred stock without any right in the owner to vote for directors. It was contended that the phrase "every stockholder," as used in section 3, should be construed to mean " 'every stockholder entitled to vote.' " It was held, however, that under this provision of the constitution all stockholders must have the right to vote for directors. We observed that "If the convention intended that only those stockholders who were given the right to vote by the charter or articles of incorporation adopted by the company were included, it would have been perfectly easy to word this section so as to convey this meaning, but instead of so wording it the convention used the language, 'every stockholder shall have the right to vote, in person or by proxy, . . . for as many persons as there are directors or managers to be elected,' and followed this with a provision as to cumulating said shares." In the case at bar it should likewise follow that since the convention failed to qualify the words "number of directors," it must have intended their natural meaning as all the directors of the corporation.

Appellants and the *amici curiae* rely upon the rule that any subject of government which is not within some constitutional inhibition may be acted upon by the General Assembly, and that constitutional provisions should be liberally construed in order that the legislative enactment may be sustained. It is true that section 3 says nothing about the number of directors which a corporation must have, except that the use of the plural in connection with cumulative voting implies there must be more than one; that it does not in terms require the whole number of directors to be elected at each regular or annual meeting; and that the classification of directors and their election for staggered terms is not expressly forbidden. It is well settled, however, that prohibitions may be found not only in the language used but also by the necessary implications of such language. The guaranty of minority representation prohibits any law which in effect defeats or nullifies it, even though such law does not in express terms attempt to nullify the right. It is not disputed that staggered elections enlarge the percentage of votes necessary to obtain representation on the board, and may result in excluding any representation for minorities which would otherwise be able to elect a director. It is likewise evident that the classification of directors and their election for staggered terms do not purport to affect the legal right of a stockholder to vote his shares cumulatively, and that the right of cumulative voting does not pretend to assure a minority a representation in any event.

It is true, as defendants urge, that the constitutional provision does not insure a voting strength which is precisely proportionate to stock ownership, and that the actual operation of the provision in a particular situation will depend upon three variable factors: the total number of shares, the number held by the stockholder, and the number of directors. But these variable factors are inherent in the language of the constitution. Their presence does not, we think, authorize us to sanction the introduction of another variable which is not inherent,—classification of directors by terms.

In determining whether the effect of classification in mathematically increasing the percentage of votes required for representation on the board is a substantial denial of the constitutional right of cumulative voting, it is appropriate to consider the mischief designed to be remedied and the purpose sought to be accomplished by the provision. Since the language to be construed is a constitutional provision, the object of inquiry is the understanding of the voters who adopted the instrument. In this connection it is appropriate to consider the historical background for the inclusion of section 3 and the debates of the members of the convention, as well as explanations of the provision published at the time. . . .

The United States Supreme Court employs the same technique in interpreting the Federal constitution. . . . While there is no such historic source as the Federalist Papers to aid in the interpretation of the Illinois constitution, we do have relevant data in the explanations which appeared in the press.

There was prevailing throughout the 1860's popular indignation at the excesses and frauds of certain railroad managements, and the press was vehement in its denunciation of the "rings" which controlled many of the railroad companies which defrauded minority stockholders. Prior to the Constitutional Convention, the moving force behind the idea of minority representation in political and corporate elections in Illinois was a group known as the Minority Representation Society of which Joseph Medill, publisher of the *Chicago Tribune* and one of the framers of the controverted constitutional provision, was a leading member.

A news item in the *Chicago Tribune* for December 31, 1869, reports the proceedings of the annual meeting of the Minority Representation Society at which Medill stated that he proposed to offer the convention a bill for minority representation, which he referred to as "proportionate representation" and which would not be confined to political matters only but which would include corporate bodies in which the minority would have their due representation.

Medill became the leading advocate of cumulative voting for both political and corporate elections, and introduced the cumulative voting provision for the election of directors soon after the convention assembled. In May, 1870, the Committee on Miscellaneous Corporations submitted a report recommending the present constitutional language. From the ensuing reported debates the intention of the framers may be gleaned.

Medill himself referred to the provision as proportional representation and in introducing the proposal, stated: "The subject of proportional representation is attracting the earnest and anxious thought of the ablest statesmen and writers in Europe as in America." (Constitutional Debates, pp. 563–564.) In expounding the section he described a system of proportional representation: "Suppose a company with a capital stock of $100,000 elect ten directors. At present, under the ordinary method of electing directors, stockholders holding five hundred and one shares elect the entire board, and those holding four hundred and ninety shares cannot elect a man to represent their interests. After these ten directors are thus elected, they can proceed to create an 'executive committee,' to run the institution, the members of which may not represent a quarter or a fifth of the stock. Thus we have the whole interests of the company controlled by $25,000 or $30,000 of stock. On the plan here proposed the holders of $49,000 by clubbing their votes together could elect four of the ten directors, and if shares to the amount of $10,000 were held by one stockholder he could elect one director to protect his interests." (Constitutional Debates, p. 1666.)

. . .

Contrary to appellants' interpretation of Medill's position, it is patent from the editorial in the *Chicago Tribune* of May 14, 1870, that he did mean that section 3 of article XI required the whole number of directors to be elected at one time. The editorial states: "In all incorporated companies every stockholder shall have the privilege of voting as heretofore, for as many Directors as are to be elected, or of casting the whole number of his shares, *multiplied by the whole number of Directors*, for any one person, or to otherwise distribute them as he pleases." (Emphasis supplied.)

. . .

Two days before ratification by the people, another emphatic editorial appeared in the *Tribune* relating to this proposed constitutional provision: "The third clause on 'Corporations' will forever prevent the confiscations of the rights of stockholders by Directors, of which the

Erie Railway is a conspicuous and infamous example. . . . Now, if the four-ninths of Erie stock actually held by the opponents of Fisk and Gould, prior to the fraudulent over-issues, had been allowed its fair representation in the Board of Directors, as provided by our new Illinois Constitution, the Gould–Fisk party, instead of electing the whole board, would only have elected five-ninths of them, while the other party would have had immediately four-ninths of them in the Board of Directors, and a minority in the Executive Committee." . . .

The fact that the constitutional provision does not expressly prohibit staggered elections does not foreclose a construction which invalidates the statute authorizing such elections. . . . A constitutional guaranty should be interpreted in a broad and liberal spirit. Courts should not apply so strict a construction as to exclude its real object and intent. As we have indicated, the general purpose of the provision, as disclosed in the debates of the constitutional convention and in contemporaneous comments and explanations in the press, was to afford a minority protection in proportion to its voting strength. In the light of such purpose and the evil sought to be remedied, the section cannot be construed to authorize a method of selecting directors which results in impairing the value of the right. That section 3 contemplates a right to vote cumulatively for the entire number of directors is also evident from the unqualified nature of its language. The second clause of the section, describing cumulative voting, provides that the stockholder shall be entitled to "give one candidate as many votes as the *number of directors* multiplied by the number of his shares." (Emphasis supplied.) This unqualified reference to "number of directors" on its face means the total number, and nothing in the remaining language of the section requires that it be construed to refer also to a smaller number resulting from classification. It must therefore follow that section 35, which provides for the classification of directors and the election of less than the entire number at any one election, is in conflict not only with the purpose of affording proportional representation but with the natural effect of the constitutional language as well.

In People ex rel. Weber v. Cohn, 339 Ill. 121, 171 N.E. 159, 161, we considered the validity of a statute providing that the directors shall fill all vacancies which may happen in the board of directors caused by death, resignation or otherwise, until the next annual meeting of the stockholders. In holding the statute to be in violation of section 3 of article XI of the constitution, we observed: "the Constitution provides all elections for directors shall be by the stockholders, etc., 'and such directors or managers shall not be elected in any other manner,' while the statute provides that the directors shall fill vacancies which happen in a board by death, resignation or otherwise. The two are inconsistent and cannot both be given effect. The stockholders have a right to direct the affairs of the corporation through directors elected by them, and they cannot be deprived of that right under the Constitution." We think a similar conclusion must follow in the case at bar. Section 35 of the Business Corporation Act, in authorizing the classification of directors, is inconsistent with the constitutional right of a stockholder to cumulate his shares through multiplying them by the "number of directors," and cannot be sustained.

Appellants emphasize the long period during which the act has been in effect. Age, however, does not immunize a statute from constitutional attack. This court does not hesitate to invalidate long standing practices under statutes where they are challenged and found offensive to the constitution. . . .

Defendants also rely on what they term a long-continued administrative construction of the statute. Even assuming that the views of the officers administering the act were authority for its validity, we cannot regard their failure to challenge the act as an administrative construction, for the reason that officers are not normally expected to question the validity of the legislation under which they act.

· · ·

[HERSEY, J., wrote an extensive dissent. His reasoning can be divided into three parts. First, he used a linguistic analysis of section 3, asserting that "[n]o significance could be ascribed to the phrase 'to be elected' if the entire board of directors had to be elected at one time." He also developed a construction of the second part of section 3, which sets forth the multiplication formula to be employed, reasoning that there can only be "candidates" in respect of the number of offices to be filled at the particular election. Multiplication of the number of shares times the number of all the directors rather than merely the number of seats at stake would "merely increase the voting strength of the minority and the majority proportionately." Finding the meaning clear, Judge Hersey would "not refer to extrinsic matters to arrive at a proper interpretation." Second, the dissent, nonetheless, points "to the contemporaneous and long continued legislative and administrative construction" of the section as consistent with staggered terms. The General Assembly, beginning immediately after the Constitution of 1870, had enacted many laws providing for classification; these included a general corporation act, railroad and building and loan corporation laws, as well as laws establishing public bodies and commissions ranging from university trustees to mosquito abatement district trustees. Furthermore, "13 states have both mandatory cumulative voting and election for staggered terms." The Model Business Corporation Act and various federal laws are parallel. Third, Judge Hersey read the constitutional debates as calling only for *some* minority representation and not as opposing the well-known practice of classification.]

COMMENT

The Montgomery Ward proxy battle of 1955 is one of the half-dozen great proxy contests of that time. It had its origins in the ultra-conservatism of Sewell Avery, its chief executive officer, then 82. His solid stubbornness was exemplified for many newspaper readers during World War II by a famous photograph of a glowering Avery being carried out of his headquarters by a group of military policemen—Avery had refused to settle a labor dispute on the basis suggested by the government which then seized the company. From 1931 to 1939 he had been a successful manager of Ward's affairs, taking it from a loss of $8,700,000 to a profit of $27,000,000. In the post-war years he made the mistake of judging that a recession would follow the wartime expansion and kept the firm's assets in cash rather than in new facilities. As a result Ward's was clearly outpaced by other retailers, most specifically Sears, Roebuck. As Ward's stock price declined, and important members of its management resigned, an opportunity was scented by various adventurous financiers and in particular by Louis Wolfson who had been building a conglomerate corporate empire. He began expending substantial sums from the treasury of that empire to acquire Ward stock and mounted the proxy fight. At the election, after the case, Wolfson was able to swerve only 30% of the vote—probably because of the large holdings of stock by conservative midwestern institutions. However, the performance by Mr. Avery in the give and take of the stockholders' meeting was such as to cause his fellow board members to obtain his resignation. Wolfson continued to be a storm center in the corporate world, at least until his conviction in 1968 of selling securities without registering them as required by federal law.[22] Mr. Wolfson's relations with Mr. Justice Fortas of the Supreme Court had adverse consequences for the latter's career.

NOTE ON CUMULATIVE VOTING

(1) Let us begin with an understanding of the basic mathematics of cumulative voting as expressed in a passage from C. Williams, Cumulative Voting for Directors 40–42 (1951)[23]:

> The most important tactical question in a cumulative voting fight is how to cumulate the votes so as to elect a maximum number of directors. A formula has been devised which is helpful, once the number of shares to be voted is known, in determining the number of shares needed to elect selected numbers of directors. This formula assumes one vote per share for each director to be elected.
>
> In the formula the following notations will be used:
>
> X = numbers of shares needed to elect a given number of directors
> Y = total number of shares at meeting
> N^1 = number of directors desired to elect
> N = total number of directors to be elected
>
> $$X = \frac{Y \times N^1}{N + 1} + 1$$
>
> Let us apply the formula to hypothetical situations. Dissident stockholder Jones wishes to be elected to an eight-man board. There are 1,500 shares outstanding, of which he expects about 900 shares to be represented at the meeting. How many of the 900 shares must Mr. Jones assemble to get elected?
>
> Apply the formula, $X = \dfrac{900 \times 1}{8 + 1} + 1$, it is seen that Mr. Jones will need 101 of the 900 shares to be elected.
>
> Now let us suppose that Mr. Jones seeks control of the company and hopes to elect five directors. According to the formula, $X = \dfrac{900 \times 5}{8 + 1} + 1$ he will need 501 shares to elect the five.

22. The above data is obtained largely from J.A. Livingston, The American Stockholder (rev.ed. 1963). See also United States v. Wolfson, 405 F.2d 779 (2d Cir. 1968).

23. Reprinted by permission of the Division of Research, Harvard Business School, Boston.

It will be at once apparent that the result of the first application of the formula is simply $\frac{1}{9}Y + 1$ and of the second, $\frac{5}{9}Y + 1$. Or changing the assumption somewhat, if five directors are to be chosen, to elect four, the formula will yield a result, $\frac{4}{16}Y + 1$.

Let us test the answers gained by the formula. Suppose in the first instance above, Mr. Jones has control of the necessary 101 shares and casts all his votes (101 × 8 = 808) for himself, and his opposition with 799 shares splits its votes over its slate of eight candidates; then each of the eight receives 799 votes and Mr. Jones' 808 votes means his election. No matter how the majority distributes its votes, Mr. Jones will have more votes than its eighth man.

Taking the second instance of eight directors and 900 total shares at the meeting, the formula indicates that Mr. Jones needs 501 shares to insure election of five men. With 501 shares and eight candidates he has 4,008 votes to distribute and can give 801 to each of his five. An opposition dividing its 3,192 votes (399 × 8) over five candidates can give each one 638 votes.

If, on the other hand, the majority group has 499 shares to the opposition's 401, the majority cannot be sure of electing the five directors needed for a majority. It has 3,992 votes (499 × 8) to divide over five candidates or 799 or 798 to each. The opposition with 3,208 votes (401 × 8) cumulated in support of but four men can give each 802 votes and hence elect four of the eight. This illustration points up the fact that with an even number of directors a situation can develop under which a clear majority of shares is inadequate to elect a majority of the board. This possibility can be obviated, of course, by having an odd number of directors.

(2) There has been a fair amount of legislation and litigation about cumulative voting. On the legislation side note the following classifications: (a) States with statutes making cumulative voting permissive, i.e., something that can be inserted in the certificate of incorporation, e.g., 8 Del.C. § 214; (b) states with constitutional or statutory provisions making cumulative voting mandatory, e.g., Illinois before 1971, Pennsylvania before 1966, and (c) states which do not provide for cumulative voting at all. It is in category (b) states that the question of conflict between cumulative voting and classification can arise. Other courts have resolved the matter in ways different from Wolfson. The courts of Pennsylvania and Arizona among others held that corporations could classify their boards of directors.[24] The latter did indicate, however, that division down to the point of one director per class would be too

---

24. Janney v. Philadelphia Transp. Co., 387 Pa. 282, 128 A.2d 76 (1956); Bohannon v. Corporation Commission, 82 Ariz. 299, 313 P.2d 379 (1957).

much. The language of the constitutional provisions differed somewhat, possibly decisively:

> *Pennsylvania Const. art. 16, § 4:* In all elections for directors
> or managers of a corporation each member or shareholder may
> cast the whole number of his votes for one candidate, or
> distribute them upon two or more candidates, as he may
> prefer.

(3) A court deciding a case of conflict between cumulative voting
and classified boards will inevitably be moved by some view of the
merits of those institutions. The case for classified boards is fairly
easily put—it provides for continuity and stability of management, as it
provides continuity for senatorial and other political bodies. The
skeptic is inclined to doubt whether there is actually the sort of
turnover among directors which calls for such a precaution and notes,
further, that with cumulative voting a long period can pass between the
time that a new group acquires voting control of the corporation and
the time that it can make its will felt through electing a majority to the
corporate board.

The Wolfson opinion and the dissent state much of the case for and
against cumulative voting. One might also mention, in favor of the
idea, the thoughts that minority representation via cumulation will
bring new ideas to the board, that it will get onto boards a watchdog
group and that it mitigates to a degree the powerful inertial position of
the "ins." To the contrary, opponents of cumulative voting argue that
a board acts as a team and that the intrusion of hostile partisans will
create disharmony, upset the working executives, lead to disclosures of
inside data and promote the interests of those with special selfish
motivations—such as "raiders" or persons anxious to sell their shares
for their nuisance value.

(4) Where cumulative voting is merely permissive only some 15%
of corporations will freely choose it.[25] The full utilization of cumulative
voting may also be impaired by several other features of modern
corporation laws such as the creation of executive committees (8 Del.C.
§ 141(c)), the filling of vacancies on the board by the remaining directors (8 Del.C. § 223), the removal of directors before expiration of their
term, especially where no showing of cause is required (but see 8 Del.C.
§ 141(k)), and the grant of the right to different classes of stock to elect
specified portions of the board. See also p. 396 infra.

(5) "Public interest" lawyers have an active concern with keeping
cumulative voting going. It is much more feasible to elect one representative of a cause to a 14–member board than to win the 51% needed
to make any dent on a noncumulatively elected board or the 20%
needed to place a representative on a 4–member board. Thus in

---

25. J. Bacon, Corporate Directorship
Practices, Membership and Committees of
the Board 7–8 (1973). According to that
source, instances of actual resort to the
cumulative voting mechanism where it is
available are rarer yet, although the consequences of its availability can be crucial in
those cases.

Coalition to Advocate Public Utility Responsibility v. Engels, 364 F.Supp. 1202 (D.Minn.1973), the Coalition sued to prevent a board from converting itself into a staggered format while a proxy fight was pending; the court agreed on the impropriety of such a maneuver, especially since the proxy materials did not reveal it.

QUESTIONS

(1) Evaluate the majority opinion in terms of the following subquestions: (a) is it persuasive as to the language of the constitutional provision? (b) does it make good use of contemporaneous and subsequent practice by the legislature and by corporations? (c) does it deal successfully with the relationship between cumulative voting in Illinois political elections and in Illinois corporate elections?

(2) In connection with question 1(a), consider the constitutional provision in Pennsylvania, quoted in paragraph (2) of the preceding note. Should the differences be regarded as determinative? Significant?

(3) Do the materials about directors in Chapter VII give a view of boards of directors that supports either position as to cumulative voting?

(4) Assuming the correctness of the result in Wolfson, how should a court deal with articles of incorporation or by-laws including provisions calling for the following: (1) removal of directors by the shareholders with or without cause; (2) election of ⅓ of the directors by some body other than the shareholders—the state, workers, bondholders, etc.; (3) a board consisting only of three directors.

PROBLEM

You are consulted by a group of shareholders in Prudential Bag Co., a rather closely held Delaware corporation. It has articles and by-laws like those in the Documentary Supplement except that they provide for cumulative voting; 1,200,000 shares of $1 par value are issued and outstanding. Your clients intend to produce a group of candidates at the next annual shareholders meeting, which is two weeks away. They believe that they can count on the following support:

120,000	shares held by individuals in their own name
15,000	shares held by a trustee
10,000	shares held by a pledgee
25,000	shares which were bought by the present owner ten days ago
170,000	total

Their intelligence sources suggest that the following lineup on behalf of management can be expected:

300,000	shares held by member of management
180,000	shares held by other individuals
50,000	shares held by a corporation which is in turn 25% owned by Prudential, a holding which gives Prudential working control
530,000	total

If your sources are correct, how many shares will be voted for each slate?

If that many votes are cast how many directors will be elected by each side?

If we take management by surprise might we pick up another seat?

If that were to happen how would the resulting impasse be resolved?

Would it be useful for the opposition group simply not to appear at the meeting?

---

3. The Relative Power of the Shareholders

The framework of power established by the typical corporation statute allocates authority more or less as follows: (a) the board manages the business of the corporation between annual elections; (b) the shareholders (1) elect directors annually, (2) may be able to remove them, at least for "cause," and (3) must approve various "fundamental changes." Some of the cases below deal further with the removal power. The Del.Code, Tit. 8, contains a fairly typical listing of basic transactions as to which shareholder assent may be necessary:

§ 109—by-law changes

§ 242(c)—amendments of the certificate of incorporation

§ 251(c)—mergers and consolidations

§ 271—sale, lease or exchange of assets

§ 275(c)—dissolution

You should examine each of these provisions noting (1) whether director approval is *also* necessary, (2) what fraction of the shareholders must approve (3) whether the transaction gives dissenting shareholders the right to be paid the value of their shares after appraisal, (4) whether the statutory norm may be varied by agreement. It is not at all clear that the fundamental changes singled out by the statute are in fact the most important ones or that those sections form a logical and coherent pattern. See Chapter XIII below.

AUTOMATIC SELF–CLEANSING FILTER SYNDICATE CO., LIMITED v. CUNINGHAME

Court of Appeal, 1906.
[1906] 2 Ch. 34.

[The Filter Company was incorporated in 1896 to exploit certain inventions for the filtration and purification of liquids. In 1902 plaintiff McDiarmid who owned 1200 of the 2700 shares caused the directors to call a shareholders meeting to sell the Company's assets. Such a resolution was passed by a vote of 1502 to 1198 but the directors refused to comply with it. The Company and McDiarmid, on behalf of himself and all other shareholders, brought a motion to compel a sale. WAR-RINGTON, J., denied the motion from which plaintiff appealed.

The relevant portions of the Company's articles of association are as follows:

"81. The company may by special resolution remove any director before the expiration of his period of office and appoint another qualified person in his stead. . . ."

"96. The management of the business and the control of the company shall be vested in the directors, who, in addition to the powers and authorities by these presents expressly conferred upon them, may exercise all such powers and do all such acts and things as may be exercised or done by the company, and are not hereby or by statute expressly directed or required to be exercised or done by the company in general meeting; but subject nevertheless to the provisions of the statutes and of these presents, and to such regulations, not being inconsistent with these presents, as may from time to time be made by extraordinary resolution, but no regulation shall invalidate any prior act of the directors which would have been valid if such regulation had not been made.

"97. Without prejudice to the general powers conferred by the last preceding clause, and to the other powers and authorities conferred as aforesaid, it is hereby expressly declared that the directors shall be entrusted with the following powers, namely, power—

"(1.) To purchase or otherwise acquire for the company any property, letters patent, rights or privileges which the company is authorized to acquire, at such price, and generally on such terms and conditions, as they think fit; also to sell, lease, abandon, or otherwise deal with, any property, rights, or privileges to which the company may be entitled, on such terms and conditions as they may think fit." . . .

"(16.) To enter into all such negotiations and contracts and rescind and vary all such contracts, and execute and do all such acts, deeds, and things in the name or on behalf of the company as they might consider expedient for or in relation to any of the matters aforesaid, or otherwise for the purposes of the company."

Since this is the only English case we consider at length it is worth mentioning that under the practice there a corporation is required, as part of its founding, to file both a memorandum of association and articles of association. The memorandum is to set forth such things as the company's name, head office, objects (or purposes) and capital stock. Other provisions relating to the company's internal affairs are contained in the articles which are more readily amendable. The Companies Acts have each contained a Table A or model set of clauses which a company may adopt. Article 96 above is very much like art. 55 of the 1862 version of Table A. However the words "by extraordinary resolution" do not appear in the Table A equivalent.[26]]

COLLINS, M.R. This is an appeal from a decision of Warrington, J., who has been asked by the plaintiffs, Mr. McDiarmid and the company, for a declaration that the defendants, as directors of the company, are bound to carry into effect a resolution passed at a meeting of the

26. For later history of this problem in English company law see L.C.B. Gower, Modern Company Law 130–33 (3d ed. 1969).

shareholders in the company on January 16. There are a number of other incidental reliefs asked—for instance, that they be ordered to affix the seal of the company, and that they may be restrained by injunction from dealing with the assets of the company in any manner inconsistent with the agreement.

The point arises in this way. At a meeting of the company a resolution was passed by a majority—I was going to say a bare majority, but it was a majority—in favour of a sale to a purchaser, and the directors, honestly believing, as Warrington J. thought, that it was most undesirable in the interests of the company that that agreement should be carried into effect, refused to affix the seal of the company to it, or to assist in carrying out a resolution which they disapproved of; and the question is whether under the memorandum and articles of association here the directors are bound to accept, in substitution of their own view, the views contained in the resolution of the company. Warrington J., held that the majority could not impose that obligation upon the directors, and that on the true construction of the articles the directors were the persons authorized by the articles to effect this sale, and that unless the other powers given by the memorandum were invoked by a special resolution, it was impossible for a mere majority at a meeting to override the views of the directors. That depends, as Warrington J. put it, upon the construction of the articles. First of all there is no doubt that the company under its memorandum has the power in clause 3(k) to sell the undertaking of the company or any part thereof. In this case there is some small exception, I believe, to that which is to be sold, but I do not think that that becomes material. We now come to clause 81 of the articles, which I think it is important to refer to in this connection. [His Lordship read the clause.] Then come the two clauses which are most material, 96 and 97, whereby the powers of the directors are defined. [His Lordship read clause 96 and clause 97(1).] Therefore in the matters referred to in article 97(1) the view of the directors as to the fitness of the matter is made the standard; and furthermore, by article 96 they are given in express terms the full powers which the company has, except so far as they "are not hereby or by statute expressly directed or required to be exercised or done by the company," so that the directors have absolute power to do all things other than those that are expressly required to be done by the company; and then comes the limitation on their general authority—"subject to such regulations as may from time to time be made by extraordinary resolution." Therefore, if it is desired to alter the powers of the directors that must be done, not by a resolution carried by a majority at an ordinary meeting of the company, but by an extraordinary resolution. In these circumstances it seems to me that it is not competent for the majority of the shareholders at an ordinary meeting to affect or alter the mandate originally given to the directors, by the articles of association. It has been suggested that this is a mere question of principal and agent, and that it would be an absurd thing if a principal in appointing an agent should in effect appoint a dictator who is to manage him instead of his managing the agent. I think that that analogy does not strictly apply to this case. No doubt for some purposes directors are agents. For whom are they agents? You have, no doubt, in theory and law one entity, the company, which might be a principal, but you have to go behind that when you look to the particular position of directors. It is by the consensus of all the individuals in the company that these directors become agents and hold their rights as agents. It is not fair to say that a majority at a meeting is for the purposes of this case the principal so as to alter the mandate of the agent. The minority also must be taken into account. There are provisions by which the minority may be over-borne, but that can only be done by special machinery in the shape of special resolutions. Short of that the mandate which must be obeyed is not that of the majority— it is that of the whole entity made up of all the shareholders. If the mandate of the directors is to be altered, it can only be under the machinery of the memorandum and articles themselves. I do not think I need say more.

One argument used by Warrington J. strongly supports that view. He says in effect: "There is to be found in these articles a provision that a director can only be removed by special resolution. What is the use of that provision if the views of the directors can be overridden by a mere majority at an ordinary meeting? Practically you do not want any special power to remove directors if you can do without them and differ from their opinion and compel something other than their view to be carried into effect." That argument appears to me to confirm the view taken by the learned judge.

The cases cited do not really apply. Indeed, I do not think that Mr. Gore–Browne, who argued this case with his usual ability and fairness, looked upon them as more than presenting some analogy, and the only case which, at first sight, appeared to me at all near this case was Isle of Wight Ry. Co. v. Tahourdin [27]; but when that is looked into, as was pointed out by Cozens–Hardy L.J., it rests upon a different statute, a statute differing in the most essential point, namely, in the limitation of the directors' authority. Therefore that case has no direct bearing on the case before us, and on these grounds, which in substance are the same grounds as those of the learned judge below, I am of opinion that this appeal fails.

COZENS–HARDY L.J. I am of the same opinion. It is somewhat remarkable that in the year 1906 this interesting and important question of company law should for the first time arise for decision, and it is perhaps necessary to go back to the root principle which governs these cases under the Companies Act, 1862. It has been decided that the articles of association are a contract between the members of the company inter se. . . . We must therefore consider what is the relevant contract which these shareholders have entered into, and that contract, of course, is to be found in the memorandum and articles. I will not again read articles 96 and 97, but it seems to me that the shareholders have by their express contract mutually stipulated that their common affairs should be managed by certain directors to be appointed by the shareholders in the manner described by other articles, such directors being liable to be removed only by special resolution. If you once get a stipulation of that kind in a contract made between the parties, what right is there to interfere with the contract, apart, of course, from any misconduct on the part of the directors? There is no such misconduct in the present case. Is there any analogy which supports the case of the plaintiffs? I think not. It seems to me the analogy is all the other way. Take the case of an ordinary partnership. If in an ordinary partnership there is a stipulation in the partnership deed that the partnership business shall be managed by one of the partners, it would be plain that in the absence of misconduct,

27. 25 Ch.Div. 320.

or in the absence of circumstances involving the total dissolution of the partnership, the majority of the partners would have no right to apply to the Court to restrain him or to interfere with the management of the partnership business. . . .

It is not a peculiar incident of co-partnership; it applies equally to cases of co-ownership. I think in some of the earlier cases before Lord Eldon[28] with reference to the co-owners of one of the theatres, he laid down the principle that when the co-owners had appointed a particular member as manager the Court would not, except in the case of misconduct, interfere with him. And why? Because it is a fallacy to say that the relation is that of simple principal and agent. The person who is managing is managing for himself as well as for the others. It is not in the least a case where you have a master on the one side and a mere servant on the other. You are dealing here, as in the case of a partnership, with parties having individual rights as to which there are mutual stipulations for their common benefit, and when you once get that, it seems to me that there is no ground for saying that the mere majority can put an end to the express stipulations contained in the bargain which they have made. Still less can that be so when you find in the contract itself provisions which shew an intention that the powers conferred upon the directors can only be varied by extraordinary resolution, that is to say, by a three-fourths majority at one meeting, and that the directors themselves when appointed shall only be removed by special resolution, that is to say, by three-fourths majority at one meeting and a simple majority at a confirmatory meeting. That being so, if you once get clear of the view that the directors are mere agents of the company, I cannot see anything in principle to justify the contention that the directors are bound to comply with the votes or the resolutions of a simple majority at an ordinary meeting of the shareholders. I do not think it true to say that the directors are agents. I think it is more nearly true to say that they are in the position of managing partners appointed to fill that post by a mutual arrangement between all the shareholders. So much for principle. On principle I agree entirely with what the Master of the Rolls has said, agreeing as he does with the conclusions of Warrington J.

When we come to the authorities there is, I think, nothing even approaching to an authority in favour of the appellants' case. Isle of Wight Ry. Co. v. Tahourdin at the utmost contained a dictum which at first sight looked in favour of appellants; but, treating it as an authority, it was an authority upon an Act which differed in a vital point from the Act which, we are now considering, because although by s. 90 of the Companies Clauses Act the directors have powers of management and superintendence very similar to those found in Table A, article 55, and in articles 96 and 97, that section contains these vital words: "And the exercise of all such powers shall be subject also to the control and regulation of any general meeting specially convened for the purpose." If those words had been found in the present Act of Parliament the appellants' case would have been comparatively clear. I see no ground for reading them into the Companies Act, 1862, or into the memorandum and articles of association of this company. For these reasons I think that the appeal must be dismissed.

---

28. See Waters v. Taylor, (1808) 15 Ves. 10; (1813) 2 V. & B. 299.

AUER v. DRESSEL

Court of Appeals, New York, 1954.
306 N.Y. 427, 118 N.E.2d 590.

DESMOND, JUDGE. This article 78 of the Civil Practice Act proceeding was brought by class A stockholders of appellant R. Hoe & Co., Inc., for an order in the nature of mandamus to compel the president of Hoe to comply with a positive duty imposed on him by the corporation's by-laws. Section 2 of article I of those by-laws says that "It shall be the duty of President to call a special meeting whenever requested in writing so to do, by stockholders owning a majority of the capital stock entitled to vote at such meeting". On October 16, 1953, petitioners submitted to the president written requests for a special meeting of class A stockholders, which writings were signed in the names of the holders of record of slightly more than 55% of the class A stock. The president failed to call the meeting and, after waiting a week, the petitioners brought the present proceeding. The answer of the corporation and its president was not forthcoming until October 28, 1953, and it contained, in response to the petition's allegation that the demand was by more than a majority of class A stockholders, only a denial that the corporation and the president had any knowledge or information sufficient to form a belief as to the stockholding of those who had signed the requests. Since the president, when he filed that answer, had had before him for at least ten days the signed requests themselves, his denial that he had any information sufficient for a belief as to the adequacy of the number of signatures was obviously perfunctory and raised no issue whatever. . . .

There was no discretion in this corporate officer as to whether or not to call a meeting when a demand therefor was put before him by owners of the required number of shares. The important right of stockholders to have such meetings called will be of little practical value if corporate management can ignore the requests, force the stockholders to commence legal proceedings, and then, by purely formal denials, put the stockholders to lengthy and expensive litigation, to establish facts as to stockholdings which are peculiarly within the knowledge of the corporate officers. In such a situation, Special Term did the correct thing in disposing of the matter summarily. . . .

The petition was opposed on the further alleged ground that none of the four purposes for which petitioners wished the meeting called was a proper one for such a class A stockholders' meeting. Those four stated purposes were these: (A) to vote, upon a resolution indorsing the administration of petitioner Joseph L. Auer, who had been removed as president by the directors, and demanding that he be reinstated as such president; (B) voting upon a proposal to amend the charter and by-laws to provide that vacancies on the board of directors, arising from the removal of a director by stockholders or by resignation of a director against whom charges have been preferred, may be filled, for the unexpired term, by the stockholders only of the class theretofore represented by the director so removed or so resigned; (C) voting upon a proposal that the stockholders hear certain charges preferred, in the requests, against four of the directors, determine whether the conduct of such directors or any of them was inimical to the corporation and, if so, to vote upon their removal and vote for the election of their successors; and (D) voting upon a proposal to amend the by-laws so as to provide that half of the total number of directors in office and, in any event, not less than one-third of the whole authorized number of directors constitute a quorum of the directors.

The Hoe certificate of incorporation provides for eleven directors, of whom the class A stockholders, more than a majority of whom join in this petition, elect nine and the common stockholders elect two. The obvious purpose of the meeting here sought to be called (aside from the indorsement and reinstatement of former president Auer) is to hear charges against four of the class A directors, to remove them if the charges be proven, to amend the by-laws so that the successor directors be elected by the class A stockholders, and further to amend the by-laws so that an effective quorum of directors will be made up of no fewer than half of the directors in office and no fewer than one third of the whole authorized number of directors. No reason appears why the class A stockholders should not be allowed to vote on any or all of those proposals.

The stockholders, by expressing their approval of Mr. Auer's conduct as president and their demand that he be put back in that office, will not be able, directly, to effect that change in officers, but there is nothing invalid in their so expressing themselves and thus putting on notice the directors who will stand for election at the annual meeting. As to purpose (B), that is, amending the charter and by-laws to authorize the stockholders to fill vacancies as to class A directors who have been removed on charges or who have resigned, it seems to be settled law that the stockholders who are empowered to elect directors have the inherent power to remove them for cause, In re Koch, 257 N.Y. 318, 321, 322, 178 N.E. 545, 546; Abberger v. Kulp, 156 Misc. 210, 212, 281 N.Y.S. 373, 376; 1 White on New York Corporations, pp. 558–559; 2 Fletcher's Cyclopedia Corporations (Perm.Ed.), §§ 351, 356. Of course, as the Koch case points out, there must be the service of specific charges, adequate notice and full opportunity of meeting the accusations, but there is no present showing of any lack of any of those in this instance. Since these particular stockholders have the right to elect nine directors and to remove them on proven charges, it is not inappropriate that they should use their further power to amend the by-laws to elect the successors of such directors as shall be removed after hearing, or who shall resign pending hearing. Quite pertinent at this point is Rogers v. Hill, 289 U.S. 582, 589, 53 S.Ct. 731, 734, 77 L.Ed. 1385, which made light of an argument that stockholders, by giving power to the directors to make bylaws, had lost their own power to make them; quoting a New Jersey case, In re Griffing Iron Co., 63 N.J.L. 168, 41 A. 931, the United States Supreme Court said: " 'It would be preposterous to leave the real owners of the corporate property at the mercy of their agents, and the law has not done so' ". Such a change in the by-laws, dealing with class A directors only, has no effect on the voting rights of the common stockholders, which rights have to do with the selection of the remaining two directors only. True, the certificate of incorporation authorizes the board of directors to remove any director on charges, but we do not consider that provision as an abdication by the stockholders of their own traditional, inherent power to remove their own directors. Rather, it provides an additional method. Were that not so, the stockholders might find themselves without effective remedy in a case where a majority of the directors were accused of wrongdoing and, obviously, would be unwilling to remove themselves from office.

We fail to see, in the proposal to allow class A stockholders to fill vacancies as to class A directors, any impairment or any violation of paragraph (h) of article Third of the certificate of incorporation, which says that class A stock has exclusive voting rights with respect to all matters "other than the election of directors". That negative language should not be taken to mean that class A stockholders, who have an absolute right to elect nine of these eleven directors, cannot amend their by-laws to guarantee a similar right, in the class A stockholders and to the exclusion of common stockholders, to fill vacancies in the class A group of directors.

There is urged upon us the impracticability and unfairness of constituting the numerous stockholders a tribunal to hear charges made by themselves, and the incongruity of letting the stockholders hear and pass on those charges by proxy. Such questions are really not before us at all on this appeal. The charges here are not, on their face, frivolous or inconsequential, and all that we are holding as to the charges is that a meeting may be held to deal with them. Any director illegally removed can have his remedy in the courts, see People ex rel. Manice v. Powell, 201 N.Y. 194, 94 N.E. 634.

The order should be affirmed, with costs, and the Special Term directed forthwith to make an order in the same form as the Appellate Division order with appropriate changes of dates.

VAN VOORHIS, JUDGE (dissenting). . . . The president of Hoe was justified in declining to call a class A stockholders' meeting pursuant to the demand of these shareholders, regardless of whether they constituted a majority of that class (cf. By–Laws, art. I, § 2) if the proposed meeting would be futile for the reason that none of the proposals could be acted upon for which the meeting was to be called. Stockholders' meetings at which illegal action is proposed to be taken are restrained by injunction. . . .

An examination of the request for a special meeting by these stockholders indicates that none of the proposals could be voted upon legally at the projected meeting. The purposes of the meeting are listed as A, B, C and D. . . .

[JUDGE VAN VOORHIS went on to dispose of three of the four purposes as follows:

(A) violated §§ 27, 60 of the New York stock corporation law entrusting the management of the business to the directors and giving them the right to choose officers.

(B) would alter the rights of common stockholders and thus could not be effectuated without a vote of the holders of common stock as a class.

(D) was regarded as having no significance separate from removal.

He discussed (C) at greater length. His disagreement rested on the following: (1) the certificate of incorporation, by giving removal for cause power to the directors, excluded the shareholders, (2) insufficient facts were alleged to make a showing of "cause" and there was danger that the removal would be based solely on policy disagreement, (3) § 60 of the stock corporation law provided a judicial removal procedure that was more appropriate. His final point relates to the capacity of the shareholders to conduct this hearing:]

If it were to develop (the papers before the court do not contain evidence of such a fact) that enough of the other directors would be disqualified so that it would be impossible to obtain a quorum for the purpose, it may well be doubted that these directors could be tried before so large a number of stockholders sitting in person (if it were possible to assemble them in one place) or that they could sit in judgment by proxy. In ancient Athens evidence is said to have been heard and judgment pronounced in court by as many as 500 jurors known as dicasts, but in this instance, if petitioners be correct in their figures, there are 1,200 class A stockholders who have signed requests or proxies, and these are alleged to hold only somewhat more than half of the outstanding shares. Since it would be impossible for so large a number to conduct a trial in person, they could only do so by proxy. Voting by proxy is the accepted procedure to express the will of large numbers of stockholders on questions of corporate policy within their province to determine, and it would be suitable in this instance if the certificate of incorporation had reserved to stockholders the power to recall directors without cause before expiration of term, as in Abberger v. Kulp, 156 Misc. 210, 281 N.Y.S. 373, but it is altogether unsuited to the performance of duties which partake of the nature of the judicial function, involving, as this would need to do if the accused directors are to be removed before the expiration of their terms, a decision after trial that they have been guilty of faithlessness or fraud. . . .

COMMENT

(1) Two other American cases are sometimes cited as bearing on the scope of the shareholders' power to intervene in management.

In Charlestown Boot & Shoe Co. v. Dunsmore, 60 N.H. 85 (1880), the corporation sued two directors for losses incurred by the business. In 1874 the corporation voted to set up a committee to act with the directors to close up its affairs and chose one Osgood for such committee. The defendants refused to act with him and continued to run the business. Allegedly they failed to insure a building that burned down with a $20,000 loss, allowed property to depreciate in value and failed to collect accounts receivable. The court said:

> The provision of the statute is, that the business of a dividend paying corporation shall be managed by the directors. The statute reads, "The business of every such corporation shall be managed by the directors thereof, subject to the by-laws and votes of the corporation, and under their direction by such officers and agents as shall be duly appointed by the directors or by the corporation." G.L., c. 148, s. 3; Gen.Stats. c. 134, s. 3. The only limitation upon the judgment or discretion of the directors is such as the corporation by its by-laws and votes shall impose. It may define its business, its nature and extent, prescribe rules and regulations for the government of its officers and members, and determine whether its business shall be wound up or continued; but when it has thus acted, the business as thus defined and limited is to be managed by its directors, and by such officers and agents under their direction as the directors or the corporation shall appoint. The statute does not authorize a corporation to join another officer with the directors, nor compel the directors to act with one who is not a director. They are bound to use ordinary care and diligence in the care and management of the business of the corporaton, and are answerable for ordinary negligence. March v. Railroad, 43 N.H. 516,

529; Scott v. Depeyster, 1 Edw.Ch. 513, 543; Ang. & Ames Corp., s. 314. There is no difference in this respect between the agents of corporations and those of natural persons, unless expressly made by the charter or by-laws. Ib., s. 315. It would be unreasonable to hold them responsible for the management of the affairs of the corporation if compelled to act with one who to a greater or less extent could control their acts. The statute not only entrusts the management of the business of the corporation to the directors, but places its other officers and agents under their direction. When a statute provides that powers granted to a corporation shall be exercised by any set of officers or any particular agents, such powers can be exercised only by such officers or agents, although they are required to be chosen by the whole corporation; and if the whole corporation attempts to exercise powers which by the charter are lodged elsewhere, its action upon the subject is void. Insurance Co. v. Keyser, 32 N.H. 313, 315. . . .

(2) In Star Line of Steamers v. Van Vliet, 43 Mich. 364, 5 N.W. 418 (1880), the shareholders had resolved to appoint a committee to hire accountants to investigate the company's affairs and accounts and to report the results. An accountant so hired sued the company for his compensation. The court held for the accountant, saying

> The court assumed that the resolution appointing the committee was a valid act of the corporation, and this is excepted to. The court did not err. The resolution was shown from the records of the corporation, and there was no evidence tending to impeach it. It purported to be a legal expression of the sense of the body of stockholders, and so stood upon the corporation records.

> Generally, no doubt, a stockholders' meeting would not be authorized to contract on such subjects, the ordinary management being with the directors; but as the purpose here was in part, at least, to investigate what had been done under the superintendence of the directors, it was competent for the holders of a majority of the stock to do what was done. Comp.Laws, § 2682. There is no ground on which the corporation can urge an intendment against the validity of the resolution, and arbitrarily deny its regularity and force. In view of the facts presented every presumption is the other way. There was no offer of proof that the stockholders present at the meeting did not hold a majority of the stock, and there was some evidence tending to show that the directors were aware of the proceeding and acquiesced. . . .

CAMPBELL v. LOEW'S, INCORPORATED

Court of Chancery, Delaware, 1957.
36 Del.Ch. 563, 134 A.2d 852.

[Control of Loew's was contested by two factions, one headed by its President, Vogel, and the other by Tomlinson. At the February 1957 shareholders' meeting a compromise was effected with each faction having 6 directors, with the board being completed by a 13th neutral party. In July, two of the Vogel directors, one Tomlinson man and the neutral resigned. On July 30th a directors' meeting attended only by five Tomlinson men purported to fill two vacancies. The Chancellor SEITZ, ruled that those elections and all other actions were invalid for lack of a seven member quorum. On July 29th Vogel, as president, sent out a notice calling a shareholder's meeting for September 12th to (1) fill director vacancies, (2) increase the board from 13 to 19 and the quorum from 7 to 10 and (3) remove Tomlinson and Stanley Meyer. Plaintiff brought an action to enjoin the meeting.

The court first rejected plaintiff's argument that the president had no power to call a meeting for these purposes (the by-law specifically empowered the president to call meetings.) The portion of its opinion that deals with shareholder powers to elect directors to vacancies and to remove them for cause follows:]

Plaintiff next argues that the stockholders have no power between annual meetings to elect directors to fill newly created directorships.

Plaintiff argues in effect that since the Loew's by-laws provide that the stockholders may fill "vacancies", and since our Courts have construed "vacancy" not to embrace "newly created directorships" (Automatic Steel Products v. Johnston, 31 Del.Ch. 469, 64 A.2d 416, 6 A.L.R. 2d 170), the attempted call by the president for the purpose of filling newly created directorships was invalid.

Conceding that "vacancy" as used in the by-laws does not embrace "newly created directorships", that does not resolve this problem. I say this because in Moon v. Moon Motor Car Co., 17 Del.Ch. 176, 151 A. 298, it was held that the stockholders had the inherent right between annual meetings to fill newly created directorships. See also Automatic Steel Products v. Johnston, above. There is no basis to distinguish the Moon case unless it be because the statute has since been amended to provide that not only vacancies but newly created directorships "may be filled by a majority of the directors then in office . . . unless it is otherwise provided in the certificate of incorporation or the by-laws . . .". 8 Del.C. § 223. Obviously, the amendment to include new directors is not worded so as to make the statute exclusive. It does not prevent the stockholders from filling the new directorships.

Is there any reason to consider the absence of a reference in the by-laws to new directorships to be significant? I think not. The by-law relied upon by plaintiff was adopted long before the statutory amendment and it does not purport to be exclusive in its operation. It would take a strong by-law language to warrant the conclusion that those adopting the by-laws intended to prohibit the stockholders from filling new directorships between annual meetings. No such strong language appears here and I do not think the implication is warranted in view of the subject matter.

I therefore conclude that the stockholders of Loew's do have the right between annual meetings to elect directors to fill newly created directorships.

Plaintiff next argues that the shareholders of a Delaware corporation have no power to remove directors from office even for cause and thus the call for that purpose is invalid. The defendant naturally takes a contrary position.

While there are some cases suggesting the contrary, I believe that the stockholders have the power to remove a director for cause. See Auer v. Dressel, 306 N.Y. 427, 118 N.E.2d 590, 48 A.L.R.2d 604; compare Bruch v. National Guarantee Credit Corp., 13 Del.Ch. 180, 116 A. 738. This power must be implied when we consider that otherwise a director who is guilty of the worst sort of violation of his duty could nevertheless remain on the board. It is hardly to be believed that a director who is disclosing the corporation's trade secrets to a competitor would be immune from removal by the stockholders. Other examples, such as embezzlement of corporate funds etc., come readily to mind.

But plaintiff correctly states that there is no provision in our statutory law providing for the removal of directors by stockholder action. In contrast he calls attention to § 142 of 8 Del.C., dealing with officers, which specifically refers to the possibility of a vacancy in an office by removal. He also notes that the Loew's by-laws provide for the removal of officers and employees but not directors. From these facts he argues that it was intended that directors not be removed even for cause. I believe the statute and by-law are of course some evidence to support plaintiff's contention. But when we seek to exclude the existence of a power by implication, I think it is pertinent to consider whether the absence of the power can be said to subject the corporation to the possibility of real damage. I say this because we seek intention and such a factor would be relevant to that issue. Considering the damage a director might be able to inflict upon his corporation, I believe the doubt must be resolved by construing the statutes and by-laws as leaving untouched the question of director removal for cause. This being so, the Court is free to conclude on reason that the stockholders have such inherent power.

I therefore conclude that as a matter of Delaware corporation law the stockholders do have the power to remove directors for cause. I need not and do not decide whether the stockholders can by appropriate charter or by-law provision deprive themselves of this right.

Plaintiff next argues that the removal of Tomlinson and Meyer as directors would violate the right of minority shareholders to representation on the board and would be contrary to the policy of the Delaware law regarding cumulative voting. Plaintiff contends that where there is cumulative voting, as provided by the Loew's certificate, a director cannot be removed by the stockholders even for cause.

It is true that the Chancellor noted in the Bruch case that the provision for cumulative voting in the Delaware law was one reason why directors should not be considered to have the power to remove a fellow director even for cause. And it is certainly evident that if not carefully supervised the existence of a power in the stockholders to remove a director even for cause could be abused and used to defeat cumulative voting. See 66 Harvard L.R. 531.

Does this mean that there can be no removal of a director by the stockholders for cause in any case where cumulative voting exists? The conflicting considerations involved make the answer to this question far from easy. Some states have passed statutes dealing with this problem but Delaware has not. The possibility of stockholder removal action designed to circumvent the effect of cumulative voting is evident. This is particularly true where the removal vote is, as here, by mere majority vote. On the other hand, if we assume a case where a director's presence or action is clearly damaging the corporation and its stockholders in a substantial way, it is difficult to see why that director should be free to continue such damage merely because he was elected under a cumulative voting provision.

On balance, I conclude that the stockholders have the power to remove a director for cause even where there is a provision for cumulative voting. I think adequate protection is afforded not only by the legal safeguards announced in this opinion but by the existence of a remedy to test the validity of any such action, if taken.

The foregoing points constitute all of the arguments advanced by plaintiff which go to the validity of the call of the meeting for the purposes stated. It follows from my various conclusions that the meeting was validly called by the president to consider the matters noticed.

I turn next to plaintiff's charges relating to procedural defects and to irregularities in proxy solicitation by the Vogel group.

Plaintiff's first point is that the stockholders can vote to remove a director for cause only after such director has been given adequate notice of charges of grave impropriety and afforded an opportunity to be heard.

Defendant raises a preliminary point that plaintiff, being only a stockholder, has no standing to make the contention that the foregoing requirements have not been met. It may be noted that the director whose removal was involved in the Bruch case was not a party in that case and yet the Court considered the issue properly raised. The same situation applied in the Auer case in New York. Moreover, on reason, there would seem no basis for telling a stockholder, particularly where cumulative voting is involved, that he has no right to challenge the legal propriety of action proposed to be taken to remove a member of the board of directors. After all, the board is managing the corporation for all the stockholders and while a director may have sufficient standing to attack the action himself, I cannot believe that a stockholder is lacking a sufficient interest to warrant legal recognition.

I am inclined to agree that if the proceedings preliminary to submitting the matter of removal for cause to the stockholders appear to be legal and if the charges are legally sufficient on their face, the Court should ordinarily not intervene. The sufficiency of the evidence would be a matter for evaluation in later proceedings. But where the procedure adopted to remove a director for cause is invalid on its face, a stockholder can attack such matters before the meeting. This conclusion is dictated both by the desirability of avoiding unnecessary and expensive action and by the importance of settling internal disputes, where reasonably possible, at the earliest moment. Compare Empire Southern Gas Co. v. Gray, 29 Del.Ch. 95, 46 A.2d 741. Otherwise a director could be removed and his successor could be appointed and participate in important board action before the illegality of the removal was judicially established. This seems undesirable where the illegality is clear on the face of the proceedings.

Defendant contends that the sufficiency of the charges or the evidence in support thereof is not for the Court to consider, citing Griffith v. Sprowl, 45 Ind.App. 504, 91 N.E. 25; New Founded Indus. Missionary Baptist Ass'n v. Anderson, La.App., 49 So.2d 342; State ex rel. Blackwood v. Brast, 98 W.Va. 596, 127 S.E. 507. These cases involved either a pertinent by-law or statute, and none involved the removal of a director. They are not contrary to the rules here announced. I conclude that plaintiff can raise the issue as to the propriety of the removal procedure.

Turning now to plaintiff's contentions, it is certainly true that when the shareholders attempt to remove a director for cause, ". . . there must be the service of specific charges, adequate notice and full opportunity of meeting the accusation   .". See Auer v. Dressel [306 N.Y. 427, 118 N.E.2d 593], above. While it involved an invalid attempt by directors to remove a fellow director for cause, nevertheless, this same general standard was recognized in Bruch v. National Guarantee Credit Corp. [13 Del.Ch. 180, 116 A. 741], above. The Chancellor said that the power of removal could not "be exercised in an arbitrary manner. The accused director would be entitled to be heard in his own defense".

Plaintiff asserts that no specific charges have been served upon the two directors sought to be ousted; that the notice of the special meeting fails to contain a specific statement of the charges; that the proxy statement which accompanied the notice also failed to notify the stockholders of the specific charges; and that it does not inform the stockholders that the accused must be afforded an opportunity to meet the accusations before a vote is taken.

Matters for stockholder consideration need not be conducted with the same formality as judicial proceedings. The proxy statement specifically recites that the two directors are sought to be removed for the reasons stated in the president's accompanying letter. Both directors involved received copies of the letter. Under the circumstances I think it must be said that the two directors involved were served with notice of the charges against them. It is true, as plaintiff says, that the notice and the proxy statement failed to contain a specific statement of charges. But as indicated, I believe the accompanying letter was sufficient compliance with the notice requirement.

Contrary to plaintiff's contention, I do not believe the material sent out had to advise the stockholders that the accused must be afforded an opportunity to defend the charges before the stockholders voted. Such an opportunity had to be afforded as a matter of law and the failure to so advise them did not affect the necessity for compliance with the law. Thus, no prejudice is shown.

I next consider plaintiff's contention that the charges against the two directors do not constitute "cause" as a matter of law. It would take too much space to narrate in detail the contents of the president's letter. I must therefore give my summary of its charges. First of all, it charges that the two directors (Tomlinson and Meyer) failed to cooperate with Vogel in his announced program for rebuilding the company; that their purpose has been to put themselves in control; that they made baseless accusations against him and other management personnel and attempted to divert him from his normal duties as president by bombarding him with correspondence containing unfounded charges and other similar acts; that they moved into the company's building, accompanied by lawyers and accountants, and immediately proceeded upon a planned scheme of harassment. They called for many records, some going back twenty years, and were rude to the personnel. Tomlinson sent daily letters to the directors making serious charges directly and by means of innuendos and misinterpretations.

Are the foregoing charges, if proved, legally sufficient to justify the ouster of the two directors by the stockholders? I am satisfied that a charge that the directors desired to take over control of the corporation is not a reason for their ouster. Standing alone, it is a perfectly legitimate objective which is a part of the very fabric of corporate existence. Nor is a charge of lack of cooperation a legally sufficient basis for removal for cause.

The next charge is that these directors, in effect, engaged in a calculated plan of harassment to the detriment of the corporation. Certainly a director may examine books, ask questions, etc., in the discharge of his duty, but a point can be reached when his actions exceed the call of duty and become deliberately obstructive. In such a situation, if his actions constitute a real burden on the corporation then the stockholders are entitled to relief. The charges in this area made by the Vogel letter are legally sufficient to justify the stockholders in voting to remove such directors. . . . In so concluding I of course express no opinion as to the truth of the charges.

I therefore conclude that the charge of "a planned scheme of harassment" as detailed in the letter constitutes a justifiable legal basis for removing a director.

I next consider whether the directors sought to be removed have been given a reasonable opportunity to be heard by the stockholders on the charges made.

The corporate defendant freely admits that it has flatly refused to give the five Tomlinson directors or the plaintiff a stockholders' list. Any doubt about the matter was removed by the statement of defendant's counsel in open court at the argument that no such list would be supplied. The Vogel faction has physical control of the corporate offices and facilities. By this action the corporation through the Vogel group has deliberately refused to afford the directors in question an adequate opportunity to be heard by the stockholders on the charges made. This is contrary to the legal requirements which must be met before a director can be removed for cause.

At the oral argument the defendant's attorney offered to mail any material which might be presented by the Tomlinson faction. This falls far short of meeting the requirements of the law when directors are sought to be ousted for cause. Nor does the granting of the statutory right to inspect and copy some 26,000 names fulfill the requirement that a director sought to be removed for cause must be afforded an opportunity to present his case to the stockholders before they vote.

When Vogel as president caused the notice of meeting to be sent, he accompanied it with a letter requesting proxies granting authority to vote for the removal of the two named directors. It is true that the proxy form also provided a space for the stockholder to vote against such removal. However, only the Vogel accusations accompanied the request for a proxy. Thus, while the stockholder could vote for or against removal, he would be voting with only one viewpoint presented. This violates every sense of equity and fair play in a removal for cause situation.

While the directors involved or some other group could mail a letter to the stockholders and ask for a proxy which would revoke the earlier proxy, this procedure does not comport with the legal requirement that the directors in question must be afforded an opportunity to be heard before the shareholders vote. This is not an ordinary proxy contest case and a much more stringent standard must be invoked, at least at the initial stage, where it is sought to remove a director for cause. This is so for several reasons. Under our statute the directors manage the corporation and each has a somewhat independent status during his term of office. This right could be greatly impaired if substantial safeguards were not afforded a director whose removal for cause is sought. The possibility of abuse is evident. Also, as the Chancellor pointed out in the Bruch case, the power of removal can be a threat to cumulative voting rights. This is particularly true where, as here, the removal is by mere majority vote.

There seems to be an absence of cases detailing the appropriate procedure for submitting a question of director removal for cause for stockholder consideration. I am satisfied, however, that to the extent the matter is to be voted upon by the use of proxies, such proxies may be solicited only after the accused directors are afforded an opportunity to present their case to the stockholders. This means, in my opinion, that an opportunity must be provided such directors to present their defense to the stockholders by a statement which must accompany or precede the initial solicitation of proxies seeking authority to vote for the removal of such director for cause. If not provided then such proxies may not be voted for removal. And the corporation has a duty to see that this opportunity is given the directors at its expense. Admittedly, no such opportunity is given the two directors involved. Indeed, the corporation admittedly refused to supply them with a stockholders' list.

To require anything less than the foregoing is to deprive the stockholders of the opportunity to consider the case made by both sides before voting and would make a mockery of the requirement that a director sought to be removed for cause is entitled to an opportunity to be heard before the stockholders vote. See the persuasive language of the dissent in Auer v. Dressel, above. But in referring to the language of the dissent I do not thereby suggest that my conclusion here is necessarily contrary to the majority decision on this point.

I therefore conclude that the procedural sequence here adopted for soliciting proxies seeking authority to vote on the removal of the two directors is contrary to law. The result is that the proxy solicited by the Vogel group, which is based upon unilateral presentation of the facts by those in control of the corporate facilities, must be declared invalid insofar as they purport to give authority to vote for the removal of the directors for cause.

A preliminary injunction will issue restraining the corporation from recognizing or counting any proxies held by the Vogel group and others insofar as such proxies purport to grant authority to vote for the removal of Tomlinson and Meyer as directors of the corporation.

The Court emphasizes that it is considering only the proxy solicitation and use aspect of this problem and is considering those only where advance authority is given to vote in a particular way. I am not called upon to consider what procedural and substantive requirements must be met if the matter is raised for consideration by stockholders present in person at the meeting.

[Finally the Chancellor disposed of various contentions regarding the solicitation of proxies by the Vogel group. He also refused to grant an injunction compelling the Vogel group to attend board meetings.]

COMMENT

Loew's Incorporated has had a history of control battles second perhaps to Alleghany's. At the time of this litigation, Loew's was an industrial empire with assets of about $250 million, including a large inventory of old films, television and radio interests, and a good deal of real estate. In 1954 it had been compelled by an antitrust decree to transfer its movie theatre properties to Loew's Theatres, Inc. However, the troubles of the movie industry after 1947 brought its Metro–Goldwyn–Mayer movie-maturing operations into a loss position. The powerful, aggressive mogul Louis B. Mayer was deposed by the president Nicholas Schenck and vowed his revenge. In long battles Mayer wore down Schenck who resigned but was able to secure the selection of Vogel, manager of Loew's Theatres to succeed him. This case represents Mayer's attempt to retake control from Vogel, although Tomlinson, a Canadian trucker and road builder, was drawn into the leadership position and was the largest single shareholder. The go-between in arranging this alliance was Stanley Meyer whose removal as director Vogel sought.

After the above decision (and other federal litigation) a shareholders' meeting was held. It resulted in a victory for Vogel, which he consolidated after he persuaded the shareholders to eliminate cumulative voting. In 1960 Loew's Inc. was renamed Metro Goldwyn Mayer, Inc. Then, a year of big losses in 1963 led to Vogel's replacement by one O'Brien. An attempt to seize control by a combination of stock purchases and proxy fighting, was made in 1967 by Philip J. Levin, a wealthy real estate developer. After his defeat he sold to Time, Inc. and Edgar Bronfman of Distillers Corp.—Seagrams who forced the replacement of the president. Quite shortly, thereafter, Loew's control changed hands again, this time through tender offers to its shareholders that resulted in a 37% interest being held by Kirk Kerkorian, another adventurous investor.[29] As of 1988 Loew's had left the movie theatre business entirely and was engaged in life insurance (CNA), cigarette-making (Lorillard), hotels and watchmaking (Bulova). The largest single owners (24%) were Robert and Preston Tisch, New York realtors.

PROBLEM

Northeast Industries, Inc. (hereafter called "Northeast") is engaged in the manufacture of brass fittings in Fairfax, New Hampshire, where it has its only factory, built in 1907. From the time that Silas Ashburton founded the firm in 1843 until 1929 Northeast prospered and the family grew wealthy. Since 1930 competition from other parts of the country has depressed its profit level so that it had losses during the depression years and, since World War II, has shown substantial earnings only during the Korean emergency. Experts in the brass industry predict a long slow decline for companies like Northeast but no immediate disaster. Northeast is the only major year-round industry in Fairfax, which is a town of about 5,000 population, and employs the bulk of its labor force.

Northeast is a Delaware corporation operating under a charter and by-laws similar to those in the Documentary Supplement except that its purpose clauses are different. It is quite closely owned. The Fairfax Savings & Trust Company holds 50,000 shares in trust for Judith and Josiah Ashburton who are in college at Bryn Mawr and Rollins respectively. 40,000 shares are owned by Marcia Ashburton, widow of Silas Ashburton III, who is now 72 years old, 30,000 shares by John Wellington Wells, 36, a relative of the Ashburtons by marriage and a New York advertising executive, 20,000 shares are held by

---

29. Most of the foregoing is from the vivid, if not excessively impartial or self-effacing account, by Vogel's counsel, L. Nizer, My Life in Court ch. 6 (1961), brought up to date by the New York Times and Moody's Manual of Industrials.

Nathan Micawber, also a collateral descendant of old Silas. The remaining authorized shares are unissued.

Micawber is a director of Northeast and takes an active part in management although he is not an officer. The other directors are all officers and have risen from the lower ranks of the Company's working and clerical force. All are residents of Fairfax. The directors have all been such at least since 1946. None of them are related to the Ashburtons; none of them own any stock in Northeast.

Special Operations, Ltd. (hereafter called "Special") has recently acquired several other companies including a borax producer and a publishing firm with a large tax loss and has engaged in various other activities of a promotional character to its very great profit. Its officers have observed that Northeast has a large inventory of brass that is very valuable currently because of bitter strikes in the brass producing industry that threaten to disrupt production for months. This inventory plus some newly installed machine tools could readily be disposed of, upon liquidation, for a price that will yield, net of all obligations, substantially more than the present worth of all of the stock of Northeast, as indicated by the expert appraisal that was made four years ago at the death of Silas Ashburton III.

Ivan Easterday, vice-president of Special, came to visit Micawber to convey Special's offer to purchase the desired assets with a deadline before the next annual meeting. Micawber, after consulting some of his fellow board members and with some of the more prominent and prosperous citizens of Fairfax, said that he could not accept this offer. According to Micawber the proposed transaction would be a betrayal of the working force and of the town. Mr. Easterday then approached John Wellington Wells who held a family conference. He, his wife and Marcia Ashburton agreed that they wanted the sale to go through and would do anything to override the opposition. Wells stated that the stock and the Company belonged to his family and that when his family needed the money he couldn't see any reason why he should be charitable to a lot of people he didn't even know. The representative of The Fairfax Savings & Trust Company indicated that he would have to consult his directors.

QUESTIONS

Along with the partner for whom you work you attend this conference. He indicates to the Wells group that he is "sure something could be done." As the two of you return to the office he outlines to you what points he wants looked up:

(1) Can the shareholders simply tell the directors to sell? It seems to me that the Cuninghame and Auer cases are relevant. Is 8 Del.C. § 141 pertinent?

(2) If we are going to tell the directors to sell what sort of mechanics do we have to go through? Article II of the by-laws should cover this. Is there any way in which the board might try to frustrate this? Can they amend the by-laws themselves? Are there limits on their right to amend? [30]

(3) What about getting rid of Micawber and his crew? Again, I think the Auer case bears on this and so does Campbell. What mechanics are involved here? Or would it be possible to "pack" the board? Article III of the by-laws

---

30. Cf. Schnell v. Chris–Craft Indus. Inc., 285 A.2d 437 (Del.1971) (discussing board's power to change date of annual meeting in such a way as to disadvantage opposition.)

tells about the board of directors. Also check 8 Del.C. §§ 141(k), 222 and 223 on this.

(4) Could we achieve any of these goals by changes in the charter and/or by-laws? Look at 8 Del.C. §§ 109, 141, 242(c)(1), 271. Also check article X of the by-laws.

(5) I am not familiar with the new 8 Del.C. § 228. What does it do to the relations between the groups?

Bibliography: On the allocation of functions to shareholders I again refer you to M. Eisenberg, The Structure of the Corporation: A Legal Analysis (1976).

4. Proxy Regulation

NOTE ON PROXIES

Somewhat artificially, we have postponed until now the question of proxy regulation. Since physical presence at annual meetings of any corporation not purely local in nature is apt to be so awkward as to discourage most shareholders, voting by proxy is the rule. Regulation of proxies and their solicitation thus takes control of the shareholder voting process at its critical point.

Recall that a proxy is basically an agency relationship whereby the shareholder constitutes the proxyholder its agent. Accordingly a proxy can be revoked at any time as can other agencies, except in those cases in which the proxy is given in order to serve the interests of the proxyholder. See Restatement, Second, Agency §§ 118, 138–39. A proxyholder is bound to obey the instructions of his principal and owes it certain duties of loyalty. Little of this learning is particularly useful here when the proxyholder is the management itself and thus is in a position of greater knowledge and power than its so-called principal. The relationship is also rather unusual since it is the agent customarily who goes and solicits the principal to establish the relation. The methods formerly used to obtain proxies were often startlingly primitive. It is told that one company placed language creating a proxy on the back of each dividend check it sent out, causing an endorsement to be a grant of a proxy unless the shareholder went to the trouble of striking it out. Matters largely stood in that position when the great depression came in 1929.

When in 1934 Congress turned its attention to abuses in the securities market that had been highlighted by the depression it included in its regulation scheme several topics that related to the internal affairs of corporations, most conspicuously that of trading by "insiders" in corporate securities and that of proxy regulation. Congress by section 14 of the Securities Exchange Act directed the new Securities and Exchange Commission,[31] to regulate this situation.

Observe that in its 1934 version the Act extended only to corporations registered on a security exchange, a relatively small number of firms. After testimony that non-listed concerns were furnishing very little information, and often inaccurately at that, Congress extended section 14 so that it now covers all companies required to register under Section 12 of the Act—an appreciably larger number. The SEC has further extended the practical effect of the rules by requiring the transmission of periodic reports by companies to their shareholders even if they do not bother to solicit proxies, a device which formerly relieved them of the obligation to report. On the other hand, the SEC has used its exempting power to raise the "floor" on the requirement of registration from $1 million in assets to $3 million in 1982 and $5 million in 1986, stating that this maintained the real value of the 1964 figure after taking inflation into account. It is very important that you understand the scope of applicability of the proxy rule. In particular you need to distinguish "registration" of a corporation under Section 12 of the 1934 Act from "registration" of a new securities issue under the 1933 Act.

The SEC has gradually developed a more precise and comprehensive system of regulation. The key portions of Rule 14a are included in the Documentary Supplement, and the following cases illuminate some of the problems which the regulation raises.[32] It may be helpful to your understanding of their framework to give a basic outline of the Rule's purposes:

(1) management solicitation of proxies is regulated so as to forbid false or misleading statements or omissions and to require inclusion of specific warnings and items of information; advance submission of proxy materials to the SEC is required;

(2) solicitation of proxies by groups challenging management is similarly regulated so as to prevent false and misleading statements and require disclosure of specified data about the persons constituting the opposition, its sources of financing, etc;

(3) the position of dissident shareholder groups relative to the management's is improved by imposing two requirements on management:

(A) that it help circulate opposition literature by either furnishing it with a list of shareholder names and addresses or mailing the literature itself upon tender of postal and other charges (Rule 14a–7).

(B) that it include in its own proxy materials proposals for consideration by shareholders, assuming that they are

31. See p. 169 supra, for an introduction to the SEC.

32. Formerly the proxy rules were numbered X–14A–, as you will see in some cases.

proper subjects for action and are not precluded by some of the specific exceptions in the Rules (see Rule 14a–8).

The latter two rules pertain to different types of shareholder insurgency. If one wants to take control of a corporation Rule 14a–8 is unavailable (due to subsection (c)(8)), and the insurgents are left with Rule 14a–7. For "cause" insurgency Rule 14a–8 is specifically tailored.

Where the federal rules are applicable, proxy contestants will not ordinarily find state law helpful except insofar as they wish to resort to state procedures for obtaining shareholder lists (as under 8 Del.C. § 220). Occasionally however, state courts provide surprises. See p. 724 infra and p. 220 supra.

SECURITIES AND EXCHANGE COMMISSION v. TRANSAMERICA CORPORATION

United States Court of Appeals, Third Circuit, 1947.
163 F.2d 511, certiorari denied 332 U.S. 847, 68 S.Ct. 351, 92 L.Ed. 418 (1948).

[Transamerica was a Delaware corporation subject to Section 14 of the Securities Exchange Act because it was registered on the New York Stock Exchange as well as those in Los Angeles and San Francisco. It had about 150,000 shareholders. In January 1946 one Lewis Gilbert, who has dedicated himself to the protection of shareholder interests, submitted to Transamerica's management four proposals for action at the stockholders' meeting in April 1946. Of these number 3 became moot when the directors amended the by-laws to move the place of annual meetings from Wilmington to San Francisco (at the center of the firm's business activities). The first proposal called for the election of Transamerica's independent public auditors by the shareholders, with a representative of the firm so elected being expected to attend each annual meeting, the second proposed to amend By–Law 47 in order to eliminate the requirement that notice of any change of the by-laws be contained in the notice of meeting and the fourth would have required that a report of the last annual meeting be sent to all stockholders. Gilbert identified proposals (1) and (2) as by-law amendments. The SEC demanded that Transamerica include these proposals in its proxy statement and when Transamerica refused, brought suit to enjoin Transamerica from soliciting or using proxies without complying with that demand. The district court ruled for the SEC on proposal (1) and for Transamerica on proposals (2) and (4). Both parties appealed.

The opinion of JUDGE BIGGS follows, in part:]

We think it will be of assistance in understanding what is involved if we deal first with the respective major contentions of each of the parties; then treat with the specific proposals involved, some of the contentions of the parties in respect to them and the applicable rulings of the court below. Respecting the major contentions of the parties, it will be observed that the decision in the case at bar must turn in some part on the interpretation to be placed on that portion of Proxy Rule X–14A–7 which provides that if a qualified security holder has given the management reasonable notice that he intends to present for action at a meeting of security holders "a proposal which is a proper subject for action by security holders" the management shall set forth the proposal and provide means by which the security holders can vote on the proposal as provided in Proxy Rule X–14A–2. Much of the briefs of the parties and most of the argument have been devoted to a discussion of what is "a proper subject" for action by the stockholders of Transamerica. Speaking broadly, it is the position of the Commission that "a proper subject" for stockholder action is one in which the stockholders may properly be interested under the law of Delaware. Transamerica takes the position that a stockholder may interest himself with propriety only in a subject in respect to which he is entitled to vote at a stockholders' meeting when every requirement of Delaware law and of the provisions of the charter and by-laws, including notice, has been fulfilled. Putting Transamerica's position in its full technical abundance, as we understand it, it says that since Section 5(8) [33] of the Delaware Corporation Law provides that a certificate of incorporation may set forth provisions which limit, regulate and define the powers and functions of the directors and stockholders, and since Article XIII of Transamerica's charter states that all the powers of the corporation shall be vested in the board of directors, the power to control corporate acts rests in the board of directors and not in the stockholders; in other words that the incorporators by the notice requirement of By–Law 47 curbed the power of the stockholders to vote on any by-law amendment of which notice was not included in the notice of meeting and in effect vested in Transamerica's board of directors the power to decide whether any proposed by-law amendment should be voted on at an annual meeting of stockholders. In short, management insists that it is entitled to use the notice requirement of By–Law 47 as a block or strainer to prevent any proposal to amend the by-laws, which it may deem unsuitable, from reaching a vote at an annual meeting of stockholders.

We will now treat specifically with Gilbert's three proposals, with some of the contentions of the parties in regard to them and with the rulings of the court below. Transamerica contends, as we have indicated, that since Article XIII of Transamerica's charter vests in the Board of Directors all powers of corporate management, not prohibited to them by the law of Delaware, this comprehensive grant renders the question of auditors not a proper subject for action by Transamerica's stockholders. The court below took the view, in our opinion, fully supportable, that the stockholders as the beneficial owners of the enterprise may prefer to consider the selection of independent auditors to review "what is no more than the trust relationship which exists between the directors and stockholders." See D.C., 67 F.Supp. at page 334. Assuredly, it is no less than this. It is necessary to go no further in order to sustain the Commission's contention that the auditing of the books of a corporation is a proper subject for stockholder consideration and action. Surely the audit of a corporation's books may not be considered to be peculiarly within the discretion of the directors. A corporation is run for the benefit of its stockholders and not for that of its managers.

Stockholders are entitled to employ watchmen to eye the guardians of their enterprise, the directors. Section 9 of the Delaware Corporation Law [34] does not militate against this view nor is it important whether Gilbert's proposal be considered as a proposal to amend the by-laws or, as the court below considered it, "a mandate from the stock-

---

33. [Ed.] Substantially the present § 102(b)(1).

34. [Ed.] Substantially the present § 141(a).

holders to the directors" to be carried into execution by following its terms. Setting to one side the notice provision of By–Law 47, to be dealt with hereinafter, the employment of independent auditors to be selected by the stockholders beyond any question is a proper subject for action by the stockholders.

As to (2), the proposal to amend By–Law 47 in order to eliminate the requirement that notice be given in the notice of any meeting of any proposed alteration or amendment of the by-laws, the court below decided in favor of Transamerica and against the Commission. As the learned District Judge pointed out, as Transamerica has contended and as has been stated herein, By–Law 47 provides that the by-laws may be altered or amended by an affirmative vote of a majority of the stock issued and outstanding and entitled to vote at any regular or special meeting of stockholders if notice of the proposed alteration or amendment is contained in the notice of the meeting. . . . The court below took the view that because notice was not given by management, management was entitled to rule out of order any proposal to amend this [sic] By-law. But Gilbert had made his intention plain. He did not intend to deny notice to the stockholders for notice would have been given if Transamerica obeyed the Commission's direction and its proxy rules. Gilbert stated to Transamerica that the proposed by-law amendment was "to be introduced only if the management again resorts to what I consider the extremely undemocratic method of trying to avoid a vote, for approval or rejection, of the other resolutions, by ruling them out of order."

That the law of Delaware will permit stockholders of a Delaware corporation to act validly on a stockholder's proposal to amend by-laws is clear beyond any doubt. . . .[35] Transamerica's charter imposes no impediment for Article X of the charter provides: "In furtherance and not in limitation of the powers conferred by statute, the board of directors is expressly authorized: (a) To make and alter the by-laws of this corporation, without any action on the part of the stockholders; but the by-laws made by the directors and the power so conferred may be altered or repealed by the stockholders." In short if it were not for the block interposed by the notice provisions of By–Law 47, it would be clear that Gilbert's second proposal would be a proper subject for stockholder action.

As to (4), the proposal to require a report of the proceeding of the annual meeting to be sent to all stockholders, we can perceive no logical basis for concluding that it is not a proper subject for action by the security holders. The security holders numbered approximately 151,000 persons holding approximately 9,935,000 shares of stock. Certainly it is proper for the stockholders to desire and to receive a report as to what transpired at the annual meeting of their company. True it may cost Transamerica $20,000 annually, but accurate information as to what transpires respecting the corporation is an absolute necessity if stockholders are to act for their joint interest. If stockholders cannot act together, they cannot act effectively.

The propriety of proposal (4) seems to us to be scarcely arguable and we conclude that no further discussion is necessary, any question of notice under By–Law 47 aside.

35. [Ed.] Citing the counterpart of the present § 109(a).

The conclusions reached by the court below in respect to Gilbert's proposals (2) and (4) may be supported only by applying the notice provision of By–Law 47 in all its strictness. Admittedly, so long as the notice provision of By–Law 47 remains in effect unless management sees fit to include notice of a by-law amendment proposed by a stockholder in the notice of meeting the proposed amendment can never come before the stockholders' meeting with complete correctness. The same would be true even if one per centum of the stockholders backed the proposed amendment. But Transamerica's position is overnice and is untenable. In our opinion Gilbert's proposals are proper subjects for stockholder action within the purview of Proxy Rule X–14A–7 since all are subjects in respect to which stockholders have the right to act under the General Corporation Law of Delaware.

But assuming arguendo that this was not so, we think that we have demonstrated that Gilbert's proposals are within the reach of security-holder action were it not for the insulation afforded management by the notice provision of By–Law 47. If this minor provision may be employed as Transamerica seeks to employ it, it will serve to circumvent the intent of Congress in enacting the Securities Exchange Act of 1934. It was the intent of Congress to require fair opportunity for the operation of corporate suffrage. The control of great corporations by a very few persons was the abuse at which Congress struck in enacting Section 14(a). We entertain no doubt that Proxy Rule X–14A–7 represents a proper exercise of the authority conferred by Congress on the Commission under Section 14(a). This seems to us to end the matter. The power conferred upon the Commission by Congress cannot be frustrated by a corporate by-law. . . .

The judgment of the court below will be modified to compel resolicitation on Gilbert's proposals (2) and (4). The court below has already ordered re-solicitation on Gilbert's proposal (1). If further re-solicitation of proposal (1) be necessary by reason of lapse of time the court below will be authorized to order such re-solicitation. It will be directed to enjoin violation of the Act and the rules by Transamerica in respect to proposals (2) and (4). In all other respects the judgment will be affirmed.

COMMENT

Lewis Gilbert, who touched off the Transamerica case together with his brother John, has for over a decade been defending the interests of the American stockholder. When he inherited a substantial estate in 1933 he attended his first shareholders' meetings and was horrified at their "disgracefully" perfunctory character. The Gilberts published an Annual Report of Stockholder activities which include episodes of their attendance at some 150 or so annual meetings. Since he holds only a few shares in any one corporation his gains from this activity are not financial but only in the nature of satisfaction at his achievements. He has pressed for convenient meeting places, for the distribution of post meeting reports, for better reporting. In particular he has pushed hard for limits on executive compensation—including a $200,000 limit on cash compensation (and $25,000 on pensions). He wants officers and directors to own stock. He favors cumulative voting. All of these things he does with vigor and persistence, being quite "unshushable". The result has not infrequently been that management has, rather than face a nasty scene, often given way and moved annual meetings to more convenient places—as did Transamerica or placed limits on its compensation, etc.[36]

MEDICAL COMMITTEE FOR HUMAN RIGHTS v. SECURITIES AND EXCHANGE COMMISSION

United States Court of Appeals, District of Columbia Circuit, 1970.
139 U.S.App.D.C. 226, 432 F.2d 659, vacated and dismissed as moot 404 U.S. 403, 92 S.Ct. 577, 30 L.Ed.2d 560 (1972).

[A. Chronology

On March 11, 1968 the Chairman of the Medical Committee for Human Rights wrote the Dow Chemical Company that his Committee had been given several shares of Dow stock. He requested that Dow submit to its shareholders the following:

"RESOLVED, that the shareholders of the Dow Chemical Company request the Board of Directors, in accordance with the laws of the State of Delaware, and the Composite Certificate of Incorporation of the Dow Chemical Company, to adopt a resolution setting forth an amendment to the Composite Certificate of Incorporation of the Dow Chemical Company that napalm shall not be sold to any buyer unless that buyer gives reasonable assurance that the substance will not be used on or against human beings."

The letter gave the following reasons:

Finally, we wish to note that our objections to the sale of this product [are] primarily based on the concerns for human life inherent in our organization's credo. However, we are further informed by our investment advisers that this product is also bad for our company's business as it is being used in the Vietnamese War. It is now clear from company statements and press reports that it is increasingly hard to recruit the highly intelligent, well-motivated, young college men so important for company growth. There is, as well, an adverse impact on our global business, which our advisers indicate, suffers as a result of the public reaction to this product.

On March 31 Dow's general counsel advised that this was too late for inclusion in the 1968 statement but promised later response for 1969.

On January 6, 1969 the Committee noted that Dow had not responded as promised.

On January 17 Dow's secretary replied that Dow intended to omit the resolution from its proxy materials, relying on an opinion of its counsel.

On February 3 the Committee replied, asserting that Dow was in error and amending its proposal so that it requested the directors to consider adopting a resolution that Dow not make napalm at all. At the same time the Committee wrote the SEC asking it to review Dow's decision if it continued to refuse.

---

36. The Man Who's Been to 2,000 Meetings, Fortune, April, 1961, p. 147.

On February 7, Dow reiterated its refusal, along with a new opinion of counsel.

On February 18 the SEC's Division of Corporate Counsel advised the parties that the SEC would not compel Dow to include the proposal.

On February 28 the Committee filed a new request and a memorandum of law.

On April 2 the SEC reaffirmed its decision.

The Committee brought an action to review this decision. The SEC moved to dismiss for want of jurisdiction. The Court denied the motion of October 13, 1969 without prejudice to its renewal on briefs and again denied it on July 8, 1970.

B.   Administrative Law Considerations

JUDGE TAMM'S opinion for the Court covers several administrative law points which are summarily treated here.

First, it denied the SEC's argument that the appeal was not filed within 60 days of the SEC order as required by § 25 of the 1934 Act.

Second, it decided that the order was one reviewable under § 25, although "it has been generally assumed that proxy decisions like the present one are not reviewable by the courts." It found that the SEC's "proxy procedures are possessed of sufficient 'adversariness' and 'formality' to render its final proxy determinations amenable to judicial review." Its concluding paragraphs on this point follow:]

On the other hand, we do see significant problems and anomalies which would result from accepting the Commission's restrictive interpretation of the jurisdictional statute. There is no doubt that the Medical Committee could obtain a judicial determination of the legitimacy of its claim through a private action against Dow Chemical in the district court; the Supreme Court held that such a remedy is implicit in section 14(a) in J.I. Case Co. v. Borak, 377 U.S. 426, 84 S.Ct. 1555, 12 L.Ed.2d 423 (1964). The essential question, then, is whether the district court is a more appropriate forum for adjudication of petitioner's claim than this court. We believe that every substantial consideration in this case leads to precisely the opposite conclusion.

Here the Medical Committee does not seek to contest any matters of fact which would require a trial de novo; rather, petitioner seeks only to have its proposal assessed by the Commission under a proper interpretation of the governing statutes and rules. The petitioner does not seek any relief which is peculiarly within the competence of the district court; instead, it seeks merely to have the cause remanded so that the Commission, in accord with proper standards, can make an enlightened determination of whether enforcement action would be appropriate. Thus we see no practical or theoretical virtues in commanding a course of action which "would result in equal inconvenience" to the petitioner, the Commission, and the overcrowded courts, and "would constitute circuitous routes for the determination of issues easily and directly determinable by review in this court." American Sumatra Tobacco Corp. v. SEC, 68 App.D.C. 77, 82, 93 F.2d 236, 241 (1937). . . .

There is also, it seems to us, an independent public interest in having the controversy decided in its present posture rather than in the context of a private action against the company. The primary and explicit purpose of section 14(a) is "the protection of investors," and the primary method of implementing this goal is through Commission regulation of proxy statements, not through private actions by individual security holders. For the small investor, personal recourse to the Commission's proxy procedures without benefit of counsel may well be the only practicable method of contesting a management decision to exclude his proxy proposal.[37] In this situation, as our recent decisions make clear, it is particularly important that the Commission look carefully at the merits of the shareholder's proposal, and that it do so pursuant to an accurate perception of the Congressional intent underlying the proxy statute. [citations omitted] Direct judicial review of Commission proxy decisions is unquestionably the most logical and efficient means of achieving this objective.

Thus, we hold that the Commission's decision in this case is presently reviewable. . . .

[Third, the court decided that the SEC action was not committed to agency discretion and thus should not be considered nonreviewable.]

There is some reason to believe that similar judicial supervision of the administrative process is needed in circumstances like the present one, in order to assure that the investing public can obtain vigorous, efficient, and evenhanded implementation of the concepts of corporate democracy embodied in the proxy rules. One published study has accused the Commission of a variety of procedural sins in its regulation of proxies, most of which could be curtailed or eliminated through judicial review. Specifically, the Commission has been charged with repeatedly violating its own established procedural principles, particularly those relating to management's burden of proof in justifying the omission of proposals; of allowing non-lawyers to decide complex legal problems raised in proxy disputes; and of affording inconsistent treatment to similar factual situations for no apparent reason.[38] Perhaps the most serious charge against the Commission's secretive decision-making, however, is all too clearly illustrated by the record in the present case: the lack of articulated bases for past decisions encourages management to file shotgun objections to a shareholder proposal, urging every mildly plausible legal argument that inventive counsel can contrive, in the hope that the Commission will accept one of them. If the Commission does agree with one of management's arguments, or if it determines not to act against the company for other reasons, the shareholder often has no idea why his proposal was deemed unworthy or what he can do to cure its defects for subsequent proxy solicitations.

37. This contention was recently presented to the Commission in a proxy contest involving the General Motors Corporation. See Cong.Rec. E–2147 (daily ed., March 17, 1970):

It must be recognized that Management's proxy statement is the only effective vehicle through which all of the shareholders can have an opportunity to express themselves, and even to hear any arguments on the questions involved. . . . [T]he cost [of conducting a competing solicitation] is virtually prohibitive except to extremely well heeled shareholders. . . .

This is no ordinary dispute with Management; it is not an effort by insurgent shareholders to seize control of the corporation. If it were so, one could justify large expenditures because the individual rewards are great and because, if successful, the insurgents could obtain reimbursement of their expenses from the company. The issues here lack that personal pecuniary bias. Denial of access to the shareholders through management's proxy solicitation, practically speaking, is total denial.

38. Clusserath, The Amended Stockholder Proposal Rule: A Decade Later, 40 N.D.Lawyer 13 (1964).

Viewed in this light, "discretion" can be merely another manifestation of the venerable bureaucratic technique of exclusion by attrition, of disposing of controversies through calculated non-decisions that will eventually cause eager supplicants to give up a frustration and stop "bothering" the agency.

Nevertheless, we recognize that there is a legitimate domain of administrative discretion in the proxy area, albeit not quite so broad as the Commission urges. As the Supreme Court has recognized, the Securities and Exchange Commission must process a formidable number of proxy statements in limited time and with insufficient manpower. Obviously not all proxy proposals can or should be given detailed consideration by the full Commission, and even the boldest advocates of judicial review recognize that the agencies' internal management decisions and allocations of priorities are not a proper subject of inquiry by the courts. However, that is definitely not what is at issue in the present case: here, the full Commission has exercised its discretion to review this controversy, and, as will be seen below, it has ostensibly acted in accord with a very dubious legal theory. The Medical Committee asks us merely to examine this allegedly erroneous legal premise and return the controversy to the Commission so that it may properly exercise its further discretion regarding the propriety and desirability of enforcement activity.

Limited and partial review to examine the legal framework within which administrative discretion must be exercised is scarcely a doctrinal innovation; it has been repeatedly sustained by the Supreme Court. [Citations omitted.] We think that Justice Frankfurter's incisive observations in Rochester Telephone Corp. v. United States, 307 U.S. 125, 136, 59 S.Ct. 754, 760 (1939), are equally appropriate here:

> Judicial relief would be precisely the same as in the recognized instances of review by courts of Commission action: if the legal principles on which the Commission acted were not erroneous, the bill would be ordered dismissed; if the Commission was found to have proceeded on erroneous legal principles, the Commission would be ordered to proceed within the framework of its own discretionary authority on the indicated correct principles.

We foresee scant possibility that such sharply circumscribed review, which depends upon the Commission's initial determination to review the staff decision will cause the destruction of informal advisory and supervisory functions which the Commission now fears. The courts, we think, are abundantly capable of distinguishing between situations in which an agency gives informal advice and situations in which it formally decides among conflicting adversary claims premised on detailed legal arguments. Moreover, experience indicates that the grim forebodings which are frequently expressed in this court regarding the possibility that a particular decision will cause irreparable disruption of the administrative process only rarely, if ever, come to pass. . . .

[The Court then discussed the merits at some length:]

III. The Merits of Petitioner's Proposal

The Medical Committee's sole substantive contention in this petition is that its proposed resolution could not, consistently with the Congressional intent underlying section 14(a), be properly deemed a proposal which is either motivated by *general* political and moral concerns, or related to the conduct of Dow's ordinary business operations. These criteria are two of the established exceptions to the general rule that management must include all properly submitted shareholder proposals in its proxy materials. They are contained in Rule 14a–8(c), 17 C.F.R. § 240.14a–8(c) (1970). . . .

Despite the fact that our October 13 order in this case deferred resolution of the jurisdictional issue pending full argument on the merits (see [p. 410, supra]), the Commission has not deigned to address itself to any possible grounds for allowing management to exclude this proposal from its proxy statement. We confess to a similar puzzlement as to how the Commission reached the result which it did, and thus we are forced to remand the controversy for a more illuminating consideration and decision. . . . In aid of this consideration on remand, we feel constrained to explain our difficulties with the position taken by the company and endorsed by the Commission.

It is obvious to the point of banality to restate the proposition that Congress intended by its enactment of section 14 of the Securities Exchange Act of 1934 to give true vitality to the concept of corporate democracy. The depth of this commitment is reflected in the strong language employed in the legislative history:

> Even those who in former days managed great corporations were by reason of their personal contacts with their shareholders constantly aware of their responsibilities. But as management became divorced from ownership and came under the control of banking groups, men forgot that they were dealing with the savings of men and the making of profits became an impersonal thing. When men do not know the victims of their aggression they are not always conscious of their wrongs. . . .
>
> Fair corporate suffrage is an important right that should attach to every equity security bought on a public exchange. Managements of properties owned by the investing public should not be permitted to perpetuate themselves by the misuse of corporate proxies.

H.R.Rep. No. 1383, 73d Cong., 2d Sess. 5, 13 (1934). See also SEC v. Transamerica Corp., 163 F.2d 511, 517, 518 (3d Cir.1947), cert. denied, 332 U.S. 847, 68 S.Ct. 351, 92 L.Ed. 418 (1948).

In striving to implement this open-ended mandate, the Commission has gradually evolved its present proxy rules. Early exercises of the rule-making power were directed primarily toward the achievement of full and fair corporate disclosure regarding management proxy materials (see, e.g., 3 Fed.Reg. 1991 (1938); 5 Fed.Reg. 174 (1940)); the rationale underlying this development was the Commission's belief that the corporate practice of circulating proxy materials which failed to make reference to the fact that a shareholder intended to present a proposal at the annual meeting rendered the solicitation inherently misleading. See Hearings on Security and Exchange Commission Proxy Rules Before the House Comm. on Interstate and Foreign Commerce, 78th Cong., 1st Sess., pt. 1, at 169–170 (1943) [hereinafter "House Hearings"]. From this position, it was only a short step to a formal rule requiring management to include in its proxy statement any shareholder proposal which was "a proper subject for action by the security holders." 7 Fed.Reg. 10,659 (1942). It eventually became clear that the question of what constituted a "proper subject" for shareholder action was to be resolved by recourse to the law of the state in which the company had been incorporated; however, the paucity of applicable state law giving content to the concept of "proper subject" led the Commission to seek guidance from precedent existing in jurisdictions which had a highly developed commercial and corporate law and to develop its own "common law" relating to proper subjects for shareholder action.

Further areas of difficulty became apparent as experience was gained in administering the "proper subject" test, and these conflicts provided the Commission with opportunities to put a detailed gloss upon the general phraseology of its rules. Thus, in 1945 the Commission issued a release containing an opinion of the Director of the Division of Corporation Finance that was rendered in response to a management request to omit shareholder resolutions which bore little or no relationship to the company's affairs; for example, these shareholder resolutions included proposals "that the anti-trust laws and the enforcement thereof be revised," and "that all Federal legislation hereafter enacted providing for workers and farmers to be represented should be made to apply equally to investors." The Commission's release endorsed the Director's conclusion that "proposals which deal with general political, social or economic matters are not, within the meaning of the rule, 'proper subjects for action by security holders.'" The reason for this conclusion was summarized as follows in the Director's opinion:

> Speaking generally, *it is the purpose of Rule X–14A–7 to place stockholders in a position to bring before their fellow stockholders matters of concern to them as stockholders in such corporation;* that is, such matters relating to the affairs of the company concerned as are proper subjects for stockholders' action under the laws of the state under which it was organized. It was not the intent of Rule X–14A–7 to permit stockholders to obtain the consensus of other stockholders with respect to matters which are of a general political, social or economic nature. *Other forums exist for the presentation of such views.*

Several years after the Commission issued this release, it was confronted with the same kind of problem when the management of a national bus company sought to omit a shareholder proposal phrased as "A Recommendation that Management Consider the Advisability of Abolishing the Segregated Seating System in the South"—a proposal which, on its face, was ambiguous with respect to whether it was limited solely to company policy rather than attacking all segregated seating, and which quite likely would have brought the company into violation of state laws then assumed to be valid. The Commission staff approved management's decision to omit the proposal, and the shareholder then sought a temporary injunction against the company's solicitation in a federal district court. The injunction was denied because the plaintiff had failed to exhaust his administrative remedies or to show that he would be irreparably harmed by refusal to grant the requested relief. Peck v. Greyhound Corp., 97 F.Supp. 679 (S.D.N.Y. 1951). The Commission amended its rules the following year to encompass the above-quoted exception for situations in which "it clearly appears that the proposal is submitted by the security holder . . . primarily for the purpose of promoting general economic, political, racial, religious, social or similar causes." 17 Fed.Reg. 11,433 (1952); see also id. at 11,431. So far as we have been able to determine, the Commission's interpretation or application of this rule has not been considered by the courts.

The origins and genesis of the exception for proposals "relating to the conduct of the ordinary business operations of the issuer" are somewhat more obscure. This provision was introduced into the proxy rules in 1954, as part of amendments which were made to clarify the general proposition that the primary source of authority for determining whether a proposal is a proper subject for shareholder action is state law. See 19 Fed.Reg. 246 (1954). Shortly after the rule was adopted, the Commission explained its purpose to Congress in the following terms:

> The policy motivating the Commission in adopting the rule . . . is basically the same as the underlying policy of most State corporation laws to confine the solution of ordinary business problems to the board of directors and place such problems beyond the competence and direction of the shareholders. The basic reason for this policy is that it is manifestly impracticable in most cases for stockholders to decide management problems at corporate meetings.

> . . . .

> . . . While Rule X–14A–8 does not require that the ordinary business operations be determined on the basis of State law, the premise of Rule X–14A–8 is that the propriety of . . . proposals for inclusion in the proxy statement is to be determined in general by the law of the State of incorporation. . . . Consistency with this premise requires that the phrase "ordinary business operations" in Rule X–14A–8 have the meaning attributed to it under applicable State law. To hold otherwise would be to introduce into the rule the possibility of endless and narrow interpretations based on no ascertainable standards.

(Senate Hearings at 118.) It also appears that no administrative interpretation of this exception has yet been scrutinized by the courts.

These two exceptions are, on their face, consistent with the legislative purpose underlying section 14; for it seems fair to infer that Congress desired to make proxy solicitations a vehicle for *corporate* democracy rather than an all-purpose forum for malcontented shareholders to vent their spleen about irrelevant matters,[39] and also realized that management cannot exercise its specialized talents effectively

---

39. See, e.g., the following colloquy, which appears in House Hearings at 162–63:

Mr. Boren. So one man, if he owned one share in A.T. & T. . . . and another share in R.C.A. . . . if he decided deliberately . . . to become a professional stockholder in each one of the companies—he could have a hundred-word propaganda statement prepared and he could put it in every

one of these proxy statements. Suppose he were a Communist.

Commissioner Purcell. That is possible. We have never seen such a case.

Mr. Boren. Suppose a man were a Communist and he wanted to send to all of the stockholders of all of these firms, a philosophic statement of 100 words in length, or a propaganda statement. . . . He could by the mere device of buying one share of

if corporate investors assert the power to dictate the minutiae of daily business decisions. However, it is also apparent that the two exceptions which these rules carve out of the general requirement of inclusion can be construed so as to permit the exclusion of practically any shareholder proposal on the grounds that it is either "too general" or "too specific." Indeed, in the present case Dow Chemical Company attempted to impale the Medical Committee's proposal on both horns of this dilemma: in its memorandum of counsel, it argued that the Medical Committee's proposal was a matter of ordinary business operations properly within the sphere of management expertise and, at the same time, that the proposal clearly had been submitted primarily for the purpose of promoting general political or social causes. (App. 9a–10a; see also id. at 19a.)   As noted above, the Division of Corporation Finance made no attempt to choose between these potentially conflicting arguments, but rather merely accepted Dow Chemical's decision to omit the proposal "[f]or reasons stated in [the company's] letter and the accompanying opinion of counsel, both dated January 17, 1969"; this determination was then adopted by the full Commission.   Close examination of the company's arguments only increases doubt as to the reasoning processes which led the Commission to this result.

In contending that the Medical Committee's proposal was properly excludable under Rule 14a–8(c)(5), Dow's counsel asserted:

> It is my opinion that *the determination of the products which the company shall manufacture,* the customers to which it shall sell the products, and the conditions under which it shall make such sales are related to the conduct of the ordinary business operations of the Company and that any attempt to amend the Certificate of Incorporation to define the circumstances under which the management of the Company shall make such determinations is contrary to the concept of corporate management, which is inherent in the Delaware General Corporation Act under which the Company is organized.[40]

In the first place, it seems extremely dubious that this superficial analysis complies with the Commission's longstanding requirements that management must sustain the burden of proof when asserting that a shareholder proposal may properly be omitted from the proxy statement, and that "[w]here management contends that a proposal may be omitted because it is not proper under State law, it will be incumbent upon management to refer to the applicable statute or case law."   19

---

stock . . . have available to him the mailing list of all the stockholders in the Radio Corporation of America.

. . .

Commissioner Purcell.   Of course, we have never seen such a case; and if such a case came before us, then we would have to deal with it and make such appropriate changes as might seem necessary. . . .

40.   App. 9a (emphasis added).   The remainder of the company's argument under Rule 14a–8(c)(5) reads as follows, in its entirety:

> Moreover, there is considerable doubt as to the efficacy of the proposed limitation in the context of the ability of the Gov-

ernment of the United States to issue a directive that the Company manufacture napalm.   Therefore, the proposed limitation could conceivably be contrary to the requirements of the Defense Production Act of 1950.

(App. 9a–10a.)   In response to this contention, the Medical Committee pointed out that "any such amendment would, of course, be subject to the requirements of the 'Defense Production Act of 1950,' as are the corporate charters and management decisions of all United States Corporations." (App. 16a.)   No rebuttal by Dow was forthcoming.

Fed.Reg. 246 (1954). As noted above, the Commission has formally represented to Congress that Rule 14a–8(c)(5) is intended to make state law the governing authority in determining what matters are ordinary business operations immune from shareholder control; yet, the Delaware General Corporation law provides that a company's Certificate of Incorporation may be amended to "change, substitute, enlarge or diminish the nature of [the company's] business." [41] If there are valid reasons why the Medical Committee's proposal does not fit within the language and spirit of this provision, they certainly do not appear in the record.

The possibility that the Medical Committee's proposal could properly be omitted under Rule 14a–8(c)(2) appears somewhat more substantial in the circumstances of the instant case, although once again it may fairly be asked how Dow Chemical's arguments on this point could be deemed a rational basis for such a result: the paragraph in the company's memorandum of counsel purporting to deal with this issue, which is set forth in the margin,[42] consists entirely of a fundamentally irrelevant recitation of some of the political protests which had been directed at the company because of its manufacture of napalm, followed by the abrupt conclusion that management is therefore entitled to exclude the Medical Committee's proposal from its proxy statement. Our own examination of the issue raises substantial questions as to whether an interpretation of Rule 14a–8(c)(2) which permitted omission of this proposal as one motivated primarily by *general* political or social concerns would conflict with the congressional intent underlying section 14(a) of the Act.

As our earlier discussion indicates, the clear import of the language, legislative history, and record of administration of section 14(a) is that its overriding purpose is to assure to corporate shareholders the ability to exercise their right—some would say their duty [43]—to control

41. Chapter 1, Title 8 Delaware Code §§ 242(a)(2), 242(d) (1968 Cum.Supp.). Cf. II L.Loss, Securities Regulation 906 (1961): "Inevitably the Commission, while purporting to find and apply a generally nonexistent state law, has been building up a 'common law' of its own as to what constitutes a 'proper subject' for shareholder action. It is a 'common law' which undoubtedly would yield, as it should, to a contrary decision of the particular state court."

42. App. 10a:

It is a well-known fact that the Company has been the target of protests and demonstrations for the past few years at its office and plant locations, and on the occasion of recruiting on college and university campuses, as well as at its annual meeting of stockholders held May 8, 1968. The various protests and demonstrations are a reflection of opposition on the part of certain segments of the population against the policy of the United States Government in waging the war in Viet Nam. Although the Dow Chemical Company was not among the 100 largest prime contractors with the Department of Defense during the 1967–68 Government fiscal year and was only 75th on the list in the 1966–67 fiscal year, it appears to have been singled out symbolically by the protesters. Under all of these circumstances it is my opinion that it clearly appears that the proposal is primarily for the purpose of promoting a general political, social or similar cause.

43. See Bayne, The Basic Rationale of Proper Subject, 34 U.Det.L.J. 575, 579 (1957):

In so far as the shareholder has contributed an asset of value to the corporate venture, in so far as he has handed over his goods and property and money for use and increase, he has not only the clear right, but more to the point, perhaps, he has the stringent duty to exercise control over that asset for which he must keep care, guard, guide, and in general be held seriously responsible.

. . . As much as one may surrender the immediate disposition of [his] goods, he can never shirk a supervisory and secondary duty (not just a right) to make sure these goods are used justly, morally and beneficially.

the important decisions which affect them in their capacity as stockholders and owners of the corporation. Thus, the Third Circuit has cogently summarized the philosophy of section 14(a) in the statement that "[a] corporation is run for the benefit of its stockholders and not for that of its managers." SEC v. Transamerica Corp., 163 F.2d 511, 517 (3d Cir.1947), cert. denied, 332 U.S. 847, 68 S.Ct. 351, 92 L.Ed. 418 (1948). Here, in contrast to the situations detailed above which led to the promulgation of Rule 14a–8(c)(2), the proposal relates solely to a matter that is completely within the accepted sphere of corporate activity and control. No reason has been advanced in the present proceedings which leads to the conclusion that management may properly place obstacles in the path of shareholders who wish to present to their co-owners, in accord with applicable state law, the question of whether they wish to have their assets used in a manner which they believe to be more socially responsible but possibly less profitable than that which is dictated by present company policy. Thus, even accepting Dow's characterization of the purpose and intent of the Medical Committee's proposal, there is a strong argument that permitting the company to exclude it would contravene the purpose of section 14(a).

However, the record in this case contains indications that we are confronted with quite a different situation. The management of Dow Chemical Company is repeatedly quoted in sources which include the company's own publications as proclaiming that the decision to continue manufacturing and marketing napalm was made not *because* of business considerations, but *in spite of* them; that management in essence decided to pursue a course of activity which generated little profit for the shareholders and actively impaired the company's public relations and recruitment activities because management considered this action morally and politically desirable. (App. 40a–43a; see also id. at 33.) The proper political and social role of modern corporations is, of course, a matter of philosophical argument extending far beyond the scope of our present concern; the substantive wisdom or propriety of particular corporate political decisions is also completely irrelevant to the resolution of the present controversy. What *is* of immediate concern, however, is the question of whether the corporate proxy rules can be employed as a shield to isolate such managerial decisions from shareholder control. After all, it must be remembered that "[t]he control of great corporations by a very few persons was the abuse at which Congress struck in enacting Section 14(a)." SEC v. Transamerica Corp., supra, 163 F.2d at 518. We think that there is a clear and compelling distinction between management's legitimate need for freedom to apply its expertise in matters of day-to-day business judgment, and management's patently illegitimate claim of power to treat modern corporations with their vast resources as personal satrapies implementing personal political or moral predilections. It could scarcely be argued that management is more qualified or more entitled to make these kinds of decisions than the shareholders who are the true beneficial owners of the corporation; and it seems equally implausible that an application of the proxy rules which permitted such a result could be harmonized with the philosophy of corporate democracy which Congress embodied in section 14(a) of the Securities Exchange Act of 1934.

In light of these considerations, therefore, the cause must be remanded to the Commission so that it may reconsider petitioner's claim within the proper limits of its discretionary authority as set forth above, and so that "the basis for [its] decision [may] appear clearly on the record, not in conclusory terms but in sufficient detail to permit prompt and effective review."

Remanded for further proceedings consistent with this opinion.

[The SEC petitioned for and obtained certiorari from the Supreme Court but the judgment was vacated and the case dismissed as moot. The basis for that action was that Dow had acquiesced (under protest) in the circulation of the Committee's proposal in 1971. The proposal obtained so small a portion of the votes that under the proxy rules Dow was not obliged to include it again until 1974. MR. JUSTICE DOUGLAS dissented. He said *inter alia:*]

While this litigation is not formally between Dow and the Medical Committee, but between the SEC and the Medical Committee, it does involve a whole panoply of substantive and procedural rights in connection with a corporation's obligation to include shareholder proposals in proxy materials. The modern super-corporations, of which Dow is one, wield immense, virtually unchecked power. Some say that they are "private governments," whose decisions affect the lives of us all. The philosophy of our times, I think, requires that such enterprises be held to a higher standard than that of the "morals of the marketplace" which exalts a single-minded, myopic determination to maximize profits as the traditional be-all and end-all of corporate concern. The "public interest in having the legality of the practices settled, militates against a mootness conclusion." . . .

There is no reason to assume Dow's antipathy to the inclusion of this shareholder proposal will be any less in 1974 than it is today. Perhaps Dow will adopt the advice given to it by the Court. But it is just as likely to decide its superior financial position makes continued litigation the preferable alternative, which may now be conducted under proxy rules more favorable to corporate management than are the present rules.

NOTE ON SHAREHOLDER PROPOSALS

Since the Medical Committee case the SEC has amended the shareholder proposal rule several times. The rule is printed in the Documentary Supplement in its current form along with parts of the old version needed to help understand the decision in that case. The SEC's actions have gone in both directions, expanding the right of access in terms of the definition of appropriate subject matter but also tightening the rule in terms of the qualifications required of the sponsor of a resolution. These reflect a continuing ambivalence about the burdensomeness of such resolutions as measured against the public significance of giving a vehicle to air these issues.

Use of the proposal rule has also been variable. To give you a general picture this Note lists the major campaigns that have been waged at a significant number of corporation meetings during the last few years. (a) There were a considerable number of resolutions provoked by the revelation of overseas bribery by U.S.-based corporations in particular exporters of jet aircraft, implicating important government figures in Japan, the Netherlands and other countries; the end result was the passage of the Foreign Corrupt Practices Act of 1976 that amended the Securities Exchange Act, the Internal Revenue Code and other federal law.   (b) In 1976–77 a number of organizations filed shareholder proposals aimed at dissuading American corporations from providing information or otherwise cooperating with the economic boycott mounted by the Arab states against Israel; this culminated in legislation forbidding such cooperation.   (c) There has been a long-continued but quite varied campaign aimed at diminishing American corporations' involvement in South Africa.   Some of them requested adherence to the Sullivan principles improving the treatment of black employees in that country.   Others called for an end to arrangements under which equipment or services were provided to the government, police or armed forces of that state.   Finally some called for complete divestiture of all operations in that country.   (d) There has been a series of attempts, focused on a smaller array of companies than the preceding three, to persuade companies to reform their practices with respect to selling powdered substitutes for mothers' milk to inhabitants of developing countries, it being alleged that sales practices were often, in context, deceptive or highly pressured.   There has now been general agreement on a set of guidelines developed by the World Health Organization.   (e) Various groups situated on the political right have sought to dissuade corporations from doing business with the Soviet Union, Peoples Republic of China, etc.   (f) Some proxy proposals have aimed at indirect targets—charitable institutions benefitting from corporate largesse.   Thus there have been proposals to bar company gifts to institutions that indulged in experiments with animals, that discriminated against recruiters from the Central Intelligence Agency or the armed forces, or that harbored Communists of the Maoist, Trotskyite or Stalinist variations.   Few of these proposals garner impressive percentages of the total vote but some of the bribery and boycott votes ran to some 30% which had an impact on management.

There has not been much useful caselaw on the meaning of the proposal rule in its amended form, although one can refer to a fairly extensive body of SEC administrative letters collected in the looseleaf services.   For one litigated case see Lovenheim v. Iroquois Brands, Ltd., 618 F.Supp. 554 (D.D.C.1985), holding that a proposal could be "significantly related" to the issuer's business if it aroused controversy; the case involved a proposal that the issuer study how its French supplier of pate de foie gras dealt with its geese, pate constituting only a very small proportion of issuer's business.   The exclusion for proposals relating to elections to office was interpreted in Rauchman v. Mobil Corp., 739 F.2d 205 (6th Cir.1984), to authorize a corporation to omit a proposal for a bylaw change that would have prevented the election to Mobil's board of citizens of OPEC countries.

SECURITIES AND EXCHANGE COMMISSION v. MAY

United States District Court, Southern District of New York, 1955.
134 F.Supp. 247, affirmed 229 F.2d 123 (2d Cir.1956).

[The SEC moved to enjoin the members of an Independent Stockholders Committee of Libby, McNeill & Libby from soliciting proxies through misleading communications. The Company was registered on the New York, Midwest and San Francisco Stock Exchanges. The SEC's complaints largely related to a letter sent out by the Committee entitled "It's Time for a Change"—after the SEC had repeatedly warned them that it was misleading. The complaints also involved a failure to disclose certain facts about the composition of the Committee and who was putting up the funds for its expenses and a failure to disclose the intention of the Committee to liquidate the Company if it won control.

On August 3 after making a formal complaint, the SEC filed its complaint. Judge Dimock denied a temporary restraining order. On August 15 CIRCUIT JUDGE LUMBARD granted the requested injunction; he also ordered postponement of the annual meeting scheduled for August 17. The Court of Appeals affirmed.

Portions of JUDGE LUMBARD's opinion dealing with the "It's Time for a Change" letter appear below. As to the other issues, the court found that two individuals were wrongfully omitted from the list of backers of the Committee and that two other substantial stockholders had been listed as supporters in some of the materials although they had repudiated the Committee. The court, however, found that the SEC had not made a sufficient showing of an intent to liquidate.]

A number of the items objected to by the Commission in the proxy materials distributed by the defendants are cast in the form of questions. Although Rule X–14A–9, 17 Code Fed.Regs. Sec. 240.14a–9 (Supp.1954), forbids in terms the use in proxy solicitation of "any statement" which is false or misleading, it would be an unrealistic strictness of interpretation which did not include within this term questions which are based upon false or misleading assumptions or which carry false or misleading implications. To hold that merely by placing a question mark at the end of a sentence the author can circumvent the requirements of fair and complete disclosure would provide an obvious escape from the salutary regulation of the Commission. Support for a broad interpretation of the word "statement" may be found in the holding of the Court of Appeals for the Second Circuit that an expression of opinion in a proxy statement may violate an injunction enforcing the SEC's proxy rules, Securities and Exchange Comm. v. Okin, 2 Cir.1943, 137 F.2d 862, 864. . . .

1. *Comparison of Libby with Other Companies.*

The Commission complains that the comparison of net earnings contained in the "Time for a Change" letter was misleading in that it compared the net earnings of Libby with those of Stokely, Van Camp, Hunt Foods, Clinton Foods, Standard Brands, Best Foods, and General Foods without explaining the differences between Libby and those companies. The comparison is also claimed to be misleading in that it implied that the present management was responsible for the earnings history during the entire period 1939–1954. These arguments do not convince me that the use of figures here is so misleading as to constitute a violation of the Commission's proxy rules. There is no contention that the figures themselves are incorrectly stated. We are all aware that comparisons are not as simple as figures sometimes make them appear. No compilation can give the true picture without substantial explanation; the very process of selection and arrangement is a form of argument. This seems to me to be a field where the Commission and the Courts must tread warily else they may unduly curb legitimate statistical debate. The Company has answered the statistical arguments of the Committee with arguments, explanations, and compilations of its own. Although a greater seasoning of explanation might be more to the taste of the bedeviled stockholder, I think the better course here is to let him compare the figures presented by both sides and give the statistical arguments what weight he wishes.

2. *Misleading Questions Implying Non–Disclosure of Information and Manipulation of Funds.*

The Commission charges and this Court finds that the following questions and statement in the "Time for a Change" letter are misleading in that they imply improper non-disclosure by the Company when no such impropriety exists:

(1) "Why isn't a full disclosure of the Company's business made to the stockholders each year?"

(2) "Are we not entitled to know how much is made or lost in the major lines—pineapple, canned fruits, canned vegetables, fruit juices, salmon, and frozen foods—and how much money is invested in the production facilities for the various items?"

(3) "Why are not the stockholders informed of the purchases and sales of capital assets?"

(4) "Only a strongly entrenched and self-perpetuating management would dare withhold from its stockholders a detailed accounting for three months operations, namely, February 27, 1954 to May 28, 1954."

The first question implied that the Company did not make a full disclosure to its stockholders of those details of its operations which it is customary for similar companies to disclose. The Company did in fact disclose in its annual reports and in its filings with the SEC such matters as it is customary for similar companies to disclose.

The second question implied that it is customary and proper to disclose to stockholders how much is made or lost in the "major lines" and how much is invested in the production facilities for each line. Clearly such disclosure is not customary.[44] In fact such details are generally guarded with care lest competitors be given information which might be harmful to some branch of the company's business.

The third question implied that it is customary to disclose to stockholders the details of the purchase and sale of particular capital assets. Clearly such disclosure is not customary.

---

44. [Ed.] In 1969 "only after a great deal of soul searching" the SEC adopted a requirement of line of business reporting.   L. Rappaport, SEC Accounting Practice and Procedure 23.1 (3d ed. 1972).

The fourth question implied that the Company withheld from its stockholders a proper accounting for the period from February 27, 1954 to May 28, 1954. I find that the Company made a proper accounting to its stockholders for this period in its annual report for the year ending in May 1955 and in its Form 10–K filed in January 1955 with the SEC and the New York, Midwest and San Francisco Stock Exchanges, and that the Committee and its members knew that such accounting had been made.

The Commission charges and I find that the following questions in the "Time for a Change" letter imply that the management was guilty of improper manipulation or mismanagement of corporate funds when there was no basis in fact for such implication:

1. "Isn't it odd that during this unaccounted for period Bridges looked around and found that nearly $4,000,000 of the Company's fixed assets were no longer in existence and had to be written off?"

2. "Why hasn't Bridges told the stockholders the status of his Pension Fund?"

3. "Where is the money and what is being done with it?"

4. "Is there $10,000,000, $15,000,000, or $20,000,000 of the stockholders' money in this Pension Fund?"

5. "How much of the stockholders' money (taken out of profit) is in the big inventory account? If it is $10,000,000, as Bridges says, it represents $3 a share of the stockholders' money. If it is $30,000,000 or $35,000,000, as has been stated, it represents nearly $10 per share of the stockholders' money."

The first item implied (a) that the period from February 27 to May 28, 1954 was unaccounted for, (b) that it was during this three month period that the whole amount of "nearly $4,000,000" was discovered to be not in existence, (c) that none of this "nearly $4,000,000" was written off prior to the three month period, (d) that there was something improper or dishonest about the transaction. The facts are (a) that the period in question was properly accounted for, as is set out above, (b) that no more than $359,333 of assets were discovered to be not in existence during the period in question, the rest having been discovered prior to that time in the course of a survey of the Company's properties begun in the fiscal year 1953, (c) that only $359,333 of assets were written off during the period in question, $3,367,719 having been written off prior to that time, (d) that there was nothing dishonest or improper about this transaction since the write-off was the result of a survey intended to make the books of the Company correspond more closely with its physical assets and was in accordance with accepted accounting practice.

Questions 2, 3, and 4, taken together, imply (a) that the Company has failed to disclose facts about the Pension Fund which it is customary and proper to disclose, (b) that there is some impropriety or dishonesty in the management of the Pension Fund. I find that (a) the Company has not failed to disclose facts about the Pension Fund which it is customary and proper to disclose, (b) that there is no basis for an insinuation of impropriety or dishonesty in the management of the Fund.

Item 5 implies that the $10,000,000 spread between the book value of the Company's LIFO inventories and their replacement cost is in some sense taken out of profit and withheld from the stockholders. This $10,000,000 is no more taken out of inventory and withheld from the stockholders than is that portion of the inventory's value which is represented on the books. It is true that amounts tied up in inventory are not available for distribution to the stockholders. This applies, however, to the total inventory value, not just the value in excess of that shown on the books. Under these circumstances the implication of question 5 is false and misleading.

. . .

Perhaps it could be argued that each or any one of these questions would not be likely by itself to influence any stockholder to execute the proxy. But taken together one after another as set forth in the "Time for a Change" letter they certainly would raise a question in the mind of the average stockholder as to whether the management of the Company was in honest and capable hands. It is clear that the questions were designed to do just that. If there were some basis for the questions then there could be no objection. But as there is no basis for asking any of them, it seems to me that the questions separately, and as a group, are grossly misleading and constitute a wilful violation of the Regulations. . . . [The Company's meeting was held on September 7 and the management prevailed. In January 1955 the Court of Appeals affirmed, adopting the opinion below. It did go on to say:

"Appellants' fundamental complaint appears to be that stockholder disputes should be viewed . . . just as are political contests . . . the assumption being that the opposing side is then at liberty to refute and thus effectively deflate the 'campaign oratory' of its adversary. Such, however, was not the policy of Congress . . . ."]

COMMENT

The views of opinions as those in SEC v. May about the proper role of the courts in dealing with misrepresentation in elections may be compared with that of the NLRB in relation to labor representation elections. One manifestation of its views occurred in Shopping Kart Food Market, 228 N.L.R.B. No. 190 (1977). That opinion, over strong dissents, overruled twenty years of NLRB case law and held that the NLRB "would no longer probe into the truth or falsity of the parties' campaign statements." The alleged falsity was a statement by a union vice president that the employer had had profits of $500,000 in a year when the evidence clearly established that no more than $50,000 was earned. The Board concluded that the old practice had injected undesirable delay, uncertainty and expense into the election process. It relied on several academic studies that cast doubt on the assumption that employees were unsophisticated and easily swayed. They showed that the votes of 81% of the employees could be predicted from their precampaign intent and their attitudes toward working conditions and unions in general. The Board reserved the right to interfere in such cases as those where forged documents are involved. The dissent found that handling 300–400 cases a year was not too burdensome and was a fair price to pay for preventing what they predicted would be an escalating barrage of misrepresentation and rough election practices. They noted the very high percentage of participation among eligible voters and the great importance of the consequences to those voting. The dissenters sharply criticized the majority's view that a freedom of speech issue—the imposition of a prior restraint—was involved in what they saw as making the speaker accountable for the impacts or effects of his speech. The ruling in Shopping

Kart was discarded after only a year in General Knit of Calif., 239 N.L.R.B. 619 (1978). However, it was reinstated by Midland Nat. Life Ins. Co., 263 N.L.R.B. 127 (1982).

A disturbing question about the constitutionality of Rule 14a–8 was raised by the dissent in a 1986 Supreme Court case. That case held that a state public utility commission could not under the First Amendment compel a regulated utility to include a third party's newsletter in its billing envelope. Justice Stevens in his dissent expressed doubt that one could distinguish Rule 14a–8, especially in cases involving political matters—such as those at stake in the Medical Committee case. Pacific Gas & Elec. Co. v. P.U.C. of Cal., 475 U.S. 1, 106 S.Ct. 903, 89 L.Ed.2d 1 (1986). Note that until its demise in 1976, the "commercial speech" exception to the First Amendment's protection was used to brush aside such arguments.

————

J.I. CASE COMPANY v. BORAK

Supreme Court of the United States, 1964.
377 U.S. 426, 84 S.Ct. 1555, 12 L.Ed.2d 423.

[Borak, owner of 2,000 shares of J.I. Case Co. common stock, brought an action attacking a merger between Case and American Tractor Corporation. One count, based on diversity, charged a violation of the directors' fiduciary duty and the second alleged violations of the Securities Exchange Act in the proxy solicitations. The trial court held that it could grant only declaratory relief as to the Act and that the Wisconsin statute as to security for costs in derivative action applied. The Court of Appeals reversed, ruling that remedial relief was available and that the Wisconsin law did not apply. The merger meanwhile was consummated. The Supreme Court limited its review on certiorari to the question:

> whether § 27 of the Act authorizes a federal cause of action for rescission or damages to a corporate stockholder with respect to a consummated merger which was authorized pursuant to the use of a proxy statement alleged to contain false and misleading statements violative of § 14(a) of the Act.

The opinion, by JUSTICE CLARK, continues:]

II.

It appears clear that private parties have a right under § 27 to bring suit for violation of § 14(a) of the Act. Indeed, this section specifically grants the appropriate District Courts jurisdiction over "all suits in equity and actions at law brought to enforce any liability or duty created" under the Act. The petitioners make no concessions, however, emphasizing that Congress made no specific reference to a private right of action in § 14(a); that, in any event, the right would not extend to derivative suits and should be limited to prospective relief only. In addition, some of the petitioners argue that the merger can be dissolved only if it was fraudulent or non-beneficial, issues upon which the proxy material would not bear. But the causal relationship of the proxy material and the merger are questions of fact to be resolved at trial, not here. We therefore do not discuss this point further.

III.

While the respondent contends that his Count 2 claim is not a derivative one, we need not embrace that view, for we believe that a right of action exists as to both derivative and direct causes.[45]

The purpose of § 14(a) is to prevent management or others from obtaining authorization for corporate action by means of deceptive or inadequate disclosure in proxy solicitation. The section stemmed from the congressional belief that "[f]air corporate suffrage is an important right that should attach to every equity security bought on a public exchange." H.R.Rep. No. 1383, 73d Cong., 2d Sess., 13. It was intended to "control the conditions under which proxies may be solicited with a view to preventing the recurrence of abuses which . . . [had] frustrated the free exercise of the voting rights of stockholders." Id., at 14. "Too often proxies are solicited without explanation to the stockholder of the real nature of the questions for which authority to cast his vote is sought." S.Rep. No. 792, 73d Cong., 2d Sess., 12. These broad remedial purposes are evidenced in the language of the section which makes it "unlawful for any person . . . to solicit or to permit the use of his name to solicit any proxy or consent or authorization in respect of any security . . . registered on any national securities exchange in contravention of such rules and regulations as the Commission may prescribe as necessary or appropriate in the public interest *or for the protection of investors.*" (Italics supplied.) While this language makes no specific reference to a private right of action, among its chief purposes is "the protection of investors," which certainly implies the availability of judicial relief where necessary to achieve that result.

The injury which a stockholder suffers from corporate action pursuant to a deceptive proxy solicitation ordinarily flows from the damage done the corporation, rather than from the damage inflicted directly upon the stockholder. The damage suffered results not from the deceit practiced on him alone but rather from the deceit practiced on the stockholders as a group. To hold that derivative actions are not within the sweep of the section would therefore be tantamount to a denial of private relief. Private enforcement of the proxy rules provides a necessary supplement to Commission action. As in antitrust treble damage litigation, the possibility of civil damages or injunctive relief serves as a most effective weapon in the enforcement of the proxy requirements. The Commission advises that it examines over 2,000 proxy statements annually and each of them must necessarily be expedited. Time does not permit an independent examination of the facts set out in the proxy material and this results in the Commission's acceptance of the representations contained therein at their face value, unless contrary to other material on file with it. Indeed, on the allegations of respondent's complaint, the proxy material failed to disclose alleged unlawful market manipulation of the stock of ATC, and this unlawful manipulation would not have been apparent to the Commission until after the merger.

We, therefore, believe that under the circumstances here it is the duty of the courts to be alert to provide such remedies as are necessary to make effective the congressional purpose. . . . It is for the federal

---

45. [Ed.] To distinguish between direct and derivative causes, see p. 461 infra.

courts "to adjust their remedies so as to grant the necessary relief" where federally secured rights are invaded. "And it is also well settled that where legal rights have been invaded, and a federal statute provides for a general right to sue for such invasion, federal courts may use any available remedy to make good the wrong done." Bell v. Hood, 327 U.S. 678, 684, 66 S.Ct. 773, 777, 90 L.Ed. 939 (1946). Section 27 grants the District Courts jurisdiction "of all suits in equity and actions at law brought to enforce any liability or duty created by this title . . . ." In passing on almost identical language found in the Securities Act of 1933, the Court found the words entirely sufficient to fashion a remedy to rescind a fraudulent sale, secure restitution and even to enforce the right to restitution against a third party holding assets of the vendor. Deckert v. Independence Shares Corp., 311 U.S. 282, 61 S.Ct. 229, 85 L.Ed. 189 (1940). This significant language was used:

> "The power *to enforce* implies the power to make effective the right of recovery afforded by the Act. And the power to make the right of recovery effective implies the power to utilize any of the procedures or actions normally available to the litigant according to the exigencies of the particular case." At 288 of 311 U.S., at 233 of 61 S.Ct. . . .

Nor do we find merit in the contention that such remedies are limited to prospective relief. This was the position taken in Dann v. Studebaker–Packard Corp., 6 Cir., 288 F.2d 201, where it was held that the "preponderance of questions of state law which would have to be interpreted and applied in order to grant the relief sought. . . . is so great that the federal question involved . . . is really negligible in comparison." At 214. But we believe that the overriding federal law applicable here would, where the facts required, control the appropriateness of redress despite the provisions of state corporation law, for it "is not uncommon for federal courts to fashion federal law where federal rights are concerned." Textile Workers Union of America v. Lincoln Mills, 353 U.S. 448, 457, 77 S.Ct. 912, 918, 1 L.Ed.2d 972 (1957). In addition, the fact that questions of state law must be decided does not change the character of the right; it remains federal. As Chief Justice Marshall said in Osborn v. Bank of United States, 9 Wheat. 738, 6 L.Ed. 204 (1824):

> "If this were sufficient to withdraw a case from the jurisdiction of the federal Courts, almost every case, although involving the construction of a law, would be withdrawn . . . ." At 819–820 of 9 Wheat.

Moreover, if federal jurisdiction were limited to the granting of declaratory relief, victims of deceptive proxy statements would be obliged to go into state courts for remedial relief. And if the law of the State happened to attach no responsibility to the use of misleading proxy statements, the whole purpose of the section might be frustrated. Furthermore, the hurdles that the victim might face (such as separate suits, as contemplated by Dann v. Studebaker–Packard Corp., supra, security for expenses statutes, bringing in all parties necessary for complete relief, etc.) might well prove insuperable to effective relief.

IV.

Our finding that federal courts have the power to grant all necessary remedial relief is not to be construed as any indication of what we believe to be the necessary and appropriate relief in this case. We are concerned here only with a determination that federal jurisdiction for this purpose does exist. Whatever remedy is necessary must await the trial on the merits.

The other contentions of the petitioners are denied.

Affirmed.

***

MILLS v. ELECTRIC AUTO–LITE COMPANY

Supreme Court of the United States, 1970.
396 U.S. 375, 90 S.Ct. 616, 24 L.Ed.2d 593.

[Shareholders of Electric Auto–Lite Co. brought suit to enjoin the voting of proxies at a meeting of Auto–Lite called to approve a merger into Mergenthaler Linotype Co. No temporary restraining order was sought and the merger was carried out. The plaintiffs then amended their complaint to have it set aside. Their complaint asserted that the proxies were misleading in stating that Auto–Lite's directors approved without disclosing that they were controlled by Mergenthaler which owned over 50% of Auto–Lite's stock. The district court ruled that the claimed defect was a material omission but read Borak to require a finding as to a causal relation between the violation of § 14(a) and the alleged injury to plaintiffs. After a hearing it concluded that, while Mergenthaler and its affiliates held 54% of Auto–Lite's shares they needed minority votes to make up the required two-thirds vote for a merger and that a causal relation was thus shown. The Court of Appeals reversed the district court, agreeing that the defect was material, but ruling that if the merger was fair it should be assumed that enough shareholders would have approved for it to pass. The Supreme Court granted certiorari, vacated the judgment of the Court of Appeals and remanded for further proceedings. JUSTICE HARLAN's opinion said the following about the requirements of finding of causation, etc.]

II

As we stressed in *Borak*, § 14(a) stemmed from a congressional belief that "[f]air corporate suffrage is an important right that should attach to every security bought on a public exchange." . . .

The decision below, by permitting all liability to be foreclosed on the basis of a finding that the merger was fair, would allow the stockholders to be bypassed, at least where the only legal challenge to the merger is a suit for retrospective relief after the meeting has been held. A judicial appraisal of the merger's merits could be substituted for the actual and informed vote of the stockholders.

The result would be to insulate from private redress an entire category of proxy violations—those relating to matters other than the terms of the merger. Even outrageous misrepresentations in a proxy solicitation, if they did not relate to the terms of the transaction, would give rise to no cause of action under § 14(a). Particularly if carried over to enforcement actions by the Securities and Exchange Commission itself, such a result would subvert the congressional purpose of ensuring full and fair disclosure to shareholders.

Further, recognition of the fairness of the merger as a complete defense would confront small shareholders with an additional obstacle to making a successful challenge to a proposal recommended through a defective proxy statement. The risk that they would be unable to rebut the corporation's evidence of the fairness of the proposal, and thus to establish their cause of action, would be bound to discourage such shareholders from the private enforcement of the proxy rules that "provides a necessary supplement to Commission action." J.I. Case Co. v. Borak, 377 U.S., at 432, 84 S.Ct. at 1560.[46]

Such a frustration of the congressional policy is not required by anything in the wording of the statute or in our opinion in the *Borak* case. . . . Use of a solicitation which is materially misleading is itself a violation of law, as the Court of Appeals recognized in stating that injunctive relief would be available to remedy such a defect if sought prior to the stockholders' meeting. In *Borak,* which came to this Court on a dismissal of the complaint, the Court limited its inquiry to whether a violation of § 14(a) gives rise to "a federal cause of action for rescission or damages," 377 U.S., at 428, 84 S.Ct. at 1558. Referring to *Def's argument* the argument made by defendants there "that the merger can be dissolved only if it was fraudulent or non-beneficial, issues upon which the proxy material would not bear," the Court stated: "But the causal relationship of the proxy material and the merger are questions of fact to be resolved at trial, not here. We therefore do not discuss this point further." *Id.,* at 431, 84 S.Ct. at 1559. In the present case there has been a hearing specifically directed to the causation problem. The question before the Court is whether the facts found on the basis of that hearing are sufficient in law to establish petitioners' cause of action, and we conclude that they are.

Where the misstatement or omission in a proxy statement has been shown to be "material," as it was found to be here, that determination itself indubitably embodies a conclusion that the defect was of such a character that it might have been considered important by a reasonable shareholder who was in the process of deciding how to vote. This requirement that the defect have a *significant propensity* to affect the voting process is found in the express terms of Rule 14a–9, and it adequately serves the purpose of ensuring that a cause of action cannot be established by proof of a defect so trivial, or so unrelated to the transaction for which approval is sought, that correction of the defect

---

46. The Court of Appeals' ruling that "causation" may be negated by proof of the fairness of the merger also rests on a dubious behavioral assumption. There is no justification for presuming that the shareholders of every corporation are willing to accept any and every fair merger offer put before them; yet such a presumption is implicit in the opinion of the Court of Appeals. That court gave no indication of what evidence petitioners might adduce, once respondents had established that the merger proposal was equitable, in order to show that the shareholders would nevertheless have rejected it if the solicitation had not been misleading. Proof of actual reliance by thousands of individuals would, as the court acknowledged, not be feasible,

see R. Jennings & H. Marsh, Cases on Securities Regulation 1001 (2d ed. 1968); and reliance on the *nondisclosure* of a fact is a particularly difficult matter to define or prove, see 3 L. Loss, Securities Regulation 1766 (2d ed. 1961). In practice, therefore, the objective fairness of the proposal would seemingly be determinative of liability. But, in view of the many other factors that might lead shareholders to prefer their current position to that of owners of a larger, combined enterprise, it is pure conjecture to assume that the fairness of the proposal will always be determinative of their vote. Cf. Wirtz v. Hotel, Motel & Club Employees Union, 391 U.S. 492, 508, 88 S.Ct. 1743, 1752, 20 L.Ed.2d 763 (1968).

or imposition of liability would not further the interests protected by § 14(a).

There is no need to supplement this requirement, as did the Court of Appeals, with a requirement of proof of whether the defect actually had a decisive effect on the voting. Where there has been a finding of materiality, a shareholder has made a sufficient showing of causal relationship between the violation and the injury for which he seeks redress if, as here, he proves that the proxy solicitation itself, rather than the particular defect in the solicitation materials, was an essential link in the accomplishment of the transaction. This objective test will avoid the impracticalities of determining how many votes were affected, and, by resolving doubts in favor of those the statute is designed to protect, will effectuate the congressional policy of ensuring that the shareholders are able to make an informed choice when they are consulted on corporate transactions.[47] . . .

III

Our conclusion that petitioners have established their case by showing that proxies necessary to approval of the merger were obtained by means of a materially misleading solicitation implies nothing about the form of relief to which they may be entitled. We held in *Borak* that upon finding a violation the courts were "to be alert to provide such remedies as are necessary to make effective the congressional purpose," noting specifically that such remedies are not to be limited to prospective relief. 377 U.S., at 433, 434, 84 S.Ct. at 1560. In devising retrospective relief for violation of the proxy rules, the federal courts should consider the same factors that would govern the relief granted for any similar illegality or fraud. One important factor may be the fairness of the terms of the merger. Possible forms of relief will include setting aside the merger or granting other equitable relief, but, as the Court of Appeals below noted, nothing in the statutory policy "requires the court to unscramble a corporate transaction merely because a violation occurred." 403 F.2d, at 436. In selecting a remedy the lower courts should exercise "the sound discretion which guides the determinations of courts of equity," keeping in mind the role of equity as "the instrument for nice adjustment and reconciliation between the public interest and private needs as well as between competing private claims." Hecht Co. v. Bowles, 321 U.S. 321, 329–330, 64 S.Ct. 587, 591–592, 88 L.Ed. 754 (1944). . . .

We do not read § 29(b) of the Act, which declares contracts made in violation of the Act or a rule thereunder "void . . . as regards the rights of" the violator and knowing successors in interest, as requiring that the merger be set aside simply because the merger agreement is a "void" contract. This language establishes that the guilty party is precluded from enforcing the contract against an unwilling innocent party, but it does not compel the conclusion that the contract is a nullity, creating no enforceable rights even in a party innocent of the

---

47. We need not decide in this case whether causation could be shown where the management controls a sufficient number of shares to approve the transaction without any votes from the minority. Even in that situation, if the management finds it necessary for legal or practical reasons to solicit proxies from minority shareholders, at least one court has held that the proxy solicitation might be sufficiently related to the merger to satisfy the causation requirement, see Laurenzano v. Einbender, 264 F.Supp. 356 (D.C.E.D.N.Y. 1966); . . .

violation.   The lower federal courts have read § 29(b), which has counterparts in the Holding Company Act, the Investment Company Act, and the Investment Advisers Act, as rendering the contract merely voidable at the option of the innocent party. . . . This interpretation is eminently sensible.   The interests of the victim are sufficiently protected by giving him the right to rescind; to regard the contract as void where he has not invoked that right would only create the possibility of hardships to him or others without necessarily advancing the statutory policy of disclosure.

The United States, as *amicus curiae*, points out that as representatives of the minority shareholders, petitioners are not parties to the merger agreement and thus do not enjoy a statutory right under § 29(b) to set it aside.[48] Furthermore, while they do have a derivative right to invoke Auto–Lite's status as a party to the agreement, a determination of what relief should be granted in Auto–Lite's name must hinge on whether setting aside the merger would be in the best interests of the shareholders as a whole.   In short, in the context of a suit such as this one, § 29(b) leaves the matter of relief where it would be under *Borak* without specific statutory language—the merger should be set aside only if a court of equity concludes, from all the circumstances, that it would be equitable to do so. . . .

Monetary relief will, of course, also be a possibility.   Where the defect in the proxy solicitation relates to the specific terms of the merger, the district court might appropriately order an accounting to ensure that the shareholders receive the value that was represented as coming to them. On the other hand, where, as here, the misleading aspect of the solicitation did not relate to terms of the merger, monetary relief might be afforded to the shareholders only if the merger resulted in a reduction of the earnings or earnings potential of their holdings. In short, damages should be recoverable only to the extent that they can be shown. If commingling of the assets and operations of the merged companies makes it impossible to establish direct injury from the merger, relief might be predicated on a determination of the fairness of the terms of the merger at the time it was approved. These questions, of course, are for decision in the first instance by the District Court on remand, and our singling out of some of the possibilities is not intended to exclude others.

COMMENT

Plaintiff's victory, it turned out, was not a satisfying one. The Court of Appeals ruling on remand, excerpted at p. 731 infra, found that the shareholders were not eligible for monetary relief as they had not demonstrated unfairness.

PROBLEM

Universal Home Products is an American-based multinational enterprise with extensive operations in Africa. It produces in Europe a dried milk

---

48. If petitioners had submitted their own proxies in favor of the merger in response to the unlawful solicitation, as it does not appear they did, the language of § 29(b) would seem to give them, as innocent parties to that transaction, a right to rescind their proxies. But it is clear in this case, where petitioners' combined holdings are only 600 shares, that such rescission would not affect the authorization of the merger.

product for infants which it has been selling in Africa. It also has extensive investments in South Africa which are held by it in the form of a joint venture with a South African firm. Both of these enterprises have been highly profitable, bolstering a rather unimpressive performance by UHP in the United States. You have agreed to do the legal work for Central Church Agencies which coordinates the proxy activities of a number of religious and educational institutions. The sixty-two member clientele of CCA holds about 2% of the stock of UHP. The directors of CCA have decided that in this proxy season they would mount a campaign to put an end to the practices of UHP in Africa which they regard as immoral. They propose to you that you draft proposals that would do two things: (a) cause UHP to get out of South Africa, and (b) stop sales of dried milk in Africa or at least substantially cut back on objectionable advertising. They specify that they regard as morally wrong using persons who dress in white uniforms resembling medical uniforms to push the powdered milk in villages not otherwise familiar with modern advertising; similarly dressed personnel appear on billboards and on television in major African cities. The advertising should, your board thinks, warn that unless the water used to make milk from the dried substance is sterile infection often results. The milk from the healthy mother is plainly superior, the staff advise you and it is largely an undue respect for western technology and a desire to be "with it" that cause Africans to purchase the commodity. You contact the legal staff of UHP and they prove to be courteous but resistant. They advise you that selling out the African investments would violate a clause in the joint venture agreement that forbids sales without the co-venturer's approval. They further assert that there are many cases in which powdered milk is urgently needed, as in the case of the mother's illness. They flatly deny some of the allegations of the CCA staff.

For a conference with the other legal advisers to CCA, you jot down the following questions that will need to be answered:

(a) Does UHP have any obligations to help us reach its shareholders with our message? To what extent will this cut our costs? Suppose that we simply appeal to our own membership and perhaps to a few other universities—can we then avoid this whole cumbersome set of rules?

(b) How can we best formulate our demands as to African matters so as to minimize the chances that we will run into trouble with the SEC in coping with the objections that UHP is sure to make?

(c) Could we also propose that UHP appoint a special committee, either composed of its directors or of outside persons that would supervise the selling of milk? That the regional advertising director who has been responsible for the present state of affairs be removed?

(d) How do we cope with the likelihood that there will be a sharp clash of views about the truth on the milk issue? Will UHP be able to enjoin us from circulating our literature? Can we try to enjoin them? Is it really constitutional for the courts to do this? Suppose that the meeting goes through and we lose, perhaps not getting our 3%, can we then sue—and what relief could we ask for?

(e) Suppose that we get less than 3% only because allies of the management at the last minute buy more stock that they try to vote against us (or perhaps management issues new stock to dilute our holdings). Could we get relief against those practices? If so, from what body? Suppose that to get our 3% we need both to disqualify that stock and some other stock reached by management through materials that they did not file with the SEC and that did not contain all the data required by its rules?

(f) Would it be useful to try to run a slate of candidates on an opposition platform? What help do we get from the proxy rules on this? Suppose we can show that there were false statements in the management's proxy materials about their candidates. Can we get any relief on that account?

(g) If we have an opportunity to comment to the SEC on revision of the proxy rules should we press for provisions that would assist us in nominating and fighting for directors in controversies such as this? What provisions might we defend as being plausible and not too burdensome?

NOTE ON PROXY EXPENSES

One of the major obstacles to the mounting of a proxy offensive against an incumbent management is the expense of reaching and persuading a large shareholding electorate. It is so great that the pro rata benefit to the shareholder group conducting the battle that may result from a change for the better in management will not usually be worth it. The sums disbursed in the case following this note were, you will observe, quite substantial. One of the largest was that reimbursed to Mr. Robert Young, the president of Alleghany, after he prevailed in the New York Central proxy battle of 1954: $1,309,000. In appealing to the shareholders for reimbursement (after originally stating that the cost would be borne by Alleghany Corporation and the 15 nominees), Young said:

> "If the expenses of only one side are to be so borne, it would seem not only more equitable, but more within the wishes of shareholders, that it be the expenses of the victors. Consequently, your board has been persuaded, and we believe rightly, that it would be a discouraging precedent to owners of other non-owner director companies for us to defray our own expenses when the benefits redound to all Central shareholders, pro rata, just as the expenses would automatically be borne if the company defrayed them." [49] The margin in favor of the reimbursement rule was 4,885,000 to 385,000 (1,000,000 of the affirmative votes belonging to the Young-Alleghany group and its allies).

These proxy expenses include some quite identifiable ones, such as the hiring of professional proxy solicitor firms, and some less identifiable costs such as the cost of hours spent by executives and employees in persuading shareholders. Some of the expenses are purely to furnish information and are indeed made mandatory by the proxy rules. Other expenses are necessitated by the opposition's tactics; the spiral of

49. Excerpt from THE AMERICAN STOCKHOLDER by J.A. Livingston. Copyright, © 1958, by J.A. Livingston. Reprinted by permission of Harper & Row Publishers, Inc. P. 134.

reply to reply and cost upon cost then mounts into the six or seven figures.[50] This is the basis of the problem here.

ROSENFELD v. FAIRCHILD ENGINE AND AIRPLANE CORP.

Court of Appeals of New York, 1955.
309 N.Y. 168, 128 N.E.2d 291.

[Plaintiff, a lawyer and holder of 25 of the company's over 2,300,000 shares, brought a derivative action to compel return of sums paid out of the corporate treasury in connection with a proxy contest:

1) $106,000—spent by the old board while still in office to defend their position
2)   28,000—paid by the new board to the old board to cover their unreimbursed expenses
3)   127,000—paid to members of the new board, after 16 to 1 ratification by the shareholders

The referee dismissed the complaint and the appellate division affirmed. The Court of Appeals split with two other judges joining in JUDGE FROESSEL's opinion, which prevailed, because of JUDGE DESMOND's concurrence, over a dissent concurred in by three judges. Extracts from these opinions follow:]

JUDGE FROESSEL. By way of contrast with the findings here, in Lawyers' Advertising Co. v. Consolidated Ry., Lighting & Refrigerating Co., 187 N.Y. 395, at page 399, 80 N.E. 199, at page 200, which was an action to recover for the cost of publishing newspaper notices not authorized by the board of directors, it was expressly found that the proxy contest there involved was "by one faction in its contest with another for the control of the corporation . . . a contest for the perpetuation of their offices and control." We there said by way of *dicta* that under *such* circumstances the publication of certain notices on behalf of the management faction was not a corporate expenditure which the directors had the power to authorize.

Other jurisdictions and our own lower courts have held that management may look to the corporate treasury for the reasonable expenses of soliciting proxies to defend its position in a bona fide policy contest. . . .

It should be noted that plaintiff does not argue that the aforementioned sums were fraudulently extracted from the corporation; indeed, his counsel conceded that "the charges were fair and reasonable", but denied "they were legal charges which may be reimbursed for". This is therefore not a case where a stockholder challenges specific items, which, on examination, the trial court may find unwarranted, excessive or otherwise improper. Had plaintiff made such objections here, the trial court would have been required to examine the items challenged.

50. For a collection of statistics showing proxy expenses in other cases ranging from $6000 to $365,000, see M. Eisenberg, The Structure of the Corporation: A Legal Analysis 109–110 (1976). Cowan, The Trench Warriors, N.Y. Times, May 29, 1988, § 3, p. 1, in describing the three main proxy solicitation firms, D.F. King, Georgeson and Carter, estimates the costs of a contested proxy fight at a corporation with 40,000 shareholders at about $1.7 million.

If directors of a corporation may not in good faith incur reasonable and proper expenses in soliciting proxies in these days of giant corporations with vast numbers of stockholders, the corporate business might be seriously interfered with because of stockholder indifference and the difficulty of procuring a quorum, where there is no contest. In the event of a proxy contest, if the directors may not freely answer the challenges of outside groups and in good faith defend their actions with respect to corporate policy for the information of the stockholders, they and the corporation may be at the mercy of persons seeking to wrest control for their own purposes, so long as such persons have ample funds to conduct a proxy contest. The test is clear. When the directors act in good faith in a contest over policy, they have the right to incur reasonable and proper expenses for solicitation of proxies and in defense of their corporate policies, and are not obliged to sit idly by. The courts are entirely competent to pass upon their *bona fides* in any given case, as well as the nature of their expenditures when duly challenged.

It is also our view that the members of the so-called new group could be reimbursed by the corporation for their expenditures in this contest by affirmative vote of the stockholders. With regard to these ultimately successful contestants, as the Appellate Division below has noted, there was, of course, "no duty . . . to set forth the facts, with corresponding obligation of the corporation to pay for such expense". However, where a majority of the stockholders chose—in this case by a vote of 16 to 1—to reimburse the successful contestants for achieving the very end sought and voted for by them as owners of the corporation, we see no reason to deny the effect of their ratification nor to hold the corporate body powerless to determine how its own moneys shall be spent.

The rule then which we adopt is simply this: In a contest over policy, as compared to a purely personal power contest, corporate directors have the right to make reasonable and proper expenditures, subject to the scrutiny of the courts when duly challenged, from the corporate treasury for the purpose of persuading the stockholders of the correctness of their position and soliciting their support for policies which the directors believe, in all good faith, are in the best interests of the corporation. The stockholders, moreover, have the right to reimburse successful contestants for the reasonable and bona fide expenses incurred by them in any such policy contest, subject to like court scrutiny. That is not to say, however, that corporate directors can, under any circumstances, disport themselves in a proxy contest with the corporation's moneys to an unlimited extent. Where it is established that such moneys have been spent for personal power, individual gain or private advantage, and not in the belief that such expenditures are in the best interests of the stockholders and the corporation, or where the fairness and reasonableness of the amounts allegedly expended are duly and successfully challenged, the courts will not hesitate to disallow them. . . .

DESMOND, JUDGE (concurring).

We granted leave to appeal in an effort to pass, and in the expectation of passing, on this question, highly important in modern-day corporation law: is it lawful for a corporation, on consent of a majority of its stockholders, to pay, out of its funds, the expenses of a "proxy fight", incurred by competing candidates for election as directors? Now that the appeal has been argued, I doubt that the question is presented by this record. . . .

Plaintiff asserts that it was illegal for the directors (unless by unanimous consent of stockholders) to expend corporate moneys in the proxy contest beyond the amounts necessary to give to stockholders bare notice of the meeting and of the matters to be voted on thereat. Defendants say that the proxy contest revolved around disputes over corporate policies and that it was, accordingly, proper not only to assess against the corporation the expense of serving formal notices and of routine proxy solicitation, but to go further and spend corporate moneys, on behalf of each group, thoroughly to inform the stockholders. The reason why that important question is, perhaps, not directly before us in this lawsuit is because, as the Appellate Division properly held, [284 App.Div. 201, 132 N.Y.S.2d 280] plaintiff failed "to urge liability as to specific expenditures". The cost of giving routinely necessary notice is, of course, chargeable to the corporation. It is just as clear, we think, that payment by a corporation of the expense of "proceedings by one faction in its contest with another for the control of the corporation" is *ultra vires,* and unlawful. Lawyers' Advertising Co. v. Consolidated Ry., Lighting & Refrigerating Co., 187 N.Y. 395, 399, 80 N.E. 199, 200. Approval by directors or by a majority stock vote could not validate such gratuitous expenditures. Continental Securities Co. v. Belmont, 206 N.Y. 7, 99 N.E. 138, 51 L.R.A., N.S., 112. Some of the payments attacked in this suit were, on their face, for lawful purposes and apparently reasonable in amount but, as to others, the record simply does not contain evidentiary bases for a determination as to either lawfulness or reasonableness. Surely, the burden was on plaintiff to go forward to some extent with such particularization and proof. It failed to do so, and so failed to make out a prima facie case.

We are, therefore, reaching the same result as did the Appellate Division but on one only of the grounds listed by that court, that is, failure of proof. We think it not inappropriate, however, to state our general views on the question of law principally argued by the parties, that is, as to the validity of corporate payments for proxy solicitations and similar activities in addition to giving notice of the meeting, and of the questions to be voted on. For an answer to that problem we could not do better than quote from this court's opinion in the Lawyers' Advertising Co. case, 187 N.Y. 395, 399, 80 N.E. 199, 200, supra: "The remaining notices were not legally authorized and were not legitimately incidental to the meeting or necessary for the protection of the stockholders. They rather were proceedings by one faction in its contest with another for the control of the corporation, and the expense thereof, as such, is not properly chargeable to the latter. This is so apparent as to the last two notices that nothing need be said in reference to them; but a few words may be said in regard to the first one, calling for proxies. It is to be noted that this is not the case of an ordinary circular letter sent out with and requesting the execution of proxies. The custom has become common upon the part of corporations to mail proxies to their respective stockholders, often accompanied by a brief circular of directions, and such custom when accompanied by no unreasonable expenditure, is not without merit in so far as it encourages voting by stockholders, through making it convenient and ready at hand. The notice in question, however, was not published until after proxies had been sent out. It simply amounted to an urgent solicitation that these proxies should be executed and returned for use by one faction in its contest, and we think there is no authority for imposing the expense of its publication upon the company. . . . it would be altogether too dangerous a rule to permit directors in control of a corporation and engaged in a contest for the perpetuation of their offices and control, to impose upon the corporation the unusual expense of publishing advertisements or, by analogy, of dispatching special messengers for the purpose of procuring proxies in their behalf."

A final comment: since expenditures which do not meet that test of propriety are intrinsically unlawful, it could not be any answer to such a claim as plaintiff makes here that the stockholder vote which purported to authorize them was heavy or that the change in management turned out to be beneficial to the corporation.

The judgment should be affirmed, without costs.

VAN VOORHIS, JUDGE (dissenting).

No resolution was passed by the stockholders approving payment to the management group. It has been recognized that not all of the $133,966 in obligations paid or incurred by the management group was designed merely for information of stockholders. This outlay included payment for all of the activities of a strenuous campaign to persuade and cajole in a hard-fought contest for control of this corporation. It included, for example, expenses for entertainment, chartered airplanes and limousines, public relations counsel and proxy solicitors. However legitimate such measures may be on behalf of stockholders themselves in such a controversy, most of them do not pertain to a corporate function but are part of the familiar apparatus of aggressive factions in corporate contests. . . .

The Appellate Division acknowledged in the instant case that "It is obvious that the management group here incurred a substantial amount of needless expense which was charged to the corporation," but this conclusion should have led to a direction that those defendants who were incumbent directors should be required to come forward with an explanation of their expenditures under the familiar rule that where it has been established that directors have expended corporate money for their own purposes, the burden of going forward with evidence of the propriety and reasonableness of specific items rests upon the directors. . . . The complaint should not have been dismissed as against incumbent directors due to failure of plaintiff to segregate the specific expenditures which are *ultra vires,* but, once plaintiff had proved facts from which an inference of impropriety might be drawn, the duty of making an explanation was laid upon the directors to explain and justify their conduct.

The second ground assigned by the Appellate Division for dismissing the complaint against incumbent directors is stockholder ratification of reimbursement to the insurgent group. Whatever effect or lack of it this resolution had upon expenditures by the insurgent group, clearly the stockholders who voted to pay the insurgents entertained no intention of reimbursing the management group for their expenditures. The insurgent group succeeded as a result of arousing the indignation of these very stockholders against the management group; nothing in the resolution to pay the expenses of the insurgent group purported to authorize or ratify payment of the campaign expenses of their adversaries, and certainly no inference should be drawn that the stockholders who voted to pay the insurgents intended that the incumbent group should also be paid. Upon the contrary, they were removing the incumbents from control mainly for the reason that they were charged with having mulcted the corporation by a long-term salary and pension contract to one of their number, J. Carlton Ward, Jr. If these stockholders had been presented with a resolution to pay the expenses of that group, it would almost certainly have been voted down. The stockholders should not be deemed to have authorized or ratified reimbursement of the incumbents.

There is no doubt that the management was entitled and under a duty to take reasonable steps to acquaint the stockholders with essential facts concerning the management of the corporation, and it may well be that the existence of a contest warranted them in circularizing the stockholders with more than ordinarily detailed information. As this court said in Lawyers' Advertising Co. v. Consolidated Ry., Lighting & Refrigerating Co., supra, 187 N.Y. at page 399, 80 N.E. at page 200: "Proper and honest corporate management was subserved by widespread notice to stockholders of questions affecting the welfare of the corporation, and there is no impropriety in charging the latter with any expenses within reasonable limits which were incurred in giving sufficient notice of a special meeting at which the stockholders would be called upon to decide these questions."

What expenses of the incumbent group should be allowed and what should be disallowed should be remitted to the trial court to ascertain, after taking evidence, in accordance with the rule that the incumbent directors were required to assume the burden of going forward in the first instance with evidence explaining and justifying their expenditures. Only such as were reasonably related to informing the stockholders fully and fairly concerning the corporate affairs should be allowed. The concession by plaintiff that such expenditures as were made were reasonable in amount does not decide this question. By way of illustration, the costs of entertainment for stockholders may have been, and it is stipulated that they were, at the going rates for providing similar entertainment. That does not signify that entertaining stockholders is reasonably related to the purposes of the corporation. The Appellate Division, as above stated, found that the management group incurred a substantial amount of needless expense. That fact being established, it became the duty of the incumbent directors to unravel and explain these payments.

Regarding the $127,556 paid by the new management to the insurgent group for their campaign expenditures, the question immediately arises whether that was for a corporate purpose. The Appellate Division has recognized that upon no theory could such expenditures be reimbursed except by approval of the stockholders and, as has been said, it is the insurgents' expenditures alone to which the stockholders' resolution of ratification was addressed. If *unanimous* stockholder approval had been obtained and no rights of creditors or of the public intervened, it would make no practical difference whether the purpose were *ultra vires*—i.e., not a corporate purpose. Kent v. Quicksilver Min. Co., 78 N.Y. 159; Capitol Wine & Spirit Corp. v. Pokrass, 277 App. Div. 184, 187, 98 N.Y.S.2d 291, 294, affirmed 302 N.Y. 734, 98 N.E.2d 704. Upon the other hand, an act which is *ultra vires* cannot be ratified merely by a majority of the stockholders of a corporation.

. . .

. . .

In considering this issue, as in the case of the expenses of the incumbents, we begin with the proposition that this court has already held that it is beyond the power of a corporation to authorize the expenditure of mere campaign expenses in a proxy contest. Lawyers' Advertising Co. v. Consolidated Ry., Lighting & Refrigerating Co., supra. That decision is not distinguishable upon the ground that those expenditures were made by the secretary of that corporation without previous authorization by its directors. That point was involved, but this court said: "Thus we have it that the publication of the last three notices was not authorized by the board of directors, *and that it could not have been lawfully authorized, even if the attempt were made. They bore upon their face sufficient notice to the plaintiff [the printer suing for printing fees] that they were of a character beyond the limit of anything which could be published in behalf of or at the expense of the corporation*" 187 N.Y. at page 400, 80 N.E. at page 201; (italics supplied). The decision was placed upon both grounds. The statement in the carefully considered opinion written by Judge Hiscock was not dictum that "it would be altogether too dangerous a rule to permit directors, in control of a corporation and engaged in a contest for the perpetuation of their offices and control, to impose upon the corporation the unusual expense". In that case, and in all of the other decisions which have been cited with the single exception of a Federal district court decision, Steinberg v. Adams, D.C., 90 F.Supp. 604, 606, the question concerned reimbursement of a management group. Moreover, with the exception of an English decision, Peel v. London & North Western Ry. Co., [1907] 1 Ch. 5, all of the appellate court cases which have been cited, and Steinberg v. Adams, were decided under the law of the State of Delaware. The Delaware law contains more latitude than in New York State, as was recognized by Judge Rifkind in his opinion in Steinberg v. Adams, supra, who said, 90 F.Supp. at page 607: "The instant case is concerned with a Delaware corporation and the law of that state determines the scope of the corporation's powers. Both parties, as I have indicated, agree that this case is governed by a less stringent rule" than the ruling by this court in Lawyers' Advertising Co. v. Consolidated Ry., Lighting & Refrigerating Co., supra. We are called upon to decide whether to abandon the rule as previously established in this State and adopt the less strict doctrine of the State of Delaware.

The Delaware cases which are cited consist of Hall v. Trans–Lux Daylight Picture Screen Corp., 20 Del.Ch. 78, 171 A. 226; Empire Southern Gas Co. v. Gray, 29 Del.Ch. 95, 46 A.2d 741, and the Federal cases applying Delaware law, Hand v. Missouri–Kansas Pipe Line Co., D.C., 54 F.Supp. 649, and Steinberg v. Adams, supra. The Hand case, supra, merely denied a preliminary injunction to restrain the management from expending corporate funds to hire professional proxy solicitors. There is a difference between hiring solicitors merely to follow up proxy notices so as to obtain a quorum, and a high pressure campaign to secure votes by personal contact. The district court in the Hand case did not attempt to decide that aspect of the case, merely ruling that it should be determined after trial, and that no irreparable injury had been shown justifying the issuance of a temporary injunction even if the practice were ultimately held to have been *ultra vires*. In Empire Southern Gas Co. v. Gray, supra, it was held that a corporation might sue to enjoin insurgents from soliciting proxies fraudulently by means of a false statement that such solicitation was being made by order of the board of directors. The case most frequently cited and principally relied upon from among these Delaware decisions is Hall v. Trans–Lux Daylight Picture Screen Corp., supra. There the English case was followed of [sic] Peel v. London & North Western Ry. Co., supra, which distinguished between expenses merely for the purpose of maintaining control, and contests over policy questions of the corporation. In the Hall case the issues concerned a proposed merger, and a proposed sale of stock of a subsidiary corporation. These were held to be policy questions, and payment of the management campaign expenses was upheld.

In our view, the impracticability of such a distinction is illustrated by the statement in the Hall case, supra, 20 Del.Ch. at page 85, 171 A. at page 229, that "It is impossible in many cases of intracorporate contests over directors, to sever questions of policy from those of persons". This circumstance is stressed in Judge Rifkind's opinion in the Steinberg case, supra, 90 F.Supp. at page 608: "The simple fact, of course, is that generally policy and personnel do not exist in separate compartments. A change in personnel is sometimes indispensable to a change of policy. A new board may be the symbol of the shift in policy as well as the means of obtaining it."

That may be all very well, but the upshot of this reasoning is that inasmuch as it is generally impossible to distinguish whether "policy" or "personnel" is the dominant factor, any averments must be accepted at their face value that questions of policy are dominant. Nowhere do these opinions mention that the converse is equally true and more pervasive, that neither the "ins" nor the "outs" ever say that they have no program to offer to the shareholders, but just want to acquire or to retain control, as the case may be. In common experience, this distinction is unreal. It was not mentioned by this court in Lawyers' Advertising Co. v. Consolidated Ry., Lighting & Refrigerating Co., supra. As in political contests, aspirations for control are invariably presented under the guise of policy or principle. . . .

The main question of "policy" in the instant corporate election, as is stated in the opinions below and frankly admitted, concerns the long-term contract with pension rights of a former officer and director, Mr. J. Carlton Ward, Jr. The insurgents' chief claim of benefit to the corporation from their victory consists in the termination of that agreement, resulting in an alleged actuarial saving of $350,000 to $825,000 to the corporation, and the reduction of other salaries and rent by more than $300,000 per year. The insurgents had contended in the proxy contest that these payments should be substantially reduced so that members of the incumbent group would not continue to profit personally at the expense of the corporation. If these charges were true, which appear to have been believed by a majority of the shareholders, then the disbursements by the management group in the proxy contest fall under the condemnation of the English and the Delaware rule.

These circumstances are mentioned primarily to illustrate how impossible it is to distinguish between "policy" and "personnel", as Judge Rifkind expressed it, but they also indicate that personal factors are deeply rooted in this contest. That is certainly true insofar as the former management group is concerned. It would be hard to find a case to which the careful reservation made by the English Judge in the Peel case, supra, was more directly applicable.

Some expenditures may concededly be made by a corporation represented by its management so as to inform the stockholders, but there is a clear distinction between such expenditures by management and by mere groups of stockholders. The latter are under no legal obligation to assume duties of managing the corporation. They may endeavor to supersede the management for any reason, regardless of whether it be advantageous or detrimental to the corporation but, if they succeed, that is not a determination that the company was previously mismanaged or that it may not be mismanaged in the future. A change in control is in no sense analogous to an adjudication that the former directors have been guilty of misconduct. The analogy of allowing expenses of suit to minority stockholders who have been successful in a derivative action based on misconduct of officers or directors, is entirely without foundation.

Insofar as a management group is concerned, it may charge the corporation with any expenses within reasonable limits incurred in giving widespread notice to stockholders of questions affecting the welfare of the corporation. Lawyers' Advertising Co. v. Consolidated Ry., Lighting & Refrigerating Co., supra. Expenditures in excess of these limits are *ultra vires*. The corporation lacks power to defray them. The corporation lacks power to defray the expenses of the insurgents in their entirety. The insurgents were not charged with responsibility for operating the company. No appellate court case is cited from any jurisdiction holding otherwise. No contention is made that such disbursements could be made, in any event, without stockholder ratification; they could not be ratified except by unanimous vote if they were *ultra vires*. The insurgents, in this instance, repeatedly announced to the stockholders in their campaign literature that their proxy contest was being waged at their own personal expense. If reimbursement of such items were permitted upon majority stockholder ratification, no court or other tribunal could pass upon which types of expenditure were "needless", to employ the characterization of the Appellate Division in this case. Whether the insurgents should be paid would be made to depend upon whether they win the stockholders election and obtain control of the corporation. It would be entirely irrelevant whether the corporation is "benefitted" by their efforts or by the outcome of such an election. The courts could not indulge in a speculative inquiry into that issue. That would truly be a matter of business judgment. In some instances corporations are better governed by the existing management and in others by some other group which supersedes the existing management. Courts of law have no jurisdiction to decide such questions, and successful insurgent stockholders may confidently be relied upon to reimburse themselves whatever may be the real merits of the controversy. The losers in a proxy fight may understand the interests of the corporation more accurately than their successful adversaries, and agitation of this character may ultimately result in corporate advantage even if there be no change in management. Nevertheless, under the judgment which is appealed from, success in a proxy contest is the indispensable condition upon which reimbursement of the insurgents depends. Adventurers are not infrequent who are ready to take advantage of economic recessions, reduction of dividends or failure to increase them, or other sources of stockholder discontent to wage contests in order to obtain control of well-managed corporations, so as to divert their funds through legal channels into other corporations in which they may be interested, or to discharge former officers and employees to make room for favored newcomers according to the fashion of political patronage, or for other objectives that are unrelated to the sound prosperity of the enterprise. The way is open and will be kept open for stockholders and groups of stockholders to contest corporate elections but if the promoters of such movements choose to employ the costly modern media of mass persuasion, they should look for reimbursement to themselves and to the stockholders who are aligned with them. If the law be that they can be recompensed by the corporation in case of success, and only in that event, it will operate as a powerful incentive to persons accustomed to taking calculated risks to increase this form of high-powered salesmanship to such a degree that, action provoking reaction, stockholders' meetings will be very costly. To the financial advantages promised by control of a prosperous corporation, would be added the knowledge that the winner takes all insofar as the campaign expenses are concerned. To the victor, indeed, would belong the spoils.

The questions involved in this case assume mounting importance as the capital stock of corporations becomes more widely distributed. To an enlarged extent the campaign methods consequently come more to resemble those of political campaigns, but, as in the latter, campaign expenses should be borne by those who are waging the campaign and their followers, instead of being met out of the corporate or the public treasury. Especially is this true when campaign promises have been made that the expenses would not be charged to the corporation.

Nothing which is said in this opinion is intended as any reflection upon the motives of the insurgent group in instigating this corporate contest, nor upon the management group. Questions of law are involved which extend beyond the persons and the corporation presently before the court. It is the established law of this State that expenditures may be incurred by management limited to informing the stockholders fully and fairly concerning the affairs and policies of the corporation, which may well include an explanation of the reasons on account of which its policies have been undertaken, nor is there any reason on account of which stockholders who have neglected to sign proxies through apathy may not be solicited so as to insure a quorum, which would ordinarily occur in instances where there is no contest, but beyond measures of this character, the purely campaign expenses of a management group do not serve a corporate purpose, and paying them is *ultra vires*. The same is true of all of the expenses of insurgent stockholders. . . .

QUESTIONS

(1) Is the issue of reimbursement of proxy expenses appropriately left to state law or is it one that ought to be included within the framework of the federal regulations?

(2) Consider the question of permitting a shareholder vote to be decisive as to reimbursement of costs. Is this a case in which having that judgment is apt to be worthwhile? If the issue is one of *ultra vires* or waste is even 16 to 1 approval irrelevant?

(3) What of the dissident shareholder who without trying to unseat management put across a proposal that turns out to be a useful improvement? Should management be able—or even be forced—to reimburse them? How can one tell whether it is "useful"? Suppose it does not quite command a majority

and thus is not enacted? What if it receives 30% of the votes cast? What if cumulative voting enables the opposition to get one seat of seven?

(4) Would it be permissible and appropriate for the SEC or a statute to place some ceiling upon the total spent for expenses by the parties? Could that ceiling apply to sums not derived from the corporate treasury?

REVIEW QUESTION

Is the treatment of the costs of proxy contests consistent with that of the costs of litigation discussed at p. 510 infra?

Bibliography: There is much material on proxies in L. Loss, Securities Regulation (2d ed. 1961) and some in his Fundamentals of Securities Regulation ch. 7D (2d ed. 1988). A specialized work on proxies is E. Aranow & H. Einhorn, Proxy Contests for Corporate Control (2d ed. 1968). There is an Annual Institute on Proxy Statements, Annual Meetings and Disclosure Documents. The "public interest" movement among shareholders is viewed favorably by Schwartz, The Public Interest Proxy Contest: Reflections on Campaign GM, 69 Mich.L.Rev. 419 (1971), and unfavorably by Manne, Shareholder Social Proposals Viewed by An Opponent, 24 Stanf.L.Rev. 481 (1972); Dent, SEC Rule 14a–8, A Study in Regulatory Failure, 30 N.Y.L.Sch.Rev. 1 (1985).

Two notes explore the Medical Committee case in detail; Proxy Rule 14a–8; Omission of Shareholder Proposals, 84 Harv.L.Rev. 700 (1971); SEC and "No Action" Decisions under Proxy Rule 14a–8, id. at 835 (1971). Some basic questions about the proxy rules are raised in M. Eisenberg, The Structure of the Corporation: A Legal Analysis pt. II (1976).

---

5. The Fiduciary Duties of Shareholders

One reads occasionally statements that, unlike directors and officers, shareholders vote their own interests and are not subject to fiduciary obligations. Such is the thrust of some of the language quoted in the Ostlind case below. In fact the full implications of such rhetoric are never drawn: it is clear, for example, that shareholders cannot receive cash bribes for casting their vote in an agreed upon way. The courts have further narrowed the scope within which a majority vote is effective by upsetting various types of votes as "fraudulent", "unfair", etc.

The issue of shareholder obligations generally comes up in one of three contexts. In the first type of case the action challenged has been taken by a shareholder vote. A merger, sale of assets, etc. must according to state law be carried by a given majority of votes; the complainant asserts that the majority did not act in a disinterested way in approving the step. Such a complaint may also involve a ratification which the shareholders are requested to give by the directors, either because the directors are unsure of what is best for the corporation or because they are aware of conflicts of interest on their part which render the transaction vulnerable to attack.[51] How often such ratification is sought will depend in part on which of the various rules on director self-dealing prevails in the jurisdiction. The second category of cases involves possible shareholder liability not for actions taken directly by the majority shareholder or shareholders but by directors acting under the control of such shareholders. Classic concepts of vicarious liability—principal-agent, joint tortfeasor, participation in a breach of trust—apply so as to make the shareholder liable. In many cases the offending director is not a beneficiary of the breach of duty and indeed may be totally judgment-proof.

The third group has to do with the exercise of the shareholder's right to sell the shares; is there a duty to exercise that right with regard to its consequences for one's fellow shareholders? That question is taken up along with other aspects of trading in shares in Chapter XI.

It is important to bear in mind that a shareholder may have control while holding significantly less than 51% of the stock; it is familiar lore that a single active, interested shareholder or a close-knit group may dominate a corporation's affairs with 40%, 30%, or even 20% or less if the remainder of the stock is held by the scattered and semioblivious shareholders so typical of the large corporation. There is no sound reason why the duties of controlling shareholders should not apply to holders of power based on a lesser percentage. Frequently the controlling shareholder will be another corporation in the same line of business. The question will then arise in the context of the parent corporation's pursuit of the best interests of its overall system at the expense of the particular subsidiary and its shareholders.

As the Transamerica case indicates, the question of fiduciary duty may arise in relations between one class of shareholders and another rather than simply between two blocks of the same class. The matter is then complicated by the rather elaborate contractual provisions that were established to regulate their relations.

OSTLIND v. OSTLIND VALVE CO.

Supreme Court of Oregon, 1946.
178 Or. 161, 165 P.2d 779.

[In 1939 Ostlind Valve Co. was founded to exploit patents obtained by Joel Ostlind on a type of valve. Until 1941 the business did not make a profit but the corporation did better in wartime making other valves for the Navy, having $54,000 due it on its contracts. It also bought tools and equipment from a machinist named Williamson. In January 1945 at the annual shareholders meeting it was reported that with peace in sight the firm's prospects in making non-Ostlind valves were not good and it was recommended that the machinery not needed to make Ostlind valves be sold. It was also stated that the corpora-

---

51. For cases involving attempted ratifications by shareholders, see pp. 220, 434 supra.

Note the limitations on ratification in Del. § 144 and the caselaw under it. P. 259 supra.

tion's interest in the Ostlind patents should be sold to a firm capable of exploiting them. It was voted to give the right to buy to one Williamson, a director, if he would match the highest competitive bid. 1468 shares out of 2000 were voted for the sale. In February the board met and stated that they had received bids of $6250, $6000 and $8497 for the machinery from outside parties. An appraiser had put a value of $8105 on it. It was carried on the books of the corporation at about $13,000. The directors resolved to sell to Williamson for $8497. All the nine directors present voted in favor except for Williamson and one Jarman who stated he expected to have an interest in the transaction. Notice of a special stockholders' meeting to confirm the sale was then sent out. Suits were filed by Joel Ostlind, owner of 215 shares, and members of his family who owned about 180 further shares, to enjoin the sale. No temporary restraining order was issued and the stockholders' meeting was held on March 9. There were then 1466 shares outstanding of which 1441 were represented. The Ostlinds and allies cast 428½ votes against the sale, and 1012½ were voted for the deal, including Williamson's 36 and Jarman's 262. The sale was carried out before the trial began and the purchasers took over the remaining work on the navy yard contract. However, the corporation's interest in the patents had not been sold. The circuit court dismissed the suits and the Supreme Court affirmed. The opinion, by JUSTICE LUSK, said the following about the shareholder action:]

We advert at this point to certain contentions put forward by counsel for the plaintiff, of doubtful pertinency to the receivership question, and which, indeed, are urged in support of a claim in the brief that the sale of the machinery and equipment should be vacated.

It is said that the sale is void, regardless of whether the transaction was fair and the consideration adequate, because it was a sale of all the assets of the corporation, which, under §§ 77–263, O.C.L.A., may be made only "with the consent of stockholders thereof holding of record as much as two-thirds of the issued capital stock of such corporation"; that Jarman and Williamson, by reason of their personal interest in the transaction, were disqualified from voting at the stockholders' meeting upon the motion to ratify the sale, and that without their votes the necessary two-thirds was wanting.

The statute applies in the case of "a sale . . . of the business, franchise and property as a whole, of any corporation." It is arguable that it does not govern here, because Ostlind Valve, Inc., still retained after the sale ownership of a one-fourth interest in patents which all the stockholders hope can be sold for $100,000 and royalties, and which the corporation proposes to sell. The reasoning of the court, however, in Matter of Timmis, 200 N.Y. 177, 93 N.E. 522, makes that a debatable conclusion.

But we need not decide the question because Jarman and Williamson were not disqualified from voting on the resolution of ratification, and, if a two-thirds vote was necessary, the resolution received it. The leading cases on the question are Gamble v. Queens City Water Co., 123 N.Y. 91, 97, 25 N.E. 201, 202, 9 L.R.A. 527, and Northwestern Transportation Co. v. Beatty, L.R. 12 App.Cas. 589. In both the court held that the personal interest of the shareholders did not disqualify them from voting, and it seems to be the accepted doctrine that, as the court said in Gamble v. Queens County Water Co., supra, in a meeting of the shareholders "each shareholder represents himself and his own [personal] interests solely, and he in no sense acts as a trustee or representative of others." . . .

Neither was the sale void, as seems to be contended by the plaintiffs, because of the fiduciary relationship which Jarman and Williamson as directors bore to the corporation, for the rule approved by the great weight of authority, including decisions of this court, is that a contract between the corporation and a director, where the director acts in good faith and the transaction is fair to the corporation, is not void but only voidable, and may be legally ratified by a meeting of the stockholders called for that purpose. . . . Such a contract, however, must be authorized by a disinterested majority of the directors. . . . And the contract will not be permitted to stand if the interested director participates in the making of it by voting for the resolution of the directors which authorizes it, at least where the vote of the interested director is necessary to carry the motion. . . . We applied this principle to a resolution of the directors fixing the compensation of one of their number for past services in Rugger v. Mt. Hood Electric Co., supra, 143 Or. at page 218, 20 P.2d at page 421. . . . In this case, as we have seen, Jarman and Williamson did not vote on the resolution of sale adopted by the directors.

It is the generally recognized rule that a stockholder may deal with the corporation if the dealing is fair and free from actual fraud; that there is no presumption of fraud in a contract between a corporation and a majority stockholder, but that such contracts will be scrutinized with much greater care than if made with a third person. . . .

We have endeavored to give the plaintiffs the benefit of this rule in our appraisal of the evidence in the case before us.

Enyart v. Merrick, 148 Or. 321, 34 P.2d 629, and Stanley v. Luse, supra, relied on by the plaintiffs, do not support their position. In the former case the court held that a director had failed to establish a valid sale to himself of stock of other stockholders, as well as his own which had been pledged to secure payment of a promissory note. In the latter a sale by a director to the corporation was annulled because it had not been ratified by the stockholders and because of concealment practiced by the director. Both decisions recognize the fiduciary character of directors toward the corporation, but neither holds that the contract of a director with the corporation is void. On the contrary, as stated above, Stanley v. Luse approves the doctrine that such contracts are voidable only and may be ratified by the stockholders.

ZAHN v. TRANSAMERICA CORPORATION

United States Court of Appeals, Third Circuit, 1947.
162 F.2d 36.

[Axton–Fisher Tobacco Company was a Kentucky corporation. It had three classes of stock, called preferred stock, Class A stock and Class B stock. We are not concerned with the preferred. The Class A stock, referred to in the charter as a common stock, was entitled to a cumulative dividend of $3.20 per share per year. The Class B stock was then entitled to $1.60 per share per year. Any further dividends declared by the directors were to be divided equally between the two classes.   Upon liquidation, the two classes were to participate as follows:

> "In the event of the dissolution, liquidation, merger or consolidation of the corporation, or sale of substantially all its assets, whether voluntary or involuntary, there shall be paid to the holders of the preferred stock then outstanding $105 per share, together with all unpaid accrued dividends thereon, before any sum shall be paid to or any assets distributed among the holders of the Class A common stock and/or the holders of the Class B common stock. After such payment to the holders of the preferred stock, and all unpaid accrued dividends on the Class A common stock shall have been paid, then all remaining assets and funds of the corporation shall be divided among and paid to the holders of the Class A common stock and to the holders of the Class B common stock in the ratio of 2 to 1; that is to say, there shall be paid upon each share of Class A common stock twice the amount paid upon each share of Class B common stock, in any such event."

Each share of Class A stock could be converted by its owner into a share of Class B. The Class A stock could be called as follows:

> "The whole or any part of the Class A common stock of the corporation, at the option of the Board of Directors, may be redeemed on any quarterly dividend payment date by paying therefor in cash Sixty dollars ($60.00) per share and all unpaid and accrued dividends thereon at the date fixed for such redemption, upon sending by mail to the registered holders of the Class A common stock at least sixty (60) days' notice of the exercise of such option. If at any time the Board of Directors shall determine to redeem less than the whole amount of Class A common stock then outstanding, the particular stock to be so redeemed shall be determined in such manner as the Board of Directors shall prescribe; provided, however, that no holder of Class A common stock shall be preferred over any other holder of such stock."

The Class B stock had the right to vote but since 1937 the Class A stock had equal voting rights because of a clause that gave them such a right when four successive defaults in quarterly dividend payments occurred. Zahn held 235 shares of Class A stock (of which he had surrendered some for redemption) and sued Transamerica on behalf of himself and other shareholders, alleging a scheme to appropriate the bulk of the company's value. The Company possessed leaf tobacco carried on its books at its "average cost" of $6,361,981 but due to wartime conditions now worth $20,000,000 on the market. Transamerica had bought Axton–Fisher stock from May 1941 on. By March 1943 it owned ⅔ of the Class A and 80% of the Class B stock. Since May 1941 it had elected a majority of Axton–Fisher's directors. On April 30 the board of Axton–Fisher, at Transamerica's behest, called the Class A stock. Most of the assets were then sold to Phillip–Morris, the preferred was paid off and the balance of the company's assets distributed to the Class B shareholders. Zahn alleged that if the Class A shareholders had participated in the liquidation they would have gotten $240 per share, instead of $80.80. The district court dismissed the complaint for failure to state a cause of action. The Court of Appeals reversed in an opinion by JUDGE BIGGS excerpted below.

JUDGE BIGGS first discussed the decision of the Court of Appeals of Kentucky in Taylor v. Axton–Fisher Tobacco Co., 295 Ky. 226, 173 S.W.2d 377, in which a holder of 9 shares of Class B stock had asserted that the company's directors had acted invalidly when they permitted Class A shareholders to rescind their surrenders of stock for redemption or to withhold their shares if not surrendered after once having called the stock. The Court held that the call of the Class A stock once passed was vested and final and could not be modified.]

The circumstances of the case at bar are *sui generis* and we can find no Kentucky decision squarely in point. In our opinion, however, the law of Kentucky imposes upon the directors of a corporation or upon those who are in charge of its affairs by virtue of majority stock ownership or otherwise the same fiduciary relationship in respect to the corporation and to its stockholders as is imposed generally by the laws of Kentucky's sister States or which was imposed by federal law prior to Erie R. Co. v. Tompkins, 304 U.S. 64, 58 S.Ct. 817, 82 L.Ed. 1188, 114 A.L.R. 1487.

The tenor of the federal decisions in respect to the general fiduciary duty of those in control of a corporation is unmistakable. The Supreme Court in Southern Pacific Co. v. Bogert, 250 U.S. 483, 487, 488, 39 S.Ct. 533, 535, 63 L.Ed. 1099, said: "The rule of corporation law and of equity invoked is well settled and has been often applied. The majority has the right to control; but when it does so, it occupies a fiduciary relation toward the minority, as much so as the corporation itself or its officers and directors." In Pepper v. Litton, 308 U.S. 295, 306, 60 S.Ct. 238, 245, 84 L.Ed. 281, the Supreme Court stated: "A director is a fiduciary. . . . So is a dominant or controlling stockholder or group of stockholders. . . . Their powers are powers in trust. . . . Their dealings with the corporation are subjected to rigorous scrutiny and where any of their contracts or engagements with the corporation is challenged the burden is on the director or stockholder not only to prove the good faith of the transaction but also to show its inherent fairness from the viewpoint of the corporation and those interested therein."

See also Hyams v. Calumet & Hecla Mining Co., 6 Cir., 221 F. 529, 537, ". . . the rule, independently of state or national antitrust statutes, is fundamental that one in control of a majority of the stock and of the board of directors of a corporation occupies a fiduciary relation towards the minority stockholders, and is charged with the duty of exercising a high degree of good faith, care, and diligence for the protection of such minority interests. Every act in its own interest to the detriment of the holders of minority stock becomes a breach of duty and of trust, and entitles to plenary relief from a court of equity.
. . .

The law of the States in this respect is illustrated by such decisions as Singer v. Carlisle, Sup., 26 N.Y.S.2d 172; Pearson v. Concord Railroad Corporation, 62 N.H. 537, 13 Am.St.Rep. 590; Miner v. Belle Isle Ice Co., 93 Mich. 97, 53 N.W. 218, 17 L.R.A. 412; Bailey v. Jacobs, 325 Pa. 187, 189 A. 320; Lofland v. Cahall, 13 Del.Ch. 384, 118 A. 1. See also 19 C.J.S., Corporations, § 764: "The directors owe a duty of managing the corporate affairs honestly and impartially in behalf of the corporation and all the stockholders . . . .." See also Restatement of the Law of Trusts, Section 170. Most of the decisions cited were rendered under circumstances in which one corporation controlled another as in the case at bar. The means of control is of course immaterial. . . .

The law of Kentucky also demonstrates the fact that those in charge of a corporation stand in a fiduciary relation to its minority stockholders. In Graham v. Tom Moore Distillery Co., D.C.W.D.Ky., 42 F.Supp. 853, 855, 856, the District Court issued an injunction against the carrying out of a contract peculiarly advantageous to a majority holder of the corporation's stock but not to the corporation. Judge Miller, quoting from Venus Oil Corporation v. Gardner, 244 Ky. 176, 50 S.W.2d 537, 538, went on to state "that it is . . . well settled by many Kentucky decisions that a person occupying a fiduciary or confidential relationship can not lawfully acquire any private interest of his own in opposition to his position of trust, and that transactions between fiduciaries and cestuis que trust are constructively fraudulent." . . .

He also said, 42 F.Supp. at page 856, that a contract entered into by such parties as were there involved, viz., between the corporation itself and the majority stockholder, is "either constructively fraudulent or absolutely void regardless of whether or not actual fraud can be spelled out of the express provisions of the contract." . . .

Other Kentucky decisions hold that public policy forbids an agent to act for his principal in a matter involving the agent's private interest, and that such a contract is void as between principal and agent. . . .

In Kirwan v. Parkway Distillery, 285 Ky. 605, 148 S.W.2d 720, 723, the Court of Appeals of Kentucky had before it the following facts. The majority shareholders of a corporation voted to dissolve it because the minority stockholders objected to a sale of the corporate assets. It appeared that the minority stockholders desired to obtain the book value of their stock in lieu of the pro-rata share of the funds remaining after the sale of the corporate assets. The minority stockholders filed a bill to restrain the dissolution. The Court of Appeals of Kentucky sustained a demurrer to the complaint, stating in part: "It is claimed that the dissolution of Bonnie Bros. corporation subsequent to the contract of sale of its assets was done for the purpose of defeating the appellants' rights to the book value of their stock which was more remunerative to them than their proportionate shares of the assets under a dissolution of the corporation. Conceding that to be true, yet the stockholders when voting strictly as stockholders were still within their legal rights. In the case of Haldeman v. Haldeman et al., 176 Ky. 635, 197 S.W. 376, it is pointed out that *there is a radical difference when a stockholder is voting strictly as a stockholder and when voting as a director. When voting as a stockholder he has the legal right to vote with a view of his own benefits and is representing himself only; but, a director represents all the stockholders in the capacity of trustee for them and cannot use his office as director for his personal benefit at the expense of the stockholders.* . . .

"To the same effect is Dudley v. Kentucky High-school, [sic] 72 Ky. 576, 9 Bush. 576. However, fraud may be an exception to these rules, but as we have already stated, no fraud is claimed or relied on in the case at bar."

In the Haldeman case, [176 Ky. 635, 197 S.W. 381], cited in the Kirwan decision, the Court said: "A stockholder occupies a position and owes a duty radically different from a director. A stockholder may in a stockholders' meeting vote with the view of his own benefit; he represents himself only. But a director represents all the stockholders; he is a trustee for them; and he cannot use his office for his personal benefit at the expense of any stockholder." . . . See also Reinhardt v. Owensboro Planning Mill Co., 185 Ky. 600, 603, 215 S.W. 523, 524, "Directors are bound to exercise nothing short of the uberrima fides of the civil law. *They must not in any degree allow their official conduct to be swayed by their private interest or welfare, unless that interest be one they have in the good of the company in common with all the stockholders.*"

In Pittsburg, C., C. & St. L. Ry. Co. v. Dodd, 115 Ky. 176, 194, 72 S.W. 822, 827, the Court said, "We go no further than to say that upon an allegation of fraud on the part of his directors, or upon an allegation of facts showing that the directors (who are also directors of another contracting corporation), *because of conflict of interest and duty, could not or ought not to act in the matter,* coupled with the further allegation showing material damage to the complaining stockholder by reason of the transaction between the two corporations, a court of equity will hear a single stockholder's complaint, and, if the charges be sustained by the proof, will grant appropriate relief."

In Covington & Lexington Railroad Co. v. Bowler's Heirs, 72 Ky. 468, 489, the Court said, "From the moment that Bowler concluded to prepare for the purchase of the road *his personal interests became antagonistic to those of the corporation, and he should have ceased to act as a director.* Instead, however, of doing so, he held on to his position, and when we contemplate his official acts in the light of subsequent events we cannot avoid the conclusion that as a member of the board of directors his influence was used for the promotion of his personal ends. *Instead of looking alone to the interests of the stockholders and creditors of the company,* their rights were not only disregarded, but deliberately sacrificed, that profit might result to him."

There can be no doubt of the general law upon this question. It is succinctly stated in Thompson on Corporations, supra, Section 1337, as follows: "Very plainly a director is disqualified from voting on matters in which he has a personal interest or on matters concerning the personal interest of a director who controls his vote. The rule is that any resolution passed at a meeting of the directors at which a director having a personal interest in the matter voted, will be voidable at the instance of the corporation or the stockholders, without regard to its fairness, where the vote of such directors was necessary to the passage of such resolution." It is clear that under the law of Kentucky the fiduciary relationship of directors is such that a court of equity will not permit them to make a profit of their trust and that directors of a corporation are required to manage and conduct their trust so as to realize whatever profit may accrue in the course of the business for the benefit of their cestuis que trust.

It is appropriate to emphasize at this point that the right to call the Class A stock for redemption was confided by the charter of Axton–Fisher to the directors and not to the stockholders of that corporation. We must also re-emphasize the statement of the court in Haldeman v. Haldeman, supra, and its reiteration in Kirwan v. Parkway Distillery, supra, that there is a radical difference when a stockholder is voting strictly as a stockholder and when voting as a director; that when voting as a stockholder he may have the legal right to vote with a view of his own benefits and to represent himself only; but that when he votes as a director he represents all the stockholders in the capacity of a trustee for them and cannot use his office as a director for his personal benefit at the expense of the stockholders.

Two theories are presented on one of which the case at bar must be decided: One, vigorously asserted by Transamerica and based on its interpretation of the decision in the Taylor case, is that the board of directors of Axton–Fisher, whether or not dominated by Transamerica, the principal Class B stockholder, at any time and for any purpose, might call the Class A stock for redemption; the other, asserted with equal vigor by Zahn, is that the board of directors of Axton–Fisher as fiduciaries were not entitled to favor Transamerica, the Class B stockholder, by employing the redemption provisions of the charter for its benefit.

We must of course treat the decision of the Court of Appeals of Kentucky in the Taylor case as evidence of what is the law of Kentucky. The Court took the position on that record that the directors at any time might call the Class A stock for redemption and that the redemption provision of the charter was written as much for the benefit of the Class B stock as for the Class A stock.[52] It is argued by Transamerica very persuasively that what the Court of Appeals of Kentucky held was that when the Class A stock received its allocation of $60 a share plus accrued dividends it received its full due and that the directors had the right at any time to eliminate Class A stock from the corporate setup for the benefit of the Class B stock.[53] It does not appear from the opinion of the Court of Appeals of Kentucky whether or not the subsequent liquidation of Axton–Fisher was brought to the attention of the Court. But it is clear from the pleading that the subsequent liquidation was not an issue in the case and from the language of the Court there is some indication that it believed that Axton–Fisher was to continue in existence because Commissioner Stanley spoke of the elimination of the Class A stock, which possessed voting rights, from the management and control of Axton–Fisher. Such surmises are hazardous, however, and are not really apposite since it is our duty to determine the law of Kentucky and not to delve into subjective mental processes. It should be noted that Commissioner Stanley stated the justiciable controversy before the Court of Appeals of Kentucky as follows: "The case presents a novel question of power of the board of directors of a corporation to rescind or modify its action in calling certain stock for redemption or retirement." This, and only this, was the question before the Court. It is notable that Commissioner Stanley said also that the acts of boards of directors "exercised in good faith and not in fraud of the rights of the stockholders" should not be interfered with by the courts and that he spoke as well of the "fair discretion" of directors to be exercised in the same manner as would be the case in the declaration of dividends, citing Smith v. Southern Foundry Co., referred to in the body of this opinion . . . .. We think that it is the settled law of Kentucky that directors may not declare or withhold the declaration of dividends for the purpose of personal profit or, by analogy, take any corporate action for such a purpose.

52. The language used as quoted supra was as follows: "We think the provision for redemption of Class A stock was made as much for the one as for the other class. If it was not, then it was very delusive."

53. The court said: "Manifestly, it was very much to the interest of the holders of Class B stock to have all these priorities, obligations and restrictions on and conditional joint control of the management eliminated. A substantial advantage was given to and acquired by the Class B stockholders . . . ."

Puppet relationship

The difficulty in accepting Transamerica's contentions in the case at bar is that the directors of Axton–Fisher, if the allegations of the complaint be accepted as true, were the instruments of Transamerica, were directors voting in favor of their special interest, that of Transamerica, could not and did not exercise an independent judgment in calling the Class A stock, but made the call for the purpose of profiting their true principal, Transamerica. In short a puppet-puppeteer relationship existed between the directors of Axton–Fisher and Transamerica.

The act of the board of directors in calling the Class A stock, an act which could have been legally consummated by a disinterested board of directors, was here effected at the direction of the principal Class B stockholder in order to profit it. Such a call is voidable in equity at the instance of a stockholder injured thereby. It must be pointed out that under the allegations of the complaint there was no reason for the redemption of the Class A stock to be followed by the liquidation of Axton–Fisher except to enable the Class B stock to profit at the expense of the Class A stock. As has been hereinbefore stated the function of the call was confided to the board of directors by the charter and was not vested by the charter in the stockholders of any class. It was the intention of the framers of Axton–Fisher's charter to require the board of directors to act disinterestedly if that body called the Class A stock, and to make the call with a due regard for its fiduciary obligations. If the allegations of the complaint be proved, it follows that the directors of Axton–Fisher, the instruments of Transamerica, have been derelict in that duty. Liability which flows from the dereliction must be imposed upon Transamerica which, under the allegations of the complaint, constituted the board of Axton–Fisher and controlled it.[54]

54. The circumstances alleged in the case at bar are suggestive of those which were before the Court of Appeals for the Seventh Circuit in Lebold v. Inland Steel Co., supra. In the Lebold case the majority stockholders forced the dissolution of the corporation and thereafter themselves continued the highly profitable business which had belonged to the corporation. This conduct of the majority stockholders resulted in their acquiring the share of the profits of the corporate business to which the minority would have been entitled had the corporation continued in existence. The dissolution of the company was carried out precisely in the manner required by the law of West Virginia.

District Judge Lindley, speaking for the court, stated in part, 125 F.2d at pages 373, 374, "What defendant might have accomplished under color of the West Virginia statute was discontinuance of the business. What it did, was to take, through form of a sale, the physical assets and the entire business of the Steamship Company. Whether we stamp the happenings as dissolution or with some other name, equity looks to the essential character and result to determine whether there has been faithlessness and fraud upon the part of the fiduciary. However proper a plan may be legally, a majority stockholder can not, under its color, appropriate a business belonging to a corporation to the detriment of the minority stockholder. The socalled dissolution was a mere device by means of which defendant appropriated for itself the transportation business of the Steamship Company to the detriment of plaintiffs. That the source of this power is found in a statute, supplies no reason for clothing it with a superior sanctity, or vesting it with the attributes of tyranny. Allied Chemical & Dye Corp. v. Steel & Tube Co. of America, 14 Del. [Ch.] 1, 120 A. 486. The books are full of instances of disapproval of such action. If it be an absorption by the dominant member of all the returns of corporate investment, or a sale of the property to oneself for an inadequate consideration, or deprivation by a syndicate formed to freeze out a minority stockholder through sale and dissolution or if the buyer and seller are the same, the right of a stockholder to vote becomes a power in trust when he owns the majority and assumes and exercises domination and control over corporate affairs. Such majority stockholders' vote 'must not be so antagonistic to the corporation as a whole as to

The *quantum* or extent of the breach of the fiduciary duty on the present record must be determined according to the law of Delaware for the reasons hereinbefore stated. The reaction of the law of Delaware to such a course as that pursued here by Transamerica is suggested by such decisions of the Supreme Court of Delaware as Bovay v. H.M. Byllesby & Co., Del.Sup., 38 A.2d 808, and Keenan v. Eshleman, 23 Del. Ch. 234, 2 A.2d 904, 120 A.L.R. 227. But whether the law of Delaware be applicable to determine the extent of the breach of fiduciary duty, or that of Kentucky or of New York, there will be found to be no substantial difference. The remedies to be afforded by the District Court of the United States for the District of Delaware, of course, must be those which may be available under the law of Delaware. See Guaranty Trust Co. v. York, 326 U.S. 99, 65 S.Ct. 1464, 89 L.Ed. 2079, 160 A.L.R. 1231, and Overfield v. Pennroad Corporation, 3 Cir., 146 F.2d 889.

As has been stated the plaintiff has endeavored to set up a "First Cause of Action" and a "Second Cause of Action" in his complaint. The first cause of action is based upon his ownership of shares of Class A stock not surrendered by him to Axton–Fisher for redemption and is asserted not only on his own behalf but also on behalf of other Class A stockholders retaining their stock. The second cause of action is asserted by him on his own behalf and on behalf of other Class A stockholders in respect to the value of the stock which was surrendered for redemption. The two alleged separate causes of action, however, are in reality one. In our opinion, if the allegations of the complaint be proved, Zahn may maintain his cause of action to recover from Transamerica the value of the stock retained by him as that shall be represented by its aliquot share of the proceeds of Axton–Fisher on dissolution. It is also our opinion that he may maintain a cause of action to recover the difference between the amount received by him for the shares already surrendered and the amount which he would have received on liquidation of Axton–Fisher if he had not surrendered his stock. . . .

[The final portion of the opinion, directed at the issue of Zahn's capacity to maintain the suit as a class action, is omitted.]

COMMENT

(1) Transamerica was "a large and powerful investment company which was dominated by the late A.P. Giannini, whose business acumen was said to be legendary." [55] Transamerica had a minority interest in the Bank of America which Giannini had founded. L.M. Giannini was approached by persons interested in an insolvent firm called Standard Commercial Tobacco Co. which wanted a loan from the Bank on the strength of its 80,000 shares of Axton–Fisher Class B. L.M. Giannini turned the situation over to Transamerica which in March 1941 purchased the shares from John M. Harlan, trustee in bankruptcy of Standard. In early 1942 it was proposed to issue a new series of preferred stock to be exchanged for the old preferred and Class A stock. The materials were processed through the SEC which, incidentally, raised an objection to non-disclosure of the Axton–Fisher tobacco inventory's liquidative

indicate that their interests are wholly outside of the interest of the corporation and destructive of the interests of the minority shareholders.' " . . .

55. Speed v. Transamerica Corp., 99 F.Supp. 808, 816 (D.Del.1951).

value. This route was abandoned, however, and at some point it was decided to liquidate Axton–Fisher. By January 1943 the OPA had placed a ceiling price on the inventory. Tax consequences were involved since liquidation could bring about a capital gain treatment. Transamerica nettled about $9,000,000 on the transaction.

(2) The court elsewhere found that the directors of Axton–Fisher were not "servile or in any sense willing to follow an improper proposal made by Transamerica . . . ." but "assumed that any request coming from Transamerica . . . should be deemed proper . . . so long as there was no obvious impropriety." [56]

(3) Other actions were brought by former holders of Axton–Fisher stock who had sold to Transamerica, alleging that Transamerica had concealed from them the appreciation of the Axton–Fisher tobacco and its intention to realize that gain by liquidation. These cases raise issues considered at p. 563 infra in connection with § 10b of the Securities Exchange Act and the SEC's rules thereunder. These plaintiffs also prevailed on the merits. The courts then had to consider issues of damages in both groups of cases. Zahn contended that he should be treated as if his A shares had gone, uncalled and unconverted, into the liquidation process and had received the benefits provided for the A shares in liquidation. The courts rejected that solution and reconstructed the liquidation as if the shares had been converted into B shares and treated as such on liquidation.[57]

QUESTIONS

(1) Does Ostlind support the proposition that shareholders have no fiduciary duty? That they have a duty corresponding to that of directors? If neither of the above, what sort of duty is involved? What is your reaction, on the strength of the cases you have seen involving shareholder ratification, e.g. Fairchild Camera, p. 434 supra, the compensation cases, pp. 333, 346 supra, etc., as to the efficacy of ratification as a means of checking indiscretions by management?

(2) What were the intentions of the draftsmen who worked out the details of the Transamerica charter governing the class A and B stock? What were the underlying understandings as to the call, the conversion and liquidation?

(3) What would a disinterested board of Axton–Fisher directors have done in this situation? Could any board in fact have been disinterested? In other words, would asking the question "what is in the best interests of Axton–Fisher as a corporation" have led to any answer?

Bibliography: Shareholders' fiduciary duties are discussed in several articles by Prof. Sneed, of which the best start is probably in The Shareholder May Vote as He Pleases—Theory and Fact, 22 U.Pitts.L.Rev. 23 (1960).

---

56. Id. at 846.

57. Speed v. Transamerica Corp., 135 F.Supp. 176 (D.Del.1955), affirmed 235 F.2d 369 (3d Cir.1956).

Chapter X

SHAREHOLDERS' DERIVATIVE SUITS

1. General Introduction

The most direct way to vindicate a fiduciary or other duty running to the corporation is through an action in the name of the corporation itself brought by authority of its directors. The board of directors commonly brings actions against outsiders and sometimes can be moved to sue a faithless executive. On the other hand, the directors may have been so related to the wrongdoer or the wrong as to be unwilling to proceed. The shareholders would have been helpless had there not been developed by the courts the device known as the shareholder's derivative suit, a relative of the older suit whereby a beneficiary of a trust might sue a third party who had injured the trust estate if the trustee were unwilling or unable to do so.[1]

Where a shareholder possesses a substantial portion of the shares of the corporation a significant recovery will redound to his or her own benefit and he or she has an incentive to pursue the matter. The problem shifts where the corporation has thousands of shareholders, none of them with more than a miniscule interest in it. Who, then, will be motivated to detect and pursue a wrong to the corporation? There seem to be two practical incentives. One has been the hope that the shareholder would be bought off by the defendants. The second is the hope of profitable employment by the attorneys who represent the plaintiff.

NOTE ON THE HISTORY OF THE DERIVATIVE SUIT

The derivative suit has a long history. Courts had to decide in connection with derivative suits issues that later became prominent in connection with non-derivative class actions. As one could consider the securities laws the first consumer protection laws (at least at the federal level) so one could consider the derivative suit the forerunner of the mass tort action. You will observe that for a long time Federal Rule 23 (and its predecessors Equity Rule 94 and Rule 38) treated the derivative and class actions together until their bifurcation in 1966. Two vignettes from the history follow.

---

1. Some States permit a derivative suit to be brought by a director, in that capacity. See, e.g. Tenney v. Rosenthal, 6 N.Y.2d 204, 189 N.Y.S.2d 158, 160 N.E.2d 463 (1959).

(1) Clarence Venner and the Turn of the Century

Venner was a member of the New York Stock Exchange and a man of mystery. He died leaving an estate of $700,000 after having sued more corporate titans than any other nonlawyer. Among his court antagonists were Atchison, Topeka & Santa Fe Railway, Union Pacific Railroad, Pullman Palace Car Company, United States Steel Corporation, J.P. Morgan & Company, New York Central Railroad, Great Northern Railway, and its powerful president, James J. Hill, the Wabash, Guaranty Trust Company, Bethlehem Steel, New York Life Insurance Company, American Telephone & Telegraph, American Hide & Leather, and many more. To Venner, the bigger the opponent, the more lucrative the triumph.

He settled a suit against the Great Northern by selling Hill, its doughty president and no pushover, 980 shares of stock, for $513,000. Venner had paid $188,587 for the shares. He received $300,000 for bonds with a face value of $30,000 by withdrawing a suit against the Union Pacific. He was accused of selling for $250,000 "worthless stock" in a paper railroad, the Nebraska Central, to the Chicago, Rock Island & Pacific Railway. Venner said he had spent $75,000 in projecting the Nebraska Central and it was profitable for the Rock Island to purchase the franchise even though it was never used.

The above facts about his triumphs are not of Venner's voluntary revealing. His own lawyer, in a suit to collect a fee, brought out the price Hill paid for the Great Northern stock. An Interstate Commerce Commission investigator gave evidence in the Rock Island case at a government hearing.

Venner was tall, heavy-set, and always impeccably dressed in expensively tailored clothes. He wore a stiff collar and his tie was embellished with a pearl stickpin. He carried his nose-glasses in a handsome silver case. His iron-gray hair and moustache carried out the impression of a purposeful man. Often he hid his identity as a litigant behind the Continental Securities Company, the General Investment Company, and the New York Central Securities Corporation, which he controlled. These companies became known among lawyers of the day as Venner's "alter egos."

On several occasions he was rebuffed by officers of the American Hide & Leather Company, when he sought information to which, as a stockholder, he was entitled. This became an issue in court. Vice Chancellor John Bentley of the Chancery Court of New Jersey, commented:

"It is true that Clarence H. Venner, in his quest for particulars, met with many obstacles and some rebuffs at the hands of the defendant's officers. Some allowances must be made, however, for the weakness of human nature. I can conceive of no monster of the jungle . . . that could [so] unsettle the nerves of a corporation director . . . as the appearance of Mr. Venner in search of information."

When the Interborough Rapid Transit Company of New York, since merged into the New York City subway system, was in financial difficulties, Venner, as a bondholder, refused to go along with a reorganization plan approved by 96 per cent of the bondholders. He demanded the appointment of a receiver. De Lancey Nicoll, one of the numerous lawyers for the IRT, said in court:

"Venner sits here on my right and has many times in court heard me expose his litigious life. Could anything be plainer than that his action either as a stockholder, bondholder, or creditor is not for the benefit of his fellow bondholders, stockholders, and creditors but entirely for himself? The higher courts have held repeatedly that in such circumstances the court is under no obligation to embarrass a company which is trying to smooth out its affairs for the benefit of the stockholders and bondholders generally."

Later, when Venner offered to withdraw his request for a receiver in the IRT case, the company's counsel immediately told the court he was taken by surprise. Venner was not withdrawing his motion at the request or suggestion of any person associated with the IRT. Counsel felt compelled to make clear that Venner had not been bought off, that no deal had been made.

When Venner attempted to join in a suit already begun against the General Baking Company in 1927, the other plaintiffs withdrew. They said they did not want to be joint plaintiffs with him. . . .

Venner's technique was to discover some legal flaw in a company's plans. He would try to stop a merger, a reorganization, or a plan of action. It would be more costly to hold up corporate plans than to buy Venner out. There is one apocryphal story: After he was well known as a bringer of "strike suits," he held up the plans of a large company over a legalism, and was invited to talk things over with the board of directors. The board listened to Venner, then asked him to retire briefly. When he returned, the chairman said he was authorized to offer Venner $10,000 for his stock—a sum which would have yielded him a handsome profit. Venner stood up and said: "Gentlemen, you forget I have a reputation to uphold."

As the years went by, a common headline was, "Venner Sues New York Central," or "Venner Against J.P. Morgan," or even more revealing, as corporations found it necessary to contest his actions, "Venner Loses Again."

Assessing Venner's work in behalf of stockholders is not easy. August Belmont, the banker, called him a "practical blackmailer." Venner started a suit for libel. But when Belmont confronted him with a demand to take the stand and be examined, Venner dropped the action.

Supreme Court Justice James C. Van Siclen, New York, said:

"No weight or virtue can be added to the court's memorandum by indulging in invectives or branding the plaintiff Venner. . . . If heretofore the judicial record and published opinions of various state and federal courts tend to establish that Venner is an artificer of litigation and a menace to corporate society, an added curse will work no cure."

But to many small stockholders and opponents of big corporations, he was a darling and a protector.[2]

(2) The Depression and the Strike Suit

Absent such a client as Venner, the driving force behind derivative suits has been the value to some lawyers of the chance to earn a fee substantially more rewarding than that to which they are accustomed. The presence of such lawyers, not unnaturally, upset members of the corporate bar. Their views were quite fully reflected in the Wood Report prepared by Franklin Wood, Esq., for Governor Thomas Dewey in 1945 which analyzed 1400 minority shareholders' suits filed in New York from 1932 to 1942 of which 573 involved publicly held corporations. This Report led to legislation curtailing shareholders' suits in New York. It has this to say at pp. 45–48 about the role of attorneys:

> Actions involving the financial affairs of large corporations in the past, as might have been expected, were principally at the suit of substantially interested investors or a few professionals, such as Venner. [In the early years of the past decade many such suits originated with semi-professional promoters on the fringes of Wall Street.] Today there is very little of either among the plaintiffs themselves. With the exception of a few lawyers' relatives or lawyer-plaintiffs, the same 'crusading' stockholder rarely appears twice, but an inexhaustible supply of the smallest of small investors have suddenly become masters of the most intricate details of corporate finance, and the most alert of sentinels to employ attorneys and attack corporate management on the slightest suspicion of a big lawsuit. Women are prominent among these one-suit students of law and finance as evidenced by the following list of cases:

> [I have omitted all of the list of 31 cases except four which you have encountered before:]

> *Augusta Winkelman v. General Motors;*
> *Celia Gallin v. National City Bank;*
> *Eva Litwin v. Guaranty Trust Company;*
> *Esther Heller v. American Tobacco Company;*

> Presumably, these stockholders flock to examine S.E.C. reports and studies, minutes of the Public Service Commission and the like for these have been the main source of information upon which stockholders' suits are based. Presumably also they are diligent students of the Law Journal and of the

2. Excerpt from THE AMERICAN STOCKHOLDER by J.A. Livingston. Copyright, © 1958, by J.A. Livingston. Reprinted by permission of Harper & Row Publishers, Inc. P. 44.

filed papers in the County Clerk's office, since, as previously observed, hardly any such suit becomes known without attracting a cloud of copies, all insistent on the sacred right of asserting corporate claims by counsel of their own choice. Beyond that point they rarely figure in the case, and on their infrequent appearances as witnesses commonly display astonishing lapses of memory, both about the reasons they brought the action and many other pertinent circumstances. It is by no means unknown for these crusaders to be so heedless of their crusade that they sell their stock during its course (as occurred midway through the trial of a recent prominent case, with the result the general trial counsel in the case was without a client until arrangement was made with another attorney and his stockholder client) or overlook the fact that they have voted for the transactions they assail, but a Providence kindly to lawyers whose fee position is thus menaced seems always to supply a qualified substitute client in the nick of time. The known existence of a pending action to protect a pro-rata six dollar interest, instead of satisfying such stockholders that action on their part is unnecessary, drives them to a lather of activity to duplicate it. Knowledge of a proposal for court-approved settlement is no less a stimulation to unnecessary activity.

This shoddy burlesque of a professional relationship to clients makes the ambulance-chaser by comparison a paragon of propriety. He at least represents a real client, with usually real injuries, and a legitimate interest in 50% of the recovery. The ambulance chaser does not need to tell his client that he is hurt, but it is questionable how many stockholder plaintiffs would recognize the diversion of a corporate opportunity. Solicitation is obviously general, but can be guarded against either by an insulating arrangement with the stockholders 'personal attorney', or by an arrangement for the attorney's virtual purchase of the stock, on terms favorable to the 'client'. While the supply of colorable situations for suit has greatly diminished since the depths of the depression, and stockholder indignation at corporate management has ceased to exist except in the imagination of their professional protectors, the supply of plaintiffs bringing suit is constantly on the increase and is only limited by injunctions against further duplicating actions. At one time the obtaining of a stockholder client presented so many difficulties that there are instances of non-existent stockholders bringing suit and of suit being maintained without the knowledge of the 'client'. Today the business of providing plaintiffs is so well systematized that a suit involving any major corporation can be depended on to be supplied with 'clients' for a dozen or more lawyers, and the expedient of admittedly purchasing stock in order to bring suit is regarded as crude and tactically unfavorable. It is apparent that the only way one of the usual stockholder plaintiffs can benefit from a recovery is from a division of fee awards, and that no stockholder in his right mind would proceed without the understanding that costs would be borne by the attorney in whose real interest suit was brought. The ten share stockholder of a large corporation is not only unlikely to conceive of bringing such an action himself, but will be induced to do so only by some assurance of (a) a strike suit settlement, or (b) a champertous arrangement by which he bears none of the expense of suit, and a division of fees in the event of a recovery. None of these are neglected in practise, and under a slogan of Social Benefit derivative actions have come to harbor as a matter of course solicitation and inducement in bringing them, champerty and maintenance in their prosecution, the brokerage of litigation in their trial, and division of fees with laymen at their conclusion. If anything remains of the policy against vexatious litigation, these actions are the worst offenders.

(3) The Situation of 1988

It is hard to understand just where the derivative suit is headed as of 1988. Both sides are reporting that things are terrible. Viewed from defendants' perspective, boards of directors are terrified by the so-called crisis in directors and officers insurance. According to them the premiums that have to be paid for insurance to protect directors and officers against liability have become intolerably high—when policies are available at all. This has led to a demand, responded to by the Delaware and other legislatures, for a diminution of the standard of care required of boards of directors and by more generous provisions on indemnification. Plaintiffs' lawyers and sympathetic academics see things differently. They say that the insurance crisis is part of a general malpractice insurance financial problem due in part to the decline in the interest rates earned by insurers' investments and by a failure of premiums in the past to cover awards made by courts years later in more inflationary times. They note that according to the statistics there is no great upsurge in derivative litigation, that any given major corporation is only hit with a derivative suit every 12 years and that there is no more litigation than is needed to keep managements reasonably honest.[3] They would then add their own worry—that new procedural rules are making corporate litigation unfeasible. Although the New York security for costs legislation that followed the

---

3. Jones, An Empirical Examination of the Incidence of Shareholder Derivative and Class Action Lawsuits, 1971–1978, 60 B.U.L.Rev. 306 (1980), who found this result with a small group of very large corporations. An insurance company study indicated that 18.5% of the corporations in its sample had been sued in 1984, up from 7.1% in 1974. See Coffee, Understanding the Plaintiff's Attorney: Implications of Economic Theory for Private Enforcement of Law through Class and Derivative Actions, 86 Colum.L.Rev. 669, 721 n. 142 (1986).

Wood Report was predicted to sound the "death knell" for derivative litigation.[4] It survived that blow and doubtless it will also survive the independent litigation committee discussed in Zapata Corp. v. Maldonado, p. 486 infra.

---

2. Distinguishing the Derivative Suit

The first question that arises in discussing derivative suits is—when is a suit derivative. Quite a few issues hinge on this, including, most conspicuously, the applicability of special legislation designed to curb derivative suits. The case of Gordon v. Elliman below raises such a question. To understand the issue you should go back to Green v. Victor Talking Machine Co., p. 36 supra. There, you will recall, the rule was laid down that the proper—indeed the only proper—plaintiff in an action to redress an injury to corporate property is the corporation itself. A shareholder like Mrs. Green has no cause of action on her or his own part, unless there has been a violation of some separate and distinct duty owing to her or him. Thus, if Mrs. Green had been in control of the corporation she should have caused it to bring the action. If she could not get action through the corporation's directors, her only recourse would be to a derivative action—one initiated by her but brought in the name of the corporation. The same rules would cover the case of where the injury to the corporation had been caused not by an outsider such as Victor but by its own officers or directors. Indeed, the derivative suit originated as a proceeding to redress such breaches; it was in effect, an action in equity somewhat on the analogy of an action to redress breaches of fiduciary duty by a trustee.[5]

The differentiation between derivative and non-derivative suits has been complicated by the emergence of the class action and in particular by the increasing frequency of class actions by shareholders asserting that they have as a class been injured in their own right. Such an action shares many characteristics of a derivative suit; both proceedings are "representative" in the sense of being conducted by one or more persons on behalf of many others. The same factual situation may give rise to causes of action of both kinds. We saw, for example, in the Old Dominion cases in Chapter III that the same fraud and deception that gave rise to a corporate cause of action might nowadays also have supported a class action by the public shareholders who purchased under the influence of misrepresentations.

The following case faces the problem of classifying as derivative or nonderivative a suit to compel the payment of dividends. It does so in

---

4. Hornstein, The Death Knell of Stockholders' Derivative Suits in New York, 32 Calif.L.Rev. 123 (1944).

5. See the historical data presented in Ross v. Bernhard, p. 472 infra.

the context of special legislation, which we examine in detail later on, designed to curb abuses of derivative actions.

GORDON v. ELLIMAN

Court of Appeals of New York, 1954.
306 N.Y. 456, 119 N.E.2d 331.

[An action was brought to compel the payment of a dividend by Ada Gordon on behalf of the Hotel Barbizon, Inc. The trial court stayed the proceedings under Section 61–b of the General Corporation Law, predecessor of the New York statute set forth in the Documentary Supplement and discussed in Section 5 of this Chapter. That law required the posting of security for costs in actions "instituted or maintained in the right of any corporation." The appellate division affirmed, as did the Court of Appeals, (4–3) in an opinion by JUDGE VAN VOORHIS.]

The test of whether an action to compel declaration of dividends and maintained in the interest of the corporation, is whether the object of the lawsuit is to recover upon a chose in action belonging directly to the stockholders, or whether it is to compel the performance of corporate acts which good faith requires the directors to take in order to perform a duty which they owe to the corporation, and through it, to its stockholders. To state the problem in this manner, is in effect, to answer it. When a dividend has lawfully been declared, the relation of debtor and creditor is created between the corporation and each stockholder for his proportion of the dividend. If the corporation refuses to pay, each stockholder may recover it in his own right in an action against the corporation. . . .

Unless a dividend has been declared, upon the other hand, no portion of the assets of the corporation has been set aside for stockholders, and no right of action inheres in them to be paid any part of the corporation's funds. It is well settled that "whether or not dividends shall be paid, and the amount of the dividend at any time, is primarily to be determined by the directors, and there must be bad faith or a clear abuse of discretion on their part to justify a court of equity in interfering; accordingly, unless fraud, bad faith or dishonesty on the party of directors can be shown, their judgment in withholding a dividend from the stockholders will be regarded as conclusive". 11 Fletcher's Cyclopedia Corporations (Perm.Ed.), § 5325. . . .

Unlike an action at law by stockholders to recover dividends that have been declared, a suit in equity to compel the declaration of dividends is in theory against recalcitrant directors to cause them to perform their duty as officials of the corporation. It has even been held in some cases that directors are indispensable parties . . .

In the leading case of Hiscock v. Lacy, 9 Misc. 578, 30 N.Y.S. 860, Judge Irving G. Vann, later of this court [said]: "Primarily, the corporation has the right, as a beneficiary of an implied trust, to call the directors to account; but, as this is not practicable while the same persons continue directors, the stockholders may commence the action in their own names, on making the corporation a party defendant."

The analogies which he draws with other kinds of stockholders' suits, leave no doubt that in Judge Vann's mind an action to compel the declaration of dividends is brought in behalf of the corporation, as in the case of actions against directors for waste or misappropriation of corporate assets. Redress is sought, not in the individual right of the minority stockholders, but through the corporation. . . . [The cited] cases hold that a demand upon a corporation to sue the directors, or proof that such a demand would be futile, is a condition precedent to the maintenance of an action to compel declaration of dividends, and no authorities are cited to the contrary. The decisions denying motions to dismiss complaints in such actions, where a majority of the directors could not be served with the summons in any jurisdiction, are later discussed. They are decided on the theory that directors who are charged with bad faith, in such a matter, should not be allowed to continue to mismanage the corporation, to the detriment of stockholders, merely by residing or keeping themselves where they are not amenable to process. Those decisions do not alter the theory or nature of the cause of action.

The idea is too restricted that derivative actions are limited to such as are brought to compel the directors to pay or restore money to the corporation. A number of specific situations instanced in Judge Vann's opinion in Hiscock v. Lacy, supra, concern other duties to be performed by the directors. In general, it may be said that an action is in the right of the corporation which invokes the equitable powers of the Supreme Court to direct the management of its affairs. This power is exercised with restraint, but, when it is brought to bear, the object is for the court to chart the course for the corporation which the directors should have selected, and which it is presumed that they would have chosen if they had not been actuated by fraud or bad faith. Due to their misconduct, the court substitutes its judgment *ad hoc* for that of the directors in the conduct of its business. That applies to the establishment of a suitable dividend policy for the corporation, as much as to anything else. A stockholder has no individual cause of action to recover dividends that have not been declared. All that he can do is to sue in equity to cause the court to perform a corporate function which the directors would have done except for their bad faith.

The situation in this respect is different from that where a contract is involved obligating the corporation to pay dividends periodically at a specified rate. Boardman v. Lake Shore & Michigan Southern Ry. Co., 84 N.Y. 157, and Koppel v. Middle States Petroleum Corp., 272 App.Div. 790, 69 N.Y.S.2d 784, were such cases. . . .

The distinction is not between preferred and common stock; it is that punctual payment of the Boardman preferred dividends was guaranteed, and that they could not have been passed if earned without violating the express promise of the corporation to pay them. They were akin to income bonds. In other words, where such dividends have been earned, they are required to be appropriated under the contract with the shareholder to the payment of dividends of this character, and, without any exercise of discretion on the part of the directors, the individual rights of each shareholder become the same as they are in the ordinary instance after a dividend has been declared by the directors. . . . The fallacy, as it seems to us, in the reasoning (e.g., 28 N.Y.U.L.Rev. 1429–1431; 28 St. John's L.Rev. 360–368) that an action such as the present is not derivative in character, consists in refusal to recognize the distinction between a case where the stockholders are vested individually with a matured right to recover against the corporation a dividend specified in amount and guaranteed to be paid by contract, as in the case of the holder of a fixed interest bearing obligation, and a situation like the present, where the stockholder possesses no individual right to recover as a creditor, and where whatever cause of action he possesses is common to all of the stockholders and depends upon the intervention of the court through the exercise of its equitable powers to direct the affairs of a corporation to the extent that they have miscarried due to misconduct by the directors. The question whether such an action can be maintained without joining all of the directors as indispensable rather than as conditionally necessary parties, is different from whether the equitable power of the Supreme Court over the affairs of the corporation can be exerted except in the right of the corporation.

It is an oversimplification to treat such an action as this as being by individual stockholders against the corporation to enforce a contract right. This assumption is based on the idea that there is an adversity of interest between the several stockholders and the corporation, that it is in the interest of the corporation to defeat such a cause of action and thereby leave more assets in the corporate treasury, that calling the directors to account for fraud or bad faith in such a matter is a superficial formality and no longer essential as an ingredient in the cause of action, that equitable intervention by the court in the management of the corporate affairs is in such case an outworn legal fiction, to cloak what is actually an action at law by individual stockholders to recover their portions of the corporation's earnings as a contractual right, and that the classification of such a cause of action with causes of action justifying the intervention of a court of equity on account of violation of trust duties by directors is unreal and should be abandoned. Until now, that has been held to be the basis for entertaining actions to compel the declaration of dividends. . . .

Nor is it correct to assume that the interest of the corporation is not involved except adversely to that of the stockholder, nor that possible personal liability on the part of directors is excluded. By what is said in this opinion, it is intended to cast no reflection upon the directors of the respondent corporation herein. It may well be that they are innocent of the charges made against them in this complaint. What is said concerning this subject is merely in order to discuss the general question of law. In the usual case where declaration of dividends is compelled, directors are not mere bystanders. They have usually sought to monopolize the earnings of the corporation by excessive salaries or collusive agreements or to manipulate the value of minority stockholdings in order to freeze them out. . . .

The idea that the corporation itself has no interest in such a question except to defeat the claims of the stockholders to additional dividends, does not accord with the facts. A corporation has an interest of its own in being well managed. . . . As was pointed out in the opinion by Presiding Justice Peck at the Appellate Division, it is in the interest of a corporation to have a sensible dividend policy which is necessary to enable it to raise new capital when needed by selling its stock. Moreover, as was also mentioned by the Appellate Division, the complaint itself alleged that this corporation has accumulated a surplus which is creating the "real hazard actually present that [Barbizon] may be cast in a heavy liability under section 102 of the Internal Revenue Code". 280 App.Div. 659, 116 N.Y.S.2d 671, 675. Inability to obtain corporate financing or being penalized under section 102 of the Internal Revenue Code, 26 U.S.C.A., are two respects, at least, which involve primarily the property and business of the corporation itself.

Equitable intervention by the court, in such cases, is not a cloak to cover what is in reality an action at law by the stockholders. This kind of action differs only from other instances of court intervention in that the immediate result is to bring about some distribution of corporate earnings to the stockholders. In other cases of intervention by the courts, the object is likewise to benefit stockholders or creditors through the corporation where the directors have been in some other manner deficient in performing their responsibility. The equitable intervention of the court in this situation, means that the court has to consider the interest of the corporation from every angle, including but not limited to its earnings, surplus, current and fixed assets and liabilities, the nature of the business and probable fluctuations in earnings and demands for new capital, competitive conditions in the industry, and so forth. These factors have to be weighed in the light of the circumstance that the stockholders are presumed to have invested their money with the expectation that they would receive a suitable return if the business prospers, and whether the directors have acted for ulterior purposes has to be considered in the light of all of these circumstances. Such a cause of action, calling upon the court to intervene in directing the affairs of the corporation due to default by the directors, is one where the court is required to act in the right of the corporation, as that phrase is used in section 61–b of the General Corporation Law.

Actions to compel payment of dividends have been described as "derivative" in opinions in courts of this State, [citations omitted.] The textwriters and the decided cases are not unanimous, . . . but a majority adhere to the view that the action is derivative. Whether the directors are indispensable parties if they cannot be served in one forum is the related but different issue which has generally been presented . . . and since the corporation pays the dividends without contribution by the directors (at least in the first instance), it has been pointed out that there is no practical reason why unavailability of the directors should preclude relief. Such a holding, based on practical considerations, does not alter the nature of the action. Directors who are not parties are not bound by the judgment, although their interest, including sometimes their ultimate liability may be indirectly affected, since the outcome depends upon an adjudication of their fraud or bad faith. If failure to serve them does not defeat the action, they may apply to be joined in order to protect their interests since their conduct is at stake.

A further word may be in order concerning the policy of section 61–b of the General Corporation Law as described in Lapchak v. Baker, 298 N.Y. 89, 80 N.E.2d 751, supra. It is not clear that secret settlements with directors was the only evil designed to be prevented by the enactment of that section. However, there is no reason to believe that the practice of buying off claims of this nature would be abandoned merely for the reason that personal claims are not presently being asserted against directors. As has been pointed out, in certain situations the personal interest of directors in such litigation may not be negligible, and, as they are ordinarily the representatives if not the owners of controlling shares, and are usually charged with conspiring to oppress the minority in this variety of litigation, they are likely to be actively interested in the result. The policy of this statute is for the Legislature to determine. It was drawn so as to apply to actions instituted in the right of the corporation, which is the type of action that the present suit is held to be.

The order appealed from should be affirmed, with costs; the questions certified answered in the affirmative.

FULD, JUDGE (dissenting).

Section 61–b of the General Corporation Law does not, in terms or in spirit, require the posting of security in every action by stockholders that challenges the conduct of directors. Concededly, it lays its burden only upon actions instituted by a shareholder "in the right" of his corporation, and yet the court is now reading into the statute a test which shifts the ground of dispute from the question of whose right is involved to that of whose conduct is attacked.

Section 61–b manifestly does not apply to actions brought by a stockholder to vindicate his personal right. Here it is alleged that the corporation has failed or refused to declare and pay dividends to which its stockholders are entitled. To me, those words plainly charge that the corporation has committed a wrong against the stockholders and, since the action is brought to redress only that wrong, it does not depend upon assertion of the right of the corporation to faithful performance of directoral duties. The plaintiff is entitled to seek—and, here is seeking—specific performance of the corporation's obligation to pay dividends upon his investment. The action is, in short, brought against the corporation as a legal entity and, if successful, will require the corporation to part with some of its assets in favor of its stockholders. I am, therefore, unable to follow the legal alchemy by which a breach of duty by the corporation—a corporate wrong—is transmuted into a corporate right.

The nub of this appeal is to divine the meaning of the statutory phrase "in the right" of the corporation. In its search for that meaning, the court has adopted an elaborate test: "whether an action to compel declaration of dividends is maintained in the interest of the corporation," the opinion reads, 306 N.Y. at page 459, 119 N.E.2d 333, turns upon whether the object of the action is to recover upon a chose in action belonging to the stockholders or whether "it is to compel the performance of corporate acts which good faith requires the directors to take in order to perform a duty which they owe to the corporation, and through it, to its stockholders."

The vice of the test is that it presupposes that every duty owed by corporate directors runs exclusively to the corporation as such and never directly to the stockholders in their personal and individual right. The law is otherwise.[6] . . .

In a very real sense, all suits against corporations—which must of necessity act through directors and officers—involve the action of the directors or of officers responsible to the directors. An indictment under the anti-trust laws or a suit based upon failure to accept goods contracted for may challenge the conduct of directors, since it is their

6. For example, in a proper case, stockholders may obtain direct redress for the directors' refusal to permit them to inspect the corporation's books or to vote or to have their stock transferred or to assert preemptive rights or to avoid a wrongful increase of stock issued to others which results in impairing their relative positions within the capital structure.

management which has resulted in the acts about which complaint is made. Rights of the government or of a supplier of merchandise, however, are certainly not to be defeated by a showing that the action or inaction on the part of the directors may also constitute a breach of their fiduciary duty to the corporation. In short, it simply is not the law that an attack on directors' conduct is, *ipso facto,* the assertion of a corporate right of action. The mere fact that the power to declare dividends resides in the directors and that a suit to compel a dividend payment challenges directors' action has no bearing on the question of whose right is involved in such a suit. We must seek elsewhere to ascertain the manner of the "right" that a court enforces when it overrules the decision of corporate directors and commands the corporation to pay dividends.

Time may have dimmed Chief Justice Marshall's pronouncement that a corporate charter is a contract with the state, see Trustees of Dartmouth College v. Woodward, 4 Wheat., U.S., 518, 4 L.Ed. 629, but it has never been doubted that it represents a contract among the shareholders and between them and the corporation. Some of the terms of the contract are expressed, others are implied, but those implied are no less important and enforcible. . . .

I can conceive of no more important or generally understood right of the stockholder in a modern corporation, where he is primarily an investor, than that of receiving dividends upon his investment. It is customary to delimit this right by express contractual language in the case of preferred stock, but the right is clearly implied in the case of common stock as well, even though the measure may be different or less certain. In essence, the stockholder has consented, by incorporation of the statutory provisions, General Corporation Law, § 27, into his contract of investment, to the management of the business by the board of directors, and this consent implies agreement that the directors in their business judgment shall determine whether corporate profits are to be distributed as dividends or retained to meet the needs of the business. But such consent does not extend to the point of absurdity; it does not give carte blanche to the directors. Broad as the business judgment rule may be, with corresponding difficulties in the way of proof of abuse, every stockholder has a right, a personal right, to have the directors exercise their discretion in good faith. If the denial of the dividend is not governed by managerial considerations, there is a breach of the contract of investment *between stockholder and corporation.*

In the present case, if the certificate of incorporation declared that dividends were to be paid on common stock when the corporation's financial situation and other conditions warrant, it would be indisputable that the stockholders had the right to, and the corporation the corresponding duty of, dividend distribution. See, e.g., Boardman v. Lake Shore & Michigan Southern Ry. Co., 84 N.Y. 157. And the corporation's *duty* does not become its *right* merely through the omission of express language in the certificate, for the law reads in the words as clearly as if they were spelled out. The right is the stockholders', whether the promise to pay the dividends is expressed or implied.

In a case such as the present, with but one class of stock outstanding, it is easy to slip into the fallacy of regarding the common and homogeneous right of the stockholders as the right of the corporation. To expose the fallacy, however, one need but consider the case in which more than one class of stock has been issued, and the shareholders have disparate and conflicting attitudes toward dividend distribution. Assume, for example, that the corporation's capital structure consists of a class of common stock carrying voting rights and effective control and a class of preferred stock entitling its holders to noncumulative dividends. The time may come when the directors, motivated by the interests of the common stockholders, decide not to pay dividends on the preferred stock. Quite obviously, the discretion of directors to declare or to omit the dividend in such an instance is of far greater moment to the preferred stockholders than in the case of common stock. The payment of a noncumulative dividend requires declaration by the directors and, if omitted, the right to it is lost. It would truly be a travesty of justice if the discretion of the directors to declare or to omit the dividend were not subject to judicial review. Such a review, however, would, of necessity, be directly concerned with the injury to the noncumulative preferred stockholders, and not to the corporation.

Since one class may urge and another resist a dividend distribution, see, e.g., Koppel v. Middle States Petroleum Corp., 272 App.Div. 790, 69 N.Y.S.2d 784, affirming Sup., 66 N.Y.S.2d 496, the controversy does not lend itself to analysis in terms of any supposed unitary "right" of the corporation as such, and it is not meaningful to say, as the Appellate Division has in this case, that the corporation and its shareholders always have identical interests, 280 App.Div. 655, 658, 116 N.Y.S.2d 671, 674.

Nor does the fact that a stockholder may sue at law for a dividend declared mean that he is enforcing the corporation's right rather than his own when he sues in equity to compel a payment. This is in essence no more than the ordinary distinction between an action for an accounting and one on an account stated. The right of a stockholder to a dividend payment is still personal to him and to his class; it is not the right of the corporation.

．．．

No one disputes the right of a corporation to sue its directors for breach of their fiduciary duties. And there is ample authority to sustain the proposition that, in cases of waste or mismanagement or other breach of duty owing directly to the corporation, only the corporation—or a stockholder in an action instituted in the right of the corporation—may sue the directors. No separate personal action may be maintained by the individual shareholder, even though he may have suffered damage through the loss in value of his pro rata interest in the corporation. See Niles v. New York Central & H.R.R.R. Co., 176 N.Y. 119, 68 N.E. 142. The only damage to the shareholders flows from the loss of corporate assets; if the corporation succeeds in its action against the directors, the pro rata loss sustained by the shareholders is made good. The assets so recovered, however—just as with other corporate assets—must be held by the corporation as a margin of safety for corporate creditors, and must not be distributed to the shareholders except under conditions which justify a dividend. Protection of the rights of creditors, then, militates against permitting individual actions by shareholders to recover their pro rata share of the loss suffered by the corporation. But, quite obviously, these considerations do not apply to an action where the avowed purpose is to compel the payment of a dividend. In such a suit, there is no recovery flowing to the corporation and there is nothing lost by the creditors, since it is clear that no dividend could be compelled which would violate the law governing dividend declarations.

For the very reason that dividend distribution is not the corporation's right but its duty, the corporation may, in a dividend action, be sued as sole defendant. . . . Nothing can be more patent than that the lone defendant in an action is not the owner of the right upon which the suit is grounded. The circumstance that no other defendant than the corporation is necessary is explainable only by recognizing that the corporation is in reality the true adversary. It is just the opposite with a suit founded upon the corporation's right. In such a case, the corporation is merely a formal defendant against which no relief is demanded. Another party must be found to fill the role of adversary to the plaintiff; in actions based on the corporation's right the plaintiff stockholder, if qualified to bring suit, merely champions the cause of the immobilized corporation.

The court, however, in its opinion, 306 N.Y. at pages 464–465, 119 N.E.2d 337, suggests that the rationale for permitting a corporation to be sued as a sole defendant in a dividend action is to prevent delinquent directors from thwarting justice by absenting themselves from the court's jurisdiction. If that were so, if that reason were valid, it would, of course, hold equally in true stockholders' derivative actions, but we know that no court has ever sanctioned a suit for waste and mismanagement against the corporation alone.

When I say that there is no corporate "right" to compel payment of dividends, I do not mean to suggest that a corporation has no financial concern or business interest in that subject. On the contrary, a corporation, viewed as a legal personality, may have a very great concern in a balanced dividend policy. Once the law has breathed life into the artificial corporate being, it becomes an entity bent on self-perpetuation and growth. It takes nourishment from the investing public and its desire for continuance and growth makes it interested in remaining solvent and in maintaining a good financial reputation. However, the corporation's interest in a sound dividend policy must not be confused with the question before us. Section 61–b requires the posting of security in only those actions brought in the corporation's "right", not in all those touching its "interest."

I do not mean to minimize the possibility that a corporation may be placed in jeopardy, by way of tax penalties or loss of access to the capital markets, through the failure of its directors to declare dividends. But I cannot too strongly emphasize that the possibility that the same act or failure to act may harm the corporation is no justification for denying the stockholder's contractual right to dividends. . . . In point of fact, the threat of harm to the corporation can be better averted without forcing recourse to the derivative action. The dangers of tax penalties for improper accumulation of surplus would disappear just as readily if the stockholders were allowed to proceed in their personal, contractual right to compel the payment of dividends. And the protection of the corporation's access to the capital market would probably be stronger if the minority shareholders have the power to compel the payment of dividends without encountering the roadblocks set up by section 61–b.

Furthermore, it seems to me self-evident that there should be a reasonable and consistent relation between the theory of the action and the relief sought. If we adhere scrupulously to the separate entity theory of corporate personality, it is both illogical and ironic to say that an action *must* be brought "in the right" of the corporation in order to deprive the corporation of part of its assets by the payment of a dividend. And we are no better off if we look at the underlying realities of the controversy. Most of the litigated cases arise in closely held corporations, when it is advantageous for the dominant group of shareholders to withhold dividends and the directors are subservient to the personal interest of this group. The reason may be simply a desire to avoid high-bracket individual taxes—which is the rationale of section 102 of the Internal Revenue Code—a consideration which may be of no weight whatever to the minority. Or there may be a more sinister purpose; the majority, entrenched in salary-paying positions in a profitable corporation, may wish to squeeze out the minority by a process of slow financial starvation. It is not persuasive in this setting to say that there is an identity of interest between the corporation, managed by majority rule, and the minority shareholders. The fundamental fact, and one that may not be blinked, is that the interest of the stockholder who sues to compel a payment of dividends is, to that extent, adverse to that of the corporation, whether the corporation is viewed as a separate person or as an instrument of the dominant group of stockholders. Thus, pragmatically as well as theoretically, a dividend action is not brought in the right of the corporation.

An action is in the right of a corporation, then, if the plaintiff asserts a right deriving from and through the corporation. Such an action "belongs primarily to the corporation, the real party in interest", and a resulting judgment or settlement "belongs to it and not the individual stockholder plaintiffs". Clarke v. Greenberg, 296 N.Y. 146, 149, 71 N.E.2d 443, 444, 169 A.L.R. 944; see, also, Horwitz v. Balaban, supra, 112 F.Supp. 99, 101; Schreiber v. Butte Copper & Zinc Co., D.C., 98 F.Supp. 106, 112. The reason is that a right of the corporation has been invaded. Since, however, a corporation has *no right to compel itself to pay a dividend*, the stockholders' right cannot possibly "derive" from it.

Several cases, as the court notes, opinion, 306 N.Y. pages 468, 469, 119 N.E.2d 339, decided in this and other jurisdictions, have held that an action to compel the declaration of dividends may be brought in the right of the corporation, . . . but in no one of them did the court consider the question whether such an action might not be brought in the personal right of the stockholder, if he chooses to frame his complaint on that theory and no other. Cf. Lydia E. Pinkham Medicine Co. v. Gove, supra, 303 Mass. 1, 20 N.E.2d 482. A far greater number of cases have sustained the action to compel the declaration of dividends on the theory that it is properly brought in the personal right of the stockholder, . . .

The majority intimates that, since suits of this character may be subject to abuse, they fall within the policy of section 61-b. While I do not share the court's apprehensions on this point, we are not here concerned with the power of the legislature to impose such a limitation on a suit to compel the payment of a dividend if it chooses to do so, but rather with whether it has done so in section 61-b. The statute as enacted does not look at the motives of the stockholder, but at the nature of the right which he asserts. If the stockholder does not proceed in the right of his corporation, as the term is generally understood in the substantive law, it is not the function of the court to extend the limitations of section 61–b to cover all cases in which there may or may not be a possibility of abuse.

Moreover, the legislative history of the section does not lend the slightest support for such an interpretation. The statute was aimed at a particular and well-perceived abuse—the so-called "strike suit," brought on behalf of a corporation against its directors or officers by persons who, since their holdings are "too small to indicate legitimate personal interest in the outcome and accordingly in the bringing of the action," realize the nuisance value of their suits and hope to be bought off by secret settlements. Wood, Survey and Report Regarding Stockholders' Derivative Suits (1944), p. 21; . . . Actions for waste or mismanagement were peculiarly vulnerable to that abuse. Since only the corporation would benefit directly from recovery, and creditors' rights might intervene, the stockholder's chance of gain would be secondhand at best. Beyond that, if his interest were fractional, his benefit would be as small as it would be remote. By inducing a secret settlement for his direct and selfish benefit, he might obtain sums wholly disproportionate to his stock interest. By the same token, faithless directors or officers, facing large personal liability and jeopardy, were tempted to enter into the secret bargain as a cheap way out.

However, since the directors are not threatened with personal liability, no such opportunities or temptations attend, or are characteristic of, a suit to compel the payment of dividends. That such actions were not the evil at which the legislation was aimed, was made clear by Governor Dewey when, in approving the legislation, he declared that it was aimed at "stockholder suit[s] *against corporation directors and officers.*" . . .

I would reverse the order of the Appellate Division and answer both certified questions in the negative.

COMMENT

The ruling in Gordon v. Elliman was in effect overruled by the amendment of § 626(a) which now speaks of a derivative suit as one ". . . brought in the right of a . . . corporation to procure a judgment in its favor." A viewpoint opposite to that in Gordon v. Elliman was taken by the Court of Appeals for the Third Circuit in construing the generally similar Pennsylvania statute.[7]

QUESTIONS

(1) Dodge v. Ford Motor Co., p. 107 supra involved a suit to compel the declaration of dividends; did the court seem to regard the action as derivative? Is Zahn v. Transamerica Corp., p. 446 supra, derivative?

(2) From the point of view of the purposes of the "strike suit" legislation involved, which of the opinions seems to have the better of it? From a conceptual standpoint?

(3) What does the theory of a derivative action necessarily indicate should be done with the proceeds of a successful suit? Where does this outcome leave the shareholder who sold his stock at a depressed price before the lawsuit began? Should this outcome prevail in a case where 95% of the stock is owned by persons who approved of the wrong? If not, what safeguards are required?

7. Knapp v. Bankers Securities Corp., 230 F.2d 717 (3d Cir.1956).

(4) What does the theory of a derivative action indicate should be the result when after one shareholder has won or lost, another shareholder complains about the same events?

(5) In the application of Federal Rule 23.1, should state conceptions about which lawsuits are derivative be taken over or should an independent appraisal be made? If the latter, what interests would the federal court try to safeguard?

Once one has distinguished the derivative suit from other types of litigation one has to go somewhat further to analyze the "nature" of a derivative suit. One helpful case in this regard is the following decision which, in the course of analyzing the need for trial by jury, in derivative actions, develops the history and theory of such actions.

ROSS v. BERNHARD

Supreme Court of the United States, 1970.
396 U.S. 531, 90 S.Ct. 733, 24 L.Ed.2d 729.

[Petitioners brought a derivative suit against the directors of their investment company, the Lehman Corporation, and its brokers, Lehman Brothers. They charged abuses on the part of those directors and of Lehman Brothers as well as specific violations of the Investment Company Act. They demanded a jury trial. The district judge held that they had a right to such trial on all issues to which the corporation would have had such a right. On interlocutory appeal, the Court of Appeals reversed, holding the cause of action entirely equitable. The Supreme Court granted certiorari and reversed, in an opinion by JUSTICE WHITE.]

We reverse the holding of the Court of Appeals that in no event does the right to a jury trial preserved by the Seventh Amendment extend to derivative actions brought by the stockholders of a corporation. We hold that the right to jury trial attaches to those issues in derivative actions as to which the corporation, if it had been suing in its own right, would have been entitled to a jury.

The Seventh Amendment preserves to litigants the right to jury trial in suits at common law—

> "not merely suits, which the common law recognized among its old and settled proceedings, but suits in which legal rights were to be ascertained and determined, in contradistinction to those, where equitable rights alone were recognized, and equitable remedies were administered. . . . In a just sense, the amendment then may well be construed to embrace all suits, which are not of equity and admiralty jurisdiction, whatever may be the peculiar form which they may assume to settle legal rights." Parsons v. Bedford, Breedlove & Robeson, 3 Pet. 433, 446, 7 L.Ed. 732 (1830).

However difficult it may have been to define with precision the line between actions at law dealing with legal rights and suits in equity dealing with equitable matters, Whitehead v. Shattuck, 138 U.S. 146, 151, 11 S.Ct. 276, 277, 34 L.Ed. 873 (1891), some proceedings were unmistakably actions at law triable to a jury. The Seventh Amendment, for example, entitled the parties to a jury trial in actions for damages to a person or property, for libel and slander, for recovery of land, and for conversion of personal property. Just as clearly, a corporation, although an artificial being, was commonly entitled to sue and be sued in the usual forms of action, at least in its own State. See Paul v. Virginia, 8 Wall. 168, 19 L.Ed. 357 (1868). Whether the corporation was viewed as an entity separate from its stockholders or as a device permitting its stockholders to carry on their business and to sue and be sued, a corporation's suit to enforce a legal right was an action at common law carrying the right to jury trial at the time the Seventh Amendment was adopted.

The common law refused, however, to permit stockholders to call corporate managers to account in actions at law. The possibilities for abuse, thus presented, were not ignored by corporate officers and directors. Early in the 19th century, equity provided relief both in this country and in England. Without detailing these developments,[8] it suffices to say that the remedy in this country, first dealt with by this Court in Dodge v. Woolsey, 18 How. 331, 15 L.Ed. 401 (1856), provided redress not only against faithless officers and directors but against third parties who had damaged or threatened the corporate properties and whom the corporation through its managers refused to pursue. The remedy made available in equity was the derivative suit, viewed in this country as a suit to enforce a *corporate* cause of action against officers, directors and third parties. As elaborated in the cases, one precondition for the suit was a valid claim on which the corporation could have sued; another was that the corporation itself had refused to proceed after suitable demand, unless excused by extraordinary conditions. Thus the dual nature of the stockholders' action: first the plaintiff's right to sue on behalf of the corporation and second the merits of the corporation claim itself.

Derivative suits posed no Seventh Amendment problems where the action against the directors and third parties would have been by a bill in equity had the corporation brought the suit. Our concern is with cases based upon a legal claim of the corporation against directors or third parties. Does the trial of such claims at the suit of a stockholder and without a jury violate the Seventh Amendment?

The question arose in this Court in the context of a derivative suit for treble damages under the antitrust laws. Fleitmann v. Welsbach Street Lighting Co., 240 U.S. 27, 36 S.Ct. 233, 60 L.Ed. 505 (1916). Noting that the bill in equity set up a claim of the corporation alone, Mr. Justice Holmes observed that if the corporation were the plaintiff, "no one can doubt that its only remedy would be at law," and inquired "why the defendants' right to a jury trial should be taken away because the present plaintiff cannot persuade the only party having [an interest in the] cause of action to sue,—how the liability which is the principal matter can be converted into an incident of the plaintiff's domestic difficulties with the company that has been wronged"? His answer was that the bill did not state a good cause of action in equity. Agreeing that there were "cases in which the nature of the right asserted for the company, or the failure of the defendants concerned to insist upon their rights, or a different state system, has led to the whole matter being disposed of in equity," he concluded that when the penalty of triple

---

8. Prunty, The Shareholders' Derivative Suit: Notes on Its Derivation, 32 N.Y.　U.L.Rev. 980 (1957), treats the development of the equitable remedy.

damages is sought, the antitrust statute plainly anticipated, a jury trial and should not be read as "attempting to authorize liability to be enforced otherwise than through the verdict of a jury in a court of common law." Although the decision had obvious Seventh Amendment overtones, its ultimate rationale was grounded in the antitrust laws.

Where penal damages were not involved, however, there was no authoritative parallel to *Fleitmann* in the federal system squarely passing on the applicability of the Seventh Amendment to the trial of a legal claim presented in a pre-merger derivative suit. What can be gleaned from this Court's opinions is not inconsistent with the general understanding, reflected by the state court decisions and secondary sources, that equity could properly resolve corporate claims of any kind without a jury when properly pleaded in derivative suits complying with the equity rules.

Such was the prevailing opinion when the Federal Rules of Civil Procedure were adopted in 1938. It continued until 1963 when the Court of Appeals for the Ninth Circuit, relying on the Federal Rules as construed and applied in Beacon Theatres Inc. v. Westover, 359 U.S. 500, 79 S.Ct. 948, 3 L.Ed.2d 988 (1959), and Dairy Queen Inc. v. Wood, 369 U.S. 469, 82 S.Ct. 894, 8 L.Ed.2d 44 (1962), required the legal issues in a derivative suit to be tried to a jury. DePinto v. Provident Security Life Ins. Co., 323 F.2d 826. It was this decision which the District Court followed in the case before us and which the Court of Appeals rejected.

Beacon and *Dairy Queen* presaged *DePinto*. Under those cases, where equitable and legal claims are joined in the same action, there is a right to jury trial on the legal claims which must not be infringed either by trying the legal issues as incidental to the equitable ones or by a court trial of a common issue existing between the claims. The Seventh Amendment question depends on the nature of the issue to be tried rather than the character of the overall action. See Simler v. Conner, 372 U.S. 221, 83 S.Ct. 609, 9 L.Ed.2d 691 (1963). The principle of these cases bears heavily on derivative actions.

We have noted that the derivative suit has dual aspects: first, the stockholder's right to sue on behalf of the corporation, historically an equitable matter; second, the claim of the corporation against directors or third parties on which, if the corporation had sued and the claim presented legal issues, the company could demand a jury trial. As implied by Mr. Justice Holmes in *Fleitmann*, legal claims are not magically converted into equitable issues by their presentation to a court of equity in a derivative suit. The claim pressed by the stockholder against directors or third parties "is not his own but the corporation's." Koster v. Lumbermens Mut. Cas. Co., 330 U.S., at 522, 67 S.Ct., at 831. The corporation is a necessary party to the action; without it the case cannot proceed. Although named a defendant, it is the real party in interest, the stockholder being at best the nominal plaintiff. The proceeds of the action belong to the corporation and it is bound by the result of the suit. The heart of the action is the corporate claim. If it presents a legal issue, one entitling the corporation to a jury trial under the Seventh Amendment, the right to a jury is not forfeited merely because the stockholder's right to sue must first be adjudicated as an equitable issue triable to the court. *Beacon* and *Dairy Queen* require no less.

If under older procedures, now discarded, a court of equity could properly try the legal claims of the corporation presented in a derivative suit, it was because irreparable injury was threatened and no remedy at law existed as long as the stockholder was without standing to sue and the corporation itself refused to pursue its own remedies. Indeed, from 1789 until 1938, the judicial code expressly forbade courts of equity from entertaining any suit for which there was an adequate remedy at law. This provision served "to guard the right of trial by jury preserved by the Seventh Amendment and to that end it should be liberally construed." Schoenthal v. Irving Trust Co., 287 U.S. 92, 94, 53 S.Ct. 50, 51, 77 L.Ed. 185 (1932). If, before 1938, the law had borrowed from equity, as it borrowed other things, the idea that stockholders could litigate for their recalcitrant corporation, the corporate claim, if legal, would undoubtedly have been tried to a jury.

Of course, this did not occur, but the Federal Rules had a similar impact. Actions are no longer brought as actions at law or suits in equity. Under the Rules there is only one action—a "civil action"—in which all claims may be joined and all remedies are available. Purely procedural impediments to the presentation of any issue by any party, based on the difference between law and equity, were destroyed. In a civil action presenting a stockholder's derivative claim, the court after passing upon the plaintiff's right to sue on behalf of the corporation is now able to try the corporate claim for damages with the aid of a jury. Separable claims may be tried separately, Fed.Rule Civ.Proc. 42(b), or legal and equitable issues may be handled in the same trial. Fanchon & Marco, Inc. v. Paramount Pictures, Inc., 202 F.2d 731 (C.A.2d Cir. 1953). The historical rule preventing a court of law from entertaining a shareholder's suit on behalf of the corporation is obsolete; it is no longer tenable for a district court, administering both law and equity in the same action, to deny legal remedies to a corporation merely because the corporation's spokesmen are its shareholders rather than its directors. Under the rules, law and equity are procedurally combined; nothing turns now upon the form of the action or the procedural devices by which the parties happen to come before the court. The "expansion of adequate legal remedies provided by . . . the Federal Rules necessarily affects the scope of equity." Beacon Theatres, Inc. v. Westover, 359 U.S., at 509, 79 S.Ct., at 956.

Thus, for example, before merger class actions were largely a device of equity, and there was no right to a jury even on issues which might, under other circumstances, have been tried to a jury. 5 J. Moore, Federal Practice ¶ 38.38[2]; 3B J. Moore, Federal Practice ¶ 23.02[1]. Although at least one post-merger court held that the device was not available to try legal issues, it now seems settled in the lower federal courts that class action plaintiffs may obtain a jury trial on any legal issues they present. . . .

Derivative suits have been described as one kind of a "true" class action. 2 W. Barron & A. Holtzoff, Federal Practice and Procedure § 562.1 (Wright ed.). We are inclined to agree with the description, at least to the extent it recognizes that the derivative suit and the class action were both ways of allowing parties to be heard in equity who could not speak at law. 3B J. Moore ¶¶ 23.02[1], 23.1.16[1]. After the rules there is no longer any procedural obstacle to the assertion of legal rights before juries, however the party may have acquired standing to assert those rights. Given the availability in a derivative action of both legal and equitable remedies, we think the Seventh Amendment preserves to the parties in a stockholder's suit the same right to a jury trial which historically belonged to the corporation and to those against whom the corporation pressed its legal claims.

In the instant case we have no doubt that the corporation's claim is, at least in part, a legal one. The relief sought is money damages. There are allegations in the complaint of a breach of fiduciary duty, but there are also allegations of ordinary breach of contract and gross negligence. The corporation, had it sued on its own behalf, would have been entitled to a jury's determination, at a minimum, of its damages against its broker under the brokerage contract and of its rights against its own directors because of their negligence. . Under these circumstances it is unnecessary to decide whether the corporation's other claims are also properly triable to a jury. Dairy Queen v. Wood, 369 U.S. 469, 82 S.Ct. 894, 8 L.Ed.2d 44 (1962). The decision of the Court of Appeals is reversed.

It is so ordered.

Decision of Court of Appeals reversed.

[MR. JUSTICE STEWART wrote a sharp dissent, joined in by THE CHIEF JUSTICE and MR. JUSTICE HARLAN. He charged the Court with wrongly combining the Seventh Amendment and the Federal Rules. "Somehow the Amendment and the rules magically interact to do what each separately was expressly intended not to do; namely, to enlarge the right to a jury trial in civil actions brought in the courts of the United States." On the contrary, the dissent urged, both instruments were concerned with *preserving* existing rights to jury trial. The dissent found that historically there had been no dual nature to the derivative suit but that "the suit has in practice always been treated as a single cause tried exclusively in equity." The dissent also disagreed on the proper reading of the cases. For example, it read *Fleitmann* "to stand for a proposition diametrically opposite to that which the Court seeks to establish." According to MR. JUSTICE STEWART, the holding there was that since the antitrust laws gave a right to a jury in all treble damage actions a derivative suit seeking such damages could not be maintained. The dissent denied the feasibility of breaking down a derivative suit into inherently "legal" or inherently "equitable" issues, stating "[t]here are only factual issues, and, like chameleons [they] take their color from surrounding circumstances." It concluded by charging that "[t]he Court's decision today can perhaps be explained as a reflection of an unarticulated but apparently overpowering bias in favor of jury trials in civil actions. It certainly cannot be explained in terms of either the Federal Rules or the Constitution."]

QUESTIONS

(1) What precisely does the Supreme Court expect the district court to do about handling the jury question when—and if—the case goes to trial?

(2) Do you agree with the opinion's view of the "nature" of a derivative suit? As a matter of history? (Noting the remark quoted from the dissent that neither the Seventh Amendment nor the Federal Rules were meant to enlarge the right to trial by jury but that the majority somehow derives that result from their combination.) Consider also the merits of the majority result in the framework of the present system of federal procedure.

(3) What are the implications of the decision and its reasoning as to the nature of the derivative suit on such questions as alignment of the complainant, the corporation and defendants for diversity purposes?

(4) What is your estimate as to how a jury would handle a negligence issue such as that in Smith v. Van Gorkom, p. 212 supra? Would the knowledge that a jury trial awaited influence the amount that you, as defendants' counsel, were willing to offer in a pretrial settlement?

3. Pre-trial Maneuvers in Derivative Actions

In derivative suits there is considerable emphasis on pre-trial motions. Protracted litigation can be embarrassing from a public relations standpoint and the hours, days or even weeks of time spent by top-level executives in depositions, courtroom testimony and other maneuvers is a costly burden for the corporation. Thus defence counsel are apt to go through a check list for possible easy dispositions, some of which are special to derivative suits. Such a list would include the following.

(a) The defence might try a motion to dismiss or for summary judgment. Here it would encounter judicial reluctance to dispose of cases prematurely before the plaintiff has had an opportunity to explore the facts through discovery processes. Another obstacle to swift disposition is the fact that, particularly in conflict of interest cases, the substantive law of corporations casts the burden of proof upon the parties defending the transaction.

(b) There may be room for objections on jurisdictional grounds. Note that since it is necessary for the corporation to be made a party to the action, the action can only be brought where both the corporation and the defendants can be reached. Delaware sought to protect its position as a forum in which not only Delaware corporations but also defendants could be conveniently reached. It did so by rejecting that part of the Uniform Commercial Code which provides that shares of stock may only be attached where the certificates embodying them are found.[9] Thus any defendant in a derivative suit in Delaware who owned any shares of the corporate party could be forced, by sequestering those shares, to choose between appearing in the action or forfeiting the shares. Shaffer v. Heitner, 433 U.S. 186, 97 S.Ct. 2569, 53 L.Ed.2d 683 (1977), held that this procedure violated the due process clause. It found that the Delaware law did not furnish any assurance that there would be the minimum contacts between the defendants and the state required by the International Shoe doctrine. It noted that the 28 individual defendants in the derivative action, each of whom was or had been an officer or director of Greyhound, had never been in Delaware

9. Compare 8 Del.C. § 324 with U.C.C. § 8–317.

and that the stock sequestered was not the subject of the litigation. Delaware responded by enacting a new law (10 Del.C. § 3114) providing that every nonresident director is to be deemed to have consented to the appointment of the registered agent of the corporation as an agent for the service of process in all actions to which the corporation is a party. In Armstrong v. Pomerance, 423 A.2d 174 (Del.1980), Delaware's court found that statute constitutional, stressing the state's interest in providing for a clear and convenient place of resolution for corporate controversies when there might be no other forum having jurisdiction over both corporation and defendants.

Then there are special questions relating to federal jurisdiction, in particular to actions that can only be based upon diversity. Speaking roughly, a corporation that refuses to prosecute an action is classed as a party defendant and aligned opposite plaintiff shareholder. Note that this affords an opening for the collusive creation of diversity. Suppose that a California corporation has a dispute with a citizen of California; the absent diversity comes into existence if a citizen of New York who is a shareholder brings a derivative suit in which the Californians are defendants.[10] The predecessors of Rule 23.1 and that Rule itself have attempted to prevent collusive behavior in this connection. There are important procedural advantages if a federal cause of action can be alleged, to which state claims can sometimes be made pendent. Finally there may be arguments about *forum non conveniens* and the related rule that the internal affairs of a corporation should only be tried in a court at its domicil.[11]

(c) Defendants would examine the statute of limitations. Some jurisdictions have shortened the limitation period quite drastically. On the other hand such doctrines as the one that concealment (or perhaps mere non-discovery) tolls the statute, have made it possible for defaults to be litigated many years after they allegedly took place.

(d) Federal Rule 23.1 requires that a complaint in a derivative suit be verified by plaintiff. The impact of this requirement was materially undercut by Surowitz v. Hilton Hotels Corp.[12] In that case, it developed during the discovery process that Mrs. Surowitz, an immigrant from Poland with a very limited knowledge of English, did not understand what the lawsuit was about. In verifying it she had relied entirely upon her son-in-law, a Harvard Law School alumnus named Brilliant. The district court dismissed but the Supreme Court reversed, finding the verification adequate.

(e) There are a number of questions about the eligibility of the shareholder to be the champion of the corporation. There are, first of all, a group of rather technical questions about one's standing as a

10. Hawes v. City of Oakland, 104 U.S. (14 Otto) 450, 26 L.Ed. 827 (1881).

11. See, e.g., Koster v. Lumbermens Mut. Cas. Co., 330 U.S. 518, 67 S.Ct. 828, 91 L.Ed. 1067 (1947). This case is also authority for the proposition that in diversity cases the requisite jurisdictional amount is calculated not by plaintiff's possible recovery but by the loss sustained by the defendant corporation.

12. 383 U.S. 263, 86 S.Ct. 845, 15 L.Ed. 2d 807 (1966).

shareholder: pledgees, holders of shares in a parent of the plundered corporation, beneficial shareholders who are not shareholders of record, etc. Then, it is clear that one who has participated in the wrong is not eligible to play the role of champion; the case law is less clear as to the status of one who takes shares from a wrongdoer without knowing about the misdeed. Then there is a basic question: should a shareholder who was not such at the time of the wrong be eligible? Note that F.R.C.P. 23.1 and § 626(b) of the New York Business Corporation Law answer this question in the negative. The contemporaneous ownership rule raises numerous technical questions—when did the wrong take place (assuming that it was not a single precisely datable theft)? what if the complaining shareholder sold stock after the wrong and then repurchased it? suppose that the corporation that was harmed is thereafter merged into another one—who is a contemporary owner? This rule throws some obstacles in the path of the lawyer seeking to commence an action but with persistence he is likely to be able to find an eligible plaintiff.

While the rule is, in terms, related to derivative suits, it has implications for a non-derivative suit by a corporation in which 100% of its shareholders would be disqualified either by their date of acquisition of their shares, or by participation in or knowledge of the wrong. Bangor Punta Operations, Inc. v. Bangor & Aroostok R.R. Co., 417 U.S. 703, 94 S.Ct. 2578, 41 L.Ed.2d 418 (1974), ordered dismissal of a suit brought by a corporation because 98.3% of its stock had been purchased—after the alleged wrongs—by another firm (Amoskeag) which knew about the wrongs when it bought the shares at a fair price. In its analysis the court rejected the argument that plaintiff's status as a railroad, and thus a public utility, should give rise to a public interest exception to the rule. A dissent joined in by four Justices doubted that Amoskeag would receive any windfall and noted that it had stipulated it would plow any recovery back into railroad improvements.

(f) The security-for-costs provisions of the New York and California statutes were intended to be a major obstacle to derivative suits. We will consider security-for-costs rules in greater depth in Section 5 of this Chapter as part of a discussion of what happens at the end of a derivative suit—including allocation of costs. We will see that the hopes of the proponents of this rule have been to a large degree disappointed.

(g) Federal Rule 23.1 and various state rules require that plaintiff allege the making of demands on the board of directors and on the shareholders. The nature of this requirement and of the associated institution, the special litigation committee of the board of directors, is explored in the cases that immediately follow.

Meanwhile, a plaintiff also has available various procedural steps with which to bedevil the defense.

(a) Plaintiff will wish to exploit all opportunities for discovery. Plaintiff will be at a disadvantage due to the other side's possession of information but may hope to compel proof of the allegations, perhaps based on no more than mere suspicion or leads supplied by some government investigation. In fact plaintiff may, along the way, come upon a windfall in the form of proof of other types of misconduct. Plaintiff has two mechanisms available: first, the regular deposition and discovery provision of the federal rules or state law and, second, the corporation law rules that afford shareholders, subject to various rules as to showing of proper purpose [13] and scope, the right to examine the documents of their corporation. This latter right may be exercised before any suit has been filed and may be used as the opening gun in the overall campaign.

(b) Plaintiff may object to defendant's counsel, in particular to defendant's being represented by past or present counsel to the corporation. This problem is explored in Marco v. Dulles below.

MAYER v. ADAMS

Supreme Court of Delaware, 1958.
37 Del.Ch. 298, 141 A.2d 458.

[Plaintiff brought an action to redress alleged wrongs suffered by Phillips Petroleum Co. in which she was a shareholder. The complaint alleged that demand on the directors would be futile—there was no challenge on this point. It further alleged that a demand on the stockholders was unnecessary since (1) a fraud was charged which the shareholders could not ratify, (2) since 100,000 stockholders were involved circularizing them would be futile and burdensome. Defendants moved to dismiss, saying that these grounds were insufficient in law. The motion relied on Rule 23(b) of the Rule of the Court of Chancery.

> "The complaint shall also set forth with particularity the efforts of the plaintiff to secure from the managing directors or trustees and, if necessary, from the shareholders such action as he desires, and the reasons for his failure to obtain such action or the reasons for not making such effort."

The Vice Chancellor granted the motion to dismiss but on appeal the Supreme Court, per CHIEF JUSTICE SOUTHERLAND, reversed. Portions of the opinion dealing with the demand requirement, follow:]

In the view we take of the case, the issue between the litigants narrows itself to this:

If the ground of the derivative suit is fraud, is demand for stockholder action necessary under the rule?

When it is said that a demand on stockholders is necessary in a case involving fraud, the inquiry naturally arises: demand to do what?

Let us suppose that the objecting stockholder submits to a stockholders' meeting a proposal that a suit be brought to redress alleged wrongs. He may do so either by attending the meeting, or, if the

---

13. In State ex rel. Pillsbury v. Honeywell, Inc., 291 Minn. 322, 191 N.W.2d 406 (1971), it was held that a shareholder could not inspect the corporate records where he had only recently acquired a few shares in order to conduct a campaign against the corporation's weapons production.

regulations of the Securities and Exchange Commission are applicable, by requiring the management to mail copies of the proposal to the other stockholders. (He is limited to 100 words of explanation. Rule X–14A–8b.) Let us further suppose—a result quite unlikely—that the stockholders approve the resolution. What is accomplished by such approval? The stockholder is about to file his suit. What additional force is given to the suit by the approval?

Let us suppose again that the proposal is disapproved by the majority stockholders—as common knowledge tells us it will ordinarily be. What of it? They cannot ratify the alleged fraud. Keenan v. Eshleman, 23 Del.Ch. 234, 2 A.2d 904, 120 A.L.R. 227; Loft, Inc., v. Guth, 23 Del.Ch. 138, 2 A.2d 225. The stockholder files his suit, which proceeds notwithstanding the disapproval.

If the foregoing is a correct analysis of the matter, it follows that the whole process of stockholder demand in a case of alleged fraud is futile and avails nothing. This appears to be the view expressed by Chancellor Seitz in Campbell v. Loew's Inc., Del.Ch., 134 A.2d 565, 567. His opinion was filed shortly before the date of the decision of the Vice Chancellor in the instant case, and had, perhaps, not been brought to the latter's attention, since the opinion below does not comment upon it. In the Campbell case demand on stockholders was excused on two grounds, first, because the stockholders could not act in time to prevent the threatened injury, and second, because "absent unanimous approval the stockholders could not ratify" illegal expenditures of corporate funds. The Chancellor said:

> "I therefore conclude from the pleadings that a demand upon the stockholders was not necessary under the facts alleged, but in any event a demand here would have been futile under the circumstances. A demand upon the stockholders implies that legally they can do something about it. Where they cannot, the Rule does not contemplate that such a useless act must nevertheless be performed."

The defendants vigorously assail this view of the matter. They say that the rule requires demand for action to be made upon the stockholders in all cases in which the board of directors is disqualified (as here) to pass upon the matter of bringing suit, because in such a case the power to determine the question of policy passes to the body of the stockholders. The stockholders may determine, when the matter is presented to them, upon any one of a number of courses. Thus, defendants say, they may authorize plaintiff's suit; they may determine to file the suit collectively—"take it over", so to speak; they may take other remedial action; they may remove the directors; and, finally, they may decide that the suit has no merit, or, as a matter of corporate policy, that it should not in any event be brought.

These answers do not impress us. As we have said, why is it "necessary" to have stockholders' approval of plaintiff's suit? Defendants say: to comply with the rule. This is arguing in a circle. The question is, does the rule make it necessary?

Again, what is gained (except, perhaps, "moral" support) by having the suit brought by a group of stockholders, however large, rather than by a single individual? A more serious objection to this suggestion is that under Delaware law the directors manage the corporation—not the stockholders. It is certainly gravely to be doubted whether the majority stockholders, as such, may take over the duties of the directors in respect of litigation. . . .

The suggestion that the directors could be removed is a suggestion that the objecting stockholder could engage in a proxy fight with the management. Of all defendants' suggestions, this seems to us to be the most unrealistic. How often is a minority stockholder equipped to take on such a formidable task? And why should a proxy fight be made a condition precedent to a minority stockholder's suit to redress an alleged fraud?

Finally it is suggested that the stockholders may (1) determine that the suit has no merit, or (2) that it is not good policy to press it.

As to the first suggestion, we think it clear that in the ordinary case the stockholders in meeting could not satisfactorily determine the probable merits of a minority stockholder's suit without a reasonably complete presentation and consideration of evidentiary facts. Perhaps some very simple cases might be handled in another manner, but they must be few. A stockholders' meeting is not an appropriate forum for such a proceeding.

The second suggestion, that the stockholders may, as a matter of policy, determine that the claim shall not be enforced and bind the minority not to sue, is really the crux of this case. If the majority stockholders have this power, there would be much to be said for defendants' argument that in case of a disqualified or non-functioning board, the stockholders should decide the matter. . . .

But a decision not to press a claim for alleged fraud committed by the directors means, in effect, that the wrong cannot be remedied. It is conceded that the wrong cannot be ratified by the majority stockholders, but it is said that refusal to sue is a different thing from ratification. Strictly speaking, this is true, but the practical result is the same. To construe Rule 23(b) as making necessary a submission of the matter to stockholders, because the stockholders have the power to prevent the enforcement of the claim, is to import into our law a procedure that would inevitably have the effect of seriously impairing the minority stockholder's now existing right to seek redress for frauds committed by directors of the corporation. This right he has always had under the Delaware law and practice. The policy of the General Corporation law for many years has been to grant to the directors, and to the majority stockholders in certain matters, very broad powers to determine corporate management and policy. But, correlatively, the policy of our courts has always been to hold the directors and the majority stockholders to strict accountability for any breach of good faith in the exercise of these powers, and to permit any minority stockholder to seek redress in equity on behalf of the corporation for wrongs committed by the directors or by the majority stockholders. We cannot believe that Rule 23(b) was intended to import into our law and procedure a radical change of this judicial policy.

It is quite true, as defendants say, that no Delaware case has ever passed upon the point, that is, whether an effort to obtain stockholder action is required. It has never been squarely raised. But over a long period of years, in many minority stockholders' suits, no defendant has apparently ever suggested the point. This, we think, is quite significant. The settled practice in Delaware has been that demand upon and refusal by the directors is sufficient, or, if the directors are disqualified to give redress, demand would be futile and is excused. Cf. Sohland v.

Baker, 15 Del.Ch. 431, 442, 141 A. 277, 282, 58 A.L.R. 693. In that case demand had been made on the directors to bring suit, but no demand had been made on stockholders. Chancellor Harrington said:

> "The corporation, having refused to institute proceedings, the only way that its rights could be brought before the court was by a bill filed by a stockholder. That the complainant, for the prevention of injustice, therefore, had the right to file the bill in the court below, seems clear."

Although the Chancellor cited and quoted from Hawes v. City of Oakland, infra, the case announcing the federal rule requiring stockholder demand, he made no mention of any such requirement under Delaware law.

We are aware that there is high authority in support of defendants' contention. See S. Solomont & Sons Trust, Inc., v. New England Theatres Operating Corp., 326 Mass. 99, 93 N.E.2d 241, holding that a majority of disinterested stockholders may in good faith determine that a cause of action for fraud against the directors shall not be enforced. There is also high authority for the view that we take, namely, that a cause of action for alleged fraud committed by the directors may be maintained by a minority stockholder without demand upon the stockholders collectively. Continental Securities Co. v. Belmont, 206 N.Y. 7, 99 N.E. 138, 51 L.R.A.,N.S., 112 and note.

Now, we observe that neither in the Massachusetts case nor in the New York case was any rule of court involved. The courts treated the question as one of substantive law. For comment on the Massachusetts rule as one of substantive law, see Pomerantz v. Clark, D.C., 101 F.Supp. 341, 343. In the Continental case, the New York Court of Appeals pointed out the difference between the power of the stockholders to ratify acts merely voidable and the lack of their power to ratify acts unlawful or against public policy. We think it clear that so far as any substantive question of law is involved the Delaware law is similar to that of New York. See Keenan v. Eshleman and Loft, Inc., v. Guth, supra (fraud cannot be ratified by the majority); Blish v. Thompson Automatic Arms Corp., 30 Del.Ch. 538, 64 A.2d 581, and Kerbs v. California Eastern Airways, Inc., 33 Del.Ch. 69, 90 A.2d 652, 34 A.L.R.2d 839 (lack of authority may be cured by stockholder action).

If, therefore, the rule were to be interpreted as defendants contend, i.e., if it contemplates that the decision to sue or not to sue in a case like this is a decision for the stockholders to make if the directors are disqualified, a serious question would arise whether the rule attempts to change substantive law. Since it could not legally have that effect, a construction leading to that conclusion should be avoided. The rule must be harmonized with substantive law.

The defendants say that it is unnecessary in this case to decide the legal effect of the action of the majority stockholders in determining that as a matter of policy no suit shall be brought. Regardless of the effect of such a determination, they say, the rule requires that they pass upon the matter because only a question of procedure is involved. One may again ask, why should a procedure be declared "necessary" if it serves no useful purpose? And how can we determine whether or not it serves a useful purpose unless we ask what results it leads to?

Defendants lay great stress upon the federal cases construing this rule. Our rule, they say, was copied (with certain omissions) from the comparable federal rule 23(b) of the Federal Rules of Civil Procedure, 28 U.S.C.A. This is certainly true. Hence, it is said that the construction placed upon the rule by the federal courts should be followed in our courts.

This brings us to a consideration of the authorities discussing or construing the federal rule.

For the history and background of the rule, see 3 Moore's Federal Practice, pp. 3489ff. Originally Equity Rule 94 (later Equity Rule 27), it derives from the decision in Hawes v. City of Oakland, 104 U.S. 450, 26 L.Ed. 827, holding that a minority stockholder must seek action by the stockholders "if necessary". The case does not undertake to decide under what circumstances such demand is necessary. We note that it did not involve any charge of fraud or wrongful personal profit against the directors.

The decision in United Copper Securities Co. v. Amalgamated Copper Co., 244 U.S. 261, 37 S.Ct. 509, 510, 61 L.Ed. 1119, contains language purporting to define the circumstances under which application to the stockholders is excused. The case involves no charge of fraud against the directors. Indicating that "as a rule" application should be made to the stockholders, Mr. Justice Brandeis added:

> ". . . unless it appears that there was no opportunity for such application, that such application would be futile (as where the wrong-doers control the corporation), or that the delay involved would defeat recovery."

Defendants treat this language as a definitive catalogue of all possible cases in which demand on stockholders is excused. We doubt that it was so intended. In the dissenting opinion of Mr. Justice Stone in Rogers v. Guaranty Trust Co., 288 U.S. 123, 53 S.Ct. 295, 302, 77 L.Ed. 652, concurred in by Mr. Justice Brandeis, it is said:

> "The directors, having failed to comply with petitioner's reasonable demand that they exercise their authority to bring this suit in the name of the corporation, petitioner was not required by general equitable principles or by Equity Rule 27 to appeal to the stockholders before bringing it, as the action complained of here was not one which the stockholders could ratify."

We note also that in the recent case of Smith v. Sperling, 354 U.S. 91, 77 S.Ct. 1112, 1114, 1 L.Ed.2d 1205, involving a charge of fraudulent waste of assets by directors, the complaint averred only that "demand on the directors would have been futile." In a footnote to the opinion it is said: "The bill therefore meets the requirements of Rule 23(b) of the Rules of Civil Procedure."

When we turn to the decisions of the lower federal courts, we find that they are far from harmonious. We shall not attempt to analyze all of them; illustrative examples will serve our purpose. . . .

We do not attempt an exhaustive analysis of all the cases cited to us. It is clear that the federal decisions are far from harmonious in construing the federal rule. They present no serious obstacle to a reasonable interpretation of our rule by this Court consonant with Delaware law and the practice of many years.

· · · ·

We are cited to only one state decision construing an equity rule similar to ours. Escoett v. Aldecress Country Club, 16 N.J. 438, 109 A.2d 277, 283.

The Supreme Court of New Jersey held that the circumstances presented excused demand upon the stockholders, but in so holding considered the history of the rule in the federal system, the federal decisions construing it, and the background of its adoption by the New Jersey Supreme Court. The Court said:

"And we do not read into the rule any blanket exemption in situations where the wrongs complained of are not subject to formal ratification by the stockholders; even there the stockholder may, before instituting his action, be profitably expected to call upon the general body of stockholders for support which may be in the form of internal corporate action or in joinder in his court action."

Referring to the background of the adoption of the rule in New Jersey in 1948, the Court said:

"The numerous stockholders' derivative actions in our State gave rise to demands that greater restrictions be imposed upon their maintenance. In 1945 the Legislature made provisions for the stockholder's posting of security for reasonable expenses (R.S. 14:3–15, N.J.S.A.) as a measure of ' "protection for corporations and their officers and directors, against 'strike suits.' " ' "

Delaware has never adopted such a statute.

With deference to the high court of our sister State of New Jersey, we are constrained, for the reasons first set forth above, to differ with its view that anything substantial can be accomplished by a demand upon stockholders in a case in which fraud is charged. Such a demand would be, in our opinion, a futile gesture.

We hold that if a minority stockholders' complaint is based upon an alleged wrong committed by the directors against the corporation, of such a nature as to be beyond ratification by a majority of the stockholders, it is not necessary to allege or prove an effort to obtain action by the stockholders to redress the wrong.

The question may be asked: In what circumstances is such demand necessary? Obviously the rule contemplates that in some cases a demand is necessary; otherwise, it would have not been adopted.

We are not called upon in this case to attempt to enumerate the various circumstances in which demand on stockholders is excused; and likewise we do not undertake to enumerate all the cases in which demand is necessary. It seems clear that one instance of necessary demand is a case involving only an irregularity or lack of authority in directorate action, . . .

The phrase "if necessary" is thus, we think susceptible of a reasonable construction that comports with Delaware law and practice.

We are accordingly compelled to disagree with the holding of the Vice Chancellor that the bill should be dismissed as to all the defendants for failure to comply with Rule 23(b). . . .

ZAPATA CORP. v. MALDONADO

Supreme Court of Delaware, 1981.
430 A.2d 779.

[In 1975 Maldonado, a stockholder of Zapata, began a derivative suit in the Delaware Court of Chancery charging ten of its officers and directors with breaches of fiduciary duty. He stated that a demand would be futile as all directors were defendants. In 1977 he began a parallel suit in the U.S. District Court for the Southern District of New York. Another shareholder sued in Texas. By 1979 Zapata's board had changed membership and it appointed an "Independent Investigation Committee" composed of two new directors to investigate this litigation. In September 1979 the Committee reported that the actions should "be dismissed forthwith as their continued maintenance is inimical to the Company's best interests . . ." The New York federal district court granted a summary judgment motion on January 24, 1980 as did the one in Texas. On March 18, 1980 the Court of Chancery denied a like motion. The Court of Appeals for the Second Circuit stayed the appeal before it pending a Delaware ruling. On May 29th the Chancery Court dismissed the suit on the ground that the federal disposition was res judicata—if sustained on appeal. However, the United States Court of Appeals for the Second Circuit ordered the federal appeal stayed pending the Delaware Supreme Court's disposition of the state appeal. Thus the litigation sat "in a procedural gridlock." The Delaware Supreme Court accepted an interlocutory appeal. It reversed the Court of Chancery and remanded for further proceedings on an opinion by JUSTICE QUILLEN.]

Thus, Zapata's observation that it sits "in a procedural gridlock" appears quite accurate, and we agree that this Court can and should attempt to resolve the particular question of Delaware law. As the Vice Chancellor noted, 413 A.2d at 1257, "it is the law of the State of incorporation which determines whether the directors have this power of dismissal. Burks v. Lasker, 441 U.S. 471, 99 S.Ct. 1831, 60 L.Ed.2d 404 (1979)". We limit our review in this interlocutory appeal to whether the Committee has the power to cause the present action to be dismissed.

We begin with an examination of the carefully considered opinion of the Vice Chancellor which states, in part, that the "business judgment" rule does not confer power "to a corporate board of directors to terminate a derivative suit", 413 A.2d at 1257. His conclusion is particularly pertinent because several federal courts, applying Delaware law, have held that the business judgment rule enables boards (or their committees) to terminate derivative suits, decisions now in conflict with the holding below.

As the term is most commonly used, and given the disposition below, we can understand the Vice Chancellor's comment that "the business judgment rule is irrelevant to the question of whether the Committee has the authority to compel the dismissal of this suit". 413 A.2d at 1257. Corporations, existing because of legislative grace, possess authority as granted by the legislature. Directors of Delaware corporations derive their managerial decision making power, which encompasses decisions whether to initiate, or refrain from entering, litigation, from 8 Del.C. § 141(a). This statute is the fount of directorial powers. The "business judgment" rule is a judicial creation that presumes propriety, under certain circumstances, in a board's decision. Viewed defensively, it does not create authority. In this sense the "business judgment" rule is not relevant in corporate decision making until after a decision is made. It is generally used as a defense to an attack on the decision's soundness. The board's managerial decision making power, however, comes from § 141(a). The judicial creation and legislative grant are related because the "business judgment" rule evolved to give recognition and deference to directors' business expertise when exercising their managerial power under § 141(a).

In the case before us, although the corporation's decision to move to dismiss or for summary judgment was, literally, a decision resulting from an exercise of the directors' (as delegated to the Committee) business judgment, the question of "business judgment", in a defensive sense, would not become relevant until and unless the decision to seek termination of the derivative lawsuit was attacked as improper . . . This question was not reached by the Vice Chancellor because he determined that the stockholder had an individual right to maintain this derivative action. _Maldonado,_ 413 A.2d at 1262.

Thus, the focus in this case is on the power to speak for the corporation as to whether the lawsuit should be continued or terminated. As we see it, this issue in the current appellate posture of this case has three aspects: the conclusions of the Court below concerning the continuing right of a stockholder to maintain a derivative action; the corporate power under Delaware law of an authorized board committee to cause dismissal of litigation instituted for the benefit of the corporation; and the role of the Court of Chancery in resolving conflicts between the stockholder and the committee.

Accordingly, we turn first to the Court of Chancery's conclusions concerning the right of a plaintiff stockholder in a derivative action. We find that its determination that a stockholder, once demand is made and refused, possesses an independent, individual right to continue a derivative suit for breaches of fiduciary duty over objection by the corporation, _Maldonado,_ 413 A.2d at 1262–63, as an absolute rule, is erroneous. The Court of Chancery relied principally upon Sohland v. Baker, Del.Supr., 141 A. 277 (1927), for this statement of the Delaware rule. _Maldonado,_ 413 A.2d at 1260–61. _Sohland_ is sound law. But _Sohland_ cannot be fairly read as supporting the broad proposition which evolved in the opinion below.

In _Sohland,_ the complaining stockholder was allowed to file the derivative action in equity after making demand and after the board refused to bring the lawsuit. But the question before us relates to the power of the corporation by motion to terminate a lawsuit properly commenced by a stockholder without prior demand. No Delaware statute or case cited to us directly determines this new question and we do not think that _Sohland_ addresses it by implication. . . .

Moreover, McKee v. Rogers, Del.Ch., 156 A. 191 (1931), stated "as a general rule" that "a stockholder cannot be permitted . . . to invade the discretionary field committed to the judgment of the directors and sue in the corporation's behalf when the managing body refuses. This rule is a well settled one." 156 A. at 193.[14]

---

14. To the extent that Mayer v. Adams, Del.Supr., 141 A.2d 458, 462 (1958) and Ainscow v. Sanitary Co. of America, Del. Ch., 180 A. 614, 615 (1935) relied upon in _Maldonado,_ 413 A.2d at 1262, contained language relating to the rule in _McKee,_ we note that each decision is dissimilar from the one we examine today. _Mayer_ held

The *McKee* rule, of course, should not be read so broadly that the board's refusal will be determinative in every instance. Board members, owing a well-established fiduciary duty to the corporation, will not be allowed to cause a derivative suit to be dismissed when it would be a breach of their fiduciary duty. Generally disputes pertaining to control of the suit arise in two contexts.

Consistent with the purpose of requiring a demand, a board decision to cause a derivative suit to be dismissed as detrimental to the company, after demand has been made and refused, will be respected unless it was wrongful.[15] . . . A claim of a wrongful decision not to sue is thus the first exception and the first context of dispute. Absent a wrongful refusal, the stockholder in such a situation simply lacks legal managerial power. Compare *Maldonado*, 413 A.2d at 1259–60.

But it cannot be implied that, absent a wrongful board refusal, a stockholder can never have an individual right to initiate an action. For, as is stated in *McKee*, a "well settled" exception exists to the general rule.

> "[A] stockholder may sue in equity in his derivative right to assert a cause of action in behalf of the corporation, *without prior demand* upon the directors to sue, when it is apparent that a demand would be futile, that the officers are under an influence that sterilizes discretion and could not be proper persons to conduct the litigation."

156 A. at 193 (emphasis added). This exception, the second context for dispute, is consistent with the Court of Chancery's statement below, that "[t]he stockholders' individual right to bring the action does not ripen, however, . . . unless he can show a demand to be futile." *Maldonado*, 413 A.2d at 1262.[16]

These comments in *McKee* and in the opinion below make obvious sense. A demand, when required and refused (if not wrongful), terminates a stockholder's legal ability to initiate a derivative action.[17] But where demand is properly excused, the stockholder does possess the ability to initiate the action on his corporation's behalf.

These conclusions, however, do not determine the question before us. Rather, they merely bring us to the question to be decided. It is here that we part company with the Court below. Derivative suits enforce corporate rights and any recovery obtained goes to the corpora-

that demand on the stockholders was not required before maintaining a derivative suit if the wrong alleged could not be ratified by the stockholders. *Ainscow* found defective a complaint that neither alleged demand on the directors, nor reasons why demand was excusable.

15. In other words, when stockholders, after making demand and having their suit rejected, attack the board's decision as improper, the board's decision falls under the "business judgment" rule and will be respected if the requirements of the rule are met. . . . That situation should be distinguished from the instant case, where demand was not made, and the *power* of the board to seek a dismissal, due to disqualification, presents a threshold issue.

For examples of what has been held to be a wrongful decision not to sue, see Stockholder Derivative Actions, supra note 5, 44 U.Chi.L.Rev. at 193–98. We recognize that the two contexts can overlap in practice.

16. These statements are consistent with Rule 23.1's "reasons for . . . failure" to make demand. See also the other cases cited by the Vice Chancellor, 413 A.2d at 1262: Ainscow v. Sanitary Co. of America, supra note 9, 180 A. at 615; Meyer v. Adams, supra note 9, 141 A.2d at 462; Dann v. Chrysler Corp., Del.Ch., 174 A.2d 696, 699–700 (1961).

17. Even in this situation, it may take litigation to determine the stockholder's lack of power, i.e., standing.

tion. Taormina v. Taormina Corp., Del.Ch., 78 A.2d 473, 476 (1951); Keenan v. Eshleman, Del.Supr., 2 A.2d 904, 912–13 (1938). "The right of a stockholder to file a bill to litigate corporate rights is, therefore, solely for the purpose of preventing injustice where it is apparent that material corporate rights would not otherwise be protected." *Sohland,* 141 A. at 282. We see no inherent reason why the "two phases" of a derivative suit, the stockholder's suit to compel the corporation to sue and the corporation's suit (see 413 A.2d at 1261–62), should automatically result in the placement in the hands of the litigating stockholder sole control of the corporate right throughout the litigation. To the contrary, it seems to us that such an inflexible rule would recognize the interest of one person or group to the exclusion of all others within the corporate entity. Thus, we reject the view of the Vice Chancellor as to the first aspect of the issue on appeal.

The question to be decided becomes: When, if at all, should an authorized board committee be permitted to cause litigation, properly initiated by a derivative stockholder in his own right, to be dismissed? As noted above, a board has the power to choose not to pursue litigation when demand is made upon it, so long as the decision is not wrongful. If the board determines that a suit would be detrimental to the company, the board's determination prevails. Even when demand is excusable, circumstances may arise when continuation of the litigation would not be in the corporation's best interests. Our inquiry is whether, under such circumstances, there is a permissible procedure under § 141(a) by which a corporation can rid itself of detrimental litigation. If there is not, a single stockholder in an extreme case might control the destiny of the entire corporation. This concern was bluntly expressed by the Ninth Circuit in Lewis v. Anderson, 9th Cir., 615 F.2d 778, 783 (1979), cert. denied, 449 U.S. 869, 101 S.Ct. 206, 66 L.Ed.2d 89 (1980): "To allow one shareholder to incapacitate an entire board of directors merely by leveling charges against them gives too much leverage to dissident shareholders." But, when examining the means, including the committee mechanism examined in this case, potentials for abuse must be recognized. This takes us to the second and third aspects of the issue on appeal.

Before we pass to equitable considerations as to the mechanism at issue here, it must be clear that an independent committee possesses the corporate power to seek the termination of a derivative suit. Section 141(c) allows a board to delegate all of its authority to a committee. Accordingly, a committee with properly delegated authority would have the power to move for dismissal or summary judgment if the entire board did.

Even though demand was not made in this case and the initial decision of whether to litigate was not placed before the board, Zapata's board, it seems to us, retained all of its corporate power concerning litigation decisions. If Maldonado had made demand on the board in this case, it could have refused to bring suit. Maldonado could then have asserted that the decision not to sue was wrongful and, if correct, would have been allowed to maintain the suit. The board, however, never would have lost its statutory managerial authority. The demand requirement itself evidences that the managerial power is retained by the board. When a derivative plaintiff is allowed to bring suit after a wrongful refusal, the board's authority to choose whether to pursue the litigation is not challenged although its conclusion—reached through the exercise of that authority—is not respected since it is wrongful. Similarly, Rule 23.1, by excusing demand in certain instances, does not strip the board of its corporate power. It merely saves the plaintiff the expense and delay of making a futile demand resulting in a probable tainted exercise of that authority in a refusal by the board or in giving control of litigation to the opposing side. But the board entity remains empowered under § 141(a) to make decisions regarding corporate litigation. The problem is one of member disqualification, not the absence of power in the board.

The corporate power inquiry then focuses on whether the board, tainted by the self-interest of a majority of its members, can legally delegate its authority to a committee of two disinterested directors. We find our statute clearly requires an affirmative answer to this question. As has been noted, under an express provision of the statute, § 141(c), a committee can exercise all of the authority of the board to the extent provided in the resolution of the board. Moreover, at least by analogy to our statutory section on interested directors, 8 Del.C. § 141, it seems clear that the Delaware statute is designed to permit disinterested directors to act for the board. Compare Puma v. Marriott, Del.Ch., 283 A.2d 693, 695–96 (1971).

We do not think that the interest taint of the board majority is per se a legal bar to the delegation of the board's power to an independent committee composed of disinterested board members. The committee can properly act for the corporation to move to dismiss derivative litigation that is believed to be detrimental to the corporation's best interest.

Our focus now switches to the Court of Chancery which is faced with a stockholder assertion that a derivative suit, properly instituted should continue for the benefit of the corporation and the corporate assertion, properly made by a board committee acting with board authority, that the same derivative suit should be dismissed as inimical to the best interests of the corporation.

At the risk of stating the obvious, the problem is relatively simple. If, on the one hand, corporations can consistently wrest bona fide derivative actions away from well-meaning derivative plaintiffs through the use of the committee mechanism, the derivative suit will lose much, if not all, of its generally-recognized effectiveness as an intra-corporate means of policing boards of directors. . . . If, on the other hand, corporations are unable to rid themselves of meritless or harmful litigation and strike suits, the derivative action, created to benefit the corporation, will produce the opposite, unintended result. . . . It thus appears desirable to us to find a balancing point where bona fide stockholder power to bring corporate causes of action cannot be unfairly trampled on by the board of directors, but the corporation can rid itself of detrimental litigation.

As we noted, the question has been treated by other courts as one of the "business judgment" of the board committee. If a "committee, composed of independent and disinterested directors, conducted a proper review of the matters before it, considered a variety of factors and reached, in good faith, a business judgment that [the] action was not in the best interest of [the corporation]", the action must be dismissed. See, e.g., Maldonado v. Flynn, supra, 485 F.Supp. at 282, 286. The issues become solely independence, good faith, and reasonable investigation. The ultimate conclusion of the committee, under that view, is not subject to judicial review.

We are not satisfied, however, that acceptance of the "business judgment" rationale at this stage of derivative litigation is a proper balancing point. While we admit an analogy with a normal case respecting board judgment, it seems to us that there is sufficient risk in the realities of a situation like the one presented in this case to justify caution beyond adherence to the theory of business judgment.

The context here is a suit against directors where demand on the board is excused. We think some tribute must be paid to the fact that the lawsuit was properly initiated. It is not a board refusal case. Moreover, this complaint was filed in June of 1975 and, while the parties undoubtedly would take differing views on the degree of litigation activity, we have to be concerned about the creation of an "Independent Investigation Committee" four years later, after the election of two new outside directors. Situations could develop where such motions could be filed after years of vigorous litigation for reasons unconnected with the merits of the lawsuit.

Moreover, notwithstanding our conviction that Delaware law entrusts the corporate power to a properly authorized committee, we must be mindful that directors are passing judgment on fellow directors in the same corporation and fellow directors, in this instance, who designated them to serve both as directors and committee members. The question naturally arises whether a "there but for the grace of God go I" empathy might not play a role. And the further question arises whether inquiry as to independence, good faith and reasonable investigation is sufficient safeguard against abuse, perhaps subconscious abuse.

There is another line of exploration besides the factual context of this litigation which we find helpful. The nature of this motion finds no ready pigeonhole, as perhaps illustrated by its being set forth in the alternative. It is perhaps best considered as a hybrid summary judgment motion for dismissal because the stockholder plaintiff's standing to maintain the suit has been lost. But it does not fit neatly into a category described in Rule 12(b) of the Court of Chancery Rules nor does it correspond directly with Rule 56 since the question of genuine issues of fact on the merits of the stockholder's claim are not reached.

It seems to us that there are two other procedural analogies that are helpful in addition to reference to Rules 12 and 56. There is some analogy to a settlement in that there is a request to terminate litigation without a judicial determination of the merits. See Perrine v. Pennroad Corp., Del.Supr., 47 A.2d 479, 487 (1946). "In determining whether or not to approve a proposed settlement of a derivative stockholders' action [when directors are on both sides of the transaction], the Court of Chancery is called upon to exercise its own business judgment." Neponsit Investment Co. v. Abramson, Del.Supr., 405 A.2d 97, 100 (1979) and cases therein cited. In this case, the litigating stockholder plaintiff facing dismissal of a lawsuit properly commenced ought, in our judgment, to have sufficient status for strict Court review.

Finally, if the committee is in effect given status to speak for the corporation as the plaintiff in interest, then it seems to us there is an analogy to Court of Chancery Rule 41(a)(2) where the plaintiff seeks a dismissal after an answer. Certainly, the position of record of the litigating stockholder is adverse to the position advocated by the corporation in the motion to dismiss. Accordingly, there is perhaps some wisdom to be gained by the direction in Rule 41(a)(2) that "an action shall not be dismissed at the plaintiff's instance save upon order of the Court and upon such terms and conditions as the Court deems proper."

Whether the Court of Chancery will be persuaded by the exercise of a committee power resulting in a summary motion for dismissal of a derivative action, where a demand has not been initially made, should rest, in our judgment, in the independent discretion of the Court of Chancery. We thus steer a middle course between those cases which yield to the independent business judgment of a board committee and this case as determined below which would yield to unbridled plaintiff stockholder control. In pursuit of the course, we recognize that "[t]he final substantive judgment whether a particular lawsuit should be maintained requires a balance of many factors—ethical, commercial, promotional, public relations, employee relations, fiscal as well as legal." Maldonado v. Flynn, supra, 485 F.Supp. at 285. But we are content that such factors are not "beyond the judicial reach" of the Court of Chancery which regularly and competently deals with fiduciary relationships, disposition of trust property, approval of settlements and scores of similar problems. We recognize the danger of judicial overreaching but the alternatives seem to us to be outweighed by the fresh view of a judicial outsider. Moreover, if we failed to balance all the interests involved, we would in the name of practicality and judicial economy foreclose a judicial decision on the merits. At this point, we are not convinced that is necessary or desirable.

After an objective and thorough investigation of a derivative suit, an independent committee may cause its corporation to file a pretrial motion to dismiss in the Court of Chancery. The basis of the motion is the best interests of the corporation, as determined by the committee. The motion should include a thorough written record of the investigation and its findings and recommendations. Under appropriate Court supervision, akin to proceedings on summary judgment, each side should have an opportunity to make a record on the motion. As to the limited issues presented by the motion noted below, the moving party should be prepared to meet the normal burden under Rule 56 that there is no genuine issue as to any material fact and that the moving party is entitled to dismiss as a matter of law.[18] The Court should apply a two-step test to the motion.

First, the Court should inquire into the independence and good faith of the committee and the bases supporting its conclusions. Limited discovery may be ordered to facilitate such inquiries. The corporation should have the burden of proving independence, good faith and a reasonable investigation, rather than presuming independence, good faith and reasonableness.[19] If the Court determines either that the

18. We do not foreclose a discretionary trial of factual issues but that issue is not presented in this appeal. See Lewis v. Anderson, supra, 615 F.2d at 780. Nor do we foreclose the possibility that other motions may proceed or be joined with such a pretrial summary judgment motion to dismiss, e.g., a partial motion for summary judgment on the merits.

19. Compare Auerbach v. Bennett, 47 N.Y.2d 619, 419 N.Y.S.2d 920, 928–29, 393

N.E.2d 994 (1979). Our approach here is analogous to and consistent with the Delaware approach to "interested director" transactions, where the directors, once the transaction is attacked, have the burden of establishing its "intrinsic fairness" to a court's careful scrutiny. See, e.g., Sterling v. Mayflower Hotel Corp., Del.Supr., 93 A.2d 107 (1952).

committee is not independent or has not shown reasonable bases for its conclusions, or, if the Court is not satisfied for other reasons relating to the process, including but not limited to the good faith of the committee, the Court shall deny the corporation's motion. If, however, the Court is satisfied under Rule 56 standards that the committee was independent and showed reasonable bases for good faith findings and recommendations, the Court may proceed, in its discretion, to the next step.

The second step provides, we believe, the essential key in striking the balance between legitimate corporate claims as expressed in a derivative stockholder suit and a corporation's best interests as expressed by an independent investigating committee. The Court should determine, applying its own independent business judgment, whether the motion should be granted. This means, of course, that instances could arise where a committee can establish its independence and sound bases for its good faith decisions and still have the corporation's motion denied. The second step is intended to thwart instances where corporate actions meet the criteria of step one, but the result does not appear to satisfy its spirit, or where corporate actions would simply prematurely terminate a stockholder grievance deserving of further consideration in the corporation's interest. The Court of Chancery of course must carefully consider and weigh how compelling the corporate interest in dismissal is when faced with a non-frivolous lawsuit. The Court of Chancery should, when appropriate, give special consideration to matters of law and public policy in addition to the corporation's best interests.

If the Court's independent business judgment is satisfied, the Court may proceed to grant the motion, subject, of course, to any equitable terms or conditions the Court finds necessary or desirable.

NOTE ON SPECIAL LITIGATION COMMITTEES AND THE DEMAND REQUIREMENT

It has been feared that the special litigation committee would destroy the derivative suit as a safeguard of corporate morality as it was once feared would be done by the security for costs statutes. The evidence at this point is mixed—certainly derivative litigation continues. Note that the Delaware version is more apt to let a suit through the filter than the version adopted in New York by Auerbach v. Bennett, 47 N.Y.2d 619, 419 N.Y.S.2d 920, 393 N.E.2d 994 (1979). The New York alternative omits what the court in Zapata calls the second step, that is, the inquiry in New York stops with ascertaining the good faith and independence of the SLC. In Lewis v. Fuqua, p. 270 supra, the Delaware court found that the connections of the one-member SLC with the corporate management were too complex and intense to enable him to give a convincing set of reasons for approving the questioned transactions. However in Kaplan v. Wyatt, 499 A.2d 1184 (Del.1985), a report was approved although one member of the committee had been on the board at the time of the questioned transaction. Note that the cost of hiring attorneys for the investigation that produced the 150 page report in that case was $500,000—exclusive of directors' and managers' time spent.

Observe the connection between the question of the SLC and its power to terminate the litigation with the question whether demand must be made on the board in the first place. Stating that the preceding case "left a crucial issue unanswered", when is a stockholder's demand upon a board of directors, to redress an alleged wrong to the corporation, excused as futile prior to the filing of a derivative suit, the court in Aronson v. Lewis, 473 A.2d 805 (Del.1984), proceeded to answer that question as follows:

> Our view is that in determining demand futility the Court of Chancery in the proper exercise of its discretion must decide whether, under the particularized facts alleged, a reasonable doubt is created that: (1) the directors are disinterested and independent and (2) the challenged transaction was otherwise the product of a valid exercise of business judgment. Hence, the Court of Chancery must make two inquiries, one into the independence and disinterestedness of the directors and the other into the substantive nature of the challenged transaction and the board's approval thereof. As to the latter inquiry the court does not assume that the transaction is a wrong to the corporation requiring corrective steps by the board. Rather, the alleged wrong is substantively reviewed against the factual background alleged in the complaint. As to the former inquiry, directorial independence and disinterestedness, the court reviews the factual allegations to decide whether they raise a reasonable doubt, as a threshold matter, that the protections of the business judgment rule are available to the board. Certainly, if this is an "interested" director transaction, such that the business judgment rule is inapplicable to the board majority approving the transaction, then the inquiry ceases. In that event futility of demand has been established by any objective or subjective standard. See, e.g., Bergstein v. Texas Internat'l Co., Del.Ch., 453 A.2d 467, 471 (1982) (because five of nine directors approved stock appreciation rights plan likely to benefit them, board was interested for demand purposes and demand held futile). This includes situations involving self-dealing directors. . . .

> However, the mere threat of personal liability for approving a questioned transaction, standing alone, is insufficient to challenge either the independence or disinterestedness of directors, although in rare cases a transaction may be so egregious on its face that board approval cannot meet the test of business judgment, and a substantial likelihood of director liability therefore exists. See Gimbel v. Signal Cos., Inc., Del.Ch., 316 A.2d 599, aff'd, Del.Supr., 316 A.2d 619 (1974); Cottrell v. Pawcatuck Co., Del.Supr., 128 A.2d 225 (1956). In sum the entire review is factual in nature. The Court of Chancery in the exercise of its sound discretion must be satisfied that a plaintiff has alleged facts with particularity which, taken as

true, support a reasonable doubt that the challenged transaction was the product of a valid exercise of business judgment. Only in that context is demand excused.

MARCO v. DULLES

United States District Court, Southern District of New York, 1959.
169 F.Supp. 622, appeal dismissed 268 F.2d 192 (2d Cir.1959).

[Plaintiff, claiming, as administrator of an estate, to own 35 shares of Blue Ridge Corporation, brought an action against former directors of that corporation and other alleged participants alleging wrongful diversion of the corporation's assets. Blue Ridge was founded in 1929 and its board consisted of two directors nominated by the banking firm of Goldman Sachs, two by Central States Electric Co. and one neutral, a senior partner of the law firm of Sullivan & Cromwell. The transactions attacked took place during 1929–33 and Sullivan & Cromwell represented the corporation and individual directors in connection therewith. Soon afterwards control of Blue Ridge passed to a new group and the board of directors changed. Blue Ridge underwent various transformations and reorganizations. Harry Marco, plaintiff's intestate, began litigation in 1936 in the state courts. Sullivan & Cromwell represented defendant directors but declined to represent Blue Ridge which, at the firm's urging, was represented by independent counsel. The suit languished but in 1955 the corporate defendant moved to disqualify Sullivan & Cromwell. The state courts took no final action on this and, in January 1958, dismissed the Marco action because of his failure to appear for pre-trial examination. In March 1958 plaintiff as administrator brought this action, based on the same claims, in the federal courts (on a diversity basis). The defendant corporation brought a new motion to disqualify Sullivan & Cromwell from representing the former directors. The motion was based on Canons 6 and 37 of the Canons of Professional Ethics:

"It is unprofessional to represent conflicting interests, except by express consent of all concerned given after a full disclosure of the facts. Within the meaning of this canon, a lawyer represents conflicting interests when, in behalf of one client, it is his duty to contend for that which duty to another client requires him to oppose.

"The obligation to represent the client with undivided fidelity and not to divulge his secrets or confidences forbids also the subsequent acceptance of retainers or employment from others in matters adversely affecting any interest of the client with respect to which confidence has been reposed."

"It is the duty of a lawyer to preserve his client's confidences. This duty outlasts the lawyer's employment, and extends as well to his employees; and neither of them should accept employment which involves or may involve the disclosure or use of these confidences, either for the private advantage of the lawyer or his employees or to the disadvantage of the client, without his knowledge and consent, and even though there are other available sources of such information. A lawyer should not continue employment when he discovers that this obligation prevents the performance of his full duty to his former or to his new client.

"If a lawyer is accused by his client, he is not precluded from disclosing the truth in respect to the accusation. The announced intention of a client to commit a crime is not included within the confidences which he is bound to respect. He may properly make such disclosures as may be necessary to prevent the act or protect those against whom it is threatened."

Portion of JUDGE BRYANT's opinion declining to disqualify counsel follow.]

I do not find that Sullivan & Cromwell represent conflicting interests in this suit within the meaning of the second paragraph of Canon 6. In this litigation that firm represents only individual defendants and none of the three corporations, Blue Ridge Corporation, Blue Ridge Mutual Fund, Inc., or Ridge Realization Corporation, who are directly or indirectly involved. Nor did Sullivan & Cromwell represent any of the corporate defendants in the litigation in the state court which preceded the present suit. In fact the firm declined to represent Blue Ridge Corporation in that action on the ground of possible conflict of interest with the directors for whom it appeared, and Blue Ridge was represented by independent counsel throughout.

There does not appear to be any inconsistency between the position which Sullivan & Cromwell took in connection with the transactions under attack and the position which it now takes upon behalf of the individual defendants. Having taken the professional position when representing the corporation and its directors that the transactions under attack were legal and proper, the firm takes the same position here. As attorneys for the former directors Sullivan & Cromwell seek to uphold the transactions entered into pursuant to their previous advice and their position is not hostile to or inconsistent with the position they previously took. They have no duty to Blue Ridge Corporation which requires them to oppose the interests of the defendants they now represent and to attempt to set aside the transactions which they advised were legal and proper, and indeed they could not properly do so. . . .

The question of whether the representation of the former directors by Sullivan & Cromwell violates the last paragraph of Canon 6 and Canon 37 is a more difficult one.

Messrs. Sullivan & Cromwell take the position that in view of the unique relationship between a corporation and its directors there can be no secrets or confidences reposed in them by the corporation which they are obligated not to divulge to the directors whom they thereafter may represent.

Their argument runs like this.—A corporation is an inanimate legal entity which can act only through and by its directors and officers. Any secrets or confidences reposed by the corporation in its general counsel are necessarily known to all of the directors since they are the only vehicles through which the corporation could have known of or expressed such confidences. Conversely, any confidences which the directors reposed in the general counsel to the corporation must have been fully known to the corporation since the directors constitute the voice and hearing of the corporation, and, indeed, its only voice and hearing. Thus there can be no secrets or confidences reposed in general counsel by the corporation which are not fully known to its directors, nor any secrets or confidences reposed by the directors which are not fully known to the corporation. From this, it is argued that the representation of the directors in this suit could not possibly involve any breach of the professional obligation not to divulge any secrets or confidences of the corporation by a firm which acted as counsel for both the corporation and its directors because no such secrets or confidences exist.

This argument does not seem to me to be valid. A corporation is a continuing entity. Boards of Directors come and go but the corporation persists. One board of directors may conceive the interests of a corporation to be quite different from a prior board. Nevertheless the professional obligation of former general counsel to the corporation persists. Its loyalty is not to the former directors alone but to the continuing corporate entity as well.

The corporation has its own files and records which it maintains continuously. While a board of directors in office has access to such files and records it by no means can be assumed that the directors know everything in the files and records of the corporation, or if they did that they retained such knowledge. There may well be secrets and confidences in the files of counsel which are in fact wholly unknown to the former directors.

It is unnecessary on a motion to disqualify for a former client to show that his former attorney is in the possession of specific secrets or confidences. As Judge Weinfeld said in T.C. Theatre Corp. v. Warner Bros. Pictures, Inc., D.C.S.D.N.Y., 113 F.Supp. 265, 268, the rule is

". . . that where any substantial relationship can be shown between the subject matter of a former representation and that of a subsequent adverse representation, the latter will be prohibited."

Judge Weinfeld goes on to say (at pages 268–269):

". . . The former client need show no more than that the matters embraced in the pending suit wherein his former attorney appears on behalf of his adversary are substantially related to the matters or cause of action wherein the attorney previously represented him, the former client."

This was specifically approved by the Court of Appeals of this circuit in Consolidated Theatres, Inc. v. Warner Bros. Circuit Management Corp., 216 F.2d 920, 924, 52 A.L.R.2d 1231, where the court pointed out that the statement, while not a rule of law purporting to define the professional obligation, measured "the quantum of evidence required for proof of the obligation".

Furthermore, the argument made by Messrs. Sullivan & Cromwell rests upon too narrow a concept of the professional relationship between lawyer and client. The words "confidence" and "confidences" as used in Canons 6 and 37 include more than specific matters of fact or information which come to the lawyer on a confidential basis. They include also intangibles arising from the very nature of the lawyer-client relationship which result from mutual discussion of the problems facing the client, consideration of the problems by counsel and the advice given thereon, the rationale of the solutions proposed and the legal techniques by which such solutions are arrived at.[20] It seems to me that this is why the courts have treated the rule formulated by Judge Weinfeld in the T.C. Theatre case as creating an "irrebuttable inference" that confidences material and relevant to the pending case were reposed in the attorney if the subject matter of the former representation is substantially related to the issues and subject matter of the current litigation. . . . .

The disclosure or use of confidences is forbidden "even though there are other available sources of such information". Canon 37. And this is true "[a]lthough all of the information obtained by the attorney from his former client may be available to his present client . . . .". Fleischer v. A.A.P., Inc., supra, 163 F.Supp. at page 551. Since here the very transactions which are the subject matter of the present litigation are the same transactions on which Messrs. Sullivan & Cromwell represented the corporation, the moving party has sufficiently established that there was "confidence" reposed by the corporation in Messrs. Sullivan & Cromwell which, in the absence of special and unusual circumstances, they would not be permitted to "divulge" or "use".

Furthermore, while the position of Messrs. Sullivan & Cromwell in this litigation is not adverse to the position which they previously took when representing the corporation, it is plainly adverse to the position which the corporation or its successor in interest takes now. Ridge Realization Corporation as the successor to and assignee of Blue Ridge Corporation with respect to these choses in action, now takes the position that these transactions should be set aside. The former directors insist that the transactions should stand. Thus Sullivan & Cromwell are presently representing the directors "in matters adversely affecting [the] interest of the client [Blue Ridge Corporation] with respect to which confidence has been reposed".

This is not to say that there may not be circumstances where the former general counsel for a corporation may properly represent directors in a minority stockholders' suit. Cf. Otis & Co. v. Penn. R. Co., D.C.E.D.Pa., 57 F.Supp. 680. If the corporate management takes the position that the transactions under attack are valid and proper and should be upheld, such representation may not be "adverse to any interest" of the corporation and such representation may be proper. But a different result would follow where, through a change in management and policy, the corporation (the former client) takes the position that the transactions should be set aside.

Thus, I am not prepared to deny the motion to disqualify upon the ground that the professional relationship between the general counsel of a corporation and the corporation and its directors is such that no confidences could have been reposed in counsel by the corporation which would bar them from subsequently representing the directors. Nor am I prepared to hold that, in the absence of special circumstances, former general counsel is free to represent former directors adversely to the interests of the corporation where the corporation itself or its successor in interest has taken the position that transactions on which the former counsel represented the corporation should be set aside.

---

20. See, also, Drinker, Legal Ethics, 104, 109, 115, which discusses the confusion that has surrounded the use of the word "confidence" in the canons and the occasional failure to comprehend that the word in context means "trust" as well as "secret".

Yet these questions are not decisive of the instant motion. There are special and unusual circumstances here which impel the conclusion that Messrs. Sullivan & Cromwell are not disqualified from representing the former directors in the present suit and that the motion to disqualify should be denied.

The first of these circumstances arises from the nature of the accusations made in the complaint.

In this case the defendant directors are being accused of what is tantamount to fraud in connection with the transactions under attack. Sullivan & Cromwell plainly were responsible for advising as to the legality of such transactions which were concededly entered into on their advice. It was their professional obligation, in so far as the facts were known to them, to vouch professionally for the legality of the transactions that were entered into. Such legality, in terms of dealings between the corporation and its directors, necessarily implied that the transactions were not tainted with fraud or impropriety.

The attempt to set aside these transactions upon the ground of fraud necessarily implies an accusation by the plaintiff not only against the directors who were clients of Messrs. Sullivan & Cromwell, but against Messrs. Sullivan & Cromwell themselves in their professional capacity as the lawyers in these transactions. Moreover, these accusations are direct as well as implied. The then senior partner of Sullivan & Cromwell is named as a defendant in the action and is alleged to have been a participant in the frauds charged. It is true that he is not expressly charged with fraud in his professional capacity. But his acts as a director cannot be separated from his acts as a member of the firm who were general counsel for the corporation. The line between the two is entirely too fine to permit the professional obligation as a lawyer and the fiduciary obligation as a director to be placed in convenient separate boxes.

It is well settled that an attorney engaged in the practice of the law is held to the same "highest standards of ethical and moral uprightness and fair dealing" when acting as a businessman or when acting as a lawyer and is subject to disciplinary action if he fails to maintain those standards in either capacity. . . . Canon 37 expressly provides that "if a lawyer is accused by his client, he is not precluded from disclosing the truth in respect to the accusation". Here the firm of Sullivan & Cromwell is being accused of fraud by plaintiff purporting to derive his cause of action from its former client Blue Ridge Corporation. The firm is entitled to use all the knowledge at its disposal to protect itself against such accusations. The accusations relieve the defendant senior partner of Sullivan & Cromwell, and Sullivan & Cromwell themselves, from any duty not to disclose or to use such confidences, if any, as may have been reposed in them in the course of the transactions under attack.

Their present position, while it may be adverse to the present interests of the former client or its successor, is not adverse to or inconsistent with the advice which they previously gave to the corporation. To defend themselves and their senior partner it is necessary and proper for Sullivan & Cromwell to do all they legitimately can to affirm the transactions upon which they are accused of fraud, and to supply all the ammunition which they have whether it came to them in confidence or not.

Thus, Sullivan & Cromwell have been relieved from their professional obligation against non-disclosure of confidences by the accusations made against them by the plaintiff which have for all practical purposes been adopted by Ridge Realization Corporation as successor to their former client, Blue Ridge. By the same token they are free from the obligation not to represent interests adversely affecting their former client in a matter in which confidence has been reposed.

While neither Canons 6 nor 37 specifically deal with representation of such interests under such circumstances, it seems to me that any bar to representation is removed when the lawyer is freed from the obligation to preserve the former client's secrets and confidences inviolate.[21] To hold otherwise would unnecessarily and unfairly restrict the directors and the firm of Sullivan & Cromwell itself from access to the legal talent most familiar with the facts of the case.

[The court went on to point out the unfairness of disqualifying counsel 22 years after the litigation began. It denied the motion.]

COMMENT

(1) The Dulles in the caption of the above case is John Foster, partner of Sullivan & Cromwell from 1920 to 1949. He was Secretary of State from 1953 to his death in 1959. He was an advisor at both the Versailles Conference in 1919 and the San Francisco U.N. Conference in 1945.

(2) The Canons cited in Marco v. Dulles have been replaced. See Model Rules 1.7, 1.9 (DR 5–105, 4–101).[22]

QUESTIONS

(1) Consider first the requirement for a demand on the directors and its purposes. What alternatives do directors have in responding to such a demand? When ought such a demand to be excused? If it is a question of being sure that a disinterested judgment as to commencing suit has been made, what standards should be applied? When should the court assume or find that the wrongdoers are so positioned as to affect the directors' reaction? Suppose that the accused directors are a minority but are old friends and colleagues of the unaffected majority?

(2) Is it possible to differentiate between the substantive and procedural aspects of the demand on shareholders requirement? For example, can one say that the shareholders may decide not to sue on a cause of action even though they could not ratify it? Under what circumstances might a court allow such a decision by the shareholders to be effective? Ought the disinterestedness of the shareholders to be decisive? Their number and distribution?

(3) Is the demand requirement like a requirement that internal remedies be exhausted? How would you evaluate the need for such a requirement in a business corporation as compared with a church or a labor union?

21. The preamble of the Canons of Professional Ethics states:

"No code or set of rules can be framed, which will particularize all the duties of the lawyer in the varying phases of litigation or in all the relations of professional life".

22. Compare with DR 1.13 the views about corporate entity as a solvent of these problems expressed in Garner v. Wolfinbarger, p. 279, supra.

(4) Is it possible that a special litigation committee might decide to sue? Recommend that the corporation bring a suit? What pressures would bear on the parties involved with the SLC if an associate of the independent law firm hired to advise the SLC turned up a "smoking gun" among the documents?

(5) When can, according to Marco v. Dulles, a lawyer for the corporation represent defendants in a derivative suit? Can ex-counsel for a corporation properly represent a complaining shareholder? Can corporate counsel who is a substantial stockholder in a corporation become the plaintiff in a derivative action? Are these questions affected by the lawyer's formerly having been a director of the company—or by the position which the lawyer took on the issues now in suit while such action was being passed on by the board? Does the case suggest that it is useful for a law firm to have a member on a client's board or the reverse? Does the Rule 1.13 (EC 5–18) principle of "allegiance to the entity" give useful guidance to the lawyer? Suppose that a group contests management's decision to dissolve the entity,—can the corporation's present or former counsel represent them?

---

4. Settlements

As appears from the quotations that introduced this chapter, one of the primary motivations for the derivative litigation of a certain type of plaintiff was the hope of obtaining a settlement on a basis that would reward the champion personally, but on the other hand, would not cost the defendants the full amount needed to give the corporation back everything of which it had been deprived. The statistics in the Wood Report indicated that a very high proportion of the derivative suits initiated were settled. Under the rules then prevailing such action could be taken privately between the parties without judicial or public intervention or even notification. The present Rule 23.1 contains requirements as to the termination of derivative actions which are designed to forestall these abuses. As the following case indicates, the presence of the Rule does not mean an end to all these problems. Note that there is still a possibility of settling a dispute *before* a complaint is filed. Such a settlement may be not unlawful (depending on rules as to self dealing, etc.) but cannot have the *res judicata* effect of a court-approved decree.

ALLEGHANY CORPORATION v. KIRBY

United States Court of Appeals, Second Circuit, 1964.
333 F.2d 327, reaffirmed after rehearing en banc, 340 F.2d 311 (1965).

Certiorari dismissed 384 U.S. 28, 86 S.Ct. 1250, 16 L.Ed.2d 335 (1966).

Rehearing denied 384 U.S. 967, 86 S.Ct. 1583, 16 L.Ed.2d 680 (1966).

[After control of Alleghany passed from the failing hands of the Van Sweringens in 1935, its affairs continued to involve disputation.

By 1949 its affairs were under the control of Robert Young and Allen Kirby (you will recall that Young used Alleghany as a vehicle for capturing control of the New York Central in one of the most famous— and expensive—proxy fights of history, see p. 433 supra). In 1949 these men arranged a transaction in which they traded to Alleghany some preferred stock of Alleghany owned by them in exchange for 48,000 shares of Investors Diversified Services, Inc. (IDS) owned by Alleghany. The exchange price was $8.1453 per share of IDS. This was what the shares had cost Alleghany in the spring of 1949. There was no real market for IDS shares but some quotations at $5.50 and later at $9.75. The shareholders of Alleghany ratified this transaction on May 3, 1950. They were advised of the cost and "market" figures and of the 1949 earnings—but not on a per share basis. By 1954 IDS stock was selling at $200 per share. "Champions on behalf of Alleghany did not long remain on the sidelines." Ten separate New York state suits were consolidated (the Zenn suit), and the firm of Pomerantz, Levy and Haudek was designated as counsel in the New York and federal courts. After various maneuvers a settlement was proposed in the New York courts. Objections were filed and hearings were held before a referee— 18 witnesses were called and 480 exhibits introduced. Meanwhile settlement hearings were held in the federal court in the so-called Breswick case. As a result the settlement offer rose to $1,000,000 in cash and then to $3,000,000 (of which Kirby was to pay $1,100,000). The settlement also involved the cancellation of another transaction whereby the Murchison brothers acquired control over IDS by giving Alleghany non-voting IDS stock in return for voting stock. Both federal and state courts approved in late 1959.

The present suit was brought in the federal district court to set aside the settlement as against Kirby alone. Young had committed suicide in 1958. It was started as a derivative suit by the Murchison brothers and became a simple corporation action when, by a proxy fight, they succeeded in displacing Kirby. It alleged (1) collusion in the settlement and (2) failure by Kirby to produce before the referee certain documents relevant to evaluation of Kirby's liability. The district court found against Alleghany on both grounds. Alleghany appealed on the second. The document chiefly involved was Exhibit 365. This consisted of a letter to Young from Purcell, Alleghany's deputy at IDS, dated July 27, 1954, i.e., during the settlement discussions. With it he enclosed various schedules. He suggested that Young note that one projection, probably completed in January 1950, had projected 1950 IDS income before taxes and non-recurring transactions at $5,992,168 ($20 per share) which figure in fact turned out to be $8,600,444. He added that "[T]his may not be too helpful as Income from Operations in 1949 was only $1,515,401." This document had not been produced at the state court hearings even though Pomerantz had demanded all IDS forecasts during 1949 and the first six months of 1950. The majority opinion by JUDGE MOORE, after a recital of the facts, went on as follows:]

The theory behind allowing a stockholder to bring a derivative stockholders' action rests upon the belief that wrongdoing directors will not voluntarily sue themselves or willingly admit their wrongful acts; hence, the right to bring a suit on behalf of the corporation is given to a stockholder. Here there were ten such suits. At this stage, if the defendant directors were fiduciaries, they certainly were not considered as such by the stockholder plaintiffs. They were under attack and entitled to defend themselves by all legal means including the right to require the plaintiffs to prove the charges made. They were, of course, under a duty to respond to all subpoenas, upon proper demand to produce all records in their possession, and to testify if called as witnesses. In the Zenn suit Kirby, although named as a defendant had not been served. He had not been subpoenaed or served with a notice to produce records in the suit itself or in the proceeding before the Referee. Nor did he testify before the Referee. Control of Alleghany's interests so far as the 1950 IDS stock exchange was concerned was in the hands of competent counsel in the derivative suits on behalf of Alleghany who had available to them all the procedural processes designed for effective pre-trial preparation. Kirby and his co-defendants were in no position to force a settlement upon the Zenn plaintiffs. These plaintiffs could have insisted upon a trial. Had they prevailed, the damages according to the theory adopted by the court could have ranged from modest amounts to astronomical figures. But even fraud cases can often be settled. A settlement is the price of peace. There is no prerequisite to the settlement of a fraud case that the defendant must come forward and confess to all his wrongful acts in connection with the subject matter of the suit. Usually such settlements are accompanied by vigorous denials of any fraud whatsoever. Yet the entire thrust of appellant's argument on this point is, in effect, directed to a proposition that Kirby was under some affirmative duty to come forward voluntarily with facts and documents possibly disclosed for the first time in this suit and of which he may or may not have had knowledge.

There can be no question that the exchange transaction perpetrated by Kirby, Young and Purcell violated fundamental legal principles against self-dealing. If the purchase of IDS was thought to be advantageous for Alleghany over a period of years, there was no justifiable reason for these officers to take this advantage away from the corporation to which they owed fiduciary duties. Nor can there be any question that the proxy statement on the basis of which stockholder ratification was sought was misleading, both in its statements and particularly in its omissions. Thus, the illegality of the exchange, the deception practiced upon the stockholders, the falsity of the Kirby statement as to the date of the exercise of the exchange offer, knowledge, either actual or imputed, of the very substantial increase in IDS earnings, the actual history of the earnings and market price of IDS stock over the period from 1950 to 1955, all these facts were available to the Zenn plaintiffs and were the basis of the charges in the stockholders' complaint. To counsel who now represent Alleghany these are "shocking facts," but they probably were equally shocking to the counsel who then were responsible for Alleghany's welfare. Alleghany could have submitted these facts to the court for determination on the merits. Through its representatives, it elected to settle. The requirement that settlements of derivative suits be upon notice to all stockholders and be subject to court scrutiny and approval was a further protection. If the settlement were approved over stockholder objection, as here, such stockholder had a right to appeal to the Appellate Division of the Supreme Court and under certain circumstances to the New York Court of Appeals. The objecting stockholder here did not exercise such rights. Having failed to pursue its remedy along normal channels, Alleghany by this action sought to have a federal district court act, in effect, in an appellate capacity to review the decisions of the Referee and the New York Supreme Court. It does this upon its theory that it has discovered certain documents which, if produced before the Referee and Supreme Court would have induced them to have disapproved the settlement.

The wrongful conduct of Kirby and his associates formed the entire basis for the Zenn suits. The Referee and the counsel for the complaining stockholders were not kept in ignorance of the facts. If their searches, aided by pre-trial discovery, did not uncover certain documents, if their inquiries fall short of obtaining the documents now brought forth by Alleghany's present counsel, or if in their judgment various documents were not introduced into evidence, these circumstances do not justify the setting aside of a settlement satisfactory to those in charge of the suit in behalf of Alleghany. Particularly is this true in the light of the bitter attack upon the settlement by the objecting stockholder. Were every settlement which had been carefully examined and judicially approved to be vacated at the behest of some subsequent corporate champion who brings forth certain documents which he claims might have so influenced the court that the settlement might not have been approved, there would be no finality to any litigation whether by settlement or by judgment.

By *a fortiori* analogy, the evidence said to have been "non-disclosed" or concealed should at least be of the character required for a new trial, namely, would it "probably have produced a different result." Helene Curtis Inds. v. Sales Affiliates, 131 F.Supp. 119, 120, aff'd 233 F.2d 148 (2d Cir.), cert. denied, 352 U.S. 879, 77 S.Ct. 101, 1 L.Ed.2d 80 (1956). So much stronger should be the evidence of fraud where a collateral attack is being made in a federal court on a state court judgment which the parties thereto did not even challenge by resorting to state appellate proceedings. Examination of the "non-disclosed" documents leads to the conclusion, also reached by the district court, that although the documents would have been admissible had they been offered before the Referee, they do not form a basis for "collaterally attacking a judgment rendered after trial or a release given pursuant to the judgment." 218 F.Supp. at 186. At most they would have been but cumulative evidence upon the basic issue of Kirby's fraud in acquiring IDS stock at a grossly inadequate price. But this fraud gave rise to the stockholders' suit and for this fraud he paid the settlement price. It is this price with which Alleghany's present counsel is dissatisfied. However, as long as there are lawyers there will be expressions of honest belief that better settlements could have been obtained had subsequent counsel been in charge initially.

Alleghany makes much of our decision in United States v. Consolidated Laundries Corp., 291 F.2d 563 (2d Cir.1961), as supporting its argument that it was not for the trial judge here to speculate concerning the effect which the "non-disclosed" documents might have had on the Referee or the Court which confirmed the report. The situation in Consolidated Laundries was quite different. Had the documents there been made available to counsel for the defense upon cross-examination, the testimony of the Government's principal witness might have been so discredited or altered that the very basis for the court's factual determinations might have been shaken and changed. Here, however, the "non-disclosed" documents merely supply additional evidence that Kirby knew or should have known that the value of the stock he was acquiring was substantially greater than the price paid. The documents would undoubtedly have given the plaintiffs in Zenn greater fire power to train upon the enemy but judging by the plaintiffs' and objectant's briefs a rather substantial barrage was laid down. Alleghany's real dissatisfaction must be based upon the Referee's and Supreme Court's decisions. There was certainly enough evidence presented to justify a rejection of the proposed settlement. Yet the stockholders suing on behalf of Alleghany, represented as they were by able counsel, chose settlement. Whatever our thoughts may be as to the merits of the derivative suits and the wisdom of the settlement, these issues are not before us.

Alleghany advances as a legal proposition that Kirby was under an affirmative duty to present facts which might aid his adversaries in establishing his liability. No authority is cited for this proposition which would require a defendant accused of fraud to make an investigation of the files of the companies involved and to tender voluntarily all relevant documents there discovered. Even then such a defendant would be in peril of having the settlement vacated if in the future other letters or documents were discovered. No support for this legal theory comes from Alleghany's citation of cases establishing the duty of self-dealing directors to make full and frank disclosure. For this failure the Zenn and Breswick suits were brought. On the merits Kirby and Young may well have obtained substantial financial benefits for themselves by wrongful self-dealing. But the *bona fides* of the 1950 stock exchange were not the issue for determination by the district court here; the issue was whether there was a sufficient basis for a federal court to nullify a settlement in a case involving fraud which had been judicially approved in the state court. . . .

Tempting though it be to retry the settlement proceeding in the New York Supreme Court and, possibly with the subconscious advantages of hindsight, to reach different conclusions and draw different inferences from those of the Referee and court therein, this is not our appellate function. The district court had to resolve the issue before it, namely, whether to vacate the State court judgment approving the settlement because of Kirby's alleged failure to produce certain documents. Essential to such resolution were such fact findings as Kirby's possession and control of the documents, his knowledge of their contents and his suppression thereof. Upon the trial, the counsel representing Alleghany had full opportunity to examine and cross-examine the principal alleged culprit, Kirby, Pomerantz (counsel for the stockholders in the Zenn suits), Graubard (counsel who so vigorously opposed the settlement), Purcell, Shipman, the various attorneys who were instrumental in bringing it to a conclusion in December, 1959, and other witnesses. After hearing these witnesses, the court found "that plaintiff has failed to establish that defendant Kirby committed a fraud upon the State court or its Referee in failing to produce documents at the hearings before the Referee which were not called for at the hearings and most of which were not in his possession but were in the possession of IDS." 218 F.Supp. at 186. In the light of the concession by plaintiff's counsel that he could not tie the financial projections sought to be introduced to Kirby's personal knowledge, the district court's refusal to speculate or infer that Kirby must have seen them cannot be characterized as "clearly erroneous." In view of this factual finding, it is unnecessary to consider the district court's alternative conclusion that plaintiff cannot collaterally attack the settlement in the State Court because "The conduct of Kirby, if fraudulent, was not extrinsic fraud as defined by New York law."

Affirmed.

FRIENDLY, CIRCUIT JUDGE (dissenting):

I can perceive no principle that would eliminate or even lessen the fiduciary obligations of directors who wish to settle a derivative action wherein they are charged with self-dealing. At least I cannot when, as here, they remain in control of the corporation, its officers, and its files relevant to the merits of the claim and consequently to the providence of the settlement. When they seek to extinguish the corporation's claim, they are dealing with the entity whose interests have been entrusted to them just as much as in the earlier transaction; I see no reason why their obligation of fair dealing and full disclosure to a court passing on the settlement should be a whit less than their previous duty to disinterested co-directors and to stockholders.

I agree nevertheless that a director thus sued is not bound actively to ferret out information that will promote the case against him or show the improvidence of a settlement to which he has persuaded a stockholder's lawyer to agree; and that insofar as the plaintiff's case here hinged upon establishing personal dereliction by Kirby with respect to the settlement hearings, this was not made out. But although the trial was largely conducted on one or the other of these theories, the complaint did not so limit the plaintiff, and on at least one occasion its counsel articulated another course which, in my view, it was entitled to pursue and which might well lead it to victory.

In examining Purcell and seeking to obtain admission of the evidence discussed below, counsel argued that "if Mr. Kirby entrusts the responsibility to some extent of his being a director of Alleghany, if he entrusts some of that responsibility to Mr. Young, then Mr. Kirby cannot avoid accepting the consequences of whatever Mr. Young may have done . . . .." When one of a group of fiduciaries accused of illegal self-dealing conceals from a court facts which pertain to the liability of his associates as well as himself, a settlement so procured is voidable as to all. A partner for whose benefit the facts were concealed can no more preserve a settlement thus obtained than the one who was on the front line. If, as the evidence shows, Young, Kirby and Purcell conspired to make an unlawful appropriation of Alleghany's investment in IDS Class A stock, which was then challenged by suit, they remained bound to the end. [JUDGE FRIENDLY then reviewed the facts relating to the Purcell–Young letter and enclosures at some length. He concluded:] As proponents of a transaction whereby they would purchase from Alleghany its cause of action against them, Young and Purcell had a duty to see that the Referee had that evidence; court approval of an advantageous bargain granted in ignorance of documents, known to Young and Purcell, showing that they had this optimistic projection in early 1950, no more finally settles the liability of themselves and Kirby than did the stockholders' approval of the underlying bargain in 1950, similarly procured without disclosure of the projection. Cf. ALI, Restatement of Torts 2d (Tent.Draft No. 10), § 551(2)(a).

Since in such complicated litigation some relevant documents will inevitably be overlooked, the undesirability of reopening judgments demands that judicial approval be final unless the undisclosed evidence is of real importance and not merely cumulative of other evidence that was received. Kirby argues, and my brothers seem to agree, that the whole matter of the complete IDS projection of 1950 earnings is a tempest in a teapot because the record before the Referee did contain a partial projection of which Young and Kirby admitted knowledge. . . .

Graubard surely did the best he could with what he had, and one may indeed wonder whether anything short of proof that Young and Kirby had received a gold plated guarantee of IDS' 1950 earnings would have swayed the Referee, who went out of his way to compliment them on their presentation to the Alleghany stockholders, as to which more below, and concluded that a trial court would give judgment in their favor. But there was an enormous difference between a paragraph in a general letter, commenting on the prospects of one department of IDS, a paragraph not even noted in the Referee's report, and proof that shortly before making the settlement, Young and Purcell had been reminded of the existence of an official company forecast in early 1950, covering all departments, which negated any fear that the anticipated quadrupling of income from mortgage operations would be cancelled out and showed instead that this would be enhanced by other divisions. There was at least a much greater chance that such evidence, developed as Graubard would have developed it, might have made some impression upon the Referee (who, because of the federal court litigations, did not file his report, dealing with a variety of claims of malfeasance, for three years after the hearings), or, if it did not, upon the Supreme Court justice who had appointed him, or, if it did not, that such evidence might have encouraged the objectors to go on to the Appellate Division, or that it might have led Judge Dimock to refuse to lift the federal court injunction that had blocked the settlement.

I cannot agree that when judicial approval of a settlement by a fiduciary has been procured by culpable nondisclosure of evidence by a confederate, the test of materiality applicable on motions for a new trial on the ground of newly discovered evidence has any relevance; indeed, in the very decision cited by the majority, Judge Kaufman carefully distinguished between newly discovered evidence *simpliciter* and the recantation of a witness, 131 F.Supp. at 120. The test should be more nearly that applied by us in United States v. Consolidated Laundries, supra, 291 F.2d 563, or by the New York courts in Matter of Lautz, 128 Misc. 710, 220 N.Y.S. 782 (Surr.Ct., Erie Co. 1927); and Boston & Maine R. R. v. Delaware & Hudson Co., 238 App.Div. 191, 196, 264 N.Y.S. 470, 477 (3d Dept. 1933)—whether there is any fair basis for thinking the undisclosed evidence *might have changed* the result. Here the evidence could well have done that.

I say this because, with full appreciation of the dangers of reliance on hindsight, Graubard's objections were so strong that almost anything more might have sufficed to tip the scales. Although my brothers seem to concede the inequity of the exchange transaction, this scarcely conveys the picture.

[JUDGE FRIENDLY then reviewed the facts bearing on the fairness of the exchange as viewed at the Alleghany directors' meeting in December 1949 and as presented to the shareholders by the proxy materials in May, 1950. He concluded:]

My brothers rightly shrink from a precedent that would make every settlement of a stockholder's suit the prelude to another in which the proceedings for approval of the settlement would be reexamined at great expense and effort. I too would regret that although, for reasons sketched below, it might be better if more such suits were tried and fewer settled so long as the procedures with respect to the approval of settlements remain as unsatisfactory as they are. But we would make no such precedent by a reversal in this case. Here we have an unusual situation. After litigation had begun, two of the principal architects and beneficiaries of the self-dealing and the subsequent settlement had their attention dramatically called to the existence of a report, clearly known to one of them and arguably to the other before the exchange, and nevertheless allowed the Referee to proceed to approval, knowing, on the most innocent construction, that this report, although eagerly sought by the objector's counsel, had not been found by him. Such cases will hopefully be rare; the instances in which the corporation or a large stockholder will seek to prosecute them will be rarer still; and the chances of success and consequent reward will not be such as to tempt the typical stockholder plaintiff save in occasional cases where it is as well to have him tempted.

I cannot at all agree with the implication in my brother Moore's opinion that standard procedures for the approval of settlements afford sufficient safeguards in the "big" case, or that they did in this one. The plaintiff stockholders or, more realistically, their attorneys have every incentive to accept a settlement that runs into high six figures or more regardless of how strong the claims for much larger amounts may be. The percentage allowance in stockholders' actions is "reduced as the amount of recovery passes the million dollar mark," 2 Hornstein, Corporation Law and Practice 253 (1959), see also Hornstein, Legal Therapeutics: The "Salvage" Factor in Counsel Fee Awards, 69 Harv.L.Rev. 658, 657–68 [sic] (1956); the income tax also plays a role; and a juicy bird in the hand is worth more than the vision of a much larger one in the bush, attainable only after years of effort not currently compensated and possibly a mirage. Once a settlement is agreed, the attorneys for the plaintiff stockholders link arms with their former adversaries to defend the joint handiwork—as is vividly shown here where the stockholders' general counsel sometimes opposed Graubard's efforts to gain information, although the settlement so vigorously defended before the Referee would have produced less than a quarter as much cash for Alleghany, $700,000, as the $3,000,000 ultimately secured through the efforts of the attorneys for the plaintiffs in the federal court litigation, unrelated to the claim here at issue, and Judge Dimock's initial refusal to lift the federal injunction. To say that "Through its representatives, it [Alleghany] elected to settle" is sheer fiction. Most of the independent Alleghany stockholders had no voice in the selection of their "representatives" or ability to evaluate the settlement these "representatives" had accepted for them. I cannot see how the attorneys proposing the settlement were any more "representative" than the attorney opposing it; the stockholders' true representative was the court, which was allowed to proceed in ignorance of vital information. Alleghany as a corporation never elected to do anything until the very end of 1959, when a directors' meeting presided over by Kirby approved the settlement. Indeed, the directors did not even provide Alleghany with independent counsel, whose supervision of the file search might have avoided the problem here presented.

This very fact, that directors accused of malfeasance have so much control over the evidence, both documentary and nondocumentary, relating to their misdeed, makes it vital for a court of equity to insist upon a high standard with respect to disclosure at settlement hearings and to subject arguments that a breach was not consequential to a most icy scrutiny. All the dynamics conduce to judicial approval of such settlements. Even when there is objection, the changes are rung on the small proportion of the stock owned by the objector whereas a curtain falls on the equally small percentage owned by the plaintiffs, who quietly annex the stock controlled by the directors and that of the inert mass. Perhaps the ultimate solution may be the appointment of government inspectors to investigate and prosecute, as is authorized in England under the Companies Act, 1948, 11 & 12 George 6, c. 38, §§ 164, 165(b)(ii), 168, 169(4), see Gower, Some Contrasts between British and American Corporation Law, 69 Harv.L.Rev. 1369, 1387–88 (1956), or, in the case of corporations trading in whose securities is subject to the Securities and Exchange Act, assignment to the SEC of an advisory role similar to that conferred by Chapter X of the Bankruptcy Act, §§ 172, 173, 222, 247. In the meanwhile, courts should enforce the most exacting standards of good faith on fiduciaries desiring to settle such serious claims of self-dealing as were here alleged. Appellant is right in reminding us of Judge Cardozo's great words, "Uncompromising rigidity has been the attitude of courts of equity when petitioned to undermine the rule of undivided loyalty by the 'disintegrating erosion' of particular exceptions." Meinhard v. Salmon, 249 N.Y. 458, 464, 164 N.E. 545, 62 A.L.R. 1 (1928). I do not believe this teaching is dead in the New York courts; and we have not hitherto demanded a state decision directly in point before enforcing that salutary principle. See Perlman v. Feldmann, 219 F.2d 173, 50 A.L.R.2d 1134 (2 Cir.), cert. denied, 349 U.S. 952, 75 S.Ct. 880, 99 L.Ed. 1277 (1955).

I would therefore reverse the judgment dismissing the complaint and, as defendants should have an opportunity to meet the evidence that was erroneously excluded, remand for further hearing. Since Kirby has regained control of Alleghany, I would instruct the judge to make provision for the continued prosecution of the action free from any control by the present directors.

[A concurring opinion by JUDGE KAUFMAN is omitted. On rehearing the Court of Appeals *en banc* affirmed by a 4–4 vote, JUDGE LUMBARD disqualifying himself because his former firm represented defendants. The Supreme Court granted, and then dismissed, a writ of certiorari.]

COMMENT

The foregoing opinion refers in several places to the law firm, Pomerantz, Levy and Haudek. This firm and successors has long been a leading representative of complaining shareholders. Its founder, Abraham L. Pomerantz (1903–1982) was the *bete noire* of corporate defendants. An article, Klaw, Abe Pomerantz is Watching You, Fortune, Feb. 1968, p. 144, described him as "a big, fast-moving friendly man who is shaped and looks rather like a giant panda. He grew up in Brooklyn, in a kosher household and his voice has a certain rabbinical resonance." His first case involved the recovery of excess compensation paid for 1929 to Charles Mitchell of the National City Bank, see p. 337 supra. He was counsel for plaintiff in many other derivative suits even though his law firm has never numbered more than a dozen lawyers and the firm's office is small and drab. Nonetheless, his earnings were estimated as over $350,000 per year on average and his fame grew to the point where even defendants hired him. On the other hand, he was for many years a socialist and was treasurer for Henry A. Wallace in the latter's 1948 campaign for president.

QUESTIONS

(1) Suppose that a derivative action is dismissed, upon payment to plaintiff of $50,000, in a state court, which is subject to no rule comparable to Rule 23.1. Can you develop a theory upon which that transaction can be attacked on general common law or equitable grounds?

(2) In the Alleghany case what is your reaction as to the critical character of the subsequently discovered document? What is it critical to—the fairness of the settlement? The fairness of the original transaction? In this connection, consider the date of the chief document. Could the document have been furnished to the shareholders consistently with Rule 14a–9 as it then stood (see p. 723 infra)?

(3) What standards are the judges using as to the level of significance to which the new evidence must rise before they will set aside the settlement? How do you respond to their comparisons with the situation that arises when the government fails to furnish evidence to a criminal defendant? Should the case have been disposed of differently if the new proceeding had been brought in the same court as that which approved the original settlement? Should the outcome have been different if the new action had been against Young rather than Kirby?

(4) Would you regard a dismissal of a derivative action because of plaintiff's failure to prosecute, refusal to respond to interrogatories or refusal to appear at a deposition as coming within the Rule 23.1 requirement that notice be given shareholders?

———

5. The Costs of Derivative Litigation

———

NOTE ON COSTS IN DERIVATIVE LITIGATION

Derivative suits tend to be expensive, involving as they do complex factual situations and elaborate legal puzzles. The same is true of their close counterparts, class actions in securities cases, some of them referred to elsewhere in this book. The following list sets forth the amounts recovered in certain cases together with the fees awarded to plaintiff's counsel—defendants' counsel fees not being available.[23]

23. These figures are from the Wood Report except for Ripley, 16 A.D.2d 260, 227 N.Y.S.2d 64 (1st Dept. 1965); Newmark v. RKO General, Inc., 332 F.Supp. 161 (S.D.N.Y.1971); Cannon, CCH Fed.Sec. L.Rep. ¶ 94,110 (S.D.N.Y.1973) (technically a class action); and Equity Funding Corp., 438 F.Supp. 1303 (C.D.Cal.1977). For compilations see Cole, Counsel Fees in Stockholders' Derivative and Class Actions—Hornstein Revisited, 6 U.Rich.L.Rev. 259 (1972); In re Warner Communications Securities Litigation, 618 F.Supp. 735, 749–50 (S.D.N.Y.1985).

	Gross Recovery	**Fees Awarded**
Litwin v. Allen (Guaranty Trust)	$ 750,000	$ 286,000
Gallin v. Nat. City Bank	1,847,943	452,500
Winkelman v. General Motors	4,500,000	795,000
Ripley v. Int'l Ry of Central Am.	16,700,000	2,105,000
Heller v. Boylan (Am. Tobacco)	1,585,000	628,000
Newmark v. RKO General	7,920,000	750,000
Cannon v. Texas Gulf Sulphur	2,800,000	580,000
Equity Funding Litigation	60,000,000	6,600,000
In re Warner Communications Securities Litigation		4,385,000

Whereas in most types of litigation the costs fall where they lie, the rules of derivative litigation are rather special. There are in essence three exceptions to the let-it-lie rule:

(1) successful counsel for plaintiff shareholder are entitled to reimbursement for costs and attorneys' fees from the corporation;

(2) defendants who successfully resist a derivative suit may be entitled to reimbursement from the corporation for the costs of their expense.

(3) a plaintiff may be required to post security for costs as a condition to maintaining a derivative action and successful defendants may be able to resort to that security for reimbursement.

The first of these rules was evolved by the courts themselves, but the second represents a combination of judicial handiwork, contractual draftsmanship and, more recently, legislation. The third is almost completely statutory. Between them they make the cost picture in derivative litigation almost wholly different from that in other actions, except that the recovery of costs by successful plaintiffs is becoming increasingly common in different types of class actions and is required in a number of important statutes such as the federal antitrust laws. The long-run trend may in fact be in the direction of the British practice of awarding costs to the prevailing party.

It is increasingly being observed that what we are dealing with here is not so much the plaintiff's attorney's fees but the attorney's fees, that what the courts need to do is find a level of fee-setting that will give attorneys an incentive to take these cases—and the right ones.[24] They in effect view plaintiff's lawyers as holding portfolios of risky investments in various derivative actions. They are thus in a better position than the stockholder of company X to invest the money (or more exactly the time) in various lawsuits knowing that enough of

---

24. Coffee, Understanding the Plaintiff's Attorney: Implications of Economic Theory for Private Enforcement of Law through Class and Derivative Actions, 86 Colum.L.Rev. 669 (1986).

them will pan out to bring them an adequate level of compensation. Thus courts begin by setting a "lodestar" figure, an amount equal to the worth of the lawyer's time aside from the riskiness of the outcome. Then there has to be added to that a risk premium for undertaking work when it is not clear that a reward will be forthcoming in any one particular case. One observes that the firms that pursue this strategy are not the firms that one regularly finds receiving large sums from clients in non-contingent litigation. They are not only different firms but they do not share many of the characteristics of corporate law firms; for one thing they tend to be much smaller.

A. Reimbursement of Plaintiff's Costs

The portion of Mills v. Electric Autolite Co. which follows details the development of the rules concerning reimbursement of plaintiffs' costs.

MILLS v. ELECTRIC AUTO–LITE CO.

Supreme Court of the United States, 1970.
396 U.S. 375, 90 S.Ct. 616, 24 L.Ed.2d 593.

[This is the same case which is set forth in part at p. 428, supra for its holding that violations of the proxy rules in soliciting votes for a merger were sufficiently causally related to the merger so that plaintiffs should have relief. The opinion by JUSTICE HARLAN goes on to say the following about attorneys' fees.]

Although the question of relief must await further proceedings in the District Court, our conclusion that petitioners have established their cause of action indicates that the Court of Appeals should have affirmed the partial summary judgment on the issue of liability. The result would have been not only that respondents, rather than petitioners, would have borne the costs of the appeal, but, we think, that petitioners would have been entitled to an interim award of litigation expenses and reasonable attorneys' fees. . . .

We agree with the position taken by petitioners, and by the United States as *amicus,* that petitioners, who have established a violation of the securities laws by their corporation and its officials, should be reimbursed by the corporation or its survivor for the costs of establishing the violation.

The absence of express statutory authorization for an award of attorneys' fees in a suit under § 14(a) does not preclude such an award in cases of this type. In a suit by stockholders to recover short-swing profits for their corporation under § 16(b) of the 1934 Act, the Court of Appeals for the Second Circuit has awarded attorneys' fees despite the lack of any provision for them in § 16(b), "on the theory that the corporation which has received the benefit of the attorney's services should pay the reasonable value thereof." Smolowe v. Delendo Corp., 136 F.2d 231, 241, 148 A.L.R. 300 (C.A.2d Cir.1943). The court held that Congress' inclusion in §§ 9(e) and 18(a) of the Act of express provisions for recovery of attorneys' fees in certain other types of suits "does not impinge the result we reach in the absence of statute, for those sections merely enforce an additional penalty against the wrongdoer."   Id. at 241.

We agree with the Second Circuit that the specific provisions in §§ 9(e) and 18(a) should not be read as denying to the courts the power to award counsel fees in suits under other sections of the Act when circumstances make such an award appropriate, any more than the express creation by those sections of private liabilities negates the possibility of an implied right of action under § 14(a).   The remedial provisions of the 1934 Act are far different from those of the Lanham Act, which have been held to preclude an award of attorneys' fees in a suit for trademark infringement.   Fleischmann Distilling Corp. v. Maier Brewing Co., 386 U.S. 714, 715, 87 S.Ct. 1404, 18 L.Ed.2d 475 (1967).   Since Congress in the Lanham Act had "meticulously detailed the remedies available to a plaintiff who proves that his valid trademark has been infringed," the Court in *Fleischmann* concluded that the express remedial provisions were intended "to mark the boundaries of the power to award monetary relief in cases arising under the Act." 386 U.S., at 721, 87 S.Ct. at 1409.   By contrast we cannot fairly infer from the Securities Exchange Act of 1934 a purpose to circumscribe the courts' power to grant appropriate remedies. . . . The Act makes no provision for private recovery for a violation of § 14(a) other than the declaration of "voidness" in § 29(b), leaving the courts with the task, faced by this Court in *Borak,* of deciding whether a private right of action should be implied.   The courts must similarly determine whether the special circumstances exist that would justify an award of attorneys' fees, including reasonable expenses of litigation other than statutory costs.

While the general American rule is that attorneys' fees are not ordinarily recoverable as costs, both the courts and Congress have developed exceptions to this rule for situations in which overriding considerations indicate the need for such a recovery.[25]   A primary judge-created exception has been to award expenses where a plaintiff has successfully maintained a suit, usually on behalf of a class, that benefits a group of others in the same manner as himself. . . .

To allow the others to obtain full benefit from the plaintiff's efforts without contributing equally to the litigation expenses would be to enrich the others unjustly at the plaintiff's expense.   This suit presents such a situation.   The dissemination of misleading proxy solicitations was a "deceit practiced on the stockholders as a group," J. I. Case Co. v. Borak, 377 U.S., at 432, 84 S.Ct., at 1560, and the expenses of petitioners' lawsuit have been incurred for the benefit of the corporation and the other shareholders.

The fact that this suit has not yet produced, and may never produce, a monetary recovery from which the fees could be paid does not preclude an award based on this rationale.   Although the earliest cases recognizing a right to reimbursement involved litigation that had produced or preserved a "common fund" for the benefit of a group, nothing in these cases indicates that the suit must actually bring

---

25. Many commentators have argued for a more thoroughgoing abandonment of the rule.   See, e.g., Ehrenzweig, Reimbursement of Counsel Fees and the Great Society, 54 Calif.L.Rev. 792 (1966); Kuenzel, The Attorney's Fee: Why Not a Cost of Litigation?   49 Iowa L.Rev. 75 (1963); McCormick, Counsel Fees and Other Expenses of Litigation as an Element of Damages, 15 Minn.L.Rev. 619 (1931); Stoebuck, Counsel Fees Included in Costs: A Logical Development, 38 Colo.L.Rev. 202 (1966); . . .

money into the court as a prerequisite to the court's power to order reimbursement of expenses. "[T]he foundation for the historic practice of granting reimbursement for the costs of litigation other than the conventional taxable costs is part of the original authority of the chancellor to do equity in a particular situation." Sprague v. Ticonic Nat'l Bank, 307 U.S. 161, 166, 59 S.Ct. 777, 780, 83 L.Ed. 1184 (1939). This Court in *Sprague* upheld the District Court's power to grant reimbursement for a plaintiff's litigation expenses even though she had sued only on her own behalf and not for a class, because her success would have a *stare decisis* effect entitling others to recover out of specific assets of the same defendant. Although those others were not parties before the Court, they could be forced to contribute to the costs of the suit by an order reimbursing the plaintiff from the defendant's assets out of which their recoveries later would have to come. The Court observed that "the absence of an avowed class suit or the creation of a fund, as it were, through *stare decisis* rather than through a decree—hardly touch the power of equity in doing justice as between a party and the beneficiaries of his litigation." Id., at 167, 59 S.Ct. at 780.

Other cases have departed further from the traditional metes and bounds of the doctrine, to permit reimbursement in cases where the litigation has conferred a substantial benefit on the members of an ascertainable class, and where the court's jurisdiction over the subject matter of the suit makes possible an award that will operate to spread the costs proportionately among them. This development has been most pronounced, in shareholders' derivative actions, where the courts increasingly have recognized that the expenses incurred by one share-holder in the vindication of a corporate right of action can be spread among all shareholders through an award against the corporation, regardless of whether an actual money recovery has been obtained in the corporation's favor. For example, awards have been sustained in suits by stockholders complaining that shares of their corporation had been issued wrongfully for an inadequate consideration. A successful suit of this type, resulting in cancellation of the shares, does not bring a fund into court or add to the assets of the corporation, but it does benefit the holders of the remaining shares by enhancing their value. Similarly, holders of voting trust certificates have been allowed reimbursement of their expenses from the corporation where they succeeded in terminating the voting trust and obtaining for all certificate holders the right to vote their shares. In these cases there was a "common fund" only in the sense that the court's jurisdiction over the corporation as nominal defendant made it possible to assess fees against all of the shareholders through an award against the corporation.

In many of these instances the benefit conferred is capable of expression in monetary terms, if only by estimating the increase in market value of the shares attributable to the successful litigation. However, an increasing number of lower courts have acknowledged that a corporation may receive a "substantial benefit" from a derivative suit, justifying an award of counsel fees, regardless of whether the benefit is pecuniary in nature. A leading case is Bosch v. Meeker Cooperative Light & Power Association, 257 Minn. 362, 101 N.W.2d 423 (1960), in which a stockholder was reimbursed for his expenses in obtaining a judicial declaration that the election of certain of the corporation's directors was invalid. The Supreme Court of Minnesota stated:

"Where an action by a stockholder results in a substantial benefit to a corporation he should recover his costs and expenses. . . . [A] substantial benefit must be something more than technical in its consequence and be one that accomplishes a result which corrects or prevents an abuse which would be prejudicial to the rights and interests of the corporation or affect the enjoyment or protection of an essential right to the stockholder's interest." Id., at 425, 427.

In many suits under § 14(a), particularly where the violation does not relate to the terms of the transaction for which proxies are solicited, it may be impossible to assign monetary value to the benefit. Nevertheless, the stress placed by Congress on the importance of fair and informed corporate suffrage leads to the conclusion that, in vindicating the statutory policy, petitioners have rendered a substantial service to the corporation and its shareholders. . . .

Whether petitioners are successful in showing a need for significant relief may be a factor in determining whether a further award should later be made. But regardless of the relief granted, private stockholders' actions of this sort "involve corporate therapeutics," and furnish a benefit to all shareholders by providing an important means of enforcement of the proxy statute. To award attorneys' fees in such a suit to a plaintiff who has succeeded in establishing a cause of action is not to saddle the unsuccessful party with the expenses but to impose them on the class that has benefited from them and that would have had to pay them had it brought the suit. . . .

Judgment of Court of Appeals vacated and case remanded to that court.

MR. JUSTICE BLACK, concurring in part and dissenting in part.

I substantially agree with Parts II and III of the Court's opinion holding that these stockholders have sufficiently proven a violation of § 14(a) of the Securities and Exchange Act of 1934 and are thus entitled to recover whatever damages they have suffered as a result of the misleading corporate statements, or perhaps to an equitable setting aside of the merger itself. I do not agree, however, to what appears to be the holding in Part IV that stockholders who hire lawyers to prosecute their claims in such a case can recover attorneys' fees in the absence of a valid contractual agreement so providing or an explicit statute creating such a right of recovery. The courts are interpreters, not creators, of legal rights to recover and if there is a need for recovery of attorneys' fees to effectuate the policies of the Act here involved, that need should in my judgment be met by Congress, not by this Court.

COMMENT

Consider the following comments on Mills from a case granting attorney's fees to a successful party in a civil rights case.[26]

> This Court-created remedy was justified as necessary to further the "corporate therapeutics" called for in Congress' strong policy favoring fair and informed corporate suffrage. The Court reasoned that the situation was not too different from the typical derivative action, where it is appropriate for the corporation to pay the attorney's

26. Lee v. Southern Home Sites Corp., 444 F.2d 143, 145 (5th Cir.1971).

fees because the corporation receives a benefit from the suit. But the benefit that the Court focused on is conferred on all shareholders in the country, and therefore established derivative action considerations do not seem to apply to the situation. Therefore the Court's decision is better understood as resting heavily on its acknowledgment of "overriding considerations," that private suits are necessary to effectuate congressional policy and that awards of attorney's fees are necessary to encourage private litigants to initiate such suits.

The generalizing implications that seemed to radiate from Mills were sharply cut back by Alyeska Pipeline Service Co. v. Wilderness Society, 421 U.S. 240, 95 S.Ct. 1612, 44 L.Ed.2d 141 (1975), which denied a general right to reimbursement of counsel fees in the absence of statute.[27] The Alyeska case in turn had an impact on the second round of the Mills litigation. The court of appeals, after remand and a trial below, determined that the merger was fair and had not damaged the minority shareholders. It was then faced with the question of counsel fees. It ruled that the Supreme Court had mandated recovery of "all fees and expenses related to the establishment of a violation of the federal securities laws" but that no further fees were recoverable since the efforts of counsel beyond that point had not produced a common benefit.[28]

QUESTIONS

(1) Do you agree with the Mills conclusion that it was appropriate to grant attorneys' fees in a cause of action under the Securities and Exchange Act, even in the face of its provisions as to attorneys' fees? Does this do more—or less—violence to the statutory structure than the creation of the substantive cause of action itself?

(2) How was the district court in Mills to go about obeying the mandate to fix a fee? How can one measure the "value" to the corporation or the stockholders of having the merger set aside? Would a court be able to apply such a technique to a suit to determine who was properly elected to the board of directors? To determine whether an amendment to the articles of incorporation was valid? To determine as in the Medical Committee case, p. 409 supra, whether the management's refusal to circulate a shareholder proposition was legal? Suppose the corporation's retained earnings turn out to be roughly equivalent to the time charges of counsel?

(3) Is the emphasis in the cases on the size of recovery justifiable? Even if the percentages applied (25–35%) produce fees on the order of $1 million or more? Should limitations along the lines of Rogers v. Hill, p. 333 supra, be imposed? Recall Judge Friendly's comments on the way in which contingent fee structures affect lawyer-client relations in settlement negotiations, p. 508 supra. Could the rules be changed to shift that relationship? Should they?

(4) Are the rules about the costs of litigation in harmony with the rules, explored at p. 433 supra, about the reimbursement of the costs of proxy fights? If there is a discrepancy does it have the effect of shifting dissident shareholders' efforts from one route to the other?

27. See also 42 U.S.C.A. § 1988 authorizing reimbursement in civil rights and certain other cases.

28. 552 F.2d 1239 (7th Cir.1977). Portions of that case dealing with "fairness" appear at p. 731 below.

B. Security for Costs Legislation

COHEN v. BENEFICIAL INDUSTRIAL LOAN CORP.

Supreme Court of the United States, 1949.
337 U.S. 541, 69 S.Ct. 1221, 93 L.Ed. 1528.

[This was a stockholder's derivative action brought in the District Court in New Jersey on the basis of diversity, in the right of Beneficial Industrial Loan Corp., a Delaware corporation doing business in New Jersey. The complaint alleged that since 1929 certain of Beneficial's managers and directors had conspired to divert its assets in excess of $100,000,000. Plaintiff, one of its 16,000 stockholders, owned 100 of its more than 2,000,000 shares; together with an intervenor with 150 shares, they held 0.0125% of the stock with a market value of $9000. During the pendency of the action New Jersey passed a statute much like New York's providing for motions to require the giving of security for costs if the plaintiffs held less than 5%, and less than $50,000, market value, of the corporation stock. The corporate defendant moved for security under that statute. The district court denied the motion, the Court of Appeals reversed and the Supreme Court granted certiorari.

The Supreme Court's opinion by JUSTICE JACKSON first disposed of the question of appealability. It then went on to deal with the constitutionality of the statute and its application in the federal courts.]

Federal Constitutional questions we must consider, because a federal court would not give effect, in either a diversity or nondiversity case, to a state statute that violates the Constitution of the United States.

The background of stockholder litigation with which this statute deals requires no more than general notice. As business enterprise increasingly sought the advantages of incorporation, management became vested with almost uncontrolled discretion in handling other people's money. The vast aggregate of funds committed to corporate control came to be drawn to a considerable extent from numerous and scattered holders of small interests. The director was not subject to an effective accountability. That created strong temptation for managers to profit personally at expense of their trust. The business code became all too tolerant of such practices. Corporate laws were lax and were not self-enforcing, and stockholders, in face of gravest abuses, were singularly impotent in obtaining redress of abuses of trust.

Equity came to the relief of the stockholder, who had no standing to bring civil action at law against faithless directors and managers. Equity, however, allowed him to step into the corporation's shoes and to seek in its right the restitution he could not demand in his own. It required him first to demand that the corporation vindicate its own rights but when, as was usual, those who perpetrated the wrongs also were able to obstruct any remedy, equity would hear and adjudge the corporation's cause through its stockholder with the corporation as a defendant, albeit a rather nominal one. This remedy born of stockholder helplessness was long the chief regulator of corporate management and has afforded no small incentive to avoid at least grosser forms of betrayal of stockholders' interests. It is argued, and not without reason, that without it there would be little practical check on such abuses.

Unfortunately, the remedy itself provided opportunity for abuse which was not neglected. Suits sometimes were brought not to redress real wrongs, but to realize upon their nuisance value. They were bought off by secret settlements in which any wrongs to the general body of share owners were compounded by the suing stockholder, who was mollified by payments from corporate assets. These litigations were aptly characterized in professional slang as "strike suits." And it was said that these suits were more commonly brought by small and irresponsible than by large stockholders, because the former put less to risk and a small interest was more often within the capacity and readiness of management to compromise than a large one.

We need not determine the measure of these abuses or the evils they produced on the one hand or prevented and redressed on the other. The Legislature of New Jersey, like that of other states, considered them sufficient to warrant some remedial measures.

The very nature of the stockholder's derivative action makes it one in the regulation of which the legislature of a state has wide powers. Whatever theory one may hold as to the nature of the corporate entity, it remains a wholly artificial creation whose internal relations between management and stockholders are dependent upon state law and may be subject to most complete and penetrating regulation either by public authority or by some form of stockholder action. Directors and managers, if not technically trustees, occupy positions of a fiduciary nature, and nothing in the Federal Constitution prohibits a state from imposing on them the strictest measure of responsibility, liability and accountability, either as a condition of assuming office or as a consequence of holding it.

Likewise, a stockholder who brings suit on a cause of action derived from the corporation assumes a position, not technically as a trustee perhaps, but one of a fiduciary character. He sues, not for himself alone, but as representative of a class comprising all who are similarly situated. The interests of all in the redress of the wrongs are taken into his hands, dependent upon his diligence, wisdom and integrity. And while the stockholders have chosen the corporate director or manager, they have no such election as to a plaintiff who steps forward to represent them. He is a self-chosen representative and a volunteer champion. The Federal Constitution does not oblige the State to place its litigating and adjudicating processes at the disposal of such a representative, at least without imposing standards of responsibility, liability and accountability which it considers will protect the interests he elects himself to represent. It is not without significance that this Court has found it necessary long ago in the Equity Rules and now in the Federal Rules of Civil Procedure to impose procedural regulations of the class action not applicable to any other. We conclude that the state has plenary power over this type of litigation.

In considering specific objections to the way in which the State has exercised its power in this particular statute, it should be unnecessary to say that we are concerned only with objections which go to constitutionality. The wisdom and the policy of this and similar statutes are involved in controversies amply debated in legal literature but not for us to judge, and, hence not for us to remark upon. The Federal Constitution does not invalidate state legislation because it fails to embody the highest wisdom or provide the best conceivable remedies. Nor can legislation be set aside by courts because of the fact, if it be such, that it has been sponsored and promoted by those who advantage from it. In dealing with such difficult and controversial subjects, only experience will verify or disclose weaknesses and defects of any policy and teach lessons which may be applied by amendment. Within the area of constitutionality, the states should not be restrained from devising experiments, even those we might think dubious, in the effort to preserve the maximum good which equity sought in creating the derivative stockholder's action and at the same time to eliminate as much as possible its defects and evils.

It is said that this statute transgresses the Due Process Clause, Amend. 14, by being "arbitrary, capricious and unreasonable;" the Equal Protection Clause by singling out small stockholders to burden most heavily; that it violates the Contract Clause, art. 1, § 10, cl. 1, and that its application to pending litigation renders it unconstitutionally retroactive.

The contention that this statute violates the Contract Clause of the Constitution is one in which we see not the slightest merit. Plaintiff's suit is entertained by equity largely because he had no contract rights on which to base an action at law, and hence none which is impaired by this legislation.

In considering whether the statute offends the Due Process Clause we can judge it only by its own terms, for it has had no interpretation or application as yet. It imposes liability and requires security for "the *reasonable* expenses, including counsel fees which may be incurred" (emphasis supplied) by the corporation and by other parties defendant. The amount of security is subject to increase if the progress of the litigation reveals that it is inadequate or to decrease if it is proved to be excessive. A state may set the terms on which it will permit litigations in its courts. No type of litigation is more susceptible of regulation than that of a fiduciary nature. And it cannot seriously be said that a state makes such *unreasonable* use of its power as to violate the Constitution when it provides liability and security for payment of *reasonable* expenses if a litigation of this character is adjudged to be unsustainable. It is urged that such a requirement will foreclose resort by most stockholders to the only available judicial remedy for the protection of their rights. Of course, to require security for the payment of any kind of costs or the necessity for bearing any kind of expense of litigation has a deterring effect. But we deal with power, not wisdom; and we think, notwithstanding this tendency, it is within the power of a state to close its courts to this type of litigation if the condition of reasonable security is not met.

The contention that the statute denies equal protection of the laws is based upon the fact that it enables a stockholder who owns 5% of a corporation's outstanding shares, or $50,000 in market value, to proceed without either security or liability and imposes both upon those who elect to proceed with a smaller interest. We do not think the state is forbidden to use the amount of one's financial interest, which measures his individual injury from the misconduct to be redressed, as some measure of the good faith and responsibility of one who seeks at his own election to act as custodian of the interests of all stockholders, and as an indication that he volunteers for the large burdens of the litigation from a real sense of grievance and is not putting forward a claim to capitalize personally on its harassment value. These may not be the best ways of precluding "strike lawsuits," but we are unable to say that a classification for these purposes, based upon the percentage or market value of the stock alleged to be injured by the wrongs, is an unconstitutional one. Where any classification is based on a percentage or an amount, it is necessarily somewhat arbitrary. It is difficult to say of many lines drawn by legislation that they give those just above and those just below the line a perfectly equal protection. A taxpayer with $10,000.01 of income does not think it is equality to tax him at a different rate than one who has $9,999.99, or to require returns from one just above and not from one just below a certain figure. It is difficult to say that a stockholder who has 49.99% of a company's stock should be unable to elect any representative to its Board of Directors while one who owns 50.01% may name the entire Board. If there is power, as we think there is, to draw a line based on considerations of proportion or amount, it is a rare case, of which this is not one, that a constitutional objection may be made to the particular point which the legislature has chosen.

The contention also is made that the provision which applies this statute to actions pending upon its enactment, in which no final judgment has been entered, renders it void under the Due Process Clause for retroactivity. While by its terms the statute applies to pending cases, it does not provide the manner of application; nor do the New Jersey courts appear to have settled what its effect is to be. Its terms do not appear to require an interpretation that it creates new liability against the plaintiff for expenses incurred by the defense previous to its enactment. The statute would admit of a construction that plaintiff's liability begins only from the time when the Act was passed or perhaps when the corporation's application for security is granted and that security for expenses and counsel fees which "may be incurred" does not include those which have been incurred before one or the other of these periods. We would not, for the purpose of considering constitutionality, construe the statute in absence of a state decision to impose liability for events before its enactment. On this basis its alleged retroactivity amounts only to a stay of further proceedings unless and until security is furnished for expense incurred in the future, and does not extend either to destruction of an existing cause of action or to creation of a new liability for past events. The mere fact that a statute applies to a civil action retrospectively does not render it unconstitutional. . . . We do not find in the bare statute any such retroactive effect as renders it unconstitutional under the Due Process Clause, and of course we express no opinion as to the effect of an application other than we have indicated.

It is also contended that this statute may not be applied in this case because the cause of action derives from a Delaware corporation and hence Delaware law governs it. But it is the plaintiff who has brought the case in New Jersey. The trial will very likely involve questions of conflict of laws as to which the law of New Jersey will apply, Klaxon Co. v. Stentor Electric Mfg. Co., 313 U.S. 487, 61 S.Ct. 1020, 85 L.Ed. 1477; Griffin v. McCoach, 313 U.S. 498, 61 S.Ct. 1023, 85 L.Ed. 1481, 134 A.L.R. 1462, and perhaps questions of full faith and credit. These are not before us now. A plaintiff cannot avail himself of the New Jersey forum and at the same time escape the terms on which it is made available, if the law is applicable to a federal court sitting in that State, which we later consider.

We conclude, therefore, that, so far as the Federal Constitution is concerned, New Jersey's security statute is a valid law of that State and the question remains as to whether it must be applied by federal courts in that State to suits brought therein on diversity grounds.

Applicability in Federal Court.

The Rules of Decision Act, in effect since the First Congress of the United States and now found at 28 U.S.C. § 1652, 28 U.S.C.A. § 1652, provides: "The laws of the several states, except where the Constitution or treaties of the United States or Acts of Congress otherwise require or provide, shall be regarded as rules of decision in civil actions in the courts of the United States, in cases where they apply." This Court in Erie R. Co. v. Tompkins, 304 U.S. 64, 58 S.Ct. 817, 82 L.Ed. 1188, 114 A.L.R. 1487, held that judicial decisions are laws of the states within its meaning. But Erie R. Co. v. Tompkins and its progeny have wrought a more far-reaching change in the relation of state and federal courts and the application of state law in the latter whereby in diversity cases the federal court administers the state system of law in all except details related to its own conduct of business. Guaranty Trust Co. of New York v. York, 326 U.S. 99, 65 S.Ct. 1464, 89 L.Ed. 2079, 160 A.L.R. 1231. The only substantial argument that this New Jersey statute is not applicable here is that its provisions are mere rules of procedure rather than rules of substantive law.

Even if we were to agree that the New Jersey statute is procedural, it would not determine that it is not applicable. Rules which lawyers call procedural do not always exhaust their effect by regulating procedure. But this statute is not merely a regulation of procedure. With it or without it the main action takes the same course. However, it creates a new liability where none existed before, for it makes a stockholder who institutes a derivative action liable for the expense to which he puts the corporation and other defendants, if he does not make good his claims. Such liability is not usual and it goes beyond payment of what we know as "costs." If all the Act did was to create this liability, it would clearly be substantive. But this new liability would be without meaning and value in many cases if it resulted in nothing but a judgment for expenses at or after the end of the case. Therefore, a procedure is prescribed by which the liability is insured by entitling the corporate defendant to a bond of indemnity before the outlay is incurred. We do not think a statute which so conditions the stockholder's action can be disregarded by the federal court as a mere procedural device.

It is urged, however, that Federal Rule of Civil Procedure No. 23 deals with plaintiff's right to maintain such an action in federal court and that therefore the subject is recognized as procedural and the federal rule alone prevails. Rule 23 requires the stockholder's complaint to be verified by oath and to show that the plaintiff was a stockholder at the time of the transaction of which he complains or that his share thereafter devolved upon him by operation of law. In other words, the federal court will not permit itself to be used to litigate a purchased grievance or become a party to speculation in wrongs done to corporations. It also requires a showing that an action is not a collusive one to confer jurisdiction and to set forth the facts showing that the plaintiff has endeavored to obtain his remedy through the corporation itself. It further provides that the class action shall not be dismissed or compromised without approval of the court, with notice to the members of the class. These provisions neither create nor exempt from liabilities, but require complete disclosure to the court and notice to the parties in interest. None conflict with the statute in question and all may be observed by a federal court, even if not applicable in state court. . . .

We hold that the New Jersey statute applies in federal courts and that the District Court erred in declining to fix the amount of indemnity reasonably to be exacted as a condition of further prosecution of the suit.

The judgment of the Court of Appeals is affirmed.

Affirmed.

MR. JUSTICE DOUGLAS, with whom MR. JUSTICE FRANKFURTER concurs, dissenting in part.

The cause of action on which this suit is brought is a derivative one. Though it belongs to the corporation, the stockholders are entitled under state law to enforce it. The measure of the cause of action is the claim which the corporation has against the alleged wrongdoers. This New Jersey statute does not add one iota to nor subtract one iota from that cause of action. It merely prescribes the method by which stockholders may enforce it. Each state has numerous regulations governing the institution of suits in its courts. They may favor the litigation or they may affect it adversely. But they do not fall under the principle of Erie R. Co. v. Tompkins, 304 U.S. 64, 58 S.Ct. 817, 82 L.Ed. 1188, 114 A.L.R. 1487, unless they define, qualify or delimit the cause of action or otherwise relate to it.

This New Jersey statute, like statutes governing security for costs, regulates only the procedure for instituting a particular cause of action and hence need not be applied in this diversity suit in the federal court. Rule 23 of the Federal Rules of Civil Procedure defines that procedure for the federal courts.

MR. JUSTICE RUTLEDGE, dissenting.

I am in accord with the dissenting opinion of MR. JUSTICE DOUGLAS in this case. . . .

. . . .

What is being applied is a gloss on the Erie rule, not the rule itself. That case held that federal courts in diversity cases must apply state law, decisional as well as statutory, in determining matters of substantive law, in particular and apart from procedural limitations upon its assertion—whether a cause of action exists. I accept that view generally and insofar as it involves a wise rule of administration for the federal courts, though I have grave doubt that it has any solid constitutional foundation.

But the Erie case made no ruling that in so deciding diversity cases a federal court is "merely another court of the state in which it sits," and hence that in every situation in which the doors of state courts are closed to a suitor, so must be also those of the federal courts. Not only is this not true when the state bar is raised by a purely procedural obstacle. There is sound historical reason for believing that one of the purposes of the diversity clause was to afford a federal court remedy when, for at least some reasons of state policy, none would be available in the state courts. It is the gloss which has been put upon the Erie ruling by later decisions, e.g., Guaranty Trust Co. of New York v. York, 326 U.S. 99, 65 S.Ct. 1464, 89 L.Ed. 2079, 160 A.L.R. 1231, which in my opinion is being applied to extend the Erie ruling far beyond its original purpose or intent and, in my judgment, with consequences and implications seriously impairing Congress' power, within its proper sphere of action, to control this type of litigation in the federal courts.

The accepted dichotomy is the familiar "procedural-substantive" one. This of course is a subject of endless discussion, which hardly needs to be repeated here. Suffice it to say that actually in many situations procedure and substance are so interwoven that rational separation becomes well-nigh impossible. But, even so, this fact cannot dispense with the necessity of making a distinction. For, as the matter stands, it is Congress which has the power to govern the procedure of the federal courts in diversity cases, and the states which have that power over matters clearly substantive in nature. Judges therefore cannot escape making the division.

It is in these close cases, this borderland area, that I think we are going too far. It is one thing to decide that Pennsylvania does or does not create a cause of action in tort for injuries inflicted by specified conduct and to have that determination govern the outcome of a diversity suit in Pennsylvania or New York. It is another, in my view, to require a bond for costs or for payment of the opposing party's expenses and attorney's fees in the event the claimant is unsuccessful. Whether or not the latter is conceived as creating a new substantive right, it is too close to controlling the incidents of the litigation rather than its outcome to be identified with the former. It is a matter which in my opinion lies within Congress' control for diversity cases, not one for state control or to be governed by the fact that the state shuts the doors of its courts unless the state requirements concerning such incidents of litigation are complied with.

In my view Rule 23 of the Federal Rules of Civil Procedure, derived from the former Equity Rules and now having the sanction of Congress, is valid and governs in the Cohen case. If, however, the State of New Jersey has the power to govern federal diversity suits within its borders as to all matters having a substantive tinge or aspect, then it may be questioned whether, in the event of conflict with some local policy, a federal court sitting in that state could give effect to the Rule's requirement that the complaint aver "that the plaintiff was a shareholder at the time of the transaction of which he complains or that his share thereafter devolved on him by operation of law . . . ." For in any strict and abstract sense that provision would seem to be as much a "substantive" one as the New Jersey requirements for bond, etc. And, if so, then it would seem highly doubtful, on any automatic or mechanical application of the substantive-procedural dichotomy, that either Congress or this Court could create such a limitation on diversity litigation, since as a substantive matter this would be for the states to control. . . .

COMMENT

(1) In reviewing the Cohen problem, consider the original New York statute, based upon the findings and recommendations of the Wood Report, which was imitated in New Jersey. There is the California statute which is *sui generis*. In the last few years a number of states have adopted security for

costs rules or adopted the cost rule of § 7.04(d) of the Revised Model Business Corporation Act. There is also a securities for costs provision in § 11(e) of the Securities Act of 1933. Please refer to the excerpts in the Documentary Supplement.

(2) The effect of the New York statute in throttling derivative litigation has not been as great as predicted. Commentators have attributed this fact to the holding in Baker v. MacFadden Publications [29] that a plaintiff, confronted with a demand that he furnish security for costs, may petition for disclosure of the shareholders' list so that he may circularize them with the suggestion that they join him. In this way he might be able to satisfy the 5%—$50,000 requirement. This tactic has caused managements to hesitate in moving for security since this may provoke circulation and publicizing of inflammatory charges they would like to keep private.[30]

(3) Three cases have construed security for costs legislation in such a way as to call for reconsideration of Cohen which, as it said, did not have the benefit of lower court gloss. The New York and Pennsylvania courts have had to deal with the problem of a derivative suitor who had not posted security because he had met the 5%—$50,000 standard. Each of them held that such a plaintiff could not be required to foot the bill for defendants' successful efforts. The Pennsylvania court found that security for expenses legislation "was not intended to discourage derivative actions generally . . . but only to prevent 'abuses attending the maintenance of such action by persons whose financial stake in the corporation is slight.' " [31]

The California statute, which as you will see is quite different from the "east coast pattern", has been interpreted to permit defendants to resort to the security fund even though they would not have been entitled to look to the corporation for reimbursement, that is, they were not directors or officers but outsiders. Beyerbach v. Juno Oil Co., 42 Cal.2d 11, 265 P.2d 1 (1954). The dissent by Carter, J., took the position that this interpretation caused the statute to violate the fourteenth amendment.

(4) While Cohen holds that state security for expenses legislation is applicable to diversity cases in the federal courts, other cases have held that such laws do not apply to actions brought in another state, including a federal district court there, even though there is such a rule in the state where the company is incorporated.[32] State security for costs legislation cannot be applied to a suit in which the underlying cause of action being asserted is based on federal law. Fielding v. Allen, 181 F.2d 163 (2d Cir.1948).

(5) Two Supreme Court cases cite Cohen in ways that may shed some light on its status. Hanna v. Plumer, 380 U.S. 460, 85 S.Ct. 1136, 14 L.Ed.2d 8 (1965), held that Federal Rule 4(d)(1) was valid and sustained service of process complying with that rule but not with Massachusetts law. In his concurrence HARLAN, J., had this to say about Cohen.

> Cohen v. Beneficial Indus. Loan Corp. held that a federal diversity court must apply a state statute requiring a small stockholder in a

---

29. 300 N.Y. 325, 90 N.E.2d 876 (1950).

30. Note, Security for Expenses in Shareholders' Derivative Suits 4 Colum. J.L. & Soc.Prob. 50 (1968) which quotes Mr. Pomerantz as saying "in most cases, the sophisticated defendant will not make the motion" (p. 65).

31. Shapiro v. Magaziner, 418 Pa. 278, 210 A.2d 890 (1965) Accord: Isensee v. Long Island Metcon Picture Co., 54 N.Y.S.2d 556 (1945).

32. Berkwitz v. Humphrey, 130 F.Supp. 142 (N.D.Ohio 1955) (the "phantom stock" case at p. 350 supra.)

stockholder derivative suit to post a bond securing payment of defense costs as a condition to prosecuting an action. Such a statute is not "outcome determinative"; the plaintiff can win with or without it. The Court now rationalizes the case on the ground that the statute might affect the plaintiff's choice of forum . . ., but as has been pointed out, a simple forum-shopping test proves too much. The proper view of Cohen is in my opinion, that the statute was meant to inhibit small stockholders from instituting "strike suits," and thus it was designed and could be expected to have a substantial impact on private primary activity. Anyone who was at the trial bar during the period when Cohen arose can appreciate the strong state policy reflected in the statute. I think it wholly legitimate to view Federal Rule 23 as not purporting to deal with the problem. But even had the Federal Rules purported to do so, and in so doing provided a substantially less effective deterrent to strike suits, I think the state rule should still have prevailed. That is where I believe the Court's view differs from mine; for the Court attributes such overriding force to the Federal Rules that it is hard to think of a case where conflicting state rule would be allowed to operate, even though the state rule reflected policy considerations which, under Erie, would lie within the realm of state legislative authority.

In Boddie v. Connecticut, 401 U.S. 371, 91 S.Ct. 780, 28 L.Ed.2d 113 (1971), the court held that a state could not constitutionally deny a divorce to an indigent incapable of paying filing and service fees. The majority opinion footnotes Cohen:

> We think Cohen v. Beneficial Industrial Loan Corp., 337 U.S. 541, 69 S.Ct. 1221, 93 L.Ed. 1528 (1949), has no bearing on this case. Differences between divorce actions and derivative actions aside, unlike Cohen, where we considered merely a statute on its face, the *application* of this statute here operates to cut off entirely access to the courts.

Mr. Justice Black, dissenting, saw more of a relation:

> There is consequently no necessity, no reason, why government should in civil trials be hampered or handicapped by the strict and rigid due process rules the Constitution has provided to protect people charged with crime.

> This distinction between civil and criminal proceedings is implicit in Cohen. . . . The Cohen case is indistinguishable from the one before us. In Cohen, as here, the statute applied to plaintiffs. In both situations the legal relationships involved are creatures of the State, extensively governed by state law. The effect of both statutes may be to deter frivolous or ill-considered suits, and in both instances the State has a considerable interest in the prevention of such suits, which might harm the very relationship the State created and fostered. Finally, the effect of both statutes may be to close the state courts entirely to certain plaintiffs, a result the Court explicitly accepted in Cohen. See id., at 552, 69 S.Ct. at 1228. I believe the present case should be controlled by the Court's thorough opinion in Cohen.

> The Court's suggested distinction of Cohen on the ground that the Court there dealt only with the validity of the statute on its face ignores the following pertinent language:

"It is urged that such a requirement will foreclose resort by most stockholders to the only available judicial remedy for the protection of their rights. Of course, to require security for the payment of any kind of costs, or the necessity for bearing any kind of expense of litigation, has a deterring effect. But we deal with power, not wisdom; and we think, notwithstanding this tendency, *it is within the power of a state to close its courts to this type of litigation if the condition of reasonable security is not met.*" Id., at 552, 69 S.Ct. at 1228. (Emphasis added.)

Rather Cohen can only be distinguished on the ground that it involved stockholders' suit, while this case involves marriage, "an interest of basic importance in our society." Thus the Court's opinion appears to rest solely on a philosophy that any law violates due process if it is unreasonable, arbitrary, indecent, deviates from the fundamental, is shocking to the conscience, or fails to meet other tests composed of similar words or phrases equally lacking in any possible constitutional precision. These concepts, of course, mark no constitutional boundaries and cannot possibly depend upon anything but the belief of particular judges, at particular times, concerning particular interests which those judges have divined to be of "basic importance." [33]

QUESTIONS

(1) Are you satisfied that today the Supreme Court would uphold the constitutionality of security for expenses legislation? In considering that issue, give effect to the interpretations grafted on to the statutes by the courts as described in (3) above and to the Supreme Court cases described in (5) above.

(2) What would the components of a satisfactory security for expenses statute be? In considering this question, compare the elements of the New York and California statutes set forth in the Supplement and attempt a synthesis of their components. Why, do you suppose, Delaware, generally sympathetic with management's problems, has not adopted such a law?

(3) Why have the federal courts, otherwise so creative in fashioning remedies, not incorporated security for costs rules into the mechanisms for enforcing federal causes of action? Does the federal system contain other elements making it less necessary to forestall strike suits?

C. Indemnification and Insurance

The origins of the indemnification of corporate officers and directors are found in common law. Perhaps the first case is D'Arcy v. Lyle.[34] D'Arcy was sent by Lyle to manage the latter's affairs in Haiti, then in the throes of violent revolution. He became involved in litigation involving adverse claims to property owned by his principal. After recovering judgment he was placed under heavy pressure by President Christophe ("an inexorable tyrant"), who jailed his lawyer, demanded that the parties settle the matter by a duel and arrested him when he tried to flee. D'Arcy finally consented to reversal of the

---

33. But see United States v. Kras, 409 U.S. 434, 93 S.Ct. 631, 34 L.Ed.2d 626 (1973) (upholding constitutionality of $50 filing fee in bankruptcy proceedings).

34. 5 Binney 441 (Pa.1813).

judgment and the entry of one admitting a debt of $3000. He sued to recover this amount from Lyle and prevailed in the Pennsylvania courts. The modern rules on indemnification of agents are crystallized in §§ 438–440 of the Restatement.

It was not at all clear what the scope of this common law rule was as it related to the corporate officers and directors. For one thing, the agency rule related to litigation involving third parties. Thus the first courts to consider the costs of directors incurred in successfully defending suits for malfeasance brought by (or on behalf of) the corporation denied any *right* to reimbursement and even questioned the corporation's power to grant it if those who controlled it so desired.

In any event, indemnification is now very much the creature of statute. As in security for costs legislation, New York was the forerunner. Delaware has, however, pulled into the lead and its legislation (8 Del.C. § 145) has been refined to the point where it is the most liberal to management. The courts have tended to be skeptical of indemnification legislation and to give it a restrictive interpretation in doubtful cases. Commentators have tended to be sharply critical of the Delaware statute.[35]

NOTE ON INDEMNIFICATION AND D & O INSURANCE

In the 1960's emphasis began to shift from indemnification by the corporation to insurance. Note that a D & O policy traditionally has two parts: (1) the corporation is insured for indemnification payments it makes to directors and officers and (2) the directors and officers are insured where the corporation does not or cannot indemnify them. Gradually such coverage became more available, even for relatively small corporations. But around 1985 there began what is termed the "D & O insurance crisis." [36] Premiums skyrocketed, deductibles were increased and coverage diminished and more and more insurance companies went out of the business until only six were left. More and more directors found themselves without coverage and quite a few resigned their jobs as a result. The reasons for the crisis are not clear. To some extent this mirrored an insurance crisis in other areas; insurers and their critics have traded charges including ones that insurance firms had been living off high interest rates on their investments and had therefore made low bids on policy premiums. It was also noted that between the time premia are paid and the time lawsuits are settled or lost there is a long time for inflation to push up costs—including legal fees. It is noted that traditional fire and automobile insurance has suffered less than medical and legal malpractice, products liability, and D & O insurance. Some data shows particular problems in the D & O field, such as increasing numbers of suits, startlingly large costs. Thus the Wyatt survey of 1984 indicated that in

35. Bishop, Sitting Ducks and Decoy Ducks: New Trends in the Indemnification of Corporate Directors and Officers, 77 Yale L.J. 1078 (1968).

36. Block, Barton & Garfield, Advising Directors on the D & O Insurance Crisis, 14 Sec.Reg.L.J. 130 (1986).

its sample of corporations 18.5% were being sued, up from 7.1% in 1974, that the average cost of defending a case had gone from $181,500 to $461,000 and the average settlement from $385,000 to $583,000. Note that this period covers a time in which the special litigation committee, p. 486 supra, became prevalent. In one year's time premiums went up from 3 to 10 times. At that, the older policies were not cheap—in 1968 Penn Central paid $305,000 for the $10 million coverage involved in the case below.

Another way insurance companies handle the risk is by reducing the coverage. Top limits have descended from $50 million to $150 million down to $10 to $25 million. Deductibles of the first few hundreds of thousands are common and risk sharing is common. Some types of losses are excluded, typically claims based on (1) short-swing profits under § 16(b), (2) libel and slander, (3) bribery, (4) excess remuneration or personal profit, (5) ERISA claims, (6) takeover and control battle claims. There have also been a string of cases—like the one that follows—in which insurers have claimed that the policy was obtained by false applications.[37]

BIRD v. PENN CENTRAL CO.

United States District Court, Eastern District of Pennsylvania, 1972.
341 F.Supp. 291.

OPINION

JOSEPH S. LORD, III, CHIEF JUDGE. This is a diversity case governed by Pennsylvania law. Plaintiffs in this action are certain named underwriters trading under the name of Lloyds of London. On July 2, 1968 they issued what we construe as two separate policies [38] providing coverage for the defendants. The Directors and Officers Liability policy (hereinafter referred to as D & O policy) provides coverage for the individual defendants, all present or past officers and/or directors of the Penn Central Company. The Company Reimbursement policy provides coverage for the defendant Penn Central Company.

There was one application [39] completed to obtain both policies. This application, which was specifically incorporated as part of the policies, was executed by defendant David C. Bevan, Chairman of the Finance Committee of the defendant corporation. It is alleged by the plaintiffs that defendant Bevan's response to Item 10 of the application was falsely made in bad faith, was material to the risk, and was justifiably relied on so as to entitle them to rescind the policy because of fraud.[40]

---

37. E.g. Shapiro v. American Home Assur. Co., 584 F.Supp. 1245 (D.Mass.1984); National Union Fire Ins. Co. of Pittsburgh, Pa. v. Continental Ill. Corp., 116 F.R.D. 252 (N.D.Ill.1987).

38. The plaintiffs contend that they issued one policy in two forms, but as more fully explained later, we have concluded that the two "forms" are two different policies with separate obligations.

39. This application was entitled "Proposal for Directors and Officers Liability and Company Reimbursement Insurance."

40. [Ed.] Judge Lord's prior opinion further described the alleged false statements as follows:

Three of the defendants, Kattau, Kirk and Annenberg, moved for summary judgment under F.R.Civ.P. 56, advancing many arguments. We rejected those arguments in an opinion filed on November 15, 1971 (334 F.Supp. 255) and denied summary judgment. In that opinion, among other things, we said that if the contract of insurance was a unitary one, with Lloyds of London and Penn Central Company the only contracting parties, the officers and directors would all be in the position of third-party beneficiaries, their rights rising no higher than those of their contracting party, Penn Central. Under this construction of the contract of insurance, if defendant Bevan's response on the application was proven fraudulent, this fraud would be imputed to his principal, Penn Central Company, regardless of the innocence of movants or other officers and directors. . . .

We said that another construction of the "policy" would consider each officer and director assured as a contracting party rather than a third-party beneficiary. We did not resolve this question of the construction of the "policy" because we said that the result would be the same in any event—if there was a material fraud in the application, and the other elements of rescission were present, the entire "policy" could be rescinded.

Having some doubts about whether our conclusion was correct if we considered the proper construction of the "policy" to be that the individual officers and directors are contracting parties, we granted reargument limited to the following questions:

(a) Was the contract of insurance a unitary contract with Penn Central as the other contracting party, or a series of individual contracts with each officer and director; (b) if the latter, is the knowledge of Bevan imputed to each individual officer and director?

Plaintiffs contend that the D & O insurance and the Company Reimbursement insurance are two forms of one policy, with Penn Central being the only contracting party. They point out there was but one application, and that a single lump sum premium was paid by the Penn Central Company. . . .

We have concluded that the Lloyds insurance package consists of two separate parts: a Company Reimbursement policy, which is a contract between Lloyds and Penn Central, and a D & O policy which is a contract between Lloyds and the directors and officers, insuring severally the distinct insurable interest of each officer and director.

A comparison of the opening sentence of both forms commands this construction:

Company Reimbursement Insurance

"In consideration of the payment of the premium and subject to all the terms of this policy, Underwriters agree with the Company (named in Item I of the Declarations) as follows:"

(1) the alleged investment by Penn Central in Executive Jet Aviation; (2) the alleged conflict of interest of certain directors who were involved in a private venture known as Penphil Corporation, and (3) the alleged illegal activities of Howard Butcher, III, a director of the railroad and a senior officer of the stock brokerage firm of Butcher & Sherrerd, which is also alleged to have been involved in such activities.

D & O Insurance

"In consideration of the payment of the premium and subject to all the terms of this policy, Underwriters agree with the Directors and Officers (named in Item I of the Declarations) as follows:"

We conclude that the Company Reimbursement insurance was a separate policy intended to protect the company's interest in the event it indemnified its officers and directors for personal liability. The D & O insurance has for its purpose the protection of the individual officer or director from personal liability, and each officer and director is a separate promisee under this policy. In addition to the preamble referred to above, various other provisions of the D & O policy lead us to this interpretation. For example, "assureds" under the D & O policy are defined in Section 4(a) as "all persons who were, now are, or shall be duly elected Directors or Officers of the Company. . . ." The Penn Central Company is nowhere referred to as an assured, while the Company Reimbursement policy refers throughout to the rights of the company. The individual nature of the protection under the D & O policy is demonstrated by Section 1 which provides that "the Underwriters will pay on behalf of the assureds or *any of them*" 95% of any claim covered by the policy. (Emphasis added.)

It is clear that if valid, when a policy such as the D & O one under consideration insures severally the distinct interests of many people, the act of one insured after issuance in breach of any condition of the policy could result in a forfeiture of only his own rights under the policy. The rights of other insureds to recover under the policy are unaffected, regardless of whether the breach involved fraud or not. . . .

The question in this case, however, does not concern the effect of one insured's breach of a condition on the rights of another insured under a valid policy, but whether the entire policy is voidable because of an alleged fraudulent act committed in the procurement of the policy.

Item 10 of the application which was the basis for both the Company Reimbursement policy and the D & O policy provides as follows:

"No person proposed for this insurance is cognizant of any act, error, or omission which he has reason to suppose might afford valid grounds for any future claim such as would fall within the scope of the proposed insurance except as follows:"

Defendant Bevan's response to this, which is alleged to have been knowingly false, and which is the basis for this rescission action, was "None known." Defendant Bevan, himself, was one of the assureds under the D & O policy. Movants argue that since the answer called for a subjective response, defendant Bevan's answer, if a misrepresentation was made, was a misrepresentation only of his own state of knowledge, but was a true response in his capacity as agent for each individual officer and director (such as movants) who would have truthfully responded "None known" to Item 10.

It is contended that defendant Bevan was acting in three capacities in signing the application: (a) as agent for Penn Central,[41] (b) as principal for his own account as one of the assureds, and (c) as agent for each of the other individual assureds. Recognizing these various capacities, movants in effect then ask us to consider defendant Bevan's single response to Item 10 as being over sixty separate responses, his own plus one representing the knowledge of each officer and director. See Bobrow v. United States Casualty Co., 231 App.Div. 91, 246 N.Y.S. 363 (Sup.Ct.1930). Thus, it is urged that plaintiffs should be able to rescind the D & O policy only as to defendant Bevan, for if he answered Item 10 fraudulently it was only in his capacity as principal for his own account. If it was held that the entire D & O policy could be subject to rescission because defendant Bevan happened to be the officer who signed the insurance application, it would be manifestly unfair to the directors and officers who are completely blameless, such as movants.

While we sympathize with movants' position, and recognize that innocent officers and directors are likely to suffer if the entire policy is voidable because of one man's fraudulent response, it must be recognized that plaintiff insurers are likewise innocent parties. Defendant Bevan was not plaintiffs' agent. Movants do not deny that he was their agent in completing the application by which the policy was obtained.

The general rule in this type of situation was stated by the Pennsylvania Supreme Court over 100 years ago.

> "Where the agent of the insured, in effecting an insurance, makes a false and unauthorized representation, the policy is void. Where one of two innocent persons must suffer by the fraud or negligence of a third, whichever of the two has accredited him, ought to bear the loss . . .." Mundorff v. Wickersham, 63 Pa. 87, 89 (1870) (dictum).

That the fraud of the agent in inducing a contract is binding on an innocent principal is a well established doctrine of agency law in other jurisdictions as well. . . .

. . .

We do not think that the fact that defendant Bevan signed the application on behalf of numerous principals including himself alters the force of this rule. It would be extremely artificial to read defendant Bevan's response to Item 10 as being multiple separate responses on behalf of himself, the company, and each of the individuals assureds under the D & O policy. No matter how the policies for Company Reimbursement insurance and D & O insurance are characterized, the simple inescapable fact is that both policies were issued on the basis of a single application, and only one response was made to Item 10 of that application. Defendant Bevan, movants' agent, made that response. As we said in our previous opinion, we construe Item 10 as being directed at gaining information regarding the nature and scope of the insured risk. If the answer to Item 10 is fraudulent, we cannot say with assurance that plaintiffs would not have acted differently before issuing the policies if they had been given a truthful response, either

---

41. In consideration of this motion, we are unconcerned with his actions as agent for Penn Central since movants are individual assureds seeking summary judgment only as to their rights as individuals under the D & O policy.

issuing the policies only if a higher premium were paid, or refusing to issue any policy at all.

Therefore, the motions for summary judgment will be denied.

COMMENT

The above opinion represents only a small part of the tumult surrounding the collapse of the Penn Central in June 1970. The Pennsylvania Railroad and its 120 years of dividends had been a center of Philadelphia's economic life. The New York Central, Commodore Vanderbilt's legacy to the American transportation system, was also an important carrier. Their merger in 1968, however, accelerated the decline which each of them had been experiencing separately and soon losses of $1 million per day were being generated by the system. The origins of this decline are various. Some are endemic to railroads in this country—and elsewhere. These include the competition of roads and airways (free, the railroads argue, from property taxes and maintenance). Others specially afflict carriers in the northeast corridor which has been losing heavy manufacturers to the south and west. The merger itself created a top heavy organization in which neither managers nor computers could communicate with each other. Observers agree that the board was not at all helpful in the declining years, that it did not ask the right questions of management. Management, under the leadership of David Bevan, relied heavily on "creative accounting" to justify maintaining dividends unsupported by cash flow. Surveying the wreckage, investigators pointed to the three episodes noted by Lloyd's. None of them really can have made a major contribution to the financial collapse. The Executive Jet Aviation episode involved an attempt to circumvent federal prohibitions on railroad control over air carriers; EJA was designed to provide "taxi" service for executives though it sought to expand its offerings. Due to lax controls, which in turn were partly due to the desire to bury Penn Central's connections with EJA, much money was spent on the personal comfort of EJA's executives, including the support of the president's current friend, "Miss Hurst Golden Shifter of 1967." Penphil was a "private investment club" in which Bevan and other Pennsylvania Railroad executives were members. It prospered greatly on investments, many of which had odd relations with diversification efforts of the railroad itself; allegedly it also benefited from banking support motivated by a desire for railroad business. Howard Butcher resigned from the board in 1968 after being accused of using secret information to sell 80,000 shares of Penn Central. Butcher & Sherrerd again boosted railroad stock from 1968 to 1970 which it then unloaded just before the collapse. Other allegations of insider trading were made against Bevan and others. Butcher had been the largest individual holder of Pennsylvania stock—his great-grandfather had been one of its first directors. One of the clients whom he guided into the stock was the University of Pennsylvania.

Apparently the litigation was ultimately settled at a cost of $2.4 million to Lloyd's. Penn Central paid $305,000 for a three year coverage of $10 million.[42]

---

42. For a journalistic overview, see J. Daughen & P. Binzen, The Wreck of the Penn Central (1971); in greater detail, Staff Report of the House Committee on Banking and Currency, The Penn Central Failure and the Role of Financial Institutions (1970–72). See also M. Schaeftler, The Liabilities of Office 169–70 (1976).

QUESTIONS

(1) As an exercise in reading 8 Del.C. § 145, read the following problems against the text. A director has been found liable to a third party to pay treble damages in an antitrust case involving the corporation. Can the board indemnify for that payment? What procedures have to be followed and what determinations made? Is the case of a fine imposed after a *nolo contendere* plea different? Suppose that the damages in question were paid to the corporation as a result of a derivative suit alleging malfeasance in office? Suppose there was no finding, but a settlement? Does § 145 cover liabilities to an outside stockholder as a result of trading by a director on the basis of inside information found illegal under Rule 10b–5?

(2) Do the mechanisms for determining whether the corporation should pay (where no court ruling is made) seem adequate to prevent abuse? Consider the role assigned to independent counsel. Is it psychologically tenable? What ties to the corporation disqualify a lawyer as not independent? Where do you suppose the drafters got the term?

(3) Under Delaware law could the corporation indemnify under subsection (f) even where you concluded under (1) above that it was not otherwise legal? Does that seem appropriate? Suppose that indemnification were given thus broadly in an antitrust case; is there a federal interest in blocking that reimbursement?

(4) Can insurance give protection beyond that provided in § 145(a) and (b)? Consider New York § 726 in comparison with Delaware. Would an insurer wish to write so wide a protective provision?

(5) Would indemnification or insurance usually be available for liabilities arising from the causes of action discussed in the Penn Central case? If you were writing insurance policies would you exclude all securities acts litigation—as is typical of lawyers' malpractice insurance? What criteria would you use to distinguish corporations you would insure from those you would not cover? Might this policy have a general effect on the conduct of business in the United States?

Bibliography: A good source on derivative suits generally is the American Law Institute, Principles of Corporate Governance (Tent.Drafts 6 and 8, 1986, 1988). See also Symposium on Shareholder Litigation, 48 L. & Contemp.Prob. 1 (Summer 1985). Where derivative litigation and federal practice intersect, look at the standard works, Moore's Federal Practice and C. Wright & A. Miller, Federal Practice and Procedure, particularly under Rule 23.1.

On indemnification one looks first at M. Schaeftler, The Liabilities of Office (1976) and the more summary treatment in The Symposium, Officers' and Directors' Responsibilities and Liabilities, 27 Bus.Law. 1, 109–164 (Spec. issue 1972).

On settlements, consult Haudek, Settlement and Dismissal of Stockholders' Actions, 22 Sw.L.J. 767, 23 id. 765 (1968–69). On attorneys' fees and related matters, see 2 G. Hornstein, Corporation Law and Practice § 732 (1959, Supp. 1968). For a sharp critique of lavishness in attorneys' fee awards, see Dawson, Lawyers' and Involuntary Clients in Public Interest Litigation, 88 Harv.L.Rev. 849 (1975).

A REVIEW PROBLEM

The following problem is designed to put together a number of issues raised in this Chapter—as well as a few substantive problems, which are largely related to the next Chapter.

J. Forsythe is a director of Trans–Missouri Railroad Corp. (TMR); both she and TMR have been clients of your firm for some time. She has just sent over to your office a letter received from two stockholders (with copies to each of TMR's other directors). It reads:

"Dear Ms. Forsythe:

This is a definitive warning to you to act promptly to straighten out a very bad situation at TMR. You will remember that in 1969 TMR, with your concurring vote, set up a 75% owned subsidiary, TMI, to develop a non-railroad diversification program, the other 25% being owned by an investment banking firm, First Transylvania. TMI made investments in a number of other corporations, preferring for sake of ease, privacy and simplicity to buy blocks of shares from their managements so as to gain control with a single purchase. Meanwhile, First Transylvania quietly picked up small packets of those securities. Since TMI always put in good managers and made new funds available, those corporations have mostly done very much better than they had been. First Transylvania has also done very nicely with its own side-investments as their market prices went up—we are sure that First Transylvania is at least $2,000,000 better off than it was. It got all of that without putting into it any of the expensive investment analysis and research that would usually be necessary since that had already been done for TMI.

You must immediately begin an action against First Transylvania; in fact you have been inexcusably neglectful of TMR's affairs since if you had been reasonably alert you would have stopped this activity a long time ago. If you do not, we will begin an action on TMR's behalf ourselves and, for good measure, will join all of you directors as defendants. You have ten days to render us a satisfactory reply.

Sincerely,
Thomas and Anne Stanner"

Ms. Forsythe tells you that she was completely unaware of First Transylvania's purchases, that there was no discussion of such activity at the time the two corporations formed TMI, and that as an outside director of TMR with an engineering background she devoted most of the time she could give TMR to its technical transportation questions. She believes she would have disapproved of those purchases by First Transylvania had she known of them and would have asked that they be stopped. However, she now puts first priority on maintaining good relations with First Transylvania as a powerful financial firm that can do much to help TMR get its somewhat shaky house in order. She states that the corporate records show Thomas Stanner has owned about 3½% of the TMR stock for many years but that the 2½% of the TMR stock has been held by Anne Stanner for only a few weeks. They both live in Ohio. Although TMR is a Delaware corporation, New York is the only place where TMR, the directors and First Transylvania could all be reached. She would like most of all to suppress the whole problem at an early stage of the litigation if that is possible or, if that is not possible, to settle the matter for a small sum which the prospective defendant would in all likelihood be willing to pay. Indeed, she would be willing to put in a few thousand dollars from her own fortune. Advise her of the likelihood of obtaining the sort of results she wants.

Chapter XI

TRANSACTIONS IN SECURITIES ALREADY ISSUED

1. Introduction

In this chapter we consider the rules affecting transactions between buyers and sellers of securities after they have been issued by the corporation and, through the underwriting process, have initially come to rest in the hands of the first investor. We are primarily concerned with rules that prevent one party to such a transaction from using a superior knowledge, or bargaining position, acquired through possession of a fiduciary position. While the purpose of these rules is not dissimilar from that of the rules in Chapter VI, they do occupy a functionally separate terrain. The rules on initial issues of stock, such as the requirement of a prospectus—do not apply to transactions that are generally not a part of the original offering process. There are, naturally, some tricky line-drawing questions. For example, if the persons selling the stock are found to be in "control" of the issuer, the Commission or the courts may extend the registration requirements of the 1933 Act to them in order to prevent them from doing indirectly what they could not do directly. In general, however, the Securities Exchange Act of 1934 with which we deal here handles a different set of situations from the 1933 Act. This is not to say that there are not curious inconsistencies and overlappings between the two.

In the present state of corporate affairs and analysis it is impossible to think intelligently about the issues of corporate governance or management without taking into account the operations of the markets on which corporate stock is traded. While examination of the detailed regulation of those markets may be left to a course called Securities Regulation and detailed understanding of operations on them to graduates of the Business School the student of Corporations must have some understanding of how those markets work. At worst one will, without such basic knowledge, fall victim to various misperceptions that are widely shared and propagated. It is all the more important to give you some of that basic knowledge now because modern law students do not bring with them much awareness of that market even though it touches their lives in various ways. In this they stand in contrast to their predecessors who were apt to have seen at first hand the functionings of the simpler markets that affected them and their families—those for real estate, livestock, cars, etc.

536

History

One starts with a group of dealers who in 1792 agreed under a buttonwood tree in downtown Manhattan to form a stock exchange. In so doing they could look back on the example of the older London institution which had its counterparts in Paris and elsewhere. It was a simple organization, the essential element of which was simply that the members would conduct their trades publicly and in one place. By doing so they made it possible for others to incorporate that price as an item of information into their own thinking about the value of the security. They also prevented individuals from being drawn into isolated, unfair transactions. Finally, the rules favored members since others were excluded from the exchange and would have to pay a member to have their transaction carried out there.

As the national economy grew so did the New York Stock Exchange—and so did its rivals, currently nine in number. By present standards, nineteenth century market behavior was wild and the risks to the uninitiated high. Bears would raid the market and drive stocks down; in the process those who had reflected their pessimism by selling stock short—in the expectation of being able to cover by buying cheaply—might be squeezed when the price went up again. At other times the price of a stock would be driven up by methods that would not bear close scrutiny; speculators would band together and sell each other stock at increasing prices while they circulated rumors about its favorable prospects. When they had succeeded in selling the stock to outsiders they would quietly move out of the market—"pull the plug"—and leave the price to drift back down to a normal level. It was possible at times to "corner" the market, i.e. to have a monopoly of all the stock anybody wished to sell. The volatility of the market was enhanced by unregulated borrowing in order to buy securities—when the stock went down the lender would want more security to maintain the original margin of stock value over the amount of the loan. This would force borrowers to sell their stock, which forced the price down, thus triggering more calls for additional security or "margin" and so on. No wonder that it was thought to be distinctly unwise and even a bit shady to be involved with the stock market.

Up to 1934 the New York Stock Exchange and its counterparts were self-governing. They established rules that governed the behaviour of the brokers and dealers who were permitted to trade on the exchange. They also set the conditions upon which they would list securities, that is, admit them to trading. Those conditions in particular forced a minimal amount of disclosure out of corporate managers. While there were periodic investigations of the stock exchanges from the turn of the century on, it was only after the great depression and the coming to light of various examples of scandalous behavior that Congress allowed the government to intrude upon this private preserve. The Securities Exchange Act of 1934 established the Securities and Exchange Commission and authorized it to regulate transactions in securities; the Act, however, contemplated a continuing role for industry self-government within the framework of the statute itself and SEC regulations. The statutory rules have been refined from time to time as new developments required. Most importantly Congress in 1975 inserted an amendment in the Exchange Act that instructed the SEC to move towards the creation of a national securities market that would tie together all of the individual markets. That has proven to be a task of considerable difficulty which is by no means completed.

As the securities markets developed during the 1980's one could observe several trends. First, was the increasing emphasis on automation. To confront the volume of paperwork that grew out of the increasing number of participants in the market and heightened expectations of speedy service it was necessary to computerize the process of entering orders, accounting for payments and preparing records of transactions. New means of communication made it possible to switch data from one person and one place to another with a speed and economy quite unavailable previously. The market reached the point where computers could be programmed so as to react automatically to changes in the market prices of securities when a certain level was reached. Another trend was the proliferation of new instruments of investments, new ways of packaging opportunities and cushioning risks. Also, in the 1980's trading in securities options or futures began. One could thus aim to make a profit or guard against loss by making a commitment to buy or sell a security or package of securities at a specified price at some future date. Significantly the seat of these operations in the United States was not in New York but in Chicago where the expertise in the buying and selling of futures in such commodities as grain and meat had been developed. The third development lay in the internationalization of the securities market; even while the SEC struggled with the task of unifying the markets within this country, linkages between the U.S. markets and those in other countries became tighter. More and more the securities of important corporations were listed on a number of markets—New York, London, Frankfurt and Tokyo for example. At any one point in the 24 hour cycle one of these markets would be open to execute orders as to such a security. More and more traders set up branches at the seats of exchanges in other countries or entered into alliances with brokerage firms there. Investors became calmer about placing their resources in other countries when that seemed to offer the best opportunities. It was particularly noticeable that U.S. securities were acquired by large numbers of foreigners, both individuals and institutions, and in increasing volumes. Thus tremors in the international early warning system about the economy of Country X could send signals to a wide variety of markets to shift holdings to Country Y or Z. The strength or weakness of X's currency became an important factor in drawing or repelling foreign investment. It became more and more difficult for states to conduct their own fiscal policy (taxation, interest rates, etc.) without taking into account the reactions of foreign investors and their governments.

The events of October 1987 illustrated the effects of all these tendencies. In particular, observers were struck by the unprecedented speed with which the markets responded to what seemed to have been at first a minor change of mood triggered by not particularly exciting developments. Computers began to talk to each other, options and futures contracts were triggered, shock waves spread from New York to London and Hong Kong. The result was a series of declines that made new records for daily drops, wiping out large quantities of paper assets and affecting thousands of lives with varying degrees of directness. Predictably there was a cry for investigation and corrective action, some steps to diminish the volatility of the market. It may be hard to distinguish that evil volatility from the market's much-praised efficiency.

Effecting Transactions

The following materials describe the course of a securities transaction on the New York Stock Exchange; the focus on the NYSE reflects the fact that it is by far the largest exchange, accounting for some 80% of the total trading volume. In the NYSE a trade is initiated by the intending buyer (or seller) instructing the broker to buy or sell so many shares. That order may tell the broker to buy or sell at the market price or to buy or sell when the stock falls or rises to a specified level. With the order the broker goes to the appropriate post on the floor of the exchange at which is found a specialist in the security in question. The specialist keeps the book on which existing buy and sell orders have been entered. The specialist matches the incoming orders with the existing ones and if there is a meeting of bid and asked declares the deal closed. Note that the specialist has another function, which is to maintain an "orderly market" in the security by buying or selling from its own inventory when there are no other buyers or sellers on the market. The specialist is not expected to interfere with basic market readjustments but should see that they are staged in orderly steps. Nowadays some transactions can be affected by the automated Designated Order Turnaround System.

On the over-the-counter market the specialist system does not prevail. However, various dealers will hold themselves out as "making a market" in this or that security, that is, as being willing to buy or sell. Thus an intended buyer of a stock quoted by NASDAQ can get in touch with such a dealer and offer to buy at the electronically posted price, thereby concluding the transaction. To be quoted, a stock must have 300 public shareholders, have two registered market makers and be issued by a firm subject to Section 12(g) of the 1934 Act. The Small Order Execution System permits some orders (under 1000 shares) to be executed automatically.

Executing the Deal

When the deal has been made by the above process, the parties are obligated to carry out their respective obligations at the time and in the manner specified in the rules of the exchange or by custom.[1] Thus the seller must make "good delivery" of the security within four business days. If the shares are held in certificate form the seller must deliver them to the broker who then delivers them to the buyer's broker. They must be endorsed by the seller either on the back of the certificate (see the form included in the Documentary Supplement) or in a separate endorsement form. The buyer's broker then can take the certificate to the issuing corporation's transfer agency and have a new certificate issued in the name of the buyer. At the same time the name of the buyer will be substituted for that of the seller in the corporation's records so that dividend checks, proxies and other items will be sent to the buyer. Note that if dividends are due to be paid in the interim they may still go to the seller as the party appearing in the records. This possibility is anticipated in the transfer practice by causing the stock to go *ex dividend* at the appropriate time, the price being diminished by the amount of the dividend which the seller rather than the buyer will receive.

If the stock is not held in the form of a certificate held in the name of the seller, other procedures apply. The stock may be held in the name of the broker or more usually of a nominee of the broker—in "street name." This arrangement makes it possible to carry out the sale by telephone instruction without the seller having to go to the safe deposit box, take out the certificate, mail or bring it to the broker, make out an endorsement, etc. All can be done by the broker in one location. Also the shares may be held by the broker through a clearing agency. The clearing agency holds a single huge certificate and recognizes the claims against that certificate of the various brokerage houses that hold such securities. A simple change on the books of the clearing agency showing that it holds x more shares in the name of Brokerage House A and x shares less in the name of Brokerage House B will suffice to effect the transfer. Note that there are disadvantages to such indirect arrangements. It takes longer for dividend checks to make their way through the chain of intermediaries and there is the possibility of error along the way. There is also the possibility that the dividends or even the underlying stock interest will be embezzled by the broker, although there are various safety devices designed to prevent such happenings or reimburse the defrauded owner, in particular insurance through SIPIC.

The seller's obligation to deliver the security is matched by the buyer's obligation to pay. The obligation to pay is also specified in some detail in the rules of the Exchange. It may be possible to borrow

---

1. Article 8 of the Uniform Commercial Code also lays down rules as to transfers of securities.

the money, from the broker or from some outside financial institution. Because of a sense that easy credit was a cause of the overextension of 1929 and hence of the collapse in the fall of that year, borrowing for the purpose of acquiring securities is regulated by the Federal Reserve Board. Along with the obligation to pay the seller comes an obligation to pay the brokers on both sides. For a long time commissions were fixed by exchange rules. That practice was challenged as violative of the antitrust laws but sustained as on the basis that the Sherman Act was impliedly repealed to that extent by the securities laws.[2] There was a great deal of pressure on the fixed commission rule, particularly on the part of large institutional customers who felt that their economic power or economies of scale justified concessions on large transactions. There was also a tendency to conduct these large transactions off the exchange through non-members, thus eroding the market position of the NYSE. In fact there were a variety of indirect concessions made by brokers in the form of extra research services, etc., in order to hold large and desirable customers. The SEC went through several successive modifications of the rules. Then in 1975 the commission schedule was repealed altogether. Consequences of that move have included volume discounts for large transactions and the emergence of discount brokers who can offer lower prices in return for not providing such traditional ancillary brokerage services as investment advice. There has always been an extra charge for deals of less than 100 shares—known as "odd lots."

The Information System

One of the most important supporting roles in the whole exchange transaction process is that of the information system. It is fair to assert that no other market is supported by as complete and current an information system as the organized securities exchanges. One starts with the fact that the transaction itself generates information. In places all over the world people follow the course of transactions on the NYSE carried by what was traditionally known as the tape. You may recall pictures in your history books of parades through lower Manhattan in which the honored visitor was showered with ticker tape. Nowadays advances in electronics enable one to call up selected quotations on one computer or to sit in a broker's office while quotations are displayed on the screen. The next morning you will find them in the daily paper. Those figures are critical items of information since they not only show what the current trading price is but also the valuation of the security by people willing to back their views with money. Much additional information is poured into the market. Some of it comes through official, regulated channels. Corporations listed on the exchanges, and now others subject to Section 12(g) of the 1934 Act, are

2. Gordon v. New York Stock Exchange, Inc., 422 U.S. 659, 95 S.Ct. 2598, 45 L.Ed.2d 463 (1975).

required to make reports annually, quarterly and upon the happening of certain specified events. See pp. 404 supra, 612 infra.

A great deal happens to information after it comes from the market or from the issuer. A whole industry has been built up to watch the market and to try to identify opportunities for profit. News about the market is studied and processed by writers for such public journals as the Wall Street Journal, Barron's, Forbes, Fortune, etc. There are private (more or less) newsletters. Brokerage firms analyze data and pass it on to their customers. Institutional investors do their own processing. There are seminars and courses at which investors and analysts can learn more about the market. This entire system has to be understood as immensely competitive, the stakes being high, both in terms of the money involved and in terms of the personal ambitions committed to the enterprise.

Market Theory

An increasing body of theory has been built up about the securities markets. A passing understanding of this learning is useful in terms of what we are trying to achieve in this course. Deductions from this theory have been used to support policy analysis and recommendations. However, expertise is not to be expected.

The core of this learning is the efficient market theory. It says, in its most technical version, that the market quickly takes account of all publicly available information about securities and reflects that data accurately in its pricing. It follows from this that no individual investor can expect regularly to make money from outguessing the market. This proposition has been checked in a substantial number of situations and found to fit the facts. There are, however, a number of cautions about that data. Most of it comes from studies of the performance of mutual funds. There are some limits on the strategies which such funds must follow. They must be largely invested in securities at any point in time; the holders of their stock will not be understanding if their holdings are kept in cash, even though they may be the sensible thing to do at that stage in the market's evolution. Mutual funds, if they are sizable, must concentrate on large issues of securities since their investments must be in issues that are large enough to allow them to limit the percentage of the issue which they own—so that they can exit fairly gracefully without upsetting the market—and that do not compel the fund to hold an extravagantly long list of securities. Some investors, not hampered by such operating rules, seem to do a bit better. Note also that the rule applies only to public information; there is evidence showing that the investor with access to inside information can regularly and systematically outperform the market. Note also that the proposition does not exclude the possibility that somebody will from time to time make a lucky hit; those investors who took their money out of the stock market in July 1929 and took the cash had a much better time in the 1930's than those who stayed with the market on the way down. It also follows that the market does not necessarily predict the future with precision. One of the items of information that goes into the pricing of securities is the current state of the collective judgment of the market about prospects; the market accurately reflects that judgment both before and after a drastic change in that judgment. One could say that the market was "efficient" in both July and December 1929. It is similarly true that the market will not reflect the likelihood of a drastic change in the fate of a security, such as a takeover. Thus the price of a security will jump quite drastically when the news of a tender offer comes out.

Particularly when writers attempt to apply efficient market analysis to other fields one should recall that the efficiency of the securities market depends on several qualities of the securities markets that are not found in other markets. These include (1) the fact that there is no built-in imbalance between buyers and sellers of securities since big and knowledgeable institutions are operating on both sides of transactions; (2) the fact that all 100 share blocks of General Motors are identical, unlike plots of real estate or used cars, so that close comparisons are possible; (3) the presence of a large number of trained and sophisticated analysts watching the market; (4) the publication of vast amounts of data relevant to the price. It is important to remember that there are markets and markets and to adjust one's theories accordingly.

Bibliography: For a description of the securities markets written as a background to a description of their regulation see Gadsby, The Federal Securities Exchange Act of 1934, ch. 2 (1967–date). For more specialized pieces read Branson, Securities Regulation after Entering and Competitive Era; The Securities Industry, SEC Policy and the Individual Investor, 75 Nw.U.L.Rev. 857 (1980); Macey & Haddock, Shirking at the SEC: The Failure of the National Market System. 1985 U.Ill.L.Rev. 315. For a handily condensed version of efficient market theory see Langbein & Posner, Social Investing and the Law of Trusts, 79 Mich.L.Rev. 72, 77–83 (1980). Application of that theory to legal issues is analyzed in Gilson & Kraakman, Mechanisms of Market Efficiency, 70 Va.L.Rev. 549 (1984). For an attempt to put the concept of "efficiency" into context see Tobin, On the Efficiency of the Financial System, Lloyd's Bank Rev. (July 1984), p. 1. There is extensive description of the securities markets (as well as normative analysis) in the Brady Report (the President's Commission's) and the SEC staff report that were provoked by the market debacle of October 1987.

2. Common Law Approaches

We come, now, to the particular point of our inquiry—the relationship between the buyer and seller of securities in regard to their unequal knowledge. First, a few questions designed to mobilize your general legal knowledge about sales and purchases:

(1) Suppose that S sells a cow to B, believing it to be barren. It is not in fact barren. What theories and what remedies are available to

S? As to which of them does it matter what B knew or might have known about the cow?

(2) Suppose that S sells a cow to B, B believing the cow to be fertile. It turns out to be barren. What theories and remedies are available to B? Assume S (a) said nothing, (b) said the cow was fertile, (c) said it "was a good cow."

(3) Which of the approaches applicable to the cow transactions are useful in approaching a sale/purchase of stock? Which are more or less useless? Why?

The following two cases illustrate the common law approaches to the problem.

———

GOODWIN v. AGASSIZ
Supreme Judicial Court of Massachusetts, 1933.
283 Mass. 358, 186 N.E. 659.

RUGG, CHIEF JUSTICE. A stockholder in a corporation seeks in this suit relief for losses suffered by him in selling shares of stock in Cliff Mining Company by way of accounting, rescission of sales, or redelivery of shares. . . .

The trial judge made findings of fact, rulings, and an order dismissing the bill. There is no report of the evidence. The case must be considered on the footing that the findings are true. The facts thus displayed are these: The defendants, in May, 1926, purchased through brokers on the Boston stock exchange seven hundred shares of stock of the Cliff Mining Company which up to that time the plaintiff had owned. Agassiz was president and director and MacNaughton a director and general manager of the company. They had certain knowledge, material as to the value of the stock, which the plaintiff did not have. The plaintiff contends that such purchase in all the circumstances without disclosure to him of that knowledge was a wrong against him. That knowledge was that an experienced geologist had formulated in writing in March, 1926, a theory as to the possible existence of copper deposits under conditions prevailing in the region where the property of the company was located. That region was known as the mineral belt in Northern Michigan, where are located mines of several copper mining companies. Another such company, of which the defendants were officers, had made extensive geological surveys of its lands. In consequence of recommendations resulting from that survey, exploration was started on property of the Cliff Mining Company in 1925. That exploration was ended in May, 1926, because completed unsuccessfully, and the equipment was removed. The defendants discussed the geologist's theory shortly after it was formulated. Both felt that the theory had value and should be tested, but they agreed that, before starting to test it, options should be obtained by another copper company of which they were officers on land adjacent to or nearby in the copper belt, that if the geologist's theory were known to the owners of such other land there might be difficulty in securing options, and that that theory should not be communicated to any one unless it became absolutely necessary. Thereafter, options were secured which, if taken up, would involve a large expenditure by the other company. The defendants both thought, also that, if there was any merit in the geologist's theory, the price of Cliff Mining Company stock in the market would go up. Its stock was quoted and bought and sold on the Boston Stock Exchange. Pursuant to agreement, they bought many shares of that stock through agents on joint account. The plaintiff first learned of the closing of exploratory operations on property of the Cliff Mining Company from an article in a paper on May 15, 1926, and immediately sold his shares of stock through brokers. It does not appear that the defendants were in any way responsible for the publication of that article. The plaintiff did not know that the purchase was made for the defendants and they did not know that his stock was being bought for them. There was no communication between them touching the subject. The plaintiff would not have sold his stock if he had known of the geologist's theory. The finding is express that the defendants were not guilty of fraud, that they committed no breach of duty owed by them to the Cliff Mining Company, and that that company was not harmed by the nondisclosure of the geologist's theory, or by their purchases of its stock, or by shutting down the exploratory operations.

The contention of the plaintiff is that the purchase of his stock in the company by the defendants without disclosing to him as a stockholder their knowledge of the geologist's theory, their belief that the theory was true, had value, the keeping secret the existence of the theory, discontinuance by the defendants of exploratory operations begun in 1925 on property of the Cliff Mining Company and their plan ultimately to test the value of the theory, constitute actionable wrong for which he as stockholder can recover.

The trial judge ruled that conditions may exist which would make it the duty of an officer of a corporation purchasing its stock from a stockholder to inform him as to knowledge possessed by the buyer and not by the seller, but found, on all the circumstances developed by the trial and set out at some length by him in his decision, that there was no fiduciary relation requiring such disclosure by the defendants to the plaintiff before buying his stock in the manner in which they did.

The question presented is whether the decree dismissing the bill rightly was entered on the facts found.

The directors of a commercial corporation stand in a relation of trust to the corporation and are bound to exercise the strictest good faith in respect to its property and business. . . . The contention that directors also occupy the position of trustee toward individual stockholders in the corporation is plainly contrary to repeated decisions of this court and cannot be supported. In Smith v. Hurd, 12 Metc. 371, 384, 46 Am.Dec. 690, it was said by Chief Justice Shaw: "There is no legal privity, relation, or immediate connexion, between the holders of shares in a bank, in their individual capacity, on the one side, and the directors of the bank on the other. The directors are not the bailees, the factors, agents or trustees of such individual stockholders." In Stewart v. Joyce, 201 Mass. 301, 311, 312, 87 N.E. 613, and Lee v. Fisk, 222 Mass. 424, 426, 109 N.E. 835, the same principle was reiterated. In Blabon v. Hay, 269 Mass. 401, 407, 169 N.E. 268, 271 occurs this language with reference to sale of stock in a corporation by a stockholder to two of its directors: "The fact that the defendants were directors created no fiduciary relation between them and the plaintiff in the manner of the sale of his stock."

The principle thus established is supported by an imposing weight of authority in other jurisdictions. [Citations omitted.]

A rule holding that directors are trustees for individual stockholders with respect to their stock prevails in comparatively few states; but in view of our own adjudications it is not necessary to review decisions to that effect. [Citations omitted.]

While the general principle is as stated, circumstances may exist requiring that transactions between a director and a stockholder as to stock in the corporation be set aside. The knowledge naturally in the possession of a director as to the condition of a corporation places upon him a peculiar obligation to observe every requirement of fair dealing when directly buying or selling its stock. Mere silence does not usually amount to a breach of duty, but parties may stand in such relation to each other that an equitable responsibility arises to communicate facts. Wellington v. Rugg, 243 Mass. 30, 35, 136 N.E. 831. Purchases and sales of stock dealt in on the stock exchange are commonly impersonal affairs. An honest director would be in a difficult situation if he could neither buy nor sell on the stock exchange shares of stock in his corporation without first seeking out the other actual ultimate party to the transaction and disclosing to him everything which a court or jury might later find that he then knew affecting the real or speculative value of such shares. Business of that nature is a matter to be governed by practical rules. Fiduciary obligations of directors ought not to be made so onerous that men of experience and ability will be deterred from accepting such office. Law in its sanctions is not coextensive with morality. It cannot undertake to put all parties to every contract on an equality as to knowledge, experience, skill and shrewdness. It cannot undertake to relieve against hard bargains made between competent parties without fraud. On the other hand, directors cannot rightly be allowed to indulge with impunity in practices which do violence to prevailing standards of upright business men. Therefore, where a director personally seeks a stockholder for the purpose of buying his shares without making disclosure of material facts within his peculiar knowledge and not within reach of the stockholder, the transaction will be closely scrutinized and relief may be granted in appropriate instances. Strong v. Repide, 213 U.S. 419, 29 S.Ct. 521, 53 L.Ed. 853; Allen v. Hyatt, 30 T.L.R. 444; Gammon v. Dain, 238 Mich. 30, 212 N.W. 957; George v. Ford, 36 App.D.C. 315. See, also, Old Dominion Copper Mining & Smelting Co. v. Bigelow, 203 Mass. 159, 194, 195, 89 N.E. 193, 40 L.R.A.(N.S.) 314. The applicable legal principles "have almost always been the fundamental ethical rules of right and wrong." Robinson v. Mollett, L.R. 7 H.L. 802, 817.

The precise question to be decided in the case at bar is whether on the facts found the defendants as directors had a right to buy stock of the plaintiff, a stockholder. Every element of actual fraud or misdoing by the defendants is negatived by the findings. Fraud cannot be presumed; it must be proved. Brown v. Little, Brown & Co., Inc., 269 Mass. 102, 117, 168 N.E. 521, 66 A.L.R. 1284. The facts found afford no ground for inferring fraud or conspiracy. The only knowledge possessed by the defendants not open to the plaintiff was the existence of a theory formulated in a thesis by a geologist as to the possible existence of copper deposits where certain geological conditions existed common to the property of the Cliff Mining Company and that of other mining companies in its neighborhood. This thesis did not express an opinion that copper deposits would be found at any particular spot or on property of any specified owner. Whether that theory was sound or fallacious, no one knew, and so far as appears has never been demonstrated. The defendants made no representations to anybody about the theory. No facts found placed upon them any obligation to disclose the theory. A few days after the thesis expounding the theory was brought to the attention of the defendants, the annual report by the directors of the Cliff Mining Company for the calendar year 1925, signed by Agassiz for the directors, was issued. It did not cover the time when the theory was formulated. The report described the status of the operations under the exploration which had been begun in 1925. At the annual meeting of the stockholders of the company held early in April, 1926, no reference was made to the theory. It was then at most a hope, possibly an expectation. It had not passed the nebulous stage. No disclosure was made of it. The Cliff Mining Company was not harmed by the nondisclosure. There would have been no advantage to it, so far as appears, from a disclosure. The disclosure would have been detrimental to the interests of another mining corporation in which the defendants were directors. In the circumstances there was no duty on the part of the defendants to set forth to the stockholders at the annual meeting their faith, aspirations and plans for the future. Events as they developed might render advisable radical changes in such views. Disclosure of the theory, if it ultimately was proved to be erroneous or without foundation in fact, might involve the defendants in litigation with those who might act on the hypothesis that it was correct. The stock of the Cliff Mining Company was bought and sold on the stock exchange. The identity of buyers and seller of the stock in question in fact was not known to the parties and perhaps could not readily have been ascertained. The defendants caused the shares to be bought through brokers on the stock exchange. They said nothing to anybody as to the reasons actuating them. The plaintiff was no novice. He was a member of the Boston stock exchange and had kept a record of sales of Cliff Mining Company stock. He acted upon his own judgment in selling his stock. He made no inquiries of the defendants or of other officers of the company. The result is that the plaintiff cannot prevail.

Decree dismissing bill affirmed with costs.

BROPHY v. CITIES SERVICE CO.

Court of Chancery of Delaware, 1949.
31 Del.Ch. 241, 70 A.2d 5.

HARRINGTON, CHANCELLOR. The question is whether the amended complaint states a cause of action against Thomas F. Kennedy, one of the defendants. Four causes are alleged, but only one seeks any relief against him. It appears that with the exception of Kennedy, the individual defendants were directors of Cities Service Company throughout the period involved in the action and constituted the controlling majority of the board. The gravamen of the charge against Kennedy is that at all times material he was employed in an "executive capacity" and as "confidential secretary" to the defendant, W. Alton Jones, a director and officer of Cities Service Company; that in those capacities "he had access to confidential information concerning Cities Service Company" and its operations and the operations of its subsidiaries. The acts of Kennedy labelled fraudulent are briefly, that by reason of his employment he knew in advance from 1932 to the date of filing the amended complaint when Cities Service Company, or its controlled subsidiaries, intended to purchase shares of Cities Service Company's stock on the open market in quantities sufficient to cause a rise in its market price; that knowing in advance when such purchases were to be made Kennedy acquired for his personal account, or for the account of his nominees, Cities Service Company's shares prior to the purchase by the company, and thereafter sold them at a profit resulting from the rise in the market price incident to the purchase by Cities Service Company; that by reason of Kennedy's employment as an executive and as the confidential secretary to an officer and director of Cities Service Company he occupied a position of trust and confidence toward the corporation, with respect to the information so acquired, and the purchase of its stock for his own account was a breach of the duty he owed to Cities Service Company.

The relief sought against Kennedy is that he be directed to account as a constructive trustee for all profits made by him from the purchase and sale of such stock, and that he be adjudged liable to Cities Service Company for the amount of such profits.

Constructive trusts depend for their existence on the wrongful conduct of a defendant causing unjust enrichment, and not on the intent of the parties. See Greenly v. Greenly, Del.Ch., 49 A.2d 126.

A mere employee, not an agent with respect to the matter under consideration, does not ordinarily occupy a position of trust and confidence toward his employer. . . . But if an employee in the course of his employment acquires secret information relating to his employer's business, he occupies a position of trust and confidence toward it, analogous in most respects to that of a fiduciary, and must govern his actions accordingly. . . .

Applying these principles, a confidential relation between Kennedy and Cities Service Company is alleged, though it does not appear that his executive and other duties related to the shaping of corporate policy with respect to the purchase of the capital stock of the corporation, or to any agency relating to its purchase. . . .

The general rule with respect to the rights and duties of a fiduciary appears in the Restatement of the Law of Restitution (§ 200, Comment a): "A fiduciary is subject to a duty to the beneficiary not to use on his own account information confidentially given him by the beneficiary or acquired by him during the course of or on account of the fiduciary relation or in violation of his duties as fiduciary, in competition with or to the injury of the beneficiary, although such information does not relate to the transaction in which he is then employed, unless the information is a matter of general knowledge. . . ."

The acquisition of its own capital stock is not ordinarily an essential corporate function, . . . and in the absence of special circumstances, corporate officers and directors may purchase and sell its capital stock at will, and without any liability to the corporation. Ordinarily an employee has the same rights. But if for some reason the corporation secretly intends to purchase large blocks of its capital stock in the market, and an employee acquires that knowledge in the course of his employment, the application of general principles would seem to require the conclusion that he cannot use that information for his own personal gain. . . . Kennedy claims that in any event no cause of action is alleged against him because it does not appear that the corporation suffered any loss through his purchase of its stock. The complaint alleges that Kennedy and other defendants used confidential and secret information "to their own advantage and to the detriment of Cities Service by acquiring shares in advance for their personal accounts . . . and selling said shares at profits resulting from the aforementioned rise of the market price incident to the purchase by Cities Service." Loss or damage to the corporation cannot be inferred from these general and indefinite allegations. The mere statement that Kennedy acquired stock and that its acquisition was "to the detriment" of the corporation is not enough. But that conclusion does not determine the case. In equity, when the breach of a confidential relation by an employee is relied on and an accounting for any resulting profits is sought, loss to the corporation need not be charged in the complaint. Cf. Loft, Inc. v. Guth, 23 Del.Ch. 138, 2 A.2d 225, affirmed. Guth v. Loft, Inc., 23 Del.Ch. 255, 5 A.2d 503; . . . Public policy will not permit an employee occupying a position of trust and confidence toward his employer to abuse that relation to his own profit, regardless of whether his employer suffers a loss. Cf. Loft, Inc. v. Guth, supra; Guth v. Loft, Inc., supra. . . .

When, therefore, a person "in a confidential or fiduciary position, in breach of his duty, uses his knowledge to make a profit for himself, he is accountable for such profit. . . ." Scott on Trusts, § 505.1, supra.

Kennedy's motion to dismiss the complaint is denied and an order will be entered accordingly.

COMMENT

(1) It is customary to divide the common law jurisdictions into three categories. First, there was the "majority rule", that directors and officers owed no special duty to either present or prospective shareholders and could deal with them at arm's length. Second, there was the "special circumstances" rule often identified with Strong v. Repide.[3] In that case the Supreme Court held that it was improper for the director, administrator general and 75% shareholder of a Philippine corporation to purchase, through a strawman, a minority interest from an outside shareholder. The insider knew that the United States government was likely to purchase the corporation's property in the Philippine Islands as part of Governor Taft's land reform program, thus causing a spectacular appreciation in its stock. The case had considerable impact, even though it was technically based on a section of the Philippine civil code, based on the Spanish Code, that forbade "insidious machinations." Third, there was the "minority rule", holding that a director or officer had a fiduciary duty to disclose facts to an outsider. One of the leading cases of this group is Hotchkiss v. Fischer.[4] There a jury found for defendant, a director and the president of the companies involved. Plaintiff was a widow from Burr Oak, Kansas, who had gone to Topeka in advance of the board meeting to find out whether the corporation would pay a dividend so that she would have enough money to hold on to the shares. The testimony as to the interview between the parties was blurred but it was clear that defendant showed her financial statements of the company. The court asserted that these did not show the

3. 213 U.S. 419, 29 S.Ct. 521, 53 L.Ed. 853 (1909).   4. 136 Kan. 530, 16 P.2d 531 (1932).

"true book value of shares" because fixed assets were carried at cost less depreciation, bonds were carried at cost, etc., and that, therefore, the statements "alone meant little so far as the true value of the corporation was concerned." The defendant, the jury found, correctly answered her questions and told her he did not know whether a dividend would be declared. She sold her shares to him for $1.25 a share and three days later a $1 per share dividend was declared. The Supreme Court of Kansas reversed, holding that a director in such negotiations "acts in a relation of scrupulous trust and confidence", subject to the closest scrutiny. It referred to section 165 of the Restatement of Trusts imposing on a trustee the duty of disclosing "all material facts" to a beneficiary with whom he deals.

It is often not easy to assign a particular state to its appropriate category. There is a distinct drift away from the "majority" rule (it may well not be one anymore). There may also be a reaching to find special circumstances more readily. Finally, the state law in recent years has been overshadowed by resort to the federal courts under Rule 10b–5.[5]

(2) The federal law we study in the next two sections has moved some, but not all, state courts to extend liability in insider trading cases beyond the bounds of the orthodox corporate opportunity doctrine towards eliminating the need for showing current corporate interest in transactions in its own stock.[6]

QUESTIONS

(1) To which of the three groups does Goodwin v. Agassiz belong? How would the Massachusetts court have dealt with the facts in Hotchkiss v. Fischer? How "special" were the facts withheld in Goodwin v. Agassiz?

(2) Is it possible, realistically, for a situation to arise in a face to face sale in which it is necessary to worry about a ruling dealing with omissions? Will the rule about half-truths cover all or substantially all of the cases?

(3) Suppose that you represent I, an officer-director of a small corporation who has been offered shares by a rather hard-pressed shareholder, X, who is unfamiliar not only with this business but with business and finance in general. In fact X is a young heir and distant relative of the founder who views the capitalist, corporationist establishment with disdain. There is really no "market" for the stock. Your client is willing to offer a price 10% above the price at which the last sale was made 18 months ago. In your client's analysis this is a fair price, based on the price/earnings ratios commonly applied to closely held companies in this line of business, as applied to the earnings of the last few years. In I's view this is a desirable transaction because I believes that the company is going to do much better in the next year than in the past. I bases that estimate on rather subjective factors: a sense that the new technical manager is much more competent than his predecessor and that the firm is close to ironing out the "bugs" that have plagued the process on which the firm relies. Can I safely buy the security? If so, what should I say to the seller—if anything? If I asks you to represent him in the negotiations will you be subject

5. State law special fact cases do still crop up, particularly in family or close corporations. E.g., Weatherby v. Weatherby Lumber Co., 94 Idaho 504, 492 P.2d 43 (1972).

6. Compare Diamond v. Oreamuno, 24 N.Y.2d 494, 301 N.Y.S.2d 78, 248 N.E.2d

910 (1969) with Schein v. Chasen, 313 So.2d 739 (Fla.1975). See also Thomas v. Roblin Industries, Inc., 520 F.2d 1393 (3d Cir.1975) (Delaware law).

to the same restraints as your client? To more restraints? Consider Rule 4.1 (DR 7–102).

(4) Is Brophy a solid, orthodox application of the concept of corporate opportunity? What would the court have done with a case in which there was no showing that the corporation was in the market to buy shares? Does the theory of corporate opportunity go so far as to cover such cases? What about cases in which an insider *sells* shares? How does that relate to the corporation's intention to issue and sell new securities?

(5) Is there any very strong reason why state law should be displaced by federal law in this area? If so, do those reasons apply in all cases—to close corporation transactions? To face to face dealings? To those not on an organized securities exchange?

---

3. Federal Regulation of Insider Trading

A. Section 16(b) of the Securities Exchange Act

Congress heard a considerable amount of testimony, when it was considering the 1933 and 1934 Acts, about the evils of trading by insiders on the basis of special knowledge not available to others. This feature appeared in conjunction with other types of market manipulations in which speculators pushed the price of a security up and down to their own benefit. The 1934 Act contains a number of provisions against manipulations. Section 16 deals with trading by "insiders" of registered firms. Subsection (a) requires reports, (b) prohibits specified "short-swing transactions", (c) deals with short selling by insiders and (d) and (e) relate to exemptions. Section 16(a) should be read in conjunction with Section 13(d), added by the tender offer legislation known as the Williams Act, p. 707 infra. That section lowers the reporting threshold in most cases to a 5% acquisition. The concern after 1973 about acquisitions of control over American industries by foreign interests, often thought to be veiled by confidential intermediaries, after 1973 led to a restudy of the problem of obtaining accurate information about the real beneficial ownership of large blocks of stock.

In dealing with Section 16(b) courts have, by and large, followed a sharp-line test, rendering good or bad intentions and knowledge immaterial; the reasoning has been that Congress chose to proscribe a certain rather arbitrarily defined set of transactions, regardless of subjective intent which would be too hard to prove or disprove. Nonetheless, a large number of interpretative questions have arisen under this statute and questions of the *bona fides* of the insiders, or more particularly of the susceptibility of particular types of transactions to being used to exploit inside information, have crept into the cases.

Read Section 16(b) with care. Some words that seem very simple and plain have given rise to much controversy. Many of these questions are technically highly intriguing and it would be easy to spend a great deal of time on these cases. However, for the nonspecialist a much more cursory knowledge will suffice to instill a sense of danger when approaching the reefs of Section 16(b). One should have a sense of alarm whenever there is a conjunction of three elements: (a) an insider relationship, (b) a pairing of a purchase and sale within six months and (c) a resulting "profit". The following text describes a few of the controversies that have arisen and points up a few unexpected dangers.

It is not always clear who qualifies as a statutory "insider" of the issuer. Take the "director or officer" branch first. Suppose that the individual is called an "assistant vice president," a title liberally bestowed by some institutions, in order to quell salary demands, it is said. Is that person an officer even though several layers removed from the top? Conversely, suppose that the title on the door is merely "personal assistant to the president," but in fact the incumbent is the *eminence grise* of the administration. Need a person who was concededly a director or officer at the time of the purchase also be one at the time of sale (or vice versa)? Opinions by the Second Circuit in the Section 16 field are generally regarded as authoritative, and that court has ruled that one need not hold such a post at both ends of the transaction.[5] Now take the 10% shareholder branch. Suppose that X, not a director or officer of the I Corporation, buys 11% of the I Corporation common stock, never previously having held any of that security, and five months later sells it. The Supreme Court recently held that X was not liable.[6] That result may be dictated by the first clause of the last sentence of Section 16(b), but there is still room to question the equity and efficiency of the resulting differentiation. It is not always clear even what the base is to which the 10% is to be applied. As a matter of fact, it may be hard to know exactly how many shares were outstanding on a given day. As a matter of law it may not be clear what securities in a complex financial structure are to be counted toward making up one "class of equity security."

Consider the term "profit". If an insider, I, buys and sells rather actively in a given period of time there are accounting questions as to whether I realized a profit. Suppose I starts with 5,000 shares, buys 1000 shares at 10, sells 1000 shares at 9, buys 1000 shares at 8 and then sells 1000 shares at 7. At the end of the period I has the same number of shares as when the trading started and is $2000 poorer (aside from any commissions and other expenses). I probably would judge the venture not a success. Nonetheless, the accounting authorized by the

5. Adler v. Klawans, 267 F.2d 840 (2d Cir.1959).

6. Foremost–McKesson, Inc. v. Provident Securities Co., 423 U.S. 232, 96 S.Ct. 508, 46 L.Ed.2d 464 (1976).

courts approves of matching the sale at 9 and the later purchase at 8 so as to realize a $1000 profit.[7]

"Purchase and sale" give rise to some rather special questions. If a person holds convertible preferred stock of a company and converts it is this a sale of the preferred? A purchase of the common? There was a substantial body of case law about this before SEC Rule 16b–9 exempted most such exchanges. Suppose that a corporation is, by the procedures called for 8 Del.C. § 251, merged into another corporation. Does the transaction result in the sale of the stock of the old corporation and the purchase of the stock of the new? The cases were not neatly consistent; the SEC's Rule 16b–7 has exempted such transactions but only as to transactions where one corporation owned 85% of the other (see p. 699, infra). Options have also given rise to considerable difficulty, centering on the SEC's Rule 16b–3 which had a rather stormy history in the courts prior to its amendment in 1960. It was stated by the courts that an earlier attempt by the SEC to exercise the exempting power granted by Section 16(b) went beyond its authority.[8] Now the Rule exempts only the receipt of the *option* (which is a security itself) and not the receipt of the *stock* when the option is exercised.

A further question can arise as to whether a transaction is one "sale" or several. For example, suppose a party has acquired 17% of the stock of a corporation and decides to dispose of it before six months are gone. It sells 7.1% and turns over the profit on that amount to the issuer. The next day it sells the remaining 9.9%, claiming that it is a separate sale and that it ceased to be a 10% shareholder at the time of the first sale. The Supreme Court has agreed.[9]

The following case shows the Supreme Court at work on Section 16(b) in a case which raises some general questions about how to construe it as well as an important specific issue.

BLAU v. LEHMAN

Supreme Court of the United States, 1962.
368 U.S. 403, 82 S.Ct. 451, 7 L.Ed.2d 403.

MR. JUSTICE BLACK delivered the opinion of the Court.

The petitioner Blau, a stockholder in Tidewater Associated Oil Company, brought this action in a United States District Court on behalf of the company under § 16(b) of the Securities Exchange Act of 1934 to recover with interest "short swing" profits, that is, profits earned within a six months' period by the purchase and sale of securities, alleged to have been "realized" by respondents in Tidewater securities dealings. Respondents are Lehman Brothers, a partnership engaged in investment banking, the brokering of securities and in securities trading for its own account, and Joseph A. Thomas, a mem-

---

7. E.g., Gratz v. Claughton, 187 F.2d 46 (2d Cir.1951).

8. Greene v. Dietz, 247 F.2d 689 (2d Cir. 1957).

9. Reliance Elec. Co. v. Emerson Elec. Co., 404 U.S. 418, 92 S.Ct. 596, 30 L.Ed.2d 575 (1972) (4–3 decision).

ber of Lehman Brothers and a director of Tidewater. The complaint alleged that Lehman Brothers "deputed . . . Thomas, to represent its interests as a director on the Tide Water Board of Directors," and that within a period of six months in 1954 and 1955 Thomas, while representing the interests of Lehman Brothers as a director of Tidewater and "by reason of his special and inside knowledge of the affairs of Tide Water, advised and caused the defendants, Lehman Brothers, to purchase and sell 50,000 shares of . . . stock of Tide Water, realizing profits which did not inure to and was not recovered by Tide Water."

The case was tried before a district judge without a jury. The evidence showed that Lehman Brothers had in fact earned profits out of short-swing transactions in Tidewater securities while Thomas was a director of that company. But as to the charges of deputization and wrongful use of "inside" information by Lehman Brothers, the evidence was in conflict.

First, there was testimony that respondent Thomas had succeeded Hertz, another Lehman partner, on the board of Tidewater; that Hertz had "joined Tidewater Company thinking it was going to be in the interests of Lehman Brothers"; and that he had suggested Thomas as his successor partly because it was in the interest of Lehman. There was also testimony, however, that Thomas, aside from having mentioned from time to time to some of his partners and other people that he thought Tidewater was "an attractive investment" and under "good" management, had never discussed the operating details of Tidewater affairs with any member of Lehman Brothers; [10] that Lehman had bought the Tidewater securities without consulting Thomas and wholly on the basis of public announcements by Tidewater that common shareholders could thereafter convert their shares to a new cumulative preferred issue; that Thomas did not know of Lehman's intent to buy Tidewater stock until after the initial purchases had been made; that upon learning about the purchases he immediately notified Lehman that he must be excluded from "any risk of the purchase or any profit or loss from the subsequent sale"; and that this disclaimer was accepted by the firm.

From the foregoing and other testimony the District Court found that "there was no evidence that the firm of Lehman Brothers deputed Thomas to represent its interests as director on the board of Tide Water" and that there had been no actual use of inside information, Lehman Brothers having bought its Tidewater stock "solely on the basis of Tide Water's public announcements and without consulting Thomas."

On the basis of these findings the District Court refused to render a judgment, either against the partnership or against Thomas individually, for the $98,686.77 profits which it determined that Lehman Brothers had realized, holding:

> "The law is now well settled that the mere fact that a partner in Lehman Brothers was a director of Tide Water, at the time that Lehman Brothers had this short swing transaction in the stock of Tide Water, is not sufficient to make the partnership liable for the profits thereon, and that Thomas

---

10. In 1956, after the purchase and sale in question, Lehman Brothers participated in the underwriting of some Tidewater bonds. Thomas handled this for Lehman and during the course of the matter discussed Tidewater affairs with the other members of Lehman.

could not be held liable for the profits realized by the other partners from the firm's short swing transactions. Rattner v. Lehman, 2 Cir., 1952, 193 F.2d 564, 565, 567. This precise question was passed upon in the Rattner decision." 173 F.Supp. 590, 593.

Despite its recognition that Thomas had specifically waived his share of the Tidewater transaction profits, the trial court nevertheless held that within the meaning of § 16(b) Thomas had "realized" $3,893.41, his proportionate share of the profits of Lehman Brothers. The court consequently entered judgment against Thomas for that amount but refused to allow interest against him. On appeal, taken by both sides, the Court of Appeals for the Second Circuit adhered to the view it had taken in Rattner v. Lehman, supra, and affirmed the District Court's judgment in all respects, Judge Clark dissenting, 286 F.2d 786. The Securities and Exchange Commission then sought leave from the Court of Appeals *en banc* to file an *amicus curiae* petition for rehearing urging the overruling of the Rattner case. The Commission's motion was denied, Judges Clark and Smith dissenting. We granted certiorari on the petition of Blau, filed on behalf of himself, other stockholders and Tidewater, and supported by the Commission. 366 U.S. 902, 81 S.Ct. 1048, 6 L.Ed.2d 202. The questions presented by the petition are whether the courts below erred: (1) in refusing to render a judgment against the Lehman partnership for the $98,686.77 profits they were found to have "realized" from their "short-swing" transactions in Tidewater stock, (2) in refusing to render judgment against Thomas for the full $98,686.77 profits, and (3) in refusing to allow interest on the $3,893.41 recovery allowed against Thomas.

Petitioner apparently seeks to have us decide the questions presented as though he had proven the allegations of his complaint that Lehman Brothers actually deputized Thomas to represent its interests as a director of Tidewater, and that it was his advice and counsel based on his special and inside knowledge of Tidewater's affairs that caused Lehman Brothers to buy and sell Tidewater's stock. But the trial court found otherwise and the Court of Appeals affirmed these findings. Inferences could perhaps have been drawn from the evidence to support petitioner's charges, but examination of the record makes it clear to us that the findings of the two courts below were not clearly erroneous. Moreover, we cannot agree with the Commission that the court's determinations of the disputed factual issues were conclusions of law rather than findings of fact. We must therefore decide whether Lehman Brothers, Thomas or both have an absolute liability under § 16(b) to pay over all profits made on Lehman's Tidewater stock dealings even though Thomas was not sitting on Tidewater's board to represent Lehman and even though the profits made by the partnership were on its own initiative, independently of any advice or "inside" knowledge given it by director Thomas.

First. The language of § 16 does not purport to impose its extraordinary liability on any "person," "fiduciary" or not, unless he or it is a "director," "officer" or "beneficial owner of more than 10 per centum of any class of equity security . . . which is registered on a national securities exchange." Lehman Brothers was neither an officer nor a 10% stockholder of Tidewater, but petitioner and the Commission contend that the Lehman partnership is or should be treated as a director under § 16(b).

(a) Although admittedly not "literally designated" as one, it is contended that Lehman is a director. No doubt Lehman Brothers, though a partnership, could for purposes of § 16 be a "director" of Tidewater and function through a deputy, since § 3(a)(9) of the Act provides that " 'person' means . . . partnership" and § 3(a)(7) that " 'director' means any director of a corporation or any person performing similar functions with respect to any organization, whether incorporated or unincorporated." Consequently, Lehman Brothers would be a "director" of Tidewater, if as petitioner's complaint charged Lehman actually functioned as a director through Thomas, who had been deputized by Lehman to perform a director's duties not for himself but for Lehman. But the findings of the two courts below, which we have accepted, preclude such a holding. It was Thomas, not Lehman Brothers as an entity, that was the director of Tidewater.

(b) It is next argued that the intent of § 3(a)(9) in defining "person" as including a partnership is to treat a partnership as an inseparable entity. Because Thomas, one member of this inseparable entity, is an "insider," it is contended that the whole partnership should be considered the "insider." But the obvious intent of § 3(a)(9), as the Commission apparently realizes, is merely to make it clear that a partnership can be treated as an entity under the statute, not that it must be. This affords no reason at all for construing the word "director" in § 16(b) as though it read "partnership of which the director is a member." And the fact that Congress provided in § 3(a)(9) for a partnership to be treated as an entity in its own right likewise offers no support for the argument that Congress wanted a partnership to be subject to all the responsibilities and financial burdens of its members in carrying on their other individual business activities.

(c) Both the petitioner and the Commission contend on policy grounds that the Lehman partnership should be held liable even though it is neither a director, officer, nor a 10% stockholder. Conceding that such an interpretation is not justified by the literal language of § 16(b) which plainly limits liability to directors, officers, and 10% stockholders, it is argued that we should expand § 16(b) to cover partnerships of which a director is a member in order to carry out the congressionally declared purpose "of preventing the unfair use of information which may have been obtained by such beneficial owner, director, or officer by reason of his relationship to the issuer. . . ." Failure to do so, it is argued, will leave a large and unintended loophole in the statute—one "substantially eliminating the great Wall Street trading firms from the statute's operation." 286 F.2d, at 799. These firms it is claimed will be able to evade the Act and take advantage of the "inside" information available to their members as insiders of countless corporations merely by trading "inside" information among the various partners.

The argument of petitioner and the Commission seems to go so far as to suggest that § 16(b)'s forfeiture of profits should be extended to include all persons realizing "short-swing" profits who either act on the basis of "inside" information or have the possibility of "inside" information. One may agree that petitioner and the Commission present persuasive policy arguments that the Act should be broadened in this way to prevent "the unfair use of information" more effectively than can be accomplished by leaving the Act so as to require forfeiture of profits only by those specifically designated by Congress to suffer those losses. But this very broadening of the categories of persons on whom these liabilities are imposed by the language of § 16(b) was considered and rejected by Congress when it passed the Act. Drafts of provisions that eventually became § 16(b) not only would have made it unlawful for any director, officer or 10% stockholder to disclose any confidential information regarding registered securities, but also would have made all profits received by *anyone,* "insider," or not, "to whom such unlawful disclosure" had been made recoverable by the company.[11]

Not only did Congress refuse to give § 16(b) the content we are now urged to put into it by interpretation, but with knowledge that in 1952 the Second Circuit Court of Appeals refused, in the Rattner case, to apply § 16(b) to Lehman Brothers in circumstances substantially like those here, Congress has left the Act as it was. And so far as the record shows this interpretation of § 16(b) was the view of the Commission until it intervened last year in this case. Indeed in the Rattner case the Court of Appeals relied in part on Commission Rule X–16A–3(b) which required insider-partners to report only the amount of their own holdings and not the amount of holdings by the partnership. While the Commission has since changed this rule to require disclosure of partnership holdings too, its official release explaining the change stated that the new rule was "not intended as a modification of the principles governing liability for short-swing transactions under section 16(b) as set forth in the case of Rattner v. Lehman. . . ." Congress can and might amend § 16(b) if the Commission would present to it the policy arguments it has to us, but we think that Congress is the proper agency to change an interpretation of the Act unbroken since its passage, if the change is to be made.

Second. The petitioner and the Commission contend that Thomas should be required individually to pay to Tidewater the entire $98,686.77 profit Lehman Brothers realized on the ground that under partnership law he is co-owner of the entire undivided amount and has therefore "realized" it all. "[O]nly by holding the partner-director liable for the *entire* short-swing profits realized by his firm," it is urged, can "an effective prophylactic to the stated statutory policy . . . be fully enforced." But liability under § 16(b) is to be determined neither by general partnership law nor by adding to the "prophylactic" effect Congress itself clearly prescribed in § 16(b). That section leaves no

---

11. Thus, § 15(b) of both H.R. 7852, and S. 2693, 73d Cong., 2d Sess. provided: "(b) *It shall be unlawful for any director,* officer, or owner of securities, owning as of record and/or beneficially more than 5 percentum of any class of stock of any issuer, and security of which is registered on a national securities exchange. . . . *(3) To disclose, directly or indirectly, any confidential information regarding or affecting such registered security,* not necessary or proper to be disclosed as a part of his corporate duties. *Any profit made by any person, to whom such unlawful disclosure shall have been made,* in respect of any transaction or transactions in such registered security within a period not exceeding six months after such disclosure *shall inure to and be recoverable by the issuer* unless such person shall have had no reasonable ground to believe that the disclosure was confidential or was made not in the performance of corporate duties. . . ." (Emphasis added.)

As to the meaning ascribed to this provision, see Hearings before the Committee on Banking and Currency on S.Res. No. 84, 72d Cong., 2d Sess., and S.Res. No. 56 and 97, 73d Cong., 1st and 2d Sess. 6555, 6558, 6560–6561; Hearings before Committee on Interstate and Foreign Commerce on H.R. 7852 and H.R. 8720, 73d Cong., 2d Sess. 135–137. These hearings seem to indicate that the provision was omitted from the final act because of anticipated problems of administration. See also Smolowe v. Delendo Corp., 2 Cir., 136 F.2d 231, 236; Rattner v. Lehman, 2 Cir., 193 F.2d 564.

room for judicial doubt that a director is to pay to his company only "any profit realized *by him*" from short-swing transactions. (Emphasis added.) It would be nothing but a fiction to say that Thomas "realized" all the profits earned by the partnership of which he was a member. It was not error to refuse to hold Thomas liable for profits he did not make.

Third. It is contended that both courts below erred in failing to allow interest on the recovery of Thomas' share of the partnership profits. Section 16(b) says nothing about interest one way or the other. This Court has said in a kindred situation that "interest is not recovered according to a rigid theory of compensation for money withheld, but is given in response to considerations of fairness. It is denied when its exaction would be inequitable." Board of Commissioners of Jackson County, Kansas v. United States, 308 U.S. 343, 352, 60 S.Ct. 285, 289, 84 L.Ed. 313. Both courts below denied interest here and we cannot say that the denial was either so unfair or so inequitable as to require us to upset it.

Affirmed.

MR. JUSTICE STEWART took no part in the disposition of this case.

MR. JUSTICE DOUGLAS, with whom THE CHIEF JUSTICE concurs, dissenting.

What the Court does today is substantially to eliminate "the great Wall Street trading firms" from the operation of § 16(b), as Judge Clark stated in his dissent in the Court of Appeals. 286 F.2d 786, 799. This result follows because of the wide dispersion of partners of investment banking firms among our major corporations. Lehman Bros. has partners on 100 boards. Under today's ruling that firm can make a rich harvest on the "inside information" which § 16 of the Act covers because each partner need account only for his distributive share of the firm's profits on "inside information", the other partners keeping the balance. This is a mutilation of the Act.

If a partnership can be a "director" within the meaning of § 16(a), then "any profit realized by him," as those words are used in § 16(b), includes all the profits, not merely a portion of them, which the partnership realized on the "inside information." There is no basis in reason for saying a partnership cannot be a "director" for purposes of the Act. In Rattner v. Lehman, 2 Cir., 193 F.2d 564, 567,[12] Judge Learned Hand said he was "not prepared to say" that a partnership could not be considered a "director", adding "for some purposes the common law does treat a firm as a jural person." In his view a partnership might be a "director" within the meaning of § 16 if it "deputed a partner" to represent its interests. Yet formal designation

---

12. The Rattner decision was rendered at a time when the Securities and Exchange Commission, pursuant to its regulatory power, provided a reporting requirement for § 16(a) which allowed a partner-director to disclose only that amount of the equity securities of the corporation in question held by his partnership and representing his proportionate interest in the partnership. Rule X–16a–3. After the Rattner decision that Rule was amended to read:

"A partner who is required under § 240.16a–1 to report in respect of any equity security owned by the partnership shall include in his report the entire amount of such equity security owned by the partnership. He may, if he so elects, disclose the extent of his interest in the partnership and the partnership transactions." 17 CFR 1961 Cum.Supp., § 240.16a–3(b). See Loss, Securities Regulation, Vol. 2, pp. 1102–1104 (1961).

is no more significant than informal approval. Everyone knows that the investment banking-corporation alliances are consciously constructed so as to increase the profits of the bankers. In partnership law a debate has long raged over whether a partnership is an entity or an aggregate. Pursuit of that will-o'-the-wisp is not profitable. For even New York with its aggregate theory recognizes that a partnership is or may be considered an entity for some purposes. It is easier to make this partnership a "director" for purposes of § 16 than to hold the opposite. Section 16(a) speaks of every "person" who is a "director." In § 3(a)(9) "person" is defined to include, *inter alia*, "a partnership." Thus, the purpose to subject a partnership to the provisions of § 16 need not turn on a strained reading of that section.

At the root of the present problem are the scope and degree of liability arising out of fiduciary relations. In modern times that liability has been strictly construed. The New York Court of Appeals, speaking through Chief Justice Cardozo in Meinhard v. Salmon, 249 N.Y. 458, 164 N.E. 545, 62 A.L.R. 1, held a joint adventurer to a higher standard than we insist upon today:

> "Many forms of conduct permissible in a workaday world for those acting at arm's length, are forbidden to those bound by fiduciary ties. A trustee is held to something stricter than the morals of the market place. Not honesty alone, but the punctilio of an honor the most sensitive, is then the standard of behavior. As to this there has developed a tradition that is unbending and inveterate. Uncompromising rigidity has been the attitude of courts of equity when petitioned to undermine the rule of undivided loyalty by the 'disintegrating erosion' of particular exceptions (Wendt v. Fischer, 243 N.Y. 439, 444, 154 N.E. 303). Only thus has the level of conduct for fiduciaries been kept at a level higher than that trodden by the crowd. It will not consciously be lowered by any judgment of this court." Id., 249 N.Y. at 464, 164 N.E. at 546.

In Mosser v. Darrow, 341 U.S. 267, 71 S.Ct. 680, 95 L.Ed. 927, we allowed a reorganization trustee to be surcharged $43,447.46 for profits made by his employees through trading in securities of subsidiaries of a bankrupt company. We made this ruling even though there was "no hint or proof that he had been corrupt or that he has any interest, present or future, in the profits he has permitted these employees to make." Id., 341 U.S. at 275, 71 S.Ct. at 684. We said:

> "These strict prohibitions would serve little purpose if the trustee were free to authorize others to do what he is forbidden. While there is no charge of it here, it is obvious that this would open up opportunities for devious dealings in the name of others that the trustee could not conduct in his own. The motives of man are too complex for equity to separate in the case of its trustees the motive of acquiring efficient help from motives of favoring help, for any reason at all or from anticipation of counterfavors later to come. We think that which the trustee had no right to do he had no right to authorize, and that the transactions were as forbidden for benefit of others as they would have been on behalf of the trustee himself.

> .　.　.　.　.　.　.　.　.　.

> ".　.　. equity has sought to limit difficult and delicate fact-finding tasks concerning its own trustee by precluding such

transactions for the reason that their effect is often difficult to trace, and the prohibition is not merely against injuring the estate—it is against profiting out of the position of trust. That this has occurred, so far as the employees are concerned, is undenied." Id., 341 U.S. at 271–273, 71 S.Ct. at 682.

It is said that the failure of Congress to take action to remedy the consequences of the Rattner case somehow or other shows a purpose on the part of Congress to infuse § 16 with the meaning that Rattner gave it. We took that course in Toolson v. New York Yankees, 346 U.S. 356, 74 S.Ct. 78, 98 L.Ed. 64, and adhered to a ruling the Court made in 1922 that baseball was not within the scope of the antitrust laws, because the business had been "left for thirty years to develop, on the understanding that it was not subject to" those laws. Id., 346 U.S. p. 357, 74 S.Ct. p. 78. Even then we had qualms and two Justices dissented. For what we said in Girouard v. United States, 328 U.S. 61, 69, 66 S.Ct. 826, 830, 90 L.Ed. 1084, represents our usual attitude: "It is at best treacherous to find in Congressional silence alone the adoption of a controlling rule of law." It is ironic to apply the Toolson principle here and thus sanction, as vested, a practice so notoriously unethical as profiting on inside information.

We forget much history when we give § 16 a strict and narrow construction. Brandeis in *Other Peoples Money* spoke of the office of "director" as "a happy hunting ground" for investment bankers. He said that "The goose that lays golden eggs has been considered a most valuable possession. But even more profitable is the privilege of taking the golden eggs laid by somebody else's goose. The investment bankers and their associates now enjoy that privilege." Id., at 12.

The hearings that led to the Securities Exchange Act of 1934 are replete with episodes showing how insiders exploited for their personal gain "inside information" which came to them, as fiduciaries and was therefore an asset of the entire body of security holders. The Senate Report labeled those practices as "predatory operations." S.Rep. No. 1455, 73d Cong., 2d Sess., p. 68. It said:

> "Among the most vicious practices unearthed at the hearings before the subcommittee was the flagrant betrayal of their fudiciary duties by directors and officers of corporations who used their positions of trust and the confidential information which came to them in such positions, to aid them in their market activities. Closely allied to this type of abuse was the unscrupulous employment of inside information by large stockholders who, while not directors and officers, exercised sufficient control over the destinies of their companies to enable them to acquire and profit by information not available to others." Id., at 55. See also S.Rep. No. 792, 73d Cong., 2d Sess., p. 9.

The theory embodied in § 16 was the one Brandeis espoused. It was stated by Sam Rayburn as follows: "Men charged with the administration of other people's money must not use inside information for their own advantage." H.R.Rep. No. 1383, 73d Cong., 2d Sess. 13.

What we do today allows all but one partner to share in the feast which the one places on the partnership table. They in turn can offer feasts to him in the 99 other companies of which they are directors. 14 Stan.L.Rev. 192, 198. This result is a dilution of the fiduciary principle that Congress wrote into § 16 of the Act. It is, with all respect, a dilution that is possible only by a strained reading of the law. Until now, the courts have given this fiduciary principle a cordial reception. We should not leave to Congress the task of restoring the edifice that it erected and that we tear down.

COMMENT

Blau v. Lehman involved the investment banking firm Lehman Brothers, which deserves some description here as an exemplar of the evolution and ultimate decline of a powerful Wall Street firm. The Lehmans, after coming from Germany, started business as cotton brokers first in Montgomery, Alabama, and then in New Orleans. They survived the collapse of the South and in 1866 moved to New York, branching out of the cotton business by acquiring a New York Stock Exchange seat in 1887. By 1914 Lehman Brothers had participated in some major underwritings including Sears, Roebuck and F.W. Woolworth, at a time when retailing firms were considered beneath notice; much of this had been done in a collaboration with Goldman, Sachs & Co. that lasted until 1925. The firm continued to prosper so that it was large enough to be a defendant in the government antitrust suit that unsuccessfully charged the Wall Street firms with a conspiracy to divide up the underwriting business.[13] It had in 1944 more than $10,000,000 capital of its own. It advised and managed two large mutual funds, Lehman Corporation, which survived its founding in the inauspicious month of September 1929, and One William Corporation named after the location of the Lehman offices. Its relationship to Lehman Corp. caused the partners to be defendants in Ross v. Bernhard, p. 472 supra. It not only underwrote securities in public offerings, (especially in the retail field where it has sponsored both Macy's and Gimbels), but also arranged private placements, handled some of its own prosperous customers and had substantial investment holdings of its own. It had widely extended research and analytical departments. Originally membership in the firm was limited to men of the family. Distinguished among these have been Herbert (Governor of New York and Senator), Irving (the Court of Appeals Judge who wrote the opinions at pp. 241 and 248 supra), and Robert (possessor of one of the greatest American private art collections). Non family members were admitted later, including General Lucius Clay who, after organizing the Berlin air lift, was allowed to reorganize the Lehman internal structure and Peter Peterson, former Secretary of Commerce. Other partners included Thomas ("an exuberant Texan") whose seat on the Tidewater Board caused the above case. Among Thomas' great coups was his early identification of Litton Industries as a spectacular growth firm (he was less fortunate with Flintkote which took 22 years to get back to the 47¼ price at which it was offered in 1936). The Hertz of the car rental service has been a Lehman partner also; it was his trading in stock of Consolidated Vultee that gave rise to the earlier Section 16(b) case discussed in Blau v. Lehman.[14]

In the 1980's conditions on Wall Street and within the firm changed drastically. The last Lehman left the firm and internal fighting between the traders and the underwriters broke out and power struggles left hard feelings within the firm even though everybody was doing extremely well financially. In 1985 the firm was sold. If you were to look for it today you would find it in Shearson Lehman Holdings which is a 60% owned subsidiary of American

---

13. United States v. Morgan, 118 F.Supp. 621, 661–63 (S.D.N.Y.1953).

14. Sources: J. Wechsberg, The Merchant Bankers ch. 7 (1966); S. Birmingham, "Our Crowd" ch. 11 (1967).

Express Company. This financial giant is the successor not only to Lehman Brothers but to other firms once well known on the street—Hayden Stone, Shearson Hammill, Loeb Rhoades, Hornblower & Weeks and Kuhn Loeb. As of 1987 it was also acquiring E.F. Hutton ("when E.F. Hutton talks everybody listens", the ads used to say). The problems of managers who cannot handle big organizations and of every-increasing needs for capital have apparently made obsolete the more personal banking firms of the past; one may be reminded of what is happening to intermediate size law firms.[15]

QUESTIONS

(1) This question tests your appreciation of the basic mechanisms of Section 16(b). Assume that the corporation is at all times registered under the 1934 Act and has 1,000,000 shares of common stock issued and outstanding. Assume further that X, who never becomes an officer or director of that corporation, trades in its stock as indicated in the following table. Is X liable for any "profit" and, if so, in what amount?

Date	Transaction	No. of Shares	Price
Oct. 1	buy	90,000	10
Nov. 1	buy	30,000	15
Dec. 1	buy	20,000	16
Dec. 15	sell	15,000	13
Jan. 1	buy	10,000	10
April 1	sell	36,000	12
April 5	sell	99,000	9

(2) Robin and Evelyn conduct a very modern marriage, complete with separate beds and brokers. They do, however, deign to file a joint income tax return because of the substantial savings involved. Robin lives in New York and Evelyn in California but they are prosperous enough to visit frequently. They each use their own funds to maintain their style of life but share, 50–50, the cost of the boarding school education of their children. Robin is a director and officer of Mod Industries, Ltd. and, on November 17, exercised a stock option under a plan to which all officers of Mod were parties. The option was exercisable for 5000 shares at 26, which on that date was 9 points below the market. On April 1 Evelyn conferred with Go–Go Investors and was told that it was time to sell all holdings of conservative securities and take a plunge into something more venturesome. Accordingly Evelyn disposed of 25,000 shares (not 10%) of Mod as well as various other securities. The general counsel of Mod has received a letter of demand from a shareholder insisting that a Section 16(b) action be filed against the couple. Advise.

REVIEW QUESTION

If the federal securities laws were being wholly revised, would there be a room for § 16(b) alongside the flexible and far-reaching tool that the courts have made out of Rule 10b–5? (the drafters of the American Law Institute's Federal Securities Code § 1714 (1980) thought so, although they would overrule a number of the cases discussed above).

15. Auletta, Greed and Glory on Wall Street: The Fall of the House of Lehman (1986).

B. Rule 10b–5

Section 10(b) of the Securities Exchange Act as implemented in Rule 10b–5 has proved to be the fountainhead of a great stream of litigation involving insider trading. It is not clear that Congress contemplated this result and, in particular, that it intended to create a private cause of action for violations of this rule. The courts have, however, quite consistently taken the stand that such a cause of action can be implied. One of the earlier cases in this sequence is Speed v. Transamerica Corp.[16] That case involved the same situation as that in Zahn v. Transamerica Corp.[17] However, it was brought by holders of Class A and Class B stock who had accepted an offer by Transamerica made in a letter of November 12, 1942 and thus were not subjected to the "call" successfully challenged in Zahn. The court held that they had a cause of action under Rule 10b–5, saying the following:

> The plan of Transamerica prior to November 12, 1942 to capture the Axton–Fisher inventory by merging, dissolving or liquidating Axton–Fisher is the crucial finding in this case. The non-disclosure of the increased earnings and increased value of the tobacco inventory in the light of the existence of such a plan constitutes a violation of subsections 1, 2 and 3 of Rule X–10B–5 of the Securities and Exchange Commission. These factors—the non-disclosures of the increased earnings and increased value of the tobacco inventory—have significance because there was such a plan.

> In my view, the facts show a violation by defendant of Rule X–10B–5, promulgated by the SEC under Sec. 10(b) of the Securities Exchange Act of 1934, 15 U.S.C.A. § 78j(b). The rule is clear. It is unlawful for an insider, such as a majority stockholder, to purchase the stock of minority stockholders without disclosing material facts affecting the value of the stock, known to the majority stockholder by virtue of his inside position but not known to the selling minority stockholders, which information would have affected the judgment of the sellers. The duty of disclosure stems from the necessity of preventing a corporate insider from utilizing his position to take unfair advantage of the uninformed minority stockholders. It is an attempt to provide some degree of equalization of bargaining position in order that the minority may exercise an informed judgment in any such transaction. Some courts have called this a fiduciary duty while others state it is a duty imposed by the "special circumstances". One of the primary purposes of the Securities Exchange Act of 1934, 15 U.S.C.A. § 78a et seq., was to outlaw the use of inside information by corporate officers and principal stockholders for their own financial advantage to the detriment of uninformed public security holders.

---

16. 99 F.Supp. 808 (D.Del.1951).   **17.** P. 446 supra.

Vagts Basic Corp. Law 3rd Ed. UCB—20

Defendant's contention that only express misrepresentations or half-truths are unlawful fails to look at the fact that an implied misrepresentation is just as fraudulent as an express one and constitutes an untrue statement of a material fact within the meaning of the governing Rule. . . . Defendant's liability for non-disclosure is not based primarily upon the provision of subparagraph 2—subparagraph 1 of the Rule makes it unlawful "To employ any device, scheme, or artifice to defraud" and subparagraph 3 outlaws "any act, practice, or course of business which operates or would operate as a fraud or deceit upon any person . . .". The three subparagraphs of this broadly remedial rule are mutually supporting and not mutually exclusive as defendant contends. Defendant's breach of its duty of disclosure accordingly can be viewed as a violation of all three subparagraphs of the Rule, i.e., (1) a device, scheme, or artifice to defraud; (2) an implied misrepresentation or misleading omission; and (3) an act, practice or course of business which operates or would operate as a fraud upon the plaintiffs.

After 1951 the number of 10b–5 cases in the lower federal courts grew rapidly and developed into a field of law accompanied by learned treatises and extensive law review commentary. The Supreme Court, even while it passed on a number of technical 16(b) problems dealt with in the preceding section, stayed away from 10b–5. Its first, rather tangential, encounter with the rule was in the 1971 decision in Superintendent of Insurance of N.Y. v. Bankers Life & Casualty Co.[18] It is true that it decided several cases such as J.I. Case Co. v. Borak, p. 425 supra, which dealt with the interpretation of other sections of the 1934 Act so as to provide private plaintiffs with relief when that particular section was silent as to its creation of a cause of action. Only in 1975 in the case which follows did the Supreme Court really take a close look at what had been created by the lower courts in the way of a body of case law. It is quite apparent that the majority of the Court did not like what it saw and was determined to cut back; one can only speculate as to whether its reaction ten years earlier might have been simply to decide that there was no implied civil remedy. Given the course of case law adjudication to date and the actual and attempted amendments by the Congress, there is now no doubt but that 10b–5 gives rise to such a cause of action.

This book selects a few cases out of this ocean of decisions with the hope that they will enable you to derive some overview of the problems and be able to guide clients away from dangerous terrain when they contemplate transactions in shares. We have thus slighted questions relating to procedural problems that come up in litigation that results from such activity. There are interesting questions of standing, of the appropriateness of individual plaintiffs to participate in a class action

18.   404 U.S. 6, 92 S.Ct. 165, 30 L.Ed.2d 128 (1971).

or act as class representative, of the right measure of damages to award, etc. The cases that follow first present the Supreme Court's underlying view of the relationship between Rule 10b–5 and the rest of the securities laws, particularly those that create private liabilities. Then we take up two cases that tackle the question of who is an "insider" or, if you prefer, what is "inside" information. Finally we ask some questions of practical importance to corporate management that is trying to comply with the rules—when is information so "material" that it must be disclosed? at what time and in what manner should it be made public? how can it be kept confidential until that time?

While the courts have poured forth precedent Congress has not been totally inactive. In 1984 it passed the Insider Trading Sanctions Act which provided for specified forfeiture penalties to be sought by the SEC; it did not, however, define the activity for which increased sanctions could be imposed. It also passed in 1970 the Racketeer Influenced and Corruption Organizations law (RICO), 18 U.S.C.A. §§ 1961–68, which, it turns out, can sometimes be applied to securities-related misbehavior and possibly even to insider trading. See Sedima S.P.R.L. v. Imrex Co., Inc., 473 U.S. 479, 105 S.Ct. 3275, 87 L.Ed. 346 (1985); cf. Moss v. Morgan Stanley Inc., 719 F.2d 5 (2d Cir.1983) (insider trading ring could be an "enterprise" under RICO). As of early 1988 Congress had draft legislation before it again, partly because of the uncertainties left by the Supreme Court's successive rulings on insider trading set forth below. The SEC meanwhile promulgated Rule 14e–3 dealing with insider trading connected with tender offers. See p. 700 infra.

Meanwhile the law professors have been busy in trying to develop a comprehensive theory of insider trading linked to the economic theory, i.e., the efficient markets hypothesis and the capital assets pricing model. Some have come out for the de-regulation of the field. They would say (a) the party on the other side of the transaction is not really injured because he or she might have sold to or bought from an ignorant trader at the same price, (b) the corporate issuer is not harmed since the obtaining of inside trading profits is a useful incentive for managers and (c) the market is not harmed but rather made more efficient because managers' trading will move the price to its appropriate level more quickly than if they are prevented from doing so.

Those who would preserve the regulation respond by arguing (a) that the entire market would become less efficient in a sense if investors perceived that inside trading was going on on a large scale because they would calculate in a new risk to their investment and ask an additional premium for accepting it,[19] (b) that corporations are harmed because managements will be motivated to do things and say

---

19. It can be argued that the very efficiency of the securities markets lulls people into thinking that they can trade on the basis of prices generated by the trading of more informed and specialized analysts and thus sets them up for special disillusionment when the inside information factor is slipped in.

things in ways that will help their securities trading rather than the shareholder wealth maximization goals they are supposed to be pursuing. The parties will also argue about whether it would be useful to take the matter out from the governmental regulatory process and remit it to the outcome of bargaining between corporations that will see to the interests of shareholders and the affected managers. It is not clear that corporations would let loose their managers' trading rapacity; you will see in some of the materials that follow evidence that firms really try to curb inside trading.

BLUE CHIP STAMPS v. MANOR DRUG STORES

Supreme Court of the United States, 1975.
421 U.S. 723, 95 S.Ct. 1917, 44 L.Ed.2d 539.

[In 1963 the United States filed a civil antitrust suit against Blue Chip Stamp Co. (Old Blue Chip) which provided trading stamps to retailers and against nine retailers who owned 90% of its stock. In 1967 a consent decree was entered. It provided for the merger of Old Blue Chip into a new corporation and the offering of a substantial part of the shares of the new company's common stock to retailers who had used the stamps but had not owned stock. The offering of stock and debentures in units was registered under the 1933 Act, and about 50% of the securities offered were sold in 1968. In 1970 plaintiff, who had been offered units but which had not bought them, brought this action under Rule 10b–5 against the old and new companies, eight of the nine shareholders and the directors. It asserted that the prospectus with which the units were offered was deliberately made over-pessimistic with the intention of discouraging retailers from buying so that the rejected units could be sold to the public at a higher price. Specifically the complaint alleged that the prospectus falsely stated that claims against New Blue Chip totalled $29,000,000 and that payments on them would consume $8,500,000 (whereas they were settled for less than $1,000,000 three months later), that the company's stamp business would be reduced and that 97.5% of stamps issued would be redeemed (whereas the true rate was under 90%). The complaint demanded $21,400,000 on behalf of the class of offerees who had relied on the false prospectus in rejecting the offer and $25,000,000 in exemplary damages. The district court dismissed the complaint for failure to state a cause of action but the Court of Appeals for the Ninth Circuit reversed. The Supreme Court granted certiorari and, in an opinion by Mr. Justice Rehnquist, reversed the judgment of the Court of Appeals.

The first section of the opinion stated the facts and the second reviewed the history of Section 10 and Rule 10b–5, noting that the courts had implied a private remedy although the statute was silent on this point. It recalled that in Birnbaum v. Newport Steel Corp., 193 F.2d 461 (2d Cir.), cert. denied 343 U.S. 956 (1952), that court held that Rule 10b–5 was limited to actual purchasers and sellers of securities. Section II concluded:]

. . . For the reasons hereinafter stated, we are of the opinion that *Birnbaum* was rightly decided, and that it bars respondent from maintaining this suit under Rule 10b–5.

III

The panel which decided *Birnbaum* consisted of Chief Judge Swan and Judges Learned Hand and Augustus Hand: the opinion was written by the latter. Since both § 10(b) and Rule 10b–5 proscribed only fraud "in connection with the purchase or sale" of securities, and since the history of § 10(b) revealed no congressional intention to extend a private civil remedy for money damages to other than defrauded purchasers or sellers of securities, in contrast to the express civil remedy provided by § 16(b) of the 1934 Act, the court concluded that the plaintiff class in a Rule 10b–5 action was limited to actual purchasers and sellers. 193 F.2d 461, 463–464.

Just as this Court had no occasion to consider the validity of the *Kardon* holding that there was a private cause of action under Rule 10b–5 until 20–odd years later, nearly the same period of time has gone by between the *Birnbaum* decision and our consideration of the case now before us. As with *Kardon,* virtually all lower federal courts facing the issue in the hundreds of reported cases presenting this question over the past quarter century have reaffirmed *Birnbaum's* conclusion that the plaintiff class for purposes of § 10(b) and Rule 10b–5 private damage action is limited to purchasers and sellers of securities. [citations omitted].

In 1957 and again in 1959, the Securities and Exchange Commission sought from Congress amendment of § 10(b) to change its wording from "in connection with the purchase or sale or any security" to "in connection with the purchase or sale of, *or any attempt to purchase or sell,* any security." (Emphasis added.) [citations omitted].

. . . . In the words of a memorandum submitted by the Commission to a congressional committee, the purpose of the proposed change was "to make section 10(b) also applicable to manipulative activities in connection with any attempt to purchase or sell any security." . . . Opposition to the amendment was based on fears of the extension of civil liability under § 10(b) that it would cause. Neither change was adopted by Congress.

The longstanding acceptance by the courts, coupled with Congress' failure to reject *Birnbaum's* reasonable interpretation of the wording of § 10(b), wording which is directed towards injury suffered "in connection with the purchase or sale" of securities, argues significantly in favor of acceptance of the *Birnbaum* rule by this Court. Blau v. Lehman, 368 U.S. 403, 413, 82 S.Ct. 451, 456, 7 L.Ed.2d 403 (1962).

Available extrinsic evidence from the texts of the 1933 and 1934 Acts as to the congressional scheme in this regard, though not conclusive, supports the result reached by the *Birnbaum* court. The wording of § 10(b) directed at fraud "in connection with the purchase or sale" of securities stands in contrast with the parallel antifraud provision of the 1933 Act, § 17(a), 15 U.S.C.A. § 77q, reaching fraud "in the offer or sale" of securities. Cf. § 5 of the 1933 Act, 15 U.S.C.A. § 77e. When Congress wished to provide a remedy to those who neither purchase nor sell securities, it had little trouble in doing so expressly. Cf. § 16(b) of the 1934 Act, 15 U.S.C.A. § 78p.

Section 28(a) of the 1934 Act, 15 U.S.C.A. § 78bb, which limits recovery in any private damage action brought under the 1934 Act to "actual damages," likewise provides some support for the purchaser-seller rule. See, e.g., A. Bromberg, Securities Law: Fraud—SEC Rule 10b–5 § 8.8, at 221 (1968). While the damages suffered by purchasers and sellers pursuing a § 10(b) cause of action may on occasion be difficult to ascertain, Affiliated Ute Citizens v. United States, supra, 406 U.S. at 155, 92 S.Ct. at 1473, in the main such purchasers and sellers at least seek to base recovery on a demonstrable number of shares traded. In contrast, a putative plaintiff, who neither purchases nor sells securities but sues instead for intangible economic injury such as loss of a noncontractual opportunity to buy or sell, is more likely to be seeking a largely conjectural and speculative recovery in which the number of shares involved will depend on the plaintiff's subjective hypothesis. [citations omitted].

One of the justifications advanced for implication of a cause of action under § 10(b) lies in § 29(b) of the 1934 Act, 15 U.S.C.A. § 78cc, providing that a contract made in violation of any provision of the 1934 Act is voidable at the option of the deceived party. [citations omitted]. But that justification is absent when there is no actual purchase or sale of securities, or a contract to do so, affected or tainted by a violation of § 10(b).

The principal express nonderivative private civil remedies, created by Congress contemporaneously with the passage of § 10(b), for violations of various provisions of the 1933 and 1934 Acts are by their terms expressly limited to purchasers or sellers of securities. [here the court referred to Sections 11(a) and 12 of the 1933 Act and Sections 9 and 18 of the 1934 Act.] . . . It would indeed be anomalous to impute to Congress an intention to expand the plaintiff class for a judicially implied cause of action beyond the bounds it delineated for comparable express causes of action.

Having said all this, we would by no means be understood as suggesting that we are able to divine from the language of § 10(b) the express "intent of Congress" as to the contours of a private cause of action under Rule 10b–5. When we deal with private actions under Rule 10b–5, we deal with a judicial oak which has grown from little more than a legislative acorn. Such growth may be quite consistent with the congressional enactment and with the role of the federal judiciary in interpreting it, see J.I. Case v. Borak, supra, but it would be disingenuous to suggest that either Congress in 1934 or the Securities and Exchange Commission in 1942 foreordained the present state of the law with respect to Rule 10b–5. It is therefore proper that we consider, in addition to the factors already discussed, what may be described as policy considerations when we come to flesh out the portions of the law with respect to which neither the congressional enactment nor the administrative regulations offer conclusive guidance.

Three principal classes of potential plaintiffs are presently barred by the *Birnbaum* rule. First are potential purchasers of shares, either in a new offering or on the Nation's post-distribution trading markets, who allege that they decided not to purchase because of an unduly gloomy representation or the omission of favorable material which made the issuer appear to be a less favorable investment vehicle than it actually was. Second are actual shareholders in the issuer who allege that they decided not to sell their shares because of an unduly rosy representation or a failure to disclose unfavorable material. Third are shareholders, creditors, and perhaps others related to an issuer who suffered loss in the value of their investment due to corporate or insider activities in connection with the purchase or sale of securities which violate Rule 10b–5. It has been held that shareholder members of the second and third of these classes may frequently be able to circumvent the *Birnbaum* limitation through bringing a derivative action on behalf of the corporate issuer if the latter is itself a purchaser or seller of securities. See e.g., Schoenbaum v. Firstbrook, 405 F.2d 215, 219 (CA2 1968), cert. denied sub nom. Manley v. Schoenbaum, 395 U.S. 906, 89 S.Ct. 1747, 23 L.Ed.2d 219 (1969). But the first of these classes, of which respondent is a member, can not claim the benefit of such a rule.

A great majority of the many commentators on the issue before us have taken the view that the *Birnbaum* limitation on the plaintiff class in a Rule 10b–5 action for damages is an arbitrary restriction which unreasonably prevents some deserving plaintiffs from recovering damages which have in fact been caused by violations of Rule 10b–5. See, e.g., *Lowenfels,* The Demise of the *Birnbaum* Doctrine: A New Era for Rule 10b–5, 54 Va.Law Rev. 268 (1968). The Securities and Exchange Commission has filed an *amicus* brief in this case espousing that same view. We have no doubt that this is indeed a disadvantage of the *Birnbaum* rule,[20] and if it had no countervailing advantages it would be undesirable as a matter of policy, however much it might be supported by precedent and legislative history. But we are of the opinion that there are countervailing advantages to the *Birnbaum* rule, purely as a matter of policy, although those advantages are more difficult to articulate than is the disadvantage.

There has been widespread recognition that litigation under Rule 10b–5 presents a danger of vexatiousness different in degree and in kind from that which accompanies litigation in general. This fact was recognized by Judge Browning in his opinion for the majority of the Court of Appeals in this case, 492 F.2d 141, and by Judge Hufstedler in her dissenting opinion when she said:

> "The purchaser-seller rule has maintained the balances built into the congressional scheme by permitting damage actions to be brought only by those persons whose active participation in the marketing transaction promises enforcement of the statute without undue risk of abuse of the litigation process and without distorting the securities market." 492 F.2d 147.

Judge Friendly in commenting on another aspect of Rule 10b–5 litigation has referred to the possibility that unduly expansive imposition of civil liability "will lead to large judgments, payable in the last analysis by innocent investors, for the benefit of speculators and their lawyers. . . ." SEC v. Texas Gulf Sulphur Co., 401 F.2d 833, 867 (CA2 1968) (concurring opinion). See also Boone and McGowan, Standing to Sue under Rule 10b–5, 49 Tex.L.Rev. 617, 648–649 (1971).

We believe that the concern expressed for the danger of vexatious litigation which could result from a widely expanded class of plaintiffs under Rule 10b–5 is founded in something more substantial than the common complaint of the many defendants who would prefer avoiding lawsuits entirely to either settling them or trying them. These concerns have two largely separate grounds.

The first of these concerns is that in the field of federal securities laws governing disclosure of information even a complaint which by

---

20. Obviously this disadvantage is attenuated to the extent that remedies are available to nonpurchasers and nonsellers under state law. . . .

objective standards may have very little chance of success at trial has a settlement value to the plaintiff out of any proportion to its prospect of success at trial so long as he may prevent the suit from being resolved against him by dismissal or summary judgment. The very pendency of the lawsuit may frustrate or delay normal business activity of the defendant which is totally unrelated to the lawsuit. . . .

Congress itself recognized the potential for nuisance or "strike" suits in this type of litigation, and in the 1934 Act amended § 11 of the 1933 Act to provide that:

"In any suit under this or any other section of this title the court may, in its discretion, require an undertaking for the payment of the costs of such suit, including reasonable attorneys' fees. . . ." (48 Stat. 881, 908.)

Senator Fletcher, Chairman of the Senate Banking and Finance Committee, in introducing Title II of the 1934 Act on the floor of the Senate, stated in explaining the amendment to § 11(e) that "[t]his amendment is the most important of all." 78 Cong.Rec. 8669. Among its purposes was to provide "a defense against blackmail suits." Ibid.

Where Congress in those sections of the 1933 Act which expressly conferred a private cause of action for damages, adopted a provision uniformly regarded as designed to deter "strike" or nuisance actions, Cohen v. Beneficial Loan Corp., 337 U.S. 541, 548–549, 69 S.Ct. 1221, 1226–1227, 93 L.Ed. 1528, that fact alone justifies our consideration of such potential in determining the limits of the class of plaintiffs who may sue in an action wholly implied from the language of the 1934 Act.

The potential for possible abuse of the liberal discovery provisions of the federal rules may likewise exist in this type of case to a greater extent than they do in other litigation. The prospect of extensive deposition of the defendant's officers and associates and the concomitant opportunity for extensive discovery of business documents, is a common occurrence in this and similar types of litigation. To the extent that this process eventually produces relevant evidence which is useful in determining the merits of the claims asserted by the parties, it bears the imprimatur of the Federal Rules of Civil Procedure and of the many cases liberally interpreting them. But to the extent that it permits a plaintiff with a largely groundless claim to simply take up the time of a number of other people, with the right to do so representing an *in terrorem* increment of the settlement value, rather than a reasonably founded hope that the process will reveal relevant evidence, it is a social cost rather than a benefit. Yet to broadly expand the class of plaintiffs who may sue under Rule 10b–5 would appear to encourage the least appealing aspect of the use of the discovery rules.

Without the *Birnbaum* rule, an action under § 10b–5 will turn largely on which oral version of a series of occurrences the jury may decide to credit, and therefore no matter how improbable the allegations of the plaintiff, the case will be virtually impossible to dispose of prior to trial other than by settlement. In the words of Judge Hufstedler's dissenting opinion in the Court of Appeals:

"The great ease with which plaintiffs can allege the requirements for the majority's standing rule and the greater difficulty that plaintiffs are going to have proving the allegations suggests that the majority's rule will allow a relatively high proportion of 'bad' cases into court. The risk of strike suits is particularly high in such cases; although they are difficult to prove at trial, they are even more difficult to dispose of before trial." 492 F.2d, at 147 n. 9.

The *Birnbaum* rule, on the other hand, permits exclusion prior to trial of those plaintiffs who were not themselves purchasers or sellers of the stock in question. The fact of purchase of stock and the fact of sale of stock are generally matters which are verifiable by documentation, and do not depend upon oral recollection, so that failure to qualify under the *Birnbaum* rule is a matter that can normally be established by the defendant either on a motion to dismiss or on a motion for summary judgment.

Obviously there is no general legal principle that courts in fashioning substantive law should do so in a manner which makes it easier, rather than more difficult, for a defendant to obtain a summary judgment. But in this type of litigation, where the mere existence of an unresolved lawsuit has settlement value to the plaintiff not only because of the possibility that he may prevail on the merits, an entirely legitimate component of settlement value, but because of the threat of extensive discovery and disruption of normal business activities which may accompany a lawsuit which is groundless in any event, but cannot be proven so before trial, such a factor is not to be totally dismissed. The *Birnbaum* rule undoubtedly excludes plaintiffs who have in fact been damaged by violations of Rule 10b–5, and to that extent it is undesirable. But it also separates in a readily demonstrable manner the group of plaintiffs who actually purchased or actually sold, and whose version of the facts is therefore more likely to be believed by the trier of fact, from the vastly larger world of potential plaintiffs who might successfully allege a claim but could seldom succeed in proving it. And this fact is one of its advantages.

The second ground for fear of vexatious litigation is based on the concern that, given the generalized contours of liability, the abolition of the *Birnbaum* rule would throw open to the trier of fact many rather hazy issues of historical fact the proof of which depended almost entirely on oral testimony. We in no way disparage the worth and frequent high value of oral testimony when we say that dangers of its abuse appear to exist in this type of action to a peculiarly high degree. The brief of the Securities and Exchange Commission, while opposing the adoption of the *Birnbaum* rule by this Court, states that it agrees with petitioners "that the effect, if any, of a deceptive practice on someone who has neither purchased nor sold securities may be more difficult to demonstrate than is the effect on a purchaser or seller." Brief, pp. 24–25. The brief also points out that frivolous suits can be brought whatever the rules of standing, and reminds us of this Court's recognition "in a different context" that "the expense and annoyance of litigation is 'part of the social burden of living under government.'" Petroleum Exploration, Inc. v. Public Service Comm'n, 304 U.S. 209, 222, 58 S.Ct. 834, 841, 82 L.Ed. 1294. The Commission suggests that in particular cases additional requirements of corroboration of testimony and more limited measure of damages would correct the dangers of an expanded class of plaintiffs.

But the very necessity, or at least the desirability, of fashioning unique rules of corroboration and damages as a correlative to the abolition of the *Birnbaum* rule suggests that the rule itself may have something to be said for it.

In considering the policy underlying the *Birnbaum* rule, it is not inappropriate to advert briefly to the tort of misrepresentation and deceit, to which a claim under § 10b–5 certainly has some relationship. [The court described the historic expansion of the common law of fraud.] These aspects of the evolution of the tort of deceit and misrepresentation suggest a direction away from rules such as *Birnbaum.*

But the typical fact situation in which the classic tort of misrepresentation and deceit evolved was light years away from the world of commercial transactions to which Rule 10b–5 is applicable.

In today's universe of transactions governed by the Securities Exchange Act of 1934, privity of dealing or even personal contact between potential defendant and potential plaintiff is the exception and not the rule. The stock of issuers is listed on financial exchanges utilized by tens of millions of investors and corporate representations reach a potential audience, encompassing not only the diligent few who peruse filed corporate reports or the sizable number of subscribers to financial journals, but the readership of the Nation's daily newspapers. Obviously neither the fact that issuers or other potential defendants under Rule 10b–5 reach a large number of potential investors, or the fact that they are required by law to make their disclosures conform to certain standards, should in any way absolve them from liability for misconduct which is proscribed by Rule 10b–5.

But in the absence of the *Birnbaum* rule, it would be sufficient for a plaintiff to prove that he had failed to purchase or sell stock by reason of a defendant's violation of Rule 10b–5. The manner in which the defendant's violation caused the plaintiff to fail to act could be as a result of the reading of a prospectus, as respondent claims here, but it could just as easily come as a result of a claimed reading of information contained in the financial pages of a local newspaper. Plaintiff's proof would not be that he purchased or sold stock, a fact which would be capable of documentary verification in most situations, but instead that he decided *not* to purchase or sell stock. Plaintiff's entire testimony could be dependent upon uncorroborated oral evidence of many of the crucial elements of his claim, and still be sufficient to go to the jury. The jury would not even have the benefit of weighing the plaintiff's version against the defendant's version, since the elements to which the plaintiff would testify would be in many cases totally unknown and unknowable to the defendant. The very real risk in permitting those in respondent's position to sue under Rule 10b–5 is that the door will be open to recovery of substantial damages on the part of one who offers only his own testimony to prove that he ever consulted a prospectus of the issuer, that he paid any attention to it, or that the representations contained in it damaged him.[21] The virtue of the *Birnbaum* rule, simply stated,

---

21. The SEC, recognizing the necessity for limitations on nonpurchaser, nonseller plaintiffs in the absence of the *Birnbaum* rule, suggests two such limitations to mitigate the practical adverse effects flowing from abolition of the rule. First it suggests requiring some corroborative evidence in addition to oral testimony tending to show that the investment decision of a plaintiff was affected by an omission or misrepresentation. SEC Brief, at 25–26.

Apparently ownership of stock or receipt of a prospectus or press release would be sufficient corroborative evidence in the view of the SEC to reach the jury. We do not believe that such a requirement would adequately respond to the concerns in part underlying the *Birnbaum* rule. Ownership of stock or receipt of a prospectus says little about whether a plaintiff's investment decision was affected by a violation of Rule 10b–5 or whether a decision was even

in this situation, is that it limits the class of plaintiffs to those who have at least dealt in the security to which the prospectus, representation, or omission relates. And their dealing in the security, whether by way of purchase or sale, will generally be an objectively demonstrable fact in an area of the law otherwise very much dependent upon oral testimony. In the absence of the *Birnbaum* doctrine, bystanders to the securities marketing process could await developments on the sidelines without risk, claiming that inaccuracies in disclosure caused nonselling in a falling market and that unduly pessimistic predictions by the issuer followed by a rising market caused them to allow retrospectively golden opportunities to pass.

While much of the development of the law of deceit has been the elimination of artificial barriers to recovery on just claims, we are not the first court to express concern that the inexorable broadening of the class of plaintiff who may sue in this area of the law will ultimately result in more harm than good. In Ultramares Corp. v. Touche, 255 N.Y. 170, 174 N.E. 441, Chief Judge Cardozo observed with respect to "a liability in an indeterminate amount for an indeterminate time to an indeterminate class" that:

> "The hazards of a business conducted on these terms are so extreme as to enkindle doubt whether a flaw may not exist in the implication of the duty that exposes to these consequences." 174 N.E., at 444. . . .

We quite agree that if Congress had legislated the elements of a private cause of action for damages, the duty of the Judicial Branch would be to administer the law which Congress enacted; the judiciary may not circumscribe a right which Congress has conferred because of any disagreement it might have with Congress about the wisdom of creating so expansive a liability. But as we have pointed out, we are not dealing here with any private right created by the express language of § 10b or of Rule 10b–5. No language in either of those provisions speaks at all to the contours of a private cause of action for their violation. However flexibly we may construe the language of both provisions, nothing in such construction militates against the *Birnbaum* rule. We are dealing with a private cause of action which has been judicially found to exist, and which will have to be judicially delimited one way or another unless and until Congress addresses the question. Given the peculiar blend of legislative, administrative, and judicial history which now surrounds Rule 10b–5, we believe that practical factors to which we have adverted, and to which other courts have referred, are entitled to a good deal of weight.

Thus we conclude that what may be called considerations of policy, which we are free to weigh in deciding this case, are by no means entirely on one side of the scale. Taken together with the precedental support for the *Birnbaum* rule over a period of more than 20 years, and the consistency of that rule with what we can glean from the intent of Congress, they lead us to conclude that it is a sound rule and should be followed.

made. Second, the SEC would limit the vicarious liability of corporate issuers to nonpurchasers and nonsellers to situations where the corporate issuer has been unjustly enriched by a violation. . . .

IV

The majority of the Court of Appeals in this case expressed no disagreement with the general proposition that one asserting a claim for damages based on the violation of Rule 10b–5 must be either a purchaser or seller of securities. However, it noted that prior cases have held that persons owning contractual rights to buy or sell securities are not excluded by the *Birnbaum* rule. Relying on these cases, it concluded that respondent's status as an offeree pursuant to the terms of the consent decree served the same function, for purposes of delimiting the class of plaintiffs, as is normally performed by the requirement of a contractual relationship. 492 F.2d, at 142.

The Court of Appeals recognized, and respondent concedes here, that a well-settled line of authority from this Court establishes that a consent decree is not enforceable directly or in collateral proceedings by those who are not parties to it even though they were intended to be benefited by it. [citations omitted.]

A contract to purchase or sell securities is expressly defined by § 3(a) of the 1934 Act, 15 U.S.C.A. § 78c(a),[22] as a purchase or sale of securities for the purposes of that Act. Unlike respondent, who had no contractual right or duty to purchase Blue Chip's securities, the holders of puts, calls, options and other contractual rights or duties to purchase or sell securities have been recognized as "purchasers" or "sellers" of securities for purposes of Rule 10b–5, not because of a judicial conclusion that they were similarly situated to "purchasers" or "sellers," but because the definitional provisions of the 1934 Act themselves grant them such a status.

Even if we were to accept the notion that the *Birnbaum* rule could be circumvented on a case-by-case basis through particularized judicial inquiry into the facts surrounding a complaint, this respondent and the members of his alleged class would be unlikely candidates for such a judicially created exception. While the *Birnbaum* rule has been flexibly interpreted by lower federal courts, we have been unable to locate a

---

22. Section 3(a)(13) of the 1934 Act, 15 U.S.C.A. § 78c(a)(13) provides:

"The terms 'buy' and 'purchase' each include any contract to buy, purchase, or otherwise acquire."

Section 3(a)(14) of the 1934 Act, 15 U.S.C.A. § 78c(a)(14) provides:

"The terms 'sale' and 'sell' each include any contract to sell or otherwise dispose of."

These provisions as enacted starkly contrast with the wording of the bill which became the 1934 Act when it emerged from committee and was presented on the Senate floor by Senator Fletcher, the chairman of the Senate Committee on Banking and Finance. See S. 2693, 73rd Cong., 2d Sess. (1934); 78 Cong.Rec. 2265. Section 3(11) of the bill as presented to the Senate provided:

"The terms 'buy' and 'purchase' each include any contract to buy, purchase, or otherwise acquire, *attempt or offer to acquire or solicitation of an offer to sell a security or any interest in a security.*" (Emphasis added.)

And Section 3(12) of the bill provided:

"The terms 'sale' and 'sell' each include any contract of sale or disposition of, contract to sell or dispose of, *attempt or offer to dispose of, or solicitation of an offer to buy a security or any interest therein.*" (Emphasis added.) During consideration of the bill on the Senate floor, the ambit of these provisions was narrowed through amendment into the present wording of Sections 3(a)(13) and (14) in which form they were enacted as a part of the Act. 48 Stat. 884. In arguing that it, as an offeree of stock, ought to be treated as a purchaser or seller for purposes of the Act, respondent is in effect seeking a judicial reinsertion of language into the Act that Congress had before it but deleted prior to passage.

single decided case from any court in the 20–odd years of litigation since the *Birnbaum* decision which would support the right of persons who were in the position of respondent here to bring a private suit under Rule 10b–5. Respondent was not only not a buyer or seller of any security but it was not even a shareholder of the corporate petitioners.

As indicated, the 1934 Act, under which respondent seeks to assert a cause of action, is general in scope but chiefly concerned with the regulation of post-distribution trading on the Nation's stock exchanges and securities trading markets. The 1933 Act is a far narrower statute chiefly concerned with disclosure and fraud in connection with offerings of securities—primarily, as here, initial distributions of newly issued stock from corporate issuers. 1 L. Loss, Securities Regulation 130–131 (1961). Respondent, who derives no entitlement from the antitrust consent decree and does not otherwise possess any contractual rights relating to the offered stock, stands in the same position as any other disappointed offeree of a stock offering registered under the 1933 Act who claims that an overly pessimistic prospectus, prepared and distributed as required by §§ 5, 10 of the 1933 Act, has caused it to allow its opportunity to purchase to pass.

There is strong evidence that application of the *Birnbaum* rule to preclude suit by the disappointed offeree of a registered 1933 Act offering under Rule 10b–5 furthers the intention of Congress as expressed in the 1933 Act. Congress left little doubt that its purpose in imposing the prospectus and registration requirements in the 1933 Act was to prevent "the high pressured salesmanship rather than careful counsel," causing inflated new issues, through direct limitation by the SEC of "the selling arguments hitherto employed." H.R.Rep. No. 85, 73d Cong., 1st Sess., 2, 8 (1933).

> "Any objection that the compulsory incorporation in selling literature and sales argument of substantially all information concerning the issue, will frighten the buyer with the intricacy of the transaction states one of the best arguments for the provision." Id., at 8.

The SEC, in accord with the congressional purposes, specifically requires prominent emphasis be given in filed registration statements and prospectuses to material adverse contingencies. . . .

Sections 11 and 12 of the 1933 Act provide express civil remedies for misrepresentations and omissions in registration statements and prospectuses filed under the Act, as here charged, but restrict recovery to the offering price of shares actually purchased:

> "To impose a greater responsibility would unnecessarily restrain the conscientious administration of honest business with no compensating advantage to the public." H.R.Rep. No. 85, 73d Cong., 1st Sess., 9 (1933).

And in Title II of the Securities Exchange Act of 1934, 48 Stat. 905–908, the same act adopting § 10(b), Congress amended § 11 of the 1933 Act to limit still further the express civil remedy it conferred. See generally James, Amendments to the Securities Act of 1933, 32 Mich.L.Rev. 1130, 1134 (1934). The additional congressional restrictions, contained in Title II of the 1934 Act, on the already limited express civil remedies provided by the 1933 Act for misrepresentations or omissions in a registration statement or prospectus reflected congressional concern over the impact of even these limited remedies on the new issues market. 78 Cong.Rec. 8668–8669. There is thus ample evidence that Congress did not intend to extend a private cause of action for money damages to the nonpurchasing offeree of a stock offering registered under the 1933 Act for loss of the opportunity to purchase due to an overly pessimistic prospectus.

Beyond the difficulties evident in an extension of standing to this respondent, we do not believe that the *Birnbaum* rule is merely a shorthand judgment on the nature of a particular plaintiff's proof. As a purely practical matter, it is doubtless true that respondent and the members of its class, as offerees and recipients of the prospectus of New Blue Chip, are a smaller class of potential plaintiffs than would be all those who might conceivably assert that they obtained information violative of Rule 10b–5 and attributable to the issuer in the financial pages of their local newspaper. And since respondent likewise had a prior connection with some of petitioners as a result of using the trading stamps marketed by Old Blue Chip, and was intended to benefit from the provisions of the consent decree, there is doubtless more likelihood that its managers read and were damaged by the allegedly misleading statements in the prospectus than there would be in a case filed by a complete stranger to the corporation.

But respondents and the members of their class are neither "purchasers" nor "sellers," as those terms are defined in the 1934 Act, and therefore to the extent that their claim of standing to sue were recognized, it would mean that the lesser practical difficulties of corroborating at least some elements of their proof would be regarded as sufficient to avoid the *Birnbaum* rule. While we have noted that these practical difficulties, particularly in the case of a complete stranger to the corporation, support the retention of that rule, they are by no means the only factor which does so. The general adoption of the rule by other federal courts in the 20–odd years since it was pronounced, and the consistency of the rule with the statutes involved and their legislative history, are likewise bases for retaining the rule. Were we to agree with the Court of Appeals in this case, we would leave the *Birnbaum* rule open to endless case-by-case erosion depending on whether a particular group of plaintiffs were thought by the court in which the issue was being litigated to be sufficiently more discrete than the world of potential purchasers at large to justify an exception. We do not believe that such a shifting and highly fact-oriented disposition of the issue of who may bring a damage claim for violation of Rule 10b–5 is a satisfactory basis for a rule of liability imposed on the conduct of business transactions. Nor is it as consistent as a straightforward application of the *Birnbaum* rule with the other factors which support the retention of that rule. We therefore hold that respondent was not entitled to sue for violation of Rule 10b–5, and the judgment of the Court of Appeals is reversed.

Reversed.

[A concurring opinion written by MR. JUSTICE POWELL, with MR. JUSTICE STEWART and MR. JUSTICE MARSHALL is omitted.]

MR. JUSTICE BLACKMUN, with whom MR. JUSTICE DOUGLAS and MR. JUSTICE BRENNAN join, dissenting.

Today the Court graves into stone *Birnbaum's* arbitrary principle of standing. For this task the Court, unfortunately, chooses to utilize three blunt chisels: (1) reliance on the legislative history of the 1933 and 1934 Securities Acts, conceded as inconclusive in this particular context; (2) acceptance as precedent of two decades of lower court decisions following a doctrine, never before examined here, that was pronounced by a justifiably esteemed panel of that Court of Appeals regarded as the "Mother Court" in this area of the law, but under entirely different circumstances; and (3) resort to utter pragmaticality and a conjectural assertion of "policy considerations" deemed to arise in distinguishing the meritorious Rule 10b–5 suit from the meretricious one. In so doing, the Court exhibits a preternatural solicitousness for corporate well-being and a seeming callousness toward the investing public quite out of keeping, it seems to me, with our own traditions and the intent of the securities laws. . . .

Certainly, this Court must be aware of the realities of life, but it is unwarranted for the Court to take a form of attenuated judicial notice of the motivations that defense counsel may have in settling a case, or of the difficulties that a plaintiff may have in proving his claim.

Perhaps it is true that more cases that come within the *Birnbaum* doctrine can be properly proved than those that fall outside it. But this is no reason for denying standing to sue to plaintiffs, such as those in this case, who allegedly are injured by novel forms of manipulation. We should be wary about heeding the seductive call of expediency and about substituting convenience and ease of processing for the more difficult task of separating the genuine claim from the unfounded one.

Instead of the artificiality of *Birnbaum,* the essential test of a valid Rule 10b–5 claim, it seems to me, must be the showing of a logical nexus between the alleged fraud and the sale or purchase of a security. It is inconceivable that Congress could have intended a broadranging antifraud provision, such as § 10(b), and, at the same time, have intended to impose, or be deemed to welcome, a mechanical overtone and requirement such as the *Birnbaum* doctrine. The facts of this case, if proved and accepted by the factfinder, surely are within the conduct that Congress intended to ban. Whether these particular plaintiffs, or any plaintiff, will be able eventually to carry the burdens of proving fraud and of proving reliance and damage—that is, causality and injury—is a matter that should not be left to speculations of "policy" of the kind now advanced in this forum so far removed from witnesses and evidence.

Finally, I am uneasy about the type of precedent the present decision establishes. Policy considerations can be applied and utilized in like fashion in other situations. The acceptance of this decisional route in this case may well come back to haunt us elsewhere before long. I would decide the case to fulfill the broad purpose that the language of the statutes and the legislative history dictate, and I would avoid the Court's pragmatic solution resting upon a 20–year–old, severely criticized doctrine enunciated for a factually distinct situation.

In short, I would abandon the *Birnbaum* doctrine as a rule of decision in favor of a more general test of nexus, just as the Seventh Circuit did in Eason v. General Motors Acceptance Corp., 490 F.2d 654, 661 (1973), cert. denied, 416 U.S. 960, 94 S.Ct. 1979, 40 L.Ed.2d 312 (1974). I would not worry about any imagined inability of our federal trial and appellate courts to control the flowering of the types of cases that the Court fears might result. Nor would I yet be disturbed about dire consequences that a basically pessimistic attitude foresees if the *Birnbaum* doctrine were allowed quietly to expire. Sensible standards of proof and of demonstrable damages would evolve and serve to protect the worthy and shut out the frivolous.

COMMENT

The approach to construction of Rule 10b–5 exemplified in the Blue Chip Stamps case occurs in several other Supreme Court cases defining the perimeter of that rule. The chief hallmarks of this method include an attempt to read together all of the liability-creating provisions of both the 1933 and 1934 Acts and to infer what Congress might have intended in putting together the two acts as a comprehensive liability scheme. In some cases this original intent approach is favorable to plaintiffs. In Herman & MacLean v. Huddleston, 459 U.S. 375, 103 S.Ct. 683, 74 L.Ed.2d 548 (1983), the Court held that the fact that plaintiffs could have sued under Section 11 of the 1933 Act, pp. 186–194 supra, did not disable them from electing to sue under 10b–5. It found the two items of legislation so different in what they demanded of, and offered to, plaintiffs that they should be available as separate options. Academics had tended to predict a holding that the more specific Section 11 remedy would be found to preempt. In Landreth Timber Co. v. Landreth, 471 U.S. 681, 105 S.Ct. 2297, 85 L.Ed. 692 (1985), plaintiffs were held entitled to sue under 10b–5 when they bought 100% of the stock of the business; the Court held that stock is stock is a security (citing § 3(a)(10) of the 1934 Act but not Gertrude Stein). Lower courts had been developing a "sale of business" doctrine that would have gone the other way.

In other cases it is the defendant that prevails as in Blue Chip. In Ernst & Ernst v. Hochfelder, 425 U.S. 185, 96 S.Ct. 1375, 47 L.Ed.2d 668 (1976), the court held that in a 10b–5 suit a plaintiff would have to allege and prove scienter on the part of defendant. This outcome was derived from contrasting Section 11 of the 1933 Act with 10b–5 to show that Congress knew how to provide for negligence liability when it chose to but had in Section 10(b) used words of "fraud" and "deceit." The Ernst and Ernst case relieved accountants from liability for an allegedly misleading statement which on plaintiff's theory they were negligent in not detecting. The actual fraud had been on the part of the corporation's chief executive officer. Plaintiff alleged that the auditors should have noted the fact that the CEO opened his own mail, which was asserted to be a suspicious indication that he was engaged in illicit activity he was trying to conceal.

CHIARELLA v. UNITED STATES

Supreme Court of the United States, 1980.
445 U.S. 222, 100 S.Ct. 1108, 63 L.Ed.2d 348.

[Chiarella was a "markup man" in the composing room of Pandick Press, a New York financial printer. In the course of that work, petitioner handled documents relating to 5 corporate takeover bids. Although the corporate names were left as blanks or aliases until the night of final printing, Chiarella was able to deduce the names. He bought stock in the target companies and sold immediately after the offers became public, thus realizing a gain of $30,000 in 14 months. When the facts came out Pandick discharged Chiarella. The SEC both filed an injunction action (settled by a consent order in which Chiarella agreed to return the gains) and indicted him for violating § 10b, Rule 10b–5 and § 32 which imposes criminal penalties for wilfull violations of the 1934 Act. He was convicted on all counts and the conviction was affirmed by the Court of Appeals. The Supreme Court granted certiorari and reversed with an opinion by MR. JUSTICE POWELL, in part as follows:]

This case concerns the legal effect of the petitioner's silence. The District Court's charge permitted the jury to convict the petitioner if it found that he willfully failed to inform sellers of target company securities that he knew of a forthcoming takeover bid that would make their shares more valuable. In order to decide whether silence in such circumstances violates § 10(b), it is necessary to review the language and legislative history of that statute as well as its interpretation by the Commission and the federal courts.

Although the starting point of our inquiry is the language of the statute, Ernst & Ernst v. Hochfelder, 425 U.S. 185, 197, 96 S.Ct. 1375, 1382, 47 L.Ed.2d 668 (1976), § 10(b) does not state whether silence may constitute a manipulative or deceptive device. Section 10(b) was designed as a catch-all clause to prevent fraudulent practices. Id., at 202, 206. But neither the legislative history nor the statute itself affords specific guidance for the resolution of this case. When Rule 10b–5 was promulgated in 1942, the SEC did not discuss the possibility that failure to provide information might run afoul of § 10(b).

The SEC took an important step in the development of § 10(b) when it held that a broker-dealer and his firm violated that section by selling securities on the basis of undisclosed information obtained from a director of the issuer corporation who was also a registered representative of the brokerage firm. In Cady, Roberts & Co., 40 S.E.C. 907 (1961), the Commission decided that a corporate insider must abstain from trading in the shares of his corporation unless he has first disclosed all material inside information known to him. The obligation to disclose or abstain derives from

> "[a]n affirmative duty to disclose material information[,] [which] has been traditionally imposed on corporate 'insiders,' particular officers, directors, or controlling stockholders. We, and the courts have consistently held that insiders must disclose material facts which are known to them by virtue of their position but which are not known to persons with whom they deal and which, if known, would affect their investment judgment." Id., at 911.

The Commission emphasized that the duty arose from (i) The existence of a relationship affording access to inside information intended to be available only for a corporate purpose, and (ii) the unfairness of allowing a corporate insider to take advantage of that information by trading without disclosure. Id., at 912, and n. 15.

That the relationship between a corporate insider and the stockholders of his corporation gives rise to a disclosure obligation is not a novel twist of the law. At common law, misrepresentation made for the purpose of inducing reliance upon the false statement is fraudulent. But one who fails to disclose material information prior to the consummation of a transaction commits fraud only when he is under a duty to do so. And the duty to disclose arises when one party has information "that the other [party] is entitled to know because of a fiduciary or similar relation of trust and confidence between them." In its *Cady, Roberts* decision, the Commission recognized a relationship of trust and confidence between the shareholders of a corporation and those insiders who have obtained confidential information by reason of their position with that corporation. This relationship gives rise to a duty to disclose because of the "necessity of preventing a corporate insider from [taking] . . . unfair advantage of the uninformed minority stockholders." Speed v. Transamerica Corp., 99 F.Supp. 808, 829 (D.Del.1951).

The Federal courts have found violations of § 10(b) where corporate insiders used undisclosed information for their own benefit. E.g., SEC v. Texas Gulf Sulphur Co., 401 F.2d 833 (CA2 1968), cert. denied, 404 U.S. 1005, 92 S.Ct. 561, 30 L.Ed.2d 558 (1972). The cases also have emphasized, in accordance with the common-law rule, that "[t]he party charged with failing to disclose market information must be under a duty to disclose it." Frigitemp Corp. v. Financial Dynamics Fund, Inc., 524 F.2d 275, 282 (CA2 1975). Accordingly, a purchaser of stock who has no duty to a prospective seller because he is neither an insider nor a fiduciary has been held to have no obligation to reveal material facts. See General Time Corp. v. Talley Industries, Inc., 403 F.2d 159, 164 (CA2 1968), cert. denied, 393 U.S. 1026, 89 S.Ct. 631, 21 L.Ed.2d 570 (1969).

This Court followed the same approach in Affiliated Ute Citizens v. United States, 406 U.S. 128, 92 S.Ct. 1456, 31 L.Ed.2d 741 (1972). A group of American Indians formed a corporation to manage joint assets derived from tribal holdings. The corporation issued stock to its Indian shareholders and designated a local bank as its transfer agent. Because of the speculative nature of the corporate assets and the difficulty of ascertaining the true value of a share, the corporation requested the bank to stress to its stockholders the importance of retaining the stock. Id., at 146, 92 S.Ct., at 1468. Two of the bank's assistant managers aided the shareholders in disposing of stock which the managers knew was traded in two separate markets—a primary market of Indians selling to non–Indians through the bank and a resale market consisting entirely of non–Indians. Indian sellers charged that the assistant managers had violated § 10(b) and Rule 10b–5 by failing to inform them of the higher prices prevailing in the resale market. The Court recognized that no duty of disclosure would exist if the bank merely had acted as a transfer agent. But the bank also had assumed a duty to act on behalf of the shareholders, and the Indian sellers had relied upon its personnel when they sold their stock. Id., at 152, 92 S.Ct., at 1471. Because these officers of the bank were charged with a responsibility to the shareholders, they could not act as market makers inducing the Indians to sell their stock without disclosing the existence of the more favorable non–Indian market. Id., at 152–153, 92 S.Ct., at 1471–1472.

Thus, administrative and judicial interpretations have established that silence in connection with the purchase or sale of securities may operate as a fraud actionable under § 10(b) despite the absence of statutory language or legislative history specifically addressing the legality of nondisclosure. But such liability is premised upon a duty to disclose arising from a relationship of trust and confidence between parties to a transaction. Application of a duty to disclose prior to trading guarantees that corporate insiders, who have an obligation to place the shareholder's welfare before their own, will not benefit personally through fraudulent use of material nonpublic information.

III

In this case, the petitioner was convicted of violating § 10(b) although he was not a corporate insider and he received no confidential information from the target company. Moreover, the "market information" upon which he relied did not concern the earning power or operations of the target company, but only the plans of the acquiring company. Petitioner's use of that information was not a fraud under § 10(b) unless he was subject to an affirmative duty to disclose it before trading. In this case, the jury instructions failed to specify any such duty. In effect, the trial court instructed the jury that petitioner owed a duty to everyone; to all sellers, indeed, to the market as a whole. The jury simply was told to decide whether petitioner used material, nonpublic information at a time when "he knew other people trading in the securities market did not have access to the same information." Record, at 677.

The Court of Appeals affirmed the conviction by holding that "[a]nyone —corporate insider or not—who regularly receives material nonpublic information may not use that information to trade in securities without incurring an affirmative duty to disclose." 588 F.2d 1358, 1365 (CA2 1978) (emphasis in original). Although the court said that its test would include only persons who regularly receive material nonpublic information, id., at 1366, its rationale for that limitation is unrelated to the existence of a duty to disclose. The Court of Appeals, like the trial court, failed to identify a relationship between petitioner and the sellers that could give rise to a duty. Its decision thus rested solely upon its belief that the federal securities laws have "created a system providing equal access to information necessary for reasoned and intelligent investment decisions." 588 F.2d, at 1362. The use by anyone of material information not generally available is fraudulent, this theory suggests, because such information gives certain buyers or sellers an unfair advantage over less informed buyers and sellers.

This reasoning suffers from two defects. First not every instance of financial unfairness constitutes fraudulent activity under § 10(b). See Santa Fe Industries Inc. v. Green, 430 U.S. 462, 474–477, 97 S.Ct. 1292, 1301–1303, 51 L.Ed.2d 480 (1977). Second, the element required to make silence fraudulent—a duty to disclose—is absent in this case. No duty could arise from petitioner's relationship with the sellers of the target company's securities, for petitioner had no prior dealings with them. He was not their agent, he was not a fiduciary, he was not a person in whom the sellers had placed their trust and confidence. He was, in fact, a complete stranger who dealt with the sellers only through impersonal market transactions.

We cannot affirm petitioner's conviction without recognizing a general duty between all participants in market transactions to forgo actions based on material, nonpublic information. Formulation of such a broad duty, which departs radically from the established doctrine that duty arises from a specific relationship between two parties, . . . should not be undertaken absent some explicit evidence of congressional intent.

As we have seen, no such evidence emerges from the language or legislative history of § 10(b). Moreover, neither the Congress nor the Commission ever has adopted a parity-of-information rule. Instead the problems caused by misuse of market information have been addressed by detailed and sophisticated regulation that recognizes when use of market information may not harm operation of the securities markets. For example, the Williams Act limits but does not completely prohibit a tender offeror's purchases of target corporation stock before public announcement of the offer. Congress' careful action in this and other areas contrasts, and is in some tension, with the broad rule of liability we are asked to adopt in this case.

Indeed, the theory upon which the petitioner was convicted is at odds with the Commission's view of § 10(b) as applied to activity that has the same effect on sellers as the petitioner's purchasers. "Warehousing" takes place when a corporation gives advance notice of its intention to launch a tender offer to institutional investors who then are able to purchase stock in the target company before the tender offer is made public and the price of shares rises. In this case, as in warehousing, a buyer of securities purchases stock in a target corporation on the basis of market information which is unknown to the seller. In both of these situations, the seller's behavior presumably would be altered if he had the nonpublic information. Significantly, however, the Commission has acted to bar warehousing under its authority to regulate tender offers after recognizing that action under § 10(b) would rest on a "somewhat different theory" than that previously used to regulate insider trading as fraudulent activity.

We see no basis for applying such a new and different theory of liability in this case. As we have emphasized before, the 1934 Act cannot be read "'more broadly than its language and the statutory scheme reasonably permit.'" Touche Ross & Co. v. Redington, 442 U.S. 560, 578, 99 S.Ct. 2479, 2490, 61 L.Ed.2d 82 (June 18, 1979), quoting SEC v. Sloan, 436 U.S. 103, 116, 98 S.Ct. 1702, 1711, 56 L.Ed.2d 148 (1978). Section 10(b) is aptly described as a catch-all provision, but what it catches must be fraud. When an allegation of fraud is based upon nondisclosure, there can be no fraud absent a duty to speak. We hold that a duty to disclose under § 10(b) does not arise from the mere possession of nonpublic market information. The contrary result is without support in the legislative history of § 10(b) and would be inconsistent with the careful plan that Congress has enacted for regulation of the securities markets. Cf. Santa Fe Industries Inc. v. Green, 430 U.S., at 479, 97 S.Ct., at 1304.

IV

In its brief to this Court, the United States offers an alternative theory to support petitioner's conviction. It argues that petitioner breached a duty to the acquiring corporation when he acted upon information that he obtained by virtue of his position as an employee of a printer employed by the corporation. The breach of this duty is said to support a conviction under § 10(b) for fraud perpetrated upon both the acquiring corporation and the sellers.

We need not decide whether this theory has merit for it was not submitted to the jury. The jury was told, in the language of Rule 10b-5, that it could convict the petitioner if it concluded that he either (i) employed a device, scheme or artifice to defraud or (ii) engaged in an act, practice, or course of business which operated or would operate as a fraud or deceit upon any person. Record, at 681. The trial judge stated that a "scheme to defraud" is a plan to obtain money by trick or deceit and that "a failure by Chiarella to disclose material, non-public information in connection with his purchase of stock would constitute deceit." Id., at 683. Accordingly, the jury was instructed that the petitioner employed a scheme to defraud if he "did not disclose . . . material non-public information in connection with the purchases of the stock." Id., at 685–686.

Alternatively, the jury was instructed that it could convict if "Chiarella's alleged conduct of having purchased securities without disclosing material, nonpublic information would have or did have the effect of operating as a fraud upon a seller." Id., at 686. The judge earlier had stated that fraud "embraces all the means which human ingenuity can devise and which are resorted to by one individual to gain an advantage over another by false misrepresentation, suggestions or by suppression of the truth." Id., at 683.

The jury instructions demonstrate that petitioner was convicted merely because of his failure to disclose material, nonpublic information to sellers from whom he bought the stock of target corporations. The jury was not instructed on the nature or elements of a duty owed by petitioner to anyone other than the sellers. Because we cannot affirm a criminal conviction on the basis of a theory not presented to the jury, . . . we will not speculate upon whether such a duty exists, whether it has been breached, or whether such a breach constitutes a violation of § 10(b).

The judgment of the Court of Appeals is

Reversed.

[The following opinions are omitted: a concurring opinion by JUSTICE STEVENS, a concurring opinion by JUSTICE BRENNAN, a dissent by CHIEF JUSTICE BURGER and a dissent by JUSTICE BLACKMUN, joined in by JUSTICE MARSHALL].

DIRKS v. SECURITIES EXCHANGE COMMISSION

Supreme Court of the United States, 1983.
467 U.S. 646, 103 S.Ct. 3255, 77 L.Ed. 911.

[In 1973 Dirks, a securities analyst and officer of a New York broker-dealer, received confidential information from Secrist, an ex-officer of Equity Funding of America. Secrist said that there were vast fraudulent activities in Equity Funding and that regulatory agencies had failed to act on complaints. Dirks investigated and found some corroborating evidence; during the same two-week period Dirks told several clients about his information. Some of them sold substantial amounts of Equity Funding securities. Shortly thereafter a sharp fall in the price of Equity Funding's stock from $26 to $15 per share produced New York Stock Exchange, SEC and grand jury action. The SEC censured Dirks for inside trading. He sought review but the Court of Appeals entered judgment against him. The Supreme Court granted certiorari and, in an opinion by JUSTICE POWELL, reversed.]

III

We were explicit in *Chiarella* in saying that there can be no duty to disclose where the person who has traded on inside information "was not [the corporation's] agent, . . . was not a fiduciary, [or] was not a person in whom the sellers [of the securities] had placed their trust and confidence." 445 U.S., at 232, 100 S.Ct., at 1116. Not to require such a fiduciary relationship, we recognized, would "depar[t] radically from the established doctrine that duty arises from a specific relationship between two parties" and would amount to "recognizing a general duty between all participants in market transactions to forgo actions based on material, nonpublic information." Id., at 232, 233, 100 S.Ct., at 1116, 1117. This requirement of a specific relationship between the shareholders and the individual trading on inside information has created analytical difficulties for the SEC and courts in policing tippees who trade on inside information. Unlike insiders who have independent fiduciary duties to both the corporation and its shareholders, the typical tippee has no such relationships. In view of this absence, it has been unclear how a tippee acquires the *Cady, Roberts* duty to refrain from trading on inside information.

A

The SEC's position, as stated in its opinion in this case, is that a tippee "inherits" the *Cady, Roberts* obligation to shareholders whenever he receives inside information from an insider:

> "In tipping potential traders, Dirks breached a duty which he had assumed as a result of knowingly receiving confidential information from [Equity Funding] insiders. Tippees such as Dirks who receive non-public, material information from insiders become 'subject to the same duty as [the] insiders.' Shapiro v. Merrill Lynch, Pierce, Fenner & Smith, Inc. [495 F.2d 228, 237 (CA2 1974) (quoting Ross v. Licht, 263 F.Supp. 395, 410 (SDNY 1967))]. Such a tippee breaches the fiduciary duty which he assumes from the insider when the tippee knowingly transmits the information to someone who will probably trade on the basis thereof. . . . Presumably, Dirks' informants were entitled to disclose the [Equity Funding] fraud in order to bring it to light and its perpetrators to justice. However, Dirks—standing in their shoes—committed a breach of the fiduciary duty which he had assumed in dealing with them, when he passed the information on to traders." 21 S.E.C. Docket, at 1410, n. 42.

This view differs little from the view that we rejected as inconsistent with congressional intent in *Chiarella*. . . .

In effect, the SEC's theory of tippee liability in both cases appears rooted in the idea that the antifraud provisions require equal information among all traders. This conflicts with the principle set forth in *Chiarella* that only some persons, under some circumstances, will be barred from trading while in possession of material nonpublic information. . . .

Imposing a duty to disclose or abstain solely because a person knowingly receives material nonpublic information from an insider and trades on it could have an inhibiting influence on the role of market analysts, which the SEC itself recognizes is necessary to the preservation of a healthy market. It is commonplace for analysts to "ferret out and analyze information," 21 S.E.C. Docket, at 1406, and this often is done by meeting with and questioning corporate officers and others who are insiders. And information that the analysts obtain normally may be the basis for judgments as to the market worth of a corporation's securities. The analyst's judgment in this respect is made available in market letters or otherwise to clients of the firm. It is the nature of this type of information, and indeed of the markets themselves, that such information cannot be made simultaneously available to all of the corporation's stockholders or the public generally.

B

The conclusion that recipients of inside information do not invariably acquire a duty to disclose or abstain does not mean that such tippees always are free to trade on the information. The need for a ban on some tippee trading is clear. Not only are insiders forbidden by their fiduciary relationship from personally using undisclosed corporate information to their advantage, but they also may not give such information to an outsider for the same improper purpose of exploiting the information for their personal gain. . . .

Thus, some tippees must assume an insider's duty to the shareholders not because they receive inside information, but rather because it has been made available to them *improperly*. And for Rule 10b–5 purposes, the insider's disclosure is improper only where it would violate his *Cady, Roberts* duty. Thus, a tippee assumes a fiduciary duty to the shareholders of a corporation not to trade on material nonpublic information only when the insider has breached his fiduciary duty to the shareholders by disclosing the information to the tippee and the tippee knows or should know that there has been a breach. As Commissioner Smith perceptively observed in *In re Investors Management Co.*, 44 S.E.C. 633 (1971): "[T]ippee responsibility must be related back to insider responsibility by a necessary finding that the tippee knew the information was given to him in breach of a duty by a person having a special relationship to the issuer not to disclose the information. . . ." Id., at 651 (concurring in result). Tipping thus properly is viewed only as a means of indirectly violating the *Cady, Roberts* disclose-or-abstain rule.

C

In determining whether a tippee is under an obligation to disclose or abstain, it thus is necessary to determine whether the insider's "tip" constituted a breach of the insider's fiduciary duty. All disclosures of confidential corporate information are not inconsistent with the duty insiders owe to shareholders. In contrast to the extraordinary facts of this case, the more typical situation in which there will be a question whether disclosure violates the insider's *Cady, Roberts* duty is when insiders disclose information to analysts. In some situations, the insider will act consistently with his fiduciary duty to shareholders, and yet release of the information may affect the market. For example, it may not be clear—either to the corporate insider or to the recipient analyst—whether the information will be viewed as material nonpublic information. Corporate officials may mistakenly think the information already has been disclosed or that it is not material enough to affect the market. Whether disclosure is a breach of duty therefore depends in large part on the purpose of the disclosure. This standard was identified by the SEC itself in *Cady, Roberts*: a purpose of the securities laws was to eliminate "use of inside information for personal advantage." 40 S.E.C., at 912, n. 15. Thus, the test is whether the insider personally will benefit, directly or indirectly, from his disclosure. Absent some personal gain, there has been no breach of duty to stockholders. And absent a breach by the insider, there is no derivative breach. As Commissioner Smith stated in *Investors Management Co.:* "It is important in this type of case to focus on policing insiders and what they do . . . rather than on policing information *per se* and its possession. . . ." 44 S.E.C., at 648 (concurring in result).

The SEC argues that, if inside-trading liability does not exist when the information is transmitted for a proper purpose but is used for trading, it would be a rare situation when the parties could not fabricate some ostensibly legitimate business justification for transmitting the information. We think the SEC is unduly concerned. In determining whether the insider's purpose in making a particular disclosure is fraudulent, the SEC and the courts are not required to read the parties' minds. Scienter in some cases is relevant in determining whether the tipper has violated his *Cady, Roberts* duty. But to determine whether the disclosure itself "deceive[s], manipulate[s], or defraud[s]" shareholders, Aaron v. SEC, 446 U.S. 680, 686, 100 S.Ct. 1945, 1950, 64 L.Ed.2d 611 (1980), the initial inquiry is whether there has been a breach of duty by the insider. This requires courts to focus on objective criteria, *i.e.*, whether the insider receives a direct or indirect personal benefit from the disclosure, such as a pecuniary gain or a reputational benefit that will translate into future earnings. Cf. 40 S.E.C., at 912, n. 15; Brudney, Insiders, Outsiders, and Informational Advantages Under the Federal Securities Laws, 93 Harv.L.Rev. 322, 348 (1979) ("The theory . . . is that the insider, by giving the information out selectively, is in effect selling the information to its recipient for cash, reciprocal information, or other things of value for himself . . . ."). There are objective facts and circumstances that often justify such an inference. For example, there may be a relationship between the insider and the recipient that suggests a *quid pro quo* from the latter, or an intention to benefit the particular recipient. The elements of fiduciary duty and exploitation of nonpublic information also exist when an insider makes a gift of confidential information to a trading relative or friend. The tip and trade resemble trading by the insider himself followed by a gift of the profits to the recipient.

Determining whether an insider personally benefits from a particular disclosure, a question of fact, will not always be easy for courts. But it is essential, we think, to have a guiding principle for those whose daily activities must be limited and instructed by the SEC's inside-trading rules, and we believe that there must be a breach of the insider's fiduciary duty before the tippee inherits the duty to disclose or abstain. In contrast, the rule adopted by the SEC in this case would have no limiting principle.

IV

Under the inside-trading and tipping rules set forth above, we find that there was no actionable violation by Dirks. It is undisputed that Dirks himself was a stranger to Equity Funding, with no preexisting fiduciary duty to its shareholders. He took no action, directly or indirectly, that induced the shareholders or officers of Equity Funding to repose trust or confidence in him. There was no expectation by Dirks' sources that he would keep their information in confidence. Nor did Dirks misappropriate or illegally obtain the information about Equity Funding. Unless the insiders breached their *Cady, Roberts* duty to shareholders in disclosing the nonpublic information to Dirks, he breached no duty when he passed it on to investors as well as to the Wall Street Journal.

It is clear that neither Secrist nor the other Equity Funding employees violated their *Cady, Roberts* duty to the corporation's shareholders by providing information to Dirks. The tippers received no monetary or personal benefit for revealing Equity Funding's secrets, nor was their purpose to make a gift of valuable information to Dirks. As the facts of this case clearly indicate, the tippers were motivated by a desire to expose the fraud. In the absence of a breach of duty to shareholders by the insiders, there was no derivative breach by Dirks. Dirks therefore could not have been "a participant after the fact in [an] insider's breach of a fiduciary duty." *Chiarella*, 445 U.S., at 230, n. 12, 100 S.Ct., at 1115, n. 12.

V

We conclude that Dirks, in the circumstances of this case, had no duty to abstain from use of the inside information that he obtained. The judgment of the Court of Appeals therefore is

Reversed.

[There was a dissent by BLACKMUN, BRENNAN and MARSHALL, JJ.]

COMMENT

(1) Not much guidance to Rule 10b–5 aficionados was afforded by the Supreme Court's ruling in Carpenter v. United States, ___ U.S. ___, 108 S.Ct. 316, 98 L.Ed.2d 275 (1987). It involved a fact situation that became well-known on Wall Street because it involved a journalist (Winans) who wrote a daily column for the Wall Street Journal entitled "Heard on the Street." The courts paid it the two-edged compliment of saying that it had enough of a following to have a potential effect of influencing the securities markets. It regularly discussed specific securities and expressed points of view about investing in them. Winans regularly interviewed corporate executives about their firms but at least in the columns involved here did not use inside corporate information. Winans entered into a scheme with two employees of the Kidder Peabody brokerage firm to trade on advance information as to what the column was going to say—in defiance of a Wall Street Journal policy to keep data confidential until publication. Trades were made on the basis of 27 columns, amassing profits of $690,000. Somebody at Kidder Peabody noticed the pattern of correspondence between the column and the trades and investigation and indictment followed. Convictions after a bench trial were affirmed by the Court of Appeals. The Supreme Court affirmed the conviction on securities law counts by an equally divided vote. Unanimously it affirmed convictions under the mail and wire fraud statutes (18 U.S.C.A. §§ 1341, 1343), ruling that the Journal's interest in the information in the column prior to publication was a property right.

(2) At least by the spring of 1988 the Supreme Court had not touched the most notorious insider trading case of all, the Boesky–Levine ring. Ivan Boesky was riding high as the most notorious arbitrageur of all, that is, he was trading in securities that were "in play" as the result of actual or impending takeover attempts. He seemed to have a charmed Midas touch turning his investments into gold. He was widely quoted in the press including a famous statement about the virtues of greed. But a long slow investigation by the SEC showed

that it was not sheer brilliance that guided his investments. An anonymous letter about two Merrill Lynch brokers in Caracas, Venezuela describing their trading led the SEC to take a close look at trades conducted by the Bahamas unit of the Swiss Bank Leu. After maneuverings about Swiss bank secrecy the SEC caught the scent of Dennis Levine, an investment banker. Pleading guilty himself, Levine agreed to repay nearly $12 million in trading profits and provided information as to his confederates. He stated, for example, that he had provided data to Boesky and had been paid off with an attache case full of cash, passed at the Harvard Club of New York. Other sources of inside data were Martin Siegel (Drexel Burnham Lambert and Kidder Peabody), David Brown (Goldman Sachs & Co.), Robert Wilkis (Lazard Freres and E.F. Hutton) and Ilan Reich (Wachtell, Lipton, Rosen & Katz). Fines, jail sentences and civil restitution as well as notoriety befell these parties. A popular movie, "Wall Street" gave a rather crude rendition of these events.

QUESTIONS

(1) The Supreme Court cases that precede this have laid to rest some of the questions about the scope of Rule 10b–5 but left others dangling. The following questions represent issues not finally determined:

(a) The owner of a tract of real estate sells it to V for 1000 shares of the stock of Corporation X. Both parties know the basic facts about Corporation X but the owner knows critical adverse facts about the supply of water to the land which the owner does not tell V.

(b) The beneficiary of a trust asserts that the trustee sold shares of stock held in the trust to a corporation in which the trustee had a major interest and that the sale price was unreasonably low.

(c) A broker dealer who is aware of adverse facts about Corporation X because of S' seat on the board of Corporation X does nothing to tell customer V about the problem so that V does not sell V's holdings of X stock. As a variant assume that V asks S, who says "don't sell".

(d) An associate in a law firm working late at night overhears two investment bankers talking about a takeover bid they are working on. A realizes that when the offer is announced there will be a major rise in the price of the target's stock and buys some.

(e) An investment banker is told by a party who is planning a takeover bid for corporation T about the plan because the offeror wants B's support and knows that B has some stock in T. B goes out and buys more T stock.

(2) Chiarella and Carpenter involve breaches of duty to a party other than the issuer of the security involved in the trading. Did (should) that party have another mode of relief—and what should the damages be in that action? Does it make sense to pile on other types of relief running to different parties?

The case that follows was a classic in its time; it gave judicial imprimatur to the SEC's theory that persons of the issuer who receive inside information from corporate officials—"tippees"—are liable under Rule 10b–5. That seems to be still good law under the Supreme Court cases above. The ruling in Ernst & Ernst, p. 578 supra, casts doubt on much of what it says about the need for showing negligence, intent, etc.

on the part of defendants. But it is still an interesting case with respect to the specificity and detail of its focus on the facts, the disclosure of the facts and what would have been the best disclosure of them.

***

SECURITIES AND EXCHANGE COMMISSION v. TEXAS GULF SULPHUR CO.

United States Court of Appeals, Second Circuit, 1968.
401 F.2d 833, certiorari denied 394 U.S. 976, 89 S.Ct. 1454,
22 L.Ed.2d 756 (1969).

[This was an action by the SEC against Texas Gulf Sulphur Company (TGS) and several of its officers, directors and employees to enjoin certain conduct by them and compel the rescission by the individuals of securities transactions conducted by them in violation of Rule 10b–5. The case was tried before Judge Bonsal who found that no insider activity was illegal before April 9, 1964 because the drilling results were not "material" until then, that the press release was not unlawful since it was not used to induce securities transactions and was not deceptive on the basis of the facts then known. Some defendants who were found liable and the SEC appealed. The Court of Appeals reversed the dismissal of the action as to several of the defendants individual and as to TGS remanded for further proceedings. Portions of the opinion of JUDGE WATERMAN relating to the press release and to the question of "materiality" are reproduced below.]

The Factual Setting

This action derives from the exploratory activities of TGS begun in 1957 on the Canadian Shield in eastern Canada. In March of 1959, aerial geophysical surveys were conducted over more than 15,000 square miles of this area by a group led by defendant Mollison, a mining engineer and a Vice President of TGS. The group included defendant Holyk, TGS's chief geologist, defendant Clayton, an electrical engineer and geophysicist, and defendant Darke, a geologist. These operations resulted in the detection of numerous anomalies, i.e., extraordinary variations in the conductivity of rocks, one of which was on the Kidd 55 segment of land located near Timmins, Ontario.

On October 29 and 30, 1963, Clayton conducted a ground geophysical survey on the northeast portion of the Kidd 55 segment which confirmed the presence of an anomaly and indicated the necessity of diamond core drilling for further evaluation. Drilling of the initial hole, K–55–1, at the strongest part of the anomaly was commenced on November 8 and terminated on November 12 at a depth of 655 feet. Visual estimates by Holyk of the core of K–55–1 indicated an average copper content of 1.15% and an average zinc content of 8.64% over a length of 599 feet. This visual estimate convinced TGS that it was desirable to acquire the remainder of the Kidd 55 segment, and in order to facilitate this acquisition TGS President Stephens instructed the exploration group to keep the results of K–55–1 confidential and undisclosed even as to other officers, directors, and employees of TGS. The hole was concealed and a barren core was intentionally drilled off the anomaly. Meanwhile, the core of K–55–1 had been shipped to Utah for chemical assay which, when received in early December, revealed an average mineral content of 1.18% copper, 8.26% zinc, and 3.94% ounces of silver per ton over a length of 602 feet. These results were so remarkable that neither Clayton, an experienced geophysicist, nor four other TGS expert witnesses, had ever seen or heard of a comparable initial exploratory drill hole in a base metal deposit. So, the trial court concluded, "There is no doubt that the drill core of K–55–1 was unusually good and that it excited the interest and speculation of those who knew about it." Id. at 282. By March 27, 1964, TGS decided that the land acquisition program had advanced to such a point that the company might well resume drilling, and drilling was resumed on March 31.

During this period, from November 12, 1963 when K–55–1 was completed, to March 31, 1964 when drilling was resumed, certain of the individual defendants . . . and persons . . . said to have received "tips" from them, purchased TGS stock or calls thereon. Prior to these transactions these persons had owned 1135 shares of TGS stock and possessed no calls; thereafter they owned a total of 8235 shares and possessed 12,300 calls.

On February 20, 1964, also during this period, TGS issued stock options to 26 of its officers and employees whose salaries exceeded a specified amount, five of whom were the individual defendants Stephens, Fogarty, Mollison, Holyk, and Kline. Of these, only Kline was unaware of the detailed results of K–55–1, but he, too, knew that a hole containing favorable bodies of copper and zinc ore had been drilled in Timmins. At this time, neither the TGS Stock Option Committee nor its Board of Directors had been informed of the results of K–55–1, presumably because of the pending land acquisition program which required confidentiality. All of the foregoing defendants accepted the options granted them.

When drilling was resumed on March 31, hole K–55–3 was commenced 510 feet west of K–55–1 and was drilled easterly at a 45° angle so as to cross K–55–1 in a vertical plane. Daily progress reports of the drilling of this hole K–55–3 and of all subsequently drilled holes were sent to defendants Stephens and Fogarty (President and Executive Vice President of TGS) by Holyk and Mollison. Visual estimates of K–55–3 revealed an average mineral content of 1.12% copper and 7.93% zinc over 641 of the hole's 876–foot length. On April 7, drilling of a third hole, K–55–4, 200 feet south of and parallel to K–55–1 and westerly at a 45° angle, was commenced and mineralization was encountered over 366 of its 579–foot length. Visual estimates indicated an average content of 1.14% copper and 8.24% zinc. Like K–55–1, both K–55–3 and K–55–4 established substantial copper mineralization on the eastern edge of the anomaly. On the basis of these findings relative to the foregoing drilling results, the trial court concluded that the vertical plane created by the intersection of K–55–1 and K–55–3, which measured at least 350 feet wide by 500 feet deep extended southward 200 feet to its intersection with K–55–4 and that "There was real evidence that a body of commercially mineable ore might exist." Id. at 281–82.

On April 8 TGS began with a second drill rig to drill another hole, K–55–6, 300 feet easterly of K–55–1. This hole was drilled westerly at an angle of 60° and was intended to explore mineralization beneath K–55–1. While no visual estimates of its core were immediately available, it was readily apparent by the evening of April 10 that substantial copper mineralization had been encountered over the last 127 feet of the hole's 569–foot length. On April 10, a third drill rig commenced drilling yet another hole, K–55–5, 200 feet north of K–55–1, parallel to the prior holes, and slanted westerly at a 45° angle. By the evening of April 10 in this hole, too, substantial copper mineralization had been encountered over the last 42 feet of its 97–foot length.

Meanwhile, rumors that a major ore strike was in the making had been circulating throughout Canada. On the morning of Saturday, April 11, Stephens at his home in Greenwich, Conn. read in the New York Herald Tribune and in the New York Times unauthorized reports of the TGS drilling which seemed to infer a rich strike from the fact that the drill cores had been flown to the United States for chemical assay. Stephens immediately contacted Fogarty at his home in Rye, N.Y., who in turn telephoned and later that day visited Mollison at Mollison's home in Greenwich to obtain a current report and evaluation of the drilling progress.[23] The following morning, Sunday, Fogarty again telephoned Mollison, inquiring whether Mollison had any further information and told him to return to Timmins with Holyk, the TGS Chief Geologist, as soon as possible "to move things along." With the aid of one Carroll, a public relations consultant, Fogarty drafted a press release designed to quell the rumors, which release, after having been channeled through Stephens and Huntington, a TGS attorney, was issued at 3:00 P.M. on Sunday, April 12, and which appeared in the morning newspapers of general circulation on Monday, April 13. It read in pertinent part as follows:

> NEW YORK April 12—The following statement was made today by Dr. Charles F. Fogarty, executive vice president of Texas Gulf Sulphur Company, in regard to the company's drilling operations near Timmins, Ontario, Canada. Dr. Fogarty said:
>
> "During the past few days, the exploration activities of Texas Gulf Sulphur in the area of Timmins, Ontario, have been widely reported in the press, coupled with rumors of a substantial copper discovery there. These reports exaggerate the scale of operations, and mention plans and statistics of size and grade of ore that are without factual basis and have evidently originated by speculation of people not connected with TGS.
>
> "The facts are as follows. TGS has been exploring in the Timmins area for six years as part of its overall search in Canada and elsewhere for various minerals—lead, copper, zinc, etc. During the course of this work, in Timmins as well as in Eastern Canada, TGS has conducted exploration entirely on its own, without the participation by others. Numerous prospects have been investigated by geophysical means and a large number of selected ones have been core-drilled. These cores are sent to the United States for assay and detailed examination as a matter of routine and on advice of expert Canadian

---

23. Mollison had returned to the United States for the weekend. Friday morning, April 10 he had been on the Kidd tract "and had been advised by defendant Holyk as to the drilling results to 7:00 p.m. on April 10. At that time drill holes K–55–1, K–55–3 and K–55–4 had been completed; drilling of K–55–5 had started on Section 2200 S and had been drilled to 97 feet, encountering mineralization on the last 42 feet; and drilling of K–55–6 had been started on Section 2400 S and had been drilled to 569 feet, encountering mineralization over the last 127 feet." Id. at 294.

legal counsel. No inferences as to grade can be drawn from this procedure.

"Most of the areas drilled in Eastern Canada have revealed either barren pyrite or graphite without value; a few have resulted in discoveries of small or marginal sulphide ore bodies.

"Recent drilling on one property near Timmins has led to preliminary indications that more drilling would be required for proper evaluation of this prospect. The drilling done to date has not been conclusive, but the statements made by many outside quarters are unreliable and include information and figures that are not available to TGS.

"The work done to date has not been sufficient to reach definite conclusions and any statement as to size and grade of ore would be premature and possibly misleading. When we have progressed to the point where reasonable and logical conclusions can be made, TGS will issue a definite statement to its stockholders and to the public in order to clarify the Timmins project."

. . .

The release purported to give the Timmins drilling results as of the release date, April 12. From Mollison Fogarty had been told of the developments through 7:00 P.M. on April 10, and of the remarkable discoveries made up to that time, detailed supra, which discoveries, according to the calculations of the experts who testified for the SEC at the hearing, demonstrated that TGS had already discovered 6.2 to 8.3 million tons of proven ore having gross assay values from $26 to $29 per ton. TGS experts, on the other hand, denied at the hearing that proven or probable ore could have been calculated on April 11 or 12 because there was then no assurance of continuity in the mineralized zone.

The evidence as to the effect of this release on the investing public was equivocal and less than abundant. On April 13 the New York Herald Tribune in an article head-noted "Copper Rumor Deflated" quoted from the TGS release of April 12 and backtracked from its original April 11 report of a major strike but nevertheless inferred from the TGS release that "recent mineral exploratory activity near Timmins, Ontario, has provided preliminary favorable results, sufficient at least to require a step-up in drilling operations." Some witnesses who testified at the hearing stated that they found the release encouraging. On the other hand, a Canadian mining security specialist, Roche, stated that "earlier in the week [before April 16] we had a Dow Jones saying that they [TGS] didn't have anything basically" and a TGS stock specialist for the Midwest Stock Exchange became concerned about his long position in the stock after reading the release. The trial court stated only that "While, in retrospect, the press release may appear gloomy or incomplete, this does not make it misleading or deceptive on the basis of the facts then known." Id. at 296.

Meanwhile, drilling operations continued. By morning of April 13, in K-55-5, the fifth drill hole, substantial copper mineralization had been encountered to the 580 foot mark, and the hole was subsequently drilled to a length of 757 feet without further results. Visual estimates revealed an average content of 0.82% copper and 4.2% zinc over a 525–

foot section. Also by 7:00 A.M. on April 13, K–55–6 had found mineralization to the 946–foot mark. On April 12 a fourth drill rig began to drill K–55–7, which was drilled westerly at a 45° angle, at the eastern edge of the anomaly. The next morning the 137 foot mark had been reached, fifty feet of which showed mineralization. By 7:00 P.M. on April 15, the hole had been completed to a length of 707 feet but had only encountered additional mineralization during a 26–foot length between the 425 and 451–foot marks. A mill test hole, K–55–8, had been drilled and was complete by the evening of April 13, but its mineralization had not been reported upon prior to April 16. K–55–10 was drilled westerly at a 45° angle commencing April 14 and had encountered mineralization over 231 of its 249–foot length by the evening of April 15. It, too, was drilled at the anomaly's eastern edge.

While drilling activity ensued to completion, TGS officials were taking steps toward ultimate disclosure of the discovery. On April 13, a previously-invited reporter for The Northern Miner, a Canadian mining industry journal, visited the drillsite, interviewed Mollison, Holyk and Darke, and prepared an article which confirmed a 10 million ton ore strike. This report, after having been submitted to Mollison and returned to the reporter unamended on April 15, was published in the April 16 issue. A statement relative to the extent of the discovery, in substantial part drafted by Mollison, was given to the Ontario Minister of Mines for release to the Canadian media. Mollison and Holyk expected it to be released over the airways at 11 P.M. on April 15th, but, for undisclosed reasons, it was not released until 9:40 A.M. on the 16th. An official detailed statement, announcing a strike of at least 25 million tons of ore, based on the drilling data set forth above, was read to representatives of American financial media from 10:00 A.M. to 10:10 or 10:15 A.M. on April 16, and appeared over Merrill Lynch's private wire at 10:29 A.M. and somewhat later than expected, over the Dow Jones ticker tape at 10:54 A.M.

Between the time the first press release was issued on April 12 and the dissemination of the TGS official announcement on the morning of April 16, the only defendants before us on appeal who engaged in market activity were Clayton and Crawford and TGS director Coates. Clayton ordered 200 shares of TGS stock through his Canadian broker on April 15 and the order was executed that day over the Midwest Stock Exchange. Crawford ordered 300 shares at midnight on the 15th and another 300 shares at 8:30 A.M. the next day, and these orders were executed over the Midwest Exchange in Chicago at its opening on April 16. Coates left the TGS press conference and called his broker son-in-law Haemisegger shortly before 10:20 A.M. on the 16th and ordered 2,000 shares of TGS for family trust accounts of which Coates was a trustee but not a beneficiary; Haemisegger executed this order over the New York and Midwest Exchanges, and he and his customers purchased 1500 additional shares.

During the period of drilling in Timmins, the market price of TGS stock fluctuated but steadily gained overall. On Friday, November 8, when the drilling began, the stock closed at 17⅜; on Friday, November 15, after K–55–1 had been completed, it closed at 18. After a slight decline to 16⅜ by Friday, November 22, the price rose to 20⅞ by December 13, when the chemical assay results of K–55–1 were received, and closed at a high of 24⅛ on February 21, the day after the stock options had been issued. It had reached a price of 26 by March 31, after the land acquisition program had been completed and drilling had been resumed, and continued to ascend to 30⅛ by the close of trading on April 10, at which time the drilling progress up to then was evaluated for the April 12th press release. On April 13, the day on which the April 12 release was disseminated, TGS opened at 30⅛, rose immediately to a high of 32 and gradually tapered off to close at 30⅞. It closed at 30¼ the next day, and at 29⅜ on April 15. On April 16, the day of the official announcement of the Timmins discovery, the price climbed to a high of 37 and closed at 36⅜. By May 15, TGS stock was selling at 58¼.

I. The Individual Defendants

A. *Introductory*

. . . . Rule 10b–5 was promulgated pursuant to the grant of authority given the SEC by Congress in Section 10(b) of the Securities Exchange Act of 1934 (15 U.S.C.A. § 78j(b)). By that Act Congress purposed to prevent inequitable and unfair practices and to insure fairness in securities transactions generally, whether conducted face-to-face, over the counter, or on exchanges, see 3 Loss, Securities Regulation 1455–56 (2d ed. 1961). The Act and the Rule apply to the transactions here, all of which were consummated on exchanges. . . . Whether predicated on traditional fiduciary concepts, see, e.g., Hotchkiss v. Fisher, 136 Kan. 530, 16 P.2d 531 (Kan.1932), or on the "special facts" doctrine, see, e.g., Strong v. Repide, 213 U.S. 419, 29 S.Ct. 521, 53 L.Ed. 853 (1909), the Rule is based in policy on the justifiable expectation of the securities marketplace that all investors trading on impersonal exchanges have relatively equal access to material information.
. . .

The essence of the Rule is that anyone who, trading for his own account in the securities of a corporation has "access, directly or indirectly, to information intended to be available only for a corporate purpose and not for the personal benefit of anyone" may not take "advantage of such information knowing it is unavailable to those with whom he is dealing," i.e., the investing public. Matter of Cady, Roberts & Co., 40 SEC 907, 912 (1961). Insiders, as directors or management officers are, of course, by this Rule, precluded from so unfairly dealing, but the Rule is also applicable to one possessing the information who may not be strictly termed an "insider" within the meaning of Sec. 16(b) of the Act. Cady, Roberts, supra. Thus, anyone in possession of material inside information must either disclose it to the investing public, or, if he is disabled from disclosing it in order to protect a corporate confidence, or he chooses not to do so, must abstain from trading in or recommending the securities concerned while such inside information remains undisclosed. So, it is here no justification for insider activity that disclosure was forbidden by the legitimate corporate objective of acquiring options to purchase the land surrounding the exploration site; if the information was, as the SEC contends, material,[24] its possessors should have kept out of the market until disclosure was accomplished. . . .

---

24. Congress intended by the Exchange Act to eliminate the idea that the use of inside information for personal advantage was a normal emolument of corporate office. See Sections 2 and 16 of the Act; . . .

B. *Material Inside Information*

An insider is not, of course, always foreclosed from investing in his own company merely because he may be more familiar with company operations than are outside investors. An insider's duty to disclose information or his duty to abstain from dealing in his company's securities arises only in "those situations which are essentially extraordinary in nature and which are reasonably certain to have a substantial effect on the market price of the security if [the extraordinary situation is] disclosed." Fleischer, Securities Trading and Corporate Information Practices: The Implications of the Texas Gulf Sulphur Proceeding, 51 Va.L.Rev. 1271, 1289.

Nor is an insider obligated to confer upon outside investors the benefit of his superior financial or other expert analysis by disclosing his educated guesses or predictions. 3 Loss, op. cit. supra at 1463. The only regulatory objective is that access to material information be enjoyed equally, but this objective requires nothing more than the disclosure of basic facts so that outsiders may draw upon their own evaluative expertise in reaching their own investment decisions with knowledge equal to that of the insiders.

This is not to suggest, however, as did the trial court, that "the test of materiality must necessarily be a conservative one, particularly since many actions under Section 10(b) are brought on the basis of hindsight," 258 F.Supp. 262 at 280, in the sense that the materiality of facts is to be assessed solely by measuring the effect the knowledge of the facts would have upon prudent or conservative investors. As we stated in List v. Fashion Park, Inc., 340 F.2d 457, 462, "The basic test of materiality . . . is whether a *reasonable* man would attach importance . . . in determining his choice of action in the transaction in question. Restatement, Torts § 538(2)(a); accord Prosser, Torts 554–55; I Harper & James, Torts 565–66." (Emphasis supplied.) This, of course, encompasses any fact ". . . which in reasonable and objective contemplation *might* affect the value of the corporation's stock or securities . . .." List v. Fashion Park, Inc., supra at 462, quoting from Kohler v. Kohler Co., 319 F.2d 634, 642, 7 A.L.R.3d 486 (7 Cir.1963). (Emphasis supplied.) Such a fact is a material fact and must be effectively disclosed to the investing public prior to the commencement of insider trading in the corporation's securities. The speculators and chartists of Wall and Bay Streets are also "reasonable" investors entitled to the same legal protection afforded conservative traders.[25] Thus, material facts include not only information disclosing the earnings and distributions of a company but also those facts which affect the probable future of the

---

25. The House of Representatives committee that reported out the bill which eventually became the Act did so with the observation that "no investor, *no speculator,* can safely buy and sell securities upon exchanges without having an intelligent basis for forming his judgment as to the value of the securities he buys or sells." H.R.Rep. No. 1383, 73d Cong., 2d Sess. (1934), p. 11. (Emphasis supplied.)

Dr. Bellemore, the Texas Gulf defendants' expert witness, has written: "The

intelligent speculator assumes that facts are available for a thorough analysis. The speculator then examines the facts to discover and evaluate the risks that are present. He then balances these risks against the apparent opportunities for capital gains and makes his decision accordingly. He is, to the best of his ability, taking calculated risks." Bellemore, Investments: Principles, Practices and Analysis 4 (2d ed. 1962).

company and those which may affect the desire of investors to buy, sell, or hold the company's securities.

In each case, then, whether facts are material within Rule 10b–5 when the facts relate to a particular event and are undisclosed by those persons who are knowledgeable thereof will depend at any given time upon a balancing of both the indicated probability that the event will occur and the anticipated magnitude of the event in light of the totality of the company activity. Here, notwithstanding the trial court's conclusion that the results of the first drill core, K–55–1, were "too 'remote' . . . . to have had any significant impact on the market, i.e., to be deemed material," [26] 258 F.Supp. at 283, knowledge of the possibility, which surely was more than marginal, of the existence of a mine of the vast magnitude indicated by the remarkably rich drill core located rather close to the surface (suggesting mineability by the less expensive open-pit method) within the confines of a large anomaly (suggesting an extensive region of mineralization) might well have affected the price of TGS stock and would certainly have been an important fact to a reasonable, if speculative, investor in deciding whether he should buy, sell, or hold. After all, this first drill core was "unusually good and . . . . excited the interest and speculation of those who knew about it." 258 F.Supp. at 282.

Our disagreement with the district judge on the issue does not, then, go to his findings of basic fact, as to which the "clearly erroneous" rule would apply, but to his understanding of the legal standard applicable to them. . . . Our survey of the facts found below conclusively establishes that knowledge of the results of the discovery hole, K–55–1, would have been important to a reasonable investor and might have affected the price of the stock.[27] On April 16, The Northern Miner, a trade publication in wide circulation among mining stock specialists, called K–55–1, the discovery hole, "one of the most impressive drill holes completed in modern times." Roche, a Canadian broker whose firm specialized in mining securities, characterized the importance to investors of the results of K–55–1. He stated that the completion of "the first drill hole" with "a 600 foot drill core is very very significant . . . anything over 200 feet is considered very significant and 600 feet is just beyond your wildest imagination." He added, however, that it "is a natural thing to buy more stock once they give you the first drill hole." Additional testimony revealed that the prices of stocks of other companies, albeit less diversified, smaller firms, had increased substantially solely on the basis of the discovery of good anomalies or even because of the proximity of their lands to the situs of a potentially major strike.

26. We are not, of course, bound by the trial court's determination as to materiality unless we find it "clearly erroneous" for that standard of appellate review is applicable only to issues of basic fact and not to issues of ultimate fact.

27. We do not suggest that material facts must be disclosed immediately; the timing of disclosure is a matter for the business judgment of the corporate officers entrusted with the management of the corporation within the affirmative disclosure requirements promulgated by the exchanges and by the SEC. Here, a valuable corporate purpose was served by delaying the publication of the K–55–1 discovery. We do intend to convey, however, that where a corporate purpose is thus served by withholding the news of a material fact, those persons who are thus quite properly true to their corporate trust must not during the period of non-disclosure deal personally in the corporation's securities or give to outsiders confidential information not generally available to all the corporations' stockholders and to the public at large.

Finally, a major factor in determining whether the K–55–1 discovery was a material fact is the importance attached to the drilling results by those who knew about it. In view of other unrelated recent developments favorably affecting TGS, participation by an informed person in a regular stock-purchase program, or even sporadic trading by an informed person, might lend only nominal support to the inference of the materiality of the K–55–1 discovery; nevertheless, the timing by those who knew of it of their stock purchases and their purchases of *short-term* calls—purchases in some cases by individuals who had never before purchased calls or even TGS stock—virtually compels the inference that the insiders were influenced by the drilling results. This insider trading activity, which surely constitutes highly pertinent evidence and the only truly objective evidence of the materiality of the K–55–1 discovery, was apparently disregarded by the court below in favor of the testimony of defendants' expert witnesses, all of whom "agreed that one drill core does not establish an ore body, much less a mine," 258 F.Supp. at 282–283. Significantly, however, the court below, while relying upon what these defense experts said the defendant insiders *ought* to have thought about the worth to TGS of the K–55–1 discovery, and finding that from November 12, 1963 to April 6, 1964 Fogarty, Murray, Holyk, and Darke spent more than $100,000 in purchasing TGS stock and calls on that stock, made no finding that the insiders were motivated by any factor other than the extraordinary K–55–1 discovery when they bought their stock and their calls. No reason appears why outside investors, perhaps better acquainted with speculative modes of investment and with, in many cases, perhaps more capital at their disposal for intelligent speculation, would have been less influenced, and would not have been similarly motivated to invest if they had known what the insider investors knew about the K–55–1 discovery.

Our decision to expand the limited protection afforded outside investors by the trial court's narrow definition of materiality is not at all shaken by fears that the elimination of insider trading benefits will deplete the ranks of capable corporate managers by taking away an incentive to accept such employment. Such benefits, in essence, are forms of secret corporate compensation, see Cary, Corporate Standards and Legal Rules, 50 Calif.L.Rev. 408, 409–10 (1962), derived at the expense of the uninformed investing public and not at the expense of the corporation which receives the sole benefit from insider incentives. Moreover, adequate incentives for corporate officers may be provided by properly administered stock options and employee purchase plans of which there are many in existence. In any event, the normal motivation induced by stock ownership, i.e., the identification of an individual with corporate progress, is ill-promoted by condoning the sort of speculative insider activity which occurred here; for example, some of the corporation's stock was sold at market in order to purchase short-term calls upon that stock, calls which would never be exercised to increase a stockholder equity in TGS unless the market price of that stock rose sharply.

The core of Rule 10b–5 is the implementation of the Congressional purpose that all investors should have equal access to the rewards of participation in securities transactions. It was the intent of Congress that all members of the investing public should be subject to identical market risks,—which market risks include, of course the risk that one's evaluative capacity or one's capital available to put at risk may exceed another's capacity or capital. The insiders here were not trading on an equal footing with the outside investors. They alone were in a position to evaluate the probability and magnitude of what seemed from the outset to be a major ore strike; they alone could invest safely, secure in the expectation that the price of TGS stock would rise substantially in the event such a major strike should materialize, but would decline little, if at all, in the event of failure, for the public, ignorant at the outset of the favorable probabilities would likewise be unaware of the unproductive exploration, and the additional exploration costs would not significantly affect TGS market prices. Such inequities based upon unequal access to knowledge should not be shrugged off as inevitable in our way of life, or, in view of the congressional concern in the area, remain uncorrected.

We hold, therefore, that all transactions in TGS stock or calls by individuals apprised of the drilling results of K–55–1 were made in violation of Rule 10b–5. Inasmuch as the visual evaluation of that drill core (a generally reliable estimate though less accurate than a chemical assay) constituted material information, those advised of the results of the visual evaluation as well as those informed of the chemical assay traded in violation of law. . . .

C. *When May Insiders Act?*

Appellant Crawford, who ordered [28] the purchase of TGS stock shortly before the TGS April 16 official announcement, and defendant Coates, who placed orders with and communicated the news to his broker immediately after the official announcement was read at the TGS-called press conference, concede that they were in possession of material information. They contend, however, that their purchases were not proscribed purchases for the news had already been effectively disclosed. We disagree.

Crawford telephoned his orders to his Chicago broker about midnight on April 15 and again at 8:30 in the morning of the 16th, with instructions to buy at the opening of the Midwest Stock Exchange that morning. The trial court's finding that "he sought to, and did, 'beat the news,'" 258 F.Supp. at 287, is well documented by the record. The rumors of a major ore strike which had been circulated in Canada and, to a lesser extent, in New York, had been disclaimed by the TGS press release of April 12, which significantly promised the public an official detailed announcement when possibilities had ripened into actualities. The abbreviated announcement to the Canadian press at 9:40 A.M. on the 16th by the Ontario Minister of Mines and the report carried by The Northern Miner, parts of which had sporadically reached New York on the morning of the 16th through reports from Canadian affiliates to a few New York investment firms, are assuredly not the equivalent of the official 10–15 minute announcement which was not

28. The effective protection of the public from insider exploitation of advance notice of material information requires that the time that an insider places an order, rather than the time of its ultimate execution, be determinative for Rule 10b–5 purposes. Otherwise, insiders would be able to "beat the news," . . . by requesting in advance that their orders be executed immediately after the dissemination of a major news release but before outsiders could act on the release. Thus it is immaterial whether Crawford's orders were executed before or after the announcement was made in Canada (9:40 A.M., April 16) or in the United States (10:00 A.M.), or whether Coates's order was executed before or after the news appeared over the Merrill Lynch (10:29 A.M.) or Dow Jones (10:54 A.M.) wires.

released to the American financial press until after 10:00 A.M. Crawford's orders had been placed before that. Before insiders may act upon material information, such information must have been effectively disclosed in a manner sufficient to insure its availability to the investing public. Particularly here, where a formal announcement to the entire financial news media had been promised in a prior official release known to the media, all insider activity must await dissemination of the promised official announcement.

Coates was absolved by the court below because his telephone order was placed shortly before 10:20 A.M. on April 16, which was after the announcement had been made even though the news could not be considered already a matter of public information. 258 F.Supp. at 288. This result seems to have been predicated upon a misinterpretation of dicta in *Cady, Roberts,* where the SEC instructed insiders to "keep out of the market until the established procedures for public release of the information are *carried out* instead of hastening to execute transactions in advance of, and in frustration of, the objectives of the release," 40 SEC at 915 (emphasis supplied). The reading of a news release, which prompted Coates into action, is merely the first step in the process of dissemination required for compliance with the regulatory objective of providing all investors with an equal opportunity to make informed investment judgments. Assuming that the contents of the official release could instantaneously be acted upon,[29] at the minimum Coates should have waited until the news could reasonably have been expected to appear over the media of widest circulation, the Dow Jones broad tape, rather than hastening to insure an advantage to himself and his broker son-in-law.[30]

II. The Corporate Defendant

Introductory

At 3:00 P.M. on April 12, 1964, evidently believing it desirable to comment upon the rumors concerning the Timmins project, TGS issued the press release quoted in pertinent part in the text at [page 591]. The SEC argued below and maintains on this appeal that this release painted a misleading and deceptive picture of the drilling progress at the time of its issuance, and hence violated Rule 10b–5(2). TGS relies on the holding of the court below that "The issuance of the release

---

29. Although the only insider who acted after the news appeared over the Dow Jones broad tape is not an appellant and therefore we need not discuss the necessity of considering the advisability of a "reasonable waiting period" during which outsiders may absorb and evaluate disclosures, we note in passing that, where the news is of a sort which is not readily translatable into investment action, insiders may not take advantage of their advance opportunity to evaluate the information by acting immediately upon dissemination. In any event, the permissible timing of insider transactions after disclosures of various sorts is one of the many areas of expertise for appropriate exercise of the SEC's rulemaking power, which we hope will be utilized in the future to provide some predictability of certainty for the business community.

30. The record reveals that news usually appears on the Dow Jones broad tape 2–3 minutes after the reporter completes dictation. Here, assuming that the Dow Jones reporter left the press conference as early as possible, 10:10 A.M., the 10–15 minute release (which took at least that long to dictate) could not have appeared on the wire before 10:22, and for other reasons unknown to us did not appear until 10:54. Indeed, even the abbreviated version of the release reported by Merrill Lynch over its private wire did not appear until 10:29. Coates, however, placed his call no later than 10:20.

produced no unusual market action" and "In the absence of a showing that the purpose of the April 12 press release was to affect the market price of TGS stock to the advantage of TGS or its insiders, the issuance of the press release did not constitute a violation of Section 10(b) or Rule 10b–5 since it was not issued 'in connection with the purchase or sale of any security' " and, alternatively, "even if it had been established that the April 12 release was issued in connection with the purchase or sale of any security, the Commission has failed to demonstrate that it was false, misleading or deceptive." 258 F.Supp. at 294. . . .

B. *The "In Connection with . . . ." Requirement*

In adjudicating upon the relationship of this phrase to the case before us it would appear that the court below used a standard that does not reflect the congressional purpose that prompted the passage of the Securities Exchange Act of 1934.

The dominant congressional purposes underlying the Securities Exchange Act of 1934 were to promote free and open public securities markets and to protect the investing public from suffering inequities in trading, including, specifically, inequities that follow from trading that has been stimulated by the publication of false or misleading corporate information releases.   . . .   Therefore it seems clear from the legislative purpose Congress expressed in the Act, and the legislative history of Section 10(b) that Congress when it used the phrase "in connection with the purchase or sale of any security" intended only that the device employed, whatever it might be, be of a sort that would cause reasonable investors to rely thereon, and, in connection therewith, so relying, cause them to purchase or sell a corporation's securities. There is no indication that Congress intended that the corporations or persons responsible for the issuance of a misleading statement would not violate the section unless they engaged in related securities transactions or otherwise acted with wrongful motives; indeed, the obvious purposes of the Act to protect the investing public and to secure fair dealing in the securities markets would be seriously undermined by applying such a gloss onto the legislative language. Absent a securities transaction by an insider it is almost impossible to prove that a wrongful purpose motivated the issuance of the misleading statement. The mere fact that an insider did not engage in securities transactions does not negate the possibility of wrongful purpose; perhaps the market did not react to the misleading statement as much as was anticipated or perhaps the wrongful purpose was something other than the desire to buy at a low price or sell at a high price. Of even greater relevance to the Congressional purpose of investor protection is the fact that the investing public may be injured as much by one's misleading statement containing inaccuracies caused by negligence as by a misleading statement published intentionally to further a wrongful purpose. We do not believe that Congress intended that the proscriptions of the Act would not be violated unless the makers of a misleading statement also participated in pertinent securities transactions in connection therewith, or unless it could be shown that the issuance of the statement was motivated by a plan to benefit the corporation or themselves at the expense of a duped investing public. . . .

Accordingly, we hold that Rule 10b–5 is violated whenever assertions are made, as here, in a manner reasonably calculated to influence the investing public, e.g., by means of the financial media, Fleischer, supra, 51 Va.L.Rev. at 1294–95, if such assertions are false or misleading or are so incomplete as to mislead irrespective of whether the issuance of the release was motivated by corporate officials for ulterior purposes. It seems clear, however, that if corporate management demonstrates that it was diligent in ascertaining that the information it published was the whole truth and that such diligently obtained information was disseminated in good faith, Rule 10b–5 would not have been violated.

C. *Did the Issuance of the April 12 Release Violate Rule 10b–5?*

Turning first to the question of whether the release was misleading, i.e., whether it conveyed to the public a false impression of the drilling situation, at the time of its issuance, we note initially that the trial court did not actually decide this question. Its conclusion that "the Commission has failed to demonstrate that it was false, misleading or deceptive," 258 F.Supp. at 294, seems to have derived from its views that "The defendants are to be judged *on the facts known to them* when the April 12 release was issued," 258 F.Supp. at 295 (emphasis supplied), that the draftsmen "exercised reasonable business judgment under the circumstances," 258 F.Supp. at 296, and that the release was not "misleading or deceptive *on the basis of the facts then known*," 258 F.Supp. at 296 (emphasis supplied) rather than from an appropriate primary inquiry into the meaning of the statement to the reasonable investor and its relationship to truth. While we certainly agree with the trial court that "in retrospect, the press release may appear gloomy or incomplete." [31] 258 F.Supp. at 296, we cannot, from the present

---

31. Examined in retrospect, the situation in Timmins at the time the release was prepared seems to offer good reason for optimism. The draftsmen of the release had full knowledge of the discoveries up to 7:00 P.M. on Friday, April 10. At that time approximately ⅔ of the ore ultimately found to exist by the time of the preparation of the April 16 "major strike" release had been discovered by 5 holes placed so as to indicate continuity of mineralization within the large anomaly. As of that time SEC experts estimated ore reserves of over 8 million tons at a gross assay value (excluding costs) of over $26 a ton. Accepting the conservative view of TGS's expert Wiles that 95.2% would be absorbed by costs, the ultimate profit could then have been estimated at more than $14,000,000. TGS experts could name very few base metal mines with a greater assay value and the court observed that bodies of much lower assay value were commercially mined. 258 F.Supp. at 282 n. 10. Roche, a mining stock specialist, added that mines with significantly lower percentages of copper and with no zinc or silver, as here, were profitably operated. On the basis of approximately one-third more data, and, for all the record shows, without any addi-

tional figures as to estimated costs, TGS announced on April 16 a major strike with over 25 million tons of ore. The trial court found that as of 7:00 P.M. on Thursday, April 9, "There was real evidence that a body of commercially mineable ore might exist." 252 F.Supp. at 282. And, by 7:00 A.M. on Sunday, April 10, eight hours before the release was issued to the press, 77.9% of the drilling in mineralization had been completed, 84.4% by 7:00 P.M. on the 12th, and 90.2% by 7 A.M. on April 13. The release did not appear in most newspapers of general circulation until later in the morning of Monday, the 13th.

The release, see [p. 591], supra, began by referring to rumored reports that the company had made a substantial copper discovery and then continued: "These reports exaggerate the scale of operations, and mention plans and statistics of size and grade of ore that are without factual basis and have evidently originated by speculation of people not connected with TGS." It then stated, purporting to give the true facts in contradiction to the rumors: "The facts are as follows." However, the "facts" disclosed relative to the Kidd–55 segment were: "Recent drilling on one property

record, by applying the standard Congress intended, definitively conclude that it was deceptive or misleading to the reasonable investor, or that he would have been misled by it. Certain newspaper accounts of the release viewed the release as confirming the existence of preliminary favorable developments, and this optimistic view was held by some brokers, so it could be that the reasonable investor would have read between the lines of what appears to us to be an inconclusive and negative statement and would have envisioned the actual situation at the Kidd segment on April 12. On the other hand, in view of the decline of the market price of TGS stock from a high of 32 on the morning of April 13 when the release was disseminated to 29⅜ by the close of trading on April 15, and the reaction to the release by other brokers, it is far from certain that the release was generally interpreted as a highly encouraging report or even encouraging at all. Accordingly, we remand this issue to the district court that took testimony and heard and saw the witnesses for a determination of the character of the release in the light of the facts existing at the time of the release, by applying the standard of whether the reasonable investor, in the exercise of due care, would have been misled by it.

In the event that it is found that the statement was misleading to the reasonable investor it will then become necessary to determine whether its issuance resulted from a lack of due diligence. The only remedy the Commission seeks against the corporation is an injunction . . . and therefore we do not find it necessary to decide whether just a lack of due diligence on the part of TGS, absent a showing of bad faith, would subject the corporation to any liability for damages. We have recently stated in a case involving a private suit under Rule 10b–5 in which damages and an injunction were sought, " 'It is not necessary in a suit for equitable or prophylactic relief to establish all the elements required in a suit for monetary damages.' " Mutual Shares Corp. v. Genesco, Inc., 384 F.2d 540, 547, quoting from SEC v. Capital Gains Research Bureau, Inc., 375 U.S. 180, 193, 84 S.Ct. 275, 11 L.Ed.2d 237 (1963).

We hold only that, in an action for injunctive relief, the district court has the discretionary power under Rule 10b–5 and Section 10(b) to issue an injunction, if the misleading statement resulted from a lack of due diligence on the part of TGS. The trial court did not find it necessary to decide whether TGS exercised such diligence and has not yet attempted to resolve this issue. While the trial court concluded that TGS had exercised "reasonable *business* judgment under the circumstances," 258 F.Supp. at 296 (emphasis supplied) it applied an incorrect *legal* standard in appraising whether TGS should have issued its April 12 release on the basis of the facts known to its draftsmen at the time of its preparation, 258 F.Supp. at 295, and in assuming that disclosure of the full underlying facts of the Timmins situation was not a viable alternative to the vague generalities which were asserted. 258 F.Supp. at 296.

near Timmins has led to preliminary indications that more drilling would be required for proper evaluation of this prospect. The drilling done to date has not been conclusive but the statements made by many outside quarters are unreliable." It was then said that, as of April 12, the release date, ". . . any statement as to size and grade of ore would be premature and possibly misleading." A definite statement "to clarify" was promised in the future.

It is not altogether certain from the present record that the draftsmen could, as the SEC suggests, have readily obtained current reports of the drilling progress over the weekend of April 10–12, but they certainly should have obtained them if at all possible for them to do so. However, even if it were not possible to evaluate and transmit current data in time to prepare the release on April 12, it would seem that TGS could have delayed the preparation a bit until an accurate report of a rapidly changing situation was possible. See 258 F.Supp. at 296. At the very least, if TGS felt compelled to respond to the spreading rumors of a spectacular discovery, it would have been more accurate to have stated that the situation was in flux and that the release was prepared as of April 10 information rather than purporting to report the progress "to date." Moreover, it would have obviously been better to have specifically described the known drilling progress as of April 10 by stating the basic facts. Such an explicit disclosure would have permitted the investing public to evaluate the "prospect" of a mine at Timmins without having to read between the lines to understand that preliminary indications were favorable—in itself an understatement.

The choice of an ambiguous general statement rather than a summary of the specific facts cannot reasonably be justified by any claimed urgency. The avoidance of liability for misrepresentation in the event that the Timmins project failed, a highly unlikely event as of April 12 or April 13, did not forbid the accurate and truthful divulgence of detailed results which need not, of course, have been accompanied by conclusory assertions of success. Nor is it any justification that such an explicit disclosure of the truth might have "encouraged the rumor mill which they were seeking to allay." 258 F.Supp. at 296.

We conclude, then, that, having established that the release was issued in a manner reasonably calculated to affect the market price of TGS stock and to influence the investing public, we must remand to the district court to decide whether the release was misleading to the reasonable investor and if found to be misleading, whether the court in its discretion should issue the injunction the SEC seeks.

[A concurring opinion by JUDGE FRIENDLY is omitted. It expressed two caveats relating to potential civil liability suits. One of them was about the possibility that the officers who received options might be liable for all damages due to that issuance (and not merely for rescission). The other had to do with the "frightening" possible consequences to the corporate issuer of recovery of damages from it with respect to its officers' negligence in connection with the press release.]

Brief concurrences by KAUFFMAN, ANDERSON and HAYS, JJ., are omitted.

A 19–page dissent by MOORE, J., concurred in by LUMBARD, J., is also omitted. Much of it dissented from the majority's treatment of the trial court's findings of fact with respect to the issue of materiality. It also took sharp issue with the majority's treatment of the "in connection with" clause.]

COMMENT

(1) On remand the district court decided that the Texas Gulf Sulphur press release was in fact misleading and was not the product of due diligence on the

part of those responsible for it.[32] In so ruling the court did note the dangers of over-optimistic reporting of mineral discoveries, which the SEC had stressed in its 1969 release on oil discoveries on the north slope of Alaska. Eventually, the private litigation that erupted in the wake of the SEC's action was resolved by a court-approved settlement on the part of TGS. This settlement divided claims into (a) "reliance" claims, those of persons who sold after the release but before full disclosure, that is, between April 12th and 16th, and (b) "non-disclosure" claims, those of persons who sold while insiders knew of the results but before the release, that is, between November and April. The release claimants received sums of $8 to $18 per share sold depending on the date they sold. Nondisclosure claimants got $3.50 a share. The total for both classes was $2.7 million. These figures can be taken as a rough and ready solution reasonable in view of the likely outcome of a trial and the costs and uncertainties of litigating to the bitter end. The settlement did not give the bar answers to the questions involved.[33]

(2) Texas Gulf Sulphur, which became Texasgulf, was taken over by Canada Development Corporation, an arm of the Canadian government dedicated to retrieving Canada's industry from foreign investors. It sued to block the tender offer on the ground that CDC's disclosure was inadequate.[34] It lost and CDC acquired working control. Texasgulf is now a subsidiary of Societe National Elf Aquitaine, a French petroleum corporation which, after being an establishment of the French government, was partially privatized in 1986.

FLAMM v. EBERSTADT

United States Court of Appeals for the Seventh Circuit, 1987.
814 F.2d 1169.

[The stock of Microdot, Inc. was trading on the New York Stock Exchange at $11¾ per share on December 2, 1975 when General Cable Corp. announced an intention to make a tender offer for those shares at $17. Microdot's stock went up to $18⅜ but began to retreat when Microdot opposed the offer through advertisements and press releases. It said that General Cable's offer was totally inadequate.

Eberstadt, CEO of Microdot and defendant in the case, complained that there would be no future growth companies if takeovers picked them all off. But Microdot also authorized Goldman, Sachs to approach other firms that might be interested—"white knights." Through December 1975 no interest was found. The stock meanwhile fell to $17. Then Northwest Industries indicated that, after all, it might be interested and on January 19th managers of the two firms met. On January 26, Northwest made an offer at $21, with the advance approval of Microdot's board. Northwest acquired the stock at $21 but later spun off Microdot.

On behalf of a class of investors who sold Microdot between December 5, 1975 and January 23, 1976 the Flamms filed a complaint alleging violations of Rule 10b–5. After trial the jury found for

32. 312 F.Supp. 77 (S.D.N.Y.1970), affirmed as modified 446 F.2d 1301 (2d Cir. 1971).

33. CCH Fed.Sec.L.Rep. ¶ 93,432 (S.D. N.Y.1972). TGS in its 1971 Report indicat-

ed that it would treat this sum as an adjustment of its 1964 earnings.

34. Texasgulf, Inc. v. Canada Development Corp., 366 F.Supp. 374 (S.D.Tex. 1973).

defendants and plaintiff appealed. The opinion of the Court of Appeals, by JUDGE EASTERBROOK, first considered the jury instructions. It disapproved of them but concluded that in any case the district court should have granted defendants' motion for summary judgment. Its opinion on the merits follows.]

II

An omission is material when there is a "substantial likelihood that, under all the circumstances, the omitted fact would have assumed actual significance in the deliberations of the reasonable shareholder"—that is, when it "would have been viewed by the reasonable investor as having significantly altered the 'total mix' of information made available." TSC Industries, Inc. v. Northway, Inc., 426 U.S. 438, 449, 96 S.Ct. 2126, 2132, 48 L.Ed.2d 757 (1976) (footnote omitted). TSC dealt with "materiality" under the proxy rules, but like every other court of appeals we have taken the definition in TSC as suitable for the term wherever it appears in securities law. . . .

Several courts of appeals have held that efforts by public corporations to arrange mergers are immaterial under this standard, as a matter of law, until the firms have agreed on the "price and structure" of the deal. Staffin v. Greenberg, 672 F.2d 1196, 1204–07 (3d Cir.1982); Reiss v. Pan American World Airways, Inc., 711 F.2d 11, 14 (2d Cir. 1983); Greenfield v. Heublein, Inc., 742 F.2d 751, 756–58 (3d Cir.1984); . . . Microdot and Northwest did not agree on the price and structure of a deal until January 24, 1976, at the earliest, the day after the period in which the last member of the class sold. On December 29, 1975, when Flamm sold, Microdot was forlornly looking for a rescuer; the most that can be said is that Microdot had authorized an investment bank to send distress signals. *Staffin* and *Reiss* treat such inquiries as immaterial.

From one perspective this conclusion is simply another cause for wonderment at the legal mind. Investors were looking at potential prices from $11.75 (if Microdot had defeated all bids) to $17 (if General Cable's bid had succeeded) to $21 (under Northwest's bid), and maybe more if a better bid were available. This is almost a 100% range. Only an addlepated investor would consider a 100% difference in price unimportant in deciding what to do. The range in this case is not unusual. Tender offers entail substantial premia compared with the prices shares carry before the bids—and afterward, should the offers be defeated. Managers who sell the firm to White Knights obtain gains in addition to those available from the initial bidders. The data may be found in [Citations omitted].

The judges who decided *Staffin, Reiss,* and similar cases did not deny that the difference between merger and no merger may be substantial. They drew instead on a different strand of the Supreme Court's reasoning in TSC, the recognition that "[s]ome information is of such dubious significance that insistence on its disclosure may accomplish more harm than good." 426 U.S. at 448, 96 S.Ct. at 2132. Our colleagues on other courts of appeals have suggested two reasons why the disclosure of ongoing negotiations may "accomplish more harm than good." One is that disclosure of ongoing negotiations may befuddle the investors, leading them to think the outcome more certain than it is. The other reason is that premature disclosure may frustrate the achievement of the firm's objective, destroying the source of the value sought to be disclosed. The cases also allude to a third rationale, the need to create a bright-line rule that will allow firms to plan corporate transactions with the assurance that they will not be condemned no matter which way they proceed on disclosure.

The first of these reasons, that disclosure may confuse investors rather than illuminate their choices, is weak. It assumes that investors are nitwits, unable to appreciate—even when told—that mergers are risky propositions up until the closing. Almost all corporate ventures, from building a new plant to angling for a merger partner, may go well or poorly, with a probability attached to each outcome. To attribute to investors a child-like simplicity, an inability to grasp the probabilistic significance of negotiations, implies that they should not be told about new plants, new products, new managers, or any of the other changes in the life of the corporation. These new events—things with potential for boom or bust—are exactly the news on which sophisticated investors make most decisions; "old" news, with settled value, already is reflected in the price of the stock and so is no news at all. Doubtless some unsophisticated investors think that negotiations for a merger are the same thing as a completed merger, but such babes in the woods are not apt to follow contested tender offers day by day. Disclosures to the market as a whole cannot be limited to what is fit for rubes. The Wall Street Journal is filled with rumors on which investors act; Rule 175, 17 C.F.R. § 230.175, allows and even encourages the disclosure of "projections" about uncertain events; any Schedule 13D filed in a tender offer will disclose a range of plans and contingent choices. These documents regularly contain statements about potential mergers, accompanied by disclaimers and cautions about risks. We do not doubt that these schedules, drafted with more haste than the prospectus used to sell newly issued stock, are correspondingly more likely to be incomplete. But some information is almost always preferable to none. Investors, who appreciate the necessary omissions, can deal with risk. And the disclosure of a fact (such as the hiring of an investment banker to hunt up a White Knight) does not invite suit just because the search turns out poorly.

The effect of premature disclosure on the probability of merger is a much more substantial concern. Investors seek monetary returns, and few want disclosure for its own sake. To the extent investors' wealth depends on withholding information, all favor that course. So a firm that is working on a valuable invention may elect not to disclose the existence of the project, let alone daily progress. Much of the value of the invention may come from stealing a march on rivals, a value that would be dissipated if the firm turned valuable information over to its investors and therefore inescapably to rivals. An investor who sells the day before the public disclosure of the invention cannot complain that he missed out on an increase in the price of the firm's stock, any more than the investor who sells the day before a favorable quarterly report of earnings or an increase in dividends may demand to receive the increase. See State Teachers Retirement Board v. Fluor Corp., 654 F.2d 843, 850 (2d Cir.1981). The famous Texas Gulf Sulphur case furnishes another illustration. TGS found the world's biggest lode of nickel. To capitalize, it had to line up the mineral rights for the whole area. If TGS had released the assays immediately, other firms (or the owners of the surface interests) could have captured the rewards of TGS's search. TGS had to keep its find secret for a while, and investors who sold their stock while TGS was silent had no complaint. See SEC

v. Texas Gulf Sulphur Co., 401 F.2d 833 (2d Cir.1968) (en banc). TGS did its investors a favor by saying as little as possible for as long as necessary. Once TGS started disclosing it had a duty not to lie, but that's another problem (which we discuss in Part III).

Negotiations for a merger present a similar problem. Some potential acquirers may demand that negotiations proceed in secrecy. They may fear that premature disclosure may spark competition that will deprive them of part of the value of their effort, so that bids in a world of early disclosure will be lower than bids in a world of deferred disclosure. One specter facing any potential buyer is the winner's curse—the prospect that the high bidder wins the auction only because he alone has placed an unrealistically high value on the assets. Negotiations in the glare of publicity may lead putative buyers to think that whenever they locate a bargain they will be preempted by some other bidder who waits in the wings, but whenever they offer too much they will be left with their "prize". The heads-I-win-tails-you-lose quality of this process will lead either to a general reduction in offers (to assure that no offer is too high) or to a refusal to offer the best price without being assured of victory. Either way, silence during negotiations may be beneficial for investors. See also Note, Rule 10b–5 and the Duty to Disclose Merger Negotiations in Corporate Statements, 96 Yale L.J. 547, 554–56 (1987). Both the New York and the American Stock Exchanges therefore suggest that listed firms postpone announcements until definitive agreements have been reached. . . .

Flamm may reply that silence is not beneficial to all investors, that there is a conflict of interest between investors who sell before the disclosure and investors who hold, thereby receiving the benefits later on. See Ronald J. Gilson, The Law and Finance of Corporate Acquisitions 977 (1986). Perhaps so, although the corporation is not required by the securities law to favor hair-trigger sellers over other investors. From a longer perspective, however, even this conflict disappears. Investors who wanted to prescribe their managers' behavior during merger discussions would favor a rule of silence until the discussions had reached agreement on price and structure. Such discussions may occur anytime during the life of the firm. Ex ante, each investor's chance of selling during that window is small. The chance of selling for "too little" is offset by an identical chance of buying at a bargain; every sale has a buyer and a seller. Over the long run, then, the prospect of selling for too little and buying a bargain are a wash, leaving only the prospect of receiving (or scaring away) beneficial opportunities to merge. All investors would prefer whichever approach maximized their anticipated wealth. The legal rule governing disclosure is like this hypothetical bargain among investors. It applies to all firms, to all investors be they buyers or sellers, at all times. In selecting a legal rule, a court must consider the effects on all investors in all firms, not just the effects on the plaintiff.

Even the unlucky investors, such as Flamm, who sell their stock in a particular firm too soon can take comfort in knowing that they do not lose the whole gain. To the extent the appearance of White Knights is predictable, the *probability* of a White Knight appearing in this contest will be reflected in the price of the stock. Most buyers during tender offer contests are arbitrageurs, professional investors who are exceptionally knowledgable. These professionals make money by taking risk—they take the risk that all bids will vanish (and the price fall here to $11.75) in exchange for the prospect of gain from the offer (here at $17) and the chance of a higher bid. When Flamm sold his stock, he passed to the arbitrageurs the risk that the price would fall to $11.75, or even to $17 (he received $17⅜); the arbitrageurs did not take the risk off Flamm's shoulders for free but were compensated by the possibility (remote as of December 29!) of a higher price. Undoubtedly many arbitrageurs had learned that Goldman, Sachs was shopping for a deal. Their bids reflected the value of a potential deal, and Flamm received this value without knowing about the prospects himself. It is not right to reply that the arbitrageurs—"speculators", transient investors—are swiping gains that "belong" to the longer-term investors such as Flamm. Arbitrageurs must compete among themselves to buy stock. The more likely the gain from a later White Knight bid, the more any given arbitrageur is willing to pay for stock. To make a profit the arbitrageur must put his hands on the stock; to acquire the stock he must outbid other arbitrageurs, who have the same end in view; the competition ultimately passes back to Flamm and the other original investors the gains from the probability of a White Knight bid, as of December 29 (or any other date), less the premium for taking risk off Flamm's hands. Premature disclosure could have reduced the chances of an acquisition by a White Knight, and therefore reduced the bids made in the market for Flamm's stock.

So silence pending settlement of the price and structure of a deal is beneficial to most investors, most of the time. We do not think that the securities laws war against the best interests of investors. Rule 10b–5 is about *fraud,* after all, and it is not fraudulent to conduct business in a way that makes investors better off—that all investors prefer ex ante and that most prefer even ex post. Cf. Dirks v. SEC, 463 U.S. 646, 653– 59, 103 S.Ct. 3255, 3260–63, 77 L.Ed.2d 911 (1983) (liability depends on a "duty" to disclose, a duty defined in part to ensure the welfare of investors as a group).

We agree, too, with the conclusion of the other circuits that the benefits of certainty supply additional support for the price-and-structure rule. If disclosure must occur at an earlier date, how much earlier? That would be fertile ground for disputation. No matter how soon the firm announced the negotiations, investors could say that it should have done so a little sooner. The pressure to advance the date of disclosure by "just a little" (at a time) would erode the benefits of deferral. No rule other than a clear one would have staying power. The time at which information should be disclosed ought to be readily ascertainable. The price-and-structure rule will leave some questions in doubt, but it is better than any alternative.

III

Although we adopt the holding of *Staffin* and *Reiss* that public corporations need not disclose ongoing negotiations until they have produced agreement on the price and structure of the deal, that does not produce immediate victory for the defendants. There is, at least potentially, a further question whether firms may deny the existence of ongoing negotiations or shade the truth.

This question has produced a conflict among the circuits. *Greenfield* holds (over a dissent by the author of *Staffin*) that a firm may deny knowledge of new corporate developments even while in the final stages of negotiation. *Levinson* explicitly rejects this part of *Green-*

field's holding, 786 F.2d at 748, while reserving judgment on the price-and-structure rule as applied to silent corporations. Flamm relies on *Levinson*. This is a difficult question—one on which our court in *Michaels* initially took the side of *Greenfield* but then amended the opinion to become neutral. See 767 F.2d at 1195–96.

The conclusion of *Levinson* is supported by the principle that he who speaks must tell the truth about important matters. The firm may be silent, leaving investors to take their chances, but may not lie; the lie may have greater adverse effect on the value of the stock than the premature truth. The conclusion of *Greenfield* is supported by the fact that unless the firm is entitled to conceal the negotiations, a demand by the Exchange to confirm or deny a rumor may flush out the truth no matter what the firm says, even though the firm is entitled to be silent and most investors would want it to be. Suppose a firm is engaged in negotiations that are best kept quiet, and the Exchange asks whether new developments account for activity in its stock. If the firm says yes and says why, the cat is out of the bag; if the firm says no, it faces liability for fraud; if the firm says "no comment" that is the same thing as saying "yes" because investors will deduce the truth. No corporation follows the CIA's policy of saying "no comment" to *every* inquiry; every firm regularly confirms or denies rumors, as the securities laws and the stock exchanges' rules require. The exchanges' rules require a response, not a refusal to respond, to inquiries. When a firm suddenly says "no comment", the inquisitor will realize that his suspicions have a foundation—yet the response may sow confusion all the same. If by hypothesis silence is the best course for investors, then it may be necessary to condone evasive answers, as the Third Circuit did in *Greenfield,* to put pursuers off the scent for a time. See also Gilson at 978–79; Note, 96 Yale L.J. at 558–64.

As Flamm describes the case, we must choose between *Greenfield* and *Levinson*. Microdot opposed General Cable's offer, issuing one press release after another. It told investors to hold their stock because $17 was inadequate and pledged to resist General Cable's bid by all available means. It cried wolf about the effect of tender offers on aggressive innovators. Flamm insists that he deduced from these statements that Microdot wanted to remain independent at any cost, even the return of the stock's price to $11.75. If the statements amount to a declaration of independence, then failure to disclose that Goldman, Sachs was beating the bushes for higher bids was an omission that made the statements materially misleading, just like the "no corporate developments" statements in *Greenfield* and *Levinson*.

Flamm offers an implausible reading of Microdot's statements, however. The test of materiality is objective, TSC, 426 U.S. at 445, 96 S.Ct. at 2130: *Michaels,* 767 F.2d at 1196, and no objectively reasonable reader of these comments would take them as denials of any interest in other bids, no matter how beneficial those bids were to Microdot's investors. The firm's management claimed to be representing the interests of investors, rather than to be pursuing a social philosophy that small is good no matter the cost to stockholders. None of the statements denied that the firm was searching for higher bids; the implication of the statement that General Cable's bid is "inadequate" is the contrary. *Levinson,* in contrast, dealt with five bald denials that the firm was attempting to arrange a merger. None of the materials Microdot issued states any view on the desirability of White Knights, for the economy in general or Microdot in particular. The only concrete advice Microdot gave its investors was not to sell, because $17 was too low. As things turned out, that was wise counsel. Flamm is hardly in a position to contend that because he rejected this advice he has been deceived.

Ours is therefore a case of silence on the subject of the omitted information. For all practical purposes, Microdot was mum on its strategy for defeating General Cable's bid. Defensive strategies include seeking White Knights as well as scorched earth and other destructive maneuvers. Microdot never announced a strategy involving moats, fences, or any tactic that would rebuff all bidders; it never announced antipathy to White Knights. At the right price, any corporation is for sale—even a corporation managed by people who say that tender offers should be illegal. A target of a tender offer is not just for sale; it is For Sale. If Flamm drew a different inference, he was unreasonable, and Flamm's errors are not grounds on which to force other investors to pay damages (which is the effect of awarding damages against Microdot). We therefore affirm the judgment without choosing between *Greenfield* and *Levinson.*

IV

Lest we seem to decide by silence, we disclaim any implication that if Microdot's omissions were material, the class would have been entitled to damages. The class asked for the difference between the price ($17 to $18⅜) that prevailed between December 5 and January 23 and the price ($21) offered by Northwest. Flamm did not offer to show that the market price was influenced by the non-disclosure at any time during the offer. If the price was uninfluenced, it must have reflected in some measure the prospect of a higher bid. Flamm's theory of damages implies that the class is entitled to keep what it got for surrendering the opportunity of a higher bid and still receive the full price of that bid—all the while avoiding risk that the price will return to the original level.

The usual measure of damages in a case under Rule 10b–5 is the difference between what the stock fetched and what it would have been worth had all of the information been disclosed. . . . (Recovery sometimes depends on the defendant's profit, but Microdot made none by deferring disclosure.) Flamm has not tried to show that the difference was other than zero, implying no recovery. . . .

To put this a little differently, this court concluded in *Mills,* 552 F.2d at 1247, that the market for the stock of widely traded firms efficiently impounds publicly available information about that firm. See also Metlyn Realty Corp. v. Esmark, Inc., 763 F.2d 826, 835 (7th Cir. 1985). This implies the adoption of the "fraud on the market" approach to liability under Rule 10b–5. . . . If the plaintiff establishes that a lie, misleading statement, or omission has affected the price of the stock, he may recover without establishing that he knew of or relied on the delict; his recovery is the difference between the actual price and the price the market would have reached if traders had been fully informed. The fraud-on-the-market theory is an important ingredient of class actions in securities cases, too, for otherwise individual differences in knowledge and reliance would make the class unmanageable. . . .

The fraud-on-the-market approach relieves the plaintiff of the need to show that he relied on or even read the misleading or incomplete disclosures; he receives a measure of damages based on the premise that actual versus "right" price is the appropriate comparison. The logic of this approach, however, implies that for widely traded securities *only* fraud on the market will establish entitlement to relief. Fraud-on-the-plaintiff won't do—not when the market price itself was unaffected and therefore "right". Flamm did not try to show that the price he received had been diminished by the omission of which he complains. If we take the fraud-on-the-market approach to its logical limit, that is dispositive against him. The competing position is that fraud on the market is just one way among many to show reliance and damages; a plaintiff who demonstrates particular reliance still may recover. Both the cases and respected scholars have vacillated between these perspectives. We need not and do not decide today whether *only* fraud on the market allows recovery in a case of this sort, and we hope that the issue will not be passed by in silence by future litigants.

Affirmed

CUDAHY, CIRCUIT JUDGE, concurring in the judgment and concurring in part:

I admire the clear and well-reasoned majority opinion which leads us through the cases and the economic theory required to come to grips with the problem before us. I have, however, important reservations and differences in perspective which require me to write separately—but not at great length.

First, I think the case could be decided, reaching the same result as the majority, on the issues of the instructions and the admission of evidence as the parties presented them.

Second, I am willing, though not eager, to go beyond the issues as presented by the parties to agree that the defendants win as a matter of law. The majority feels that this approach requires the adoption of a bright-line test (agreement on price and structure) . . .

I understand the majority's preference for a bright-line rule. If the secrecy of merger negotiations is in most investors' ultimate best interest (a plausible premise though not necessarily one carved in stone), there is certainly an argument for keeping them quiet until agreement in principle is reached. (And, of course, here we are apparently considering only the welfare of investors.) My problems with the majority's conclusion are primarily procedural—not necessarily substantive. We have heard no argument on the important issues which the majority boldly decides based on its own—no doubt well-informed—notions of how the corporate world turns. The Securities and Exchange Commission might have given us *its* views, had it not thought this a case about instructions and evidence. I do not think it is necessary—or wise—to be so bold. I would merely hold that on the specific facts of this case there has been no nondisclosure or misrepresentation from which a reasonable jury could conclude that the securities laws had been violated. . . .

Third, I believe at several points in the majority opinion the moral underpinnings of the law are at risk in the sweep of the economic analysis. For example, in its generally approving discussion of Greenfield v. Heublein, Inc., 742 F.2d 751 (3d Cir.1984), the majority speaks kindly of lying in the interest of maintaining the secrecy of merger negotiations. Such an analysis may be economically rational and may tend to maximize investors' wealth but it does seem to raise a few old-fashioned questions of corporate morality. Without pursuing the matter here, I do not think it is the place of the courts to undermine business morality even in the name of shareholder wealth maximization.

Fourth, I think the majority opinion is interesting and generally correct in most of its observations about fraud-on-the-market theory. Although their activities are not directly relevant, chartists and tape-readers find all they need to know about securities in their price (and sometimes in their volume of trading). True "technicians" eschew balance sheets, news, rumors and information of any kind outside the price as a distraction from the real, true and complete information discounted in the price attained in an efficient market. Perhaps, this is the right approach to security analysis (although I am certainly not suggesting that this is what the majority has in mind). But the securities laws were not written by market technicians and they put an emphasis on telling the truth and the whole truth about securities. Again I believe this is a moral dimension which may or may not contribute to wealth maximization in the context of an efficient market. It is important that we not lose sight of the moral underpinnings of the law in our concern for its economic consequences.

COMMENT

In 1988 the Supreme Court decided another merger negotiation—10b–5 case, Basic Incorporated v. Levinson, ___ U.S. ___, 108 S.Ct. 978, 99 L.Ed.2d 194. It is a less incisive look at the topic than is afforded by the contrasting opinions in Flamm v. Eberstadt. Basic had been talking on and off for two years (1976–78) with another corporation about the possibility of a merger. On three occasions it issued public statements to the effect that nothing was going on. Then in December 1978 came an announcement that there was an offer and two days later one that it had been approved. A class action was brought on behalf of those who sold after the first denial and before the correct statement. The Supreme Court reversed and remanded for further proceedings. It refused to apply a simple, rigid bright-line test—"the agreement-in principle as to price and structure" formula—and instructed the trial court to start with a general test—what would the impact of disclosure have been on the "reasonable investor"? It stressed the applicability of its decision in a proxy case—TSC Industries v. Northway, Inc., p. 719 infra. It also said that one could establish a presumption of reliance on the basis of the fraud-on-the-market theory that is discussed near the end of the Flamm opinion.

NOTE ON INFORMATION POLICY AND INSIDE TRADING

One has to put the question of inside trading into the context of general policies about provision of information to those trading on the securities markets. The chief instruments of control over that information flow are the annual and quarterly reports regulated and required by the provisions of the Exchange Act. But information has a way of popping up between quarters; Rule 13a–11 requires prompt reporting on Form 8–K of certain events (changes in control, acquisition or disposition of important assets, etc.). But many events are not specified and are thus left to the issuer's discretion. Particularly with the takeover movement it turns out that there is information that is important to securities prices that does not originate with the issuer. Sometimes other rules smoke out this data, for instance the acquisition of 5% of a corporation's stock, etc., dispositions of stock under § 16(a), etc. But here there are many possibilities left uncovered.

A preliminary question is *when* must data be announced by the issuer. The courts recognize four factual situations: (1) if a corporation is aware that insiders are trading on the basis of data unpublished but known to them, (2) if a corporation is aware the misleading rumours are circulating, (3) if there is strong reason not to report a fact because it will interfere with the corporation's business or (4) none of the above facts is present. Texas Gulf Sulphur and Flamm both refer to issues of this kind. Bear in mind the realism in the Stock Exchange Manual that follows about the likelihood that attempts to maintain confidentiality will fail if many people are let in on the secret, as is necessarily the case with tender offers, etc. The Chiarella history reinforces that learning.

Then comes the question of *how* the disclosure is to be made. The Texas Gulf Sulphur court seemed to be telling issuers something about (a) through what media and at what times disclosure is to be made and (b) how the release is to be written. The following represents TGS' attempt to obey that mandate the next time they made a strike in 1975.

Izok Lake

At Izok Lake, 225 miles north of Yellowknife in the Northwest Territories and about 25 miles south of the Hood River occurrence reported last year, Texasgulf Canada has drilled high grade sulphide mineralization that includes zinc, copper, lead and silver values, and gold in one hole in a deeper zone. Over 575 mining claims have been staked by Texasgulf in the area. Twenty-nine holes have been drilled to depths of about 500 feet establishing mineralization over a thousand feet along strike open on both ends with assays now available on 18 holes. Drilling began with 7 holes from the lake ice. Since breakup of the ice, drill sites have been confined to a small island 400 feet long.

Definition of the mineralization beyond the island must be done either from barges or platforms in the lake or from the lake ice after freeze-up. The mineralized structure appears to be highly contorted, and there is wide variation between sections. Drilling and assaying to July 22 are not adequate to interpret the structure or to estimate tonnage and grade. Drilled lengths may not represent true thicknesses because of structural contortions.

An additional six holes have been drilled on sections 2800E and 3000E. Five of these had good sulphide intersections, one with 250 feet of mineralization, but assays are not yet available.

Assays of mineralized holes available from Izok Lake to July 22 follow:

Hole No.	Grid Location	Direction and Dip	Assay Length (feet)	Grade			
				% Zn	% Cu	% Pb	oz. Ag
1	2200E	N	20.3	15.17	0.85	1.60	1.18
	650S	−60°	17.2	6.46	0.20	1.32	1.53
3	2200E	S	45.7	18.89	1.58	1.04	1.60
	340S	−60°					
4	2400E	S	10.4	19.06	0.31	2.87	2.47
	40S	−60°					
5	2000E	S	66.5	16.04	2.68	1.35	2.25
	270S	−45°					
6	2000E	S	76.7	18.55	0.64	2.46	1.93
	270S	−70°					
8	2725E	S	9.5	25.54	0.84	0.43	0.49
	293S	−45°	20.1	12.74	1.28	1.78	0.98
9	2725E	N	62.3	9.46	—	—	—
	293S	−45°					
12	2066E	N	22.0	21.14	3.50	1.49	1.67
	550S	−45°					
13	2600E	N	25.1	27.06	2.19	2.28	1.79
	550S	−70°	45.0	—	—	—	3.72
14	2600E	N	7.3	26.59	1.26	2.66	2.88
	550S	−90°	76.9	28.40	1.37	5.82	3.49
			130.3	17.02	2.41	3.03	2.00
15	2600E	N	233.3	18.02	2.55	1.39	1.57
	740S	−55°					
16	2600E	N	194.5	26.59	1.96	4.86	2.57
	740S	−70°					
17*	2600E	N	93.7	21.3	1.60	3.12	2.81
	740S	−80°	25.0*	0.04	1.52	4.20	23.41
18	2600E	N	3.3	34.83	0.57	9.85	15.1
	940S	−80°					

* Gold assays 0.09 oz. per ton over the 25 feet.

New York Stock Exchange Manual

(Reprinted as an Appendix to Flamm v. Eberstadt, p. 604 supra).

202.00 Material Information

202.01 Internal Handling of Confidential Corporate Matters

Unusual market activity or a substantial price change has on occasion occurred in a company's securities shortly before the announcement of an important corporate action or development. Such incidents are extremely embarrassing and damaging to both the company and the Exchange since the public may quickly conclude that someone acted on the basis of inside information.

Negotiations leading to mergers and acquisitions, stock splits, the making of arrangements preparatory to an exchange or tender offer, changes in dividend rates or earnings, calls for redemption, and new contracts, products, or discoveries are the type of developments where the risk of untimely and inadvertent disclosure of corporate plans are most likely to occur. Frequently, these matters require extensive discussion and study by corporate officials before final decisions can be made. Accordingly, extreme care must be used in order to keep the information on a confidential basis.

Where it is possible to confine formal or informal discussions to a small group of the top management of the company or companies involved, and their individual confidential advisors where adequate security can be maintained, premature public announcement may properly be avoided. In this regard, the market action of a company's securities should be closely watched at a time when consideration is being given to important corporate matters. If unusual market activity should arise, the company should be prepared to make an immediate public announcement of the matter.

At some point it usually becomes necessary to involve other persons to conduct preliminary studies or assist in other preparations for contemplated transactions, e.g., business appraisals, tentative financing arrangements, attitude of large outside holders, availability of major blocks of stock, engineering studies and market analyses and surveys. Experience has shown that maintaining security at this point is virtually impossible. *Accordingly, fairness requires that the company make an immediate public announcement as soon as disclosures relating to such important matters are made to outsiders.*

The extent of the disclosures will depend upon the stage of discussions, studies, or negotiations. So far as possible, public statements should be definite as to price, ratio, timing and/or any other pertinent information necessary to permit a reasonable evaluation of the matter. As a minimum, they should include those disclosures made to outsiders. Where an initial announcement cannot be specific or complete, it will need to be supplemented from time to time as more definitive or different terms are discussed or determined.

Corporate employees, as well as directors and officers, should be regularly reminded as a matter of policy that they must not disclose confidential information they may receive in the course of their duties and must not attempt to take advantage of such information themselves.

In view of the importance of this matter and the potential difficulties involved, the Exchange suggests that a periodic review be made by each company of the matter in which confidential information is being handled within its own organization. A reminder notice of the company's policy to those in sensitive areas might also be helpful.

A sound corporate disclosure policy is essential to the maintenance of a fair and orderly securities market. It should minimize the occasions where the Exchange finds it necessary to temporarily halt trading in a security due to information leaks or rumors in connection with significant corporate transactions.

While the procedures are directed primarily at situations involving two or more companies, they are equally applicable to major corporate developments involving a single company.

QUESTIONS

(1) Read the TGS press release, p. 591 supra. Is any part of it an affirmative misstatement? If not, what makes it misleading? If it had been submitted to you for clearance how would you have rewritten it? Is the Itzok Lake disclosure the right way to go about it? Do you understand what its implications for the investor in TGS stock is? (Is that the question?)

(2) What is the test of "materiality" as to undisclosed information which emerges from the case? Is it the same as is used in dealing with the press release branch of the case? Is it the same test as appears in the cases applying § 11 of the Securities Act (p. 186 supra)? Is it the same question as arises in the context of Rule 14a–9 forbidding misstatements in proxy solicitations? Could one link it to a specific figure relating to its impact on the securities market—if the data not disclosed would, when disclosed, likely have caused a 5% shift in the price of the security? Incidentally, are there any unanswered questions emerging from the way the price of TGS stock behaved after K–55–1 was found?

(3) If you think of a tender offer in terms comparable to TGS when in the process does the plan to make a tender offer reach a stage comparable to that of K–55–1? When the analysts within the offering corporation deliver a report to the directors of that corporation? When investment bankers are consulted as to the terms of the plan? When they formulate a definitive plan for an offer? When first negotiations with the board of the target are opened? Is this a matter that ought to be handled by a special, targeted SEC rule rather than left to the courts?

Bibliography: The most comprehensive treatment of Rule 10b–5 and other antifraud rules is A. Bromberg & L. Lowenfels, Securities Fraud and Commodities Fraud (1982, loose-leaf) (5 volume coverage). For a short treatment by an expert see L. Loss, Fundamentals of Securities Regulation ch. 9 (2d ed. 1988)—his fuller treatment in Securities Regulation ch. 6C and 9C (2d ed. 1961, Supp. 1969) is still valuable for its completeness. See also the American Law Institute, 2 Federal Securities Code § 1603 (1980) for a compact restatement. For a general theoretical attack on insider trading prohibitions see Manne, Insider Trading and the Stock Market (1966). For contrasting views of the impact of market theory on insider trading rules see Cox, Insider Trading and Contracting: A Critical Response to the "Chicago School," [1986] Duke L.J. 628; Carlton & Fischel, The Regulation of Insider Trading, 35 Stanf.L.Rev. 857 (1983); Seligman, The Reformulation of Federal Securities Law Concerning Nonpublic Information, 73 Geo.L.J. 1083 (1985); Wang, Trading on Material Nonpublic Information on Impersonal Stock Markets, 54 So.Calif.L.Rev. 1217 (1981).

---

4. Sales of Control

The ultimate, most complex, type of case or controversy about sales of stock is that which arises when the holder of a majority (or controlling minority) of the shares of stock sells that control in a transaction from which the other shareholders are excluded. Some commentators have suggested that such a transaction is inherently illegal, stating as their basic theoretical ground, either that (a) control is an asset of the corporation held in trust and cannot be sold by private parties or (b) there is a right on the part of all shareholders to be given an equal pro rata opportunity to offer their shares to the party seeking control. Before we tackle the ultimate question, it is a useful review exercise to see how many situations involving a transfer of control can be solved by doctrines we have already encountered.

A REVIEW

Suppose that you are the owner of 35% of the stock of Prudential Bag Co. There is no other shareholder bloc with more than 5%. You are a director and a majority of the other directors were nominated by you. You are approached by Mephisto, Inc., a company with a rather doubtful financial reputation. Which of the following transactions would be illegal? Why?

(1) "Sell me your stock at $10 and vote my directors into office. Tell the others to sell to me at $5, saying that's the price you're getting."

(2) "Sell me your stock at $10 and vote my directors in. Transmit my offer at $5 to the other shareholders."

(3) "Sell me your stock at $10 and vote my directors in. We will forget buying stock from the others."

(4) "Have the company sell me its assets." You reply, "I won't do that but I will sell you control over it with my 35% stock interest."

(5) "Sell me your stock for cash, I'm not interested in buying all those corporate assets."

(6) "Sell me your stock for $10 per share and resign and go away. I'll get it back by selling off the company's assets."

(7) "Sell me the shares at $10 and resign and go away." (Mephisto says nothing more but there's a faint smell of brimstone in the air).

(8) Switch the facts so that you have only stock and no directorships. Does this alter the results in (6) and (7)?

(9) Now switch the facts so that you have only directorships and no stock. You are offered $500,000 to resign *seriatim,* voting in M and M's friends. Assume no reason to suspect looting.

(10) Suppose you have both stock and directorships and are offered $1,000,000 for both (the market for the stock being $500,000).

Now consider two leading cases in this field.

———

PERLMAN v. FELDMANN

United States Court of Appeals, Second Circuit, 1955.
219 F.2d 173, certiorari denied 349 U.S. 952, 75 S.Ct. 880, 99 L.Ed. 1277 (1955).

CLARK, CHIEF JUDGE. This is a derivative action brought by minority stockholders of Newport Steel Corporation to compel accounting for, and restitution of, allegedly illegal gains which accrued to defendants as a result of the sale in August, 1950, of their controlling interest in the corporation. The principal defendant, C. Russell Feldmann, who represented and acted for the others, members of his family,[35] was at that time not only the dominant stockholder, but also the chairman of the board of directors and the president of the corporation. Newport, an Indiana corporation, operated mills for the production of steel sheets for sale to manufacturers of steel products, first at Newport, Kentucky, and later also at other places in Kentucky and Ohio. The buyers, a syndicate organized as Wilport Company, a Delaware corporation, consisted of end-users of steel who were interested in securing a source of supply in a market becoming ever tighter in the Korean War. Plaintiffs contend that the consideration paid for the stock included compensation for the sale of a corporate asset, a power held in trust for the corporation by Feldmann as its fiduciary. This power was the ability to control the allocation of the corporate product in a time of short supply, through control of the board of directors; and it was effectively transferred in this sale by having Feldmann procure the resignation of his own board and the election of Wilport's nominees immediately upon consummation of the sale.

The present action represents the consolidation of three pending stockholders' actions in which yet another stockholder has been permitted to intervene. Jurisdiction below was based upon the diverse citizenship of the parties. Plaintiffs argue here, as they did in the court below, that in the situation here disclosed the vendors must account to the non-participating minority stockholders for that share of their profit which is attributable to the sale of the corporate power. Judge Hincks denied the validity of the premise, holding that the rights involved in the sale were only those normally incident to the possession of a controlling block of shares, with which a dominant stockholder, in the absence of fraud or foreseeable looting, was entitled to deal according to his own best interests. Furthermore, he held that plaintiffs had failed to satisfy their burden of proving that the sales price was not a fair price for the stock per se. Plaintiffs appeal from these rulings of law which resulted in the dismissal of their complaint.

The essential facts found by the trial judge are not in dispute. Newport was a relative newcomer in the steel industry with predominantly old installations which were in the process of being supplemented by more modern facilities. Except in times of extreme shortage Newport was not in a position to compete profitably with other steel mills for customers not in its immediate geographical area. Wilport, the purchasing syndicate, consisted of geographically remote end-users

---

35. The stock was not held personally by Feldmann in his own name, but was held by the members of his family and by personal corporations. The aggregate of stock thus had amounted to 33% of the outstanding Newport stock and gave working control to the holder. The actual sale included 55,552 additional shares held by friends and associates of Feldmann, so that a total of 37% of the Newport stock was transferred.

of steel who were interested in buying more steel from Newport than they had been able to obtain during recent periods of tight supply. The price of $20 per share was found by Judge Hincks to be a fair one for a control block of stock, although the over-the-counter market price had not exceeded $12 and the book value per share was $17.03. But this finding was limited by Judge Hincks' statement that "[w]hat value the block would have had if shorn of its appurtenant power to control distribution of the corporate product, the evidence does not show." It was also conditioned by his earlier ruling that the burden was on plaintiffs to prove a lesser value for the stock.

Both as director and as dominant stockholder, Feldmann stood in a fiduciary relationship to the corporation and to the minority stockholders as beneficiaries thereof. . . . His fiduciary obligation must in the first instance be measured by the law of Indiana, the state of incorporation of Newport. . . . Although there is no Indiana case directly in point, the most closely analogous one emphasizes the close scrutiny to which Indiana subjects the conduct of fiduciaries when personal benefit may stand in the way of fulfillment of trust obligations. In Schemmel v. Hill, 91 Ind.App. 373, 169 N.E. 678, 682, 683, McMahan, J., said: "Directors of a business corporation act in a strictly fiduciary capacity. Their office is a trust. Stratis v. Andreson, 1926, 254 Mass. 536, 150 N.E. 832, 44 A.L.R. 567; Hill v. Nisbet, 1885, 100 Ind. 341, 353. When a director deals with his corporation, his acts will be closely scrutinized. Bossert v. Geis, 1914, 57 Ind.App. 384, 107 N.E. 95. Directors of a corporation are its agents, and they are governed by the rules of law applicable to other agents, and, as between themselves and their principal, the rules relating to honesty and fair dealing in the management of the affairs of their principal are applicable. They must not, in any degree, allow their official conduct to be swayed by their private interest, which must yield to official duty. Leader Publishing Co. v. Grant Trust Co., 1915, 182 Ind. 651, 108 N.E. 121. In a transaction between a director and his corporation, where he acts for himself and his principal at the same time in a matter connected with the relation between them, it is presumed, where he is thus potential [sic] on both sides of the contract, that self-interest will overcome his fidelity to his principal, to his own benefit and to his principal's hurt." And the judge added: "Absolute and most scrupulous good faith is the very essence of a director's obligation to his corporation. The first principal duty arising from his official relation is to act in all things of trust wholly for the benefit of his corporation."

In Indiana, then, as elsewhere, the responsibility of the fiduciary is not limited to a proper regard for the tangible balance sheet assets of the corporation, but includes the dedication of his uncorrupted business judgment for the sole benefit of the corporation, in any dealings which may adversely affect it. . . .

Although the Indiana case is particularly relevant to Feldmann as a director, the same rule should apply to his fiduciary duties as majority stockholder, for in that capacity he chooses and controls the directors, and thus is held to have assumed their liability. Pepper v. Litton, supra, 308 U.S. 295, 60 S.Ct. 238. This, therefore, is the standard to which Feldmann was by law required to conform in his activities here under scrutiny.

It is true, as defendants have been at pains to point out, that this is not the ordinary case of breach of fiduciary duty. We have here no fraud, no misuse of confidential information, no outright looting of a helpless corporation. But on the other hand, we do not find compliance with that high standard which we have just stated and which we and other courts have come to expect and demand of corporate fiduciaries. In the often-quoted words of Judge Cardozo: "Many forms of conduct permissible in a workaday world for those acting at arm's length, are forbidden to those bound by fiduciary ties. A trustee is held to something stricter than the morals of the market place. Not honesty alone, but the punctilio of an honor the most sensitive, is then the standard of behavior. As to this there has developed a tradition that is unbending and inveterate. Uncompromising rigidity has been the attitude of courts of equity when petitioned to undermine the rule of undivided loyalty by the 'disintegrating erosion' of particular exceptions." Meinhard v. Salmon, supra, 249 N.Y. 458, 464, 164 N.E. 545, 546, 62 A.L.R. 1. The actions of defendants in siphoning off for personal gain corporate advantages to be derived from a favorable market situation do not betoken the necessary undivided loyalty owed by the fiduciary to his principal.

The corporate opportunities of whose misappropriation the minority stockholders complain need not have been an absolute certainty in order to support this action against Feldmann. If there was possibility of corporate gain, they are entitled to recover. In Young v. Higbee Co., supra, 324 U.S. 204, 65 S.Ct. 594, two stockholders appealing the confirmation of a plan of bankruptcy reorganization were held liable for profits received for the sale of their stock pending determination of the validity of the appeal. They were held accountable for the excess of the price of their stock over its normal price, even though there was no indication that the appeal could have succeeded on substantive grounds. And in Irving Trust Co. v. Deutsch, supra, 2 Cir., 73 F.2d 121, 124, an accounting was required of corporate directors who bought stock for themselves for corporate use, even though there was an affirmative showing that the corporation did not have the finances itself to acquire the stock. Judge Swan speaking for the court pointed out that "The defendants' argument, contrary to Wing v. Dillingham [5 Cir., 239 F. 54], that the equitable rule that fiduciaries should not be permitted to assume a position in which their individual interests might be in conflict with those of the corporation can have no application where the corporation is unable to undertake the venture, is not convincing. If directors are permitted to justify their conduct on such a theory, there will be a temptation to refrain from exerting their strongest efforts on behalf of the corporation since, if it does not meet the obligations, an opportunity of profit will be open to them personally."

This rationale is equally appropriate to a consideration of the benefits which Newport might have derived from the steel shortage. In the past Newport had used and profited by its market leverage by operation of what the industry had come to call the "Feldmann Plan." This consisted of securing interest-free advances from prospective purchasers of steel in return for firm commitments to them from future production. The funds thus acquired were used to finance improvements in existing plants and to acquire new installations. In the summer of 1950 Newport had been negotiating for cold-rolling facilities which it needed for a more fully integrated operation and a more marketable product, and Feldmann plan funds might well have been used toward this end.

Further, as plaintiffs alternatively suggest, Newport might have used the period of short supply to build up patronage in the geographical area in which it could compete profitably even when steel was more abundant. Either of these opportunities was Newport's, to be used to its advantage only. Only if defendants had been able to negate completely any possibility of gain by Newport could they have prevailed. It is true that a trial court finding states: "Whether or not, in August, 1950, Newport's position was such that it could have entered into 'Feldmann Plan' type transactions to procure funds and financing for the further expansion and integration of its steel facilities and whether such expansion would have been desirable for Newport, the evidence does not show." This, however, cannot avail the defendants, who— contrary to the ruling below—had the burden of proof on this issue, since fiduciaries always have the burden of proof in establishing the fairness of their dealings with trust property. . . .

Defendants seek to categorize the corporate opportunities which might have accrued to Newport as too unethical to warrant further consideration. It is true that reputable steel producers were not participating in the gray market brought about by the Korean War and were refraining from advancing their prices, although to do so would not have been illegal. But Feldmann plan transactions were not considered within this self-imposed interdiction; the trial court found that around the time of the Feldmann sale Jones & Laughlin Steel Corporation, Republic Steel Company, and Pittsburgh Steel Corporation were all participating in such arrangements. In any event, it ill becomes the defendants to disparage as unethical the market advantages from which they themselves reaped rich benefits.

We do not mean to suggest that a majority stockholder cannot dispose of his controlling block of stock to outsiders without having to account to his corporation for profits or even never do this with impunity when the buyer is an interested customer, actual or potential, for the corporation's product. But when the sale necessarily results in a sacrifice of this element of corporate good will and consequent unusual profit to the fiduciary who has caused the sacrifice, he should account for his gains. So in a time of market shortage, where a call on a corporation's product commands an unusually large premium, in one form or another, we think it sound law that a fiduciary may not appropriate to himself the value of this premium. Such personal gain at the expense of his coventurers seems particularly reprehensible when made by the trusted president and director of his company. In this case the violation of duty seems to be all the clearer because of this triple role in which Feldmann appears, though we are unwilling to say, and are not to be understood as saying, that we should accept a lesser obligation for any one of his roles alone.

Hence to the extent that the price received by Feldmann and his codefendants included such a bonus, he is accountable to the minority stockholders who sue here. Restatement, Restitution §§ 190, 197 (1937); Seagrave Corp. v. Mount, supra, 6 Cir., 212 F.2d 389. And plaintiffs, as they contend, are entitled to a recovery in their own right, instead of in right of the corporation (as in the usual derivative actions), since neither Wilport nor their successors in interest should share in any judgment which may be rendered. See Southern Pacific Co. v. Bogert, 250 U.S. 483, 39 S.Ct. 533, 63 L.Ed. 1099. Defendants cannot well object to this form of recovery, since the only alternative, recovery for the corporation as a whole, would subject them to a greater total liability.

The case will therefore be remanded to the district court for a determination of the question expressly left open below, namely, the value of defendants' stock without the appurtenant control over the corporation's output of steel. We reiterate that on this issue, as on all others relating to a breach of fiduciary duty, the burden of proof must rest on the defendants. . . . Judgment should go to these plaintiffs and those whom they represent for any premium value so shown to the extent of their respective stock interests.

The judgment is therefore reversed and the action remanded for further proceedings pursuant to this opinion.

SWAN, CIRCUIT JUDGE (dissenting).

With the general principles enunciated in the majority opinion as to the duties of fiduciaries I am, of course, in thorough accord. But, as Mr. Justice Frankfurter stated in Securities and Exchange Comm. v. Chenery Corp., 318 U.S. 80, 85, 63 S.Ct. 454, 458, 87 L.Ed. 626, "to say that a man is a fiduciary only begins analysis; it gives direction to further inquiry. To whom is he a fiduciary? What obligations does he owe as a fiduciary? In what respect has he failed to discharge these obligations?" My brothers' opinion does not specify precisely what fiduciary duty Feldmann is held to have violated or whether it was a duty imposed upon him as the dominant stockholder or as a director of Newport. Without such specification I think that both the legal profession and the business world will find the decision confusing and will be unable to foretell the extent of its impact upon customary practices in the sale of stock.

The power to control the management of a corporation, that is, to elect directors to manage its affairs, is an inseparable incident to the ownership of a majority of its stock, or sometimes, as in the present instance, to the ownership of enough shares, less than a majority, to control an election. Concededly a majority or dominant shareholder is ordinarily privileged to sell his stock at the best price obtainable from the purchaser. In so doing he acts on his own behalf, not as an agent of the corporation. If he knows or has reason to believe that the purchaser intends to exercise to the detriment of the corporation the power of management acquired by the purchase, such knowledge or reasonable suspicion will terminate the dominant shareholder's privilege to sell and will create a duty not to transfer the power of management to such purchaser. The duty seems to me to resemble the obligation which everyone is under not to assist another to commit a tort rather than the obligation of a fiduciary. But whatever the nature of the duty, a violation of it will subject the violator to liability for damages sustained by the corporation. Judge Hincks found that Feldmann had no reason to think that Wilport would use the power of management it would acquire by the purchase to injure Newport, and that there was no proof that it ever was so used. Feldmann did know, it is true, that the reason Wilport wanted the stock was to put in a board of directors who would be likely to permit Wilport's members to purchase more of Newport's steel than they might otherwise be able to get. But there is nothing illegal in a dominant shareholder purchasing from his own corporation at the same prices it offers to other customers. That is what the members of Wilport did, and there is no proof that Newport suffered any detriment therefrom.

My brothers say that "the consideration paid for the stock included compensation for the sale of a corporate asset", which they describe as "the ability to control the allocation of the corporate product in a time of short supply, through control of the board of directors; and it was effectively transferred in this sale by having.Feldmann procure the resignation of his own board and the election of Wilport's nominees immediately upon consummation of the sale." The implications of this are not clear to me. If it means that when market conditions are such as to induce users of a corporation's product to wish to buy a controlling block of stock in order to be able to purchase part of the corporation's output at the same mill list prices as are offered to other customers, the dominant stockholder is under a fiduciary duty not to sell his stock, I cannot agree. For reasons already stated, in my opinion Feldmann was not proved to be under any fiduciary duty as a stockholder not to sell the stock he controlled.

Feldmann was also a director of Newport. Perhaps the quoted statement means that as a director he violated his fiduciary duty in voting to elect Wilport's nominees to fill the vacancies created by the resignations of the former directors of Newport. As a director Feldmann was under a fiduciary duty to use an honest judgment in acting on the corporation's behalf. A director is privileged to resign, but so long as he remains a director he must be faithful to his fiduciary duties and must not make a personal gain from performing them. Consequently, if the price paid for Feldmann's stock included a payment for voting to elect the new directors, he must account to the corporation for such payment, even though he honestly believed that the men he voted to elect were well qualified to serve as directors. He can not take pay for performing his fiduciary duty. There is no suggestion that he did do so, unless the price paid for his stock was more than its value. So it seems to me that decision must turn on whether finding 120 and conclusion 5 of the district judge are supportable on the evidence. They are set out in the margin.[36]

Judge Hincks went into the matter of valuation of the stock with his customary care and thoroughness. He made no error of law in applying the principles relating to valuation of stock. Concededly a controlling block of stock has greater sale value than a small lot. While the spread between $10 per share for small lots and $20 per share for the controlling block seems rather extraordinarily wide the $20 valuation was supported by the expert testimony of Dr. Badger, whom the district judge said he could not find to be wrong. I see no justification for upsetting the valuation as clearly erroneous. Nor can I agree with my brothers that the $20 valuation "was limited" by the last sentence in finding 120. The controlling block could not by any possibility be shorn of its appurtenant power to elect directors and through them to control distribution of the corporate product. It is this "appurtenant power" which gives a controlling block its value as such

---

36. "120. The 398,927 shares of Newport stock sold to Wilport as of August 31, 1950, had a fair value as a control block of $20 per share. What value the block would have had if shorn of its appurtenant power to control distribution of the corporate product, the evidence does not show."

"5. Even if Feldmann's conduct in cooperating to accomplish a transfer of control

to Wilport immediately upon the sale constituted a breach of a fiduciary duty to Newport, no part of the moneys received by the defendants in connection with the sale constituted profits for which they were accountable to Newport."

block. What evidence could be adduced to show the value of the block "if shorn" of such appurtenant power, I cannot conceive, for it cannot be shorn of it.

The opinion also asserts that the burden of proving a lesser value than $20 per share was not upon the plaintiffs but the burden was upon the defendants to prove that the stock was worth that value. Assuming that this might be true as to the defendants who were directors of Newport, they did show it, unless finding 120 be set aside. Furthermore, not all the defendants were directors; upon what theory the plaintiffs should be relieved from the burden of proof as to defendants who were not directors, the opinion does not explain.

The final conclusion of my brothers is that the plaintiffs are entitled to recover in their own right instead of in the right of the corporation. This appears to be completely inconsistent with the theory advanced at the outset of the opinion, namely, that the price of the stock "included compensation for the sale of a corporate asset." If a corporate asset was sold, surely the corporation should recover the compensation received for it by the defendants. Moreover, if the plaintiffs were suing in their own right, Newport was not a proper party. . . . I would affirm the judgment on appeal.

ESSEX UNIVERSAL CORPORATION v. YATES

United States Court of Appeals, Second Circuit, 1962.
305 F.2d 572.

LUMBARD, CHIEF JUDGE. This appeal from the district court's summary judgment in favor of the defendant raises the question whether a contract for the sale of 28.3 per cent of the stock of a corporation is, under New York law, invalid as against public policy solely because it includes a clause giving the purchaser an option to require a majority of the existing directors to replace themselves, by a process of seriatim resignation, with a majority designated by the purchaser. Despite the disagreement evidenced by the diversity of our opinions, my brethren and I agree that such a provision does not on its face render the contract illegal and unenforceable, and thus that it was improper to grant summary judgment. Judge Friendly would reject the defense of illegality without further inquiry concerning the provision itself (as distinguished from any contention that control could not be safely transferred to the particular purchaser). Judge Clark and I are agreed that on remand, which must be had in any event to consider other defenses raised by the pleadings, further factual issues may be raised by the parties upon which the legality of the clause in question will depend; we disagree, however, on the nature of those factual issues, as our separate opinions reveal. Accordingly, the grant of summary judgment is reversed and the case is remanded for trial of the question of the legality of the contested provision and such further proceedings as may be proper on the other issues raised by the pleadings.

Since we are in agreement on certain preliminary questions, this opinion constitutes the opinion of the court up to the point where it is indicated that it thenceforth states only my individual views.

The defendant Herbert J. Yates, a resident of California, was president and chairman of the board of directors of Republic Pictures

Corporation, a New York corporation which at the time relevant to this suit had 2,004,190 shares of common stock outstanding. Republic's stock was listed and traded on the New York Stock Exchange. In August 1957, Essex Universal Corporation, a Delaware corporation owning stock in various diversified businesses, learned of the possibility of purchasing from Yates an interest in Republic. Negotiations proceeded rapidly, and on August 28 Yates and Joseph Harris, the president of Essex, signed a contract in which Essex agreed to buy, and Yates agreed "to sell or cause to be sold" at least 500,000 and not more than 600,000 shares of Republic stock. The price was set at eight dollars a share, roughly two dollars above the then market price on the Exchange. Three dollars per share was to be paid at the closing on September 18, 1957 and the remainder in twenty-four equal monthly payments beginning January 31, 1958. The shares were to be transferred on the closing date, but Yates was to retain the certificates, endorsed in blank by Essex, as security for full payment. In addition to other provisions not relevant to the present motion, the contract contained the following paragraph:

"6. Resignations.

Upon and as a condition to the closing of this transaction if requested by Buyer at least ten (10) days prior to the date of the closing:

(a) Seller will deliver to Buyer the resignations of the majority of the directors of Republic.

(b) Seller will cause a special meeting of the board of directors of Republic to be held, legally convened pursuant to law and the by-laws of Republic, and simultaneously with the acceptance of the directors' resignations set forth in paragraph 6(a) immediately preceding will cause nominees of Buyer to be elected directors of Republic in place of the resigned directors."

Before the date of the closing, as provided in the contract, Yates notified Essex that he would deliver 566,223 shares, or 28.3 per cent of the Republic stock then outstanding, and Essex formally requested Yates to arrange for the replacement of a majority of Republic's directors with Essex nominees pursuant to paragraph 6 of the contract. This was to be accomplished by having eight of the fourteen directors resign seriatim, each in turn being replaced by an Essex nominee elected by the others; such a procedure was in form permissible under the charter and by-laws of Republic, which empowered the board to choose the successor of any of its members who might resign.

On September 18, the parties met as arranged for the closing at Republic's office in New York City. Essex tendered bank drafts and cashier's checks totalling $1,698,690, which was the 37½ per cent of the total price of $4,529,784 due at this time. The drafts and checks were payable to one Benjamin C. Cohen, who was Essex' banker and had arranged for the borrowing of the necessary funds. Although Cohen was prepared to endorse these to Yates, Yates upon advice of his lawyer rejected the tender as "unsatisfactory" and said, according to his deposition testimony, "Well, there can be no deal. We can't close it."

Essex began this action in the New York Supreme Court, and it was removed to the district court on account of diversity of citizenship. Essex seeks damages of $2,700,000, claiming that at the time of the aborted closing the stock was in actuality worth more than $12.75 a share.[37] Yates' answer raised a number of defenses, but the motion for summary judgment now before us was made and decided only on the theory that the provision in the contract for immediate transfer of control of the board of directors was illegal *per se* and tainted the entire contract. We have no doubt, and the parties agree, that New York law governs.

Appellant's contention that the provision for transfer of director control is separable from the rest of the contract can quickly be rejected. We see no significance in the fact that the contract gave Essex only an option to have the directors replaced, rather than providing directly for such a transfer of control, and the most elementary application of the parol evidence rule forbids us to entertain Essex' argument that there is a factual issue as to whether the transfer clause was central to the negotiations or only an afterthought.

On the face of the contract the sale of stock and the transfer of director control are but two aspects of a single transaction; the provision for the latter in paragraph 6 states that it is to be "a condition to the closing of this transaction." A matter so practically important as achieving immediate rather than deferred acquisition of control over the day-to-day operations of the corporation in which Essex was making such a substantial investment cannot be dismissed as a mere "incidental provision."

The terms of the contract thus express the unwillingness of Essex to pay the agreed price if Yates did not bring about the transfer of directorships, and surely no court would have forced it to make payment in that event. Since Yates could thus not have chosen to excise the hypothetically illegal term of the contract to make the provision for the sale of stock enforceable, it would be unjust to allow Essex the option of waiving it to make the sale enforceable should it suit its purposes to do so. See 6 Corbin, Contracts § 1521 at 1006 (1951).

We are strongly influenced by those New York cases holding invalid agreements to sell stock because accompanied by illegal agreements for the transfer of management control even though they contain no indication that the issue of separability was explicitly raised. See Manson v. Curtis, 223 N.Y. 313, 119 N.E. 559 (1918); Fennessy v. Ross, 90 Hun 298, 35 N.Y.S. 868; 5 App.Div. 342, 39 N.Y.S. 323 (1st Dept. 1896). Accordingly, we hold the provision regarding directors inseparable from the sale of shares, and proceed to a consideration of its legality.

Up to this point my brethren and I are in agreement. The following analysis is my own, except insofar as the separate opinions of Judges Clark and Friendly may indicate agreement.

It is established beyond question under New York law that it is illegal to sell corporate office or management control by itself (that is, accompanied by no stock or insufficient stock to carry voting control). McClure v. Law, 161 N.Y. 78, 55 N.E. 388 (1899); Ballantine v. Ferretti, 28 N.Y.S.2d 668, 678–680 (N.Y.County Sup.Ct.1941); see Manson v. Curtis, 223 N.Y. 313, 119 N.E. 559 (1918). The same rule apparently applies in all jurisdictions where the question has arisen. E.g., Guernsey v. Cook, 120 Mass. 501 (1876); Reed v. Catlett, 228 Mo.App. 109, 68

---

37. In 1959, while this action was pending, the stock was sold to another party for ten dollars a share.

S.W.2d 734 (1934); see Hill, The Sale of Controlling Shares, 70 Harv.L. Rev. 986, 998 (1957); Berle, "Control" in Corporate Law, 58 Colum.L. Rev. 1212 (1958). The rationale of the rule is undisputable: persons enjoying management control hold it on behalf of the corporation's stockholders, and therefore may not regard it as their own personal property to dispose of as they wish. Any other rule would violate the most fundamental principle of corporate democracy, that management must represent and be chosen by, or at least with the consent of, those who own the corporation.

Essex was, however, contracting with Yates for the purchase of a very substantial percentage of Republic stock. If, by virtue of the voting power carried by this stock, it could have elected a majority of the board of directors, then the contract was not a simple agreement for the sale of office to one having no ownership interest in the corporation, and the question of its legality would require further analysis. Such stock voting control would incontestably belong to the owner of a majority of the voting stock, and it is commonly known that equivalent power usually accrues to the owner of 28.3% of the stock. For the purpose of this analysis, I shall assume that Essex was contracting to acquire a majority of the Republic stock, deferring consideration of the situation where, as here, only 28.3% is to be acquired.

Republic's board of directors at the time of the aborted closing had fourteen members divided into three classes, each class being "as nearly as may be" of the same size. Directors were elected for terms of three years, one class being elected at each annual shareholder meeting on the first Tuesday in April. Thus, absent the immediate replacement of directors provided for in this contract, Essex as the hypothetical new majority shareholder of the corporation could not have obtained managing control in the form of a majority of the board in the normal course of events until April 1959, some eighteen months after the sale of the stock. The first question before us then is whether an agreement to accelerate the transfer of management control, in a manner legal in form under the corporation's charter and by-laws, violates the public policy of New York.

There is no question of the right of a controlling shareholder under New York law normally to derive a premium from the sale of a controlling block of stock. In other words, there was no impropriety *per se* in the fact that Yates was to receive more per share than the generally prevailing market price for Republic stock. . . .

The next question is whether it is legal to give and receive payment for the immediate transfer of management control to one who has achieved majority share control but would not otherwise be able to convert that share control into operating control for some time. I think that it is.

Of course under some circumstances controlling shareholders transferring immediate control may be compelled to account to the corporation for that part of the consideration received by them which exceeds the fair value of the block of stock sold, as well as for the injury which they may cause to the corporation. In Gerdes v. Reynolds, 28 N.Y.S.2d 622 (N.Y.County Sup.Ct.1941), the purchasers of control of an investment company proceeded immediately to loot the corporation of its assets, and the court required the sellers to account on the theory that the circumstances of the sale put them on notice of the buyers' evil intentions. The court found the price paid grossly in excess of the calculable fair value of a controlling interest in the corporation, and found the differential to be payment for the immediate control which, foreseeably, the buyers used to the detriment of the corporation and its other shareholders.   . . .

In Perlman v. Feldmann, 219 F.2d 173, 50 A.L.R.2d 1134 (2 Cir.), cert. denied, 349 U.S. 952, 75 S.Ct. 880, 99 L.Ed. 1277 (1955), this court, in a decision based only nominally on Indiana law, went beyond this rule to hold liable controlling shareholders who similarly sold immediate control even in the absence of illegitimate activity on the part of the purchasers. Our theory was basically that the controlling shareholders in selling control to a potential customer had appropriated to their personal benefit a corporate asset: the premium which the company's product could command in a time of market shortage.   . . .

A fair generalization from these cases may be that a holder of corporate control will not, as a fiduciary, be permitted to profit from facilitating actions on the part of the purchasers of control which are detrimental to the interests of the corporation or the remaining shareholders. There is, however, no suggestion that the transfer of control over Republic to Essex carried any such threat to the interests of the corporation or its other shareholders.

Our examination of the New York cases discussed thus far gives us no reason to regard as impaired the holding of the early case of Barnes v. Brown, 80 N.Y. 527 (1880), that a bargain for the sale of a majority stock interest is not made illegal by a plan for immediate transfer of management control by a program like that provided for in the Essex–Yates contract.   . . .

. . .

To be sure, in Barnes v. Brown no term of the contract of sale *required* the seller to effectuate the immediate replacement of directors, as did paragraph 6 of the Essex–Yates contract, but Judge Earl stated that "I shall assume that it was the understanding and a part of the scheme that he should do so." 80 N.Y. at 536. Although the court might have decided the case by pointing out that under the parol evidence rule either party could have ignored what was at best a collateral oral agreement for the replacement of directors and enforced the written contract for the sale of the stock as it read, it chose not to do so but explicitly upheld the legality of the transfer of directorships.   . . .

Given this principle that it is permissible for a seller thus to choose to facilitate immediate transfer of management control, I can see no objection to a contractual provision requiring him to do so as a condition of the sale. Indeed, a New York court has upheld an analogous contractual term requiring the board of directors to elect the nominees of the purchasers of a majority stock interest to officerships. San Remo Copper Mining Co. v. Moneuse, 149 App.Div. 26, 133 N.Y.S. 509 (1st Dept. 1912). The court said that since the purchaser was about to acquire "absolute control" of the corporation, "it certainly did not destroy the validity of the contract that by one of its terms defendant was to be invested with this power of control at once, upon acquiring the stock, instead of waiting for the next annual meeting." 149 App. Div. at 28, 133 N.Y.S. at 511.   . . .

The most troublesome, and most recent, of the relevant New York decisions, one not cited below, is Benson v. Braun, 8 Misc.2d 67, 155 N.Y.S.2d 622 (Nassau County Sup.Ct.1956). That case was a derivative action by minority shareholders seeking to recover an alleged premium received by the sellers of a majority share interest for transferring control over the board of directors in the manner provided for in the Essex–Yates contract; there was, however, no such explicit contractual provision. The complaint, sustained earlier by the Appellate Division, 286 App.Div. 1098, 145 N.Y.S.2d 711 (2d Dept.1955), alleged that this premium had been for the immediate transfer of control under circumstances raising a reasonable suspicion that the purchasers intended to loot the corporation. At the trial, the court found no reason for the sellers to have suspected looting, but went on to say that it was necessary to determine "whether the price paid for the stock is so great that it can be explained in no other way than as a payment for resigning from office." 8 Misc.2d at 71, 155 N.Y.S.2d at 627. Although the court found that the price could be justified in terms of the fair value of the stock, the fact that it made the inquiry suggests that the opposite factual conclusion would have resulted in liability. The court's approach may, however, be explained in terms of the principle, evolved earlier in this discussion, that an accounting will be required in any case where the transfer of control works to the detriment of the corporation or its other shareholders. The court pointed out the absence of any resultant harm, and stated that

> "The rules restricting free alienability of controlling stock have been developed, as earlier noted, to prevent injury and injustice to the corporation and its stockholders. When these restrictive rules have been applied their thrust has been at those found to be responsible for injury to the corporation, its shareholders or creditors." 8 Misc.2d at 73, 155 N.Y.S.2d at 629.

The payment of a large premium for resigning (alleged to be $800,000 in Benson v. Braun) is, of course, relevant to the question whether the sellers had any reason for suspecting that the purchasers had improper intentions in acquiring control. See Gerdes v. Reynolds, 28 N.Y.S.2d 622, 658 (N.Y.County Sup.Ct.1941). Such an interpretation best comports with the line of New York authority as we have traced it.

To be sure, § 16(a) of the Investment Company Act of 1940, 54 Stat. 813, 15 U.S.C.A. § 80a–16(a), prohibits replacement of more than one-third of the directors of a registered investment company other than by shareholder vote, and some authorities contend that the same principle should be enforced as to all corporations. . . . Investment companies, whose assets consist of more or less liquid securities, present a special temptation to looters, and in the judgment of Congress a special prophylactic rule is needed to protect shareholders from the consequences of secret transfers of management control. It is doubtful, however, that such a restriction is necessary or desirable in the case of an industrial corporation such as Republic; in any event, I can find no indication that the New York courts would impose it.

The easy and immediate transfer of corporate control to new interests is ordinarily beneficial to the economy and it seems inevitable that such transactions would be discouraged if the purchaser of a majority stock interest were required to wait some period before his purchase of control could become effective. Conversely it would greatly hamper the efforts of any existing majority group to dispose of its interest if it could not assure the purchaser of immediate control over corporation operations. I can see no reason why a purchaser of majority control should not ordinarily be permitted to make his control effective from the moment of the transfer of stock.

Thus if Essex had been contracting to purchase a majority of the stock of Republic, it would have been entirely proper for the contract to contain the provision for immediate replacement of directors. Although in the case at bar only 28.3 per cent of the stock was involved, it is commonly known that a person or group owning so large a percentage of the voting stock of a corporation which, like Republic, has at least the 1,500 shareholders normally requisite to listing on the New York Stock Exchange, is almost certain to have share control as a practical matter. If Essex was contracting to acquire what in reality would be equivalent to ownership of a majority of stock, i.e., if it would as a practical certainty have been guaranteed of the stock voting power to choose a majority of the directors of Republic in due course, there is no reason why the contract should not similarly be legal.[38] Whether Essex was thus to acquire the equivalent of majority stock control would, if the issue is properly raised by the defendants, be a factual issue to be determined by the district court on remand.

Because 28.3 per cent of the voting stock of a publicly owned corporation is usually tantamount to majority control, I would place the burden of proof on this issue on Yates as the party attacking the legality of the transaction. Thus, unless on remand Yates chooses to raise the question whether the block of stock in question carried the equivalent of majority control, it is my view that the trial court should regard the contract as legal and proceed to consider the other issues raised by the pleadings. If Yates chooses to raise the issue, it will, on my view, be necessary for him to prove the existence of circumstances which would have prevented Essex from electing a majority of the Republic board of directors in due course. It will not be enough for Yates to raise merely hypothetical possibilities of opposition by the other Republic shareholders to Essex' assumption of management control. Rather, it will be necessary for him to show that, assuming neutrality on the part of the retiring management, there was at the time some concretely foreseeable reason why Essex' wishes would not have prevailed in shareholder voting held in due course. In other words, I would require him to show that there was at the time of the contract some other organized block of stock of sufficient size to outvote the block Essex was buying, or else some circumstance making it likely that enough of the holders of the remaining Republic stock would band together to keep Essex from control.

Reversed and remanded for further proceedings not inconsistent with the judgment of this court.

[A concurring opinion by JUDGE CLARK is omitted.]

FRIENDLY, CIRCUIT JUDGE (concurring).

Chief Judge Lumbard's thoughtful opinion illustrates a difficulty, inherent in our dual judicial system, which has led at least one state to authorize its courts to answer questions about its law that a Federal court may ask. Here we are forced to decide a question of New York

---

38. The fact that under the Essex–Yates contract only 37½% of the price of the stock was to be paid at the closing and the balance was not to be fully paid for twenty-eight months is irrelevant to this case. There is no indication that Essex did not have sound financial backing sufficient to discharge properly the obligation which had been incurred.

law, of enormous importance to all New York corporations and their stockholders, on which there is hardly enough New York authority for a really informed prediction what the New York Court of Appeals would decide on the facts here presented, see Cooper v. American Airlines, Inc., 149 F.2d 355, 359, 162 A.L.R. 318 (2 Cir., 1945); Pomerantz v. Clark, 101 F.Supp. 341 (D.Mass.1951); Corbin, The Laws of the Several States, 50 Yale L.J. 762, 775–776 (1941), yet too much for us to have the freedom used to good effect in Perlman v. Feldmann, 219 F.2d 173 (2 Cir.), cert. denied, 349 U.S. 952, 75 S.Ct. 880, 99 L.Ed. 1277 (1955).

I have no doubt that many contracts, drawn by competent and responsible counsel, for the purchase of blocks of stock from interests thought to "control" a corporation although owning less than a majority, have contained provisions like paragraph 6 of the contract *sub judice*. However, developments over the past decades seem to me to show that such a clause violates basic principles of corporate democracy. To be sure, stockholders who have allowed a set of directors to be placed in office, whether by their vote or their failure to vote, must recognize that death, incapacity or other hazard may prevent a director from serving a full term, and that they will have no voice as to his immediate successor. But the stockholders are entitled to expect that, in that event, the remaining directors will fill the vacancy in the exercise of their fiduciary responsibility. A mass seriatim resignation directed by a selling stockholder, and the filling of vacancies by his henchmen at the dictation of a purchaser and without any consideration of the character of the latter's nominees, are beyond what the stockholders contemplated or should have been expected to contemplate. This seems to me a wrong to the corporation and the other stockholders which the law ought not countenance, whether the selling stockholder has received a premium or not. Right in this Court we have seen many cases where sudden shifts of corporate control have caused serious injury; . . .

To hold the seller for delinquencies of the new directors only if he knew the purchaser was an intending looter is not a sufficient sanction. The difficulties of proof are formidable even if receipt of too high a premium creates a presumption of such knowledge, and, all too often, the doors are locked only after the horses have been stolen. Stronger medicines are needed—refusal to enforce a contract with such a clause, even though this confers an unwarranted benefit on a defaulter, and continuing responsibility of the former directors for negligence of the new ones until an election has been held. Such prophylactics are not contraindicated, as Judge Lumbard suggests, by the conceded desirability of preventing the dead hand of a former "controlling" group from continuing to dominate the board after a sale, or of protecting a would-be purchaser from finding himself without a majority of the board after he has spent his money. A special meeting of stockholders to replace a board may always be called, and there could be no objection to making the closing of a purchase contingent on the results of such an election. I perceive some of the difficulties of mechanics such a procedure presents, but I have enough confidence in the ingenuity of the corporate bar to believe these would be surmounted.

Hence, I am inclined to think that if I were sitting on the New York Court of Appeals, I would hold a provision like Paragraph 6 violative of public policy save when it was entirely plain that a new election would be a mere formality—i.e., when the seller owned more than 50% of the stock. I put it thus tentatively because, before making such a decision, I would want the help of briefs, including those of *amici curiae,* dealing with the serious problems of corporate policy and practice more fully than did those here, which were primarily devoted to argument as to what the New York law has been rather than what it ought to be. Moreover, in view of the perhaps unexpected character of such a holding, I doubt that I would give it retrospective effect.

As a judge of this Court, my task is the more modest one of predicting how the judges of the New York Court of Appeals would rule, and I must make this prediction on the basis of legal materials rather than of personal acquaintance or hunch. Also, for obvious reasons, the prospective technique is unavailable when a Federal court is deciding an issue of state law. Although Barnes v. Brown, 80 N.Y. 527 (1880), dealt with the sale of a majority interest, I am unable to find any real indication that the doctrine there announced has been thus limited. True, there are New York cases saying that the sale of corporate offices is forbidden; but the New York decisions do not tell us what this means and I can find nothing, save perhaps one unexplained sentence in the opinion of a trial court in Ballantine v. Ferretti, 28 N.Y.S.2d 668, 682 (Sup.Ct.N.Y.Co.1941), to indicate that New York would not apply Barnes v. Brown to a case where a stockholder with much less than a majority conditioned a sale on his causing the resignation of a majority of the directors and the election of the purchaser's nominees.

Chief Judge Lumbard's proposal goes part of the way toward meeting the policy problem I have suggested. Doubtless proceeding from what, as it seems to me, is the only justification in principle for permitting even a majority stockholder to condition a sale on delivery of control of the board—namely that in such a case a vote of the stockholders would be a useless formality, he sets the allowable bounds at the line where there is "a practical certainty" that the buyer would be able to elect his nominees and, in this case, puts the burden of disproving that on the person claiming illegality.

Attractive as the proposal is in some respects, I find difficulties with it. One is that I discern no sufficient intimation of the distinction in the New York cases, or even in the writers, who either would go further in voiding such a clause, see Berle, "Control" in Corporate Law, 58 Colum.L.Rev. 1212, 1224 (1958); Leech, Transactions in Corporate Control, 104 U.Pa.L.Rev. 725, 809 (1956) [proposing legislation], or believe the courts have not yet gone that far, see Baker & Cary, Corporations: Cases and Materials (3d ed. unabr. 1959) 590. To strike down such a condition only in cases falling short of the suggested line accomplishes little to prevent what I consider the evil; in most instances a seller will not enter into a contract conditioned on his "delivering" a majority of the directors unless he has good reason to think he can do that. When an issue does arise, the "practical certainty" test is difficult to apply. The existence of such certainty will depend not merely on the proportion of the stock held by the seller but on many other factors—whether the other stock is widely or closely held, how much of it is in "street names," what success the corporation has experienced, how far its dividend policies have satisfied its stockholders, the identity of the purchasers, the presence or absence of cumulative voting, and many others. Often, unless the seller has nearly 50% of the stock, whether he has "working control" can be determined only by an election; groups who thought they had such control have experienced unpleasant surprises in recent years. Judge Lumbard correctly recognizes that, from a policy standpoint, the pertinent question must be the buyer's prospects of election, not the seller's—yet this inevitably requires the court to canvass the likely reaction of stockholders to a group of whom they know nothing and seems rather hard to reconcile with a position that it is "right" to insert such a condition if a seller has a larger proportion of the stock and "wrong" if he has a smaller. At the very least the problems and uncertainties arising from the proposed line of demarcation are great enough, and its advantages small enough, that in my view a Federal court would do better simply to overrule the defense here, thereby accomplishing what is obviously the "just" result in this particular case, and leave the development of doctrine in this area to the State, which has primary concern for it. . . .

NOTE ON PREMIUMS FOR SALE OF CONTROL

(1) In Birnbaum v. Newport Steel Corp.,[39] minority shareholders in Newport sought to hold members of the Feldmann group liable under Rule 10(b)–5. Their complaint alleged a fact not stated in Perlman, that in August 1950 Feldmann as president of Newport, rejected a profitable offer by Follansbee Steel Corporation for a merger, that rejection being followed by a misleading letter to the Newport shareholders. The Court of Appeals rebuffed this attempt and dismissed the complaint, holding as follows:

> section [10(b)] was directed solely at that type of misrepresentation or fraudulent practice usually associated with the sale or purchase of securities rather than at fraudulent mismanagement of corporate affairs, and that Rule X–10B–5 extended protection only to the defrauded purchaser or seller. Since the complaint failed to allege that any of the plaintiffs fell within either class, the judgment [of dismissal] was correct . . .

The Birnbaum ruling has been much disputed and somewhat eroded by a series of Court of Appeals cases but was resoundingly reaffirmed in Blue Chip Stamps v. Manor Drug Stores, p. 566, supra.

(2) The district court in Perlman, on remand, had the task of determining "the value of the defendant's stock without the appurtenant control over the corporation's output of steel."[40] After extensive expert testimony the court found an enterprise value of $15,825,777.53. The calculations involved primarily the steel division and a woodworking division plus some real estate, etc. The steel division had a net book value of $12,753,237, and foreseeable average net earnings after taxes of $1,475,021.63, which, capitalized at 5.5 times, led to a capitalized earnings figure of $8,112,619. The court gave a weight of 60% to earnings and 40% to net book value; it thus evaluated the steel division at $9,968,866.20. By a similar process it valued the woodworking division (Caswell–Runyan) at $1,573,439.33. Miscellaneous assets were valued on different bases to arrive at the total. Dividing this

---

39.　193 F.2d 461, 464 (2d Cir.1952).　　　　**40.**　154 F.Supp. 436 (D.Conn.1957).

figure by the 1,078,491.4 shares issued and outstanding produced a value of $14.67 a share. The defendants had sold 398,927 shares for $20.00 a share or a bonus of $5.33 a share or a total premium of $2,126,280.91. However, the court awarded a lesser amount of damages. 36.99% of the shares—those held by Wilport—were ruled to be ineligible to recover. This reduced the recovery to $1,339,769.62 to be divided among the eligible plaintiffs. Note that this method of allocating the recovery, mandated by the Court of Appeals, departs from the normal, logical result deriving from the theory of the derivative suit.

(3) Transactions in the control of investment companies raise peculiar problems. The assets of an investment company are particularly vulnerable to looting since they can be quickly, quietly and anonymously liquidated. Some spectacular cases along this line, in which looters paid the purchase price for control (of such companies) by pilfering the companies' treasuries when they got control of them and keeping the rest for themselves, did much to get the premium doctrine on its way.[41] This particular problem has been largely foreclosed by provisions of the federal Investment Company Act of 1940 which require that the securities be kept in the custody of a reliable and disinterested third party.[42] Another problem is more difficult. As stated in Essex Universal Corp. v. Yates, at p. 624 supra, § 16(a) of the Act requires a shareholder vote if more than $\frac{1}{3}$ of the directors are replaced. However, effective control over the typical investment company is vested not in its board of directors but in its investment manager which, pursuant to a management contract, handles the company's portfolio. This manager is typically an investment banking firm which originated and sponsored the enterprise. It is not in theory possible to gain a profit by assigning the manager's contract rights since Section 15 of the Act says that the contract must be terminable on assignment. However, the realities seem to be that the directors are likely to vote to approve a new contract with a new manager if requested by the outgoing manager. Rosenfeld v. Black, decided by Judge Friendly (recall his concurrence in Essex Universal Corp. v. Yates, at p. 630 supra), held that in such a situation the outgoing manager could not retain a fee paid to it by its replacement in connection with such a transfer. This case may be fundamentally indistinguishable from a Ninth Circuit case that held it proper for those who controlled an incorporated investment manager to sell their stock therein to another group.[43]

(4) The record has been barren for the last two decades in the matter of sales of control. There have been a scattering of cases in

---

41. E.g., Gerdes v. Reynolds, 28 N.Y.S.2d 622 (1941).

42. 15 U.S.C.A. § 80a–16.

43. SEC v. Insurance Securities, Inc., 254 F.2d 642 (9th Cir.1958); Rosenfeld v. Black, 445 F.2d 1337 (2d Cir.1971).

The Securities Act Amendments of 1975 added subsection 15(f) to the Investment Company Act which permits the adviser to receive "any amount or benefit in connection with" a transfer of interests in the adviser. However, it sets two conditions: (A) that for three years after transfer 75% of the board must be outsiders and (B) that there can be no "unfair burden" imposed on the company.

which claims have been made that the sellers were negligent in their choice of buyer; the courts regard this as stating a cause of action.[44] There have also been a few rather crass sale-of-office cases in which the block of stock held by the sellers of directoral control was less than 10%.[45] Those courts which have been asked to adopt a sweeping "equal opportunity rule" have uniformly declined to do so, saying that such a change would be drastic and fundamental and hence should be left to the legislature.[46]

A close observer notes that sales of control may be more subtle nowadays. In conjunction with a takeover the collaboration of incumbent management is very useful, sometimes essential. Their duty is to act impartially, as in the advice they give. To do so under corrupt influence would be clearly illegitimate. But the matter can be shrouded in ambiguity. Thus in Singer v. Magnavox Co.,[47] the Delaware Supreme Court noted that when a tender offer was made for the target company's stock at $8 per share the incumbents stated that they were "shocked by the inadequacy of the offer." When the offer went to $9 per share, accompanied by a two year employment contract at their then salary level for the incumbent officers, the board recommended acceptance. Technically, this would not be a sale of office in any case since the incumbents remained, at least as officers, but the problem in principle seems to be the same.

QUESTIONS

(1) Is Perlman v. Feldmann explicable in terms of a theory other than one making sales of control *per se* unlawful? If not, can you state what the Perlman v. Feldmann theory is, i.e., how far it goes? Does Essex represent a retreat from Perlman?

(2) Does the way in which the Perlman court handles the damages question shed any light on the theory which it used to resolve the merits?

(3) Suppose that your client X owns a block of shares with effective director control going along with it and has been asked by a potential purchaser to sell for $15 per share. X has a sense that this is substantially above the price at which shares have been traded on the over-the-counter market lately, which prices have been at about $10–12. X states however that the market is thin and erratic and not a very reliable guide. X would like to accept this offer if it is safe to do so. X asks (a) whether it is legal to sell on this basis and (b) what terms and conditions about change of control can be acquiesced in if the buyer insists.

(4) Operating Co. is a closely-held corporation that has prospered greatly in the past few years. On an original investment of $100 per share, the corporation has expanded to the point where it has a book value of over $4000 a share and an appraiser might put a like value on those shares. However, Operating

44. Cf. Doleman v. Meiji Mutual Life Ins. Co., 727 F.2d 1480 (9th Cir.1984).

45. Petition of Caplan, 20 A.D.2d 301, 246 N.Y.S.2d 913 (1st Dept.1964) (sale of control by lawyer-financier Roy Cohn with 3% of outstanding stock held unlawful).

46. Zetlin v. Hanson Holdings, Inc. 48 N.Y.2d 684, 421 N.Y.S.2d 877, 397 N.E.2d 387 (1979).

47. 380 A.2d 969 (Del.1977). This case was overruled by Weinberger v. UOP, Inc., p. 739 infra.

has never split its shares to make them more marketable nor has it publicized its activities. Hence there is, effectively, no market for its stock; there have been one or two distress sales at around $1,000. Finally, a group of stockholders who owned about 85% of Operating's stock formed a new corporation, Holding, Inc., and exchanged their Operating shares for Holding shares at a ratio of 100 Holding shares for 1 Operating share. Through their investment banking connections they developed wide publicity in the investing community and obtained a listing for Holding on one of the national securities exchanges. Soon Holding shares were selling at $50 each, although Holding had no significant assets other than its Operating stock. The shareholders in Holding refused to permit the minority shareholders of Operating to exchange their shares for Holding shares and the minority aggrieved, brought suit. In your judgment, do they have a valid claim that the majority breached a fiduciary duty owed them? Do any of the foregoing cases, or their theories, support this claim? [48]

(5) A law firm is contemplating selling its practice at a price which represents an appreciable margin over and above the fair market value of the lease on its office, its library and its business equipment. Do the preceding materials suggest that accepting such a price would be inappropriate?

Bibliography: There is a significant body of theoretical literature on sales of control. The theory was first advanced in A. Berle & G. Means, The Modern Corporation and Private Property 244 (1933) and developed by Berle in his "Control" in Corporate Law, 58 Colum.L.Rev. 1212 (1958). There is a large mass of material in Leech, Transactions in Corporate Control, 104 U.Pa.L.Rev. 725 (1956). Andrews, Stockholders' Right to Equal Opportunity in the Sale of Shares, 78 Harv.L.Rev. 505 (1965), propounds a provocative theory, which has been explicitly rejected by several courts as too "radical". At the opposite end of the spectrum, Easterbrook & Fischel, Corporate Control Transactions, 91 Yale L.J. 698 (1982), take the position that "any attempt to require sharing simply reduces any likelihood that there will be any gains to share."

---

48. The facts in this question are modeled on Jones v. H.F. Ahmanson & Co., 81 Cal.Rptr. 592, 460 P.2d 464 (1969).

Chapter XII

FINANCIAL TRANSACTIONS OF THE GOING CONCERN

1. Introduction

In the pursuit of its explicit or implicit corporate strategy a corporation is constantly dealing with a flow of funds from external sources (issues of stock, borrowings) into other resources (inventory, plant, etc.) which in turn generate cash earnings that can either be recycled into acquisitions of more resources or returned to the outside sources (dividends to shareholders, repurchases of stock, interest on or repayments of debt). Responsibility for different portions of this process is divided among officers of the firm. There will normally be some financial officer responsible for the procurement of funds, the forecasting of needs and the setting of repayment policies. In large concerns an elaborate forecasting and programming budgetary system is a necessity. The process of preparing the budget may involve various levels of management, with estimates and requests for funds coming up through channels. The financial staff must, of course, work very closely with the officer or officers in charge of the investment process since they must know of the needs for funds enough in advance to program adequately. Financial officers must also be prepared to do battle with those production experts who have an insatiable desire for funds and to make them justify their requisitions in terms of the cost/benefit relationship of the funds they require.

The budgeting process at one corporation in the chemical industry was described as follows by a court in deciding a case in which the forecasts were made public and turned out in one year to be far off the target.[1] It is well to remember that the forecasting is still an art, not a science, and is subject to as many hazards as weather predictions.

E. Preparation of Monsanto's Principal Internal Documents Reflecting Results and Estimates

27. The principal internal documents that provided management with the factual information upon which to base operational and financial decisions, and that were the basis for the public statements

---

1. Dolgow v. Anderson, 53 F.R.D. 664, 675–676 (S.D.N.Y.1971), affirmed 464 F.2d 437 (2d Cir.1972). Compare Beecher v. Able, 374 F.Supp. 341 (S.D.N.Y.1974), find-ing that predictions of Douglas Aircraft's earnings had been made and released without due diligence.

were the "Corporate Long–Range Plans," the yearly "Budgets," the quarterly "Budget Reviews," and the various "Capital Appropriation Requests," described below. At the end of each month, there was also prepared a monthly financial results report for the Board of Directors and Executive Committee.

The Corporate Long–Range Plan

28. The "Corporate Long–Range Plan," which covered a period of five years, and was revised annually, represented a consolidation of individual five-year plans by each of Monsanto's Divisions. Preparation of these Division plans involved determinations by the General Manager of the Division and his staff in the Marketing, Purchasing, Personnel, Treasury and Engineering Departments of the Division, as well as consultations with outside experts. The Division plans were each reviewed by top corporate officers prior to their consolidation by the financial planning staff into the Corporate Long–Range Plan, which was also reviewed by top officers prior to presentation to the Board of Directors.

29. Corporate Long–Range Plans were the product of many people, starting from "front-line salesmen" and were ultimately presented to the Board of Directors so that its members' judgments could be incorporated into future company plans.

The Budgets and Budget Reviews

30. At the end of each year, each Division of Monsanto prepared a budget for the next year indicating, among numerous other operating data, budgeted sales and earnings of the Division Work on the budgets began in August or September and was completed in December. After the initial Division budget was prepared, it was reviewed by the Division Budget Committee, the Division Operating Committee and then the Corporate Budget Committee. Thereafter, the budgets of the individual Divisions were consolidated into an over-all Corporate Budget, which was then reviewed by the Corporate Budget Committee and, finally, presented to the Monsanto Board of Directors as the "Approved Corporate Budget" for the next ensuing year.

31. The preparation of the Budget involved the work and judgment of many people from every department of each Division with regard to raw cost and price data; Marketing made an estimate of pounds and price determined primarily from discussions with customers; Manufacturing calculated how much it would cost to make these products; and Accounting assessed overhead, research and other charges.

32. A quarterly "Budget Review" was regularly prepared at the end of the first and second quarters of each year but not the other quarters because of duplication with the procedures for the budget itself. The budget reviews included forecasts of sales and earnings, as

of that time, by each Division, as well as for Monsanto on an overall basis, for the balance of the year.

Capital Appropriation Requests

33. During the three-year period 1964–1966 Monsanto made capital outlays of over $700 million for plant and equipment. Each sizable capital project was described in an "Appropriate [sic] Request" which set forth the capital requirement need, the anticipated return on investment and the payout period. Each appropriation request was reviewed with, and approved by, the Corporate Executive Committee and also by Monsanto's Board of Directors. Preparation of an Appropriation Request involved estimates by Engineering, Treasury, Accounting and other groups within the Division of such factors as costs, time of completion, technical innovations and developments required, and overheads required to handle the new production. These figures were reviewed by the Division Operating Committee before presentation to the Executive Committee and the Board, to be sure that projected prices, capacities and costs were accurate.

Note that for these purposes the chief financial officer is not concerned so much with income as with cash flow. Consider the following "statements of changes in financial position and changes in working capital" which is sometimes referred to as a cash flow statement. Note how it undoes the work of accrual and deferral and puts together current items and capital items, dividends, loans, etc. The idea that depreciation and amortization could be additions to working capital may seem a strange one. The reason that they are is that they were subtracted in calculating net income—the first line of the statement—but do not in fact involve outflows of cash.

Cabot Corporation Consolidated Statements of Changes in Financial Position and Changes in Working Capital

Changes in Financial Position

Years ended September 30	1976	1975
Sources of working capital:		
Income from continuing operations	$ 29,373,000	$ 15,750,000
Charges and (credits) to income which do not currently affect working capital		
Depreciation, amortization and depletion	26,943,000	24,864,000
Deferred income taxes	9,265,000	8,513,000
Equity in net income of affiliated companies	(1,486,000)	(50,000)
Total working capital provided by continuing operations	64,095,000	49,077,000

Changes in Financial Position

Years ended September 30	1976	1975
Discontinued operations		
Provision for anticipated net loss on disposal of discontinued operations		$ (23,000,000)
Related deferred income tax benefits		(16,700,000)
Total working capital absorbed by discontinued operations		(39,700,000)
Total working capital provided by operations	$ 64,095,000	9,377,000
Disposals of plant assets and investments, net book value	6,359,000	115,690,000
Dividends received from affiliated companies	490,000	313,000
Advanced payments on future oil and gas production	1,917,000	5,087,000
Increase in long-term debt	3,992,000	37,398,000
Total sources of working capital	76,853,000	167,865,000
Applications of working capital:		
Property, plant and equipment	44,270,000	64,846,000
Investments	2,012,000	555,000
Decrease in long-term debt	24,582,000	81,816,000
Cash dividends	5,334,000	4,907,000
Other, net	(7,019,000)	2,272,000
Total applications of working capital	69,179,000	154,396,000
Increase in working capital	$ 7,674,000	$ 13,469,000

Changes in Working Capital

	1976	1975
Increase (decrease) in current assets:		
Cash	$ 3,156,000	$ (2,167,000)
Time deposits and marketable securities	(2,109,000)	404,000
Accounts and notes receivable	21,929,000	(12,709,000)
Inventories	5,873,000	6,469,000
Total increase (decrease) in current assets	28,849,000	(8,003,000)
Increase (decrease) in current liabilities:		
Notes payable to banks	5,401,000	(773,000)
Current portion of long-term debt	(908,000)	(11,966,000)
Accounts payable and accruals	12,783,000	(5,294,000)
U.S. and foreign income taxes	3,899,000	(3,439,000)
Total increase (decrease) in current liabilities	21,175,000	(21,472,000)

Changes in Financial Position

Years ended September 30	1976	1975
Increase in working capital	$ 7,674,000	$ 13,469,000

Working capital at September 30	$144,834,000	$137,160,000

The accompanying notes are an integral part of these financial statements.

———

In planning for the future the corporate management will need to make out a working capital or cash flow budget stating projections rather than past history. The budget will have to take into account the exact times of the needs for funds, since it is disastrous not to have the cash when needed but quite expensive to have cash on hand when it is not needed.

The role of the corporation lawyer in this process varies. Legal controls over the uses of a corporation's resources are scant; in particular corporation laws have little to say about it, other than penalizing an occasional spectacular abuse of judgment in investing a firm's funds as spectacular. It is true that § 13(b)(2) of the Securities Exchange Act, motivated by the discovery of widespread illicit payments to foreign officials, introduced a requirement that an issuer subject to § 12 have adequate books, records and accounts and maintain a system of internal accounting controls sufficient to provide reasonable assurances that assets cannot be used without management's approval. Of course the acquisition of a new plant may involve the law of real property, sales, etc. On the other hand, legal rules, either of corporation law or of closely related bodies, govern rather intensively the input of funds into the system and their outflow back to investors. Some of them are quite rigid and specific in character as to what is to be done while others merely develop the concept of full and fair disclosure. Lawyers specializing in this area need a working familiarity with the realities of finance and the accounting techniques used to measure the flows of funds and the success thereof.

Below we consider the legal implications of flows of funds into and out of a corporation in four categories: (1) as respects the inflow of funds arising from the sale of additional issues of stock by the corporation (over and above the original issue problems analyzed in Chapter VI). This section includes a brief treatment of problems arising from an issue of stock that is preferred; (2) as respects the inflow of funds arising from the sale of new issues of bonds or indebtedness; (3) outflows caused by the payment of dividends and (4) outflows caused by the repurchase of corporate stock.

Bibliography: The financial policy of corporations is investigated from legal and business perspectives in V. Brudney & M. Chirelstein, Cases and Materials on Corporate Finance (3d ed. 1987). For business background, consult such textbooks as R. Brealey & S. Myers, Principles of Corporate Finance (2d ed.

1984). There is a journal, The Financial Executive, published by the Financial Executives Institute.

---

2. Additional Issues of Stock

In Chapter VI we considered the basic problems of the issuance of stock in connection with the founding of the firm. These problems included both the regulation of such issues under the federal Securities Act of 1933 and state blue sky laws and corporation law rules about the integrity of capital. The issuance of more stock after the first issue involves all of these problems plus some further ones that pertain to the maintenance of a fair relationship between the holders of the initially issued stock and the newcomers. To illustrate, suppose that a corporation at its creation issued 10,000 shares of stock at $10 per share—its par value. It acquired a single asset for $100,000 and sold it for $150,000. It would then have a balance sheet like this:

	Assets	Liabilities & Proprietorship	
Cash	$150,000	Capital stock	$100,000
		Retained earnings	50,000
			$150,000

Suppose that the firm wishes to expand so as to go through a new acquisition and sale cycle, for which it needs $200,000. Plainly it would be unfair to the original investors to raise $50,000 of new capital by selling another 5,000 shares at the par value of $10 per share. The new investors would have a share of control, and a financial interest amounting to ⅓, of a $200,000 enterprise for a contribution of only ¼ of that amount. Conversely, the rights of the old-timers would be "diluted" from $15 per share to $13.33. It would seem plain that the newcomers ought to be paying $15 per share for these privileges. Normally, this would be achieved by issuing the stock at $15 per share, so that the newcomers would only receive 3,333 shares for the needed $50,000. The extra $5 per share would be credited to an account called "paid in capital" or something of that nature. Of course, the above problem is artificial in that there is a precise cash measure of the firm's worth. A conventional cost-oriented balance sheet of the typical corporation would show the costs of the assets less depreciation in some cases, which could vary widely from present value. Determining the worth per share, as opposed to the book value per share, is a matter involving effort and sophisticated judgment as to which reasonable men might differ—just as valuation turns out to be controversial in other contexts we explore.

Several different approaches might be taken to this problem. The first would be rather rigid and absolutistic. The law might forbid new issues without the express consent of all the existing shareholders. This rule would parallel the understanding as to the admission of new members to a partnership—the *delectus personae* principle discussed in Chapter II. The closest that corporation law has come to this has been the preemptive rights rule. This rule stated that each present stockholder had a right to his *pro rata* share of the new issue. Thus each holder of three shares of stock in the example above would be entitled to subscribe to one share of new stock. This rule originated in 1807 in a classic case, Gray v. Portland Bank,[2] which drew heavily upon partnership analogies. Delaware Law (§ 102(b)(3)) now eliminates such rights unless they are expressly set forth in the articles of incorporation; before 1967 preemptive rights could be deleted only by express language. The latter is probably still the more common statutory solution to the problem.

With or without preemptive rights, some corporations achieve a like effect by use of a "rights offering." In such an offering the firm seeks additional capital by sending each shareholder a warrant representing his proportional right to subscribe to the new offering. To continue with the above example, if each shareholder who held 1,000 shares would get a warrant showing a right to subscribe to $333\frac{1}{3}$ shares at the offering price. The holder has a choice whether to exercise the rights by sending a check for the $5,000 needed plus the warrant for the rights to the agency handling the transaction for the company. If not, the rights can be sold to somebody who wants to exercise them. Nobody would desire to exercise rights unless they were valuable so that a firm would ordinarily issue the rights at a price somewhat below what it felt that the stock could be sold for on the market. Since maintaining proportionality usually involves the issuance of fractional shares there is generally some agency that will round things off by buying and selling fractions. An underwriting firm may be engaged to stand by to purchase and sell to outsiders any shares not bought by the shareholders. The mechanism is somewhat cumbersome and involves some risks of misjudgment and failure but for companies with large bodies of fairly contented shareholders it is a fairly serviceable means of raising funds, especially in such firms as utilities which have recurrent needs for expansion.

Another way in which the issuance of new shares may be restricted is by the limit set in the articles of incorporation upon the number of shares of stock outstanding. Examine the certificate of incorporation for such a limit. Unlike most European corporation laws, the law of Delaware (§ 161) and of most American jurisdictions allows for the device of shares authorized but not outstanding, to the extent of the gap between what is issued and what is authorized by the articles. In this gap the directors are authorized to move, subject always to the application to this special area of the general corporation law fiduciary rules. If the corporation's needs go beyond this point, there will have to be an

2. 3 Mass. 363 (1807).

amendment of the articles, subject to the shareholder vote requirements (Del. § 242) and to the concomitant proxy regulations, if applicable. The lawyer's opinion as to the issuance of shares, which is typically required in this context, has to be based upon a search through the minutes of shareholders and director's meetings to determine the legality of the authorizations thus given.

One is left, then, by the modern rules free of precise and formal restraints and subject only to flexible fiduciary standards, controlling new stock issuance on the basis of such factors as the fairness of the judgment of the need and the appropriate pricing of the issue, as balanced against the impact of the transactions on existing shareholders. That impact is magnified if there are only a few shareholders and their relative shares of control in the enterprise would be drastically shifted by the new issue. The following case deals with such a problem.

HYMAN v. VELSICOL CORP.

Appellate Court of Illinois, First District, 1951.
342 Ill.App. 489, 97 N.E.2d 122.

KILEY, JUSTICE. This is an action to restrain the directors of Velsicol Corporation from carrying out a plan of recapitalization and to nullify acts already done pursuant to the plan. A master in chancery recommended a decree dismissing the suit for want of equity. The chancellor sustained exceptions to the master's report and entered a decree in favor of plaintiff. Defendants have appealed.

Plaintiff is a research chemist. In 1930 he was employed by the Pure Oil Company. During the latter part of 1930 he spoke to defendant Regenstein, his cousin, about inventions he had made in the petroleum field. He wanted capital for exploitation of the inventions. At the time Regenstein was owner of two-thirds of the stock of defendants, Arvey and Transo Corporations, referred to hereinafter as Arvey and Transo. It was decided that the two corporations would provide the capital necessary for plaintiff's purposes.

In 1931 the Velsicol Corporation was organized. Its authorized capital was $20,000 and its authorized stock 200 shares. Arvey and Transo each paid in $8,000 in cash for 80 shares of the stock. Plaintiff assigned two applications for patents to Velsicol in consideration of the issuance to him of the remaining 40 shares. The original Velsicol officers were defendant Regenstein, president, plaintiff Hyman, vice president and F.P. Schneider, secretary-treasurer. The original directors were plaintiffs, Regenstein, Schneider, Sidney Blum and Henry Degginger. Schneider was a stockholder in Transo and Blum and Degginger were shareholders in Arvey. In 1940 Degginger was succeeded on the board of directors by defendant A.R. Jameson.

Velsicol's sales increased from $1,021 in 1932 to $4,096,356 in 1945. Except for 1935 ($2,114) it had no net profit until 1940. Beginning in 1940 its net profit before federal taxes ranged from $44,002 to $353,347. Prior to 1939 Transo and Arvey each advanced to Velsicol, for building and operating purposes, $264,000. Non-interest bearing notes covered the advances until January 1, 1944 when two 4% per annum demand notes for $264,000 each were given.

Plaintiff was the managing vice president of the business from its inception. His salary ranged from $40 per week in 1931 to $600 per week in 1945 and 1946. From 1943 to 1946 he drew expenses of over $8,000 per year. In 1943 he sought a greater proportion of stock interest. In 1946 he refused to assign certain applications for patents covering insecticides, referred to as "1068," to Velsicol until his interest was increased. The dispute over this event resulted in plaintiff's resignation from Velsicol September 13, 1946. Schneider succeeded him in office. On October 15th Velsicol sued plaintiff to compel assignment of the "1068" patent applications. The following day plaintiff resigned as director of Velsicol. In November he brought about the organization of a Delaware corporation to do business in Denver, Colorado, for the manufacture and sale of insecticide "1068". Velsicol's suit to compel assignment of the patent applications covering "1068" was successful. 405 Ill. 352, 90 N.E.2d 717.

Early in December the directors of Velsicol decided on a plan of recapitalization for the company. Due notice of a special meeting of the stockholders, to be held December 16, 1946, was given to plaintiff. At the meeting resolutions for the recapitalization program, passed by the directors, were submitted to the stockholders for approval. These decreased the par value of Velsicol stock from $100 to $10 per share and increased the number of shares from 200 to 2000; amended the charter to authorize 100,000 shares of common stock, $10 par value; authorized issuance of 68,000 additional shares to the stockholders so that 70,000 shares would be outstanding, representing $700,000 capital; provided for purchase of these additional shares by cash or "by credit against sums owing by this corporation on outstanding notes"; and that the subscriptions should be paid for in full before 5:00 P.M. on December 27, 1946. The resolutions were approved by the stockholders. Plaintiff did not attend the meeting. His proxy voted against the resolution.

In due course subscription warrants for the pre-emptive rights were issued. Transo and Arvey each surrendered their demand notes and each paid $8,000 in cash to exercise in full their rights for 27,200 shares each of the additional stock. Plaintiff had the right to subscribe for 340 shares of the $10 par value stock for each share of the $100 par value stock held by him. He did not exercise his rights to purchase the 13,600 shares at $10 per share. He filed this suit on the day fixed by resolution for expiration of the time within which rights had to be exercised.

Plaintiff's suit charged, among other things, that the plan of reorganization was the design of an oppressive majority of stockholders and directors to decrease his interest in Velsicol, was not adopted in the interest of Velsicol but in defendants' interests and was fraudulent and a violation of the fiduciary obligation of the majority. The chancellor confirmed the master's report in most respects. Contrary to the master, however, the chancellor found the plan of recapitalization inequitable and motivated by the desire only to oppress and defraud plaintiff; that the burden of proving the transaction was in good faith and fair rested on defendants; and that they had failed to make that proof. This contrariety is the crux of the case.

It is not disputed that the majority stockholders were entitled to control the policy of the corporation, that when plaintiff became a stockholder he agreed to the majority's ruling, that he had notice of the stockholders' meeting and that the resolutions received the requisite vote at the meeting. We think that, if the circumstances justified the recapitalization and if the plan was legal and fair, the questions of defendants' state of mind with respect to plaintiff and as to the effect of the plan on his interests are immaterial.

We consider it unnecessary to decide whether the majority was the fiduciary of the plaintiff in the transactions or whether plaintiff or defendant had the burden of proving good faith and fairness. We think that the plaintiff's testimony shows clearly that the plan was legal and not unfair and, for the reasons given hereinafter, that the plaintiff is not entitled to the relief sought.

In 1931 plaintiff had the inventions and Regenstein, through Arvey and Transo, had the money. Between 1935 and 1938 a plant was built in Marshall, Illinois and put into operation with more than $500,000 of Arvey's and Transo's money. In 1941 and 1942 plaintiff discussed with Regenstein the capitalization of these loans. After notes were given, covering the loans, plaintiff suggested their capitalization through the issuance of preferred stock. He thought this was a wise tax move. He brought up the subject of capitalization again in 1945 and in 1946. At no time did he have a "concrete plan". In early 1946, when Velsicol borrowed money, the First National Bank suggested that the notes be subordinated or capitalized. It is apparent that the idea of recapitalization was common to all concerned.

There was no question about the validity of the notes held by Arvey and Transo. Under their terms the holders could demand payment whenever they decided to do so. . . . Arvey and Transo had, in 1946, subordinated payment of their notes to facilitate Velsicol's borrowing an additional $675,000. The method of capitalizing the notes was the prerogative of the majority of the directors and stockholders, who in this case were substantially the same because of Regenstein's majority interest in Transo and Arvey corporations. At the stockholders' meeting there was no discussion of the resolutions, yet plaintiff was represented by an attorney as proxy. There was no recommendation of a substitute plan of recapitalization, though plaintiff had discussed such a plan with his attorney. Plaintiff's preferred stock idea was not proposed. Assuming the recapitalization was prudent business, we see no reason for concluding that the method was not sound. We see no reason for deciding that the stock split or new par value was clearly out of line. Steven v. Hale–Haas Corp., 249 Wis. 205, 23 N.W.2d 620, 768. What difference did it make to plaintiff that the stock was split and the par value reduced instead of issuing the new stock at the original par?

We think it must be admitted that the recapitalization was timely. Plaintiff, who had been general manager since the inception of the corporation, had resigned as vice president, as manager and as director. About thirty of the fifty technical employees had left Velsicol with plaintiff to establish the competing Hyman corporation. As a result of these events a reorganization of the management and personnel was necessary. We think that the directors were justified in presenting the plan at the time it was done. This is aside from the question of Velsicol's financial distress, a question argued here but which we need not decide because the reasons given above are sufficient for the conclusion of timeliness.

At the stockholders' meeting there was no complaint about the stock split, the new par value or the period of time within which preemptive rights had to be exercised. Plaintiff does not claim that he was not given his pro rata share of the preemptive rights. He says that he had not the $136,000 cash and that defendants knew this fact, and that the unreasonably short period of time between the date of the meeting and the date on which preemptive rights expired was designed to oppress him. Notice of the meeting, with copies of the resolutions, was sent to him on December 3rd. He knew he was in a minority position. Had he been interested in attempting to raise the money, he had from the time he received the notice to do so. It is clear from the record that he was not interested in raising the money. He thought the new management would not succeed. He was "primarily" interested in the newly formed, competing, Hyman corporation. He testified that if he had had the money at the time, he did not know whether he would have exercised his preemptive rights. There is no merit in plaintiff's contention that the par value for the new stock was insignificant compared to the true value. The directors were not required to recommend the stock at a price equivalent to the "true value". Moreover his express attitude renders the contention unimportant. . . .

We think that the right which plaintiff had to a proportionate share of the new stock issue at the new par value was respected in this case by the issuance to him of the additional stock, arising from the stock split, and the issuance to him of subscription warrants. . . By the issuance of the additional stock and the preemptive rights to plaintiff he was given the opportunity to protect his pro-rata interest in the corporation. The defendants were not to blame for his failure to obtain the money necessary for him to avail himself of his preemptive rights. Scheirich v. Otis–Hidden Co., 204 Ky. 289, 264 S.W. 755.

It is our conclusion that the reorganization plan, including the price at which the new stock was issued, was not an abuse of the discretion vested in the majority stockholders or directors and was not fraudulently oppressive. Steven v. Hale–Haas Corp., 249 Wis. 205, 231, 23 N.W.2d 620, 768. For the reasons given the decree is reversed and the cause is remanded with directions to enter a decree in conformity with the recommendations of the master.

Decree reversed and cause remanded with directions.

BURKE, P.J., and LEWE, J., concur.

BENNETT v. BREUIL PETROLEUM CORP.

Court of Chancery of Delaware, 1953.
34 Del.Ch. 6, 99 A.2d 236.

[This was an action originally brought to restrain issuance of stock but, after the discovery that it had already been issued, to cancel it. The corporate and other defendants moved to dismiss and for summary judgment.

The Corporation was organized in 1949 to engage in crude oil production. Plaintiff Bennett and Breuil (a defendant) were the chief parties in it—of the 1,000,000 $1 par shares issued and outstanding,

Bennett held 423,500 and Breuil 562,000 with his close relatives holding some 5000 more. Evidently relations between the two deteriorated. In 1952 and 1953 offers were allegedly made by Breuil to buy plaintiff's shares. The values assigned were in one case $2.95 per share in cash and then $2.35 per share on 4% 15 year corporate debentures. Defendants denied the second offer. In 1953 a stockholders meeting authorized amendments to the certificate of incorporation (a) changing the $1 par value to $.40, (b) reducing the capital account from $1,000,000 to $400,000, (c) increasing the authorized shares to 2,000,000, (d) denying preemptive rights and (e) authorizing the issuance pro rata of rights for the 1,000,000 additional shares at $.40 per share. It was alleged that the further shares were needed to raise additional needed capital. Plaintiff admitted that the corporation was not in good condition but asserted that the majority caused the stock to be issued to force him out of the company.

The opinion, by CHANCELLOR SEITZ, continues as follows.]

As a starting point it must be conceded that action by majority stockholders having as its primary purpose the "freezing out" of a minority interest is actionable without regard to the fairness of the price. . . . The corporate defendant and its controlling stockholders say that this is a sheer dispute over a matter of business judgment and is for the Board of Directors and stockholders to resolve, not the court.

Let us first consider which side has the burden and the extent thereof. I believe that plaintiff has the burden of proving bad faith or improper motive because I believe defendants are entitled to start with a presumption of good faith. I cannot agree with plaintiff that merely because Breuil is the controlling stockholder, the burden of showing good faith and proper purpose is shifted to the defendants. I say this because I do not believe that Breuil is on "both sides of the transaction" in the sense that he has an adverse personal interest. . . . .

Defendants say the plaintiff makes charges and does not set forth any facts. I cannot agree. It seems to me that plaintiff has set forth a legally recognized claim and the pleadings and affidavits have raised a substantial factual dispute as to the legal propriety of the motives of the corporate defendant and its controlling stockholder which can only be resolved by a hearing. . . .

Plaintiff's second grievance is that the shares have a value substantially in excess of 40¢ a share, to-wit, a value of $2.50–$3 per share. In support of this claim plaintiff points out that the corporate defendant's principal asset consists of the ownership of 525,784 shares of the capital stock of Kingwood Oil Company, being approximately 59% of the outstanding shares. The balance sheet of the defendant for 1952 shows that the Kingwood shares were carried on the corporate defendant's books at 65¢ per share but have a book value according to Kingwood's books of $3.88 per share. Moreover, Kingwood stock is selling over the counter at approximately $4 to $5 per share, although in small amounts. Plaintiff alleges and defendants deny that the stock could be sold at a premium. Plaintiff also emphasizes that the principal officers of Kingwood are substantially the same as the corporate defendant's and that the Kingwood operations are under the control of Breuil.

The following quotation from the minutes of the stockholders' meeting referring to statements by the corporate representatives probably best states defendants' position on this point:

"Mr. MacFarland and Mr. Sullivan referred to the losses suffered by the Corporation from its inception, the uncertainty and hazards of the oil production industry, the sharp decline in Kingwood's production during the last two years and the fact that no market exists for Breuil Petroleum Corporation stock and they stated that, considering all factors, they believed the price to be fair. They further stated that no stockholder should complain as each stockholder was offered shares on the basis of one for one at the par value price."

It would serve no useful purpose at this stage to enter into a protracted and detailed summary and analysis of the various affidavits filed. They raise a serious and substantial question as to whether or not the 40¢ per share stock price was not grossly inadequate. This conflict cannot be fairly resolved by this court on a motion for summary judgment.

The complaint does not charge fraud in so many words but it alleges that the price is more than six times less than its fair value. This charge when considered in conjunction with the affidavits and the surrounding circumstances certainly makes out, pleading-wise, a case of constructive fraud. . . . I conclude that plaintiff need not show actual fraud. But it will be plaintiff's burden to show constructive fraud at the trial.

I cannot agree with defendants' contention that 8 Del.C. § 152, making the directors' judgment as to the value of property, etc., received for stock conclusive in the absence of a showing of actual fraud, applies to this case. I say this because that Section deals with the judgment of the directors as to the value of property received for stock. Our case involves the value of stock issued for cash.

Defendants also say that 8 Del.C. § 157, which authorizes the issuance of rights and options, applies to the rights here involved. . . . § 157 is not pertinent to the question of the value placed on the shares themselves—the issue here. It applies to the value placed on the rights, apart from the stock itself—not the issue here. . . . But defendants say plaintiff has not been injured, even assuming that the price is grossly inadequate, because he is being offered his pro rata share of the additional shares. This argument is wide of the mark. I say this because plaintiff has the right not to purchase as well as the right to purchase. But his right not to purchase is seriously impaired if the stock is worth substantially more than its issuing price. Any other purchase at that price obviously dilutes his interest and impairs the value of his original holdings. Defendants suggest that though he could not assign his right, he could borrow thereon. This does not impress me as being a substantial answer especially in the case, as here, of a closely held corporation where no dividends have ever been paid and where plaintiff had only 15 days to decide. . . . A corporation is not permitted to sell its stock for a legally inadequate price, at least where there is objection. Plaintiff has a right to insist upon compliance with the law whether or not he cares to exercise his option. He cannot block a sale for a fair price merely because he disagrees with the wisdom of the plan but he can insist that the sale price be fixed in accordance with legal requirements.

Defendants insist that plaintiff's complaint is premature because the unsubscribed stock may not be issued illegally. The answer is that any subscription dilutes plaintiff's interest if he is correct in his contention concerning the value of the stock. Thus, if plaintiff is correct, Breuil's subscription alone shows injury.

The individual defendants also claim that the corporation may not issue par value stock at a price above par over stockholder objection. Thus, they say the stock in issue could not have been issued at what plaintiff claims is its fair price. This argument is premised upon an aspect of the common-law preemptive rights doctrine adopted in some states. See 13 Am.Jur. Corporations, § 190. Under the amendment here validly adopted the preemptive rights are now only of such a character as the majority of the stockholders see fit to give. Therefore, assuming but by no means deciding that the rule contended for by defendants would be applicable in Delaware despite our statute,[3] and prior decision, the fact remains that this judicially created characteristic of preemptive rights was abolished by the stockholders when they amended the charter. It can now afford the defendant stockholders no comfort.

Defendants also challenge plaintiff's right to maintain this action because they claim that plaintiff has improperly joined a personal action with a derivative one. Plaintiff claims that he is suing in his personal right and that this is not a derivative action. This is now a complaint for cancellation on two grounds, viz., issuance for improper purpose and for inadequate consideration. Assuming that the first ground is personal to plaintiff, nevertheless, I am persuaded that the second is derivative because cancellation of the "new" shares is sought to remedy a direct injury to the corporation consisting of the issuance of stock in violation of legal requirements as to consideration. . . .

[The court denied defendants' motions.]

COMMENT

Rules about the issuance of new securities that affect the rights of the existing stock were put to severe tests by the so-called "Poison pill" that developed as a response to the threat of takeovers. The leading case is Moran v. Household International, Inc., 500 A.2d 1346 (Del.1985), which upheld the issuance by the board of directors of "Rights" in the following form. A 48 page "Rights Agreement" gave the stockholders Rights that were triggered by the happening of either of two events: (1) the announcement of a public tender offer for 30% or more of Household's stock or (2) the purchase of 20% or more of that stock. In the event that either triggering event took place each share of common stock would have the right to buy $1/100$ of a share of preferred for $100 that had extensive voting rights; a particular feature was the "flip-over," the extension of the preferred stock's rights into any merged corporation used in a takeover. Shareholders protested that this was an abuse of the powers vested in the directors under §§ 151 and 157 because the issuance was not a legitimate financing device and the rights had no economic value. The Delaware court sustained this as a reasonable exercise of the business judgment of the directors, noting that no immediate takeover offer was in sight and observing that there were advantages to the greater security offered to management by such protection. "Poison pills" thereafter became a popular defensive device for fearful corporate managements.

3. 8 Del.C. § 154.

PROBLEM

The directors of United Knitwear observed with concern and surprise that the price at which their company's stock was traded on the over-the-counter market was moving upward from $16 to $17.50 per share. Nothing in the affairs of this fairly prosperous but quite conservative and stable enterprise called for such a jump. This mystery was clarified when the president received a call from Lowell Learmont who advised that he had acquired a large packet of Knitwear Stock and that he intended to acquire more. Learmont asked whether any of the directors or other shareholders would be willing to sell their shares and whether they would consent to giving him a seat on the board. Learmont has a reputation of moving in on companies he acquires, ruthlessly lopping off executives he regards as unnecessary, and often liquidating enterprises he cannot turn around. A hasty directors' meeting was called at Knitwear and you as counsel were summoned to attend.

From the rather confused deliberations the following facts emerged:

(a) Learmont's ownership is presently probably between 15% and 20% and he has the resources to acquire some 5% to 10% more, although there are some rumours to the effect that he is currently pressed for cash.

(b) At present 10% of the stock is held by the Thomas family which is represented by two of the 7 members of the board and 10% by a trust for members of the other founding family. 5% is held by two other directors. Three hold no stock at all. The remaining 60% –65% not held by Learmont is fairly widely distributed among perhaps 1000 shareholders.

(c) There is some chance that at the next shareholders meeting Learmont might be able to rally the support of enough public shareholders to outvote the incumbents and their sympathizers. The failure of the firm to improve its earnings at a time when some of its rivals have has alienated some holders.

(d) Two members of the board have long had a plan to diversify the firm into specialty lines not as vulnerable to competition, particularly foreign competition. The majority of the board has never been willing to spend the money needed for the acquisition of such companies or their assets.

(e) The balance sheet of Knitwear when worked out would probably look roughly like this:

Assets		Liabilities	
Cash	1,000,000	Current liabilities	750,000
Receivables	800,000	Long term bank loan	1,000,000
Inventory	1,500,000	Capital (400,000 shares	2,000,000
Plant	3,000,000	of $5 par)	
	$6,300,000	Retained earnings	2,550,000
			$6,300,000

(f) The Thomas family would be willing to buy some more stock, perhaps 25,000 to 35,000 shares, but would want two more seats on the board. They would be willing to pay not more than $17.50.

The directors decided to meet 2 days later to consider alternative courses of action. One would be to issue new shares to all shareholders hoping that Learmont will not be able to raise the funds to buy his share. The other would be to issue the shares to the Thomas family thus cementing their control.

The following questions seem to need researching:

(1) Is Learmont entitled to preemptive rights under our articles and under the Delaware statute? If so, can we, nonetheless prevail by following our first plan and "swamping" him? Would it matter what price we assigned to the shares? Are there any cumbersome procedural obstacles to this approach?

(2) What about a sale to the Thomas family only—if there are no preemptive rights? Will there be any problems with pricing the shares at the Thomas' stipulated level? What directors should participate in voting for this? Is it important to "build a record" for this action? If so, what are the elements of that record?

Bibliography: See Note, Judicial Control over the Fairness of the Issue Price of New Stock, 71 Harv.L.Rev. 1133 (1958). The sources cited on the original issue of stock in the bibliographies in Chapter VI are generally relevant here.

NOTE ON PREFERRED STOCK

(1) Preferred stock, sharing features of both indebtedness and common stock, has its place in the armory of the corporate financier. It has the merit of not requiring fixed payments of principal or interest as does a bond while not diluting control as would the issuance of common. Some corporate purchasers may prefer it for tax reasons (the inter-corporate dividend credit) although the issuer cannot deduct an interest expense. The ingenuity of financiers has even created adjustable rate preferred which can fulfill the financial requirements normally met by the use of commercial paper and which has the further advantages of providing corporate holders with a substantial tax advantage and of providing better debt/equity ratios to banks and other financial institutions. To increase the strain on the concept that these are preferred stock some of them are collateralized to provide greater safety to the holder. On the other hand, dividend rates on preferred stock necessarily tend to be higher than interest rates on fixed indebtedness. Thus the use of preferred stock must be approached with caution. If it is decided that preferred is to be used the task of drafting its terms must also be approached with care. Common stock, as the residual element in a corporation's structure, tends to define itself. The rights of the preferred must, on the other hand, be spelled out. The certificate of incorporation in the Documentary Supplement contains in its Paragraph Fourth compact but carefully drafted provisions creating issues of preferred stock. You should consider that paragraph alongside the comments that follow.

(2) A critical point to be covered is that of dividends. The draftsmen must not only state the percent rate of dividends but must also cover other points with care. They must remember that, absent protective provisions, preferred stock is in a vulnerable position, getting little protection from statutory or decisional law. A vital issue is whether dividends are "cumulative." If dividends are not cumulative a failure of the directors to declare them is fatal—that year's dividend is gone forever. If dividends are cumulative they pile up if not paid and

no dividends can be paid on the common until all of those arrearages on the preferred have been cleared away. Non-cumulative dividends turned out to be subject to hazards beyond the corporation's inability to earn the dividend; a management might bypass the preferred dividend even in a year when earnings fully covered it. For example, suppose a corporation with a certificate like our sample earns $1,000 a year for 5 years. This is twice as much as is needed to service the preferred's 5% dividend but no dividends were declared on the preferred. Naturally, no dividends could be declared on the common either. Then in the sixth year the corporation earns $2,000. The directors declare a $500 dividend on the preferred and $5000 on the common. According to most courts this is legal in the case of a non-cumulative preferred. The New Jersey courts sought to remedy this gap in the preferred's protection by, in effect, making the stock cumulative if earned and not reinvested in fixed assets. The New Jersey doctrine has been largely rejected elsewhere. In a notable opinion [4] by Judge Jerome Frank, former SEC Commissioner and presumably no foe of the small shareholder, the entirely non-cumulative nature of such preferred stock was affirmed as follows:

> Here we are interpreting a contract into which uncoerced men entered. Nothing in the wording of that contract would suggest to an ordinary wayfaring person the existence of a contingent or inchoate right to arrears of dividends. The notion that such a right was promised is, rather, the invention of lawyers or other experts, a notion stemming from considerations of fairness, from a policy of protecting investors in those securities. But the preferred stockholders are not—like sailors or idiots or infants—wards of the judiciary. As courts on occasions have quoted or paraphrased ancient poets, it may not be inappropriate to paraphrase a modern poet, and to say that "a contract is a contract is a contract." To be sure, it is an overstatement that the courts never do more than carry out the intentions of the parties: In the interest of fairness and justice, many a judge-made legal rule does impose, on one of the parties to a contract, obligations which neither party actually contemplated and as to which the language of the contract is silent. But there are limits to the extent to which a court may go in so interpolating rights and obligations which were never in the parties' contemplation. In this case we consider those limits clear.

4. Guttman v. Illinois Cent. R.R., 189 F.2d 927 (2d Cir.1951). The New Jersey rule, sometimes called the "Cast Iron Pipe Doctrine" after Bassett v. United States Cast Iron Pipe and Foundry Co., 74 N.J.Eq. 668, 70 Atl. 929 (Ch.1908), affirmed 75 N.J. Eq. 539, 73 Atl. 514 (Err. & App.1909), was reaffirmed in Sanders v. Cuba RR., 21 N.J. 78, 120 A.2d 849 (1956).

Sometimes a preferred stock is specifically stated to be cumulative if earned. For such a contractual provision, see Kern v. Chicago & East. Ill. R.R., 6 Ill.App.3d 247, 285 N.E.2d 501 (1972) (revenues of subsidiary not "earned" by parent that issued preferred).

In sum, we hold that, since the directors did not "abuse" their discretion in withholding dividends on the non-cumulative preferred for any past years, (a) no right survived to have those dividends declared, and (b) the directors had no discretion whatever to declare those dividends subsequently.

From the point of view of the preferred stockholders, the bargain they made may well be of a most undesirable kind. Perhaps the making of such bargains should be prevented. But, if so, the way to prevent them is by legislation, or by prophylactic administrative action authorized by legislation, as in the case of the S.E.C. in respect of securities, including preferred stocks, whether cumulative or non-cumulative, issued by public utility holding companies or their subsidiaries. The courts are not empowered to practice such preventive legal medicine, and must not try to revise, extensively, contracts already outstanding and freely made by adults who are not incompetents.

A preferred stock may be made "participating," that is, it may receive a portion of the corporation's earnings over and above the specified rate. This is a rather rare occurrence; for an example examine the provisions of the Axton–Fisher Class A stock involved in Zahn v. Transamerica Corp., p. 446 supra.

Finally, remember that dividends on the preferred may not be paid if payment would violate the restrictive provisions of state law. Some state laws permit dividends on the preferred to be paid on a basis somewhat more liberal than that relating to dividends on common.

(3) The sum paid in to the corporation in exchange for the issuance of the preferred is part of its capital and is not "due" to be repaid at any specific point. On the other hand, it is generally assumed that it will not remain outstanding forever. On the one hand, the "principal" may be reduced by redemption, that is, by the deliberate action of the corporation in calling it. Review the complications involved in the call of the Axton–Fisher Class A stock detailed at p. 447 supra. The statutory provisions (e.g., 8 Del.C. § 243) as to the funds available for redemption must be strictly observed. It is, incidentally, unclear whether common stock can be redeemed though it can plainly be repurchased if the holder will sell. On the other hand the "principal" may be returned to the preferred shareholders in the event of a liquidation; indeed they are entitled to recover that before the common gets anything at all. Clauses differ in significant detail as to the amount of the liquidation preferences (the model sets it at par but others, such as the Axton–Fisher Class A, involve a premium) and as to the events which bring the liquidation preference into play (some clauses would include a reorganization under the Bankruptcy Act or a merger and others would not). Some preferred stock issues provide for a "sinking fund", that is, for the appropriation of funds for the periodic repurchase of specified portions of the issue.

(4) Preferred stock ordinarily has only limited voting rights such as those granted in our model's Paragraph Second Alternative Fourth. This sort of limitation caused trouble under the former Illinois Constitution's requirement that every share have a vote (pp. 366 and 374 supra). In some cases you will find a statute (e.g., 8 Del.C. § 242(c)) that requires a majority vote of every class affected, thus overriding contractual silence or even a statement. Despite such provisions it happens that majority approval has been won for changes that sharply and adversely affected the right of a preferred stock almost to the point of class suicide.

(5) Convertibility is an important feature of some preferred stock issues—notably absent from our model certificate provisions. The availability of the convertibility feature is a major attraction for prospective purchasers of the preferred; on the other hand it may pose a substantial threat of dilution to the common stockholders and, hence, may need to be disclosed under the "earnings per share" provisions of Opinion No. 15 of the Accounting Principles Board.[5] The drafting of convertibility provisions can be very tricky indeed. In particular the creation of provisions that will safeguard the preferred against dilution of its rights requires thought. It is not enough simply to say that one share of preferred is convertible at the holder's option into 5 of common if the relative portion of the equity represented by 5 shares of common has been reduced by stock dividends, stock splits or other transactions.

QUESTIONS

(1) Which of the following issues of stock are cumulative: (a) the Class A stock in Zahn v. Transamerica, p. 446, supra; (b) the preferred in Paragraph Second Alternative Fourth of the Model Certificate of Incorporation? Why was the Class A stock in Zahn not entitled "preferred"? In the case of a merger what rights, if any, do the holders of the preferred created by the Model Certificate possess?

(2) What conflicts of interest exist between the holders of the common stock of a corporation and of its preferred? Do you think that the directors of a corporation can successfully balance out those interests? How should directors elected by the preferred vote in such questions? What differences of opinion about accounting matters might one expect to arise as between those classes? What kind of preferred stock is most acutely affected by such differences? Does it, for example, matter whether an item of income is regarded as "extraordinary"? Whether an item is properly accrued in a given year or deferred to the next?

Bibliography: A principal source is Buxbaum, Preferred Stock–Law and Draftsmanship, 42 Calif.L.Rev. 243 (1954). For discussion of dilution questions see Kaplan, Piercing the Corporate Boilerplate: Anti–Dilution Clauses in Convertible Securities, 33 U.Chi.L.Rev. 1 (1965); Katzin, Financial and Legal Problems in the Use of Convertible Securities, 24 Bus.Law. 359 (1969). Some-

---

5. Discussed briefly at p. 349 supra in connection with stock options.

what similar problems are treated in Klein, The Convertible Bond: A Peculiar Package, 123 U.Pa.L.Rev. 547 (1975).

---

3. Corporate Borrowing

Corporate borrowing plays a critical role in the finance of corporations and hence in corporate legal practice. In 1986 corporations issued $355 billion of new bonds, $231 billion of which was in public offerings.[6] This amounted to more than 5 times the amount of stock issued. This is a great deal more than in the past—in 1975 the new debt issue figure was only $42.75 billion. Some of the increase in borrowing has to do with the needs of corporations that are paying vast sums to buy the stock of other firms. Some of it arises from leveraged buy outs in which the managements of corporations borrow to buy the publicly held stock of a firm to take it private. The term "junk bond" has come into common use to describe debt issues that are not secured and do not have the credit rating that was once expected of publicly issued debt securities. The purist would say that since they are unsecured they are really "junk debentures." Conservatives are concerned about the implications of this much indebtedness as to the strength of the corporate issuers and wonder how they will react to adversity when debt equity ratios are often in the range of 10 to 1 rather than the more traditional 2 to 1 for industrial firms. However, investors seem to have adapted to this new frame of reference and thus far the rate of default has not been momentous.

Much of the corpus of legal rules applicable to corporate borrowing comes from areas outside of corporation law. Corporation law itself contains some rules, with which you are now generally familiar, that apply to borrowings:

(1) A borrowing must be authorized. This, particularly with larger loans, calls for formal board of directors' action. However, the matter may be found to have been delegated to corporate officers. See p. 306 supra.

(2) If a mortgage of all the corporate assets is involved, some state statutes require shareholder consent. Note that while 8 Del.C. § 271 says that sales *en bloc* of corporate assets need such approval, § 272 explicitly says that mortgages do not.

(3) Borrowings are subject to rules about "thin incorporation" discussed at p. 159 supra.

(4) Generally speaking, loans to corporations represent "securities" and are subject to the rules of the Securities Act and the Securities

---

6. Fed.Res.Bull., Nov. 1987 A 34; compare id. Jan. 1977, A 36.

Exchange Act. The Trust Indenture Act, discussed below, complements these rules.

Outside of the corporation law field, a review would touch upon the following categories of rules as being particularly relevant.

(1) Public utility regulation statutes, the Interstate Commerce Act for example, require commission approval for the consummation of borrowings by utilities.

(2) Uniform Commercial Code rules, in particular articles 3 and 8 on commercial paper and investment securities, govern corporate borrowings and the instruments emerging from borrowings. The rules of article 9 concerning transactions secured by personal property apply.

(3) The law of real property mortgages applies to corporate transactions. These mortgages can be exceedingly complex, as when they involve such aggregation of items as a gas pipeline, a public utility network, etc.

(4) The federal Bankruptcy Code, including particularly the chapters governing corporate reorganizations and compositions, and creditors rights rules under state law ultimately govern the collectibility of corporate indebtedness.

(5) Legislation designed to protect the borrower is apt not to be applicable to corporate obligors. The usury statutes normally do not apply to corporations (quite a few cases have involved incorporation designed solely to circumvent the usury laws). Since corporations are not consumers, consumer loan legislation is inapplicable. Note, however, that the important margin rules limiting the amount that can be borrowed on the security of marketable securities, do apply to borrowings by corporations.

(6) Certain legal rules are designed to protect the lender against unwise extensions of credit. Aside from general concepts of the law of negligence there are elaborate rules in many states pertaining to investments eligible for the money of savings banks, insurance companies, trustees, etc.[7] These rules to some degree codify considerations or rules of thumb which lending officers would use in any event:

(a) they may limit the percentage of the institution's funds which can be loaned to any one borrower;

(b) they may require that the interest payable on the loan per year be no more than a specified percentage of the borrower's average annual earnings over the past several years.

(c) they may require that the principal be "covered", e.g., by requiring that specific security amounting to X times the principal be provided or by requiring that net income plus depreciation be sufficient to amortize the loan within its term.

7. For a particularly ornate example see N.Y.Ins. Law Art. 14.

These rules may also further other state interests, such as those which require insurance companies to invest within the state amounts related to the premiums derived from insuring risks within that state. Modern security theory would say that such rules are misdirected because real investment safety is found in the diversification of a portfolio of investments rather than the qualities of any one particular holding.

The documents embodying a lending transaction start with a simple promissory note and range upwards in complexity. The crowning achievement of the financial lawyer is the corporate mortgage or deed of trust. The inventors of this document adapted the simple mortgage contract to the needs of large bond issues sold to the general public and covering extensive aggregates of property—railroad, telephone, electric or gas systems—and lasting for long periods of time. They took the ordinary mortgage and, instead of trying to give each lender a fractional interest in it, had the mortgagee be a trustee, usually a corporate one, who held the mortgagees' interests in trust for those who would be from time to time holders of the bonds. The trustee would exercise the rights and powers of the holders on their behalf. It would collect and pay out the interest, permit new bond issues upon an adequate showing that the pro rata security would not be diminished, permit substitution of one type of collateral for another, make the borrower live up to its covenants and, in case of trouble, institute foreclosure procedures or other legal actions. The individual bondholder retained only a right to sue the debtor for the sum due but no right to enforce the indenture. In the course of time indentures grew to the point where they may cover 300 to 400 pages. If an indenture does not relate to the issue of secured indebtedness it can be somewhat simpler and shorter. Then it needs only to define the terms of the notes or debentures to be issued, set forth the promises of the debtor (typically called covenants and relating to such matters as the creation of other debt, the creation of security interests or liens on the debtor's property, the payment of dividends, etc.) and authorize or require the trustee to take various steps. Attempts have been made to standardize and simplify the indenture, most prominently by an American Bar Foundation group.

The format of the indenture is now very largely controlled by the Trust Indenture Act of 1939 for, where it applies, that Act requires that its limitations be set forth in *ipsissimis verbis* in the contract. We will not attempt the discouraging task of acquiring a specialist's knowledge of the very complex and involuted provisions of that law. The 1939 Act has a coverage parallel to that of the Securities Act of 1933 so that if a bond or debenture issue is offered to the public it must also be qualified under the 1939 Act. The Trust Indenture Act was the product of investigations that concluded that indentures did not adequately protect security holders during the 1929–1933 crash but were rather written so as to shield the trustee from liability. Some of that history is reflected in the case that follows. The inadequacies of earlier practice were put forcefully in the famous words of Chief Justice Stone who referred to ". . . those who serve nominally as trustees, but [are] relieved, by clever legal devices, from the obligation to protect those whose interests they purport to represent." He went on, sadly to note "[t]here is little to suggest that the Bar has yet recognized that it must bear some burden of responsibility for these evils." [8]

UNITED STATES TRUST CO. v. FIRST NAT. CITY BANK

Appellate Division, First Department, New York 1977.
57 A.D.2d 285, 394 N.Y.S.2d 653.

[In 1973 Equity Funding Corporation of America collapsed in a spectacular disaster involving much deceit and oversight. In 1971 Equity Funding had issued $38,500,000 of 5½% Convertible Subordinated Debentures under an Indenture between itself and defendant First National City Bank as Trustee. The defendant resigned as Trustee on the date Equity Funding filed a petition for reorganization under Chapter X of the Bankruptcy Act. Plaintiff succeeded it as trustee. Plaintiff then brought this suit charging defendant with misconduct as trustee. The lower court granted defendant's motion to dismiss certain causes of action but denied others. It also denied plaintiff's motion for partial summary judgments. Both parties appealed. Portions of the opinion on appeal, by JUSTICE SILVERMAN, follow.]

B. Defendant's Motions The Revolving Credit Agreement

The first nine causes of action in the complaint relate to property and monies received by defendant as an individual creditor under a "Revolving Credit Agreement." The Revolving Credit Agreement dated as of June 29, 1972, was entered into by the defendant as agent for itself and three other banks. Under the Revolving Credit Agreement these four banks agreed to make loans to Equity Funding up to a maximum of $75,000,000. Defendant's share of the total lending commitment was about 47%. The Revolving Credit Agreement contained a provision whereby Equity Funding was required to pay a commitment fee of ½% per annum on unused portions of the loan commitment. To the extent that the loan was availed of, Equity Funding was to pay interest at a fluctuating rate equal to or greater than the base rate (also apparently sometimes referred to as the prime rate). Equity Funding had the right to repay and reborrow. Repayment was required to be made in quarterly installments between September 30, 1976 and June 30, 1980, with provisions under which the lenders could require earlier payments in certain contingencies. The advances under the Revolving Credit Agreement were evidenced by a "grid note," a promissory note on which notations of advances and repayments would be made. On June 29, 1972 the banks advanced $41,000,000 to Equity Funding under the Revolving Credit Agreement. Additional advances of $5,000,000 each were made on or about October 10, 1972 and February 20, 1973, making total advances under the Revolving Credit Agreement of $51,000,000.

----

8. Stone, The Public Influence of the Bar, 48 Harv.L.Rev. 1, 9 (1934).

The Indenture's Sharing Provision § 613; Definition of Security

Six of the first nine causes of action (the First, Third, Fifth, Seventh, Eight, and Ninth) rest largely on § 613(a) of the Indenture, a provision required by § 311 of the Trust Indenture Act. In essence, the provision requires that the Trustee hold in a special account for the benefit of the Trustee individually and of the holders of the Debentures any amounts or property received by the Trustee in reduction of amounts owed or as security for the Trustee's individual creditor claim after four months prior to a default under the Indenture.

Section 613(b) of the Indenture, also required by the Trust Indenture Act, provides, however, that:

"(b) There shall be excluded from the operation of Subsection (a) of this Section a creditor relationship arising from

(1) the ownership or acquisition of securities issued under any indenture, or any security or securities having a maturity of one year or more at the time of acquisition by the Trustee."

It is the contention of the defendant that the Revolving Credit Agreement and the grid note constitute a "security or securities" with the requisite maturity; and that, therefore, any payments received with respect to the Revolving Credit Agreement and the grid note were not subject to the sharing provisions of § 613(a) of the Indenture. Special Term agreed with defendant and therefore dismissed the causes of action resting on § 613(a).

The Indenture and the Trust Indenture Act referred the definition of the term "security" back to the definition in the Securities Act of 1933, § 2, 15 U.S.C.A. § 77b; [Trust Indenture Act § 303, 15 U.S.C.A. § 77ccc(1)]. The Securities Act of 1933 provides in relevant part:

"When used in this subchapter, unless the context otherwise requires—

(1) the term 'security' means any note, . . . evidence of indebtedness, . . . or, in general, any interest or instrument commonly known as a 'security' . . .."

The federal courts have frequently had to consider "the vexing question how far instruments bearing the form of promissory notes are securities within the anti-fraud provisions of the Securities Act of 1933 and the Securities Exchange Act of 1934." Exchange National Bank of Chicago v. Touche Ross & Co., 544 F.2d 1126, 1127 (2d Cir.1976). They have arrived at results with different rationales. The state of these authorities is summarized by Judge Friendly in the *Exchange National Bank* case, supra. In that case, Judge Friendly further said on p. 1133:

"As will be seen, courts have shrunk from a literal reading that would extend the reach of the statutes beyond what could reasonably be thought to have been intended in these two great pieces of legislation and would produce a seemingly irrational difference in the scope of their anti-fraud provisions."

The federal courts have paid great attention to the introductory phrase "unless the context otherwise requires" in the effort to give an appropriate and just meaning to the definition of "security" in particular cases.

The context with which we are concerned is the Trust Indenture Act and particularly its provision with respect to "preferential collection of claims against obligor," § 311, 15 U.S.C.A. § 77kkk.

The federal cases cited to us arose primarily out of the anti-fraud provisions of the Securities Act. No case has been cited to us involving the definition of "security" as used in the Trust Indenture Act.

These acts are remedial statutes and they should of course be given a reading consistent with their remedial purpose.

To include a particular instrument within the definition of "security" under the anti-fraud provisions of the Securities Act brings the transaction within the protection of that Act. To include a particular instrument as a "security" within the meaning of § 311 of the Trust Indenture Act (and the corresponding § 613[b] of the Trust Indenture) would exclude the transaction from the protection of that Act.

The introductory section of the Trust Indenture Act on "necessity for regulation" (§ 302, 15 U.S.C.A. § 77bbb) declared that

> "[T]he national public interest and the interest of investors in notes, bonds, debentures, evidences of indebtedness, and certificates of interest or participation therein, which are offered to the public, are adversely affected—"
>
> . . .
>
> "(3) when the trustee . . . has any relationship to or connection with the obligor . . . or holds, beneficially or otherwise, any interest in the obligor . . ., which relationship, connection, or interest involves a material conflict with the interests of such investors . . .."

And the Act further provided that:

> "[I]t is hereby declared to be that policy of this subchapter, in accordance with which policy all the provisions of this subchapter shall be interpreted, to meet the problems and eliminate the practices, enumerated in this section, connected with such public offerings."

We must determine the application of the statute and of § 613(b) of the Indenture in the light of this congressionally mandated canon of interpretation.

So interpreted, we do not think that the Revolving Credit Agreement and the grid note issued thereunder constitute "securities," with respect to which payments are exempt from the provisions of § 311 of the Trust Indenture Act (15 U.S.C.A. § 77kkk), or the corresponding § 613(a) of the Indenture. As is apparent from the heading of § 311, that section is aimed at "preferential collection of claims" against the obligor. The word "preferential" here of course is used in obvious analogy to the provisions of the Bankruptcy Act with respect to "preferences" made within four months prior to bankruptcy. The section is intended to protect the debenture holders against conflicts of interest arising out of the Debenture Trustee's "relationship to or connection with the obligor," in particular its relationship as a creditor of the obligor. In that context, we think that the exclusion of "securities" held by the Indenture Trustee from the sharing requirements of § 311 was primarily intended to cover the case where the Indenture Trustee holds some securities out of a large public issue and where the Indenture Trustee's securities are treated the same as the vast majority of securities held by others and there is little or no opportunity or incentive for the Indenture Trustee to favor its individual interests over those of the debenture holders. Here the Revolving Credit Agreement and the grid note represent a debt owed to four banks; and the Indenture Trustee, the defendant in this case, was the managing agent of those four banks in connection with that loan. The loan was individually negotiated between defendant and Equity Funding; arrangements could be and were individually made for the protection of the defendant when insolvency was imminent (see, e.g., the Northern Life Insurance stock transaction referred to below).

Thus, the relationship seems to be one where there is at least a substantial opportunity for the Indenture Trustee to favor its individual interest over those of the debenture holders, and thus the protections and restrictions of the Act should be applicable.

Of somewhat less importance perhaps is the fact that the Revolving Credit Agreement was in some sense a provision for interim financing in that Equity Funding was required to prepay the debt to the extent of net cash proceeds received by Equity Funding from the sale or issuance of any note, debenture, or other evidence of indebtedness, with certain exceptions, or from the sale or other disposition not in the ordinary course of business, of assets of Equity Funding (Revolving Credit Agreement § 2.05). Nor do we think that for our purposes the Revolving Credit Agreement and the grid note should be deemed a "security" because the $41,000,000 advance under the Revolving Credit Agreement was used almost entirely for the purpose of acquiring a large investment, to wit, the stock of Northern Life Insurance Company.

Accordingly, we hold that the Revolving Credit Agreement, the grid note, and the indebtedness evidenced thereby were not "securities" within the meaning of § 613(b) of the Indenture and the corresponding § 311(b) of the Trust Indenture Act, and that the Special Term was in error in dismissing the causes of action based on § 613(a) of the Trust Indenture on the ground that they were "securities."

.   .   .

Second, Fourth, Sixth, Seventh, Eighth, and Ninth Causes of Action— Breach of Common Law Fiduciary Duties

The transactions attacked in the First, Third, and Fifth causes of action under § 613(a) of the Indenture are also attacked in the Second, Fourth, and Sixth causes of action, respectively, as a breach of the defendant Trustee's fiduciary duty, at a time when defendant knew Equity Funding was in danger of insolvency.

In the Seventh, Eighth, and Ninth causes of action, plaintiff attacks the failure of defendant to declare a default and accelerate the maturity of the Debentures until May 1, 1973, which was more than four months after the collection of collateral interest under the Revolving Credit Agreement on December 31, 1972, thus taking those payments out of the reach of § 613(a) of the Indenture. The complaint alleges that the filing by Equity Funding of a petition for reorganization on April 5, 1973 was an "Event of Default" under the Indenture; that thereupon defendant as Trustee could have accelerated the maturity of the Debentures; and that the non-payment of the accelerated principal would have been a default, bringing within the reach of § 613(a) of the Indenture all payments made after four months prior thereto. The complaint further alleges that on or about April 3, 1973, defendant delivered to Equity Funding a notice declaring that Events of Default had occurred under the Revolving Credit Agreement and accelerating the maturity of the indebtedness under the Revolving Credit

Agreement; but that although the defendant could have similarly accelerated the maturity of the Debentures, it did not do so until May 1, 1973. This failure by defendant is alleged to be a breach of its obligation to use the same degree of care and skill as a prudent man would exercise in the conduct of his own affairs, and willful misconduct or negligence, and a breach of its fiduciary duties to the debenture holders.

. . .

Defendant also contends that its duties as Trustee were circumscribed by the Indenture, that they were purely contractual duties, and that the defendant was not really a trustee within the rules imposing fiduciary liability on trustees.

This precise contention was made and rejected in Dabney v. Chase National Bank, 196 F.2d 668 (2d Cir.1952). There the court had before it an indenture executed before the Trust Indenture Act and governed by the preexisting law of New York. The court held in an opinion by Judge Learned Hand that notwithstanding very narrow definitions of the trustee's duties in the indenture, the trustee was still liable for breach of its fiduciary obligation of loyalty. In his opinion, Judge Hand said:

> "[T]he duty of a trustee, not to profit at the possible expense of his beneficiary, is the most fundamental of the duties which he accepts when he becomes a trustee. It is a part of his obligation to give his beneficiary his undivided loyalty, free from any conflicting personal interest; an obligation that has been nowhere more jealously and rigidly enforced than in New York where these indentures were executed." (p. 670)

Speaking of some language in Hazzard v. Chase National Bank, 159 Misc. 57, 84, 287 N.Y.S. 541, 570, aff'd 257 App.Div. 950, 14 N.Y.S.2d 147, aff'd 282 N.Y. 652, 26 N.E.2d 801 (1940), that seemed to suggest that an indenture trustee's rights and duties were defined not by the fiduciary relationship but exclusively by the terms of the agreement, Judge Hand said:

> "That language we read only as criticism of practices that had grown up, and not as asserting that the courts of New York had given any countenance to the notion that, so far as a corporation sees fit to assume the duties of an indenture trustee, it can shake off the loyalty demanded of every trustee, corporate or individual. We can find no warrant for so supposing; and, indeed, a trust for the benefit of a numerous and changing body of bondholders appears to us to be preeminently an occasion for a scruple even greater than ordinary; for such beneficiaries often have too small a stake to follow the fate of their investment and protect their rights." (p. 671)

Defendant argues that the Trust Indenture Act has changed this rule, and that by giving its blessing to a corporate trustee also having the status of an individual creditor, the Act in essence made the rule of the *Dabney* case inapplicable to indentures governed by the Trust Indenture Act. We do not agree. We do not think that the Trust Indenture Act was intended in any way to take away from debenture holders any protections which they had before the Act.

And we think that the language of both the Trust Indenture Act § 323(b) (15 U.S.C.A. § 77www) and § 510 of the Indenture expressly preserve any rights of the debenture holders under the law prior to the enactment of the Trust Indenture Act. The Trust Indenture Act § 323, provides in part:

> "The rights and remedies provided by this subchapter shall be in addition to any and all other rights and remedies that may exist under the Securities Act of 1933, or the Securities Exchange Act of 1934, or the Public Utility Holding Company Act of 1935, or otherwise at law or in equity. . . ."

Section 510 of the Indenture provides in part:

> "No right or remedy herein conferred upon or reserved to the Trustee or to the Holders is intended to be exclusive of any other right or remedy, and every right and remedy shall, to the extent permitted by law, be cumulative and in addition to every other right and remedy given hereunder or now or hereafter existing at law or in equity or otherwise."

In our view, the motion to dismiss for failure to state a cause of action was properly denied as to the Second, Fourth, and Sixth causes of action, and erroneously granted as to the Seventh, Eighth, and Ninth causes of action.

COMMENT

This case is but one of many arising from the tangled affairs of Equity Funding Corp. of America. That firm was founded in 1960 in Los Angeles to sell a life insurance-mutual fund package that was supposed to provide "synergism," through economics of selling a package and through the hope that increases in the value of the mutual fund shares would pay the premiums. The firm was committed to lending money to its investors. Equity Funding seemed to prosper greatly but it later turned out that a large proportion (some 80%) of the insurance policies and program loans were wholly fictitious. The fictions were concealed from four accounting firms that at one time or another audited the activities of Equity Funding and its affiliates by an elaborate scheme involving many employees and several computers. Computer printouts of record-holders were falsified and supposedly random spot checks were frustrated by coding devices that ensured that only real accounts would be selected for review. The system avoided collapse for a good many years until a former employee revealed the deception (causing further problems by choosing a Wall Street investment analyst who passed the news on to various institutional investors).[9] This episode gave rise to Dirks v. SEC, p. 583 supra.

QUESTIONS

(1) The preceding case raises questions regarding the potential conflicts of interest between a bank acting as a lender to the debtor and acting as a trustee under an indenture. What are the types of conflicts which might be expected to arise? Why does the Act exclude "securities" from the scope of the § 613 restriction on action in the case of potentially preferential collection of the debtor's assets? Why does the Act not simply forbid banks that are lenders to the debtor from being trustees? Do other services provided by banks—acting as

---

9. For general reading see Dead Souls in the Corporation, New Yorker, Aug. 22, 1977, p. 35; Robertson, Those Daring Young Con Men of Equity Funding, Fortune, Aug. 1973, p. 81. See also Herman, Equity Funding, Inside Information, and the Regulators, 21 U.C.L.A.L.Rev. 1 (1973); In re Equity Funding Corp. of America Securities Litigation, 438 F.Supp. 1303 (C.D.Cal.1977).

a trustee under a pension fund, checking accounts, advisory services—give rise to serious potential conflicts?

(2) The court refers to the pre-Act history of trust indenture litigation and to cases such as Hazzard that suggested that the terms of a trust indenture could then override trust law. Would such a result necessarily flow from the general law of trusts? Could an imaginative court have written an opinion that struck down a clause that, for example, relieved a trustee from liability for mere negligence, as opposed to willful misconduct?

(3) It is uniformly held that no fiduciary duty is owed by corporate management to the holders of debt (even if very thinly secured). Could a case be made for the contrary outcome? Suppose that the Class A stock in Zahn v. Transamerica, p. 446 supra, had been debentures. Why should debenture holders get worse treatment?

Bibliography: It is still hard to outdo Stetson, Preparation of Corporate Bonds, Mortgages, Collateral Trusts and Debenture Indentures in Some Legal Phases of Corporate Financing, Reorganization and Regulation (1917), for a description of lawyers' functions in corporate debt issues. See, e.g., Kennedy & Landau, Debt Financing and Corporate Trust Administration, 22 Bus.Law. 353 (1967); Rodgers, The Corporate Trust Indenture Project, 20 Bus.Law. 551 (1965). The latter item described an endeavor by the American Bar Foundation to streamline the paperwork surrounding corporate borrowings. For business aspects, see, e.g., P. Hunt, C. Williams & G. Donaldson, Basic Business Finance Chs. 11–15, 18, 20, 25 (4th ed. 1971). R. Brealey & S. Myers, Principles of Corporate Finance ch. 22 (2d ed. 1984); McDaniel, Bondholders and Stockholders, 13 J.Corp.L. 205 (1988), argues the case for fiduciary duties to bondholders.

---

4. Dividend Law and Policy

NOTE ON DIVIDEND POLICY AND LAW

In casebooks of the preceding generation it was normal to devote substantial space to a treatment of dividend law. The problems seemed challenging and realistic and they afforded an opportunity to explore all sorts of questions about law and accounting; after all, if dividends can only be declared out of "surplus" or "net earnings" one must work one's way through all of the corporation's accounts to get to that bottom line figure. Various things have conspired to displace dividend law from that position. For one thing there are very few cases in the field and for another the statutory rules have been relaxed to the point that few boards of directors are inhibited from paying as much in dividends as their business judgment thinks is tolerable. While omission of the topic would leave a conceptual and practical gap in the student's training in corporation law it seems appropriate to curtail its treatment.

(1) Three interests shape dividend law and practice. Overall there is a public interest in dividend policy in the large. Shareholders

obviously want to be rewarded for their investment through receipt of dividends. Creditors want their capital "cushion" to be preserved intact for protection in case the corporation runs into adversity.

Corporation law of course does not purport to deal with the public interest. To a large extent the interests of investors and management, operating through the market, will fulfill that interest. Managers should retain for reinvestment within the corporation as much as they judge can earn a rate of return under their control that is at least equivalent to what shareholders could get by reinvesting in projects of a similar level of risk outside the corporation. There is a temptation to squirrel away more than that—the temptations that go with empire-building, with creating as large a corporate edifice as possible for one to be at the head of. But there is also a danger, particularly in periods when tender offers are ripe. Offerors are drawn powerfully to corporations with large amounts of uncommitted cash on hand—those funds can be used to pay for buying its shares or for use in connection with the next acquisition. Thus the pressures probably wind up at a fairly optimal balanced level, though the business press recounts abuses in both directions. At times the tax laws have tilted dividend policy, particularly in the smaller corporation. When private individuals paid tax at considerably higher levels than did corporations there was a temptation to retain earnings within the corporation so as to avoid a second tax; those savings might be made more enduring by selling the shares (capital gains were taxed at lower rates than dividends) or by dissolving the corporation. This effect was counterbalanced by tax rules that imposed special penalties on corporations that retained earnings but could not prove that they had a sensible business purpose for doing so. In other countries such as the Federal Republic of Germany tax rules that forego part of the tax on distributed earnings have clearly been motivated, at least in part, by a desire to see more funds flowing into the securities markets for reallocation to branches of industry most in need of additional capital.[10]

(2) Stockholder motivations for wanting dividends are obvious in one sense—it is the dividends that are the reward for their investment. But things get complicated. Theory says that what a shareholder should be interested in is the total wealth represented by the shares, including the increase in their value which is due to the retention and reinvestment of earnings in order to earn yet more for their shares. If a shareholder is impatient with the dividend distribution it is always possible to sell the shares to somebody who can wait. Life is not as simple as that. Steady and reliable dividends attract some investors— the $9 dividend paid by the old AT & T for many years was relied upon by many investors who needed income. Many episodes attest to the drastic reconsideration the stock market gives to a stock when its dividend is omitted or cut.[11] And in some cases there is no market for

10. H. Gumpel & C. Boettcher, Taxation in the Federal Republic of Germany 518 (2d ed. 1969).

11. In Cady, Roberts & Co., 40 S.E.C. 907 (1961), the first case establishing "tippees'" liability under Rule 10b–5, p. 579

the security and its holders are at the mercy of the judgment of the directors as to what they should be paid. That judgment could be warped by such considerations as the fact that the managers are receiving ample funds through salaries.

Thus there is a sprinkling of litigation in which the shareholders of corporations sue for dividends, alleging an abuse of directors' discretion. One important case in the field of inadequate dividends is Dodge v. Ford Motor Co., p. 107 supra, which you should now re-examine as a dividend case. Gordon v. Elliman, p. 462 supra, is another case in that area. Curiously there are also cases in which shareholders complain that too much is being paid. *Prima facie,* it is hard to understand why shareholders would complain about a payout of too much money of which they got their pro rata shares. In the one case,[12] the allegation was that the parent, owning 80% of the subsidiary's stock, knew that the antitrust authorities would compel divestiture of the subsidiary and decided that it would first strip the subsidiary of its liquid assets so that, once independent it would present no competitive threat. In the other,[13] it was charged that the parent took funds out of the subsidiary and invested them in profitable new oil ventures conducted directly by the parent whereas a disinterested board running the subsidiary would have kept the money and pursued those opportunities for itself. Neither claim prevailed although in each case one judge voted for the complainants.

(3) A word about the mechanics of dividend payment. Dividends arise when they are voted by the board. They then become for the first time an enforceable obligation of the corporation. In a corporation of any size the directors will declare that the dividend is payable to the shareholders as of record on a given date shortly after that meeting. Sometimes with automated equipment, the names and addresses of the shareholders are copied off, the multiplication of the number of shares times the dividend per share is effected, checks are processed, enveloped and mailed. Upon the record date, shares are traded on the exchanges "ex dividend", that is, the dividend will go to the seller who was the registered owner on that date and not to the buyer.[14] An appropriate reduction will be made in the price of the stock. With numerous shareholders there will almost inevitably be some who will prove to be untraceable. State law may provide for the escheat of such

supra, the tip involved a halving of the dividend of Curtis–Wright Corp. from $.625 per share to $.375. A representative of the respondent brokerage firm was a director; he telephoned the news to the firm during a recess in the meeting. The firm sold several thousand shares at 11:15–11:20 a.m. at prices of 40¼ to 40⅜. When the news was officially published on the Dow Jones tape at 11:48 a.m. trading was suspended until 2 p.m. and the afternoon's trading ranged from 34⅛ to 37.

12. American District Tel. Co. v. Grinnell Corp., 33 A.D.2d 769, 306 N.Y.S.2d 209 (1969). See also Gabelli & Co., Inc., Profit Sharing Plan v. Liggett Group Inc., 479 A.2d 276 (Del.1984).

13. Sinclair Oil Corp. v. Levien, 280 A.2d 717 (Del.1971).

14. This process should remind you of the treatment of shareholders' voting rights in cases of purchases shortly before meetings. See p. 370 supra.

sums, which may be large enough to promote a major dispute between states over the privilege.[15]

(4) Creditors' interests have historically been protected by rules putting ceilings on dividends in terms related to the firms assets less liabilities and capital or to its earnings. Those rules have evolved over time and range considerably in detail and sophistication. Consider the former Indiana law allowing dividends

> "out of the surplus earnings or net profits or surplus paid in cash." [16]

The Delaware statute once said dividends could be paid

> "only out of surplus or net profits arising from the business of the company." [17]

It then said:

> "(1) out of its net assets in excess of its capital . . . or (2) in case there shall be no such excess, out of its net profits for the fiscal year then current and/or the preceding fiscal year."

Examine the present 8 Del.C. § 170 in conjunction with §§ 154, 242, 243, 244.

The Model Business Corporation Act formerly limited distributions to "the unreserved and unrestricted earned surplus of the corporation" plus (if the adopting state so chose) "the unreserved and unrestricted net earnings of the current fiscal year and the next preceding fiscal year taken as a single period." The current version (§ 6.40) forbids distributions if after giving effect thereto the corporation would not be able to pay its debts as they become due in the ordinary course of business or its total assets would be less than the sum of its total liabilities plus amounts due to the holders of preferred shares.

These statutes raise substantial interpretative problems. Let us consider the following skeleton balance sheet.

Assets		Liabilities	
Cash	5,000	Notes payable	10,000
Accounts receivable	10,000	Proprietorship: Capital	30,000
Investments	10,000	Capital surplus	10,000
Inventory	10,000	Earned surplus	10,000
Plant	25,000		$60,000
	$60,000		

Another way of conceptualizing this situation is to visualize two columns, one of assets and the other of accounting measuring blocks:

---

15. Standard Oil Co. v. New Jersey by Parsons, 341 U.S. 428, 71 S.Ct. 822, 95 L.Ed. 1078 (1951).

16. Indiana Acts of 1929, ch. 215, § 12.

17. For case law concerning earlier versions of the statute, see Kingston v. Home Life Ins. Co. of Am., 11 Del.Ch. 258, 101 A.

898 (Ch.1917), affirmed per curiam, 11 Del. Ch. 428, 104 A. 25 (1918), and Morris v. Standard Gas & Elec. Co., 31 Del.Ch. 20, 63 A.2d 577 (1949). The Delaware dividend statute was originally borrowed from New Jersey and cases from that jurisdiction may be relevant.

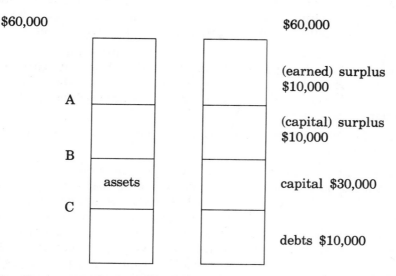

$60,000 $60,000

A

(earned) surplus
$10,000

(capital) surplus
$10,000

B

assets   capital $30,000

C

debts $10,000

As the asset column shrinks the possibility of paying dividends under various tests is cut off. Some tests come into play at point "A" when earned surplus is exhausted. Point "B" is operative under tests that speak of "surplus". Below point "C" the corporation is insolvent in the bankruptcy sense and vulnerable to being adjudicated bankrupt. The distribution would not pass the Model Act test, either. Any further distribution is a fraudulent conveyance recoverable under the bankruptcy act.

(5) Observe some of the questions arising from the face of the balance sheet:

(a) Since the balance sheet is prepared according to generally accepted accounting principles the assets are shown at their cost, less depreciation. If we have an appraiser's statement that the plant is now worth, i.e., is readily saleable at, $40,000, which figure governs?

(b) Should the capital surplus account, representing the price paid by the shareholders for their shares, over the par or stated value thereof, be useable? Suppose that it resulted from a charter amendment reducing the par value of each share?

(c) Suppose that it had been discovered that on the original issuance of the stock there had been some "watering" so that there had been a capital deficit of $3,000. Is the dividend-paying potential of the corporation reduced accordingly?

(d) Suppose that the corporation has been doing badly so that the earned surplus account shows a $25,000 deficit. This year, however, has been much better and has shown a net income of $15,000. Can a "nimble dividend" be paid? Does it matter whether the net income results entirely from a sale at a profit of a large item of corporate property—a transaction not likely to be repeated.

(e) Suppose that the corporation instead of owning a factory, has as its sole asset a mine that is being used up. Must the capital be kept intact at its original figure corresponding to its original cost?

(f) Suppose that the item "investments" represents the cost of a controlling stock interest in a subsidiary that has had earnings at year's end not yet distributed as a dividend. Can these sums be included in measuring the parent's capacity to pay? Suppose that the subsidiary has accumulated only net losses?

(6) The state corporation law may or may not provide an answer to any of such questions.

A once hotly debated issue was the first-mentioned, whether the assets should be treated at their book value or cost. Many students slogged through Randall v. Bailey, a 1940 case [18] which held that it was lawful to declare a dividend that was permissible only through writing the corporation's main asset, the Bush Terminal on the Brooklyn waterfront up to an appraised value. The writeups took place in 1915 and 1918 when war-time freight traffic towards Europe was heavy. The dividends in question were paid in 1928–32 when circumstances differed again. The court considered the evidence of professional appraisers as well as the status of the corporation's property tax assessments (protested by the company) it concluded that the reappraisals were reasonable. It then examined the statute in effect which spoke of "value" and concluded that the dividend was lawful. Some courts operating under different statutes have gone the other way. The situation in a current case would depend on the statute in part. Thus the Model Act § 6.04 allows use of "fair valuation" to meet the test. It might also depend in part on attitudes towards valuation. As a result of inflation the accounting profession and the SEC have somewhat softened their stance on writeups. The authorities now call for the provision of inflation-adjustment information alongside the regular cost-based figures. This data is addressed, of course, to a different need—the provision of the data needed to evaluate an investment under conditions of changing price levels, but it does at the minimum take something of the shadow off reappraisals, once thought to be merely the tool of unscrupulous speculators.

(7) With the softening of legal rules about distributions to shareholders the need of the creditor to protect itself becomes more apparent. When a knowledgeable institutional creditor presents a prospective borrower with a loan agreement or when counsel for underwriters of a public bond or debenture craft the mortgage or indenture they would likely include a covenant restricting the payment of dividends. These clauses are aimed very specifically at protecting the interests of the lender. Examine the following clause:

> SECTION 6.07. The Company will not, except as provided below in this Section, (a) declare or pay any dividend or make

---

18. Randall v. Bailey, 288 N.Y. 280, 43 N.E.2d 43 (1942).

any distribution on its Common Stock or to its Common stock-holders (other than dividends or distributions payable in shares of Common Stock of the Company), or (b) purchase, redeem or otherwise acquire or retire for value any shares of its stock, except shares acquired upon the conversion thereof into, or in exchange for, other shares of stock of the Company, or (c) permit a Subsidiary to purchase, redeem or otherwise acquire or retire for value any shares of stock of the Company, unless after giving effect to such dividend, distribution, purchase, redemption or other acquisition, the accumulated consolidated net income of the Company and its Subsidiaries earned subsequent to December 31, 1986 plus the sum of $15,000,000 shall exceed the sum of (i) the aggregate of all dividends and other distributions on its capital stock (other than dividends or distributions payable in shares of Common Stock of the Company . . .) expended by the Company subsequent to December 31, 1986, and (ii) the excess, if any, of the aggregate amount of expenditures made by the Company or any Subsidiary subsequent to December 31, 1986 for the purchase, redemption or other acquisition or retirement for value of any shares of capital stock of the Company over the sum of (A) the net proceeds of the sale after December 31, 1986 of stock of the Company, and (B) the net proceeds of the sale after December 31, 1986 of any indebtedness of the Company (including the Debentures) which has thereafter been converted into shares of stock of the Company.

Note also the following definition of consolidated earned income:

The term "consolidated net income" shall mean all net income (or net deficit) of the Company and its Subsidiaries, appearing on a consolidated income statement of the Company and its Subsidiaries as reported to its stockholders and accompanied by a certificate of a firm of independent public accountants. Such income shall include nonoperating income, and shall be after deducting all expenses and charges of every proper character, all as determined in accordance with generally accepted accounting principles.

PROBLEM

The corporation's prospects for the future have been assessed by its managers as highly favorable. They note that the real estate around the plant has appreciated in value due to the construction of new highways in the area and that enough spare land could be sold to realize a $2,500,000 gain. That sum, together with some additional financing, could then be invested in expanding a newer factory in an area where costs are lower. If these plans materialize the firm should be able to catch an expanding market in which its competitors are already substantially increasing their earnings, paying dividends and seeing their market values increase. The president would like to resume paying dividends after a three year hiatus. He knows or suspects that a number of the shareholders are getting restless about their interception.

The partner for whom you work is both a director of and general counsel to the firm. She asks you whether a declaration of a small cash dividend would be lawful under Delaware law and under the company's 1985 indenture covering its debenture issue (the dividend clause is identical with that set forth at p. 670 supra except that it does not contain the words "plus the sum of $15,000,000.") She would also like to know about the legality of a stock dividend. Finally she would like to have a list of the considerations which may be relevant to the question of the advisability of some sort of dividend from a business point of view.

NOTE ON STOCK DIVIDENDS

Students are often confused by the term "stock dividends"; properly this refers only to dividends paid in stock and not to dividends paid in cash to the holders of stock. In fact it refers only to dividends paid by company X in the form of stock of company X and not to dividends paid by X in stock of company Y. Payment in the stock of another corporation occurs at such times as when a corporation is "spinning off" a part of its business which it no longer finds congenial or which the antitrust division will no longer permit it to retain. For example, Textron, Inc. in 1953 distributed one share of Indian Head Mills, Inc. for every ten shares of Textron held by its shareholders; Standard Oil of Indiana from 1948 on distributed shares of Standard Oil of New Jersey which it had received as the result of the sale of some of its foreign properties and could not retain.[19] Legally this is in much the same category as the famous (and presumably much appreciated) dividend paid in bottles by Park & Tilford Distillers after the droughty years of World War II.

A stock dividend, however, involves no reduction of the assets of the corporation. It does not in fact even change the relative positions of the shareholders for if a corporation with 1,000,000 shares equally divided among 1,000 owners issues a stock dividend of 1% each shareholder now has 1,010 shares which is still $1/10$ of 1%. Why do companies then go to the trouble involved in stock dividends? Primarily it seems to serve a psychological function, giving shareholders a tangible sign that their investment has increased even though the increase is still "locked in." Thus directors will often intersperse stock dividends with regular dividends when an earnings increase they regard as temporary seems to call for some recognition of that prosperity without setting a precedent for cash drains. Similarly a long delay in paying dividends while funds are used for needed capital investments may cause shareholder unrest that receipt of new certificates may slightly assuage. If the firm is paying a cash dividend and keeps

---

19. These examples appear in P. Hunt, C. Williams, & G. Donaldson, Basic Business Finance, ch. 23 (1958).

paying at the same rate per share after the stock dividend, each shareholder's receipts will of course go up.

One should compare stock dividends with the closely related phenomenon of a "stock split." [20] In a split, for example, each shareholder might receive twice as many shares as he or she previously possessed. The motivation for a split would typically be a desire to make trading in the stock easier; since shares are most cheaply and easily traded in multiples of 100, the price per share may reach such a point that the price per 100 shares and accordingly of the typical trade may be out of reach for the small investor. A split can remedy such a situation, also making it easier for holders to realize part of their gains by selling off some of their investments. If the proportions are adjusted a split and a stock dividend can come to look very much alike. The differences between a split and a dividend include:

(a) A split requires an amendment of the articles of incorporation to change the par or stated value of each share. A stock dividend does not unless the number of shares required to effectuate the dividend would be greater than the number authorized but not outstanding.

(b) Accounting treatment differs as between the two modes. In a stock split, there may, at the simplest, be no change at all, if there is a simple subdivision of X shares to make 2X shares, with the capital stock remaining constant. A stock dividend inevitably entails a transfer from earned surplus to capital of some amount. Just what that amount should be is a matter of some dispute. A fairly strong logical case can be made for the proposition that the transfer should be no more than the par or stated value per share times the number of shares issued as a dividend. Indeed, state law requires no more. However, there is high accounting authority for the claim that in some cases an amount equal to the *fair market value* of the shares so issued must be capitalized. To illustrate the book entries, suppose that a corporation issues as a dividend 10,000 shares of its $1 par stock then trading on an organized exchange at $12½ per share. The entry should be either:

(a)			(b)		
dr. earned surplus	$10,000		dr. earned surplus	$125,000	
		OR			
cr. capital stock	10,000		cr. capital stock		10,000
			capital surplus		115,000

The reasoning behind the accounting view is expressed in the following paragraphs from the American Institute of Certified Public Accountants: [21]

20. A reverse stock split is also possible. In such a case the par or stated value per share is increased and the number of shares reduced. Consequently those with small holdings find themselves with fractional shares. For example, the holder of 63 shares after a 100 to 1 reduction in number of shares has only $^{63}/_{100}$ths shares. Such holders can then be involuntarily bought out under many state laws. See Teschner v. Chicago Title & Trust Co., 59 Ill.2d 452, 322 N.E.2d 54 (1974), appeal dismissed 422 U.S. 1002, 95 S.Ct. 2623, 45 L.Ed.2d 666 (1975).

21. Acct.Res.Bull. No. 43, Ch. 7B (1953).

AS TO THE ISSUER

Stock Dividends

10. As has been previously stated, a stock dividend does not, in fact, give rise to any change whatsoever in either the corporation's assets or its respective shareholders' proportionate interests therein. However, it cannot fail to be recognized that, merely as a consequence of the expressed purpose of the transaction and its characterization as a *dividend* in related notices to shareholders and the public at large, many recipients of stock dividends look upon them as distributions of corporate earnings and usually in an amount equivalent to the fair value of the additional shares received. Furthermore, it is to be presumed that such views of recipients are materially strengthened in those instances, which are by far the most numerous, where the issuances are so small in comparison with the shares previously outstanding that they do not have any apparent effect upon the share market price and, consequently, the market value of the shares previously held remains substantially unchanged. The committee therefore believes that where the circumstances exist the corporation should in the public interest account for the transaction by transferring from earned surplus to the category of permanent capitalization (represented by the capital stock and capital surplus accounts) an amount equal to the fair value of the additional shares issued. Unless this is done, the amount of earnings which the shareholder may believe to have been distributed to him will be left, except to the extent otherwise dictated by legal requirements, in earned surplus subject to possible further similar stock issuances or cash distributions.

11. Where the number of additional shares issued as a stock dividend is so great that it has, or may reasonably be expected to have, the effect of materially reducing the share market value, the committee believes that the implications and possible constructions discussed in the preceding paragraph are not likely to exist and that the transaction clearly partakes of the nature of a stock split-up as defined in paragraph 2. Consequently, the committee considers that under such circumstances there is no need to capitalize earned surplus, other than to the extent occasioned by legal requirements. It recommends, however, that in such instances every effort be made to avoid the use of the word *dividend* in related corporate resolutions, notices, and announcements and that, in those cases where because of legal requirements this cannot be done, the transaction be described, for example, as a *split-up effected in the form of a dividend.* . . .

. . .

13. Obviously, the point at which the relative size of the additional shares issued becomes large enough to materially influence the unit market price of the stock will vary with individual companies and under differing market conditions and, hence, no single percentage can be laid down as a standard for determining when capitalization of

earned surplus in excess of legal requirements is called for and when it is not. However, on the basis of a review of market action in the case of shares of a number of companies having relatively recent stock distributions, it would appear that there would be few instances involving the issuance of additional shares of less than, say 20% or 25% of the number previously outstanding where the effect would not be such as to call for the procedure referred to in paragraph 10.

14. The corporate accounting recommended in paragraph 10 will in many cases, probably the majority, result in the capitalization of earned surplus in an amount in excess of that called for by the laws of the state of incorporation; such laws generally require the capitalization only of the par value of the shares issued, or, in the case of shares without par value, an amount usually within the discretion of the board of directors. However, these legal requirements are, in effect, minimum requirements and do not prevent the capitalization of a larger amount per share.

The New York Stock Exchange has established a similar requirement for companies it lists [22]:

Exchange Listing Policy

The Exchange, in authorizing the listing of additional shares to be distributed pursuant to a stock dividend (or a stock split-up, whether or not effected through the technique of a stock dividend) representing less than 25% of the number of shares outstanding prior to such distribution will require that, in respect of each such additional share so distributed, there be transferred from earned surplus to the permanent capitalization of the company (represented by the capital stock and capital surplus accounts) an amount equal to the fair value of such shares. While it is impracticable to define "fair value" exactly, it should closely approximate the current share market price adjusted to reflect issuance of the additional shares.

Applicability of Exchange Policy: This policy does not apply to distributions representing 100% or more of the number of shares outstanding prior to the distribution. As to distributions of 25% or more, but less than 100%, the Exchange will require capitalization at fair value only when, in the opinion of the Exchange, such distributions assume the character of stock dividends through repetition under circumstances not consistent with the true intent and purpose of stock split-ups.

QUESTIONS

(1) Modern analysts of dividend law take a very pessimistic view of statutes designed to restrict payments in order to protect the interests of creditors. They note that given the right to reduce capital, etc., the protection of dividend statutes is illusory. They go from there to recommend the elimination of protection above the fraudulent conveyance level—as in the Revised Model

22. N.Y.S.E. Company Manual A-235.

Business Corporation Act. Given the efforts of sophisticated drafters to write covenants restricting dividends, should not an effort be made to improve, rather than eliminate, statutory protection for those who cannot write their own clauses? How would such clauses look?

(2) What are the primary arguments for and against the use of current market or other values for the purpose of calculating the amounts available for dividends? Are you convinced one way or the other?

(3) Does the AICPA's argument (in ¶ 10) about the perceived effect of stock dividends convince you? Is it undermined by findings, consistent with efficient market theory, that the securities markets discount their effect?

Bibliography: On dividend policy and shareholder interests see Brudney, Dividends, Discretion and Disclosure, 66 Va.L.Rev. 85 (1980); Fischel, Law and Economics of Dividend Policy, 67 Va.L.Rev. 699 (1981). B. Manning, A Concise Textbook on Legal Capital Ch. IV (2d ed. 1981) covers the distribution rules. See also Current Issues on the Legality of Dividends from a Law and Accounting Perspective: A Task Force Report, 39 Bus.Law. 289 (1983). For a review of the problems in connection with valuation and price-level adjustment see Siegel, Accounting and Inflation, 29 U.C.L.A.L.Rev. 271 (1981). The old classic was D. Kehl, Corporate Dividends (1941).

---

5. Stock Repurchases

American corporation law has accepted the purchase by a corporation of its own shares and has thereby opened the door to a series of problems avoided by British law so long as it adhered to the rule of Trevor v. Whitworth,[23] outlawing such acquisitions. See 8 Del.C. §§ 160, 243. The possible purposes of a repurchase cover a wide range: (a) the corporation may wish to have shares available for such ends as the fulfillment of employee stock option or bonus plans or the acquisition of other assets (and the alternative of issuing new stock may be cumbersome or undesirable); (b) the shareholder may wish to withdraw his or her investment but not be able to find a purchaser on the open market, (c) the management of the corporation, having excess liquid funds on hand, may prefer to "shrink" its size in this way rather than by a dividend, i.e., *pro rata* distribution; (d) the controlling group within the corporation may wish to eliminate the particular shareholder from a position in the power structure of the corporation or may wish to prevent the shares from falling into the hands of a buyer it finds undesirable; (e) if the corporation has issued several classes of securities it may wish for financial reasons to retire a senior class; (f) it may be easiest to tidy up messy situations with fractional shares by having the corporation buy up the fragments; (g) "open end" investment companies are obligated to repurchase their shares on demand at

---

23. 12 App.Cas. 409 (1887); see L. Gower, Modern Company Law 111–15 (3d ed. 1969). The Companies Act of 1985 now permits repurchases. See R. Pennington, Company Law 210 (5th ed. 1985).

the current *pro rata* value of the investment assets of the firm; (h) the fulfillment of the corporation's duty to pay dissenting shareholders with "appraisal rights" the value of their shares requires a repurchase, or (i) management may wish to reduce the number of shareholders to the point where the corporation will no longer be subject to Sections 12, 14 and 16 of the Exchange Act. Some of these purposes (especially (d) and (i)) can raise serious questions about the consistency of management's maneuvers with proper fiduciary standards.

A repurchase of stock is similar to a dividend in that it involves a diminution of corporate assets. It differs most conspicuously in that it entails a shift in the relative proportions of ownership. Observe that if a corporation has 3 equal shareholders, a repurchase of A's shares may redound indirectly to the benefit of B and C, since they now each own 50% rather than 33⅓% of the enterprise (even though a somewhat shrunken one). Accordingly a repurchase is limited by rules designed to protect the capital of the corporation. These rules are not always precisely parallel to those involving dividends; observe, for example, the differences between 8 Del.C. § 170 on dividend sources and § 160 on repurchases. Note that 8 Del.C. § 253 allows repurchases to be carried out for certain specified purposes even though a dividend or repurchase for other ends would not be permissible. The Revised Model Business Corporation Act equates dividends and repurchases as "distributions" and makes them subject to the same insolvency test. §§ 6.31, 6.40.

The question of the appropriate source for a repurchase is complicated by a further question of timing. Suppose that on January 1, 1986 a corporation agreed to repurchase X's stock on the happening of a certain event (say X's reaching the age of 60). That event took place on July 1, 1987 and on August 1 X tenders the stock. The corporation refuses to buy and on November 1 X brings suit. As of which of the dates is the corporation's financial capacity to repurchase the shares to be tested? This is important because repurchase agreements, particularly in close corporations, may be part of a long term arrangement that the parties rely on very heavily. Indeed an agreement may call for repurchases in installments. A famous New York case, Topken, Loring, & Schwartz, Inc. v. Schwartz,[24] said (1) that since a corporation might not have surplus when performance of its duty to repurchase fell due it might be relieved of its duty and, therefore, (2) that the corporation could not compel the shareholder-employee to perform his duty to tender the shares to it since there was no consideration and no mutuality of promises. This case has been overruled by a later New York statute.[25] The present case law seems to require that the corporation meet the financial tests as of the time when its payment(s) become(s) due. This has meant a rejection or overlooking of the argument that the corporation is merely meeting an obligation that

24. 249 N.Y. 206, 163 N.E. 735 (1928). **25.** N.Y.Bus.Corp.L. § 514(b).

was incurred as of the date of the agreement.[26] Accordingly, one who relies upon a stock repurchase contract must live with the possibility that the corporation will be disabled from performing when the time comes.

Accounting for transactions in a corporation's own shares—in treasury stock—produces some complexities. First of all, take the question of accounting for the acquisition of the treasury stock. The credit, to cash, is plain enough; but what about the debit? If it were the stock of another corporation it would clearly be proper to create an asset to balance the expense. But it is a bit hard to carry a corporation's own stock as its asset: stock is after all only a set of claims upon the corporation issuing it. This may not seem entirely true if the stock is just a small fraction of the corporation's total and if it is readily marketable. If General Motors holds 1000 shares of its own stock which it intends to use to satisfy obligations under a stock option or purchase program, that looks rather like an asset. The approved method is to carry the treasury stock, at its cost to the company, as a deduction from the net worth section on the right hand side of the balance sheet. In the cost method the whole cost is taken as a deduction from the overall equity section; in the par method an amount equal to the par value of the shares is deducted from capital and the rest from earned surplus. As far as subsequent dividends or repurchases are concerned, the earned surplus available has been reduced to the extent of the cost—either by deducting that cost from earned surplus or by labelling it restricted. The treatment of subsequent resales of treasury stock raises issues suitable for an advanced course. Note, however, that the accounting profession has firmly stated that the corporation does not realize income from such transactions. Instead of selling the stock again the company may cancel or retire the shares; this is in effect a reduction of capital. This is covered by special statutory provisions—in Delaware by § 244.

Two kinds of repurchases of stock by the corporation that issued it involve obvious questions of fiduciary duties. One is referred to as "going private." In such a case, the corporation makes an offer for the stock held by the public, non-management, shareholders. If the offer succeeds the corporation is controlled by its insiders. It may be possible to get the corporation out from under the reporting, proxy etc. rules that come with liability to registration under § 12 of the 1934 Act. The sharp decline in the stock market between 1973 and 1974 first gave rise to an efflorescence of such activity. A much-cited case [27] involved Wells, Rich, Greene Inc., an advertising firm best known for the flamboyant style of its founder and chief executive, Mary Wells Lawrence. She and other executives had originally received shares for an average of 30 cents each. Then the insiders and the corporation sold shares to the public in 1968 at $17.50 per share and again in 1971

---

26. See Herwitz, Installment Repurchase of Stock, 79 Harv.L.Rev. 303 (1965).

27. Kaufmann v. Lawrence, 386 F.Supp. 12 (S.D.N.Y.1974), affirmed 514 F.2d 283 (2d Cir.1975).

at $21.75. Thereafter, although the company prospered and its earning per share went from $1.02 to $2.04, the price of its stock on the American Exchange fell to 5½. Then an offer was made under which the corporation would repurchase its own shares in exchange for a package of $3 in cash and $8 principal amount of 10% subordinated debentures for each share. In the judgment of the marketplace the package was worth about $6. Litigation ensued. Commentators went so far as to suggest that such transactions should be prohibited. In the 1980's the language shifted to the "leveraged buy out." In those transactions it was typically not the corporation itself but the managers themselves or a corporate vehicle controlled by them that did the purchasing. The net result would be the same; instead of a publicly held corporation there was one directly or indirectly owned by the management group. The tendency of such transactions to overreach the public shareholder and obtain for them too low a price was moderated by the tendency for auctions to arise in which an excessively low bid by the insiders would be outcome by third parties.

The other special type of share repurchase is almost the reciprocal of going private—"greenmail." In such cases management causes the corporation to buy out a shareholder they find threatening or obnoxious. The next case involves such a situation.

POLK v. GOOD

Supreme Court of Delaware, 1986.
507 A.2d 531.

[This case came on appeal from a decision of the Court of Chancery approving settlement and dismissal of derivative actions against Texaco, its directors and certain investors (the Bass group). The parties had agreed on the basis of defendants' payment of $700,000 in attorneys' fees plus litigation expenses, modification of a voting agreement described below and the provision of certain discovery. The Supreme Court, in an opinion by JUSTICE MOORE, affirmed, first stating the facts:]

A.

The Bass Group's Purchases, the Getty Acquisition and Texaco's Buyout.

In 1982, the Bass group began buying shares of Texaco, and by the end of 1983 had acquired almost 5% of the corporation's outstanding common stock. During this period Bass had urged Texaco to acquire shares of its own stock by either a self-tender or open market purchases. Texaco rejected the idea, but relations between the parties remained cordial. There was no indication that Bass was pressuring the corporation to act.

In January 1984, Texaco became involved in one of the biggest corporate acquisitions in history, when it bought Getty Oil Company (Getty) at a cost of over $10 billion. The Texaco management was consumed with such tasks as obtaining government and shareholder approval of the transaction, selling off expendable assets to refinance the debt incurred, integrating the two huge companies, and dealing with the inevitable litigation.

While Texaco was acquiring Getty, the Bass group continued buying Texaco stock on the open market, and by January 30, it held about 9.9% of the corporation's outstanding shares. Bass also kept urging Texaco to repurchase its own shares. Moreover, the group indicated that it might obtain up to 20% of Texaco, hinting at a possible tender offer. Rumors appeared in the financial press that the Bass group would join with Pennzoil, an adversary of Texaco in the Getty acquisition, to break up Texaco and force a divestiture of Getty. All of this concerned Texaco, which, in the midst of the Getty acquisition, would be vulnerable in warding off a hostile shareholder group whose actions might be contrary to the best interests of a majority of the company's stockholders. Although the Bass group was still openly supportive of existing Texaco policy, both the management and the financial community expected Bass to maximize its financial advantage at this critical time.

On February 28, the Bass group suggested a joint venture with the company which would combine some Texaco shares and real estate assets of the Bass group with certain oil reserves of Texaco. Corporate management studied and rejected the plan, considering it nothing more than a means for Bass to realize $68 per share for its stock, a value which greatly exceeded Texaco's market price, and one which management considered excessive. Fearing that rejection of the proposal would trigger some hostile Bass move, Texaco consulted its investment banker, The First Boston Corporation, and its outside corporate counsel. The company and its advisors all concluded that a substantial immediate threat to the corporation's best interests existed, and that the most effective way of meeting the danger was to acquire the Bass stock.

The parties opened negotiations for a repurchase. Bass initially sought $68 per share, but eventually dropped its price to an "absolute bottom" of $55. Texaco's chairman, John K. McKinley, announced a top purchase price of $50. On March 5, the parties reached an agreement in principle for a sale at $50 per share, representing a premium of $1⅝ over $48⅜, the market price on March 2, the previous trading day. The Bass group was to receive one half of the proceeds in cash. The other half would be in the form of a new issue of preferred stock with voting rights, similar to the common, in order to provide tax benefits and assurance of the new securities' marketability for the group. However, because one of the reasons behind the repurchase was to prevent a disruption of Getty's assimilation into Texaco, the Bass group volunteered, after the price for its stock was set, to vote the preferred shares as the Texaco board directed. This offer was accepted.

On March 6, the proposal was submitted to the Texaco board, 10 of whose 13 members were outside directors. First Boston informed the board that the premium was reasonable and at the low end of the range other companies were paying in similar transactions, and that the $50 price was consistent with the long-term value of the company. Texaco's legal counsel advised that the corporation had the power to repurchase the shares, and that such action would be protected under Delaware's business judgment rule. The directors unanimously approved the repurchase. The Bass group received approximately $650 million in cash and 12.6 million shares of the preferred voting stock, which now comprised about 5% of the total voting power of Texaco's outstanding shares. The sellers agreed not to acquire any more Texaco stock for a period of ten years, during which time they would vote their shares in accordance with the board's recommendations.

[The opinion continued with a discussion of Delaware law:]

A Delaware corporation has the power to deal in its own stock, 8 Del.C. § 160(a) and may acquire a dissident's shares provided the transaction is free from fraud or unfairness. Kors v. Carey, Del.Ch., 158 A.2d 136 (1960). Unless the primary or sole purpose was to perpetuate the directors in office, such an acquisition will be sustained if, after reasonable investigation, a board has a justifiable belief that there was a reasonable threat to the corporate enterprise. Unocal Corporation v. Mesa Petroleum Co., Del.Supr., 493 A.2d 946, 953–55 (1985); Cheff v. Mathes, Del.Supr., 199 A.2d 548, 554, 556 (1964); compare Bennett v. Propp, Del.Supr., 187 A.2d 405 (1962). When properly accomplished, such matters are protected by the business judgment rule. Unocal, 493 A.2d at 954; Pogostin v. Rice, Del.Supr., 480 A.2d 619, 627 (1984).

However, as we noted in *Unocal*, a company repurchasing its shares to eliminate a perceived danger must meet certain threshold standards to come within the ambit of the business judgment rule. The first problem is a potential conflict of interest. Thus, in *Unocal* we held that:

> [i]n the face of this inherent conflict directors must show that they had reasonable grounds for believing that a danger to corporate policy existed because of another person's stock ownership . . . However, they satisfy that burden "by showing good faith and reasonable investigation . . ." . . . Furthermore, such proof is materially enhanced as here, by the approval of a board comprised of a majority of outside independent directors who have acted in accordance with the foregoing standards. Unocal, 493 A.2d at 955.

Finally, the board's action must be reasonable in relation to the threat posed, based on an analysis of the perceived danger and its effect on the corporation and its stockholders. Id.

Here, the presence of the 10 outside directors on the Texaco board, coupled with the advice rendered by the investment banker and legal counsel, constitute a *prima facie* showing of good faith and reasonable investigation. See Moran v. Household International, Inc., Del.Supr., 500 A.2d 1346, 1356 (1986); see also, Smith v. Van Gorkom, Del.Supr., 488 A.2d 858, 872–73 (1985). With 10 of the 13 directors being independent, the plaintiffs thus bore a heavy burden of overcoming the presumptions thus attaching to the board's decisions. . . .

The events occurring from the outset of the Bass group's acquisition of Texaco stock, up to the repurchase, created reasonable grounds for a justifiable belief by the directors that there was a threat to Texaco. The payment of a premium of approximately 3% over market seems reasonable in relation to the immediate disruptive effect and the potential long-term threat which the Bass group posed. Clearly, that was a benefit to the company and most of its stockholders.

IV.

Thus, we turn to the various challenges of the objectors.

1. *The law governing the repurchase.*

Appellants contend that *Kors, Cheff,* and *Bennett v. Propp,* should not be interpreted to permit "greenmail," and should be limited to those instances where dissident shareholders threaten to interfere with the day-to-day business operations of a company.[28]   They argue that these cases do not sanction the repurchase at a premium of shares of those who threaten such activities as proxy fights and tender offers— the exercise of legitimate corporate "democratic processes".   However, our recent decision in *Unocal* completely rejects that thesis, and we need not repeat it here.   *Unocal,* 493 A.2d at 953–55.   The Chancellor's conclusions were entirely consistent with the principles stated in *Unocal.*

[The court then disposed of several other objections to the settlement, including the argument that there was insufficient consideration for it because the voting agreement had already been modified and thus was moot, that the board was not disinterested because they had bought the Bass group's vote, that the notice of the settlement was inadequate and that there were errors of fact in the Chancellor's settlement decision.]

COMMENT

The struggle between Texaco and Pennzoil over the assets of Getty Oil led to a series of court victories by Pennzoil that ultimately induced Texaco to seek the shelter of a federal bankruptcy court and then to accept a settlement in 1988 of $3 billion to end the litigation.   A major role in that settlement was played by Carl Icahn, another important takeover specialist of the 1980's.   It is not clear that any part of Texaco's management's operations in this sequence of events in fact benefited Texaco's shareholders, who saw large parts of their stake in the corporation vanish.[29]

Two of the cases cited in the principal case bear comment.   Cheff v. Mathes was long the principal case on what had not yet come to be termed "greenmail." [30]   There the court exonerated directors who had bought back their corporation's stock from an acquirer who had a reputation of being a liquidator of companies.   There was evidence to the effect that the problems of the corporation were not primarily due to the threat of acquisition—FTC proceedings were pending against the company and its chief executive (who was afterwards sentenced to 6 months imprisonment for contempt) and the firm's sales and profits had been decreasing.   The Unocal case involved a somewhat different type of repurchase.   Unocal made an offer to buy back its shares that was extended to all its shareholders but one.   That one party was Mesa Petroleum, the instrumentality of T. Boone Pickens, a major formulator of acquisitions in the oil business.   The court held that this exclusion did not render the offer illegal.

In the 1987 tax legislation, Congress imposed a 50% excise tax on profits derived through greenmail, which is defined to involve a hostile tender offer. Int.Rev.Code § 5881.

---

28. As we observed in *Unocal,* the term "greenmail" refers to the practice of buying out a takeover bidder's or dissident's stock at a premium that is not available to other shareholders. *Unocal,* 493 A.2d at 956, n. 13.

29. S. Coll, The Taking of Getty Oil (1987).

30. 41 Del.Ch. 494, 199 A.2d 548 (1964).

QUESTIONS

(1) Does a comparison between the high sale price to the public and the low repurchase really prove that anything was wrong with the repurchase? If so, is there any reason *a priori* to believe that the flaw was in the repurchase rather than the sale? Is there a strong inference that there was a failure of disclosure somewhere? Why should an advertising firm such as Wells, Rich go public in the first place? What dangers do outside investors face?

(2) Are public shareholders really free to reject a tender offer slightly above the current market quotation? Assume they share the insiders' view that the market strongly undervalues the security. What perils and disadvantages do they face if the offer is generally successful and most shares are tendered?

(3) Are the potential abuses of "going private" or greenmail sufficiently great to cause one to consider generally outlawing repurchases by the corporation? If so, do the same considerations apply to purchases by management individually? If not, would you favor some less sweeping restraint on repurchases—in terms of either (a) distinguishing between purposes, (b) imposing a requirement that the opportunity be made available pro rata to all shareholders, or (c) establishing special valuation proceedings?

PROBLEM

Refer back to the problem on p. 651, supra. Suppose that the board of directors of United Knitwear, after examining the proposition that more of the company's stock be issued to prevent Learmont's taking of control and rejecting it for some reason, now ask you to consider whether it would be lawful to buy his stock. Indirectly and tentatively, he has indicated a willingness to sell 50,000 shares at $20.00 per share.

Bibliography: On stock repurchases, see Israels, Corporate Purchase of Its Own Share—Are There New Overtones? 50 Cornell L.Q. 620 (1965). D. Herwitz, Business Planning 414–557 (1966), covers a wide range of tax, accounting and other aspects of repurchases. On the accounting side see Rudolph, Accounting for Treasury Shares under the Model Business Corporation Act, 73 Harv.L.Rev. 323 (1959); Hackney, Financial Provisions of the Model Business Corporation Act, 70 Harv.L.Rev. 1357, 1392 (1957). For critical views of the "going private" phenomenon, see Brudney, Equal Treatment of Shareholders in Corporate Distributions and Reorganizations, 71 Calif.L.Rev. 1072, 1106 (1983); Lowenstein, Management Buyouts, 85 Colum.L.Rev. 730 (1985). On "greenmail", see Bradley & Rosenzweig, Defensive Stock Repurchases, 99 Harv.L.Rev. 1377 (1986), and Macey & McChesney, A Theoretical Analysis of Corporate Greenmail, 95 Yale L.J. 13 (1985).

Chapter XIII

FUNDAMENTAL CHANGES—IN STRUCTURE AND CONTROL

1. Introduction

This chapter deals with two related but quite distinct subjects—changes in corporate structure and changes in corporate control. By changes in structure we mean alterations in the basic legal documents creating the corporation and in the rights that flow therefrom. These include amendments of the articles of incorporation, mergers, etc. By changes in control we refer to operations that end with a different group of people being in control of the firm than previously. This can happen through a structural change as where one corporation is merged into another. It can also happen without a change in structure as where an acquisitive purchaser buys up enough of its stock to control its affairs. We begin with a basic introduction to the mechanical alternatives that are open to one bent on acquiring control.

The basic model of corporation law balances (1) the power of the directors to manage the business of the corporation, typically expressed as in 8 Del.C. § 141(a), and (2) the power of the shareholders to veto certain fundamental changes, typically mergers, charter amendments, dissolution and sales or leases of substantially all the assets of the corporation. The broad theory seems a sensible one: shareholders have neither the time nor the expertise to manage or supervise the day-to-day operations of the firm but such basic changes ought to interest them enough so that they will be induced to think about them. If intelligent and informed investors were to hammer out a fully negotiated contract with management it seems likely that they would fix upon a more or less similar pattern, reserving veto powers over major decisions. In fact, a partnership agreement, (including one resting on the suppletory provisions of the Uniform Act) would typically require consent of the partners—all of the partners—to changes in the mode of operations, such as a shift in the area of the partnership's line of business. Indeed, there is historical evidence to suggest that any change in the charter was thought, like a change in any other contract, to require the assent of every contracting party, i.e. every shareholder. That is clearly not now the law—the contract creating the corporation preserves the right of the state to amend the corporation laws and the charter and also the right of specified majority shareholder votes to do

684

so.[1] As part of the price of being compelled to allow such changes to take place, the shareholders may be allowed a right to "drop out" by way of appraisal procedures explained below. This makes their situation more comparable to partners who individually have a right to "drop out" by virtue of the dissolution privilege.

You should now examine the Delaware sections on fundamental changes as follows:

(1) mergers and consolidations (§§ 251–262)

(2) sales and leases of assets (§ 271)

(3) charter amendments (§§ 241–246)

(4) dissolution (§§ 273–284)

Read them critically and with the following comments and questions in mind. Delaware law distinguishes "mergers" (in which corporation X vanishes into pre-existing corporation Y which continues to exist) from "consolidations" (in which existing corporations X and Y vanish into new corporation Z). The statutory provisions seem longer than they really are since § 251 differs from 252, 254, 255, 256, 257, and 258 basically only in that they relate to mergers of different types of corporations—domestic (Delaware) vs. foreign, non-stock vs. for profit. For simplicity's sake, we will deal with § 251 unless otherwise stated. Pay special heed to the "short merger" provisions of § 253 which permit a parent corporation holding 90% of the stock of a subsidiary to merge the subsidiary into itself in rather summary fashion, dealing fairly abruptly with the minority.

In reading these statutes bear in mind some broader perspectives, first, that the fiduciary concepts of fairness, self-dealing, etc. are not absent from this field and second that the federal proxy-disclosure requirements are brought into play by these voting requirements.

QUESTIONS

(1) Fill in the following matrix, using the Delaware statutes:

type of transaction	vote required	appraisal?
mergers		
sales		
amendments		
charter		
dissolution		

(2) Does the above pattern make sense—should the voting requirements be as they are now? Formerly Delaware law required a two-thirds majority for mergers—was this preferable? Should appraisal rights be afforded in other situations?

(3) Is the list of major changes complete? Should it include *mortgages* of substantially all the assets as well as sales? Does it make sense to include charter amendments but not by-law changes? The federal Investment Compa-

1. The history is reviewed in Manning, The Shareholder's Appraisal Remedy: An   Essay for Frank Coker, 72 Yale L.J. 223, 246–260 (1962).

ny Act in effect requires shareholder approval before there can be a replacement of more than ⅓ of the board of directors.[2] Would this be a good addition to the list? Should the shareholders have a vote on dividend payments—as they do in Germany? On changes of auditors?

2. Changes in Structure and Changes in Control

There is a close but rather complex relationship between changes in structure to which the preceding section introduces you and changes in control, specifically to activities popularly termed "takeovers" in which control over an existing corporation (Target) is acquired by another person (Raider) or persons or another corporation.[3] A takeover may be effected without a change in structure, where Raider buys a majority of the voting shares of Target or it may involve a change in structure, where Raider causes a merger of Target into his own Raidercorp. Incidentally, a change in structure, such as a change of the charter to broaden the purpose clauses, may have no change of control effect.

Takeovers are a special subject in and of themselves and a full appreciation of their importance would require treatment from several perspectives. An antitrust expert is concerned about their tendencies to diminish competition by increasing the concentration of the industry in question into a lesser number of large enterprises. With a historical bent, that expert might point to the successive waves of mergers that peaked in 1897–1901, in 1925–30 and in 1966–68. The tax lawyer would emphasize the impact of tax considerations on the incidence of takeovers and on the forms which they take. Others would look at the impact of takeovers on the communities in which the target company had its headquarters and other activities. They would debate whether takeovers, and the threat of their happening, do in fact discipline corporate executives and replace somnolent managers; others would tend to see the typical situation as one in which reckless conquistadors displace hard-working and faithful stewards of the investors' and employees' interests.

Corporation law provides one with only a limited set of tools for grappling with takeovers. It is concerned chiefly with the protection of the investors in the corporations that are involved and to some degree with the situation of their creditors. Its chief tools are the fiduciary and the disclosure principles. There are also a number of formal

2. § 16(a) of the Investment Company Act of 1940, 15 U.S.C.A. § 80a–16(a).

3. Three terms need to be kept separate. "Takeover" is used here to refer to all transactions in which the voting control over a corporation passes from one party to another. A takeover may involve a "merger", which is a specific statutory device. It may also involve a "tender offer" which, as section 3 of this Chapter expounds, is an offer to purchase stock of the target company from the public.

requirements which may or may not contribute significantly towards the protection of those interests. The lawyer is very much involved with questions relating to the choice among different means, usually involving some structural change, whereby the change of control can be carried out.

Thus as Raider starts to make plans to get control of Target he or she will run through a list of possible alternatives, some of which will include structural changes and some of which will not.

(1) Raider may buy for cash enough stock of Target to get control from (a) a group related to Target's management or (b) from the public or (c) from both.

(2) Raider may buy the stock but instead of cash may offer shares of stock of Raidercorp, perhaps in excess of those presently authorized by Raidercorp articles of incorporation and unissued.

(3) Raider may merge Target into Raidercorp.

(4) Raider may buy the assets of Target for cash; Target may then be dissolved.

(5) Raidercorp may buy the assets of Target for stock of Raidercorp. Target may then dissolve.

(6) Raider could institute a proxy campaign to get control of Target's board of directors.

Considerable ingenuity is invested in selecting the optimum route, sometimes with a view to avoiding the impact of the shareholder vote and appraisal right requirements. There may be a number of steps involved, sometimes requiring several shareholder actions—observe that approval of the shareholders of Raidercorp may also be required.

Exercise

To fully understand the comparison between the different modes of obtaining control listed above you should now work through the steps involved in each of them, assuming Delaware law applies. It may be easier for you to do "before and after" diagrams for each transaction comparable to that which I have done below for a merger.

Before Merger

R shareholders   T shareholders
   ↓   ↓
R corporation   T corporation
   ↓   ↓
R assets   T assets

After Merger

R   T shareholders
         ↓
RT corporation
         ↓

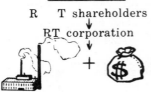

[A6954]

The following two cases represent different approaches to a basic question: will the courts always respect the characterization which the managers of a "take-over" choose to apply to the transactions they have designed or will they recategorize them according to their own perception of the underlying "reality"?

FARRIS v. GLEN ALDEN CORPORATION

Supreme Court of Pennsylvania, 1958.
393 Pa. 427, 143 A.2d 25.

COHEN, JUSTICE.   We are required to determine on this appeal whether, as a result of a "Reorganization Agreement" executed by the officers of Glen Alden Corporation and List Industries Corporation, and approved by the shareholders of the former company, the rights and remedies of a dissenting shareholder accrue to the plaintiff.

Glen Alden is a Pennsylvania corporation engaged principally in the mining of anthracite coal and lately in the manufacture of air conditioning units and fire-fighting equipment.   In recent years the company's operating revenue has declined substantially, and in fact, its coal operations have resulted in tax loss carryovers of approximately $14,000,000.   In October 1957, List, a Delaware holding company owning interests in motion picture theaters, textile companies and real estate, and to a lesser extent, in oil and gas operations, warehouses and aluminum piston manufacturing, purchased through a wholly owned subsidiary 38.5% of Glen Alden's outstanding stock.[4] This acquisition enabled List to place three of its directors on the Glen Alden board.

On March 20, 1958, the two corporations entered into a "reorganization agreement," subject to stockholder approval, which contemplated the following actions:

1.   Glen Alden is to acquire all of the assets of List, excepting a small amount of cash reserved for the payment of List's expenses in connection with the transaction.   These assets include over $8,000,000

4. Of the purchase price of $8,719,109,
$5,000,000 was borrowed.

in cash held chiefly in the treasuries of List's wholly owned subsidiaries.

2.   In consideration of the transfer, Glen Alden is to issue 3,621,703 shares of stock to List.   List in turn is to distribute the stock to its shareholders at a ratio of five shares of Glen Alden stock for each six shares of List stock.   In order to accomplish the necessary distribution, Glen Alden is to increase the authorized number of its shares of capital stock from 2,500,000 shares to 7,500,000 shares without according pre-emptive rights to the present shareholders upon the issuance of any such shares.

3.   Further, Glen Alden is to assume all of List's liabilities including a $5,000,000 note incurred by List in order to purchase Glen Alden stock in 1957, outstanding stock options, incentive stock options plans, and pension obligations.

4.   Glen Alden is to change its corporate name from Glen Alden Corporation to List Alden Corporation.

5.   The present directors of both corporations are to become directors of List Alden.

6.   List is to be dissolved and List Alden is to then carry on the operations of both former corporations.

Two days after the agreement was executed notice of the annual meeting of Glen Alden to be held on April 11, 1958, was mailed to the shareholders together with a proxy statement analyzing the reorganization agreement and recommending its approval as well as approval of certain amendments to Glen Alden's articles of incorporation and bylaws necessary to implement the agreement.   At this meeting the holders of a majority of the outstanding shares, (not including those owned by List), voted in favor of a resolution approving the reorganization agreement.

On the day of the shareholders' meeting, plaintiff, a shareholder of Glen Alden, filed a complaint in equity against the corporation and its officers seeking to enjoin them temporarily until final hearing, and perpetually thereafter, from executing and carrying out the agreement.

The gravamen of the complaint was that the notice of the annual shareholders' meeting did not conform to the requirements of the Business Corporation Law, 15 P.S. § 2852–1 et seq., in three respects: (1) It did not give notice to the shareholders that the true intent and purpose of the meeting was to effect a merger or consolidation of Glen Alden and List; (2) It failed to give notice to the shareholders of their right to dissent to the plan of merger or consolidation and claim fair value for their shares, and (3) It did not contain copies of the text of certain sections of the Business Corporation Law as required.[5]

By reason of these omissions, plaintiff contended that the approval of the reorganization agreement by the shareholders at the annual meeting was invalid and unless the carrying out of the plan were enjoined, he would suffer irreparable loss by being deprived of substantial property rights.[6]

5.   The proxy statement included the following declaration: "Appraisal Rights.

"In the opinion of counsel, the shareholders of neither Glen Alden nor List Industries will have any rights of appraisal or similar rights of dissenters with respect to any matter to be acted upon at their respective meetings."

6.   The complaint also set forth that the exchange of shares of Glen Alden's stock

The defendants answered admitting the material allegations of fact in the complaint but denying that they gave rise to a cause of action because the transaction complained of was a purchase of corporate assets as to which shareholders had no rights of dissent or appraisal. For these reasons the defendants then moved for judgment on the pleadings.[7]

The court below concluded that the reorganization agreement entered into between the two corporations was a plan for a *de facto* merger, and that therefore the failure of the notice of the annual meeting to conform to the pertinent requirements of the merger provisions of the Business Corporation Law rendered the notice defective and all proceedings in furtherance of the agreement void. Wherefore, the court entered a final decree denying defendants' motion for judgment on the pleadings, entering judgment upon plaintiff's complaint and granting the injunctive relief therein sought. This appeal followed.

When use of the corporate form of business organization first became widespread, it was relatively easy for courts to define a "merger" or a "sale of assets" and to label a particular transaction as one or the other. [citations omitted.] But prompted by the desire to avoid the impact of adverse, and to obtain the benefits of favorable, government regulations, particularly federal tax laws, new accounting and legal techniques were developed by lawyers and accountants which interwove the elements characteristic of each, thereby creating hybrid forms of corporate amalgamation. Thus, it is no longer helpful to consider an individual transaction in the abstract and solely by reference to the various elements therein determine whether it is a "merger" or a "sale". Instead, to determine properly the nature of a corporate transaction, we must refer not only to all the provisions of the agreement, but also to the consequences of the transaction and to the purposes of the provisions of the corporation law said to be applicable. We shall apply this principle to the instant case.

Section 908, subd. A of the Pennsylvania Business Corporation Law provides: "If any shareholder of a domestic corporation which becomes a party to a plan of merger or consolidation shall object to such plan of merger or consolidation . . . such shareholder shall be entitled to . . . [the fair value of his shares upon surrender of the share certificate or certificates representing his shares]." Act of May 5, 1933, P.L. 364, as amended, 15 P.S. § 2852–908, subd. A.[8]

for those of List would constitute a violation of the pre-emptive rights of Glen Alden shareholders as established by the law of Pennsylvania at the time of Glen Alden's incorporation in 1917. The defendants answered that under both statute and prior common law no preemptive rights existed with respect to stock issued in exchange for property.

7. Counsel for the defendants concedes that if the corporation is required to pay the dissenting shareholders the appraised fair value of their shares, the resultant drain of cash would prevent Glen Alden from carrying out the agreement. On the other hand, plaintiff contends that if the shareholders had been told of their rights as dissenters, rather than specifically advised that they had no such rights, the resolution approving the reorganization agreement would have been defeated.

8. Furthermore, section 902, subd. B provides that notice of the proposed merger and of the right to dissent thereto must be given the shareholders. "There shall be included in, or enclosed with . . . notice [of meeting of shareholders to vote on plan of merger] a copy or a summary of the plan of merger or plan of consolidation, as the case may be, and . . . a copy of subsection A of section 908 and of subsections B, C and D of section 515 of this act." . . .

This provision had its origin in the early decision of this Court in Lauman v. Lebanon Valley R.R. Co., 1858, 30 Pa. 42. There a shareholder who objected to the consolidation of his company with another was held to have a right in the absence of statute to treat the consolidation as a dissolution of his company and to receive the value of his shares upon their surrender.

The rationale of the Lauman case, and of the present section of the Business Corporation Law based thereon, is that when a corporation combines with another so as to lose its essential nature and alter the original fundamental relationships of the shareholders among themselves and to the corporation, a shareholder who does not wish to continue his membership therein may treat his membership in the original corporation as terminated and have the value of his shares paid to him. . . .

Does the combination outlined in the present "reorganization" agreement so fundamentally change the corporate character of Glen Alden and the interest of the plaintiff as a shareholder therein, that to refuse him the rights and remedies of a dissenting shareholder would in reality force him to give up his stock in one corporation and against his will accept shares in another? If so, the combination is a merger within the meaning of section 908, subd. A of the corporation law. . . . '

If the reorganization agreement were consummated plaintiff would find that the "List Alden" resulting from the amalgamation would be quite a different corporation than the "Glen Alden" in which he is now a shareholder. Instead of continuing primarily as a coal mining company, Glen Alden would be transformed, after amendment of its articles of incorporation, into a diversified holding company whose interests would range from motion picture theaters to textile companies, Plaintiff would find himself a member of a company with assets of $169,000,000 and a long-term debt of $38,000,000 in lieu of a company one-half that size and with but one-seventh the long-term debt.

While the administration of the operations and properties of Glen Alden as well as List would be in the hands of management common to both companies, since all executives of List would be retained in List Alden, the control of Glen Alden would pass to the directors of List; for List would hold eleven of the seventeen directorships on the new board of directors.

As an aftermath of the transaction plaintiff's proportionate interest in Glen Alden would have been reduced to only two-fifths of what it presently is because of the issuance of an additional 3,621,703 shares to List which would not be subject to pre-emptive rights. In fact, ownership of Glen Alden would pass to the stockholders of List who would hold 76.5% of the outstanding shares as compared with but 23.5% retained by the present Glen Alden shareholders.

Perhaps the most important consequence to the plaintiff, if he were denied the right to have his shares redeemed at their fair value, would be the serious financial loss suffered upon consummation of the agreement. While the present book value of his stock is $38 a share after combination it would be worth only $21 a share. In contrast, the shareholders of List who presently hold stock with a total book value of $33,000,000 or $7.50 a share, would receive stock with a book value of $76,000,000 or $21 a share.

Under these circumstances it may well be said that if the proposed combination is allowed to take place without right of dissent, plaintiff would have his stock in Glen Alden taken away from him and the stock of a new company thrust upon him in its place. He would be projected against his will into a new enterprise under terms not of his own choosing. It was to protect dissident shareholders against just such a result that this Court one hundred years ago in the Lauman case, and the legislature thereafter in section 908, subd. A, granted the right of dissent. And it is to accord that protection to the plaintiff that we conclude that the combination proposed in the case at hand is a merger within the intendment of section 908, subd. A.

Nevertheless, defendants contend that the 1957 amendments to sections 311 and 908 of the corporation law preclude us from reaching this result and require the entry of judgment in their favor. Subsection F of section 311 dealing with the voluntary transfer of corporate assets provides: "The shareholders of a business corporation which acquires by sale, lease or exchange all or substantially all of the property of another corporation by the issuance of stock, securities or otherwise shall not be entitled to the rights and remedies of dissenting shareholders. . . ." [citation omitted.]

And the amendment to section 908 reads as follows: "The right of dissenting shareholders . . . shall not apply to the purchase by a corporation of assets whether or not the consideration therefor be money or property, real or personal, including shares or bonds or other evidences of indebtedness of such corporation. The shareholders of such corporation shall have no right to dissent from any such purchase." [citation omitted.]

Defendants view these amendments as abridging the right of shareholders to dissent to a transaction between two corporations which involves a transfer of assets for a consideration even though the transfer has all the legal incidents of a merger. They claim that only if the merger is accomplished in accordance with the prescribed statutory procedure does the right of dissent accrue. In support of this position they cite to us the comment on the amendments by the Committee on Corporation Law of the Pennsylvania Bar Association, the committee which originally drafted these provisions. The comment states that the provisions were intended to overrule cases which granted shareholders the right to dissent to a sale of assets when accompanied by the legal incidents of a merger. See 61 Ann.Rep.Pa.Bar Ass'n 277, 284 (1957). Whatever may have been the intent of the *committee*, there is no evidence to indicate that the *legislature* intended the 1957 amendments to have the effect contended for. But furthermore, the language of these two provisions does not support the opinion of the committee and is inapt to achieve any such purpose. The amendments of 1957 do not provide that a transaction between two corporations which has the effect of a merger but which includes a transfer of assets for consideration is to be exempt from the protective provisions of sections 908, subd. A and 515. They provide only that the shareholders of a corporation which acquires the property or purchases the assets of another corporation, *without more*, are not entitled to the right to dissent from the transaction. So, as in the present case, when as part of a transaction between two corporations, one corporation dissolves, its liabilities are assumed by the survivor, its executives and directors take over the management and control of the survivor, and, as consideration for the transfer, its stockholders acquire a majority of the shares of stock of the survivor, then the transaction is no longer simply a purchase of assets or acquisition of property to which sections 311, subd. F and 908, subd. C apply, but a merger governed by section 908, subd. A of the corporation law. To divest shareholders of their right of dissent under such circumstances would require express language which is absent from the 1957 amendments.

Even were we to assume that the combination provided for in the reorganization agreement is a "sale of assets" to which section 908, subd. A does not apply, it would avail the defendants nothing; we will not blind our eyes to the realities of the transaction. Despite the designation of the parties and the form employed, Glen Alden does not in fact acquire List, rather, List acquires Glen Alden, cf. Metropolitan Edison Co. v. Commissioner, 3 Cir., 1938, 98 F.2d 807, affirmed sub nom., Helvering v. Metropolitan Edison Co., 1939, 306 U.S. 522, 59 S.Ct. 634, 83 L.Ed. 957, and under section 311, subd. D [9] the right of dissent would remain with the shareholders of Glen Alden.

We hold that the combination contemplated by the reorganization agreement, although consummated by contract rather than in accordance with the statutory procedure, is a merger within the protective purview of sections 908, subd. A and 515 of the corporation law. The shareholders of Glen Alden should have been notified accordingly and advised of their statutory rights of dissent and appraisal. The failure of the corporate officers to take these steps renders the stockholder approval of the agreement at the 1958 shareholders' meeting invalid. The lower court did not err in enjoining the officers and directors of Glen Alden from carrying out this agreement.

Decree affirmed at appellants' cost.

ORZECK v. ENGLEHART

Supreme Court of Delaware, 1963.
41 Del.Ch. 361, 195 A.2d 375.

WOLCOTT, JUSTICE. This is an appeal by the plaintiff, a stockholder of Olson Brothers, Incorporated (formerly Bellanca Corporation) from an order of the Vice Chancellor denying her motion for summary judgment on the first two causes of action asserted in the complaint.

The complaint challenges the validity of the purchase by Bellanca Corporation (now Olson Brothers, Incorporated) from the defendants, C. Dean Olson and H. Glenn Olson, of all of the capital stock of seven California corporations engaged in the egg business in California.

Bellanca Corporation for many years was in the business of manufacturing airplanes. In recent years it ceased this business and had been used as a holding company by its president. It had in fact become an "empty shell". For more than three years prior to March, 1961, it

---

9. "If any shareholder of a business corporation which sells, leases or exchanges all or substantially all of its property and assets otherwise than (1) in the usual and regular course of its business, (2) for the purpose of relocating its business, or (3) in connection with its dissolution and liquida- tion, shall object to such sale, lease or exchange and comply with the provisions of section 515 of this act, such shareholder shall be entitled to the rights and remedies of dissenting shareholders as therein provided." Act of July 11, 1957, P.L. 711, 15 P.S. § 2852–311, subd. D.

had engaged in no business operations, had been delisted by the American Stock Exchange, but had accumulated large losses available for Federal tax loss carry-over purposes.

In March, 1961, negotiations began between Bellanca and the Olsons looking toward the purchase by Bellanca of all the outstanding stock of the California corporations. On April 5, 1961, Bellanca's directors accepted an offer to sell this stock to Bellanca, and a written agreement was entered into on April 25, 1961, to effectuate the purchase.

The agreement fixed the purchase price at $5,150,000, and directed that it be paid by Bellanca to the Olsons as follows: (1) 150,000 shares of Bellanca's stock at its par value of $1.00; (2) payment of one-half the recovery by Bellanca in certain litigation with Bankers Life and Casualty Company, and (3) the balance payable over a period of 12 years with interest at 2½% annually commencing four years from April 25, 1961.

By the agreement of purchase the Olsons also were granted stock options to purchase at par 1,250,000 shares of Bellanca for a period of 10 years, and the individual defendant, Morris L. Sullivan, was granted an option as a "finder's fee" to purchase 75,000 shares of Bellanca stock at par, and further 2% of Bellanca's profits before taxes for five years, and 3% of the profits after taxes for five years.

The agreement of purchase has long since been consummated by the parties, and Bellanca actually acquired all the stock of the seven California corporations. As a result, it now appears that the Olson brothers are in control of the affairs of Bellanca.

Thereafter, Bellanca, then owning all of the stock of the seven California corporations in the egg business, went through a so-called short-form merger pursuant to 8 Del.C. § 253, and changed its name to Olson Brothers, Incorporated. It now conducts the egg business in California and is controlled and its affairs directed by the Olson brothers. . . .

The basic fact in this cause is that the transaction complained of was the purchase by one corporation of all of the stock of seven other corporations. On its face there is nothing illegal in this. On the contrary, it is specifically authorized by 8 Del.C. § 123. Once the acquisition has been made the purchasing corporation thereafter has the status of a stockholder of the corporation whose shares it has purchased and nothing more. In other words, the purchasing corporation is not the owner of the assets of the other corporation, but is merely a stockholder with all the incidents of such. Nor do the corporate identities merge by reason solely of the purchase by one of all of the other's stock. Owl Fumigating Corp. v. California Cyanide Co., 3 Cir., 24 F.2d 718; Fidanque v. American Maracaibo Co., 33 Del.Ch. 262, 92 A.2d 311.

Despite this, however, plaintiff argues that the end result of the acquisition by Bellanca of all the stock of the California corporations has been to merge Bellanca into them, and put Bellanca in the egg business. Thus, it is argued, a merger has in fact taken place of the apparent purchasing corporation into the apparent selling corporation without compliance with the merger provisions of the Delaware Corporation Law, including the right of a dissenting stockholder to withdraw from the enterprise and be paid the value of his stock.

While the argument made may have a surface plausibility, it nevertheless is contrary to the uniform interpretation given the Delaware Corporation Law over the years to the effect that action taken in accordance with different sections of that law are acts of independent legal significance even though the end result may be the same under different sections. The mere fact that the result of actions taken under one section may be the same as the result of action taken under another section does not require that the legality of the result must be tested by the requirements of the second section.

For example, in Federal United Corp. v. Havender, 24 Del.Ch. 318, 11 A.2d 331, the former Supreme Court held that accumulated dividends on preferred stock could be extinguished by merger of two corporations under 8 Del.C. § 251, although earlier, in Keller v. Wilson & Co., 21 Del.Ch. 391, 190 A. 115, the same Court had held that the same result could not be achieved legally by amendment to a corporate charter under 8 Del.C. § 242.

Similarly, in Heilbrunn v. Sun Chemical Corporation, 38 Del.Ch. 321, 150 A.2d 755, and in Hariton v. Arco Electronics, Inc., Del., 188 A.2d 123, this Court held that the reorganization of two corporations through the medium of a sale of assets from one to the other pursuant to 8 Del.C. § 271, and the subsequent absorption of one by the other did not constitute a merger so as to make it mandatory that the provisions of the merger statute be complied with, including the right of a dissenting stockholder to an appraisal.

In speaking of the sale of assets statute and the merger statute, we said:

"They are, so to speak, of equal dignity, and the framers of a reorganization plan may resort to either type of corporate mechanics to achieve the desired end. This is not an anomalous result in our corporation law."

In Fidanque v. American Maracaibo Co., supra, the Court of Chancery held that the purchase by one corporation of all the outstanding stock of another corporation did not amount to a *de facto* merger of the two corporations, for the reason that ownership of stock in one corporation by another does not create an identity of interest between the two corporations and make one the owner of the property of the other.

It is true that the Vice Chancellor in the Fidanque case laid stress on the absence of any agreement for the liquidation or dissolution of the selling corporation, but we think the point not decisive of the question. The plan in the Heilbrunn case to effect a reorganization by the sale of assets in fact required the dissolution of the selling corporation, but we held that fact did not make the transaction a merger.

The effect of the cited cases is to make it plain that the general theory of the Delaware Corporation Law is that action taken under one section of that law is legally independent, and its validity is not dependent upon, nor to be tested by the requirements of other unrelated sections under which the same final result might be attained by different means.

Thus it is that we think the transaction here complained of was a valid purchase of stock by Bellanca Corporation under the authority of 8 Del.C. § 123, which has independent legal significance unrelated to the merger sections.

We do not intend to be understood as holding that the doctrine of *de facto* merger is not recognized in Delaware. Such is not the case for it has been recognized in cases of sales of assets for the protection of creditors or stockholders who have suffered an injury by reason of failure to comply with the statute governing such sales. Drug, Inc. v. Hunt, 5 W.W.Harr. 339, 168 A. 87, and Finch v. Warrior Cement Corp., 16 Del.Ch. 44, 141 A. 54. In the case before us the statute has been complied with and a stockholder has no ground to claim injury.

Plaintiff argues, however, that this cause is different because the selling corporations have actually taken over and absorbed the purchasing corporation. The argument is founded upon Farris v. Glen Alden Corporation, 393 Pa. 427, 143 A.2d 25, in which the Supreme Court of Pennsylvania held a sale of assets to be a *de facto* merger upon the challenge of a stockholder of the purchasing corporation, and permitted him appraisal rights under the merger sections of the Pennsylvania Business Corporation Law.

We note that the Supreme Court of Pennsylvania has rejected the theory, firmly embodied in the Delaware Corporation Law, of the independent legal significance of action taken under one section of that law, as opposed to other sections. If that is the holding in the Farris case, as we think it is, we decline to accept it as persuasive. . . . [Affirmed.]

COMMENT

(1) The arrangement between List and Glen Alden was, in spite of everything, completed on April 21, 1959 on terms substantially similar. Since 1959 the combined enterprise has disposed of the coal properties. Glen Alden acquired Schenley by first buying 86% of its stock via a tender offer and then pushing through a merger in May 1971 under 8 Del.C. § 251. The tender offer in 1968 was at $53.33 per share of common and the package given each common share as a result of the merger was $5 in cash and $30 principal amount of Glen Alden 7½% debentures, valued somewhere between $25 and $30. The rash of litigation that followed from this merger illustrates the variety of ways in which a merger can be attacked.[10] One lawsuit charged that the merger was unfair in violation of Delaware law, a second that it was inadequately disclosed in violation of Rule 10b–5, a third and fourth that transactions in connection with the tender offer violated Rule 10b–5 and a fifth sought to gain via appraisal a larger sum than that given in the merger.

Glen Alden in turn became the cornerstone of Rapid American Corp., the creation of another acquisitive "conglomerateur", Meshulam Riklis. As of 1988 it retained the alcoholic beverage business plus several chains of retail stores and some manufacturing—McGregor apparel and Faberge fragrances. All of this adds up to sales of about $1.9 billion. Riklis has also found time to promote the career of his wife Pia Zadora as singer and actress.

(2) List Industries was the creature of one A.A. List whose activities as an acquisitor brought him into litigation fairly often. In Menzel v. List, he was found to have purchased, in good faith, a Chagall painting that had been seized by the Nazis from its original owners in Belgium. In List v. Fashion Park he

---

10. David J. Greene & Co. v. Schenley Indus. Inc., 281 A.2d 30 (Del.Ch.1971); Voege v. Smith, 329 F.Supp. 180 (S.D.N.Y. 1971); SEC v. Glen Alden Corp., CCH Fed. Sec.L.Rep. ¶ 92,280 (S.D.N.Y. August 7, 1968); Penn Mart Realty Co. v. Becker, 300 F.Supp. 731 (S.D.N.Y.1969); Loeb v. Schenley Indus. Inc., 285 A.2d 829 (Del.Ch.1971).

initiated and lost a 10b–5 action against parties who had bought shares of a corporation from him at $18 and then sold them at a profit when it merged and its shareholders got $50 per share. He had the cold comfort of being told by the courts that he was too sophisticated and well advised to benefit from disclosure concepts that protect the uninitiated.[11]

(3) Glen Alden was followed by derivative litigation asserting that those who managed the merger that misfired should be liable for the costs thereof. The New York courts held that the advice of "eminent counsel" that the deal was lawful shielded the directors who reasonably relied thereon.[12]

(4) The case was also followed by an amendment of the pertinent Pennsylvania statute so that it now reads as follows:

> The shareholders of a business corporation which acquires by purchase . . . substantially all of the property of another corporation by the issuance of shares . . . with or without assuming the liabilities of such other corporation, shall be entitled to [appraisal rights] if, but only if, such acquisition shall have been accomplished by the issuance of voting shares . . . to be outstanding immediately after the acquisition sufficient to elect a majority of the directors . . . .[13]

(5) Olson Farms, Inc., by contrast, in contrast to Glen Alden, seems to be quietly pursuing a local business in California making egg cartons rather than eggs, for a relatively modest $100 million in sales in 1987.

(6) The Delaware reports continue to bring cases reiterating the "equal dignity" rule in different contexts such as the poison pill case Moran v. Household Int'l Inc., 490 A.2d 1059, 1077 (Del.Ch.), aff'd, 500 A.2d 1346 (Del.1985). See also Field v. Allyn, 457 A.2d 1089 (Del.Ch.), aff'd, 467 A.2d 1274 (Del.1983).

QUESTIONS

(1) One commentator has suggested that Glen Alden is distinguishable on its facts from Orzeck and the Delaware cases it cites. What would that distinction be? Are the Delaware and Pennsylvania statutes significantly different as they relate to Glen Alden?

(2) Suppose that the objection to the transaction had come from a shareholder of List Industries rather than Glen Alden—would it have had the same force and effect? Did the fact that List was, as part of the plan, to be dissolved weigh in the consideration? The fact that "List" was to remain in the name of the continuing corporation? Suppose that Glen Alden had acquired the stock of List rather than its assets?

(3) What is a "merger" anyhow? Neither the Pennsylvania nor Delaware statutes define it. Is it relevant that the Internal Revenue Code § 368(a)(1) speaks of a "reorganization" which includes "a statutory merger or consolidation" but also an acquisition of stock? Is it a useful test to ask whether the steps taken have led to a situation in which the accountants would require the filing of consolidated reports?

11. Menzel v. List, 49 Misc.2d 300, 267 N.Y.S.2d 804 (1966), affirmed 28 A.D.2d 516, 279 N.Y.S.2d 608 (1st Dept.1967); List v. Fashion Park, 340 F.2d 457 (2d Cir.1965).

12. Gilbert v. Burnside, 13 A.D.2d 982, 216 N.Y.S.2d 430 (2d Dept.1961), aff'd

mem. 11 N.Y.2d 960, 229 N.Y.S.2d 10, 183 N.E.2d 325 (1962). See p. 277 supra.

13. Penn.Bus.Corp.L., 15 P.S. § 1311F.

(4) Is the way to tidy up the issue of availability of appraisal not to redefine "merger" but to extend the scope of the appraisal remedy to other transactions? If so, how would you define the transactions, including List–Glen Alden, to which that right should be extended?

(5) Would the List–Glen Alden situation have been affected by the passage of the Pennsylvania statute excerpted in paragraph (4) of the Comment?

NOTE ON SOME OTHER PROBLEMS AFFECTING CHOICE OF MEANS

As appears from the *de facto* merger cases, the choice of means may be affected by the desire to avoid the formality of a stockholders' meeting or the drain of the cash payments entailed by appraisal rights. There are various other considerations that affect this choice which will be sketched briefly below. The area is so complex that its thorough analysis belongs more properly in an advanced course, in particular one that can blend a treatment of tax problems together with corporate matters.

(1) **Liability Problems.** Suppose that A Corporation is obligated on certain guarantees as to the performance of equipment it has sold which are potentially very great in amount but which are hard to assign a present value in probabilistic terms. B Corporation might reasonably be wary of assuming these liabilities. Different consequences would follow from the use of different routes. A statutory merger would make the combined AB Corporation and all of the assets, whether formerly A's or B's, liable to execution for A's or B's old debts. If the method used is such that A continues as a separate entity with its old assets, although under B's control, then the liability usually continues to attach only to A's assets. Some rather more difficult problems occur if A Corporation sells its assets to B. As a matter of general theory it would seem that A Corporation would continue to be liable and B Corporation would not be. But this poses problems in the real world. A Corporation is apt to be liquidated. Some safeguards are provided by the liquidation provisions of corporation law (8 Del.C. §§ 275, 278–282). These are likely to be inadequate, particularly in the case of claims that are unknown at the time of liquidation. Thus old creditors of A Corporation will wish to pursue B. They can attempt various approaches. For one, the provisions of the Uniform Fraudulent Conveyances Act would cover a transfer made without equivalent consideration. Failure to comply with the bulk sales rules in Article 6 of the Uniform Commercial Code may provide an opening. They can argue a de facto merger along the lines of the Glen Alden case, an argument that would usually be attractive only in the case of an assets for stock situation. Various courts have gone further than this. In products liability cases courts have tended to hold B Corporation liable where it holds itself out as a successor to A Corporation, producing the

same equipment at the same plant with the same personnel—regardless of the form of succession.[14]

These considerations operate in reverse when it is a question of keeping the benefit of a desirable contract—a patent license, etc. In such a case merging into the favored corporation seems the right choice. Of course, the other party may be very unhappy about the change in its obligations brought about by a merger. To take an *expansio ad absurdum,* suppose that a sparkplug company had signed a contract to supply the requirements of a little firm making 500 beachbuggies a year and now discovers that Chrysler has merged "into" that firm. Obviously a court would tend to relieve it of its obligations thereunder.

(2) Minority Interests. Certain types of transactions produce a situation in which the acquiror may be faced with a contentious and objectionable minority. If B Corporation acquires 75% of the stock of A Corporation it faces a captive 25% minority interest in what is now its subsidiary. This sets the stage for controversies about inter-corporate transactions such as those in Chelrob v. Barrett.[15] If there is a statutory merger B winds up with a substantial minority of former A shareholders who, if they form a cohesive bloc, may cause trouble for the B management.

(3) Federal Securities Regulation. If the corporations involved come up to the relevant jurisdictional yardsticks, the Securities Exchange Act of 1934 or the Securities Act of 1933 may apply in one or more of the following ways:

(a) A merger normally calls for the approval of the shareholders, which can only be obtained by proxy solicitation that must comply with section 14 of the 1934 Act and the regulations thereunder. Other shareholder approvals—for charter amendments, sales of assets etc. likewise must be solicited by materials which provide the data called for in the regulations.

(b) Purchases of stock will commonly require compliance with the "tender offer" provisions of Section 13(d) and 14(d)–(f) added by the Williams Act to the 1934 Act. See Section 2 below.

(c) The amalgamating transaction may qualify as a "purchase" or a "sale" in such a way as to trigger liabilities under Section 16(b) of the Exchange Act on the part of statutory insiders if they are responsible for matchable transactions. This matter is complicated by the existence of SEC Rule 16b–7 which exempts some transactions, those involving the existing 85% ownership of one corporation by another, and thus implies that in general a merger involves a purchase of one

---

14. See Turner v. Bituminous Cas. Co., 397 Mich. 406, 244 N.W.2d 873 (1976); Cyr v. B. Offen & Co., Inc., 501 F.2d 1145 (1st Cir.1974); Conn v. Fales Division of Mathewson Corp., 835 F.2d 145 (6th Cir.1987); Juenger & Schulman, Assets Sales and Products Liability, 22 Wayne L.Rev. 39 (1975).

15. P. 248 supra.

security and the sale of another. The case law has taken a pragmatic view of such " 'unorthodox' transactions." It has sought to distinguish among different types of mergers according to the degree of likelihood that inside information will be abused. In particular, the courts have been dismayed at the thought that a rigid classification of mergers as sale-purchases would enable the management of the target company to entrap an unsuccessful tender offeror into an involuntary sale. Thus if R Corporation bought 20% of the stock of Target, Inc. and Target, Inc., over R's objection, merged into Z, it would seem harsh to compel R to forfeit to Target–Z all of the gains on its 20%.[16]

(d) Liabilities under Rule 10b–5 for trading on inside information can crop up in any of these types of transformation; the plaintiff must, inter alia, prove that any loss was connected with a "purchase" or "sale" and that defendant was under a duty not to use the data. Since 1980 Rule 14e–3 bans use of inside data coming from issuer or offeror. P. 563 supra.

(e) The 1933 Act may cover the merger. If the transaction takes the form of an offer to corporation X's stockholders to exchange their stock of corporation X for that of corporation Y, the offer of Y's stock would be an offer to sell a security and may have to comply with the registration and prospectus provisions. Furthermore, the 1933 Act has been ruled by the SEC to extend to occasions, such as a merger, at which there is submitted to security holders a proposal that requires such holders to elect whether or not to exchange the securities they now have for a new or different security. However, the same Rule 145 that so defines the terms "sale" and "offer to sell" also provides that registration under the Securities Act may be effectuated by complying with the informational requirements of the proxy rules under the 1934 Act.

(4) **Antitrust Aspects.** An acquisition of a significant firm raises questions under the Clayton Act of 1914, as fortified by the amendments of 1950. Since 1950 it has been irrelevant under the anti-merger statute which form is used so that this important aspect of mergers and other acquisitions can, with a fair degree of neatness, be left to the antitrust law course. It is through the antitrust laws that it becomes most clear that mergers and other acquisitions are not simply matters of private maneuvering but affect public policy in a very important way. However, since 1981 enforcement of antitrust policy has been much relaxed.

(5) **Taxation.** One of the most complex topics taught in law school is the taxation of mergers and acquisitions. Suffice it for present purposes to note that taxation, unlike antitrust, does have a very direct bearing on the choice between alternative acquisition routes. A basic

---

16. See, e.g., Kern County Land Co. v. Occidental Petroleum Corp., 411 U.S. 582, 93 S.Ct. 1736, 36 L.Ed.2d 503 (1973); American Standard, Inc. v. Crane Co., 510 F.2d 1043 (2d Cir.1974). Note that similar anal-ysis would seem to apply to a situation in which Corporation S sold its assets to Corporation X for X's stock and then liquidated, distributing the X stock to its shareholders.

question is whether the transaction can be fitted into one of the tax free categories of mergers described in the Internal Revenue Code. Note that some tax materials sometimes use the term "merger" more sweepingly than the Delaware or other corporation laws. More commonly, they refer to "reorganizations," again in a way that does not quite match corporate terminology.

The seller is apt to push in the direction of fashioning the deal so as to qualify as a type A, B or C merger so as to spare taxes; the acquirer on the other hand will prefer a transaction in which the transferor's gains are recognized and the acquirer has a new and higher basis. This divergence of interests injects into the negotiations a factor that can be traded off for a higher (or lower) price or other concessions. These issues are developed extensively in courses on advanced taxation and business planning.

Meanwhile, sales and stamp tax costs may be an appreciable factor in the economics of a proposed transaction.

(6) **Accounting Aspects.** Of late, a considerable amount of attention has been focused on accounting for mergers. Again the issues are too complex for explanation here and the most we can do is indicate the nature of the questions. The chief controversies have centered around the differences between "purchase" and "pooling" accounting treatment. If Corporation A buys the assets of Corporation B for cash, A will, plainly, carry those assets on its books at the amount of cash it laid out. The same would seem to follow if A issues shares of its stock (noting the valuation problems we have seen in connection with such cases as See v. Heppenheimer, p. 143 supra). On the other hand, if A and B amalgamate through an ordinary merger they are treated as if they were now one bigger corporation in the shoes of its predecessors; their asset accounts are "pooled" at the previous cost-based figures and the earned surplus accounts will also be "pooled" (subject to legal rules about the capital stock accounts needed to reflect the amount of stock issued to effect the merger). The subsequent performance of the new firm's earnings will obviously be affected by the difference between the depreciation required to amortize the old or new cost figures—if, in fact, amortization is permissible, and it may not be as to intangible assets. The difference between accounts set up on a purchase and on a pooling basis may be very substantial and the difference may have much to do with whether the transaction will go through. The matter has been complicated by the acceptance by the accounting profession of the idea that some transactions that formally are purchases are really poolings of interest (shades of Farris v. Glen Alden Corp.). The inability of the profession to fix upon lines of definition between the two concepts that can be easily defended by accountants in concrete cases has much befuddled the issue.[17]

17. See Fiflis, Accounting for Mergers, Acquisitions and Investments, in a Nutshell, 37 Bus.Law. 89 (1981).

NOTE ON TECHNIQUES OF RESISTING TAKEOVER

(1) A management that gets the message that a takeover is in the wind must carefully consider its response. It may decide to acquiesce in the operation. If the members of the management are also holders of its stock they may find that the price is right. Management of a family enterprise may be aging or the second generation may be interested in doing something else and the offer may be positively attractive. In their role as managers, the incumbents may feel that they are as good as the takers-over and will survive in the struggle to get to the top of the combined enterprise. They may look with eagerness for a chance to expand their horizons, to be able to play for higher stakes with bigger chips. The legal and ethical problems enter when the advantages that lead managements to accept or further the take-over are not shared with the stockholders, their beneficiaries. You will recall the Perlman v. Feldmann [18] problem. Less obvious possibilities for abuse arise when the management is given guarantys of employment for the future in the new enterprise or a handsome retirement allocation; it will often be hard to determine whether their emoluments represent anything more than a fair market price for those services.

(2) On the other hand, management may experience a strong negative reaction. That feeling may stem from (a) fear for their positions, (b) a sense that these arrangements are such that their own stockholdings would lose value or, (c) a sense that the strategy which they have created for "their" enterprise would be discarded and something repulsive put in its stead. Such perceptions may be right or wrong, strong or weak, unanimously held or subject to controversy. If management is moved to act on those perceptions, it will, of course, advise its stockholders not to accept the offer. It might also consider other modes of resistance.

(a) The management may buy up shares of its own corporation. This has several effects: it puts shares of stock into hands friendly to existing management and out of the hands of the "enemy" and it drives up the price which the raider will have to pay. Management may buy shares with its own resources, including borrowed funds. It may also use the corporation's treasury. Such actions are subject to financial limitations and to fiduciary restraints explored at pp. 676–683 supra. The ultimate use of management's purchasing power is to buy out the wielder of the threat itself, as was done in Polk v. Good, p. 679 supra, thus ending the threat (through what has come to be known as "greenmail").

(b) Management may cause the corporation to issue and sell new shares. Lodged in friendly hands, these shares will support management; at the least, the opposition will have to spend more money acquiring the desired proportion of the corporation's stock. Recall the

18. See p. 618 supra.

problems, such as preemptive and fiduciary restraints, of these activities referred to at pp. 642, 652 supra. The effectiveness of such issuance can be enhanced by attaching special voting privileges and other unusual rights that come to exist in the face of a takeover offer. These are "poison pills."

(c) Management has the advantage of controlling the proxy machinery. The inertial power of being the incumbents plus the power to spend money from the corporate treasury in soliciting proxies (see p. 433 supra) is the equivalent of the ownership of a large block of shares. That inertial power might also be enhanced, if the incumbents are forehanded enough, by such devices as a staggered board of directors or a requirement in the articles of incorporation that mergers and other major changes be approved by large majority votes of the stockholders. The term "shark repellent" is attached to these arrangements.

(d) Management may make commitments that will render the proposed take over impossible or undesirable. A target corporation might enter into a line of business in competition with the threatening firm so that it would then be able to say that a merger between the target firm and the aggressor would violate the anti-merger provisions of the Clayton Act. Long-term commitments for the purchase of the firm's supplies or the sale of its products might frustrate the purpose of the intended take over. Of course, such arrangements might be subject to attack if they could be shown not to have a significant motivation in terms of the prosperity of the corporation.

(e) Management could arrange for a merger with some other corporation which it happened to prefer. This would create a new enterprise that would be bigger and more difficult to gain control over. It might be engaged in a line of business that was so parallel to the acquiror's as to create antitrust problems as mentioned in (d) above. It might even create some risk of the seller's being entrapped in a Section 16(b) violation though the case law has not favored this idea. P. 700 supra.

(f) Management may resort to the courts. Even if it is not ultimately successful there its action may take so much time or cost so much money as to discourage the prospective suitor. The causes of action that might be asserted would include violations of the Clayton Act, violations of the tender offer requirements of the Williams Act, violations of other provisions of the securities laws, including Rule 10b–5, and the proxy rules.

Resort to any of these devices by target management raises issues about its compatability with their fiduciary duties. The problem has two prongs. First, directors and officers are "interested" in a real sense whenever their incumbency is threatened. This is true even if they have arranged for themselves "golden parachutes" which will make their situation in case of a takeover as financially comfortable as if the status quo continued—a device justified as enabling them to make decisions with detachment. Second, if shareholder-wealth-maximization is the overriding goal for a corporation, how can they resist a substantial premium for those shareholders? Thus there are some who would say that managers may never take action for the purpose of resisting a proposed takeover but should remain entirely neutral. Others would allow management the right to help shareholders make the best possible bargain. On this theory managers should give the shareholders the best possible insight into the alternatives and may, if they see advantage to it, invite a "white knight" to make a better bid for the firm's assets. The argument against this activity is that raiders will be discouraged from making the best possible bids for corporations if they know that others may get a free ride on their research into the target company and then outbid them. Still others would say that management is free to use its judgment in deciding whether the offer is the best possible solution, taking into account both shareholder wealth maximization and the interests of the workforce, the community, etc. If we were to pursue in detail each of the methods we outline below we would come to see that each represents somewhat different risks of injury to shareholder interests and that some may have positive contributions to corporate welfare.

3. Takeovers and Tender Offers

We now proceed to survey the field of takeovers in general, first raising some general economic and political issues before we look at tender offer legislation in particular. Takeovers tend to come in waves. Historians identify the first as coming around the end of the 19th century. It involved the consolidation of relatively small businesses of a local bent into much larger national industries. Several achieved near-monopoly postures. The Standard Oil, American Tobacco and U.S. Steel mergers were among the impressive outcomes. The paper merger that failed in See v. Heppenheimer, p. 143 supra, reminds one that there were failures too. These mergers aroused political opposition which was reflected in the first proceedings under Section 2 of the Sherman Act and, after the wave had subsided, the antimerger provisions of the Clayton Act of 1914 (15 U.S.C.A. § 18). The next wave came in the 1920's and tended to bring about the creation of countervailing second and third firms in fields where the first wave had created leaders. The Bethlehem and Republic steel firms, for example, balanced out against U.S. Steel. It turned out that the Clayton Act had mechanical problems which the courts were unwilling to help with. The third wave came in the 1960's and its thrust was to some extent dictated by the antitrust laws which had been strengthened by the Celler–Kefauver Amendment to the Clayton Act in 1950 and were enforced with some rigor. The acquisition thrust tended to go in the direction of conglomerate acquisitions which since they did not enhance market control within a market were not deemed to violate the Clayton

Act. The value of these acquisitions was thought to lie in the fact that they enabled expert managers to bring their talents to bear on unrelated types of businesses (along with access to funds). The idea that there was an undifferentiated ability to manage always aroused some skepticism. There are a good many instances in which those acquisitions were undone, though often at a profit.[19]

A new wave began in the 1970's that is a bit hard to categorize, perhaps because we do not have enough distance from it. The motivation now seems to have been the profit that raiders perceived that they could make because of discrepancies between the market value of securities and the underlying value of the assets they represented. Why there were such "premia" is open to dispute. It is widely asserted that they represented perceptions that the incumbent managements were inefficient, that is, unable to make the most effective use of the assets they managed. Other explanations included references to the existence of considerable inflation which, those theorists asserted, was not adequately taken into account in pricing stock. This explanation, incidentally, flies in the face of some versions of efficient market theory. Whatever the reason, takeover entrepreneurs were able to offer truly phenomenal prices to the shareholders of their targets, offers that they often felt they could not refuse. In 1985 the total capital stock of the companies subject to tender offers came to some $180 billion (up from $12 billion in 1975). The actual or potential presence of tender offers set the tone for all stock market activities and a statutory proposal to abolish the income tax deduction for indebtedness incurred in connection with takeovers was asserted to be a significant factor in the stock market break of October 1987. In turn that development in the securities market unsettled the takeover market. It is too early to judge how much it will do to change the calculations of acquiring firms; of course transactions then under way were drastically affected by the general price declines and some proved to be losers. But a few months later one found offers beginning to revive, including but not limited to offers by foreigners who found the lower prices in dollars coupled with lower prices for the dollar itself made American acquisitions seem highly attractive.

The observer notices that these waves of acquisitions have evolved in terms of the methods employed. Before the 1970's most acquisitions were through mergers or asset acquisitions. As you have observed, these required the consent and cooperation of the target's management. Once in a while a program of stock acquisition plus a proxy fight was attempted as in the case of Wolfson v. Avery, p. 374 supra. In the 1960's tender offers to public shareholders became more frequent to the point that they were regulated by the Williams Act, discussed below. 1975 is often given as the date of the first hostile takeover—that of International Nickel, or at least the first one in which a respectable

19. Porter, From Competitive Advantage to Corporate Strategy, Harv.Bus.Rev., May–June 1987, p. 43.

investment banking firm took part. Hostile takeovers became increasingly frequent. Of course, the prospect of a hostile takeover makes management much more anxious than the possibility that somebody will come along with an attractive offer that they can either accept or reject. The hostile takeover brought into the game a number of actors independent of the two corporations' managements. It became necessary to have an investment banking firm handle the matter from the acquirer's point of view. That firm would give advice about tactics and pricing, would help in acquiring the shares and in the later part of the period would even provide some of the financing needed (or at least assist in organizing the financing by others). The target firm would need to have advice about the acceptability of the offer (recall the suggestion in Smith v. Van Gorkom, p. 212 supra, that the failure to get such advice amounted to negligence). Both sides would need large teams of lawyers to advise and arrange and, if necessary, to litigate. Meanwhile arbitrageurs developed, that is, persons who would buy the stock of target firms either after the offer was announced or anticipation of such an offer. All of these actors had an interest in encouraging takeovers and thus were prone to suggest to potential offerors where they could find good targets. They were also very involved with inside information of great potential effect on securities prices and sometimes slipped over the line in terms of the applicable laws. See pp. 587–588.

In the midst of all this excitement and publicity what was happening to the public interest? One version was that all was well, that acquisitions could not happen unless the buyers knew they would be able to manage better than the incumbents for otherwise they could not offer the handsome premia that it would take to dislodge the shares from the public. Even when the raiders broke up the firm's assets, chopped the working force and reduced the scale of operations, they were said to be doing a necessary, if unpleasant, job of restructuring. Critics assailed this position. They said that the interests of groups other than shareholders were being disregarded in the process; they pointed to workers, communities and consumers as sufferers in the process. Others noted that the time framework within which shareholders made decisions was very short. Thus managers were forced to worry about the next quarterly financial statements and were unable to make the investments in research, development and plant modernization that competition with foreign firms required. Some noted that when the decline of the dollar made exporting more profitable many American firms had so cut their manufacturing facilities that they were unable to take advantage of the new opportunities. Indeed the whole looming presence of potential takeovers distracted managements from their real job of managing their assets. Nowhere was this clearer than in the case of the Texaco versus Pennzoil battle over Getty Oil, a battle which caused the combined market value of the two firms' securities to decline since the assets of neither were being optimally managed. Another byproduct of the takeover wave was the increasing tendency to substitute debt for equity in financial structures. Much of the cost of acquiring firms was paid for by issuing bonds, "junk bonds" as they came to be known. It was thought that this practice creates financial structures that are top-heavy with debt and hence are vulnerable if the firm experiences a stretch of adversity.

All of these considerations make takeovers a matter of more than private interest and there have been agitations since 1968 going on to the present for statutory intervention at the state or federal level. Most of these have been directed at the tender offer mechanism and are billed as being designed to protect shareholders. They do however at times show signs of being inspired by the interests of managers and occasionally openly say that they allow managers to take non shareholder wealth maximizing interests into account.

We thus turn to the Williams Act, the presently governing federal law on tender offers. It added sections 13(d)–(e) and 14(d)–(f) to the Exchange Act. You should first examine those sections. In general they are in harmony with the disclosure philosophy characterizing the 1933 and 1934 Acts. The following aspects of the Williams Act should be taken into account.

(a) The Act does not define a tender offer. The courts and the Commission have wrestled with the definitional problem, bearing in mind that the coercive pressures that the Act seeks to counteract occur only when there are a fair number of offerees who find it difficult to coordinate their response. There is some analogy to the concept of public offer under the Securities Act of 1933 in respect of sales but the analogy should not be pushed too far. One major case, Hanson Trust PLC v. SCM Corp., 774 F.2d 47 (2d Cir.1985), said that there was no tender offer when Hanson made 5 privately negotiated purchases and one on the open market—the sellers being sophisticated and the premium small. The related question is whether private purchases are so factually linked with the public offer that they come under the Act.

(b) The Act imposes disclosure obligations on the person or persons making the offer, including filing with the SEC. These obligations come into play, generally, once 5% of the equity security in question has been purchased (compare the requirements of § 16(a) of the Exchange Act, p. 551 supra. There are of course questions of fact about what aggregations of individual holdings are to be counted as being held together.

(c) Section 14(e) of the Act outlaws falsehoods, misleading statements or deceptive or manipulative acts by any person in connection with the offer, or with any solicitation in opposition to the tender, as by a rival bidder or by target management resisting displacement. However, it has been held that no private right of action in favor of a tender offeror claiming to be frustrated arises from Section 14(e), the court reasoning that "the sole purpose of the Williams Act was the protection of investors confronted with a tender offer." [20] The Supreme Court has

---

20. Piper v. Chris–Craft Industries, Inc., 430 U.S. 1, 97 S.Ct. 926, 51 L.Ed.2d 124 (1977). Compare Rondeau v. Mosinee Paper Corp., 422 U.S. 49, 95 S.Ct. 2069, 45

also held that the term " 'manipulative acts' under § 14(e) requires misrepresentation or nondisclosures"; this was in the context of an allegation that target management had colluded with the offeror to substitute for the first tender offer a second one less advantageous to the shareholders, though better for management.[21]

We now consider the leading Supreme Court case on the relationship of the Williams Act to the legislation which the states passed dealing with tender offers. It is the second of two, dealing with somewhat different statutes.

CTS CORPORATION v. DYNAMICS CORPORATION OF AMERICA

Supreme Court of the United States, 1987.
___ U.S. ___, 107 S.Ct. 1637, 95 L.Ed.2d 67.

[In 1986 Indiana enacted a corporation law revision including a Control Share Acquisition Chapter. It applied to any corporation incorporated in Indiana unless it amended its articles of incorporation or bylaws to opt out. It applied only to "issuing public corporations" defined as businesses incorporated in Indiana and having (1) two or more shareholders, (2) its principal place of business, principal office or substantial assets in Indiana and (3) more than 10% of its shares owned by Indiana residents or more than 10,000 Indiana shareholders. The Act focuses on the acquisition of "control shares" in such a corporation. An entity acquires control shares if it acquires shares that would bring its voting power to or above any of three thresholds—20%, 33⅓% or 50%. It would gain the voting rights for those shares only "to the extent granted by resolution approved by the shareholders of the issuing public corporation." That involves a majority vote of the disinterested shareholders holding each class of stock. The acquiror can require the holding of a special meeting within 50 days by filing a statement and agreeing to pay the meeting expenses. If shareholders do not vote to restore voting rights to the control shares they may be redeemed by the corporation at fair market value.

On March 10, 1986 Dynamics Corporation of America (Dynamics) owned 9.6% of the common stock of CTS Corporation, an Indiana corporation. On that day Dynamics announced a tender offer for another million CTS shares that would have brought its ownership up to 27.5%. On the same day it filed a suit in the U.S. District Court for the Northern District of Illinois alleging securities laws violations by CTS. On March 27, the CTS directors elected to be governed by the Indiana Act and on March 31, Dynamics amended its complaint to allege that the Act was pre-empted by the Williams Act and violated the Commerce Clause. The District Court ruled in favor of Dynamics and the Court of Appeals affirmed. The Supreme Court noted probable jurisdiction and in an opinion by JUSTICE POWELL affirmed.]

The first question in this case is whether the Williams Act preempts the Indiana Act. As we have stated frequently, absent an

L.Ed.2d 12 (1975), denying injunctive relief for failure of offeror to comply with Act, where irreparable injury was not shown.

21. Schreiber v. Burlington Northern, Inc., 472 U.S. 1, 105 S.Ct. 2458, 86 L.Ed.2d 1 (1985).

explicit indication by Congress of an intent to pre-empt state law, a state statute is pre-empted only

> " 'where compliance with both federal and state regulations is a physical impossibility . . .,' Florida Lime & Avocado Growers, Inc. v. Paul, 373 U.S. 132, 142–143 [83 S.Ct. 1210, 1217, 10 L.Ed.2d 248] (1963), or where the state 'law stands as an obstacle to the accomplishment and execution of the full purposes and objectives of Congress.' Hines v. Davidowitz, 312 U.S. 52, 67 [61 S.Ct. 399, 404, 85 L.Ed. 581] (1941). . . ."
> Ray v. Atlantic Richfield Co., 435 U.S. 151, 158, 98 S.Ct. 988, 994, 55 L.Ed.2d 179 (1978).

Because it is entirely possible for entities to comply with both the Williams Act and the Indiana Act, the state statute can be pre-empted only if it frustrates the purposes of the federal law.

A

Our discussion begins with a brief summary of the structure and purposes of the Williams Act. Congress passed the Williams Act in 1968 in response to the increasing number of hostile tender offers. Before its passage, these transactions were not covered by the disclosure requirements of the federal securities laws. See Piper v. Chris–Craft Industries, Inc., 430 U.S. 1, 22, 97 S.Ct. 926, 939–940, 51 L.Ed.2d 124 (1977). The Williams Act, backed by regulations of the Securities and Exchange Commission (SEC), imposes requirements in two basic areas. First, it requires the offeror to file a statement disclosing information about the offer, including: the offeror's background and identity; the source and amount of the funds to be used in making the purchase; the purpose of the purchase, including any plans to liquidate the company or make major changes in its corporate structure; and the extent of the offeror's holdings in the target company.

Second, the Williams Act, and the regulations that accompany it, establish procedural rules to govern tender offers. For example, stockholders who tender their shares may withdraw them during the first 15 business days of the tender offer and, if the offeror has not purchased their shares, any time after 60 days from commencement of the offer. 15 U.S.C. § 78n(d)(5); 17 CFR § 240.14d–7(a)(1) (1986). The offer must remain open for at least 20 business days. 17 CFR § 240.14e–1(a) (1986). If more shares are tendered than the offeror sought to purchase, purchases must be made on a pro rata basis from each tendering shareholder. 15 U.S.C. § 78n(d)(6); 17 CFR § 240.14(8) (1986). Finally, the offeror must pay the same price for all purchases; if the offering price is increased before the end of the offer, those who already have tendered must receive the benefit of the increased price. § 78n(d)(7).

B

The Indiana Act differs in major respects from the Illinois statute that the Court considered in Edgar v. MITE Corp., 457 U.S. 624, 102 S.Ct. 2629, 73 L.Ed.2d 269 (1982). After reviewing the legislative history of the Williams Act, Justice White, joined by Chief Justice Burger and Justice Blackmun (the plurality), concluded that the Williams Act struck a careful balance between the interests of offerors and target companies, and that any state statute that "upset" this balance was pre-empted. Id., at 632–634, 102 S.Ct., at 2635–2636.

The plurality then identified three offending features of the Illinois statute. Justice White's opinion first noted that the Illinois statute provided for a 20–day precommencement period. During this time, management could disseminate its views on the upcoming offer to shareholders, but offerors could not publish their offers. The plurality found that this provision gave management "a powerful tool to combat tender offers." Id., at 635, 102 S.Ct., at 2637. This contrasted dramatically with the Williams Act; Congress had deleted express precommencement notice provisions from the Williams Act. According to the plurality, Congress had determined that the potentially adverse consequences of such a provision on shareholders should be avoided. Thus, the plurality concluded that the Illinois provision "frustrate[d] the objectives of the Williams Act." Ibid. The second criticized feature of the Illinois statute was a provision for a hearing on a tender offer that, because it set no deadline, allowed management " 'to stymie indefinitely a takeover,' " id., at 637, 102 S.Ct., at 2638 (quoting MITE Corp. v. Dixon, 633 F.2d 486, 494 (CA7 1980)). The plurality noted that " 'delay can seriously impede a tender offer,' " 457 U.S., at 637, 102 S.Ct., at 2638 (quoting Great Western United Corp. v. Kidwell, 577 F.2d 1256, 1277 (CA5 1978) (per Wisdom, J.)), and that "Congress anticipated that investors and the takeover offeror would be free to go forward without unreasonable delay," 457 U.S., at 639, 102 S.Ct., at 2639. Accordingly, the plurality concluded that this provision conflicted with the Williams Act. The third troublesome feature of the Illinois statute was its requirement that the fairness of tender offers would be reviewed by the Illinois Secretary of State. Noting that "Congress intended for investors to be free to make their own decisions," the plurality concluded that " '[t]he state thus offers investor protection at the expense of investor autonomy—an approach quite in conflict with that adopted by Congress.' " Id., at 639–640, 102 S.Ct., at 2639 (quoting MITE Corp. v. Dixon, supra, at 494).

C

As the plurality opinion in MITE did not represent the views of a majority of the Court, we are not bound by its reasoning. We need not question that reasoning, however, because we believe the Indiana Act passes muster even under the broad interpretation of the Williams Act articulated by Justice White in MITE. As is apparent from our summary of its reasoning, the overriding concern of the MITE plurality was that the Illinois statute considered in that case operated to favor management against offerors, to the detriment of shareholders. By contrast, the statute now before the Court protects the independent shareholder against both of the contending parties. Thus, the Act furthers a basic purpose of the Williams Act, " 'plac[ing] investors on an equal footing with the takeover bidder,' " Piper v. Chris–Craft Industries, 430 U.S., at 30, 97 S.Ct., at 943 (quoting the Senate Report accompanying the Williams Act, S.Rep. No. 550, 90th Cong., 1st Sess., 4 (1967)).

The Indiana Act operates on the assumption, implicit in the Williams Act, that independent shareholders faced with tender offers often are at a disadvantage. By allowing such shareholders to vote as a group, the Act protects them from the coercive aspects of some tender offers. If, for example, shareholders believe that a successful tender offer will be followed by a purchase of nontendering shares at a depressed price, individual shareholders may tender their shares—even if they doubt the tender offer is in the corporation's best interest—to protect themselves from being forced to sell their shares at a depressed price. As the SEC explains: "The alternative of not accepting the tender offer is virtual assurance that, if the offer is successful, the shares will have to be sold in the lower priced, second step." Two–Tier Tender Offer Pricing and Non–Tender Offer Purchase Programs, SEC Exchange Act Rel. No. 21079 (June 21, 1984), [1984 Transfer Binder] CCH Fed.Sec.L.Rep. ¶ 83,637, p. 86,916 (footnote omitted) (hereinafter SEC Release No. 21079). See Lowenstein, Pruning Deadwood in Hostile Takeovers: A Proposal for Legislation, 83 Colum.L.Rev. 249, 307–309 (1983). In such a situation under the Indiana Act, the shareholders as a group, acting in the corporation's best interest, could reject the offer, although individual shareholders might be inclined to accept it. The desire of the Indiana Legislature to protect shareholders of Indiana corporations from this type of coercive offer does not conflict with the Williams Act. Rather, it furthers the federal policy of investor protection.

In implementing its goal, the Indiana Act avoids the problems the plurality discussed in MITE. Unlike the MITE statute, the Indiana Act does not give either management or the offeror an advantage in communicating with the shareholders about the impending offer. The Act also does not impose an indefinite delay on tender offers. Nothing in the Act prohibits an offeror from consummating an offer on the 20th business day, the earliest day permitted under applicable federal regulations, see 17 CFR § 240.14e–1(a) (1986). Nor does the Act allow the state government to interpose its views of fairness between willing buyers and sellers of shares of the target company. Rather, the Act allows shareholders to evaluate the fairness of the offer collectively.

D

The Court of Appeals based its finding of pre-emption on its view that the practical effect of the Indiana Act is to delay consummation of tender offers until 50 days after the commencement of the offer. 794 F.2d, at 263. As did the Court of Appeals, Dynamics reasons that no rational offeror will purchase shares until it gains assurance that those shares will carry voting rights. Because it is possible that voting rights will not be conferred until a shareholder meeting 50 days after commencement of the offer, Dynamics concludes that the Act imposes a 50–day delay. This, it argues, conflicts with the shorter 20–business-day period established by the SEC as the minimum period for which a tender offer may be held open. 17 CFR § 240.14e–1 (1986). We find the alleged conflict illusory.

The Act does not impose an absolute 50–day delay on tender offers, nor does it preclude an offeror from purchasing shares as soon as federal law permits. If the offeror fears an adverse shareholder vote under the Act, it can make a conditional tender offer, offering to accept shares on the condition that the shares receive voting rights within a certain period of time. The Williams Act permits tender offers to be conditioned on the offeror's subsequently obtaining regulatory approval. There is no reason to doubt that this type of conditional tender offer would be legitimate as well.

Even assuming that the Indiana Act imposes some additional delay, nothing in *MITE* suggested that *any* delay imposed by state regulation, however short, would create a conflict with the Williams Act. The plurality argued only that the offeror should "be free to go forward without *unreasonable* delay." 457 U.S., at 639, 102 S.Ct., at 2639 (emphasis added). In that case, the Court was confronted with the potential for indefinite delay and presented with no persuasive reason why some deadline could not be established. By contrast, the Indiana Act provides that full voting rights will be vested—if this eventually is to occur—within 50 days after commencement of the offer. This period is within the 60–day maximum period Congress established for tender offers in 15 U.S.C. § 78n(d)(5). We cannot say that a delay within that congressionally determined period is unreasonable.

Finally, we note that the Williams Act would pre-empt a variety of state corporate laws of hitherto unquestioned validity if it were construed to pre-empt any state statute that may limit or delay the free exercise of power after a successful tender offer. State corporate laws commonly permit corporations to stagger the terms of their directors.

By staggering the terms of directors, and thus having annual elections for only one class of directors each year, corporations may delay the time when a successful offeror gains control of the board of directors. Similarly, state corporation laws commonly provide for cumulative voting. By enabling minority shareholders to assure themselves of representation in each class of directors, cumulative voting provisions can delay further the ability of offerors to gain untrammeled authority over the affairs of the target corporation.

In our view, the possibility that the Indiana Act will delay some tender offers is insufficient to require a conclusion that the Williams Act pre-empts the Act. The longstanding prevalence of state regulation in this area suggests that, if Congress had intended to pre-empt all state laws that delay the acquisition of voting control following a tender offer, it would have said so explicitly. The regulatory conditions that the Act places on tender offers are consistent with the text and the purposes of the Williams Act. Accordingly, we hold that the Williams Act does not pre-empt the Indiana Act.

III

As an alternative basis for its decision, the Court of Appeals held that the Act violates the Commerce Clause of the Federal Constitution. We now address this holding. On its face, the Commerce Clause is nothing more than a grant to Congress of the power "[t]o regulate Commerce . . . among the several States . . .," Art. I, § 8, cl. 3. But it has been settled for more than a century that the Clause prohibits States from taking certain actions respecting interstate commerce even absent congressional action. See, e.g., Cooley v. Board of Wardens, 12 How. * 299, 13 L.Ed. 996 (1852). The Court's interpretation of "these great silences of the Constitution," H.P. Hood & Sons, Inc. v. Du Mond, 336 U.S. 525, 535, 69 S.Ct. 657, 663, 93 L.Ed. 865 (1949), has not always been easy to follow. Rather, as the volume and complexity of commerce and regulation has grown in this country, the Court has articulated a variety of tests in an attempt to describe the difference between those regulations that the Commerce Clause permits and those regulations that it prohibits.

A

The principal objects of dormant Commerce Clause scrutiny are statutes that discriminate against interstate commerce. The Indiana Act is not such a statute. It has the same effects on tender offers whether or not the offeror is a domiciliary or resident of Indiana. Thus, it "visits its effects equally upon both interstate and local business," Lewis v. BT Investment Managers, Inc., supra, 447 U.S., at 36, 100 S.Ct., at 2015.

Dynamics nevertheless contends that the statute is discriminatory because it will apply most often to out-of-state entities. This argument rests on the contention that, as a practical matter, most hostile tender offers are launched by offerors outside Indiana. But this argument avails Dynamics little. "The fact that the burden of a state regulation falls on some interstate companies does not, by itself, establish a claim of discrimination against interstate commerce." Exxon Corp. v. Governor of Maryland, 437 U.S. 117, 126, 98 S.Ct. 2207, 2214, 57 L.Ed.2d 91 (1978). Because nothing in the Indiana Act imposes a greater burden on out-of-state offerors than it does on similarly situated Indiana offerors, we reject the contention that the Act discriminates against interstate commerce.

B

This Court's recent Commerce Clause cases also have invalidated statutes that adversely may affect interstate commerce by subjecting activities to inconsistent regulations. E.g., Brown–Forman Distillers Corp. v. New York State Liquor Authority, 476 U.S. ___, ___, 106 S.Ct. 2080, ___, 90 L.Ed.2d 552 (1986); Edgar v. MITE Corp., 457 U.S., at 642, 102 S.Ct., at 2640–2641 (plurality opinion of White, J.); Kassel v. Consolidated Freightways Corp., 450 U.S. 662, 671, 101 S.Ct. 1309, 1316–1317, 67 L.Ed.2d 580 (1981) (plurality opinion of Powell, J.). The Indiana Act poses no such problem. So long as each State regulates voting rights only in the corporations it has created, each corporation will be subject to the law of only one State. No principle of corporation law and practice is more firmly established than a State's authority to regulate domestic corporations, including the authority to define the voting rights of shareholders. See Restatement (Second) of Conflict of Laws § 304 (1971) (concluding that the law of the incorporating State generally should "determine the right of a shareholder to participate in the administration of the affairs of the corporation"). Accordingly, we conclude that the Indiana Act does not create an impermissible risk of inconsistent regulation by different States.

C

The Court of Appeals did not find the Act unconstitutional for either of these threshold reasons. Rather, its decision rested on its view of the Act's potential to hinder tender offers. We think the Court of Appeals failed to appreciate the significance for Commerce Clause analysis of the fact that state regulation of corporate governance is regulation of entities whose very existence and attributes are a product of state law. As Chief Justice Marshall explained:

> "A corporation is an artificial being, invisible, intangible, and existing only in contemplation of law. Being the mere crea-

ture of law, it possesses only those properties which the charter of its creation confers upon it, either expressly, or as incidental to its very existence. These are such as are supposed best calculated to effect the object for which it was created." Trustees of Dartmouth College v. Woodward, 4 Wheat. 518, 636, 4 L.Ed. 518 (1819).

See First National Bank of Boston v. Bellotti, 435 U.S. 765, 822–824, 98 S.Ct. 1407, 1439–1441, 55 L.Ed.2d 707 (1978) (Rehnquist, J., dissenting). Every State in this country has enacted laws regulating corporate governance. By prohibiting certain transactions, and regulating others, such laws necessarily affect certain aspects of interstate commerce. This necessarily is true with respect to corporations with shareholders in States other than the State of incorporation. Large corporations that are listed on national exchanges, or even regional exchanges, will have shareholders in many States and shares that are traded frequently. The markets that facilitate this national and international participation in ownership of corporations are essential for providing capital not only for new enterprises but also for established companies that need to expand their businesses. This beneficial free market system depends at its core upon the fact that a corporation— except in the rarest situations—is organized under, and governed by, the law of a single jurisdiction, traditionally the corporate law of the State of its incorporation.

These regulatory laws may affect directly a variety of corporate transactions. Mergers are a typical example. In view of the substantial effect that a merger may have on the shareholders' interests in a corporation, many States require supermajority votes to approve mergers. By requiring a greater vote for mergers than is required for other transactions, these laws make it more difficult for corporations to merge. State laws also may provide for "dissenters' rights" under which minority shareholders who disagree with corporate decisions to take particular actions are entitled to sell their shares to the corporation at fair market value. By requiring the corporation to purchase the shares of dissenting shareholders, these laws may inhibit a corporation from engaging in the specified transactions.

It thus is an accepted part of the business landscape in this country for States to create corporations, to prescribe their powers, and to define the rights that are acquired by purchasing their shares. A State has an interest in promoting stable relationships among parties involved in the corporations it charters, as well as in ensuring that investors in such corporations have an effective voice in corporate affairs.

There can be no doubt that the Act reflects these concerns. The primary purpose of the Act is to protect the shareholders of Indiana corporations. It does this by affording shareholders, when a takeover offer is made, an opportunity to decide collectively whether the resulting change in voting control of the corporation, as they perceive it, would be desirable. A change of management may have important effects on the shareholders' interests; it is well within the State's role as overseer of corporate governance to offer this opportunity. The autonomy provided by allowing shareholders collectively to determine whether the takeover is advantageous to their interests may be especially beneficial where a hostile tender offer may coerce shareholders into tendering their shares.

Appellee Dynamics responds to this concern by arguing that the prospect of coercive tender offers is illusory, and that tender offers generally should be favored because they reallocate corporate assets into the hands of management who can use them most effectively.[22] See generally Easterbrook and Fischel, The Proper Role of a Target's Management in Responding to a Tender Offer, 94 Harv.L.Rev. 1161 (1981). As indicated supra, Indiana's concern with tender offers is not groundless. Indeed, the potentially coercive aspects of tender offers have been recognized by the Securities and Exchange Commission, see SEC Release No. 21079, p. 86,916, and by a number of scholarly commentators, see, e.g., Bradley & Rosenzweig, Defensive Stock Repurchases, 99 Harv.L.Rev. 1377, 1412–1413 (1986); Macey & McChesney, A Theoretical Analysis of Corporate Greenmail, 95 Yale L.J. 13, 20–22 (1985); Lowenstein, 83 Colum.L.Rev., at 307–309. The Constitution does not require the States to subscribe to any particular economic theory. We are not inclined "to second-guess the empirical judgments of lawmakers concerning the utility of legislation," Kassel v. Consolidated Freightways Corp., 450 U.S., at 679, 101 S.Ct., at 1321 (Brennan, J., concurring in judgment). In our view, the possibility of coercion in some takeover bids offers additional justification for Indiana's decision to promote the autonomy of independent shareholders.

Dynamics argues in any event that the State has " 'no legitimate interest in protecting the nonresident shareholders.' " Dynamics relies heavily on the statement by the MITE Court that "[i]nsofar as the . . . law burdens out-of-state transactions, there is nothing to be weighed in the balance to sustain the law." 457 U.S., at 644, 102 S.Ct., at 2641. But that comment was made in reference to an Illinois law that applied as well to out-of-state corporations as to in-state corporations. We agree that Indiana has no interest in protecting nonresident shareholders *of nonresident corporations.* But this Act applies only to corporations incorporated in Indiana. We reject the contention that Indiana has no interest in providing for the shareholders of its corporations the voting autonomy granted by the Act. Indiana has a substantial interest in preventing the corporate form from becoming a shield for unfair business dealing. Moreover, unlike the Illinois statute invalidated in MITE, the Indiana Act applies only to corporations that have a substantial number of shareholders in Indiana. See Ind.Code § 23–1–42–4(a)(3) (Supp.1986). Thus, every application of the Indiana Act will affect a substantial number of Indiana residents, whom Indiana indisputably has an interest in protecting.

D

Dynamics' argument that the Act is unconstitutional ultimately rests on its contention that the Act will limit the number of successful tender offers. There is little evidence that this will occur. But even if

---

22. It is appropriate to note when discussing the merits and demerits of tender offers that generalizations usually require qualification. No one doubts that some successful tender offers will provide more effective management or other benefits such as needed diversification. But there is no reason to assume that the type of conglomerate corporation that may result from repetitive takeovers necessarily will result is more effective management or otherwise be beneficial to shareholders. The divergent views in the literature—and even now being debated in the Congress— reflect the reality that the type and utility of tender offers vary widely. Of course, in many situations the offer to shareholders is simply a cash price substantially higher than the market price prior to the offer.

true, this result would not substantially affect our Commerce Clause analysis. We reiterate that this Act does not prohibit any entity—resident or nonresident—from offering to purchase, or from purchasing, shares in Indiana corporations, or from attempting thereby to gain control. It only provides regulatory procedures designed for the better protection of the corporations' shareholders. We have rejected the "notion that the Commerce Clause protects the particular structure or methods of operation in a . . . market." Exxon Corp. v. Governor of Maryland, 437 U.S., at 127, 98 S.Ct., at 2215. The very commodity that is traded in the securities market is one whose characteristics are defined by state law. Similarly, the very commodity that is traded in the "market for corporate control"—the corporation—is one that owes its existence and attributes to state law. Indiana need not define these commodities as other States do; it need only provide that residents and nonresidents have equal access to them. This Indiana has done. Accordingly, even if the Act should decrease the number of successful tender offers for Indiana corporations, this would not offend the Commerce Clause.

IV

On its face, the Indiana Control Share Acquisitions Chapter even-handedly determines the voting rights of shares of Indiana corporations. The Act does not conflict with the provisions or purposes of the Williams Act. To the limited extent that the Act affects interstate commerce, this is justified by the State's interests in defining the attributes of shares in its corporations and in protecting shareholders. Congress has never questioned the need for state regulation of these matters. Nor do we think such regulation offends the Constitution. Accordingly, we reverse the judgment of the Court of Appeals.

[In a concurring opinion JUSTICE SCALIA stated that he "did not share the Court's apparent high estimation of the beneficence" of the Indiana statute but said that a "law can be both economic folly and constitutional." JUSTICE WHITE wrote a dissent joined in part by JUSTICES BLACKMUN and STEVENS. He argued that the law would "effectively prevent minority shareholders in some circumstances from selling their stock to a willing tender offeror" and thus was preempted by the Williams Act. He further found that the act was designed to permit shareholders to determine whether the target company would be liquidated or removed from Indiana and thus represented a tendency toward "economic Balkanization" that was prohibited by the Commerce Clause.]

QUESTIONS

(1) Define just what the alternatives facing target corporation shareholders are and what consequences may follow. You may find it helpful to sketch this out as a decision-tree. What information does the shareholder have to possess in order to make an intelligent estimate of the risks and benefits of each alternative?

(2) In what sense did the Williams Act result in a "careful balance"? Just why did the state legislation in Edgar v. MITE Corp. upset that balance while that in CTS Corp. v. Dynamics Corp. did not? What would be the most efficacious (and constitutional law for a state to pass if it was specifically

concerned with the dismissal of workers or the closing of corporate headquarters within its jurisdiction?

(3) Is there room in tender offer litigation for some recognition of the adversary process in defining what "truth" is? For example, suppose that an offeror incorrectly summarizes some facts about the target company that are specially within the knowledge of current management, e.g., progress on its technical developments. Ought the incumbents or shareholders to be entitled to an injunctive remedy or ought the main avenue of relief to be the right of reply by informed insiders? What should be the role of predictions as to future earnings, business, etc.? Is information about the offeror or its plans for the target company at all material to shareholders who are being asked to surrender their stake in the target company for cash?

(4) Suppose that a commercial bank has for a long time had the target company as its client, in the process acquiring a great deal of information about the company. Is it free to act on behalf of the offeror? Such action might take such forms as offering analytical advice, lending money to finance purchases, acting as depositary? Would it make a difference if the bank had previously performed functions for *both* corporations? What of the role of a law firm that has been counsel for the target company—either as its general counsel or as a special consultant for its tax or antitrust problems?

Bibliography: R. Gilson, The Law and Finance of Corporate Acquisitions (1986) represents a course-length casebook treatment. A. Fleischer, Tender Offers: Defenses, Responses and Planning (1983, suppl.) and M. Lipton & E. Steinberger, Takeovers and Freezeouts (1984, with suppl.), give up-to-date practical coverage. The controversy over defensive tactics by targets is reviewed in Johnson & Siegel, Corporate Mergers: Redefining the Role of Target Directors, 136 U.Pa.L.Rev. 315 (1987). Langevoort, The Supreme Court and the Politics of Corporate Takeovers: A Comment on CTS Corp. v. Dynamics Corp. of America, 101 Harv.L.Rev. 96 (1987), reviews the state of takeover legislation. M. Salter & W. Weinhold, Merger Trends and Prospects (U.S. Dep't of Commerce, 1980) sets the historic background. There are numerous journalistic accounts of particular takeovers (such as S. Coll, The Taking of Getty Oil (1987)). There is a periodical, Mergers and Acquisitions, devoted to this topic.

---

4. Fundamental Changes and Minority Rights— Introductory

The problems of self dealing by insiders or of fairness to the shareholders that we have discussed in other contexts recur in particularly troubling form in connection with these fundamental changes. A change may be used to shift control to some party's advantage or to shift the financial benefits from one party to the other. This can be true of any of the modes of transformation. Consider the following possibilities.

1. All of a corporation's assets are sold to another corporation controlled by insiders of the seller. The transfer benefits the insiders if the sale price is not adequate.

2. A corporation is merged into another one on terms which provide that a disproportionately large share of the benefits enures to the other firm's shareholders.

3. A corporation's articles of incorporation are amended so as to permit a new issue of shares that will strengthen incumbent management's voting power.

4. A prosperous corporation is dissolved at such a time that only an inside group is in a position to continue the business and take over its assets.

5. A corporation's articles are amended so as to cut off the accumulated arrears in dividends owing to the holders of shares of cumulative preferred stock.

There are three basic lines of inquiry counsel should explore when acting for a group of shareholders feeling themselves threatened or aggrieved by a major change. Of course, approaches differ both in terms of the realities of the particular situations and of the mechanisms chosen.

(1) *Voting Protection.* Must the matter be submitted to the shareholders for approval under the provisions studied in sections 1 and 2? If so, does the protesting group have enough votes to block the step, by itself or with the aid of others to whom it can appeal? What help can they get from the proxy rules to circulate their own opposition material or to attack managements as misleading or inadequate?

(2) *Substantive Remedy.* Can we enjoin the proposed transaction (or set it aside) as substantively in violation of duties owed the shareholders? Is the relevant test fraud, unfairness or what? Is the test to be lowered because of the existence of an appraisal remedy?

(3) *Appraisal Remedy.* Does the relevant statute provide for an appraisal right in connection with the proposed transaction? If so, what steps must be taken to protect that right against waiver? What help can they get from the proxy rules in circulating their own opposition material or in attacking management's as misleading or inadequate?

-----

5. Voting Rights in Fundamental Changes

To start with voting questions, let us remember that if state law calls for a vote the federal proxy rules may cover mergers and like transactions. Indeed two of the major proxy cases, Borak and Mills, at pp. 425–428 above, are merger cases; you should reexamine them from that point of view. There is a special Item 14 in the schedule to Rule 14a which specifies what must be told the shareholders. Note that in the case of a merger—and of other transactions—proxy materials must be sent out to *two* groups of shareholders whose needs for information must be satisfied, although it is possible to do it in one document.

TSC INDUSTRIES, INC. v. NORTHWAY, INC.

Supreme Court of the United States, 1976.
426 U.S. 438, 96 S.Ct. 2126, 48 L.Ed.2d 757.

[In early 1969 National Industries, Inc. (National) bought 34% of the voting securities of TSC Industries, Inc. (TSC) from TSC's founder and his family. In October 1969 the boards of the two companies approved a proposal to sell all TSC's assets to National in return for National securities and then to liquidate TSC and distribute those securities to the TSC shareholders. The proxy solicitation for shareholder approval succeeded and the plan was carried out. Northway, a TSC shareholder, began an action against TSC and National, claiming violation of the proxy rules. When Northway moved for summary judgment on defendants' liability, the district court denied the judgment but granted leave to appeal. The Court of Appeals for the Seventh Circuit reversed, holding some omissions of fact were material as a matter of law. The Supreme Court granted certiorari and reversed the Court of Appeals in an opinion written by MR. JUSTICE MARSHALL.

The opinion first expresses a general philosophy about "materiality," a portion of which follows:]

In formulating a standard of materiality under Rule 14a–9, we are guided, of course, by the recognition in *Borak* and *Mills* of the Rule's broad remedial purpose. That purpose is not merely to ensure by judicial means that the transaction, when judged by its real terms, is fair and otherwise adequate, but to ensure disclosures by corporate management in order to enable the shareholders to make an informed choice. See *Mills*, supra, at 381, 90 S.Ct., at 620. As an abstract proposition, the most desirable role for a court in a suit of this sort, coming after the consummation of the proposed transaction, would perhaps be to determine whether in fact the proposal would have been favored by the shareholders and consummated in the absence of any misstatement or omission. But as we recognized in *Mills*, supra, at 382, n. 5, 90 S.Ct., at 620, such matters are not subject to determination with certainty. Doubts as to the critical nature of information misstated or omitted will be commonplace. And particularly in view of the prophylactic purpose of the Rule and the fact that the content of the proxy statement is within management's control, it is appropriate that these doubts be resolved in favor of those the statute is designed to protect. *Mills*, supra, at 385, 90 S.Ct., at 622.

We are aware, however, that the disclosure policy embodied in the proxy regulations is not without limit. See id., at 384, 90 S.Ct., at 621. Some information is of such dubious significance that insistence on its disclosure may accomplish more harm than good. The potential liability for a Rule 14a–9 violation can be great indeed, and if the standard of materiality is unnecessarily low, not only may the corporation and its management be subjected to liability for insignificant omissions or misstatements, but also management's fear of exposing itself to substantial liability may cause it simply to bury the shareholder in an avalanche of trivial information—a result that is hardly conducive to informed decisionmaking. Precisely these dangers are presented, we think, by the definition of a material fact adopted by the Court of Appeals in this case—a fact which a reasonable shareholder *might* consider important. . . .

The general standard of materiality that we think best comports with the policies of Rule 14a–9 is as follows: an omitted fact is material if there is a substantial likelihood that a reasonable shareholder would consider it important in deciding how to vote. This standard is fully consistent with *Mills* general description of materiality as a requirement that "the defect have a significant *propensity* to affect the voting process." It does not require proof of a substantial likelihood that disclosure of the omitted fact would have caused the reasonable investor to change his vote. What the standard does contemplate is a showing of a substantial likelihood that, under all the circumstances, the omitted fact would have assumed actual significance in the deliberations of the reasonable shareholder. Put another way, there must be a substantial likelihood that the disclosure of the omitted fact would have been viewed by the reasonable investor as having significantly altered the "total mix" of information made available.

The issue of materiality may be characterized as a mixed question of law and fact, involving as it does the application of a legal standard to a particular set of facts. In considering whether summary judgment on the issue is appropriate, we must bear in mind that the underlying objective facts, which will often be free from dispute, are merely the starting point for the ultimate determination of materiality. The determination requires delicate assessments of the inferences a "reasonable shareholder" would draw from a given set of facts and the significance of those inferences to him, and these assessments are peculiarly ones for the trier of fact. Only if the established omissions are "so obviously important to an investor, that reasonable minds cannot differ on the question of materiality" is the ultimate issue of materiality appropriately resolved "as a matter of law" by summary judgment.

[The opinion then discusses the specific claims as to omissions in the proxy material. The first one involved National's control of TSC. While the proxy statement revealed National's 34% ownership and the fact that five of ten TSC directors were National nominees, it did not point out that the chairman of TSC's board was president of National and the chairman of TSC's executive committee was National's executive vice president. The Court found that it could not say that these additional facts were material as a matter of law. It came to the same conclusion as to the omission of the fact that in other SEC filing National indicated that it "may be deemed to be the parent of TSC."

The second issue concerned the omission of a letter from the investment bankers who gave the basic opinion on fairness. The opinion, according to the proxy statement, took into account, inter alia, "the substantial premium over current market values represented by the securities being offered to TSC shareholders." That premium could be deduced from materials setting forth the November 7, 1969 closing prices—5 days before the issuance of the proxy statement—as follows:

	TSC Preferred	TSC Common
National B. Pfd. (at 16⅝)........	$9.98 (.6 sh.)	$8.31 (.5 sh.)
National Warrant (at 5¼)	5.25	7.88 (1½ war.)
Total.........................	$15.23	$16.19
Less TSC Market (pfd. 12) (com. 13¼)	12.00	13.25
Premium......................	3.23	2.94
Premium expressed as a percentage of TSC Market.............	27%	22%

In its letter of two weeks later the Hornblower firm revealed that its judgment as to fairness had assumed that the warrants would settle to a value of $3.50 rather than $5.25, with results as follows:

	TSC Preferred	TSC Common
National B. Pfd. (at 16)	$9.60 (.6 sh.)	$8.00 (.5 sh.)
National Warrant (at 3.50)	3.50	5.25 (1½ war.)
Total.........................	$13.10	$13.25
Less TSC Market (pfd. 11) (com. 11⅝)	11.00	11.63
Premium......................	2.10	1.62
Premium expressed as a percentage of TSC Market.............	19%	14%

The Court analyzed the omission as follows:]

It would appear, however, that the subsequent communication from the Hornblower firm, which the Court of Appeals felt contained "bad news," contained nothing new at all. At the TSC board of directors meeting held on October 16, 1969, the date of the initial Hornblower opinion letter, Blancke Noyes, a TSC director and a partner in the Hornblower firm, had pointed out the likelihood of a decline in the market price of National Warrants with the issuance of the additional Warrants involved in the exchange, and reaffirmed his conclusion that the exchange offer was a fair one nevertheless. The subsequent Hornblower letter, signed by Mr. Noyes, purported merely to explain the basis of the calculations underlying the favorable opinion rendered in the October 16th letter. "In advising TSC as to the fairness of the offer from [National]," Mr. Noyes wrote, "we concluded that the warrants in question had a value of approximately $3.50." On its face, then, the subsequent letter from Hornblower does not appear to have contained anything to alter the favorable opinion rendered in the October 16th letter—including the conclusion that the securities being offered to TSC shareholders represented a "substantial premium over current market values."

The real question, though, is not whether the subsequent Hornblower letter contained anything that altered the Hornblower opinion in any way. It is rather whether the advice given at the October 16th meeting, and reduced to more precise terms in the subsequent Hornblower letter—that there may be a decline in the market price of the National Warrants—had to be disclosed in order to clarify the import of the proxy statement's reference to "the substantial premium over current market values represented by the securities being offered to TSC stockholders." We note initially that the proxy statement referred to the substantial premium as but one of several factors considered by Hornblower in rendering its favorable opinion of the terms of exchange.

Still, we cannot assume that a TSC shareholder would focus only on the "bottom line" of the opinion to the exclusion of the considerations that produced it.

TSC and National insist that the reference to a substantial premium required no clarification or supplementation, for the reason that there was a substantial premium even if the National Warrants are assumed to have been worth $3.50. In reaching the contrary conclusion, the Court of Appeals, they contend, ignored the rise in price of TSC securities between early October 1969, when the exchange ratio was set, and November 7, 1969—a rise in price that they suggest was a result of the favorable exchange ratio's becoming public knowledge. When the proxy statement was mailed, TSC and National contend, the market price of TSC securities already reflected a portion of the premium to which Hornblower had referred in rendering its favorable opinion of the terms of exchange. Thus, they note that Hornblower assessed the fairness of the proposed transaction by reference to early October market prices of TSC Preferred, TSC Common, and National Preferred. On the basis of those prices and a $3.50 value for the National Warrants involved in the exchange, TSC and National contend that the premium was substantial. Each share of TSC Preferred, selling in early October at $11, would bring National Preferred Stock and Warrants worth $13.10—for a premium of $2.10, or 19%. And each share of TSC Common, selling in early October at $11.63, would bring National Preferred Stock and Warrants worth $13.25—for a premium of $1.62, or 14%. We certainly cannot say as a matter of law that these premiums were not substantial. And if, as we must assume in considering the appropriateness of summary judgment, the increase in price of TSC's securities from early October to November 7 reflected in large part the market's reaction to the terms of the proposed exchange, it was not materially misleading as a matter of law for the proxy statement to refer to the existence of a substantial premium.

There remains the possibility, however, that although TSC and National may be correct in urging the existence of a substantial premium based upon a $3.50 value for the National Warrants and the early October market prices of the other securities involved in the transaction, the proxy statement misled the TSC shareholder to calculate a premium substantially in excess of that premium. The premiums apparent from early October market prices and a $3.50 value for the National Warrants—19% on TSC Preferred and 14% on TSC Common—are certainly less than those that would be derived through use of the November 7 closing prices listed in the proxy statement— 27% on TSC Preferred and 22% on TSC Common. But we are unwilling to sustain a grant of summary judgment to Northway on that basis. To do so we would have to conclude as a matter of law, first, that the proxy statement would have misled the TSC shareholder to calculate his premium on the basis of November 7 market prices, and second, that the difference between that premium and that which would be apparent from early October prices and a $3.50 value for the National Warrants was material. These are questions we think best left to the trier of fact.

[In a final section the opinion minimized the significance of omissions as to purchases of National stock by National and by a mutual fund with personal ties to National. In the absence of evidence of coordination and manipulation, the court found that this omission could not be said to be material as a matter of law.]

NOTE ON DISCLOSURE IN MERGER PROXY MATERIALS

(1) The disclosure concepts developed under the securities laws are under special strains where the votes of securities holders are solicited in connection with a merger or other basic change. Such transactions are apt to be complex, arguably too complex to be thoroughly explained to all shareholders as distinguished from those who have expert advice. The SEC has helped, but only modestly, by specifying in Item 14 of Schedule 14A some items that must be disclosed. The case law, as exemplified by the preceding opinion, has generally not afforded very specific guidance. It does indicate a strong emphasis on disclosure of conflicts of interest and other problems of moral risk.[23]

(2) An important issue with respect to merger proxy materials has concerned the use of current value appraisals of assets of the corporations being merged. The SEC has wavered on this issue.[24] Appraisals are not called for in Item 14 of the proxy rules. Until 1976 Rule 14a–9 frowned on "predictions as to specific future market values, earnings or dividends." Note that essentially valuation must be considered as a question of prediction. Then the SEC went into court with an amicus brief calling for a disclosure of appraisal values. Gerstle v. Gamble– Skogmo, Inc., 478 F.2d 1281 (2d Cir.1973). It argued that failure to disclose bona fide third party offers to buy property for more than book value was misleading. It drew upon the Transamerica litigation (p. 563 supra) which involved seriously undervalued inventory. As Judge Friendly noted,

> the Commission's policy against disclosure of asset appraisals in proxy statements has apparently stemmed from its deep distrust of their reliability, its concern that investors would accord such appraisals in a proxy statement more weight than would be warranted, and the impracticality, with its limited staff, of examining appraisals on a case-by-case basis to determine their reliability.

The ruling in Gamble–Skogmo was that the merger proxy statement was misleading in that it did not disclose that Gamble–Skogmo had firm offers to buy the billboards that were owned by General Outdoor Advertising, the intended merger partner. The SEC later proposed new rules on predictions. In 1976 the word "earnings" was deleted from Rule 14a–9. Rule 175, referred to in Flamm v. Eberstadt, p. 604 supra, now declares that "forward-looking" statements shall not be deemed fraudulent unless made without reasonable basis or in bad

23. See, e.g., Gould v. American–Hawaiian S.S. Co., 535 F.2d 761, 773–774 (3d Cir. 1976).

24. See T. Fiflis & H. Kripke, Accounting for Business Lawyers ch. XII (2d ed. 1977).

faith.   This includes projections of income, expenses, dividends, etc., statements of plans and statements about future economic prospects.[25]

(3) Lynch v. Vickers Energy Corp., 383 A.2d 278 (Del.1977) found inadequacy of disclosure with respect to facts curiously similar to those at stake in TSC.   The inadequate disclosure was in a tender offer and was judged according to Delaware state law standards.   The circular in which the offer was made stated that the target company's assets, chiefly oil and gas reserves, were "not less than $200,000,000 . . . and could be substantially higher."   The Court held that the duty to disclose all germane facts required disclosure of an estimate by a vice-president of the target company who was a qualified geologist fixing the net asset value at $250 million (or $20 per share) and suggesting a possible value as high as $300 million.   Further inadequacy of disclosure was found in the failure to state that Vickers had, prior to its tender offer of $12 per share, authorized open market purchases at up to $15.   The circular did accurately state that acquisitions in fact had been at an average price of $11.50 per share.   On remand, 402 A.2d 5 (Ch. 1979).

QUESTIONS

(1) Review in your mind other contexts where "materiality" appears (as in Rule 10b–5 or Section 11 of the Securities Act).   How does the context of a merger proxy statement affect the shape of that idea?   If the merger is contested is there room for the idea that the opposition should be required to ventilate their ideas through an adversary process?   Could that idea be applied fairly to the TSC case?

(2) Were you the trier of fact on remand, which way would you decide?   Is the decision of Hornblower to write the letter evidence of the materiality of the facts revealed by it?   Could the original statement have been rephrased so as to give fair warning of the possible developments?   What impact would you expect a recommendation by investment bankers to have on the shareholders' vote?   Was there any connection between the banker and TSC that might affect the integrity of the advice?   Would that be endemic to all bankers or could it be guarded against by appropriate safeguards?

(3) Would you find appraisals of the assets of TSC and Northway helpful?   Could Hornblower in fact give an opinion on fairness without implicitly setting values on assets?   Would you expect the SEC to have "approved" such appraisals?   Is the SEC's position on appraisals here consistent with its recent call for inflation-adjustment figures in annual reports?   (See p. 670 supra)

---

25. For a case illustrating the dangers of publishing a projection that turns out to be far off the mark, see Beecher v. Able, 374 F.Supp. 341 (S.D.N.Y.1974), involving an earnings projection in a prospectus of Douglas Aircraft Co.

6. Fairness and Fundamental Change

NOTE ON FAIRNESS IN MERGERS AND OTHER CHANGES

(1) The question of fairness as it arises in mergers and other basic changes can be looked at from three different aspects. First, there is the financial issue. Are the shareholders in each corporation (or in each class) being given a fair equivalent in value to what they are giving up? In a merger situation one has the appraisal problem, doubled. One must decide what the value of stock of corporation A is and then what the value of stock of corporation B is, and, third, compare the two to see whether there is an economic equivalent. In a sale of assets there is, obviously, a question of the adequacy of the price received in cash or otherwise. In amendments of the certificate of incorporation that affect rights as between classes of stock there is a question whether what is to be surrendered is equivalent to what is returned. These questions become very difficult to decide when the discrepancies are not wide and obvious.

(2) Then, there is a question of fairness as it relates to retroactivity. As we saw previously in A.P. Smith Mfg. Co. v. Barlow, p. 114 supra—the reservation of the right to amend a charter is qualified by most courts with some conception that certain rights are too "vested" to be tampered with. Just where this line runs is highly uncertain but counsel should be alert to emphasize this aspect of any transaction they wish to question.

(3) Finally, there is the aspect of motivation. If the controlling group in a corporation carries out a change with the sole purpose of eliminating or neutralizing an awkward minority should that motivation vitiate the transaction even if the minority receives a payment reasonably equivalent to the value of the investment they are forced to surrender? The situation blurs when a colorable corporate purpose for the change can be demonstrated by the majority.

(4) The problem of fairness of course implicates a conflict of interest and, thus, problems explored in Chapter VII. These conflicts can include positions held in both corporations involved in a merger, disproportionate holdings of the stock of the two corporations in a merger or of the classes of stock involved in a recapitalization, etc. It also appears that a law firm may be afflicted by conflicts of interest problems: Messrs. Sullivan & Cromwell felt obliged to withdraw from representation of one of two corporations as soon as negotiations for their merger began, although not at the time when the corporations were independently thinking of such a step. The Court of Appeals

indicated its approval of that step.[26] Just what sort of representation of a target corporation in the past disqualifies a firm from representing a raider remains unclear.

(5) Note the relationship between the questions of fairness and those of voting rights and the appraisal remedy. A court may find its eagerness to tackle a complex question of fairness dwindling if it learns that a large majority of the shareholders, adequately informed of their rights, voted in favor of the change. Likewise a sense that a minority had an adequate "out" through the appraisal remedy may discourage close consideration of the merits. Indeed that may, specifically or by implication, be the meaning of the statute granting the right. These tendencies may be reflected either in a rule that unfairness will not be considered—or not unless it amounts to "fraud"—or in a mere tendency to skimp on the thoroughness of the review. Note that there is a question of state-federal relationships in that questions of informed consent via the proxy system are allocated in general to the federal system whereas the appraisal mechanism and questions of substantive fairness remain in state hands.

Three principal cases follow. The first, Santa Fe, deals with the question whether Rule 10b–5 creates a federal fairness remedy as distinct from a federal falsehood or nondisclosure remedy. The second, Mills II, discusses fairness in the financial sense. The third, Weinberger v. UOP, Inc., discusses fairness in both financial and motivational dimensions. Observe that the U.S. Supreme Court in Santa Fe discussed Delaware precedents now several steps removed.

SANTA FE INDUSTRIES, INC. v. GREEN

Supreme Court of the United States, 1977.
430 U.S. 462, 97 S.Ct. 1292, 51 L.Ed.2d 480.

[In 1936 Santa Fe acquired 60% of the stock of Kirby Lumber Corporation (Kirby), a Delaware corporation, which block it gradually increased to 95%. In 1974 Santa Fe resorted to the short form merger provisions (§ 253) of Delaware law. It obtained independent appraisals of Kirby's assets and submitted them to Morgan, Stanley & Company, an investment banking firm, for an opinion as to the fair market value of Kirby stock. The physical assets were valued at $320 million (or $640 for each of 500,000 shares). Morgan Stanley set a value of $125 per share and the minority shareholders were actually offered $150 per share. Transactions in the 1968–73 period had ranged from $65 to $92.50 a share. The merger transaction, carried out through a new corporation specially set up for the purpose, took effect on July 31, 1974. Minority shareholders of Kirby, instead of resorting to their appraisal remedy, brought suit to set aside the merger or recover what they claimed to be a fair value of $772 for the Kirby shares (arrived at by adding the pro rata value of Kirby's land and timber to the $150). They alleged that Santa Fe's course of conduct violated Rule 10b–5.

---

26. Kohn v. American Metal Climax, Inc., 458 F.2d 255, 268–69 (3d Cir.1972).

The district court dismissed the complaint for failure to state a claim but a divided Court of Appeals reversed. The Supreme Court granted certiorari and, in an opinion by MR. JUSTICE WHITE, reversed. Part II of the opinion reviewed the language of the Rule.]

III

It is our judgment that the transaction, if carried out as alleged in the complaint, was neither deceptive nor manipulative and therefore did not violate either § 10(b) of the Act or Rule 10b–5.

As we have indicated, the case comes to us on the premise that the complaint failed to allege a material misrepresentation or material failure to disclose. The finding of the District Court, undisturbed by the Court of Appeals, was that there was no "omission" or "misstatement" in the Information Statement accompanying the notice of merger. On the basis of the information provided, minority shareholders could either accept the price offered or reject it and seek an appraisal in the Delaware Court of Chancery. Their choice was fairly presented, and they were furnished with all relevant information on which to base their decision.[27]

We therefore find inapposite the cases relied upon by respondents and the court below, in which the breaches of fiduciary duty held violative of Rule 10b–5 included some element of deception.[28] Those cases forcefully reflect the principle that "[s]ection 10(b) must be read flexibly, not technically and restrictively" and that the statute provides a cause of action for any plaintiff who "suffer[s] an injury as a result of deceptive practices touching its sale [or purchase] of securities . . . .." Superintendent of Insurance v. Bankers Life & Casualty Co., 404 U.S. 6, 12–13, 92 S.Ct. 165, 169, 30 L.Ed.2d 128 (1971). But the cases do not support the proposition, adopted by the Court of Appeals below and urged by respondents here, that a breach of fiduciary duty by majority

27. In addition to their principal argument that the complaint alleges a fraud under clauses (a) and (c) of Rule 10b–5, respondents also argue that the complaint alleges nondisclosure and misrepresentation in violation of clause (b) of the Rule. Their major contention in this respect is that the majority stockholder's failure to give the minority advance notice of the merger was a material nondisclosure, even though the Delaware short-form merger statute does not require such notice. Brief for Respondents, at 27. But respondents do not indicate how they might have acted differently had they had prior notice of the merger. Indeed, they accept the conclusion of both courts below that under Delaware law they could not have enjoined the merger because an appraisal proceeding is their sole remedy in the Delaware courts for any alleged unfairness in the terms of the merger. Thus the failure to give advance notice was not a material nondisclosure within the meaning of the statute or the Rule. Cf. TSC Industries, Inc. v. Northway, Inc., 426 U.S. 438, 96 S.Ct. 2126, 48 L.Ed.2d 757 (1976).

28. The decisions of this Court relied upon by respondents all involved deceptive conduct as part of the Rule 10b–5 violation alleged. Affiliated Ute Citizens v. United States, 406 U.S. 128, 92 S.Ct. 1456, 31 L.Ed. 2d 741 (1972) (misstatements of material fact used by bank employees in position of market maker to acquire stock at less than fair value); Superintendent of Insurance v. Bankers Life & Cas. Co., 404 U.S. 6, 9, 92 S.Ct. 165, 167, 30 L.Ed.2d 128 (1971) ("seller [of bonds] was duped into believing that it, the seller, would receive the proceeds"). Cf. SEC v. Capital Gains Research Bureau, 375 U.S. 180, 84 S.Ct. 275, 11 L.Ed.2d 237 (1963) (injunction under Investment Advisers Act of 1940 to compel registered investment adviser to disclose to his clients his own financial interest in his recommendations).

We have been cited to a large number of cases in the Courts of Appeals, all of which involved an element of deception as part of the fiduciary misconduct held to violate Rule 10b–5. [citations omitted.]

stockholders, without any deception, misrepresentation, or nondisclosure, violates the statute and the Rule.

It is also readily apparent that the conduct alleged in the complaint was not "manipulative" within the meaning of the statute. Manipulation is "virtually a term of art when used in connection with securities markets." *Ernst & Ernst,* 425 U.S., at 199, 96 S.Ct., at 1384. The term refers generally to practices, such as wash sales, matched orders, or rigged prices, that are intended to mislead investors by artificially affecting market activity. See, e.g., § 9 of the 1934 Act, 15 U.S.C.A. § 78i (prohibiting specific manipulative practices); . . . (Rule 10b–6, also promulgated under § 10(b), is "an antimanipulative provision designed to protect the orderliness of the securities market during distributions of stock" and "to prevent stimulative trading by an issuer in its own securities in order to create an unnatural and unwarranted appearance of market activity"); 2 A. Bromberg, Securities Law: Fraud § 7.3 (1975); 3 L. Loss, Securities Regulation 1541–70 (2d ed. 1961); 6, id., at 3755–3763 (2d ed. Supp.1969). Section 10(b)'s general prohibition of practices deemed by the SEC to be "manipulative"—in this technical sense of artificially affecting market activity in order to mislead investors—is fully consistent with the fundamental purpose of the 1934 Act "to substitute a philosophy of full disclosure for the philosophy of caveat emptor . . .." Affiliated Ute Citizens v. United States, 406 U.S. 128, 151, 92 S.Ct. 1456, 1471, 31 L.Ed.2d 741 (1972), quoting SEC v. Capital Gains Research Bureau, 375 U.S. 180, 186, 84 S.Ct. 275, 279, 11 L.Ed.2d 237 (1963). Indeed, nondisclosure is usually essential to the success of a manipulative scheme. 3 L. Loss, supra, at 1565. No doubt Congress meant to prohibit the full range of ingenious devices that might be used to manipulate securities prices. But we do not think it would have chosen this "term of art" if it had meant to bring within the scope of § 10(b) instances of corporate mismanagement such as this, in which the essence of the complaint is that shareholders were treated unfairly by a fiduciary.

IV

The language of the statute is, we think, "sufficiently clear in its context" to be dispositive here, *Ernst & Ernst,* 425 U.S., at 201, 96 S.Ct., at 1385; but even if it were not, there are additional considerations that weigh heavily against permitting a cause of action under Rule 10b–5 for the breach of corporate fiduciary duty alleged in this complaint. Congress did not expressly provide a private cause of action for violations of § 10(b). Although we have recognized an implied cause of action under that section in some circumstances, Superintendent of Insurance v. Bankers Life & Cas. Co., supra, 404 U.S. at 13 n. 9, 92 S.Ct. at 169, we have also recognized that a private cause of action under the antifraud provisions of the Securities Exchange Act should not be implied where it is "unnecessary to ensure the fulfillment of Congress' purposes" in adopting the Act. Piper v. Chris–Craft Industries, 430 U.S., at 40–42, 97 S.Ct., at 949. Cf. J.I. Case Co. v. Borak, 377 U.S. 426, 431–433, 84 S.Ct. 1555, 12 L.Ed.2d 423 (1964). As we noted earlier, . . . the Court repeatedly has described the "fundamental purpose" of the Act as implementing a "philosophy of full disclosure"; once full and fair disclosure has occurred, the fairness of the terms of the transaction is at most a tangential concern of the statute. Cf. Mills v. Electric Auto–Lite Co., 396 U.S. 375, 381–385, 90 S.Ct. 616, 620–622, 24 L.Ed.2d

593 (1970). As in Cort v. Ash, 422 U.S. 66, 78, 80, 95 S.Ct. 2080, 2087, 2090, 45 L.Ed.2d 26 (1975), we are reluctant to recognize a cause of action here to serve what is "at best a subsidiary purpose" of the federal legislation.

A second factor in determining whether Congress intended to create a federal cause of action in these circumstances is "whether 'the cause of action [is] one traditionally relegated to state law . . . .' " Piper v. Chris–Craft Industries, Inc., 430 U.S., at 40–42, 97 S.Ct., at 949, quoting Cort v. Ash, 422 U.S., at 78, 95 S.Ct., at 2087. The Delaware Legislature has supplied minority shareholders with a cause of action in the Delaware Court of Chancery to recover the fair value of shares allegedly undervalued in a short-form merger. . . . Of course, the existence of a particular state law remedy is not dispositive of the question whether Congress meant to provide a similar federal remedy, but as in *Piper* and *Cort,* we conclude that "it is entirely appropriate in this instance to relegate respondent and others in his situation to whatever remedy is created by state law." . . .

The reasoning behind a holding that the complaint in this case alleged fraud under Rule 10b–5 could not be easily contained. It is difficult to imagine how a court could distinguish, for purposes of Rule 10b–5 fraud, between a majority stockholder's use of a short-form merger to eliminate the minority at an unfair price and the use of some other device, such as a long-form merger, tender offer, or liquidation, to achieve the same result; or indeed how a court could distinguish the alleged abuses in these going private transactions from other types of fiduciary self-dealing involving transactions in securities. The result would be to bring within the Rule a wide variety of corporate conduct traditionally left to state regulation. In addition to posing a "danger of vexatious litigation which could result from a widely expanded class of plaintiffs under Rule 10b–5," Blue Chip Stamps v. Manor Drug Stores, 421 U.S. 723, 740, 95 S.Ct. 1917, 1927, 44 L.Ed.2d 539 (1975), this extension of the federal securities laws would overlap and quite possibly interfere with state corporate law. Federal courts applying a "federal fiduciary principle" under Rule 10b–5 could be expected to depart from state fiduciary standards at least to the extent necessary to ensure uniformity within the federal system.[29] Absent a clear indication of congressional intent, we are reluctant to federalize the substantial portion of the law of corporations that deals with transactions in securities, particularly where established state policies of corporate regulation would be overridden. As the Court stated in *Cort v. Ash,* supra, "Corporations are creatures of state law, and investors commit their funds to corporate directors on the understanding that, except where federal law *expressly* requires certain responsibilities of directors

---

[29]. For example, some States apparently requires a "valid purpose" for the elimination of the minority interest through a short-form merger, whereas other States do not. Compare Bryan v. Brock & Blevins Co., 490 F.2d 563 (CA5), cert. denied, 419 U.S. 844, 95 S.Ct. 77, 42 L.Ed.2d 72 (1974) (merger arranged by controlling stockholder for no business purpose except to eliminate 15% minority stockholder violated Georgia short-form merger statute) with Stauffer v. Standard Brands, Inc., 41 Del. Ch. 7, 187 A.2d 78 (Sup.Ct.1962) (Delaware short-form merger statute allows majority stockholder to eliminate the minority interest without any corporate purpose and subject only to an appraisal remedy). Thus to the extent that Rule 10b–5 is interpreted to require a valid corporate purpose for elimination of minority shareholders as well as a fair price for their shares, it would impose a stricter standard of fiduciary duty than that required by the law of some States.

with respect to stockholders, state law will govern the internal affairs of the corporation." 422 U.S., at 84, 95 S.Ct., at 2091 (emphasis added).

We thus adhere to the position that "Congress by § 10(b) did not seek to regulate transactions which constitute no more than internal corporate mismanagement." Superintendent of Insurance v. Bankers Life & Cas. Co., 404 U.S., at 12, 92 S.Ct., at 169. There may well be a need for uniform federal fiduciary standards to govern mergers such as that challenged in this complaint. But those standards should not be supplied by judicial extension of § 10(b) and Rule 10b–5 to "cover the corporate universe." [30]

The judgment of the Court of Appeals is reversed, and the case is remanded for further proceedings consistent with this opinion.

So ordered.

[MR. JUSTICE BRENNAN dissented, "for substantially the reasons stated" in the opinions of the Court of Appeals, and JUSTICES BLACKMUN and STEVENS concurred, except that they declined to join in Part IV.]

QUESTIONS

(1) Do you concur in the Supreme Court's reading of the scope of 10b–5? Is the result, in any case, compelled or strongly suggested by the Blue Chip Stamps case, p. 566 supra?

(2) Is the subject-matter of this case one that strongly calls for federal displacement of state corporation law, i.e., can it be distinguished from other breaches of fiduciary duty by corporate management? Recall that a typical "going private" transaction involves two stages—first, an acquisition of stock either on the market or by a general tender offer and, second, a merger to create 100% ownership. Which of those two stages is more suitable for regulation consistent with the general philosophy of securities regulation and the institutions that have been developed to enforce it? How severely should "force out" mergers be discouraged? Are there arguments to be made for the proposition that they terminate situations fraught with other dangers of unfairness?

(3) Consider the Delaware short form merger statute. Does it seem objectionable? Do you have suggestions as to how it might be recast or how a federal rule on the topic might be structured?

(4) Could federal courts preserve a role for 10b–5 on the theory that nondisclosure hinders exercise of state remedies by appraisal or suit?

---

30. Cary, Federalism and Corporate Law: Reflections Upon Delaware, 83 Yale L.J. 663, 700 (1974) (footnote omitted). Professor Cary argues vigorously for comprehensive federal fiduciary standards, but urges a "frontal" attack by a new federal statute rather than an extension of Rule 10b–5. He writes, "It seems anomalous to jigsaw every kind of corporate dispute into the federal courts through the securities acts as they are presently written." Ibid. See also Note, Going Private, 84 Yale L.J. 903 (1974) (proposing the application of traditional doctrines of substantive corporate law to problems of fairness raised by "going private" transactions such as short-form mergers).

MILLS v. ELECTRIC AUTO–LITE CO.

United States Court of Appeals, Seventh Circuit, 1977.
552 F.2d 1239.

[The Supreme Court reversed a prior ruling of the Seventh Circuit and remanded for further proceedings on the theory that the proxy materials with respect to the merger between Mergenthaler Linotype Company (Mergenthaler) and Electric Auto–Lite Company (Auto–Lite) were misleading even though it had not been established that but for the deception the merger would not have been approved. Portions of that opinion are set forth at p. 431, supra and other portions relating to the award of attorneys' fees at p. 512, supra. The district court then concluded that the merger should not be rescinded but that the merger had been unfair to plaintiffs who should have damages of $1,233,918. On appeal, the Court of Appeals reversed in an opinion by JUDGE SWYGERT:]

II

The district court considered two possible theories of damages in attempting to follow the Supreme Court's mandate: (1) to compensate plaintiffs for the reduction of the earnings potential of their holdings in Auto–Lite as a result of the merger; or (2) an award based on a determination of the fairness of the terms of the merger at the time it was approved. It rejected the use of the first theory under the circumstances of this case and adopted the second. We shall evaluate both whether the district court was erroneous in its choice of remedies and whether it correctly applied the second theory.

In order to perform this evaluation, it is first necessary to describe the merger terms. They called for the minority Auto–Lite shareholders to receive 1.88 preferred shares of Eltra for each share of Auto–Lite common that they held and the Mergenthaler shareholders to receive one common share of Eltra for each share of Mergenthaler common that they held. Eltra preferred shares were convertible into common shares on a one-to-one basis for the first two years following the merger and on a slightly decreasing basis for the next three years. At the time of the merger Mergenthaler common paid a dividend of $1 per share and Auto–Lite common paid a dividend of $2.40 per share. Under the merger terms Eltra common was to pay a dividend of $1 per share and Eltra preferred a dividend of $1.40 per share. The dividend received by the Auto–Lite minority shareholders was therefore increased as a result of the merger by twenty-three cents for each share of Auto–Lite that they had held, because $1.88 \times \$1.40 = \$2.63$.

The preferred Eltra stock was clearly worth more than Eltra common because it paid a higher dividend and represented a more secure investment if the new corporation encountered financial difficulties, yet was convertible into common stock. During the month following the merger, the average market value of Eltra preferred was $31.06 per share. Consequently the Auto–Lite minority shareholders received stock worth $58.39 on the market for each share of Auto–Lite that they had previously held, because $1.88 \times \$31.06 = \$58.39$. The average market value of Eltra common for this month was $25.25 per share. Since the Mergenthaler shareholders received one share of Eltra common for each share of Mergenthaler common, the Auto–Lite shareholders received stock for each share of Auto–Lite that they held worth $58.39/$25.25 = 2.31 times as much on the market as the stock that the Mergenthaler shareholders received for each share of Mergenthaler that they held. We therefor hold that the exchange ratio for the merger was effectively 2.31 to 1.

III

A theory of damages based on the "reduction of the earnings or earnings potential" of the Auto–Lite minority shareholders caused by the merger is an attempt to discern, by looking at the postmerger performance and activities of the Auto–Lite subsidiary in comparison to the other components of Eltra, whether the value placed on the Auto–Lite shares at the time the merger took place was fair to those shareholders. Plaintiffs contend that the postmerger record of Eltra demonstrates the unfairness of the merger in two significant ways: first, by showing that Eltra appropriated for use in its other divisions liquid assets held by Auto–Lite prior to the merger; and second, by showing that Eltra continually siphoned off Auto–Lite's postmerger earnings.

Even if plaintiffs' assertions are true, they cannot form the basis for an award of damages. Plaintiffs assume that it would be unfair to the former minority Auto–Lite shareholders if, after the merger, the Eltra management "weakened" the Auto–Lite divisions by shifting liquid assets or earnings to other divisions. This assumption is incorrect. After the merger the former Auto–Lite shareholders had become Eltra shareholders and had no more interest in the Auto–Lite divisions than any other Eltra shareholder. Therefore, they could not be injured by intra-corporate transfers of assets designed to strengthen the corporation as a whole. The interests of the former Auto–Lite shareholders and former Mergenthaler shareholders coincided after the merger, and the Eltra management could not possibly take actions that benefitted "its" shareholders at the expense of the Auto–Lite shareholders.

[Here the court distinguished cases where defendants had realized demonstrable profits, at plaintiff's expense, through misrepresentation.] But whether the exchange of Auto–Lite stock for Eltra stock profited Mergenthaler at the expense of the Auto–Lite minority shareholders is precisely the issue we are trying to resolve. Damages must be based on evidence that the Auto–Lite minority shareholders were not paid a fair price and the fact that Eltra shifted assets away from Auto–Lite following the merger is not satisfactory evidence of unfairness at the time the merger was consummated.

Plaintiffs ignored the only theory on which relief based on the postmerger performance of Eltra might be granted. If the ratio of the postmerger earnings of the Auto–Lite subsidiary of Eltra to the postmerger earnings of the Mergenthaler subsidiary were unusually high given the terms of the merger, it would be evidence that those terms were unfair to the Auto–Lite minority shareholders. This is true not because the former Auto–Lite minority shareholders are entitled to any percentage of the earnings of the Auto–Lite subsidiary after the merger, but because a high ratio would indicate that in retrospect the merger terms underestimated Auto–Lite's value as an enterprise.

Eltra's financial records show that for the ten year period beginning in 1963 and ending in 1972 the Auto–Lite divisions earned

$122,501,632 while the Mergenthaler divisions earned $58,827,595. Before the merger Auto–Lite had 1,159,265 shares outstanding while Mergenthaler had 2,698,822 shares outstanding. Arguably, therefore, Auto–Lite would have had average yearly earnings per share of $10.57 between 1963 and 1972 if there had been no merger because its average yearly earnings would be $122,501,632/10 = $12,250,163 and $12,250,163/1,159,265 = $10.57. By the same reasoning, Mergenthaler's average yearly earnings per share for the same period would be $2.18 because $58,827,595/10 = $5,882,759 and $5,882,759/2,698,822 = $2.18. The ratio of $10.57 to $2.18 is 4.85, indicating that the actual effective exchange ratio of 2.31 underestimated the value of Auto–Lite in comparison to Mergenthaler.

An award of damages based on the comparative postmerger earnings of Auto–Lite and Mergenthaler, however, depends upon the assumption that the two subsidiaries continued to function independently after the merger was consummated. If the assets or operations of the two subsidiaries were commingled, it would be improper to utilize the postmerger performance of either one as evidence that at the time of the merger Auto–Lite was a stronger company than the merger terms indicated, because Auto–Lite's increase in earnings following the merger might have been the result of input from Mergenthaler that it would not have received without the merger.

The district court held that there was substantial commingling of the assets and operations of Auto–Lite and Mergenthaler during the period following the merger. It found that the plaintiffs' statistics failed to measure the change in the quality of management that flowed to the Auto–Lite divisions of Eltra as a consequence of the merger or the economies of scale that the merger produced. It also found the statistics to be misleading because the postmerger Eltra statements underestimated the expenses of the Auto–Lite divisions, making the earnings of those divisions appear higher than they really were. These findings are supported by substantial evidence and we affirm them.

Given the fact that significant commingling occurred, the postmerger earnings of Auto–Lite and Mergenthaler cannot supply a reliable guide to whether the merger terms were fair to the Auto–Lite minority shareholders. Even in the absence of commingling, postmerger evidence can only create a rebuttable inference of unfairness because it is impossible to know with certainty whether the increase in earnings of one partner to a merger should have been predictable at the time the merger took place. In this case the ratio of the earnings per share of the two companies for the four years prior to and including 1963 were all at or below the effective exchange ratio of 2.31 to 1.[31] Plaintiffs have not shown that the management of Mergenthaler should have known in 1963 that Auto–Lite's earnings were going to increase faster than Mergenthaler's during the next decade. The more plausible inference is that, insofar as Auto–Lite's business became more productive because of factors unrelated to commingling, they were unforeseeable at the time the merger was consummated. Accordingly, we hold that the district court did not abuse its discretion in refusing to award damages based on post-merger data.

31. Plaintiffs assert that the ratio of Auto–Lite's earnings per share to Mergenthaler's earnings per share was 2.2 in 1960, 1.0 in 1961, 1.5 in 1962, and 2.33 in 1963. Defendants assert that the ratio was 1.0 in 1961, 1.27 in 1962, 1.79 in the fiscal year 1963, and 1.90 in the calendar year 1963. They do not provide figures for 1960.

IV

A

The district court based its award of damages on an assessment of the fairness of the merger terms at the time the merger took place. It evaluated five criteria in making this assessment: (1) the market value of each corporation's stock; (2) each corporation's earnings; (3) the book value of each corporation's assets; (4) the dividends that each corporation paid on its stock; and (5) other "qualitative factors" indicating the strength of each corporation. The court found market value to be an unreliable criterion and discounted the importance of dividends. It found that the comparative earnings and book values of each corporation were significant and demonstrated that the merger terms were unfair to the Auto–Lite minority. The court did not indicate what significance it was attributing to "qualitative factors."

Based on these findings the court held that the merger would have been fair if the Auto–Lite minority shareholders had received the equivalent of 2.35 shares of Eltra common for each share of Auto–Lite that they held and Mergenthaler shareholders had received one share of Eltra common for each share of Mergenthaler that they held. It also found that the effective exchange ratio for the actual merger, where the Auto–Lite minority shareholders received 1.88 shares of Eltra preferred for each share of Auto–Lite common that they held, was 2.25 to 1 in terms of Eltra common. It then awarded damages of $1,233,918.35 to plaintiffs based on the differential of .10 between the effective exchange ratio of 2.25 to 1 and the fair exchange ratio of 2.35 to 1.[32]

32. The district court used the following method of reaching the figure of $1,233,918.35:

(1) Since each share of Auto–Lite was exchanged for the equivalent of 2.25 shares of Eltra common while each share of Mergenthaler was exchanged for one share of Eltra common, the holder of one share of Auto–Lite received 67.38 percent of the interest in Eltra distributed for one share of Auto–Lite and one share of Mergenthaler, because $2.25/(2.35 + 1) = .6738$.

(2) If a fair exchange ratio of 2.35 had been employed, the holder of one share of Auto–Lite would have received 70.15 percent of the interest in Eltra distributed for one share of Auto–Lite and one share of Mergenthaler, because $2.35/(2.35 + 1) = .7015$.

(3) Since $70.15 - 67.38 = 2.77$, the Auto–Lite minority shareholders were unfairly deprived of 2.77 percent of the combined value of an Auto–Lite share and a Mergenthaler share for each share of Auto–Lite that they held.

(4) In July 1963, the month following the merger, the average market value of the Eltra stock that was distributed for one share of Mergenthaler was $25.25 and the average market value of the Eltra stock

that was distributed for one share of Auto–Lite was $58.39. Accordingly, the combined value of one share of Mergenthaler and one share of Auto–Lite was $25.25 + $58.39 = 83.64.

(5) 2.77 percent of $83.64 is $2.317. Since there were 532,500 minority shares of Auto–Lite, the total damages were $532,500 \times \$2.317 = \$1,233,918.35$.

The district court's method of calculation was mathematically unsound. First, there was an arithmetic error in step one because $2.25/(2.25 + 1)$ is .6923 rather than .6738. The more fundamental error, however, lies in the court's premise in steps 3, 4, and 5 that the 2.77 percent figure could be multiplied by the combined market value of one share of Auto–Lite and one share of Mergenthaler to calculate the per share dollar loss which the Auto–Lite shareholders had suffered. It is circular reasoning to use the market value generated by the actual merger. If a different exchange ratio had been employed, the market value of Eltra stock undoubtedly would have been different. Moreover, the mathematical significance of the 2.77 percent figure is questionable.

What the court should have done, if its differential of .10 were correct, was simply

B

The district court discounted the significance of the comparative market values of Auto–Lite and Mergenthaler stock during the five year period preceding the merger because it found that purchases of Auto–Lite stock by Auto–Lite itself and by Mergenthaler, and of Mergenthaler stock by the American Manufacturing Company, made market value an unreliable indicator during that period of the true worth of the two parties to the merger. Defendants challenge the district court's assessment while plaintiffs contend that it was correct, at least for the period after 1960. We agree with defendants.

The district court's holding depends upon the validity of two premises: first, that the inter- and intra-company purchases substantially affected the market value of either corporation's stock immediately prior to the merger and second, that any effect which these purchases did have caused the price of Auto–Lite stock to fall relative to the price of Mergenthaler stock. We find neither premise to be supported by the evidence. [The opinion noted (1) that most purchases of Auto–Lite stock by Auto–Lite itself or by Mergenthaler took place before the six months preceding the merger, (2) there was no manipulation directly before the merger, (3) the price ratio of the stocks did not change during the period when there were purchases, (4) there were more purchases of Auto–Lite than of Mergenthaler, tending to push Auto–Lite's price upward.]

We therefore hold that the inter- and intra-company transactions did not unfairly distort the relative market prices of Auto–Lite and Mergenthaler for purposes of determining the fairness of the merger. We must now decide what period of time should be used in calculating a price ratio between each corporation's stock. Since prices from the period immediately preceding the merger are the most likely to reflect the actual value of each corporation at the time the merger was consummated, we begin with a presumption that a short period is appropriate. Accordingly, we hold that the average market value for approximately the six month period preceding the merger should be used unless there are special factors indicating that this period is unreliable. Six months is long enough so that very short term price fluctuations will not play an unfairly important role and short enough so that the calculated ratio does not reflect business conditions that have substantially changed as of the time of the merger.

In this case the ratio between the average price of Auto–Lite and the average price of Mergenthaler during 1963 prior to the formulation of the merger terms in late May was 2.1. Our confidence that this figure accurately reflects the relative worth of the two corporations is bolstered by the fact that the ratio for 1962 was also 2.1 and was 2.0 for 1961. The similarity of these numbers is evidence that the ratio immediately preceding the merger was not the result of a short term anomaly caused either by the merger itself or by other factors.

[The court rejected plaintiffs' argument that 1958–60 market prices were a more valid measure, noting that Auto–Lite's business was eroding.]

multiply the differential by the number of minority Auto–Lite shares to calculate the number of additional Eltra common shares that should have been distributed to plaintiffs to make the merger terms fair.

C

After finding that market value provided an inaccurate measure of the true worth of Auto–Lite and Mergenthaler, the district court determined whether the merger terms were fair on the basis of comparative earnings and book value. Given our conclusion that market prices were an accurate gauge of actual value, we must decide whether the other criteria on which the district court relied should properly be considered in evaluating whether the merger was fair.

We hold that when market value is available and reliable, other factors should not be utilized in determining whether the terms of a merger were fair. Although criteria such as earnings and book value are an indication of actual worth, they are only secondary indicia. In a market economy, market value will always be the primary gauge of an enterprise's worth. In this case thousands of shares of Auto–Lite and Mergenthaler were traded on the New York Stock Exchange during the first part of 1963 by outside investors who had access to the full gamut of financial information about both corporations, including earnings and book value. If we were to independently assess criteria other than market value in our effort to determine whether the merger terms were fair, we would be substituting our abstract judgment for that of the market. Aside from the problems that would arise in deciding how much weight to give each criterion, such a method would be economically unsound.

D

We turn now to a determination of whether the merger terms were fair, based on the comparative market price of each corporation's stock during the first part of 1963. The simplest method of resolving this issue would be to compare the price ratio, in this case 2.1, to the effective exchange ratio, which we have previously established as 2.31. Under this framework the merger would be fair since the effective exchange ratio gave the Auto–Lite minority shareholders more Eltra stock than they were entitled to in the judgment of the market.

This method of calculation, however, assumes that the new corporation that results from a merger is worth exactly as much as the sum of what its two component parts were worth before the merger. As Professors Brudney and Chirelstein have cogently pointed out, this assumption is usually false because a merger produces a synergistic effect resulting in the merged corporation being worth more than the sum of the two old corporations. Brudney & Chirelstein, Fair Shares in Corporate Mergers and Takeovers, 88 Harv.L.Rev. 297, 308–09 (1974). They demonstrate that fairness requires that minority shareholders be compensated not only for the market value of their shares in the old corporation but also for the share of the synergism generated by the merger that is proportionate to the interest that those shares represented in the combined premerger value of the two old corporations. Id. at 313–25.

We adopt the approach formulated by Professors Brudney and Chirelstein and will attempt to apply it to this case. At the time of the merger there were 532,550 minority shares of Auto–Lite and 2,698,822 shares of Mergenthaler outstanding. During the first part of 1963 the average market price of Auto–Lite was $52.25 per share and the average market price of Mergenthaler was $24.875 per share. Thus, the premerger value of the minority holdings in Auto–Lite was 532,550 × $52.25 = $27,825,737 and the premerger value of Mergenthaler was 2,698,822 × $24.875 = $67,133,197. The combined premerger value of the two corporations was $27,825,737 + $67,133,197 = $94,958,934.[33]

In the month following the merger, Eltra common stock had an average market value of $25.25 per share. Eltra preferred stock had an average market value of $58.39 per 1.88 shares, the amount of stock which Auto–Lite shareholders had received for each share of Auto–Lite that they had held. The postmerger value of Eltra was therefore (2,698,822 × $25.25) + (532,550 × $58.39) = $68,145,255 + $31,095,-594 = $99,240,849. The difference between the combined premerger value of Auto–Lite and Mergenthaler and the postmerger value of Eltra, which was $99,240,849 − $94,958,934 = $4,281,915, can be attributed to the synergism generated by the merger.

According to the fairness formula devised by Professors Brudney and Chirelstein, the minority shareholders of Auto–Lite should have received Eltra stock worth at least as much as the premerger market value of their holdings in Auto–Lite and a share of the synergism produced by the merger proportionate to the percentage of the combined premerger value of Auto–Lite and Mergenthaler which their holdings represented. The premerger value of the Auto–Lite minority shares was $27,825,737, which represented 29.3 percent of $94,958,934, the combined premerger value of Auto–Lite and Mergenthaler. Thus, to satisfy the constraints of fairness, the Auto–Lite minority shareholders should have received stock worth at least $27,825,737 + (.293 × $4,281,915) = $29,080,338. This would be equivalent to 1,151,696.5 shares of Eltra common at $25.25 per share. Had this many shares been distributed to the Auto–Lite minority shareholders, the exchange ratio would have been 1,151,696.5/532,550 = 2.16 to 1.

The Auto–Lite minority shareholders actually received preferred stock worth $58.39 on the market for each share of Auto–Lite that they had held. As a group, their Eltra holdings were worth 532,550 × $58.39 = $31,095,594. This was $31,095,594 − $29,-080,338 = $2,015,256 more than fairness required. This result can be expressed in terms of Eltra common shares. Since the effective exchange ratio of the merger was 2.31 to 1, the property given the Auto–Lite minority was worth 2.31 − 2.16 = .15 shares of Eltra common per share of Auto–Lite more than what a fair amount would have been.

We therefore hold that the terms of the merger were fair and that plaintiffs should recover no damages. A numerical example may help to show the justice of this result. In early 1963, an Auto–Lite shareholder with one hundred shares and a Mergenthaler shareholder with 210 shares each owned stock worth approximately $5225. After the merger, the former Auto–Lite shareholder had 188 shares of Eltra preferred worth approximately $5839 while the former Mergenthaler shareholder had 210 shares of Eltra common worth approximately

---

33. Although Mergenthaler owned more than half of the Auto–Lite stock, this holding should not be independently counted as part of the combined value of the two corporations because it was already reflected in the value of Mergenthaler stock.

$5302. Both individuals benefitted from the merger, but the former Auto–Lite minority shareholder benefitted more.

QUESTIONS

(1) Be sure that you understand the Brudney & Chirelstein formula the court uses. If corporation A has a "value" of $10,000,000 and B has one of $20,000,000 and the planners predict a value of $40,000,000 for the new AB firm how should the benefits be allocated between A's and B's shareholders? Are you skeptical of the assumption that synergism normally results from a merger? How does the formula differ from an arm's length test? Why is it preferable? Could it be generalized to non-merger situations tainted by conflicts of interest?

(2) Note the court's strong preference for market values. Is it right in discounting other indicia in this case? Can you visualize other types of situations in which the market would not be a fair guide? Suppose corporation B is not traded on a public securities market while A is traded on the New York Stock Exchange? Suppose that A made a tender offer slightly above the then market a year ago which obtained 70% of B's stock which has been inactive on the market ever since.

(3) Recall the earlier history of the Mills litigation which originated in a disclosure question under the federal proxy rules. Assuming that there was a significant failure to disclose, is the outcome calculated to remedy that deficiency? Does a shareholder who was misled have any incentive to pursue his remedies if the upshot is like Mills No. 2? Is the question of fairness discussed in Mills No. 2 basically one of federal or of state law?

PROBLEM

Review the opinion in Farris v. Glen Alden Corp.,[34] for what it says about the question of the fairness of the attempted transaction. Consider also these additional facts, drawn from a related case,[35] which shed some light on the problem:

    (a) The $63,500,000 book value attributed to Glen Alden "reflected unrealistically excessively depreciated values on the numerous pieces of improved property owned by [it] and did not reflect any valuation for the $14,000,000 tax loss carry-over. It likewise did not include the value of coal selt a waste from mining operations utilized to make steam. . . . In 1958, after the agreement herein was proposed, the selt was sold for $2,000,000."

    (b) "In 1956 Glen Alden made a redetermination of its coal properties for federal income tax purposes and found it alone to be $49,650,000."

    (c) Glen Alden and List Industries engaged a nationally known business consulting firm to render an opinion as to whether an exchange of 4 shares of Glen Alden for 5 of List would be correct. It recommended an exchange of 5 shares for 6, valuing List at $35.7 million and Glen Alden at $17.9 million. "It based its valuation by capitalizing its forecast of earnings of List Industries

34. P. 688 supra.

35. Gilbert v. Burnside, 197 N.Y.S.2d 623, 628–9 (1954).

for 1958, its anticipated cash generation flow by Glen Alden and also factors arrived at by an examination of the market performance of stocks of companies said to be respectively comparable to the two enterprises."

(1) Do the facts as stated in the Pennsylvania case or the New York case or both give one a sufficient basis for passing on the fairness of the transaction?

(2) Compare the facts the courts give with the analysis used in Delaware appraisal cases. What additional data about List and Glen Alden would the appraiser have to have to do the job the Delaware courts expect? What use would a Delaware appraiser make of the information that can be extracted from the opinions?

WEINBERGER v. UOP, INC.

Supreme Court of Delaware, 1983.
457 A.2d 701.

[The Signal Companies, Inc. (Signal) is a diversified, technically based corporation. Its stock is publicly traded on the New York and other stock exchanges. In 1974, after selling off a subsidiary, Signal looked for a use for its cash surplus. It hit upon UOP, also a diversified industrial corporation. UOP's stock was trading on the New York Stock Exchange at just under $14 per share. As a result of a cash tender offer and a purchase by Signal of 1,500,000 shares of UOP's authorized but unissued stock, Signal acquired in the spring of 1975 50.5 percent of the stock of UOP at $21 per share. Of UOP's board six were Signal's nominees. After searching for other investment candidates, Signal in 1978 decided to acquire the remaining 49.5 percent of UOP's stock. The study leading up to the acquisition was made by two Signal officers, Arledge and Chitiea, who were also directors of both Signal and UOP. Although they concluded that UOP shares were a good investment at up to $24, Signal ultimately proposed a merger at $21 per UOP share. At the UOP board meeting a Lehman Brothers opinion letter finding $21 to be a fair price was available but not the Arledge–Chitiea report. The merger was accepted by the UOP board with Signal's directors abstaining from voting. The merger was submitted to the May 1978 annual meeting of UOP's shareholders. 56 percent of the minority shares voted, 51.9 percent in favor of the merger and 4.1 percent against—with Signal's holdings a total of 76.2 percent for and 2.2 percent opposed. The merger became effective on May 26, 1978. Plaintiff, a former UOP shareholder, brought a class action challenging the merger. The Chancellor, finding the terms fair, entered judgment for defendants. On appeal and after rehearing en banc, the Supreme Court reversed and remanded in an opinion by JUSTICE MOORE:]

II.

A.

A primary issue mandating reversal is the preparation by two UOP directors, Arledge and Chitiea, of their feasibility study for the exclusive use and benefit of Signal. This document was of obvious significance to both Signal and UOP. Using UOP data, it described the advantages to Signal of ousting the minority at a price range of $21–$24 per share. Mr. Arledge, one of the authors, outlined the benefits to Signal: [36]

Purpose Of The Merger

(1) Provides an outstanding investment opportunity for Signal— (Better than any recent acquisition we have seen.)

(2) Increases Signal's earnings.

(3) Facilitates the flow of resources between Signal and its subsidiaries—(Big factor—works both ways.)

(4) Provides cost savings potential for Signal and UOP.

(5) Improves the percentage of Signal's "operating earnings" as opposed to "holding company earnings".

(6) Simplifies the understanding of Signal.

(7) Facilitates technological exchange among Signal's subsidiaries.

(8) Eliminates potential conflicts of interest.

Having written those words, solely for the use of Signal, it is clear from the record that neither Arledge nor Chitiea shared this report with their fellow directors of UOP. We are satisfied that no one else did either. This conduct hardly meets the fiduciary standards applicable to such a transaction.

.   .   .

The Arledge–Chitiea report speaks for itself in supporting the Chancellor's finding that a price of up to $24 was a "good investment" for Signal. It shows that a return on the investment of $21 would be 15.7% versus 15.5% at $24 per share. This was a difference of only two-tenths of one percent, while it meant over $17,000,000 to the minority. Under such circumstances, paying UOP's minority shareholders $24 would have had relatively little long-term effect on Signal, and the Chancellor's findings concerning the benefit to Signal, even at a price of $24, were obviously correct. Levitt v. Bouvier, Del.Supr., 287 A.2d 671, 673 (1972).

Certainly, this was a matter of material significance to UOP and its shareholders. Since the study was prepared by two UOP directors, using UOP information for the exclusive benefit of Signal, and nothing whatever was done to disclose it to the outside UOP directors or the minority shareholders, a question of breach of fiduciary duty arises. This problem occurs because there were common Signal–UOP directors participating, at least to some extent, in the UOP board's decision-making processes without full disclosure of the conflicts they faced.[37]

36. The parentheses indicate certain handwritten comments of Mr. Arledge.

37. Although perfection is not possible, or expected, the result here could have been entirely different if UOP had appointed an independent negotiating committee of its outside directors to deal with Signal at arm's length. See, e.g., Harriman v. E.I. duPont de Nemours & Co., 411 F.Supp. 133 (D.Del.1975). Since fairness in this context can be equated to conduct by a theoretical, wholly independent, board of directors acting upon the matter before them, it is unfortunate that this course apparently was neither considered nor pursued. Johnston v. Greene, Del.Supr., 121 A.2d 919, 925 (1956). Particularly in a parent-subsidiary context, a showing that the action taken was as though each of the contending parties had in fact exerted its bargaining power against the other at arm's length is strong evidence that the transaction meets the test of fairness. Getty Oil Co. v. Skelly Oil Co., Del.Supr.,

B.

In assessing this situation, the Court of Chancery was required to:

> examine what information defendants had and to measure it against what they gave to the minority stockholders, in a context in which "complete candor" is required. In other words, the limited function of the Court was to determine whether defendants had disclosed all information in their possession germane to the transaction in issue. And by "germane" we mean, for present purposes, information such as a reasonable shareholder would consider important in deciding whether to sell or retain stock.

· · ·

. . . Completeness, not adequacy, is both the norm and the mandate under present circumstances.

Lynch v. Vickers Energy Corp., Del.Supr., 383 A.2d 278, 281 (1977) (*Lynch I*). This is merely stating in another way the long-existing principle of Delaware law that these Signal designated directors on UOP's board still owed UOP and its shareholders an uncompromising duty of loyalty.

· · ·

Given the absence of any attempt to structure this transaction on an arm's length basis, Signal cannot escape the effects of the conflicts it faced, particularly when its designees on UOP's board did not totally abstain from participation in the matter. There is no "safe harbor" for such divided loyalties in Delaware. When directors of a Delaware corporation are on both sides of a transaction, they are required to demonstrate their utmost good faith and the most scrupulous inherent fairness of the bargain. Gottlieb v. Heyden Chemical Corp., Del.Supr., 91 A.2d 57, 57–58 (1952). The requirement of fairness is unflinching in its demand that where one stands on both sides of a transaction, he has the burden of establishing its entire fairness, sufficient to pass the test of careful scrutiny by the courts. . . .

There is no dilution of this obligation where one holds dual or multiple directorships, as in a parent-subsidiary context. Levien v. Sinclair Oil Corp., Del.Ch., 261 A.2d 911, 915 (1969.) Thus, individuals who act in a dual capacity as directors of two corporations, one of whom is parent and the other subsidiary, owe the same duty of good management to both corporations, and in the absence of an independent negotiating structure or the directors' total abstention from any participation in the matter, this duty is to be exercised in light of what is best for both companies. Warshaw v. Calhoun, Del.Supr., 221 A.2d 487, 492 (1966). The record demonstrates that Signal has not met this obligation.

C.

The concept of fairness has two basic aspects: fair dealing and fair price. The former embraces questions of when the transaction was timed, how it was initiated, structured, negotiated, disclosed to the directors, and how the approvals of the directors and the stockholders

267 A.2d 883, 886 (1970); Puma v. Marriott, Del.Ch., 283 A.2d 693, 696 (1971).

were obtained. The latter aspect of fairness relates to the economic and financial considerations of the proposed merger, including all relevant factors: assets, market value, earnings, future prospects, and any other elements that affect the intrinsic or inherent value of a company's stock. Moore, The "Interested" Director or Officer Transaction, 4 Del.J.Corp.L. 674, 676 (1979); Nathan & Shapiro, Legal Standard of Fairness of Merger Terms Under Delaware Law, 2 Del.J.Corp.L. 44, 46–47 (1977). See Tri–Continental Corp. v. Battye, Del.Supr., 74 A.2d 71, 72 (1950); 8 Del.C. § 262(h). However, the test for fairness is not a bifurcated one as between fair dealing and price. All aspects of the issue must be examined as a whole since the question is one of entire fairness. However, in a non-fraudulent transaction we recognize that price may be the preponderant consideration outweighing other features of the merger. Here, we address the two basic aspects of fairness separately because we find reversible error as to both.

D.

Part of fair dealing is the obvious duty of candor required by *Lynch I*, supra. Moreover, one possessing superior knowledge may not mislead any stockholder by use of corporate information to which the latter is not privy. Lank v. Steiner, Del.Supr., 224 A.2d 242, 244 (1966). Delaware has long imposed this duty even upon persons who are not corporate officers or directors, but who nonetheless are privy to matters of interest or significance to their company. Brophy v. Cities Service Co., Del.Ch., 70 A.2d 5, 7 (1949). With the well-established Delaware law on the subject, and the Court of Chancery's findings of fact here, it is inevitable that the obvious conflicts posed by Arledge and Chitiea's preparation of their "feasibility study", derived from UOP information, for the sole use and benefit of Signal, cannot pass muster.

The Arledge–Chitiea report is but one aspect of the element of fair dealing. How did this merger evolve? It is clear that it was entirely initiated by Signal. The serious time constraints under which the principals acted were all set by Signal. It had not found a suitable outlet for its excess cash and considered UOP a desirable investment, particularly since it was now in a position to acquire the whole company for itself. For whatever reasons, and they were only Signal's, the entire transaction was presented to and approved by UOP's board within four business days. Standing alone, this is not necessarily indicative of any lack of fairness by a majority shareholder. It was what occurred, or more properly, what did not occur, during this brief period that makes the time constraints imposed by Signal relevant to the issue of fairness.

The structure of the transaction, again, was Signal's doing. So far as negotiations were concerned, it is clear that they were modest at best. Crawford, Signal's man at UOP, never really talked price with Signal, except to accede to its management's statements on the subject, and to convey to Signal the UOP outside directors' view that as between the $20–$21 range under consideration, it would have to be $21. The latter is not a surprising outcome, but hardly arm's length negotiations. Only the protection of benefits for UOP's key employees and the issue of Lehman Brothers' fee approached any concept of bargaining.

As we have noted, the matter of disclosure to the UOP directors was wholly flawed by the conflicts of interest raised by the Arledge–

Chitiea report. All of those conflicts were resolved by Signal in its own favor without divulging any aspect of them to UOP.

This cannot but undermine a conclusion that this merger meets any reasonable test of fairness. The outside UOP directors lacked one material piece of information generated by two of their colleagues, but shared only with Signal. True, the UOP board had the Lehman Brothers' fairness opinion, but that firm has been blamed by the plaintiff for the hurried task it performed, when more properly the responsibility for this lies with Signal. There was no disclosure of the circumstances surrounding the rather cursory preparation of the Lehman Brothers' fairness opinion. Instead, the impression was given UOP's minority that a careful study had been made, when in fact speed was the hallmark, and Mr. Glanville, Lehman's partner in charge of the matter, and also a UOP director, having spent the weekend in Vermont, brought a draft of the "fairness opinion letter" to the UOP directors' meeting on March 6, 1978 with the price left blank. We can only conclude from the record that the rush imposed on Lehman Brothers by Signal's timetable contributed to the difficulties under which this investment banking firm attempted to perform its responsibilities. Yet, none of this was disclosed to UOP's minority.

Finally, the minority stockholders were denied the critical information that Signal considered a price of $24 to be a good investment. Since this would have meant over $17,000,000 more to the minority, we cannot conclude that the shareholder vote was an informed one. Under the circumstances, an approval by a majority of the minority was meaningless. *Lynch I,* 383 A.2d at 279, 281; Cahall v. Lofland, Del.Ch., 114 A.2d 224 (1921).

Given these particulars and the Delaware law on the subject, the record does not establish that this transaction satisfies any reasonable concept of fair dealing, and the Chancellor's findings in that regard must be reversed.

E.

Turning to the matter of price, plaintiff also challenges its fairness. His evidence was that on the date the merger was approved the stock was worth at least $26 per share. In support, he offered the testimony of a chartered investment analyst who used two basic approaches to valuation: a comparative analysis of the premium paid over market in ten other tender offer-merger combinations, and a discounted cash flow analysis.

In this breach of fiduciary duty case, the Chancellor perceived that the approach to valuation was the same as that in an appraisal proceeding. Consistent with precedent, he rejected plaintiff's method of proof and accepted defendants' evidence of value as being in accord with practice under prior case law. This means that the so-called "Delaware block" or weighted average method was employed wherein the elements of value, i.e., assets, market price, earnings, etc., were assigned a particular weight and the resulting amounts added to determine the value per share. This procedure has been in use for decades. See In re General Realty & Utilities Corp., Del.Ch., 52 A.2d 6, 14–15 (1947). However, to the extent it excludes other generally accepted techniques used in the financial community and the courts, it is now clearly outmoded. It is time we recognize this in appraisal and other stock valuation proceedings and bring our law current on the subject.

While the Chancellor rejected plaintiff's discounted cash flow method of valuing UOP's stock, as not corresponding with "either logic or the existing law" (426 A.2d at 1360), it is significant that this was essentially the focus, i.e., earnings potential of UOP, of Messrs. Arledge and Chitiea in their evaluation of the merger. Accordingly, the standard "Delaware block" or weighted average method of valuation, formerly employed in appraisal and other stock valuation cases, shall no longer exclusively control such proceedings. We believe that a more liberal approach must include proof of value by any techniques or methods which are generally considered acceptable in the financial community and otherwise admissible in court, subject only to our interpretation of 8 Del.C. § 262(h), infra. See also D.R.E. 702–05. This will obviate the very structure and mechanistic procedure that has heretofore governed such matters. . . .

Fair price obviously requires consideration of all relevant factors involving the value of a company. This has long been the law of Delaware as stated in *Tri–Continental Corp.*, 74 A.2d at 72:

> The basic concept of value under the appraisal statute is that the stockholder is entitled to be paid for that which has been taken from him, viz., his proportionate interest in a going concern. By value of the stockholder's proportionate interest in the corporate enterprise is meant the true or intrinsic value of his stock which has been taken by the merger. In determining what figure represents this true or intrinsic value, the appraiser and the courts must take into consideration all factors and elements which reasonably might enter into the fixing of value. Thus, market value, asset value, dividends, earning prospects, the nature of the enterprise and any other facts which were known or which could be ascertained as of the date of merger and which throw any light on *future prospects* of the merged corporation are not only pertinent to an inquiry as to the value of the dissenting stockholders' interest, but *must be considered* by the agency fixing the value. (Emphasis added.)

This is not only in accord with the realities of present day affairs, but it is thoroughly consonant with the purpose and intent of our statutory law. Under 8 Del.C. § 262(h), the Court of Chancery:

> shall appraise the shares, determining their *fair* value exclusive of any element of value arising from the accomplishment or expectation of the merger, together with a fair rate of interest, if any, to be paid upon the amount determined to be the *fair* value. In determining such *fair* value, the Court shall take into account *all relevant factors* . . . (Emphasis added)

. . .

It is significant that section 262 now mandates the determination of "fair" value based upon "all relevant factors". Only the speculative elements of value that may arise from the "accomplishment or expectation" of the merger are excluded. We take this to be a very narrow exception to the appraisal process, designed to eliminate use of *pro forma* data and projections of a speculative variety relating to the completion of a merger. But elements of future value, including the nature of the enterprise, which are known or susceptible of proof as of the date of the merger and not the product of speculation, may be considered. When the trial court deems it appropriate, fair value also includes any damages, resulting from the taking, which the stockholders sustain as a class. If that was not the case, then the obligation to consider "all relevant factors" in the valuation process would be eroded. We are supported in this view not only by *Tri–Continental Corp.,* 74 A.2d at 72, but also by the evolutionary amendments to section 262.

Prior to an amendment in 1976, the earlier relevant provision of section 262 stated:

> (f) The appraiser shall determine the value of the stock of the stockholders . . . The Court shall by its decree determine the value of the stock of the stockholders entitled to payment therefor . . .

The first references to "fair" value occurred in a 1976 amendment to section 262(f), which provided:

> (f) . . . the Court shall appraise the shares, determining their fair value exclusively of any element of value arising from the accomplishment or expectation of the merger. . . .

It was not until the 1981 amendment to section 262 that the reference to "fair value" was repeatedly emphasized and the statutory mandate that the Court "take into account all relevant factors" appeared [section 262(h)]. Clearly, there is a legislative intent to fully compensate shareholders for whatever their loss may be, subject only to the narrow limitation that one can not take speculative effects of the merger into account.

Although the Chancellor received the plaintiff's evidence, his opinion indicates that the use of it was precluded because of past Delaware practice. While we do not suggest a monetary result one way or the other, we do think the plaintiff's evidence should be part of the factual mix and weighed as such. Until the $21 price is measured on remand by the valuation standards mandated by Delaware law, there can be no finding at the present stage of these proceedings that the price is fair. Given the lack of any candid disclosure of the material facts surrounding establishment of the $21 price, the majority of the minority vote, approving the merger, is meaningless.

The plaintiff has not sought an appraisal, but rescissory damages of the type contemplated by Lynch v. Vickers Energy Corp., Del.Supr., 429 A.2d 497, 505–06 (1981) (*Lynch II*). In view of the approach to valuation that we announce today, we see no basis in our law for *Lynch II*'s exclusive monetary formula for relief. On remand the plaintiff will be permitted to test the fairness of the $21 price by the standards we herein establish, in conformity with the principle applicable to an appraisal—that fair value be determined by taking "into account all relevant factors" [see 8 Del.C. § 262(h), supra]. In our view this includes the elements of rescissory damages if the Chancellor considers them susceptible of proof and a remedy appropriate to all the issues of fairness before him. To the extent that *Lynch II,* 429 A.2d at 505–06, purports to limit the Chancellor's discretion to a single remedial formula for monetary damages in a cash-out merger, it is overruled.

While a plaintiff's monetary remedy ordinarily should be confined to the more liberalized appraisal proceeding herein established, we do not intend any limitation on the historic powers of the Chancellor to grant such other relief as the facts of a particular case may dictate. The appraisal remedy we approve may not be adequate in certain cases, particularly where fraud, misrepresentation, self-dealing, deliberate waste of corporate assets, or gross and palpable overreaching are involved. Cole v. National Cash Credit Association, Del.Ch., 156 A. 183, 187 (1931). Under such circumstances, the Chancellor's powers are complete to fashion any form of equitable and monetary relief as may be appropriate, including rescissory damages. Since it is apparent that this long completed transaction is too involved to undo, and in view of the Chancellor's discretion, the award, if any, should be in the form of monetary damages based upon entire fairness standards, i.e., fair dealing and fair price.

Obviously, there are other litigants, like the plaintiff, who abjured an appraisal and whose rights to challenge the element of fair value must be preserved. Accordingly, the quasi-appraisal remedy we grant the plaintiff here will apply only to: (1) this case; (2) any case now pending on appeal to this Court; (3) any case now pending in the Court of Chancery which has not yet been appealed but which may be eligible for direct appeal to this Court; (4) any case challenging a cash-out merger, the effective date of which is on or before February 1, 1983; and (5) any proposed merger to be presented at a shareholders' meeting, the notification of which is mailed to the stockholders on or before February 23, 1983. Thereafter, the provisions of 8 Del.C. § 262, as herein construed, respecting the scope of an appraisal and the means for perfecting the same, shall govern the financial remedy available to minority shareholders in a cash-out merger. Thus, we return to the well established principles of Stauffer v. Standard Brands, Inc., Del. Supr., 187 A.2d 78 (1962) and David J. Greene & Co. v. Schenley Industries, Inc., Del.Ch., 281 A.2d 30 (1971), mandating a stockholder's recourse to the basic remedy of an appraisal.

III.

Finally, we address the matter of business purpose. The defendants contend that the purpose of this merger was not a proper subject of inquiry by the trial court. The plaintiff says that no valid purpose existed—the entire transaction was a mere subterfuge designed to eliminate the minority. The Chancellor ruled otherwise, but in so doing he clearly circumscribed the thrust and effect of *Singer*. Weinberger v. UOP, 426 A.2d at 1342–43, 1348–50. This has led to the thoroughly sound observation that the business purpose test "may be . . . virtually interpreted out of existence, as it was in *Weinberger* ".[38]

The requirement of a business purpose is new to our law of mergers and was a departure from prior case law. See Stauffer v. Standard Brands, Inc., supra; David J. Greene & Co. v. Schenley Industries, Inc., supra.

In view of the fairness test which has long been applicable to parent-subsidiary mergers, Sterling v. Mayflower Hotel Corp., Del. Supr., 93 A.2d 107, 109–10 (1952), the expanded appraisal remedy now available to shareholders, and the broad discretion of the Chancellor to fashion such relief as the facts of a given case may dictate, we do not

---

38. Weiss, The Law of Take Out Mergers: A Historical Perspective, 56 N.Y.U.L. Rev. 624, 671, n. 300 (1981).

believe that any additional meaningful protection is afforded minority shareholders by the business purpose requirement of the trilogy of *Singer, Tanzer,*[39] *Najjar,*[40] and their progeny. Accordingly, such requirement shall no longer be of any force or effect.

The judgment of the Court of Chancery, finding both the circumstances of the merger and the price paid the minority shareholders to be fair, is reversed. The matter is remanded for further proceedings consistent herewith. Upon remand the plaintiff's post-trial motion to enlarge the class should be granted.

. . .

Reversed and remanded.

NOTE ON THE APPRAISAL REMEDY AND FAIRNESS

As the List and Weinberger cases indicate, there is now an intense interrelation between fairness questions and the appraisal process. This was not so in the early days of the appraisal remedy. The generally agreed upon version of the history of appraisal is that it was introduced by legislation on the theory that shareholders were parties to the contract created by the corporate charter and that they were entitled not to have the contract changed on them without their consent. Appraisal, then, was a no-fault right to bail out of the transformed corporation simply because one didn't like the transformation. This still can be the outcome in certain situations, that is, where a corporation is merged into another on an exchange of securities basis a shareholder who does not want to go along can start the appraisal process. Compare the rights which a partner can exercise if the affairs of the partnership are being managed in a way unacceptable to that partner—the delectus personae principle, the right to initiate dissolution, etc. See p. 28 supra.

The appraisal remedy has come under fire from different directions. It is noted that the events which trigger appraisal are defined very differently in the laws of the 50 states and that all of them are rather arbitrary. Recall that in Farris v. Glen Alden the two state laws in question made appraisal available under quite different circumstances. A merger, a charter amendment, a sale of assets, a dissolution, etc. can, from a practical economic sense, be either overwhelmingly important or wholly trivial.

Another challenge became stronger as efficient market theory developed. Why should a shareholder get appraisal if the shares of stock that are held after the transaction are marketable and can be simply sold by the dissatisfied? Modern corporation statutes like Delaware's (§ 262(b)) except some transactions on that basis although the definitions of the market exception vary from state to state.

Note that the steps that have to be taken to preserve and exercise one's appraisal rights are elaborately defined by statute and need to be

---

39. Tanzer v. International General Industries, Inc., Del.Supr., 379 A.2d 1121, 1124–25 (1977).

40. Roland International Corp. v. Najjar, Del.Supr., 407 A.2d 1032, 1036 (1979).

followed with precision. The process itself is somewhat expensive and has generally been judged to be unsatisfactory. The Court in Weinberger (p. 739) refers to "the so-called 'Delaware block' or weighted average method" as having been used for decades. It then goes on to rule that it is now outmoded. To give you a flavor of the way in which the Delaware block worked consider in summary the facts in Application of Delaware Racing Ass'n, 42 Del.Ch. 406, 213 A.2d 203 (1965). The case involved a corporation which owned Delaware Park, a track used for thoroughbred horse racing. The method of appraisal involved use of (1) asset value—the appraised value of the racing plant, (2) the market value of the shares, (3) the earnings value of the shares, measured by a five year average of the firm's earnings per share capitalized by a multiplier of 15.2 by the appraiser and 10 by the Vice Chancellor and (4) a dividend value of $0 since there were no dividends. The four values were weighted—according to a rather arbitrary formula:

Asset value	$5,996.00 × 25%	$1,499.00
Market value	$1,305.00 × 40%	$ 522.00
Earnings value	$1,201.19 × 25%	$ 300.30
Dividend value	$ 0 × 10%	
		$2,321.30

While evaluation according to earnings has been the center of modern financial analysis the particular version represented in the Delaware block is subject to special criticism. In See v. Heppenheimer, p. 143 supra, the court criticizes valuation of property as consideration for stock issuance in terms that take future earnings into account. The Delaware block takes only past earnings—the five years' average—into account. But what if there is a distinct upward swing to the track of the earnings over the five years? Surely intelligent commercial evaluators would take that very much into account and therefore there is a conservative bias to the Delaware method.

NOTE ON "FAIRNESS" IN FUNDAMENTAL CHANGES OTHER THAN MERGERS

While each of the three cases here set forth on fairness involves a merger, the issue arises in other types of basic changes as well. A sale of assets or a dissolution could be attacked as being unfair to a minority, if, for example, the buyer of the asset were an "insider" as to the selling and dissolving corporation. A special set of circumstances surrounds the issue of fairness in amendments to the charter or articles of incorporation. In particular there is a set of cases involving the ability of a corporation to cut off accrued preferred dividends. To set the situation, imagine a corporation that has had a rough time financially for some years. It has an issue of cumulative preferred stock, and arrears of dividends have built up to an oppressive degree. The corporation is now in better circumstances and has realized some earnings. The management foresees the day coming when it can pay dividends on its common but notes that it would have to pay off the arrears on the preferred first and that may take a long time. It proposes a recapitalization plan under which the arrearages are cut off; the preferred stockholders obtain in return either shares of common stock or of a new preferred minus the vexing arrearages. The preferred casts its vote under the pressure of the fact that the management, generally controlled by the common (except in cases where the preferred is given voting rights by the charter after arrearages reach a certain point), will not declare any dividends on the preferred unless the demands of the common are met. Thus the preferred will very likely give the requisite class vote (examine § 242(c) of the Delaware law for the vote required).

Dissident preferred holders have attacked recapitalizations on several grounds. They have asserted a "vested rights" theory under which no adverse change to such rights is legitimate—especially if it had not been authorized by antecedent legislation. They have also asserted the unfairness of the transaction.[41]

In the courts' responses an important role has been played by the interaction between the amendment and merger clauses. It has proved to be advantageous to choose the merger route. Sometimes the merger statute calls for a lesser vote than the amendment statute. After having asserted the vested rights doctrine in sweeping terms in a series of recapitalization cases that astonished the corporate world, the Delaware courts then astounded it by turning around and permitting a cancellation of preferred stock arrearages in a merger with a corporation set up for that purpose.[42] They thus created the doctrine that different sections of the Delaware corporation law have independent legal significance and that things impermissible under one can be done under another. It is much the same problem as that over which the Pennsylvania courts and those of Delaware have disagreed with respect to appraisal rights (see pp. 688–696 supra).

More recent amendment problems have arisen in connection with reverse stock splits in which the number of shares is reduced and their par or stated value increased, thus permitting the involuntary squeeze out of small shareholders who are left with fractional shares. This is a route to the goal [43] of going private and eliminating numbers of small shareholders.

---

41. The judicial history is recounted in Bove v. Community Hotel Corp. of Newport, R.I., 105 R.I. 36, 249 A.2d 89 (1969). For a study of the impact of preferred stock amendments see Conard, Manipulation of Share Priorities, The Record of 79 Listed Securities, 8 Vand.L.Rev. 55 (1954). For an argument favoring preservation of the priority of preferred claims, see Brudney, Standards of Fairness and the Limits of Preferred Stock Modifications, 26 Rutgers L.Rev. 445 (1973).

42. The forceful verbs come from the opinion in Hottenstein v. York Ice Machinery Corp., 136 F.2d 944, 950 (3d Cir.1943), a case in which the court concluded that the Erie doctrine obliged it to follow suit.

43. See Teschner v. Chicago Title & Trust Co., 59 Ill.2d 452, 322 N.E.2d 54 (1974) and the comments on "going private," p. 678 supra.

QUESTIONS

(1) Consider the rejection of a business purpose test in Weinberger. How often will it occur in a publicly held corporation that the majority owner will not have some plausible purpose other than sheer malicious enjoyment at cutting out the minority? Should it be sufficient as a business purpose that there will be an end to the expense and nuisance of reporting on the subsidiary's affairs as required by exchange rules and by the 1934 Act?

(2) Consider possible justifications for a merger aimed at eliminating a minority interest. What if the minority has consistently been obstructionist, perhaps to the point where a director so acting might be removed for cause? Suppose that there are continuing and apparently irreconcilable differences about dealings between the parent and the subsidiary and these quarrels produce not only expensive litigation but business paralysis?

(3) You will recall the argument, p. 616 supra, that it is wrong for the holder of a controlling stock interest in a corporation to obtain a premium upon the sale of the block to others. In the light of that argument, how would you react to the fairness of the following transaction? Corporation X has two classes of common stock, possessing identical rights except that each share of Class A common has one vote but Class B common stock has no vote except as to mergers, amendments of the articles and other fundamental changes. To simplify the financial structure of Corporation X it is proposed that a single new class of common stock be substituted for both A and B common. Each share of Class B common is to be exchanged for one of the new shares; each share of Class A would receive 1.25 shares of the new in recognition of the surrender of its voting preference. Or suppose the opposite case—a recapitalization will leave most shareholders with a voteless common stock.

(4) How does Weinberger deal with the ban put by § 262(k) on appraisals of classes of stock that had been listed on a national securities exchange or held by more than 2000 shareholders? Does this mean that the quasi appraisal remedy is available where appraisal is not? Is the approach of § 262(k) vulnerable to analysis in economic terms, that is, might the ability to sell one's shares on the market not be enough to guarantee the fairness of one's cash-out?

Bibliography: An up-to-date review of appraisal law is Kanda & Levmore, Appraisal Remedy and the Goals of Corporate Law, 32 U.C.L.A.L.Rev. 429 (1985). Important on the issue of financial fairness is Brudney & Chirelstein, Fair Shares in Corporate Mergers and Takeovers, 88 Harv.L.Rev. 297 (1974). A classic on fairness especially outside of the merger field is Lattin, Minority and Dissenting Shareholders' Rights in Fundamental Changes, 23 Law & Contemp. Prob. 307 (1958).

Chapter XIV

THE CLOSE CORPORATION

1. Introduction

With the close corporation we almost come a full circle to Chapter II, for we are dealing with corporations that have been structured so as to resemble as closely as possible a partnership. A basic question about any close corporation is whether it should be incorporated at all. Questions of liability and continuity may push the entrepreneurs away from a partnership towards incorporation. Tax factors may push in the other direction. This is a suitable point to look again at Chapter II and the problem at the end of that chapter.

Some of the older cases found it objectionable to confuse partnership and corporate structures. To let one of the classic cases speak for itself: [1]

> . . . The law never contemplated that persons engaged in business as partners may incorporate, with intent to obtain the advantages and immunities of a corporate form, and then, Proteus-like, become at will a copartnership or a corporation, as the exigencies or purposes of their joint enterprise may from time to time require. The policy of the law is to the contrary. If the parties have the rights of partners, they have the duties and liabilities imposed by law, and are responsible in solido to all creditors. If they adopt the corporate form, with the corporate shield extended over them to protect them against personal liability, they cease to be partners, and have only the rights, duties, and obligations of stockholders. They cannot be partners inter sese and a corporation as to the rest of the world. Furthermore, upon grounds of public policy, the doctrine contended for cannot be tolerated, as it renders nugatory and void the authority of the Legislature—a co-ordinate branch of the government—established by the Constitution, in respect to the creation, supervision, and winding up of corporations.
> . . .

More recent case law has been more sympathetic to the close corporation. Aside from paying less attention to the conceptual problems, judges fail to see how changes in the internal structuring of a corpora-

---

1. Jackson v. Hooper, 76 N.J.Eq. 599, 75 Atl. 568 (Err. & App.1910). The case involved two corporations, one organized in England and one in Illinois, marketing the Encyclopedia Britannica.

tion are likely to have an adverse effect on outsiders and hence to be a matter of public policy. Modern corporate legislation has been much more accommodating to the needs of the close corporation. The Delaware statute is an example of this; it sets the tone for its Subchapter XIV on the topic with a section (§ 354) that forbids a court to follow the philosophy set forth in the above quotation. The rest of the subchapter spells out various ways in which participants in small corporations can shape their arrangements to suit their needs. In fact, Delaware law is not as prominent in this sector as it is with such corporations as the Fortune 500 since those who are incorporating small businesses in, say, New York or Illinois will seldom find it expedient or economical to file their papers in Delaware. Thus the Close Corporation Supplement provisions of the Model Business Corporation Act [2] may prove more the trend-setters in this field and, as incorporated into state statutes, more intensively explicated by the courts.

In the 1950's and 60's the focus of this Chapter would have been upon the problems encountered by drafters of corporate papers—and those who have to make them work when dissension emerges—in accommodating their clients' needs with the demands of rather rigid statutes, rigidly applied. Now, in the more advanced states, that is no longer a significant problem. Significant problems peculiar to the close corporation do remain but their focus is somewhat different. The questions now are in terms of whether and how one should use those opportunities thus opened by a permissive statute. Note that some permissive statutes have been interpreted to require quite strict compliance with the terms of such permissions.[3]

The chief problems peculiar to the close corporation which we discuss below can be grouped as follows:

(1) *Shifts in Control:* The group of entrepreneurs forming a close corporation may reject one or all of the underlying assumptions that the law typically makes about the allocation of control in an ordinary corporation.

(a) That management is consigned to the hands of the board of directors. It may be unnecessarily cumbersome to have a board at all where all concerned are shareholder-managers.

(b) That decisions by the board or the shareholders are taken by a majority vote of those present at a meeting with a quorum (with some

---

2. See 4 Model Business Corporation Act Annotated (3d ed. 1986—Suppl.)

3. For example, in Ling & Co. v. Trinity Sav. & Loan Ass'n, 470 S.W.2d 441 (Tex. Civ.App.1971), restrictions on stock transfer were held invalid because they did not meet the Texas law's requirements (a) that they be set forth in a "conspicuous" manner and (b) that the corporation have no more than 20 shareholders. New York courts have repeatedly held *by laws* invalid when they attempted to include provisions which the statute permits if set forth in the *charter.* E.g., Model, Roland Co. v. Industrial Acoustics Co., 16 N.Y.2d 703, 261 N.Y.S.2d 896 (1965); In re William Faendrich, Inc., 2 N.Y.2d 468, 161 N.Y.S.2d 99, 141 N.E.2d 597 (1957). But see Zion v. Kurtz, 50 N.Y.2d 92, 428 N.Y.S.2d 199, 405 N.E.2d 681 (1980), interpreting Delaware law to uphold shareholder agreement that limited board of director action in ways that could have been accomplished by charter provisions under § 351.

exceptions for major changes). Some minority shareholders may insist upon the security against changes in direction afforded by having the right to veto decisions; hence requirements of unanimity or near unanimity in decision-making are common.

(c) That decisions by the shareholders will be made by those having a majority in interest of the equity investment of the corporation. Close corporation founders may wish to arrange matters so that persons contributing skill and effort rather than cash have a larger say in matters. The drafter may try to accommodate this either by agreements affecting how votes are to be cast or by arranging the stock structure of the corporation, through non-voting stock or the like, so as to achieve the desired balance. See pp. 368–371, supra, for some related problems.

(d) That decisions will be made as they come up by directors or shareholders exercising their then current best judgment. Participants in close corporations often want commitments to safeguard their interests. For example, they may insist upon long-term assurances of a job and a salary. Jones v. Williams, p. 318, supra, involved a long-term contract giving editorial policy control to one person. It was challenged unsuccessfully on grounds of public policy based on a statute like 8 Del. C. § 141 giving control to the board of directors. Desires for long-term commitments may also relate to policies on dividends versus reinvestment, use of particular sources of services or supplies, etc. Some members may seek to enter into alliances with others by which they are committed to voting as a bloc rather than according to their current interests or views.

(2) *Provisions on Transfers:* Whereas a public corporation seeks to make its stock as marketable as possible, the members of a close corporation operate on the assumption, implied by the very term itself, that the membership is limited, that changes in ownership will be important, even traumatic, because they bring with them changes in the personal, operating relationships among the venturers. One side of the coin is the drafting of restrictions upon transfers of interests in the enterprise, approximating the disposition of Section 18 of the Partnership Act—the delectus personae. The other side of the coin is the provision of some sort of partial substitute for the ready market available for shares of publicly owned enterprises so that, in the event of death, disability or disagreement, one of the member's interests can be bought out by the others. There may need to be a complex option, first refusal or contingency clause accompanied by valuation provisions.

(3) *Dispute–Resolution Clauses:* The combination of (a) clauses requiring actual or virtual unanimity before changes in policy can be made with (b) clauses or conditions preventing the dissentient member from selling out provides a fertile seedbed for disputes. Lawyers attempt to cope with clauses calling for arbitration or other third party dispute resolution or for dissolution of the strife-ridden enterprise.

While these are the major areas of special close corporation interest it is also worth recalling that a number of issues discussed in the preceding chapters take on a different aspect when a close corporation is involved.

(1) While "piercing the veil" problems (Chapter IV, supra) arise most commonly in connection with corporations having but a single shareholder, they occur quite often in connection with close corporations also. The same is true of related undercapitalization problems discussed at p. 159, supra.

(2) Much of the federal regulation discussed above, in particular the proxy rules under Section 14 and the short swing insider trading rules under Section 16, does not apply to close corporations, for reasons set out at pp. 403, 404. With a little care, the close corporation's planners can ordinarily escape the registration requirements of the Securities Act through one of the exemptions it provides. See p. 170 supra. Note, however, that Rule 10b–5 usually covers close corporation transactions since its interstate commerce requirements are easily met.

(3) In general it is close corporations that are most careless of the formalities prescribed for directors' and shareholders' meetings so that lawyers are most apt to have to unravel procedural messes in close corporation cases, sometimes relying on the active or tacit consent of all of the small body of shareholders. See p. 202, supra.

(4) The rules about fiduciary obligations explored in Chapters VII and VIII take on a different coloration in the close corporation context. Distinctions between officers and directors on the one hand and shareholders on the other, see p. 385 supra, tend to lose all significance where the same actors play all roles as they typically do in a corporation with two to ten members. The likelihood increases that personal motivations and feelings will interfere with the objective performance of fiduciary duties. In particular one observes the likelihood that one faction within the corporation will attempt to oust another, a process that has come to be known as squeezing out or freezing out the dissident. Those devices, such as a contrived merger or a recapitalization, that have been used in connection with "going private" or with eliminating public shareholders of a partially owned subsidiary may be employed in such internal warfare.[4]

One of the opening questions about a close corporation is its definition. The modern statutes that give special treatment to these creatures normally define them in one or more of the following ways: (1) by barring their securities from the exchanges or the organized over-the-counter market, (2) by requiring them to make explicit the restrictions on transfer of shares by appropriate agreements, properly filed, and by notations on the stock certificates, and (3) by limits on the permissible number of shareholders. For an example, see 8 Del.C.

---

4. For a close dissection of such transactions see F. O'Neal, Squeeze–Outs of Minority Shareholders: Expulsion or Oppression of Business Associates (1975). A classic example is Matteson v. Ziebarth, 40 Wash.2d 286, 242 P.2d 1025 (1952).

§ 342.   None of these restrictions prevent a close corporation from being very big in terms of assets, earnings, employees and other indicia. Indeed, the Ford Motor Company before 1956 could have qualified as such.   Note that none of the American statutes have accepted the concept that there ought to be two distinct types of corporations under different statutes.   In the German system, quite widely copied in other civil law countries, there are two quite distinctly different types of corporations, the Aktiengesellschaft (public) and Gesellschaft mit beschrankter Haftung (private).   A corporate name must contain either the abbreviation AG or GmbH and changes from one form to the other are transactions almost as complex as mergers.[5]

One sub-category of the close corporation poses somewhat special problems: the corporation that has two (or three or four) stockholders each of which are themselves corporations.   These intercorporate creations are generally known as joint ventures and sometimes as incorporated joint ventures to distinguish them from contractual joint ventures in which no separate entity is established to pool the collaborators' efforts and assets.   You will recall (p. 32 supra) that the joint venture terminology has been employed to minimize the adverse impact of obsolescing rules about the *ultra vires* nature of corporate partnerships. This type of close corporation is immune to problems of death and generational succession but not to quarrels and conflicts of interest. Additionally, such collaboration can arouse the interest of the antitrust authorities if the parents are sufficiently important.

Working with close corporations is quite a different experience from counseling the public enterprise.   While personal factors are not wholly out of the picture in even the biggest corporation's executive suite, they are very much in the forefront in the typical close corporation.   Effective operations and rational decision-making may be hard to maintain amid the personal tensions that can arise between the temperamental entrepreneurs with their own interests at stake—often bound together or fatally divided by marital or family ties—in a way not typical of the bureaucratic functionary in the multi-divisional regime.   In this aspect corporation law gets tied together with estate planning and domestic relations and the corporation lawyer becomes a personal counselor and confidante.[6]   This personal factor, combined with the possibility of witnessing truly spectacular growth and success, make the work of the close corporation lawyer appealing to many. Additionally, the lawyer for a close corporation is characteristically less able to rely upon specialists' support in handling the other problems of the enterprise—its tax, real estate, consumer protection, environmental, etc. problems.   Thus the role involves being general counsel in the broadest sense.   One fears that close corporation counseling is not

---

5. DeVries & Juenger, Limited Liability Contract—the GmbH, 64 Colum.L.Rev. 866 (1964).

6. For a treatment of the estate planning aspects of the close corporation, see

H. Zaritsky, Tax Planning for Family Wealth Transfers ¶¶ 6.05–6.07 (1985).

always optimal. For example, Assessing the Utility of Wisconsin's Close Corporation Statute: An Empirical Study, [1986] Wisc.L.Rev. 811, reports that only 5% of corporation papers filed used the new close corporation law.

PROBLEM

As a lawyer in a small mid-western city you have known long and well Edam, Gouda and Kranz who have been involved in various branches of the dairy business. Edam is about 30 and has a reputation for great skill in the technical aspects of the industry. In business matters, however, you know Edam to be rather naive and no match for the trading instincts of Gouda. Recently they have decided that the time had come when Americans could produce high quality cheese for the gourmet market in competition with imports from Europe. They have agreed, after discussions to some of which you were a party, to form a small corporation to make and market this product. Edam and Gouda would leave their present employments with respectively, a major dairy concern and a wholesale food distributor to devote themselves to the enterprise. They can each put in $25,000. Kranz, who is Gouda's uncle and has retired from a prosperous business career, is willing to invest $50,000; he expects to keep an active eye on the firm's affairs but not to be involved in regular operations, particularly because he spends winters in the South. He will not be on the board of directors and the third board member will be a local banker, Warbucks, whose goodwill they are anxious to cultivate and whose judgment they trust.

The three individuals have specifically agreed that Edam and Gouda should draw minimum salaries of $10,000 per year and that these jobs should be contractually guaranteed to them indefinitely. Kranz has agreed to receive only a 25% share of the voting power in the enterprise and only one third of the profits even though he will furnish half of the funds invested in it. The parties wish the articles of incorporation and the by-laws to be amended only by a unanimous vote of the parties. Edam suggests that this ought to apply to all actions of the shareholders, especially the election of directors. There should be no transfers of stock without the consent of the others.

While you were starting to work on drafts of the necessary documents, Gouda and Kranz call upon you at your office and advise you that they also want to have a private agreement drafted by you under which Gouda and Kranz would commit themselves to vote their shares together, or, in case of disagreement, as Warbucks decides that they should. Gouda and Warbucks would be bound to exercise their votes on the board of directors in the same way.

As they leave your office you sort out in your mind the questions that the situation raised in your mind and jotted them down on a pad as follows:

(1) Ought I to get involved in this side deal that Gouda and Kranz are cooking up? Must we tell Edam?

(2) If I do draft such a clause will it hold up? What procedures and precautions must we follow?

(3) How can things best be arranged to give Kranz only the agreed-on share of control and earnings?

(4) Can we really guarantee job tenure by a binding contract?

(5) Are the proposed 100% consent requirements valid?

(6) Does the no-transfer change present problems?

(7) Does it make a difference to any of these questions whether we incorporate in Delaware or organize in this state which generally copies Delaware but has not yet gotten around to enacting close corporation provisions such as 8 Del.C. §§ 341–356? Are there any other considerations involved in making this choice?

(8) The clients seem to agree that what they want to do is incorporate. Are there any reasons for thinking that it would be simpler and more efficient for them to do all of this as a partnership?

Coming in to the office today, you start to cope with these questions.

---

2. Rearranging Control of the Corporation

RINGLING v. RINGLING BROS.–BARNUM & BAILEY COMBINED SHOWS, INC.

Court of Chancery of Delaware, 1946.
29 Del.Ch. 318, 49 A.2d 603, modified 29 Del.Ch. 610, 53 A.2d 441 (1947).

[The defendant corporation was incorporated in Delaware; its 7 directors were to be elected cumulatively. It had 1000 shares of authorized and issued stock which, at the time here involved was owned or controlled as follows.[7]

Edith Conway Ringling, petitioner (315 shares)
Aubrey B. Haley, defendant (315 shares)
John Ringling North, defendant (370 shares)

About September 15, 1941 Edith Ringling and Aubrey Haley (then Ringling) executed a "Memorandum of Agreement." The agreement recited various facts about the ownership of stock in the corporation, then tied up in various collateral deposit and voting trust arrangements which were to end on October 22, 1947 or earlier. It also referred to a 1934 agreement between the two parties. The agreement then continued as follows:

"NOW, THEREFORE, in consideration of the mutual covenants and agreements hereinafter contained the parties hereto agree as follows:

"1. Neither party will sell any shares of stock or any voting trust certificates in either of said corporations to any other person whomsoever, without first making a written offer to the other party hereto of all of the shares or voting trust certificates proposed to be sold, for the same price and upon the same terms and conditions as in such proposed sale, and allowing such other party a time of not less than 180 days from the date of such written offer within which to accept same.

"2. In exercising any voting rights to which either party may be entitled by virtue of ownership of stock or voting trust

---

7. [Ed.] This statement of facts is compounded from elements of both the Chancellor's and the Supreme Court's statements.

certificates held by them in either of said corporations each party will consult and confer with the other and the parties will act jointly in exercising such voting rights in accordance with such agreement as they may reach with respect to any matter calling for the exercise of such voting rights.

"3. In the event the parties fail to agree with respect to any matter covered by paragraph 2 above, the question in disagreement shall be submitted for arbitration to Karl D. Loos, of Washington, D.C., as arbitrator and his decision thereon shall be binding upon the parties hereto. Such arbitration shall be exercised to the end of assuring for the respective corporations good management and such participation therein by the members of the Ringling family as the experience, capacity and ability of each may warrant. The parties may at any time by written agreement designate any other individual to act as arbitrator in lieu of said Loos.

"4. Each of the parties hereto will enter into and execute such voting trust agreement or agreements and such other instruments as, from time to time they may deem advisable and as they may be advised by counsel are appropriate to effectuate the purposes and objects of this agreement.

"5. This agreement shall be in effect from the date hereof and shall continue in effect for a period of ten years unless sooner terminated by mutual agreement in writing by the parties hereto.

"6. The agreement of April 1934 is hereby terminated.

"7. This agreement shall be binding upon and inure to the benefit of the heirs, executors, administrators and assigns of the parties hereto respectively."

Because the corporation's indebtedness was paid off in 1943, the voting trust ended and the agreement took effect then. The parties voted together at the 1943, 1944, and 1945 meetings and elected 5 of the 7 directors each time. Before the 1946 meeting, however, dissension emerged. Karl Loos, an attorney, attempted to mediate the disputes. Finally, invoking his powers under the agreement, he gave instructions as to how the parties were supposed to vote their shares. Haley as proxy for Mrs. Haley refused to vote for an adjournment of the meeting, as instructed, Loos then ordered all the stock to be voted for a slate of 5 directors (Edith C. Ringling, Aubrey B. Haley, James A. Haley, Robert Ringling and William P. Dunn, Jr.). More precisely the 2205 votes each lady had (315 times 7 vacancies) were to be cast as follows:

Mrs. Ringling:
882 for herself
882 for her son Robert
441 for Mr. Dunn

Mrs. Haley:
882 for herself
882 for her husband
441 for Mr. Dunn

Although Mrs. Ringling complied, Mr. Haley tried to cast his wife's votes:

  1103 for his wife
  1102 for himself

Meanwhile Mr. North voted his 2590 votes (370 shares)
  864 for Mr. Woods
  863 for Mr. Griffin
  863 for himself

The Chairman ruled that the 5 candidates named by Mr. Loos were elected—and Messrs. Woods and North. The Haley–North group insisted that Mr. Griffin, not Mr. Dunn was elected. After a rather chaotic director's meeting, Mrs. Ringling began this action under § 31 (now § 225) of the Delaware law.

The opinion by VICE CHANCELLOR SEITZ recited the facts and determined that Delaware law applied. It continued as follows:]

Having concluded that the Delaware law must be applied to test the validity of this Agreement, it is next pertinent to examine defendants' contentions that the Agreement is unenforceable under Delaware law because it is only "an agreement to agree", or because it involves an attempted delegation of irrevocable control over voting rights in a manner which is against the public policy of this state.

Do we have here only "an agreement to agree", by which defendants mean that there exists no legally enforceable obligation?

Preliminarily, I think it clear that the mutual promises contained in the Agreement constitute sufficient consideration to support it. The mutual restraints on the actions of the parties with respect to the sale and voting of their stock comply with the consideration requirements of contract law.

Did the parties only agree to agree? Certainly the parties agreed to agree as to how they would vote their stock, but they also provided that they would be bound by the decision of a named person in the event they were unable to agree. Thus, an explicitly stated consequence follows their inability to agree. This consequence is conditioned upon the existence of a fact which is objectively ascertainable by the so-called arbitrator as well as a court of equity, namely, that the parties are in disagreement as to how their stock should be voted. The Agreement to agree has, therefore, provisions which are capable of being enforced with respect to particular facts. Moreover, the very nature and object of the Agreement render it impossible for the parties to do more than agree to agree, and to provide an enforceable alternative in the event no agreement is reached.

Defendants urge that no standard is provided in the Agreement for the guidance of the parties in reaching an agreement and that the purposes and policies which should guide them are not set forth and cannot be foretold. The Agreement does perhaps leave something to be desired in the way of explicitly setting forth the function and purpose of the Agreement for the guidance of the parties. However, I think it clear that the same language which is expressed as the standard by which the arbitrator should act must necessarily be read as the governing standard for the parties. This language provides: ". . . Such arbitration shall be exercised to the end of assuring for the respective corporations good management and such participation therein by the members of the Ringling family as the experience, capacity and ability of each may warrant. The parties may at any time by written agreement designate any other individual to act as arbitrator in lieu of said Loos."

It is quite evident that no agreement could set forth explicit guides to govern the parties because it is impossible in the nature of things to anticipate all the various subjects on which the vote of the stockholders might be required. Moreover, there is no reason to believe that the arbitrator would be expected to apply a different guiding principle in arriving at a decision than that which would guide the stockholders who agreed to submit to such arbitration.

I conclude that the Agreement is sufficiently definite in terms of the duties and obligations imposed on the parties to be legally enforceable on the state of facts here presented.

Turning to defendants' second objection, is the Agreement invalid as an attempted delegation of irrevocable control and voting rights in a manner which is against the public policy of this state? The answer to the question must depend upon the answer to two questions of a more explicit character, namely:

(1) Is the Agreement a voting trust agreement in which event it would admittedly be invalid for failure to comply with the statutory requirements of this state governing voting trusts?

(2) If not a voting trust agreement, is it, nevertheless, invalid as being against public policy because of the provision that the parties shall be bound by the instructions of the arbitrator as to how they shall vote in the event of a disagreement?

Section 18 of our General Corporation Law, Rev.Code 1935, § 2050, provides the exclusive method for creating voting trusts of stock of a Delaware corporation, Appon et al. v. Belle Isle Corporation et al., Del. Ch., 46 A.2d 749, affirmed by Supreme Court of Delaware, September 13, 1946. Does the present Agreement create a voting trust as that term is employed in Section 18? This court in Peyton v. William C. Peyton Corporation et al., 22 Del.Ch. 187, 199, 194 A. 106, 111 (reversed on other grounds 23 Del.Ch. 321, 7 A.2d 737, 123 A.L.R. 1482), has thus described a voting trust: "A voting trust as commonly understood is a device whereby two or more persons owning stock with voting powers, divorce the voting rights, thereof from the ownership, retaining to all intents and purposes the latter in themselves and transferring the former to trustees in whom the voting rights of all the depositors in the trust are pooled." See also Aldridge v. Franco–Wyoming Oil Co., 24 Del.Ch. 126, 7 A.2d 753, affirmed 24 Del.Ch. 349, 14 A.2d 380.

Does the present Agreement fall within the limitations of the quoted definition? I think not. The stockholders under the present Agreement vote their own stock at all times which is the antithesis of a voting trust because the latter has for its chief characteristic the severance of the voting rights from the other attributes of ownership. See in re Chilson, 19 Del.Ch. 398, 168 A. 82. In the cases where the parties to the present Agreement cannot reach an accord as to how they will vote, and are directed by the arbitrator as to how they shall vote their shares, the substance of the matter may be said not to differ in effect from a voting trust situation. However, considering the whole Agreement, there is this substantial distinction. Voting trustees have continuous voting control for the period of time stipulated in the agreement of trust. While here, the right of the arbitrator to direct the vote is limited to those particular cases where a stockholder's vote is called for and the parties cannot agree. True, the arbitration provision gives teeth to the Agreement but the parties desired that they should have the initial choice to determine policy in so far as it was determined by the vote of their shares and that a third party identified as an arbitrator should only resolve a conflict. In a voting trust as generally understood, the trustees in the very first instance determine policy and implement it by their votes.

This Agreement is actually a variation of the well-known stock pooling agreement and as such is to be distinguished from a voting trust. As is stated in 5 Fletcher Cyc. Corp. (Perm.Ed.) § 2064, at page 199, "Such agreements are distinct from voting trusts, and are not controlled by the same principles." See also Creed v. Copps, 103 Vt. 164, 152 A. 369, 71 A.L.R. p. 1289. It is my conclusion that the present Agreement is not a voting trust within the meaning of that term as used in Section 18 of our General Corporation Law and as a consequence, is not invalid for failure to comply with the provisions thereof.

Does the provision for arbitration constitute such a severance of voting control from ownership as to violate some public policy of this state with respect thereto?

The law with respect to agreements of the general type with which we are here concerned is fairly stated as follows in 5 Fletcher Cyc. Corp. (Perm.Ed.) § 2064, at page 194: "Generally, agreements and combinations to vote stock or control corporate action and policy are valid, if they seek without fraud to accomplish only what the parties might do as stockholders and do not attempt it by illegal proxies, trusts, or other means in contravention of statutes or law."

The principle of law stated seems to be sound and I think it is applicable here with respect to the legality of the Agreement under consideration. In the first place, there is no constitutional or statutory objection to the Agreement and defendants do not seriously challenge the legality of its objects. Indeed, in my opinion the objects and purposes of the Agreement as they are recited in the Agreement are lawful in principle and no evidence was introduced which tended to show that they were unlawful in operation.

The only serious question presented under this point arises from the defendants' contention that the arbitration provision has the effect of providing for an irrevocable separation of voting power from stock ownership and that such a provision is contrary to the public policy of this state. Perhaps in no field of the law are the precedents more varied and irreconcilable than those dealing with this phase of the case.

By adhering to strict literalism, it can be said that the present Agreement does not separate voting rights from ownership because the arbitrator only directs the parties as to how they shall vote in case of disagreement. However, recognizing substance rather than form, it is apparent that the arbitrator has voting control of the shares in the instances when he directs the parties as to how they shall vote since, if the Agreement is to be binding, they are also bound by his direction. When so considered, it is perhaps at variance with many, but not all of the precedents in other jurisdictions dealing with agreements of this general nature. [Citations omitted].

To the extent that the precedents elsewhere are based on questions other than public policy, they are inapplicable here. As to those cases which strike down agreements containing provisions which have the effect of severing voting control from ownership because of some judicially constructed public policy, I am not satisfied that the invocation of such a sanction is justified. See White v. Snell, 35 Utah 434, 100 P. 927; 5 Fletcher Cyc.Corp. (Perm.Ed.) § 2065, at page 212 et seq. As the California Court said in Smith et al. v. San Francisco & N.P. Ry. Co. et al., 115 Cal. 584, 47 P. 582, 587, 588, 35 L.R.A. 309, 56 Am.St.Rep. 119: ". . . 'Public policy' is a term of vague and uncertain meaning, which it pertains to the lawmaking power to define, and courts are apt to encroach upon the domain of that branch of the government if they characterize a transaction as invalid because it is contrary to public policy, unless the transaction contravenes some positive statute or some well-established rule of law."

No controlling Delaware precedent has been cited. The case of Aldridge v. Franco–Wyoming Oil Co., supra, relied upon by defendants, dealt only with the question of whether or not the particular Agreement before the court was or was not a voting trust agreement. The court was not called upon, as I am here, to determine whether or not the public policy of Delaware invalidates an agreement of the general type here involved (not being a voting trust), without regard to statutory law. In re Chilson, supra, actually turned on the question of the existence of an irrevocable proxy in the absence of a property interest in the holder. In view of the sweeping assumptions made in the case, it is not clear that it can be considered as having to do with anything more than a simple proxy situation—a very different situation from the contractual arrangement here involved.

Directing attention to the present Agreement, what vice exists in having an arbitrator agreed upon by the parties decide how their stock shall be voted in the event they are unable to agree? The parties obviously decided to contract with respect to this very situation and to appoint as arbitrator one in whom both had confidence. The cases which strike down agreements on the ground that some public policy prohibits the severance of ownership and voting control argue that there is something very wrong about a person "who has no beneficial interest or title in or to the stock" directing how it shall be voted. Such a person, according to these cases, has "no interest in the general prosperity of the corporation" and moreover, the stockholder himself has a duty to vote. See Bostwick et al. v. Chapman et al. (Shepaug Voting Trust Cases), 60 Conn. 553, 24 A. 32. Such reasons ignore the realities because obviously the person designated to determine how the shares shall be voted has the confidence of such shareholders. Quite naturally they would not want to place such power over their investment in the hands of one whom they felt would not be concerned with the welfare of the corporation. The objection based on the so-called duty of the stockholders to vote, presumably in person, is ludicrous when considered in the light of present day corporate practice. Thus, precedents from other jurisdictions which are based on reasons which have, in my opinion, lost their substance under present day conditions cannot be accorded favorable recognition. No public policy of this state requires a different conclusion.

Once it be concluded that no constitutional or statutory objection to the validity of the present Agreement exists, as I have found, then I think the objection to its legality must be based not on some abstract public policy but on fraud or illegality of purpose. Since no such fraud or illegality has been shown, defendants' objections must fall.

Defendants say that even if the Agreement is valid under the statutes and public policy of this state, it is, nevertheless, to be governed by "principles applicable to proxy delegations and, hence, would be revocable." Defendants go on to show how, in their opinion, the alleged proxy was revoked and conclude therefrom that the Agreement was not violated. It is perfectly obvious that the construction of the Agreement contended for by defendants, if accepted, would in effect render it meaningless. The answer to this contention of the defendants must be that we are not here concerned with a proxy situation as between the parties to the Agreement on one hand, and the arbitrator Loos on the other. The Agreement does not contemplate such a proxy either in form or in substance.

Defendants make several contentions based on the theory that we are here dealing with an Agreement containing an arbitration provision and that such a provision will not be specifically enforced in this state. Although Loos is referred to in the Agreement as an arbitrator, it is evident that this Agreement does not possess the characteristics which go to make up an arbitration Agreement. Here the action by the arbitrator, so-called, constitutes one of the principal, if not the principal feature of the Agreement. Obviously no Agreement was needed as to the action to be taken by the parties so long as they agreed. Under this Agreement, the arbitrator is *not* given both sides of a conflict and required to resolve the issue. The *fact* of the conflict gives to him the power to direct how the stock shall be voted without necessarily being bound by the facts which controlled the decisions of the parties, although both operate pursuant to the same general standard. Moreover, the so-called arbitrator is not called upon to resolve a conflict which would otherwise be decided by a court. The parties agreed to a specific procedure and made it an integral part of the contract itself—not something over and above the contract—which is the only way they could secure the objective they obviously sought in making the Agreement, namely, that the stock would be voted jointly. The principles of law governing arbitration agreements as set forth in Electrical Research Products, Inc. v. Vitaphone Corp., 20 Del.Ch. 417, 171 A. 738, are, therefore, inapplicable. Nomenclature when inconsistent with the objects and purposes of an agreement should not be permitted to control. Consequently, I have not felt bound by the use of the words "arbitration" and "arbitrator" in the Agreement.

Other contentions made with respect to the invalidity of the Agreement based on the premise that it constituted an arbitration agreement must fall in the light of my conclusion that it was not such an arbitration agreement as is governed by the principles of law relied upon by defendants. Moreover, I cannot agree with the defendants that the validity of this Agreement must in some way be adversely affected by the fact that it provides for a possible further agreement by way of a voting trust. . . .

I conclude that the stock held under the Agreement should have been voted pursuant to the direction of the arbitrator Loos to the parties or their representatives. When a party or her representative refuses to comply with the direction of the arbitrator, while he is properly acting under its provisions (as did Aubrey B. Haley's proxy here), then I believe the Agreement constitutes the willing party to the

Agreement an implied agent possessing the irrevocable proxy of the recalcitrant party for the purpose of casting the particular vote. Here an implied agency based on an irrevocable proxy is fully justified to implement the Agreement without doing violence to its terms. Moreover, the provisions of the Agreement make it clear that the proxy may be treated as one coupled with an interest so as to render it irrevocable under the circumstances. . . .

It is the opinion of the court that the nature of the Agreement does not preclude the granting of specific performance, e.g., see Clark v. Dodge, 269 N.Y. 410, 199 N.E. 641. Indeed, the granting of such relief here is well within the spirit of certain principles laid down by our courts in cases granting specific performance of contracts to sell stock which would give the vendee voting control. See G.W. Baker Mach. Co. v. United States Fire Apparatus Co., 11 Del.Ch. 386, 97 A. 613; Francis et al. v. Medill, 16 Del.Ch. 129, 141 A. 697. Obviously, to deny specific performance here would be tantamount to declaring the Agreement invalid. Since petitioner's rights in this respect were properly preserved at the stockholders' meeting, the meeting was a nullity to the extent that it failed to give effect to the provisions of the Agreement here involved. However, I believe it preferable to hold a new election rather than attempt to reconstruct the contested meeting. In this way the parties will be acting with explicit knowledge of their rights.

A meeting of the stockholders should be held before a master to be appointed by this court pursuant to the provisions of Section 31 of the General Corporation Law, Rev.Code 1935, § 2063. It is conceivable that prior to such meeting the parties to the Agreement will be able to agree as to how they will vote their stock, since such a possibility was lost prior to the meeting here reviewed through certain unfortunate happenings having nothing to do with the merits of the policy disagreement. It is obviously to the advantage of both parties to avoid the necessity for calling upon the arbitrator to act, and he will only act if the parties are unable to agree and action by him is requested. It must and should be assumed that the so-called arbitrator, if called upon to act, will bring to bear that sense of duty and impartiality which doubtless motivated the parties in selecting him for such an important role. In any event, the master in conducting the election will be bound to recognize and to give effect to the Agreement here involved, if its terms are properly invoked.

A decree accordingly will be advised.

[On appeal, the Delaware Supreme Court modified the order. First, it concluded that the agreement did not by implication give either party the right to vote the others' shares, although this would have been a more effective means of enforcing the arbitrator's decision. It then discussed the defendants' contention that the agreement was illegal because voting power in a Delaware corporation could be "irrevocably separated from the ownership of the stock" only by an agreement complying, as this did not, with § 18 (now 218) of the Delaware law.

JUDGE PEARSON's opinion states:]

In our view, neither the cases nor the statute sustain the rule for which the defendants contend. Their sweeping formulation would impugn well-recognized means by which a shareholder may effectively confer his voting rights upon others while retaining various other rights. For example, defendants' rule would apparently not permit holders of voting stock to confer upon stockholders of another class, by the device of an amendment of the certificate of incorporation, the exclusive right to vote during periods when dividends are not paid on stock of the latter class. The broad prohibitory meaning which defendants find in Section 18 seems inconsistent with their concession that proxies coupled with an interest may be irrevocable, for the statute contains nothing about such proxies. The statute authorizes, among other things, the deposit or transfer of stock in trust for a specified purpose, namely, "vesting" in the transferee "the right to vote thereon" for a limited period; and prescribes numerous requirements in this connection. Accordingly, it seems reasonable to infer that to establish the relationship and accomplish the purpose which the statute authorizes, its requirements must be complied with. But the statute does not purport to deal with agreements whereby shareholders attempt to bind each other as to how they shall vote their shares. Various forms of such pooling agreements, as they are sometimes called, have been held valid and have been distinguished from voting trusts. [Citations omitted.]

We think the particular agreement before us does not violate Section 18 or constitute an attempted evasion of its requirements, and is not illegal for any other reason. Generally speaking, a shareholder may exercise wide liberality of judgment in the matter of voting, and it is not objectionable that his motives may be for personal profit, or determined by whims or caprice, so long as he violates no duty owed his fellow shareholders. Heil v. Standard G. & E. Co., 17 Del.Ch. 214, 151 A. 303. The ownership of voting stock imposes no legal duty to vote at all. A group of shareholders may, without impropriety, vote their respective shares so as to obtain advantages of concerted action. They may lawfully contract with each other to vote in the future in such way as they, or a majority of their group, from time to time determine. . . .

Reasonable provisions for cases of failure of the group to reach a determination because of an even division in their ranks seem unobjectionable. The provision here for submission to the arbitrator is plainly designed as a deadlock-breaking measure, and the arbitrator's decision cannot be enforced unless at least one of the parties (entitled to cast one-half of their combined votes) is willing that it be enforced. We find the provision reasonable. It does not appear that the agreement enables the parties to take any unlawful advantage of the outside shareholder, or of any other person. It offends no rule of law or public policy of this state of which we are aware.

Legal consideration for the promises of each party is supplied by the mutual promises of the other party. The undertaking to vote in accordance with the arbitrator's decision is a valid contract. The good faith of the arbitrator's action has not been challenged and, indeed, the record indicates that no such challenge could be supported. Accordingly, the failure of Mrs. Haley to exercise her voting rights in accordance with his decision was a breach of her contract. It is no extenuation of the breach that her votes were cast for two of the three candidates directed by the arbitrator. His directions to her were part of a single plan or course of action for the voting of the shares of both parties to the agreement, calculated to utilize an advantage of joint action by them which would bring about the election of an additional director. The actual voting of Mrs. Haley's shares frustrates that plan to such an extent that it should not be treated as a partial performance of her contract.

Throughout their argument, defendants make much of the fact that all votes cast at the meeting were by the registered shareholders. The Court of Chancery may, in a review of an election, reject votes of a registered shareholder where his voting of them is found to be in violation of rights of another person. Compare: In re Giant Portland Cement Co., Del.Ch., 21 A.2d 697; In re Canal Construction Co., 21 Del. Ch. 155, 182 A. 545. It seems to us that upon the application of Mrs. Ringling, the injured party, the votes representing Mrs. Haley's shares should not be counted. Since no infirmity in Mr. North's voting has been demonstrated, his right to recognition of what he did at the meeting should be considered in granting any relief to Mrs. Ringling; for her rights arose under a contract to which Mr. North was not a party. With this in mind, we have concluded that the election should not be declared invalid, but that effect should be given to a rejection of the votes representing Mrs. Haley's shares. No other relief seems appropriate in this proceeding. Mr. North's vote against the motion for adjournment was sufficient to defeat it. With respect to the election of directors, the return of the inspectors should be corrected to show a rejection of Mrs. Haley's votes, and to declare the election of the six persons for whom Mr. North and Mrs. Ringling voted.

This leaves one vacancy in the directorate. The question of what to do about such a vacancy was not considered by the court below and has not been argued here. For this reason, and because an election of directors at the 1947 annual meeting (which presumably will be held in the near future) may make a determination of the question unimportant, we shall not decide it on this appeal. If a decision of the point appears important to the parties, any of them may apply to raise it in the Court of Chancery, after the mandate of this court is received there.

An order should be entered directing a modification of the order of the Court of Chancery in accordance with this opinion.

NOTE ON THE HISTORY OF THE RINGLING ENTERPRISE

The following resume of the history of the Ringling family enterprise is included partly because it sheds some light on the case itself, partly because it illustrates the problems likely to be encountered by any draftsman who seeks to establish regulations for a close corporation that will last far into the future and partly just because it's quite a story.

The first Ringling show was mounted in 1882 at Mazomanie, Wisconsin, by the sons of August Rüngeling, an immigrant German harness-maker. John, "emperor of dutch comedians," did a dance in wooden shoes while Charlie and Alf provided the music and Al juggled plates. The circus prospered and acquired equipment (starting with a rather moth-eaten hyena) and by the 1890's began to invade Barnum country, i.e., New England, and when Bailey died in 1906, the brothers bought control of Barnum & Bailey. From 1906 to 1929 the Ringling circus was "supremely uppermost"; these were the traditional days of the tented show, enormous trains moved with Prussian staff precision, animal smells, freaks and popcorn. The cash register reflected this prosperity.

During this era John held the center of the ring, particularly after 1926 when his older brother Charles died. John was a flamboyant hustler who carried his risk-laden tactics into other areas of business (picking up oil-wells, banks, etc.) into art collecting (stocking a large museum in Sarasota, Florida) and domestic life (managing a wealthy widow he had met at a roulette table, with whom he litigated intensively over her dower rights). In 1929 he overreached himself. He had neglected to renew the lease on Madison Square Garden and found himself preempted by a smaller rival. His characteristic response was to buy them out, borrowing $1,700,000. By 1932 he was in default on the loan. The circus was turned over to a newly formed Delaware corporation and managed by a relative outsider Sam Gumpertz. John's position declined: he was divorced from Emily after long battles, had to evade creditors in over 100 lawsuits and finally succumbed to a heart attack in 1936. Despite all the problems, his estate was valued at $23,500,000.

John was childless and left behind a model of what estate planning ought not to be. The Florida government had claims as a legatee under the will as well as claims for taxes. Meanwhile, the family was at odds. There were 3 sets of heirs: (1) Charles had left a ⅓ interest to his wife, Edith Conway Ringling, and their son Richard. (2) Ida Ringling North, a sister of John, Charles and the other first-generation circus Ringlings, and her son John voted a ⅓ interest as executors of John's estate, although John had disinherited them and doubtless had meant to oust them as executors, too. John Ringling North was the most shrewd and ambitious member of the cast. (3) Aubrey Ringling voted a ⅓ interest which had passed to her from Alf via her late husband Richard. In 1937 a series of transactions took place that resulted in a John Ringling North regime. North, as executor of the estate, was able to refinance the debt incurred in 1929 by John Ringling by borrowing from Manufacturers Trust Company. A voting trust was set up to last as long as the indebtedness. Under this arrangement North was to name 3 directors, the ladies (Edith and Ida) 3 and Manufacturers Trust 1. The ladies consented to this, although they had over 60% of the stock, because North as executor arranged the loan. Dunn the seventh director (and a bank Vice President) cast his seventh vote so as to install North as circus President.

North brought the circus out of the doldrums, started to pay dividends and paid off the corporation's debts. Meanwhile the ladies were discontent, despite the dividends, nourishing a feeling that the Norths were too power-hungry. Edith's son Robert wanted to rise above his position as senior vice president. Aubrey (shortly to be married to one Haley, an accountant who came to audit the company's affairs and stayed . . .) was also discontent. In 1941, seeing the end of the voting trust in sight, they signed the agreement described in the case and in 1943 when the trust ended, they took control, electing 5 of the 7 members (including Mr. Dunn who changed sides). Robert replaced North as President and Haley became First Vice President. However, their administration was shattered by the holocaust at Hartford on July 6, 1944 when the Big Top burnt down, causing 168 deaths and 487 injuries. Robert was not present and Haley was faced with the task of keeping the company going. The circus never considered bankruptcy as an alternative and worked out a "Hartford Arbitration Agreement" under which it agreed to pay all damage claims approved by a committee by allocating 100% of its net profits until the total (about $4 million) was paid. Meanwhile involuntary manslaughter charges were filed against Haley and other executives on the scene at the time: They pleaded *nolo contendere* and received enough time before sentencing to reorganize the circus for the 1945 season. Then Haley received a prison sentence from which he emerged on December 24, 1945 full of resentment at Robert because he felt that Robert really shared the blame but had escaped by the accident of his temporary absence, because Robert had not supported him strongly at the sentencing procedures and because Robert had not visited or written to him in prison (North had done both). North had meanwhile filed a derivative suit against the managers responsible for the disaster.

This was the state of events when the above case broke out. After it had ended, North took the offensive in order to end the stalemate. He was aided by the facts that (1) Robert had fallen ill and (2) North's derivative action had succeeded at the trial level. He was able, by shuttling back and forth between the two other groups, to work out an arrangement by which the Haleys sold out to the Ringlings and the Norths so as to give the Norths working control and the presidency. The Norths controlled the firm until 1967 when it was sold for over $10 million—the closing was held in the Colosseum in Rome—to Roy Hofheinz, owner of the Houston Astrodome, and the Felds, theatrical representatives. It was then sold to Mattel, the toy manufacturer, which resold it to the Felds in 1982.[8] Sic transit. . . .

BENINTENDI v. KENTON HOTEL, INC.

Court of Appeals of New York, 1945.
294 N.Y. 112, 60 N.E.2d 829.

[In 1928 three men, plaintiff Benintendi, defendant Dondero and one Schiffino, formed Kenton Hotel, Inc. to replace a partnership that had been running a lodging home in the Bowery in New York city under a leasehold. The 100 shares of capital stock went 25% to Benintendi and 37½% each to Dondero and Schiffino. In 1935 difficulties arose about Schiffino's behaviour in allegedly buying, in his wife's name, a competing leasehold interest in the hotel premises. After long maneuvers in 1941 Schiffino's stock was bought by the other two

----

8. The foregoing is based on Ringling Wrangling, Fortune, July 1947, p. 114; H. North & A. Hatch, The Circus Kings (1960) (by J.R. North's brother); N.Y. Times, Nov. 12, 1967, p. 82, col. 3.

shareholders. In the meantime, Schiffino's lawyer had suggested that unanimity of action should be a governing principle. That idea was carried out in 4 amendments to the corporation's by-laws adopted at a meeting of March 11, 1941—the date of the sale of Schiffino's stock. Those amendments read:

"Art. I. Section 4. Voting: At all meetings of the stockholders whether regular or special and whether or not in any other manner or percentage as provided by law, or regulated by statute, in general or for any specific vote, or any specific question, no resolution shall be adopted except by a unanimous vote of the stock of the Corporation issued and outstanding. Save, however, unless at least thirty days' notice of the meeting, has been given by registered mail, addressed to the stockholders of record, in which event the unanimous vote of the stock present in person or by proxy shall be sufficient."

"Art. II. Section 2. How Elected: At the annual meeting of Stockholders, the three persons receiving a unanimous vote of all the stock of the Corporation issued and outstanding shall be directors."

"Art. II. Section 10. Voting at Meetings of the Board of Directors: No resolution of the Corporation at any meeting, whether regular or special, shall be adopted except by the unanimous vote of the three directors duly elected as provided herein. However, should any director become incapacitated or die or absent himself from such meeting, then the two remaining directors may adopt any resolutions necessary to the carrying on of the business of the Corporation at any meeting duly called, provided that at least thirty days' notice by registered mail, directed to the last known address of the directors of such meeting and of the resolutions to be amended and to be voted upon is given to all directors."

"Art. VIII. Section 1. How Amended: These By–Laws may be altered, amended or repealed by the affirmative vote of the stockholders representing all of the issued capital stock at an annual or at a special meeting called for that purpose, but provided that a written notice shall have been sent to the stockholders of record by registered mail, at his last known post office address, at least ten days before the date of such annual or special meeting, which notice shall state the alterations, amendments or changes which are proposed to be made in such By–Laws. Only such changes as shall have been specified in the notice shall be made. If, however, all the stockholders shall be present at any regular or special meeting, either in person or by proxy, then these By–Laws may be amended by a unanimous vote, without any previous notice."

Benintendi then owned ⅓ and Dondero ⅔ of the stock. There was an agreement that Dondero should devote twice as much time (and receive twice the salary) as Benintendi. In June 1942 controversy broke out between the parties and Benintendi sued to prevent Dondero from conducting any meetings or taking actions in violation of the amendments of March 11, 1941. The trial court found the facts in favor of Benintendi, but found the first two by-laws above invalid. The Appellate Division affirmed. The Court of Appeals divided, the majority in an opinion by JUDGE DESMOND finding only the fourth by-law valid. Portions of that opinion follow:]

In striking down the by-law (No. 2 above) which requires unanimous stock vote for election of directors, Special Term properly relied upon Matter of Boulevard Theatre & Realty Co., 195 App.Div. 518, 186 N.Y.S. 430, affirmed 231 N.Y. 615, 132 N.E. 910. This court wrote no opinion in that case. The Appellate Division had ruled, however, that a provision in the Boulevard Theatre's certificate of incorporation requiring unanimous vote of all stockholders to elect directors, violated section 55 of the Stock Corporation Law, Consol.Laws, c. 59, which says that directors shall be chosen "by a plurality of the votes at such election." We think it unimportant that the condemned provision was found in the certificate of incorporation in the Boulevard Theatre case, and in a by-law in the present case, or that the attack on the provision is in this case made by a stockholder who agreed to vote for it and did vote for it. In 1897 a similar by-law was invalidated in Matter of Rapid Transit Ferry Co., 15 App.Div. 530, 44 N.Y.S. 539. The device is intrinsically unlawful because it contravenes an essential part of the State policy, as expressed in the Stock Corporation Law. An agreement by a stockholder to vote for certain persons as directors is not unlawful (Clark v. Dodge, 269 N.Y. 410, 415, 199 N.E. 641) since the directors are still, under such an agreement, elected by a plurality of votes, as the statute mandates. But a requirement, wherever found, that there shall be no election of directors at all unless every single vote be cast for the same nominees, is in direct opposition to the statutory rule—that the receipt of a plurality of the votes entitles a nominee to election.

Although not covered by the Boulevard Theatre case, or any other decision we have found, the by-law (No. 1 above) which requires unanimous action of stockholders to pass any resolution or take any action of any kind, is equally obnoxious to the statutory scheme of stock corporation management. The State, granting to individuals the privilege of limiting their individual liabilities for business debts by forming themselves into an entity separate and distinct from the persons who own it, demands in turn that the entity take a prescribed form and conduct itself, procedurally, according to fixed rules. As Special Term pointed out in this case, the Legislature, for reasons thought by it to be sufficient, has specified the various percentages of stock vote necessary to pass different kinds of resolutions. For instance, sections 36 and 37 of the Stock Corporation Law require an affirmative two-thirds vote for changing the capitalization, while section 102 of the General Corporation Law, Consol.Laws, c. 22, empowers the holders of a majority of the stock to force the directors to dissolve the corporation, and section 103 of that law gives the same power to holders of half the stock, if there be a deadlock on the question of dissolution. Any corporation may arrive at a condition where dissolution is the right and necessary course. The Legislature has decided that a vote of a majority of the shares, or half of them in case of a deadlock, is sufficient to force a dissolution. Yet under the by-laws of this corporation, the minority stockholder could prevent dissolution until such time as he should decide to vote for it. Those who own all the stock of a corporation may, so long as they conduct the corporate affairs in accordance with the statutory rules, deal as they will with the corporation's property (always assuming nothing is done prejudicial to creditors' rights). They may, individually, bind themselves in advance to vote in a certain way or for certain persons. But this State has decreed that every stock corporation chartered by it must have a representative government, with voting conducted conformably to the statutes, and the power of decision lodged in certain fractions, always more than half, of the stock. That whole concept is destroyed when the stockholders, by agreement, by-law or certificate of incorporation provision as to unanimous action, give the minority interest an absolute, permanent, all-inclusive power of veto. We do not hold that an arrangement would necessarily be invalid, which, for particular decisions, would require unanimous consent of all stockholders. See for instance, Ripin v. United States Woven Label Co., 205 N.Y. 442, 98 N.E. 855; Tompkins v. Hale, 284 N.Y. 675, 30 N.E.2d 721. In Tompkins v. Hale, supra, the stockholders of a "cooperative apartment house" had agreed in writing that such leases could be canceled and surrendered only if all the stockholder-tenants concurred. That is a far cry from a by-law which prohibits any nonunanimous determination on any corporate question.

The by-law numbered 3 in our list above makes it impossible for the directors to act on any matter except by unanimous vote of all of them. Such a by-law, like the others already discussed herein, is, almost as a matter of law, unworkable and unenforcible for the reason given by the Court of King's Bench in Hascard v. Somany, 1 Freeman 504, in 1693: "primâ facie in all acts done by a corporation, the major number must bind the lesser, or else differences could never be determined." The directors of a corporation are a select body, chosen by the stockholders. By section 27 of the General Corporation Law, the board as such is given the power of management of the corporation. At common law only a majority thereof were needed for a quorum and a majority of that quorum could transact business. Ex parte Willcocks, 7 Cow. 402, 17 Am.Dec. 525. Section 27 modifies that common-law rule only to the extent of permitting a corporation to enact a by-law fixing "the number of directors necessary to constitute a quorum at a number less than a majority of the board, but not less than one-third of its number." Every corporation is thus given the privilege of enacting a by-law fixing its own quorum requirement at any fraction not less than one-third, nor more than a majority, of its directors. But the very idea of a "quorum" is that, when that required number of persons goes into session as a body, the votes of a majority thereof are sufficient for binding action. See for example, Harroun v. Brush Electric Light Co., 152 N.Y. 212, 46 N.E. 291, 38 L.R.A. 615, as to a quorum of the Appellate Division. Thus, while by-law No. 3 is not in explicit terms forbidden by section 27, supra, it seems to flout the plain purpose of the Legislature in passing that statute. We have not overlooked Section 28 of the General Corporation Law, the first sentence of which is as follows: "Whenever, under the provisions of any corporate law a corporation is authorized to take any action by its directors, action may be taken by the directors, regularly convened as a board, and acting by a majority of a quorum, except when otherwise expressly required by law or the by-laws and any such action shall be executed in behalf of the corporation by such officers as shall be designated by the board." Reading together Sections 27 and 28 and examining their legislative history (see L.1890, Ch. 563; L.1892, Ch. 687; L.1904, Ch. 737), we conclude that there never was a legislative intent so to change the common-law rule as to quorums as to authorize a by-law like the one under scrutiny in this paragraph. A by-law requiring for every action of the board not only a unanimous vote of a quorum of the directors, but of all the directors, sets up a scheme of management utterly inconsistent with Sections 27 and 28.

Before passing to a consideration of the fourth disputed by-law, we comment here on a view expressed in the dissenting opinion herein. The dissenting Judges conclude that, while the two by-laws first herein discussed are invalid as such because violative of statutes, the courts should, nevertheless, enforce as against either stockholder the agreement made by both of them and which finds expression in those by-laws. The substance of that stockholders' agreement was, as the dissenting opinion says, that neither stockholder would vote his stock in opposition to the stock of the other. Each stockholder thus agreed that he would conform his opinion to that of his associate on every occasion, or, absent such accord, that neither would vote at all on any occasion. We are at a loss to understand how any court could entertain a suit, or frame a judgment, to enforce such a compact . . .

The fourth by-law here in dispute, requiring unanimity of action of all stockholders to amend the by-laws, is not, so far as we can find, specifically or impliedly authorized or forbidden by any statute of this State. Nor do we think it involves any public policy or interest. Every corporation is empowered to make by-laws, General Corporation Law, § 14, subd. 5, and by-laws of some sort or other are usually considered to be essential to the organization of a corporation. But a corporation need not provide any machinery at all for amending its by-laws—and for such an omission it could not be accused of an attempt to escape from the regulatory framework set up by law. A corporation, to function as such, must have stockholders and directors, and action and decision by both are required for the conduct of corporate business. The State has an interest in seeing to it that such "private laws" or by-laws as the corporation adopts are not inconsistent with the public law and not such as will turn the corporation into some other kind of entity. But, once proper by-laws have been adopted, the matter of amending them is, we think, no concern of the State. We, therefore, see no invalidity in by-law numbered 4 above.

The judgment should be modified in accordance with this opinion, and, as so modified, affirmed, without costs.

[Portions of the dissenting opinion by JUDGE CONWAY follow:]

The owners of 100% of the stock of a corporation may do with it as they will, even to giving it away, provided the rights of creditors are not involved and the public policy of the State is not offended. [citations omitted]

The general rule could be no more succinctly stated than in Matter of American Fibre Chair Seat Corp., Lehman, J., 265 N.Y. 416, 421, 193 N.E. 253, 255 (where there was unanimous stock action), as follows: "Where no rights of third parties are involved and no public policy of the state violated, the courts will give effect to the agreement of the stockholders and the corporate resolution."

In Ripin v. United States Woven Label Co., supra, the charter of the corporation provided that the number of directors should not be changed except by unanimous consent of all the stockholders and that provision was held to be a valid and binding limitation on the power of the corporation, notwithstanding the provisions of the then section 21 of the Stock Corporation Law, which declared that the number of directors might be increased or reduced by holders of a majority of the stock. The decision rested upon the express provisions of section 10 of the General Corporation Law: "The certificate of incorporation of any corporation may contain any provision for the regulation of the business and the conduct of the affairs of the corporation, and any limitation upon its powers, or upon the powers of its directors and stockholders, which does not exempt them from the performance of any obligation or the performance of any duty imposed by law." [205 N.Y. 442, 98 N.E. 856] This, despite the fact that it was not made to appear that all of the stockholders had agreed that the number of directors should not be changed except by their unanimous consent.

In Clark v. Dodge, supra, Crouch, J., we said, 269 N.Y. at pages 415, 416, 199 N.E. at page 642: "If the enforcement of a particular contract damages nobody—not even, in any perceptible degree, the public—one sees no reason for holding it illegal, *even though it impinges slightly upon the broad provision of section 27.* Damage suffered or threatened is a logical and practical test, and has come to be the one generally adopted by the courts. See 28 Columbia Law Review, 366, 372. Where the directors are the sole stockholders, there seems to be no objection to enforcing an agreement among them to vote for certain people as officers. There is no direct decision to that effect in this court, yet there are strong indications that such a rule has long been recognized. The opinion in Manson v. Curtis, 223 N.Y. 313, 325, 119 N.E. 559, 562, Ann.Cas.1918E, 247, closed its discussion by saying: 'The rule that all the stockholders by their universal consent may do as they choose with the corporate concerns and assets, provided the interests of creditors are not affected, because they are the complete owners of the corporation, cannot be invoked here.' That was because all the stockholders were not parties to the agreement there in question. So, where the public was not affected, 'the parties in interest, might, by their original agreement of incorporation, limit their respective rights and powers,' even where there was a conflicting statutory standard. Ripin v. United States Woven Label Co., 205 N.Y. 442, 448, 98 N.E. 855, 857." (Emphasis supplied.)

In Little v. Garabrant, 90 Hun 404, 35 N.Y.S. 689, opinion by Parker, J., later Ch. J. of this court, aff'd on opinions below in 153 N.Y. 661, 48 N.E. 1105, it was held that with the consent of all the stockholders and with no rights of creditors involved, the corporate assets might be *given away.* The court there said, pages 407, 408 of 90 Hun, page 691 of 35 N.Y.S., after stating the rule and the reason for it: "As one of the results of this rule, Mr. Morawetz, in his work on Corporations (section 625), asserts that: 'If the directors of a corporation apply the funds of the company to their own use, or misapply them in any manner, the excess of authority, as between the directors and the corporation, may be cured by the unanimous consent or ratification of the stockholders.' "

Clearly nothing could be more against public policy or the public interest than larceny or conversion and yet unanimous consent or ratification validates even such acts.

Despite that power of 100% of the stockholders, they may not write into a certificate of incorporation nor adopt in by-laws provisions contrary to applicable statutes. Since corporations are creatures of statute, their charters and by-laws must conform to the will of the creating power. Ripin v. United States Woven Label Co., supra; Matter of Boulevard Theatre & Realty Co., 195 App.Div. 518, 186 N.Y.S.

430, affirmed 231 N.Y. 615, 132 N.E. 910; Lorillard v. Clyde et al., 86 N.Y. 384. For that reason we think that the amendments to article I, section 4, and article II, section 2, were beyond the power of the stockholders since they contravene General Corporation Law, sections 102 and 103, and Stock Corporation Law, sections 35, subd. c, 36, 55, 86(b), 105, subd. c.

The amendment to article II, section 10, appears to be proper under General Corporation Law, sections 27 and 28. Those sections are in part as follows and show clearly by the portions we have italicized that the amendment was permissible:

"27. Directors; qualifications; powers of majority.

"The business of a corporation shall be managed by its board of directors, all of whom shall be of full age and at least one of whom shall be a citizen of the United States and a resident of this state. *Unless otherwise provided* a majority of the board at a meeting duly assembled shall be necessary to constitute a quorum for the transaction of business and the act of a majority of the directors present at such a meeting shall be the act of the board. The by-laws may fix the number of directors necessary to constitute a quorum at a number less than a majority of the board, but not less than one-third of its number. . . . (Emphasis supplied.)

"28. Acts of directors.

"Whenever, under the provisions of any corporate law a corporation is authorized to take any action by its directors, action may be taken by the directors, regularly convened as a board, and acting by a majority of a quorum, *except when otherwise expressly required by law or the by-laws and any such action* shall be executed in behalf of the corporation by such officers as shall be designated by the board. Any business may be transacted by the board at a meeting at which every member of the board is present, though held without notice." (Emphasis supplied.)

The amendment to article VIII, section 1, is not forbidden by any statute.

The question is then presented whether the *agreement* between the parties as to the manner in which they would vote their stock may be specifically enforced through the injunctive process of an equity court *in forbidding a breach of it by Dondero* even though validity may not be accorded to the first two attempted amendments. We think it may. Benintendi and Dondero agreed together as to the manner in which they would vote their respective stock interests. To implement their agreement they chose a method forbidden by statute. The agreement, however, was valid without the method chosen. Both of the parties have lived up to and under that agreement for more than a year. We granted specific performance of an agreement in Clark v. Dodge, supra, to vote for a single-named director—certainly a more drastic limitation upon the power of a stockholder than the limitation here.

In New England Trust Co. v. Abbott, supra, the court dealt with a by-law assented to by all of the stockholders. In upholding it as a *binding contract*, the court said [162 Mass. 148, 38 N.E. 433]: "The defendant contends that these by-laws are void. We have not found it necessary to consider that question, and we express no opinion upon it. We think that the case may well stand on the ground that the defendant's testator entered into an agreement with the plaintiff to do what the plaintiff now seeks to compel his executor to do. It is manifest that a stockholder may make a contract with a corporation to do or not to do certain things in regard to his stock, or to waive certain rights, or to submit to certain restrictions respecting which the stockholders might have no power of compulsion over him. In Adley v. Whitstable Co., 17 Ves. 315, 322, Lord Eldon says: 'It has been frequently determined that what may well be made the subject of a contract between the different interests of a partnership would not be good as a by-law. For instance, an agreement among the citizens of London that they would not sell except in the markets of London would be good; yet it has been declared by the legislature that a by-law to that effect is void.' See, also, Davis v. Proprietors [of the Second Universalist Meetinghouse], 8 Metc., Mass., 321; Bank of Attica v. Manufacturers' & Traders Bank, 20 N.Y. [501] 505; 6 Cook, Stocks & S. § 408."

We think that the emphasis should be placed upon the fact that this is an appeal to the equity power of the court. That power may be invoked in a proper case to ameliorate the rigors or rigidity of the law. Equity ofttimes alleviates hardship and prevents injustice in a specific case where the law is unable to do so since it speaks in terms of general rules. The distinction was well pointed out in Breslin v. Fries Breslin Co., supra [70 N.J.L. 274, 58 A. 316] (a case involving 100% stock action), as follows: "In the eye of the *law*, corporations are entities separate and distinct from their constituent members, and not bound by the individual acts of the latter. The law deals with the corporation as an artificial person. *Equity* realizes that this legal entity is but a legal fiction. Looking through the form, it discerns the substance. It finds that a stock corporation is, in essence, an aggregation of individuals—a statutory partnership—with assignable membership and limited liability of the members; and so the doctrine of equitable estoppel applies fully to all the internal concerns of stock companies. Saving, so far as public policy and the interest of creditors and other third parties are concerned, none of which is involved in the present case, the stockholders may bind themselves *inter sese* and in favor of the corporation by their own acts and agreements; and what will bind all the stockholders with respect to an obligation from the company to one of its members will bind the company as such."

There are here no rights of creditors involved. A totality of stockholders may agree among themselves as to how they shall or shall not vote shares of stock owned by them. They may by agreement waive or relinquish as between themselves statutory rights where such waiver or abandonment is not contrary to the public interest. There is here no question of public policy. The State does not need the assistance or leadership of Dondero in vindicating its public policy. . . .

COMMENT

(1) In considering the Ringling situation one would now consult 8 Del.C. § 218 as to voting trusts. See p. 368, supra. One would also have to take into account the increasingly more hospitable attitude towards voting trusts that emerges from the more recent cases. See, e.g., Oceanic Exploration Co. v. Grynberg, 428 A.2d 1 (Del.1981).

(2) Benintendi was quite promptly overruled by New York statute. The current rules are set forth in §§ 616 and 709 of the New York Business

Corporation Law, which as to shareholders and directors respectively provide (1) that the certificate of incorporation may provide for a higher than majority quorum requirement; (2) that it may require a higher than majority vote to transact business; (3) that such clauses may only be deleted by a "super majority" vote and (4) that warning of the existence of such provisions must be noted on the shares.

QUESTIONS

(1) What is the difference between the relief ordered by the Chancellor and by the Supreme Court? Is that difference dictated by different views of the compatability of voting agreements with public policy? By concepts about the specific enforceability of personal contracts such as agency agreements? Compare Jones v. Williams, p. 318, supra, and §§ 14H, 118, 139 of the Restatement, Second, Agency? Could you draft an amended version of the agreement that the courts would enforce as written without running afoul of voting trust problems? Could you do the same for an arrangement involving 20 shareholders?

(2) Consider the public policy aspects of the Ringling situation. Is it clear that there are no dangers from the use of this type of agreement? Would it be any different if one shareholder signed because of an explicit promise of employment by the corporation? Because of a cash payment? Are agreements by directors to vote together or in a specified way any more vulnerable? Does this depend on whether one believes shareholders are fiduciaries or are free to vote as they please? Suppose that the corporation is operating under shareholder management, as permitted by § 351; would that mean that stricter rules applicable to directors should apply to the shareholders?

(3) Does the shareholder who is not a party to such a voting agreement have a complaint? Suppose that he was not told about it when he bought his shares even though the seller knew of its existence? Recall question (4) on p. 635. Suppose that the majority shareholders had exchanged their stock for voting trust certificates rather than into a holding corporation and had achieved similar financial results. Would that strengthen or weaken the case for the excluded shareholders?

(4) Given the phrasing and policy of the then existing New York law, do you agree with the majority's choice as to which provisions it chose to sustain? Does the present New York arrangement in Paragraph (2) of the Comment seem warranted? Noting that it does not exclude publicly held corporations except as noted in clause (4), do you see any dangers from application to such enterprises? Would charter provisions for an unusually low quorum cause problems? Do the current Delaware provisions (§§ 141(b), 215(c), 216 as well as Subchapter XIV) permit such actions.

3. Drafting Arrangements on Stock Transfers—For or Against

ARON v. GILLMAN

Court of Appeals of New York, 1955.
309 N.Y. 157, 128 N.E.2d 284.

[Plaintiff and one Dora Ostroff, each represented by counsel, agreed in writing that:

> (1) that if either should wish to sell his or her stock while both were alive, the price should be the "actual value" as determined by arbitration; but (2) that when either should die, the stockholdings of the deceased should be sold to, and purchased by, the other stockholder at the "book value of said stock" to "be determined by the most recent audit of the books of the Corporation provided such audit has been made not more than sixty days before the death of such" stockholder.

On August 19–21st 1953, an audit took place, reflecting the corporation's position as of July 31st. Dora Ostroff died on September 21st. Samuel Ostroff, Dora's administrator, refused to perform. He did offer to buy Aron's ⅓ of the stock for $100,000 or sell Dora's share (⅔) for $200,000. Plaintiff began this action for specific performance against Samuel and, after Samuel's death, against his administrators. Special Term granted specific performance at a price of $186,222.30. Both parties appealed, plaintiff urging that the value was incorrect. The Appellate Division affirmed (2–1) and plaintiff appealed to the Court of Appeals which modified and affirmed the decision below in an opinion by JUDGE FROESSEL.]

As the case now comes before us, only two items—inventory and taxes—are in dispute. How are they to be evaluated under the agreement which describes this method for determining the value of the stock: "book value . . . determined by the most recent audit"? Before discussing them in particular, however, it may be helpful to look more closely at the term "book value" without further definition.

There appears to be no agreement among the decisions or textbook writers on a complete and authoritative definition of the term "book value". At least two principles seem to emerge from the better reasoned authorities: (1) the book entries must be correct and complete, and not made to defeat an outstanding claim, and (2) accepted accounting principles should not be entirely disregarded, see Steinbugler v. William C. Atwater & Co., 289 N.Y. 816, 47 N.E.2d 432. Thus, where interest, which had accrued on notes held by a bank had not been posted on the books and was not yet payable, it was held that the interest should nevertheless be included as an asset in determining book value of the bank's stock, Elhard v. Rott, 36 N.D. 221, 162 N.W. 302. And where the parties were aware that several assets which were listed at substantial sums on the books of a bank had no actual value, it was held that they should be eliminated from the computation of book value, Gurley v. Woodbury, 177 N.C. 70, 97 S.E. 754.

Although when the peculiar asset "good will" has been in issue it has quite consistently been excluded from book value unless actually recorded at some value on the books [citations omitted], not all unrecorded intangible assets have been so excluded. In Hollister v. Fiedler, 22 N.J.Super. 439, 92 A.2d 52, where the book value of stock of an insurance business had been calculated without considering the value of the corporation's expiration and renewal books and records, the court held that such information, of conceded value in the insurance business, should be included in determining the stock's book value; otherwise, according to the court, the result would be inaccurate, inequitable and unintended by the parties to the stock purchase agreement.

So, if abnormal depreciation has been taken on the books for income tax purposes, the court in finding book value may go outside the books and determine a different rate of depreciation. Hagan v. Dundore, 187 Md. 430, 50 A.2d 570. In the last-mentioned case, the court also held that the labor cost invested in outstanding contracts of the corporation should be included in a computation of book value, even though no ledger entries indicated either the amount or value of that labor, see, also, Rubel v. Rubel, Miss., 75 So.2d 59, 67–68. And in Succession of Warren, 162 La. 649, 110 So. 891, the court held that disputed claims by the government for taxes on the income of previous years should be included as liabilities in determining book value even though the claims might never have to be paid.

In the instant case, the parties have not contended themselves with the mere use of the term "book value", but have themselves defined it, namely, that it should be determined according to the most recent audit of the corporation's books. Webster (New International Dictionary, 2d ed., Unabridged, 1950) defines "audit" as a "formal or official examination and verification of accounts, vouchers and other records", and as "an account as adjusted by auditors". Thus the very purpose of an audit is to verify and reconcile the book entries of a business according to proper accounting practice, and to see that they are accurate.

We now turn to the two specific problems presented in the instant case. First, as to the inventory: Among the current assets listed in the balance sheet of July 31, 1953, is "Merchandise Inventory—Estimated ...... 12,001.15". It will be noted the amount is "estimated". At the trial the accountant testified that this figure was submitted to him by Dora Ostroff, president of the corporation; he did not know the correct figure and did not audit this item. It was conceded by plaintiff, however, that, on July 31, 1953, the actual inventory value amounted to $51,058, nearly $40,000 more. Nevertheless, plaintiff contends that we should take the inventory figure at $12,001.15 simply because it is the figure appearing on the books, and despite the fact that it is concededly erroneous. We are not obliged to follow blindly entries in books that are indisputably untrue. The courts below were therefore correct in holding that the concededly accurate $51,058 inventory figure should be used for determining book value in place of the arbitrary and erroneous guess of $12,001.15 which was supplied to the accountant by the corporation's president.

Second, as to taxes: The audit in question speaks as of July 31, 1953. At the foot of the balance sheet appears the following: "Note: Subject to Federal and State Income Taxes & year-end adjustments." The same notation appears at the bottom of the statement of income, profit and loss. And on the schedule of surplus account, net profit for

January 1, 1953, to July 31, 1953, is listed at $81,951.20, but this figure is stated to be "Exclusive of Provision for Federal Income & Excess Profits Tax & New York State Franchise Tax".

Plaintiff contends that before book value was determined by the courts below, the indicated provision for State and Federal income taxes should have been deducted. Defendants, on the other hand, insist that no such allowance should be made for income taxes because no figures therefor appear on the books, and because the corporation was not actually liable for taxes on 1953 income until the end of the taxable year—December 31, 1953. The difference, in practical result, is substantial. If the taxes are disregarded, the book value of intestate's stock would be, as the trial court found, $186,222.30 (assuming that the true inventory figure rather than the inaccurate estimate is used), whereas, if both State and Federal income taxes are first deducted, the book value thereof would, we are told, be approximately $132,000—a difference of over $53,000.

It is well settled that in construing the provisions of a contract we should give due consideration to the circumstances surrounding its execution, to the purpose of the parties in making the contract, and, if possible, we should give to the agreement a fair and reasonable interpretation, 3 Corbin on Contracts, pp. 78–79, 88–91, 115; 3 Williston on Contracts, pp. 1780–1788. In the instant case the parties attempted to arrange a method whereby the survivor should buy out the other's interest in the corporation. At the execution of the agreement, no one knew which party would be the survivor, or at what time he would be obliged to purchase. The price was to be book value as determined by the most recent audit; but obviously in such a serious agreement involving the transfer of many thousands of dollars of stock, the parties must have intended by this provision to establish a fairly stable and predictable valuation basis.

The position maintained by defendants, however, namely, a complete ignoring of the income taxes until actually payable, would mean an arbitrary, capricious and widely fluctuating purchase price, depending on the time of the last audit. For example, if that audit took place one day before the taxes became payable, by defendants' theory no income taxes at all should appear in the computation of book value. But if the audit should take place a few days later, book value would have suddenly dropped by an amount equal to the income taxes for the entire year. Such a result is manifestly unreasonable from both a practical and theoretical point of view.

Clearly it makes no sense to charge the entire year's burden of income taxes to the income of the last month preceding termination of the taxable year. On the contrary, sound accounting practice requires that each dollar of income as it is earned throughout the year should bear its proportionate share of the costs of the enterprise, including the tax burden, [citations omitted]. For this reason interim audits made during the taxable year should include an estimate of the income taxes applicable to the period in question. The mere fact that an item is not yet legally due and payable does not mean that it may be ignored as a liability, [citations omitted] nor does it mean that the item may not be included in a computation of book value. [citations omitted]

Moreover, judicially, we must recognize that income taxes are continuing and reasonably predictable charges against corporate income. Their influence pervades modern business. Rare indeed is the corporation or businessman who is not acutely aware of their incidence and effect upon its or his operations. Under such circumstances, to accept defendants' argument that these taxes must be ignored because they were not yet "liabilities" would be to subject our reason to what Mr. Justice Cardozo termed "the tyranny of labels". Snyder v. Com. of Massachusetts, 291 U.S. 97, 114, 54 S.Ct. 330, 335, 78 L.Ed. 674. If a corporation, such as here, has earned a given net income over the first seven months of its tax year, it is only reasonable that the tax which will be payable on that income should be included in a determination of its financial position in terms of book value. The success or failure of the business thereafter is a risk the purchaser assumes.

In sum, then, the corrected inventory figure, conceded by plaintiff to be accurate, was properly allowed by the courts below. As for the estimated income taxes, they should have been deducted before reaching the final book value figure. The agreement called for book value as determined by audit; the audit, in turn, was expressly made subject to Federal and State income taxes, and prior to the contemplation of any controversy. No question is raised as to the integrity of the accountant who made the audit—indeed, he was selected by defendants' intestate herself. Good accounting practice required an estimation of those taxes for the seven-month period, and, although the actual computations did not appear on the corporate books, those computations should have been made by the trial court and deducted from the corporate earnings prior to determining book value.

Any other result would be unreasonable. It would require plaintiff to pay to defendants over $53,000 extra for the stock, notwithstanding that at the end of the year he would be obligated either to pay out that same amount again in taxes on income attributable to the first seven months of the year, or to account for loss of that income in some other way. In other words, he would have to pay out an extra $53,000 in order to receive an income tax liability of equal amount. And, to make matters worse, the seriousness of this anomaly would vary tremendously depending upon when the applicable audit had taken place.

Accordingly, the judgment appealed from should be modified so as to take into account the estimated State and Federal income taxes in the computation of book value. In all other respects the judgment should be affirmed with costs. Since no finding was made below as to what the book value of the stock would be when the inventory is valued at $51,058 and when the estimated taxes applicable to the January 1– July 31 income are included, the case should be remitted to the Supreme Court for computation of that figure.

The judgment of the Appellate Division should be modified in accordance with this opinion and, as so modified, affirmed, with costs.

DESMOND, JUDGE (dissenting).

.   .   .

In every New York case we have found, the bare phrase "book value" has been taken and defined to mean what it is popularly supposed to mean, that is, the assets shown on the books less the liabilities shown on the books, [citations omitted].

Book value "is reached by estimating all the assets as they appear upon the corporate books, and deducting all the liabilities and other matters required to be deducted by law". . . . As tersely put in White on New York Corporations (Vol. 7, § 7.26): "Book value means

the value of the stock as shown on the books of the corporation. . . .
Book value is determined by deducting liabilities from assets." With
that settled, we turn to the two items here in dispute: that is, taxes and
inventory.

The latest audit contained no liability figure for income taxes
which could not, of course, be computed accurately until the year
ended. However, the report of audit contained a note that the figures
were "Subject to Federal and State Income Taxes & year-end adjustments". While, by such an audit, those taxes were not, in the fullest
sense, "determined", nevertheless, the note, apparently made as a
routine accounting practice, showed that the auditor (and the corporation) considered that its net worth was lessened by accrued income
taxes. Of course, the final amount of those taxes, dependent on future
months' earnings and losses, could not be fixed until the end of the
year. However, they could be estimated. We, therefore, consider it
reasonable to say that the "book value" of this corporation, according to
the "most recent audit", necessarily involved a deduction for the
estimated amount of taxes to become due on business already done.

As to inventory, the audit stated the value thereof as "Estimated
. . . . . . $12,001.15", a figure submitted to the accountant at the time of
the audit, by Miss Ostroff, the president, whose estate is now insisting
that the larger figure of $51,058 be used because a postdeath inventory
produced that latter figure. We think that, in the absence of fraud or
mathematical error, the book figure was the one to use. These parties,
taking their chances as to which should die first, chose to make book
value, as shown on the latest audit, the measure of price. It is entirely
beside the point that the use of such figures turned out to be "unfair"
to one or the other. As our courts long ago noted, a sale at book value
is always "unfair" in the sense that book value, as to a going concern, is
always more or less than, never equal to, actual or market value,
[citations omitted]. This corporation took inventory at intervals but
had no running or continuous inventory. When the auditor came
around, Miss Ostroff gave him an estimate of inventory and he put it on
the books. At the trial, plaintiff's counsel conceded that the actual
figure, after Miss Ostroff's death, was much higher than the book
figure, but such a concession could not change the contract's test of
"book value" as determined by latest audit. If, despite such a contract,
there has to be a new physical inventory, and, likewise, a new, true
valuation of every other asset and liability, then the phrase "book
value" has no meaning and the convenient arrangements carefully
worked out by the parties and their counsel in the written agreement
comes to naught.

I have found no case where the New York courts have failed to
carry out such an agreement according to its precise terms, see Druck-
lieb v. Sam H. Harris, Inc., 209 N.Y. 211, 102 N.E. 599, and Surrogate
Griffith's opinion in Re Estate of Reben's Will, Sur., 115 N.Y.S.2d 228,
237. In Steinbugler v. William C. Atwater & Co., 289 N.Y. 816, 47
N.E.2d 432, supra, when the "book value" was computed, it was found
that stocks (in other corporations) owned by defendant Atwater were on
the Atwater books at cost, which was concededly much higher than
actual value. Atwater's accountant then attempted to write these
values down, but the courts, including this court, refused to permit it.
So the cost figures stood although, like the inventory value here, they

were "concededly erroneous" in the sense that they did not represent actuality.

The judgment should be modified accordingly, without costs.

NOTE ON DRAFTING CLAUSES ON STOCK TRANSFERS IN CLOSE CORPORATIONS

(1) Originally the chief questions about a clause on stock transfers centered about its quality as a restriction on transferability. Cases considered at length whether a given clause operated as an unreasonable restraint on alienation. The following excerpts from a New York case [9] indicate the dimensions of this issue as well as the tendency of more recent cases to look favorably on clauses that are not totally unjustifiable.

> Section 176 of the Personal Property Law, which is identical with section 15 of the Uniform Stock Transfer Act, provides that "there shall be no restriction upon the transfer of shares" represented by a stock certificate "by virtue of any by-law of such corporation, or otherwise, unless the . . . restriction is *stated* upon the certificate." (Emphasis supplied.) In order to comply with this statutory mandate, the corporation printed the words, "Issued subject to restrictions in sections 28, 29, and 30 of the By-laws," on the side of the certificate. The plaintiffs maintain that this is not a proper "statement," that the restriction must be set out verbatim or in substance. There is no such prescription in the statute, and the courts have found noncompliance only where the stock certificate gives no notice whatever of the restriction sought to be enforced. . . . The word "stated" sanctions a notation indicating where the restriction appears and permits incorporation by adequate reference. In other words, a restriction is sufficiently "stated" by a legend noting that the stock is "issued subject to restriction" and specifying where its full text may be found. . . . In this connection, it is significant that, where the legislature wished the words of a restriction or its substance to be actually printed on the certificate, it used language to express that thought. Thus, section 66 of the Stock Corporation Law recites that, "If a stockholder shall be indebted to the corporation, the directors may refuse to consent to a transfer of his stock until such indebtedness is paid, provided *a copy of this section or the substance thereof is written or printed upon the certificate of stock.*" (Emphasis supplied.)

> Since, then, the legend on the certificate meets the statute's requirements, we turn to the validity of the by-law restriction.

---

9. Allen v. Biltmore Tissue Corp., 2 N.Y.2d 534, 161 N.Y.S.2d 418, 141 N.E.2d 812 (1957).

The validity of qualifications on the ownership of corporate shares through restrictions on the right to transfer has long been a source of confusion in the law. The difficulties arise primarily from the clash between the concept of the shares as "creatures of the company's constitution and therefore . . . essentially contractual choses in action" (Gower, Some Contrasts between British and American Corporation Law, 69 Harv.L.Rev. 1369, 1377) and the concept of the shares as personal property represented so far as possible by the certificate itself and, therefore, subject to the time-honored rule that there be no unreasonable restraint upon alienation. While the courts of this state and of many other jurisdictions, as opposed to those of England and of Massachusetts . . . have favored the "property" concept . . . the tendency is, as section 176 of the Personal Property Law implies, to sustain a restriction imposed on the transfer of stock if "reasonable" and if the stockholder acquired such stock with requisite notice of the restriction.

The question posed, therefore, is whether the provision, according the corporation a right or first option to purchase the stock at the price which it originally received for it, amounts to an unreasonable restraint. In our judgment, it does not.

The courts have almost uniformly held valid and enforcible the first option provision, in charter or by-law, whereby a shareholder desirous of selling his stock is required to afford the corporation, his fellow stockholders or both an opportunity to buy it before he is free to offer it to outsiders. . . . The courts have often said that this first option provision is "in the nature of a contract" between the corporation and its stockholders and, as such, binding upon them. . . .

(2) Nowadays the questions tend to center more around the problems in putting together a clause that is agreeable and fair to the parties and will prove to be workable if the time comes when it must operate.

First of all, one must decide which type of clause is called for. At their simplest, there are clauses flatly forbidding transfers or conditioning them on the consent of the other entrepreneurs—individually or through the board of directors. These clauses are the most likely to encounter objections as restraining alienation and they offer no recompense to the party subject to the restraint. The drafters attention is apt, therefore, to turn to other forms that involve in effect a deflection of a transfer rather than a prohibition. In the right-of-first-refusal form the party wishing to sell must first offer at that price to the other shareholder(s) or the corporation before gaining clearance to others. In the option form the other shareholders have an option, arising on certain stated events, to buy the stock at a specified price. Sometimes the clause mandates the purchase and sale at a specified event or it may give the holder a right to demand that the others buy him out.

If these more complex provisions are selected, the drafter must be clear about who is to exercise the choice involved and about what events other than choice: death, disability, retirement, deadlock, etc. are to bring the rights and duties into operation. It may turn out that quite different provisions ought to be applied to different events; for example, recall that in Aron v. Gilman one price formula was to be applied in cases where one of the parties chose to sell and a different one in case of death. The mechanisms, such as the length of time given in which to elect whether or not to match an outsider's offer, need to be made as nearly exact and frictionless as possible. If the corporation itself is to be a purchaser special problems arise from the fact that a corporate repurchase is subject to rules about surplus, etc. See pp. 676–683 supra. In order to be effective as against outsiders, the restrictions ought to be referred to on the stock certificates (see § 8–204 of the Uniform Commercial Code). It may also be advisable to place annotations on the stock transfer records (apt to be primitive in the case of a close corporation) that will cause the corporate secretary to refuse to carry out a transfer when requested to do so.

(3) Finally, there comes the difficult and all-important question of price. This clause must balance out the interest of the departing shareholder in having a fair price (or perhaps the interest of the survivors or heirs) against the interest of the remaining shareholders in having a continuing enterprise that is financially viable. At the time of drafting the agreement it will very likely not be apparent who is going to be the survivor. Furthermore all parties if they are members of a family may feel a strong interest in the firm's survival. Thus it may be necessary to integrate with the price provision arrangements having to do with life insurance or delayed installment payments, etc. Note some of the commoner methods used for setting a price:

(a) Mutual Agreement. If the parties can agree on a price that is obviously most satisfactory. However, any price thus set will rapidly become obsolete. The parties may find it possible to agree upon reasonably prompt changes but the problem may become a difficult one if the parties' interests begin to show clear divergence. Some commentators think that it may be psychologically upsetting to have the issue of price brought up repeatedly by renegotiation clauses.

(b) Market or Offer. By definition a close corporation has no market price. A bona fide offer by an outsider may from time to time offer a benchmark but usually only one that is appropriate in connection with a right of first refusal clause.

(c) Book value. The preceding case illustrates some of the problems with a book value clause. Over time the book value will diverge quite drastically from a current value. Thus in Jones v. Harris [10] a clause calling for sale of a 10% stock interest in two corporations in the broadcasting business at its book value of $25,936.33 was enforced even though there was strong evidence that the corporations had a value of $2,500,000 at the time of sale and even though the corporations were during the litigation sold for $3,225,000 cash. The book value is on the other hand reasonably susceptible to easy and precise calculation— though there are distinct limitations as the preceding case indicates (especially when one recalls the amount of flexibility inherent in the generally accepted accounting principles under which the basic calculations are made).

(d) Appraised Value. A much closer approximation to actual present value can be achieved by an able and experienced appraiser. This can however, be rather expensive and time consuming. The clause needs to be quite precise about who the appraiser or appraisers are to be or who is to pick them and how. It may be wise to be quite specific about the standards which they are to apply.

(4) Where it is the close corporation that repurchases stock courts have in some cases found a fiduciary duty not to purchase only the stock of one favored members but to offer an equal opportunity to all shareholders. Donahue v. Rodd Electrotype Co. of New England, Inc., 367 Mass. 578, 328 N.E.2d 505 (1975). Compare p. 635 supra.

(5) Most of these arrangements are made at the start of a corporate enterprise and have the assent of all parties. Additional retroactivity problems arise if a restriction is subsequently imposed, as by a by-law amendment, following a less than unanimous action.[11]

QUESTIONS

(1) The two equal co-owners of a small corporation that makes a scientific research device that is unpatented but hard to duplicate have agreed in principle that upon the death of the first of them the other will have a right and obligation to buy the decedent's interest at "book value." The chief assets of the firm consist of a factory which the two purchased about 7 years ago and refurbished largely with their own efforts and those of their assistant plus an inventory of components and finished parts which they have, for tax purposes, been carrying on a "LIFO" basis for at least 5 years. The corporation is presently the beneficiary of life insurance policies to the extent of $50,000 on the life of each of them (the cash surrender value of each policy is about $5,000). The two have been allowing themselves salaries of $12,000 each and putting back the balance of the cash flow into expansion. You represent the senior of the two as they start to hammer out the details of the arrangements. Would you advise your client to press for modifications or clarification of the agreement in principle and, if so, in what respects?

10. 6 Wash.2d 559, 388 P.2d 539 (1964). See also In re Mather's Estate, 410 Pa. 361, 189 A.2d 586 (1963) (upholding option at $1 a share when actual value over $1,000).

11. See, e.g., Tu–Vu Drive–In Corp. v. Ashkins, 61 Cal.2d 283, 38 Cal.Rptr. 348, 391 P.2d 828 (1964); Sandor Petrol. Corp. v. Williams, 321 S.W.2d 614 (Tex.Civ.App. 1959); B & H Warehouse, Inc. v. Atlas Van Lines, Inc., 490 F.2d 818 (5th Cir.1974) (Delaware law).

(2) Suppose that, for some reason, the co-owners referred to in (1) above decided to have the "buy-sell" arrangement provide that the sale was to take place at the price most recently agreed upon between the parties. For four consecutive years the two sat down and worked out a mutually satisfactory figure. In the fifth year your client became ill and his condition gradually grew worse over the next three years. His junior colleague first evaded and then refused to renegotiate a price even though it became apparent each year that the firm was growing more profitable and was expanding. Your client died recently and the junior seeks to enforce her right to buy at the 3 year old price. You are aware that she has given a large firm in the field an option to buy 100% of the corporation's stock at a price nearly four times that which she would have to pay your client's estate. The executor consults you for advice as to whether he can resist the co-venturer's claim.

---

4. Devices for Coping With Internal Dissension

JACKSON v. NICOLAI–NEPPACH CO.

Supreme Court of Oregon, 1959.
219 Or. 560, 348 P.2d 9.

[The Nicolai–Neppach Co. was a close corporation engaged in the manufacture, at Portland, Oregon, of such lumber products as sash, doors, cabinets and store fixtures. The business began in 1866 and was incorporated in 1887. In 1928 C.E. Cowdin was president, general manager and principal shareholder; in that year Herbert Jackson was hired as employee; in 1931 he married Cowdin's secretary Eva Jackson. In 1945 Herbert Jackson and his brother Arthur Jackson made arrangements to buy the stock of Nicolai–Neppach Co. for $180,000 payable over twelve years.[12] Payment was completed in 1949. At that time the stock of the corporation was allocated: 25 to Herbert, 25 to Arthur and 1 to Mr. Rankin, the company's attorney, in trust for the Jacksons. (The by-laws required directors to be shareholders). Herbert (president), Arthur (secretary and treasurer) and Mr. Rankin (vice president) were the directors. Business continued prosperously and harmoniously. In 1950 Arthur died and his wife, the plaintiff in this case, inherited his shares. Rankin resigned and delivered ½ share to Herbert and ½ to Hazel. Hazel and Eva were elected to fill the vacancies on the board; Herbert assigned Eva 1 share so that she could qualify. Thus at the time of the suit the shareholders were Herbert (24½), Eva (1) and Hazel (25½). Herbert was the active manager of the corporation and the only shareholder on salary.

In 1952 there was the first sign of tension. Hazel came to the stockholders meeting with an attorney, demanding a by-law change to add a fourth director so that she could have equal representation with Herbert (and Eva). She also suggested that a $12,000 dividend would

12. [Ed.] The purchase was made through a corporation called the Jackson Company. The court states that it "changed its corporate name to Nicolai–   Neppach Co." It does not make clear what the relations between the two corporations were.

be appropriate but the matter was postponed for further study of needed repairs.

At the 1953 stockholders meeting plaintiff Hazel, with counsel, again moved for a 4 directors board; there was some confusion as to what happened but the court accepted the version in the minutes that the 3 directors were reelected. At the directors meeting a dividend of $7,650 was agreed upon; motions to raise Herbert's salary from $13,750 to $20,000 or $15,000 were lost by 1–1 votes, Herbert abstaining.

In 1954, the meeting failed to approve either an increase in the size of the board or Eva's motion to name three lawyers as directors. Under the by-laws the old directors continued in office. The directors agreed on a $3,825 dividend. Herbert invited the directors to inspect the plant but they declined saying they were not qualified.

In 1954 net earnings were only about $8,250 and there was talk of liquidating. In April 1955 plaintiff began this suit for involuntary liquidation. At the shareholders meeting in November 1955 the motion to increase the number of directors was defeated again. A $12,750 dividend was declared by the directors. On Hazel's motion Herbert's salary was increased $3,000. In 1956 there was again a deadlock on naming directors. A dividend of $25,000 was declared and Herbert's increased salary was reapproved.

1956 was a prosperous one. The firm had 65 employees, many with long tenures. Herbert's testimony about the company's future was optimistic. Hazel's counsel conceded that "[W]e are not undertaking to charge the management with oppression or mismanagement or any illegal acts." However, plaintiff asserted a right under the statute to liquidation, without showing detriment to the stockholders.

The statute [13] reads as follows:

"(1) The circuit courts shall have full power to liquidate the assets and business of a corporation:

"(a) In an action by a shareholder when it is established:

"(A) That the directors are deadlocked in the management of the corporate affairs and the shareholders are unable to break the deadlock, and that irreparable injury to the corporation is being suffered or is threatened by reason thereof; or

"(B) That the acts of the directors or those in control of the corporation are illegal, oppressive or fraudulent; or

"(C) That the shareholders are deadlocked in voting power, and have failed, for a period which includes at least two consecutive annual meeting dates, to elect successors to directors whose terms have expired or would have expired upon the election of their successors; or

"(D) That the corporate assets are being misapplied or wasted."

The circuit court, after a hearing, dismissed and plaintiff appealed. The Supreme Court's opinion by JUSTICE ROSSMAN, after reviewing the facts, analyzed the history of ORS 57.595 as derived from the Model Business Corporation Act which in turn was taken haec verba from the Illinois statute enacted in 1951. It noted that before 1951 the Illinois

13. [Ed.] Oregon Bus.Corp.L., O.R.S. 57.595(1)(a)(C).

cases had held that dissolution could not be granted if the corporation was solvent. The opinion continued as follows:]

The shareholder deadlock provisions of the Illinois Business Corporation Act, of the Model Business Corporation Act, and of the Oregon Business Corporation Law are clearly couched in language of permission. It is incredible that the many able lawyers who worked from time to time on these three identical acts would have used such phraseology to express a mandate. The statute contemplates that the court of equity shall take jurisdiction once a requisite showing of fact is made and contemplates further that having taken jurisdiction it will bring its discretion to bear in granting or refusing to grant equitable relief. The very fact that the legislature has made the remedy of liquidation a matter of discretion for the courts is a mandate to us to use discretion, and we would not be carrying out the legislative will by simply decreeing liquidation as a matter of course once the jurisdictional facts and nothing more are proven. The common law rule was thought to be an insufficient safeguard of the rights of the half-owner of a corporation who happened to be out of power. The drafters of the shareholder deadlock provision apparently thought that any statutory rule which provided for liquidation as a matter of law would insufficiently safeguard the rights of the half-owner who happened to be in power. As we read the statute its intent is to obligate the courts to thread their way from case to case without the assistance of sweeping generalizations.

In arguing for liquidation of the Nicolai–Neppach Company, appellant places her principal reliance on Strong v. Fromm Laboratories, 1956, 273 Wis. 159, 77 N.W.2d 389, which construed the shareholder deadlock provision of the Wisconsin business corporation law, Wis.Ann. Stat. 180.771(1)(a)(4). Wisconsin had adopted the Model Business Corporation Act and the shareholder deadlock provision is in every material respect identical to our own, ORS 57.595(1)(a)(C). In the Strong case the Supreme Court of Wisconsin decreed liquidation of a prospering corporation, and it is appellant's argument that the decision ought to be followed here. We think, however, that the facts of the Strong case and the reasoning of the Wisconsin court set the case apart from the one that is before us.

Strong v. Fromm Laboratories was an action by Harland Strong, trustee of 50 per cent of the share of Fromm Laboratories, Inc., for liquidation of the company. Fromm Laboratories was a Wisconsin corporation created in 1933 by Edward and Walter Fromm and Dr. Robert Gladding Green. Strong represented the Green interests. The Fromm interests owned the other 50 per cent stock interest. The company manufactured vaccines used in the fur farming business and at the time of the petition for dissolution was prosperous. However, the corporation had never paid a dividend. Dr. Green drew a salary as active director of the laboratories and the Fromms were salaried officers. The by-laws of the corporation provided that only stockholders were to be directors. Moreover, as stated in the opinion [273 Wis. 159, 77 N.W.2d 391]:

> "The by-laws . . . contain no provision permitting the members of the board of directors to fill a vacancy on the board. Instead, such by-laws expressly provide that, in the case a vacancy should occur on the board of directors, the board shall call a special meeting of the stockholders for the

purpose of filling such vacancy, and that *until such vacancy is filled the board 'shall transact no other business than to authorize the calling of the special meeting' for the purpose of filling the vacancy."*

Dr. Green died in 1947. By will he left his stock in trust to Strong for the benefit of his niece Gale Green. The trust was to last until Strong should sell the stock. The Fromms were granted first purchase rights. Green had also entered into an inter vivos written agreement with the Fromms, granting them a first option to purchase his stock, which was to be binding on his estate. The Fromms apparently made no move to purchase the Green interest. Strong had a disagreement with the Fromms which became acute in 1951.

The by-laws of the corporation called for a board of four directors. Although Wisconsin law requires an annual election of directors (Wis. Ann.Stat. 180.32(2)), no meeting of stockholders was held, after a single meeting to elect Dr. Green's successor in 1947, until the year 1953. The 1953 stockholders meeting was "abortive." A vote on only one director was taken which resulted in a tie. In 1954 another shareholders meeting was called. Strong cast his share for himself as director and "against any other candidate for director"—doing this because all of the other eligible shareholders were members of the Fromm party and Strong, as trustee, could not assign any of his shares to an ally. The Fromms cast their votes for three other shareholders and declared Strong's negative ballot a nullity, but the Supreme Court held that it was valid, and deadlocked the election.

On the above facts the trial court denied dissolution but the Supreme Court reversed with orders to liquidate the company. To an argument that there was no showing of benefit to the stockholders the court replied as follows:

"Because of the extensive research made by the committee of eminent Wisconsin corporation lawyers who sponsored the 1953 addition of par. 4 of section 180.771(1)(a) to our new corporation code, we must assume that its members were familiar with the New York and Minnesota deadlock statutes and court decisions interpreting the same, and that they preferred to word the Wisconsin statute so as not to make dissolution or liquidation, because of a stockholders' deadlock, contingent upon a finding that the same will be beneficial to stockholders. We, therefore, hold that whether or not a liquidation of Fromm Laboratories, Inc., will be beneficial or detrimental to the stockholders is not a material factor to be considered in exercising the power of liquidation conferred by par. 4 of section 180.771(1)(a) Stats."

The further argument was made that the power of dissolution was discretionary by statute, "and that there was no abuse of discretion on the part of the trial court in refusing to exercise such power." The opinion of the Supreme Court makes it clear that reversal was based on abuse of discretion rather than absence of discretion, and furthermore, that the primary reason for which dissolution was granted was lack of a legally functioning board of directors—a situation not present in Nicolai–Neppach Company. We quote from the relevant paragraphs of the opinion:

"Section 180.30, Stats., provides that, 'The business and affairs of a corporation shall be managed by a board of directors.' The by-laws of Fromm Laboratories, Inc. expressly prohibit the board of directors of such corporation from transacting any business after a vacancy occurs on the board, except to call a meeting of the stockholders to elect a successor director, until such vacancy has been filled. This by-law was undoubtedly adopted for the purpose of insuring that neither the Green nor Fromm interest should be able to manage the corporate business, in the event of the death of a director, as a result of having two members to the other's one among the other three members of the board. We thus have a situation where, ever since Dr. Green's death on September 6, 1947, the board of directors has been without legal power to manage the business of the corporation. The fact that the two directors representing the Fromm faction have usurped such power and may have capably exercised the same is wholly beside the point.

. . .

"In the instant case there is no *alternative corrective remedy*, other than that provided by section 180.771(1)(a) 4, Stats., which will permit Fromm Laboratories, Inc., to function and be legally managed as required by section 180.30, Stats., and the corporate by-laws. It, therefore, was an abuse of discretion for the trial court not to have decreed a liquidation."

The by-laws of Nicolai–Neppach Co. provide that the board of directors shall consist of three members "who shall hold office until the next annual meeting and until their successors are elected and have qualified." At a time long before any dispute arose, the incorporators, Herbert and Arthur Jackson and C.E. Cowdin, construed this provision to mean that the directors were "to hold office until the next annual meeting of stockholders, *or* until their successors were duly elected and qualified." This appears from the "Incorporators' Certificate of Election" of August 31, 1945, which appears in the company minute book. Moreover, ORS 57.185 provides that:

". . . Each director shall hold office for the term for which he is elected and until his successor shall have been elected and qualified, unless removed in accordance with the provisions of the by-laws."

ORS 57.141 provides that:

". . . The bylaws may contain any provisions for the regulation and management of the affairs of the corporation not inconsistent with law or the articles of incorporation."

Therefore, whether by act of the legislature or by virtue of the by-laws of the company—which, it is unnecessary to decide—the board of directors of Nicolai–Neppach Co. in office at the time of the deadlock continued to function legally thereafter. Strong v. Fromm Laboratories held, on the other hand, that under Wisconsin law the by-laws of a company may be drawn so as to paralyze effectively the corporate function. In addition, the by-laws of Nicolai–Neppach Co., by requiring three directors, indicate that the stockholders of that concern placed a higher value on effective corporate action than on equal representation of their equal interests while the by-laws of Fromm Laboratories, by requiring four directors, indicate that the stockholders insisted on equal representation even at the risk of deadlock.

Appellant argues that we can not consider benefit to the stockholders as a factor in decreeing or withholding liquidation since the shareholder deadlock provision of our statute fails to require it, citing the language of Strong v. Fromm Laboratories which we have quoted above. She notes that Virginia, which has adopted section 90 of the model act, changed the shareholder deadlock provision to require "That as shown by the proceedings at any meeting of the stockholders the stockholders are deadlocked in voting power and that irreparable injury to the corporation is being suffered or is threatened by reason thereof. . . ."

Benefit to the shareholders is a condition precedent to the granting of dissolution on the grounds of shareholder deadlock in some jurisdictions, notably New York. The New York Gen.Corp.Law, ch. 23, § 103, provides:

"Unless otherwise provided in the certificate of incorporation, if a corporation has an even number of directors who are equally divided respecting the management of its affairs, or if the votes of its stockholders are so divided that they cannot elect a board of directors, the holders of onehalf of the stock entitled to vote at an election of directors may present a verified petition for dissolution of the corporation as prescribed in this article."

Section 117 provides that the court must make a final order dissolving the corporation if upon application it appears that a dissolution "will be beneficial to the stockholders or members and not injurious to the public. . . ." In re Radom & Neidorff, 1954, 307 N.Y. 1, 119 N.E.2d 563, 566, denied dissolution of a corporation on facts outlined by Justice Fuld in a dissenting opinion:

". . . Neidorff died in 1950, at which time respondent, through inheritance, acquired her present 50% stock interest in the business. Since then, all has been discord and conflict. The parties, brother and sister, are at complete loggerheads; they have been unable to elect a board of directors; dividends have neither been declared nor distributed, although the corporation has earned profits; debts of the corporation have gone unpaid, although the corporation is solvent; petitioner, who since Neidorff's death has been the sole manager of the business, has not received a penny of his salary—amounting to $25,000 a year—because respondent has refused to sign any corporate check to his order. More, petitioner's business judgment and integrity, never before questioned, have been directly attacked in the stockholder's derivative suit, instituted by respondent, charging that he has falsified the corporation's records, converted its assets and otherwise enriched himself at its expense. . . ."

The appellate division, 282 App.Div. 854, 873, 124 N.Y.S. 424, 922, dismissed the petition and this was affirmed in the court of appeals by a four to three vote. The majority said that "The prime inquiry is, always, as to necessity for dissolution, that is, whether judicially-imposed death 'will be beneficial to the stockholders or members and not injurious to the public.' "

If the Wisconsin court, in ruling that benefit to the stockholders is not a material factor to be considered in proceedings for dissolution, had in mind the "benefit" that exists by virtue of mere solvency, which apparently was that contemplated by the New York Court of Appeals in

In re Radom & Neidorff, we tend to agree with its position. If, on the other hand, it means to suggest that we can not consider actual benefits to the stockholders in the form of such matters as payment of regular and substantial dividends, then we can not accept its viewpoint. We must remember that Strong v. Fromm Laboratories was a case in which the complainant was receiving no dividends from the company while the faction in power were drawing substantial salaries. We think that actual benefit to the stockholders is a factor which may properly be considered in determining whether dissolution is to be granted. We say this not because we think the petitioner in such cases has a duty to be satisfied in spite of himself, but because we must consider the rights of the 50 per cent interest which is in control of the company as well as that which is out of control.

Appellant argues that because the director deadlock provision of our act, ORS 57.595(1)(a)(A), requires a showing of "irreparable injury to the corporation" before the court can liquidate a company by reason of a deadlocked directorate which the shareholders can not break, and because such a requirement is absent from the shareholder deadlock provision, a further reason is thus provided why we can not consider benefit or detriment to the stockholders. We do not understand the statute in this way. We can not equate "irreparable injury" and "benefit to the shareholders." The former is a much more restrictive idea. The absence of a requirement of "irreparable injury" from the jurisdictional facts which must be proven in a petition for dissolution by reason of shareholder deadlock certainly does not indicate that we must dismiss from our consideration of the equities of the case any showing of actual benefit to the stockholders from the operation of the company. We think that it is only persuasive of the fact that "irreparable injury" is not properly a decisive factor. We take note of the fact that the shareholder deadlock provision did not appear in the 1950 revision of the model act. It was added to the 1953 revision after Illinois had included such a provision in its Business Corporation Act. To this extent, therefore, Section 90 is not made up of integrated subsections, and reasoning from one subsection to another must therefore be done with caution.

[A discussion of two cases under a New Jersey statute saying corporations "may be dissolved" in case of shareholder deadlock is omitted. In both cases, there was paralysis of the corporate operation.]

Appellant also cites and relies upon the reasoning of a scholarly article by Carlos L. Israels, "The Sacred Cow of Corporate Existence— Problems of Deadlock and Dissolution," 19 U. of Chic.L.Rev. 778 (1952). It is Mr. Israels' position that courts should be reluctant to "put themselves in business" by reviewing the equities of cases involving deadlock among shareholders, and that the model act is susceptible of a mechanical and "pragmatic" interpretation. Mr. Israels apparently would permit dissolution whenever the jurisdictional facts are proven. If we assume, arguendo, that a mechanical rule is desirable, if only from the standpoint of facility of administration, we have nevertheless already expressed our view that the statute contemplates that courts shall consider the equities of the individual case. If this were not true, the shareholder deadlock provision would have been expressed in terms of mandate rather than permission.

Viewed in this light we do not think that appellant has made out a case for liquidation of the Nicolai–Neppach Co. While her sole purpose in introducing the minute book of the corporation into evidence was to show deadlock and failure of the stockholders to elect a board of directors, the minute book as well as other evidence furnishes us with a broader view of the activities of the company. Even so, there is nothing in evidence which persuades us to enter an order winding up the company. We think that the plaintiff has not only the burden of proof to establish jurisdictional facts under the shareholder deadlock provision, but the further burden of proving equitable grounds for dissolution. She has failed to meet that burden.

The evidence before us is that Herbert Jackson has refused to allow the board of directors to be increased to four members—which would certainly result in further deadlock—and that he has refused to consider liquidation of the company. We do not think that it is lack of equity for a stockholder who is in control of a deadlocked company to refuse to vote against his own interests, even though the effect is to perpetuate him in office. The evidence shows affirmatively that Herbert Jackson has ably administered the company for the benefit of all of the stockholders, and that he has agreed to the distribution of profits in dividends in so far as they were not required for the repair or development of the plant. These profits have been substantial. The plant employs about 65 men and there is a public interest in preserving it as a going concern.

The evidence shows, moreover, that Hazel Jackson has an effective weapon of corporate management through her control over Herbert Jackson's salary. The power to fix officers' salaries is vested in the stockholders by virtue of the by-laws. There is thus no danger, so long as the company remains prosperous, that the incumbent management will be able to siphon off profits of the corporation through salaries rather than dividends.

We need not decide at what point we would hold that dissolution must be granted as a matter of right. Traditionally a court of equity will not interfere with the exercise of business discretion by the directors and officers of a company. Perhaps this is a branch of the law where we will find it necessary to do so under proper circumstances. But such circumstances are not present in this case. The proper solution of the impasse reached in Nicolai–Neppach Co. appears to be for one of the two shareholders to purchase the other's shares. We think an equitable adjustment will be reached by denying rather than granting dissolution in this case. To decree liquidation would give Hazel Jackson a club to hold over the head of Herbert Jackson. To deny liquidation imposes upon each party a certain amount of burden and uncertainty so long as their differences continue. There is a possibility that Hazel and Herbert Jackson may compose their differences amicably—it does not appear so far that either has attempted to oppress or unfairly deal with the other. If they can not settle their disagreement, then we think that denial of relief at the present time may well lead to a fairer buy-sell agreement than the remedy of enforced liquidation, a remedy which might destroy the going concern value of the plant and give both parties an unduly small return for the value of their investment.

The judgment of dismissal is affirmed.[14]

---

14. In Baker v. Commercial Body Building, 264 Or. 614, 507 P.2d 387 (1973), the Court refused to grant dissolution at the request of a 49% shareholder even though it recognized that some oppression had taken place. It defended its ruling in the

NOTE ON DISPUTE RESOLUTION IN THE CLOSE CORPORATION

(1) When the drafters of a closed corporation's documents insert provisions preventing non-unanimous action and impeding transfers of the discontented party's stock, the stage is institutionally set for intense conflict.[15] The fuel is provided by inter-personal dynamics of a complex sort that interweave economic and psychic forces. At times frustration breaks out in a crude form. From Tennessee comes this report of the reaction of one member of a two-man firm when faced with a bill in equity brought by the other (Rymon) to make him repay excessive advances from the firm's treasury:

> "just before the bill was filed, he made a violent attack upon Rymon with a heavy stick, inflicting wounds, which made it necessary for Rymon to go to a hospital. Other circumstances exist which show bad feelings between the two men . . ." [16]

In other places parties are more apt to resort to the subtle cruelties and harassments that can only be learned through prolonged business or family intimacy: refusals to sign documents, insulting corporate resolutions, etc. Curiously, the evidence indicates that firms can often continue to be effectively and profitably run even in the presence of a level of behind-the-scenes turbulence rivalling that of the house of Atreus. It is related that two Bostonians refused to speak to each other for decades, communicating by messenger only, but still coined money hand over fist. Sometimes even violence coexists with careful, honest and successful management.[17]

Increasingly both commentators and practitioners have become aware of the analogies between close corporations and families on the psychological level—especially when they are family corporations. There have been attempts to apply the learning generated by the alternative dispute resolution (ADR) school of thought to intracorporate disputes. The thrust of this learning is to diminish the role of hardline rule-oriented litigation and enhance the role of mediators and conciliators who can ease the pressures and tensions generated by the combination of personal and economic clashes. What is not so clear is whether any communicable skill emerges from this lore.[18]

(3) The careful drafter is aware of the possibility that disputes will arise and would like to do something about it. Two approaches seem to develop: the first is by interposing some form of third-party presence

principal case as not based on a "robber baron" theory.

15. Levinson, Conflicts that Plague Family Business, Harv.Bus.Rev., March–April 1971, p. 90.

16. Nashville Packet Co. v. Neville, 144 Tenn. 698, 235 S.W. 64 (1921).

17. Stott Realty Co. v. Orloff, 262 Mich. 375, 247 N.W. 698 (1933).

18. Solomon & Solomon, Using Alternative Dispute Resolution Techniques to Settle Conflicts Among Shareholders of Closely Held Corporations, 22 Wake Forest L.Rev. 105 (1987); Corneel, Dealing with Conflicts in Family Corporations, 15th Ann.Inst. on Estate Planning ch. 18 (1981).

between the two camps and the second is to terminate the relationship. Each has its problems.

Among third party solutions, the most obvious one is arbitration. This has had a somewhat paradoxical history. Courts were originally sensitive to incursions upon their domain and refused to enforce clauses calling for arbitration of controversies that were justiciable. Statutes, conspicuously in New York, directed the courts to enforce arbitration clauses in cases otherwise justiciable. Then cases came to the courts in which a party sought to use a clause providing for arbitration of any arbitrable controversy between them to oust the opposing director. The New York Court of Appeals found that while shareholders might in some cases be able to remove a director no suit for such removal would be possible. Therefore, it said, the dispute was not justiciable and therefore not arbitrable.[19] The present Civil Practice Law § 7501 now makes clauses "enforceable without regard to the justiciable character of the controversy." Thus, at least in New York, the problems of using arbitration clauses are not ones of coping with an overly rigid legal system. Rather they are questions of the inherent limits of arbitration as a system. Fairly plainly, one cannot continually resort to arbitration for the settlement of day-to-day business decisions; it is far too slow and expensive. Even with rarer and more significant decisions, most arbitrators would feel out of their depth in deciding between reasonable alternatives proposed by the parties if they affected questions, say, as to the selection of managerial personnel or the investment of large sums in new equipment. Also, there may be issues which the parties would not have wished to have an arbitrator decide. It has been suggested, for example, that in the New York case referred to the parties would not, had they been asked, have included an authorization to have an arbitrator remove one of them for cause.

(4) A variant of the arbitrator is the neutral director (referred to in 8 Del.C. §§ 352 and 353).[20] A neutral director would have a more continuous relation to the corporation and would come to know its business and its managers better. Such a director would be capable of breaking deadlocks arising in complex business areas, unlike an outsider brought in to settle one controversy. By the same token such a director would be very much caught up in the emotional cross-currents between the parties. It might not be easy to find a person of competence willing to undertake such a thankless (and potentially liability-producing) task. On the other hand, a friend or counselor of the family might be more willing to take the job if asked by all concerned, at a time when passions were not running deep.

(5) If the parties cannot resolve critical problems by themselves or with the aid of others, it is time to consider a parting of the ways. Not infrequently both parties come to desire this and it is just a matter of settling on a price. That task is fraught with the difficulties discussed

19. Matter of Burkin (Katz), 1 N.Y.2d 570, 136 N.E.2d 862, 154 N.Y.S.2d 898 (1956).

20. This statute was carried over from California. See Calif.Corp.Code § 308.

above in connection with the drafting of a transfer restraint or "buy out" clause, except that the question is not an abstract future one but a very present one with the lines clearly drawn between the two sides. On the other hand, it may be that each party wants to remain and oust the other or that one party may refuse to consent to dissolution or sale as a tactical maneuver to maximize a bargaining position, much as one spouse will refuse a divorce. If the parties do not agree, the matter comes before a court for dissolution. As Jackson v. Nicolai–Neppach indicates, the powers of the court depend very much upon what the statute authorizes or directs it to do. If the statute leaves the court some discretion, it may have to consider such questions as the following: (a) if dissolution is granted, how will that affect the position of the parties, say the active manager vis-a-vis the passive investor? Since dissolution implies an auction of the property or something like it, who will be in a position to buy it up—and will the price be fair? (b) Will dissolution destroy intangible "going-concern" values and reduce the firm to its bare bones? (c) Will dissolution adversely affect third parties, employees or customers?

(6) A majority of the shareholders and directors can, absent deadlock clauses, generally obtain dissolution simply by taking the steps provided in the voluntary dissolution provisions (e.g., 8 Del.C. § 275). These actions are then subject only to the generalized fiduciary controls against abuses discussed at p. 725 supra. Other devices, sometimes collectively referred to as "squeeze outs", can be used by a majority to compel one party to sell out or minimize his role in the enterprise. Thus they might reduce his relative position in the corporation by issuing new stock to others or they might merge the corporation into another so that the objector winds up only with nonvoting stock in the surviving enterprise. The degree to which courts will upset such maneuvers is explored at pp. 642, 725 supra. Cutting the salary of a shareholder-employee or interfering with responsibilities or perquisites may achieve like results. One of the functions of the special clauses in a close corporation agreement is to safeguard against these devices.

(7) The break up of a close corporation causes special problems for its legal counsel. Having represented all the interests involved and very likely not even having had occasion to distinguish among them, counsel is now confronted by contending factions and a choice as to whom to represent. At this point analysis in terms of loyalty to the corporate entity seems not particularly useful although some cases have held that a lawyer for the corporation is entitled to go on representing those who control it against shareholders now adverse to them. Some lawyers are tempted to act as "lawyers for the situation", to use a phrase of Justice Brandeis', but there are many pitfalls along this path. In one case a lawyer became even more deeply embroiled by buying one side's shares at a time when the other side had been

negotiating for their purchase. The Delaware court held this a breach of a fiduciary duty running to each of the venture's members.[21]

QUESTIONS

(1) Suppose that a court had been asked to dissolve the Ringlings' corporation under a deadlock statute such as that in Oregon. Should it have taken into account the risk that absent the family's managerial talents, the circus might have fallen apart, throwing employees out of work and depriving the public of the greatest show on earth? How could it balance that against the needs and wishes of the family? What weight would you give to the testimony of a psychiatrist that the mental health of one member of the family would be seriously impaired if that person had to continue to collaborate with the others?

(2) Suppose that one of the ladies had decided that the circus ought to be dissolved and had persuaded Mr. Loos. Could she have seen her wishes carried out? Assume the present Delaware statute and the provisions of the charter and ladies' agreement set forth in the case at pp. 757–758 supra?

(3) Was Mr. Loos basically an "arbitrator"? Did it matter for the purposes of the Delaware courts? Or was he closer to being a provisional director?

(4) Suppose that a corporation's directors are divided regularly 6 to 3 but because of a unanimity clause such as that in the Benintendi case, supra, p. 768, there is a continuing deadlock. Can the provisional director statute (8 Del. C. §§ 352, 353) be used in such a situation?

Bibliography: The major work in this field is F. O'Neal, Close Corporations: Law and Practice (3d ed., O'Neal & R. Thompson 1985) which largely supersedes not only the earlier editions but also his other books and articles. See also W. Painter, Corporate and Tax Aspects of Closely Held Corporations (1971), and on New York, Kessler, Drafting a Shareholders Agreement for a New York Close Corporation, 35 Fordham L.Rev. 625 (1967), and Certificate of Incorporation for a New York Close Corporation: A Form, 33 id. 541 (1965). L. Sarner, Organizational Problems of Small Business (1961) is a compact and useful summary, in the series published by the A.L.I.–A.B.A. Joint Committee on Continuing Legal Education. See Note, Joint Venture Corporations; Drafting the Corporate Papers, 78 Harv.L.Rev. 393 (1964), as to that type of close corporation. A helpful small business bibliography is assembled in Jackson, Small Business Development and Management, Harv.Bus.Rev. Sept.–Oct. 1977, p. 182.

---

21. Opdyke v. Kent Liquor Mart, Inc., 40 Del.Ch. 316, 181 A.2d 579 (1962). In Nanfito v. Tekseed Hybrid Co., 341 F.Supp. 240, 247 n. 6 (D.Neb.1972), affirmed 473 F.2d 537 (8th Cir.1973), the judge denounced the "chameleon-like practice" of a lawyer who represented both parties in a stock purchase.

*

GLOSSARY *

AFFILIATE—An affiliate is a corporation directly or indirectly related to one or more other corporations by stockholdings or other means of control. It includes a parent or a subsidiary but also firms under common control.

APPRAISAL RIGHT—Some statutes give shareholders who dissent from fundamental changes, such as mergers, the right to demand cash for their stock, the price being set by a court-appointed appraiser.

ARBITRAGE (ARBITRAGEUR)—Arbitrage is the practice of trading so as to take advantage of price discrepancies between the same securities on different markets (e.g., New York and Tokyo) or between equivalent (e.g., convertible) securities. § 16(e) permits exemption of such trading from the "short-swing" trading prohibition. The term is also used, but loosely, to cover traders such as Ivan Boesky who acquire the stocks of corporations targeted for takeovers.

ARTICLES OF ASSOCIATION—In the British practice, the articles of association make up part of the constitutive agreement of a corporation. For details see Automatic Self–Cleaning Filter Syndicate Co. v. Cuninghame (p. 385).

ARTICLES OF INCORPORATION—The basic publicly filed constitutive document of a corporation is sometimes referred to as its "articles of incorporation"—more or less interchangeably with "certificate of incorporation" or, more informally, "charter."

BLUE SKY—State statutes regulating the sale of securities are commonly known as "blue sky laws," one state legislator having asserted that securities salesmen would sell the blue sky itself if left unregulated.

BOND—A bond is a debt obligation, usually issued in series and secured by a mortgage or other lien. The fact that it is secured distinguishes it from a debenture (q.v.).

BONUS STOCK—Bonus stock is stock issued by a corporation without valid consideration. Distinguish a stock bonus (q.v.).

BOOK VALUE—The book value of a share of stock is equal to the sum of the proprietorship accounts (capital, capital surplus and retained earnings) divided by the number of shares. Since these figures are, ultimately, based on assets at cost less liabilities the term "value" is really a misnomer.

* Further terminological guidance can be found in Barron's Dictionary of Finance and Investment Terms (J. Downes & J Goodman eds. 1985).

BROKER—A broker is, in general usage, one who handles sales and purchases of securities. More technically, a broker is an agent in effecting a trade for a customer, as distinguished from a dealer who buys from or sells to a customer for the dealer's own account.

BY–LAWS—The by-laws are a document constituting internal regulations of the corporation. Unlike the articles, or certificate of incorporation, they need not be filed.

CALL, CALLABLE—If a corporation can, at its option, redeem its own stock by paying a stipulated price for it, that stock is referred to as "callable" and the action of notifying the holders is known as a "call." Also, if X agrees to sell to Y 100 shares of stock of corporation A upon Y's demand (i.e., gives him an option), Y is said to have a "call." A "call" may be transferable.

CAPITAL, STATED CAPITAL, WORKING CAPITAL—Capital is, in corporate accounting, an item on the right hand side representing the contributions of the shareholders. It is not itself an asset, although one frequently hears non-technical references to "capital assets," etc. If an asset is contributed to a corporation in return for shares the balance sheet will reflect both the asset and its counterweight which is likely to be capital. Where par stock is used capital equals the number of shares times the par value of each share. Where no par stock is used the amount per share designated by the directors becomes the capital, often the "stated capital." "Working capital" is the amount arrived at by subtracting current liabilities from current assets. It thus shows how much cash and near-cash a firm has to conduct operations with.

CERTIFICATE OF INCORPORATION—The basic, publicly filed, constitutive document of a corporation is sometimes referred to as its "certificate of incorporation"—more or less interchangeably with "articles of incorporation" or, more informally, "charter."

CHARTER—The term "charter" is used as a more informal and unofficial equivalent of articles of incorporation or certificate of incorporation to describe the basic constitutive document of a corporation.

CLOSE(D) CORPORATION—A close or closed corporation is one with only a few shareholders, most or all of whom participate in management. It is customary for the organizers of such corporations to include special provisions in its constitutive documents (see Chapter XIV) and modern corporation laws increasingly provide for that.

CLOSING—The formal completion of a transaction previously agreed upon, for example, the sale of stock or extension of a loan, is referred to as a "closing."

CONGLOMERATE—A corporation or group of affiliated corporations engaged in distinct lines of business is known as a "conglomerate." It is a term of antitrust more than of corporation law.

CONSOLIDATION—If two or more corporations merge into a new corporation formed at that time, that is referred to as a "consolidation" as distinguished from a merger in which one of the existing corporations is the surviving entity. See "merger."

CONTROL—A person is said to "control" a corporation if he can cause it to do what he wishes. Majority stock ownership normally carries with it such control and an incumbent management may have effective control with much less than 50%. The concept appears in various legal rules, including statutes and may be stated in general terms requiring somebody to find existence or non-existence of control as a fact or it may be defined in arbitrary terms such as 50% ownership, etc.

CONVERTIBLE—A security is referred to as convertible if its owner has the right to convert it into a different type of security. Most typically the convertible security is a preferred stock or a debenture.

CORPORATE OPPORTUNITY—When a person in a fiduciary relationship to a corporation takes to himself or herself a chance for the corporation to engage in a profitable venture that is known as diverting a "corporate opportunity." For such an act to be unlawful may require a showing that the corporation was interested in, and capable of, undertaking such an enterprise.

CUMULATIVE DIVIDENDS—A preferred stock is referred to as "cumulative" if it is provided that its dividends when left unpaid in a given year accumulate so that before dividends may be paid upon the common stock in a subsequent year not only that year's preferred dividends but the arrears built up in previous years must be paid.

CUMULATIVE VOTING—When it is provided that each shareholder may take a number of votes, equal to the number of shares owned times the number of directorships to be filled and cast all of them for one candidate or distribute them among several, as he or she chooses, that is cumulative voting. Its purpose is to afford some membership on the board to minority interest.

DEALER—Legal usage distinguishes between a broker (q.v.) who acts as an agent in conducting purchases and sales for others and a dealer who trades for its own account.

DEBENTURE—A debenture is a debt obligation of a corporation, usually issued in series and usually not secured by a mortgage or other lien. It is normally issued under—and defined by—an indenture, which term it is important to distinguish.

DE FACTO—The term "de facto" is usually attached to "corporation" so as to indicate that, while not formed in sufficiently full compliance with the legal requirements to be a de jure corporation, the entity is invulnerable except against direct attack by the state in quo warranto proceedings. In other words, plaintiffs or defendants in private actions cannot rely on the defect. Irregularly chosen directors or officers may also have de facto status.

DERIVATIVE SUIT—A derivative suit, often referred to as a stockholder's or shareholder's suit, is one to assert a legal right of the corporation brought by one of its shareholders (or sometimes a director). Some definitions also require that it be one brought to recover a judgment for the corporation.

DISCOUNT—A share of stock or a bond or debenture is sold at a discount if the price is less than the par or stated value. Sales at a discount by a corporation of its own securities, particularly its stock, are generally not lawful but subsequent sales between other parties are not so limited. With respect to debt obligations a discount serves the function of increasing the rate of interest above that paid periodically.

DIVIDEND—A sum paid to a shareholder by a corporation in respect of its stock, whether common or preferred is termed a "dividend." Dividends may be in cash, in property (including the stock of other corporations) or in stock of the corporation itself, in which latter case it is properly referred to as a "stock dividend."

DIVISION—A "division" refers to an operation of a corporation that it kept somewhat separate for administrative purposes but is not separately incorporated.

EMPLOYEE STOCK OWNERSHIP PLANS—Under stock bonus plans employees acquire interests in the employer company which contributes to the plan either shares of its stock or cash to buy such shares. Employee stock ownership plans (ESOP's) finance such acquisitions of the firm's stock through borrowings. Tax benefits are available to ESOP's that qualify according to the Internal Revenue Code.

EQUITY SECURITY—An "equity security" is one that represents a shareholder's interest rather than a creditor's, i.e., the term is used in contradistinction to a "debt security." The borderline is somewhat difficult to draw at times but factors pointing to an equity security include entitlement to dividends (not interest), a right to vote, an absence of a right to a return of the amount contributed at a fixed date. The term appears in the Securities Exchange Act of 1934.

EXECUTIVE COMMITTEE—A corporation may establish one or more executive committees consisting of members of its board of directors who may carry out large parts of the functions attributed to the board as a whole.

FREEZE OUT—When the controlling interests in a corporation eliminate the minority shareholding interests the process is referred to as a "freeze out." The means employed may include a merger, a recapitalization through a charter amendment or the withholding of dividends for a long period.

GOING PRIVATE—"Going private" refers to the process whereby the controlling group within a corporation that has sold stock to the public reacquires all, or the bulk of that stock.

GOING PUBLIC—"Going public" refers to the process whereby a company first distributes its stock to the public and thereby ceases to be a close corporation. It requires either compliance with the registration and prospectus provisions of the Securities Act of 1933 or the availability of one of its exemptions.

GREENMAIL—If a corporation purchases some of its own stock from an outside party and pays a premium above its market value, in particular because the management is afraid of that party's potential use of the stock's voting power, there is said to be "greenmail."

HOLDING COMPANY—A holding company is a corporation that holds a controlling interest in the stock of one or more other corporations. It is roughly equivalent to parent, but the term implies that there are several subsidiaries.

INCORPORATORS—The persons who organize a corporation and who execute its articles of incorporation are called incorporators.

INDENTURE, INDENTURE TRUSTEE—It is customary to issue debt securities—bonds or debentures—under a contract termed an indenture, between a corporation and an "indenture" trustee who is to protect the interests of the various security holders. These indentures when connected with a public offering of the securities are regulated by the federal Trust Indenture Act of 1939. An indenture may also constitute a mortgage, pledge or deed of trust.

INSIDER, INSIDER TRADING—A person who has special access to information concerning a corporation, because of financial interests or a role in management is referred to as an "insider." Such persons are subject to special restrictions in using such data in trading in securities. The term is specially defined in Section 16 of the Securities Exchange Act of 1934 which limits short term transactions by such parties.

INSOLVENCY, INSOLVENT—A person may be "insolvent" in one or both of two senses: in the equity sense, meaning unable to pay one's debts as they come due or in the bankruptcy sense, meaning having a lesser amount of assets than of liabilities.

INTERLOCKING—Interlocking directors are those who hold seats on the boards of two corporations in particular on the boards of corporations that do business with each other. Such a position may invalidate or cast doubt upon such a transaction.

INVESTMENT COMPANY—An investment company is one which holds the securities of other companies as investments, i.e., for the returns thereon and the increments in their growth, rather than for control. It differs in this regard from a holding company (q.v.). An investment company thus customarily gathers in funds through the sale of its securities to investors which it then reinvests in other companies' securities. It, at least in theory, renders two services to its investors—diversifying their holdings and providing them with sophisticated management expertise. Publicly held investment companies are regulated by the federal Investment Company Act of 1940.

JOINT VENTURE—A partnership limited either in time or in scope is frequently referred to as a joint venture, particularly when the parties involved are corporations.

LEVERAGE—If a corporation has a high proportion of debt obligations as compared to equity it is said to be highly "leveraged." One effect of leverage is to cause the earnings left over for the common stock to fluctuate sharply since the returns to the debt obligations (and preferred stock) are fixed. Another effect is to give the common stock control over a very substantial enterprise for relatively very little investment. Similar effects can be achieved by building up tiers of holding companies.

Leverage is hard to understand without an example. Take a firm with assets of $1,000,000 and try two possible capitalizations: (1) a no-leverage version with only equity and (2) a high-leverage version with $100,000 equity and $900,000 debt. Assume a good year with $180,000 earnings before interest and a bad year with only $50,000. Further assume $100 par shares of common and 6% interest on the debt. Observe the results.

	High Leverage		No Leverage	
	Good Year	Bad Year	Good Year	Bad Year
Total Earnings	$180,000	$50,000	$180,000	$50,000
Interest	54,000	54,000	0	0
Left for Common	126,000	(4,000)	180,000	50,000
Earnings per share	$126.00	$(4.00)	$18.00	$5.00

LISTED—A security is "listed" on a stock exchange in order to be admitted to trading. The issuing corporation must comply with the requirements of the exchange, which include signing a listing agreement. Before the Securities Exchange Act was amended in 1964 such listing was a step that made a security subject to the reporting, proxy and insider trading provision of the Act.

LOW PAR—Stock that is issued at a price appreciably above its par value is referred to as low par. The par values may be as low as $1 or even 1¢. The practice gives the entrepreneurs great flexibility in pricing later issue of stock and has from time to time been advantageous in minimizing stock transfer taxes.

MARGIN—If one purchases or owns a security but pledges the security in order to secure part of the purchase price one is said to hold it "on margin." The proportion of the value of the security which one can borrow is fixed from time to time by the margin requirements of the

Federal Reserve Board acting under Section 7 of the Securities Exchange Act of 1934.

MEMORANDUM OF ASSOCIATION—In English practice the name and other vital details as to a corporation are embodied in its memorandum of association which is filed as an official record—other matters pertaining to its internal organization belonging in the articles of association.

MERGER—When two or more existing corporations are brought together so that one of them emerges as the surviving entity that is a merger. Distinguish a consolidation (q.v.) in which a newly created corporation is the survivor.

MUTUAL FUND—An investment company (q.v.) may be "closed end", in which case there is a fixed quantity of its stock outstanding, or "open end", in which case it stands ready to repurchase its stock on demand (redemption) and may issue more such stock. The term mutual fund is generally associated with the open end variety.

NIMBLE DIVIDEND—A nimble dividend is one paid under an authorization, contained in the Delaware law and Model Act (as an option), to pay dividends from the previous period's net income, even though there is a cumulative negative in the surplus account.

NO PAR—Stock issued without a par value, as is permitted under modern corporation laws, is referred to as no par stock. The counterpart of the consideration received is allocated between stated capital and capital surplus at the directors' discretion.

OFFICER—A corporate agent at a high level is referred to as an "officer." State corporation law may designate certain positions as being filled by officers, usually the president, secretary and treasurer, but the corporation may designate others as officers for its own internal purposes and for the sake of the prestige attached. Whether or not a person is an "officer" may be critical under the short-swing trading provisions of Section 16(b) of the Securities Exchange Act.

OPTION—See "stock option."

OVER THE COUNTER MARKET—The over-the-counter market for securities embraces transactions not carried out on one of the organized securities exchange. Increasingly, the over-the-counter market has become organized and coordinated with quotation services and other devices to enable buyers and sellers to locate one another and follow price movements.

PAR—The standardized value attributed by law to a share of stock is known as its par value. Issues at a price lower than par are illegal and subject the recipient to liability to make up the difference. The inflexibility of the par value system has led to the use of low par shares, at a par value well below that of the issue, and of no par stock authorized by more recent corporation laws. The counterpart of the par value times the number of shares is credited to the corporation's capital account.

PARENT—A corporation which owns all of the stock of another corporation or enough to control it is known as its "parent."

PHANTOM STOCK—It has become common for a corporation to create, as a compensation device, a phantom stock plan. Under such a plan the beneficiaries receive, not actual stock, but cash in amounts geared to the earnings and appreciation of a hypothetical block of the corporation's stock. Such plans are regarded as alternatives to stock options. For details see Chapter VIII.

POISON PILL—A corporation fearing an unfriendly takeover may distribute to its present shareholders a new class of stock or other voting rights or options that, in the event of a hostile takeover can exercise voting and other rights that will make the acquisition less attractive.

PREEMPTIVE RIGHT—The right of existing shareholders to subscribe to a sufficient portion of any subsequent issue of stock to maintain their relative proportional ownership of the stock of the corporation is referred to as the "preemptive right." Whether or not such a right exists depends upon state law and the certificate of incorporation.

PREFERRED STOCK—A preferred stock is one that has priority over the common stock as to the payment of its dividends and the repayment of the sum originally paid in (usually termed the liquidation preference). The dividend is usually subject to an upper limit (though there are issues of participating preferred that share in further earnings along with the common). Dividends may or may not be cumulative (q.v.). In general no voting rights attach to preferred stock except that (a) the right to elect some directors may be given in the event of failure to pay dividends for a specified period and (b) there is a right to vote on fundamental changes affecting the preferred.

PREMIUM—When the price at which a security is sold is greater than some benchmark such as par value, the difference is referred to as a premium. With a debt obligation a premium serves as the counterpart of a discount, lowering the overall interest rate below the periodic or coupon rate of interest. The term is also used in discussions of sales of controlling stock interests, the theory being advanced that a seller of stock may not legally retain a premium above the proportionate share of the investment value of the corporation since the premium represents a price for the sale of control, a corporate asset.

PRIVATE PLACEMENT—If securities are sold by the issuer to a limited number of sophisticated persons in such a way as to be exempt from registration under § 4(2) of the Securities Act of 1933 that is referred to as a private placement—as distinguished from a public offering.

PROMOTER—One who participates in the organization of a corporation, and the assembling of resources for it, is termed a promoter. Promoter's liability may refer to the liability incurred by those who deal with the corporation in its formative stages without fully disclosing the profits they are making. A promoter may also become liable for obligations undertaken on behalf of the as yet nonexistent corporation. The SEC rules require disclosure of specified data as to the issuer's promoters in the prospectus and registration statement.

PROSPECTUS—A prospectus is a document furnished to a prospective purchaser of a security to give him or her the data needed to make a decision thereon. Unless an exemption applies, the form of the prospectus is prescribed by SEC regulations. A copy of the prospectus is included in the registration statement (q.v.) filed with the SEC.

PROXY—A proxy is a power given by a shareholder to another person to vote his (or her) share(s) of stock. It is basically a principal agent relationship and is subject to the principles of the law of agency as modified by special state statutes, or judicial rules and by federal regulations under § 14 of the Securities Exchange Act. A proxy is set forth in the Documentary Supplement.

PROXY STATEMENT—The proxy (q.v.) itself is usually accompanied by a proxy statement which is expected to give the person solicited to give a proxy the information needed for intelligent choice. Its contents are extensively regulated by § 14 of the Securities Exchange Act and the rules issued thereunder.

PUBLIC OFFERING—When securities are sold or offered to a number of persons in such a way that the exemption offered by Section 4(2) of the Securities Act of 1933 to private placements (q.v.) is not available the transaction is termed a public offering.

PUBLIC UTILITY HOLDING COMPANY—A corporation that owns controlling interests in the stock of corporations that are public utilities (i.e., gas or electric companies) is referred to as a public utility holding company. Such corporations are subject to regulation by the SEC under the Public Utilities Holding Company Act of 1935.

QUO WARRANTO—"Quo warranto" is an ancient writ used to test the legality of a use of a public power. It is used to raise the question whether a corporation was validly organized or whether it has the legal power to conduct the business in which it is engaged.

QUORUM—When the number of directors or the number of shares required to be present or represented at a meeting in order to conduct business are present or represented the quorum requirement is satisfied. The pertinent quorum requirements may usually be found in the by-laws, subject to limits in corporation statutes or by common law.

RECAPITALIZATION—By amending the certificate of incorporation so as to change the rights of one or more classes of stock a recapitalization may be effected. Normally a recapitalization implies a reduction of the par or stated value or of the number of shares thereby diminishing capital and eliminating an accumulated earnings deficit. Arrears of cumulative preferred dividends may also be eliminated.

REDEEM, REDEEMABLE, REDEMPTION—A corporation may repurchase its own securities, in which case it is said to redeem them. Securities, typically preferred stock, which provide for such action are said to be "redeemable." In this sense "redeemable" and "callable" are substantially equivalent.

REGISTRATION—The term "registration" appears in the federal securities rules in two different, and confusing, senses. An issue of securities must, with some exemptions, be registered under the Securities Act. An issuer, i.e., the company issuing the securities, must register if it meets the terms of section 12 of the Securities Exchange Act. Registering under one Act does not satisfy the requirements of the other.

REGISTRATION STATEMENT—If an offering of securities is not exempt, the Securities Act requires the issuer to file with the SEC a registration statement setting forth the data pertinent to the decision whether or not to buy such a security. The registration statement includes the prospectus (q.v.) but also other data that need not be furnished each offeree.

REORGANIZATION—The term "reorganization" is often loosely used to cover a number of types of rearrangements of corporate financial structures achieved through different devices. Those may include mergers, consolidations, sales or exchanges of stock, insolvency proceedings or amendments of the articles of incorporation. The Internal Revenue Code uses such an expansive meaning in describing transactions that may be free from tax.

SECURITIES EXCHANGE—A securities exchange is an organized market on which securities can be traded easily and conveniently and which generates a steady flow of price data. The New York Stock Exchange and the American Stock Exchange are the principal exchanges and there are regional exchanges as well. Exchanges are subject to special regulation under the 1934 Act.

SECURITY OR SECURITIES—The Securities and Securities Exchange Acts affect transactions in "securities" which are very broadly defined in the Acts and by the courts that have had occasion to interpret the terms. Almost any arrangement that takes A's money and gives it to B to manage for his or her benefit may be deemed to be a security. Thus cases have held that securities arose from transactions under which A bought a tract of orange grove which B was to manage along with the rest of the grove or in which A bought mink, beaver or livestock which B was to raise, breed and sell with other creatures. A security need not involve any of the engraved paper which is so characteristic of the formal type of a security such as a share of stock, a bond or a debenture.

SECURITY FOR COSTS—By a statute such as those in New York, California and New Jersey, a shareholder bringing a derivative suit may be required to post security for costs. This obligation may be contingent on his failure to show ownership of a specified quantity of stock or to demonstrate a likelihood of success. In this context "costs" refers to the attorney's fees of the defense of the action, not merely to court costs.

SHARK REPELLENT—The term shark repellent encompasses various devices usually in a corporation's articles of incorporation that make it more difficult to take control of it. For example, the articles might be amended to require more than fifty per cent (a supermajority) shareholder approval for mergers and other basic changes.

SHORT MERGER—Some corporation laws provide that if a corporation holds a very high proportion, say 90%, of the stock of another it may merge that corporation into itself in a rather summary manner. This is known as a "short merger". The minority interest need not vote on the matter and may be entitled only to a cash payment of the value of its shares.

SHORT SALE—A short sale results when a person sells a security without owning it. Delivery of the security to the buyer is effected by borrowing it from another party. The seller does this on the estimate or gamble that the price of the security will go down and that it will be possible to "cover," i.e., buy the security at a lower price and restore it to the lender. Regulations under the Securities Exchange Act of 1934 limit the extent to which short sales can be made. They are thought of as speculative devices calculated to cause market declines. They were instruments in the older days of "bear raids" in which profits were made by causing sharp declines in the price of the security put under attack by rumours and other devices.

SHORT SWING—Short swing transactions in securities are those in which a purchase and sale or sale and purchase by the same person occur within a six month period. Such transactions are subject to Section 16 of the Securities Exchange Act of 1934.

SQUEEZE OUT—A transaction in which certain stockholders are forced out of a corporation by others is referred to as a "squeeze out" (or sometimes "freeze out"). This is a problem primarily in the case of close corporations.

STAGGER SYSTEM—Where the board of directors is divided into several groups or classes and the term of office of those classes expires at different annual meetings, rather than having the whole board come up for reelection each year, that is known as the "stagger system." A nine member board might, for example, be divided into three classes, one group of three being elected each year.

STOCK BONUS—When a corporation grants one of its executives shares of its stock as a reward—often measured in terms of corporate earnings—for his efforts, that is a "stock bonus."

STOCK DIVIDEND—When a corporation issues shares of its stock to its existing shareholders without consideration that is called a "stock dividend." Such distributions, usually a symbolic substitute for a cash dividend, are sometimes hard to distinguish from a stock split (q.v.). In a stock dividend the par or stated value of each share is unchanged but the total number of shares, and therefore the amount of the corporation's capital stock, are increased.

STOCK OPTION—A right, at the holder's choice, to purchase stock is known as a stock option, in particular an option issued by the issuing corporation to an officer or employee in order to compensate him for his work or give him an incentive for further effort. Income tax advantages, varying from time to time, have attached to this method of compensation, provided various limitations are observed.

STOCK SPLIT—When par or stated value of a corporation's shares of stock is divided and the number of shares correspondingly increased, there is said to be a "stock split." The purpose is generally to reduce the cost of a share and thus of the 100 share lot which is the normal unit of trading and thereby make the stock more readily marketable. There are problems in distinguishing a split from a stock dividend (q.v.).

STREET NAME—If certificates of stock are registered in the name of a broker or of a nominee for a broker they are referred to as being held in "street name."

SUBORDINATE—A debt security is referred to as "subordinate" or "subordinated" if its constitutive document provides that its principal or interest or both will not be repaid until some other class of indebtedness has been repaid. Such a security may provide much the same sort of "cushion" to the holders of other debt securities as does a class of preferred stock, while still maintaining the tax deductibility of the interest payments thereon.

SUBSIDIARY—A corporation controlled by another corporation is referred to as a subsidiary. Some are wholly owned but others are only majority owned or less.

SURPLUS—Surplus is an extraordinarily misleading term. In most contexts it means "excess," "too much." In a corporate accounting context it is simply what is left over after liabilities and capital have been subtracted from assets. It does not mean, therefore, that the corporation has cash on hand to pay a dividend, although no dividend can be paid if there is no surplus. Surplus is broken down into several categories: "earned surplus," now referred to as retained earnings, "revaluation surplus," the result of revaluing assets—to the extent that is allowed—and capital surplus, now referred to by its clumsier but truer designation: capital contributed for shares in excess of their par value. The accounting profession has been trying to avoid use of "surplus" altogether.

SURPLUS, CAPITAL—Capital surplus is a proprietorship account on the books of a corporation, arising from such transactions as the sale of stock at a price above the par or stated value, from the reduction of the par or stated value of stock, from gains on the purchase and sale by the corporation of its own stock. It is to be distinguished from earned surplus which arises from the conduct of the corporation's business.

"TAKEOVER", TAKEOVER BID—If an individual or a corporation or some group of either of them gain control over another corporation by buying its stock or otherwise this is referred to as a "take over". If they make an offer to the target company as shareholders to buy their shares this is known as a takeover bid or more commonly as a "tender offer."

TENDER OFFER—If an individual or a corporation or some group of either of them makes to the shareholders of a target company over which they seek to gain control an offer to buy their shares of stock that is known as a tender offer. Such offers have since 1968 been regulated by the Williams Act (Sections 13(d) and 14(d)–(f) of the 1934 Act).

THIN INCORPORATION—A corporation is termed "thin" if its capitalization is so inadequate in relation to its obligations and risk as to be vulnerable to challenge by its creditors—or by the Internal Revenue Service.

TIP, TIPPEE—In the case law relating to obligations with respect to the purchase and sale of securities, the transmission of inside knowledge not publicly available at the time is referred to as a "tip" and its recipient as a "tippee." It is equivalent to a "leak" (the term "leakee" has never taken hold).

TRANSFER AGENT—A corporation with widely traded securities will have a transfer agent, generally a bank, to manage transfers. The transfer agent issues new certificates upon the surrender of old ones and maintains the current list of security-holders. It requires appropriate documentation of the right to transfer the securities. Typically it also mails dividend or interest checks.

TREASURY STOCK—Stock that has been repurchased by the corporation issuing it and has not been cancelled is referred to as "treasury stock".

TRUST INDENTURE—It is customary to issue debt securities—bonds or debentures—under a trust indenture between a corporation and an indenture trustee who is to protect the interests of the various security holders. Trust indentures connected with a public offering of securities are regulated by the federal Trust Indenture Act of 1939. A trust indenture may also constitute a mortgage, pledge or deed of trust.

ULTRA VIRES—An action outside of the power granted to a corporation by its charter is referred to as *ultra vires* and may be invalid depending upon the rules in force in the state in question.

UNDERWRITER—The Securities Act defines an underwriter as one who purchases securities from an issuer with a view to their resale or distribution and regulates transactions by such underwriters. Under that definition one may be an underwriter without intending to be one. In general usage the term is reserved for those who make a regular business of distributing securities.

VOTING TRUST—A voting trust, as distinguished from an ordinary trust in which the res is stock, is one in which the trustee holds only the voting rights and not the full legal title including the right to transfer the stock. Courts divided as to the legality of voting trusts at common law but statutes now generally provide for and limit them.

WARRANT—A corporation may issue, usually to make the issue of some other security more attractive, warrants which are negotiable documents giving the owner an option to purchase stock of the corporation at a specified price.

WATERED STOCK—If stock is issued for a consideration less than that called for by legal requirements it is referred to as "watered." The reference is to the nineteenth century practice of persuading livestock to drink large quantities of water before they were weighed and sold.

WHITE KNIGHT—After a hostile tender offer has been made for the stock of a corporation and has been judged inadequate or unacceptable by the management of the target, that management may seek out a more appealing offeror, termed a white knight.

WORKING CAPITAL—Working capital is the difference between a firm's current assets and its current liabilities. It is frequently used as a measure of a firm's liquidity and capacity to meet its obligations as they fall due.

INDEX

†